The French Revolution

A volume
in
THE DOCUMENTARY HISTORY
of
WESTERN CIVILIZATION

The French Revolution

Edited by

PAUL H. BEIK

MACMILLAN

First published in the United States 1970
First published in the United Kingdom by
The Macmillan Press Ltd. 1971

Published by
THE MACMILLAN PRESS LTD
Associated companies in New York Toronto
Dublin Melbourne Johannesburg and Madras

SBN 333 07911 6

Printed in the United States of America.

Contents

Introduction

THE FRENCH REVOLUTION lives in the consciousness of world opinion as a reference point for change. It retains a remarkable contemporaneity, product of the passage from a traditionalistic, aristocratic society toward one whose contours are the focus of today's contestations. What began to be visible in the wreckage of the old regime at the end of the eighteenth century was not yet today's world; one may not ask of one era that it be another. Many of the projections of the revolution did not come to pass— for example, the vision of a society of small independent producers— and although our political and social vocabulary owes much to the revolutionary era its terms have been buffeted since then by many contexts. Yet the evolution, even distortion, of terms was to do honor to the importance of the issues raised but not solved at the end of the eighteenth century, and some of the revolution's principles—for example, the sovereignty of the people and national self-determination—have gone from triumph to triumph. What the revolution possessed, owing to the breakdown of authority and the struggle for the succession on the part of contending groups and programs, was intensity, seriousness, and variety. The revolution never spoke with one voice except in the claims of its competing children and their descendants. It was a collective experience, unplanned, a clashing of wills and purposes. It remains a point of reference because of this, because the attackers and defenders brought out problems of political organization and social justice and, when these needed backing, propositions about the nature and prospects of man.

Such a revolution could not fail to be an international event, a "challenge" to the institutions and conceptions of Europe and, to a lesser degree, of America, and a "struggle" over their future— to use the metaphors of Robert R. Palmer. The French were not alone in making this challenge, nor were they the first to do so, and they never claimed that the principles at stake in the struggle applied only to France. Where the French Revolution was unique was in its combinations of men and circumstances, its timing, its stages, and its methods. And since France was by many indexes the most powerful, advanced, and influential country in Europe, the French experience in all its intensity became the model that overshadowed the others and gave its name to the era.

The earliest decision in the making of this book of documents about the revolution was to concentrate on this French experience rather than on the international, in order to make room for the fullest possible expression of what the French thought was happening to them or ought to happen. These events and prospects were long considered, and for some are still thought to have been, primarily political. Certainly the revolution was a political effort of great staying power, brought on by the failure of those in charge of the absolute monarchy to make reforms without losing the initiative and authority essential to government; it became a political effort to replace absolutism by some form of representative institutions, an effort that lasted for ten years before its temporary diversion into other channels by Napoleon. This central theme encompassed many technical problems of a growing political science; but what is most interesting in the experience is its core, the linking of government to society, which in the given circumstances produced some half-dozen possibilities. The least drastic change would have been a representative system guaranteeing the old social system as long as its defenders, preponderant in the Estates General, wished to preserve it. The next possibility, recommended by men such as Jean Joseph Mounier and his fellow Anglophiles, featured strong royal authority and a legislature of two chambers in an effort to conciliate the aristocracy and contain the lower classes; the Anglophiles, while hoping for the support of all propertied and educated people, including nobles and clergy, in reality deprived the aristocracy of the guarantees that most of them wanted. Other positions followed, both logically and as the products of events. There were Constitutionalists, followers of Lafayette or of Antoine Barnave and his friends, two wings that came together as Feuillants in later, adverse times in a futile effort to check the democratic avalanche before its weight became overwhelming. The Constitutionalists at first opposed some of the Anglophile brakes on popular enthusiasm, although they agreed with the Anglophiles in wanting to limit the suffrage and in regarding representation as a political function best reserved for persons of tested capacity, the most obvious test being possession of property. Under the pressure of events, some of the Constitutionalists tended to evolve backward toward the Anglophile political position. Both groups were left behind by the revolution, but it would be an error to assume that their social and political preferences died out in France during the Terror; many of the Anglophiles and Constitutionalists survived in disguise or in silence, to emerge after Thermidor as royalists or moderate republicans.

Meanwhile, owing to the violent overthrow of the monarchy in wartime conditions and under the threat of counterrevolution, moderates had to give way, throughout two-thirds of the period of the Convention, to democrats of varying degrees of egalitarianism. Girondin and Mountain deputies, some of them secretly reluctant, competed with each other in the presence of the powerful, spontaneous revolutionary movement of the sans-culottes, which, with its sincere but unsophisticated notions of direct democracy and social justice, and by virtue of the efforts of neighborhood leaders to take power in its name, threatened their leadership and at times the very existence of the Convention. Representative government in the crisis of the war and its hardships, complicated by yearnings for a better life awakened by the unusual, habit-destroying circumstances of the revolution, could be reconciled with order and with swift wartime decisions only by new theories of revolutionary government; these amounted to dictatorship in the name of unimpeachable values, and these means were resorted to during the Terror.

The succession of political changes during the revolution, if it can be described systematically, must nevertheless be explained historically by combinations of circumstances. Nor did political programs fail to evolve with these circumstances. One cannot, for example, appreciate either the meaning or the dynamics of the revolution without awareness of the effects of the counterrevolution, which, moreover, itself tended to evolve, as did its opponents in the fight. The partisans of absolute monarchy, few and without influence in 1789, were predominant in the emigration in 1795 at the time of Louis XVIII's Declaration of Verona and were soon to be reinforced by intellectuals such as Joseph de Maistre, whose doctrines represented the maturing of a reactionary position inexplicable without the experience of the revolution. At the other extreme, another process of maturation was taking place as François

Noël Babeuf concluded that the partitioning of properties was not enough. By 1797, when de Maistre became famous and Babeuf was executed, the problems confronting a moderate republican within France, or a moderate royalist, or a radical Jacobin, were by no means the same as they had been in, say, the summer of 1792. The revolutionary spectrum was, if not kaleidoscopic, at least not static.

To many historians and others who use it as a point of reference, the revolution was most significant for what it did to the control of resources, over which the hold of the aristocracy was diminished and that of the middle classes and richer peasants was increased. Similarly the possession of property took on added importance as an influence on one's position in life, because advantages which in the old regime had been reserved by law for certain groups were abolished, with the result that the society was no longer one of legalized privileges; indeed it was no longer, in principle, one of groups having different sets of rights but one of equal individuals so far as the law was concerned. This social revolution is to be found everywhere in the documents assembled in the present collection, not only in the more obvious classical expressions such as the Declaration of the Rights of Man and the reforms of the night session of August 4, 1789, and not only in such master works as Sieyès's famous pamphlet of January, 1789, or Mounier's of the following month, or in still later expressions by Chapelier, Roland, Robespierre, and others. One can, in addition, find the contours of the social revolution in the protests of its critics, de Maistre and the more moderate Pierre Victor Malouet and Jacques Mallet du Pan on the right, and men on the left such as Jacques Roux and Jacques Hébert, who had learned the language of the sans-culottes, and Babeuf, in whose moral condemnation of the dominant forces of the revolution a form of revolutionary socialism had crystallized. Everywhere on the political spectrum will be found social aspirations and attitudes more or less consciously formulated as doctrines, because that was what the political struggle was about.

Nor was the social side of the revolution altogether materialistic. It is impossible to mistake the moral fervor of a Condorcet, a Robespierre, or a Saint-Just, which has more to do with the dignity of man than with changes of ownership. This respect for the individual is a dominant note in the revolution, testified to even by conservatives in their varying shades, a Rivarol, a Malouet, a Mallet du Pan. The revolution as a contest over values reached its quintessence in disputes over the nature of man and the nature of religion. Man's capabilities and his place in history provided an issue visible whenever it was necessary to call upon overpowering premises. At the extremes of those represented here are de Maistre, with his view of man's weakness and need for help, and the dechristianizers, with their celebration of man's powers, but there were many nuances concerning religion. Robespierre's report of May 7, 1794, and Chemin's *Théoanthropophile Manual* of 1796 illustrate positions between atheism and Christianity.

It is natural to ask, "What of those who left no traces on paper, who cared little for politics, whose social aims did not extend much beyond material things, or whose values did not encompass much more than family and community loyalties and routine practices?" There is no penetrating that mass, who expressed themselves mainly by action or abstention, but perhaps never before had there been such swiftly growing consciousness of them, of the people, on the part of the literate and reflective minority. The present collection of documents is drawn from the literate minority of observers and contestants, with an eye to the principal shadings of opinion; from expressions identifiable by author, time, and place. These are documents by persons who took stands, and that is why their spectrum is, to begin with, political. This established, one notices that they cared deeply about society and values; theirs was a social politics; and one notices, again and again, that they were drawn into taking stands about the people and their potentialities. If I have had any special leaning, it has been toward such expressions, and toward the presentation of a full spectrum of opinions about this question of the people, so vital to politics, society, and values.

This, then, is a book about the revolution that people thought was happening, or were trying to make happen. There was another revolution that was happening in spite of them—or, rather, through the instrumentality of their wills and aspirations—but above them and beyond the reach of any man or group, a grand total, so to speak, out of control: in short, the revolution of facts, of conditions and institutions; of statistics when it comes to documents. That revolution, with which French scholars have been concerning themselves to good effect, and particularly since Georges Lefebvre broadened the subject of the inquiry to include all social levels and the provinces as well as the center, is no less human than the revolution of the participants and observers. I have taken care to record the latter's awareness of it but have had to renounce its statistical side, along with the international revolution, and along with laws, constitutions, and descriptive accounts that are readily available elsewhere, in order to devote this volume to the consciousness of contemporaries and to their conflicts of will and purpose. Those represented here are all French, it should be added, except for Joseph de Maistre, Mallet du Pan, and Mme. de Staël, who have special claims. Of course there cannot be an account of the evolution of each person, although in this respect Robespierre has been somewhat favored; in general, however, each has been called upon at a moment significant for him and for the revolution. And since there is not enough room for a spectrum for each year or period, I have emphasized certain problems at each stage: the conflict of the aristocracy with the officials of the absolute monarchy as public discussion increased offstage; the monarchy's loss of control and the failure of a moderate coalition to take charge; the rise and interaction of counterrevolution and democracy; certain key reforms, though here it was necessary to renounce comprehensiveness; the conflict of popular aspirations with the necessities of war and the ideologies of the leaders; the accumulation of competing views and the hazards of attempts to achieve stability. One could devote many pages to a search for an ideal periodization of the revolution; much of the pleasure of working with historical materials consists of such exercises of judgment; I have not deprived the reader of this pleasure but have simply placed the documents in chronological order and have provided a few headings and a substantial chronology of events to go with them.

Naturally these documents are of varying lengths. Wherever possible, they have been included in their entirety. There are, however, superb pieces that are really small books, such as Condorcet's presentation of the so-called Girondin constitution to the Convention, Robespierre's report of May 7, 1794, and No. 35 of Babeuf's *Tribun du peuple*. In such cases, it has been necessary to adopt various devices, depending on the material. That of Condorcet is the most unusual, for, owing to the nature of the material, no effort has been made to represent all of the major ideas; rather, certain of the most significant passages, long enough to be self-contained, have been selected. In the case of Robespierre's May 7 report, as in that of Sieyès's *What Is the Third Estate?* mentioned earlier, and a number of other writings, the whole structure of the argument has been retained. In the case of Babeuf's

No. 35 and a few other works, it has been possible to use the conclusion, or most of it, as a distinct entity. In every case, the headnote explains what has been done unless no cuts have been made. Most of these documents have not before been translated into English, and most of those that have been translated have been presented in truncated versions, and frequently in translation by nineteenth-century writers whose punctuation and choice of words now seem rather far removed from the original French in spirit and sometimes in literal meaning. In any case, all of the documents with the single exception of Louis XVIII's Declaration of Verona appear here in new translations. The accomplishment of this considerable task would have taken twice as long without the talent and efficiency of Doris Beik, my wife, who prepared preliminary drafts of them all, which I then revised with an eye to historical circumstances and usages, so that the translations are our joint effort, the greater contribution being hers and the responsibility mine.

In sum, this is a book about the meaning of the revolution to those who were going through it, and about its problems, viewed from the principal points of view of that time and place, and with attention to the stages through which the revolution passed. It abstains from comprehensiveness and is intended as a companion volume to other studies while standing on its own as a body of literature representing a variety of attitudes in the participants and onlookers.

I

Crown, Parlement, and Aristocracy

---

1. November 19, 1787: Chrétien François de Lamoignon on Principles of the French Monarchy

A still photograph of the occasion of November 19, 1787, would show Louis XVI meeting with the Parlement of Paris. The king might be shown declaring that a government loan of some 420 million *livres* was henceforth to be considered as registered by the parlement. Among the preliminaries to this act was a speech by the Keeper of the Seals, M. de Lamoignon, explaining the need for the loan and, along the way, reiterating the formal doctrine of the monarchy concerning its own authority, as stated in the document printed below.

If the picture of November 19, 1787, were in the form of a movie sequence, Lamoignon's speech would be seen to follow a short opening statement by the king, and to be followed by a long discussion, including a shocking protest by the Duke of Orléans when the king ordered registration without taking a vote of the members of the parlement. Awkwardly, Louis XVI insisted that his will had to prevail. If extended through several years, the film would show a series of confrontations between the crown and the parlements, with the government's need for money raising questions of tax reforms and the problems of how to tax effectively raising questions of political procedures. In Lamoignon's statement of principles and in the following documents, the nature of the monarchy becomes the subject of formal pronouncements. Much more than political doctrine was at stake, however, for political procedures could influence the further development of French society, with obvious implications for the future roles of its various groups. What has come to be called modernization was an economic and social fact in France at the end of the old regime, and was not to be coped with unless the question of political modernization was raised. The king and his ministers might guide France into the future, but powerful aristocratic groups for whom the parlements were more and more acting as spokesmen were extremely reluctant to entrust them with this task. The situation was not as yet revolutionary, because in spite of many potentially dangerous economic and social conditions and an intellectual climate that was encouraging more and more independence of mind in what was coming to be called public opinion, the official government had not yet lost control of the situation. The years 1787 and 1788 have sometimes been called the prerevolution, because debates among the powerful and socially influential were under way but had not yet paralyzed the government's ability to keep order.

The portion of M. de Lamoignon's speech dealing with the principles of the monarchy is taken from pp. 5–6 of *Séance royale tenue en parlement, le 19 novembre 1787* (s.l.n.d., 42 pp. in 8°).

Speech of M. de Lamoignon, Keeper of the Seals of France, During the Royal Session of the Parlement on November 19, 1787.

. . . THESE PRINCIPLES, universally recognized by the Nation to be true, attest that to the King alone belongs the Sovereign power in his kingdom;

That he is accountable only to God for the exercise of the supreme power;

That the bond uniting the King and the Nation is by its nature indissoluble;

That interests and duties that are reciprocal between the King and his subjects do nothing else than to assure the perpetuity of this union;

That the Nation's interests require that the rights of its Chief suffer no alteration;

That the King is Sovereign Chief of the Nation and one with the Nation;

Finally, that the legislative power resides in the person of the Sovereign, independently and without partition.

Gentlemen, such are the unchangeable principles of the French Monarchy. The King has by no means derived them from a source that can be suspect to his Parlement. His Majesty found them literally consecrated in your decree of March 20, 1766, whose words I have merely repeated to you here.

It follows from these long-standing national maxims attested to by every page of our history that the right to summon the Estates General belongs to the King alone;

That he alone must judge whether such convocation is useful or necessary;

That to administer his kingdom he has need of no extraordinary powers; that a King of France could find in the representatives of the three orders of the state only a more extensive council composed of members chosen from a family of which he is the Chief and concerning whose remonstrances and grievances he will always be the supreme arbiter.

Gentlemen, this prerogative of the Crown that you have all sworn to defend will always enable the King to look upon the Estates General of his kingdom as merely *the great days* of the love of the French for their Sovereign. . . .

2. *April 17, 1788: Louis XVI to a Deputation from the Parlement of Paris*

In the winter and spring of 1787–1788, the Parlement of Paris continued to resist the king's will, in spite of the exiling of the Duke of Orléans to his country estates and the imprisonment of the parlementary *conseillers* Fréteau and Sabatier and Louis XVI's reiteration of his willingness to call the Estates General by 1791. Various exchanges took place between the parlement and the court, but the parlement was meanwhile preparing lengthy remonstrances concerning the royal session of November 19, 1787. These were presented to the king on April 13, 1788. Louis XVI then summoned a deputation of the parlement to Versailles on April 17, 1788, and in a setting of pomp and severity, surrounded by his brothers, the princes of the blood, his ministers, and various courtiers, read the parlement's deputation the following lecture. The source is *Remontrances du Parlement de Paris au XVIIIᵉ siècle publiées par Jules Flammermont. Vol. III, 1768–1788* (Paris, 1898), pp. 735–736.

Louis XVI to the
Grande Députation du Parlement,
April 17, 1788.

I HAVE READ your remonstrances and I wanted to respond to them with such clarity that you could not doubt my intentions or fail to take them into account.

It was superfluous to speak to me about the law concerning registration and the liberty of suffrage. When I meet with my parlement, it is to listen to discussion of the law that I bring there and to decide for myself about the registration with all the facts before me; that is what I did on November 19 last.

I listened to the deliberations.

There is no need to sum them up except when I am not present at your deliberations; on such occasions only the majority view can acquaint me with the outcome.

When I am present, I judge the sense of the meeting for myself.

If the majority in my parlement were able to go against my will, the monarchy would be no more than an aristocracy of magistrates, as harmful to the rights and interest of the Nation as to those of the Sovereign.

It would indeed be an odd constitution that would reduce the will of the King to the equivalent of the opinion of one of his officers and would force the legislator to have as many wills as there were different deliberations in the various courts of justice of his kingdom.

I must protect the Nation from such a misfortune.

The session of November 19 was completely lawful.

The deliberations were complete because all of the opinions were heard.

The opinions were not recounted because I was present.

There is no need to determine anything by voting when the vote must not be allowed to prevail.

There was a judgment because whenever I hold a session of my parlement for a matter of administration or legislation the only possible judgment is that which I command.

I therefore was obliged to reject your decree and I forbid you to take such measures in the future. To remove from your register an error that I choose to attribute only to a moment of deception and misjudgment is to purify the register, not to alter it.

How many useful laws that serve as daily guides to your deliberations does France not owe to the authority of its kings, who had them registered not only without regard for a plurality of votes but even against such a plurality and in spite of the resistance of the parlements!

These principles must be the basis of your conduct. I will never permit even their slightest infraction.

3. May 4, 1788: Repeated Remonstrances of the Parlement of Paris in Response to the King's Statement of April 17

After the king's rebuke to their delegation on April 17, 1788, the Parlement of Paris prepared additional remonstrances, which were completed on April 30 and delivered to the King on May 4. These remonstrances—given below, from Flammermont, *op. cit.*, pp. 736–743, with the deletion of eight paragraphs of illustrative material,[1] and the shortening of three others—came at a crucial time when the struggle between the crown and the parlements was reaching a climax. Louis XVI's response was to be the *lit de justice* of May 8, which reorganized the parlements and deprived them of any political role. But the final struggle between the crown and the aristocracy in the summer of 1788 was destined to be won by the aristocracy, whose prize was to be an earlier opening of Pandora's box, the Estates General.

April 30, 1788 (Delivered to the King on May 4, 1788) Iterative Remonstrances of the Parlement of Paris in Response to the King's Statement of April 17, 1788.

THE RESPONSE of Your Majesty on the seventeenth of this month is distressing; but the resolution of your parlement is not broken. Excesses of despotism being the only recourse for the enemies of the Nation and of truth, they are not afraid to use this means. Their success presages the greatest misfortunes. To forestall them, if possible, will be the objective of your parlement's zeal to the very end. Its silence would betray the most vital interests of Your Majesty by delivering the kingdom to all the abuses of arbitrary power. Such, in effect, would be the consequences of the maxims whose value has been misrepresented to Your Majesty. If your ministers were to succeed in applying them, our kings would no

---

1. As in other documents of this collection, deletions will be indicated by three ellipsis points, and deletions extending beyond one paragraph will also be indicated by extra space.

longer be monarchs, but despots; they would no longer rule by law, but by force, over slaves instead of subjects.

The behavior of ambitious ministers is always the same. To extend their power under shelter of the King's name is their objective; to slander the magistracy is their means. Faithful to this old and evil method, they attribute to us the senseless project of establishing in the kingdom an aristocracy of magistrates. But what is the moment they have chosen for this imputation? The moment when your parlement, enlightened by the facts, and retracing its steps, proves that it is more attached to the rights of the Nation than to its own precedents.

The French constitution appeared to be forgotten. The assembling of the Estates General was treated as a chimera. Richelieu and his cruelties, Louis XIV and his glory, the Regency and its disorders, the ministers of the late King and their hardheartedness seemed to have obliterated permanently from people's minds and hearts the very name of the Nation. The ministry had overlooked nothing in its efforts to undermine the French Nation: terror, enthusiasm, corruption, indifference—all of the conditions designed to make people abandon themselves. But the parlement remained. It was thought to be overcome by the apparently universal lethargy; this was an error. Abruptly warned about the condition of the finances, forced to take cognizance of two disastrous edicts, it grows anxious, it ceases to deceive itself, it judges the future by the past, and it sees only one resource for the Nation: the Nation itself. Soon, after mature and wise reflection, it comes to a decision, and it gives the world the unheard-of example of an ancient assembly, an official body connected with the very roots of the state, which returns from itself to its fellow citizens a power of great importance that it had applied on their behalf but without their formal consent for a century. In response to its courage: immediate success. On July 6 it calls for the Estates General; on September 19 it formally proclaims its own incompetence; on November 19 Your Majesty himself announces the Estates General; two days later he promises it and sets the time limit within which it will meet; his word is sacred. Nowhere in the world, nowhere in history, can one find a single empire in which the King and the Nation have made so much peaceful progress in so little time, the King toward justice, the Nation toward liberty! The Estates General will therefore be assembled! The Estates General will come once more into its rights! We can demand that your ministers say to whom the King owes this great project, to whom the Nation owes this great benefit! And your ministers dare accuse us in the presence of the people, in the presence of the King, of aspiring to aristocratic power! . . .

No, Sire, no aristocracy in France, but no despotism; such is the constitution; such also is the will of your parlement and the interest of Your Majesty.

Let us grant for a moment the maxims deceitfully recommended to Your Majesty to the effect that the royal will alone determines the judgment in matters of administration and legislation and that the consequences in the last analysis clarify the principle.

The heir to the crown is named by law; the Nation has its rights; the peerage has its rights; the magistracy is irremovable; each province has its customs, its special rights; each subject has his constitutional judges; every citizen has his property; if he is poor he at least has his liberty.

But we dare to ask: what are the rights, what are the laws that could resist claims announced by your ministers in the name of Your Majesty?

Your Majesty's will alone is to determine the judgment in matters of legislation! It could, therefore, by means of a law, dispose of the crown, choose its heir, cede its provinces, deprive the Estates General of the right to grant taxes, change the nature of the peerage, make the magistracy removable, change the customs, turn the courts upside down, invest itself with the right of judging or of choosing judges in civil and criminal cases; declare itself, finally, co-proprietor of the property of its subjects and master of their liberty. . . .

Will it be said that the King will never abuse the right that is attributed to him, that he will always be just, that his laws and decrees will always respect the rights of everyone, from his oldest son down to the least significant of his subjects? Your parlement, Sire, will be forced to reply that the hypothesis is untenable, that kings are men, and that there is no infallible man. And it is precisely because it is not given to kings to be ceaselessly on guard against mistakes or enticements, and in order not to abandon the Nation to the harmful effects of inappropriately advised acts of will, that the constitution requires, for the laws, the verification of the courts; and for taxation a preliminary grant by the Estates General, in order to be sure that the will of the King will conform to justice and his demands to the needs of the state.

The right of freely consenting to taxation does not make the Estates General into an aristocracy of citizens; the right of freely verifying the laws does not make the parlements into an aristocracy of magistrates. Government is in the hands of aristocrats, but your parlement does not aspire at all to govern. In its judgments it is subject to the laws and its own will is nothing; it pronounces, but the law has decided. . . .

There is, to be sure, a tendency to popularize a maxim to the contrary: it is claimed that property, life, liberty, and the honor of the citizens are in the hands of the King. If he is present, it is said, he issues the decree; if he is absent, he can change it. Slavery itself did not employ a baser language, but at least your ministers have not yet pushed things to that point.

Is it a question of taxes? It is for the Nation to grant them. The liberty of the Estates General has not yet been subject to doubt.

Is there question of a law? It is the responsibility of the courts to examine it freely, but since the right of verifying the laws is not the same as that of making them, the courts can neither compel nor supersede the will of the King; your parlement, Sire, has already professed this truth, and will repeat it as often as your ministers try to obscure it.

In accordance with their own system, moreover, the extent of the plurality was not known to Your Majesty on the day of the session. It is inconceivable that the ministers should distinguish between the sense of the meeting and the plurality, as if the plurality were not the sense of the meeting, and that they should want to persuade Your Majesty that from having heard separate opinions Your Majesty was able to judge independently what a synthesis of all the separate opinions would amount to. As if they were ignorant of the fact that early expressions of opinions are sometimes modified after the arguments of later speakers have been presented.

If your parlement had rejected useful laws, it would be necessary to pity humanity without making the King a despot, without destroying the constitution, without establishing slavery *by the system of the unique will.* . . .

* * *

Would it be permissible for the parlement, in its turn, to use as arguments against the enemies of the right of verification the host of harmful laws which owed their origin to *lits de justice?* To go back no further than the Regency, if since that time our laws, our customs, the public fortune, all of the estates and companies, and most families have experienced so many shocks, are they not the sad fruits of arbitrary power manifested in the *lits de justice?* If the taxes have merely augmented expenditures, is this not an effect of the security that *lits de justice* inspired in the ministers? If economy has now come to be taken seriously, has this development not coincided with the inability of the ministers to count on this same device? The reign of the late King—why do we remain silent about it? History would testify, if the parlement did not, that this reign was marked by many *lits de justice* and also by excessive taxation, borrowing, and waste.

Vainly, as a tactic to justify despotism, fears for the legislator are professed. *He will then have as many wills as there are courts in the kingdom.* Such is the objection of your ministers. The answer is in history and in the laws. A general oath, that of the coronation, binds its sovereign to all of France. But the King does not reign over all of the provinces by virtue of a single legal title. In Normandy, in Brittany, in Guyenne, in Languedoc, in Provence, in Dauphiné, in Alsace, in Burgundy, in Franche-Comté, in conquered territories, in annexed territories, different conditions govern obedience. In Béarn the first article of the customary law is an oath by the King to respect privileges; this oath is renewed at each reign, by the King in person, before the deputies of the estates of this province, after which the province renders its oath to the King. You yourself, Sire, have renewed yours. The will of the King, in order to be just, must consequently vary according to the provinces; it is not the courts that bind him, but principles. Beneficent chains solidifying legitimate power! Each province has demanded a parlement for the defense of its particular rights. These rights are not chimeras and these parlements are not vain institutions. Otherwise the King could say to Brittany: *I take away from you your Estates;* to Guyenne: *I rescind your capitulations;* to the people of Béarn: *I do not intend to take an oath to you any longer;* to all the provinces: *your liberties are chains for the legislator; your parlements oblige him to vary his volitions; I abolish your liberties; I destroy your parlements.* It is certain that then the will of the King could be uniform. But, Sire, may your parlement be permitted to express alarm about this! Would it be just? Would it be prudent? And finally, would it be possible for your ministers to have formed such projects? Such is assuredly neither the intention nor the interest of Your Majesty.

For your parlement, its principles—or, rather, Sire, those of the state—which are given into its care, are unchangeable. It is not in its power to alter its conduct.

Sometimes magistrates are called upon to sacrifice themselves for the sake of the laws, but such is their honorable and perilous condition that they must cease to exist before the Nation ceases to be free.

4. December 12, 1788: Memoir of the Princes

The Memoir of the Princes was sent to the king by the princes of the blood on December 12, 1788, at the close of the second Assembly of Notables. The Notables had been summoned by Necker on November 6 in the hope of winning support for the doubling of the representation of the Third Estate in the Estates General, but they took a firmly "aristocratic" stand, refusing to endanger the dominance of the nobles and clergy in the Estates; of the six working committees into which the Notables divided, only one—chaired by Monsieur, Louis XVI's next younger brother, the Count of Provence—agreed to "doubling," and it said nothing about permitting vote by head. The Memoir of the Princes was not signed by Provence, who at this time was trying to maintain a reputation for moderation. Called by Georges Lefebvre "the best manifesto of the aristocracy,"[1] this Memoir was almost certainly the work of Antoine Jean Auget, baron de Montyon, who had held many government offices and was closely associated with the Count of Artois, Louis XVI's youngest brother. Montyon's traditionalistic, mildly liberal, aristocratic constitutionalism was characteristic of eighteenth-century aristocratic and parlementary critics of absolute monarchy. He was, however, to be one of the few to hold to this point of view through the revolution; most of the great nobles, including the princes for whom he prepared the Memoir in 1788, and including Provence, who at that time posed as considering it too

1. Georges Lefebvre, *The Coming of the French Revolution*, translated by R. R. Palmer (Princeton, 1947), p. 58.

reactionary, were to abandon aristocratic constitutionalism for a revived absolutism. The Memoir of the Princes anticipates some of the arguments of the right during the revolution and of rightist historiography since the revolution.

The source is "Mémoire présenté au roi par monseigneur comte d'Artois, M. le prince de Condé, M. le duc de Bourbon, M. le duc d'Enghein et M. le prince de Conti," in *Archives parlementaires de 1787 à 1860. Recueil complet des débats législatifs et politiques des chambres françaises . . . sous la direction de M. J. Mavidal . . . et de M. E. Laurent. Première série (1787–1799)*, Vol. I, second edition (Paris, 1879), pp. 487–489.

WHEN YOUR MAJESTY forbade the Notables to give their attention to the Prince of Conti's Memoir, Your Majesty declared to the *princes of the blood that if they should wish to make suggestions useful to his service and that of the state, they could address themselves to him.*

The Count of Artois, the Prince of Condé, the Duke of Bourbon, the Duke of Enghien, and the Prince of Conti believe it to be their duty to respond to this invitation of Your Majesty.

It is indeed the responsibility of the princes of the blood, who by their rank are the foremost of your subjects, and by their situation and profession your born counselors, and by their rights committed to defending yours; it is especially their responsibility to speak the truth to you, and they believe that they also owe you an accounting of their sentiments and thoughts.

Sire, the state is in peril; your person is respected, for the virtues of the monarch assure him the homage of the nation; but, Sire, a revolution in the principles of government is being prepared; it is being induced by the fermentation of minds. Institutions reputed to be sacred, and by means of which this monarchy has prospered for many centuries, are being transformed into problematical questions or even criticized as acts of injustice.

The writings that have been published during the Assembly of Notables, the memoirs that have been sent to the undersigned princes, the demands formulated by various provinces, cities, or corporations; the objectives and style of these demands and memoirs: it all announces, all proves that there is a system of reasoned insubordination and scorn for the laws of the state. Every author assumes the attributes of a legislator; eloquence or skill in writing, even unsupported by education, information, and experience, seem to be qualification enough for reforming the constitutions of empires: whoever sets forth a bold proposition, whoever proposes to change the laws, is sure to have readers and partisans.

The disastrous progress of this agitation is such that opinions which some time ago would have appeared to be the most reprehensible seem today to be reasonable and just; and what today makes respectable people most indignant will perhaps within a short time pass as conventional and legitimate. Who can say where the recklessness of opinions will stop? The rights of the throne have been questioned; the rights of the two orders of the state divide opinions; soon property rights will be attacked; inequalities of wealth will be presented as an object for reform; already it has been proposed that feudal rights be abolished as a system of oppression, a remnant of barbarism.

It is from these new systems, from the project of changing the rights and the laws, that has come the pretension announced by some groups in the Third Estate to obtain for this order two votes in the Estates General, while each of the first two orders would continue to have only one.

The undersigned princes will not repeat what several committees [of the Notables] have exposed, the injustice and danger of an innovation in the composition of the Estates General, or in the manner of convoking it; the multitude of claims that would result; the ease, if the votes were counted by head and without distinction of orders, of jeopardizing through the seduction of some members of the Third Estate the interests of that order, which are better protected under the present constitution; the destruction of the equilibrium so wisely established among the three orders, and of the independence of each of them.

It has been indicated to Your Majesty how important it is to preserve the only manner of convoking the Estates General that is constitutional, the manner consecrated by laws and customs, the distinction between orders, the right to deliberate separately, and the equality of the votes, these unalterable bases of the French monarchy.

It has not been concealed from Your Majesty that to change the form of the letters of convocation for the Third Estate only, and to call to the Estates General two deputies from this order, even while giving them only one vote, as in the past, would be an intermediate, indirect way of accepting the claims of the Third Estate, which, alerted by this first success, would not be inclined to be satisfied with a concession having no result or real benefit so long as the number of deputies was increased without the number of votes being changed.

Your Majesty has also seen that the joining of two deputies to make one vote can, through differences in their opinions, nullify their vote, and that if the nullified vote is declared a negative one, according to the custom accepted in the various bodies, the means of resistance against the demands of the government are increased.

These principles have been expounded and their demonstration appears to have been definitive.

It remains only for the undersigned princes to express the feelings inspired by their attachment to the state and to Your Majesty.

They cannot hide the fear for the state that would be inspired in them by the success of the pretensions of the Third Estate and the fatal consequences of the proposed revolution in the constitution of the Estates: they see in these a deplorable future; they see in these any king changing the nation's law according to his opinions or attachments: a superstitious king giving the clergy several votes; a warlike king lavishing them on the nobles who have followed him into battle; the Third Estate, which at the present moment would have obtained a preponderance of votes, punished for its success by these variations: each order, according to the period, oppressor or oppressed; the constitution corrupted or vacillating; the nation always divided, and therefore always weak and unhappy.

But there are still other misfortunes that are more pressing. In a kingdom where civil dissension has not existed for a long time, it is only with sorrow that one uses the word schism: one would, however, have to anticipate this event if the rights of the first two orders were subjected to any alteration; in that case, one of these orders, or perhaps both, might disavow the Estates General and refuse to confirm their own degradation by appearing in the assembly.

Who can doubt that one will at least see a great number of gentlemen attacking the legality of the Estates General, making protests, having them registered in the parlements, making them known even to the assembly of the Estates? In that event, in the eyes of a part of the nation, what would be decreed in this assembly would no longer have the force of a national resolution; and what confidence would not be inspired in people's minds by protests that would tend to spare them from paying the taxes imposed by the Estates? And so this assembly so yearned for and so necessary would only be a source of trouble and disorder.

But even if Your Majesty were to experience no obstacles to the execution of his wishes, could his noble, just, and humane soul decide to sacrifice, to humiliate this brave, ancient, and respectable nobility that has shed so much blood for the *patrie* and for its kings, that placed Hugh Capet on the throne, that tore the scepter from the hands of the English in order to offer it to Charles VII, and was able to make the crown secure for the founder of the present dynasty?

While speaking for the nobility, the princes of the blood speak for themselves; they cannot forget that they are a part of the nobility, that they must not be dissociated from it; that their first title is that of gentleman: that was said by Henry IV, and they like to repeat the expressions of his noble sentiments.

Let the Third Estate cease, then, to attack the rights of the first two orders; rights which, no less ancient than the monarchy, must be as unalterable as its constitution; let it limit itself to requesting a reduction in the taxes by which it may be overburdened: then the first two orders, recognizing, in the third, citizens who are dear to them, could, by the magnanimity of their feelings, renounce prerogatives that have a monetary interest as their object, and consent to bear the public charges in the most perfect equality.

The undersigned princes ask to set the example for all those sacrifices that could contribute to the good of the state, and to the strengthening of the union of the classes that compose it.

Let the Third Estate foresee what, in the last analysis, could result from the infringement of the rights of the clergy and nobility, and from the confusion of the orders.

As a consequence of the general laws that govern all political constitutions, the French monarchy would necessarily degenerate into despotism, or would become a democracy: two kinds of revolution opposed to each other, but both disastrous.

Against despotism the nation has two barriers, Your Majesty's interest and his principles, and Your Majesty can be assured that true Frenchmen will always resist the idea of a government irreconcilable with the size of the state, the number of its inhabitants, the national character, and the innate sentiments that have always bound them and their fathers to the idea of a sovereign as to the idea of a benefactor.

The undersigned princes do not want to carry these reflections further; they have spoken only with sorrow about the misfortunes menacing the state; they will take more satisfaction in turning their attention to its resources.

Your Majesty, by his virtues rising above the commonplace viewpoints of sovereigns who are jealous and ambitious for power, has made concessions to his subjects not demanded by them; he has appealed to them to exercise a right whose use they had lost and almost forgotten. This great act of justice imposes very large obligations on the nation; it must not refuse to devote itself to a king who has devoted himself to it. The expenses of the state, sanctioned by the will of the public, must be supported with less regret; the royal power, better regulated and consequently more impressive and more paternal, must find zealous defenders in the magistrates, who in difficult times have always been the supports of the throne, and who know that the rights of kings and of the *patrie* are combined in the eyes of good citizens.

It will appear again with energy, this noble sentiment that has always marked the French people, this love for the person of their King, this affection that in monarchies is one of the resources of the government, and is fused with patriotism; this passion, this enthusiasm that has produced among us so many heroic and sublime actions, so many efforts and sacrifices that the laws could not have demanded.

The undersigned princes take pleasure in speaking to Your Majesty with the voice of sentiment; it seems to them that they should never speak otherwise to their sovereign.

Sire, all your subjects view you as a father; but it is particularly appropriate for the princes of the blood to give you this title; you have displayed these paternal sentiments to each of them, and their very recognition of this encourages the solicitations they make of Your Majesty.

Deign, Sire, to listen to the plea of your children, dictated by the most affectionate and respectful interest, and by the desire for public tranquillity and for maintenance of the power of the King who is most worthy of being loved and obeyed because he wants only the happiness of his subjects.

Signed: CHARLES PHILIPPE, LOUIS JOSEPH de BOURBON, LOUIS HENRI
     JOSEPH de BOURBON, LOUIS ANTOINE HENRI de BOURBON,
     LOUIS FRANÇOIS JOSEPH de BOURBON.

II.

The Surge of Opinion

---

5. January, 1789: Sieyès,
What Is the Third Estate?

This is the most famous pamphlet of the deluge that accompanied the writing of the *cahiers* and the preparations for the Estates General. It was written late in 1788, at the time of the meeting of the second Assembly of Notables, by a priest, Emmanuel Joseph Sieyès (1748–1836), and published anonymously in January, 1789. The first edition was a pamphlet of 127 pages. There were two more editions in 1789 and many later ones, including English and German translations. Nevertheless the pamphlet became rare in the nineteenth century, and in 1888 the Société de l'Histoire de la Révolution Française sponsored a critical edition, *Qu'est-ce que le Tiers État? par Emmanuel Sieyès précédé de l'Essai sur les privilèges. Édition critique avec une introduction par Edme Champion.*

Abbé Sieyès was both a major figure in the revolution and a theorist of representative government and political and social individualism whose influence on French thought was lasting. *What Is the Third Estate?* is a splendid document whose assumptions and arguments have great significance for contemporary history, social as well as political. Space limitations have necessitated cutting, but an effort has been made to include the key passages from each of the six chapters and to preserve all of the principal arguments. Deletions within a paragraph or within two adjoining paragraphs have been indicated by the usual device of placing three dots in the text. Where the deletion amounts to at least one whole paragraph, an extra line of space has been left between the passages. The source used is the Edme Champion edition.

What Is the Third Estate?

[Quotation after title omitted]
THE PLAN of this essay is fairly simple. We have three questions to ask:

1. What is the Third Estate? Everything.
2. What has it been thus far in the political order? Nothing.
3. What does it demand? To become something.

You will see whether the answers are correct. We shall then examine the measures that have been tried, and those that must be taken, in order for the Third Estate to become, in fact, *something*. Thus we shall say:

4. What the ministers have *attempted*, and what the privileged classes themselves *propose* in its favor.

5. What *should* have been done.

6. Finally, what *remains* to be done so that the Third may take its rightful place.

Chapter I. The Third Estate Is a Complete Nation

What is needed for a nation to exist and prosper? *Private* enterprise and *public* functions.

Private enterprise can be reduced to four categories. . . . Who sustains them? The Third Estate.

All public functions can likewise, under present circumstances, be classified under four well-known designations, Sword, Robe, Church, and Administration. It would be superfluous to examine them in detail in order to show that the Third Estate everywhere makes up nineteen-twentieths of them, with this difference, that it is burdened with everything really irksome, with all the duties that the privileged order refuses to undertake. Only the lucrative and honorific positions are held by members of the privileged order. Is that to their credit? For that it would be necessary either that the Third Estate had refused to take these posts or that it was less competent to carry out their functions. We know what the situation is; nevertheless the Third has been excluded. . . .

It is enough at this point to have made it plain that the pretended usefulness of a privileged order for public service is only vain imagination; that without it all that is tiresome in such service is done by the Third; that without it the higher positions would be infinitely better filled; that they should naturally be the prize and reward for talent and recognizable services; and that if the privileged have succeeded in usurping all the lucrative and honorific posts, it is both an injustice shocking to the majority of citizens and a betrayal of the public interest.

Who, then, would dare to say that the Third Estate does not contain everything needed to form a complete nation? It is like a strong, robust man one of whose arms is still enchained. If the privileged order were removed, the nation would not be something less, but something more. So, what is the Third Estate? Everything, but an everything shackled and oppressed. What would it be without the privileged order? Everything, but an everything free and flourishing. Nothing can function without it; everything would function infinitely better without the others. It is not enough to have shown that the privileged, far from being of use to the nation, can only enfeeble and harm it; it must still be proved that the noble order[1] is not in the social organization at all; that it can indeed be a *burden* to the nation but cannot be part of it. . . .

The noble order is no less a foreigner in our midst because of its *civil* and *public* prerogatives.

What is a nation? A body of associates living under a *common* law and represented by the same *legislature*.

Is it not all too certain that the noble order has privileges, exemptions, even rights distinct from the rights of the great body of citizens? Thereby it is apart from the common order, the common law. Thus its civil rights already make it a separate people in the great nation. It is truly *imperium in imperio*.

1. I am not speaking of the clergy. To my mind, it is not an order but a profession charged with a public service. (And it is precisely for this reason that it means something to us. If the clergy were only an *order*, it would not be a real thing. There are in a political society only private and public professions. Except for those, there are only fanciful tales or dangerous chimeras.) In this case, it is not the person who is privileged but the function, which is very different. If there are useless benefices in the Church, that is an abuse. All ecclesiastics must be of service, either in public instruction or in religious services. Because, before being admitted to the clergy, it is necessary to go through a long series of tests, that is no reason for regarding this body as a separate *caste*. This word can only mean a class of men without functions, and without usefulness, and who merely by existing enjoy personal privileges. According to this point of view, the true one, there is only one order, the nobility. That is truly a people apart, but a false people who, not being able, for lack of useful organs, to exist by itself, attaches itself to a real nation, like those vegetal tumors that can live only on the sap of plants, which they overtax and dry out. The Clergy, the Robe, the Sword, and the Administration are four classes of public representatives that are necessary everywhere. Why in France are they accused of *aristocracisme*? It is because the noble caste has usurped all the good posts; it has made them into patrimonial property, which it exploits, not in the spirit of social law but for its private profit.

As for its *political* rights, it exercises them separately also. It has its own representatives, who have no mandate of any kind from the people. . . .

The Third therefore includes everything that belongs to the nation; and everything not of the Third cannot be regarded as being of the nation. What is the Third? Everything.

CHAPTER II. WHAT HAS THE THIRD ESTATE BEEN UNTIL THE PRESENT TIME? NOTHING

. . . People are not free by virtue of privileges, but by virtue of the rights that belong to all.

If the aristocrats should, even at the cost of this liberty (thereby showing themselves to be unworthy of it), try to keep the people in a condition of oppression, the people will dare to ask by what right they do so. If the answer is by right of conquest, it must be admitted that this is going rather far back. But the Third need not fear to go back to past ages. It can appeal to the year preceding the conquest, and since it is today too strong to let itself be conquered, its resistance will no doubt be more effective. Why should it not send back to the forests of Franconia all those families who keep up the foolish pretension of being descendants of the race of the conquerors and of having succeeded to their rights? . . .

Let us pursue our objective. The Third Estate must be understood to mean all the citizens who belong to the common order. Everyone privileged by law, in whatever manner, is not of the common order, takes exception to the common law, and consequently does not belong to the Third Estate. As we have already said, a common law and a common representation are what make *one* nation. . . .

But here we have to consider the Third Estate less in its civil status than in its relations with the constitution. Let us examine its relation to the Estates General.

Who have been its so-called representatives? Persons who have been ennobled or temporarily privileged. It is even the case that these false deputies have not always been freely elected by the people. Sometimes in the Estates General, and nearly everywhere in the Provincial Estates, representation of the people is regarded as a right pertaining to certain public functions or offices. . . .

* * *

Sometimes people seem to be astonished at hearing complaints of a triple *aristocracy* of Church, Sword, and Robe. One could wish that this were only a manner of speaking, but the expression must be taken literally. If the Estates General are the interpreters of the general will and have by this token legislative power, is it not a clear case of aristocracy so long as the Estates General are merely a *clerical-noble-judicial* assembly?

To this frightening truth add the fact that, in one way or another, all the branches of executive power have also come into the hands of the class that peoples the Church, the Robe, and the Sword. A kind of fraternal spirit makes the nobles prefer each other to the rest of the nation, and in all things. The usurpation is complete; they actually reign.

Let history be read with a view to discovering whether the facts confirm or deny this assertion, and you will become convinced, as I have been, that it is a great mistake to believe that France is subject to a monarchical regime.

Delete from our annals a few years of Louis XI and Richelieu and several moments in the career of Louis XIV, when there was pure despotism, and you will believe you are reading the history of a *courtly* aristocracy. It is the court that has ruled, and not the monarch. It is the court that makes and unmakes, appoints and discharges ministers, creates and dispenses positions, and so on. And what is the court if not the head of this immense aristocracy that covers all parts of France, and which, through its members, attains to everything and everywhere has a hand in the essentials of all parts of the public business? And so the people in their complaints have been accustomed to distinguishing the monarch from the actual wielders of power. They have always regarded the king as a man so obviously deceived and so defenseless in the midst of an active and all-powerful court that they have never thought to blame him for all the evil done in his name.

Let us sum up: the Third Estate has not had up to the present time real representatives in the Estates General. Therefore its political rights are nonexistent.

Chapter III. What Does the Third Estate Demand?
To Become Something

One must not judge its demands from isolated observations of a few authors more or less educated about the rights of man. The Third Estate is still very backward in this respect, by which I mean not only in comparison with those who have studied the social order, but even in comparison with the mass of commonly held ideas that form public opinion. One can only come to appreciate the real complaints of this order by studying the formal demands addressed to the government by the large municipalities of the kingdom. What does one see there? That the people want to be *something*, and actually, they ask very little. They want to have real representatives in the Estates General, meaning deputies *drawn from their order*, who are capable of being interpreters of their wishes and defenders of their interests. But what would be the use of their being present in the Estates General if interests contrary to theirs were to predominate! Their presence would only sanction the oppression of which they would be the eternal victims. Therefore, it is indeed certain that they cannot come to the Estates General to vote unless they can have *influence at least equal to that of the privileged*, and they demand a number of representatives equal to those of the other two orders together.[2] Finally, this equality of representation would become perfectly illusory if each chamber had its separate vote. The Third therefore demands that the votes be taken *by head and not by order*. There you have the essence of the claims that have seemed to alarm the privileged, because the latter have thought their mere acceptance sufficient to make reform of abuses unavoidable. The real intention of the Third Estate is to have in the Estates General an influence *equal* to that of the privileged. I repeat, can the Third demand any less? And is it not clear that if its influence is less than equal it cannot hope to escape from its political nonexistence and become *something?*

But what is really unfortunate is that the three articles of the Third Estate's claim are not sufficient to give it the equality of influence that it cannot in fact do without. In vain will it get an equal number of representatives drawn from its order: the influence of the privileged will infiltrate and dominate even within the sanctuary of the Third. Who has the offices, the employment, the patronage to give? On which side is there need for protection? Which side has the power to protect? . . . And the nonprivileged

2. This second demand has just been granted, without comment concerning the third and with an outright refusal of the first. But is it not clear that the one cannot work without the other? They form a whole. To destroy one is to annul all three. We will say later whose business it is to pronounce on everything concerning the constitution.

who would seem from their talents to be the most suitable to uphold the interests of their order, are they not from childhood indoctrinated with a superstitious or compulsory respect for the nobility? It is well known how easy it is for men in general to submit to all the practices that can be useful to them. They think constantly of bettering their lot; and when personal industriousness does not advance them by honest means it impels them into false ways. Some ancient people or other, in order to accustom their children to violent or dexterous exercises, withheld food until they had succeeded or made an effort. In the same way, among us, the most capable class of the Third Estate has been forced, in order to obtain the necessities, to devote itself to the purposes of the powerful. This part of the nation has thereby come to compose something like a great antechamber where, occupied ceaselessly with what its masters say or do, it is always ready to sacrifice everything for the advantages it hopes to gain from the good fortune of pleasing them. . . .

In addition to the power of the aristocracy, which in France controls everything, and of that feudal superstition that still degrades most people's minds, there is the influence of property: this is natural; I do not reject it; but one must agree that it is still completely to the advantage of the privileged and that there is good reason to fear that they will benefit from its powerful support at the expense of the Third Estate. . . .

1. FIRST DEMAND

That the representatives of the Third Estate be chosen only from among citizens who really belong to the Third.

We have already explained that in order to belong to the Third in actuality it is necessary not to have been tarnished by any kind of privilege. . . .

It is argued, in addition, that to restrict the free choice of the voters is damaging to their liberty; I have two replies to make to this alleged difficulty. . . . Without doubt, the constituents must be left their entire liberty, and it is for that very reason that it is necessary to exclude from their number all the privileged, who are too much accustomed to dominating the people overbearingly.

My second reply is straightforward. You cannot have, in any fashion, a liberty or a right without limits. In all countries, the law has fixed upon certain characteristics without which one can be neither a voter nor eligible for office. Thus, for example, the law must determine the age below which one will be considered unsuitable for representing one's fellow citizens. Similarly women everywhere, for better or worse, are kept from this sort of representation. It is an established fact that a vagabond, a beggar, cannot be charged with the political mandate of the people. Would a servant or anyone dependent upon a master, or an unnaturalized alien, be allowed to appear among the nation's representatives? Thus political liberty, like civil liberty, has its limits. It is only a question of knowing whether the condition of noneligibility upon which the Third insists is as essential as all those that I have just indicated. Now the comparison is entirely in its favor; for a beggar, an alien, can be without any interest opposed to the interest of the Third. Whereas the noble and the ecclesiastic are in the nature of things partisans of the privileges from which they profit. . . .

As a result of these principles, members of the Third Estate who are too closely connected with the members of the first two orders must not be entrusted with the confidence of the commoners. . . . I demand especially that attention be given to the numerous agents of feudality.[3]

It is to the odious remains of this barbarous regime that we owe the division that still exists, unfortunately for France, among three orders hostile to each other. All would be lost if the mandatories of feudalism were able to usurp the function of representing the commoners.

In the eyes of some, the argument that we have just refuted was rescued by the observation that the Third Estate lacked members with enough enlightenment, courage, and so on, to represent it, and that it was necessary to seek help from the nobility. . . . This strange assertion does not merit an answer. Consider the classes *available* within the Third Estate—and like everyone else I mean by available classes those with sufficient wealth to receive a liberal education, cultivate their reason, and take an interest in public affairs. Those classes have no other interest than that of the rest of the people. See if they do not contain enough citizens

3. Innumerable vexations perpetrated by these agents still desolate the countryside. It can be said that the privileged order is followed by a retinue as damaging as itself. The tax collector, with his hundred arms, weighs no more heavily upon the people.

who are educated, honest, and worthy in every way to be good representatives of the nation. . . .

2. SECOND DEMAND OF THE THIRD

That its deputies be equal in number to those of the two privileged orders.

. . . Political rights, like civil rights, must be attached to the quality of citizen. This legal property is the same for all without regard to the greater or lesser amount of real property composing the fortune or possession of each individual. Every citizen who fulfills the conditions determined for electors has a right to be represented, and his representation cannot be a fraction of the representation of another. This right is unitary; all exercise it equally, just as all are equally protected by the law to whose making they have contributed. How can it be maintained, on the one hand, that the law is the expression of the general will, in other words of the plurality, and claimed at the same time that ten individual wills can balance a thousand particular wills? Does this not leave the way open to lawmaking by the minority, which is obviously contrary to the nature of things? . . .

In terms of population, it is well known what a great superiority the third order has over the first two. No more than anyone else do I know the exact relationship, but like everyone I will allow myself to make an estimate. . . .

Thus in all there are somewhat less than two hundred thousand privileged of the first two orders [footnote omitted]. Compare this number to twenty-five or twenty-six million and judge for yourself. . . .

In the days of Philip the Fair, a few good towns sufficed to provide for a chamber for commoners in the Estates General.

Since that time, feudal servitude has disappeared and the countryside has produced a numerous population of *new citizens*. Cities have grown in numbers and size. . . .

Think of how the former relationship of the orders to each other has changed from two sides at once; the Third, which had been reduced to nothing, has reacquired through its industry a portion of what the abuses of the stronger had taken from it.

Instead of demanding the return of its rights, it has consented to pay for them; they have not been restored to the Third, but sold back to it. But finally, in one way or another, it can take possession of them. It must not be ignorant of the fact that today it is the national reality whereas it used to be only the shadow; that during this long transformation the nobility has ceased to be the monstrous feudal reality that could oppress with impunity and is now its mere shadow, and that in vain this shadow still seeks to frighten an entire nation.

3. THIRD AND LAST DEMAND OF THE THIRD ESTATE

That the Estates General vote not by orders but by head. . . . There are surely abuses in France; these abuses benefit someone: it is scarcely the Third Estate to which they are advantageous, but it is certainly the Third to which they are harmful. Now I ask whether, given this state of affairs, it is possible to destroy any abuse as long as the *veto* is left in the hands of those who profit from it. All justice would be powerless; everything would have to wait upon the pure generosity of the privileged. Would that be what one thinks of as social order? . . . But could the three orders as they are now constituted join together to vote by head? That is the real question. No. According to true principles, they cannot vote *in common* either by head or by orders. Whatever proportion you adopt among them, it cannot fulfill the objective that is proposed, which would be to link together the totality of representatives by *one* common will. No doubt this assertion needs development and proofs: permit me to postpone them to the sixth chapter. . . .

CHAPTER IV. WHAT THE GOVERNMENT HAS ATTEMPTED AND WHAT THE PRIVILEGED PROPOSE TO DO FOR THE THIRD

. . . It is notable that the cause of the Third has been defended with more zeal and force by writers who are priests and nobles than by the nonprivileged themselves.

In the sluggishness of the Third Estate, I have seen only the characteristic silence and fear of the oppressed, which offers one proof more of the reality of the oppression. . . . I am not astonished that the first two orders have provided the earliest defenders of justice and humanity. The *talents* are related to the exclusive use of the intelligence and to habits of long duration:

there are a thousand reasons why members of the Third Estate must eventually excel; but *enlightenment* in the realm of public morality must first appear among men who are well positioned to grasp the major social relations and in whom natural initiative has been less commonly spoiled; for there are sciences having to do as much with the spirit as with the mind. . . .

Certainly the first two orders have good reason to restore the rights of the Third. One should not try to avoid the facts; the guarantee of public liberty can only be found where the real strength lies. We can only be free along with the people and with their aid.

If a consideration of such importance is beyond the reach of most of the French, owing to their frivolousness and narrow egoism, at least they cannot fail to be impressed by the changes in public opinion. The empire of reason is extended farther every day; more and more it requires the restitution of the rights that have been usurped. Sooner or later it will be necessary for all classes to be included within the boundaries of the social contract. Will the innumerable advantages of this development be reaped or will they be sacrificed to despotism? That is the true question. During the night of barbarism and feudality, the true relationships among men were destroyed, all nations overturned, all justice corrupted; but with the coming of dawn gothic absurdities must flee and the remains of outmoded ferocity must crumble to nothing. This much is certain. But will we merely change evils or will social order, in all its beauty, take the place of the former disorder? . . .

The privileged do not tire of saying that everything is equal among the orders from the moment that they renounce pecuniary exemptions. If everything is equal, what do they fear in the demands of the Third? Do they imagine that it wished to harm itself in attacking a common interest? If everything is equal, why all these efforts to prevent it from overcoming its political nullity?

Everything is equal! It is, then, from a spirit of equality that the Third has been sentenced to the most dishonorable exclusion from all positions and offices with the least distinction? It is from a spirit of equality that an excess of tribute has been wrenched from the Third in order to amass this prodigious quantity of resources of all kinds destined exclusively for what is called *the impoverished nobility?*

In all of the relationships that take place between our privileged and a man of the people, is not the latter assured of being oppressed with impunity precisely because if he dares to demand justice he has recourse only to the privileged? . . .

It is proposed that there be vote by head concerning taxes and everything related to them. No doubt it is desired that thereafter the orders retire to their chambers as to impregnable fortresses, where the commoners will deliberate without success and the privileged will revel without fear, while the minister will remain the master. But can anyone believe that the Third will fall into this trap? The requirement that voting of taxes be the last action of the Estates General will make it necessary to agree beforehand on a procedure for all the deliberations.

Different interests have had time to group themselves within the order of the nobility. They are on the verge of dividing into two parties. Those most closely related to the three or four hundred most distinguished families long for the establishment of an upper chamber like that of England; their pride is nourished by the hope of being no longer indistinguishable from the rank and file of gentlemen. Thus the higher nobility would gladly consent to see the rest of the nobles associating with ordinary citizens in a house of commons.

The Third will protect itself above all against a system that would at the very least tend to fill its chamber with people who have an interest so contrary to the common interest; against a system that would force it back into unimportance and oppression. In this respect there exists a very real difference between England and France. In England there are no privileged nobles except those to whom the constitution grants a part of the legislative power.[4]

All other citizens are mingled together, their interest being the same, since there are no privileges to group them into distinct

4. The lords of the upper chamber do not even form a distinct *order*. There is in England only a single order, the nation. The member of the chamber of peers is a great mandatary named by the law to exercise a part of the legislative power together with the highest judicial functions. He is not a man privileged by right of *caste* without regard to political functions, since the younger brothers of a peer do not share in his privileges. . . .

orders. If, then, it is desired to join the three orders in France into one, it will be necessary first to abolish every kind of privilege. It will be necessary for the noble and the priest to have no other interest than the common interest and to enjoy, by force of the law, no rights but those of simple citizens. Failing that, you will have joined the three orders together in vain; they will always be three heterogeneous substances impossible to amalgamate. Let no one accuse me of upholding the distinctions between the orders, which I regard as the worst possible creation from the point of view of the good of society. There would be only one thing worse: to amalgamate the orders *in name* while leaving them *really* separate by the maintenance of privileges. That would consecrate forever their victory over the nation. The public safety requires that the common interest of society be maintained somewhere in pure and unmixed form. And it is for this reason, the only good, the only national reason, that the Third will never lend itself to the confusion of the three orders in a so-called house of commons. . . .

I do not deny that the English constitution is an astonishing artifact considering the time when it was established. However, and although people are always ready to mock a Frenchman who does not prostrate himself before it, I will make bold to say that instead of seeing in it the simplicity of good order, I see there only a prodigious scaffolding of precautions against disorder.[5] . . .

No people, it is said, has done better than the English. And yet when that is granted, must the products of the art of politics at the end of the eighteenth century be no more than they were able to be in the seventeenth? The English were not beneath the level of the enlightenment of their time: let us not remain beneath the enlightenment of our time. That is the way to imitate while

---

5. In England the government is the subject of a continuous combat between the ministry and the aristocracy of the opposition. The nation and the king have there almost the appearance of simple spectators. The king's policy consists of always taking the side of the stronger party. The nation fears both parties equally. For its safety it is necessary that the combat continue; it therefore supports the feebler party in order to prevent its complete annihilation. But if the people, instead of allowing the management of its affairs to serve as a prize in this contest of gladiators, wished to take part in management itself by means of true representatives, can anyone believe in good faith that the great importance that is today attached to the *balance* of the powers would not disappear with an order of things that alone makes it necessary?

showing oneself to be worthy of good models. Above all, let us not be discouraged at finding nothing in history that can meet our needs. The true science of the state of society does not date from very long ago. Men constructed huts before being able to build palaces. There are good reasons why social architecture was slower in its progress than that multitude of arts that went so well with despotism.

Chapter V. What Should Have Been Done —Relevant Principles

[Quotation at head of chapter omitted]

In every free nation, and every nation must be free, there is only one way to terminate the differences which arise concerning the constitution. It is not to notables that one must have recourse but to the nation itself. If we are lacking a constitution, one must be made; the nation alone has the right to do so. If we have a constitution, as some insist, and it provides, as they claim, for the National Assembly to be divided into three deputations sent by three orders of citizens, the fact cannot be avoided, at least, that there exists, on the part of one of these orders, a claim so strong that it is impossible to take another step until it has been settled. Now whose responsibility is it to judge the validity of such claims? . . .

It is impossible to create a body for a purpose without giving it an organization, a structure, and laws that will oblige it to carry out the functions for which it is intended. This is what is called the *constitution* of this body. Without it, clearly, the body cannot exist. Thus it is also evident that every government that is established must have its constitution; and what is true of government in general is also true of all the parts that compose it. . . .

But who can say according to what design or interest a constitution could have been given to the *nation* itself? The nation exists before all else and is the origin of all else. Its will is always legal; it is itself the law. Before it and above it, there is only *natural* law. If we wish to form an exact idea of the succession of *positive* laws that can emanate only from the nation's will, we see in the first rank the *constitutional* laws, themselves divided into two parts: those regulating the organization and functions of the *legislative* corps and those determining the organization and functions of the various *active* corps. These laws are called *fundamental,* not in the sense of being capable of independence of the national will but because the bodies that exist and act by virtue of them cannot interfere with them. In each of its parts, the constitution is not the creation of the constituted power but of the constituent power. . . .

Not only is the nation not subject to a constitution, but it *cannot* be and *must* not be so subject, which amounts to repeating that it is not. . . .

In the first place, a nation can neither alienate nor deny itself the right to will: and whatever its will may be, it cannot lose the right to change it whenever its interest demands. In the second place, who is there to whom the nation could bind itself? . . . One must conceive of the nations upon the earth as individuals existing outside of the social bonds, or, as is sometimes said, in a state of nature. . . .

With the help of these explanations, we may answer the question that we set ourselves. It is evident that the parts of what you believe to be the French constitution are not in agreement with each other. Who, then, should resolve their differences? The answer is the nation, independent as it necessarily is of all positive forms. . . .

The *ordinary* representatives of a people are charged with exercising, according to the constitutional forms, that part of the common will that is essential to the maintenance of a good administration. Their power is limited to governmental affairs.

Extraordinary representatives will have whatever new powers the nation wishes to give them. Since a great nation cannot itself literally assemble every time that extraordinary circumstances might demand it, it must on these occasions confide to extraordinary representatives the necessary powers. . . .

The privileged, as one can see, have good reason to confuse ideas and principles in this manner. They will uphold today with intrepidity the contrary of what they asserted six months ago. At that time there was but a single cry in France: we had no constitution and we demanded that one be written.

Today not only do we have a constitution but if one is to believe the privileged it contains two excellent and unattackable dispositions.

The first is the division of the citizens into orders; the second is the equality of influence, for each order, in the formation of the national will. We have certainly already proved sufficiently that even if all these things did amount to a constitution the nation would still be capable of changing them. . . .

Individual wills are the only elements of the common will. It is not possible either to deprive the greatest number of the right to concur in its formation or to decree that ten wills are worth only one, whereas ten others are worth thirty. These are contradictions in terms, veritable absurdities.

If one abandons for a single instant this self-evident principle that the common will is the judgment of the plurality and not that of a minority, it is useless to speak in terms of reason. By the same token, one could decide that the will of a single person shall be called the plurality, and there is no longer any need either for the Estates General or for the national will, and so on . . . for if one will can be worth ten, why can it not be worth a hundred, a million, twenty-five millions? . . . Let us conclude that all principles are in perfect agreement that (1) only an extraordinary representation can change the constitution or give us one, and so on; (2) this constituent representation must be formed without regard to distinctions of orders. . . .

Thus there is no difficulty concerning the question what should have been done. The nation should have been convoked to send to the capital as deputies extraordinary representatives with a special mandate to regulate the constitution of the ordinary National Assembly. . . .

Chapter VI. What Remains to Be Done. Development of Several Principles

The time is past when the three orders, thinking only of defending themselves against ministerial despotism, were ready to join forces against the common enemy. Although it is impossible for the nation to profit from the present circumstances or to take a single step toward an improved social order without the Third Estate sharing in the benefits, nevertheless the pride of the two higher orders is irritated at seeing the great municipalities of the kingdom demand even the smallest part of the political rights that belong to the people. What did they want, then, these privileged who are so ardent to defend their superabundance, so prompt to prevent the Third Estate from obtaining the merest necessities of this kind? Did they mean for the regeneration of which they are so proud to be only for themselves? And did they wish to use the always unfortunate people only as a blind instrument for the extension and consecration of their aristocracy? . . .

In vain the Third Estate expected the collaboration of all classes to restore its political rights and the fullness of its civil rights; fear of seeing the abuses reformed inspires in the first two orders an alarm that outweighs their desire for liberty. Between liberty and a few odious privileges, they have chosen the latter. In their hearts they have discovered an affinity for the favors of servitude. Today they fear those very Estates General for which they called not long ago with so much ardor. . . .

For the Third Estate, moreover, it is no longer a question of being better off or remaining as it was. Circumstances no longer permit this choice; it is now a case of advancing or losing ground; of either abolishing or recognizing and legalizing iniquitous and antisocial privileges. Now it must be obvious how senseless it would be to consecrate, at the end of the eighteenth century, the abominable remains of feudalism. . . .

In vain one may close one's eyes upon the revolution that time and the force of things have operated; it is no less real. Formerly the Third Estate was made up of serfs and the noble order was everything. Today the Third is everything, and nobility is a word. But into the shelter of this word has slipped a new and intolerable aristocracy; and the people have every reason to want no more aristocrats.

In this situation, what remains for the Third to do if it wishes to take possession of its political rights in a manner useful to the nation? There are two means to this end. According to the first option, the Third should meet separately and not collaborate with the nobility and clergy at all, either voting by order or by head. . . . The Third alone, it may be said, cannot form the *Estates General*. Eh! So much the better! It will form a *National Assembly*. [Footnote omitted] . . .

I say that the deputies of the clergy and nobility have nothing in common with the national representation, that no alliance is possible of the three orders in the Estates General, and that, being unable to vote *in common*, they can do so neither by *order* nor by *head*. . . .

There is, according to a maxim of universal law, *no greater default than the absence of power*. As is well known, the nobility is deputized neither by the clergy nor by the Third. The clergy has no powers entrusted to it by the nobles or the commoners. From this it follows that each order is a distinct nation, which has no more competence to interfere in the affairs of the other orders than the Estates General of Holland or the Council of Venice, for example, has to vote in the Parliament of England. . . .

One must see in the light of the above that according to strict rule it is perfectly useless to seek a relationship or proportion by which each order must concur in the formation of the general will. This will cannot be *one* as long as you allow three orders and three representations to persist. . . .

It is an established fact that the deputies of the clergy and nobility are not representatives of the nation; they are thus incompetent to vote in its name. . . .

There you have enough to demonstrate the obligation that the Third Estate is going to have to form by itself alone a National Assembly, and to authorize, in the name of reason and equity, the claim that this order may have to deliberate and vote for the entire nation without exception. . . .

I have announced, for the Third, two means of securing the place in the political order that is due it. If the first, which I have just presented, appears to be a bit brusque; if it is thought that time should be allowed for the public to accustom itself to liberty; if it is believed that national rights, evident though they are, still have need, being under dispute even by the smallest possible minority, of a sort of legal judgment that, in a manner of speaking, solidifies them and consecrates them by a final sanction, I am certainly in favor of this; let us appeal the affair to the tribunal of the nation, the sole competent judge concerning all differences pertaining to the constitution. This is the second means open to the Third. . . .

* * *

I would terminate here my memoir on the Third Estate if I had undertaken only to suggest forms of conduct. . . . But I also set out to develop principles. . . .

It is necessary, in the first place, to understand clearly what is the object or end of the representative assembly of a nation; it cannot be different from what the nation itself would propose if it were able to meet and confer together in the same location. What is the will of a nation? It is the result of putting together all of the individual wills, as the nation is the assemblage of the individuals. It is impossible to conceive of a legitimate association that does not have for object the common security, the common liberty, and in the last analysis the public welfare. . . .

Let us observe that in the hearts of men there are three kinds of interests: (1) the kind wherein they resemble each other, which marks the proper limits of the common interest; (2) the kind for which an individual allies himself to several others only, which is a corporate interest; and (3) the kind for which each individual isolates himself, thinking only of himself, which is personal interest. The interest that unites a man to all of his co-associates is evidently the object of the will of all, and that of the common assembly. The influence of personal interest must have no place in the common assembly, and that is what happens, for its diversity provides its own remedy. The great difficulty arises from the kind of interest that unites a citizen to only a few others. This kind of interest permits them to concert their efforts, to league together; for its sake projects dangerous to the community are conceived and the most dangerous enemies of the public are formed. History is full of this truth.

Let no one be astonished, therefore, that the social order so rigorously requires that ordinary citizens not be permitted to organize themselves into *corporations*, and even insists that the holders of executive mandates, who in the very nature of things form true *corporate* bodies, renounce, while in office, election to the legislature.

Thus, and not otherwise, the common interest is assured dominance over private interests. Only on these conditions can one envisage the possibility of founding human associations based on the general advantage of the associates, and thereby account for the *legitimacy* of political societies.

The same principles impress upon us with no less force the necessity to constitute the representative assembly itself according to a plan that will not permit it to form an *esprit de corps* and degenerate into an aristocracy. . . .

But when, instead of paying homage to these first principles, so clear and certain, the legislator, on the contrary, himself creates corporations within the state, recognizes all those that are formed, and consecrates them with the power at his disposal; when finally he dares to call upon the most eminent, and consequently the most harmful, to share, under the appellation of *orders*, in the national representation, one is convinced that one is seeing an evil principle striving to spoil everything, ruin everything, and overturn all relationships among men. . . .

We know the real purpose of a National Assembly; it is not called to serve the private interests of citizens but only to consider their affairs all at once from the point of view of the common interest. Let us deduce from this fact the natural consequence that the right to be represented belongs to citizens only by virtue of the qualities common to them all, and not by virtue of those qualities that differentiate them.

The advantages which differentiate citizens from each other are *beyond* the essentials of citizenship. Inequalities of property and industriousness are like inequalities of age, sex, height, and so on. They do not detract from the *equality* of citizenship. These individual advantages are without doubt under the protection of the law; but it is not up to the legislator to create advantages of this nature, to give privileges to some and refuse them to others. The law grants nothing; it protects what already exists, up to the point where what exists begins to harm the common interest. At that point only are limits placed on individual liberty. . . .

The interests in relation to which citizens resemble each other are therefore the only ones that they can treat in common, the only ones concerning which and in the name of which they can claim political rights—that is, an active part in the formation of the social law—and therefore the only ones which endow a citizen with the quality of being *representable*. . . . It follows that corporate interests, far from having an influence in the legislature, can only arouse its suspicions; corporate interests are as opposed to the business of a legislature as they are foreign to its mission.

These principles become all the more rigorous when there is reference to privileged corporations and orders. I mean by privi-

leged any man who is outside of the common law, either because
he claims not to be subject *in its entirety* to the common law, or
because he claims to have *exclusive* rights. A privileged class is
harmful, not only by its *esprit de corps* but by its very existence.
The more it has obtained of these favors necessarily contrary to the
common liberty, the more it is essential to keep it separate from the
National Assembly. The privileged would be *representable* only
by virtue of his quality as a citizen; but in him this quality is
destroyed, he is outside of citizenship, and he is the enemy of rights
held in common. To give him a right to representation would
amount to a manifest contradiction in the law; the nation would not
have been able to submit to this except by an act of servitude
impossible to conceive.

I know that such principles will appear *extravagant* to most
readers. . . . My own role is that of all patriot writers; it consists
of presenting the truth. Others will approach it to a greater or
lesser degree according to their strength and to circumstances, or
may well draw farther away out of dishonesty; in that case we will
endure what we cannot prevent. If everyone were to think *the
truth*, there would be no difficulty about making even the greatest
changes if they offered socially useful objectives. What better can
I do than to aid with all my strength to spread this truth that pre-
pares the way? In the beginning it is ill-received; little by little it
makes its way into people's minds, public opinion takes shape, and
finally one begins to see *in practice* principles that one had at first
treated as insane chimeras. Concerning almost all kinds of prejudices, if writers had not been willing to pass for fools, the world
would today be less *wise*.

I meet everywhere the kind of moderates who would like the
steps toward truth to be made one at a time. I doubt their understanding when they speak in this way. They confuse the progress
of the administrator with that of the philosopher. The former
advances as best he can; provided he moves in the right direction,
one can only praise him. But this route must have been explored
to its end by the philosopher. He must have arrived at the terminus;
otherwise he would be unable to guarantee that this is really the
route that leads to that end. . . .

One would have to have a poor idea of the progress of reason to
imagine that a whole people must remain blind to its own interests
and that the most useful truths, existing only in a few people's heads,

must be revealed only to the extent that an able administrator needs to call upon them for the success of his operations. In the first place, this view is false because it is impossible to implement. In the second place, is it not known that the truth penetrates only very slowly into a large mass such as a nation? Must we not allow time for those whom the truth irritates to grow accustomed to it, for young people who receive it avidly to become something, and for old people to become nothing at all? In a word, must one await harvest time before sowing? It would never come.

Besides, Reason has no love for mystery; it acts only by means of a great expansion; only by striking everywhere does it hit the mark, because that is how that power of opinion is formed to which one must perhaps attribute most changes that are truly advantageous to mankind. . . .

Meanwhile it is impossible to say what place two privileged corporations should occupy in the social order: one may as well ask what place can be assigned, in the body of an invalid, to the malignant fluid that is undermining his health and tormenting him. It must be *neutralized;* the health and functioning of all the organs must be re-established sufficiently so that no more morbific combinations will form, capable of contaminating the most essential principles of vitality.

6. *February, 1789:*
Mounier on the Estates General

Jean Joseph Mounier (1758–1806) achieved prominence in Dauphiné in 1788 and at Versailles in the National Assembly in 1789. He was President of the National Assembly during the "October days" of 1789, but shortly thereafter went home to Grenoble from which he eventually escaped abroad. Mounier was a merchant's son whose well-to-do parents gave him a good education and bought him the office of royal judge in the common court of Grenoble. In 1788 he became a spokesman for prominent residents of Dauphiné, both noble and nonnoble, in their resistance to the government's efforts to discipline the parlement, and when the Estates General were summoned he became a deputy from Dauphiné and drafted the mandate that he and his fellow deputies took to Versailles. His book *Nouvelles observations sur les États-Généraux de France* (s.l., 1789, 284 pp.) was published toward the end of February, 1789, about a month after Sieyès's *Qu'est-ce que le Tiers État?* At Versailles, Mounier became the leader of the group known as Anglophiles because of their support for a royal veto and a legislature of two chambers; he was still, as in Dauphiné, trying to reconcile all classes in a program that would limit the absolute monarchy without making the nobles and clergy counterrevolutionary or relying very much on the unpropertied and uneducated masses. Mounier's final chapter of the *Nouvelles observations*, pp. 266–282, in which he may have been replying to Sieyès's more radical argument, is a fine example of how the situation appeared to a moderate early in 1789, and will serve as a description of Mounier's position in August and September, when he was most prominent, except that by then he was willing to be less specific about requirements for membership in the upper chamber. A few deletions of illustrative material and repetitions, amounting to about two pages, have been made.

I SHALL NOT BE so foolish as to think that the fundamental bases of the constitution must be laid down slowly; we must profit from the favorable moment, for liberty is like fortune; it easily escapes from the indolent. People who have glimpsed it and been too cowardly to fly to meet it are condemned to eternal regret and to the world's scorn. Frenchmen, make haste to build the foundations of a constitution in the torrent of despotism while its flow is still diminished!

But once the rights of the monarch and of the people have been solemnly announced, it then becomes very important, for the preservation of these rights, to make the formation of new laws more difficult, to guarantee the prerogatives of the crown, and to choose other means which, without binding the sovereignty so tightly that it cannot act, nevertheless maintain the constitution and forestall too frequent and hasty changes. . . .

Order and peace cannot exist in a large kingdom if the prince does not have at his disposal great power with which to see that the laws are obeyed. The executive power must therefore be entirely in the hands of the monarch: but this power would not be enough to guarantee the independence of the crown and the maintenance of its prerogatives. When the constitution has been finished, it is essential, in order to make impossible all changes prejudicial to the rights of the throne, that no law be established without the free consent of the royal authority and that a refusal on the part of the prince be able to defeat any proposal.

There is no hiding the fact that France cannot expect to enjoy forever the good fortune it is experiencing today. How can one hope for the continuation in future centuries of this unity of will and sentiments that exists between the monarch and the people? If ministers were to abuse the royal authority, might not the conflicts of the two powers, of the prince and of the representatives of the people deliberating in a single body, become too frequent, and might not the rights of the throne be insufficiently guaranteed?

The power of the monarch is so essential to the happiness of the people and it is of such great importance to impede everything that might alter the constitution that the creation of two chambers seems to me to be necessary; one would be formed of representatives of the nation, and the other by a supreme magistrature that the nation itself would have established. No law would be valid without the consent of the prince and of the two chambers.[1]

After having demonstrated the danger of the separation of the orders, one is aware that such separation must not be proposed for the two chambers. Neither would I propose to proportion the representation of the three orders; although joining them together forestalls the harmful effects of mutual suspicion and rivalry, it does not prevent them from calculating their respective strengths, and I would never believe the reconciliation to be really sincere among rivals who were forever obliged to prepare for attack or defense.

After having destroyed all pecuniary privileges, abolished exclusions that have been in operation against nonprivileged citizens, and subjected all the prince's subjects equally to the authority of the laws, we must, if we wish to enjoy liberty for any length of time, renounce this unfortunate mistrust that divides the orders; and we must see in a gentleman merely a citizen who has been decorated, who is as interested as the most obscure of men in resisting arbitrary power, demanding good laws, and remaining free.

Then, as in the early Estates General, the people will be able to choose for their representatives citizens of the upper orders when they have merited their confidence; but it would be futile and dangerous to wish to assign a certain number of deputies to each order; for since the members of the first two orders would already be able to represent the people, such an added precaution would only serve to maintain their *esprit de corps* and to make it all the

---

1. The provincial estates being charged with nothing but administration, there would be many inconveniences and no advantages in dividing them into two chambers.

more dangerous in that they would always have, by this means, a more advantageous representation.

Would it not be more just, more in conformity with true principles, if no attention were paid to a citizen's rank, and if, to be admitted to the chamber of representatives, he needed no other title than the confidence of the inhabitants of a district? In that case, all of the French would consider themselves to be brothers and the barbarous designations of *commoners* and *Third Estate* would disappear. One would recognize only noble or ecclesiastical or nonnoble citizens; all would have the same right to the votes of electors.

Since gentlemen ordinarily enjoy larger fortunes and have more leisure and independence, they would be able to devote themselves with success to the study of administration and could hope to distinguish themselves by their patriotism in the national assemblies; that being the case, they could be elected in large numbers, and since their nomination would not be compulsory, no one would have the right to complain of it; they would not be elected as nobles but as citizens; they would owe the preference with which they were being honored to their enlightenment and their virtues and not to their birth, since all citizens could compete for the same selection. It is thus that the baronets or knights, the squires, and the gentlemen defend the interests of the people in the Commons of England, without their social positions ever making them suspect to their constituents.[2]

The first chamber should be formed of members as interested in supporting the rights of the crown as in opposing despotism. It should be neither in the dependence of the monarch nor in that of the representatives of the people. The princes of the blood belong to the fatherland; they are the guardians of the throne to which they have the right to succeed; they have an interest in opposing arbitrary power; the princes of the blood who, a number of times, have voted in the Estates General, could be birthright members in the upper chamber; the same right would be granted the chancellor, the hereditary peers, and the marshals of France. To them would be added a number of members of the clergy and nobility elected in the various parts of the kingdom.

Deputies of the higher courts of justice could be permitted to

2. If one were to insist on maintaining a proportion in the representation of the orders, it would then become indispensable, in order to prevent the inconveniences of their separation, to give an equal influence to the privileged and to the commoners in the two chambers.

meet with that chamber and voice opinions when it was necessary to examine the inconveniences or advantages of new laws.

Every man who was a noble, were it for a single day, would be eligible to the upper chamber; even an ordinary citizen could be appointed to the peerage if the monarch thought him worthy of it. It would indeed be absurd that anyone who acquired sufficient glory to honor his family should be less honored than his descendants and that the king should be unable to place in the first rank a citizen who should have merited the promotion by outstanding virtues or important services.

Thus the first chamber would not be at too great a distance from the other citizens, since by being ennobled any subject of the monarch could be admitted, and since the brothers and the children of the members could vote only in the chamber of representatives. [Footnote omitted.]

It would even be possible to grant to the holders of several important offices—for example, to a certain number of state councilors—the right to sit in the upper chamber, and these places could be occupied by nonnoble citizens; for in forming the constitution it will be agreed that it is a violation of the social pact to exclude from office citizens who are not favored by birth and fortune.[3]

There will be no reason for alarm at the power conferred upon the upper chamber if it is remembered that, being created by the constitution, it will place no obstacles in the way of the reestablishment of order and the reform of abuses.

In order not to give this chamber too much of an aristocratic tendency, it should be kept smaller than that of the representatives; it could have the right to consent to taxes or oppose them, but it should not have the right to propose them or to make any change in the laws on this subject, which would always be written in the chamber of representatives. It is known that this device is the great resource of the English Commons.[4]

3. One must not insist that places or employment be guaranteed to the Third Estate; they must be satisfied by not being excluded.
4. Since one must guard oneself against malignity, I shall make the observation that it would take a great deal of ignorance and bad faith to find any resemblance between this first chamber and the Cour Plénière proposed in the month of May, 1787 [sic], which caused so much indignation in the French people. Circumstances and our present situation would not permit identification of the upper chamber in France with the upper chamber in England. But how could it be compared with the Cour Plénière? It would

According to what we have just said, it is easy to see that the upper chamber would not be a device for representing the upper orders, since all citizens would be represented in the second chamber; therefore there would not be the inconveniences of the separation of the orders, which, by destroying the union among citizens, leaves them without defense against the efforts of despotism; but the first chamber would be devoted to the defense of the rights of the crown and the maintenance of the constitution.

These two chambers would procure for France an invaluable advantage, one of the best assets to be found in the constitution of England; this would be the judgment of state crimes following their denunciation and prosecution in the chamber of representatives. . . .

I must present some thoughts that may allay the fears of those who might believe public liberty to be in danger if the representatives of the people were to be chosen indiscriminately from all classes, the privileged as well as the other citizens.

Would not the confidence of the inhabitants of a district—that is, of all the orders joined together for the elections—be a sure guarantee of the integrity of a gentleman elected to the Estates General? . . .

The representatives exercise only a power that comes from the electors. When all classes participate in the elections, it is the people who are made powerful, since it is the master of the choices. To limit the number of those to whom it can give its confidence is to diminish its rights and curtail its liberty.

Finally, the French will not have a beneficial and durable constitution until the time when there will no longer exist any differences of interest between the nobles and the other citizens; when the people will be able, without inconvenience, to call upon gentlemen to represent them; when persons who live on independent means and have no profession will try to merit their suffrage, and will not blush to present themselves as candidates and run the risk of not

---

not be created until after the reform of the principal abuses and the re-establishment of the public liberty. It could not destroy the latter, since it would never have the right of decision without the consent of the representatives of the people, whereas the Cour Plénière, entirely formed of members chosen by the royal authority, and closely dependent upon it, would have been the sole depositary of the rights of the nation and would have had no other power but that of sacrificing them to despotism.

being elected, and will be eager to serve their *patrie* without any salary. Only then will our national assemblies be able to meet as frequently as needed to safeguard the well-being of twenty-four million people.

Those who would like to oppose such a division of the chambers as I have proposed must reflect that the separation of the orders would have all of the inconveniences, as well as additional ones that would be much worse, and would not have any of the same advantages. But whatever one's judgment concerning this proposition, I believe that I have at least proved that the coming Estates General will be useless if the orders are not joined together and the votes counted by head. They will determine after that the forms to be followed in the future.

Since it is clear that deliberation by head can alone procure a constitution for us, we must therefore either accept this form or resign ourselves to remaining slaves of the ministers and the aristocracy. Good citizens will not think it possible to hesitate. They will judge that to become free they must risk the so-called inconveniences of deliberation by head; that the worst of evils is to languish in servitude after having had the hope of liberty: but they will soon be convinced that these inconveniences are only chimeras; that under a beneficent and beloved king, under a minister who has merited the public confidence, the representatives of the nation can desire neither anarchy nor the dishonor of the throne.

Have those happy days come, then, that I have so much desired, when the royal authority would have a more solid support than the terror inspired by arbitrary orders, when the monarch would no longer be reduced to wishing impotently for the happiness of his people, when their common well-being would rest on the foundation of a wise constitution? Would we be worthy of possessing it? Ah! If one listens to the voice of private interest, how many obstacles will stand in the way of its establishment! What efforts will be concerted to stifle it at birth! How many men are saying that they are satisfied with the present constitution; that is, that they are satisfied with not having one at all! How many men have an interest in keeping all the abuses; so many courtiers, so many lesser agents of despotism, and those who are getting rich from the finances, and this so numerous army of men of the law, who encircle the frightful labyrinth of our legislation and who profit from its obscurity! . . .

* * *

Will those for whom fate has reserved the splendors of rank and fortune be so blinded by prosperity as to fear better laws? Would they not find any advantage in a constitution which, while denying them the means of harming the liberty of their fellow citizens, would shelter their own from any attack? Do they not understand, then, that the most elevated posts in a country subjected to a despotic regime can guarantee neither honor nor property nor life? Has not injustice often chosen its victims from among the most illustrious persons? Is there a single family that cannot cite such cases among its members?

But I see that you count sufficiently on the favors of the strong so that you do not fear their unreliability; would you forget the interest of your brothers or your children? Do you believe it possible to assure them permanent possession of the places and the wealth that you are enjoying today, and do you wish, in opposing the public welfare, to become the artisans of the misfortune of your descendants?

If you are insensitive to all the ills of other men, reflect on what you are. The brilliance that surrounds you, the slaves that you make tremble with a glance, the base protégés who flatter your passions, can they make you happy, then? With your scorn of the opinion of a dishonored people, with your belief that you are above criticism, what restraint guarantees you against corruption? Whatever your power may be, are you not always obliged to crawl in the presence of men more powerful than you? And in spite of the brilliant appearances that are imposing to the multitude, what are you other than decorated slaves to whom their masters allow liberty to oppress more feeble slaves?

Know the price of a constitution; it will not deprive you in any way of the advantages that are derived from birth and wealth: but the ordinary citizen will be less humiliated; he will fear the laws and not men; the esteem of your fellows will become for you a thousand times more precious; you will attempt to merit their love and their respect; you will be virtuous, you will be distinguished, and above all you will be free.

7. March 1, 1789:
Parish Cahiers of Écommoy and Mansigné

To read even a few *cahiers* is to enter a world of labyrinthine complexity and variety, much of which was to be swept away by the revolution, to be remembered with hostility or affection and named the old regime as soon as awareness of change caught up with events. The *cahiers* suggest this world, and although they do not tell everything about it they remain one of the most comprehensive sets of observations ever collected about any society. The difficulty lies in making use of these sources, which reflect in variety the world that produced them. One can read and read, accumulating impressions, or await the results of computerized questioning; but meanwhile a particular *cahier*, like any document, can provide the satisfaction of knowing that this much, at least, existed.

To begin with the parish *cahiers* of Écommoy and Mansigné is to seek the grass roots in a part of the old province of Maine, in west central France, part of which became the department of the Sarthe during the revolution. In the center of the Sarthe is Le Mans, which is a little more than halfway between Paris and Nantes. Écommoy and Mansigné are in the farming country below Le Mans, an area of mainly small holdings, walled or hedged, producing various grains and some wine. In 1789 they were electoral districts at the lowest level; they were parishes, each with some five hundred or fewer households, whose taxpaying heads of families were entitled to write a *cahier* and send it with several delegates to the more important meeting at Château-du-Loir, to the southeast of them, where all local *cahiers* would be combined into a general *cahier* and all local delegates would choose deputies to represent the Third Estate of the Château-du-Loir electoral district in the Estates General at Versailles. Château-du-Loir was the chief town of a *sénéchaussée*, and the old low-level judicial jurisdictions called *sénéchaussées* and *bailliages* had been made the electoral districts for the Estates General for all three estates. The *cahiers* of Écommoy and Mansigné below are from *Cahiers de doléances du tiers état de la sénéchaussée de Château-du-Loir pour les États Généraux de 1789, publiés par Paul Bois* (Gap, 1960), pp. 26–28, 33–36. They have been chosen for translation because they were neither very conservative nor very radical and were apparently not much influenced by the "model" *cahiers* that were circulating in their area.

Écommoy. Cahier.

1. That the people of mortmain possess a large part of the landed property of our parish, without any help on their part even in times of calamity for the relief of the poor who are in great numbers here.[1]

2. The leases which the men of mortmain give reduce the worth of farms rented from them to well below their true value, and in addition they require payment in advance of huge gratuities, an abuse very detrimental especially in the parishes where the land tax is arbitrary.

3. We beg the king to remove from the clergy the liberty of taxing itself, wanting it to be taxed in the same way as the Third Estate.

4. We likewise desire that all nobles exploiting their domains be taxed in the same way as the Third Estate, and other privileged people as well.

5. That in this parish there is a postmaster who exploits a large number of fields, some his own and some farmed on shares, for which he is not made to pay the land tax, and it is demanded that he be included in the taxes of the Third Estate.

6. It would be very important if the Assembly of the Estates General would concern itself with the salt tax the more so as it forces even the poor to take salt and it would be desirable for it to be reasonable in price.

7. One finds no less burdensome the taxes that are levied generally on all the beverages indispensable to the life of man.

8. And as the maintenance of the main roads is very onerous, it is desired that the responsibility of the parish be limited.

9. In short, we would hope, if it were possible, for everything to be brought together into one and the same tax.

Determined at Écommoy, this March 1, 1789.

[Articles added, probably after reviewing the *cahier*]

10. That without the men of mortmain and the nobles and all the privileged being included in the taxes, it seems inescapable that the Third Estate could not by itself make up the deficit and fulfill the intentions of His Majesty.

11. It would be desirable also that finance be suppressed, con-

---

1. This is a reference to Church properties whose revenues went elsewhe and were not at the disposal of the local curé.—Editor.

sidering that it involves much money when these gentlemen ply their trade, whether for [the taxing of] noble properties in the possession of commoners or for the hundredth *denier* and collateral inheritors and also the office of process-server-appraiser in view of the trouble that it causes in family inheritances, and especially in cases where there is a minority it often involves more money than the inheritance itself.

Mansigné. Cahier.

The inhabitants of Mansigné observe and remonstrate:

1. That since the first two orders of the State do not admit as their deputies persons of a different order, the Third Estate must also choose its deputies to the Estates General only from its own order; in acting otherwise one would diminish noticeably the influence of the Third Estate and increase that of the clergy and nobility; for whatever confidence one might have in the sentiments of the nobles whom the Third Estate elected as deputies, it would be possible for the deputies, or each one individually, to prefer the interests of their order to those of their constituents.

2. That the deputies of the Third Estate, whether in the Assembly of the three Estates of the Province, or in the Estates General, must insist that the votes be counted by head and not by order. For if they were counted by order, either of two things could happen: either the combined votes of the two orders would prevail over those of the Third, or a single order could prevent by its opposition the result of the deliberations of the two others.

In the first case, the interests of the clergy and nobility being linked together more closely than with those of the Third Estate, to which they are often actually opposed, it could happen that the influence of the Third would become worthless, or nearly worthless; especially in matters of taxation, and also in matters concerning the liberty of individual citizens.

In the second case, a single order being able to oppose the deliberations of the other two joined together, affairs could drag on inconclusively; it would be possible for there to be no agreement on the most essential matters, such as taxes or legislation, and for everything to remain in disorder and confusion, as has happened in most of the preceding assemblies of the Estates General.

3. That the honors possessed by the first two orders must be preserved but that the Third must not be debased nor fall into the

humiliating position it occupied in the last Estates General in 1614; the deputies of this order must be effective in their opposition to any such humiliation in case there should be any attempt to renew it.

4. That the debts of the State must be paid off, but that the Estates General must first look into the actual state of the finances, in order to give advice both concerning the taxes necessary for acquitting the debts and meeting the other needs of the State, and concerning the most simple and least onerous means of collecting those taxes.

The real, or land, tax, and that on objects of consumption (except those of basic necessity) are the fairest and the most natural. The personal tax is the most unjust, the worst of all, because it is impossible to make an assessment proportionate to the means and faculties of each of the taxpayers.

5. That the Estates General must not grant any tax or subsidy unless beforehand all other matters that must be dealt with in the Estates relative to the reformation of abuses, to legislation or otherwise, have been agreed upon and defined, and certain and effective resolutions have been taken on all of them; except, however, for the granting of a temporary tax in a case of urgent and essential necessity.

6. That one must demand and insist that the Assembly of the Estates General henceforth be held periodically and that the interval from one assembly to the next be set in the coming assembly.

7. That taxes not be granted in perpetuity nor for long periods of time but only for the interval from one assembly of the Estates to that which will follow immediately.

8. That the clergy, instead of taxing themselves via the *décime*, pay, like the other orders of the State, the twentieth tax on their property or such other real tax as might be substituted for the twentieth; without any distinction or prerogative in that respect.

The clergy do not constitute a corps extraneous to the State; they are its citizens like the other two orders, and they must support its expenses in proportion to the property they possess.

Besides, clergymen are incorporated for the enlightenment of the people, for teaching them as much by their actions and example as by their words, and they will never succeed better in securing the confidence of the people and in fulfilling their spiritual function than by giving, through their justice and their disinterestedness, unequivocal proofs of their patriotism.

That if, notwithstanding these reasons, it were impossible to get the clergy to pay the same property tax as the other citizens, one must insist effectively that in each diocese the amount of *décimes* with which the diocese is charged, and the revenue of each benefice that is is assessed, be shown, in order that each taxpayer who might claim unjust treatment be able to claim overassessment.

The curés, especially those who enjoy moderate revenues and are at the head of a numerous flock, should, having regard to their obligations and to the number of poor in their parishes, be taxed more moderately than any other beneficiary.

However, in the present state of affairs most of the curés have no idea of the amount of *décimes* due from their diocese, nor the total revenues of the benefices of the diocese, do not know to what point they can be taxed, and consequently cannot appeal to have their taxes reduced.

9. Ecclesiastical property was originally destined for the subsistence of the clergy and the poor.

In many country parishes, the clergy possess tithes and other substantial assets; since he does [they do] not reside in the area, most of the revenues from these benefices leave the parishes and are consumed elsewhere. From that arises the poverty of the countryside, the lack of resources for procuring work for the poor; thus public roads are neglected, and for a part of the time unusable; hence, finally, the difficulty of transporting merchandise or commodities to neighboring markets.

It would therefore be reasonable for a portion of the revenues from these ecclesiastical properties, the amount to be determined in the Estates General, to be used in the places where the benefices are located, for public works in which the poor of the area would be employed.

10. That gleaning on the part of vicars be absolutely abolished in the parishes where it still exists, and that the tithe collectors be obliged to pay livings to vicars in sufficient number, taking into consideration the number of inhabitants in the parishes even where the said tithe collectors are not accustomed to paying livings.

And since in a number of parishes there are several tithe collectors who have their legal actions committed to different tribunals, it is demanded that all privileges of this sort cease and that the curé and inhabitants be able to proceed against the tithe collectors before the royal judge of the area in question in order to be able to sue in the courts where the said tithe collectors would have their cases committed.

11. That there be given to the provincial administrations the same degree of stability and the same functions as in the Estates of provinces that have Provincial Estates; and that the Third always have in these administrations a number of representatives chosen from its order equal to that of the other two orders combined.

12. That every office and employment whose usefulness would not be recognized be suppressed, while allowing the present holders to retain during their lifetimes the honors attached to the said offices; and that the price be reimbursed to them not on the basis of financial receipts but on the basis of its evaluation under the terms of the Edict of 1771.

13. That the salt tax especially—that tax most disastrous of all for the people—be abolished and converted into some other equivalent tax, the collection of which would be simpler, less of a burden to the people, and less expensive: or if present circumstances rule out this suppression, that at least all possible alleviations be brought to it, and that the people cease to be subjected to odious visits and searches on the part of its employees.

14. The nobles have the privilege of exploiting their domains to the extent of two plows' work without paying the land tax; but as a greater or lesser area can be farmed with two plows according to the nature of the terrain, and the strength and number of work animals, there often result from this ambiguity substantial abuses to the detriment of inhabitants subject to the land tax.

It would therefore be interesting to determine the number of *arpents* of land that nobles can exploit without being subject to the land tax.

15. The horse guards are exempt from the head tax and have in addition the privilege of being taxed *ex officio*. Their exemption from the head tax should be set at a positive sum and they should, without preference for the surplus, pay the land tax along with others subject to it, proportionately to the land they farm.

There are several other subjects and abuses about which the said inhabitants would have been able to make their observations and remonstrances if the scarcity of time had not hindered them, and which can be made by their deputies to the assembly of the seneschalsy of Château-du-Loir, who are given full powers in this respect.

8. March 14, 1789:
Cahier of the Nobility of Crépy

When nobles elected their deputies to the Estates General, they did so in a single meeting for the entire electoral district (*bailliage* or *sénéchaussée*). The *bailliage* of Crépy-en-Valois, in the Paris basin about 28 miles north and slightly east of the capital, had been a part of the old *comté* of Valois from which the line of French kings prior to the Bourbons took its name. Besides being an administrative center, Crépy had many religious institutions, including several important churches, two convents, two priories, and a *collège*. The following *Cahier de la noblesse du bailliage de Crépy* (s.l.n.d., 15 pp.) was published as a pamphlet.

THE DEFENSE of the country is the principal duty of the Nobility. Summoned today along with the other Orders to seek a remedy for the ills that threaten the Kingdom, it will take care to respond to the views of a benevolent monarch.

Loyalty, patriotism, and love for its King will dictate its resolutions.

It has no intention, in seeking the happiness and glory of the State, except the most fraternal cooperation with the other Orders, and the sacrifices that will give notice of its zeal.

Imbued with these sentiments, the Order of the Nobility declares that it renounces all pecuniary privileges, with special reservation only of honorific distinctions and prerogatives, which are a true form of property confirmed by the laws of the monarchy; but that, in order not to obstruct any suffrages, it is essential that voting be by Order.

And in case the assembled representatives of the Nation should decide otherwise on this subject or propose to establish a new constitution, it is of utmost necessity, in order to preserve the liberty of the three Orders, that, although assembled together according to a majority vote taken separately by each of the Orders, each of the aforesaid Orders be free to withdraw in order to deliberate separately on the points that will concern it particularly, and that the majority of votes in each of the Orders be set at three-fourths.

And considering that the Estates General, assembling to regenerate the constitution of the monarchy, is going to concern itself with great questions that must be deliberated with all the wisdom owing to the Nation in view of its confidence in its deputies, [the Order of the Nobility] draws up its complaints and petitions as follows:

1. That no general and permanent law may be decreed except with the consent of the three Orders, under the express sanction of the paternal authority of the King. Consequently, the draft of every law proposed shall be made available so that each deputy may take a copy of it, ponder it separately, weigh its advantages and disadvantages, and so that it can be adopted only after a delay proportionate to its importance.

2. That the Estates General consider how to make the capitalists pay taxes in proportion to their affluence and luxury.

3. That Nobility no longer be purchasable; that it be obtainable only through useful and distinguished services.

4. That venality of offices be suppressed; that the civil and criminal code be reformed; and that it is important for another penalty to replace that of banishment, which only gives the criminal a new theater for his crimes.

5. That the *capitaineries* be suppressed; that in preserving the game preserves, there be made a law which, contrived with sagacity, checks the abuses which arouse almost universal complaints.

6. That in preserving for the gentlemen of mortmain this same property, they may permit hunting only by guards clothed with their identifying shoulder belts.

7. That there be made a regulation concerning seigneurial monopolies which, in repressing the abuses of the obligations involved, does not attack property rights.

8. That rights concerning tolls, justified or usurped, be, after mature consideration, redeemed or suppressed.

9. That to improve cultivation and give to a greater number of families an easier subsistence, the same [renting] farmer not be permitted to work more than an amount of land requiring four plows, unless a larger amount belongs to the same proprietor and is all a part of the same farm.

10. That the leases granted by usufructuaries, holders of benefices, or heirs of entailed properties run their full terms, notwithstanding transfers of the properties.

11. That, in order to prevent the threatened scarcity of wood, new plantings be encouraged by exemption from all taxes for thirty years.

12. That the lot of curates and vicars conform more to the decency and obligations of their status.

13. That needy Nobility find in the assistance of the Nation the return for services that their ancestors rendered to the *patrie*, and that presentation by the Provincial Estates (about which more will be said later), who are incorruptible judges of the resources of the three Orders, be the governing consideration in admissions to the military schools, House of Saint-Cyr, and other such establishments.

14. That beneficed clergymen be held to a more strict residence, their absence being a formal breach of the intention of the founders, who concerned themselves with the poor.

15. That the salaries of Governors, provincial military commanders, and so on, result in advantage to the provinces, which their presence must invigorate.

16. That begging be suppressed, and that indigence be prevented by useful work projects.

17. That since a passion for gambling has made dangerous progress in spite of police regulations, there be pronounced rigorous penalties against the offenders; observing that there is a sort of gambling still more dangerous, although it is authorized by the State, the gambling of the royal lottery. By its devices, it seems to reach fortunes of all sizes; this game sets traps for the greed of men already wealthy; the decision of chance often upsets their contrivances and punishes them, but it presents an insidious kind of hope to the indigent, and through the caprices of fortune the ruin of this speculator is achieved.

18. That the periodical return of the Estates General, recognized as necessary, be fixed at an interval of three years.

19. That an intermediary commission be established, chosen from among the deputies of the three Orders of the Estates General, and that the very limited powers that will have been conferred upon it lawfully cease at the periodic return every three years.

20. That the Provincial Estates contemplated by His Majesty himself for the good of his people be established at an early date and organized in such a manner that, "to form a lasting bond between the individual administration of each province and the

general legislation, they have a close relationship with the intermediary commission of the Estates General."

21. That henceforth the Estates General enjoy the constitutional
right to determine the appanages of the Princes by means of a
pension suitable to the dignity of their rank.

22. That in case of the misfortune of a regency or a minority
the law require that the Estates General be convoked immediately.

23. That the King's domains can be alienated but never exchanged, and that the possession of things already alienated be
confirmed.

24. That the King alone have the right to dispense pardons and
pensions, that their volume be determined, and that these under-
takings be made public every year, so as to announce to the Nation
the justice of the Sovereign and the recompenses for merit.

25. That the Estates General see about the replacement of the salt
tax by a means less onerous for the people.

26. That for the sake of the liberty and ease of commerce,
which is languishing under the vexatious annoyances caused by the
customs barriers, the latter be suppressed, and that the tariff walls
which [so-called] foreign provinces establish in the midst of the
Kingdom be moved back to its farthest frontiers.

27. That no loan may be floated without the agreement of the
three Orders.

28. That no tax or subsidy may be consented to except by the
three Orders, and then only until the following session of the
Estates General.

29. That after a mature examination of the debt of the clergy,
the Estates General concern itself with ways to pay it off.

30. That *lettres de cachet* be suppressed, as damaging to the
liberty of citizens, who must be protected, restrained, and punished
by the law.

31. That the liberty of the press have limits that reassure the
citizen concerning his individual tranquillity, and the public concerning the general good.

32. That the Estates General discuss the question of the utility
of granaries of abundance in each province.

33. That since the failures and bankruptcies that have caused
very frequent disorders for several years seem to have been encouraged by impunity, by stays of execution, and by the commissioners to whom jurisdiction over these failures has been given,
private considerations that too often have sheltered criminals from

the opprobrium with which they should be covered, it is essential that such offenses against the State or against society be repressed by the judges who have legal jurisdiction over them.

34. That the Nation, alarmed by the dimly known state of the finances, cannot, however, despair of the fate of the *patrie* when it is summoned to provide for its security. The wasteful mismanagement of the finances can have come only from the incompetence or unfaithfulness of the almost ephemeral ministers who, through criminal abuse of their power, have taken advantage of the King's goodness, disrupted the provinces, and armed citizens against citizens.

That, being justifiably indignant against them, the Nation would have the right to investigate their conduct; but that, learning from its King to practice clemency, it stifles its resentment, limiting itself to demanding, in order to prevent similar abuses, that the ministers henceforth be responsible to the Nation for their administration.

35. That a remedy is only a palliative when it is administered without complete knowledge of the evil.

That it is therefore necessary that the present state of the finances, the proceeds of the subsidies already established, the absolutely necessary expenses, the total *deficit*, its origin and its causes, be submitted to the examination of the Estates General, in order to stabilize each department, economize in all branches of the administration, and take the most effective measures for assuring their management; that only on these conditions will the deputies to the Estates General be able to acknowledge the national debt and consent finally to the taxation that must be entailed only by the urgent needs of the *patrie*.

Signed: LE DESMÉ DE SAINT-ÉLIX [et al.]

Extract from the Minutes of the Assembly

We, Grand Bailiff d'Épée, and nobles, holders of fiefs, or domiciled in the *bailliage* of Crépy;

Observing that, individual liberty being a prerogative that man acquires at birth, it is his own and of his nature except for the portion which he has sacrificed, by order of the law, for the security of society.

That the constitutional laws of the State are the conditions to which each of its members has subscribed;

But that if these same laws are subject to alteration the State is then in danger;

That the Nation has the right to keep watch over the preservation of those that it has established for the maintenance of each and all of its members, and for the glory of the monarchy.

That this surveillance can be carried out only by the periodical return of the Estates General.

We entrust to our representative the power to implement our demands, to uphold our rights with the zeal merited by our confidence and the importance of the general good of the *patrie*.

But we impose on him the special charge of demanding individual liberty, limited by the laws that the Estates General will set, and by the periodic return of the aforesaid Estates at a time which they will determine.

And in the absence of these two points, irrevocably enacted, we annul and withdraw all of the power that we have entrusted to him.

The said minutes dated March 14, 1789, and signed as above by all the gentlemen composing the said Assembly.

9. March 26, 1789:
Cahier *of the* Clergy *of* Troyes

When the members of the First Estate elected their deputies to the Estates General, they did so for the most part in one stage, like the nobles. The parish priests, almost all of whom were commoners in their social origins, met with the bishops in an assembly for the electoral district (*bailliage* or *sénéchaussée*), to write a *cahier* expressing their wishes and elect the deputies who were to carry this document to the Estates General. At this electoral meeting were also delgates from communities of regular clergy and from the canons.

In the case of the *bailliage* of Troyes, whose center was the city of that name—a city with a distinguished medieval past and beautiful churches, located on the upper Seine somewhat less than 100 miles to the east and south of Paris—the principal assembly of the clergy took place on March 26, 1789, at which time the following document was written: *Cahier des pouvoirs et instructions des députés de l'ordre du clergé du bailliage de Troyes, assemblé dans la même ville, le 26 mars*

1789 (s.l.n.d., 22 pp.). In translation from the printed version, a number of articles treating Church affairs in detail have been omitted.

THE CLERGY of the *bailliage* of Troyes, devoted, like all the Clergy of the kingdom, as much to the *patrie* as to religion, and accustomed at all times to set an example of the respect, attachment, and fidelity due to the Sovereign, especially charges its deputies to the Estates General to bear to the foot of the throne, in the National Assembly, the homage of the sentiments with which it is imbued and the tribute of the vows it makes for the preservation of the sacred person of the King, the prosperity of the royal family, the strengthening of the ruling branch, and the maintenance of the monarchy.

Eager to cooperate with the other orders in the fulfillment of the paternal views that His Majesty had in convoking the Estates General, the Clergy of the *bailliage* of Troyes expects that these same deputies, worthy in every respect of its confidence, will not neglect any of the articles of the present *cahier*, as expressing the general will of the Clergy of the *bailliage*, but will submit them, nevertheless, to the enlightened judgment of the majority of the representatives of the nation, posing as an invariable maxim that all individual interests must be entirely subordinated to the general interest.

Objectives Common to the Three Orders

1. The distinction of the three orders will be maintained in the French government, just as it has existed since the beginning of the monarchy.

2. The preference of the Clergy of the *bailliage* of Troyes would be for the Estates General to deliberate by head for taxation only, and by order for all other subjects; but it believes it must rely in this matter on the wisdom of the Estates General.

3. The ancient and fundamental laws of the Kingdom shall be collected in a code which forever assures to the nation its purely monarchical government.

4. No law shall be regarded as constitutional which has not been consented to by the nation, in its Estate General, and sanctioned by the King.

5. For the convocation of the Estates General, there shall be legislation, in an invariable form, which assures to all members of the

hree orders representation conforming to the rule made for the
resent convocation, with liberty for all the curés, at whatever
istance they may be, to be present at the assemblies convoked for
at purpose.

6. The return of the Estates General shall be periodical, and fixed
r not more than five years.

7. In all the provinces of the Kingdom, there shall be established
ovincial Estates, composed after the fashion of the Estates
eneral, which shall be entrusted exclusively with the admin-
ration and jurisdiction now in the hands of assigned commis-
ners.

8. Reform of the civil and criminal code.

9. The Estates General shall pronounce on the venality of judi-
l mandates or offices: they shall suggest means for bringing closer
ether the judges and those coming under their jurisdiction, for
duating the subordinate tribunals, and for remedying the slow-
s and costliness of procedures.

0. No citizen shall be vulnerable to deprivation of his natural
ge, nor to removal from his jurisdiction, [and the deputies are]
bolish, consequently, every contrary right and privilege.

1. In order to give commerce the credit which it needs, [the
uties are] to assign exclusively to consular jurisdictions the
nizance of failures and bankruptcies; to suppress decrees order-
stays of execution, and areas of exemption; and to arrange for all
he corporations in cities to be summoned to concur in the
ination of officials of the consular jurisdictions.

. [The deputies are] to restrict seigneurial justice to those acts
e which are necessary on the spot, such as affixing seals to
ments, making inventories, and police matters; to suppress the
s of process-server-appraiser and clerk-recorder in the
tryside, their functions being abusive and vexatious; to oblige
e officers of justice to reside in the locality.

Individual liberty for all the subjects of the Kingdom; con-
ntly suppression of *lettres de cachet*, and assurance of the
t due to letters entrusted to the postal service.

he Estates General authorizes the redemption of quitrent and
dues, the Clergy should be free to reinvest the money from
in landed property, and consequently the Declaration of
hould be revoked or restricted to alienation alone.

Before voting for any tax whatever, [the deputies are] to
and consolidate the debt of the nation; to ascertain and deter-

mine the expenses of the state; to establish an invariable order in each department; and to pass decrees concerning all the demands of the nation.

15. To adopt preferably the tax whose collection will be the easiest and least onerous.

16. Whatever the tax adopted, it shall not be granted except for a limited time; it shall be generally and proportionately borne by all individuals of the three orders, while taking into consideration the debts of the Clergy.

17. The Estates General shall advise concerning means of making capitalists and merchants pay taxes in a manner that is least arbitrary and most just.

18. The assessment and collection of taxes shall be entrusted only to the Provincial Estates, which will deposit receipts directly into the Royal Treasury, after paying for things that are the responsibility of the government in each province.

19. In order to simplify the tax collections and their costs, there will be only one tax administration for all three orders.

20. The consent of the nation, assembled in the Estates General, shall be required for all borrowing, just as it is for all taxation.

21. To establish, for the paying off of the national debt, a reserve fund which shall not be diverted, under any pretext whatever, to any other purpose.

22. To suppress the excise and salt taxes as disastrous for the people.

23. To extinguish the functions and offices harmful to the well-being of the administration; to include their reimbursement in the body of the debts.

24. To restrict the rights of inspection and fix them at an invariable rate.

25. The Administration of the Domains to be reformed; the Administration of Waters and Forests to be entrusted to the Provincial Estates; tariff barriers and customs to be withdrawn to the borders of the Kingdom to facilitate the liberty of interior commerce.

26. To advise as to means of modifying the treaty of commerce with England, if it is not judged best to abolish it.

27. To give agriculture back the hands that manufacturing and spinning take from it in the rural areas.

28. To establish sumptuary laws on luxury items, and especially on too great a number of servants.

be concerned with the regeneration of morals and with
ation of agriculture, commerce, and the arts.

see to the supplying of manure and feed necessary to
e, through the conservation of common pastures; to forbid
ng of them among individuals; and to fix the quota to
serve for the needs of the communities.

the municipalities be preserved in the cities and in the
de; let the three orders be eligible to them; let their
ations be uniform and as economical as possible; let the
e precedence in them when the seigneurs are not present

remedy the abuses in the formation of the militia and in
istration of the common carriers.

e financial accounts, national and provincial, shall be made
ery year, and the ministers shall be accountable to the
eneral for their management.

preserve for the nobility its honorific privileges.

e Estates General shall set aside an annual sum for pensions
ilitary men and for the widows of officers; the Estates
are requested to examine scrupulously all the pensions
granted.

rit and talent combined with irreproachable conduct shall
Third Estate the right to be admitted to military ranks
offices of the magistracy.

Objectives Relative to the Clergy

ome of the more technical and detailed clauses have been

e Catholic, apostolic, and Roman religion shall be the only
ht, professed, and publicly authorized; its services and
shall be uniform throughout the Kingdom.

e Edict of 1787 concerning non-Catholics shall be sub-
the Estates General for revision.

e ordinances, statutes, and decrees for the sanctification of
and holidays shall be renewed and sanctioned by the
eneral.

restore to the Clergy national and provincial councils;
force the Diocesan Synods; to suppress the general as-
f the Clergy and the chambers of the tithes.

e King shall be entreated to have regard in the nomination

of bishops, less for birth than for virtue and merit, and to choos
bishops, as much as possible, from among the Clergy born in th
province of the vacant Chair, and experienced in the pastoral min
istry.

42. Bishops shall be required to reside in their dioceses, and t
visit them according to the Holy Canons. . . .

45. The observance of the Holy Canons shall be obligatory con
cerning plurality of benefices up to the amount of fifteen hundre
livres, and residence shall be equally obligatory for every ecclesi
astic without exception, when he is provided with a benefice o
the same value. . . .

49. To keep the religious orders, and to make their member
useful to the state by employing them as ministers or in the edu
cation of the young, or in the service of hospitals; and in orde
to destroy the kind of degradation attached to the mendicant orders
to endow these monks sufficiently, and, that being the case, subjec
them to the authority of the bishop for the service of the diocese
and to revoke the committee of the Regulars. . . .

53. Once the Clergy is subjected to the same taxes as the othe
subjects of His Majesty, it seems just that they enjoy the same privi
leges in the administration and exploitation of their property, tha
henceforth every edict, declaration, law, and decree to the contrar
be revoked, and that the Declaration of 1749 be confined to alien
ation alone.

54. Restitution of the tithe to the curés, as true proprietors, o
improvement of the parishes, whose endowment shall not be les
than fifteen hundred *livres* in the country, and in the cities twenty
four hundred *livres;* in which sums, whether in the city or in th
country, the property of the curés, whether in the nature of patri
mony or endowment, shall not be included, even if they should b
able to oppose only a former possession to the present holder o
this property.

55. There shall be provided, through consolidation of benefices
an amelioration of the incomes of country parishes whose tithe
do not enable them to enjoy a revenue of fifteen hundred *livres*
There shall be provided by the same means the endowment o
city parishes, raised to at least twenty-four hundred *livres;* no
counting a progressive increase to take account of local circum

:d and determined by the Diocesan Synod, a situation
lso apply in country parishes. . . .

ession of all edicts and declarations hindering liberty
itical rights, and especially the Declaration of 1656;
lently, the curés have a right to organize, to meet in
induct their affairs, without the present demand doing
prejudicing that set out above, Article 5.
ve to the present possessors of tithes, other than the
table indemnity, in cases where they would cede

ippress all privileges and exemptions relative to the

clesiastic, secular or regular, or even a graduate, shall be
th a benefice-parish before the age of at least thirty
fter having exercised the functions of the holy ministry
of five years.
r ecclesiastic, not excepting graduates, shall be declared
possess a benefice of more than a thousand *livres* if
istituted in Holy Orders. . . .

claim precedence after the Bishop in religious and
:mblies. . . .

offices of municipal officials be suppressed and the
municipalities be named each year, both progressively,
ion, and by ballot, publicly in the City Hall.
:eigneur and the curé of each parish shall form with two
f the municipality a tribunal of peace, to prevent
to reconcile the contesting parties. . . .

der to eliminate begging, the poor in each parish shall
y at works of charity, and each province shall provide
e workshops. . . .

ery city of the *bailliage*, there will be formed a bureau
r the spiritual and temporal needs of prisoners, and steps
n to keep debtors from being confused with criminals.
: Estates General believes liberty of the press to be a con-

sequence of individual liberty, at least let there be established penalties against authors of books contrary to religion and good morals, or against any printer of anonymous works. . . .

As there are some articles in the present *cahier* that could be prejudicial or contrary to the rights, prerogatives, and property of some of the members of the Assembly, it has been unanimously agreed that all the signatures placed at the end of the said *cahier* will be able to harm no one; and that all corporations, communities, and benefice holders would be able to submit to the deputies of the Estates General their opposition and protests against the articles that can hurt or prejudice them. Made, read, approved, and decreed in the said Assembly of the Clergy of the *bailliage* of Troyes, April 3, 1789, by the authorized Commissioners.

[Signatures]

III.

The Loss of
Royal Initiative

10. June 16, 1789:
Barentin's Memorandum on the Crisis
in the Estates General

Charles Louis François de Paule de Barentin (1738–1819) was Keeper of the Seals in succession to Lamoignon, whose ill-fated Cour Plénière had been the high point of the crown's efforts to resist the aristocracy. Barentin was closely associated with the comte d'Artois and others at the court who were hostile to Necker in the weeks following the opening of the Estates General. As the delay over verification of powers by the deputies lengthened, the tension mounted, and more and more people, especially in aristocratic circles, turned to the idea of some form of royal session as a means of breaking the deadlock. But what solution should the king impose? It was of enormous importance to France's future whether Louis XVI used his authority in support of the aristocratic position that representative institutions should be keyed to the traditional society by means of the traditional Estates General voting by order, or of some other solution that would give more weight to the representatives of the Third Estate. Barentin's confidential memorandum of June 16, 1789, asked for by the king two days before, was the advice of a man who was to be very influential in the final outcome, the royal session of June 23, 1789. It has been translated from the document published under the direction of Georges Lefebvre by the Institut d'Histoire de la Révolution Française de la Faculté des Lettres et Sciences Humaines de Paris, in Part II of Volume I, of *Recueil de documents relatifs aux séances des États-Généraux mai-juin 1789* (Paris, 1962), pp. 157–160.

THE KING, on receiving the decree and the memoir from the Third Estate, responded to its Dean that he would make his intentions known to the Chamber of the Third. Thus His Majesty has announced an answer; he must make it.

Even if he had not promised to do so, the present situation of the Estates General requires urgently that the King indicate his position, and he would not be able to remain silent any longer without taking the risk of seeing his Crown's rights compromised and his authority destroyed, or without perhaps being forced to dissolve the Estates General, which would become a misfortune all of whose dangers cannot be foreseen, and which it is necessary to prevent.

What in fact is the state of affairs? The Nobility, considering the Estates to be in existence from their opening day, thought it possible to constitute itself and proceed to the verification of the powers of its deputies by distinguishing those of its own deputies, on which it felt that it alone was competent to pronounce, from those of the deputations which concerned the three orders. With regard to the latter, in accordance with the plan of conciliation proposed by Your Majesty's commissioners, by its own acknowledgment the Nobility judged that they should be sent to the commissioners of the three orders, subject to final decisions by His Majesty, in the event of difficulties.

The Clergy, faithful to the preference for mediation which has animated it, has not constituted itself. It has accepted purely and simply the overture of conciliation, but the fact must be faced that it finds itself in a most embarrassing situation, which is made even worse by the desertion of a part of its members; if this continues, if as a result of seductive arguments, of promises of improvement in the lot of the curates, of conviction that the King approves of their ranging themselves on the side of the Third, which the silence of Your Majesty seems to warrant, the majority were to range itself definitively on the side of the Third, what would become of the rest of the Clergy? There would be efforts to subject it to the opinion of the majority, it would refuse to fall in with this, and the scission would be made, perhaps irremediably.

The Chamber of the Third by the organization of its members raises the most unreasonable pretensions, along with opinions most incompatible with the power of the King. Overexcited heads are all the more heated by the presence of the public, and the people themselves draw from this democratic school maxims that are destructive of the principles of the Monarchy, and whatever the name this chamber eventually takes, it will regard itself in fact as the national chamber. The locale strengthens this idea, and the roll call of the *bailliages* that it has presumed to make no longer leaves room for doubt as to its views. And so there you have the Estates General, as a result of a false notion, concentrated in a single order. The Chamber of the Third also seeks to abolish all distinctions among the orders, and, advancing along a line as dangerous as it is consistent, after having become accustomed to hitherto unknown expressions such as *petition, honorable members, commons, amendment*, and *address*, is not afraid to designate the first two orders as privileged classes.

And so here we are transported to England, and the Estates General convoked by Your Majesty transformed into the Commons. Such rapid progress announces sufficiently what the royal authority will lose if it is not deployed, if the King does not show himself; if he does not assert his authority over the gentlemen who wish to establish a constitution, on the assumption that we do not have one; if he does not encourage those who, still attached to sound principles, do not dare show themselves; if he does not, finally, reassure the timid, or those uncertain of his wishes, who hesitate in the face of His Majesty's silence.

It is not enough that he does not formally approve the word Commons, that he merely calls the third order the Chamber of the Third; it is necessary to forbid openly those labels that cannot be viewed with indifference when one is aware of the pernicious, and even seditious, principles being retailed in the hall of the Third.

Any further delay in clearing these matters up would be reproached as feebleness even by loyal and moderate men, and that is the most damaging vice of a monarchical government. It must always be just, but firm, and a king of France must above all develop a pronounced character, and one capable of dominating the destroyers of legitimate authority.

Moreover, what evils would not be portended by an inactivity whose every instant is to be feared? Interminable debates about the existence of the Estates: the Chamber of the Third will declare that it alone represents them; the nobility and clergy will vigorously oppose this; there will then be two or three Estates Generals— or, rather, there will exist none at all.

What will then be the condition of the finances? How will the debts of the state be paid? How will taxes be collected in the midst of the general turmoil of which France is the theater?

Will it be said that the Chamber of the Third, having taken form, will negotiate with the King, that it will zealously pursue its aims, and that it will thus force the other two orders to adhere to the law as indicated by the multitude? Admitting the possibility of this plan, what sacrifices would not be attached to it? The overthrow of the constitution, at most the partition of the legislative authority, hindrances of all kinds to a power that ought not to be troubled by anything, and finally, as one of the spectators imbued with new principles was not afraid to say some days ago in the assembly hall, the King would be nothing more than the *decorated part of the nation.*

It is time for the King to teach his people that he will not let himself be robbed of a power that he cannot and does not wish to abandon, that the separation of the three orders is one of the fundamental laws of the monarchy, that it is based on the most formal ordinances, that it was consecrated by the Estates General itself in 1560, and that to mix the orders among themselves or alter them would shake the throne.

It would be vain to argue that the Estates General of 1789 cannot resemble those early ones; they must be established on the same bases, and any change in their organization or in their way of voting can only result from agreement of the will of the King and of the nation. That is expressly recorded in the council minutes of the twenty-seventh of December last and in the speeches at the opening of the Estates. The double representation of the Third, which it owes to the goodness of the King, was not a commitment to vote by head. That order would in that case have too marked an influence, and would be absolute master of all the deliberations. This increase in representatives which it is misusing today had its origin in the progress of commerce and agriculture and the increase in population since the last Estates General; and those are not acting in good faith who try to oppose twenty-three million men to the small number of individuals who make up the other two orders. If one is to use population as the point of departure, one should also take into account the total amount of property, especially with respect to taxes, and then the interest of the first two orders, as a result of their property, should surpass even that of the Third.

Everything thus calls upon Your Majesty, everything presses him to make his intentions known, and to forestall the disorders in the Estates General which would result from his silence were it to last any longer. The Clergy is already alarmed by it and dreads its results; the Nobility, if it is abandoned, will be discouraged, and if, left to itself, it finally joins as a whole or in part with the Chamber of the Third, this would be to the detriment of Your Majesty, and all the orders of your state, in league against the royal power, would substitute for it a new constitution which, under the pretext of preventing abuses of authority, would eclipse them, and thus would prepare for France misfortunes whose duration and effects it would be impossible to calculate. But even if one rejects that idea and considers the present situation only politically with Your Majesty having to decide between the Clergy and the Nobility on the one hand and the Third on the other, to which does his interest oblige him to give preference? To the first two orders without doubt, for whom he will always be, in the last analysis, the Master, because he has sure means of binding them to him, whereas the Third Estate will see its advantage in being unrestricted by any salutary law, in freeing itself from obligations to the other two orders, and in escaping from contracts that it has been persuaded to view as humiliating; and it will believe itself happier if it can manage to participate in the administration. It will become aware of its error too late, that its constituents, most of whom are not proprietors, have abused its confidence, and instead of a paternal authority, the people of the countryside, truly worthy of Your Majesty's protection, will be subjected to a new yoke, and will see that they have been deceived, because after having been promised that they would pay less, they will pay as much; the benevolent and necessary authority that their lords used to exercise will have been alienated from them; they will no longer receive from them the same assistance, because their reciprocal ties will have been broken; royal power will be destroyed, the upper Clergy discredited in public opinion; the Clergy of the second order, proud of having participated in the administration, will neglect its duties; the humiliated Nobility will live on its lands without credit, and will no longer regard the inhabitants as its children; the poor will be more than ever to be pitied, and what is called the high Third will alone profit from this revolution, and will have usurped rights whose abuse will soon force their destruction, without monarchical authority being able to regain them.

Such are the reflections, Sire, which my duty, my respect, and my attachment to Your Majesty's person have prescribed that I put before you. I beg you to weigh them, and to consider that the time has come when you must assemble your council and consult it. I will take care not to believe that my opinion must prevail, but I would have had to reproach myself for not warning Your Majesty of a danger which seemed pressing to me, and for not indicating the only remedy that I foresee, which is to profit from the enlightenment of those whom you honor with your confidence, and of the magistrates who, called by Your Majesty to form the Estates General, have the capacity to judge the present situation and to review for him the true principles of the monarchy.

11. June 22, 1789:
Montmorin's Testimony in Support of Necker

As the Barentin memoir of June 16, 1789, has shown, there was a growing conviction in court circles that the king should intervene to end the deadlock over voting in the Estates General. The action of the Third Estate's representatives on June 17 in declaring themselves to be the National Assembly was a direct challenge to the royal authority as traditionally conceived and also an embarrassment to Necker and the moderate liberals of Anglophile persuasion, who were now threatened with a unicameral legislature instead of the two chambers for which they had been hoping as a compromise solution. June 17 endangered Necker's position as a conciliator popular with the Third Estate. He now had to look to a royal session that would undo the Third Estate's action, but his plan for the royal session was liberal and Anglophile in tendency, recommending two chambers and eligibility of commoners to high offices in the future and, for the present, joint deliberations of the Estates on questions of general interest. Necker's memoir, which was the subject of important council meetings on June 19, 20, 21, and 22, has been lost. The document printed below is that of Armand Marc, comte de Montmorin de Saint-Hérem, the Minister of Foreign Affairs, who supported Necker's position in the council meetings and in this memoir to the king written just prior to the last meeting, which took place on June 22, the day before the royal session. The source is *Recueil de documents*, Vol. I, Part II, pp. 199–201.

June 22, Versailles

SIRE,

The object on which Your Majesty is going to deliberate definitively this morning is so important, the decision he will make can have such far-reaching consequences, that my attachment for the person of Your Majesty forces me to set them before him again prior to the moment when he will make this final decision.

Your Majesty assembled the Estates General because the parlements announced their incompetence with respect to taxes and loans; Your Majesty himself declared in the month of July of last year that neither the one nor the other could henceforth take place without the nation's consent; all collection of taxes thus becomes impossible without this condition, and no loan could be successful without it because the lenders wish to see a pledge assured of their confidence, and because this pledge would not exist if there were no tax returns.

The Estates General once assembled, as they are today, their consent becomes indispensable for the continuation even of the present taxes, and if they dispersed without having consented to them, collection would present so many difficulties that it would become impossible. However, Your Majesty's revenues are expended in advance, the royal treasury cannot continue the most essential payments and provide the expenditures that the famine requires except by means of credit devices which for nearly a year have resembled a kind of miracle; the separation of the Estates General would make all these methods disappear, the sources on which the royal treasury draws would be entirely dried up, payments of all kinds would be suspended, Your Majesty could not provide for the immense outlays that the maintenance of a great part of his kingdom requires; one could [not] foresee to what point the alarms and anxieties would be increased, nor the excesses they would bring about; however Your Majesty would be without the means to repress them, for the truth must not be concealed from him, even pay for the troops would be lacking.

This is the setting in which it is proposed to Your Majesty to sustain the old constitution with a firm hand, and in which he is told that he will be sustained by it; I certainly give full credit to the sentiments and courage that prompt this advice, but I daresay to Your Majesty, those who give it are not familiar with the true state of affairs, or at least do not view it realistically.

I am certainly very far from approving, or excusing, the conduct of the Third Estate; no one in the world condemns it more than I, or is more afflicted by it, but however extravagant, and however criminal it may be, the public judges it very differently;

sustained by this opinion, the Third will not depart from the course it has set for itself; it will grow still more embittered toward the first two orders, it will disobey the orders of Your Majesty, and Your Majesty will have compromised his authority uselessly; he will be forced to dissolve the Estates General, and Your Majesty has seen what would be the consequences of that; perhaps the Third would not even let itself be disbanded, and as a result the disorder and troubles would be at their height, and Your Majesty has seen what means would remain to him for repressing them.

The plan that is being proposed to Your Majesty is noble and great and seems to me to be the only one worthy of the character and goodness of Your Majesty; it can without doubt fail to impress the assembly, but it could not fail to impress the nation. It is feared that the first two orders may refuse to submit to it; I like to believe that this fear would prove groundless, but in any case, it would not be the entire membership of these two orders that would retire; the majority of the clergy would hasten to conform to the wishes of Your Majesty, and a part of the nobility, perhaps a greater part than people realize, would follow this example; strengthened by those remaining around you and by the love and admiration of the nation, Your Majesty would go forward and would scarcely hear the murmurs of those who would be discontented.

Apparently little importance is given to the parish priests; I confess, Sire, that I think very differently; they are the ones who influence the people most directly and arouse them at will.

People have spoken to Your Majesty of the parlements; I will not recall to Your Majesty how dangerous their help would be, what force would be acquired by these bodies that Your Majesty has learned to know all too well, but I will say that they would be useless to Your Majesty; the magistracy has no force except through opinion, and certainly it would not have it on this occasion.

I believed, Sire, that I had to bring these reflections to the attention of Your Majesty before the council announced for this morning. They are dictated by the purest attachment to the person of Your Majesty, and by the most ardent zeal for his glory. These, Sire, are the only sentiments in my soul; I wish he were able to read therein; he would see how deeply serious they are, and how far I am from any factional spirit and from any attachment foreign to the true interests of Your Majesty.

Deign, Sire, to receive with benevolence this proof of my absolute devotion to the person of Your Majesty and the homage of deep respect with which I am, Sire, the very humble and very obedient servant and subject of Your Majesty, De Montmorin.

12. June 23, 1789:
Louis XVI at the Royal Session
of the Estates General

The royal session of June 23, 1789, was of utmost gravity in the history of the revolution. It represented a position taken formally and in detail on the great issues of the time, and taken freely, by Louis XVI. As the last uncoerced decision on the part of the king, it became the rallying point of the counterrevolution, justifying in his own mind and the queen's their subsequent behavior and remaining for more than a quarter of a century the ideal of the aristocracy: what they would have attained if the revolution had been stopped at the first stage below absolutism. The June 23 documents are perhaps the best evidence of what such a victorious aristocratic revolution would have meant. Later, after years of anger and frustration, there was to be a revival of absolutism as a political idea, and the aristocratic position in favor of representative government keyed to the old society of Estates was to lose favor in official circles of the counterrevolution. June 23 represented a defeat for Necker, who until the council meeting of the previous evening had hoped that the king would remain above the struggle between the aristocracy and the commoners and impose a solution that would protect aristocratic social distinctions and property rights while giving representatives of the Third Estate real political power at least equal to that of the aristocracy. The royal session took place in the meeting room of the Estates General at Versailles and lasted not much longer than half an hour. Louis XVI first read a short speech, following which a declaration containing fifteen articles having to do with future conduct of the Estates General was read on his behalf. Then the king spoke again briefly at the start and after the conclusion of a reading of a reform program of thirty-five articles. The account which follows is from *Recueil de documents*, Vol. I, Part II, pp. 274–284. The king's opening remarks have been omitted.

Declaration of the King Concerning
the Present Session of the Estates General

Art. 1. It is the King's will that the former distinction of the three orders of the State be preserved in its entirety, as essential to the constitution of his kingdom, that the deputies, freely elected by each of the three orders, forming three chambers, deliberating by order, and being able, with the approval of the Sovereign, to agree to deliberate in common, alone be considered as forming the body of representatives of the nation; consequently, the King has declared void the decisions made by the deputies of the order of the Third Estate on the seventeenth of this month, as well as those which may have resulted from them, as illegal and unconstitutional.

Art. 2. His Majesty declares valid all powers verified or to be verified in each chamber, concerning which no objection has been raised or will be; His Majesty orders that information concerning this matter be exchanged among the orders.

As for powers which could be contested in each order, and concerning which the interested parties might appeal, the ruling for the present session *only* of the Estates General shall be as ordered below.

Art. 3. The King rescinds and annuls as unconstitutional, contrary to the letters of convocation, and opposed to the interest of the State, the restrictions of powers which, by curtailing the liberty of deputies to the Estates General, would prevent their adopting forms of deliberation by order, separately, or in common when this is decided upon by separate votes of the three orders.

Art. 4. If, contrary to the intention of the King, any deputies have taken the rash oath not to deviate from some particular form of deliberation, His Majesty leaves it to their consciences to consider whether the arrangements that he is going to make deviate from the letter or spirit of the obligations they have undertaken.

Art. 5. The King permits deputies who believe themselves to be restricted by their mandates to request new powers of their constituents; but His Majesty enjoins them to remain, meanwhile, in the Estates General, in order to be present at all deliberations on urgent affairs of state and give consultative opinions concerning them.

Art. 6. His Majesty declares that in subsequent sessions of the Estates General he will not permit *cahiers* or mandates ever to be considered imperative; they must be only simple instructions, entrusted to the consciences and free opinions of the deputies chosen.

Art. 7. His Majesty, having for the safety of the State exhorted the three orders to assemble, during this session of the Estates only, to deliberate in common upon matters of general utility, wishes to make known his intentions concerning procedure.

Art. 8. Specifically excepted from the matters which may be treated in common shall be those pertaining to the ancient and constitutional rights of the three orders, the manner of constituting the next Estates General, feudal and seigneurial property, and the useful rights and honorific prerogatives of the first two orders.

Art. 9. The particular consent of the clergy shall be necessary for all provisions which could pertain to the interests of religion, ecclesiastical discipline, and the administration of secular and regular orders and bodies.

Art. 10. Resolutions made jointly by the three orders concerning the contested powers, following petitions to the Estates General by the interested parties, shall be determined by a plurality of votes; but if two-thirds of the members of one of the three orders should protest the decision of the assembly, the matter shall be referred to the King for definitive settlement by His Majesty.

Art. 11. If, with a view to facilitating the union of the three orders, they desire that decisions taken in common be valid only when passed by a two-thirds majority, His Majesty is disposed to authorize this procedure.

Art. 12. Matters which shall have been decided in the assemblies of the three orders united together shall be reconsidered on the following day if one hundred members of the assembly so request.

Art. 13. The King desires that in such a case, and in order to bring about conciliation, the three chambers separately begin to appoint a commission made up of whatever number of deputies they judge suitable, to prepare the form and composition of the conference bureaus which are to deal with the various matters.

Art. 14. The general assembly of deputies of the three orders shall be presided over by presidents chosen by each of the orders, according to their customary rank.

Art. 15. Good order, decency, and even liberty of suffrage require that His Majesty forbid, as he expressly does, any person other than the members of the three orders composing the Estates General to be present at their deliberations, whether they hold them in common or separately.

Discourse of the King

I wish also, Gentlemen, to draw your attention to the various benefits I am granting to my people. It is not my intention to confine your zeal to the circle that I am going to trace, for I shall adopt with pleasure any other view of public welfare that may be proposed by the Estates General. I can say, without self-deception, that never has a king done so much for any nation; but what other can have deserved it more because of its sentiments than the French nation? I shall not hesitate to say it: those who, by exaggerated pretensions or irrelevant objections, would still retard the effect of my paternal intentions, would make themselves unworthy to be considered French.

Declaration of the Intentions of the King

Art. 1. No new tax shall be established, no old one shall be extended beyond the term stated by law, without the consent of the representatives of the nation.

Art. 2. Newly established taxes, or old ones that have been extended, shall be effective only until the next session of the Estates General.

Art. 3. Because loans can become the necessary occasion for increasing taxes, none shall be contracted without the consent of the Estates General, on condition that always, in case of war or other national danger, the Sovereign have the power to borrow, without delay, to the amount of one hundred million. For it is the King's formal intention never to make the safety of the State dependent upon anyone.

Art. 4. The Estates General shall examine with care the condition of the finances, and shall request all information necessary to inform them thoroughly.

Art. 5. The statement of revenues and expenditures shall be made public annually, in a form proposed by the Estates General and approved by His Majesty.

Art. 6. The sums assigned to each department shall be determined in a fixed and invariable manner, and the King subjects to this general rule even the funds destined for the maintenance of his household.

Art. 7. In order to assure this stability of the various expenditures of the State, the King desires that dispositions suitable to the achievement of this objective be recommended to him by the Estates General, and His Majesty will adopt them if they are in accord with the royal dignity and with the indispensable rapidity of the public service.

Art. 8. The representatives of a nation, faithful to the laws of honor and integrity, will commit no offense against the public confidence, and the King expects them to assure and strengthen the confidence of creditors of the State in the most authentic manner.

Art. 9. After the formal intentions announced by the clergy and the nobility of renouncing their pecuniary privileges have taken the form of resolutions, the King intends to sanction them, and to allow no more privileges or distinctions of any kind in the payment of monetary taxes.

Art. 10. In order to consecrate so important a resolution, the King desires that the name of *taille* be abolished in his kingdom, and that this tax be joined either to the *vingtièmes* or to any other territorial assessment, or that it be eventually replaced in some way, but always according to proportions that are just, equal, and without distinction of status, rank, or birth.

Art. 11. The King desires that the right of *franc-fief* be abolished as soon as the revenues and fixed expenditures of the State are exactly balanced.

Art. 12. All property, without exception, shall be respected at all times, and His Majesty expressly includes under the name of property the tithes, *cens, rentes,* feudal and seigneurial rights and duties, and, in general, all rights and prerogatives, useful or honorific, attached to lands and fiefs or belonging to persons.

Art. 13. The first two orders of the State shall continue to enjoy exemption from personal obligations, but the King will approve of the Estates General's providing means of converting such obligations into pecuniary contributions, and of all orders being equally subject to them thereafter.

Art. 14. His Majesty intends to determine, with the advice of the Estates General, what positions and offices shall in the future conserve the privilege of conferring and transmitting nobility; nevertheless, according to the right inherent in his crown, His Majesty will grant patents of nobility to those of his subjects who, by services rendered to the King and to the State, show themselves worthy of this reward.

Art. 15. The King, desiring to assure the personal liberty of all citizens in a solid and durable manner, invites the Estates General to seek and to propose to him the most suitable means of reconciling the abolition of the warrants known as *lettres de cachet* with the maintenance of public security and the precautions necessary to safeguard in certain cases the honor of families, to repress promptly the first indications of sedition, and to guarantee the state against the effects of criminal communications with foreign powers.

Art. 16. The Estates General shall examine and make known to His Majesty the most suitable means of reconciling liberty of the press with the respect due to religion, morals, and the honor of citizens.

Art. 17. There shall be established in the several provinces or *généralités* of the kingdom provincial estates composed in the ratio of two-tenths clergy, some of whom will necessarily be chosen from the episcopal order, three-tenths nobility, and five-tenths Third Estate.

Art. 18. The members of these provincial estates shall be freely elected by the respective orders, and a property qualification shall be necessary to be an elector or to be eligible.

Art. 19. The deputies to these provincial estates shall deliberate in common on all matters, according to the usage observed in the provincial assemblies that these estates shall replace.

Art. 20. An intermediate commission, chosen by these estates, shall administer the affairs of the province during the interval between sessions, and these intermediate commissions, becoming solely responsible for their administration, shall have as delegates only persons chosen by them or by the provincial estates.

Art. 21. The Estates General shall propose to the King their views on all other aspects of the internal organization of the provincial estates, and on the choice of forms applicable to the election of members of these assemblies.

Art. 22. Apart from the administrative matters for which the provincial assemblies are responsible, the King will entrust to the provincial estates the administration of hospitals, prisons, poorhouses, foundling hospitals, the inspection of the expenditures of cities, the supervision of the maintenance of forests, of the storage and sale of wood, and of other matters that could be more usefully administered by the provinces.

Art. 23. Disputes that have arisen in provinces where old estates still exist, and objections raised against the constitutions of these assemblies, shall be considered by the Estates General, and they shall inform His Majesty concerning just and wise provisions suitable for the establishment of order and stability in the administration of these same provinces.

Art. 24. The King invites the Estates General to seek appropriate means of exploiting his domains in the most advantageous fashion and likewise to propose to him their recommendations of suitable actions concerning indentured domains.

Art. 25. The Estates General shall concern themselves with the project, conceived long ago by His Majesty, of transferring the tariffs to the frontiers of the kingdom, in order that the most perfect freedom may prevail in the internal circulation of national or foreign merchandise.

Art. 26. His Majesty desires that the harmful effects of the tax on salt and the importance of its revenue be carefully discussed, and that in any case there at least be proposed means of making its collection less irritating.

Art. 27. His Majesty desires also that the advantages and disadvantages of the *aides* and other taxes be carefully examined, but without losing sight of the absolute necessity of assuring an exact balance between the revenues and the expenditures of the State.

Art. 28. According to the wish manifested by the King in his declaration of September 23 last, His Majesty will give serious attention to projects presented to him relative to the administration of justice, and to means of perfecting the civil and criminal laws.

Art. 29. The King desires that the laws promulgated during the session, and according to the advice or desire of the Estates General, experience no delay or impediment in their registration and execution throughout his kingdom.

Art. 30. His Majesty desires that the use of the *corvée* for the construction and maintenance of roads be abolished in his kingdom entirely and forever.

Art. 31. The King desires that abolition of the right of *main-morte*, of which action His Majesty has set an example in his domains, be extended to all France, and that means be proposed to him for providing the indemnity due seigneurs who possess this right.

Art. 32. His Majesty will inform the Estates General without delay of the regulations which he is preparing in order to restrict the *capitaineries* and give in this connection, which is related very closely to his personal enjoyment, a new proof of his love for his people.

Art. 33. The King invites the Estates General to consider all aspects of the drafting of militia, and to consider means of reconciling what is due the defense of the State with the alleviations that His Majesty would like to procure for his subjects.

Art. 34. The King desires that all provisions for public order and beneficence that shall have been authorized by His Majesty on behalf of his people during the present session of the Estates General—among others, those relating to personal liberty, equality of taxation, and the establishment of provincial estates—never be subject to change without the consent of the three orders given separately. His Majesty places them, in advance, in the category of national properties for which he wishes to provide, along with all other properties, the greatest possible security.

Art. 35. His Majesty, having called upon the Estates General to concern itself, in concert with him, with important matters of public utility, and with everything that can contribute to the happiness of his people, declares in the clearest possible manner that he wishes to preserve, completely and without the slightest impairment, the institution of the army, as well as complete authority, administration, and power over the military such as French monarchs have continuously enjoyed.

The King's Closing Speech

Gentlemen, you have just heard the summation of my inclinations and views; they are consistent with my earnest desire to serve the public welfare and if, by a misfortune which I am far from anticipating, you should abandon me in so worthy an undertaking, I will effect by myself the happiness of my people;

by myself I will assume the role of their true representative and, knowing your *cahiers*, knowing the perfect accord that exists between the most general wishes of the nation and my beneficent intentions, I will have all the confidence that so rare a harmony must inspire, and I will advance toward the goal I wish to attain with all the courage and resolution it must inspire in me.

Consider, Gentlemen, that none of your projects, none of your resolutions, can have the force of law without my special approval; in this way I am the natural guarantor of your respective rights, and all the orders of the State can rely upon my equitable impartiality. Any distrust on your part would be a great injustice. Thus far I am the one who has been doing everything for the happiness of my people, and it is perhaps rare for the only ambition of a sovereign to consist of getting his subjects to understand each other and cooperate at last in accepting the benefits he gives them.

I order you, Gentlemen, to separate immediately, and to go tomorrow morning to the chambers allotted to your respective orders to resume your sessions. Accordingly, I order the Grand Master of Ceremonies to have the halls prepared.

13. August 2, 1789:
Rivarol on the Meaning of July 14

Antoine de Rivarol, in his mid-thirties at the outbreak of the revolution, had made a brilliant conquest of Parisian society as a very young man by virtue of his extraordinary wit and intelligence. If much of his talent was expended in conversation, Rivarol nevertheless won a prize of the Berlin Academy in 1784, and praise from Frederick the Great, for his essay on the universality of the French language; and works such as his irreverent treatment of the literary figures of the day in his *Petit Almanach de nos grands hommes* (1788) won him much notoriety. Without having given any advance notice of political interests or social conscience, Rivarol became in 1789 an excellent journalist, at first a contributor to and then the principal author of the *Journal politique-national*, which appeared three times a week in 1789 and 1790. Rivarol's views were conservative, and he was forced to emigrate in 1792, to continue his sporadic but intelligent critiques of the revolution, together with a few promising but unfinished literary projects, until his death in Berlin in 1801. The following is from one of his *résumés* of events, published in the *Journal politique-national No. 10. Dimanche 2 août 1789.* It is a commentary on June 23, July 14, and the peasant *jacquerie* that was at that moment irreversibly revolutionizing the countryside.

Continuation of the New Résumé

The Court is at fault before the Nation for having surrounded the peaceful deputies of the people with threatening soldiers; for having divided the sovereign by setting the executive power against the legislative power; for having started the civil war by inciting the defenders of the state against its restorers. The whole conduct of the ministry proves that it had neither foreseen nor understood what an Estates General should be when granted after so many prayers, after so many causes for discontent, after such long-established depredations. In having a *Declaration of Rights* pronounced by His Majesty, and in forcing the Estates General to sanction it, the order of things was reversed; it was the Estates General's place to make the Declaration and it was the King's place to sanction it: and so the National Assembly seized the executive power the very same day that the King seized the legislative power; and royal authority, abandoned by the Army, rendered void in public opinion, and in collision with the mass of an enormous population, broke like a glass.

The errors of the National Assembly are no less obvious, although more necessary; in arming Paris, it endangered equally the King's head, the life of his subjects, and public liberty. One has only to imagine for a moment that the Army had obeyed, or even after the defection of the Army, one has only to imagine that the King had resisted the insolent claims of Paris, one has only, I say, to follow this supposition in one's thoughts if indeed one can bear the image of the horrible consequences it presents. Happily the King disconcerted his enemies by offering them no resistance; and without doubt, if Charles I had done as much, Cromwell would have lost. The National Assembly must therefore make a choice and confess that there was in all this either imprudence or treason: imprudence if Paris was armed without being sure of the Army; treason if the Army had been won over before Paris was incited to rise. Now that the National Assembly can count the King as being nothing, it must count Paris as being everything; time will tell us whether it has gained from the exchange. However that may be, an immense people has deserted its workshops, the courts are closed, the regiments no longer have officers, and France, under arms, is waiting for a *constitution*, that peaceful product of laws, as if it were threatened by a raid on its coasts or an invasion of barbarians. The truth is that the National Assembly cried for help without being able either to guarantee or to forestall the consequences.

The mistakes of the capital—or, rather, its crimes—are too well known: it has already given posterity subject matter for tragedies and the enemies of liberty terrible arguments. Gentle and sensitive souls want nothing more to do with benefits that one must purchase with so many crimes and at the cost of an anarchy whose end cannot be foreseen. It is, some will say, the fault of despotism, which leaves no door open to liberty except insurrection: I agree; but was it necessary, barbarous city, when the troops had been retired, when the National Assembly came to tell you how well it was satisfied with the King's latest session, was it necessary to require that your Prince, that the descendant of your sixty kings, come to humble himself within your walls? Why not have received him as he came himself, good-natured and unarmed? Did you know whether, in the midst of this forest of lances and bayonets, some monster or madman such as may be found among you in more peaceful times would place you in mourning and under eternal infamy?[1] But Paris wanted to brag; it wanted to show its King, deprived of any display of power or sign of majesty, its breast bristling with iron.

This crime against royalty was followed by numberless outrages against humanity. Vainly the King demanded at the City Hall, as a return for so much compliance on his part, that all those whom public outcries designated as victims be delivered to the courts; in vain he implored for his subjects not an act of grace but ordinary justice; in vain was the city illuminated and the opening of the theaters arranged; it was in the first moments of this false peace that the people of Paris—ruler, judge, and executioner—after several obscure murders which we pass over in silence, dragged Messieurs *Foulon* and *Berthier* into the Place de Grève, and subjected them to tortures and to a death the

1. This fear is not groundless. A shot from a gun, from an unknown hand, mortally wounded a woman of the people, very near the King's carriage.

example of which is found only among the most ferocious peoples on earth, or in the most disastrous periods of history. M. *Foulon*, grown old in public service and well known for his talents, was the father-in-law of M. *Berthier*, the Intendant of Paris. He was handed over by the peasants of his lands to the Parisian rabble. He was accused, without any proof, of having said once in his life that *the people were born to eat hay*. This proverbial sentence would not have led to his death if he had not been nominated as one of the ephemeral Ministers who succeeded M. *Necker*. That was his real crime. It has been observed that this same rabble, who are moved every day by the Passion of *Jesus Christ*, assigned to this unfortunate Minister the same ordeal, as if derision and impiousness added something to vengeance. He was crowned with thorns; and when, overcome with torture and fatigue, he asked for something to drink, they offered him vinegar. His head, carried through the streets of Paris, was taken the same day to his son-in-law, who was making his way toward the capital, in the midst of a crowd of peasants and armed bourgeois. Forced to kiss this bloodstained head, M. Berthier was soon afterward massacred under the windows of that same City Hall which vainly demanded mercy of the tigers over whom it was no longer master. The soldier who tore out the heart of M. Berthier, to present it still bleeding to Messieurs Bailly and La Fayette, proved to these new sages that the people taste liberty, like strong liqueurs, only to become drunken and wild. Woe to those who stir the depths of a nation! There is no century of light for the populace; it is not French, or English, or Spanish: the populace is always, and in every country, the same, always cannibalistic, always anthropophagous. Remember, Deputies of the French, that when one arouses the people one always gives them more energy than is needed to attain one's intended objective, and that this surplus of strength soon carries them beyond all limits. You are at this moment about to give firm laws and a permanent constitution to a great nation, and you want this constitution to be preceded by a pure and simple Declaration of the Rights of Man. Legislators, founders of a new order of things, you wish to set marching ahead of you the metaphysics that ancient legislators always had the wisdom to hide in the foundations of their structures. Ah! Do not be more learned than Nature. If you want a great people to enjoy the shade and take nourishment from the fruits of the tree that you plant, do not leave the roots uncovered. Beware lest men to whom you have spoken only about their rights and never about their duties, lest men who no longer need to fear royal authority, who understand nothing about the legislative operations of a National Assembly and have conceived exaggerated hopes for it, wish to pass from natural equality to social equality, from hatred of ranks to hatred of governmental powers, and lest, with their hands reddened from the blood of the nobles, they wish also to massacre their magistrates. The people need everyday truths and not abstractions; and when they leave behind them a long slavery, liberty must be presented to them with precaution and little by little, just as one is sparing of nourishment to those famished crews that one often meets in the middle of the ocean on voyages of long duration. Finally, do not forget, Deputies of France, that if kings destroy themselves for wanting to rule too much, legislative assemblies ruin themselves no less for wanting to introduce too many changes.

Besides, why disclose to the world purely speculative truths? Those who will not misuse them are those who know them as you do; and those who have not known how to think of them for themselves will never understand them and will abuse them always. Far from saying to the people that Nature has made all men equal, tell me on the contrary that it has made them very unequal; that one is born strong and another feeble; that one is healthy and another frail; that all are not equally clever and alert; and that the chief task of a well-ordered society is to make equal by laws those whom Nature has made so unequal in abilities.[2] But do not let them, because of that, believe that people's conditions are equal; you know, you can even see, what misfortunes result from this false idea once the people are preoccupied with it. At the first rumor that was spread concerning the abolition of feudal dues, the peasants wished neither to wait for nor to hear of the National Assembly's distinguishing between real and personal obligations; they have marched in throngs toward the abbeys, toward the châteaux, toward all the places where the archives of the nobility and the titles to ancient possessions are located. Fire, bloodshed, ruin, and death have

2. M. *de La Fayette*, in a sketch of a constitution read in the National Assembly, said on the contrary that Nature made men equal and that society made them unequal. His speech, in which it is claimed that M. Marmontel had a hand, depends on this principle so false and so fatal to societies.

everywhere marked the trail of these unmuzzled tigers; France is no more than a vast deathtrap, as formidable to foreigners as to its own inhabitants; and you are today forced to beg for help against these madmen from the very same regular troops whose disobedience you have praised too much to be able to hope ever to make them obey you.

IV.

The Defeat of a Moderate Coalition

---

14. *August 4, 1789:*
Night Session of the
National Assembly

The evening session of the National Assembly on August 4, 1789, which lasted until two o'clock in the morning of August 5, was one of the most famous events of the revolution, and became known for the renunciation, in an atmosphere of excitement and enthusiasm, of privileges of the aristocracy, Church, provinces, and municipalities. What was done was in part the product of planning by a minority of liberal leaders who were aware of the peasant revolts sweeping the country, of the dangers to the Assembly if repression were to be carried out by regular armies under the command of the king, and of the need not only to appease the peasantry but to do so without losing support of the liberals among the nobles and clergy who had thus far supported the revolution. Although the session of August 4 was the product of a calculated maneuver, neither the maneuver nor the response it elicited could have occurred without a backlog of problems that needed clearing up if there was to be national unity and equal citizenship; there was awareness of both the peasant crisis and the need to take a stand on matters of principle before the revolution could go forward to the making of a declaration of rights and a constitution. It is often pointed out that the detailed implementation between August 5 and 11 was less generous than the resolutions of the famous evening session, and this is of course true, but August 4 remains the crucial breakthrough toward a major reorganization of society, the Church, and political subdivisions, as well as citizenship and constitutional government.

Available reports of what was said on the night of August 4 are too lengthy to be repeated here in full. The opening speeches are given below, followed by the final resolutions. The source is *Archives parlementaires*, vol. VIII (Paris, 1875), pp. 343–345, 350.

August 4, 1789. National Assembly

Evening session.

The bureaus having met at six o'clock for the election of their presidents and secretaries and for the nomination of an archivist for the Assembly, and of replacements for the new ministers in the committees of which they had been members, the Assembly did not open its general meeting until eight o'clock.

THE PRESIDENT first requests the reading of the *project for a decree on the security of the kingdom*, which had been sent to the editing committee.

M. TARGET reads it as follows:

"The National Assembly, considering that, while it is single-mindedly occupied with securing the well-being of the people on the bases of a free constitution, troubles and violence affecting various provinces are spreading alarm in people's minds and seriously damaging the sacred rights of property and security of persons;

"That these disorders can only slow up the work of the Assembly and serve the criminal projects of the enemies of the public welfare;

"Declares that the already existing laws are still in effect and must be enforced until such time as the authority of the nation annuls or modifies them;

"That the taxes, in such forms as they have had, must continue to be collected according to the terms of the decree of June 17 last, until that authority has established taxes and forms less burdensome to the people;

"That all the customary payments and obligations must be honored as in the past until otherwise ordered by the Assembly;

"That, finally, the laws established for the security of persons and property must be universally respected.

"The present declaration shall be sent to all the provinces, and the priests requested to make it known to their parishioners and to recommend obedience to it."

M. LE VICOMTE DE NOAILLES. The aim of the project for a decree that the Assembly has just heard is to halt the disturbances in the provinces, assure public liberty, and confirm the legitimate rights of proprietors.

But how can one hope to accomplish this aim without knowing

what is the cause of the insurrection that is taking place in the kingdom, and how can it be remedied without applying the remedy to the evil that is causing the agitation?

The communities have made demands: it is not a constitution that they have desired; they have expressed this wish only in the *bailliages:* what have they asked for, then? That the *aides* be suppressed; that there no longer be subdelegates; that seigneurial dues be made less burdensome or redeemed.

For more than three months these communities have seen their representatives give their attention to what we call, and to what is in fact, the public business; but to them the public business seems above all to be what they desire and what they hope ardently to obtain.

Given all the differences of opinion that have existed among the representatives of the nation, the country people have distinguished only the persons acknowledged by them, who were working for their welfare, and the powerful figures who were opposing it.

Given this state of affairs, what has happened? They have believed it necessary to arm themselves against the use of force, and today they no longer know any restraint: and so, as a result of this tendency, the kingdom is drifting between the alternative of the destruction of society and that of a government that will be admired and imitated by all Europe.

This government, how can it be established? By means of public tranquillity. This tranquillity, how can one hope for it? By calming the people, by showing them that they are not being resisted except where something of value to them must be preserved.

In order to achieve this so necessary tranquillity, I propose:

1. That it be announced, before the proclamation projected by the committee, that the representatives of the nation have decided that taxes shall be paid by all individuals in the kingdom in proportion to their incomes;

2. That all public burdens shall in the future be supported equally by all;

3. That all feudal dues shall be redeemable by the communities, either for cash or via redemption payments according to a price arrived at with justice; that is, according to the income of an average year calculated on the basis of a ten-year period;

4. That seigneurial labor services, mortmains, and other personal servitudes shall be abolished without redemption.

Just then another noble deputy, M. le duc d'Aiguillon, proposes to express in more detail the resolution advanced by the previous speaker; his conception of it follows:

M. LE DUC D'AIGUILLON. Gentlemen, there is no one who does not groan at the spectacle of the horrible scenes in France. These popular uprisings, which served the purpose of consolidating liberty when culpable ministers wished to deprive us of it, have become an obstacle to this very liberty at the present moment, when the views of the government seem to be in harmony with our desires for the public welfare.

It is not only brigands who, with arms in their hands, wish to enrich themselves in the midst of calamities: in several provinces the whole people forms a kind of league for the destruction of the châteaux, the ravaging of the lands, and especially for the seizure of the archives where the title deeds to feudal properties are kept. It seeks to throw off at last a yoke that has for many centuries weighed it down; and it must be admitted, Gentlemen, this insurrection, although criminal (for all violent aggression is criminal), can be provided with some excuse by the vexations of which it is the victim. The proprietors of fiefs, of seigneurial lands, are, it must be stated, only very rarely guilty of the excesses of which their vassals complain; but their agents are often pitiless, and the unfortunate cultivator, subject to the barbarous remains of feudal laws that still exist in France, laments the constraints of which he is the victim. There is no hiding the fact that these rights are a property, and every property is sacred; but they are burdensome on the people, and everyone agrees concerning the continual irritation that they cause.

In this century of enlightenment, when salutary reason has recaptured its empire, during this fortunate epoch when, gathered together for the public welfare and freed from all selfish interests, we are going to work for the regeneration of the state, it seems to me, Gentlemen, that it would be necessary, before establishing the constitution that is so ardently desired and for which the nation is waiting, it would be necessary, I say, to prove to all the citizens that our intention, our hope, is to anticipate their desires, to establish as promptly as possible this equality of rights that must exist among all men and which can alone assure them of liberty. I do not doubt that the proprietors of fiefs, the seigneurs of landed properties, far from denying this truth, are disposed to sacrifice their rights for the sake of justice. They have already renounced their privileges, their pecuniary exemptions, and at this moment one cannot demand the outright renunciation of their feudal rights.

These rights are their property. They are, for some individuals, their only fortune; and equity forbids that the abandonment of any property be demanded without provision for a just indemnity for the proprietor, who sacrifices his own convenience to the public welfare.

In view of these weighty considerations, Gentlemen, and in order to make the people aware that you are attending efficiently to their dearest interests, my wish would be that the National Assembly declare that taxes shall be supported equally by all citizens in proportion to their abilities, and that henceforth all feudal dues of fiefs and seigneurial properties shall be redeemed by the vassals of these same fiefs and lands, if they wish to do so; that the redemption be paid at a rate fixed by the Assembly; and my estimate, my opinion, is that this should be at about a thirtieth, because of the indemnity to be granted.

It is according to these principles, Gentlemen, that I have written the following decree, which I have the honor to submit to your judgment, and which I beg you to take under consideration.

"The National Assembly, considering that the first and most sacred of its duties is to make individual and private interests cede to the general interest;

"That the taxes would be much less burdensome for the people if they were distributed equally over the whole citizenry according to their abilities to pay;

"That justice requires that this exact proportion be observed;

"Decrees that the corporations, towns, communities and individuals who have up to the present enjoyed individual privileges and personal exemptions shall in future bear all taxes, all public charges, without any distinction, either in the amount of the taxes or in their manner of collection.

"The National Assembly, considering, further, that feudal and seigneurial dues are also an onerous form of tax, which harms agriculture and desolates the countryside;

"Being unable, nevertheless, to deny that these dues are a

genuine property right and that all forms of property are inviolable;

"Decrees that these dues shall in future be redeemable at the will of those subject to them, at the rate of one-thirtieth or at whatever other rate shall be judged most equitable for each province by the National Assembly according to the rates which shall be presented to it.

"The National Assembly orders, finally, that all of these dues shall be maintained and collected exactly as in the past until their complete redemption."

These two motions, presented with the most intense interest in the fate of the inhabitants of the rural areas, whose ills they should alleviate while calming their effervescence and fulfilling their hopes, are received with inexpressible transports of joy.

ONE OF THE MEMBERS OF THE ASSEMBLY suggests with emotion how touching it would be for all citizens to learn that whereas yesterday the members of the commons solicited the zeal of the National Assembly against violence at the expense of the persons and properties of the nobles, today the latter in a generous move of reciprocity gave to all classes of the French people so marked a proof of their patriotism.

M. DUPONT DE NEMOURS. Universal disorder has taken possession of the state by virtue of the inaction of all the agents of power; no political society can exist for a single moment without laws and courts to guarantee liberty, security of persons, and the safeguarding of property. I insist on the necessity of maintaining and not abandoning the laws, however imperfect, which have as their purpose the conservation of the social order.

M. Dupont calls attention to the fact that the courts charged with the maintenance of public tranquillity in conformity with these laws exist legally as well as in fact as long as they have not been abolished;

That it is not possible for representatives of the nation to reform legislation until after they have determined how, according to the constitution itself, new laws are to be proposed, adopted, and executed;

And that it is essential that calm, peace, and justice, re-established throughout the empire, make it unnecessary for the National Assembly to have any other concern than that which is inseparable from the task with which it is occupied, of choosing and decreeing the parts of this wise and durable constitution.

In consequence, he makes the following motion:

To declare that every citizen is obliged to obey the laws and to respect the liberty, security, and property of the other citizens;

That the courts must act without interruption for the execution of these laws;

And that the bourgeois militias and all military forces are enjoined by them, as well as by the wishes of the representatives of the nation, to intervene forcefully for the re-establishment of peace and order and for the protection of persons and property on every occasion when they may be called upon by the municipalities and civil magistrates.

M. LEGUEN DE KÉRANGAL, DEPUTY FROM LOWER BRITTANY. Gentlemen, a great question has concerned us today; the declaration of the rights of man and of the citizen has been judged necessary. The abuse that the people is making of these same rights presses you to explain them and to set with a skilled hand the limits that it must not overstep; it will surely hold itself in check.

You would have prevented the burning of the châteaux if you had been more prompt to declare that the terrible weapons that they contained and which have been tormenting the people for centuries were to be destroyed by a forced redemption that you were going to order.

The people, impatient to obtain justice and tired of oppression, is eager to destroy these title deeds, monuments to the barbarism of our ancestors.

Let us be just, Gentlemen: let us gather those title deeds that outrage not only decency but even humanity. Let us gather those title deeds that humiliate the human race by requiring that men be hitched to a plow like work animals. Let us gather those title deeds that oblige men to pass their nights beating the swamps so that the frogs will be prevented from troubling the sleep of their voluptuous seigneurs.

Who among us, Gentlemen, in this century of enlightenment, would not make a funeral pyre in expiation of these infamous parchments and would not lift the torch to make of them a sacrifice on the altar of the public welfare?

Gentlemen, you will not return calm to agitated France until you have promised the people that you are going to convert into monetary payments, redeemable at will, all the feudal dues of whatever kind; that the laws you are going to promulgate will abolish every trace concerning which they have just complaints. Tell them that you recognize the injustice of these rights acquired in times of darkness and ignorance.

For the sake of peace, hasten to give these promises to France; a universal cry is making itself heard; you have not a moment to lose; each day of delay occasions new burnings; the fall of empires is announced with less commotion. Do you wish to give laws only to a devastated France? . . .

[M. de Kérangal's speech becomes a rather detailed attack on feudal dues. He is enthusiastically applauded, and then speaker after speaker comes forward, and the proposed renunciations turn to all kinds of privileges having to do with the Church and with provinces and towns, as well as with the nobility and rural life.]

The session having continued rather far into the night, the President, after having consulted the wishes of the Assembly, suspends this flow of patriotic declarations in order to reread the principal points that have been made and have them decreed by the Assembly, except for the final writing; this action is taken at once with unanimous support, subject to reservations required by the oaths and mandates of some constituencies.

The following are the articles decreed:

Abolition of the condition of serf and of mortmain in whatever form it exists.

The right to redeem seigneurial dues.

Abolition of seigneurial jurisdictions.

Suppression of exclusive hunting rights, and rights to keep pigeons and rabbits.

A tax in money in place of the tithe.

Possible redemption of all tithes of whatever kind.

Abolition of all pecuniary privileges and immunities.

Equality before taxes of all kinds, retroactive to the beginning of the year 1789, according to regulations to be passed by the provincial assemblies.

Admissibility of all citizens to civil and military offices.

Declaration on the forthcoming establishment of free justice and of suppression of venality of offices.

Abandonment of particular privileges held by provinces and

towns. Declaration by deputies having imperative mandates that they will write to their constituents to secure their agreement.

Abandonment of the privileges of a number of cities: Paris, Lyons, Bordeaux, and so on.

Suppression of the right of *déport* and *vacat*, of annates, and of plurality of benefices.

Abolition of pensions obtained without qualifications.

Reformation of *jurandes*.

A medal to be struck to commemorate the memory of this day.

A solemn *Te Deum*, and a deputation from the National Assembly to the King to take him the homage of the Assembly and the title of *Restorer of French Liberty*, with the invitation to be present at the *Te Deum*.

Cries of *Vive le Roi*, public expressions of joy taking many forms, mutual felicitations of the deputies and the people present terminate the session.

15. August 20–26, 1789: Declaration of the Rights of Man and of the Citizen

The Declaration of the Rights of Man and of the Citizen was a product of both theory and fact. The National Assembly interrupted its consideration of these principles to take account, between August 4 and 11, of the fact of the peasant revolution, and when they returned to vote the following articles between August 20 and 26, they composed and arranged them, as Georges Lefebvre has shown unforgettably, in awareness of the old regime that they were combating and of material interests and political considerations in the new one that they were shaping. The Declaration leaves much unsaid concerning the intentions of its authors, both in the way of practical implementations that were to prove disappointing and cause difficulties, and in the way of a general social philosophy that envisaged liberty and equality insuring justice in an individualistic society. Both the realism and the faith were to be expressed in their subsequent actions. The document as presented below was translated from *Déclaration des droits de l'homme et du citoyen, décrétés par l'Assemblée nationale dans les séances des 20, 21, 23, 24, et 26 août 1789, acceptés par le Roi* (Paris, Goujon, s.d.), a poster of 1789 reproduced photographically for the Exposition des Droits de l'Homme of 1969.

Preamble

The representatives of the French people, organized as a national assembly, considering that ignorance, neglect, and scorn of the rights of man are the sole causes of public misfortunes and of corruption of governments, have resolved to display in a solemn declaration the natural, inalienable, and sacred rights of man, so that this declaration, constantly in the presence of all members of society, will continually remind them of their rights and their duties; so that the acts of the legislative power and those of the executive power, being subject at any time to comparison with the purpose of any political institution, will be better respected; so that the demands of the citizens, based henceforth on simple and incontestable principles, will always contribute to the maintenance of the constitution and the happiness of all.

Consequently, the National Assembly recognizes and declares, in the presence and under the auspices of the Supreme Being, the following rights of man and citizen:

Article 1. Men are born and remain free and equal in rights; social distinctions can be established only for the common benefit.

2. The aim of every political association is the conservation of the natural and imprescriptible rights of man; these rights are liberty, property, security, and resistance to oppression.

3. The source of all sovereignty is located in essence in the nation; no body, no individual can exercise authority which does not emanate from it expressly.

4. Liberty consists in being able to do anything that does not harm another person. Thus the exercise of the natural rights of each man has no limits except those which assure to the other members of society the enjoyment of these same rights; these limits can be determined only by law.

5. The law has the right to forbid only those actions harmful to society. All that is not forbidden by the law cannot be hindered, and no one can be forced to do what it does not order.

6. The law is the expression of the general will; all citizens have the right to concur personally or through their representatives in its formation; it must be the same for all, whether it protects or punishes. All citizens being equal in its eyes are equally admissible to all honors, positions, and public employments, according to

their capabilities and without other distinctions than those of their virtues and talents.

7. No man can be accused, arrested, or detained except in cases determined by the law, and according to the forms which it has prescribed. Those who solicit, draw up, execute, or have executed arbitrary orders must be punished; but any citizen summoned or seized by virtue of the law must obey instantly; he renders himself culpable by resisting.

8. The law must establish only penalties that are strictly and clearly necessary, and no one can be punished except in virtue of a law established and published prior to the offense and legally applied.

9. Every man being presumed innocent until he has been declared guilty, if it is judged indispensable to arrest him, all severity that is not necessary for making sure of his person must be severely repressed by the law.

10. No one may be disturbed because of his opinions, even religious, provided that their public demonstration does not disturb the public order established by law.

11. The free communication of thoughts and opinions is one of the most precious rights of man: every citizen can therefore freely speak, write, and print: he is answerable for abuses of this liberty in cases determined by the law.

12. The guaranteeing of the rights of man and citizen necessitates a public force; this force is therefore instituted for the advantage of all, and not for the private use of those to whom it is entrusted.

13. For the maintenance of the public force, and for the expenses of administration, a tax supported in common is indispensable; it must be assessed on all citizens in proportion to their capacities to pay.

14. Citizens have the right to determine for themselves or through their representatives the need for taxation of the public, to consent to it freely, to investigate its use, and to determine its rate, basis, collection, and duration.

15. Society has the right to demand an accounting of his administration from every public agent.

16. Any society in which guarantees of rights are not assured nor the separation of powers determined has no constitution.

17. Property being an inviolable and sacred right, no one may be deprived of it unless public necessity, legally determined,

clearly requires such action, and then only on condition of a just and prior indemnity.

16. September 1, 1789:
Mirabeau on Royal Authority

Honoré Gabriel, comte de Mirabeau (1749–1791), the most celebrated orator of the revolution, cannot be classified with any of the groups on the political spectrum, indistinct though they were, and evolving. He must be placed a bit to the left of the Anglophiles, although like them he was anxious to preserve the king's authority and not to make a complete break with tradition, and a bit to the right of Lafayette and Duport and Barnave and the various leaders who were to be associated as Feuillants, although he was quicker than they to see the dangers of a unicameral legislature and a suspensive veto for the king. The document that follows is the printed version of his speech of September 1, 1789, advocating an absolute veto for the king, a cause which he shared with the Anglophiles and in which he was to share their defeat ten days later when the suspensive veto was voted by the National Assembly. Nevertheless the Assembly voted that this speech should be printed. Mirabeau explains in a footnote that has been omitted from the first page that he cannot repeat everything that he said orally but that he can guarantee that whatever is here was said in the Assembly. We must, of course, assume that printed speeches, whether delivered or not, may contain arguments that the speaker wished he had said; but that is part of their interest. The pamphlet is *Discours de M. le comte de Mirabeau sur la sanction royale* (s.l.n.d., 26 pp.). No deletions have been made in the argument about the royal veto. Two footnotes in which Mirabeau comments on conditions of debate in the National Assembly, and several paragraphs advocating tax reform, a law code, and annual assemblies, with which Mirabeau provided a change of pace in the middle of his speech, have been omitted.

Session of September 1

MESSIEURS,

In the best organized monarchy, the royal authority is always the subject of fears on the part of the best citizens; he whom the law places above everyone else easily becomes a rival to the law. Powerful enough to protect the constitution, he is often tempted to destroy it. The consistent progress that the authority of kings has everywhere made has only too clearly taught the necessity of keeping an eye on them. This distrust, salutary in itself, naturally leads us to want to contain such a fearful power. A secret fear estranges us in spite of ourselves from the means with which it is necessary to arm the supreme head of the nation in order that he may fulfill the functions that are assigned him.

However, if one considers coolly the principles and nature of monarchical government instituted on the basis of the sovereignty of the people; if one examines attentively the circumstances that give rise to it, it will be seen that the monarch must be considered rather as the protector of the people than as the enemy of their welfare.

Two powers are necessary to the existence and functioning of a political body: that of willing and that of acting. By the first, society establishes rules for guiding it toward its objective, which is without doubt the good of all. By the second, these rules are executed, and the public force serves to make the society triumph over the obstacles that this execution may meet in the opposition of individual wills.

In a great nation these two wills cannot be exercised by the nation itself; that is why representatives of the people are needed to exercise the faculty of willing, or the legislative power; that is why, also, another kind of representative is needed for the exercise of the faculty of acting, or the executive power.

The larger the nation is, the more important it is that this latter power be active; that is why there is needed a single supreme chief, a monarchical government, in great states where upheavals and dismemberments would be infinitely to be feared if there did not exist a force that was adequate for keeping all the parts together and directing their activity toward a common center.

Both of these powers are equally necessary, equally valued by the nation. It is remarkable, however, how the executive power, acting on the people continually, is in a more immediate relationship with them; and how important it is for the people that this power, charged with the responsibility of maintaining an equilibrium and preventing the biases and preferences toward which the minority tends ceaselessly at the expense of the majority, have constantly available a sure means of maintaining itself.

This means exists in the right of the supreme head of the

nation to examine the acts of the legislative power and give to them or withhold from them the sacred character of law.

Called upon by his very nature to be at once executor of the law and protector of the people, the monarch could be obliged to turn the public force against the people if his intervention were not an essential part of the legislative process, declaring the laws to be in harmony with the general will.

This prerogative of the monarch is especially important in every state where the legislative power must be entrusted to representatives owing to the complete inability of the people to exercise it themselves.

Because in the nature of things the choice of representatives does not necessarily fall to the most worthy but to those whose situation, wealth, and particular circumstances designate them as being able most willingly to sacrifice their time to the public business, there will always result from the selection of these representatives of the people a kind of aristocracy of fact which, ceaselessly tending to acquire a legal character, will become hostile both to the monarch, whom it will wish to equal, and to the people, whom it will always seek to hold down.

From this condition springs the natural and necessary alliance between the Prince and the people against every form of aristocracy; an alliance based on the fact that, having the same interests and fears, they must have the same objective and consequently the same will.

If on the one hand the grandeur of the Prince depends on the prosperity of the people, the welfare of the people depends mainly on the tutelary power of the Prince.

It is thus not at all for his selfish interest that the monarch intervenes in legislation but precisely for the interest of the people; and it is in this sense that one can and must say that the royal sanction is not at all the prerogative of the monarch but the property, the domain, of the nation.

Thus far I have spoken in terms of an order of things toward which we are progressing rapidly, I mean an organized and constituted monarchy; but since we have not yet achieved this order of things, I must explain myself very frankly. I think that the right to suspend, and even halt, the action of the legislature must belong to the King when the constitution is finished and there will merely be a question of maintaining it. But this right to call a halt, this *veto*, cannot be in effect while the problem at hand is the creation of the constitution: I cannot conceive how one could dispute a people's right to give itself the constitution by which it wished to be governed henceforth.

Therefore let us examine only whether the constitution that is in process of being made should include the royal sanction as an integral part of the legislature.

Certainly to anyone who only views the matter superficially there will come to mind great objections to the idea of a *veto* applied by anyone at all to the wishes of the people's representatives. When one pictures the National Assembly composed of its true components presenting to the Prince the fruit of its deliberations, voting by head, and offering him the product of the freest and most enlightened discussion and of all the knowledge it has been able to gather, it seems that you have there all that human caution can require for the verification of—I do not say only the general will, but the general reason; and without doubt from this abstract point of view it seems to violate good sense to accept as true the idea that a single man may have the right to respond: "I take issue with this will, this general reason." This idea becomes even more shocking still when it must be accepted as constitutional that the man armed with this terrible *veto* will also be armed with the whole public force without which the general will can never be assured of execution.

All of these objections disappear before the great truth that without a right to resist in the hands of the holder of the public force this force could often be laid claim to and employed in spite of him to implement wishes contrary to the general will.

Now, to demonstrate by an example that this danger would exist if the Prince were to be despoiled of the *veto* over all the proposals of legislation that the National Assembly would present to him, I demand only that you imagine a poor choice of representatives and two internal regulations already proposed and authorized by the example of England; namely:

The exclusion of the public from the national chamber on the simple request of a member of the Assembly, and the prohibition of newspaper reports of its deliberations.

These two regulations once obtained, it is evident that it would be a short step to the expulsion of any member who might be indiscreet, and with the terror of despotism of the Assembly acting against the Assembly itself, it would take only a short time, and a little cleverness under a weak prince, to establish *legally* the domination of twelve hundred aristocrats, reduce the royal authority to nothing but the passive instrument of their desires, and plunge the people once more into that condition of degradation that always accompanies the servitude of the Prince.

The Prince is the perpetual representative of the people, as the deputies are its representatives elected at stated periods. The rights of the one, like those of the others, are only based on their utility to those who have established them.

No one objects to the *veto* of the National Assembly, which is, in effect, merely a right of the people entrusted *to its representatives* in order to oppose any proposition that might tend to re-establish ministerial despotism. Why complain, then, about the *veto* of the Prince, which is also merely a right of the people *entrusted especially to the Prince*, because the Prince is as interested as the people in preventing the establishment of aristocracy.

But, someone says, the deputies of the people in the National Assembly, being clothed with power for only a limited time and having no share of the executive power, cannot abuse the use of their *veto* with anywhere near as harmful results as would be obtained by an irremovable Prince opposing a just and reasonable law.

In the first place, if the Prince does not have the *veto*, who will prevent the representatives of the people from prolonging their term in office and before long making it permanent? (This is the way the Long Parliament overturned political liberty in Great Britain, and not, as you have been told, by the suppression of the Chamber of Peers.) Who will prevent their even appropriating the part of the executive power that disposes of offices and favors? Will they lack pretexts to justify this usurpation? Appointments are so scandalous! Favors are so unworthily degraded! And so on.

In the second place, the *veto*, whether of the Prince or of the deputies of the National Assembly, has no other virtue than to halt a proposition: there cannot therefore result from a *veto*, of whatever sort, anything except the inaction of the executive in this regard.

In the third place, the *veto* of the Prince can without doubt be opposed to a good law; but it can protect against a bad one, the existence of which is incontestably a possibility.

In the fourth place, suppose that indeed the Prince's *veto* prevents the establishment of the law wisest and most advantageous to the nation; what will happen *if the* ANNUAL *return of the National Assembly is as solidly assured as is the crown on the head of the Prince who wears it;* that is, if the annual return of the National Assembly is assured by an *authentically constitutional* law, which forbids, on pain of the conviction for imbecility, the proposing or granting of any kind of tax or the establishment of the military force for more than one year? Suppose that the Prince has made use of his *veto;* the Assembly will determine first if that use does or does not have consequences harmful to liberty. In the second case, the difficulty raised by the *veto* being nonexistent or of only slight importance, the National Assembly will vote the tax and the army for the usual term, and in consequence everything will remain as usual.

In the first case, the Assembly will have various means of influencing the King's will; it will be able to refuse taxes; it will be able to refuse the army: it will be able to refuse both, or simply vote them only for a very short period. Whichever of these means the Assembly adopts, the Prince, threatened with the paralysis of the executive power at a specified time, has no other means than to appeal to his people by dissolving the Assembly.

If in that case the people then return the same deputies to the Assembly, will it not be necessary for the Prince to *obey?* For that is the true word, whatever idea has previously been given him of his supposed sovereignty, when he ceases to be united in opinion with his people, and the people are informed.

Supposing now that the right of *veto* has been taken from the Prince and the Prince is obliged to sanction a bad law; in this case you have no other hope than in a general insurrection, of which the best outcome you could hope for would probably be more damaging to the representatives of the people than the dissolution of their Assembly. But is it really certain that this insurrection would damage only the unworthy representatives of the people? I also see in it a resource for the partisans of ministerial despotism. I see in it the imminent danger that the public peace will be troubled and perhaps violated; I see in it the almost inevitable conflagration that we have had to fear for too long in a state where a necessary but so rapid revolution has left germs of division and hatred that only the strengthening of the constitution by the uninterrupted labors of the Assembly can stifle.

You can see, Gentlemen, that I have in every case assumed the permanence of the National Assembly, and I have even drawn from it all my arguments in favor of the royal sanction, which to me seems to be the impregnable rampart of political liberty, provided the King can never persist in his *veto* without dissolving the Assembly, nor dissolve without immediately convoking another, because the constitution must never permit the social body to be without representatives; provided that a constitutional law declare all taxes and even the army legally nullified three months after the dissolution of the National Assembly; and provided, finally, that the responsibility of the ministers be always exercised with the most inflexible rigor, and even if public affairs should not be improved each year through the progress of the public reason, would not a glance at the imposing extent of our duties be sufficient to convince us that we should decree annual National Assemblies? . . .

What! say those whom great power frightens because they know how to judge it only by its abuses, the royal *veto* would be unlimited! There would be no time determined by the constitution when this *veto* could no longer hinder the legislative power? Would not that government be a despotism where the King could say: "Such is the will of my people, but mine is the opposite, and it is mine that shall prevail"?

Those who are agitated by this fear propose what they call a *suspensive veto:* in other words the King will be able to refuse his sanction to a project of law of which he disapproves; he will be able to dissolve the National Assembly, or wait for another one; but if this new Assembly presents to him for a second time the same law that he has already rejected, he will be obliged to accept it.

Here is their reasoning in all its force. When the King refuses to sanction a law that the National Assembly proposes to him, it must be supposed that he judges this law to be contrary to the interests of the people, or to usurp the executive power that resides in him and that he must defend: in this case he appeals to the nation and it names a new legislature, making its wishes known to the new representatives; thus the nation pronounces judgment, and the King must submit or he will be denying the authority of the supreme tribunal to which he himself had appealed.

This objection is very specious, and I only came to understand its falsity after examining all aspects of the question; but it has already been made apparent, and will be brought out still more in the course of the discussion, that:

1. It supposes falsely that it is impossible for a second legislature to fail to report accurately the wishes of the people.

2. It supposes falsely that the King will be tempted to prolong his *veto* against the known will of the nation.

3. It supposes that the *suspensive veto* has no inconveniences, whereas in several respects it has the same inconveniences as if the King were granted no *veto* at all.

It was necessary to make the crown hereditary so that it would not be a perpetual cause of upheavals; from that has resulted the necessity of making the person of the King irreproachable and sacred, without which the throne could never have been sheltered from the ambitious. Now, what power is not already in the hands of a hereditary and inviolable chief? The refusal to enforce execution of a law that he judged contrary to his interests, of which he is guardian as chief of the executive power—would this refusal be enough to justify removal of his high prerogatives? That would be destroying with one hand what you had built with the other; that would be associating a precaution aimed at peace and security with the means most likely to arouse endlessly the most terrible storms.

Pass from this consideration to the instruments of power, which must be in the hands of the nation's chief. Twenty-five million men whom he must command! All points of an area of thirty thousand square leagues over which his power must be ceaselessly ready to protect or forbid, and there are those who would claim that this chief, legitimate holder of the means that this power demands, could be forced to execute laws to which he had not consented! But through what frightful troubles, through what convulsive and bloody insurrections do they wish to make us pass in order to combat his resistance? When the law is under the safeguard of public opinion, it becomes truly imperious for the chief you have armed with the whole public force; but when can one count on this empire of public opinion? Is it not when the chief of the executive power has himself given his consent to the law and when this consent is known to all citizens? Is it not then and only then that public opinion places the law irrevocably above him and forces him, on pain of becoming an object of horror, to execute what he has promised; for his consent as chief of the executive power is nothing else than a solemn engagement to execute that law to which he has just given his sanction.

And let it not be said that the generals of armies are depositaries of very great powers and are nevertheless obliged to obey orders from above whatever they may think of the nature of these orders. The generals of armies are not hereditary chiefs, their persons are not inviolable, their authority ceases in the presence of the superiors whose orders they execute, and, if one were to push the comparison further, one would be forced to agree that they are usually very poor generals who execute arrangements to which they have not given their approval. There you have the dangers that you are going to run, and for what? Where is the real effectiveness of the *suspensive veto?*

Does it not require, as in my system, that certain precautions against the royal *veto* be taken in the constitution? If the King upsets the precautions, will he not place himself easily above the law? Your formula is thus useless in terms of your own theory, and I am proving it to be dangerous in terms of mine.

One can only imagine two cases in which there will be refusal of the royal sanction.

One is the case where the monarch would judge that the proposed law would damage the interests of the nation, and the other is the case where, misled by his ministers, he would resist laws that were contrary to their personal views.

Now, in both of these cases would not the King or his ministers, being deprived of the faculty of preventing the law by the peaceful means of a legal *veto*, have recourse to illegal and violent resistance, according to whether they attached greater or less importance to the law? Can anyone doubt that they would have prepared their means very much in advance? For it is always easy to forecast the amount of attachment that the legislative power will have for its law. It would thus be possible for the legislative power to find itself forcibly restricted at the moment indicated by the constitution for overcoming the royal *veto;* whereas if this *veto* remains always possible, illegal and violent resistance, having become useless to the Prince, can no longer be employed without making him in the eyes of the whole nation a rebel against the constitution, a circumstance which soon makes such resistance infinitely dangerous for the King himself and especially for his ministers. Note especially that this danger is no longer the same when the Prince has only resisted a law to which he has not consented.

In this latter case, since violent and illegal resistance can always be supported by plausible pretexts, the insurrection of the executive power against the constitution always finds partisans, especially when it is the monarch's doing. With what facility did not Sweden return to despotism for having wanted its King, although hereditary, to be nothing but the passive and blind instrument of the senate's will?

Let us not, then, arm the King against the legislative power by making him foresee even an instant when his consent would be made unnecessary and when as a result he would be nothing but a blind and coerced executor. Let us admit that the nation will find more security and tranquillity in laws expressly consented to by its chief than in resolutions he had no share in making, and which would contrast sharply with the military power with which he would under any circumstances have to be endowed. Let us admit that as soon as we have placed the crown in a designated family and made it the patrimony of its eldest sons, it is imprudent to alarm them by subjecting them to a legislative power whose means of enforcement remains in their hands and in whose meetings, nevertheless, their opinions would be scorned. This scorn eventually becomes associated with the person, and the despositary of all the forces of the French Empire cannot be scorned without the greatest danger.

It follows from these considerations, which are based on the human heart and on experience, that the King must have the power to make the National Assembly face re-election. This kind of action is necessary in order to preserve for the King a legal and peaceable means of securing, in his turn, laws that he would judge useful for the nation, and that the National Assembly would resist. Nothing would be less dangerous, for it would certainly be necessary for the King to rely on the will of the nation if, to get a law accepted, he had recourse to the election of new members; and when the nation and the King join in desiring a law, the resistance of the legislative corps can have only two causes: either the corruption of its members, in which case their replacement is a benefit; or a doubt concerning public opinion, and in that case the best means of clarifying the situation is certainly the election of new members.

Gentlemen, I sum up in a single word: yearly meetings of the National Assembly; yearly renewal of support for the army; yearly renewal of taxation; responsibility of ministers; and the royal sanction, without written restrictions, but perfectly limited in fact, will be the Palladium of the national liberty and the most precious exercise of the liberty of the people.

17. September 4, 1789:
Abbé Grégoire on the Royal Veto and the Legislature of Two Chambers

Abbé Henri Grégoire, born in 1750 and destined to live until 1831, had been one of the leaders of the deputies of the clergy when they joined the deputies of the Third Estate in June, 1789, and had played a prominent part in the resistance to the court and the aristocracy on June 20 and July 14. His name remains associated with many causes: the defense of the civil and political rights of the Jews, opposition to slavery, defense of the constitutional Church, cultural projects such as the Institute, opposition to "vandalism"—he is said to have coined the word—and eventually resistance to Napoleon and persistence in his own liberal ideas under the Restoration. His speech on September 4, 1789, against the Anglophile constitutional measures, *Opinion de M. Grégoire, curé d'Embermenil, député de Nanci, sur la sanction royale, à la séance du 4 systembre*, was printed in the *Procès-Verbal de l'Assemblée nationale, imprimé par son ordre*. Deuxième Livraison, Tome Quatrième (Paris, s.d.). His appeal was that of a man who was well known, if rather radical for that period, and who argued in everyday terms accessible to a great many people. The opinions of men like Grégoire prevailed over those of Mirabeau and of Jean Joseph Mounier, the Anglophile leader whose views have already been illustrated in Document 6. Mounier and Lally-Tollendal had spoken on August 31 for the Constitutional Committee, and Mounier and others spoke again in September, but the Anglophiles had lost the majority.

GENTLEMEN,

The Royal Sanction, in my opinon, is only the act by which the Prince declares that a decree has come from the Legislature, and promises to have it executed. His function amounts to the promulgation of the law.

Has he, by virtue of his high rank, the right to share the legislative power? No, for he can have only those rights that are accorded him by the constituent power; consequently the King (I do not say the Sovereign—henceforth this term will signify the Nation) can be an integral part of the Legislature only through a concession freely granted by the body from which all the rights of the crown emanate—namely, the people.

On the basis of this principle, the King cannot therefore refuse his consent to the law; but if one takes into account the influence of the passions, perhaps it is necessary to grant him a prerogative which, being necessary for political tranquillity, is reconcilable with the rigor of the principle that I have just established. Thus the royal *veto* can be envisaged only as a matter of convenience and utility. The question is therefore reduced to knowing whether it is important for the sake of the national good to arm the King with the absolute or suspensive right to oppose a law.

Charged by our mandates with rejuvenating the Constitution, or creating a new one on the ruins of the old, we are exercising at this moment the constituent power; thus, even if the right of refusing the law were accorded to the august Delegate of the Nation, his refusal could never be opposed to the Constitution.

I am going to try to prove, Gentlemen, that you do not have the right to accord the Prince an absolute *veto;* that even if you had the right, you should not do so, and that it is in the Prince's interest for him not to have it.

1. You would exceed your powers in according him an unlimited *veto;* for you do not have the right to compromise, still less to alienate, the liberty of your constituents: if the representatives of the Nation and the King are not in agreement on the acceptance or rejection of a decree, there is only one tribunal competent to judge at the highest level of jurisdiction; this tribunal is that which creates kings, that of the people, before whom all private interests disappear. Now, if the King had the absolute *veto*, he would be judge and litigant, and the national liberty could find itself in a struggle with despotism.

Besides, you *cannot* make an irrevocable covenant for posterity, nor bind those who will come after you, and you have scarcely more authority over the liberty of future generations than over the liberty of past generations. Therefore you would try in vain to bend future men under the yoke of slavery, for the people would always have the right to break the chains that you would have tried vexatiously to impose on them.

2. If you had the right to accord the Prince an unlimited *veto*,

it would be imprudent to do so; for if the law is agreeable or immaterial to the King, he will sanction it without difficulty; but in that case what good does the right to say *I am opposed* do him? It would be, in that case, only the illusory faculty of preventing someone from doing what would be agreeable to him. Or the law will displease the Prince, and then the will of an entire Nation will be sacrificed to the will of a single person; would this one man therefore be less accessible to error and corruption, he alone, than twenty-four millions of his fellows? Prove to me that the King is, if not infallible, at least more enlightened than the sum total of the people; guarantee to me an unbroken succession of princes whose ever-present integrity and always moderate and wise inclinations will never be at odds with reason, with the result that their individual interest will never clash with the national interest.

Unfortunately kings are men. Truth reaches their thrones only with difficulty, withered by courtiers and often accompanied by lies. Unfortunately kings, badly brought up for the most part, have tumultuous passions. One of the most deeply rooted in the human heart and one of the most ardent is the thirst for power, and the urge to extend its empire. A king capable of dominating through the superiority of his genius, like Louis XIV, who did everything to satisfy his vanity, and who always thought of himself before his people; such a king, by virtue of the absolute *veto*, will rapidly encroach upon the legislative power, through the facility of directing alone the lever of the executive power, which is always in operation. You will have a despot.

A feeble king will be subjugated by his agents, interested in invading the unlimited power of a master whom they will have enslaved in order to rule in his name, and you will then have the most absurd *veto*, as well as the most formidable—that of the Ministers. The King whom you have decorated with so beautiful a title, and the Ministers whom he has honored with his confidence, must without doubt reassure yours; but we are laying the foundations of an edifice that can last for centuries. Our Constitution, our legislation, must be independent of the moral qualities of the head of the Nation; they must be unassailable under a scoundrel, under a Nero—that is to say, under Louis XI—as well as under a good prince, a Henri IV—that is to say, a Louis XVI.

The partisans of the absolute *veto* give us effective means of overcoming persistent refusals of the Royal Sanction. Such are popular insurrection, the ascendancy of opinion, and the refusal to pay taxes.

What logic—to wish to raise a barrier in order to give oneself the pleasure of destroying it through violent means!

Is the ascendancy of national opinion irresistible? Does not experience testify that tyrants of all centuries were deaf to the cries of reason, and braved opinion?

Insurrection is one misfortune opposed to another misfortune; in anticipating evil, we exempt ourselves from remedying it.

The refusal to pay taxes would be a scourage which, through a counterstroke, would strike all citizens, and soon the political corps would be deprived of movement and life. Besides, would it not be illusory to say to the King, you have the right to accept or reject our laws; but nevertheless if you refuse to accede to our will, we will be able to force you to do so by drying up the public treasury?

Will they never stop telling us that our mandates stipulate the Royal Sanction? Have they even defined those terms? Have they distinguished between the unlimited and the suspensive *veto*? No, the right to distinguish between the authority allowed the King and that which the Nation reserves for itself is reserved for your wisdom.

Will they never stop objecting to us that formerly in France, and even now in most European governments, the King has a portion of the legislative authority, and that the King of England has the absolute *veto?*[1] I am examining less what is done in other

1. M. de Lolme and other writers who have praised the English Constitution so much should have cited it not as the best possible, but as one of the best in existence. That is the opinion that all Europe will soon have, when the French have finished theirs. Does *religious liberty* exist in a country where Catholics are harassed? Have the English the *liberty of commerce* when almost all branches of trade are subject to onerous and sometimes ridiculous regulations? Do they have *individual liberty*, when the law of *habeas corpus* is violated on the simple affirmation of someone who claims payment of a debt, even imaginary; when the slightest pretext of a maritime armament authorizes the impressment of sailors?

The English are not governed directly by the arbitrary authority of the King and his Ministers, but by the arbitrary will of a parliament whose members have often purchased the votes of the electors and have then sold their own votes to the Court. The notorious election of Middlesex in which Mr. Wilkes, elected and rejected three times, was finally admitted some years later, proves only too well the corruptive influence of the ministry.

Are the English people truly represented? The Upper House is composed only of members admitted to take seats through the right of birth or of rank, and not through the free choice of their fellow citizens; out of about six million inhabitants in Great Britain, 5,700 persons choose half of the Commons, as Mr. *Burgh* proves in his *Political Researches*. There is therefore an

countries than what should be done. Too often the history that is invoked is an arsenal from which each takes arms of all sorts, because it offers examples of every kind. A multiplicity of facts, instead of supporting a principle, often only indicates in many cases the violation of principles; and often one cites as an example to follow something that should be considered only as an abuse to reform.

3. It is in the King's interest not to have the absolute *veto;* for if the law is wise, it will necessarily be advantageous to the Prince, whose true happiness is inseparable from that of the Nation. If the law is bad, the King will incur no blame, and the Nation will be able to blame only itself for the error.

But a National Assembly can err. The prestige of eloquence, the effervescence of enthusiasm, or other causes can overbalance it through a too brusque movement, and divert it from its true objectives; it is then that a limited opposition to the law can be of service. This suspensive *veto* is only an appeal to the people, and people, assured that they will have the final decision, will not become incensed; whereas the absolute *veto*, restraining and suffocating national liberty under the scepter of despotism, would perhaps lead to insurrection.

Therefore a barrier is needed against precipitous decisions, but this barrier must be neither insurmountable nor permanent; after a determined lapse of time, the obstacle placed by the Prince must be removed by the will of the people.

There are even political circumstances in which the suspensive *veto* accorded the Prince would threaten the Nation's liberty. For example, in the interval between the present session and the following one, will not the antipatriots whose party is dispersed but not destroyed foment new troubles? They will cabal in a base manner, that is to say, worthy of them; in an atrocious manner, that

---

extreme inequality in the exercise of the right of suffrage and of representation. Of the fifty-two counties, twelve send only one representative each. Sheffield, with more than thirty thousand souls, and Birmingham and Manchester, with seventy to eighty thousand, do not send any deputies to Parliament, while the universities, and even simple hamlets, furnish two legislators to the state.

It is known also that the English Constitution is unjust to Scotland and Ireland, whose inhabitants do not have as keen an attachment to their *patrie* as the English. It must be admitted, however, that in spite of these faults, the English Constitution has been a rampart of liberty against the assaults of despotism, and the nearness of this rival nation which has so many claims to our esteem is one of the causes for the revival of liberty among us.

is to say, worthy of them. They will buy corrupt men, subjugate the weak, mislead the ignorant, and perhaps bring us misfortunes of incalculable extent and duration.

On the assumption that permanence and unity will characterize our National Assemblies, I declare my support for the suspensive *veto*, which, being only an appeal to the people, leaves their rights intact; but I oppose with all my strength the absolute *veto*, which would reduce the Nation to a subordinate role, whereas it is everything, and would become the most terrible arm of despotism.

V.

The Power of
the National Assembly

---

18. October 10, 1789:
Talleyrand on Ecclesiastical Property

Charles Maurice, duc de Talleyrand-Périgord, was to live until 1838 and to be more famous as a diplomat of the Napoleonic, Restoration, and July Monarchy eras than for his career during the revolution. Talleyrand was prominent during the revolution, however, as the young Bishop of Autun—he was in his mid-thirties in 1789—who as a deputy of the clergy to the Estates General favored the joining together of the three orders, shared in the writing of the Declaration of the Rights of Man, strongly supported using the property of the Church to defray part of the government's debts, and, when there was opposition to the Civil Constitution of the Clergy, consecrated the bishops who had been elected. It is well known that Talleyrand was intelligent, worldly, and more interested in Church administration than in religion. He had been general agent of the French clergy before the revolution and in addition was interested in property and investments as an individual. The document that follows, *Motion de M. l'évêque d'Autun, sur les biens ecclésiastiques. Du 10 octobre 1789* (Versailles, s.d. [1789], 24 pp.), pp. 1–10, is the first part of Talleyrand's introduction to the motion on Church property. One footnote has been omitted and two have been shortened. Not included are Talleyrand's masterful but lengthy recommendations (pp. 10–15) for allocating funds to payment of the State's obligations and the actual articles of the motion (pp. 16–24).

Motion of M. l' Évêque d' Autun
on Ecclesiastical Property.
October 10, 1789.

THE STATE for a long time has been at grips with very great needs: none of us is unaware of it; great measures are therefore necessary to provide for these needs. Ordinary means are exhausted; the people are under pressure from all sides; truly the very lightest tax increase would be insupportable to them. It must not even be thought of. Extraordinary expedients have just been attempted, but they are chiefly destined for the special needs of this year, and more are needed for the future, more are needed for the entire re-establishment of order. There is one that is vast and decisive, and that, in my opinion (for otherwise I would reject it), can be allied with a strict respect for property: this resource seems to me to be bound up with ecclesiastical property.

The Clergy on several occasions, and in this Assembly, has given proof of its devotion to the public good too memorable to permit one to think that it will not courageously consent to the sacrifices that the urgent needs of the State solicit of its patriotism.

Already a great operation on the property of the Clergy seems inevitable in order to re-establish in a suitable fashion the situation of those who have been completely despoiled by the abandonment of the tithes.

Already, for this reason alone, the members of the Clergy who enjoy revenue from landed property have without doubt foreseen the impending necessity for a considerable change in these properties; and while those who have incomes from tithes are perhaps not without anxiety about their replacement, one cannot doubt that in everyone's eyes a powerful consideration will be to see that this same revolution can satisfy their common rights and still work directly for the public safety.

It is not a question here of a contribution to the expenses of the State proportionate to that of other properties: that could never have appeared to be a sacrifice. What is in question is a transaction of a quite different importance to the Nation. I go into specifics.

I do not believe that it is at all necessary to discuss at length the question of ecclesiastical properties.

What seems to me to be certain is that the Clergy is not a proprietor in the manner of other proprietors, since the properties from which it benefits (and which it cannot dispose of) have been given not for the advantage of persons but for the performance of functions.

What is certain is that the Nation, possessing a very extended empire over all corporate bodies existing within its confines, if it has not the right to destroy the entire corps of Clergy, because this body is indispensable to organized religion, can certainly destroy particular aggregations of this corps if it judges them harmful or simply useless, and that this right over their existence entails necessarily a very extensive right over the disposition of their properties.

What is no less sure is that the Nation, for the very reason that it is protector of the wishes of the founders, can, and even must, suppress benefices that have come to have no functions; that, in consequence of this principle, it has the right to give to the useful ministers and channel to the service of the public interest the proceeds of properties of this nature which are at the present time vacant, and can designate for the same purpose those that become vacant in due course.

Up to this point, there is no difficulty, and nothing that could even be called very unusual; for one has seen, in all ages, religious communities extinguished, rights to benefices suppressed, ecclesiastical properties returned to their intended purposes and applied to public establishments; and without a doubt, the National Assembly has the necessary authority to decree similar operations if the well-being of the State demands them.

But can it also reduce the incomes of living beneficiaries and make use of a part of this revenue?

I know that men of imposing authority, men not suspect of any private interest, have refused it this power: I know all the plausible arguments in favor of those in possession.

But in the first place it is necessary at this moment to start from a point of fact: this question has already been decided by your decrees concerning the tithes.

Moreover, I confess that to me the reasons used for the contrary opinion have seemed to give rise to several responses: there is a very simple one that I wish to submit to the Assembly.

However inviolable may be the possession of a property that is guaranteed to us by the law, it is clear that this law cannot change the nature of the property in guaranteeing it; that when it is a question of ecclesiastical property, it can only assure to each current beneficiary the enjoyment of what has been truly accorded him by its foundation deed. Now, everyone knows that all the foundation deeds of ecclesiastical properties, as well as the various laws of the Church that have explained the meaning and spirit of these titles, tell us that only the part of these properties that is necessary to the decent subsistence of the beneficiary belongs to him [footnote omitted]; that he is only the administrator of the rest, and that this remainder is actually given to the unfortunate, or for the maintenance of churches. If therefore the Nation conscientiously assures to each beneficiary, whatever the nature of his benefice, this decent subsistence, it will not be taking his individual property; and if at the same time it takes charge, as it without doubt has the right to do, of the administration of the remainder; if it takes responsibility for the other obligations attached to these properties, such as the maintenance of hospitals, charity workshops, repairs of churches, expenses of public education, and so on; if especially it has recourse to this property only in a time of general calamity, it seems to me that all the intentions of the founders will be fulfilled, and that full justice will be found to have been strictly done.[1]

So, to recapitulate, I believe that the Nation, principally in a period of general distress, can, without injustice, (1) dispose of the properties of the different religious communities that it believes ought to be suppressed, subject to assuring each of the monks who are still alive the means of subsistence; (2) redirect to its own profit, henceforth, but always in keeping with the general spirit of the founders, the revenues of all benefices which are no longer performing functions and are vacant, and count upon, similarly, those of all the other benefices of the same nature as they fall vacant; (3) reduce by some proportion the present revenues of beneficiaries when they exceed a certain sum, while taking responsibility for a part of the obligations attached to these properties.

1. One is always correct in saying, in ordinary language, that the properties were given to the Church: which has never meant anything, if not that these properties have been, to the discharge of the State, destined for the use of religion, the maintenance of the temples, the relief of the poor, and, finally, for works of public benefit, and they must always fulfill this intended objective. One is also correct in saying that they were given irrevocably; for, save for a formal clause of reversion, they are irrevocably assigned for this purpose, whatever fate may befall the particular corps they were assigned to at first. . . .

For all of these operations, present or future, which I shall merely indicate here, and in which I can see no violation of property rights, since they fulfill all the intentions of the founders; by all of these moves, I say, the Nation could, I think, while assuring the Clergy two-thirds of the present ecclesiastical revenue, except for the successive reduction to a certain fixed sum of this revenue, legitimately dispose of the totality of ecclesiastical properties, funds, and tithes. The total revenue of the Clergy being, according to current estimates, 150 millions,[2] 80 in tithes and 90 [sic] in landed property, this would be 100 millions reducible by successive extirpations to 80 or 85, which would be, at this time, assured to the Clergy through a special claim on the primary revenues of the State and of which the portion allotted to each beneficiary would be paid to him quarterly, in advance and on the premises. I specify these particulars and this special privilege because, organized religion being an objective of highest priority, its necessary expenses must be the first to be paid; and its ministers being, by indissoluble ties, bound to their condition, they must never be permitted to experience anxiety about the collection of their revenue. These 100 millions, by virtue of their origin, would give—or, rather, would conserve for each of the titular bishops, to whom they would be proportionally distributed—citizenship rights in the political assemblies.

I cannot persuade myself that anyone will find this sum of 100 millions, which one day will be reduced to 80 or 85, too considerable if it is remembered that there exist at this moment, insofar as one can estimate, from 70 to 80,000 ecclesiastics already appointed, for whom subsistence must be assured, since it has been guaranteed them by law; that within this number of ecclesiastics more than half make up the respectable body of parish priests, of whom the Assembly surely wants the least affluent to be assured of 1,200 livres, in addition to a suitable lodging, and of whom some must have much more. It is impossible, above all, for me to conceive of such a sum as appearing to be too considerable when it is understood how much good must result for the Nation from the plan that I am going to propose.

In the estimate of income from the landed property of the Clergy, the houses and enclosures that are dwelling places for some of its

2. This is about the average of the various known evaluations.

members, and notably of the religious communities that are going to be suppressed, have not been included; but although their product has been impossible to estimate readily, these properties nevertheless have considerable value. It would be proper, I think, to apply the sums obtained from such of them as may be sold to investments or government securities that would add to the present allotment of 100 millions a supplement that could be judged indispensable in view of the large number of present members of the Clergy. As they died one by one, this supplement would be returned to the Nation, as well as everything in excess of the 80 or 85 millions to which it will be decreed that the ecclesiastical income will one day be reduced.

There is also another kind of property which has not been included in the evaluation of income from the property of the Clergy, and which should not have been so included because the possession has never been part of its revenues: I mean the quarter of woods reserved for the Clergy. The profit from the cuttings of these reserves was designated for meeting expenses of reconstruction and repairs of religious or ecclesiastical houses, or was invested for the profit of the benefice when there were no repairs to make. In this matter, Gentlemen, the honor of individual clergymen as well as the interest of creditors in good faith solicits you to perform an act of justice: what would be involved would be the sequestration, for the number of years you would judge proper, of the income from the sale of these quarters of reserved forests, and its application to payment of the debts of benefices and beneficiaries proportionate, for the beneficiaries, to the diminution of revenue they will have suffered, and according to the rule that your prudence will suggest to you for that purpose.

Here now is the manner in which I conceive that the plan I have just described would be executed, and the ever-memorable advantages that would result from it for the State.

It has not been lost sight of that the tithes have been returned to the Nation by the Clergy. The Assembly has, it is true, decreed their abolition; but it also decreed that they would still be collected for a certain length of time. Well, they will still be collected for a time, but for the benefit of the Nation, and also with the option of converting them into pecuniary payments. I say for some time still; for by means of the operations of a sinking fund, whose first moneys will be very considerable, as will soon be explained, it will not be long before it will be possible to suppress them entirely, either without redemption or at least with an inconsiderable redemption.

To these 80 millions of tithes collected for the Nation would be added by the Nation another 20 millions, in order to complete the 100 millions needed for the Clergy. With the deaths of an indicated number of the present titular bishops, who will not be replaced, this expense of 20 millions will decrease imperceptibly.

At the same time, all of the landed properties of the Clergy would be put on sale.[3] Their revenues can be estimated at approximately 70 millions, perhaps more.

It will perhaps be said that there does not exist in France a sum of free currency in the form of available capital sufficient to represent the price of all this property, and that the value of the other landed estates would be depreciated for a long time by the continuing competition of this multitude of new properties thrown onto the market.

The answer is simple. Since the product of these sales would be destined to reimburse public debts, the shortest way to arrive at the same objective will be to grant immediately to the creditors of the State the right to bid for and themselves acquire these properties, and to give in payment their government securities, estimated at 5 percent for the perpetual annuities and at 10 percent for the lifetime annuities; so that, to pay the price of a property for which the bidding would rise to 100,000 *livres* the buyer could, if he chose, deliver 100,000 *livres* in silver, or the receipt acknowledging redemption of a lifetime annuity of 10,000 *livres*, or else that for a perpetual annuity of 5,000 *livres*, with the arrears for the current semester. Thus no one, I think, will doubt that the public creditors will hasten to make this kind of exchange; and this competition of numerous purchasers, combined with all the other holders of actual currency, will unquestionably carry the price of these properties at least to a capitalization at thirty times their annual revenues. Seventy millions of revenue will therefore give a capital of 2,100,000,000 *livres*. . . .

3. One could, if pressing needs did not permit delay, and if particular circumstances occasioned some postponement of sales, mortgage, from that moment, a part of the landed property of the Clergy, against loans which would no longer take the form of perpetual annuities or of annuities for life. *Annuities* seem to me to be the only form of borrowing that must be authorized in the future. . . .

19. October 15, 1789:
Mirabeau, a Secret Memoir

Following the "October [5–6] days" in 1789, which took the king and eventually the Assembly to Paris, the Anglophile leaders, Mounier and his friends, were discredited, and the leadership of the revolutionaries had clearly fallen to Lafayette, Mirabeau, and the "triumvirate" of Barnave, Duport, and Alexandre de Lameth, whose brother Charles was also associated with this group. Mirabeau's behavior during the October days had appeared to fluctuate between support of the insurrection and support of the crown; he was widely suspected of having plotted with the Duke of Orléans for the overthrow of Louis XVI, and he took pains to scoff at such rumors. It may have been under prodding from his friend La Marck, who was a great aristocrat closely associated with the Austrian and French courts, that Mirabeau tried to make his loyalty to Louis XVI clear in the secret memoir of October 15, 1789, a document which La Marck gave to the king's brother, Provence, the future Louis XVIII, who read it and apparently approved of most of it but refused to pass it on to Louis XVI, on the grounds that the King was incapable of the resolution necessary to carry out Mirabeau's plan. Mirabeau himself may not have been as serious as he appears to be in this memoir; he was undoubtedly making a tactical move to strengthen his position with the court; nevertheless the memoir is a remarkable document in view of his undoubted wish to mediate between the monarchy and the revolution and his later efforts first to maintain leadership in the Assembly and become a minister, and later to guide the royal family's counterrevolutionary efforts in a series of secret memorandums. The source is *Correspondance entre le Comte de Mirabeau et le Comte de la Marck pendant les années 1789, 1790 et 1791. Recueillie, mise en ordre et publiée par M. Ad. de Bacourt.* Vol. I (Paris, 1851), pp. 364–382. The last two pages, a concluding recommendation that the project be undertaken at once and in secrecy, have been omitted.

THE KING was not free not to come to Paris; and whether the National Assembly was or was not free to follow him, it at least lacked the power to hold him back.

Is the King free in Paris? He is, in the sense that no other will takes the place of his, but he is certainly not free to leave Paris, nor to choose his personal guards; he does not even have direct control over the militia to whom his safety is entrusted.

The National Assembly is unimpeded in Paris in its deliberations, but it would not have the power to transfer itself to another city of the kingdom; it does not even have the power to guarantee to a deputy of the nation any more liberty than he has.

The King's position is evidently harmful to the success of the revolution. The state of affairs is not such that the decrees of the Assembly and the sanction or acceptance of the monarch, which are indivisible, can be regarded as the result of constraint, as the enemies of the revolution never stop repeating to the people. But this state of affairs serves as a pretext for disobedience; it leads to protests, gives hope and furnishes means for seducing the best intentioned citizens, and can serve as a screen for enterprises of the parlements and the nobility. Two protests are already known, the will of several provinces is uncertain, and the obedience of some of the military commanders is doubtful. That is enough to show how important it is for the safety of the State that no excuse be left for the ill-intentioned, if one wants the revolution to be consummated peacefully.

Will the King at least have in Paris the most complete personal safety? Situated as he is, even minor catastrophes could compromise this safety! It is threatened by movements from outside, commotions within, divisions in the factions, faults due to zeal, those due to impatience, and above all by the violent conflict of the capital and the provinces.

If Paris has great strength, it also contains great causes of disorder. Its agitated populace is irresistible: winter is coming; food supplies can be lacking; bankruptcy might appear suddenly; what will Paris be in three months? Certainly a hospital, possibly a theater of horrors. Is it to such a place that the head of the nation must entrust his existence and all our hopes?

The ministers have no powers. A single one, who always had enthusiasts rather than a party, still has some popularity. But his resources are well known; he has just revealed himself completely. His truly empty head has dared only to bolster several parts of an edifice that is collapsing on all sides: he wishes to prolong the agony until the moment he has selected for his political retirement, and when, as in 1781, he thinks he can leave an alleged balance between revenues and expenditures, and some millions in the royal treasury. His devices may succeed or fail but in any case the success will not extend beyond several months, and this destructive financier leaves a breathing spell for Paris only by ruining the kingdom.

That is not a conjecture; it is a result which can be reduced to an arithmetical demonstration.

What will become of the nation after this useless attempt which makes bankruptcy inevitable? Today we are only weary and discouraged; it is the moment of despair that must be dreaded.

The provinces have not split apart, but they are watching each other; a muffled discord heralds storms. Commerce in provisions is interrupted more and more. The number of malcontents grows as an unavoidable result of even the most just decrees of the Assembly. A nation is, in the last analysis, only what its work is. The nation is getting out of the habit of work. The public force is dependent on opinion and on the State's revenues; all the bonds of opinion have dissolved, and only the direct taxes are any longer being paid, and those only in part, whereas half of our taxes are indirect. Several years would be needed to replace what six months have just destroyed, and the people's impatience, stimulated by their poverty, is manifested on all sides.

A still more disastrous event is on the way: the National Assembly, so ill-conceived in its principle, composed of factions so little homogeneous and so laboriously combined, sees confidence in its work diminishing every day. The best intentions do not make up for errors; it has been led away from its own principles by the fatal irrevocability it has bestowed on its first decrees, and, daring neither to contradict itself nor to retrace its steps, it has made one more obstacle of its own power. The respect inspired by a great name and a great revolution, seen from afar, and the hope that is so necessary to all people sustain it still; but each day a portion of public opinion breaks away from this great cause which required the most personal collaboration of all the parts of the empire. To the people are revealed only the almost inevitable errors of a too numerous legislative body, whose steps are uncertain and whose apprenticeship is incomplete, instead of showing them to what extent its errors will be easy to correct in the next legislature. A muffled commotion is gathering force; it can undo in a day the gains of the greatest labors; the body politic is collapsing in dissolution; a crisis is needed to revive it; it needs a transfusion of new blood.

The only way to save the State and the nascent constitution is to put the King in a position which will permit him to form an immediate coalition with his people.

Paris for a long time has been swallowing up all the taxes of the kingdom. Paris is the seat of the fiscal regime loathed by the provinces; Paris has created the debt; Paris, through its disastrous speculation, has ruined the public credit and compromised the nation's honor. Must the National Assembly also look only at this city and lose the whole kingdom for it? Several provinces fear that it dominates the Assembly, and directs its work. Paris asks only for financial transactions; the provinces consider only agriculture and commerce. Paris is only angry about money; the provinces demand laws. The dissensions between Paris and the provinces are well known; at the slightest incident they will explode.

What decision remains to be made, then? Is the King free? His liberty is not complete; it is not recognized.

Is the King safe? I do not believe so. Can even Paris save itself through its own efforts? No: Paris is lost if it is not restored to order, if it is not constrained to moderation. Its consumption puts it at the mercy of the rest of the kingdom, and its inevitable downfall would result from the prolongation of its tyrannical anarchy, which is to the interest only of its chiefs, whether deceived or deceivers, who have by their own excesses exceeded all measure.

Will the National Assembly terminate its session without being troubled by the commotions which a thousand events are preparing for us? He would be very rash who would put up a bond guaranteeing it!

Unless someone succeeds in guiding public opinion into other channels, in enlightening the people concerning their true interests, in preparing, through instructions given to the constituents, the disposition of the next legislature, will the State regain peace, the army its strength, the executive power its action, the monarch his real rights, the exercise of which is indispensable for public liberty? Or will the monarchy be shaken to its foundations and very probably dismembered—in other words, dissolved? It is easy to forecast from what has been done everything to be dreaded.

Therefore other measures must be taken; all the facts indicate this result.

Several measures can be mentioned, but some of them would unleash the most frightful evils, and I recall them only to turn the King from them, as from his inevitable downfall.

To withdraw to Metz or to any other frontier would be to declare war on the nation and abdicate the throne. A king who is the only protector of his people does not flee from his people; he appeals to them to judge his conduct and principles, but he does not break with one blow all the ties which unite him with them, he does not arouse all possible distrust against him, he does not put himself into the position of being unable to return to the bosom of his estates except by armed force, or of being reduced to beg foreigners for help.

And who can calculate to what point the exaltation of the French nation could be carried if it saw its King abandon it in order to join with outlaws and become one himself, or to what extent it could prepare for resistance and defy the forces he would recruit? I myself, after such an event, would denounce the monarch.

To retire into the interior of the kingdom, and convoke all of its nobility, would be no less dangerous an expedient.

Justly or not, the entire nation, which in its ignorance confuses nobility and patriciate, will for a long time regard gentlemen as a group as its most implacable enemies. The abolition of the feudal system was an atonement owing for ten centuries of delirium. The commotion could have been diminished, but it is too late, and the decree is irrevocable. To join forces with the nobility would be worse than to cast oneself into a foreign and enemy army; would be to choose between a great people and a few individuals; between peace and civil war with excessively unequal forces.

In such a resolution, where would the safety of the King be? A corps of nobility is not an army which can fight; it is not a province which can fortify itself. Even before coming together, would not the greatest part of this nobility be destroyed, slaughtered? Would not its possessions be wiped out? Were it to be called together only to secure its agreement to the greatest sacrifices, the mortal blow would be struck before one could explain oneself and be understood; and if one wished to conserve for the nobility all that universal opinion, all that a more enlightened reason has destroyed of its exemptions and privileges, can one believe that peace and taxes could be reestablished in a nation deprived by that act alone of the most precious and justified of its hopes?

To withdraw in order to regain liberty, to denounce the Assembly to the people and break off all connection with it, would be a less violent measure than the first two that were mentioned, but not less perilous; it would jeopardize the safety of the King; it would open up civil war as well, because a large portion of the provinces wants to support the decrees of the Assembly; because among its numerous faults there are more errors of administration than of principle, and because the people cannot doubt that basically the Assembly is very favorable to their interests; because the enlightened part of this nation knows that it is necessary to obey provisionally even the errors of a legislative body, or no sort of constitution would ever be established. The King would then have on his side neither the nobility, to whose passions he would not subscribe, nor his people, whose projects he would not adopt; or, rather, this first measure, not being able to exist by itself, would lead to many others, and one would fall into one of the disastrous possibilities whose danger I have just indicated.

It is certain, besides, that a great revolution is needed to save the kingdom, that the nation has rights, that it is on the way toward recovering all of them, and that it is necessary not only to reestablish but to consolidate them; that only a national convention can regenerate France; that the Assembly has already made several laws that are indispensable and must be adopted, and that there is no safety for the King and for the State except in the closest possible alliance between the Prince and the people.

All the measures that I have just reviewed being, therefore, rejected, here is what I think of the last one that is being proposed, and which is certainly not without danger; but one must not suppose it possible to escape from great peril without taking some risks, and now the time has come for statesmen to use their entire strength to prepare for, to moderate, to direct, and to limit the crisis, and not to prevent its taking place, which is completely impossible, nor even to postpone it, which would only make it more violent.

This last course of action is workable by simple measures. These measures would doubtless be prepared down to the smallest detail. They would not be explained to those who were to use them until the time for action. The Ministry is not well-intentioned enough, or at least may not be presumed so, for one to be able to confide in it. What is at stake is a last resort for the public welfare and the very safety of the King. All would be lost if any indiscretion revealed a plan which ignorance of its objective and its results could cause to be regarded as a conspiracy, when its sole object is the safety of the State; therefore one must not expose the project to anyone but those who would be directly charged with carrying it out. Once the leaders were selected, moreover, they should have an absolutely free hand concerning means and the choice of other agents; and truly, our misfortune is such that the same secrecy must be used in doing good as the enemies of the country use in harming it.

Here are the principal conclusions:

The King's departure would be prepared for, and [also] the opinion of the provinces, already determined in part by events easy to foresee.

It is impossible that the King's lack of liberty, if he wishes to make use of it, not be established by refusals or by insulting precautions.

It is impossible that the militia of Paris not overstep its true functions, if one wishes to limit it to what it is supposed to be.

It is impossible that, if one tried to reconcile the complete liberty of the King with even his sojourn in the capital, and if he demanded the support of the legislative body, the true position of the King should not be immediately disclosed and that the National Assembly should not see its own safety, its own existence, compromised in the heart of Paris. That would not be creating a new order of things; it would be stating what already exists.

Neither is it difficult to foresee that, during whatever delay the King's departure will require, one will witness new protests by the parlements, or by cities, or by corporations, whose evil intentions will in one sense help the public cause, and will demonstrate more and more the necessity for changing the King's position.

The motive for the King's departure would thus be sufficiently prepared for; public safety would make it an obligation.

Various means would be used to insure that the safety of the departure would not even be doubtful.

His guard would be systematically dispersed.

There are a thousand pretexts for arranging the sudden organization of a corps of ten thousand men, composed solely of national regiments which would be transported in three days to a point almost equally distant by 20 to 25 leagues from Rouen and from Paris.

If, as is almost impossible to believe, the provinces were to misunderstand a step on which the common safety depends, reliable and faithful leaders would be ready to form a second line capable of containing the malcontents and of cutting the communications of the suspect cantons. This precaution would gain time for enlightening the people, and public opinion would soon be the real army.

It would be very easy to make these moves without the concurrence of the ministers and through particular influences on the garrisons.

These precautions taken, the King could openly leave the château and withdraw to Rouen.

He would choose that city or its environs because it is at the center of the kingdom, because a military position, taken respective to this point, commands an immense amount of navigation, disposes of the food supplies of the only center of resistance that must really be considered, and would change this resistance to benedictions if the beneficence of the King, his efforts, his personal sacrifices succeeded in bringing abundance there; again, Rouen is necessary because such a choice indicates that there is no project for flight and that there is only a desire to become reconciled with the provinces, because Normandy is very densely populated, and because its inhabitants have more tenacity than the rest of the French; finally because it is very easy to unite this province in a coalition with Brittany and Anjou, which would be sufficient to constitute an irresistible force.

Before the King's departure, a proclamation addressed to all the provinces would be held ready, in which the King would say, among other things: that he is casting himself into the arms of his people; that violence was done him at Versailles; that in a manner of speaking a close watch was kept on him in Paris; that he was not at liberty to go and come, which is a right every citizen has, and must have, and he would furnish proofs of this; that he knew that this position served as a pretext for malcontents to refuse to obey the decrees of the National Assembly and the sanction given by him to these decrees, which could compromise a revolution in which he takes as much interest as the most ardent friends of liberty;

That he wishes to be inseparable from his people, and that his choice of Rouen proves it without a doubt;

That he is the first King of his lineage to formulate the plan of investing the nation with all its rights, and that he has persisted in this plan in spite of his ministers and the advice which corrupts princes;

That he has adopted without reservation such-and-such decrees of the National Assembly, that he renews his sanction and approval, and that his sentiments regarding this will be invariable;

That certain other decrees do not appear to him to be even advantageous enough to his people, that certain others have perhaps not been reflected on sufficiently, and that in this respect he desires the nation to return freely to a new examination, without, however, intending to damage provisional obedience or allow it to be damaged;

That he is going to summon to him the National Assembly in order to continue its labors, but that he will soon convoke a new convention to judge, confirm, modify, and ratify the operations of the first Assembly;

That he desires above all that the public debt be sacred, that this point is one of those on which he cannot compromise, because they are questions of the national honor and consequently of his own;

That neither does he believe that he can compromise on the existence of the parlements, which he has always regarded as his people's greatest scourge, and which the National Assembly has without doubt delayed too long in destroying;

That it is time to instruct the nation that these bodies, which pretend never to have been more than a barrier against kings, are no less enemies of the nation than of the monarch; that their interest and their ambition account for their apparent supervision; that their real design, manifested by their alliance with the nobility, with all the malcontents, with all the enemies of the public cause, is to base their power on anarchy, to destroy the bonds of obedience in order to diminish the authority of the King; to support when needed this authority in order to oppose that of the nation, and to favor, through this equilibrium and these struggles, the judicial aristocracy, which, of all the forms of corrupt government, would clearly be the most tyrannical;

That he personally will submit to the greatest sacrifices, that it is no longer a question of promising economies without realizing them, that he will live as a simple individual, that a million is enough for his expenses as a man and father of a family, that he asks for nothing more, that he wants only a single table for himself and his family, that all the luxury of the throne must be transferred to the improvement of the civil government and to the wise magnificence of truly national expenditures;

That the State's creditors will no longer be lured with false promises; that, forced to resign himself to some delays, he asks that at least they be given as security all that the nation has available; that in order to get out of the inextricable labyrinth of the finances, he is going to order the summoning of all the State's creditors to find out the total of the debt, and will order the formation of a syndicate of these same creditors to negotiate with them and present them with something other than uncertain, ruinous operations which can only alarm the nation more and more;

That, personally determined to make every sacrifice, he does not believe that the same economy measures can be applied to all of the salaries accorded for a long time to a crowd of citizens who today have only this means of existence, and that he urges the nation to consider that it is not in ruining, in driving to despair, so many thousands of individuals that one succeeds in re-establishing public peace. That, besides, he calls upon his people to bear witness to the personal conduct he has always had, that he will conquer them not by arms but by his love; that he entrusts his honor and his safety to French loyalty; that he desires only the well-being of the citizens; and that he himself is nothing more than a citizen.

This declaration of a good king, this manifesto of peace, very firm but very popular, would be carried by emergency couriers into all the provinces, and all the commanders would be warned to hold themselves in readiness.

Another proclamation would be taken to the National Assembly, to announce the departure of the King, his choice of destination, and to ask it to deliberate on whether it should not go there itself. He would reveal in his letter to the Assembly his motives for leaving Paris.

The Assembly would unquestionably go to the place indicated by the King, if it was free to do so. If, after having deliberated, it did not have that freedom, the session would by that alone be terminated in law if not in fact.

If the Assembly continued to deliberate after its lack of liberty had been established, its subsequent deliberations would bear all the marks of the same violence.

If the Assembly decided to continue its sessions in Paris in spite of the decree in which it declared itself inseparable from the monarch, such a decision would be determined only by fear and by the absence of liberty. But henceforth this same cause, being influential on all subsequent deliberations, would soon be revealed and known in the provinces; the constraint would be established by individual avowals of members of the Assembly, by their correspondence, by the hostile behavior of Paris, and there would be an occasion for the convoking of a legislature. In any case, the King, whether through his present ministry, or through another that he would choose immediately, would take new measures.

Proclamations would be issued one after another, and the King would instruct his people as to their true interests.

The creditors having been summoned and syndicated, it would be easy to take very useful measures in collaboration with them.

The current mentality of the National Assembly would necessarily change, in part because of the change of public opinion in the provinces.

If a few cantons resisted, the executive power, authorized by the National Assembly, woud deploy all its forces.

Everywhere good citizens would join the King's cause, and it would soon be seen how respect and devotion for a good prince who never wanted to do anything except good, and who is himself more unhappy than his people, can influence a faithful and generous nation. . . .

20. January 28, 1790:
A Petition to the National Assembly
from Leaders of Jewish Communities

French Jews numbered about 30,000 in 1789. Most of them lived in the east, in Alsace and Lorraine, or in the south, around Bordeaux and Avignon. There were only about 500 Jews in Paris. Unlike the 700,000 or so Protestants in France, whose legal existence had finally been recognized in 1787, the Jews had no statute granting them rights as a group. Individual Jews had in a few cases received specific privileges, and some Jewish communities, especially those of Bordeaux, had been granted certain rights, but there was no uniformity. In spite of the leadership of men like Robespierre, Clermont-Tonnerre, Duport, and Abbé Grégoire, who insisted that the principles of the revolution required equal rights for Jews as individuals, it was not until September 27, 1791, only three days before the closing of the National Assembly, that all Jews were voted the rights of citizens. Anti-Semitic prejudices, particularly in the east, coupled with fears of Jewish economic competition, account for the delay. The lack of uniformity in existing conditions and privileges of Jews in various parts of France was also a factor, together with differences of view among Jews themselves— for example, concerning the desirability of retention of the corporate organization of the Jewish communities, generally opposed by the French revolutionaries with their vision of an individualistic society.

The following document[1] was produced as a Jewish response to the National Assembly's debates of December 21, 23, and 24, 1789, which raised the problem of Jewish citizenship but failed to solve it. It has been attributed to a lawyer, Jacques Godard, but was in any case signed by leaders of the Jewish communities in France. Space is lacking for inclusion of the full 107 pages of this important brochure, most of which is taken up with replies to the anti-Jewish arguments of the period, but some of the early pages (11–20) and the main part of the conclusion (97–103) combine a statement of principles with a summary of existing disabilities. The early passages are separated from the later one by a space.

. . . Let us begin with the principles that imperiously demand the elevation of the Jews to the rank of CITIZENS.

A first principle is that all men domiciled in an empire, and living as subjects of that empire, must participate without distinctions in the same title and enjoy the same rights. They must all have the title and possess the rights of CITIZENS.

Through being *domiciled*, in fact, and through their condition as *subjects*, they contract the obligation to serve the *patrie;* they serve it in reality; they contribute to the support of the public force: and the public force owes an equal protection and an equal distribution of benefits to all who unite to form it. It would be an extreme injustice if it did not render to all, in the same proportion, what it receives from all, and if some were favored by it to the prejudice of the others. These ideas do not need further development; their obviousness is evident to all minds.

There is only one thing more to examine at this stage: are the Jews who live in France, or are they not, *domiciled* there? Do they or do they not live there as *subjects of France?*

Assuredly, it is unthinkable to regard them as FOREIGNERS; whether because they would be absolutely unable to assign themselves to another *patrie;* whether because they are born, become established, and have their families in France; whether because in certain cities they even have separate neighborhoods assigned to them; or whether, finally, because they pay all the taxes to which the French are subject, in addition to the other taxes that they are still made to pay separately.

Then Jews are therefore not *foreigners* in France. They are

1. Pétition des Juifs établis en France, adressée à l'Assemblée nationale, le 28 janvier 1790, sur l'ajournement du 24 décembre 1789 (Paris, Imprimerie de Prault, 1790. Pp. iv, 107).

subjects of this empire; and consequently, they are and must be *citizens*. For in a State, whatever it be, one recognizes only two classes of men, *citizens* and *foreigners*. Those who are not in the second class must be in the first. The Jews, once again, are therefore and must be CITIZENS.

In truth, they are of a religion condemned by that which is dominant in France. But the time is past when it was accepted that only the dominant religion gave the right to advantages, to prerogatives, to lucrative and honorable positions in society. For a long time this maxim, worthy of the Inquisition, was used against the Protestants; and the Protestants had no civil rights in France. Today, they have just been re-established in possession of civil rights; they are on the same footing as the Catholics in everything; the intolerant maxim that we have just recalled will no longer be applicable against them. Why should it continue to be used as an argument against the Jews?

In general, civil rights are entirely independent of religious principles. And all men of whatever religion, of whatever sect they may belong to, whatever form of worship they practice, provided that their cult, their sect, and their religion are not offensive to the principles of a pure and severe morality, all of these men, we say, since they can all equally serve the *patrie*, defend its interests, and contribute to its splendor, must equally share the title and the rights of citizens.

What would result from a contrary system, in virtue of which it would only be the single dominant religion, and others whose dogmas more or less resembled it, that could confer this title and these rights? The result would be the acceptance of the principle that force must prevail over weakness and the greater number over the lesser; whereas social rights must be calculated and measured only by justice.

The result would be that, in countries where it is not the Catholic religion that is dominant, the Catholics could be subjected legally to all the injustices with which the Jews are burdened today.

The result would be permission either to violate consciences or to seduce them. For you violate them by using persecution to force individuals to forswear their cults; you seduce them by offering them more advantages in the dominant religion than in their own. And you know that violence is no more permitted here than seduction. You know that in matters of belief it is to the evidence alone and not to force that man must submit his reason. You know that through force you would gain only indifferent people or hypocrites, and that in such conquests religion would have more to complain about than to applaud. You know, finally, that the Jew is attached to his religion, as you are to yours, and that injustices are no more permitted against him than they would be against you yourselves; that it is from itself and only itself that the conscience can receive its inspirations; that no being on earth has the right to command it; and that it is only God who can call men to account for their opinions relative to Him, and for the form under which they render homage to Him.

It will be permitted to the Jews to point out that no religion would have the right to assume dominion over another unless it could offer, in favor of the excellence of its origin, that irresistible evidence whose light must strike and convince all minds at the same time; but that, if it is impossible to assume that it has such evidence for all, it is equally impossible for it to be obligatory for all citizens; that, if it is impossible for it to oblige them all, then it is not a crime not to believe what it teaches; and that, if it is not a crime, there can be no penalty pronounced against those who refuse to submit to its dogmas.

And so the word *tolerance*, which, after so many centuries and so many *intolerant* acts, appears to be a word for humaneness and reason, is no longer suitable to a nation that wishes to affirm its rights on the eternal basis of justice. And America, to whom politics will owe so many useful lessons, has rejected it from its code as a term that tends to compromise individual liberty and to sacrifice certain classes of men to other classes.

To *tolerate*, in fact, is to suffer what one would have the right to prevent; and the dominant religion which, alone perhaps, as opposed to other religions, must have ministers recognized by the nation and a cult paid for by it, does not have the right to keep another from rising humbly beside it. Now the necessary consequence of this principle is that since different religions all have equal rights, it would be contradictory for there to be one of them which could give a right of pre-eminence over another, relative to the functions of citizens.

If one wishes to be even more convinced of this truth, let him reflect on the nature of these functions. They consist in paying to the State the taxes which are the price for tranquillity and for public safety; in defending the *patrie* as much in case of internal strife as in outside wars; in collaborating through the use of one's talents, intelligence, and virtues for the glory of the nation. Now in order to fulfill all these duties, is it necessary to be of one religion or another, to adopt or to reject this or that dogma? When men, united for the common defense, serve the public interest with equal ardor, are they going to be asked what they believe or what they do not believe? In a word, does anyone worry about the nature of their dogmas? Does it not matter more what they do than what they believe? Consequently, can their form of worship, whatever it is, be the measure of the rights that must be accorded them?

Thus, two incontestable principles assure the Jews the rights of citizens.

First, their qualification as *subjects of the kingdom* by itself assures them this right; we have proved it.

Their particular religion cannot deprive them of it; we have just established this.

Therefore it is a necessary consequence of true principles that they be declared CITIZENS; and it is impossible that they not be so declared. . . .

The Jews are no longer, it is true, exposed to all the odious treatments under which they formerly groaned.

One no longer says to them, as under the reign of Dagobert I and Léon l'Ifaurien, that it is necessary to choose between baptism and death.

One no longer takes from them, as was done in other times, their children under the age of puberty, in order to raise these children in the principles of the Catholic religion.

There is no longer that atrocious and absurd barbarism, customary under the feudal regime, of first forcing the Jews to be converted, and then confiscating their property after they had been converted, as a kind of indemnity for the enormous head taxes that they had formerly had to pay, simply for being *Jews*.

They are no longer burned, they are no longer legally massacred; they are no longer made to submit, on certain days of the year, to ceremonies as cruel as they were degrading.

But they are treated like slaves, and with even more scorn.

But in certain cities, they are relegated to segregated neighborhoods where they are made to live in narrow and unhealthy houses.

But they are crushed under arbitrary taxes. They are made to pay a *protection* duty,[2] on the one hand; a *habitation* duty,[3] on the other; a *reception* duty.[4] And all these duties[5] still exist, and are, at this very moment, claimed. [Footnote omitted.]

But, finally, with the exception of certain of them who have received special privileges from the government, or who have, in their favor, letters patent, all are deprived of the faculty of exercising an art, of embracing a profession, of acquiring and possessing real estate. If some of them, in Alsace, acquire a refuge, soon a Catholic appears, who, without right of relationship, but through the sole right of oppression, exercises against them a redemption called *redemption by preference*. All, finally, without exception, all, everywhere, are deprived of the faculty of being eligible for public employment and for offices in a society of which they are members.

And it is when such a state of affairs still exists; it is when so many injustices are still united against them, that some people dare to say that the National Assembly has adjourned indefinitely the question of their fate! It is when this assembly is attacking all prejudices, destroying all abuses, fixing the rights of men and regulating at the same time their duties; it is, finally, when it is regenerating the entire kingdom; it is in the midst of all these circumstances, and carried along by the impulse it has itself generated, that certain people want it to stop at the sight of the prejudices and the abuses which are denounced to it; that these people would like it to fail to recognize the rights of one class of men, to exempt other men from their duties, and to condemn to perpetual misery fifty thousand individuals whose shackles it is in the assembly's power to break immediately. . . .

2. The Jews of Metz pay to the King a *protection* duty, ceded to the house of Brancas, which runs annually to the sum of TWENTY THOUSAND LIVRES. The Jews of the ancient Alsatian sovereignty also pay the King a special *protection* fee.
3. The *habitation* duty is one that the Jews of the ancient Alsatian sovereignty pay to the lords of the lands where they live.
4. The *reception* duty is one that the Jews pay, in a part of Alsace, to the nobles who permit them to live on their lands. It is independent of the right of *habitation*. This duty must be paid by each child who wishes to establish his dwelling in the place that has been chosen by his father.
5. When the Jews went to Strasbourg on business, they paid three *livres* a day to the city. But, since 1784, the King, who, through an infinity of excellent special laws, prepared the present revolution, suppressed that duty, as well as all the other fees that were body tolls.

21. May 29, 30, 1790:
Debate on the Civil Constitution
of the Clergy

Toward the end of May, 1790, the National Assembly was concluding its discussion of the Civil Constitution of the Clergy, although there were to be six more weeks of voting on the individual articles before the final adoption on July 12. Already on November 2, 1789, the Assembly had decreed that Church properties belonged to the nation. On November 27, 1790, the Assembly was to order all clergy to take an oath of allegiance to the nation, the law, and the king.

Jean-de-Dieu Ramond de Cucé, Archbishop of Aix, who was to emigrate to England after the Civil Constitution of the Clergy, was a highly respected spokesman against the proposed legislation on May 29. Jean Baptiste Treilhard's reply on May 30 is a good expression of the point of view of the proponents of the plan. Trielhard was a member of the Assembly's Ecclesiastical Committee who was to have a long career, serving in the Convention and Council of Five Hundred and, briefly, as a Director, and in Napoleon's Council of State. The source is the *Moniteur*'s account of the sessions, in *Réimpression de l'ancien Moniteur seule histoire authentique et inaltérée de la Révolution française depuis la réunion des États-Généraux jusqu'au consulat (mai 1789-novembre 1799)* Vol. IV (Paris, 1847), pp. 491–492, 498–500. Dots in the text are from the *Moniteur* except where two paragraphs of historical illustrations have been omitted from Treilhard's speech. These are indicated by a space.

Session of May 29

THE ARCHBISHOP OF AIX. Does the ecclesiastical committee know what a useful influence religion has on citizens? It is the curb which checks the wicked; it is the support of the virtuous. Religion is the seal on the declaration which assures man his rights and liberty: it is unalterable in its dogmas; its ethics cannot change; and its doctrine will always be the same. The committee wants to recall the clergy to the purity of the primitive Church. It is not bishops, successors to the apostles, it is not pastors charged with preaching the Gospel who can reject this procedure: but since the committee is recalling us to our duty, it will allow us to remind it of our rights and of the sacred principles of ecclesiastical power. It is necessary, therefore, to remind it of the indispensable authority of the Church; it is a question of the truths of religion: I am going to recite them with all the resoluteness that is proper in ministers of the Lord. Jesus Christ gave his mission to the apostles and his successors for the sake of the well-being of the faithful; he did not entrust it to magistrates, nor to a king: it is a question of an order of things which magistrates and kings must obey. The mission that we have received by way of ordination and consecration goes back as far as the apostles. It is being proposed to you today to abolish a part of the ministers, to divide their jurisdiction; it was established and limited by the apostles; no human power has the right to interfere with it. [Murmurs arise.]

I must make the observation that it is a question of purely spiritual jurisdiction. Abuses have been introduced; I do not claim the contrary; I deplore it as others do; but the spirit of the primitive Church is always there to curb them. It is the canons and traditions of churches, and not the abuses, that we insist upon: it is only by virtue of councils that one can effect the dismemberment of a province. Observe that I speak only of the spiritual; the Church alone can govern that; it alone can determine its relationships. A bishop cannot have jurisdiction over a foreign bishopric; to suppress a part of it would be to abolish the administration of the Church for the faithful. The jurisdiction of the parish priests is limited by the bishops; except by virtue of their orders, no change can be made. It is to matters of ecclesiastical discipline that it is desired to extend your power. We are certainly astonished to see disappear in this way the holy canons and title deeds of the Church. . . . It is possible for some retrenchments to be made in the Church; but the Church must be consulted, and it would be sacrilegious to deprive it of its administration. Without doubt, it is necessary to reform the abuses and bring about a new order of things. We think that the ecclesiastical power must do everything possible to conciliate your wishes with the interests of religion; but it is with considerable pain that we look upon the culpable designs for making episcopal authority disappear.

If you do not have recourse to the authority of the Church, you are disregarding that Catholic unity which forms the constitution of the empire. In any case, we cannot renounce the forms prescribed by the councils. We propose, therefore, that you consult the Gallican Church by means of a national council. That is where the power rests which must watch over the sacred trust of faith;

that is where, instructed in our duties and our vows, we will conciliate the interests of the people with those of religion. We are here, then, to place in your hands the declaration of our sentiments. We request most respectfully of the King and the National Assembly that they permit the convocation of a national council. If this proposition is not adopted, we declare that we cannot participate in the deliberation.

Session of May 30

M. TREILHARD. The principles of the former French government had corrupted all classes of citizens, and the clergy, in spite of the virtues of some of its members, had not been able to resist the influence of a bad constitution. Establishments without any purpose, useless men highly salaried, useful men without recompense . . . such are the evils of the present organization of the clergy. The discussion opened on the decree presented to you by the ecclesiastical committee. Are the proposed changes useful? Have you the right to order them? These are the only subjects of this discussion.

Are these changes useful?

Some dioceses, some priests, had very narrow territories; others very widespread ones. You see an aged pastor, burdened with work disproportionate to his strength, receive a bare living of 700 *livres*. Near him stands a sumptuous building; it belongs to a rich benefice holder without functions, who brings together for his own use enough resources for two hundred private individuals. Would one not suppose that chance alone had momentarily produced this disorder? Well! It has existed for two hundred years. It has defenders; habit makes everything legitimate, and even slavery has found some apologists. There is no doubt that the changes are advantageous. I restrict myself to examining whether those that you have proposed are suitable. It is agreed that the benefices must be extended enough to occupy the holder, but not enough to overwhelm him. A new division will moreover be very useful to the faithful, to pastors, and to religion. I do not go into whether you ought to adopt the details of the project; they will be discussed in due course. I apply myself only to the bases. One must abolish benefices without functions, so useless, abusive, and dangerous for religion that no one will rise to defend them. The uselessness of the collegiate chapters is no less recognized; for a long time their suppression was checked. Perhaps the cathedral chapters will find some defenders; but their apologists are thinking more of what these establishments were in the beginning than what they are today. In the first centuries, the bishop had priests near him who were necessary to him for the administration of his diocese. These priests who made up the cathedral chapter molded the councils of the bishop; today they are his rivals; formerly they worked with the bishop for the tranquillity of families; today they trouble them by a mass of litigation: they used to work at ecclesiastical administration; today they occupy themselves by reciting a few prayers, and their uselessness is so notorious that one represents laziness with the emblem of a canon. It is true that the cathedral chapters add to the pomp of the worship; but when seminaries have been established in the bishops' places of residence, one will have the same pomp with greater utility. Therefore, no motive justifies the preservation of the cathedral chapters. The basis of the first point is therefore just.

The second heading presents the objectives of a reform of the manner of providing for the carrying out of ecclesiastical duties. A change is urgent, and the bases for this division of the report could not be attacked. God forbid that I seek to inculpate anyone; but is it not evident that the method of proceeding by elections will assure to the Church the pastor who will be best fitted for such important duties? An individual with the power of conferring a benefice cannot choose as well as the faithful themselves the man most worthy of the respect of the people: thus formerly it was the people who elected the pastors. The first who was named after Jesus Christ, Saint Matthew, was elected by all the disciples, numbering seventy-two. Two persons had been selected, and chance decided between them. The honorable member who said yesterday that pastors were only elected by lot therefore said only half the truth. As long as this so holy discipline was maintained, the Church had good pastors; when it was destroyed, great positions came to be entrusted to incompetent hands. When incompetence led to disgust, both for the duties that had to be fulfilled and for the office that had to be occupied, vicars-general were established; but they were more anxious to solicit favors than to merit them, and the cares of the dioceses rested on obscure secretaries who, after long labors, had to content themselves with obtaining a small pension or a tiny benefice. How can these abuses be destroyed? How can the old order of things which created the splendor of the Church be re-established? By elections entrusted to the people. It is said that these elections would occasion factions; but how many profane motives determined the ancient choices! . . . Let us throw a veil over the past: my objective, in this discussion, is neither to hide the defects nor to engage in criticism of the old regime. It was said yesterday that some non-Catholics would compete in the elections. I respond (1) that in the present state of affairs a number of non-Catholics nominate to benefices, even to some involving the care of souls; (2) one could demand of all electors that they state that they profess the Catholic religion. . . . I believe I have shown that the changes proposed are useful and that they are based on principles that should lead to good reforms.

It is time to examine whether you have the right to order these changes.

Yes, you have the right to do so. Far from harming religion, you will do it the most worthy homage by assuring to the faithful the most upright, virtuous ministers. He who believes that this would be a wound inflicted on religion has a very false idea of religion. He who, regretting various abuses, fears to see the administration of the public cult purified by religious reforms is the true enemy of religion. That is the kind of man who would destroy it, if it were not entirely divine, if the gates of hell could prevail against it. . . . I am going to try to indicate the limits of temporal and spiritual authority. My discussion will be based on the most simple truths and on the most authentic facts. Nothing is more opposed to temporal authority than spiritual jurisdiction. Temporal authority is established for the peace of society, to assure the well-being of individuals in this life. Spiritual jurisdiction has as its sole objective the salvation of the faithful; it is entirely spiritual in its faith and its objectives.

Jesus Christ, after his resurrection, said to his apostles: "Go, instruct the nations. . . . As my father sent me, I send you also. . . . Receive the Holy Spirit. Those for whom you remit sins will have their sins remitted." There you see the only qualification possessed by the apostles: "Instruct, and administer the sacraments." The most virtuous of the priests, Fleury, in his discourse on ecclesiastical history, reduces spiritual jurisdiction to the instruction of the faithful and the administration of the sacraments: such is the doctrine of the Church of France. Pastors do not, therefore, have jurisdiction except over spiritual affairs, and over what concerns salvation. . . . Religion emerged in a state of perfection from the hands of its founder. The apostles were at first travelers: Saint John later lived in Jerusalem, and Saint Paul in Antioch. But we must take care not to conclude that territories were assigned them; that the name of bishop signified anything but *guardian*. This name, which comes from the Greek, does not pertain to religion; it expressed a civil function. The word *diocese* was likewise employed to indicate the portions into which a state or a province was divided. The Church never recognized a particular division of provinces and dioceses. Historic monuments prove it. This division is contrary to dogma and faith. The apostles were appointed for the whole world. . . . The Holy Spirit was not responsible for the administrative districts that have been established and whose vices no one can hide.

If the division of the dioceses is not part of the dogma and of the faith, neither does the election of pastors belong to faith or dogma. I have already said that Saint Matthew was elected by his disciples: all the faithful concurred then in the election of the seven deacons. . . .

It is necessary to return to the principle: spiritual jurisdiction only embraces faith and dogma. All that is discipline and supervision belongs to temporal authority. The changes proposed touch neither faith nor dogmas; they can therefore belong to temporal power. Let us have no more claims that religion is lost; let it be recognized that we are attacking only abuses which must appear monstrous even to those who profit from them. Let the ministers of the Church be heard in this discussion; I demand this. It is necessary to profit from their enlightenment and experience: but when the sovereign believes a reform necessary, nothing can oppose it. A state can recognize or not recognize a religion; all the more reason why it can declare that it wants a certain establishment to exist in a certain place, in a certain manner. The right of the sovereign is entirely foreign to faith and dogma. . . .

Permit me to stop for a moment. If the fathers who were present at the councils were among you, if they were interrogated on the reforms whose necessity is impressed on all hearts, would there be a single one who would rise to say: this appertains only to us; if you wish to make these reforms, we will leave this assembly? That would be to abandon the public cause; that would be to dare, by rash declarations, to put religion in danger and the state in peril because the nation wanted to reform useless ministers and pay suitable salaries to useful ones. Would you recognize in this language the moral content of our religion, and should we be surprised at the aspersions which the impious and the infidels permit themselves if such were the sentiments of its apostles? Suppose that twenty-one bishops are instituted and that the parishes are re-organized, and you will say: we do not wish to deliberate; we will not ordain the priests, we will not install the curates, we will not follow the bishops; and you will interrupt your religious functions; and in order to defend temporal interests, you will abuse the ministry that you have received from religion, and you will compromise the interests of religion and of the state.

I resume the arguments which determine the rights of the sovereign. If sovereigns have sometimes let others besides themselves exercise these rights, they have not been able to lose them. These rights have been re-established by several decrees. In our time, in 1764, the temporal authority stated that a too powerful religious body would cease to exist.

How could anyone say that the sovereign could not, without hurting dogmas and faith, order that one prelate would suffice for a territory of a certain area and that this prelate should remain there? . . . I halt; for if I said more to support the principles of your committee, I would underestimate the wisdom of this assembly, I would be lacking respect for the Church, which always seeks the greatest possible good of religion. Your decrees will not harm this holy religion; they will recall it to its primitive purity, and you will truly be Christians of the Gospel. I know that at the time of the famous Declaration of the Clergy, the Pope refused to give bulls for the consecration of thirty bishops; but he was a foreigner and an enemy of Louis XIV. Do not fear such opposition on the part of French pastors, on the part of all those who have a spark of patriotism and virtue and who cannot better serve religion than by concurring in the execution of your wise decrees. There will no longer be any but French; all good citizens, united by a desire for the common good, will have but one soul and one will.

I conclude that the bases of the work of the committee should be adopted.

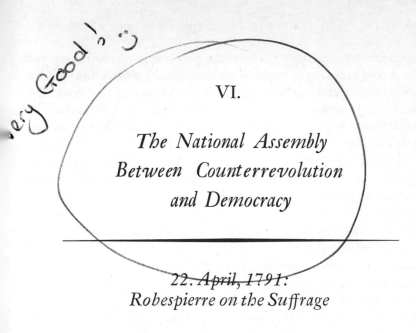

VI.

The National Assembly Between Counterrevolution and Democracy

22. April, 1791:
Robespierre on the Suffrage

With considerable popular support—for example, from the Commune of Paris—and reinforced by the views of Condorcet, Marat, and others, Robespierre had in 1790 and early 1791 opposed the property qualification for voters and attempted to influence the National Assembly and its Constitutional Committee in this sense. The following document is a speech he was unable to get permission to deliver to the Assembly, and finally at the end of March, 1791, published, and, early in April, distributed to the popular societies and other groups. Although this speech was never delivered in the Assembly, it attracted much attention and greatly strengthened opposition to the silver mark. Robespierre himself used some of its materials in later speeches. The document contains social material and passages about the meaning of the revolution and its place in history, as well as a classic list of arguments against the property qualification for voting. Robespierre was always very careful about the publication of his works. The source in this case is *Discours à l'Assemblée nationale, sur la nécessité de révoquer les décrets qui attachent l'exercice des droits du citoyen à la contribution du marc d'argent, ou d'un nombre déterminé de journées d'ouvriers, par Maximilien Robespierre* (Paris, Imprimerie nationale, 1791, 24 pp.). The only omissions made in translation affect illustrative materials in the late pages and the draft decree at the end, rather than the structure and arguments of the speech.

MESSIEURS,

I questioned, for a moment, whether I should propose to you my ideas concerning the provisions you appear to have adopted. But I saw that it was a question of defending the cause of the nation and of liberty, or of betraying it by my silence; and I wavered no longer. I have even undertaken this task with a confidence all the more firm in that the imperious passion for justice and the public welfare which imposed it on me were common to us both and it is your own principles and authority that I invoke in their favor.

Why are we gathered in this temple of the laws? Without doubt, to give to the French nation the exercise of the imprescriptible rights which belong to all men. This is the purpose of every political constitution. If it fulfills this aim, it is just and free; if it opposes this aim, it is nothing but a conspiracy against mankind.

You recognized this truth yourselves, in a striking manner, when you decided, before beginning your great work, that a solemn declaration must be made of the sacred rights that serve as the immutable foundations upon which that work must rest.

"All men are born and remain free, and are equal before the law."

"Sovereignty resides essentially in the nation."

"The law is the expression of the general will. All citizens have the right to concur in its making, either by themselves or through their freely elected representatives."

"All citizens are eligible to all public offices, without any other distinction than that of their virtues and talents."

These are the principles that you have consecrated: it will now be readily seen which are the measures that I wish to combat; it will be sufficient to test them against these immutable laws of human society.

Now, 1. Is the law the expression of the general will when the greater number of those for whom it is made can have no hand whatever in its making? No. And yet to deny such men as do not pay a tax equal to three days' wages the right even to choose the electors whose task it is to name the members of the legislative assembly—what is this but to deprive a majority of the French completely of the right to make the laws? This provision is therefore essentially unconstitutional and antisocial.

2. Are men equal in rights when some are endowed with the exclusive faculty of eligibility to the legislative body or to other public institutions, and others merely with that of electing them, while the rest are deprived of all these rights at once? No. Yet such are the monstrous distinctions drawn between them by the decrees that make a man active or passive, or half active and half passive, according to the varying degrees of fortune that permit him

to pay three days' wages, ten days' wages in direct taxes, or a silver mark. All these provisions are, then, essentially unconstitutional and antisocial.

3. Are men admissible to all public employments, with no other distinctions than virtues and talents, when inability to pay the required tax excludes them from every public office without regard for the virtues and talents that they possess? No. All these provisions are therefore essentially unconstitutional and antisocial.

4. And again, is the nation sovereign when the majority of the persons composing it is deprived of the political rights which constitute sovereignty? No. And yet you have just seen that these same decrees deny them to the majority of the French. What, then, would your Declaration of Rights amount to if these decrees were allowed to continue? An empty formula. What would the nation become? A slave; for liberty consists of obeying laws one has given oneself, and slavery of having to submit to the will of another. What would your constitution become? A veritable aristocracy. For aristocracy is the condition in which one part of the citizens is sovereign and the rest subjects. And what an aristocracy! The most intolerable of all: that of the rich.

All men *born* and *domiciled* in France are members of the political society called the French nation; that is to say, they are French citizens. They are so by the nature of things and by the first principle of the law of nations. The rights attached to this title do not depend on the fortune that each man possesses, nor on the portion of the taxes to which he is subject, because it is not taxes that make us citizens; it is citizenship that obliges one to contribute to public expenditure in proportion to one's means. Now, you may give laws to citizens—but you may not annihilate them as citizens.

The upholders of the system that I am denouncing have themselves realized this truth, for, not daring to challenge the title of citizen in those whom they condemn to political disinheritance, they have confined themselves to evading the principle of equality presupposed by citizenship by drawing a distinction between active and passive citizens. Counting on the ease with which men may be governed by words, they have tried to distract us by proclaiming, in this new formula, the most flagrant violation of the rights of man.

But who can be so stupid as not to perceive that such a phrase can neither change the principle nor resolve the difficulty, since to declare that certain citizens are not to be active, or to say that they shall no longer exercise the political rights attached to the title of citizen, is exactly the same thing in the idiom of these subtle politicians. Well, I shall still demand of them by what right they may thus reduce their fellow citizens and constituents to inactivity and paralysis; and I shall not cease to protest against this insidious and barbaric expression which will soil both our law code and our language if we do not hasten to efface it from them both, in order that the word "liberty" itself may not become insignificant and derisory.

What need I add to such self-evident truths? Nothing for the representatives of the nation whose opinions and wishes have already anticipated my demand; but I still must reply to the deplorable sophisms by means of which the prejudices and ambitions of a certain class of men seek to buttress the disastrous doctrine that I am opposing. It is to them alone that I am going to speak.

The people! Persons who have nothing! The dangers of corruption! The example of England, and of other nations supposedly free; these are the arguments that are being used against justice and reason.

I should not have to answer more than one word: the people, this multitude of men whose cause I am defending, have rights with the same origin as yours. Who has given you power to deprive them of these rights?

The general interest, you say! But is anything of general interest except what is just and honest? And does not this eternally valid maxim apply especially to the social order? And if the aim of society is the good of all, the preservation of the rights of man, what must one think of those who wish to base it on the power of a few individuals and on the abasement and nullity of the rest of mankind! Of what sort, then, are these lofty politicians who applaud their own genius when, by virtue of laborious subtleties, they have finally succeeded in substituting their futile fantasies for the unchangeable principles that the eternal legislator has himself engraved in the hearts of men!

England! Well, what does England matter to you with her vicious constitution, which may well have appeared free to you when you were reduced to the basest servitude but which must finally cease to be acclaimed from ignorance or mere habit? The free peoples! Where are they? What does history tell you of those whom you honor with this name if not that they are agglomerations of men more or less removed from the ways of reason and nature, more or less enslaved, under governments established by chance, ambition, or violence? Is it, then, to copy slavishly the errors or injustices that have so long degraded and oppressed the human race that eternal Providence has summoned you alone since the origin of the world to re-establish on earth the empire of justice and liberty, in the heart of the most vivid enlightenment that has ever instructed the public reason, in the midst of the almost miraculous circumstances that it has seen fit to assemble, in order to assure you the power to give man his happiness, his virtues, and his basic dignity[?]

Do they appreciate the full seriousness of this sacred mission —those whose only answer to our just complaints is to say coldly: "With all its vices, our constitution is still the best that has ever existed"? Have twenty-six million men entrusted you with the fearful responsibility of safeguarding their destiny in order that you may lightheartedly leave in this constitution fundamental vices which undermine the very foundations of the social order? Could it not be said that the reform of a great number of abuses and the enactment of several useful laws are so many concessions to a people that asks nothing further for itself? No. All the good that you have done was a duty of the most serious kind. Failure to do all the good that you can would be a breach of trust; the harm that you would be doing would be a crime against the nation and against humanity. And more: if you do not do everything for liberty, you will have done nothing. There are not two ways of being free: one must be so entirely or become a slave again. The least resource left to despotism will soon restore its power. Yes, already it surrounds you with its seductive influences; soon it will overwhelm you with its power. Oh, you who are proud to have attached your names to a great change and are not too concerned whether it is sufficient to assure the happiness of mankind, do not be deceived; the din of praise that novelty and superficiality have produced will soon die away; posterity, comparing the greatness of your obligations and the immensity of your resources with the fundamental vices of your work, will say of you, with indignation: "They could have made men happy and free, but they did not wish to; they were unworthy."

But, you will say, the people! Those who have nothing to lose! They will be able, like us, to exercise all the rights of citizenship.

People who have nothing to lose! How unjust, how false is this proud, crazy language in the sight of truth!

These men of whom you speak are apparently men who live, who subsist in the heart of society, with no means of living or subsisting. For if they have such means, they have, it seems to me, something to lose or to preserve. Yes, the rough clothing that covers me, the humble retreat where I buy the right to withdraw and to live in peace; the modest wage with which I nourish my wife, my children; these are not, I admit, lands, châteaux, or coaches-and-pairs; all that is called *nothing*, perhaps, by luxury and opulence; but it is something to humanity; it is a sacred property—as sacred, no doubt, as the brilliant possessions of the rich.

I will say more! My liberty, my life, the right to obtain protection or vengeance for myself and for those who are dear to me, the right to repel oppression and to exercise freely all the faculties of my mind and heart; all these so good belongings, the first that nature has bestowed on man—are they not placed, like your own, under the protection of the laws? And yet you say that I have no interest in these laws; and you wish to deprive me of the share that I must have, as you must, in the administration of public affairs, and for no other reason than that you are richer than I! Ah! If the balance should cease to be equal, should it not favor the citizens of lesser fortune? Have not the laws been framed and the public authority been established to protect the weak against injustice and oppression? To place the public authority entirely in the hands of the rich is therefore to flout all the principles that govern society.

But the rich and powerful have reasoned otherwise. By a strange abuse of words, they have restricted the general notion of property to their own narrow usage; they have called themselves the only proprietors; they have claimed that proprietors alone are worthy of the name of citizen; they have labeled their private interest the general interest, and to insure the success of this claim they have appropriated for themselves the whole social power. And we! O frailty of men! We who claim to recall them to principles of equality and justice, we are seeking, without realizing it, to build our constitution on these same absurd and cruel prejudices.

But what is, after all, the rare merit in paying a silver mark or some other tax to which you attach such exalted privileges? If you make a larger contribution to the public treasury than

I, is it not because society has favored you with greater pecuniary advantages? And, if we wish to press the point further, what is the cause of this extreme inequality of fortunes that concentrates all wealth in the hands of a few? Is it not bad laws, bad government, and in the last analysis all the vices of corrupted societies? Now, why must the victims of these abuses be punished again for their misfortune by the loss of their dignity as citizens! I do not covet the unequal portion that you have received, since this inequality is a necessary or an incurable evil; but do not take from me, at least, the inalienable property of which no human law can deprive me. Permit me even at times to be proud of an honorable poverty, and do not seek to humiliate me by arrogantly presuming to monopolize the title of sovereign while leaving me only that of subject.

But the people! But corruption!

Ah! Cease, cease to profane the stirring, sacred word of "people" by linking it to the idea of corruption. What kind of man is it who, among persons equal in rights, dares to declare his fellows unworthy to exercise theirs so that he may despoil them to his own advantage! And indeed, if you allow yourselves to base such a sentence on a mere suspicion of corruptibility, what a terrible power you are arrogating to yourselves to judge humanity! And where will your proscriptions end!

But should they fall on those who do not pay the silver mark or on those who pay much more! Yes, in spite of all your prejudice in favor of such virtues as come with wealth, I venture to believe that you will find as many in the poorest class of citizens as in the wealthiest! Do you honestly believe that a hard, laborious life engenders more vices than one of comfort, luxury, and ambition? And have you less faith in the probity of our artisans and peasants, who, according to your requirements, will almost never be active citizens, than in that of traders, courtiers, and those whom you call great lords, who, following the same requirements, would be so six hundred times over? I wish to avenge just once those whom you call the *people* for the sacrilegious slanders.

But are you capable of appreciating this, and of knowing men, you who, since the development of your powers of reasoning, have judged them only according to the absurd ideas of despotism and feudal pride; you who, accustomed to its strange jargon, have found it easy to degrade the greater part of the human

species by using terms such as *canaille* and *populace;* you who
have revealed to the world that there were men without birth,
as if not all living men had been born; as if there were not
gens de rien who were men of worth, and *d'honnêtes gens,
des gens comme il faut,* men of respectability and distinction,
who were the vilest and most corrupt of all mankind. Ah! Doubtless
you may be permitted to render the people less than the justice
that is due them. For myself, I call upon all those whose nobility
and sensitivity of soul has brought them close to the people
and made them worthy of knowing and loving equality to bear
witness that, in general, there is nothing so just and good as
the people so long as they are not angered by excessive oppression;
that they are grateful for the least mark of concern shown
them; for the slightest good done them, and even for the ill
that is not done them; that it is among the people that you
find, under what we consider a coarse exterior, frank and upright
souls and a good sense and energy for which you would search
vainly for a long time in the class that despises them. The
people demand only what is necessary; they want only justice
and tranquillity; the rich lay claim to everything; they wish
to invade everything and to dominate everything. Abuses are
the handiwork and domain of the rich, the scourge of the people.
The interest of the people is the general interest, that of the
rich a particular interest; and you wish to make the people
nothing and the rich all-powerful!

Will you now answer me with those time-worn accusations
which have continuously been leveled at the people ever since
they shook off the yoke of despotism, as if the people as a
whole could be charged with a few local and particular acts
of vengeance carried out at the beginning of an unexpected
revolution in which, finally taking breath after so long an oppression, it was in a state of war with all its tyrants? No, was
there ever a time that gave more striking proofs of the people's
natural goodness than that when, armed with irresistible might,
it stopped all at once of its own accord and returned to calm
at the summons of its representatives? Oh you who are so relentless
toward suffering humanity and so indulgent toward its oppressors,
consult history, look around you, count the crimes of tyrants,
and judge between them and the people.

No, let us be clear, let us understand from the very efforts
made by the enemies of the revolution to slander the people

to their representatives and to slander you to the people, to suggest to you measures for stifling their voice, or weakening their energy, or misdirecting their patriotism, to keep them in ignorance of their rights by hiding your decrees from them; from the unwavering patience with which they have borne all their misfortunes and awaited a happier state of things—from all this let us understand that the people are the sole support of liberty. Well, then, who could tolerate the idea of seeing them despoiled of their rights by the very revolution that is due to their courage and to the tender and generous devotion with which they have defended their representatives! Is it to the rich and the great that you owe this glorious insurrection that saved France and yourselves? These soldiers who turned their weapons to the service of the aroused nation, were they not men of the people? Those who had been leading them against you, to what classes did they belong? Was it, then, to help you defend its rights and its dignity that the people fought at that time, or was it to give you the power to crush them? Was it to fall under the yoke of an aristocracy of wealth that the people helped you break the yoke of the feudal aristocracy?

Until now, I have adopted the language of those who seem to mean by the word "people" a separate class of men, one with whom they associate an idea of inferiority and contempt. It is now time for more precise expressions, in recalling that the system we are combating proscribes nine-tenths of the nation and that it excludes even from the list of those whom it labels active citizens great numbers of men whom even the prejudices based on pride used to respect for their distinctions of education, industry, and even fortunes.

Such is, in fact, the nature of this institution that it leads to the most absurd contradictions, and while taking wealth as the measure of the rights of citizenship, it departs from this very rule by attaching them to what are called direct taxes, although it is evident that a man who pays substantial indirect taxes may enjoy a larger fortune than one who is subject only to a moderate direct tax. But how could anyone have thought to make the sacred rights of man dependent on the changing nature of financial systems, on the variations and diversities that our system presents in the different parts of the same state? What sort of system is it where a man who is a citizen in one part of France ceases to be one either in part or in whole if he moves to another place, and where a man who is one today will no longer be one tomorrow if his fortune suffers a reverse!

What sort of system is it in which an honest man, despoiled by an unjust oppressor, sinks into the class of the *helots* while his despoiler is raised by this very crime into the ranks of the citizens; in which a father, as the number of his children increases, sees with a growing certainty that he will not be able to leave them this title along with their feeble shares of his divided patrimony; in which all sons in half the kingdom can have no *patrie* until the deaths of their fathers! Finally, what is the worth of my superb prerogative of belonging to the sovereign body if the assessor of taxes has the power to deprive me of it by reducing my contribution by a *sou* and if it is subject both to the caprices of men and to the inconsistency of fortune! . . .

But see, I beg you, what bizarre consequences result from a great error of this kind. Forced by basic notions of equity to seek means of palliating it, you have accorded soldiers, as recompense after a certain period of service, the rights of active citizen. You have accorded them as a mark of distinction to the ministers of religion when they cannot fulfill the pecuniary conditions required by your decrees; you will still grant them in analogous cases, from like motives. Now, all these dispositions, so just in their objectives, are so many inconsistencies and infractions of the first constitutional principles. How, in fact, have you who have suppressed all privileges been able to establish as privileges for certain persons, and for certain professions, the exercise of the rights of citizen? How have you been able to compensate by changing a property that belongs essentially to everyone? Moreover, if the clergy and the soldiers are not the only ones who deserve well of the *patrie*, must not the same reason force you to extend the same privilege to the other professions? And if you reserve it for merit, how have you been able to make it the special preserve of wealth? . . .

"If only he still lived!" we have said several times, in associating the idea of this great revolution with that of a great man who helped bring it about. "If only he still lived, this sensitive and eloquent philosopher whose writings have developed among us those principles of public morality that have made us worthy to conceive of plans for regenerating our country!" Ah, well, if he were still alive, what would he see? The sacred rights of man which he defended violated by the nascent constitution, and his name erased from the list of citizens. . . .

These heroes were not unaware, and we sometimes ourselves repeat, that only upon moral standards can liberty be solidly established. Now, what morals can a people have in whose country the laws seem calculated to stir the thirst for wealth into the most furious activity? And what surer means can the laws take of irritating this passion than to stigmatize honorable poverty and to reserve for wealth all the honors and all the power? To adopt such an institution, what else is it than to force even the noblest ambition, that which seeks glory in serving the *patrie*, to take refuge in the midst of cupidity and intrigue and to make of the constitution itself a corrupter of virtue? . . .

After that, how could you boast of bringing about the rebirth among us of that public spirit upon which the regeneration of France depends when, making the majority of the citizens alien to concern for public affairs, you condemn them to concentrate all their thoughts and affections on the objectives of personal interest and pleasure; that is to say, when you pile egotism and frivolity on the ruins of useful talents and generous virtues, which are the sole guardians of liberty, there will never be a lasting constitution in any country where it will be, so to speak, the domain of one class of men, and will only be a matter for indifference to the others, or a subject of jealousy and humiliation. If attacked by adroit and powerful enemies, it must succumb sooner or later. Already, GENTLEMEN, it is easy to foresee all the fatal consequences which would result from the dispositions of which I speak, if they were to persist. Soon you will see your primary and elective assemblies deserted, not only because these very decrees deny admission to the majority of citizens, but also because most of those whom they summon, such as persons paying three days' wages in taxes, having the right to vote but not to be elected themselves to the offices filled by the confidence of the citizens, will not hasten to abandon their businesses and their families in order to frequent assemblies to which they can bring neither the same hopes nor the same rights as the more well-to-do citizens, unless some of them go there to sell their votes. . . .

Does not the universe, moreover, know that your true will,

that your true decree even, is the prompt revocation of the measures of which I speak; and that it is indeed the opinion of the majority of the national assembly that I am defending when I attack them? I make this declaration, therefore: such decrees do not even need to be formally revoked; they are essentially void, because no human power, not even yours, was competent to inscribe them. The power of the representatives, of the mandataries of a people, is necessarily determined by the nature and objective of their mandate. Now what is your mandate? To make laws to re-establish and solidify the rights of your constituents. It is therefore not possible for you to deprive them of these same rights. Take careful note: those who chose you, those by whom you exist, were not taxpayers of the silver mark, of three, or of ten days' wages in direct taxes; it was all the French—that is, all men born and domiciled in France, or naturalized—paying any tax whatever. . . .

It inheres only in the essentially infallible Being to be immovable; to change is not only a right but a duty for every human will that has failed. Men who decide the fate of others are less than anyone exempt from this universal obligation. But it is the misfortune of a people passing rapidly from servitude to liberty to transfer to the new order of things, without being aware that it is doing so, the prejudices of the old which it has not yet had the time to discard; and it is certain that this system of the absolute irrevocability of the decisions of the legislative body is nothing else than an idea borrowed from despotism. Authority cannot retreat without compromising itself, it was said, although in fact it had sometimes been forced to draw back. This maxim was actually good for despotism, whose oppressive power could be sustained only by illusions and terror; but the tutelary authority of the nation's representatives, based both on the general interest and on the strength of the nation itself, can repair a disastrous error without running any risk other than of awakening the sentiments of confidence and admiration which encompass it; it can be compromised only by an invincible perseverance in measures contrary to liberty and rejected by public opinion. There are some decrees, however, which you cannot repeal, namely those to be found in the Declaration of the Rights of Man, because it was not you who made these laws; you only announced them. It is to the immutable decrees of the eternal legislator placed in the reason and hearts of all men before you ever inscribed them in your code that I appeal against the dispositions which infringe them and must disappear before them. . . .

23. June 14, 1791:
Chapelier on Organizations of Workers

The deputy Isaac René Guy Le Chapelier came from Brittany, where he had been a successful lawyer. He was deputy for the Third Estate from the *sénéchaussée* of Rennes and was one of the most vigorous supporters of the revolution in its early years, being one of the founders of the Breton Club, which became the Jacobins, and President of the National Assembly during the night session of August 4, 1789. He was to have misgivings about the radical course of the revolution after the king's flight in June, 1791, and was probably one of those who wanted to revise the constitution in a conservative direction. Here we see him a week before the king's flight, successfully introducing legislation characteristic of the economic and social individualism that he shared with many of his fellow deputies. The source is *Réimpression de l'ancien Moniteur*, Vol. VIII (Paris, 1847), pp. 661–662, 663.

National Assembly. Presidency of M. Dauchy.
Session of Tuesday, June 14.

M. CHAPELIER: I come, in the name of your constitutional committee, to report to you a violation of the constitutional principles which suppress corporations, a violation from which originate great dangers for public order. Several people have tried to recreate the abolished corporations by forming assemblies of arts and crafts, in which there have been named presidents, secretaries, syndics, and other officers. The object of these assemblies, which are spreading in the kingdom and which have already entered into correspondence with each other, is to force contractors, the former masters, to increase the wage for a day's work; to hinder workers and the individuals who employ them in their workshops from making their own private agreements; to make them sign registers acknowledging the obligation to comply with the rates for a day's work set by these assemblages, and with other rules that they take the liberty of making. Violence is used to enforce these rules; workers are forced to leave their shops, even when they are satisfied with the wages that they are receiving; they want to empty the workshops; and already several workshops have revolted, and various disturbances have been caused.

The first workers who assembled obtained permission to do so from the municipality of Paris. In this respect the municipality seems to have been in error. All citizens must without doubt be permitted to assemble; but citizens of certain professions should not be permitted to assemble for their so-called common interests; there is no longer a corporation in the State; there is nothing more than the particular interest of each individual, and the general interest. No one is permitted to suggest to citizens an intermediate interest, to separate them from the public welfare by a corporate spirit.

In order to obtain the authorization of the municipality, the assemblies in question have introduced specious motives; they are said to be intended for providing aid for needy workers of the same profession, persons who are ill or out of work; these funds for assistance have proved useful; but let no one be mistaken about this claim: it is for the nation, it is for public officials acting in its name, to furnish work for those who need it in order to exist, as well as help for the disabled. Private distribution of relief, when it is not dangerous because of poor administration, tends at the least to cause corporations to spring up again; it necessitates frequent meetings of people of the same profession, the nomination of syndics and other officers, the making of rules, the exclusion of those who would not submit to these rules; thus would arise privileges, masterships, etc., etc. Your committee believed it was urgent to prevent the progress of this disorder. These unhappy societies have, in Paris, been succeeded by a society established under the name *Society of Duties.* Those who did not fulfill the duties and live up to the rules of this Society were plagued in every way. We have the strongest reasons for believing that the establishment of these assemblies was encouraged, in the minds of the workers, not so much with the object of making daily wages increase by their union as with the secret intention of fomenting troubles.

It is therefore necessary to return to the principle that it is for independent agreements among individuals to determine the daily wage of each worker; it is then up to the worker to maintain the agreement that he has made with the one who employs him. Without examining what a reasonable wage for a day's work should be, and acknowledging only that it should be a little larger than it is at present [murmurs], and what I have just said is utterly true, because in a free nation wages must be large enough so that those who receive them are above that absolute subordination produced by deprivation of needs of prime necessity, which is almost slavery; it is thus that English workers are paid more than French workers; I said, then, that, without determining here the precise rate of the day's work, a figure which must result from agreements freely made between individuals, the constitutional committee believed it obligatory to submit to you the following decree project, which has for its objective as much the preventing of coalitions formed by workers in order to increase wages as the preventing of those formed by entrepreneurs in order to lower wages.

Art. I. The extinction of all kinds of corporations of citizens of the same station and profession being one of the fundamental bases of the French constitution, it is forbidden to re-establish them *de facto*, under any pretext or under any form whatsoever.

II. The citizens of the same station or profession, contractors, shopkeepers, workers, and *compagnons* of whatever art, shall not, when they meet together, designate any president, secretary, or syndic, keep registers, make bylaws or resolutions, or formulate rules about their so-called common interests.

III. It is forbidden for any administrative or municipal corporation to receive any document or petition designated as coming from a social category or profession, or to make any response to it; and they are enjoined to declare invalid any deliberations that may be concluded in this way and to watch carefully in order that no sequel or implementation may result from them.

IV. If, contrary to the principles of liberty and of the constitution, citizens allied to the same professions, arts, and crafts have deliberated and made agreements among themselves leading to concerted refusal, or to the granting only at a set price, of assistance to their industry or their enterprise, the said deliberations, supported or not by an oath, are declared unconstitutional and prejudicial to liberty and the Declaration of the Rights of Man, and of no effect; the administrative and municipal corporations are obliged so to declare them; the originators, leaders, and instigators who have incited, drawn up, or presided over them shall be cited before the police tribunal, at the demand of the prosecutor of the commune, and sentenced to a fine of 500 *livres*, and suspended for a year from the exercise of all their rights as active citizens, and from entry into the assemblies.

V. All administrative and municipal corporations are forbidden, on pain of their members having to answer personally, to employ, admit, or allow to be admitted to the practice of their professions in any public works those entrepreneurs, workers, and *compagnons* who may instigate or sign the said deliberations or agreements except in cases where, on their own initiative, they may present themselves to the office of the police tribunal to retract them or disavow them.

VI. If the said deliberations or conventions, posted or distributed by circular letters, contained any threats against the entrepreneurs, artisans, or foreign workers and day laborers who might come to work in that place, or against those who accept an inferior salary, all authors, instigators, and signatories of the acts or writings will be punished with a fine of 1,000 *livres* each, and three months in prison.

VII. If the individual liberty of entrepreneurs and workers was attacked by threats or violence on the part of these coalitions, the authors of the violence shall be prosecuted as disturbers of the public peace.

VIII. Gatherings of workers whose objective is to obstruct the liberty given by the constitution to labor and industry, and to oppose in this manner police regulations or the execution of judicial decisions, shall be regarded as seditious gatherings and punished accordingly.

[After discussion] . . . The various articles proposed by M. Chapelier are successively put to a vote and decreed.

24. June 20, 1791:
Louis XVI on the Subject of His Flight

The flight of the royal family through an unguarded door of the Tuileries Palace on the night of June 20, 1791, their arrest at Varennes in eastern France on June 21, and their humiliating return to captivity in the palace by the Seine on June 25 dramatized questions of extreme gravity. The monarchy was confronted with the possibility of a republic; the makers of the constitution were faced with the possibility of revision in a democratic direction; into France's foreign policy there suddenly intruded the possibility of armed foreign intervention; and relations of State and Church, already plagued by increasing resistance to the Civil Constitution of the Clergy and the punitive backlash which it was exciting, were worsened by the king's counterrevolutionary effort and its failure. For the king and queen, who had considered themselves as being under coercion ever since the failure of the king's program of June 23, 1789, and therefore felt justified in resorting to extraordinary means, the flight was a carefully planned act of policy. The king's position was argued in detail in a remarkable document which he signed and left behind on June 20, translated below from the *Archives parlementaires*, Vol. XXVII (Paris, 1887), pp. 378–383. The main body of the Declaration, containing all of the king's political and constitutional arguments, has been retained, together with the conclusion. For lack of space, several pages concerning the discomforts, dangers, and lack of freedom of the royal family have been omitted.

Declaration of the King Addressed to All the French upon His Departure from Paris.

. . . The convocation of the Estates General, the doubling of the deputies of the third estate, the King's efforts to eliminate all difficulties which could delay the assembling of the Estates General and those which arose after its opening, all the retrenchments which the King had made in his personal expenses, all the sacrifices which he made for his people in the session of June 23; and finally, the union of the orders, effected by the King's wish, a measure which His Majesty then deemed indispensable for the functioning of the Estates General, all his anxiety, all his efforts, all his generosity, all his devotion to his people—all have been misjudged, all have been misrepresented.

It should be remembered that when the Estates General, assuming the name of the National Assembly, began to occupy itself with the constitution of the kingdom, factions had the cleverness to have memoirs sent from various provinces, and there were movements in Paris designed to make the deputies disregard one of the principal clauses contained in all their *cahiers*; namely, that *the making of the laws should be done in concert with the King.* In violation of this clause, the Assembly placed the King entirely outside the constitution by refusing him the right to grant or to withhold his sanction to articles which it regards as constitutional, reserving to itself the right to include in that category those which it considers suitable; and for those regarded as purely legislative, reducing the royal prerogative to a right of suspension until the third legislature, a purely illusory right as so many examples prove only too well.

What remains to the King other than a vain semblance of royalty? He has been given 25 millions for the expenses of the civil list; but the grandeur of the household he must maintain to do honor to the dignity of the crown of France, and the charges which were rejected above, ever since the time when the sums were regulated, must absorb all of it.

He has been left the usufruct of some of the crown domains, subject to several troublesome formalities. These domains are only a small part of those that the kings have owned from the most remote times, and from the patrimonies of His Majesty's ancestors, which they joined to the crown. One is not afraid to say that if all these lands were joined together, they would exceed by a great deal all the sums allocated for the maintenance of the King and his family, and that in that case it would cost the people nothing for this entry.

A matter difficult for the King to discuss is the attention paid to the separation, in the arrangements for finances and all other elements, of the services rendered to the King personally and those to the State, as if these matters were not truly inseparable, and the services rendered to the person of the King were not also that of the State.

Let us next examine the several branches of the government.

JUSTICE

The King has no share in making the laws; he has simply the right to obstruct, up to the third legislature, matters which are not regarded as constitutional, and to request the National Assembly to apply itself to such-and-such matters, without having the right to make a formal proposal about it. Justice is rendered in the name of the King; the provisions of the judges are dispatched by him; but this is only a matter of form, and the King has only the nomination of the royal commissioners, newly created offices, which have only a part of the functions of the former procurers general, and are only designed to maintain the execution of the forms: all the public part falls on another officer of justice. These commissioners are for life and not revocable, while the functions of judges last only six years. One of the latest decrees of the Assembly has just deprived the King of one of the finest prerogatives attached everywhere to royalty: that of pardoning and of commuting punishments. However perfect laws may be, it is impossible for them to foresee all cases; and it will then be the jurors who will really have the right to pardon, in applying as they see fit the sense of the law, even though it appears to be the opposite. Besides, how much this provision lessens the royal majesty in the eyes of the people, who for so long have been accustomed to turn to the King with their needs and difficulties, and to seeing in him the common father who can relieve their afflictions!

INTERNAL ADMINISTRATION

It is entirely in the hands of the departments, districts, and municipalities, jurisdictions which are too numerous and which impede the working of the machine, and may often thwart one another. All these bodies are elected by the people, and are not under the jurisdiction of the government, according to the decrees, except for their execution or for that of the particular orders consequent upon it. They have, on the one hand, no favors to expect from the government; and on the other, the ways of punishing or of repressing their faults, since they are established by decrees, are so complicated in form that it would need very extraordinary cases to be able to use them; which reduces to almost nothing the surveillance the ministers can have on them. Moreover, these bodies have acquired little influence and esteem. The Societies of the Friends of the Constitution (about which we will speak later), who are not accountable, are a great deal stronger than they are, and from that, the government's action is of no effect. Since their establishment, there have been several occasions upon which, whatever good will they had for maintaining good order, they did not dare make use of the means the law gave them, through fear of the people aroused by other instigations.

The electoral bodies, although they have no initiative of their own, and are restricted to elections, are a real force by virtue of their numbers, their biennial term, and the fear natural to

men, and especially to those who have no fixed state, of displeasing
those who can help or harm.

The disposition of the military forces is, according to the
decrees, in the hands of the King. He has been declared the
supreme head of the army and navy; but all the work of forming
these two forces has been done by committees of the Assembly
without the participation of the King; everything, down to the
slightest regulation of discipline, has been done by them; and
if there remains for the King a third or a fourth of the nominations,
according to the occasions, this right becomes almost illusory
because of the obstacles and the oppositions without number
which everyone permits himself against the King's choices. He
has been known to have been obliged to redo all the work
of the general officers of the army, because these choices were
displeasing to the clubs. In yielding in this way, His Majesty
did not wish to endanger the honest and brave military men,
and expose them to the violence which would surely have been
used against them, too many examples of which have been seen
already. The clubs and administrative bodies meddle with internal
military details, which must be completely foreign, even to the
latter, who have only the right to call for public force when
they think there is a need for it. They have made use of this
right, sometimes even to upset the dispositions of the government
concerning the distribution of the troops; so that it has happened
several times that they were not where they should be. It is
to the clubs only that one must attribute the spirit of revolt
against officers and military discipline which is spreading in many
regiments, and which, if it is not dealt with effectively, will
cause the destruction of the army. What becomes of an army
when it no longer has leaders or discipline? Instead of being
the power and safeguard of a state, it becomes then its terror
and scourge. How the French soldiers, when their eyes have
been opened, will blush at their conduct, and look with horror
on those who have perverted the good spirit which reigned
in the French army and navy! Those arrangements are disastrous
which have encouraged soldiers and sailors to frequent the clubs!
The King has always thought that the law should be equal
for all; the officers who are in the wrong must be punished;
but they must be punished, like subalterns, according to the
dispositions established by law and rules; all doors must be open,
in order that merit can be apparent and can advance; all the

welfare that one can provide the soldiers is just and necessary, but there cannot be an army without officers and without discipline, and there will be no officers and discipline as long as the soldiers believe themselves entitled to judge the conduct of their leaders.

FOREIGN AFFAIRS

Appointment to ministerial posts at foreign courts and the conduct of negotiations have been reserved to the King; but the King's liberty, in these choices, is just as nonexistent as for those of officers in the army; an example of it was seen in the last appointment. The revision and confirmation of treaties, which is reserved to the National Assembly, and the appointment of a diplomatic committee absolutely nullify the second provision. The right to make war would only be an illusory right, because a king who is not or does not wish to be a despot would have to be mad to attack another kingdom point-blank, when the wishes of the nation were opposed to it, and when the nation would grant no funds in support of it. But the right to make peace is another thing entirely. The King, who is only one with the whole nation, who cannot have any other interest than the nation's, knows its rights, needs, and resources, and does not fear therefore to make commitments which seem to him right for assuring its welfare and its tranquillity; but when it is necessary for treaties to be submitted for revision and confirmation to the National Assembly, no power will consent to make engagements which can be broken by others than those with whom it contracted; and moreover, all powers are concentrated in this Assembly; besides, is it possible to entrust the secret of the frankness one puts into negotiations to an Assembly whose deliberations are of necessity public?

FINANCES

The King declared, even before the convocation of the Estates General, that he recognized the right of the Assemblies of the nation to grant subsidies, and that he no longer wished to tax the people without their consent. All the *cahiers* of the deputies to the Estates General were in agreement to put the re-establishment of the finances foremost among matters to be dealt with by that assembly; some had imposed restrictions concerning what articles were to be decided upon first. The King eliminated the difficulties which such restrictions might have occasioned, by taking matters into his own hands and granting, in the session of June 23, everything that had been desired. On February 4, 1790, the King himself urged the Assembly to take effective action on such an important matter: it only went into the matter late, and then in a way which can only seem faulty. There is still no exact statement of receipts and expenditures, and concerning the resources which can make up the deficit, the Assembly has permitted itself to indulge in hypothetical calculations. It hastened to destroy taxes which, in truth, weighed heavily on the people, but which yielded assured resources; it replaced them by an almost unique tax, the exact collection of which will perhaps be very difficult. Ordinary taxes are at present greatly in arrears, and the emergency fund of the first 1,200,000,000 of *assignats* is almost exhausted. The expenses of the departments of war and the navy, instead of diminishing, have increased, without including the expenses which the necessary armaments have occasioned during the last year. For the administration of this department, the machinery has been greatly expanded, by entrusting the receipts to district administrations. The King, the first one who was not afraid to make public the accounts of his financial administration, and who had manifested the wish that the public accounts be established as a regulation of the government, has been rendered, if that is possible, even more extraneous to this department than to others, and the prejudices, jealousies, and recriminations against the government have been even more widespread on this subject. The regulation of funds, the collection of taxes, the assessment among the departments, the rewards for services rendered have all been removed from the King's supervision; there remains for him only some fruitless appointments, and not even the distribution of some gratuities to help the indigent. The King recognizes the difficulties of this administration; and if it were possible that the governmental machinery could operate without his direct surveillance on the administration of the finances, His Majesty would regret only not being able to cooperate more to establish a stable order which could succeed in the lessening of taxes (an objective which it is well known His Majesty has always ardently desired, and which could have been executed save for the expenses of the war in America), and of having no longer the distribution of aid for the relief of the unfortunate.

Finally, according to the decrees, the King was declared to be the supreme head of the administration of the kingdom; other subsequent decrees have regulated the organization of the ministry so that the King, whom that must concern more directly, nevertheless can change nothing without new decisions of the Assembly. The system of the leaders of the dominant party has been so well followed, of arousing such mistrust for all the agents of the government, that it becomes nearly impossible today to fill the administrative positions. No government can operate or subsist without mutual confidence between administrators and administered; and the last rules proposed in the National Assembly on the penalties to be inflicted on ministers or agents of the executive power who were prevaricators, or were judged as having overreached the limits of their power, must give rise to all sorts of anxieties. (These penal provisions extend even to subordinates, which destroys all subordination, inferiors not being able to judge the orders of the superiors who are responsible for what they command.) These regulations, because of the multiplicity of precautions and the kinds of misdemeanors indicated in them, tend only to inspire mistrust instead of the confidence which would be so necessary.

This form of government, so vicious in itself, is becoming still more so for several reasons. (1) The Assembly, through its committees, constantly exceeds the limits it has prescribed for itself; it devotes itself to matters dealing only with the internal administration of the kingdom and with that of justice, and thus it acquires all authority; through its Committee on Investigations it even exercises a veritable despotism, more barbarous and insufferable than any ever known to history. (2) There exist in almost all the cities, and even in some towns and villages of the kingdom, associations known under the name of Friends of the Constitution; contrary to the tenor of the law, they do not tolerate any others not affiliated with them; they thereby constitute an immense corporation, more dangerous than any that formerly existed. Without being authorized to do so, and even in defiance of all decrees, they deliberate on all questions of the government, correspond among themselves upon all matters, make and receive denunciations, post decrees, and have acquired such a preponderance that all the administrative and judicial bodies, without even excepting the National Assembly itself, usually obey their orders.

The King does not think it possible to govern a kingdom of such great extent and importance as France through the means established by the National Assembly, such as they exist at present. His Majesty, in granting to all decrees, without distinction, a sanction which he well knew could not be refused, was in so doing motivated by a desire to avoid all discussion, which experience had shown him to be useless to say the least; he feared, moreover, that he would be suspected of wishing to retard or to bring about the failure of the efforts of the National Assembly, in the success of which the nation took so great an interest; he placed his confidence in the wise men of that Assembly, who recognized that it is easier to destroy a government than to reconstruct one on entirely different bases. They had several times felt the necessity, at the time of the announced revision of the decrees, of providing a force of action and of coercion necessary to any government; they also recognized the utility of inspiring for this government and for the laws, which must assure the prosperity and condition of everyone, a confidence such that it would bring back into the kingdom all those citizens, for some of whom, discontent, and, for most of whom, fears for their lives and their properties have forced to expatriate themselves.

But the closer one sees the Assembly approaching the end of its labors and the wiser heads losing their influence, the more one sees a daily increase in dispositions which can only make difficult or even impossible the conduct of the government, and which cause it to be distrusted and disfavored; the other regulations, instead of applying healing balm to the wounds which still bleed in several provinces, only increase the worries and sharpen the discontentments. The spirit of the clubs dominates and pervades everything; the thousand slanderous and incendiary newspapers and pamphlets, distributed daily, are simply their echoes, and prepare minds for the way in which they wish to lead them. The National Assembly has never dared remedy that license, so far removed from true liberty; it has lost its influence and even the force which it would need to retrace its steps and change whatever it would seem desirable to correct. One can see from the spirit which prevails in the clubs, and from the manner in which they are making themselves masters of the new primary assemblies, what is to be expected from them; and if they show any inclination to revise anything, it is in order to destroy the remainder of the monarchy and to establish a metaphysical and philosophical government which would be impossible to operate.

Frenchmen, is that why you sent your representatives to the National Assembly? Would you want the anarchy and despotism of the clubs to supplant the monarchical government under which the nation has prospered for fourteen hundred years? Would you want to see your King overwhelmed with insults and deprived of his liberty, while he devotes himself entirely to the establishment of yours?

Love for their kings is one of the virtues of the French, and His Majesty has received personally evidences of this too touching ever to be forgotten. The rebels were well aware that so long as this love remained their work could never succeed; they felt, likewise, that in order to enfeeble it, it was necessary, if possible, to destroy the respect that has always accompanied it; and that is the source of the outrages which the King has experienced during the past two years, and of all the ills which he has suffered. His Majesty would not here review the distressing picture of these if he did not wish to make known to his faithful subjects the spirit of these rebels who are rending the bosom of their *patrie* while pretending to desire its regeneration. . . .

In view of all of these facts and the impossibility of the King's being able to do the good and prevent the evil which is being committed, is it surprising that the King has sought to recover his liberty and find security for himself and his family?

Frenchmen, and especially you Parisians, you inhabitants of a city which the ancestors of His Majesty were pleased to call the good city of Paris, beware of the suggestions and lies of your false friends. Return to your King; he will always be your father, your best friend. What pleasure will he not take in forgetting all his personal injuries, and in seeing himself again in your midst, when a constitution, which he will have accepted freely, will cause our holy religion to be respected, the government to be established on a firm foundation and to be useful by its actions, the property and position of every person to be disturbed no longer, the laws no longer to be violated with impunity, and, finally, liberty to be established on firm and immovable foundations.

Paris, June 20, 1791.   *Signed*: Louis

* * *

The King forbids his Ministers to sign any order in his name until they have received further instructions; he enjoins the Keeper of the Seal of State to send it to him as soon as he shall be so ordered in his name.

Paris, June 20, 1791.   *Signed*: Louis

25. *August 11, 1791:*
Barnave on Representative Government and the Social Order

Antoine Barnave was twenty-eight in 1789, a young deputy from Grenoble who at first was a supporter of Mounier but moved beyond him to support the unicameral legislature and the suspensive veto and the other clauses of the Constitution of 1791. Barnave was one of the outstanding orators of the National Assembly, a maker of striking phrases who in the early years seemed very radical. This remained the case as long as he was primarily concerned, along with his associates Duport and the Lameth brothers, about dangers from the king and the aristocracy, but by 1791 he had misgivings about dangers from the left. The episode of Varennes, in which he participated as one of the commissioners sent by the Assembly to escort the royal family back to Paris, rallied him to the defense of the revolution as it had been up to that point, as is shown in the document below, a leading example of that effort at consolidation. Barnave and his friends also secretly advised the court and hoped to amend the constitution in the direction of something like the ideas of Mounier in 1789. This effort failed, and Barnave, after going home to Grenoble, was to be arrested, brought to Paris, and guillotined in 1793. Before his death, he wrote a remarkable manuscript which was published in 1845 as *Introduction à la Révolution française,* a work comparable in the breadth of its vision to Condorcet's manuscript produced under rather similar circumstances. The speech below is from *Journal des États-Généraux convoqués par Louis XVI, le 27 avril 1789; aujourd'hui Assemblée nationale permanente, ou Journal logographique . . . par M. Le Hodey.* (Paris, 1791) Vol. XXXI, pp. 377–384. The date, August 11, 1791, is that of one of the important debates on revision of the constitutional provisions for election of members of the legislature. There is a motion on the floor to increase substantially the property requirement for electors; that is, for the men who, after being chosen by active citizens, would themselves choose the deputies to the legislature.

National Assembly, Session of
Thursday, August 11, 1791.

M. BARNAVE:

I maintain that the proposal put forth by M. Roederer [to close the discussion] is not a regular motion, but a means by which he intends to fight the committee's proposal, a proposal which I defend. The true means of upholding, in the integrity of its principles, the constitution that has been decreed is to set it on pure and unshakable foundations. It shows a poor understanding of the means to establish liberty to search for it in what destroys it. It is not enough to want to be free; it is still necessary to know how to be free. [Murmurs on the far left; applause everywhere else.]

I will speak briefly on this question [interruption]: for after the success of the deliberation, which I anticipate without anxiety in view of the good will of the assembly, all that I want, and I state it emphatically, is to have expressed my opinion on a matter the defeat of which would bring about sooner or later, and perhaps too soon, the loss of our liberty; on a matter concerning which those men who have pondered more or less about governments, and who are at least guided by a calm and impartial sense, cannot hesitate over a proposal that can have only some temporary disadvantages which I will soon prove to be essentially demolished by the lapse of time that separates us from the moment of its execution.

All those who have opposed the opinion of the committee have shared this fundamental error in their means; they have confused democratic government and representative government. It is because of this that they have mistakenly identified the rights of the people with the position of elector, which is merely a public function to which no one has a right, and which society assigns as its interest prescribes.

In democratic countries, one can with seriousness examine from the point of view of the rights of man the question of the quota of property or of tax contribution necessary to constitute the citizen and give him the right to vote in public assemblies; but where the government is representative, and especially where there exists an intermediate degree of electors, because it is on behalf of the entire society that each elects, the society in whose name and for whose sake the election takes place has the basic right to determine the conditions under which it wishes the choices to be made on its account by certain individuals. If there exist individual rights among the political rights in your constitution, that of active citizen is such a right; your committees have not proposed that you alter it.

The function of elector is not a right; once again, it is for everyone that any one person exercises it; it is for everyone that the active citizens name the electors; it is for the sake of the entire society that they exist; it is for society alone to determine the conditions under which one can be an elector, and those who are deeply ignorant of the nature of representative government as well as its advantages ceaselessly come before us to present models of the governments of Athens and Sparta. Aside from the difference in population, in area, and in all the political distinctions between these states and ourselves, have they then forgotten that pure democracy did not exist in these little republics, that it did not exist in Rome during the waning of its liberty except through an institution infinitely more faulty than any for which one can reproach representative government? Have they forgotten that the Lacedemonians had the right to vote in public assemblies only because the Lacedemonians had slaves and that it was by sacrificing not political rights but civil rights, the individual rights of the majority of the population of the territory, that the Lacedemonians, and the Romans themselves, had put pure democracy in the place of representative government, still unknown in that epoch of the world.

I demand of those who come to us with comparisons of those governments with our own whether they wish to purchase liberty at such a price. I demand of those who ceaselessly profess here metaphysical ideas of liberty, because they have no real ideas of liberty, of those who ceaselessly plunge us into clouds of theory, because the essential, fundamental notions of governments are absolutely unknown to them; if, when they come before this assembly to set pure democracies against the representative government for whose sake I will shortly demonstrate that the decree which we propose to you is indispensably necessary; I demand of them once again whether they have forgotten that which experience proves, that the pure democracy of a part of the people can exist only through the civil, political, effective, and absolute slavery of the other part of the people.

Now I say that representative government, the first, the freest, the most noble of governments, has only one trap to avoid, has only one failure to fear: that is corruption. I say that for representative government to be eternally good, eternally free, there is only one anxiety, one care to consider when it is constituted, and that is the purity and so far as possible the incorruptibility of the electoral body. But, Gentlemen, if there lies the true base of representative government, it follows that every form which, for whoever has eyes to see, clearly tends to subject the election of representatives to the influence of the government itself or of rich citizens is by that very fact equivalent to the complete destruction of representative government.

You have been shown from different points of view the three advantages that should be found in electoral assemblies. First, enlightenment; and it is impossible to deny that, not in the case of any particular individual but in that of a large number of men, a certain amount of wealth, a certain tax contribution, is to a degree an indication of more extensive enlightenment. The second guarantee lies in the interest in public affairs on the part of the one whom society has charged with the making of its choices. And then the last guarantee lies in the independence of fortune which, in placing the individual above need, more or less places him beyond the reach of corruption.

These three means of achieving liberty, these three guarantees that the electoral assemblies can give to the nation in the persons of the electors who compose them—I do not look for them in the superior class, for it is there, without a doubt, that along with the independence of the enlightened one would find too easily motives that are personal and interests stemming from private ambitions that are removed from the public interest, and also means of corruption which, while different from those stemming from need, often are all the more alarming for liberty.

Gentlemen, you have established, at least through custom, that the electors would not be paid; and it is recognized, by each of us, that the very large number of members whom, for the maintenance of public liberty, you have introduced into the electoral assemblies would make very expensive, quite apart from other difficulties, the payment that would be accorded to them. Now I say, however, that from the moment the elector is without sufficient property to refrain from working for a certain period of time and to pay the expenses of his transportation to the place of the election, one of these three things must happen, that he forego the election, that he be paid by the state; or else, finally, that he be paid by the person who wishes to be elected. [Sharp applause.]

Those, Gentlemen, are material means which it is impossible to contest because they arise from facts known to everyone. It is certain either that you will come to one of the three abuses that I am presenting to you or else that the law permitting a person who pays ten days of tax to be an elector will not be enforced; in other words, that no one will in fact be elected who is not much more wealthy. Those who would offer the remedy as a response to my objections would be supporting by that very act the proposal of the committees to enact into law what practice and custom require and necessitate.

Although in general more wealth is required to be chosen an elector, there slips in, nevertheless, a kind of man who has not the qualities that your committees would like to require, but who is very far from belonging to that pure class of artisans and farmers that I would see with as much pleasure as any other in the electoral assemblies. Among the electors who are chosen without paying thirty or forty days of labor, it is not the worker without credit, it is not the farmer, it is not the honest artisan, endlessly given over to the work his needs necessitate, who is going to exercise the function of elector: it is a number of men animated and driven by intrigue who go about peddling in the primary assemblies the principle of turbulence and the desire for change with which they are inwardly consumed; these are men who, for the very reason that they have nothing, and do not know how to find in honest work the subsistence that they lack, seek to create a new order of things that can substitute intrigue for probity, a little wit for good sense, and an ever-active private interest for the stable general interest of society. [Sharp applause.]

If I wished to support with examples the proposition I have just stated, I would certainly not go very far to look for them; I would ask the members of this assembly who have upheld the opposing viewpoint: those members of the electoral bodies who are known to you, who are very close to you, those who do not pay taxes worth thirty or forty days of work, are they laborers? No. Are they farmers? No. Are they publicists, journalists? Yes. [Sharp applause.]

As soon as the government is determined, as soon as, by an established constitution, the rights of each individual are regulated and guaranteed (and that is the moment I hope we are going to reach), then there is no longer any difference of interest between men who live by their property and those who live by honest work. Then there remain in society only two opposed interests, the interest of those who want to preserve the existing state of affairs because they see in it well-being combined with property, existence with work; and the interest of those who wish to change the existing state of affairs because there is no resource for them except in a succession of revolutions; because they are beings who fatten and grow, as it were, in troubled times, like maggots in putridity. [Sharp applause.] Well, it is true that in an established constitution, all who are honest, all who want well-being and peace, have essentially the same interest. Everything depends on placing the common interest in the hands of those who, in that very extensive class, have enlightenment, somewhat more of a personal interest that deters them from corruption, and finally the necessary guarantee that will provide everyone with the certainty that their common interests will be well defended.

Therefore I want the electors to be taken from this general class, but from this same class I want chosen those who have, or show promise of having, a certain enlightenment, who are not easily deceived; those who, in this common interest that they share with everyone, find enough advantages, and who have a way of life to preserve that is important enough so that they will not sacrifice it for the personal advantages of those who would pit against the common interest they have with society the particular interest of corruption: for it is necessary for the one who elects on behalf of society to be attached to the social interest by his property in such a way that it is not easy to offer him through corruption an interest greater than that which binds him to the common and general interest. To the extent that you stray from this principle you will fall, as I have assured you, into the only abuse of representative government: your elections will be corrupt. Does anyone flatter himself that there will always prevail this ardent and pure zeal for liberty that animates the least affluent citizens in a time of revolution? Is it not known that in peaceful times an alliance is always formed between the poorest class and the government or the opulence

that is its source of livelihood? Poverty, extreme poverty, in
the electoral corps, will have no other effect than to place wealth,
extreme wealth, or corruption into the legislative corps; and you
will see happen in France what occurs daily in England in borough
elections where the electors are generally very poor: sometimes
the election will not even be managed by means of money,
a method which would at least limit corruption because of its
very high cost, but will be purchased with pots of beer, as
is done in England by a very great many members of Parliament.

Let us return, then, to the principal point, which is not to
seek representation in either of the two extreme classes, neither
among extremely rich men nor among extremely poor men, but
in the middle class; and let us see whether that is where the
committee has placed it.

It results from calculations that have been made for you that
to be an elector it would be necessary to pay taxes equivalent
to forty days of work; that is, according to local estimates,
it would be necessary to have from 120 *livres* to 240 *livres*
of revenue, either from property or from industry. Now, I do
not think that one can seriously say that that is taking from
too high a class those who must make choices on behalf of
society; those who make the choices, I have already said, must
elect in a place other than that of their habitation, since the
election is done in France by departments; consequently they
will find themselves with two alternatives, either to be absent
from the electoral assembly from the necessity of working and
the impossibility of defraying the expenses, or to seek dishonest
support. If you want your liberty to be lasting, set it on foundations
based on reason, on calculations that no one can dispute. And
let us not be detained by trivial considerations, for fear of displeasing for a moment a few individuals who will themselves
recognize the purity of our principles and the effectiveness of
our provisions as soon as they have examined them. As you
have been told, the decree that we are proposing to you does
not have to be executed immediately. There will be an interval
of two years. The new system of taxation, by increasing the
quantity of direct taxes to be paid by individuals, will play
a part in this last. The passage from the one to the other tax,
and the two years that will elapse, will calm people's minds
and will revive the taste for and habit of working; those who
of necessity must concern themselves with it, above all, will

so encourage in all classes true notions of government and of what makes for constitutional stability that you would not even have to fear their discontent if you did not offer them in the same decree an equivalent as honorable as and more honorable than what you are taking from them; I mean the perspective of a national representation. For, Gentlemen, it is almost universally agreed (and it is on that basis that the objection to our opinion is founded), it is almost universally agreed that the citizens who do not pay forty days' work in taxes are almost never named electors, but that they are honored, that they are satisfied, to have the possibility of being electors; that it is less the actual enjoyment of the right than the possession of the right that gives them satisfaction. Now, if it is a question of honor, if it is a question of the possibility of arriving at an honorable rank, I ask whether the one that you are presenting to them, whether the career that you are opening to them by suppressing the silver mark, by thus making it possible for all to be admitted to the legislature, does not give them more stature, will not place them more on a level with their fellow citizens, does not tend more than anything else to efface in France this class distinction for which we are reproached, is not really much more in harmony with the principle of equality, since under its terms each individual becomes eligible to represent the entire nation; and since it is agreed that the inconveniences lie not in reality but in opinion, I ask whether the provision we are adding does not do much more to improve opinion than our changing of provisions does to damage it.

It is evident, Gentlemen, that it is not from motives that find easy favor with legislators, from motives capable, perhaps, of obtaining popularity for a day but for which the nation would reproach you eternally, that you must act at the moment of determining our constitution once and for all. I too want to keep it unchanged, I too want it to be eternal, and it is for that reason that I invite you not to incorporate in it imprudent provisions whose bad effects would soon cause the entire nation to recognize the necessity for a new national convention.

For the constitution to be durable, it must above all be good; your committees have had the obligation of presenting to you clearly their views on this matter and they have done so completely in the materials that they have laid before you. It is not necessary to ascribe to them ulterior projects when you see with what frankness they have presented their opinions to you. They will not propose to you dispositions beyond those that they have presented to you, but I declare to you that what is here proposed is the view of all the members, the only real and direct guarantee of the conversation of France's liberty, tranquillity, and prosperity. [Applause]

26. September 8, 1791:
Marie Antoinette on
Ending the Revolution

Marie Antoinette was thirty-six when she wrote this letter, which was a secret document intended to save the monarchy and the inheritance of her children and the dignity of her husband's position and place in history. She had been married for twenty-one years, and most of that time had paid little attention to politics, but with the coming of the revolution and the terrible responsibility she felt herself to be carrying, in view of her husband's indecisiveness, she began to play a political role for which her understanding, though not her will, was poorly prepared. Marie Antionette had had much to do with the plans for the escape in June, which turned into a catastrophe. She did not give up, but her renewed efforts contributed to new catastrophes. The letter below, to her brother the emperor of Austria, is from *Marie Antionette. Lettres; recueil des lettres authentiques de la reine, publié pour la Société d'histoire contemporaine par Maxime de la Rocheterie et le Marquis de Beaucourt*, Vol. II (Paris, 1896), pp. 284–304. Although the document is long, only minor cuts have been made in its first half lest the tone and the casting about for solutions be interfered with. It has been possible to eliminate a number of repetitions from the second half without destroying the thread of the argument or deleting any of the principal points.

Marie Antoinette. Memoir
[to Leopold II] September 8, 1791.

To PUT AN END to the troubles of the French revolution depends on the Emperor.

There is no longer any possibility of conciliation.

Armed force has destroyed everything; only armed force can repair the damage.

The King has done everything to avoid civil war, and he is still very much convinced that civil war can correct nothing, and that it must end by destroying everything.

The leaders of the revolution rightly judge that their constitution cannot last. It is sustained by the personal interests of all those who are dominant in the departments, the municipalities, and the clubs. A part of the people is deceived and follows the opinions of those who dominate; but all educated people, peaceful bourgeois, and in general the majority of the citizens in all walks of life are fearful and discontented.

If there takes place opposition on the part of the great powers, if the language of the powers is reasonable, if their assembled forces are imposing, and if there is no civil war, one ventures to guarantee that a general revolution will be effected in all the cities and that there will be no difficulty about a return to order.

But if there is a civil war, the powers, with all their forces, will dominate only in the areas where their armies are located. The distant provinces will be divided; those which have been oppressed will want to avenge themselves, those which have dominated will certainly feel that they must risk everything. There will be massacres for the sake of vengeance; there will be massacres to gain twenty-four hours and have time to flee. Everyone is armed; it will be a most deplorable state if crime and murder are brought into people's houses and no citizen is sure of living from one day to the next. . . .

That is not the intention of the Emperor, and yet it is what will inevitably happen if civil war is provoked or breaks out, and once it has started, foreign war will not make it stop.

That is why the King has never wished to consent to projects for the entry of the princes.

Whatever their relationships and their hopes, he felt that their initiative would cause civil war, and that, once ignited, a civil war could not for a long time be put out.

The King wants neither civil war by itself nor civil war mixed with foreign war.

A regency has been proposed; the King refuses it. What would be its effect?

The princes would give orders and prohibitions to the departments and municipalities; the National Assembly would issue contrary orders. The princes would make appointments to posts in the army; they would win a part of the regiments; the other part would support the Assembly, authorized in the name of the King; the Assembly would make appointments as well as the princes. Regiments would find themselves in distant towns in the interior of the kingdom, far from the areas where the foreign forces could keep order. There would be discord in the provinces, in the cities, in all parts of the kingdom. The war would be man to man in each state. Everywhere there would be combat, pillaging, and massacres.

The revolution must not be destroyed merely to make another. How many offices and favors have been distributed from the first moment, in virtue of these new powers! How much activity there has been on the part of all the interested factions with an eye to seducing the people and the army! What would happen if the army associated with the princes were alienated from the King? That is not their intention; but personal interests, once set in motion, will not call a halt to their projects. The King must not let his power be compromised by the very undertaking that should recover it for him. . . .

The premature convocation of the parlements and the Estates General by the sole authority of the princes, and without the authority of the King, multiplies all the difficulties and for no return gives tangible advantages to the leaders of the revolution.

Is it not realized that the King is no longer anything if, without his presence and before he can speak and act by himself, the separate orders of the Estates General are recalled, the parlements are re-established, and in mustering the French army all the appointments and ranks are filled?

The eyes of the people must not be accustomed to seeing any other power than that of the King take a prominent place in the state.

If it is not the King who governs, if some other authority can overshadow his, the government loses its strength and its dignity.

It is only the legitimate power, when it has recovered its force and freedom of action, that does not arouse personal jealousy and rivalry. The nation is in a state of disunion susceptible to all kinds of disturbances; it will be forever in a state of upheaval if any but the royal authority reunites and represses all the factions.

The King declares that he will be unable to recognize any rank, any office of the army that is not filled by his free and voluntary choice.

The King reserves for himself decisions about the form in which he would like to re-establish the parlements.

And, in what concerns the Estates General, he believes that there is a political procedure to follow according to circumstances, and it is no longer possible to do what circumstances may advise if one has immediately convened the Estates General, as a first move, before having examined all the opportunities or the difficulties that the King, his liberty recovered and his power regained, can find in the general arrangements and in the alteration in his position.

There are questions of such importance that they well deserve that time be taken to think about them.

Where, in any nation, has there been an example of an assembly which has committed like outrages, and which the King has not dissolved when he has had the power to do so?

If one assumes that the King will get back his power, is it possible for him to keep, under one form or another, the very Assembly that is responsible for the complete downfall of the state?

It is possible that one may be forced to do so by the dictates of higher wisdom, but it is impossible for the princes to be permitted to decide the question in the early stages of the war.

The King has not been at all free; will he not, when he is free, be able to distinguish the decrees within the competence of the Estates General from those which are beyond their powers; the useful laws from those that have only brought destruction; and finally the establishment of taxes, which can be regarded as indispensable, from all other objectives.

Can he not differentiate between the sanctions he grants, those he refuses, and those that he defers? Can he not proclaim the laws after having dispersed the Assembly (that was the established custom in France from the first assemblies of the Champ-de-Mars down to the last Estates General) and give himself time before convoking another one? One discusses in council the most practical forms; one sees which are more or less difficult; one weighs the probabilities; in the meantime one builds up the public force; one does useful things; one accustoms the nation to the comforts of peace and quiet; one gives time to sensible men to spread their opinions, which become public opinion, and one is able to find a more peaceful form of assembly that no longer menaces the foundations of the monarchy.

Is it wished to throw a plan of government haphazardly at a nation at the only time perhaps when even the cleverest man cannot know what the form is that best suits it?

How can one recognize what may be suitable for the state of a nation whose most feeble faction dominates in a delirium, and whom fear has subjugated entirely?

The sentiment of habitual and daily things which seemed to form not only the constitution of the state but also that of each class, profession, and family has not been preserved.

Everything has been torn up and destroyed without arousing surprise and indignation on the part of most people.

There is no public and positive opinion in a nation that has no sentiment.

What has become of all the habits? Where is the citizen who has not been robbed of his employment, deprived of his standing, injured in his possessions, tormented in the very secrecy of his conscience?

What customary right has not been banned, what customary obligation not broken?

Insurrection and popular riots have been used to destroy all the established forms. They could not be used to give new habits to the entire nation, and one cannot, in the space of two years devoted to destruction, create, maintain, and consolidate habits.

It is necessary to allow it time to breathe for a moment after so many troubles and agitations; it is necessary to let it pick up its habits and customs again before judging what circumstances demand or allow.

It is not a question only of the safety of France; it is a question of the tranquillity of Europe.

It is apparent what the astonishing undertaking of the leaders of the revolution was. It was not a simple revolt against the government of France; it was an insurrection against all established governments. Its principles tended to arouse all nations against all sovereigns.

These principles call for an equality that destroys all authority, for a licentiousness that leaves no haven for liberty, for a corruption that tarnishes both morals and laws.

There are in this revolution some lures for the people; and, in every nation, men of all conditions who have as yet learned nothing from experience can believe that they are gaining advantages from this strange overturn of orders and ranks.

A propaganda club has been established whose emissaries have had a most perceptible influence on the troubles of the Brabant. These emissaries have made attempts, in Switzerland and Holland, at Turin, at Rome, and in Spain.

All possible surveillance of the authorities in each state was needed to forestall their effects.

Is it desired to renew disurbances in a nation in which the oldest institutions are disappearing without regret or astonishment and which can tolerate without indignation destruction, usurpations, and crimes of all kinds?

It cannot be concealed that there is forming among the émigrés a party spirit of which they themselves are not aware. They have experienced so many injustices that it is very natural for them to give way to their resentments. The remarks circulated on every side indicate their sentiments. If they insist on returning home with a thirst for a vengeance other than that of the laws, they will arouse against them the same kind of fury that animates them. Hates are always reciprocal, and civil war will march in the footsteps of foreign troops. If the émigrés return armed, they will add nothing to the strength of the allied powers, and the civil war that they will bring with them is the one thing that can prevent success.

It is of vital interest to Europe, to France, and to themselves that the émigrés return to their native land only after peace has been established and that they give their confidence to the only authority that can dispel all the factions and prevent the return of the same troubles and calamities.

That must be the aim of the King, of the princes, and of all citizens; it must be the aim of all the powers interested in preventing the return of a similar revolution, and that is what the King proposes to the Emperor.

The Emperor must be the judge of a matter that concerns him; and if these ideas seem to him to be correct, the thing to do now is to consider the way in which they can be carried out.

The means depend on him and on his negotiations with the powers which unite with him to deliver Europe from the danger which threatens the power of all sovereigns, the constitutions of all governments, and the peace and quiet of all states.

There must be no civil war.

If possible, foreign war must be avoided. Therefore it is necessary that it be the united powers whose demands bring about the needed changes and who display forces suitable for the support of their demands.

The declaration of the united powers can restore to the King his rank and authority, and the King, sustained by the concurrence of the united powers, must restore peace and order to France.

The united powers must declare that they do not want to interfere in the domestic government of France in what does not affect the relations of France with them;

That they wish to deal only with the King, when he is free, and will make no treaty with the present Assembly of France, nor with the Estates General, nor with the princes, brothers of the King, nor with members of the royal family of France, nor with any Frenchman;

That they will address their manifesto only to the King, and will change nothing in the formalities of ordinary correspondence with him, with confidence that pending the King's liberation publication by means of printing, supported by the combined engagement of their forces, will leave no cause for doubt or ignorance about their intentions;

That they will accept no answer to the demands contained in their manifesto unless it comes from the King of France, and in due form, while reserving the right to assess, taking account of circumstances, the degree of liberty he will have regained, and the amount of confidence that they may consequently have in his responses.

It is not a matter of indifference to the united powers whether France, in its position on the continent, is a republic or a monarchy, in view of its extent and population.

It must be a monarchy, in order that they may maintain with it the kind of relations that are necessary to the equilibrium of Europe.

They must declare that they recognize that France is a monarchy; that the crown is hereditary from male to male in the reigning dynasty; that the King's person is inviolable, without, in any case and under any pretext whatever, there being the possibility of the King's being suspended from his functions or deprived of his power, and without any possibility of a regency or council being named without his complete, entire, and free consent.

Therefore the united powers must demand the freedom of the King, the honor and dignity of his crown, his re-establishment in the inalienable exercise of his royal functions, and the annulment or revocation of all decrees that specify instances of deposition from the throne or compulsory abdication, as well as of all decrees that violate either his hereditary rights or the perpetuity of his powers, or the inviolability of his person.

There is nothing that can interest the united powers more than the longstanding or more recent treaties that they have contracted with France. . . .

In case of the repeal of some treaty, made by the King involuntarily and under compulsion, the injured powers, appealing to the terms of the treaty, have the right to declare war, and to regard as void and illegal the alteration made without the free and unconstrained will of the King of France. . . .

There exists, by a kind of tacit agreement among the various powers, a ratio of armed force that corresponds to the disparity in their means, and this ratio is one of the basic foundations of their mutual relations, and determines the alliances and treaties that preserve the peace of Europe. It is impossible for the united powers to see without fear a single nation, and a nation as powerful as France, increase its armed force to a prodigious degree without any proportion or limit with respect to the other nations. No sovereign in Europe increases his troops, to a discernible degree, without the interested powers demanding the reason for it. It was such a demand that was the occasion for the Seven Years' War among all the states of Europe.

There have been levied, clothed, armed, and equipped up to four million men in France, independent of the line troops, whose peacetime level is one hundred and fifty, and the war footing two hundred and fifty thousand men and more, without counting the officers and troops allocated to the navy, and the sailors and merchant marine. They have even condemned all citizens under sixty years of age to serve in the National Guard, or submit to announced penalties. . . . A single nation could be regarded as the enemy of all Europe if it could attack all other nations with impunity. It is this armed force that keeps the King imprisoned, that constitutes the power that was used to destroy royalty, that can combine with popular movements, and that, guided by an aroused people, or by the desire for conquest, can suddenly oblige an assembly which has no force by itself, and for whom popularity is law, to declare war; no state can be secure near a people so powerfully armed and in a state of insurrection.

The united powers must announce that they will follow the rules established for warfare. It is known that cities, even if fortified, in which the bourgeois were armed, would be liable to all the rights of war. . . .

The united powers must declare that they will regard as armed not only all those who carry weapons as National Guards, but will also regard all the bourgeois and inhabitants of the cities of France as under arms in the person of the National Guards who represent them, and with whom they are associated, and as subject because of this fact to all the rigors of the law of warfare. They must end by declaring that the cities which refuse to disarm will answer to God and men for the evils they draw down upon themselves and that the united powers are trying to prevent by the present declaration. The united powers cannot be tranquil if France ceases to be a monarchy, if each municipality has an armed force at its disposal, if all the powers, alienated from the King, form a veritable republic; and the King cannot maintain with them the kind of relations that interest them when there remains no way for him to prevent or to repress disorders. It must not be the intention of the powers to meddle with the domestic administration of France; they respect all the forms of government out of self-interest and the right of of each power to conserve its own government; they will limit themselves to demanding that there be returned to the King what pertains in all countries to the center and exercise of power, the means without which he cannot reassure the united powers against the return of the same disorders. . . .

The united powers must take into account that the position of the King, his power and his dignity, and the relationships that depend on them, cannot be firmly re-established if factions can dictate laws which, on the pretext of regulating the exercise of his authority, deprive him of all the necessary means. The united powers must require that, in accordance with the principles and fundamental laws of the French monarchy, no law or constitution may be re-established in France except through the concurrence of his free, complete, entire will, and that there be no possibility of specifying a limit to the free declaration of his will.

The united powers cannot view without concern the spreading within a great European nation of principles of anarchy and confusion destructive to all governments. One cannot fail to see what these principles are when the deplorable state of France proves, better than all arguments, their excesses and dangers. The powers must recognize that this is a question of the greatest interest not only for all sovereigns, but for all orders, states, and classes of citizens in all nations, and in republics as well as monarchies. . . .

It seems impossible that the nation should be without misgivings, and that it should consent to losing all its resources because an immoderate and improvident assembly has destroyed at one and the same time the King's authority and its own. The Assembly is not the nation; forms of government can be disturbed or suspended; the nation remains, and, being more realistic about the danger, it can appreciate its real interests. It was the time-honored method of the kings of France to appeal to the good cities. It is probable that the cities, in order to redeem themselves from the misfortunes of the war, will entreat the King to take back his power and play a mediating role. The desire for public safety can restore to him the love of the people. All the anxieties, all the fears will rally to his authority; upon his head will rest all hopes. His sufferings will be recalled, and those of the Queen, and their courage in the terrible days of October 5 and 6. All the crimes of the revolution will be remembered. It is possible that there will arise a terrible cry against their authors, against all the violent men who have been placed in office. Those frightened men will try to save themselves by flight, and the communal assemblies will no longer be composed of the same members, dominated by the same force, and governed by the same sentiments.

The revolution will be effected in the interior of each city; it will be effected by the approach of the war and not by the war itself. The King, his powers restored, will be entrusted with negotiations with the foreign powers, and the princes will return, in the general tranquillity, to reassume their ranks at his court and in the nation.

VII.

War and Revolution

27. January 11, 1792:
Robespierre on War

At the Jacobin Club on January 2 and 11, 1792, Robespierre made a major statement in his campaign to oppose the coming of war. Like most of Robespierre's speeches, this one was long, so long that on January 2, after attacking Brissot's prowar statements, he broke off because of the lateness of the hour, promising to supplement his remarks in another meeting. He resumed on the eleventh, delivering what was really another full-dress speech, which the club ordered printed, together with the speech of the second, and distributed to the members of the club and the legislature and the affiliated clubs. The following is Robespierre's speech of the eleventh as it was printed after that of January 2 as pp. 45–76 of *Discours de Maximilien Robespierre sur la guerre* (s.l.n.d., 76 pp.), of which the second part is entitled *Suite du discours de Maximilien Robespierre, sur la guerre, prononcé à la Société des amis de la constitution, le 11 janvier 1792, l'an quatrième de la révolution.* Of its 24 paragraphs, two on pp. 49–52 and five on pp. 56–61, which are detailed comments on the conduct of the executive, have been omitted, and there are also several deletions of illustrative or rhetorical statements. The major arguments of the speech have all been retained.

Is it true that a new ministerial sleight of hand has misled the friends of liberty concerning the true objectives of their enemies' plans? . . .

Is it a case of knowing whether the war should be offensive or defensive; whether an offensive war has more or fewer inconveniences; whether the war should be started in fifteen days or in six months? Not at all; it is a question, as we have proved, of recognizing the plot woven by the internal enemies of our liberty who provoke us to war, and of choosing the best means of check-mating them. Why throw a veil over this essential objective? Why be afraid even to touch so many powerful enemies, who must be unmasked and defeated? Why preach confidence when it is out of the question? I too demand war; but I will tell how and on whom it must be waged.

Everyone seems to agree that there is in France a powerful faction which directs the maneuverings of the executive power with the objective of reviving ministerial influence at the expense of national sovereignty: the leaders of this intrigue have been identi-fied; their plan has been unfolded; the whole of France has, on a fatal occasion, become acquainted with their character and their principles. I have also examined their system; I have seen in the conduct of the court a consistently followed plan for destroying the rights of the people and reversing, as much as possible, the work of the revolution: it proposed war, and I have shown how that pro-posal is related to this system; I did not believe that it wished to ruin the émigrés, dethrone their protectors, the foreign princes who made common cause with the court and professed exclusive loyalty to it at the very moment when it was at war with the French people; their language and their conduct were too blatantly in con-cert with the court; the rebels were too openly its satellites and friends; it had too constantly favored their efforts and their in-solence; it reached the point of granting them striking proofs of its protection by shielding them from the decree voted against them by the National Assembly; the court had at the same time accorded the identical favor to internal enemies who were more dangerous[1]; everything indicated to even the least discerning of observers the existence of the court's plan to trouble France internally and ex-ternally in order to recapture in the midst of disorder and terror a power fatal to nascent liberty.

The intentions of the court being obviously suspect, what decision should have been made on the war proposal? Applaud, worship, preach confidence, and give millions? No; it was necessary to examine it scrupulously, determine the motives behind it, foresee its consequences, take stock of oneself, and adopt the measures most

1. Robespierre refers here to the king's vetoes of the Legislative Assembly's decrees of November 9 against the émigrés and November 29 against non-juring priests.—Editor.

appropriate for disrupting the designs of the enemies of liberty while assuring the safety of the state.

Such is the spirit in which I have entered this discussion: I have preferred this point of view to presenting a brilliant picture of the advantages and marvels of a war terminated by a universal revolution; the conduct of this war was to be in the hands of the court; the court could not fail to regard it as a means of achieving its objective; I have proved that to attain this objective it did not even need to make war immediately and take the field; that it was sufficient to its purposes to have war desired, to have it regarded as necessary, and to secure authorization to undertake at once all the preparations for war.

To assemble a great army under the colors, to distribute the troops to various camps in order to bring them more easily to idolatry of the supreme commander of the army and to passive obedience by separating them from the people and occupying them exclusively with military ideas; to give great importance and great authority to the generals judged most appropriate for arousing the enthusiasm of the armed citizens and for serving the court; to increase the ascendancy of the executive power, which flourishes especially when it appears responsible for the defense of the state; to turn people away from their domestic cares and preoccupy them with external security; to achieve the triumph of royalism, moderatism, and Machiavellianism, whose chiefs are military nobles; to prepare in this way for the ministry and its faction the means of extending from day to day their usurpations of national authority and of liberty—there lies the supreme interest of the court and of the ministry. Well, this interest would be satisfied; their objective would be attained from the moment their war proposals were adopted. . . .

Instead of recounting emphatically so many platitudes about the miraculous effects of the Declaration of Rights and the winning of world liberty; instead of reciting to us the exploits of the people who have conquered their own liberty from their own tyrants, it was necessary to consider our own circumstances and the effects of our own constitution. Is it not to the executive power alone that it gives the right to propose war, to make preparations for it, to direct it, to suspend it, to slow it down, to accelerate it, to choose the moment and perfect the means for making it? How will you overcome all the obstacles? Will you preserve this same

constitution even when thus far you have been unable to muster
enough energy to have it applied? Moreover, how will you oppose
the many specious motives with which the executive power will
confront you? What will you respond when it tells you, when the
foreign princes prove to you with authentic documents, that they
have dispersed the gatherings, that they have taken every measure
needed to make them incapable of attempting any hostile move
against you? What legitimate pretext will remain to you when they
have given you the satisfaction demanded by the executive power
in the name of the nation? It is true that soon they will be able
to recommence in secret the same maneuvers; it is true that they
will be able to arrange a favorable occasion for renewing your
alarms and for undertaking a serious war or a simulated one,
directed by our government itself; but before this new intrigue
comes into the open, how will you establish the truth about it?
What possibilities will you have of acting? Some wish to attack
the émigrés and the German princes; others wish to declare war on
Leopold; some want it to start tomorrow; others consent to wait
until the preparations are made, or until the winter is over;
finally, others refer to the patriotism of the minister and to the
wisdom of the executive power, in whom they maintain we must
have complete confidence. But in the midst of all these diverse opinions it will always be the executive power alone which will decide; it
is the nature of the affair that determines this outcome; it was up
to you not to get involved in a system which entails of necessity
all these inconveniences, and which puts us at the mercy of the
court and the ministry. Well, then! Do you not see that the executive power is already gathering the fruits of the adroitness with
which it lured you into its traps? You ask whether it wants war,
when it will declare war; what does all this matter to it? What does
it matter to you yourselves? It already enjoys advantages from war;
and it is true to say, in this sense, that the war has already
started for you. Has not the executive already assembled armies
which are at its disposal? Has it not already received solemn
evidence of confidence and idolatry on the part of our representatives? Has it not obtained millions, at a time when corruption is
the most dangerous enemy of liberty? Has it not violated our laws
and gained a victory over our principles in giving prematurely to
two of its generals extraordinary honors which are an expression
of the spirit and prejudices of the old regime? Has not another
general obtained the command of our armies, a command from

which he was excluded both by the sacred and demanding functions he had just abandoned and by the constitution? . . . [2] The violation of the principles upon which liberty depends, the decadence of the public spirit are calamities more terrible than the loss of a battle, and they are the first fruits of the ministerial plan I have combated. What can one anticipate for the public spirit from a war begun under such auspices? The very victories of our generals would be more disastrous than even our defeats. Yes, whatever may be the outcome of this plan, it can only be fatal. Will the émigrés resign themselves to dispersing without coming back? That would be the most favorable hypothesis and the least likely. All the glory from it would belong to the court and its partisans; and henceforth they would crush the legislative body with their ascendancy; surrounded by the enormous forces which they have assembled, objects of enthusiasm and of universal confidence, they can pursue with unbelievable facility the project of raising their power imperceptibly above the remains of a feeble and poorly consolidated liberty. The likelihood of peace that they seem to offer us, is it not merely a perfidious game concerted with our external enemies, either to calm the anxieties of the patriots by concealing their ardor for war or to defer the war to a more favorable time? . . .

What was it necessary to do then, and what can one still do? It was necessary to persist in the first measure,[3] since the safety of the state required it and the will of the nation demanded it, and since the opposite course compromised the liberty and authority of the representatives. It was necessary to uphold the constitution, which formally denies the executive the right to nullify in an absolute manner the decrees of the legislative corps, and especially to deprive it of the power to save the state. To whom does it fall to defend the principles of the constitution when they are attacked? Who is its legitimate interpreter if not the representatives of the people, unless one prefers to say it is the people themselves? Now, I think that the court intriguers and all the enemies of the people would not like to have the people as a tribunal any more than they would the people's delegates. The legislative corps was

2. This is a reference to Lafayette. The two other generals mentioned were Rochambeau and Luckner, who had been made Marshals of France.—Editor.
3. This is a reference to the Legislative Assembly's measure of November 9, 1791, against the émigrés, which Louis XVI had vetoed.—Editor.

therefore able, and was under the obligation, to declare the *veto* contrary to the safety of the people and to the constitution. This vigorous action would have stunned the court; it would have disconcerted the league of our enemies and terrified all the tyrants. You would also have seen those who wish to lead both the people and the monarch to the same ruin lose all their daring and all their resources, which are based only on the influence of their party in the National Assembly; they would not have dared attempt a useless and terrible struggle against it; or if they had dared, public sentiment emphatically declared, the public interest, the indignation inspired by the audacity of the rebels and the protection given them, and the genius of the nation at last awakened on this happy occasion by the virtue of its representatives and the supreme interest of the public safety would have assured victory to the National Assembly, and this would have been a victory of reason and liberty: that was one of those incomparable occasions that Providence presents to men in the history of revolutions and which they cannot with impunity overlook; since in the last analysis it is necessary, sooner or later, for the combat between the court and the National Assembly to take place—or, rather, since for a long time a mortal combat between them has been going on—it was necessary to seize that occasion, and then we would not have had to fear seeing the executive power degrade and master our representatives, condemn them to a shameful inactivity, or give them leeway only to augment its own power and favor its secret views; henceforth we would not have been menaced with the misfortune of seeing all patriotic efforts frustrated by the powerful action of intrigue and by the forces of inertia, ignorance, weakness, and cowardice.

What could have been done at that time—can it still be done? Perhaps, with fewer advantages and less facility: the representatives of the people are never without the right to save them; they can never renounce this right; I still think that they have enough influence with the people to make them know their true interest, when it is in good faith that they defend that interest, and even that the people's good sense, enlightened by that sacred interest, goes further sometimes in this respect than the wisdom of its representatives; I even think that the public view of the causes and aim of the proposed war is already clear enough to indicate that the people desire to see the National Assembly return to a resolution more useful to their interests and less favorable to the criminal plans of their enemies. However, I do not overlook the fact that this policy could encounter difficulties of another kind; that men retrace their steps with difficulty; that sometimes even by virtue of being right one becomes insufferable and almost suspect; and that in remaining always invariably attached to the truth and to the only principles that can save the *patrie* one exposes oneself to attacks from all the prudent, from all the moderates, from all those privileged beings who know how to reconcile truth with lies, liberty with tyranny, vice with virtue.

I shall therefore take care not to propose this severe course of action, not to assume this inflexible sternness; I am compromising; I am asking to yield.

I shall not therefore concern myself with this *veto* put forth in the king's name by men who care very little for the king but who detest the people and would like to bathe in the blood of the patriots in order to rule. But I say that given the position in which this *veto* and the events which have followed it have placed the National Assembly and the nation, there remains only one means of achieving peaceful and constitutional security; it is for the Legislative Assembly to reassume a character that will be all the more imposing because the Assembly has up to now left more advantages to the ministers and to their valets; it is for it to understand that its enemies, like those of the people, are the enemies of equality; that the only friend, the only upholder of liberty, is the people; it is for it to be proud and inexorable with the ministers and the court; responsive and respectful with the people; it is for it to hasten to support the laws which concern the interests of the most unfortunate citizens and which repel the pride and cupidity of those who are called the great; it is for it to hasten to do justice to the people's complaints, of which the Constituent Assembly was too neglectful; it is for it to counter the power of intrigue, of gold, of force, of corruption with the power of justice, of humanity, of virtue; it is for it to make use of the immense means at its disposal to lift the public spirit and rekindle patriotism to the degree of those first days when liberty was conquered for a moment, the public spirit without which liberty is only a word, and in the presence of which all assaulting foreign and domestic forces will break themselves against the foundations of the French constitution. I will cite only one example: your army is being worked upon; if you feel very secure about that, if all that has been happening recently, if even the trips and the cajoleries of your new minister do not arouse your suspicions, you are deceiving yourselves cruelly;

the army is being given officers appropriate for restoring in it vile sentiments of royalism and idolatry, under the specious pretexts of order, honor, and monarchy. Well, then! Use your legislative authority to give the soldiers advantages which the principles of the constitution, in conformity with military discipline, assured them, and which the interest of the military patricians of the Constituent Assembly took away from them; consult the military code and your principles, and the army will belong to the people and to you. I will say no more about this. It is well enough known, without my saying it, by what means the representatives of the people can serve them, honor them, elevate them to the level of liberty, and force pride and all the vices to bow before them with respect. Everyone knows that if the National Assembly displays this kind of character, we will have no more enemies. It would therefore be useless for my opponents to try to reject those measures under the pretext that they would be too simple, too generous: one is not exempted from fulfilling a sacred duty by seeking to replace it with an illusory and pernicious supplement. When a capricious invalid refuses a beneficial remedy, and then another, and when he says, "I wish to get well using poison," if he dies, it is not the remedy one must hold responsible, it is the invalid. Let the people, awakened, encouraged by the energy of their representatives, regain that attitude which for a moment made all their oppressors tremble; let us conquer our internal enemies; let us make war on the conspirators and on despotism, and then let us march against Leopold; let us march against all the tyrants of the earth: it was on this condition that a new orator, who at the last session upheld my principles while pretending to oppose them, demanded war; it was to this condition, and not to the cry for war and to the commonplaces about the war, already for a long time familiar to this assembly, that he owed the applause with which he was honored.[4]

It is on this condition that I myself clamor for war. What do I say? I go much further than my adversaries themselves; for if this condition is not fulfilled, I still demand war; I demand it not as a wise thing to do, not as a reasonable decision, but as an act of despair; I demand it on another condition which doubtless is understood between us; for I do not think that the advocates of war wished to deceive us; I demand it just as they describe it to us; I demand it just as the spirit of liberty would declare it,

4. The speaker was Jean Baptiste Louvet.—Editor.

just as the French people would make it themselves, and not as vile intriguers could want it, or as ministers and generals, even patriots, could make it for us.

Frenchmen! Men of July 14, who knew how to win liberty without guide or master, come, let us form this army which must free the world. Where is the general who, imperturbable defender of the people's rights, eternal enemy of tyrants, will never breathe the poisoned air of the courts, whose austere virtue is attested by the hatred and the disgrace of the court; this general, whose hands, not dirtied by innocent blood or by the shameful gifts of despots, are worthy to carry before us the sacred banner of liberty? Where is he, this new Cato, this third Brutus, this hero yet unknown? Let him recognize himself by these qualities; let him come; let us put him at our head. Where is he? Where are they, those heroes who on July 14, dashing the hope of the tyrants, placed their weapons at the feet of the alarmed *patrie?* Soldiers of Château-Vieux, approach. Come guide our victorious efforts. Where are you? Alas! One could more easily cheat death of its prey than despotism of its victims! Citizens who, the first, displayed your courage under the walls of the Bastille, come, the *patrie,* liberty summon you to the first ranks. Alas! One finds you nowhere; poverty, persecution, the hatred of our new despots has dispersed you. . . .

Come, at least, national guardsmen, you who are particularly devoted to the defense of our frontiers in this war with which a perfidious court threatens us, come. What! You are not yet armed? What! For two years you have been demanding arms, and you do not have them? No! You have been refused clothing, you are condemned to wander without an objective, from region to region, an object of scorn to the ministry and of derision to the insolent nobles who pass you in review in order to enjoy your distress. Never mind, come; we will combine our resources to buy you arms; we will fight naked, like the Americans—come. But shall we wait to overthrow the thrones of the despots of Europe, shall we wait for orders from the War Office? Shall we consult, for this noble enterprise, the genius of liberty or the spirit of the court? Shall we be guided by these same patricians, these eternal favorites, in the war declared in our midst between the nobility and the people? No. Let us march by ourselves against Leopold; let us take counsel only of ourselves. But what now! Here come all the orators of war to stop me; there is M. Brissot who tells me that it is necessary for *M. le comte de Narbonne* to manage all this business; that it is neces-

sary to march under the orders of *M. le marquis de La Fayette.*
That it is the executive power which has the right to lead the
nation to victory and to liberty. Ah! Frenchmen! This single word
has broken the whole spell; it has destroyed all my plans. Farewell
liberty of the peoples. If all the scepters of all the German princes
are broken, it will not be by such hands. Spain will be for some
time yet slave to the superstition of royalism and prejudices. The
Stathouder and his wife are not yet dethroned; Leopold will continue to be the tyrant of Austria, of Milan, of Tuscany, and we will
by no means soon see a Cato and Cicero replace the pope and
cardinals in the conclave. I say with frankness, if the war, as I have
presented it, is unfeasible, if it is the war of the court, of the
ministers, of the patricians, of the intriguers, which we must accept,
far from believing in universal liberty, I do not even believe in
yours; and the most prudent course we can follow is to defend it
against the perfidy of interior enemies, who delude you with pleasant illusions.

I sum up, then, calmly and sadly. I have proved that the war
in the hands of the executive power was only a means of overturning the constitution, only the climax of a profound plot woven
to compromise liberty. To promote this war project, under whatever pretext, is therefore to damage the cause of liberty. All the
patriotism in the world, all the commonplaces of politics and morals
do not change the nature of things, nor the inevitable result of the
proposed step. To preach confidence in the good intentions of the
executive power, to justify its agents, to call for public approval
for its generals, to represent lack of confidence as a *shocking state
of affairs,* as a means *of disturbing the harmony of two powers
and the public order,*[5] was therefore to deprive liberty of its last
resource, the vigilance and energy of the nation. I had to contest
this system; I have done so; I did not want to injure anyone; I
wished to serve my country by refuting a dangerous opinion; I
would have opposed it even if it had been proposed by the being
who is most dear to me.

In the horrifying situation into which despotism, weakness, imprudence, and intrigue have led us, I take counsel only from my
heart and my conscience; I wish to have attention only for the
truth, complaisance only for misfortune, respect only for the
people. . . . If the moment for liberty had not yet arrived, we

5. The italicized expressions are from Brissot's speech of December 30,
1791.—Editor.

would have the patient courage to wait for it; if this generation was destined only to squirm in the mire of vices into which despotism has plunged it; if the theater of our revolution can show to the eyes of the world only prejudices at grips with prejudices, passions with passions, pride with pride, egoism with egoism, perfidy with perfidy, the new generation, purer, more faithful to the sacred laws of nature, will begin to cleanse this earth soiled with crime; it will bring not the peace of despotism or the shameful ferment of intrigue, but the sacred flame of liberty, and a sword for exterminating tyrants; it is this new generation that will raise up the throne of the people, set up altars to virtue, break the pedestal of charlatanism, and overturn all the monuments of vice and servitude. Sweet and tender hope of humanity, nascent posterity, you are not foreign to us; it is for you that we are confronting all the blows of tyranny; it is your happiness that is the prize for our painful combats; often discouraged by the obstacles surrounding us, we feel the need for throwing ourselves into your arms; it is to you that we entrust the task of finishing our work, and the destiny of all the generations of men who must rise from nothingness! . . .

28. January 20, 1792: Brissot on War

At the end of 1791 and in early 1792, when Brissot and Robespierre were contesting each other's views on foreign policy in a series of speeches, Jacques Pierre Brissot had behind him the more varied career. He was thirty-eight to Robespierre's thirty-four. He had been a prolific writer on law and politics in the 1780s, had been a journalist in London, one of the founders of the Société des Amis des Noirs, and had been in America. On the other hand, he had also been in financial tangles and been imprisoned in the Bastille for a political brochure, and although he had founded perhaps the first of the newspapers of the revolution, the *Patriote français*, he had not been elected deputy until the Legislative Assembly. Brissot at this time was just coming into his own at the Jacobins and in the Assembly. He and the Brissotins were to win the war argument and take an early lead in the Convention after the overthrow of the monarchy, but the war and wartime conditions were to put them to a severe test and lead to their overthrow in the crisis of May

31–June 2, 1793. The speech below is from the pamphlet version as
ordered published by the Jacobin Club where it was delivered:
*Société des amis de la constitution, séante aux Jacobins, à Paris. Troi-
sième discours de J. P. Brissot, député, sur la nécessité de la guerre;
prononcé à la société, le 20 janvier 1792* (s.l.n.d., 18 pp.). Four paragraphs of the conclusion have been omitted. They note that Robespierre
is almost alone in his position, and assure the audience that Brissot has no
hard feelings.

SIRS,

Convinced that the discussion in the National Assembly and in
this society had clarified completely the question of war, I did
not imagine that by reproducing the same arguments anyone would
force me to reappear in the arena. I would have disdained both
the sophisms and the insinuations on the lips of the ministry's
partisans; but it is a patriot and a brother who demands these
clarifications and it is my duty to furnish them. I will fulfill it
with the propriety suitable to every man who respects himself and
the society before which he speaks.

I will not repeat here the arguments I developed the day before
yesterday in the National Assembly, because my speech should be
distributed to you in your next session. I will tell you only that I
tried to prove two important points.

1. That the emperor was in a state of open hostility toward
France, and that it was as much a matter of our safety as of our
dignity to attack him should he fail to give us such satisfaction
as to dissipate all our anxieties.

2. That the emperor had constantly violated the treaty of May 1,
1756, that it was necessary to put an end to it without delay,
since it was onerous to France from every point of view, and that,
above all, it was impossible to preserve the liberty of France as
long as this treaty existed.

I come now to the arguments which were presented to me from
this tribunal by M. Robespierre, and which I have not yet refuted.

The question which divides us can perhaps be reduced to very
simple terms, and I copy the very terms of my adversary: *What
position*, he said, *should we take in the circumstances in which we
find ourselves?*

To determine this position, we must be acquainted with these
circumstances. Well, we are in hostile circumstances, offensive ones;
therefore it is necessary—I do not say to attack, but to defend
ourselves; and since in defending ourselves it suits us better to make

enemy territory rather than our own the theater of the war, it is therefore necessary to hasten to carry the war beyond the Rhine.

Will anyone dare to deny these hostile circumstances? Will anyone deny that the émigrés had succeeded in assembling forces at Worms, at Coblenz, in arming them, in provisioning them? Will anyone deny that they threatened us with an imminent invasion? Will anyone deny that the electors granted them not only asylum but considerable material aid, which they collected from the various princes who had an interest in maintaining the fires of discord in the interior of France?

Given this situation, does it not become an absolute necessity, in order to stop these assemblages, these menaces, these approaching hostilities, for France to deploy its forces and in its turn to crush its imprudent neighbors?

She succeeded, the assemblages were dispersed; success proved the excellence of this move, and the firmness that France displayed in this operation, while astonishing Europe, convinced its peoples and sovereigns that France was not without means, that she was not reduced to impotence by anarchy, as her detractors everywhere repeat.

But would not France lose all the advantages that she should expect from this great development if she were to fail to complete it and if, after having frightened the petty princes who dared to insult her, she did not take the same attitude toward the great powers who were secretly inciting the electors?

The emperor is the leading offender. He showed his hostility to the French nation by refusing at first to disperse the assemblages, by promising troops to the electors, and above all by urging and then forming with various other powers a league against France; the existence of this league is proved by his letters, by a memorandum, by various treaties, by the notifications concerning it to the diet of Ratisbon. He is consequently in a state of hostility against France.

Would it not now be senseless to remain quietly on the defensive, to let this crowned coalition be formed tranquilly abroad, to let the emperor assemble his forces in order to fall upon us at the moment which suits him best? I will not cease to repeat this dilemma to which no reply has yet been given.

Either the emperor wishes to attack us or he wishes only to frighten us. If he wishes to attack us, it is sheer madness not to anticipate him, since by anticipating him we have a thousand advantages, since by waiting for him we lose them all.

If the emperor wishes only to frighten us, it is in order to force us to spend enormous sums in preparations and armaments, an expenditure which exhausts us; it is in order to leave us with a perpetual reason for anxiety, to keep up the hopes of the malcontents, and thereby the disorders, and thereby to bring about bankruptcy, and so on.

In this case, does not good sense indicate that an end must be brought to this ruinous game, that an outright war would be less dangerous, less costly, than these preparations for war? Therefore we must either demand of the emperor such satisfaction as will set our minds at rest, as will enable us to disarm, or we must force him by arms.

What answer is given to this pressing dilemma? The court of France wishes war, and we must beware of its secret intentions.

And I say, Gentlemen, I say that the court does not want war. I said it on the very day when the king gave his famous speech of December fourteenth; all that display did not seduce me; from then on I foresaw that on the fifteenth of January there would be no proposal of war. I persisted in my prediction although all the satellites of the ministry seemed to have been given instructions to talk in warlike terms, and my prediction was verified; for, Gentlemen, you saw the minister of foreign affairs bring you soothing letters announcing the submission of the electors. You saw him publish a proclamation manifesting his fears about unexpected aggression. You heard him, in his last speech, preaching peace.

A new trick! someone cries. The court still wants war, but it is changing tactics to make you accept it more readily.

But this trick would be useless, and even stupid; for if the court wants war, why does the king not come and propose it to the National Assembly?

I dare to guarantee that two-thirds of this assembly would receive that proposition with enthusiasm. Why, then, since the court is sure of making—is sure of having—war when it wants it, why would it have the madness to take a long, tortuous, uncertain route? Why would it pretend not to want it, in order to make us want it, when we do want it, when the general desire has been clearly indicated? Why would it disdain to profit from the fruit of its maneuvers when this fruit is in its hands? Why would it postpone the moment for it? Why would the members of the assembly who are devoted to the court take a position in opposition to the very war that the court desires?

Let us go further, and let us see whether the other acts of the court prove that it wants war. If the king wants war, what must he do? Multiply all the means that can make it necessary. Thus, since it is assumed that he is in concert with the refugees of Coblenz, with the electors, with the emperor, why did he not request them secretly not to break up the assemblages, to continue the military exercises, to irritate the French, to affront their territory? By what madness does he combine these contradictions? He wants war, he is in agreement with the electors! And these electors disperse the assemblages, chase away the émigrés, give satisfaction to France, and take away every pretext for war from the king, who wants it in agreement with them! He wants the war, and the emperor, his brother-in-law, his secret support, who must want it with him, and must make it for him, who should profit from every pretext to get it declared, hasten the preparations, and set his troops marching; this emperor forces the electors to disperse the assemblages, leaves his troops inactive, makes no movement, and of his own accord seeks peace! Is there not an obvious contradiction between the will for war that is being attributed to the king, and his actions? Is there not a mystery here to which the interpretation of my opponent can offer no solution?

On the other hand, this whole mystery is easily explained in my interpretation: *neither the court of France nor the emperor wants war; they have only wanted to frighten us.*

In order to frighten us, they have had to propose it to us with a bang; they have had to propose it in order to arouse apprehension in the minds of enlightened patriots; they have had to propose it in order to make themselves popular among the troops.

They must today alter their language because they are about to be taken at their word; they must change it because war does not suit them; and that is something easy to demonstrate.

Leopold must be opposed to it; ten volcanoes are alight under his feet; a spark can make them into one big flame.

The court of France itself must fear the outcome of this war; what suits it is the triumph of the aristocracy and of Leopold. And this triumph is uncertain; the court sees that Leopold's armies are insufficient for his own needs; that his finances are crumbling; that his will is indecisive; it knows that the confederated princes have neither the power nor the means nor the good faith necessary for assuring the success of this coalition that has been embarked upon. The court knows that it has a reliable backer in Leopold; but it also knows that it is impossible to calculate the effects of a war, the effects of a universal conflagration. It trembles at the thought that at the first cannon shot the Brabant can erupt and overthrow its old regime; it knows that discontented Vienna can take advantage of this moment to manifest its dissatisfaction: and who can assure our court that Leopold's throne will not be overturned? Who can assure it that the audacity of the French troops can be held within limits by its orders? Who can assure it that the French will not overstep the limits that it will set for them? Who can assure it that even if the French respect its wishes the foreigners will not dare to disregard them? When Louis XVI assembled the notables, did he foresee the fall of the Bastille? To what mortal is the power given to read the future and indicate to the revolution the time and the country in which it must halt? Volcanoes are everywhere in readiness; again, only a spark is needed to bring about a universal explosion. *It is not for patriotism to fear its consequences; it threatens only thrones.*

The courts of Europe see only too well the consequences of the French revolution; they plainly see that *kings are ripe*, and their policy must be to delay the moment when the fruit must fall. Well, war would hasten this moment; they must therefore avoid it.

But at the same time as they are forced to avoid it, they must pretend not to fear it; they must affect haughtiness toward France, try to badger her, sow discord in her breast, frighten her from abroad with coalitions impossible to achieve; and they very well know this impossibility; but what does it matter? If they have aroused terror, they will have succeeded; but their hopes have been dashed.

This maneuver was without success, and why? Because the kings misjudged France and the spirit of liberty. They believed, from the aristocratic press (and they read only that), from the lying stories of vile flatterers, that France was without soldiers, without money, without means, and they insulted it with brilliance; they believed that France was directed by a handful of malcontents, and this handful is composed of twenty-five million men; they believed that love of liberty was only a vain word, that it would give way to fear, and they insulted this spirit of liberty.

Repulsed with firmness, there they are, forced to give way, forced to render homage to your independence, to obey your demands. What do you see in this conduct? Ineptitude and chastisement on the side of insolence; resoluteness and success on the side of justice.

As I have already said to you, Gentlemen, what do the petty calculations of a few individuals matter to a great nation? What does it matter to it to know what they want or what they do not want; to be acquainted with all the threads of the intrigues which take place in their offices, all the passions of the scoundrels or of the corrupt women who direct them? A great nation must have under its eyes only two great objects, *principles* and *force*.

However, I must deal with an objection that has been presented to me.

If the courts of France and of Vienna, the argument runs, do not want war at present, it is because they are not prepared; they want it only in the spring. I agree; but what is the inference? *That war must be made now.* We are sure of success in attacking first; all the advantages await us on enemy territory; all the disasters will follow us to our own doorsteps: also, Gentlemen, all that can be said on this question can be reduced to this threefold point of view: the emperor wants war, or he does not want it until spring, or he does not want it at all.

If he wants it, we must forestall him; if he wants it only next spring, we must still hasten to forestall him; if he does not want it at all, we must force him, by declaring war on him, to give us all the satisfactions needed to dissipate our anxieties and put us in a position to terminate this armaments race. Thus in all three cases war is necessary.

You see now that we are not free to want or not to want war. It is not offensive war on our part, for we are being attacked; our security is in danger if the coalition materializes; and if it does not materialize, it is still causing us expensive anxieties.

It has been claimed that it would be better to have this war within France rather than outside. That is like saying that it is better to encounter at home fire, pestilence, and all possible afflictions rather than to forestall them and repel them on enemy territory; it is to forget what is owed to our fellow citizens on the frontiers, onto whose heads all of these calamities are being called.

It has been said that war is indeed to be desired, but a *people's war* and not a war of paid soldiers.

This is a great idea, but is it feasible, is it good for the people? It means that one wishes to tear all the people away from their homes, from their businesses; it means that one has everywhere the means to provision and arm them; it means that one has need of this unlimited crusade of millions of men in order to repulse several thousand men; it means that with a throng of men who are courageous but who are not accustomed to arms, who have no experienced leaders, one is more sure of success than with troops who are disciplined, armed, and accustomed to fatigue; it means, in a word, sending the people to be butchered. Like everyone else, I admired the apostrophe of M. Robespierre; but I will say to him in his own words *that the destiny of empires is not decided by rhetorical flourishes.*

The executive power responsible for directing the war inspires fear: it is desired to take this responsibility away from it.

Certainly people's fears of the executive power are well founded; they derive from its nature and background. The people have no control over the ministry, and it was truly criminal of those who revised the constitution to have deprived the people of its influence in this way; in so doing they sowed anarchy and distrust.

However, allegiance has been sworn to this constitution, and it must be obeyed: it places the direction of the army in the king's hands; it must remain there, but with surveillance of its use and with public knowledge of all his actions.

The army must therefore be organized according to the decrees, comply with the discipline decreed, and obey the generals named by the king. It is necessary either to proceed in this way or to break the constitution.

It has been said repeatedly that war would place great forces at the disposal of the executive power, which it could abuse.

And I have already replied that this was an insult to our soldiers, to our national volunteers. I have replied that the court could seduce a few generals, a few officers, but that it would not seduce the soldiers, our national guard. I cited Bouillé, deserting alone, Arnold, deserting alone. . . .

I said that great treasons were henceforth impossible, and I like to believe that the fears of M. Robespierre would be repudiated in our camps.

It has been said that there was a desire to billet and encamp the soldiers in order to bring them around more easily to idolatry for the supreme head of the army.

But these camps have been established for a long time, and this idolatry has not appeared, and those who have visited the camps know that the soldier loves liberty and the revolution above everything.

And those who are familiar with the quick results of the progress of reason, and the influence of writings and public opinion, which are becoming more enlightened each day, see that this idolatry for a man will soon run its course.

We have been told that instead of occupying ourselves with war, it would be better to set our own country in order, throw a light on the finances, etc., etc. And all these commonplaces were and are still today preached by the ministry. It also remarked to us day before yesterday *that the most auspicious war would entail the very greatest calamities.*

It is very odd to see M. Robespierre today, while following the same line as the ministry, maintain, however, that he is going in the opposite direction, and claim that only those support him who combat him.

Like M. de Lessart, he says to us: "What will you reply to the executive power when it tells you, when it proves to you, by authentic records, that the princes have dispersed the assemblages? What legitimate pretext will you still have to make war?"[1]

Most certainly we do not, in spite of these parallels, accuse M. Robespierre of collaborating with the ministry; but let him at least try to believe that no such collaboration exists between this ministry and those who openly combat it, who vigorously denounce the vices and abuses of its administration.

This idea brings me back to some insinuations about the purity of my intentions which mar the speeches of M. Robespierre. They are out of character, I like to believe; for I have observed him, I have known his personality and character, and maliciousness never had a place there. If there are disguised poisons in his speeches, I will attribute them only to the suggestions of men of whom he is not sufficiently mistrustful.

M. Robespierre boasts that he can speak freely about the ministers, *because he is not seeking profit for himself or for his friends.*[2]

And I too can give my opinion freely for not only am I not speculating on the ministry, but I have even renounced relations of any kind with men I had known before their promotions to the ministry. If, in the course of private conversations with friends,

1. See the *Discours* of M. Robespierre, page 52.
2. See the *Discours,* page 8.

I may sometimes have revealed my hope of seeing enlightened patriots appointed to the ministry, is this wish, then, so great a crime that it was necessary to betray the outpourings of friendship and vehemently denounce it? Must we, then, be condemned to never having any but ignorant or corrupt ministers? Is it desired, then, to condemn the government to eternal inaction, and the French people to their ruin? For such is the destination to which we are being led by those who do not wish to see patriots promoted to the ministry. What! If the court were hesitating between a Jacobin and a moderate, it would be a crime to want the balance tipped toward our brother, and especially toward a man who has rendered the greatest services to the cause of liberty!

A patriot elevated to the ministry either supports the cause of the people or betrays it; if he supports it, he contributes to the public prosperity; if he betrays it, is not public opinon there to denounce him?

M. Robespierre still reproaches me for having sent some *certificates of patriotism*[3] to two ministers. He has misread me; I said that a plebeian ministry, to crush the aristocrats, had to unite with patriots, and, to crush the patriots, had to unite with moderates. What a certificate of patriotism! Parting from this supposition, he exclaims: *How sweet and pleasant the routes of patriotism have become for M. Brissot!*[4]

Defamatory writings, threats, daggers, and, what is still more grievous, oblique attacks in the guise of abused friendship—these are the flowers strewn upon the path I follow.

Insinuation is the weapon of the malicious; it is therefore not at all fitting on the part of a patriot. If I have deviated from correct principles, if I am guilty, let M. Robespierre set forth a positive act; I call on him to do so, he and all those who can hear me.

I have my own conscience; it alone has sustained me in all the combats that I have engaged in for some time; but I confess, this consolation leaves me when I see myself not openly torn to shreds but brushed with an air of secrecy, by a man who has a right to public esteem. For some time he has incessantly announced to you the revelation of great conspiracies. Let him dare finally to lift the veil; let him exhibit in broad daylight these dark plots; let him dare say whether I am involved in them—here I am, ready to reply; let him finally stop waving the sword of denunciations over a man

3. See the *Discours*, p. 8.
4. See the *Discours*, p. 13.

who, like him, has a right to say of himself: *integer vitae scelerisque purus*.

Yes, Gentlemen, this head is, like his, the execration of the partisans of tyranny; it must fall when liberty falls, for tyrants do not forgive men of principles, because these men are unchangeable.

But I blush for having gone on so long about these denunciations.

However, I must say a word about the capital crime which seems to me to have most violently excited the hatred of my adversaries; it is that of not tearing to pieces every day the king and his ministers, and the generals, and above all M. Lafayette.

Gentlemen, denunciation has always seemed to me to be too precious a weapon to be misused every minute. The saviors of ministers are precisely their perpetual denouncers, or those who denounce them without proofs.

Important facts, overpowering proofs, those are what I have always believed it essential to collect in order to denounce ministers. Since my entry into the legislature, I have given eight speeches; let anyone cite for me a single one in which I have not energetically unmasked the plots and abuses of various ministers! Has a single one of my facts been discredited since? Let my denunciation concerning the colonies be read; and have the colonials and their protectors, the ministers, dared to reply?

It is thus, Gentlemen, that denunciations are honored, are made useful. Ah! Let us beware of those overexcited men who speak of nothing but daggers, blood, and gallows, and for the least of misdeeds: those men disparage and do harm to the people, and strengthen the cause of the ministers.

Do you want to know the signs by which one can, among these declaimers, distinguish the true friends of the people from their enemies? By energy, and not by passion; by surveillance, and not by slander; by facts, and not by hypotheses; by proofs, and not by suspicions; by *character* above all—that is to say, by vigorous perseverance in a policy dictated by reason alone; and this word will teach you to be suspicious of those men who go swiftly from one extreme to another, break the statues they have put up, tear apart today what they flattered the day before. True patriotism does not have this triviality or these inconsistencies.

It is according to these principles that I acted in my relations with M. Lafayette. I saw him once in all the months before the Saint Bartholemew of July 17; I saw him, and that was in order to maintain in him a few breaths of liberty, and it was to keep him from surrendering to the enticements of men who had sworn our ruin. Heaven is my witness that never did I have any other intentions; that never was there any other motive involved in my behavior. I saw him, above all, at the moment when an unexpected event made it possible to give to the French constitution a great characteristic which it lacked, the only one which would have corrected all its faults. I believed Lafayette great enough to rise to the level of his destiny, and strong enough to raise us to ours. He promised it to me; he deceived me. I have publicly broken with him, and I have not seen him again since. . . .

That is without doubt enough, Gentlemen, to enlighten you concerning my conduct and behavior and the principles which guide me. These are not mere words, they are facts, recorded everywhere, repeated in all my writings and in my conduct for the past four years. . . .

Events are coming to my aid; the electors have yielded; the emperor will yield, I dare to predict; thus we will have done well to deploy a great force in order to oblige him to recognize our rights, and to deprive the malcontents of this support. . . .

29. April 27, 1792:
Malouet, a Conservative View
of the Revolution

Pierre Victor Malouet at the outbreak of the revolution was a veteran administrator approaching fifty, Intendant of the Navy at Toulon, in charge of the nonmilitary management of the naval base, a post he had held since 1781. Prior to that he had served in the administration of the colony of Saint-Domingue and had acquired property there. In 1789 he became a deputy of the Third Estate to the Estates General. He supported the revolution to the point advocated by Mounier and the Anglophiles but no further; nevertheless, he remained in the National Assembly to the end, spoke out courageously as often as he was able, and only emigrated when his life was in danger after the insurrection of August 10, 1792. Besides many speeches and pamphlets, he published books on slavery and on colonial administration. Malouet until his forced emigration maintained social relations with the court—he insisted on calling on the king and queen immediately after Varennes—and with a number of the king's ministers; but in the emigration his closest friends were conservative liberals such as Mounier, and liberal conservatives such as Mallet du Pan, men who were regarded, as he was, as reactionaries by the republicans and as dangerous radicals by most of the émigrés. Malouet returned to France under the Consulate and once more took up his administrative career, but he was disgraced for opposing Napoleon's invasion of Russia. He died in 1814 as Minister of the Navy under Louis XVIII. The document below is a pamphlet, *Réponse de M. Malouet à M. . . .* (s.l.n.d., 16 pp.). The first three paragraphs and the postscript have been omitted.

April 27, 1792

. . . As LONG ago as the month of June, 1789, and very often since, in the course of our discussions, I have foretold all the misfortunes with which the present generation, and perhaps the following one, was to be afflicted. And now we have a war; it can be disastrous for Europe and for us. If we are successful, the revolution is bound to be extended to the north and south; if we are beaten, if foreign armies penetrate into the kingdom, conquest, dismemberment, the temporary return of an arbitrary government, and soon new troubles, new revolutions; in all cases, much blood spilled, fortunes overturned, general bankruptcy: these are the probable results of three or four false premises about *sovereignty, equality, liberty, the general will,* and what is called *the nation.* It seems as if men are destined, in all times, to grow passionately enthusiastic over absurdities; but I am indeed mistaken if we are not approaching the time when their rule will end. Believe me, this great epoch will be forever memorable in the annals of the human race, and so many crimes and horrors, so many sad ordeals from fanaticism of all kinds will not be lost for our descendants. Here is what I base my hopes on: follow me with attention, for I want to put you on guard against the persuasiveness of my views, which I myself at first considered illusory, and which I have adopted only after profound reflection.

I have just told you that three or four false premises can overturn the world, as they have overturned France. Well! The happiness of society depends on three or four truths which the present revolution is going to make evident to all, and which will become ineffaceable hereafter.

During a long succession of centuries, ignorance and superstition favored despotism and corrupted all the political institutions that were useful and wise at their origin; for all peoples, during the first period of their civilization, set out with a paternal government, reserved for themselves all the rights that were important for their safety, and allowed only the necessary distinctions and authority.

Wars, conquests, and the barbarism into which Europe was plunged until the renaissance of letters confused all rights and obscured all ideas concerning the social order. For two centuries, and particularly during the present one, the progress of the human mind in the speculative sciences has surpassed that of the scholars of antiquity; but its thrust, too long repressed, has, when finally released, passed the limits that nature permitted us to attain but not to exceed without danger.

It was bound to happen that man, in obtaining enlightenment, after having long suffered the yoke of all the tyrannies and all the prejudices, making for a second time the conquest of the moral and political truths to which the happiness of his social existence is connected, did not know how to halt at the point of utmost correctness and precision of each of these truths.

This aberration is inevitable when enlightenment progresses in the midst of bad morals, exalted passions, increased needs, and corrupting arts. If, in this state, philosophy, by research and repeated efforts, overthrows the foundations of superstition and despotism, the philosophers themselves will go beyond their objective; they will pull up the wheat and the tares. The doctrine that will free man from all his shackles will have the most proselytes; the most daring systems will excite the most enthusiasm: it is no longer only the errors, the old abuses that one wants to root out; the first trial of liberty is to abuse it. Each makes for himself a justice according to his own liking, and sanctions the morals of his passions, the means of his independence. Such are the general propensities that have produced the most astonishing revolution of which we have knowledge. I say the most astonishing, for one cannot impute it to one chief, to one powerful man; never were there fewer among us who were outstanding for their influence, their talents, or their character; such a revolution would therefore have been impossible, in spite of the vices of the government, if the French had not been predisposed to it by their enlightenment and their corruption. Look even to the majority of those who uphold the old order of things, and see if they do not participate in the mania for new systems, and if the exaggerations of self-esteem and the spirit of independence do not manifest themselves in the most divergent parties.

Now follow the simultaneous influence of learning and corruption on the events to which we are witnesses. Sound philosophy had said that it was necessary to purge religion of its abuses; that the princes were instituted for the people and not the people for the princes; that the law could not be the arbitrary will of any man.

These great truths, passing more or less rapidly through all the ranks of society, had taken root deeply, and all the political and religious lies had no more support. But these truths could produce good effects only insofar as they were collected and sanctioned by virtuous men invested with a considerable power of repression, and only if the bonds on public reason were not loosened without at the same time tightening those on passion and vice. What has the absence of this condition necessarily produced? Precisely what you see: every excess, the irresistible empire of passions and vices. They have said: Religious fanaticism has devastated the world, let us proscribe all religious opinions. Despotism has oppressed us for a long time, let us seize all powers. Political distinctions have humiliated us, let us destroy all distinctions. Unjust laws have burdened us, let us abrogate all the laws. Tyranny is a scourge, hence license is a benefit. Force is in the number of arms, let us place sovereignty there. Have no doubt about it, that is what is called today national wish, the *general will*. For such is the will of each individual, reduced to his depraved instinct, and they have the extravagance to believe that such a collection of men is a nation, and that by putting *reason* and *liberty* on their ensigns the irruption of their passions forms a political system endorsed by reason and liberty. But the preceptors of the human race, *experience, misfortune*, and *necessity*, will soon reappear with all the authority that great catastrophes always give them; and as nations have until now been able to impute their troubles only to ignorance, to oversights, and to the violation of their rights, they will not be long in learning that these rights have limits beyond which there is another abyss.

They will recognize that an aggregate of men without morality is not and cannot be a nation, but only a more or less formidable horde. And such is the difference between a disastrous revolution of the present time and those that have preceded us that, in a barbarous century, the fear, want, and misery that follow a great overturn cause to be accepted unconditionally the power which presents itself to make repairs; while in an enlightened century the cessation of delirium causes the truths and principles that had been abused to be put back in their places. Yes, I have hopes for a consoling future, and I announce it to all the ambitions, to all the blind vanities which take offense at it, and they will be subjugated like that ferocious demagogy which rules today. The imperishable truths of which we are possessed will emerge more dazzling from the dark clouds with which they are surrounded; we may still be subjected for a long time to domination by force, but systematic despotism is destroyed and will never again have our respect; no longer will any but cowards and hypocrites bow before it; all pure consciences reject it forever.

Here, then, I dare to predict, is what will remain of all this:

1. In the first place it will be established that the French revolution, for having been directed by depraved and incompetent men, is bringing about the subversion of the laws, of morals, of religion, and of all legal authority.

2. That it was not necessary to destroy, but to reform.

3. That, instead of being made free and happy, the people have been made ferocious and miserable.

4. That liberty exists only under the empire of the laws and of good morals; that license produces tyranny, and immorality all kinds of crimes; that France no longer presents anything but a spectacle of license and immorality.

5. That a constitution that favors or that cannot repress such an order of things is untenable.

6. That a great empire cannot continue without a concentrated authority, without a political hierarchy; that equality is admissible only in small societies.

7. That of all governments, the most easily corrruptible and most oppressive is democracy.

8. That representative government in a great nation is a true democracy when the choices of the people are not limited to the class of proprietors independent of all salary, and when the influence of the people is immediate and continuous on their judges, their administrators, and their representatives.

9. That it is the public reason and not the general will that must dictate the laws, inasmuch as the public reason has characteristics of justice and of reliance on evidence that cannot be possessed by the general will, which is often a lie or an error, or a passion, and which can never be perceived with sureness; that it is obvious, from the small number of citizens who are to be found at

elections, that the majority of the nation is silent, and that the minority alone acts; that in this way all those who command, counsel, and menace in the name of the general will are impostors and tyrants when they clearly offend the public reason.

10. That perfidious maneuvers and the most culpable ineptitude have destroyed our finances, commerce, and colonies.

11. That the first need of the people is not merely to be free, but to be governed; that there is no longer any government, liberty, peace, or safety for anyone when the unbridled multitude is continually agitated by the most furious demagogues, libelists, and informers.

12. That monarchical government consists of a well-regulated action of one over all, and that the easy resistance of all to the central authority is anarchy.

13. That the constitution is violated in its fundamental principles not by those whom one calls its enemies but by those who call themselves *its friends;* that liberty and equality thus constituted are reduced to the violent exercise of the right of the strongest over the priests, nobles, and incessantly over all those who own something.

14. That the furors of the organized and federated clubs, combined with the disorganization of the troops, are a conflagration that threatens all Europe; that all governments must unite to save themselves from it; that the evil is without a remedy if justice and reason do not unite with force for the re-establishment of the fundamental principles of all societies.

Well, these fundamental principles long forgotten and unrecognized but today inviolably established are:

1. Security and property, which call for sovereignty; that is to say, the necessity for a supreme power that resists individual wills and liberties in everything that could be harmful to security and property.

2. That this supreme power must receive its direction only from those who have an interest in its being just and yet repressive; for security and property cannot exist where there is not exact justice and continuous repression against those who attack it in any manner whatever.

3. That the absolute power of one man would be reasonable only in a society that recognized only one single proprietor.

4. That the influence of nonproprietors on the supreme power would be reasonable only in a society that would not recognize any proprietors.

5. That there exist, therefore, political distinctions, inequalities of fact and of rights in a society.

6. That anything added to these distinctions by usurpations of pride and cupidity could not destroy what the distinctions have of utility and rationality.

7. That the principles of morality and religion, in their purity, are as necessary to society as good laws if the usurpations of pride and cupidity are to be combated.

8. That immorality would contribute more to re-establishing than to extirpating fanaticism and superstition.

9. That monarchical government, in its primitive simplicity, is the only one that can maintain the liberty and prosperity of a great people, and that everything that is harmful to the strength, unity, and authority of this government, in its protective action, must be abrogated. Everything that guarantees the people security and property, by the free consent of the proprietors to the laws and taxes, must be preserved.

That is, I hope, where we will end.

You are going to ask me what would be the form of government resulting from the principles that I have established, and how a government, concentrated thus, could be reconciled with liberty.

But you know very well that the liberty of honest men cannot be reconciled with that of rogues, intriguers, libelists, and all trouble-makers; that in order to protect the former effectively it is necessary to repress all the others, and there you have precisely the government resulting from the principles I have set.

From the moment it is established that the law cannot be the will of any individual, that the power which maintains it is not the property of any man, the law and the power that maintains it must have the very greatest energy.

An absolute government is odious only by its partiality when there is preference given to persons and wills, and when some always have the advantages of command and influence, others always the burdens of obedience.

But if the government is absolute only by the maintenance of the law, without preference to persons and wills, the society is then in a state of protection and liberty, which is the most desirable, the only desirable condition.

Therefore do not ask me first for a free government, before I am assured of its justice and its power; for I have need, before all else, of justice and protection; this need of every citizen is his first right acquired by means of the social compact.

First, then, I want a superior power that guarantees my social existence; my second wish is for it not to disturb that existence, and I search then for the necessary precautions to keep this supreme power from becoming tyrannical.

Placed in a great society, I have no wish to expose myself to the storms and factions of popular government; the tribunes of the demagogues, the large and small senates of five or six thousand cities and towns recall to me all the horrors of anarchy; I want a single leader, a monarch who commands, who governs according to fundamental laws, and whose power is recognized, punctually respected, and obeyed in all parts of the empire. My first wish fulfilled, the second must also be, for I do not wish to be oppressed.

Thus I am obliged to search for measures to keep the monarch from being a despot.

What must be done is to establish barriers which are at the same time supports and limits to his power.

These barriers are the laws independent of all individual wills and superior to the agents of the power and will of the monarch.

These laws must be neither dictated by public opinion in the sense of a misguided and corrupted general will nor contrary to public opinion in the sense of a general will that is enlightened and rectified by the felt interest of the social body.

Thus the laws must be proposed and drafted only by men having the habit and means of observing public opinon and its lapses as well as the felt interests of society and its needs.

They can be accepted and recognized as the expression of the general will only by men who have a felt interest in conserving its soundness and in making it prevail.

From which it follows that not only all those who have vicious habits and interests but also all those who are not essentially interested in the general harmony of society must be excluded from every kind of influence on the proposing and making of the laws.

The proposing and accepting of the laws not being able to be a right common to all, it seems that the first function cannot be better performed than by the prince and his council, who are the government; and the second by the representatives of the people, who have recognized the necessity for a government.

These representatives, being chosen from among the proprietors and invested with their confidence, are also the depositaries of their rights, and to exercise them without disturbing the activities of the government they should limit themselves to consenting, rejecting, and accusing.

They consent to the laws and the expenditures, or they reject them; they accuse the agents, or they approve them.

Those who accuse cannot judge; and when it is a question of judging the agents of the government, it must be done by a power independent of the government.

Thus there should be two classes of representatives, one of whom accuses, while the other judges breaches of trust on the part of holders of public offices; any other action of the people and its representatives on the public powers alters them, thwarts them, or usurps them.

Thus the whole active part of the government should be separated from the people and from its representatives.

That is what results from the principles I have proposed: it is a monarchical government which effectively protects the liberty and security of persons and property.

30. July 7, 1792:
Marat, a Radical View
of the Revolution

Jean Paul Marat, at the outbreak of the revolution a doctor in his mid-forties who had also been a writer on political and scientific subjects, ambitious and bold but controversial and not altogether successful, became famous after 1789 for his newspaper *L'Ami du peuple*. He was one of the earliest journalists to appeal directly to the sans-culottes both by his stance as their defender and by the violence of his language and proposals; his appeal was democratic but also extremely revolutionary; he continually called for the blood of the people's enemies and built a reputation for being early in the field with denunciations of leaders who were to fall from favor. He was undoubtedly a force in the revolution, and was much imitated—for example, by

Jacques Hébert, creator of *Père Duchesne*. After his assassination by Charlotte Corday on July 13, 1793, Marat became one of those revolutionary martyrs whose cult expressed the genuine revolutionary fervor of the sans-culottes in their great days when their power had to be reckoned with. Marat disappeared from the scene when that power was still on the rise, and it is impossible to say how he would have responded to the problems it entailed. The selection which follows is No. 667 of *L'Ami du peuple*, of July 7, 1792, translated from *Oeuvres de Marat* (*L'Ami du peuple*) *recueillies et annotées par A. Vermorel* (Paris, 1869), pp. 203–210. The first two paragraphs, which are introductory, have been omitted.

The Objectives of the Revolution
Completely Unattained by the People.

. . . At all times men have been tigers toward one another. Under the old regime we had for masters both the despot and his agents and valets, who robbed us and oppressed us as they wished, but the law left us a natural defense and allowed us to complain. Under the new regime the law that should defend us serves only to oppress us: we no longer have masters, but we groan under the iron rod of our own representatives and are abandoned defenseless to the mercies of our own agents; and, what is the height of the horror, they crush us in the name of justice, they load us with irons in the name of liberty; they prevent us from unmasking the traitors who misuse our powers in order to ruin us; they punish us for resisting the liars who abuse our forces for the purpose of oppressing us; they make it a crime for us to defend ourselves in a natural way, they forbid us to grumble, they go so far as to prohibit complaints. Thanks to the perfidious institutions of our agents in power, never had we as much cause for complaint in our former tyrants as we have today in the barbarism of our own delegates. Senseless beings that we are! Shall we, then, waste our whole lives in forestalling attacks by our enemies within and without, in defending ourselves against the assaults of our public officials, and in groaning under the blows of our oppressors, only to fall, finally, exhausted by night vigils, annoyances, chagrin, and misery, after having suffered under the so-called regime of liberty a hundred times more misfortunes than we had to fear under despotism?

Let us not be afraid to repeat it, we are farther from liberty than ever: for not only are we slaves, but we are slaves legally, as a consequence of the perfidy of our legislators, who have become the accomplices of a rehabilitated despotism.

It is folly to persist longer in wanting to recapture a good already too far removed from us; the people are dead, and for them liberty is lost forever. But before leaving the performance let us consider the stage for a while longer from the back of the theater where we are situated; let us examine the acting of the players, the responses of the spectators, and let us seek the principal reasons for the opposition to the establishment of liberty among us, after we had momentarily overcome despotism.

Cast a glance at the theater of the State. Only the decorations have changed, but there are still the same actors, the same masks, the same plots, the same forces: still a despot surrounded by collaborators, still vexatious and oppressive ministers; still a single legislator; still unfaithful and prevaricating agents of authority; still greedy, fawning, oppressive, and scheming courtiers; still petty careerists, brazen intriguers, cowardly hypocrites; still men consumed by the thirst for gold and deaf to the call of duty, of honor, and of humanity—pursuing the favors of fortune in defiance of justice and trying to seize all of the offices at the expense of merit. Today the principal actors are behind the curtain; it is there that they plot at their ease with those who play the parts before our eyes. Most of the latter have already disappeared, new actors have come forward to play the same roles; they will disappear in their turn; others will take their places, and will likewise be replaced, without anything having changed in the play of the political machine so long as the people are neither clairvoyant enough to balk the cheats who deceive them nor courageous enough to punish the scoundrels who have deluded them. But what can one expect of the people so long as our moral standards have not changed? And what remedy is there against the deep-rooted corruption that has penetrated all ranks?

The first and major reason for the impotence of our efforts to establish liberty may be seen in the very nature of the revolution.

Pushed to despair by excesses of tyranny, peoples have tried a hundred times to break their bonds.

They are always successful when the entire nation revolts against despotism. This case is extremely rare, but nothing is more common than to see the nation split into two parties, one of which declares itself for and the other against the despot.

When each of these parties is composed of a variety of classes of society, the one which declares itself against the despotism succeeds rather easily in crushing it, because in that case there are more advantages for the attackers in overthrowing it than there are for the defenders in maintaining it. That was the case with the Swiss, the Dutch, the English, and the Americans.

But that never happens when the plebeians—that is, the lower classes of the nation—are alone in the struggle against the upper classes. At the outbreak of the insurrection, they at first crush all opposition by their sheer numbers, but whatever advantage they have won, they always end by succumbing: for, being always deficient in knowledge, arts, wealth, arms, leaders, and operational plans, they are without means of defense against conspirators full of finesse, asuteness, and guile, against the ever-present schemers who have at their disposal wealth, arms, munitions, all the responsible positions, all the means provided by education, politics, fortune, and authority. This is precisely the case of the French revolution; for it is not true that the entire nation rose in revolt against the despot, since he remained at all times surrounded by his subalterns, by the nobility, the clergy, the judges, the financiers, the capitalists, the scholars, and the literary figures and their followings. If men of the lower classes who were educated, well-to-do, and given to intrigue took part at first against the despot, that was only in order to turn against the people after having won their confidence and made use of their force to put themselves in the places of the privileged orders they had proscribed. Thus the revolution has been made and sustained only by the lowest classes of society, by the workers, the artisans, the retailers, the farmers, by the plebeians, by those unfortunates whom the rich impudently call the rabble, and whom the insolent Romans called their proletarians. But what one would never have imagined is that it was made only for the sake of small landowners, men of the legal profession, and practitioners of chicanery.

The objectives of the revolution have been missed completely. Since it was made against despotism, it was necessary to begin by suspending the despot and his agents from all their functions, by entrusting the government to representatives of the people, by decreeing that there would be an interregnum for the entire time that the constitution was not yet made. Once completed, it would have been presented to the prince, who would have been declared dethroned if he had refused to swear obedience to the new laws and fidelity to the nation. Nothing could have been easier for the representatives of the people on the day following the taking of the Bastille. But, for that, it was necessary for them to have purposes and character. Now, far from being statesmen, they were almost all merely adroit swindlers who sought to sell themselves, vile intriguers who flaunted their false civic-mindedness in order to be bought at a higher price. And so they began by securing the prerogatives of the crown before ruling on the rights of the people. They did more, they began by restoring to the prince the supreme executive power, by making him the arbiter of the legislator, by charging him with the execution of the laws, and by abandoning to him the keys of the public treasury, the management of the national property, the command of the fleets and armies, and the disposal of the public force, in order to assure him the means of opposing more effectively the establishment of liberty and of overturning more easily the new order of things.

That is not all; the representatives of the people robbed, in the name of the nation, the clergy of its possessions, the nobility of its titles, the financial world of its positions, and the privileged orders of their prerogatives, but instead of striking down these flunkies of despotism by declaring them unfit for any posts, they left them a thousand means of re-establishing themselves in its favors: then, content to share their pre-eminence and associate themselves with their wealth, they banded together with them in selling themselves to the despot.

The first representatives of the people must therefore be considered as the mainstays of the counterrevolutionaries and as the people's most deadly enemies.

At least, if the people had known their rights, if they had known how to appraise the perfidious conduct of their envoys and appreciate the necessity of checking their unfaithful delegates at their first false step, of repressing bad citizens with vigor, of getting rid of traitors, and of reserving for themselves the full exercise of sovereignty in the sanctioning of the laws—but they did not even think of ways to keep from being put back under the yoke. Instead of arming themselves completely, they permitted only a part of the citizens to be armed; then they abandoned themselves to the good faith of their agents, and they did with the enemies of the revolution precisely the opposite of what should have been done. Far from attacking them without delay and crushing them without granting them any respite, they took a defensive posture and by this false measure stupidly renounced all their advantages: for the worst that can happen to plotters is not to be successful in every attempt; in failing, they do not lose anything but time; for hardly have they been thwarted than they recommence with new outlays, at the cost only of planning their measures better than the first time; now it is impossible always to be on one's guard, and often the least negligence becomes fatal. Judge where the carelessness and the inertia of the people must lead.

Those who wish to reassure us about our agonizing situation attribute our misfortunes *to the lack of enlightenment of the people,* and I share this view so long as they do not make it the exclusive reason. Then, in order to animate us with the hope that lies deep in their hearts, they add *that it is in the nature of things for the progress of reason to be slow and gradual.* That is true for the small number of men who think, but there is no progress, or reason, or enlightenment for the mass of the people, although they sometimes appear to renounce certain prejudices—or, rather, to change them. The tricks of an adroit and profound Machiavellianism escape them and always will escape them; they lack and always will lack the shrewdness to discover the traps of their enemies, and political discussions have always been, are, and always will be beyond their reach.

Assuming them to benefit from the most favorable course of circumstances, they will never be in a condition to analyze a decree, to perceive what there is about it that is specious, to deduce its consequences, to foresee its sequel, and to predict the effects. If a touching example of this sad truth were needed here, I would say that in spite of the perpetual speechmaking of our patriotic societies and the deluge of writings with which we have been inundated for three years, the people are farther removed from appreciating what it is suitable for them to do in order to resist their oppressors than they were on the first day of the revolution. Then they abandoned themselves to their natural instincts, to the simple good sense which had enabled them to find the right means of bringing their implacable enemies to their senses.

Since then, indoctrinated by a host of sophists paid to hide under the guise of public order the blows struck against their sovereignty, to cover with the cloak of justice the outrages against their rights, to present to them as means of assuring liberty the measures taken to destroy it; lured by a crowd of hypnotists interested in concealing from them the dangers that threaten them, in feeding them false hopes, in recommending calm and peacefulness to them; misguided by a crowd of charlatans interested in praising the false patriotism of the most unfaithful public functionaries, in assigning pure intentions to the most formidable schemers, in slandering the best citizens, in treating as factions the friends of the revolution, as seditious the friends of liberty, as brigands the enemies of tyranny; in disparaging the wisdom of the measures proposed to assure the triumph of justice, in passing off as fairy tales the plots hatched against the *patrie*, in lulling the people with flattering illusions; in hiding, under the deceptive image of happiness, the precipice where they seek to drag them; deceived by public officials united in a coalition with traitors and conspirators to restrain their indignation, to smother their resentment, curb their zeal, and fetter their audacity by ceaselessly preaching to them confidence in their magistrates, submission to the constituted authorities, and respect for laws;[1] finally, deceived by their perfidious representatives who lulled them with the hope of avenging their rights, of assuring their sovereignty, of establishing the reign of liberty and justice, they allowed themselves to be caught in all the traps. There they are, enchained in the name of the laws by the legislator and tyrannized in the name of justice by the trustees of authority! There they are, slaves constitutionally! And today, when they have renounced their natural good sense to abandon themselves to the perfidious speeches of so many impostors, they are far from regarding as their most mortal enemies their cowardly mandataries purchased by the court, their unfaithful delegates who have sold their most sacred rights, their dearest interests, and all those scoundrels who have abused their confidence in order to sacrifice them to their former tyrants; they are far from regarding as the source of all their ills the fatal decrees that have deprived them of the sovereignty, that have reunited in the hands of the monarch all powers, that have made illusory the declaration of rights, that have put the people back in chains and riveted its irons. They are far from trampling underfoot this monstrous constitution for the maintenence of which they are going forth foolishly to be slaughtered on enemy territory. They are far from sensing that the only way to establish their liberty and to assure their peace and quiet was to rid themselves without pity of traitors to the *patrie* and to drown in their own blood the leaders of the conspirators.

1. It is this superstitious respect for the disastrous decrees, this rash oath to maintain the constitution which has ruined everything; today, when the people are slaves constitutionally, one knows very well that blind submission to oppressive laws can only rivet their irons forever.

VIII.

The Responsibilities of the Convention

31. November 19, 1792:
Petitioners vs. Roland
on Price-Fixing

Among the pieces of business in the National Convention on November 19, 1792, was the reading of an address concerning the cost of living, brought in by a delegation of the electoral corps of Seine-et-Oise. This was followed by the reading of a statement on the same subject by the Minister of the Interior, Jean Marie Roland de La Platière, whose point of view was quite different from that of the delegation. Roland was then fifty-eight years of age, with a long career behind him as an inspector of manufactures, which included substantial writings on economic and technological development. He and his wife were very closely associated with the leading Girondins. These selections are from the *Archives parlementaires*, Vol. LIII, pp. 475–477. Dots in the text represent the punctuation of the original rather than cuts in the documents.

A deputation from the electoral corps of Seine-et-Oise is admitted to the bar.

The speaker for the deputation expresses himself as follows:

Citizens, the first principle that we should state to you is this one: *Liberty of commerce in grains is incompatible with the existence of our Republic* . . . Of what is our Republic composed? Of a small number of capitalists and a large number of poor . . . Who engages in the commerce in grains? This small number of capitalists . . . Why do they engage in commerce? To enrich themselves. How can they enrich themselves? Through the increase in the price of grain in the resale that they make to the consumer.

But you will also observe that this class of capitalists and proprietors, being through unbounded liberty masters of the price of grain, are masters also of the price of a day's work; for each time that there is need for a worker, ten present themselves, and the rich have a choice; moreover, this choice falls on him who demands the least: it sets his wages and the worker submits to necessity because he has need for bread and because this need cannot be postponed. This small number of capitalists and proprietors is therefore master of the wages for a day's work. The unlimited liberty of commerce in grain makes them also masters of the means of subsistence of prime necessity. Sordid interest does not permit them to take into account any rule other than that of their avidity. There results from this a frightening disproportion between the price of a day's work and the prices of commodities of prime necessity. The day's wage is from 16 to 18 *sous*, while wheat is 36 *livres* for a *setier* weighing from 260 to 270 pounds, each pound being 16 ounces. The day's wage therefore is not enough to live on. Whence comes inevitably the oppression of every individual who lives by means of the work of his hands.

But if this class which lives by means of the work of its hands is the largest; if, summoned through legal equality to participation in the making of the laws, it is still the one and only power in the State, how may it be assumed that it can endure an order of things that wounds it, crushes it, and takes away from it both subsistence and life?

Legislators, do not be frightened by the severity of this truth: it is not the truths brought into the open that make revolutions, it is those that are stifled. The unlimited liberty of commerce in grain is oppressive for the most numerous class of the people. The people therefore cannot endure it. It is thus incompatible with our Republic. We go even further: this unlimited liberty is contrary to the will of the people. The countless insurrections that it has produced, the general outcry, the will manifested on all sides make this plain enough to you, and this reason alone is enough to forbid it; for the law is the expression of the general will. This truth was appreciated by the Legislative Assembly (*the law of the sixteenth of September is a proof of it*); but we must tell you it did not go far enough, and this partial measure, if it were prolonged, would do very great harm. If there is no more liberty, there can no longer be commerce; one can no longer count on the grain trade to provision the departments that have insufficient food; and if one can no longer count on it, it must not be endured, for it is odious and immoral . . . and yet it is necessary to procure provisions for the departments!

Here we arrive at a second truth. *The law must provide for the provisioning of the Republic and the subsistence of everyone*. What rule should it follow in that? See to it that there is grain; that the invariable price of this grain always be in proportion to the wages for a day's work; for if the price of grain varies, the day's wages being invariable, there can be no proportion between the two. Well, if there is no proportion, the most numerous class will inevitably be oppressed: an absurd state of affairs that cannot last for very long.

Legislators, these are therefore reliable truths; there must be a fair proportion between the price of grain and a day's wage. It is up to the law to maintain this proportion, to which unlimited liberty is an obstacle.

What are the means that must be used? That is the last point we have to develop for you . . . The fact must not be concealed from you, legislators; any partial method is in this matter dangerous and unavailing; no halfway measures, for it is those that will ruin us; it is those on which the economists count to have their system of limitless liberty prevail. If commerce is to be relied on, its liberty must be complete, and at the first restriction commerce must be destroyed; otherwise it will act only to take from you and not to provide for you; it will exist only for your ruin: such would be the effect of the law of September 16, this so necessary law that would become so pernicious if you did not finish the work that has been started. Suppress as of today all those unequal measures that maintain ignorance and favor monopoly. Order that all grain be sold by weight. Set a *maximum* price; put it for this year at 9 *livres* the quintal, a medium price, equally good for the farmer and the consumer. Order that in other years it be fixed in the same proportion, according to the relation of the output of an *arpent* of land to the cost of production: a relationship to be determined by persons chosen by the people.

Prohibit commerce in grain to anyone other than bakers and millers, who will not themselves be able to purchase until after the inhabitants of the communes have done so, and at the same price, and who will be obliged to carry on their commerce openly. Order that the measurers will not be permitted to buy for more than three months' consumption; that each farmer shall be obliged to sell his grain himself in the market nearest to his domicile, and not be allowed to sell it by means of displays and through the medium of measurers, transporters, or auctioneers; and finally that the grain remaining at the end of the market shall be recorded by the municipalities, put in reserve, held for the next market, and put on sale first. Break up the large aggregations of rented land that concentrate in culpable hands considerable quantities of grain. Order that no one may rent more than 120 *arpents*, a measure of 22 feet per rod; that no proprietor may exploit more than a single farmstead and that proprietors will be obliged to lease any others in their possession; that no one may collect rent in grain; and, finally, that no one will be permitted to be at one and the same time a miller and a farmer. Then place the responsibility for provisioning each part of the Republic in the hands of a central administration chosen by the people, and you will see that abundance of grain and a just relationship of its price to that of a day's work will restore tranquillity, happiness, and life to all citizens.

We are, *adds the orator*, peaceful citizens, supporters of the laws, who think that order can only be produced and preserved by justice, and who come to tell you so. Our blood belongs to the *patrie*, our submission to the laws, and our opinions to ourselves. The law and our courage permit us to make our views known, and duty orders us to do so; we have now accomplished this duty; our confidence in you, legislators, makes us believe that we will not have done so in vain.

THE PRESIDENT: When the people suffer, their representatives share their grief; the assembly is going to suspend its useful labors in order to give its attention to the important objective of your petition; it has already received such enlightenment as it has been able to procure, and it will without delay take remedial action. [Applause.] I confer on you the honors of the session.

A MEMBER: I demand the printing of this petition and its distribution to the Committee of Public Assistance.

THE PRESIDENT: The Minister of the Interior has just submitted to the Convention a letter relative to the matter of subsistence. I believe that it will perhaps be useful to acquaint the assembly with it before it takes action on the petition of the electoral corps of the Department of Seine-et-Oise; one of the secretaries is going to read it to you.

MAILHE, SECRETARY, reads this letter and the documents that accompany it; they are as follows:

Paris, November 18, 1792, Year I of the French Republic, letter from the Minister of the Interior to the National Convention on the problem of subsistence, followed by some observations sent by him to the municipality of Paris, by the proclamation of the executive council relative to this subject, and by the covering letter to the Convention about this proclamation.

A Citizen to the President of the National Convention:

I divest myself of the title of minister because it tends to curtail the liberty of the man to whom it is given and because I believe it useful to the public good to employ, at this moment, all the rights of a citizen and a free man to attack prejudices whose effects would be disastrous for France.

The Committee on Agriculture and Commerce has presented a draft decree that seems to me very harmful in the light of some experience in administration as well as my travels in Europe to study the character of nations, their commercial relations, and in particular the origin and progress of that spirit which wishes to make, and indeed must make, of private interests the elements of the public interest. Everything—both the history of England and our own, the great ideas of Turgot and the disastrous errors of Necker—proves that the government has never meddled in any commerce, in any manufacture, in any enterprise, without doing so at enormous cost and in competition with private individuals and always to the disadvantage of everyone; that whenever it has wished to interfere in the business of private individuals, to make regulations about the form or the manner of disposing of properties and modifying them at will, it has put shackles on industry and increased the cost of labor and of the objects that labor produces.

This rule applies to the subject of subsistence more particularly than to any other because it is of utmost necessity, because it occupies a great number of individuals, and because there is not a single person who is not interested in it. Restrictions herald, summon, prepare, increase, and spread distrust, and yet confidence is the only means of keeping an administration functioning in a free country. Force, whatever coercive means one conceives, can be used only in moments of crisis, in convulsions, in violent and precipitate moments; but in a succession of works, in a continuity of operations, the use of force necessitates its continued use; it establishes the need for more force, and multiplies and aggravates it ceaselessly, so that soon it would be necessary to arm half the nation against the other half. Such will always be the effect of decrees that have as their aim to constrain what justice and reason wish to and must leave free.

Now every declaration demanded, especially in the matter of subsistence, will be false and will entail violence.

Every order to take here or there such-and-such quantity, to sell in one place and not in another, at such a time for these, and at such a time for those; everything that establishes constraints will lead to arbitrariness and will become vexatious.

The proprietor worries at first, then grows disgusted; he ends by being indignant: then the people can become irritated and revolt. The source of prosperity would dry up and France would become the prey of long and cruel agitations. A decree which brings with it coercion and encourages violence is a terrible weapon, of which malevolence soon takes advantage. Already that of last September 16 which orders an inventory of grain and authorizes the use of force in its execution is spreading alarm and fostering uprisings. If there is another restriction, another provocation on the part of the enforcing authority, I no longer know, I no longer conceive of a human power capable of halting the disorders.

It is not sufficiently realized that in administration as in mechanics a multiplicity of wheels impedes movement, retards or lessens the effect, and that for want of a rational plan, based on the history of the facts, on the results of combinations, and on the availability of moral and physical means, a code becomes overburdened with rules of which some are meant to rectify others.

There result complications, which invite comments, and the application becomes as hazardous as it is difficult. Inconveniences of this nature are infinitely serious in the case of legislation about subsistence, which then becomes an arsenal of murderous weapons, seized by all factions.

President of the representative body of a great people, show that the great art is to do little, and that government, like education, consists principally in foreseeing and preventing evil of a negative kind, in order to leave to the faculties their full development, for it is on this liberty that all forms of prosperity depend. Perhaps the only thing that the assembly can permit itself in the matter of subsistence is to announce that it can do nothing, that it abolishes all shackles, that it declares the most complete liberty concerning the circulation of commodities; that it in no way determines action, but that it is very active indeed against whoever would curtail this liberty. The glory and the safety of the Convention seem to me to be related to this act of justice and reason, because it seems to me that the peace and happiness of the nation depend on it.

There are many topics that I would like to discuss, and time and space are too scarce, but I have here some observations that I thought it necessary to address to the municipality of Paris, together with the proclamation of the executive council and my covering letter for the proclamation to the Convention; they will serve to develop my ideas. They seemed to me to merit attention sufficiently to justify my astonishment when the committee charged with a project relevant to the destiny of France avoided hearing my testimony on an administrative problem about which it is important to collect opinions and weigh arguments in order to guarantee against error and misunderstanding.

I submit to the wisdom of the assembly my remonstrances on the subject of my greatest concern: I owe them to the assembly as a citizen, and it is under this title that I offer it this homage.

Signed: ROLAND

32. December 12, 1792: An Attack on the Slave Trade

The question of slavery, so simple that no equivocation would seem possible in view of the Declaration of the Rights of Man, nevertheless troubled the revolutionaries and turned a merciless searchlight on one group after another as problems associated with colonial interests, the value of the colonies to France, colonial government, rivalry with England, rights of mulattoes and freed slaves, the slave trade, the navy, agricultural methods in the sugar islands, and tax revenues became involved. All this had been foreshadowed by the crusading on the eve of the revolution of the Société des Amis des Noirs, founded in 1787, which demanded immediate abolition of the slave trade and gradual suppression of slavery itself. Every stage of the revolution and all parts of the spectrum of opinions had to take account of these problems, and it was not until February 4, 1794, that slavery was finally abolished without qualifications by the Convention.

The pamphlet *Benj. Sig. Frossard à la Convention nationale, sur l'abolition de la traite des Nègres. Paris, le 12 décembre 1792, l'an premier de la République françoise*, was the work of a Protestant theologian of Swiss origin who had become a pastor at Lyon in the years before the revolution. He knew and was known by antislavery circles in both England and France, was associated with the Société des Amis des Noirs, and in 1788 published an attack on slavery, a work in French, in two volumes, with a shocking engraving that was a revelation to most of his readers, the interior of a slave ship. Frossard's pamphlet of December, 1792, calls attention by its date to the slowness of the revolutionaries to act, even on the question of the slave trade, and, by its arguments, to the kind of opposition he and his friends faced. Space is lacking for the full 32-page pamphlet, but pp. 1–3, below, introduce the author's principles, and pp. 23–32, which follow the space, answer the objections of opponents.

Legislators,

On the memorable day when you welcomed with rapture those generous Englishmen who came to swear before you that they would soon be republicans, Kersaint proposed to you a decree abolishing the trade in Negroes. You returned this motion, which was so worthy of you, to your committees on Commerce and Colonies.

Permit a citizen who in less prosperous times dared to raise his voice against the oppression under which Europe retains numerous peoples[1] to offer you the homage of his work, to place under your special protection the unfortunate people whose cause he pleads, to solicit, in a word, in their favor the application of that law of nature which binds together societies and individuals, and which is like the peristyle of the magnificent temple that you are raising in honor of liberty and morals. I speak of the Africans whom our fellow citizens tear from their native land

1. In a work in 2 volumes in octavo, printed in 1788, having for title: *The Cause of the Negro Slaves and of the Inhabitants of Guinea Carried to the Tribunal of Justice, of Religion, and of Politics, or, History of the Trade and of the Slavery of the Negroes, Proofs of Their Illegitimacy, Means of Destroying Them Without Harming Either the Colonies or the Colonists.*

This work can be found in Paris at Gattey, Bookstore of the Palais-Royal, and Guessier Junior, Printer-Bookseller, Quai des Augustins; at Lyon, Chez Vatar la Roche.

Citizens who wish to contemplate all the horror that the trade in Negroes inspires in sensitive hearts must read the eloquent works of Clarkson, Condorcet, Brissot, Lanthenas, Grégoire, Clavière, Bancal, etc.

in order to condemn them, in distant regions, to all the horrors of the most unjust slavery.

The trade in Negroes is the greatest crime that a government can tolerate and that a man can commit; for it assumes and encourages every kind of atrocity. Its successes are scourges, its lapses the benefits of Providence. Through it, the human race has become a merchandise; and—the greatest affront to our nature—what is esteemed in the victim of this commerce is only physical vigor without any regard for intellectual faculties; without supposing even that he can have a soul.

I shall not undertake, LEGISLATORS, to arouse your sensibilities in favor of the inhabitants of Guinea. Your hearts have been more than sufficiently afflicted by all the disorders that have brought our glorious regeneration, without lacerating them still more by the description of the most execrable of assaults and by the cruel idea that those guilty of them are men, your fellow citizens, your brothers in the natural and social order. Besides, there is not one of you who has not often deplored this violation of natural and human rights. The cause of the Blacks has been victorious in the National Convention, as in public opinion. The Declaration of Rights pronounced the liberation of Guinea. It said: "All men are born and remain free." And this great truth, engraved in all hearts in characters of fire, victorious over all the efforts that despotism has made to efface it, which has become, through the most memorable revolution, the principle of the code that you are preparing, condemns every Frenchman barbarous enough to propagate slavery and tyranny in any country whatever. . . .

All projects which tend to sacrifice particular interests for the general interest are destined to find numerous contradictors. You experience this, LEGISLATORS, in the great work of our regeneration; but you oppose with the noblest courage the calculations of egoism and the sophistry of cupidity. You will follow the same course during the time, without a doubt very near, when the tranquillity of France will permit you to work for that of Africa. At that time, awaited with the keenest solicitude by all the humanitarian circles of Europe, persons with an interest in the commerce in Negroes will seek to parry the blows with which your justice and your humanity will threaten them, by frightening you with apparently insurmountable objections.

They will tell you that the trade, in other times known as *piracy*, is as ancient as the world. But because a crime has been propagated from century to century, has it for all that changed its character?

They will claim that the Negroes exported from Africa are only prisoners of war or criminals whom they save from the final penalty, whose capital punishment is commuted to slavery. Even if that were true, does a crime become legitimate as soon as it prevents another crime? Besides, slave traders here confound cause and effect. To be exact, they should not say, "We are reducing to slavery only captives and criminals," but, "It is because we buy slaves that there are so many captives and so many criminals."

They declare that if the trade is abolished it will be necessary to abandon the colonies. That is a sophism refuted by experience; but even if that objection were true, is there a choice to make when an interest is contrary to justice, to men's rights, and to humanity?

They will allege that if they do not have the means of increasing the numbers of their slaves, they will be unable to extend the arable land area. What! Because the population of a country is not in proportion to its area, it will therefore be permissible for the proprietors of uncultivated lands to raid neighboring regions, to remove the inhabitants, put them in irons, force them to fertilize arid lands, and at what price? At the price of their liberty, of the most arbitrary punishments, often of experiencing the most dire need. The planters wish to increase their revenues: well, let them treat their Negroes with fraternity; let them seek to replace the dead through births, let them make agrarian work easier; then they can render immense areas fruitful without multiplying the victims of colonial greed.

Concerning these methods, they will object that there exists in the islands no normal ratio between black men and women, which impedes population growth. Without doubt, this is true of slaves newly imported, since only a third of the *cargo* is composed of women; but nature soon re-establishes an equilibrium, and the Creoles are born in a proportion fixed by immutable laws.

They will add that the abolition of the trade in Negroes will ruin our commerce with Africa. But if the commerce that will replace it becomes both legitimate and more lucrative, to what will this difficulty be reduced? That, however, will be the necessary consequence of the abandoning of this piracy, and of its replacement by justifiable exchanges of our merchandise with the natural products of Africa.

Doubtless they will not dare to add that this brigandage forms a nursery for sailors, since it has been proved that it destroys more sailors in a year than two years of all the maritime commerce combined.

Nor will they dare to invoke the laws which authorize it; for an abuse, however ancient it may be, does not cease to be an abuse; and the French revolution, LEGISLATORS, has destroyed abuses that had long been maintained by more deeply rooted habits, by much older laws, and by much more formidable defenders.

They will not dare to solicit again that you *regulate* this commerce rather than *abolish* it, because they know very well that if you were to order the traders to provide the sailors and transported slaves with the space and the nourishment that the laws specify for criminals sent to people deserted lands,[2] the trade in Negroes would be abolished on the spot, since otherwise the shipowners could only lose money. Moreover, will it be possible to regulate this commerce according to laws of justice and honor as long as it is so criminal both in its *particulars* and in its *effects?*

Lastly, they will not dare hereafter to attribute to the Friends of the Blacks the criminal project of provoking the slaves in America to rebellion against their masters, however illegitimate their enslavement is, since we have stated in speeches and in our numerous writings that it is important not to confuse the trade in Negroes, the immediate abolition of which all good men demand and hope for, with the slavery to which they are subjected, which without doubt must be destroyed only by imperceptible degrees, in order not to sacrifice either public order or individual property. But I know of no title on which one can base in perpetuity the privilege of tearing the Negroes from

2. Ordinarily slave ships are loaded with two or more men per ton; but according to the regulations relative to criminals transferred to Botany Bay, no more than one man per two tons can be taken aboard. When the Chevalier Dolben proposed three years ago to the Parliament of England the provisional law against loading more than three Negroes per two tons, all of the shipowners cried that it was better to abandon the trade. However, the regulation passed, and they continue it.

the heart of their families and native land. We never had the right to dispose of the inhabitants of Guinea; and if we had acquired it, should the French nation exercise it by means of such crimes?

But what they will without doubt repeat to you several times, LEGISLATORS, is that if you abolish the trade in Negroes, England, appropriating it almost exclusively,[3] will continue it to the detriment of our commerce, of our navy, and of our colonies. The same objection is on the lips of all the English shipowners. They cause our competition to be feared in the British senate at the same time as we in France are threatened with theirs. Neither of these two nations, if one believes the advocates of the trade, will dare to be generous, for fear that the other will profit from this occasion to cease being so. In your hands, LEGISLATORS, is the answer to this objection so often repeated by the planters of the two nations. You alone can form that sacred coalition so much desired by all the philanthropists. Set the example; and, soon reintegrated in the privileges of nature and of society, England will not be able to perpetuate in its distant domains principles of despotism that would be its dishonor and its ruin. Knowing the rights of man and citizen, she will henceforth dare neither to permit nor even to tolerate the most odious violation of the laws that unite nations and individuals.

Yes, LEGISLATORS, declare infamous all citizens who henceforth allow themselves to commit such crimes; then it will not be in vain that you give to the rest of Europe the signal for the liberation of Guinea. By this means you will force the Chamber of Peers of Great Britain, still so far removed from the true principles of liberty, to sanction the decree voted by the Commons in the last session; and this noble example will add the greatest splendor to the triumph that your courageous works will assure you.

Do not doubt, LEGISLATORS, even if you should establish our happiness on the rock of ages; even if the constitution that you are going to give to the French Republic should transmit to the most distant posterity both your name and your good

3. Will it be for deliveries to us, or to her? In the first case, it will be fitting to prevent the furtive introduction of additional Negroes into our islands. In the second case, there is no reason to assume that she will import into her own colonies over and above what the planters ask for annually; that is to say, beyond their needs.

deeds, there will be something lacking in your glory if you do not ban a commerce made to dishonor both the citizen who profits from it and the nation that tolerates it, if you let live within the new edifice that you raise upon the ruins of all the old abuses this monstrous portion of the aristocratic regime that you have just crushed—if, in a word, you authorize the French to transmit to Guinea all the germs of destruction. But I am saying something blasphemous; for here doubt alone is blasphemy. Ah! One would have to be very ignorant of the principles upon which all of your laws are established in order to be anxious about the fate of the peoples who are dependent upon your legislative wisdom! The same senate that has just broken the chains of so many European nations will without doubt extend this system of liberty to the Negroes of America. You will prepare them for this benefit by abolishing the trade that is ravaging their *patrie;* you will teach the colonists that opulence or disorderly management are not in your eyes sufficient justification for the perpetuation of despotism; and you will no longer permit luxury articles exported from our islands to cost annually the lives of more than 100,000 Africans; and why? For the sole reason that their deaths or their servitude nourishes our cupidity.

In this way, LEGISLATORS, you will give an unlimited extension to this maxim that nature has engraved in all hearts, but whose sacred characters despotism has for several centuries veiled. "All men are born and remain free and equal in rights."

In this way, you will generalize for all countries and all societies those laws of justice and order by which you are uniting French citizens; you will no longer permit what is called in your *patrie* brigandage and assassination to become, below the equator, a simple commercial speculation; and far from sanctioning any practice contradictory to this sublime rule, the foundation of all moral duties: "Do not do to others anything except what you would want done to you," the code that you will decree will tend to imprint it more firmly in the hearts of all citizens.

In this way, you will prevent the French character, so loyal, so generous, from being perverted in foreign climates by a traffic tending to make it hard and cruel. For he who equips a slave ship, he who commands it, he who buys its cargo, he who condemns that cargo to eternal enslavement—in short, all those pirates—must have hearts cruelly callous to permit themselves such outrages. Man is not made to exercise an absolute control over his fellows. Habit alone can surmount the repugnance that nature inspires in him at this prospect; and this same habit makes him necessarily arrogant, irascible, and cruel; that is to say, hardly fit to fulfill worthily the duties of a citizen in his native land.

In this way, you will instruct the colonists that the most scorned of men are always worthy of our fraternity, provided that they are not contemptible; and that it is to no purpose that they have vast domains or immense debts—for this is not in your eyes a permit authorizing them to carry carnage and slavery into all regions where their cruel agents penetrate.

In this way, finally, you will proscribe forever the crimes inseparable from this odious traffic in human beings; these unjust wars that we provoke, and in which one prisoner costs the lives of ten combatants; these domestic abductions which the most savage tribes scarcely permit themselves; these acts of despotism we encourage in the monarchs of Africa; these arbitrary condemnations that we dictate in order to multiply the guilty; above all, the crime endlessly renewed of assaulting the liberty of our fellow beings, of forcing them to leave *patrie*, possessions, family, and friends, in order to serve an inhuman master, without having been guilty of any crime, without having consented to the transaction, without having received the price for their future labor.

No disposition is better calculated to honor a free and generous nation. The United States of America pronounced the abolition of the trade at the very moment of casting off the shameful yoke of English despotism. Great Britain, up to now our rival in power, will decree it as soon as she becomes our emulator in republican virtues. The trade in Blacks, this bloody invention of avarice, must disappear before the regenerative aspect of liberty. Its proscription is the only way to announce to Guinea that at last France has no more tyrants. Everywhere our victorious armies establish the wills of nations on the mutilated thrones of kings. And that says much for our glory. But it is not enough, liberators of the world, to break the scepter of tyranny in Europe; it is still your task to overthrow in Africa and in the Colonies the despotism of greed. Such is the imperious order of public opinion, of the morality of peoples, of the sacred law of nations, of immortal liberty. Certainly it will not be in the assembly that most respects the supreme power of these eternal principles that the cause of the Africans will be pleaded in vain. You will sustain it with all the force of your eloquence, regenerators of the national felicity, intrepid protectors of oppressed peoples. After having founded French prosperity on liberty, equality, and virtue, you will direct toward the dark regions of colonial slavery these rays of truth that disperse all kinds of tyranny as the morning sun dissipates the night mists. You will proscribe this system of oppression and bloodshed which costs the barbarian who perpetuates it so many crimes, and the sensitive man who deplores it so many tears, and the unfortunate who is its victim so much suffering. The nations whose gaze is upon you, who admire you and prepare to imitate you, will recognize that if reason, intellect, and courage are enough to enable the French Republic to re-establish nations in the sovereignty that kings had usurped, it is through justice, morals, fraternity, and the exercise of all the social virtues that you will consolidate the work of universal regeneration. And through this profound respect for individual liberty, this proscription of every calculation founded on murder and enslavement, this abolition of all usages contrary to the rights of nations or of individuals, you will cause your political principles to be cherished, you will tear out the last roots of feudal aristocracy, and you will merit, finally, the glorious title of LIBERATORS OF THE TWO WORLDS.

33. February 15, 1793: Condorcet Presents His Constitution to the Convention

The Marquis Jean Antoine Nicolas Caritat le Condorcet is well known as an aristocrat and a philosophe who during the revolution became a democratic theoretician of representative government and the principal author of the so-called Girondin constitution which was presented to the Convention on February 15 and 16, 1793. The constitution, like Condorcet himself, became a victim of the Girondin-Mountain struggle. It was set aside by the Convention, vilified by the leaders of the Mountain, replaced by the Jacobin constitution of 1793, and given little notice by subsequent generations. Condorcet himself, who died in prison in

.1794, is much better known for the remarkable *Esquisse d'un tableau historique des progrès de l'esprit humain* (1794), which he wrote while outlawed and in hiding during the Terror. His speech of February 15, 1793, introducing the constitutional project is, however, remarkable in its own right and much less accessible. Not only does it represent an immense effort to solve the theoretical problems of creating a representative democracy; it is also, despite its complexity, a document expressing awareness of the contingencies of the revolutionary crisis and of many of the problems that were to defeat the efforts of Robespierre and the leaders of the Mountain. Condorcet's speech and the constitution, as printed by order of the Convention, total 48 pages each. There can be no question of reproducing here in their entirety even Condorcet's introductory remarks, but their importance as the high point of his life and of his effort to apply the product of his thought to the demands of the revolution, together with the relative neglect that this document has suffered, justifies inclusion of several key passages. Those selected are not descriptions of the contours of the constitution but, rather, reflections on problems of representation and of the revolution. They have been translated from *Plan de constitution présenté à la Convention nationale, les 15 et 16 février 1793, l'an II de la République. Imprimé par ordre de la Convention nationale* (Paris, Imprimerie nationale, 1793) [Part I] *Exposition des principes et des motifs du plan présenté . . . par le Comité de constitution*, pp. 1–2, 5–7, 9–13, 30–33, 46–48. The passages have been given headings describing their contents, and are separated from each other by extra space.

Opening Remarks; the Political Task

To GIVE to a territory of twenty-seven thousand square leagues, inhabited by twenty-five million individuals, a constitution which, based solely on the principles of reason and justice, assures to the citizens the maximum possible enjoyment of their rights; to assemble the parts of this constitution in such a way that the necessity of obedience to the laws and of the submission of individual wills to the general will leaves in existence and uncurtailed the sovereignty of the people, the equality of the citizens, and the exercise of natural liberty: such is the problem that we had to resolve.

Never did a people freer from all prejudices, more emancipated from the yoke of their ancient institutions, offer a better occasion for following, in the making of their laws, only the general principles consecrated by reason; but never, either, did the disturbance caused by so complete a revolution, never did a more active ferment aroused in people's minds, never did the weight of a more dangerous war, never did greater dislocations in the public economy seem to oppose to the establishment of a constitution more numerous obstacles.

The new constitution must be suitable to a people in whom a revolutionary movement is coming to completion, and yet it must also be suitable for a peaceful people; the constitution must, in calming the agitation without enfeebling the activity of the public spirit, permit this movement to subside without making it more dangerous, repressing it without perpetuating it by ill-conceived or uncertain measures which would transform this temporary fever into a spirit of disorganization and anarchy.

On Consulting the People's Will via Referendum

In examining the workings of a deliberative assembly, one easily sees that the discussions that take place in it have two very distinct objectives. Discussion takes place there concerning the principles that must serve as a basis for the decision on a general question; that question is examined in its various parts, and the consequences that would result from different ways of deciding it are indicated. Up to that point, people have all sorts of opinions, all different from each other, and no one opinion has a majority of the votes. Thereafter comes a new discussion: in proportion as the question is clarified, opinions draw nearer and combine with each other; a small number of more general opinions is formed, and soon the question under discussion is reduced to a certain number of more simple questions, clearly posed, on which it is possible to consult the will of the assembly; and one would have attained the point of perfection for this kind of operation if those questions were such that each individual, in responding yes or no to each of them, had truly uttered his wish.

The first kind of discussion does not assume a meeting of men in the same assembly; it can take place as well by the printed word as by the spoken word; perhaps even better.

The second kind of discussion, on the other hand, could not take place between isolated men without interminable delays; the one is sufficient for men who seek only to be enlightened and to form opinions for themselves; the other can be useful only to those who are obliged to pronounce or to prepare a common decision.

Finally, when these two discussions are completed, the moment comes to make a decision; and if the purpose of the questions to be responded to by rising or remaining seated, by adoption or rejection, by yes or by no, is clearly determined, it is evident that the decision is as much an expression of everyone's opinion whether they vote together or separately, by voice vote or by ballot.

Thus the first kind of discussion no more belongs to a deliberative assembly than to isolated men, no more to an assembly with public powers than to a private group.

The second stage of discussion is only possible in a deliberative assembly, and, to be properly conducted, requires a single assembly. It would be almost impossible without an exchange of views in an assembly created for that purpose to prepare the way for decisions by formulating the questions in a clear way, permitting an immediate decision either by this or by any other assembly.

The final decision can be made by votes in separate assemblies, provided that these questions, posed in a manner to be resolved by a simple yes or no answer, be irrevocably fixed. Then all discussion in these assemblies becomes superfluous: it suffices for there to have been time enough to examine the questions in silence or to discuss them freely in private societies. The objection that in that case the citizens have not been able to take part in the totality of the discussion—that all have not been able to be heard by all—can have no force.

For it is not necessary, in order to decide with full knowledge of the facts, to have read or heard on each subject everything that all other men charged with that same decision have been able to think; it is not necessary to have heard them in preference to others, who may have been able to diffuse more light; it is enough not to have been deprived of any means of instruction, and to have been able to use these means freely. It is up to each individual to choose the method of enlightening himself that best suits him, to adjust the study that he is obliged to make of a question to his own education and intelligence. And certainly experience has proved that men who would like to have read everything written on a subject and heard everything that could have been said about it would in the end make themselves incapable of any decision.

But in order to form a general will from the particular wills of several isolated assemblies, it is necessary that these wills be expressed on a question definitively posed, and everyone knows to what extent the manner of posing a question can influence the outcome of a decision.

One must therefore regard as illusory the right of decision left to separate assemblies in every case where the form in which the question is posed can influence their will, or even determine it in some way. This method of deciding must therefore not be applied to all kinds of decisions; but it must be reserved for those where, no matter how a proposition may have been posed, it is really possible to fulfill the purpose for which the assemblies were consulted by giving a yes or no answer. One must therefore have recourse to this method only for some propositions; in cases where the refusal to accept a proposition would mean its entire rejection even when only one part of it was objected to, that refusal still expresses the will that one wished to know about when posing the question.

Dangers and Benefits of Consulting Assemblies of the People

The bringing together of citizens in primary assemblies must be considered more a means of reconciling peace with liberty than a danger to public tranquillity. These assemblies, formed of men occupied with peaceful concerns and useful work, cannot be troubled unless a too lengthy session reduces them to a residue of idlers and thereby makes them dangerous, or unless, in leaving them to their own devices, one exposes them to letting themselves be led astray. And so we have neglected no means of conserving all the natural utility of these assemblies, and of forestalling the influence of intrigue.

First, those assemblies in which citizens exercise their rights as members of the sovereign by accepting or rejecting a constitution, by responding to the questions that are put to them in the name of the national representation, by formulating demands concerning the laws and thereby obliging the legislative corps to undertake a considered examination, those assemblies in which the participating citizen votes not for himself alone but for the entire nation, are entirely distinct, both by their form and by their distribution over the territory, from those in which the same citizens could be called upon to deliberate as members of one of the territorial divisions; hence their attention can be devoted only to questions for the consideration of which the law stipulates their convocation.

Since these same assemblies do not act each for itself but as parts of a whole, never being convoked except to pronounce on questions already set, no discussion should be authorized in them. The citizens who compose them can, to be sure, freely discuss in the meeting place of the assembly, during the interval between the proposing of a question and the decision, the subjects that are submitted for their judgment; but at such times the officers of the assembly exercise no function. This discussion necessarily preserves a private character, and one can neither interfere with the decision nor delay it, since that kind of voluntary meeting, when it does take place, is absolutely distinct from the assembly where the decision must be made.

Localized spontaneous demands and voluntary private gatherings, assuming of their own accord a public character not sanctioned by the law, or municipal or section assemblies which transform themselves into primary assemblies: that is what we wanted to replace by regular and legal demands, by assemblies convoked in the name of the law and exercising, according to legally established procedures, precise and well-defined functions.

By the very nature of things, when individual demands make themselves heard, when the people, agitated by unavoidable anxieties, especially during the birth of a constitution, on the heels of a revolution, either assemble in crowds or respond to these anxieties in assemblies convoked for other reasons, the representatives of the people find themselves placed between two dangers. A facility that could be taken for weakness encourages intrigue and factions, debases the laws, corrupts the national spirit, and leads to a resistance that can bring about insurrections: these insurrections, which can be dangerous for liberty, are always dangerous for peace, and almost necessarily bring misfortunes to some people. If that state of anxiety persists in the people, continual movements place in the way of the tranquillity so necessary to public prosperity ever-recurring obstacles; and, on the contrary, if the people themselves grow weary of these movements, soon the established authorities learn to defy their spiritless and timid demands; and their petitions, tranquilly deposited on some desk or other, serve only to prove their indifference and to encourage the desire to abuse it. Those irregular demands also have the inconvenience of maintaining among the citizens dangerous errors about the nature of their rights, or of the sovereignty of the people, or of the various powers established by the law.

Finally, there would result a real inequality among the various parts of the republic. In fact, both improperly made claims and the insurrections or the inconveniences that can result from them have a greater force if the place where they occur is the site of the national government, or is nearby, or if the center of agitation is in a city that is richer or more important because of its location and the numerous institutions that have been established there; in such cases certain parts of the territory, because they contain those cities, or because other local circumstances tempt people to conciliate them, and make people afraid of alienating them, may exercise on the entire republic an influence contrary to equality among all the parts of the country—an equality whose most scrupulous conservation is so forcefully demanded by the law of nature, justice, common welfare, and general prosperity.

The procedure proposed by the committee for making demands appears to forestall all of these inconveniences.

An ordinary citizen can request his primary assembly to demand that any law whatever be subjected to a new examination, or to ask that there be provided, through a new law, a remedy to some disorder that he has noticed. The only requirement is that fifty other citizens sign with him not a statement that the proposition is just but one to the effect that it merits submission to a primary assembly.

The primary assembly has the right to convoke, for the purpose of examining the proposition that it has itself admitted, all the assemblies of one of the territorial divisions. If the will of the majority in these assemblies agrees with that of the original primary assembly, then the assemblies of the next higher territorial division are convoked; and if the will of the majority in them still concurs, the assembly of the people's representatives for the whole nation is obliged to examine not the proposition itself but only whether it ought to concern itself with that proposition. If it refuses, all of the primary assemblies in the country are convoked on the same question, still that of whether such a subject ought to be taken under consideration; and then either the will of the majority in the primary assemblies declares itself in favor of the opinion of the national representatives, and the proposition is rejected, or that majority expresses a contrary view, and the central assembly, which appears in consequence to have lost the national confidence, must be renewed. The new law, which is the result of the demand made by the primary assemblies, is subject to the same contestation and the same censure; with the result that never can the will of the people's representatives or that of the citizens become immune to correction by the general will.

The same rules are observed if there is a question whether to call a Convention charged with presenting to the people a new constitution or a revision of the old one; but it is necessary that the Convention, which will of necessity be directed by the national spirit, have, in any case, the power to present a whole new constitution. It would be absurd for the number of articles that it could reform or correct to be restricted; for the manner of changing them can compel changes in a great number of others; and in a work that must offer a systematic ensemble, every change must entail a general examination in order to harmonize all the parts with the new element introduced into the system.

If the majority desires a Convention, the assembly of national representatives will be obliged to support it. A refusal on its part to convoke the primary assemblies is therefore the only case in which the right of insurrection may be legitimately employed, and then the motive for it would be so clear, so universally felt, and the movement that would result from it would be so general, so irresistible, that this refusal, contrary to a positive law dictated by the nation itself, is beyond all probability. These forms, which an urgent concern can render very prompt, assure nevertheless sufficient mature consideration and force individuals to reflect on the question. The demands of the territorial divisions would all have an equal authority, since they would lead with an equal force, and with all the force of the law, to consultation of the whole people. There would be no pretext for disorderly movements, since such movements could not exist unless they were composed of a part of the people against the whole people, whose decision they would obviously appear to be seeking to prevent or to render useless. No system of intrigue that did not encompass the entire republic could hope for success. The body of national representatives, subject to a legal renewal, could not, in a case of refusal to examine, become the object of resentment; for either the national will would back the decision of the representatives or that body would cease to exist and would thereby cease to incite anxiety. Finally, the execution of provisional laws guarantees public tranquillity; and if, on the one hand, very precise knowledge of the will of an imposing majority crushes all the factions, awareness of a feeble majority, by calling attention to the dangers involved in opposing it, is still enough to rally all the good citizens, all the true patriots, to it, and to cause them to join forces through the momentary sacrifice of their personal opinions.

Besides, a Declaration of Rights adopted by the people, that exposition of the conditions to which each citizen consents in order to enter into the national association, and of the rights that he recognizes in all the others, that limit imposed by the general will on the enterprises of the social authorities, that pact that each of them is pledged to maintain with respect to individuals, is still a powerful protection for liberty and equality, and at the same time a sure guide for the citizens when they formulate demands. . . .

Equality of Political Rights

Whom does the constitution recognize as having the faculty of exercising the political rights that men have received from nature, and which, like all other rights, are derived essentially from qualities of men as sensitive beings susceptible to moral ideas and capable of reasoning? The publicists are divided on this question between two opposing opinions. Some have regarded the exercise of political rights as a kind of public function for which conditions based on common utility could be required. They have believed that the exercise of the rights of all could be entrusted exclusively to a portion of the citizens so long as that portion had no interest in abusing that trust and could have no motive for doing so, and above all on the condition that there would be reason to believe that they would better exercise those rights for the public utility. They have thought that there would be no real injustice in this distinction if these privileged men were not able to make laws for themselves alone, especially if the exclusion established by law could in some measure be regarded as voluntary, owing to the existence of easy ways to avoid it on the part of those who might wish to do so.

Others thought, on the contrary, that political rights should belong to all individuals with complete equality; and that if one could legitimately subject their exercise to conditions, the only acceptable ones would be those necessary to establish that a given man belonged to a certain nation, and not to another, and, in case all citizens could not vote in the same place, to determine to what assembly each individual should belong.

Until now, all free peoples have accepted the first opinion. The constitution of 1791 also conformed to it; but the second opinion appeared to us more in keeping with reason, with justice, and even with a truly enlightened policy. We did not believe that it was legitimate to sacrifice a natural right recognized by the most simple reasoning to considerations the reality of which is at least uncertain. We felt that it was necessary either to limit ourselves to insignificant distinctions without any real object or to give to these exclusions a dimension to which an egalitarian, generous, and just people could consent without dishonoring itself.

We did not believe that it was possible, in a nation enlightened concerning its rights, to propose to half of the citizens to abdicate a part of those rights, nor that it was useful to the public tranquillity to separate a people actively occupied with political interests into two parts, of which one would be everything and the other nothing, by virtue of the law, in spite of the will of nature, which, in creating men, wanted all of them to be equal. In ancient times nations were a composite of families for whom a common origin was assumed, or who at least dated back to a first union. Political rights were hereditary, and it was through legal adoption that new families became affiliated. Nowadays it is by territory that nations are distinguishable, and it is the inhabitants of this territory who are naturally the members of each association.

It has been claimed that political rights should appertain only to landed proprietors. But in observing the present order of societies, one can base this opinion only on one argument; one can say that they alone exist on the territory in an independent manner and cannot be excluded from it by the arbitrary will of another. Now, while admitting the pertinence of this reasoning, one sees, in the first place, that it may be used with equal force in favor of those who, through a convention, have acquired the right thus to exist on the territory in an independent manner for a determined period; and if one admits this consequence, one sees the force of this argument diminish little by little, and the limits of the time during which one would require this independence to last to be impossible to fix except in an uncertain and purely arbitrary manner. It would even be seen before long that the point where this kind of independence ceases is no longer marked clearly enough to serve as a basis for such an important distinction as the enjoyment or deprivation of political rights. The condition of dependence that does not permit the belief that an individual obeys his own will could still doubtless be a motive for exclusion. But we did not believe it possible to assume the existence of such a condition of dependence under a truly free constitution and in the midst of a people whose love of equality is the distinctive characteristic of the public spirit. Social relationships that would support such humiliation cannot persist among us, and must soon take another form. Finally, since the entire code of our laws consecrates civil equality, is it not better that political equality also reign there completely and serve to disperse what remains of that dependence, rather than that the dependence should to some extent be sanctioned by our new laws?

Other considerations have added the final touch to our conclusion. Such is the difficulty of fixing the limits where, in the chain of dependencies that the social order entails, there begins the condition that renders an individual of the human race incapable of exercising his rights. Such is the fear of making still more dangerous the dependence of certain classes of men who would escape from exclusion; that of giving for the future a pretext for new exclusions; and finally that of separating a great number of individuals from the social interest and making them indifferent or even hostile to a liberty that they could not share. Thus we believed that the public interest, in accord with justice, permitted us to refrain from sullying our legal system by any stain of inequality, and for the first time on earth to conserve in the institutions of a great people the entire equality of nature.

In small states public security can compel considerable restrictions of the exercise of political rights. In such states there can be fear that resident foreigners who share political rights may exercise a dangerous influence, and that they may wish to play the role of citizens in order to carry out projects contrary to the interest of the nation that has allowed them to share its rights. And the more neighboring peoples differ in opinions, customs, and principles, the more fear is justifiable; but it becomes void for a territory such as that of France, especially under this so wise system of a single republic already unanimously adopted by the National Convention.

Thus every man twenty-one years of age, born in France or having declared his intention of settling here, is admitted, after one year of residence on the territory, to the enjoyment of all the rights of a French citizen; and three months of previous residence will give him the power to exercise them in the place where he will have established his home. An absence of six years not caused by public service will compel, as a prerequisite to renewed exercise of the rights of citizenship, a new residence of six months.

We believed that we should limit the austerity of the law to these simple police precautions, necessary in order not to make admission to the right of citizenship arbitrary, not to expose it to contestations, and for the sake of uniform principles throughout the republic.

Every citizen shall be eligible to all of the positions to be filled by elections.

Only the age of twenty-five years will be a requirement. This interval between admission to citizenship rights and the age of eligibility for holding public office provides the time necessary for judging new citizens, observing their conduct, and recognizing their principles. . . .

Concluding Remarks; Tactics and Principles

Given these salutary arrangements, we may expect that exaggerated enthusiasm and excessive suspicion will disappear, as well as party passions and the fear of factions, the pusillanimity for which all agitation is the dissolution of the State, and the anxiety that suspects tyranny as soon as it perceives order and peace. In every great society that experiences a revolution, men are of two kinds. The one kind is busy with public affairs from interest or from patriotism, appears in all the disputes of opinion, enters all the factions, and supports all the different parties; one would think them the entire nation, while often they are only a feeble portion of it. The other kind, committed to their work, retained in their personal occupations from necessity or from liking for peace and quiet, love their country without seeking to govern it, and serve the *patrie* without wishing to make their opinions or their parties dominant in it. Forced either to split into factions and give their confidence to the leaders of opinion or to be reduced to inactivity and silence, they have need of a constitution to show them in a sure manner what their interest is, and what their duties are, in order that they may learn without difficulty toward what ends they should unite their efforts; and from the moment that their imposing mass is finally in motion toward this common end, the active portion of the citizens ceases to appear to be the whole people. From that moment, individuals are no longer anything and the nation alone exists. Thus it must be expected that all those whose vanity, ambition, or greed requires troubles, all those who fear that the establishment of a peaceful order will once more immerse them in the crowd, lost to public esteem; all those who can be something in a party, and can be nothing in a nation; it must be expected that all those men will unite their efforts in order to retard, to trouble, perhaps to prevent, the establishment of a new constitution. They will be seconded by those who regret some portion of what the revolution has destroyed, who say that the formation of a republic founded on equality is impossible, because they fear to see it established, and by those men, more guilty still, who have calculated that only the long duration of our divisions could give to our foreign enemies victories fatal to liberty.

Thus the intriguers of all descriptions, the aristocrats of all degrees, the conspirators at all levels will have but one will hostile to the establishment of a new constitution, and will employ the same means and speak the same language. If they cannot attack an arrangement too obviously useful or wise, they will accuse those who have proposed or defended it of having secret intentions; for it is easier to cause a suspicion to arise than to destroy a reasonable argument, and even less talent is needed to launch a slander than to construct a sophism.

But the Convention will destroy these shameful hopes; it will hasten to present to the people a constitution worthy of itself and of them; it will know how to distinguish the traps with which its route will be zealously strewn.

The citizens, who all feel the necessity of having, finally, a set of stable laws, will unite with the Convention; they are not unaware that the glory of the Convention, and the fate, for the rest of their lives, of the men who compose it are linked to the success of this great act of the national will. It is on this basis that the nation, that Europe, that posterity will judge our intentions and our conduct. This idea will sustain their confidence, and they will pronounce with their reason alone on the plan that your wisdom must submit to their sovereign authority.

As for us, we present our work to you with the confidence of men who have sought for that which was useful and just, without passion, without prejudices, without party spirit, without any return for themselves of interest or of vanity, but with that distrust of ourselves rightly inspired in us both by the difficulty of such a task and by all those difficulties inherent in the present circumstances.

The sovereignty of the people, the equality of all men, the unity of the republic—such are the principles which, ever present in our thoughts, guide us in the choice of the arrangements we have adopted, and we have believed that the constitution best in itself, the one most in conformity to the present spirit of the nation, would be that in which these principles would be respected.

Frenchmen, we owe you the whole truth. A constitution simple and well combined, and accepted by you, would not be enough to assure your rights. You will experience neither peace, nor well-being, nor even liberty, if submission to the laws that the people will have adopted is not for every citizen the first of his duties; if this scrupulous respect for law which characterizes free peoples does not extend even to those laws in need of reform for the sake of the public interest; if, charged with choosing the trustees of all authority, you yield to slanderous murmurs instead of listening to the voice of renown; if an unjust suspicion condemns the virtues and talents to retirement and to silence; if you believe the accusers instead of judging the accusations; if you prefer the mediocrity that envy spares to the merit that it enjoys persecuting; if you judge men according to sentiments that are easy to pretend, and not according to a conduct that is difficult to sustain; if, finally, through culpable indifference, citizens do not exercise with calm, with zeal, and with dignity the important functions that the law has imposed on them. Where would liberty and equality be if the law that regulates the rights common to all were not uniformly respected? And what peace, what happiness could a people hope for whose imprudence and negligence would abandon its interests to incapable or corrupt men? On the other hand, whatever faults a constitution may contain, if it offers means of reforming itself to a people who support the laws, to citizens concerned with the interests of the *patrie* and responsive to the voice of reason, soon those faults will be corrected, even before they have been able to do harm; thus nature, which has willed that each people be the arbiter of its laws, has made it, equally, the arbiter of its own welfare.

34. March 10, 1793:
Danton on Crisis Measures

Georges Jacques Danton at the time of this session of the National Convention was in his early thirties and famous for having, as Minister of Justice following the overthrow of the monarchy on August 10, 1792, rallied opinion in the Legislative Assembly and the public to resist the advancing Prussians. By virtue of his office, he had also had a large share of the responsibility for not stopping the September massacres. Danton had given up the ministry to be a Parisian deputy to the Convention, where he found the Girondins cool to his advances and moved toward the Mountain politically. Although haunted by rumors of mismanagement of funds and to some extent by the September massacres, Danton was to go on to become a member of the first Committee of Public Safety, an institution for which, along with the Revolutionary Tribunal, he helped prepare the way in the speeches of March 10, given at a time of crisis when news reports of defeats in Belgium were coming in and there was an atmosphere of mounting tension in the assembly. On this occasion Danton spoke several times. His two principal interventions are given below, separated by bracketed material explaining the course of the debate. The source is the *Réimpression de l'ancien Moniteur*, Vol. XV (Paris, 1847), pp. 679–680, 683. Danton's speeches were seldom prepared in advance. He seized a moment when he wanted to accomplish something and improvised with great effect, imposing his powerful voice and personality.

National Convention. Gensonné, President.
Continuation of the Session of
Sunday, March 10.

DANTON: The general considerations which have been presented to you are true; but it is less a question at this time of examining the causes of the disastrous events which can afflict you than it is of applying the remedy with rapidity. When the building is on fire, I do not direct myself to the scoundrels who carry off the furniture, I put out the fire. I say that you should be convinced more than ever, by reading Dumouriez's dispatches, that you have not a moment to lose to save the republic.

Dumouriez had conceived a plan which does honor to his genius. I must render him a justice even more striking than that which I paid him recently. Three months ago he announced to the executive power, to your committee of general defense, that if we were not audacious enough to invade Holland in the middle of winter, and to declare on England without delay the war which she had been waging against us for a long time, we would double the difficulties of the campaign by allowing the enemy forces time to deploy. Since this stroke of genius was ignored, we must correct our faults.

Dumouriez is not discouraged; he is in the middle of Holland; he will find munitions there; to overcome all our enemies, he needs only Frenchmen, and France is full of citizens. Do we wish to be free? If we no longer wish it, let us perish, for we have all sworn to do so; if we do wish it, let us all march to defend our independence. Your enemies are making their utmost efforts. Pitt well knows that having everything to lose he must spare nothing. Let us take Holland, and Carthage is destroyed, and England can no longer exist except for liberty. Let Holland be conquered for liberty, and the commercial aristocracy itself, which dominates the English people at this time, will rise against the government which will have dragged it into this war of despotism against a free people. It will overthrow the stupid ministry that believed that the talents of the old regime could stifle the genius of liberty which hovers over France. When this ministry is overthrown by the interests of commerce, the party for liberty will show itself, for it is not dead; and if you hasten to fulfill your obligations, if your commissioners set out at once, if you give a hand to the foreigners who long for the destruction of every form of tyranny, France is saved and the world is free.

Send forth your commissioners, then; support them by your energy, let them set out this evening, this very night. Let them say to the wealthy class: the aristocracy of Europe, overwhelmed by our efforts, must pay our debt, or you must pay it; the people have only their blood; they pour it forth unstintingly. Come, unfortunates! pour forth your riches. [Lively applause is heard.] Look, citizens, at the beautiful destiny that awaits you. What! You have a whole nation for a lever, reason for a fulcrum, and you have not yet overturned the world! [The applause redoubles.] For that, character is needed and the truth is that it has been lacking. I set aside all passions; they are completely alien to me, except passion for the public good.

In more difficult circumstances, when the enemy was at the gates of Paris, I said to those who were then governing: your discussions are despicable; I know only the enemy, let us beat the enemy. [New applause] You who make me tired with your selfish arguments, instead of concerning yourselves with the safety of the republic, I repudiate you all as traitors of the *patrie*. I lump you all together. I said to them: well! what does my reputation matter to me! Let France be free, and my name can be tarnished! What does it matter to me to be called a drinker of blood! Very well, let us drink the blood of the enemies of mankind if we must; let us fight, let us win liberty.

There are those, it would seem, who fear that the departure of the commissioners will weaken one or another part of the Convention. Vain terrors! Use your energy everywhere. The best service of all is to announce to the people that the terrible debt which weighs on them will be liquidated at the expense of their enemies, or that the rich will pay it before long. The condition of the nation is grievous; the currency in circulation is no longer in balance; the day's wages of the worker are below the cost of living; a great corrective measure is needed. Let us conquer Holland, let us revive the republican party in England, let us set France on the march, and we will go gloriously to posterity. Fulfill these great destinies: no debates, no quarrels, and the *patrie* is saved.

[After Danton's speech there was a lengthy discussion, in which he took part, of the behavior of certain generals at the front and of how best to determine whether their conduct was harmful to the nation and, if so, how to judge them. There was also an intense discussion of the need for a revolutionary tribunal, and some decisions were made on this subject, but the Convention, without completing the organization of the tribunal, voted to terminate the session. At this point Danton rushed to the tribune and with the following speech secured agreement that the Convention should merely adjourn until that evening.]

DANTON, rushing to the tribune: I call on all good citizens not to leave their posts. [All the members sit down, and a great stillness reigns over the assembly.] What! Citizens, at the moment when our position is such that if Miranda were beaten, and that is not impossible, Dumouriez, surrounded, would be obliged to lay down his arms, you could disperse without deciding on the great measures required by the public safety! I appreciate how important it is to take judicial measures for the punishment of counterrevolutionaries, for it is for them that this tribunal is necessary; it is for them that this tribunal must take the place of the supreme tribunal that is the vengeance of the people. The enemies of liberty present a bold front; everywhere infiltrated, they are everywhere *provocateurs*. Seeing virtuous citizens busy in their homes, and artisans occupied in their workshops, they are stupid enough to believe themselves in the majority. Well! Tear them yourselves from the popular vengeance; humanity demands this of you.

Nothing is more difficult to define than a political crime. But if a man of the people, for a particular crime, receives punishment for it at once; if it is so difficult to deal with a political crime, is it not necessary that emergency laws, taken outside of the social body, frighten the rebels and reach the guilty? Here the safety of the people demands great means and awe-inspiring measures. I do not see a middle course between the usual forms and a revolutionary tribunal. History bears witness to this truth; and since members of this assembly have been so bold as to recall those bloody days lamented by every good citizen, I will say, speaking for myself, that if a tribunal had existed then, the people, who have been so often and so cruelly blamed for those days, would not have steeped them in blood; I will say, and I will have the backing of all who witnessed these movements, that no human power was in a position to halt that overflowing of national vengeance. Let us profit from the faults of our predecessors.

Let us do what the Legislative Assembly did not do; let us inspire terror to dispense the people from doing so; let us organize a tribunal, not the best, for that is impossible, but the least bad that we can manage, in order that the power of the law may weigh heavily on the heads of all its enemies.

This great work finished, I remind you of the armies, of the commissioners you must send out, of the ministry you must organize; for we cannot hide from the fact, we must have ministers; and the Naval Ministry, for example, in a country where anything can be created—because all the elements are available, with all the qualities of a good citizen—has not created a navy; our frigates have not set out, and England takes our corsairs. Well! The time has come, let us be prodigal of men and money, let us use every means in the national power, but let us put the direction of these means only into the hands of men whose necessary and habitual contact with you assures you of the over-all pattern and execution of the measures which you have planned for the public welfare. You are not a constituted body, for you can yourselves constitute everything. Take care, citizens, you are responsible to the people for our armies, for their blood, for the *assignats*; for if defeats so weakened the value of this money that the means of existence were reduced to nothing in the people's hands, who could halt the effects of their resentment and of their vengeance? If, from the moment I demanded them of you, you had created the necessary forces, today the enemy would already be pushed back far beyond our frontiers.

I demand therefore that the revolutionary tribunal be organized at once, that the executive power, in the new organization, receive the means of action and the energy necessary to it. I do not demand that nothing [*sic*] be disorganized, I propose only means of improvement . . . [break in *Moniteur* text].

I demand that the Convention judge my reasoning on its own merits and scorn the injurious and punitive insults to which I have been subjected. I demand that as soon as the measures for general security have been taken, your commissioners part at once; that the objection no longer be raised that they sit on one or another side of this room. Let them go out into the departments, let them inspire the citizens, let them restore in them the love of liberty; and if they regret not having a hand in the writing of useful decrees, or not being able to oppose bad decrees, let them remember that their absence has contributed to the safety of the nation.

I sum up, then; this evening organization of the tribunal, organization of the executive power; tomorrow military movement;

tomorrow let your commissaries set out; let all France arise, spring to arms, march on the enemy; let Holland be invaded; let Belgium be free; let the commerce of England be ruined; let the friends of liberty in this country triumph; let our arms, everywhere victorious, bring deliverance and well-being to other peoples, and let the world be avenged.

[Danton descends from the tribune to the accompaniment of vigorous applause. The assembly adjourns its various propositions. The session is adjourned. It is seven o'clock.]

35. May 10, 1793:
Robespierre on Constitutional Principles

It is well known that in the debates leading to the adoption of the Jacobin constitution of 1793 Robespierre's speech of May 10, 1793, was very influential and that many of his proposals went into the new constitution. The document below, consisting of the introductory portion of this speech, has been selected because of its statements about principles of government, relations of government and society to each other, and the place of the French Revolution in history, and because these statements were made when they were, during the contest with the Girondins and before the coming of the Terror. The source is the version printed under the auspices of the Jacobin Club, *Société des amis de la liberté et de l'égalité séante aux Jacobins, rue Saint-Honoré. Discours de Maximilien Robespierre sur la constitution. De l'Imprimerie patriotique et républicaine* . . .(n.d., 34 pp.), pp. 1–10. These pages are the same as the version adopted by the editors of the *Oeuvres de Maximilien Robespierre*, Vol. IX (Paris, 1958), pp. 495–498, except for two misplaced lines that the editors of the *Oeuvres* have relocated in the ninth paragraph, and another difference of one word that does not affect the translation.

MAN IS BORN for happiness and for liberty, and everywhere he is a slave and unhappy. The purpose of society is the conservation of his rights and the perfection of his being, and everywhere society degrades and oppresses him. The time has come to recall him to his true destiny; the progress of human intelligence has brought about this great revolution, and it is upon you that the duty of accelerating it is especially imposed.

In order to fulfill your mission, you must create precisely the opposite of what has existed previously.

Until now, the art of governing has been nothing but the art of despoiling and enslaving the many for the profit of the few, and legislation has been the means of organizing these acts of aggression into a system. Kings and aristocrats have practiced their profession very well; it is now time for you to practice yours, which is to say, to make men happy and free by means of laws.

To give government the necessary strength so that citizens always respect the rights of other citizens, and to do it in such a way that the government can never itself violate them: there, in my opinion, is the twofold problem that the legislator must seek to resolve. The first seems to me very easy. As for the second, one would be tempted to regard it as insoluble if one searched for explanations only in past and present events without going back to their causes.

Examine history and you will see everywhere magistrates oppressing the citizenry and governments devouring sovereignty. Tyrants speak of sedition; the people complain of tyranny when they dare to complain about what is happening, as they do when excessive oppression revives their energy and spirit of independence. May it please God that they preserve these always! But the reign of the people is for a day; that of tyrants embraces centuries.

I have heard much about anarchy since the revolution of the fourteenth of July, 1789, and especially since the revolution of the tenth of August, 1792; but I maintain that it is not anarchy that is the malady of political bodies, but despotism and aristocracy. I find, in spite of what has been said about it, that it is only in this much-slandered period that we have had the beginnings of laws and of government, in spite of the disturbances that have taken place, which are nothing but the last convulsions of expiring royalty and the struggles of an unfaithful government against equality.

Anarchy reigned in France from Clovis to the last of the Capets. What is anarchy if not the tyranny that makes nature and law descend from the throne in order to place men there!

The ills of society never come from the people, but from the government. How could this not be the case? The interest of the people is the public good; the interest of the man in office is a private interest. In order to be good, the people need only to prefer themselves to that which is not themselves;

in order to be good, the magistrate must sacrifice himself for the people.

If I deigned to respond to absurd and barbarous prejudices, I would point out that it is power and opulence that produce pride and all the vices; that it is labor, mediocrity, and poverty that are the guardians of virtue; that the wishes of the weak aim only at justice and the protection of beneficial laws; that the weak esteem only the passion for uprightness; [that the passions of the man who is powerful tend to overrule just laws or to create tyrannical ones;][1] I would say, finally, that need on the part of citizens is the equivalent of crime on the part of governments. But I establish the basis of my system by a single argument.

Government is established to make the general will respected; but men who govern have individual wills, and every will seeks to dominate. If they use for this purpose the public force with which they are armed, the government is nothing but the scourge of liberty. Conclude, then, that the first objective of every constitution must be to defend public and individual liberty against the government itself.

It is precisely this objective that the legislators have forgotten; they have all concerned themselves with the power of the government; none has thought of means to restore it to its basic purpose. They have taken infinite precautions against insurrection of the people, and they have encouraged with all their power the revolt of the people's delegates. I have already indicated the reasons for this. Ambition, force, and perfidy have been the legislators of the world. They have enslaved even human intelligence, by corrupting it, and have made it an accomplice of man's misery. Despotism has produced corruption of morals, and corruption of morals has sustained despotism. In this state of affairs, it is up to each to sell his soul to the strongest to legitimize injustice and share the tyranny. Then reason is only madness; equality is anarchy; liberty is disorder; nature is illusion; recollection of the rights of humanity is revolt. Then there are prisons and scaffolds for virtue, palaces for debauchery, tyrants and triumphal chariots for crime. Then there are kings, priests, nobles, bourgeois, rabble; but no people, and no men.

---

1. Bracketed material is not in the orginal pamphlet; part of it is there, but misplaced and meaningless; as shown above, it was reconstructed by the editors of the *Oeuvres de Robespierre*, Vol. IX.—Editor.

Consider even those among the legislators whom the increase of public enlightenment seems to have forced to render some homage to principles; see whether they have not employed their cleverness to evade these principles when they could no longer reconcile them with their personal views. See if they have done otherwise than to vary the forms of despotism and the nuances of aristocracy. They have ostentatiously proclaimed the sovereignty of the people, and have enchained them; while indeed acknowledging that magistrates are agents, they have treated them as the people's rulers and as their idols. All have agreed upon the assumption that the people are senseless and unruly, and the public functionaries essentially wise and virtuous. Without seeking examples among foreign nations, we would be able to find very striking ones in the midst of our revolution and even in the conduct of the legislatures that have preceded us. See with what cowardice they flattered royalty; with what imprudence they preached blind confidence in corrupt public officials; with what insolence they disparaged the people; with what barbarousness they assassinated them. Consider, however, on which side were to be found the civic virtues. Recall the generous sacrifices of the poor, and the shameful avarice of the rich; recall the splendid devotion of the soldiers, and the infamous betrayals of the generals; the invincible courage, the magnanimous patience of the people, and the cowardly egotism, the odious perfidy of its mandataries.

But let us not be too astonished at so many injustices. At the outset of so great an upheaval, how could they respect humanity, cherish equality, believe in virtue? We—unfortunates!— we are raising the temple of liberty with hands still branded with the irons of slavery. What was our former education if not a continual lesson in egotism and senseless vanity? What were our customs and our supposed laws if not the code of impertinence and servility, where scorn for men was subject to a kind of tariff and measured by degrees according to rules as bizarre as they were numerous? To scorn and be scorned; to grovel in order to dominate, slaves and tyrants, by turns; now on one's knees before a master, now trampling the people underfoot; such was our destiny, such was our ambition, all of us such as we were, *men well born or men well educated, honorable persons and persons of breeding, men of law and financiers, men of the robe or men of the sword.* Should one be astonished, then, if so many stupid merchants, so many egotistical bourgeois still preserve for artisans that insolent disdain that the nobles lavished on the bourgeois and merchants themselves? Oh! Such noble pride! Oh, such a fine education! That, however, is why the great destiny of the world is being held back! That is why the heart of the *patrie* is being torn by traitors! That is why the ferocious satellites of the European despots have ravaged our harvests, set fire to our cities, massacred our women and children; the blood of three hundred thousand French has already flowed; the blood of three hundred thousand others will perhaps still flow in order that the simple laborer may sit in the senate at the side of the rich grain merchant; in order that the artisan may vote in the assemblies of the people at the side of the illustrous wholesale merchant, or the conceited lawyer, and that the intelligent and virtuous poor person may retain the bearing of a man in the presence of someone imbecile, corrupt, and rich! Madmen! You who call for masters, in order not to have equals, do you believe, then, that the tyrants will adopt all the calculations of your sad vanity and your cowardly avidity? Do you believe that the people who conquered liberty, who shed their blood for the *patrie* while you were sleeping in indolence, or while you were secretly conspiring, will let themselves be enchained, starved, and slaughtered by you? No. If you do not respect humanity, justice, or honor, at least give some thought to your treasures, which have no other enemy than the public misery which you aggravate so unwisely. But what incentive can reach these haughty slaves? The law of truth, thundering in corrupt hearts, resembles the sounds which reverberate in tombs and which never awaken the corpses.

You, then, for whom liberty, for whom the *patrie*, is dear, take upon yourselves unaided the task of saving it; and since the urgent necessity for its defense has seemed to demand all of your attention at a moment when it is also desired to construct in haste the edifice of the constitution of a great people, establish it at least upon the eternal base of truth. Pose first this incontestable maxim: *that the people are good, and that their delegates are corruptible; that it is to the virtue and the sovereignty of the people that we must look for safeguards against the vices and despotism of the government.* . . .

IX.

The Convention and
the Sans-Culottes

36. June 25, 1793:
Roux Before the Convention

This document, which is the account in the *Moniteur* of the appearance of Jacques Roux before the Convention and the members' reception of him and of the delegation he led, is related to conditions of life among the Parisian sans-culottes, and especially among the very poor of the Gravilliers section around the church on the Rue Saint-Martin known as Saint-Nicolas-des-Champs, where Jacques Roux was vicar. Roux was a provincial priest who had secured an appointment in Paris and been shocked by the terrible conditions of the urban poor. He has been pictured in many histories as wild and ignorant, a leader—the one most often mentioned—of the *enragés*, neighborhood demagogues who, with little understanding of the economic causes of the people's distress or of the political possibilities, encouraged primitive impulses in the lower classes to attack shopkeepers, engage in witch hunts for traitors, and overthrow the Convention because it contained men who were middle-class, educated, and different. The elements of truth in this stereotype fall short of the complexities of places such as the Gravilliers section and the mentalities of their residents, which are difficult to reconstruct from their sparse traces and were generally misunderstood by historians before Albert Soboul and others set the example for sociological urban history. Manifestations such as Roux's visit to the Convention, no doubt imperfectly reported, and Roux himself as an interpreter of the sentiments of largely illiterate parishioners do indicate the existence of a popular movement that was spontaneous and powerful and had to be coped with by the Convention: a movement, indeed, without which the French Revolution would have been much different. Jacques Roux is generally credited with sincerity. His stock of ideas about society and politics is perhaps beyond our reach, though he was not an uneducated man and he published a number of sermons that were very popular and widely disseminated. He was regarded as a threat by the Convention's leaders, including Robespierre, and they successfully put him out of action, although not without adopting many of the demands of the sans-culottes. Roux was one of those who called for terror and were eliminated by the Terror in the hands of the Convention. He was condemned to death by the Revolutionary Tribunal in January, 1794, and committed suicide upon hearing the verdict. The account below is from the *Réimpression de l'ancien Moniteur*, Vol. XVI (Paris, 1847), pp. 747–748.

National Convention. Collot d'Herbois Presiding.
Session of Tuesday Evening.

. . . A delegation from the Gravilliers section, together with some citizens from the Bonne-Nouvelle section and from the Cordeliers club, is received at the bar.

JACQUES ROUX, *speaker for the delegation:* Mandataries of the people, for a long time you have been promising to put an end to the people's misfortunes; but what have you done about them? [Fierce mutterings.] You have just drawn up a constitution for which you are going to seek the people's sanction. In it have you banned speculation? No. In it have you declared a penalty against hoarders and monopolists? No. Well! We declare to you that you have not finished your work. You who inhabit the Mountain, worthy sans-culottes, will you remain forever inert at the summit of this immortal rock? Take care: the friends of equality will not be the dupes of the charlatans who wish to besiege them with famine, of those vile hoarders whose shops are the haunts of crooks. But, it is said, who knows how things will turn out? [Mutterings] It is thus that, through fear of counterrevolution, they try to raise the price of commodities: but do they not know that the people want liberty or death? What is the aim of these speculators who grab up manufactured goods and commercial and agricultural products if not to drive the people to despair and oblige them to throw themselves into the arms of despotism? How much longer will you permit these rich egotists to go on drinking from their golden goblets the purest blood of the people?

If you should show unconcern for the rooting out of speculation and hoarding, such cowardice would make you guilty of the crime of lèse-nation. You must not fear to incur the hatred of the rich—that is to say, of the wicked; you must sacrifice everything to the welfare of the people. What you should fear is that you will be accused of having discredited the paper money, and of having thus prepared the way for bankruptcy. [There are murmurs in all parts of the hall.] Without doubt, there are ills inseparable from great revolutions, and our intention is to make all the sacrifices necessary to the maintenance of liberty; but the people remember that they have already been betrayed twice by two legislatures. It is time that the sans-culottes, who have broken the scepter of tyrants, bring down every kind of tyranny. Let a prompt cure be found for our pressing ailments! How, legislators, do you expect a person who has only 600 *livres* of revenue to subsist if you do not stop speculation by a constitutional decree which cannot be repealed by a legislature. It is possible that we will not have peace for another twenty years; the enormous expenditures of the war . . . [Loud murmurs on the left] Deputies of the Mountain, lay the foundations for the prosperity of the republic; do not terminate your career in ignominy. [Renewed and louder murmurs]

A citizen of the delegation: I assert that this is not the petition to which the Gravilliers section gave its assent.

It is demanded that the speaker be placed under arrest.

Several members: No, no, he must be heard.

The speaker continues: The oppressed sans-culottes from the departments are going to arrive; we will show them these pikes which overthrew the Bastille, these pikes which broke the Statesmen faction, these pikes which destroyed the rottenness of the Committee of Twelve, and then we will accompany them to the sanctuary of the laws, and we will show them the side that wished to save the tyrant, and that which pronounced his death sentence.

All the petitioners except the speaker, who remains at the bar, are admitted to the honors of the session.

THURIOT: You have just heard professed in this tribune the monstrous principles of anarchy; this man has coldly assembled all the words that were used in this petition; he has calculated to what point crime could be extended; I wish to state that Coburg would not have spoken any differently; if he had gold to distribute, he could not have chosen a better agent than the orator you have just heard, who wishes to dishonor Paris. What! He wants it believed that everything is hopeless! Despicable orator for anarchy, why not also tell the people that the son must cut the throat of his father, and the mother plunge a dagger into the breast of her daughter! Citizens, he has risen against the aristocracy of nobles; but he has not spoken to you about the priestly caste. You will not learn without astonishment that this man is a priest, a worthy rival to the fanatics of the Vendée. But the hope of the tyrants will still be disappointed; we will save Paris, whose ruin was sought; we will save the republic; and monsters like you will die of rage.

I demand that the president order this man to retire, and that the committee on legislation be charged with making a report on provisional means of lowering the prices of consumer goods.

ROBESPIERRE: You have easily grasped the perfidious intentions of the speaker; he wants to make the patriots suspected of moderatism, which would lose them the confidence of the people. I am informed that this speech is not an expression of the wishes of the Gravilliers section. I was pleased to see it repudiated at the bar of the Convention.

BILLAUD-VARENNES: This man is all the more suspect in that he went to several sections and to the Cordeliers club in order to disparage the Constitution; the indignant patriots asked him if he had read it, and he was obliged to confess that he was not acquainted with it.

LEGENDRE: I demand that this man be ejected; there are patriots in his section; they will know how to do him justice.

This proposition is adopted. The speaker retires.

37. September 2, 1793:
Section des Sans-Culottes, Social Views

The Section des Sans-Culottes was the forty-seventh of the forty-eight sections. It was located south of the Seine (and thus on the Left Bank), opposite the Île-Saint-Louis, in the eastern part of what is today the 5th arrondissement. Of their petition, *Liberté, égalité ou la mort. Section des Sans-Culottes. Adresse à la Convention nationale*, a product of the deliberations of the section on September 2, 1793, Albert Soboul has written: "At no other moment in the revolution does one find so concise and striking a formulation of the popular social ideal. . . ."[1] The document was printed but Soboul concludes that it was apparently not presented to the Convention, perhaps out of caution because of its views on the property.[2] The translation is from the copy in the Bibliothèque Nationale, with no deletions.

REPRESENTATIVES OF THE PEOPLE,

How long will you permit royalism, ambition, egoism, intrigue, and avarice, allied with fanaticism, to surrender our frontiers to tyranny and to spread devastation and death everywhere? How long will you permit hoarders to spread famine over the whole surface of the republic in the culpable hope of making patriots cut each other's throats and of re-establishing the throne, with the aid of foreign despots, on their bloody cadavers? Make haste, time is getting short . . . The whole world is looking at you, humanity reproaches you for the ills that are devastating the French Republic; and posterity will forever curse your names in centuries to come unless you move promptly to find a remedy . . . Make haste, representatives of the people, to expel from the armies all former nobles, and priests, magistrates of the *parlements*, and financiers from all administrative and judiciary functions, to fix invariably the prices of commodities of prime necessity and of all raw materials, as well as the wages for labor, the profits of industry, and the gains from commerce; you have the right and the powers to do so . . . But wait!—you will be told by the aristocrats, the royalists, the moderates, and the intriguers. That is an injury to property rights, which must be sacred and inviolable . . . No doubt, but do they not know, those scoundrels, do they not know that property rights have no limits except people's physical needs? Do they not know that no one has the right to do what can harm another? What is more harmful than the arbitrary power to place on the essentials of life a price to which seven-eighths of the citizens cannot attain. . . . Do they not know, finally, that each of the individuals who compose the republic must employ his intelligence and his strength for its benefit and shed up to his last drop of blood for it: the republic for its part must assure all of them the means of procuring for themselves the commodities of prime necessity in sufficient quantity to maintain their existence. . . .

1. Albert Soboul, *Les Sans-culottes parisiens en l'an II* (Paris, 1962), p. 469.
2. *Ibid.*, p. 163.

Have we not, you will say, directed against hoarders a terrible law? Representatives of the people, do not deceive yourselves. . . . That decree, by forcing all who have considerable stocks of things of prime necessity to declare them, favors the hoarders more than it destroys hoarding; for it places all their merchandise under the safeguard of the nation, leaving them free to sell at whatever price pleases their cupidity. Consequently, the general assembly of the Section of the Sans-Culottes, considering that it is the duty of all citizens to propose the measures that they have judged most proper for recreating abundance and public tranquillity, orders that the convention be requested to decree:

1. That former nobles may not exercise any military functions, or possess any public offices of any nature whatsoever; that former magistrates of the parlements, financiers, and priests be dismissed from all administrative or judiciary functions;

2. That all commodities of prime necessity be stabilized at prices taking account of their different qualities and based on the years called former years, from 1789 up to and including the year '90;

3. That raw materials also be stabilized in such a way that the profits of industry, the wages for labor, and the gains from commerce, which shall be kept at reasonable levels by law, may place the skilled worker, the cultivator, and the tradesman within reach of procuring for himself not only the necessities indispensable for existence but also all that can add to the enjoyment of life;

4. That all cultivators who through mishap have no harvest be compensated by the public treasury;

5. That there be allotted to each department a sum sufficient to keep the price of commodities of prime necessity the same for all individuals who compose the French Republic;

6. That the sums allotted to the departments be used to abolish inequalities in the prices of commodities and articles of prime necessity caused by transportation throughout the whole extent of the French Republic, which must procure the same advantages for each of its children;

7. That rent contracts be revoked and returned to their levels of the common years which you will choose for setting the invariable *maximum* for commodities and articles of prime necessity;

8. That a *maximum* for fortunes shall be fixed;

9. That the same individual shall not be allowed to possess more than one *maximum*;

10. That no one may rent more land than is needed for a number of plows to be determined;

11. That the same citizen may have no more than one workshop or one store;

12. That all those who have merchandise or land in their names be recognized as proprietors.

The Section of the Sans-Culottes thinks that these measures would bring back abundance and tranquillity, would gradually eliminate the too great inequality of fortunes, and would increase the number of proprietors.

Extract from the register of the deliberations of the Section of the Sans-Culottes, session of Monday, September 2, 1793, year II of the Republic, one and indivisible.

After the reading of the above address, whose principles the assembly had carefully discussed and whose basic propositions it had decreed, the assembly approved the above wording; it orders that copies be printed to the number of 500, sent by the commissioners to the forty-seven other sections, and addressed to all the communes of the department of Paris, with an invitation to adhere to it and to name commissioners to present these propositions at the National Convention.

DESCHAMPS, vice-president
For certified copy, AUGER, secretary

38. November 7, 10, 1793: Dechristianizing

The phenomenon of dechristianization, which had its most noticeable manifestations in the Festival of Reason in the Cathedral of Notre-Dame on 20 Brumaire, An II (November 10, 1793), and in the behavior of many former clergy, as shown in the document which follows, has psychological, social, and political aspects that make it far more complicated than it appears to be at first glance. The subject of religion and the revolution viewed broadly involves much more than what happened to the Church as an institution during this period, or even the balance sheet containing the contributions of the clergy and Catholics generally to the revolution and the steps by which the Church and many clergy came to be counterrevolutionary; there is also the question to what extent and in what manner revolutionaries became anticlerical, anti-Christian, or antireligious, and there is even the question of whether the revolutionary movement was itself a religious phenomenon. Behind such words as "reason" and *"patrie,"* sentiments of revolutionary or religious enthusiasm are not easy to define or to distinguish from each other, particularly when one thinks of social gradations and the influences of different life experiences on consciousness. There is also the matter of political manipulation to consider. These complexities do not detract from the importance of the behavior of the Convention in November, 1793; rather, they heighten the interest of such documents as the *Procès-verbal de la Convention nationale. Imprimé par son ordre.* Vol. XXV (Paris, An II), of which pp. 47–50 and 128–131 have been translated below.

From the Procès-verbal for 17 brumaire, an II.
(November 7, 1793)

. . . The President read a letter addressed to him by the constituted authorities of the department and commune of Paris, the text of which follows:

Citizen-President,

The constituted authorities of Paris precede into your presence the former bishop of Paris, and his former clergy, who come of their own volition to render energetic and sincere homage to reason and eternal justice.

Signed, CHAUMETTE, MOMORO, Provisional President, LULIER, Solicitor General of the Department of Paris, PACHE.

They ask to be admitted. —Granted.

MOMORO, President of the delegation, says:

Citizen-legislators,

The Bishop of Paris and several other priests, guided by reason, come into your midst to divest themselves of the quality which superstition had placed upon them; this great precedent, we are sure, will be followed by their colleagues. Thus it is that the accomplices of despotism will become its destroyers; thus it is that in a short while the French Republic will have no other cult than that of liberty, equality, and truth: a cult drawn from the bosom of nature, and which, thanks to your work, will soon be the universal cult.

    Signed, MOMORO, Provisional President.

    Gobet, Bishop of Paris, begs the representatives of the people to listen to his declaration.

    Born plebeian, I had in my soul at an early age the principles of liberty and equality. Called to the Constituent Assembly by the wish of my fellow citizens, I did not wait for the Declaration of the Rights of Man to recognize the sovereignty of the people. I had more than one occasion to make a public profession of political faith in this respect, and since that time all of my opinions have been arrayed under this high standard. From that moment the will of the sovereign people became my supreme law and my first duty was submission to its orders: it was this will which elevated me to the position of Bishop of Paris, and which summoned me at the same time to three others. I obeyed by accepting that of this great city, and my conscience tells me that in complying with the wishes of the people of the Department of Paris I did not deceive them; that I have used the influence lent me by my title and position only to increase in them their attachment to the eternal principles of liberty, equality, and morality, necessary foundations for every truly republican constitution.

    Today when the revolution is moving with long strides toward a happy conclusion, since it is conducting all opinions to a single political center, today when there must no longer be any other public and national worship than that of liberty and holy equality, because the sovereign wills it thus; consistent to my principles, I submit to its will and I come here to declare to you openly that from today I renounce the exercise of my functions as a clergyman of the Catholic form of worship; the citizens here present, my vicars, join with me: consequently we return to you all our titles.

    May this example serve to consolidate the reign of liberty and equality. *Long live the Republic.*

    Signed: GOBET, DENOUX, LABOREY, DELACROIX, LAMBERT, PRIQUELER, VOISARD, BOULLIOT, GENAIS, DESLANDES, DHERBÈS, MARTIN, called SAINT-MARTIN

[Many other priests came forth with similar declarations.]

From the Procès-Verbal for 20 Brumaire, An II
(November 10, 1793).

THE CONSTITUTED authorities of Paris present themselves at the bar; the attorney of the Paris Commune is their spokesman, and says:

The People have just made a sacrifice to Reason in the former metropolitan church; they come to offer another in the sanctuary of the Law. I request that the Convention admit them.

Upon the motion of a member, the Convention votes admission.

The procession begins with a group of young musicians; they are followed by young republicans, defenders of the *patrie;* they sing a patriotic hymn, repeated in chorus, to very lively applause.

A large group of republicans, wearing the cap of Liberty, move forward shouting *Long live the Republic! Long live the Mountain!* The People and the members of the Convention mingle their voices with those of these republicans.

The numerous musicians make the vaults resound with the beloved melodies of the revolution. A procession of young republican girls, dressed in white, girded with a tricolored ribbon, their heads wreathed with garlands of flowers, precede and encircle Reason. She is a young woman, the ideal of feminine beauty: on her head is the Liberty bonnet; from her shoulders floats a blue cloak, and in her right hand she holds a pike, upon which she leans. Seated in an armchair of simple construction decorated with garlands of oak leaves, she is carried by four citizens; her imposing and gracious mien commands respect and love.

These two sentiments are manifested with the greatest enthusiasm; the cries of *Long live the Republic* are redoubled; bonnets and hats fly into the air; the People give themselves up to cries of purest joy.

The goddess of Reason is placed before the bar, opposite the president. The attorney of the Commune of Paris speaks as follows:

Citizen-legislators, you have seen that fanaticism has released its hold; it has abandoned its former place to Reason, to Justice, and to Truth; its squinting eyes were unable to bear the brilliance of the light, and it has fled. We have seized the temples it abandoned to us; we have regenerated them.

Today all the People of Paris entered beneath the gothic vaults which had resounded for so long with the voice of falsehood, and which, for the first time, reverberated with the shouts of Liberty. There we offered a sacrifice to Liberty, to Equality, to Nature; there we cried, *Long live the Mountain,* and the Mountain heard us, for it came to join us in the Temple of Reason. We have not offered our sacrifices to empty images, to lifeless idols; no, we have chosen a masterpiece of Nature to represent her, and this sacred image has enflamed all hearts. A single vow, a single cry, was heard everywhere. The People said: No more priests, no other gods than those Nature offers us.

We, the People's magistrates, have received this vow; we bring it to you from the Temple of Reason; we come into that of the Law to celebrate Liberty again. We ask of you that the former metropolitan cathedral of Paris be dedicated to Reason and to Liberty. Fanaticism has abandoned it; rational beings have become masters of it: sanctify their property.

This speech was loudly applauded.

The president answered:

The Assembly sees with the greatest satisfaction the triumph that Reason has made today over superstition and fanaticism; it is going to go as a body, surrounded by the People, to the temple that you have just dedicated to this goddess, in order to celebrate with them this august and memorable festival: it is its work and the news of a victory that have kept it from attending thus far.

A member puts in the form of a motion the demand of the citizens of Paris that the metropolitan cathedral be henceforth the Temple of Reason.

A member requests that the goddess of Reason place herself at the side of the president.

The attorney of the Commune conducts her to the desk. The president and the secretaries give her the fraternal kiss in the midst of applause.

She sits at the side of the president.

A member demands that the National Convention march in a body, in the midst of the People, to the Temple of Reason, to sing the hymn of Liberty there.

This proposal is passed.

The Convention marches with the People to the Temple of

Reason in the midst of general enthusiasm and joyful acclamations.

Having entered the Temple of Reason, they sing the following hymn, with words by Chénier, a representative of the People, and with music by Gossec:

> Descend, O Liberty, daughter of Nature:
> The People have recaptured their immortal power;
> Over the pompous remains of age-old imposture
> Their hands raise thine altar.
> Come, vanquishers of kings, Europe gazes upon you;
> Come, vanquish the false gods.
> Thou, holy Liberty, come dwell in this temple;
> Be the goddess of the French.
> Thy countenance rejoices the most savage mountain,
> Amid the rocks harvests grow:
> Embellished by thy hands, the harshest coast,
> Embedded in ice, smiles.
> Thou doublest pleasures, virtues, genius;
> Under thy holy standards, man is always victorious;
> Before knowing thee he does not know life;
> He is created by thy glance.
> All kings make war on the sovereign People;
> Let them henceforth fall at thy feet, O goddess;
> Soon on the coffins of the world's tyrants
> The world's peoples will swear peace.
> Warrior liberators, powerful, brave race,
> Armed with a human sword, sanctify terror;
> Brought down by your blows, may the last slave
> Follow the last king to the grave.

39. November, 1793: Père Duchesne, His Plebeian Appeal

Jacques René Hébert was one of those who found their vocations in the revolution. Hébert found his talent, which was that of a journalist and was superior to his ability as a political leader, which fell short of his ambition. The real Hébert is hard to find behind the mythical figure he used as his spokesman and the name of his newspaper, *Père Duchesne*, mythical because he was already known to the crowds at plebeian fairs in Paris, the way the puppet Guignol is still known to French children, as a corrector of injustice. Père Duchesne was a fierce and honest sans-culotte stove merchant whose foul language, great angers, and great joys as he surveyed the scene of the revolution became known, through Hébert's talent, to some 10,000 readers, or purchasers—many of whom read aloud to others—of the paper. Hébert—himself an educated man of bourgeois origin who in his youth had failed to find a profession and, from living among the lower classes, had learned their language and aspirations and hates—followed Marat's example and became an even better reflection of the mentality of the crowds. His fame carried him only as far in politics as the assistantship to the prosecutor of the Commune of Paris, but by expressing sans-culotte views he and the Hébertists were able, in the fall and winter of 1793 to 1794, to challenge the leadership of the Jacobin politicians of the Convention, vulnerable in the great city, as the Girondins had been. The Hébertists were not the only leaders of the sans-culottes, but they were among those who exacerbated the problem, already posed, of the relationship of the national representation to the city population: they contributed to the coming of the Terror, and it was used against them in March, 1794, when Hébert and his close associates were guillotined.

As Père Duchesne appears below, in No. 313, in late November or possibly early December 1793 (the issues of the paper are not dated), he is speaking to an audience of sans-culottes whose power has won a number of concessions from the Convention but whose relationship to the national political leaders has not been fully worked out. This issue of *Père Duchesne* has been chosen from the many of that winter because of the author's way of communicating with his audience, which was the source of his strength but was to be his undoing; the radical political, social, and religious posture of Hébert and others like him was attracting unfavorable attention from the leaders of the Mountain, who disapproved of it and were threatened by it. François Chabot, a former Capucin monk who had become one of the more violent members of the Mountain, was already in prison; he was suspected of embezzlement in collaboration with his wife's brothers, who were Austrian barons, but he was also, like Hébert, considered a potential leader of radical opposition to Robespierre and the Committee of Public Safety. Hébert at this time had been warned that the Robespierrists were out to get him too. Here is the title page of Hébert's No. 313: *La grande Colère du père Duchesne, contre le frocard Chabot, qui veut mesurer tous les Sans-Culottes à son aulne, et qui fait courir le bruit par les autrichiens qui lui graissoient la patte, que les meilleurs Jacobins vont siffler la linotte avec lui, et que le marchand de fourneax [sic] sera bientôt mis à l'ombre, comme s'il existoit encore un comité des douze. Sa grande joie de voir que la mine est éventée, et que tous les fripons qui ont volé et pillé le peuple, vont avoir les ongles rognés. Je suis le véritable père Duchesne, foutre!* (s.l.n.d., 8 pp.).

The Great Anger of Père Duchesne Against the Monk Chabot,
Who Wants to Measure All the Sans-Culottes According
to His Own Bushel, and Who Spreads Rumors Started by the
Austrians Who Grease His Palm That the Best Jacobins
Are Going to Be Jailed Along with Him, and That the Merchant
of Stoves Will Soon Be Put in the Shade, as if There
Still Existed a Committee of Twelve. His Great Joy to See
That the Mine Is Discovered, and That All the Rogues
Who Have Robbed and Plundered the People Are Going
to Have Their Nails Chewed. I Am the Genuine
Père Duchesne, foutre![1]

IF THE ARISTOCRATS were as strong as they are sly, it is ten to one, *foutre,* that for a long time now they would have had their foot on our throat. They are not so stupid as to squabble among themselves like the Sans-Culottes; they don't eat the white of each other's eyes as we do; they are united not like brothers but like robbers who need each other to steal from the passers-by and join forces when they pull a job. They all have a single wish, to cut our throats. Never have they been known to betray each other, nobody gives away the show, because for them it's either counterrevolution or the guillotine. And so, *foutre,* for their own interest, for their lives even, they are obliged to walk straight along the path of crime.

Thunder of God, can it be that the love of patriotism is not as powerful in the souls of republicans as the hatred of liberty in counterrevolutionaries? Have not the Sans-Culottes a thousand times more reason to uphold their cause than the aristocrats to defend despotism? What would become of us all, such as we are, if the crowned brigands could force us to give in. The *jean-foutres* who play both ends against the middle, can they flatter themselves that they would be spared? They would be the first to be stretched, for no one would do them the favor of shortening them. Their score would be settled and the vile slaves commanded by Coburg would begin by giving each of these jackasses a horse's nightcap; in other words, they would first be given a rope around the neck and then suspended at all the street corners. You will not escape either, you cowardly villains who after having fattened yourselves

1. Literally, in vulgar usage, fuck, or semen, but the exclamatory form common in the eighteenth century is difficult to translate, and so the French has been retained.—Editor.

on the blood of the people change sides when you have your hands full. You will be so many milch cows for our tyrants, and they will kill you like bears, in order to have your skin.

It grates on me to see a bunch of swindlers build castles in Spain, sacrifice honor and country, and defy the national razor to become rich. What good is wealth? He who has much gold and *assignats*, can he dine twice? Ah, *foutre*, if one could read the inner souls of all the buggers who have piled coin on coin to garnish their strongboxes; if one could know the anxieties of all these niggards who would kill a louse to have its skin, if one saw them always on the lookout and never sleeping except with one eye open, paralyzed to the marrow of their bones at the least noise, calling for mercy when they hear some decree bawled out against monopolizers, tearing their hair when an effort is made to force the rich to loose their purse strings to help their country, burying their gold, dying of fright at the very name of the revolutionary army—is there anywhere in the world such a punishment? What a difference, *foutre*, between the lot of this miserable creature and that of the brave Sans-Culotte who lives from day to day by the work of his hands! As long as he has a loaf of four pounds in his bread bin and a glass of spirits, he is happy. From early morning, he is bright as a pinch mark, and at break of day he takes up his tools while singing the carmagnole; when he has worked hard all day, he goes in the evening to relax at the section, and when he appears among his brothers he is not regarded as a werewolf and he does not see every Tom, Dick, and Harry whisper and point at him as an aristocrat, a moderate. One holds out his hand to him; another slaps him on the shoulder while asking him how goes it. He has no fear of being denounced; he is never threatened with domiciliary visits. He goes everywhere with his head high. In the evening when he enters his garret, his wife leaps on his neck, his little brats come to caress him, his dog jumps to lick him. He recounts the news he has learned in his section. He is joyful as a bugger as he tells about a victory over the Prussians, the Austrians, the English; he relates how a traitorous general, a Brissotin, has been guillotined; by citing the example of the rogues, he makes them promise to be good citizens always and to love the republic above all things. He then sups with the appetite of a bugger, and after his meal he entertains his family by reading to them "The Great Anger or the Great Joy of Père Duchesne." His wife laughs herself hoarse while listening to the disputes of my Jacqueline with the religious bigots who weep for their ousted saints. The little brats split their sides on hearing the "buggers" and the *"foutre's"* with which I lard my discourses. Ah! what a joker he must be, Père Duchesne, says the tall son. He has big mustaches, cries the little girl. Does he hurt little children, says the younger brother; yes, *foutre*, cries the papa, he carries them away in his great pocket when they wet the bed, and when they are very good and shout long live the republic, he hugs them and gives them some almond biscuits and spice bread.

There is the life, there are the enjoyments of the true Sans-Culotte. Having thus passed the day, he goes to bed tranquilly and snores all night long; whereas, *foutre*, the surveillance committee goes to pay a visit at midnight to the onetime nobles, nobles of the robe, and financiers. You should hear the cries of the whole brood when Monsieur Skinflint or Monsieur Pinchpenny is requested to do his packing in a shoe and leave his gilded apartment and his feather bed to go and try out the equality of the grand hotel of beans otherwise known as Madelonettes.

Can it be, *foutre*, that when one is free to choose between these two one can take the wrong path? But, as they say, it is the opportunity that makes the thief. A Sans-Culotte in office is surrounded, like Saint Anthony, by a million devils. One presents him with heaps of gold, the other handfuls of *assignats;* once the first step is taken, my poor Job will go no farther without limping, until he has broken his neck. Nearly always some she-devil in furbelows excites the employer on her sofa. Is it not true, lascivious Chabot, that one does not resist such a trial; you can tell us all about it, as well as you, popinjay Bazire, and you too, Julien the apostate of Sans-Culotterie, you who have just made a hole in the moon. What then was your hope, miserable featherbrains? So close to port, and you have been shipwrecked?

The same *jean-foutres* who have greased your palms and who have found the real Jacobins impervious are in despair at seeing the mine exposed, and are seeking, like Samson, to bury themselves along with the patriots under the ruins of the temple. They are spreading the rumor that Père Duchesne has been denounced by Chabot. Everywhere I am greeted with these remarks; already there has even been a rumor that I am in prison. I have laughed at this with all my heart and I have asked whether there still exists a Committee of Twelve. But, *foutre*, there is no fire without smoke. You threaten me, infamous monk, in order to frighten me and prevent me from blabbing about you. You are furious that I will no more let myself be Chaboted than I have let myself be Brissoted. It was not for nothing, I see now, that you so many times offered me soup and a cutlet in order to acquaint me with your gypsy. I was not anxious to have my fortune told. I did not fall into the snare; for I do not trust monks any more than converted Austrians. Moreover, I defy you to cast reflections on me. I am ironclad, and anyone can turn and return my stoves, examine my whole life, and can see whether I am a genuine republican. Meanwhile, perfidious monk, I will no more overlook your hood than I will old Roland's horned head. The wine is drawn, one must drink it, *foutre*.

40. February 5, 1794 (17 Pluviôse, An II): Robespierre's Report on the Principles of Political Morality

This selection is one of Robespierre's major speeches. On November 18, 1793, he had delivered a long statement on foreign policy. Now he turned to a formal summation on domestic affairs which was nothing less than a doctrine of what the revolution was about and what its objectives should be, a statement in which he attempted to define as clearly as possible both constitutional government and revolutionary government, and in so doing revealed his convictions about the nature of man and of the good society. Although Robespierre obviously meant this speech to be a serene and permanent codification of revolutionary purposes, its later passages give way to more immediate concerns and indicate what pressures he and the Committee of Public Safety were under; the speech changes its character and becomes a political offensive that is as revealing in its way as the earlier passages are in theirs. In the following, translated from *Rapport sur les principes de morale politique qui doivent guider la Convention nationale dans l'administration intérieure de la République, fait au nom du Comité de salut public, le 18 [sic] pluviôse, l'an 2ᵉ de la République, par Maximilien Robespierre. Imprimé par ordre de la Convention nationale* (Paris, Imprimerie nationale [s.d.], 31 pp. in 8°), the entire statement of principles, amounting to the first half of the pamphlet, has been retained, and also its seven concluding paragraphs. Between these two major parts of the speech, a few scattered passages and one block of seven pages of denunciation of the tactics of enemies of the revolution have been omitted; they add little to the charges that have not been omitted, but their existence testifies to Robespierre's growing concern with varieties of opposition.

CITIZENS, representatives of the people,

Some time ago we presented to you the principles of our foreign policy; we come before you today to develop the principles of our domestic policy.

After having for a long time proceeded by chance and as we were carried along by the actions of contending factions, the representatives of the French people have finally displayed character and produced a government. A sudden change in the success of the nation announced to Europe the regeneration which had taken place in the national representation. But to this very moment when I am speaking, we were, it must be admitted, guided through such stormy circumstances more by a love of the good and by awareness of the needs of our country than by an exact theory and precise rules of conduct, which we had not the leisure even to sketch.

It is time to state clearly the purpose of the revolution and the point which we wish to attain. It is time for us to render an accounting to ourselves both of the obstacles which still separate us from that objective and of the means which we must adopt to attain it: a simple and important consideration which appears never to have been grasped. Indeed, how could a cowardly and corrupt government have dared to conceive of it? A king, a proud senate, a Caesar, a Cromwell must first of all cover their designs with a religious veil, compromise with every vice, caress every party, destroy that of men of probity, oppress or deceive the people in order to attain the aim of their perfidious ambition. If we had not had a greater task to accomplish, if our only concern were with the interests of a faction or to create a new aristocracy, we could have believed, like certain writers who are even more ignorant than they are depraved, that the plan of the French revolution was to be found in the works of Tacitus and Machiavelli, and sought the duties of the representatives of the people in the history of Augustus, of Tiberius, or of Vespasian, or even in that of certain French legislators; for, apart from a few trifling shades of perfidy or cruelty, all tyrants resemble each other.

For our part, we come today to let the whole world share your political secrets, so that all friends of the *patrie* may rally at the voice of reason and public interest; so that the French nation and its representatives may be respected in all the countries of the world to which knowledge of their true principles may penetrate; so that the intriguers who always seek to supplant other intriguers may be judged by public opinion according to reliable and clear rules.

Every precaution must be taken in advance to place the interests of freedom in the hands of truth, which is eternal, rather than in those of men, who change; so that if the government forgets the interests of the people or falls into the hands of corrupt men, according to the natural course of things, the light of acknowledged principles will reveal their treasons, and so that every new faction will see that such crimes mean its own death.

Happy the people that can attain this stage! For whatever new outrages are plotted against them, what resources are not presented when public reason is the guarantee of liberty!

What is the objective toward which we are reaching? The peaceful enjoyment of liberty and equality; the reign of that eternal justice whose laws are engraved not on marble or stone but in the hearts of all men, even in the heart of the slave who has forgotten them or of the tyrant who disowns them.

We wish an order of things where all the low and cruel passions will be curbed, all the beneficent and generous passions awakened by the laws, where ambition will be a desire to deserve glory and serve the *patrie;* where distinctions grow only out of the very system of equality; where the citizen will be subject to the authority of the magistrate, the magistrate to that of the people, and the people to that of justice; where the *patrie* assures the well-being of each individual, and where each individual shares with pride the prosperity and glory of the *patrie;* where every soul expands by the continual communication of republican sentiments, and by the need to merit the esteem of a great people; where the arts will embellish the liberty that ennobles them, and commerce will be the source of public wealth and not merely of the monstrous riches of a few families.

We wish to substitute in our country morality for egotism, probity for honor, principles for usages, duties for good manners, the empire of reason for the tyranny of fashion, contempt for vice for contempt for misfortune, pride for insolence, character for vanity, the love of glory for the love of money, good people for good company, merit for intrigue, genius for wit, the truth for pretentiousness, the charm of happiness for the boredom of sensuality, the grandeur of man for the pettiness of the great; a magnanimous, powerful, happy people for one that is amiable, frivolous, and miserable; in a word, all the virtues and miracles of the republic for all the vices and absurdities of the monarchy.

We wish, in a word, to fulfill the intentions of nature and the destiny of humanity, realize the promises of philosophy, and acquit providence of the long reign of crime and tyranny. We wish that France, once illustrious among enslaved nations, may, while eclipsing the glory of all the free peoples that ever existed, become a model to nations, a terror to oppressors, a consolation to the oppressed, an ornament of the universe; and that, by sealing our work with our blood, we may witness at least the dawn of universal happiness—this is our ambition, this is our aim.

What kind of government can realize these prodigies? A democratic or republican government only; these two terms are synonymous notwithstanding the abuse of common language; for aristocracy is no more the republic than is monarchy. A democracy is not a state where the people, always assembled, regulate by themselves all public affairs, and still less one where one hundred thousand portions of the people, by measures that are isolated, hasty, and contradictory, would decide the fate of the whole society: such a government has never existed and could not exist except to return the people to despotism.

A democracy is a state where the sovereign people, guided by laws of their own making, do for themselves everything that they can do well, and by means of delegates everything that they cannot do for themselves.

It is therefore in the principles of democratic government that you must seek the rules of your political conduct.

But in order to found democracy and consolidate it among us, in order to attain the peaceful reign of constitutional laws, we must complete the war of liberty against tyranny and weather successfully the tempests of the revolution; such is the aim of the revolutionary government that you have organized. You must therefore still regulate your conduct by the stormy circumstances in which the republic finds itself, and the plan of your administration should be the result of the spirit of the revolutionary government combined with the general principles of democracy.

And what is the fundamental principle of a democratic or popular government; in other words, what is the mainspring which supports it and gives it motion? It is virtue; I speak of the public virtue which produced so many prodigies in Greece and Rome, and which should produce still more wonderful prodigies in republican France; of that virtue which is nothing else than love of the *patrie* and its laws.

But as the essence of the republic or of democracy is equality, it follows that love of one's country necessarily includes love of equality.

Again, it is true that this sublime passion supposes a preference for the public interest over all private considerations; whence it results that love of country still supposes or produces all the virtues; for what are they but a strength of soul which makes possible such sacrifices, and how could the slave of avarice or ambition, for example, sacrifice his idol to his country's welfare?

Not only is virtue the soul of democracy, but it can exist in no other government. In a monarchy, I know of only one individual who can love his country, and who for this does not even need virtue; it is the monarch. The reason is that of all the inhabitants of his dominions the monarch alone has a *patrie*. Is he not sovereign at least in practice? Does he not assume the prerogative of the people? And what is the *patrie* if it is not the country where one is a citizen and a member of the sovereign?

By a natural consequence of this principle, in aristocratic states the word *patrie* means nothing for any but the patrician families who have usurped the sovereignty.

It is only in democracies that the state is truly the *patrie* of all the individuals who compose it, and can count as many defenders of its cause as there are citizens. This is the source of the superiority of free people over all others. If Athens and Sparta triumphed over the tyrants of Asia, and the Swiss over the tyrants of Spain and Austria, no other cause need be sought.

But the French are the first people in the world who have established true democracy by calling all men to equality and to full enjoyment of the rights of citizenship; and that is, in my opinion, the true reason why all the tyrants leagued against the republic will be vanquished.

There are from this moment great conclusions to be drawn from the principles that we have just laid down.

Since virtue and equality are the soul of the republic, and your aim is to found and to consolidate the republic, it follows that the first rule of your political conduct must be to relate all of your measures to the maintenance of equality and to the development of virtue; for the first care of the legislator must be to strengthen the principles on which the government rests. Hence all that tends to excite a love of country, to purify moral standards, to exalt souls, to direct the passions of the human heart toward the public good must be adopted or established by you. All that tends to concentrate and debase them into selfish egotism, to awaken an infatuation for trivial things, and scorn for great ones, must be rejected or repressed by you. In the system of the French revolution, that which is immoral is impolitic, and that which tends to corrupt is counterrevolutionary. Weakness, vices, and prejudices are the road to monarchy. Carried away, too often perhaps, by the force of ancient habits, as well as by the tendency of human nature to be attracted by false ideas and pusillanimous sentiments, we have much less need to defend ourselves from excesses of energy than from excesses of weakness. The most dangerous shoal that we have to avoid is not perhaps warmth of zeal but rather that lassitude which ease produces and a distrust of our own courage. Therefore tighten continually the spring of republican government, instead of letting it run down. I need not say that I am not here justifying any excess. The most sacred principles may be abused; the wisdom of government should take account of circumstances, time its measures, choose its means; for the manner of preparing for great accomplishments is an essential part of the talent for producing them, just as wisdom is itself an attribute of virtue.

We do not claim to model the French Republic after that of Sparta; we wish to give it neither the austere manners nor the corruption of a cloister. We have just presented to you the essence of the moral and political principle of a popular government. You have, therefore, a compass to direct you through the tempest of the passions and the whirlwind of the intrigues that surround you. You have the touchstone with which you can test all your laws, all the propositions that are laid before you. By comparing them always with this principle, you may henceforth avoid the rock on which large assemblies usually split, the danger of being taken by surprise, and of hasty, incoherent, and contradictory measures. You can give to all your actions the systematic unity, the wisdom, and the dignity that should characterize the representatives of the first people of the world.

There is no need to detail the obvious consequences of the principle of democracy; it is the principle itself, simple yet fruitful, which deserves to be developed.

Republican virtue may be considered in relation to the people and in relation to the government: it is necessary in both. When the government alone lacks it, there remains the resource of the people's virtue; but when the people themselves are corrupted, liberty is already lost.

Fortunately virtue is natural in the people, aristocratic prejudices notwithstanding. A nation is truly corrupt when, after having, by degrees, lost its character and liberty, it passes from democracy to aristocracy or monarchy; this is the death of the political body by decrepitude. When, after four hundred years of glory, avarice at length drove from Sparta the moral standards and laws of Lycurgus, Agis died in vain to restore them; Demosthenes in vain thundered against Philip; Philip found in the vices of degenerated Athens advocates more eloquent than Demosthenes. There is still as great a population in Athens as in the time of Miltiades and Aristides, but there are no more Athenians. What does it matter that Brutus has killed the tyrant? Tyranny still lives in people's hearts, and Rome survives only in the person of Brutus.

But when, by prodigious efforts of courage and reason, a people breaks the chains of despotism to make trophies to liberty out of the pieces; when, by the force of moral vigor, they rise, in some manner from the arms of death, to resume all the strength of youth; when, by turns sensitive and proud, intrepid and docile, they can be checked neither by impregnable ramparts nor by innumerable armies of tyrants leagued against them, and yet of themselves they stop before the image of the law; if they do not rise rapidly to the height of their destiny, it can only be the fault of those who govern them.

Besides, there is a sense in which it may be said that to love justice and equality the people need no great virtue; it is sufficient that they love themselves.

But the magistrate is obliged to sacrifice his interest to that of the people, and the pride of office to equality. The law must speak with special authority to those who are its organs. The power of the government must be felt by its own agents to keep all its parts in harmony with the law. If there is a representative body, a primary authority constituted by the people, it is the duty of that body to superintend and repress continually all public functionaries. But what will keep *it* within proper bounds other than its own virtue? The more exalted this source of public order is, the purer it must be; the representative body must therefore begin by subjecting all its own private passions to a general passion for the public good. Happy the representatives when their glory and their own interests attach them as much as their duty to the cause of liberty.

Let us deduce from all this an important truth: that the character of a popular government is to place its confidence in the people and be severe toward itself.

Here the development of our theory would stop if you had only to pilot the vessel of the republic in fair weather; but the tempest howls, and the revolutionary condition in which you now find yourselves imposes another task upon you.

This great purity of the principles of the French revolution, the very sublimity of its aim, is precisely what constitutes our strength and our weakness; our strength because it gives us the ascendancy which truth has over imposture, and the rights of the public interest over private interests; our weakness, because it rallies against us all the vicious men, all those who in their hearts meditated the plundering of the people, and all those who wish their former plunderings to go unpunished, and all those who have rejected liberty as a personal calamity, and those who have embraced the revolution as a trade and the republic as a prey: hence the defection of so many ambitious and greedy men who since the point of departure have abandoned us on the road, because they had not undertaken the journey to arrive at the same goal. It would appear that the two opposite geniuses who have been represented as disputing the empire of nature are combating in this great epoch of human history to shape irrevocably the destiny of the world, and that France is the theater of this fearsome contest. Externally all the despots surround you; internally all the friends of tyranny conspire; they will conspire until crime is deprived of all hope. It is necessary to annihilate both the internal and external enemies of the republic or perish with its fall. Now, in this situation your first political maxim should be that one guides the people by reason, and the enemies of the people by terror.

If the driving force of popular government in peacetime is virtue, that of popular government during a revolution is both *virtue and terror:* virtue, without which terror is destructive; terror, without which virtue is impotent. Terror is only justice that is prompt, severe, and inflexible; it is thus an emanation of virtue; it is less a distinct principle than a consequence of the general principle of democracy applied to the most pressing needs of the *patrie.*

It has been said that terror is the spring of despotic government. Does yours, then, resemble despotism? Yes, as the swords that flash in the hands of the heroes of liberty resemble those with which the satellites of tyranny are armed. Let the despot govern his debased subjects by terror; he is right as a despot: conquer by terror the enemies of liberty and you will be right as founders of the republic. The government of the revolution is the despotism of liberty against tyranny. Is force only intended to protect crime? And is it not the destiny of lightning to strike prideful heads?

Nature imposes on every physical and moral being the law of self-preservation; crime butchers innocence in order to reign, and innocence struggles with all its might in the grip of crime. Let tyranny reign a single day and not one patriot will survive on the morrow. How much longer will the madness of despots be called justice, and the justice of the people barbarism or rebellion? How tenderly oppressors are treated and how pitilessly the oppressed! Nothing more natural: whoever does not abhor crime cannot love virtue.

Yet one or the other must be crushed. Indulgence for the royalists, cry certain people. Mercy for the villains! No! Mercy for innocence, mercy for the weak, mercy for the unfortunate, mercy for humanity!

The protection of society is due only to peaceable citizens: there are no citizens in the republic except the republicans. The royalists and conspirators are nothing but foreigners to the republic —or, rather, enemies. This terrible war of liberty against tyranny— is it not indivisible? Are not internal enemies the allies of external enemies? The assassins who rip to pieces the interior of the *patrie*, the intriguers who purchase the consciences of mandataries of the people; the traitors who sell them; the mercenary journalists paid to dishonor the cause of the people, to kill public virtue, to fan the flame of civil discord, and bring about a political counterrevolution by means of a moral one—all these men, are they less guilty or less dangerous than the tyrants they serve? All those who interpose their parricidal leniency between these villains and the avenging sword of national justice resemble those who would throw themselves between the satellites of the tyrant and the bayonets of our soldiers; all the transports of their false sensibility appear to me nothing but sighs for the success of England and Austria. . . .

* * *

With such affable weakness we are still being duped by words! How the aristocracy and the moderates still govern us by the murderous maxims to which they have accustomed us!

Aristocracy defends itself better by intrigues than patriotism defends itself by its services. The revolution is being run legalistically, and conspiracies against the republicans are treated as if they were the lawsuits of private persons. Tyranny kills and liberty sues; and the code framed by the conspirators themselves is the law by which they are judged. . . .

To punish the oppressors of humanity is clemency, and to pardon them is uncivilized. The severity of tyrants has nothing but severity for its principle; that of a republican government is founded on beneficence.

And so misfortune to him who would dare to direct against the people the terror which should be applied only to their enemies! Misfortune to him who, confusing the inevitable errors of patriotism with the premeditated crimes of treason or the attempts of conspirators, lets the dangerous intriguer escape and pursues the peaceful citizen! Death to the villain who dares abuse the sacred name of liberty, or the fearful weapons intended for her defense, in order to carry mourning or death to the hearts of patriots! This abuse has existed, it cannot be doubted. It has certainly been exaggerated by the aristocracy; but if in the whole republic there were but one virtuous citizen persecuted by the enemies of liberty, the duty of the government would be to search for him anxiously and avenge him promptly and energetically. . . .

How shortsighted it would be to regard a few victories achieved by patriotism as the end to all our dangers. Examine our real situation, and you will see that your vigilance and energy are more necessary than ever. A secret opposition everywhere hinders the operations of the government; the fatal influence of foreign courts, though hidden, is no less active and no less damaging. One senses that crime, intimidated, has only covered its tracks with more cunning.

The internal enemies of the French people are divided into sections which are like two army corps. They march under banners of different colors, and by different roads; but they march toward the same objective; this objective is the disorganization of the popular government and the ruin of the Convention; that is, the triumph of tyranny. One of these two factions is pushing us toward feebleness, the other toward excesses. The one wishes to transform liberty into a bacchante, the other into a prostitute.

Subordinate intriguers, frequently even good citizens who have been misled, take one or the other side; but the chiefs belong to the cause of royalty or aristocracy and always cooperate against the patriots. Swindlers, even when at war with one another, hate each other less than they detest all honest men. The *patrie* is their prey; they fight to divide it, but they band together against those who defend it.

One of these factions has been called the moderates; there is perhaps more wit than truth in the appellation of *ultra-revolutionaries* by which the others have been designated. This appellation, which can in no case be applied to men of good intentions who are sometimes carried by zeal or ignorance beyond the bounds of good revolutionary policies, does not characterize exactly the perfidious men who are paid by tyrants to compromise by false or damaging applications the sacred principles of our revolution. . . .

What is the remedy for all these evils? We know of no other than the development of that general principle of the republic—virtue.

Democracy perishes from two kinds of excess, the aristocracy of those who govern or contempt on the part of the people for the authorities that they themselves have established, a contempt which makes each coterie, or each individual, try to get control of the public force, and which leads the people, through an excess of disorder, either to annihilation or to the despotism of one man.

The double task of the moderates and the false revolutionaries is to bandy us eternally between these two shoals.

But the representatives of the people can avoid them both, for the government is always capable of being just and wise, and when it has these characteristics it is certain of the confidence of the people.

It is very true that the aim of all our enemies is to dissolve the Convention; it is true that the tyrant of Great Britain and his allies promise their parliament and their subjects to deprive you of your energy and of the public confidence which it has earned for you, and that this is the first instruction given to all their agents.

But there is a truth which should be regarded as a maxim in politics, that a great body having the confidence of a great people can only be destroyed by its own misconduct. Your enemies are aware of this; therefore do not doubt that they are trying above all to awaken among you all the passions which can help their sinister designs.

What can they do against the national representation unless they succeed in influencing the adoption of impolitic measures which may furnish pretexts for their criminal declamations? They must therefore necessarily wish to have two kinds of agents, one of which seeks to degrade it by their speeches, while the other, in its very bosom, will strive to deceive it in order to compromise its glory and the interests of the republic. . . .

They had at first adopted the policy of aiming straight for their objective by slandering the Committee of Public Safety; at that time they predicted openly that the committee would collapse under its painful burdens; but the victories and good fortune of the French people defended it. Since that time they have adopted the tactic of praising it while attempting to paralyze it and destroy the fruits of its labors. All these vague declamations against the necessary agents of the committee, all the plans of disorganization disguised under the appellation of reforms already rejected by the Convention and again brought forward with a strange affectation; this eagerness to praise intrigues that the Committee of Public Safety has had to thwart; this terror inspired in good citizens, this indulgence with which conspirators are treated, this whole system of imposture and intrigue whose principal author is a man you have expelled from among you—all this is directed against the National Convention and tends to realize the wishes of all the enemies of France.

It is since the time when this system was announced in libelous writings and began to be put into practice that aristocracy and royalism have begun to raise their insolent heads, that patriotism has again been persecuted throughout the republic, that the national authority has experienced an opposition of which intriguers were beginning to lose the habit. Moreover, even if these indirect attacks had had no other inconvenience than to divide the attention and energy of those who have to bear the immense burden with which you have entrusted them, and to distract them too often from great measures of public safety and preoccupy them with counteracting dangerous intrigues, they could still be considered as a diversion useful to our enemies.

But let us be reassured; this is the sanctuary of truth; here sit the founders of the republic, the avengers of humanity, the destroyers of tyrants.

Here, to destroy an abuse it is sufficient to point it out. It is enough for us to appeal, in the name of our country, from the persuasions of self-love or the weakness of individuals to the virtue and glory of the National Convention.

We call for a solemn discussion of all aspects of these anxieties and of everything that can influence the progress of the revolution. We conjure it to permit no private and hidden interest to usurp here the place of the general will of the assembly and the inde-structible power of reason.

We shall limit ourselves today to proposing that you sanction with your formal approbation the moral and political truths on which your internal administration and the stability of the republic should be founded, as you have already sanctioned the principles of your conduct toward foreign nations; you will thereby reassure all good citizens, you will deprive the conspirators of hope; you will assure your further progress and will confound the intrigues and calumnies of the kings; you will do honor to your cause and to your character in the eyes of all peoples.

Give to the French people this new pledge of your zeal in protecting patriotism, of your inflexible justice toward the guilty, and of your devotion to the cause of the people. Order that the principles of political morality that we have just developed be pro-claimed in your name within and beyond the borders of the republic.

41. February 26, March 3, 1794: Saint-Just on the Ventôse Decrees

In 1789, Louis Antoine de Saint-Just, son of a retired cavalry officer, was twenty-two. In 1791, at twenty-four, he published a book called *Esprit de la révolution et de la constitution de France*. The next year, at twenty-five, he was elected to the Convention, where his first speech was an indictment of Louis XVI. During the Terror, Saint-Just was as tireless and unbending as Robespierre, whom he admired and whom he resembled in having a vision of a democratic society that entailed not merely a free play of all the existing social forces by way of a democratic suffrage but the creation of a kind of new personality capable of maintaining such a society. Saint-Just expressed these ideas in a manuscript that was not published until after his death, his *Institutions républicains*, a more radical conception of the tasks of the revolution than his *Esprit* of 1791. Besides serving as a representative on mission, Saint-Just bore a great part of the political burden of maintaining the ascendancy of the Committee of Public Safety in the Convention and that of the Convention in Paris and in the country at large. In the documents below, he is to be seen introducing social legislation that the historian Mathiez regarded as the key to the long-range program of the Robespierrists, the Ventôse decrees, one of the most controversial aspects of the Terror, difficult to interpret but extremely important because of the problem of how to retain and use political power in the circumstances of 1794. Saint-Just speaks twice, once on 8 Ventôse (February 26) and again on 13 Ventôse (March 3), and on each occasion introduces a decree. The source is the pamphlet printed by order of the Convention, recording the speeches and the decrees: *Rapports de Saint-Just, au nom des comités de salut public et de sûreté générale, et décrets de la Convention nationale, relatif aux personnes incarcérées. Des 8 et 13 Ventôse, l'an 2 de la République française une et indivisible. Imprimés par ordre de la Convention nationale* (s.l.n.d., 23 pp.). Pages 1–5, 7, and 10–23, which have been translated, contain the basic argument; the passages deleted are condemnations of other regimes in history that were more bloody than the Terror, or of the motives of the Indulgents.

You HAVE DECREED, the fourth of this month, that your two committees joined together of Public Safety and General Security should make you a report on the detentions, on the most concise methods of recognizing and freeing innocent persons and persecuted patriots, as well as of punishing the guilty.

I do not wish to deal with this question before you as if I were accuser or defender, or as if you were judges: for the detentions did not originate in judicial relations, but in the question of security for the people and the government. I do not wish to speak of the storms of a revolution as if they were a dispute of orators, and you are not judges, and you do not have to make up your minds in terms of a civil interest, but in terms of the safety of the people, which takes precedence over us.

It is still necessary to be just; but instead of being so in accordance with a particular interest, it is necessary to be so according to the public interest.

You therefore have less occasion to decide concerning what matters to such-and-such an individual than to decide concerning what is important to the Republic; less responsibility to make concessions to private views than to make universal views triumph.

The detentions encompass several political questions: they have to do with the constitution and strength of the sovereign; they have to do with republican values, with virtues or vices, with the happiness or the distress of future generations; they have to do with your economy through the idea that you find suitable to hold concerning wealth and possessions; principles forgotten until today, unrecognized relationships, yet without which our Republic would be a dream from which the awakening would be its breakup. The detentions are related to the progress of reason and justice. Review the periods which brought them about. One has proceeded, with respect to the rebellious minority, from scorn to suspicion, from suspicion to setting examples, from setting examples to the terror.

To the detentions is linked the defeat or the triumph of our enemies. I do not know how to express my thought by halves; I am without indulgence for the enemies of my country; I know only justice.

It is perhaps not possible to treat the detentions with any solidity or fruitfulness, or even to make myself comprehensible, without at the same time surveying our situation.

Does an empire sustain itself by its own weight, or must there be a profoundly conceived system of institutions to give it harmony? A society whose political relationships are unnatural, where interest and avarice are the hidden motors of many men thwarted by opinion and who try to corrupt everything in order to evade justice—must not such a society make the utmost efforts to purify itself if it wishes to survive? And those who wish to prevent it from purifying itself, do they not wish to corrupt it? And those who wish to corrupt it, do they not wish to destroy it?

In a monarchy, there is only one government; in a republic, there are, in addition, institutions, whether for exerting pressure on moral standards, whether for stopping corruption of the laws or of men. A state where these institutions are lacking is only an illusory republic; and since in such a case each person means by his liberty the independence of his passions and of his avarice, the spirit of conquest and egoism is established among the citizens, and the private idea that each forms of his own liberty, according to his interest, produces the slavery of all.

We have a government; we have this commonplace of Europe which consists of powers and a public administration; *the institutions that are the soul of the Republic* we lack.

We do not have civil laws that consecrate our well-being, our natural relationships, and destroy the elements of tyranny; a part of the youth is still brought up by the aristocracy, which is powerful and opulent; the foreigner, who has tried to corrupt talent, still seems to want to wither our hearts. We are inundated with writings: there intolerant and fanatical atheism is deified; one would think that the priest had become an atheist and that the atheist had become a priest: there is no need to speak further about this! We need energy, and delirium and weakness are proposed to us.

The foreigner has only one means of destroying us: it is to pervert us and corrupt us, since a republic can be based only on nature and on morals. It is Philip who stirs Athens; it is the foreigner who wishes to re-establish the throne, and who responds to our words, which fly away, by great crimes which remain with us.

When a republic has tyrants for neighbors and is agitated by them, it needs strong laws; it has no use for gentle treatment of the partisans of its enemies, or even of indifference.

It is the foreigner who officiously defends criminals.

The natural agents of this perversity are the men who, from motives of vengeance and personal interests, make common cause with the enemies of the Republic.

You wanted a republic; if you did not at the same time want what is needed to constitute it, the people will be buried under its wreckage. What constitutes a republic is the total destruction of what is opposed to it. There are complaints about revolutionary measures; but we are moderates in comparison with all the other governments. . . .

The monarchy, jealous of its authority, swam in the blood of thirty generations; and you would hesitate to show yourselves severe against a handful of guilty? Those who demand liberty for the aristocrats do not want the Republic, and fear for them. It is a glaring sign of treason, the pity that is shown for crime in a Republic that can be founded only on inflexibility. I defy all those who speak in favor of the imprisoned aristocracy to expose themselves to a public accusation in a tribunal. Can the voices of criminals and of men depraved and corrupt be counted in judging their fellows? . . .

Our aim is to create an order of things such that a universal bent toward the good is established; such that the factions suddenly find themselves flung onto the scaffold; such that a vigorous energy disposes the spirit of the nation toward justice; such that we obtain in the interior the calm necessary for establishing the happiness of the people; for it is only, as in the time of Brissot, the aristocracy and the intriguers who bestir themselves; the popular societies are not agitated, armies are calm, the people work; it is thus entirely enemies who are agitating, and who are agitating to overthrow the revolution. Our objective is to establish a sincere government, such that the people will be happy; such, finally, that with wisdom and eternal providence alone presiding at the founding of the Republic, it will no longer be shaken every day by a new atrocity.

Revolutions proceed from weakness to audacity and from crime to virtue. It is not necessary that one boast of establishing a solid empire without difficulties; it is necessary to wage a long war on all pretensions, and as human interest is invincible, it is rarely by other means than the sword that the liberty of a people is founded.

At the start of the revolution, indulgent voices were raised in favor of those who combated it: this indulgence which spared a few of the guilty then has since cost the lives of 200,000 men in the Vendée; this indulgence has obliged us to raze cities, has exposed the *patrie* to total ruin, and if today you were to allow yourselves to give way to the same weakness, it would eventually cost you thirty years of civil war.

It is difficult to establish a republic other than by the inflexible censuring of all crimes. Never would Précy, never would Larouerie and Paoly have created a faction under a jealous and rigorous government. Jealousy is necessary to you: you have not the right to be either merciful or sensitive where treason is involved; you are not working on your own account but for the people. Lycurgus had this idea in his heart when, after having established the well-being of his country with a pitiless rigidity, he exiled himself.

To see the indulgence of some, one would believe them to be the owners of our destinies, and the pontiffs of liberty. Our history, since last May, is an example of the terrible extremities to which indulgence leads. At that time Dumouriez had evacuated our conquered territories; the patriots in Frankfurt had been stabbed. Custine had delivered Mayence, the Palatinate, and consequently the course of the Rhine: Calvados was aflame; finally the Vendée was triumphant; Lyon, Bordeaux, Marseille, Toulon had revolted against the French people. Condé, Valenciennes, Le Quesnoy had been surrendered; we were undergoing misfortunes in the Pyrenees, at Mont-Blanc. All the world was betraying you, and no one seemed any longer to take responsibility for governing the state and commanding the troops except to surrender them and prey upon what was left. The fleets were betrayed; the arsenals and vessels in ashes; the money debased, foreigners masters of our banks and our industry, and the greatest of our misfortunes of that time was a tendency to fear to use the authority necessary to save the state; with the result that the conspiracy of the Right had broken in advance by means of an outrageous trap the weapons with which you would one day have been able to combat them and punish them: these are the weapons that they still want to break.

The constitution rallied the sovereign. You mastered fortune and victory, and you finally deployed against the enemies of liberty the energy that they had deployed against you: for, while to you scruples about defending the country would be suggested, Précy, Charette, and all the conspirators were blowing out the brains of those who were not of their opinion and refused to join their forces; and those who were trying to unnerve us do nothing and propose nothing to unnerve our enemies; to listen to them, one would believe that Europe is tranquil and is levying no troops against us; to listen to them, one would believe that the frontiers are as peaceful as our public squares.

Citizens, they want to bind you and to brutalize us in order to make our defeats easier. To see with what indulgence they talk to you about the fate of the oppressors, one would be tempted to believe that they are scarcely embarrassed at the prospect of our being oppressed.

Such is the behavior of the new factions; they are not audacious, because there exists a tribunal capable of delivering sudden death; but they lay siege to all the principles and wither the body politic. Long since they attacked us by main force; today they want to undermine us through maladies of languidness: for that is the character of the Republic since it degenerated from the tautness to which it was carried by the punishment of Brissot and his accomplices; in those days you were conquerors everywhere; in those days the cost of living fell and the exchange regained some value.

The pace of the revolutionary government that had established the dictatorship of justice has slackened; one might think that the hearts of the guilty and of their judges, frightened by the examples that have been set, have come to a secret understanding in order to put justice on ice and escape from its effects.

One might think that each, frightened by his conscience and by the inflexibility of the laws, has said to himself: We are not virtuous enough to be so terrible; philosopher legislators, take pity on my weakness; I do not dare to say to you, I am vicious; I prefer to say to you, you are cruel.

It is not with such maxims that we will acquire stability. I have told you that the system of the Republic was linked to the destruction of the aristocracy.

In fact, the force of things perhaps leads us to results about which we have not thought. Opulence is in the hands of a rather large number of enemies of the revolution; need places working people in a position of dependence on their enemies. Do you think that an empire can exist if its civil relationships develop into new forms that are in opposition to the form of government? Those who half make revolutions only dig their own graves. The revolution is teaching us to recognize the principle that he who has shown himself to be an enemy of his country cannot be a proprietor there. We still need some strokes of genius if we are to be saved.

Is it, then, to safeguard the enjoyments of their tyrants that the people shed their blood on the frontiers, and that all families are in mourning for their children? You will acknowledge this principle: that he alone has rights in our country who has cooperated in its liberation. Abolish the begging that dishonors a free state; the property of patriots is sacred, but the goods of conspirators are there for all the unfortunate. The unfortunate are the powers of the earth; they have the right to speak as masters to the governments which neglect them. These principles are subversive of corrupt governments; they would undermine yours if you were to let it be corrupted: destroy injustice and crime, then, if you do not want them to destroy you.

It is also necessary to call to your attention ways of providing a solid basis for democracy and representation. The governmental machinery and all that is intermediary between the people and you is stronger than you and the people.

If you pass a general law that calls the whole nation to arms, your law is carried out and the whole nation takes up arms. If you issue a decree against a general, against a particular abuse of government, you will by no means always be obeyed. This condition comes from the feebleness of the legislation, from its vicissitudes, and from dishonorable propositions in favor of the aristocracy, which corrupt opinion. It comes from the impunity of the bureaucrats and from the fact that in the popular societies the people are spectators of the bureaucrats instead of judging them; from the fact that a thousand intrigues are competing with the agencies of justice, which do not dare to strike. The more the bureaucrats put themselves in the people's place, the less democracy there is. When I attend the meeting of a popular society, when my eyes are on the people who applaud and who are seated in the second row, what reflections afflict me! The society of Strasbourg, when Alsace was lost to the enemy, was composed of bureaucrats who scorned their duties. It was a central committee of accountable agents who, disguised as patriots, made war on the revolution. Put everything in its place; equality is not in powers useful to the people, but in men; equality does not consist in everyone's having pride, but in everyone's having modesty.

I dare to say that the Republic would soon be flourishing if the people and their representatives had the principal influence, and if the sovereignty of the people were purged of the aristocrats and officials who seem to usurp it in order to acquire impunity. *Is there any hope of justice when the evildoers have the power to condemn their judges,* says William: let nothing evil be either pardoned or unpunished in the government, and justice will be more fearful to enemies of the Republic than terror alone. How many traitors have escaped a terror which merely talks who would not escape from a justice which weighs crimes in its hand! Justice condemns enemies of the people and partisans of tyranny among us to eternal slavery. Terror lets them hope for an end to it; for all tempests come to an end, and you have seen this; justice condemns civil servants to integrity; justice makes the people happy and consolidates the new order of things; terror is a two-edged weapon which some have used to avenge the people and others to serve tyranny; terror has filled the prisons, but the guilty are not punished; the terror has passed by like a thunderstorm. Do not look for lasting severity in the public character except from the strength of institutions; a dreadful calm always follows our tempests, and we are also always more indulgent after terror than before it.

The authors of this depravity are the indulgent who do not bother to call anyone to account because they are afraid that the same would be done to them; thus, through a tacit transaction among all the vices, the *patrie* finds itself sacrificed to the interests of individuals instead of all private interests being sacrificed to the interest of the *patrie*.

Marat had some good ideas about representative government which I regret he took away with him; only he could have expressed them; only necessity will permit their being heard from the lips of another.

There has been a revolution in government; it has not by any means penetrated to the level of civil affairs. The government is based on liberty, but civil relationships depend on the aristocracy, which forms between the people and you an intermediate rank of enemies of liberty: can you remain far from the people, your only friend?

Compel the intermediaries to a rigorous respect for the national representation and for the people. If these principles could be adopted, our country would be happy, and Europe would soon be at our feet.

How long will we go on being dupes, both of our domestic enemies through misguided indulgence and of the foreign enemies whose projects we encourage through our feebleness?

Spare the aristocracy, and you will prepare fifty years of troubles for yourselves. *Dare*—this word contains the whole policy of our revolution.

The foreigner wishes to reign over our country through discord; let us stifle that discord by sequestering our enemies and their partisans. Let us return war for war: our enemies cannot resist us much longer; they make war on us in order to destroy each other. *Pitt wants to destroy the house of Austria, the latter wants to destroy Prussia, all of them together want to destroy Spain; and this frightful and false alliance wants to destroy the European Republics.*

As for you, destroy the rebel faction; toughen liberty; avenge the patriot victims of intrigue; make good sense and modesty the order of the day; do not permit there to be an unhappy or poor person in the state: it is only after paying this price that you will have made a real revolution and a true republic. Ah! Who would be grateful to you for the misfortune of the good and the good fortune of the wicked?

Decree

The National Convention, after having heard the joint report of the Committees of Public Safety and General Security, decrees that the Committee of General Security is invested with the power to set free all imprisoned patriots. Every person who demands his liberty shall give an accounting for his conduct since the first of May, 1789.

The property of the patriots is inviolable and sacred. The property of persons recognized as enemies of the revolution shall be sequestered for the profit of the Republic; those persons shall be detained until the peace, and thereafter banished in perpetuity.

The report as well as the present decree shall be printed and sent immediately, by special messengers, to the departments, the armies, and the popular societies.

Certified by the inspector,
[Signature] s. e. MONNEL

Report on the Method of Execution
of the Decree Against the Enemies of the Revolution,
Made in the Name of the Committee of Public Safety,
by Saint-Just, 13 Ventôse, Year II of the Republic.
Printed by Order of the National Convention.

CITIZENS,

I present to you, in the name of the Committee of Public Safety, the method of execution of the decree issued the eighth of this month against the enemies of the revolution.

It is very generally felt that the whole wisdom of government consists in reducing the party opposed to the revolution and in making the people happy at the expense of all the vices and of all the enemies of liberty.

The way to strengthen the revolution is to turn it to the profit of those who support it and to the ruin of those who combat it.

Identify yourselves in your minds with the secret aspirations of all hearts; leap over the intermediary ideas that separate you from the objective toward which you tend. It is better to hasten the progress of the revolution than to follow after it and be at the mercy of all the plots that embarrass and fetter it. It is up to you to determine its plan and to precipitate its results for the benefit of humanity.

Let the rapid course of your policies sweep up all of the foreign intrigues. When you strike a great blow, it reverberates on the thrones and in the hearts of all kings. Laws and measures of detail are pinpricks that hardened imperviousness does not feel.

Make yourselves respected by announcing with pride the destiny of the French people; avenge the people for twelve hundred years of crimes against their ancestors.

The people of Europe are being deceived about what is happening in our country; your discussions are misrepresented, but strong laws are not to be misrepresented; they penetrate foreign countries with the suddenness of an inextinguishable flash of light.

Let Europe learn that you want no more unfortunates, and no more oppressors on French territory; let this example bear fruit in the whole world; let it propagate the love of virtue and happiness. Happiness is a new idea in Europe.

DECREE

The National Convention, on the basis of the report of the Committee of Public Safety, decrees:

Article I. All the communes of the Republic will prepare lists of the indigent patriots resident therein, with their names, ages, professions, and the number and ages of their children. The district directories will send these lists to the Committee of Public Safety in the shortest possible time.

II. When the Committee of Public Safety has received these lists, it will make a report on the means of indemnifying all these unfortunates from the properties of the enemies of the revolution, according to the table that the Committee of General Security will have presented to it, and which will be made public.

III. Consequently, the Committee of General Security will give precise orders to all the committees of surveillance of the Republic, so that, within a time limit that it will set for each district according to its remoteness, these committees shall report to it respectively the names and the conduct of all the prisoners since the first of May, 1789. It will do the same for those who will be detained later.

IV. The Committee of General Security will add instructions to the present decree to facilitate its execution.

Certified by the inspector.
[Signed] MONNEL

42. May 7, 1794 (18 Floréal, An II):
Robespierre's Report on
Religious and Moral Ideas
and Republican Principles

It would be difficult to choose between Robespierre's report of February 5, 1794, on the Principles of Political Morality, and this report of May 7, 1794, on Religious and Moral Ideas and Republican Principles. They are the two most comprehensive statements of his principles, designed to be so, but at the same time both are like action photographs of political acts, caught and held forever in their juxtaposition of the loftiest principles with the coldest, most merciless attacks on his opponents. This latter aspect of the speeches cannot be overlooked, and it is perhaps misleading to omit chiefly passages of this kind, but both speeches are so lengthy that some omissions have been necessary. With this qualification, one may say that the principal ideas have been retained in this major document as in its predecessor. In the case of the present report of May 7, 1794, this form of presentation has been somewhat more difficult but, it is hoped, just as effective. In addition to some—though by no means all—attacks on opponents, certain passages in praise of martyrs of the revolution, and a number of historical references, have been omitted; the deletions have been indicated by dots in the text and, where a whole paragraph or more is affected, by extra spacing; whereas, to avoid confusion, the dots placed by Robespierre himself for rhetorical effects have been omitted. The source is the speech as printed by order of the Convention: *Convention nationale. Rapport fait au nom du Comité de salut public, par Maximilien Robespierre, sur les rapports des idées religieuses et morales avec les principes républicains, et sur les fêtes nationales. Séance du 18 floréal, l'an second de la République française une et indivisible* (Paris, s.d., 45 pp.). The pages translated are 1–7, 9, 11–12, 13–14, 15, 16–20, 21–31, 34, 35.

CITIZENS,

It is in prosperity that peoples, as well as individuals, should, in a manner of speaking, retire within themselves to listen, with passions stilled, to the voice of reason. The moment in which the clamor of our victories resounds throughout the world is therefore one in which the legislators of the French Republic should, with new solicitude, watch over themselves and their country, and strengthen the principles upon which its stability and its happiness must depend. We come today to submit for your consideration profound truths which are essential to the welfare of mankind, and to propose to you measures which are their natural result.

The moral world, far more than even the physical world, seems full of contrasts and enigmas. Nature tells us that man was born to be free, and the experience of centuries shows him to be a slave. His rights are written in his heart, and his humiliation in history. The human race reveres Cato, and bends beneath the yoke of Caesar. Posterity honors the virtue of Brutus but accepts it only in ancient history. The centuries and the earth are the legacy of crime and tyranny; liberty and virtue have had only a momentary existence on a few points of the globe. Sparta shines like a flash of lightning across the enormous darkness.

But do not say, O Brutus, that virtue is a phantom! And you, founders of the French Republic, take care not to despair of mankind, or to doubt for one instant the success of your great enterprise!

The world has changed, it must change again. What is there in common between what *is* and what *was?* Civilized nations have succeeded the wandering savages of the deserts; fertile harvests have taken the place of the ancient forests that once covered the globe. A world has appeared beyond the limits of the world; the inhabitants of the earth have added the seas to their immense domain. Man has conquered the very lightning and redirects its course. Compare the imperfect language of hieroglyphics with the miracles of printing, or the voyage of the Argonauts with that of La Pérouse; calculate the distance between the astronomical observations of the Asian Magi and the discoveries of Newton, or between the sketch traced by the hand of Dibutade, and the pictures of David.

Everything has changed in the physical order; everything must change in the moral and political order. Half the revolution of the world is already accomplished; the other half must be achieved.

Man's reason still resembles the globe he inhabits; half of it is plunged in darkness when the other is enlightened. The peoples of Europe have made astonishing progress in what are called arts and sciences, and they seem in ignorance of the first notions of public morality. They know everything except their rights and their duties. What is the origin of this mixture of genius and stupidity? The explanation is that to seek to become expert in the arts, we need only to follow our passions, whereas to defend our rights and respect those of others we must vanquish passions. There is still another reason, which is that the kings who decide the destiny of the world fear neither great mathematicians, nor great painters, nor great poets, but dread stern philosophers and defenders of humanity.

The human race, however, is in a state of violence which cannot last. Human reason has, for a long time, been marching against thrones, with slow steps and along roads that are winding but sure. Genius menaces despotism even when it seems to caress it; today despotism is scarcely guarded any longer except by habit and by terror, and above all by the support it receives from the league of the wealthy and of all the subaltern oppressors who shrink from the imposing character of the French revolution.

The French people seem to have outdistanced by two thousand years the rest of the human race; one is tempted to consider the French as a different species in the midst of mankind. Europe is on its knees before the shadows of the tyrants whom we are punishing.

In Europe a peasant, an artisan, is an animal tamed for the pleasures of a noble; in France the nobles seek to transform themselves into peasants and artisans, and cannot even obtain that honor.

Europe does not see how one can live without kings, without nobles; and we how one can live with them.

Europe lavishes its blood to fasten the chains of mankind, and we shed ours to break them. . . .

Yes, this delightful land which we inhabit, and which nature caresses with special affection, is made to be the domain of liberty and of happiness; this sensitive and proud people were indeed born for glory and for virtue. O my country! If fate had placed my birth in a distant and foreign region, I would have addressed to heaven unceasing wishes for your prosperity; I would have shed tears of sensibility at the recital of your struggles and your virtues; my attentive soul would have pursued with restless ardor all the events of your glorious revolution; I would have envied the destiny of your citizens; I would have envied that of your representatives. I am French, I am one of your representatives. O sublime people! Receive the sacrifice of my whole being: happy is he who is born in your midst! Still happier he who can die for your well-being!

O you to whom your country has confided its interests and its power, what can you not achieve with it and for it! Yes, you can show the world the unprecedented spectacle of democracy established in a vast empire. Those who, in the infancy of the public law, and on the breast of servitude, have babbled contrary maxims, did they foresee the prodigies that have been performed in the past year? Is what you still must do any more difficult than what you have done? Who are the statesmen who can serve you as teachers or models? Must you not do precisely the contrary of everything that has been done before you? The art of government has been until our day the art of deceiving and corrupting men: it must be nothing other than that of enlightening them and making them better.

There are two kinds of egotism: one, base and cruel, which isolates a man from his fellows, which seeks an exclusive well-being purchased by the misery of others; the other kind, generous and beneficent, which blends our happiness with the happiness of all, which attaches our glory to that of our country. The first forms oppressors and tyrants; the second defenders of mankind. Let us follow its healthy impulse; let us cherish the repose purchased by glorious labors; let us not at all fear the death that crowns them, and we will consolidate the happiness of our country, and even our own.

Vice and virtue shape the destiny of the earth; they are the two conflicting geniuses which dispute its empire. The sources of both are in the passions of men. According to the direction given to his passions, man lifts himself to the skies or plunges into a slimy abyss. Now the objective of all social institutions is to direct men toward justice, which is at once public happiness and private happiness.

The only foundation of civil society is morality! All of the associations which are making war on us are based on crime: in the eyes of truth they are nothing but hordes of polished savages and disciplined brigands. To what, then, is this mysterious science of politics and legislation reduced? To inserting into the laws and into the administration the moral truths that have been relegated to the books of philosophers, and to applying to the conduct of peoples the everyday notions of probity which everyone is obliged to adopt for his private conduct; that is to say, to employ as much skill in forming the reign of justice as governments have hitherto employed in being unjust with impunity or urbanity.

And so observe how much artifice kings and their accomplices have used to avoid the application of these principles, and to obscure every notion of right and wrong! How perfect was the good sense of that pirate who answered Alexander, "They call me a robber because I have only one ship; and you, because you have a fleet, are called a conqueror!" With what effrontery they make laws against theft while they are invading the public fortune! Assassins are condemned in their name, and they assassinate millions of men by war and poverty. . . .

What conclusion should be drawn from what I have just said? That immorality is the basis of despotism, as virtue is the essence of the republic.

The revolution, which tends to establish it, is simply the passage from the reign of crimes to that of justice; hence the unceasing efforts of the kings leagued against us, and of all the conspirators, to perpetuate among us the prejudices and vices of the monarchy.

All who regretted the passing of the old regime, all who threw themselves into the career of the revolution only to effect a change of dynasty have labored from the beginning to check the progress of public morality. . . .

They could not say to the people, the son of the tyrant, or another Bourbon, or one of the sons of King George would make you happy; but they said, You are miserable. They drew for the people the picture of the very famine which they themselves were seeking to bring about; they told them that eggs and sugar were not abundant. They did not tell them that liberty was of some worth; that the humiliation of their oppressors and all the other effects of the revolution were not benefits to be scorned; that they were still in the heat of the battle; that only the ruin of their enemies could secure their happiness; but all this the people sensed. In short, they could not enslave the French people by force or by their own consent, and they tried to enchain them by means of subversion, revolt, and corruption of their morals.

They raised immorality not merely into a system but into a religion. They attempted to extinguish all natural religious sentiments by their example as well as by their precepts. In their hearts the wicked wished that not a single good man would be left on earth, so that they would never meet with a single accuser, and would be able to breathe in peace. They went in search of whatever serves as the support of morality in people's minds and hearts, in order to eliminate it and stifle the invisible arbiter that nature has hidden there. . . .

* * *

What was the aim of those who, in the midst of the conspiracies which surrounded us, in the midst of the perplexities of such a war, at the very moment when the torches of civil discord were still smoking, suddenly attacked with violence all forms of religious worship and set themselves up as the fiery apostles of the void and the fanatical missionaries of atheism? What was the motive of that great operation plotted in the darkness of night, without the knowledge of the National Convention, by priests, by foreigners, and by conspirators? . . .

They were serving the cause of the kings leagued against us, of the kings who had themselves predicted these events and successfully taken advantage of them to excite against us by manifestoes and public prayers the fanaticism of the peoples. . . .

Consult only the good of the *patrie* and the interests of mankind. Every institution, every doctrine which consoles and which elevates souls should be welcomed; reject all those which tend to degrade and corrupt them. Reanimate, exalt all of the generous sentiments and all of the great moral ideas which your enemies have tried to destroy; draw together by the charm of friendship and the ties of virtue the men they have attempted to separate. Who, then, gave you the mission of announcing to the people that the Divinity does not exist, O you who are enamored of this arid doctrine but were never enamored of the *patrie?* What advantage do you find in persuading mankind that a blind force presides over their destiny and strikes crime and virtue at random, and that the soul is only a faint breath which is extinguished at the gates of the tomb?

Will the idea of his nothingness inspire man with pure and more elevated sentiments than that of his immortality? Will it inspire more respect for his fellows and for himself, more devotion to his country, more audacity with which to resist tyranny, more contempt for death or for sensuality? You who regret a virtuous friend, you love to think that the noblest part of his being has escaped death! You who weep over the coffin of a son or of a wife, are you consoled by him who tells you that nothing remains of them but a vile dust? Unhappy victim expiring under the blows of an assassin, your last sigh is an appeal to eternal justice! Innocence on the scaffold makes the tyrant pale in his triumphal chariot: would virtue have this ascendancy if the tomb made equals of the oppressor and the oppressed? Wretched sophist! By what right do you come to wrest the scepter of reason from the hands of innocence, to place it in the hands of crime, to cast a funereal veil over nature, to make misfortune despair, to make vice rejoice, to sadden virtue, to degrade humanity? The more a man is endowed with sensibility and genius, the more he clings to ideas which reinforce his being and elevate his heart; and the doctrine of such men becomes that of the universe. Ah, how could those ideas not be truths? At least I cannot conceive how nature could have suggested to mankind fictions more useful than all the realities; and if the existence of God and the immortality of the soul were only dreams, they would still be the most sublime conceptions of the human mind.

I need not observe that there is no question here of attacking any particular philosophical opinion, or of denying that a given philosopher may be virtuous whatever his opinions, or even in spite of them by the strength of a happy disposition, or a superior reason. It is a question here of considering atheism only in relation to the needs of the nation, and as linked to a system of conspiracy against the republic.

For what do they matter to you, legislators, the various hypotheses by which certain philosophers explain the phenomena of nature? You may leave those subjects to the everlasting disputes in which they are involved: it is not as metaphysicians or theologians that you must envisage them. In the eyes of the legislator whatever is useful to the world, and good in practice, is truth.

The idea of the Supreme Being and the immortality of the soul is a continual recall to justice; it is therefore social and republican. Nature has implanted in man the feelings of pleasure and pain, which oblige him to flee from physical objects that are harmful to him and to seek those which are suitable to his condition. The masterpiece of society would be to create in him, for questions of morals, a swift instinct which, without the tardy aid of reasoning, would impel him to do good and avoid evil; for the individual reason, led astray by the passions, is often merely a sophist who pleads their cause, and the rule of conduct prescribed by man can always be attacked by man's self-love. Now, what produces or replaces this precious instinct, what makes up for the insufficiency of human authority, is the religious sentiment which imprints in people's souls the idea of a sanction given to the precepts of morality by a power superior to man. And so I know of no legislator's ever recommending national atheism; I know that even the wisest of them have been willing to blend a few fictions in with the truth, either to strike the imaginations of ignorant peoples or to attach them more firmly to their institutions. Lycurgus and Solon had recourse to the authority of oracles; and Socrates himself, in order to impress truth upon the minds of his fellow citizens, thought it necessary to persuade them that he was inspired by a familiar genius.

You will not conclude from all this, no doubt, that it is necessary to deceive men in order to instruct them, but only that you are happy to be living in a century and in a country whose enlightenment leaves you no other task to fulfill than that of recalling men to nature and to the truth.

You will take care not to break the sacred tie that unites them to the author of their being. It is enough even that this opinion has prevailed among a people for its destruction to be dangerous. For, the motives to duty and the bases of morality being necessarily linked to this idea, to efface it is to make the people immoral. From the same principle it results that one must never attack an established mode of worship except with prudence and a certain delicacy, lest a sudden and violent change should appear to be an attack on morality, and even a dispensation from common honesty. What is more, he who can replace the Deity in the system of social life is in my eyes a prodigy of genius; he who without having replaced it only seeks to banish that idea from men's minds seems to me a prodigy of stupidity or perversity.

What had the conspirators substituted for that which they were destroying? Nothing except chaos, emptiness, and violence. They despised the people too much to take the trouble of persuading them; instead of enlightening them, they only wished to irritate, alarm, or deprave them. . . .

. . . It will be useful to glance at this period [immediately preceding our revolution] if only to explain more fully some of the phenomena which have since occurred.

For a long time acute observers were able to perceive symptoms of the present revolution. Every important event tended toward it; even individual affairs of some importance became connected with political intrigues. Men of literary reputation, by virtue of their influence on public opinion, were beginning to have influence in public affairs. The most ambitious had formed a sort of coalition, which was increasing their importance; they appeared to be divided into two sects, one of which stupidly defended the clergy and despotism. The more powerful and celebrated was that known as Encyclopedists. It included a few estimable men and a great number of ambitious charlatans. Several of its leaders had become important personages in the state: anyone ignorant of this sect's influence and policies would have an incomplete idea of the prelude to our revolution. In political questions, they always fell short of doing justice to the rights of the people; in treating moral questions they went much further than the destruction of religious prejudices. Their *coryphaei* sometimes declaimed against despotism, and they were pensioned by despots; at one moment they wrote books against the court, and at another dedications to kings, treaties for courtiers, and madrigals for courtesans; they were proud in their writings and servile in the antechambers. This sect propagated with much zeal the opinion of materialism, which was the prevailing doctrine among the wellborn and the clever. To them we owe in great part this form of practical philosophy which, reducing egotism to a system, views human society as a contest of guile, success as the rule of right and wrong, honesty as a matter of taste or good manners, and the world as the patrimony of adroit swindlers. I have said that this sect and its imitators were ambitious; the commotions which announced a great change in the political order of things had been able to enlarge their views. It has been remarked that many among them had intimate connections with the House of Orléans; and the English constitution was, in their opinion, the masterpiece of politics and the *maximum* of social well-being.

Among those who, at the time of which I am speaking, were celebrated as literary men and philosophers, there was a man who by his nobleness of soul and greatness of character showed himself worthy of being the teacher of mankind. He attacked tyranny openly; he spoke with rapture of the Deity; his manly and dignified eloquence painted, in glowing colors, the charms of virtue and defended those consoling dogmas which reason supplies to support the human heart; the purity of his doctrine, drawn from nature and from a profound hatred of vice, as well as his invincible scorn for the intriguing sophists who usurped the name of philosophers, drew upon him the hatred and persecution of his rivals and of his false friends. Ah! If he had been a witness of this revolution whose precursor he was and which has placed him in the Panthéon, who can doubt that his generous soul would have embraced with transport the cause of justice and equality? But what have his cowardly adversaries done for this cause? They have opposed the revolution from the moment they feared that it would raise the people above all private vanities; some have employed their talents to dilute republican principles and corrupt public opinion; they have prostituted themselves to factions, and especially to the Orléans party; the others have taken refuge in a cowardly neutrality. In general the men of letters have dishonored themselves in the course of this revolution; and, to the eternal shame of the talented, the reason of the people has by itself borne the whole burden.

Vain and trivial men, blush, if it is possible. The prodigies which have immortalized this period of human history have been performed without you and in spite of you; good sense without intrigue and genius without education have carried France to this degree of elevation which terrifies your meanness and confounds your nothingness. This artisan has shown himself proficient in knowledge of the Rights of Man, while that maker of books, half republican in 1788, stupidly defended the cause of kings in 1793. This peasant was shedding the light of philosophy in the countryside when the academician Condorcet—formerly a great geometrician, so they say, in the opinion of men of letters, and a great man of letters in the opinion of geometricians, since a timid conspirator, despised by all parties—was laboring continually to obscure it by the profusion of his perfidious and mercenary rhapsodies.

You have no doubt been struck with the tenderness with which so many men who have betrayed their country have embraced the sinister opinions which I now combat. . . . What is the origin of this singular agreement of principles among so many men who appeared to be divided? Must it be attributed merely to the care taken by the deserters of the cause of the people to hide their treachery behind pretended zeal against what they called religious prejudices, as if they wished to compensate for their indulgence toward aristocracy and tyranny by declaring war against the Deity?

No, the conduct of those artful personages was no doubt connected with more profound political views; they sensed that to destroy liberty it was necessary to favor by all means whatever tended to justify egotism, to dry up the heart, and to efface the idea of that sublime morality which is the only rule by which the public reason judges the defenders and the enemies of humanity. They joyfully embraced a system which, confounding the destinies of the good and the wicked, leaves no other distinction between them than the precarious favors of fortune, and no other arbiter than the right of the strongest and the most cunning.

You wish to attain a much different objective; you will therefore follow a contrary policy. But is there no danger of reawakening fanaticism and giving an advantage to the aristocracy? No, if we adopt the measures which wisdom dictates, it will be easy for us to avoid this danger.

Enemies of the people, whoever you may be, the National Convention will never favor your perversity. Aristocrats, whatever specious appearance you may wish to hide behind today, in vain would you seek, in the name of our censure against the authors of a criminal plot, to accuse sincere patriots who could only have been led into indiscretions by their hatred of fanaticism. You do not have the right to accuse; and national justice, in the midst of these storms excited by factions, knows how to distinguish errors from conspiracy. It will seize with a sure hand all the perverse intriguers and will not strike a single man of worth.

Fanatics, expect nothing from us! To recall men to the pure cult of the Supreme Being is to strike a mortal blow at fanaticism. All fictions disappear before truth and all follies vanish before reason. Without constraint, without persecution, all sects should blend of their own accord in the universal religion of nature. We will therefore advise you to maintain the principles that you have hitherto manifested. Let religious liberty be respected, for this is the triumph of reason; but let it not disturb public order, and let it in no way become a means of conspiracy. If counterrevolutionary malignity hides behind this pretext, repress it; and place your confidence, besides, in the power of principles, and in the very force of circumstances.

Ambitious priests, do not expect, then, that our labors tend to re-establish your empire; such an enterprise would even be beyond our power. You are your own assassins, and men do not come back to life morally any more than they do physically.

And besides, what is there in common between priests and God? Priests are to morality what charlatans are to medicine. How different is the God of nature from the God of priests! Nothing so nearly resembles atheism as the religions they have constructed. By misrepresenting the Supreme Being they have, insofar as it was in their power to do so, annihilated Him; they have made of Him sometimes a ball of fire, sometimes an ox, sometimes a tree, sometimes a man, sometimes a king. The priests have created God after their own image: they have made Him jealous, capricious, greedy, cruel, and implacable. They have treated Him as the mayors of the palace once treated the descendants of Clovis in order to reign in his name and put themselves in his place. They have relegated Him to the heavens as to a palace, and have only called Him down upon earth to demand for their benefit tithes, riches, honors, pleasures, and power. The true high priest of the Supreme Being is nature; his temple the universe; his cult virtue; his festivals the joy of a great people assembled under his eyes to tighten the gentle bonds of universal fraternity, and to present Him the homage of pure and feeling hearts.

Priests, by what title have you proved your mission? Have you been more just, more modest, more the friends of truth than other men? Have you cherished equality, defended the rights of peoples, abhorred despotism, and thrown down tyranny? It is you who have said to kings: *You are the images of God on earth; from Him alone you derive your power.* And the kings have answered you: *Yes, you are truly the messengers of God; let us unite to divide the spoils and the adoration of mortals.* The scepter and the miter have conspired to dishonor heaven and to usurp the earth.

Let us leave the priests and return to the Divinity. Let us attach morality to eternal and sacred foundations; let us inspire in man that religious respect for man, that deep sentiment of his duties, which is the only guarantee of social well-being; let us nourish it by all our institutions; let public education be, above all, directed toward this end. You will without doubt impress on it a lofty character, analogous to the nature of our government and to the sublimity of the destinies of the republic. You will feel the necessity of rendering education general and equal for all the French. It is no longer a question of forming gentlemen but citizens: the *patrie* alone has the right of rearing its children; it cannot confide this trust to the pride of families or to the prejudices of individuals, which provide eternal nourishment to aristocracy and to a domestic federalism that contracts souls by isolating them and destroys, together with equality, all the foundations of the social order. But this great object is foreign to the present discussion.

There is, however, one kind of institution which must be considered as an essential part of public education, and which necessarily belongs to the subject of this report: I wish to speak about national festivals.

Assemble men together and you will make them better; for men assembled together will seek to please each other, and thus will only be able to please each other by those qualities which make them

estimable. Give a great moral and political motive to their meeting
and the love of what is right will enter their hearts along with the
sentiment of pleasure; for men do not meet together without
pleasure.

Man is the greatest object that exists in nature; and the most
magnificent of all spectacles is that of a great people assembled. One
never speaks without enthusiasm of the national festivals of Greece;
yet they had scarcely any other purpose than games that displayed
the strength and agility of the body—or, at most, the talents of
poets and orators. But Greece was there; there was a spectacle
greater than the games: it was the spectators themselves; it was the
people who had vanquished Asia, whom republican virtues had
sometimes elevated above ordinary humanity; the great men were to
be seen who had saved and glorified their *patrie:* fathers showed
their sons Miltiades, Aristides, Epaminondas, Timoleon, whose
presence alone was a living lesson of magnanimity, justice, and
patriotism.

How easy it would be for the French people to give to such
assemblies a broader objective and greater significance. A system of
well-organized national festivals would be at once the most gentle
of fraternal ties and the most powerful means of regeneration.

Institute general and most solemn festivals for the whole republic;
institute particular and local festivals which are days of rest and
which replace those that circumstances have destroyed.

Let all of them tend to awaken those generous sentiments which
are the charm and ornament of human life, and induce enthusiasm
for liberty, the love of country, and respect for the laws. Let the
memory of tyrants and traitors be here consigned to execration;
let that of the heroes of liberty and the benefactors of mankind
here receive the just tribute of public gratitude; let the festivals
draw their interest, and even their names, from the immortal
events of our revolution, and from the objects most sacred and most
dear to the hearts of men; let them be embellished and distinguished
by emblems analogous to their immediate aims. Let us invite to our
festivals both nature and all the virtues; let all of them be celebrated
under the auspices of the Supreme Being; let them be so consecrated; let them be opened and closed with homage to his power
and goodness.

You will lend your sacred name to one of our most glorious
festivals, O daughter of nature, mother of happiness and glory, only
lawful sovereign of the world, dethroned by crime, you to whom

the French people have restored your empire, and who give them in return a *patrie* and morals, august Liberty! You will share our sacrifices with your immortal companion, gentle and holy Equality. We will have a festival to Humanity, Humanity debased and trampled upon by the enemies of the French Republic. It will be an illustrious day when we celebrate the festival of the human race, that fraternal and sacred banquet to which, crowned by victory, the French people will invite the immense family whose honor and imprescriptible rights they alone defend. We will also celebrate all the great men of every age and every country who have freed their *patrie* from the yoke of tyrants and who by wise laws have founded liberty. You will not be forgotten, illustrious martyrs of the French Republic! You will not be forgotten, heroes who died for its cause! Who could forget the heroes of my country? France owes them liberty, and the universe will owe them its liberty. . . .

Misfortune to him who seeks to extinguish this sublime enthusiasm, and to stifle, by destructive doctrines, that moral instinct of the people which is the basis of all great actions! It is your duty, representatives of the people, to secure the triumph of those truths which we have been developing. . . .

X.

The Search for Stability After Thermidor

---

43. June 23, 1795:
Boissy d'Anglas on a New Constitution

It is not so much François Antoine Boissy d'Anglas who matters in the presentation of the following document, although he presented it to the Convention, speaking for the Committee of Eleven that prepared the Constitution of the Year III (1795). Boissy d'Anglas was one of the leaders of the Thermidorian Convention and of the Council of Five Hundred in the early years of the Directory; it had, indeed, been he who was presiding over the Convention on 1 Prairial, An III (May 20, 1795), to be faced with a bloody head on a pike during the last insurrection of the sans-culottes. It was he who was chosen by the committee to make the presentation of the constitution on June 23, 1795, an event which led to a month of discussion before the constitution was passed without all of the committee's recommendations in it. What is important in the following document is not any description of particular clauses; the commentary that Boissy d'Anglas delivered is 63 pages long without a listing of the clauses of the constitution. It is the fact that this document expresses the point of view of the majority of the Committee of Eleven that makes it important: one may say very important, for the Committee was expressing very well the current mood and hopes and ideas of the Thermidorian Convention and its explanation of why, having tolerated the Terror and accepted the Jacobin Constitution of 1793, it was embarking on a new course. What follows is a selection of eight passages from the speech, separated from each other by extra spacing, and chosen with an eye to their expression of the Committee's attitude concerning where they were in the revolution, and the main lines, as well, of their political and social philosophy. The document is *Discours préliminaire au projet de constitution pour la République française, prononcé par Boissy d'Anglas, au nom de la Commission des onze, dans la séance du 5 messidor, an 3. Imprimé par ordre de la Convention nationale* (Paris, Messidor, An III), pp. 2–3, 4–5, 10, 12–14, 21–25, 29–33, 36–38, 40.

. . . For six years, victims of the turmoils of the revolutions that have rent our unfortunate country, eyes fixed on an end that seemed to flee from us, weapons in our hands in order to conquer the liberty that everything conspired to tear from us, checked by all the prejudices, combated by all the vices, tormented by all the passions, we have labored more to destroy than to build; we have yielded more to popular impulse than we have directed it; we have fought more for the existence of France than for its welfare. At last the happy time has come when, ceasing to be the gladiators of liberty, we can be its true founders. I no longer see in this assemblage the scoundrels who used to sully it; the domes of this temple no longer ring with their bloody shouts, their perfidious propositions. Our deliberations are no longer paralyzed by the tyranny of the decemvirs, no longer distracted by the demagoguery of their accomplices. Their numerous fierce satellites, disarmed, vanquished, imprisoned, will no longer have the insolence to bring their daggers here and point out their victims among you. Only crime inhabits the prisons; industry and innocence have gone forth from them to revive agriculture and put new life into commerce. The flags suspended from our walls remind us of our victories, promise us more of them, and testify to the impotence of the kings united in a coalition against us. The ambassadors seated within these walls indicate to you the wish of the sanest part of Europe to see us end our labors worthily and take again among its states the elevated rank that belongs to us. I will by no means say, however, that all is tranquil around us, that all the factions are extinguished, that all hatreds have ceased, that all immoral men have disappeared, that all the careerists have been discredited, that all the ferocious men have suppressed their plots; but I will say that the French people have the tranquillity of strength; that they are fatigued, but not discouraged, by this long, terrible struggle of crime against virtue; that they know all their enemies; that after having already vanquished them, they have learned the secret of always defeating them; that they have no more than one weapon to use against their separate or concerted efforts, and this weapon is a wise, strong constitution. . . .

* * *

The French Revolution, which delirious ignoramuses ventured to call the work of a handful of factious writers; this revolution which they thought to destroy by gibes, corruption, intrigue, conspiracy, and sly and hidden maneuvers; this revolution which has over-whelmed all its enemies, and which has survived its own excesses, its own frenzies, is not the work of a few individuals but the result of enlightenment and civilization; it is the fruit of time and phi-losophy; it is the daughter of that heavenly art which multiplies with such rapidity and preserves for future generations all the conceptions of genius. Its principle was placed in the hearts of all men. Error, despotism, superstition, and ignorance hindered its development for a long time; but when the torch of the sciences, of the arts, and of reason came to dissipate these shadows, it was born in the light and, assuming an invincible force, soon inflamed all souls with the triple love for justice, liberty, and equality. . . .

It is painful for me to retrace for you its picture [that of the Terror]. Why can I not tear out these shameful, bloody pages of our history, and hide from the scrutiny of posterity those horrible times when France, bristling with prisons, covered with scaffolds, inundated with blood, torn apart by civil war, mutilated in its richest cities, in its most celebrated monuments, saw devastation and death hover over all of its communes! Why can I not bury in the shadows of oblivion those days when innocence was so many times massacred, families dispersed, decency outraged, fortunes handed over for pillaging, all talents, all virtues turned into crimes, and when the people's representatives themselves, condemned to being passive witnesses of so many heinous crimes, awaited each day the moment when their executioners would come to give orders for their torture!

But what am I saying? Citizens, far from veiling these mournful images, let us recall them ceaselessly; let these somber jails, these ferocious committees, these bloodthirsty Jacobins never leave our memories, and let these sad and terrible memories, like those protective lighthouses placed on our coasts for the safety of travelers, serve as a signal for statesmen, for friends of liberty in all countries and all times, for avoiding the shoals of anarchy, false patriotism, and the fanaticism of demagogues. . . .

. . . Oh! How different is this position from that of the two assemblies that preceded us! Whatever their principles may have been, they were forced to encourage the enthusiasm that knew no limits: we are permitted to listen to reason which wants no excesses. Because they were at war with the throne, which they undermined and which threatened them, and were always preoccupied with the destruction of two powerful corporations whose wealth and prestige made their overthrow as difficult as it was dangerous, the spirit of destruction had to preside over their system; the spirit of organization must direct ours. They had neither the time to choose nor the option of choosing the instruments and means available to them to fight their enemies; everything directs us to choose, and nothing hinders us from choosing our means and our instruments, and from brushing aside all that may be impure or dangerous. The institutions which were the most useful to them for defending the spirit of liberty, for electrifying the people, and for vanquishing despotism were for the same reason destructive of the new government that they had just established. And we who have just experienced the vice of these institutions, and who have nothing further to hope for in the way of aid from them, we can replace them with sound institutions whose continual effect is the maintenance of order and tranquillity. Finally, the Constituent and Legislative Assemblies, always fearful of the strength and vengeance of a rival power placed opposite and almost over them, believed themselves forced to promote the enthusiasm and even the excesses of patriotism and love for equality. Although they wished to dampen this zeal, they would have been afraid to extinguish it; in purging their defenders, they would have believed they were diminishing their strength; and it was only after the fall of the throne that the most enlightened representatives of the people, released from one peril, became aware of another and began to open their eyes to the dangers of the institutions created for their protection which could not fail before long to turn against their own authors. But this new peril escaped the notice of many people: circumstances were different but passions were still the same; the vibration of spirits was not ready to subside; royalty existed no longer, but its name still frightened, and the people, accustomed to applauding the patriotism of those who had attacked the old government, following the same impulsion, still treated as enemies those who wanted to consolidate the new government, while regarding as friends all those who sought to overthrow it through blind zeal or a baneful and perfidious ambition.

These moments have passed; we have traversed centuries of

errors, and today we can, profiting from our faults, from the misfortunes of the people, and from the crimes of our tyrants, attach ourselves to principles alone, and deduce from them all their consequences.

It is in this spirit, representatives of the people, that, according to your orders, we have examined the constitution of 1793 and have tried carefully to save all of it that could be useful and to modify or to change everything that could be contrary to your sole objective, the safety, liberty, and glory of the French people; but it is our duty to state to you that that constitution, conceived by ambitious men, drafted by schemers,[1] dictated by tyranny, and accepted through terror, is nothing other than the express preservation of all the elements of disorder, the instrument designed to serve the avidity of greedy men, the interest of turbulent men, the pride of the ignorant, and the ambition of usurpers. We declare to you with complete unanimity that that constitution is nothing other than the organization of anarchy, and we expect from your wisdom, patriotism, and courage that, instead of allowing yourselves to be deceived by vain words, you will be capable, after having immolated your tyrants, of burying their odious work in the same tomb that has swallowed them. . . .

. . . The Convention has reached the time when, rising above all private interests, false views, and petty ideas, it must abandon itself fearlessly to the impulse of its own enlightenment; it must have the courage to guarantee itself against the illusory principles of an absolute democracy and an equality without limits, which are incontestably the most formidable stumbling blocks in the way of true liberty.

Civil equality, in fact, is all that a reasonable man can claim. Absolute equality is a chimera; for it to exist, there would have to be

1. Saint-Just and Hérault-Séchelles were the principal drafters of the constitution of 1793. The principles of the first are well known, and those of the second will be appreciated after the reading of the letter that he wrote to the Society of Jacobins of Newbrissac, 2 Frimaire, An II. It is in the hands of the Committee of General Security and will appear with other pieces of the same kind; in the meantime I must cite this passage: "Good revolutionary taxes, good patriotic loans, without having established which I will not leave here, will soon restore the philosophical level of nature, and will consolidate in reality that equality which would be nothing but a dream of men of good will, a formula of phrasemakers, and an ATROCIOUS *joke for so many thousands of men* if its implementation had not been effected and consecrated."

absolute equality in intelligence, virtue, physical strength, education, and fortune for all men.

To no purpose would wisdom exhaust itself in attempting to create a constitution if ignorance and lack of interest in order had the right to be received among the guardians and administrators of this edifice. We must be governed by the best; the best are those who are best educated and most interested in the maintenance of the laws: now, with very few exceptions, you find such men only among those who, owning a piece of property, are devoted to the country that contains it, to the laws that protect it, to the tranquillity that maintains it, and who owe to this property and to the economic security it provides the education that has made them capable of discussing with wisdom and exactitude the advantages and inconveniences of the laws that determine the fate of their native land. The man without property, on the other hand, requires a constant exercise of virtue to interest himself in a social order that preserves nothing for him, and to resist actions and movements that hold out hopes to him. One must assume him to be possessed of very sophisticated and profound conceptions for him to prefer genuine good to apparent good, and future interests to immediate interests. If you give men without property political rights without reservations, and if they ever find themselves on the benches of the legislature, they will excite unrest or allow it to be excited without fearing its effects; they will establish or allow to be established taxes disastrous for commerce and agriculture, because they will not have appreciated, or feared, or foreseen the deplorable results; they will precipitate us, finally, into violent convulsions like those from which we are barely recovering, the woes of which will be felt for so long everywhere in France.

A country governed by proprietors is an organized community; one governed by nonproprietors is in a state of nature. The ancients recognized this truth in their brilliant allegories when they said that Ceres, who was the goddess of agriculture and consequently of property, had been the first to build cities, organize societies, and give laws to peoples. We therefore propose that you decree that to be eligible for the legislative corps one must possess landed property of some kind. You will determine whether the value of this property should be fixed, or whether, as we have thought, its amount being always relative to the fortune of the proprietor, the guarantee is not the same whatever its extent. This will not be interference with the liberty of elections; the aim is to present to the electors, to present to the social body a means of refining the choices; it is a guarantee of a sort, a pledge of responsibility that society as a whole requires when it is going to invest one of its members with the function of stipulating in its name.

But we did not believe it possible to restrict the right of citizenship, to propose to the majority of the French, or even to any portion of them, that they renounce this august characteristic. All have fought equally and with the same courage for the enfranchisement of the social corps; all must therefore be a part of it. The guarantee that society demands when it is going to delegate one of its powers is a result of its collective right, of its general will; it is after it has been organized that it deliberates on the conditions it will require from its magistrates; its interest is then its guiding principle, and it can have no other; but when it assembles to exercise this original function, it is composed of members all of whom are equal; it cannot expel any of them from itself. The stipulation of property is not the basis of the association, of which each man is equally a part regardless of what he possesses. The poverty of the indigent has the same right to protection as the opulence of the rich, and the industry of the artisan as the harvest of the cultivator. Besides, would it be prudent, would it be advantageous to tranquillity to separate a people into two parts, one of which would clearly be subject, while the other would be sovereign? Could this usurpation fail to arm the oppressed portion against that which would oppress it, and would this not establish in the state an eternal source of division which would end by overthrowing your government and your laws? In cutting off from the social corps so numerous a portion of men, would you not be condemning them to consider themselves as without a *patrie*, and would you not be making them perpetual satellites of the first brigand who could present himself to them as capable of avenging their outrage?

We have, however, investigated whether there were not some exceptions indispensably necessary and rigorously just for the exercise of political rights. We believed that every citizen must, in order to exercise them, be free and independent; thus the man in domestic service seemed to us to be neither one nor the other; he in fact no longer possesses his natural independence; he has exchanged for some form of wages a portion of his liberty; he is subjected to another man, whose opinions and thoughts he will borrow in spite of himself and whose influence in public deliberations he would thereby double. He therefore loses temporarily the exercise of a citizen's rights. The same will be true in the future of anyone who will be unable to read or write, or who will not have learned a mechanical art. A man is truly free in fact only when he has in his own work the means of supporting his existence; a man is truly independent only when he has need of no one to enlighten him concerning his duties and to convey his ideas for him. Since the use of printing, the faculty of knowing how to read must be regarded as a sixth sense, the development of which alone can make us truly men and consequently citizens. Finally, the obligation imposed on each person to learn a mechanical profession is a splendid homage rendered to civil equality; it amounts to removing forever the odious distinctions taken from the distinctions between the estates; it means enlarging for the whole nation the sources of its wealth by adding to the extent of its industry; it means wresting man from vice and from the boredom which in most cases afflicts him only because he is not occupied.[2] Beggars and vagabonds are not part of the social corps: the former because they are dependents, the latter because they do not belong to any country. Finally, bankrupts are indebted to the whole society; they have betrayed the first duty it imposes, that of respecting one's pledges; they are to be presumed to be of bad faith. To decree that no citizen may exercise [political] rights unless he is inscribed on the list of taxpayers is not to hinder their exercise either, but is to confirm the principle that every member of society must contribute to its expenses, however small his fortune may be. . . .

. . . I will pause only briefly to remind you of the unavoidable dangers of a single assembly; to help me I have your own history, of which you are all aware. Who better than you could tell us what can be, in a single assembly, the influence of an individual, how the passions which can enter there, the divisions that can arise there, the intrigues of factions, the audacity of scoundrels, the eloquence of orators, and that false public opinion which is so easy to arouse can incite movements that nothing halts, can occasion a precipitation that nothing restrains, and can produce decrees that may cause a people to lose its happiness and its liberty if they are maintained, and the national representation to lose its strength and reputation if they are rejected?

2. It is useless to observe that this disposition cannot be applied to the present generation, whose education has been abandoned to the indifference of the old regime.

In a single assembly tyranny meets opposition only in its first steps; if an unexpected circumstance, an enthusiasm, a popular misconception enables it to clear a first obstacle, it encounters no more of them; it arms itself with all the strength of the nation's representatives against the nation itself; it enthrones terror on a unique and solid foundation, and the most virtuous men are before long forced to appear to sanction crimes, to let rivers of blood flow before they are able to create a successful conspiracy that can overthrow the tyrant and re-establish liberty.

There cannot be a stable constitution where there exists in the legislative body only a single, unique assembly; for if there can be no stability in decision-making, it is very evident that there will be none in the constitution that will serve as its base. As there will be no permanent laws, there will be no political habits; as there will be no political habits, there will be no national character, and then nothing will any longer defend the constitution that the people will have sworn to. If some members whose views are opposed grow impatient, that will be enough to cause the assembly, finding itself suddenly perturbed, without knowing why, to be led involuntarily to attack and destroy the constitution. The division of the legislative corps into two sections ripens all of the deliberations by obliging them to pass through two different stages; that is the guarantee that the rules outlined for each of them for making laws will be respected by both of them. The first will make its decisions more carefully, knowing that they will be subject to revision by the second; the second, warned by the errors of the first and the causes that will have produced them, will take precautions in advance against an erroneous judgment whose principle it will understand; it will not dare to reject a decision presented to it with the seal of justice and with general approbation; it will not dare to adopt one opposed by this same justice, this same public opinion. If the matter is questionable, from the acceptance by one section and the rejection by the other will come a new discussion, and if one should sometimes persist in an ill-founded refusal, as is constitutionally possible, there can be no comparison between the danger of having one good law less and that of having one bad law more; we will still have attained in this respect the highest degree of perfection of which human institutions are capable. . . .

A chamber of hereditary peers is a product of feudal pride designed to preserve the privileges of the great and to defend the authority of the throne. It cannot be an integral part of a Republic. A senate for life is an aristocratic institution no less contrary to the sacred principles that have prepared our revolution than to those of the public interest. We propose only to divide the legislative body into two councils, both elected by the people for the same period of time and differing from each other only in the number and age of their members. One, called the Council of Five Hundred, will be charged with proposing the laws; the other, called the Council of Elders and composed of two hundred and fifty members, will have the right to examine them, and a law will not be perfect until it has been accepted by this latter chamber. There is certainly nothing in this system resembling a peerage or a senatorial aristocracy. . . .

One of the greatest modern publicists, Samuel Adams, wrote *that there was no good government, no stable constitution, no assured protectors for the laws, liberty, and property of the people without the balance of the three powers.* It is this principle that we propose to you for employment in your midst. We have talked to you about the legislative power: with the two powers that it contains we must associate in our organization that charged with executing the laws. The executive must be independent of the legislative power without ever oppressing it: it must be subject to the law, the presumed expression of the people's will, without ever being subject to the legislator. The independence of the executive power must not arouse in you any distrust: forget the impression made on you by older forms of expression which have since changed their meaning entirely. Formerly the executive power was the force of the throne; today it will be that of the Republic. You have always attacked it and weakened it because you wanted to overthrow the throne that threatened you. Today you must strengthen it, since your aim is no longer to destroy, but to preserve, the government; you must encompass it with strength, consideration, and prestige; you must take far away from it everything that might oppress and debase it, for it is also the depository of a considerable portion of the people's strength. We have examined carefully whether we should have it elected directly by the citizens; we have found too many disadvantages in such an election to propose it to you. We feared that, being elected by all, it would acquire too great a power relative to the legislative body, each member of which is named by only part of the citizens. And as it must be responsible and susceptible to being brought to trial, we feared that it would profit from the support of all the votes that had elected it to escape from all prosecution. In having it elected by two sections of the national representation, we thought to provide guarantees against these disadvantages, and we saw in this procedure the advantage of fostering more amicable relations between these two authorities. It is enough for liberty that these powers be independent: now the executive power, although elected by the people's representatives, will not be subordinate to them, since they will not be able to revoke it but only to bring it to trial, according to forms established for the representatives themselves; that is, by means of a decree issued like any law.

We propose that you constitute the executive power of five members, renewed by one-fifth every year, and that you call it a directory. This combination concentrates the force of the government sufficiently for it to be rapid and firm, and divides it sufficiently to rule out any pretension of one of the directors to tyranny. . . .

However, whatever glamour, whatever strength we were proposing that you give to the directory charged with the supreme executive function, we believe we have set enough limits to its power to reassure you concerning the abuses of that power that it might be tempted to commit. It will execute all the laws; but it will never propose any. It cannot be summoned or revoked by the legislative body; but if it violates its trust, it can be accused by it before a national court, elected directly by the people. It orders and regulates expenditures from the funds granted by the legislative power; but the national treasury which pays on its writs is absolutely independent of it. That treasury is named by the Legislative Assembly, which supervises and directs it, and, its only function being to conserve the public funds without ever having them at its disposal, there can never be on its part any peculation. The directory will rightly have command of the military forces on land and sea, of all such forces possessed by the Republic; but in no case will it be able to have them commanded by one of its own members: finally, the disposition of the public force guarding the very sessions of the national representation must certainly be its responsibility; but in case the legislative body should fear some disturbance, some conspiracy, some great attack against liberty, it could transfer this guard from the jurisdiction of the directory into its own by declaring the country in danger, and in that case it would be under the orders of the Council of Elders, who, however, would keep it only until the re-establishment of tranquillity.

You will easily conceive, citizens, that this opposition of interests, this diversity of functions, and this division of powers must be insurmountable barriers to the ambition of men mad enough to aspire to tyranny. The cooperation of these three powers will give us wise laws, slowly conceived and rapidly executed: and as the rights of each one of them are enclosed within well-placed limits, which promise them no advantages in the attacks which they might launch against each other, everything must guarantee to you, citizens, that they will balance each other without colliding, and will supervise each other without fighting. . . .

44. July, 1795:
Louis XVIII, Declaration of Verona

Louis XVI's younger brother Provence had left for the border on June 20, 1791, the same night that Louis XVI and Marie Antoinette took the less fortunate route toward Varennes. A still younger brother, Artois, was already abroad by this time. With the execution of Louis XVI on January 21, 1793, Provence assumed the title of regent, the new king being Louis XVII, who was still a boy and was being held prisoner in Paris, like his mother, Marie Antionette, who was to be executed on October 16, 1793. When Louis XVII died on June 8, 1795, the regent assumed the title of Louis XVIII, which he bore with considerable dignity during many years of adversity until his actual attainment of the throne on French soil in 1814. In 1795, however, Louis XVIII had some reason to believe that the situation in France was developing in the direction of a restoration of the monarchy, and he was, moreover, surrounded by people whose attitudes toward the revolution had been growing more and more intransigent, whose image of the old regime in France had been growing more and more idealized, and who, to the extent that they went in for philosophizing, tended to be under the influence of a kind of neo-absolutism that was maturing in the minds of many émigrés and was soon to find its most imposing expression in the works of Louis de Bonald and Joseph de Maistre. Although many factors other than doctrine contributed to the failure of the royalists to bring about a restoration and thereby to enable France to enter the nineteenth century without the Napoleonic adventure, an indisputably important fact was the difference in attitudes between Louis XVIII and most of the émigrés, on the one hand, and, on the other hand, persons actually living in France, most of whom, even the royalists, favored or were at least resigned to some aspects of the revolution. Louis XVIII's intransigence in the Verona declaration made it very difficult for royalists in France to win converts; it embarrassed the constitutional monarchists and left moderates no choice except between the Directory and what came to be called neo-Jacobinism. Louis XVIII's Declaration of Verona may have been completed on June 24, 1795, the date assigned to it by some historians. The document translated for publication in the British *Annual Register* of 1795 is dated July, 1795, on its last page. Pages 254–257, somewhat more than the first half of the Declaration, containing its main assertions about the nature of the revolution and the kind of restoration needed in France, appear below.

Proclamation of Louis XVIII

Louis, by the grace of God, King of France and Navarre,
To all our subjects, greeting.

In depriving you of a king, whose whole reign was passed in captivity, but whose infancy even afforded sufficient grounds for believing that he would prove a worthy successor to the best of kings, the impenetrable decrees of Providence, at the same time that they have transmitted his crown to us, have imposed on us the necessity of tearing it from the hands of revolt, and the duty of saving the country, reduced, by a disastrous revolution, to the brink of ruin.

The fatal conformity which subsists between the commencement of our reign and the commencement of the reign of the fourth Henry, operates as an additional inducement with us to take that monarch for our model, and imitating, in the first instance, his noble candour, we shall now lay open our whole soul before you. Long, too long have we had to deplore those fatal circumstances which imperiously prescribed the necessity of silence; but now that we are allowed to exert our voice, attend to it. Our love for you is the only sentiment by which we are actuated; our heart obeys with delight the dictates of clemency; and since it has pleased Heaven to reserve us, like Henry the Great, to reestablish in our empire the reign of order and the laws, like him we will execute this divine task, with the assistance of our faithful subjects, by uniting kindness with justice.

Your minds have, by dreadful experience, been sufficiently informed of the extent and origin of your misfortunes. Impious and factious men, after having seduced you by lying declamations, and by deceitful promises, hurried you into irreligion and revolt. Since that time a torrent of calamities has rushed in upon you from every side. You proved faithless to the God of your forefathers; and that God, justly offended, has made you feel the weight of his anger; you rebelled against the authority which he had established, and a sanguinary despotism, and an anarchy no less fatal, have alternately continued to harass you with incessant rage.

Consider an instant the origin and progress of the evils with which you are overwhelmed. You first consigned your interests to faithless representatives, who, by betraying the confidence which you had reposed in them, and violating the oaths which they had taken, paved the way for their rebellion against their king, by treachery and perjury towards you: and they rendered you the instruments of their passions, and of your own ruin. You next submitted to the despotic sway of gloomy and austere tyrants, who contested with each other, while the contest was marked by mutual massacres, the right of oppressing the nation; and they imposed upon you an iron yoke. You afterwards permitted their blood-stained sceptre to pass into the hands of a rival faction, which, in order to secure their power, and to reap the fruits of their crimes, assumed the mask of moderation, which sometimes it lifts up, but which it dares not yet venture wholly to throw aside; and you have changed sanguinary despots, whom you abhorred, for hypo-critical despots whom you despise. They conceal their weakness beneath an appearance of mildness, but they are actuated by the same ambition which influenced the conduct of their predecessors. The reign of terror has suspended its ravages, but they have been replaced by the disorders of anarchy. Less blood is shed in France, but greater misery prevails. In short, your slavery only changed its form, and your disasters have been aggravated. You have lent a favourable ear to the calumnious reports that have been propagated against that ancient race which, during so long a period, reigned as much in your hearts as over France: and your blind credulity has increased the weight of your chains, and prolonged the term of your misfortunes. In a word, your tyrants have overthrown the altars of your God and the throne of your king, and have com-pleted the sum of your wretchedness.

Thus impiety and revolt have been the cause of all the torments you experience: in order to stop their progress you must dry up their source. You must renounce the dominion of those treacherous and cruel usurpers who promised you happiness, but who have given you only famine and death: we wish to relieve you from their tyranny, which has so much injured you, to inspire you with the resolution of shaking it off. You must return to that holy religion which had showered down upon France the blessings of Heaven. We wish to restore its altars; by prescribing justice to sovereigns and fidelity to subjects, it maintains good order, ensures the triumph of the laws, and produces the felicity of empires. You must restore that government which, for fourteen centuries, constituted the glory of France and the delight of her inhabitants; which rendered our country the most flourishing of states, and yourselves the happiest of people: it is our wish to restore it. Have not the various revolutions which have occurred augmented your distress, since the period of its destruction, and convinced you that it is the only government that is fit for you?

Give no credit to those rapacious and ambitious men, who, in order to violate your property and to engross all power, have told you that France had no constitution, or, at least, that its constitution was despotic. Its existence is as ancient as the monarchy of the Franks; it is the produce of genius, the master-piece of wisdom, and the fruit of experience.

In composing the body of the French people of three distinct orders, it traced with precision that scale of subordination without which society cannot exist. But it gives to neither [sic] of the three orders any political right which is not common to all. It leaves all employments open to Frenchmen of every class; it affords equal protection to all persons and to all property; and by this means, in the eye of the law, and in the temple of justice, all those inequalities of rank and fortune disappear, which civil order necessarily introduces among the inhabitants of the same empire.

These are great advantages; but there are others still more essential. It subjects the laws to certain specific forms prescribed by itself; and the sovereign himself is equally bound to the observance of the laws, in order to guard the wisdom of the legislature against the snares of seduction, and to defend the liberty of the subject against the abuse of authority. It prescribes conditions to the establishment of imposts, in order to satisfy the people that the tributes which they pay are necessary for the preservation of the state; it confides to the first body of the magistracy the care of enforcing the execution of the laws, and of undeceiving the monarch, if he should chance to be imposed upon; it places the fundamental laws under the protection of the king and of the three orders, for the purpose of preventing revolutions, which are the greatest calamities that the people can possibly sustain; it has adopted a multiplicity of precautions in order to secure to you the advantages of a monarchical government, and to screen you from its dangers. Do not your unexampled misfortunes, as much as its venerable antiquity, bear testimony of its wisdom? Did your ancestors ever experience the evils which you have borne, since the hands of ignorant and obstinate innovators have overthrown their constitution? It was the common support of the cottage of the poor, and the palace of the rich; of personal freedom, and of public safety; of the rights of the throne, and of the prosperity of the state. The moment it was overthrown, property, safety, freedom, all ceased to exist. No sooner did the throne become a prey to usurpers, than your fortunes were seized by plunderers: the instant the shield of royal authority ceased to protect you, you were oppressed by despotism, and sunk into slavery.

To that ancient and wise constitution, whose fall has proved your ruin, we wished to restore all its purity which time had corrupted; all its vigour which time had impaired: but it has itself fortunately deprived us of the ability to change it. It is our holy ark; we are forbidden to lay rash hands upon it; it is your happiness and our glory; it is the wish of all true Frenchmen; and the knowledge we have acquired in the school of misfortune; all tend to confirm in our mind the necessity of restoring it entire. It is because France is dear to us, that we are anxious to replace her under the beneficent protection of a government, the excellence of which has been proved by so long a continuance of prosperity. It is because we feel it to be our duty to quell that spirit of system making, that rage for innovation which has been the cause of your ruin, that we are anxious to renovate and confirm those salutary laws which are alone capable of promoting a general unity of sentiment, of fixing the general opinion, and of opposing an insurmountable barrier to the revolutionary rage, which every plan of a change in the constitution of our kingdom would again let loose upon the public.

But while the hand of time gives the stamp of wisdom to the institutions of man, his passions are studious to degrade them; and they place either their own work on the side of the laws, with a view to weaken their effect, or make it usurp the place of the laws, in order to render them useless. In those empires which have attained the highest pitch of glory and prosperity, abuses most generally prevail, because in such states they are the least likely to attract the attention of those who govern. Some abuses had therefore crept into the government of France, which were not only felt by the lower class of people, but by every order of the state. The deceased monarch, our brother and sovereign lord and master, had perceived and was anxious to remove them; in his last moments he charged his successor to execute the plans which he had in his wisdom conceived, for promoting the happiness of that very people who suffered him to perish on the scaffold. On quitting the throne, from which crime and impiety had hurled him, to ascend that which Heaven had reserved for his virtues, he pointed out to us our duties in that immortal will, the inexhaustible source of admiration and regret. The King! that martyr! submissive to the God who had made him a king, followed his example without a murmur, in rendering the instrument of his punishment a trophy of his glory, and in attending to the welfare of his people at the very time when they were completing the sum of his misfortunes! What Louis XVI could not effect, we will accomplish! . . .

45. November 30, 1795:
Babeuf's Le Tribun du peuple, No. 35

The "Conspiracy of the Equals" of François Noël Babeuf and his associates took place in 1796 and led to their arrest in that year and to the execution of Babeuf in 1797. Thus in 1796 and 1797, along with the mature expressions of a social philosophy justifying absolute monarchy and the group-oriented society of the old regime, there appeared out of the same revolutionary tempering a communist conspiracy. The element of conspiracy was real, although its prospects for success were minuscule; what is perhaps more important in the realm of methods is that Babeuf and his innermost circle of friends took for socialism the idea of dictatorship that they had seen in practice in the revolution. What is most important in the realm of objectives is that Babeuf, at least, was extraordinarily alienated, not only from the society that was being left behind but from that which was emerging in the revolutionary years, and that this alienation took the form of a communist version of equality backed by an extreme moral fervor. Again, it is not the chance of success that counts, or the small number of persons who shared his views, but the crystallization of an idea that was to have a history. Babeuf had arrived at this point at the age of thirty-four or thirty-five, in 1794 or 1795, from a peasant background, from a profession of *feudiste* before the revolution (a worker in manorial records to justify the income-producing claims of gentry landlords), from a reading of the philosophes, from continually frustrated attempts to hold office in the revolution and spread the idea of the agrarian law (the partition of properties), with poverty and personal difficulties pursuing him, and with a background of periods in jail. That Babeuf passed from the agrarian law to socialism, however, is clear from his newspaper, *Le Tribun du peuple ou le défenseur des droits de l'homme, par Gracchus Babeuf* (Paris, Imprimerie du Tribun du peuple), of which No. 35, dated Paris, *9 frimaire, an 4 de la République* (November 30, 1795), has been drawn upon below for the principal passages of its climax, a section called (in the table of contents) "Précis du grand Manifeste à proclamer pour rétablir l'égalité de fait." The pages translated are 83–85, 92–93, and 101–107. Spaces have been left between these passages. Dots in the text within the passages are Babeuf's. No. 35 is paged consecutively with other issues and consists of pp. 53–108.

. . . They are mistaken who believe that I agitate with a view to substituting one constitution for another. We have much more need of institutions than of constitutions. The constitution of '93 merited the applause of all good men only because it prepared the way for institutions. If through it that objective had proved unattainable, I would have ceased admiring it. Every constitution that will permit the continuation of the old inhuman and abusive institutions will cease exciting my enthusiasm; any man who, summoned to regenerate his fellow creatures, will drag along painfully in the old routine set by earlier legislation, whose barbarism consecrates the existence of happy and unhappy people, will not be in my eyes a legislator; he will not inspire my respect.

Let us work first to establish good institutions, plebeian institutions, and we will always be sure that a good constitution will come afterward.

Plebeian institutions must assure the *common happiness*, the equal sufficiency of all the co-associates.

Let us recall some of the fundamental principles developed in ur last number, in the article: "About the War of the Rich and ｅ Poor." Repetitions of this kind are in no way boring to all ｅ whom they concern.

ｅ have laid down a principle[1] that *perfect equality* has its in primitive law; that the social pact, far from damaging ural right, must merely give to each individual the guarantee s right will never be violated; that in consequence there

du Peuple, No. 34, pp. 11ff.

should never have been institutions which favor inequality and cupidity, which permit the necessities of some people to be seized in order to provide an overabundance for others. That, however, the contrary had come about; that absurd conventions had been introduced into society, and had protected inequality and permitted the despoiling of the majority by the minority; that there were epochs when the final consequences of these deadly social rules were that the whole of the wealth of the community became concentrated in the hands of a few; that peace, which is natural when all are happy, then inevitably became troubled; that the masses, no longer being able to exist, finding everything out of their reach, encountering only merciless hearts in the class which has monopolized everything—these consequences set the time for those great revolutions, fixed those memorable periods predicted in the book of Time and Destiny when a general upheaval in the system of property becomes inevitable, when the revolt of the poor against the rich is so necessary that nothing can prevent it.

We have shown that from '89 we were at this point, and that it is for that reason that the revolution broke out then. We have shown that since '89, and notably since '94 and '95, the heaping up of calamities and public oppression had made especially urgent the majestic upheaval of the people against its despoilers and oppressors.

Tribunes are needed, in such circumstances, to sound the first alarms and to awaken and signal all their brothers who suffer. The first to display enough energy to mount an all-out attack on the oppressors are recognized and endorsed by the oppressed. . . .

"Is it the *agrarian law* that you want?" will cry a thousand respectable voices. No, it is more than that. We know what invincible argument could be used against that. We would be told, with reason, that the agrarian law can last only for a day; that from the morrow of its establishment inequality would return. The Tribunes of France who have preceded us have conceived better the true system of social well-being. They have felt that it could only exist in institutions capable of assuring and of maintaining unalterably an *equality of fact*. . . .

Let the people proclaim its manifesto. Let it define democracy as it intends to have it and such as it must exist according to pure principles. Let it prove there that democracy is the obligation of those who have too much to make up all that is lacking to those who do not have enough! That the whole *deficit* that is found in the fortune of the latter comes only from what the others have stolen from them! Stolen legitimately, if you wish; that is to say, with the assistance of brigand laws which, under recent regimes as well as under the most ancient ones, have authorized all the thefts; with the assistance of laws such as all those existing at this moment; with the assistance of laws according to which I am forced, in order to live, to unfurnish my household each day, to carry to all the thieves whom they protect, everything, to the last rag which covers me! Let the people declare that it intends to have restitution for all these thefts, for these shameful confiscations by the rich from the poor. This restitution will be as legitimate, no doubt, as that to the émigrés. We want from the re-establishment of democracy, first, that our rags, our old furnishings be returned to us, and that those who have taken them from us hereafter be made incapable of recommencing such outrages. Next we want from democracy what all those who have conceived some just idea of it have made us see that they wanted.

Must there be, in order to re-establish the rights of the human race and put an end to all our wrongs, must there be necessary a *retreat to the* SACRED MOUNTAIN *or a* PLEBEIAN VENDÉE? Let all the friends of *Equality* make their preparations and consider themselves already warned! May each be touched by the incomparable beauty of this enterprise. Israelites to rescue from Egyptian slavery!—to lead to possession of the lands of Canaan! . . . What expedition was ever more worthy of animating great courage? The God of Liberty, let us be sure of it, will protect those Moseses who will wish to direct it. He promised it to us, without the instrumentality of Aaron, with whom we have no more to do than with his vicarial college. He promised it to us, without any miraculous appearance in the burning bush. Let us ignore all these marvels, all this stupidity. The inspirations of the republican divinities appear very simply, under the auspices of nature (the supreme God) by way of the hearts of republicans. It has therefore been revealed to us that while new Joshuas will struggle one fine day on the plain, without need for the sun to be stopped, several, instead of a legislator of the Hebrews, will be on the veritable *Plebeian Mountain*. They will inscribe there, under the dictation of eternal justice, the Decalogue of holy humanity, of sans-culottism, of imprescriptible equity. We will proclaim, under the protection of our hundred thousand lances and our pieces of artillery, the veritable first code of nature, which should never have been infringed.

We will explain clearly what is the *common welfare, the aim of society*.

We will prove that the lot of no man should have become worse in passing from the natural to the social state.

We will define property.

We will prove that the soil is no one's, but belongs to all.

We will prove that any of it that an individual hoards beyond what can nourish him is a social theft.

We will prove that the so-called right of *alienability* is an infamous attack causing ruin or death to the people.

We will prove that *heredity by families* is a no less great horror; that it isolates all the members of the association and makes of each household a little republic which can only conspire against the great one, and consecrate inequality.

We will prove that everything that a member of the social body has *below* sufficiency for his needs of every kind and every day is the result of a despoiling of his individual natural property, made by the monopolizers of the common property.

That, from the same result, all that a member of the social body has *above* sufficiency for his needs of every kind and every day is the result of a theft made from the other co-associates, which deprives, necessarily, a certain number of them of their share in the common properties.[2]

That all the most subtle reasonings cannot prevail against these unalterable truths.

That superiority of talent and industry is only a chimera and a specious decoy which has always been unduly useful to the plots of conspirators against equality.

That the differences in value and merit in the products of men's work are based only on the opinion that certain men have attached to them and have known how to make prevail.

That it is without doubt wrong for opinion to have evaluated the day's work of a watchmaker at twenty times that of a plowman.

That it is nevertheless with the aid of this false estimate that the

2. The social state brought to perfection: "Let all have enough, and no one have too much." J. J. Rousseau. This sentence cannot be pondered upon too much.

income of the artisan watchmaker has put him within reach of acquiring the patrimony of twenty workers at the plow, whom he has, by this means, expropriated.

That all the proletarians became thus only as the result of the same combination in all other relationships of such proportions, but all stemming from the one basis of differences in value established among things by the sole authority of opinion.

That there is absurdity and injustice in the claim of a greater recompense for him whose work demands a higher degree of intelligence and more concentration and mental strain; that that in no way extends the capacity of his stomach.

That no reason can justify a recompense exceeding sufficiency of individual needs.

That neither is the value of intelligence more than a matter of opinion and that it must perhaps still be examined whether wholly natural and physical strength is not just as valuable.

That the intelligent people are the ones who have given such a high price to the conceptions of their brains, and that, if it had been the strong who had jointly regulated things, they would doubtless have established that the value of the arms is as great as that of the head, and that fatigue of the whole body could be said to offset that of the thinking part alone.

That, without the positing of this equalization, one gives to the most intelligent and industrious a warrant for monopolizing, a right to despoil with impunity those who are less so.

That it is in this way that the equilibrium of affluence in society is destroyed and overturned, since nothing is better proved than our great maxim: *that no one succeeds in having too much without causing others to have too little.*

That all our civil institutions, our reciprocal transactions are merely acts of perpetual brigandage authorized by absurd and barbarous laws, under cover of which we are occupied only with exploiting each other.

That our society of rogues drags along in the wake of its atrocious primordial conventions all kinds of vices, crimes, and misfortunes against which a few good men band together in vain in order to make war on them, but a war that they cannot win because they do not attack at all the root of the evil, and because they apply only palliatives drawn from the reservoir of false ideas about our organic depravity.

That it is clear from all that precedes that everything those possess who have more than their individual quota of the goods of society is theft and usurpation.

That it is therefore just to take it back from them.

That the very person who would prove that by the effect of his natural strength alone he is capable of doing as much as four, and who consequently would demand the remuneration of four, would be no less a conspirator against society, because he would upset the equilibrium by this means alone, and would destroy precious equality.

That wisdom commands urgently that all co-associates repress such a man, prosecute him as a social scourge, restrict him at least to doing the work of a single person, that he may exact only the recompense of a single person.

That it is our species alone that has introduced this murderous foolishness of distinctions of merit and of value, and that also it is only our species that knows the resulting misfortune and privations.

That there must not exist deprivation of the things nature gives to all, produces for all, unless this deprivation results from unavoidable accidents of nature, and that in that case they must be supported and shared equally by all.

That the productions of industry and genius also become the property of all, the domain of the entire association, from the very moment when the inventors and workers have realized them; because they are only the returns from earlier inventions of genius and industry, from which these inventors and these new workers have profited in social life, and which have aided them in their discoveries.

That since accumulated knowledge is the domain of all, it must therefore be equally distributed among all.

That a truth ill-advisedly contested out of bad faith, prejudice, or thoughtlessness is that this equal distribution of knowledge among all would make all men nearly equal in capacity and even in talent.

That education is a monstrosity when it is unequal, when it is the exclusive heritage of a part of the association, since it then becomes, in the hands of this part, an accumulation of machines, a stock of weapons of all kinds, with the aid of which this first part combats the other which is disarmed, and succeeds easily, consequently, in strangling it, deceiving it, despoiling it, and enslaving it under the most shameful bonds.

That there is no truth more important than that which we have already cited, and which a philosopher has proclaimed in these terms: *Discourse as much as you please on the best form of government; you will have done nothing as long as you have not destroyed the seeds of cupidity and ambition.*

That it is necessary, therefore, for social institutions to lead to the point of depriving every individual of the hope of ever becoming richer, more powerful, or more distinguished by his learning than any of his equals.

That it is necessary, speaking more precisely, to succeed in *enchaining fate;* in making the fate of each co-associate independent of chance and circumstances, fortunate and unfortunate; *in assuring to everyone and to his posterity, however numerous, sufficiency, but nothing more than sufficiency;* and in closing to everyone all possible routes to the attainment at any time of more than an individual quota of the products of nature and of labor.

That the only way to achieve this is to establish *a common administration;* to suppress private property; to assign each man to the skill, to the industry, that he knows; to oblige him to deposit its output in kind in the communal warehouse; and to establish a simple administration of distribution, an administration of sustenance which, keeping track of all individuals and of all things, will see that the latter are distributed with the most scrupulous equality and will have them delivered to the residence of each citizen.

That this government, proved by experience to be practicable, since it is the one administered for the twelve hundred thousand men of our dozen armies (what is possible in a small way is possible in a large way)—that this government is the only one from which there can result universal happiness, unalterable, unadulterated; *the common happiness, aim of society.*

That this government will do away with the boundaries, the hedges, the walls, the locks on the doors, the disputes, the lawsuits, the thefts, the murders, all crimes; the courts, prisons, gallows, punishments, the despair caused by all these calamities; envy, jealousy, insatiability, pride, fraud, duplicity, lastly all the vices; with, moreover (and this point is without doubt the essential), the cankerworm of anxiety that is general, specific, and perpetual within each of us, concerning our fate of the morrow, of the next month, of the next year, of old age, and the fate of our children and of their children.

Such is the summary outline of this terrible manifesto that we will offer to the oppressed mass of the French people, and of which we give them the first sketch so that they may have a foretaste of it. People! Awaken to hope, cease to remain numb and plunged in discouragement; . . . Brighten at the vision of a happy future. Friends of kings! Lose any idea that the wrongs you have inflicted on this people will subject them indefinitely to the yoke of a single person. And you, patricians! Rich people! Republican tyrants! Renounce all of you together and at the same time your oppressive speculations on this nation which has not entirely forgotten its oaths to liberty. A prospect more agreeable than everything with which you entice it appears before its eyes. Guilty rulers! At the moment when you believe you can, without danger, lay your heavy iron hand upon this virtuous people, it will make you feel its superiority, it will free itself from all your usurpations and chains, it will recover its primitive and sacred rights. For too long you have played upon its magnanimity; for too long you have insulted its suffering. . . .

"The people," you say, "are without vigor; they suffer and die without daring to complain." The annals of the republic will not be soiled by such a humiliation! The word French will not go down to posterity accompanied by such degradation. Let this writing be the signal, be the flash of lightning which reanimates and revitalizes all that formerly had warmth and courage, all that burned with an ardent flame for the public welfare and perfect independence! Let the people take from it the first true idea of EQUALITY! Let these words: *equality, equals, plebeianism* be the rallying words of all the friends of the people. Let the people subject to discussion all the great principles; let battle be joined on the famous chapter of this *equality* properly named, and on that of PROPERTY! Let them savor its morality precisely this time, and let it ignite in them a flame that will be sustained until their work has been entirely completed! Let them overthrow all those old barbarous institutions and substitute for them those dictated by nature and eternal justice. Ah, yes, all the wrongs of the people are at their peak; they can become no worse! They can be rectified only by a complete overthrow. May this atrocious war of the rich against the poor therefore take at last a less ignoble coloration. May it cease to have this character of total audacity on one side and total cowardice on the other! May the unfortunate at last respond to their aggressors! . . . Let us profit from the fact that they have pushed us to the limit. Let us advance without detours, like men who are aware of their own strength. Let us march openly to EQUALITY. Let us keep in view the *purpose of society;* let us keep in view the *common happiness!* . . .

Treacherous or ignorant! You cry that it is necessary to avoid civil war, that one must not hurl the torch of discord among the people? . . . And what civil war is more revolting than that which discloses all assassins on one side and all defenseless victims on the other? Can you make it a crime for someone to wish to arm the victims against the assassins? Is it not better to have a civil war with both parties able to defend themselves? Let our newspaper be accused, then, of being a brand of discord, if that is someone's wish. So much the better; discord is worth more than a horrible harmony in which one is strangled by hunger. Let the factions grapple with one another; let it be determined if the rebellion is partial, general, imminent, distant; we are still satisfied! Let the *Sacred Mountain* or the *Plebeian Vendée* take form in one place or in each of the 86 departments! Let there be conspiracy against oppression, on a scale large or small, secretly or openly, in a hundred thousand secret meetings or in a single one; it matters little to us, so long as there is conspiracy and so long as remorse and fears hereafter perpetually haunt the oppressors. We have given the signal very loudly in order that many may notice it; in order to summon many accomplices; we have given them well-justified motives and some idea of the method, and we are almost sure that there will be conspiracy. Let tyranny see whether it can hinder us. . . . The people, they say, have no guides. Let some appear, and let the people, from that moment, break their chains and conquer bread for themselves and for all future generations. Let us repeat again: All evils are at their height; they can become no worse; they can be rectified only by a total overturn!!! Let everything therefore be intermingled! . . . Let all the elements become confused, mixed up, and in conflict! . . . Let everything return to chaos and from the chaos come forth a new and regenerated world!

"Come, let us after a thousand years change these stupid laws."
                    Paris, 9 Frimaire, Year IV of the Republic
                    G. BABEUF, *Le Tribun du peuple*

46. December 6, 1795:
Mallet du Pan After Vendémiaire

Jacques Mallet du Pan was a journalist and political analyst who wrote steadily about European and French affairs through the 1780s and 1790s to his death in England in 1800. Mallet du Pan was a Swiss and a citizen of Geneva, but he wrote about the French Revolution with the passion of a member of the family. He lived in Paris as the principal political writer of the *Mercure de France,* narrating the political scene week by week, from the mid-1780s until he left the country on a secret mission for Louis XVI in 1792, and he knew everyone of importance. After his diplomatic mission he continued to report from Berne and, finally, London, partly as a journalist and partly as a news analyst for various governments, with the help of agents in France and in the European centers most sensitive to French and international affairs. Mallet du Pan was a moderate royalist, a very close friend of Malouet, Mounier, and others of Anglophile political views. Charles Saladin was a Swiss friend of Mallet du Pan, a fellow Genevan who was resident in England, where he had married an English girl, Elizabeth Egerton. Mallet du Pan's letters to him were informal and very outspoken, but Mallet du Pan knew that through Saladin his analyses reached government circles. The letter that follows is from *Lettres de Mallet du Pan à Saladin-Egerton (1794–1800) publiées par Victor van Berchem* (Geneva, 1896) [*Extrait de Pages d'histoire dediées à M. Pierre Vaudier, Professeur à l'Université de Genève*], pp. 24–29.

Mallet du Pan to Saladin-Egerton

Berne, December 6, 1795

I RECEIVED your friendly letter of the tenth of November only day before yesterday, my dear Saladin; this interval is discouraging, it is one of the causes of my silence. This country furnishes almost no subject for correspondence; besides, your father keeps you informed and you learn of the events of both France and Europe before my letters reach you.

I am happy to receive your assurance that in your circle I am not regarded entirely as a Jacobin. That, nevertheless, is the opinion that men who I must presume have influence with your ministers have tried to give about me. Cardinal Retz said with rare sagacity indeed that one has more difficulty living with men of one's own party than with outsiders.

The aristocracy has its terrorists: I see little difference between Marat and some magistrates of the French parlements. Their fury must be pardoned on account of their ineptitude and their ignorance of affairs; but that foreigners should allow themselves to be drawn into these movements, that they should let themselves be influenced by men who, far from rescuing people in great need, would spoil the finest causes—that is something that I can scarcely understand.

My opinions are and will always be invariable. You ask me how I reconcile a moderate monarchy with the suppression of the nobility. Alas! My dear friend, I am as far from reconciling them as you. France has perhaps fifty years of these troubles before returning to the only government that suits it; this is a revolution of *principles*, like the Reformation; powerful interests have arisen which will oppose for a long time yet a complete restoration. I love liberty insofar as it is compatible with public safety and national character. If I had to be the legislator of France, do you believe that I would throw this fickle, turbulent, babbling, presumptuous people, so susceptible to being misled by the magic of fine words, into national assemblies? Do you think that I would loosen restraints that in fact cannot be too tight, and that I would set up a monarch without an intermediate hierarchy between his throne and the people?

The question of the day is not knowing what would be the best monarchy to establish in France. It would not be, in my opinion, that dissolute, variable, arbitrary government of 1789; or that ministerial bureaucracy, or that satrapy of Versailles substituted for a true aristocracy, or especially those insolent courts of justice usurping the veto over the king and fomenting troubles every year by their *decrees*. One could restore the full royal authority while moderating its exercise through institutions analogous to the national genius and the national constitution, and in maintaining, more carefully than was ever done, that hierarchy of ranks so prostituted in France before the revolution.

But we are not at that point; we cannot, with our legs broken, leap with full force on a monstrous revolution that has overturned in France all the elements of the social order. It is a question of deciding first not what monarchy one will have but if one will have a monarchy. That is the point of departure; what is important above all, in Europe as much as in France, is to end a revolution whose principles and application will eternally threaten the public tranquillity, is to end the Republic which is nothing but a perpetual revolution.

But are we sufficiently the masters of our instruments to succeed in that? Is it our wishes or our capabilities that must be considered? Where are our means for re-establishing that pure monarchy to which reason perhaps tells us to aspire? Do they exist in foreign armies? You do not think so, and I do not believe that there exists a minister insane enough to attempt yet again by this means an absolute counterrevolution. Do they exist in the wigs of the magistrates of the old parlements gathered at Verona, in the pamphlets of d'Antraigues and other firebrands, in the counterrevolutionary Maratists of Condé's army? Is it the repressed and almost finished Vendée that holds out hope? Is it the infantile conspiracies that are being made in Switzerland, on which immense sums are lavished and which are entrusted to adventurers worthy of Bedlam?

No, my dear Saladin, it is necessary to abandon all these castles in Spain, all these poorly digested novels. You can no longer, without waiting for perhaps twenty years and for the total extinction of France—you can no longer remake a monarchy, overthrow the Republic, and close the revolutionary abyss without the help of those in the interior who want to return to royalty. Now, as nineteen-twentieths of those men want a conditional royalty, limited by means of a national representation of the proprietors, with guarantees for the future, and with the consecration of some of the results of the revolution, it is certainly necessary either to make use of them, while submitting to their terms, or to leave the enterprise to another generation.

Do not deceive yourself, and count on this factual truth that hardly *one* monarchist in *a thousand* wants the return of the old regime: some are resolved to preserve a measure of liberty; the greatest number dread the émigrés as much as the Jacobins; all who have participated in the revolution to the extent of one thought, one action, or one speech shudder at being delivered to the vengeance of the counterrevolutionaries whose speeches, whose publications, and whose conduct have *widely diffused* this sentiment of terror. The senseless declaration of the King has crowned it; his feebleness, his remoteness, and his imbecile councilors have silenced his partisans; there remain none. All the pure and sensible royalists who exist, even those who fear the dissensions of a mixed monarchy, are nevertheless in agreement with the partisans of that kind of limited royalty, because they cannot do without them and because they have the good sense to perceive that in order to *dethrone* the republican power and spirit, which have much deeper roots than most people think, one is obliged not to frighten all those whose safety, lives, and civil existence require guarantees against an absolute monarch controlled by the émigrés.

This sentiment, so widespread and so strong, was dominant in the sections. You judge them incorrectly, and I see that in London people have been very ill-informed about their sources of energy, their objectives, and the character of the actors. I have corresponded since the middle of June with the principal chiefs of this movement— a movement indicated as soon as the Convention opened an abyss before itself by decreeing that the primary assemblies should meet, and toward which Europe has shown an inattentiveness as fatal as it is inconceivable. I certify to you that the re-establishment of the monarchy was the central objective of the operations; this would have been attained, without any doubt, if the Convention had been forced to renounce the idea of re-election, and with the coming of a new legislative corps. But to achieve that, it was not necessary to go beyond a moral and political offensive and entrust themselves, as some sections did, to harebrained agitators, sent from outside, who led them into a hostile insurrection with 3,000 guns and 400 quintals of powder as their only resources, with neither chiefs nor a plan of *war*, against an authority that had command of the arsenals, of the public treasury, and of 20,000 soldiers.

Certainly, my friend, those who named as deputies men such as Messieurs d'Ambray, Morellet, de Bonnières, Portalis, and so on, were as good royalists as the bloody nonentities who have not been ashamed to rejoice at the catastrophe of the fifth of October. Contemptible creatures! It was only *constitutionalists*, they say! In their horrible madness, they prefer the return of the Jacobins. Well! They will be satisfied; their relatives, their friends will once more fall under the axe; the sans-culotte revolution will run its course and the émigrés will then be able to laugh at their ease. Those ferocious beasts have closed my soul to all pity.

Yes, the Jacobins are at the door: given back their liberty, they are reopening their clubs, conspiring, threatening; Barère walks in the Palais-Royal, Tallien and the regicidal faction direct maneuvers; the Directory peoples the courts, the administrations, the commissions, and all the positions with them. They alone have unity of sentiments, views, and aims; they alone have audacity. The apathy of honest men, the tranquillity of the people, born of their poverty, which forces them to concern themselves only with the means of subsisting, the general isolation, the terror inspired by October 5, the divisions of the royalists, their insufficient courage, their lack of leadership and cooperation, to the point of exterior reverses, are pushing the Jacobins ahead under full sail.

The government has changed only for form's sake: the regicidal majority, dominant in the Legislative Corps and to be reckoned with in the Five Hundred, represents the former Convention; the Directory is its Committee of Public Safety. The constitution is only a word devoid of sense—arbitrariness and the revolutionary regime rule in fact; before long you will see them in full and legal exercise of power. This machine cannot work without such a motive power; there is no middle ground—it must either shake to pieces or have terrorism and the concentration of the powers to hold it together.

The greatest part of the new Third and 160 former Conventionals form the minority of the Legislative Corps. These are royalists of *opinion*, who must not be confused with the party of moderate republicans or with the *conspiratorial* royalists. Timid, unknown to each other, without a fixed plan, without means, they are reduced to observing, and to gropings that will destroy them. The universal will of these royalists rejects the king of Verona and destines the crown for the Duke of Angoulême.

We are seeing splendid successes on the part of the Austrians who are in Alsace; but since yesterday, the bad news is being announced that M. de Vins, stormed along his front, is in full retreat toward Lombardy; tell Malouet, I beg you, that I am no longer receiving any news from him.

47. 1794, 1795, 1796:
Joseph de Maistre
on Reason, Monarchy, and Aristocracy

Joseph de Maistre was the most famous continental counterrevolutionary publicist, author of the book *Considérations sur la France* (1797), which became a classic of its kind, rivaling Burke's earlier *Reflections on the Revolution in France* (1790). Although de Maistre was not French but was a resident of Savoy who was driven out by the advancing French armies in 1793 and spent the years 1802–1817 in Russia as Sardinian minister to St. Petersburg, his education had been shaped by the French cultural diffusion of the Enlightenment and he was a master of French prose. By virtue of his prominent counterrevolutionary role he was, moreover, deeply involved with France and the revolution emotionally and intellectually and was indebted to them for his career and reputation as a spokesman for traditional values. During the crucial years 1794, 1795, and 1796, as he was maturing the views that were to make him famous, de Maistre recorded many of his ideas in a manuscript which he called *Étude sur la souveraineté* and which remained unpublished until after his death in 1821. The following passages, of which the first two are short chapters with their own titles and the last is part of a chapter that has been given an identifying heading in brackets, are from pp. 375–378, 411–416, and 430–435 of *Oeuvres complètes de J. de Maistre. Nouvelle édition contenant ses oeuvres posthumes et toute sa correspondance inédite.* Vol. I (Lyon, 1884). The author left a note in his papers saying that these materials had never been revised, although he had drawn on some of them in his published writings.[1] Joseph de Maistre is included in this collection because he was a leading intellectual in French émigré circles, because there is need to emphasize the fact that the thought of such men did not originate in the Restoration (which is to say that the revolution, which placed all the older ideas on trial, was an intellectual event of the first magnitude), and because he illustrates once more the fact that an important aspect of the revolution was the counterrevolution.

Chapter X of Book I. Concerning the National Soul

HUMAN REASON reduced to its individual strength is completely insignificant, *not only for the creation but also for the conservation of any religious or political association,* because it produces only disputes, and because man, for his guidance, needs not problems but beliefs. His cradle must be surrounded with dogmas; and when his reason awakens, he must find all his opinions ready-formed, at least on matters related to his conduct. There is nothing so important for him as *prejudices.* Let us not take this word in a bad sense. It does not necessarily signify false ideas, but only, according to the full sense of the word, opinions adopted before any examination. Now opinions of this kind are man's greatest need, the veritable essentials of his happiness and the Palladium of empires. Without them, he can have neither cult, nor morality, nor government. For man must have a state religion as well as state policies;

1. *Loc. cit.,* p. 311.

or, rather, it is necessary that religious and political dogmas intermingled form together a *universal* or a *national reason* strong enough to check the aberrations of individual reason, which is, by its nature, the mortal enemy of any association whatever, because it produces only divergent opinions.

All known peoples have been happy and powerful in proportion to their obedience to that national reason which is nothing but the annihilation of individual dogmas and the absolute and general reign of the national dogmas—in other words, of useful prejudices. Let each man, in the matter of worship, depend on his individual reason: immediately you will see anarchy of beliefs arise, which is the annihilation of religious sovereignty. Similarly, if each makes himself a judge of the principles of government, immediately you will see civil anarchy arise, which is the annihilation of political sovereignty. The government is a veritable religion: it has its dogmas, its mysteries, its ministers; to destroy it or to subject it to the discussion of each individual is the same thing; it lives only by the national reason; that is to say, by the political faith, which is a *symbol*. Man's first need is for his nascent reason to be bent under this double yoke, for it to be crushed, for it to be lost in the national reason, so that it may change its individual existence into another, common existence, as a river that rushes into the ocean exists forever in the mass of the waters, but without a name and without a distinct reality.[2]

What is *patriotism?* It is that national reason about which I am speaking, it is individual *abnegation*. Faith and patriotism are the two great miracle-workers of the world. Both are divine: all their actions are prodigies; beware of speaking to them about examining, choice, discussion: they will tell you that you blaspheme; they know only two words: *submission* and *belief*: with these two levers they lift the universe; their very errors are sublime. These two children of Heaven confirm their origin to all eyes in creating and in conserving; but if they happen to be united, to mingle their forces and together take possession of a nation, they exalt it, they make it divine, they increase its strength a hundredfold. One will

2. Rousseau said that one should not talk about religion to children and that the task of choosing one should be left to their reason. This maxim can be placed alongside another one: "The constitution of man is a work of nature; that of the state is a work of art" (*Social Contract*). No more is necessary to establish that Jean Jacques, so superficial under a vain appearance of profundity, had not the least idea about human nature and true political bases.

see a nation of five or six million men establish on the barren rocks of Judea the most superb city of superb Asia,[3] resist shocks that would have pulverized nations ten times more populous, brave the torrent of the centuries, the sword of conquerors, and the hatred of peoples, astonish the masters of the world[4] by its resistance, finally outlive all the conquering nations, and still after forty centuries display its deplorable remains to the eyes of the astonished observer.

One will see another people, having left the deserts of Asia, become in the wink of an eye a prodigious colossus; travel over the universe, a sword in one hand and the Koran in the other, breaking empires in its triumphal march, redeeming the evils of war through its institutions. Great, generous, and sublime, it will shine at the same time through reason and imagination; it will bring the sciences, the arts and poetry to the midnight of the middle ages; and so finally, from the Euphrates to the Guadalquivir, twenty prostrated nations will bend their heads under the peaceful scepter of Haroun-al-Raschid.

But this sacred fire that animates nations, is it you that can kindle it, insignificant man? . . . What! You can give a common soul to several million men? . . . What! You can make only one will from all those wills? Reunite them under your laws? Press them around a single center? Give your thought to men who do not yet exist? Make yourself obeyed by future generations and create those venerable customs, those conservative *prejudices*, fathers of laws and stronger than laws?—Hush.

Chapter 13 of Book I. Necessary Clarification

I must forestall an objection. In reproaching human philosophy for the wrongs it has done us, does one not risk going too far and being unjust in its regard, in going to the opposite extreme?

Without a doubt, one must guard against enthusiasm; but it seems that in this respect there is a sure rule for judging philosophy. It is useful when it does not leave its sphere; that is to say, the circle of the natural sciences: in this area all its attempts are useful, all its efforts merit our recognition. But as soon as it sets foot in the moral world, it must remember that it is no longer on

3. "*Hierosolyma longe clarissima urbium orientis, non Judaeae modo.*" Plin. *Hist. Nat.* 5, 14.
4. Joseph, *Bell. Jud.* 6, 9.

its own ground. It is general reason that holds the scepter in this circle; and philosophy—that is to say, individual reason—becomes harmful and consequently guilty if it dares to contradict or question the sacred laws of that sovereign—that is, the national dogmas: therefore its duty, when it transports itself into the empire of that sovereign, is to act in the same sense. By means of this distinction whose exactitude I do not believe it possible to contest, one knows what attitude to take to philosophy: it is good when it remains within its own domain or when it enters the territory of a superior empire only in the role of ally and even subject; it is detestable when it enters there as a rival or enemy.

This distinction serves to judge the century in which we are living and the one that preceded it; all the great men of the seventeenth century are especially remarkable for a general attitude of respect and submission toward all the civil and religious laws of their country. You will not find in their writings anything rash, anything paradoxical, anything contrary to the national dogmas, which are for them facts, maxims, and sacred axioms that they never call into question.

What distinguishes them is an exquisite good sense whose prodigious merit is well perceived only by men who have escaped the influence of false modern taste. As they address themselves always to the conscience of the readers, and as the conscience is infallible, it seems that one has always thought what they have thought, and minds given to sophistry complain that one finds *nothing new* in their works, whereas their merit lies precisely in investing in brilliant colors those general truths which are of all countries and all places, and on which depends the happiness of nations, families, and individuals.

What is today called a *new idea, a bold thought, a great thought* would almost always be called in the dictionary of writers of the last century, *criminal audacity, delirium,* or *outrage:* the facts show on which side reason is to be found. [Footnote omitted.]

I know that philosophy, ashamed of its appalling successes, has made the decision to disavow loudly the excesses of which we are the witnesses; but it is not thus that one escapes the censure of the sages. Fortunately for humanity, harmful theories are rarely to be found united in the same men in sufficient strength to lead to their practical consequences. But what does it matter to me that Spinoza lived tranquilly in a village in Holland? What does it matter to me that Rousseau, feeble, timid and eccentric, never had

the will or the power to excite sedition? What does it matter
to me that Voltaire defended Calas in order to be written about in
the gazettes? What does it matter to me that, during the frightful
tyranny that has burdened France, the philosophers, trembling for
their heads, have shut themselves up in a prudent solitude? Because
they have established maxims capable of giving birth to all sorts of
crimes, those crimes are their work, since the criminals are their
disciples. The most guilty, perhaps, of them all has not feared to
boast publicly that *after having obtained great successes for reason,
he had taken refuge in silence when it had become impossible to
listen to reason;*[5] but the successes of *reason* were only the intermediate state through which it was necessary to pass in order to
arrive at all the horrors that we have seen. Philosophers! You will
never exculpate yourselves, by pitying yourselves for the effect,
from having produced the cause. *You detest crimes,* you say. *You
have not killed.* Ah, well! *You have not killed:* that is the only praise
one can give you. But you have made others kill. It is you who said
to the people: *"The people, sole author of political government, and
distributor of the power confided in whole or in part to its
magistrates, is eternally in the right to interpret its contract—or,
rather, its gifts—to modify its clauses, to annul them, or to establish
a new order of things."*[6] It is you who have said to them:
*"The laws are always useful to those who possess and harmful to
those who have nothing: from which it follows that the social state
is advantageous to men only so long as they all have something
and no one has too much."*[7] It is you who have said to them:
*"You are sovereign: you can change your laws at will, even your
best fundamental laws, even the social pact; and if it pleases you
to do ill to yourself, who has the right to keep you from it?"*[8]
All the rest is only a consequence. The execrable Lebon, the
executioner of Arras, the monster *who stopped the blade of the guillotine ready to fall on the heads of his victims in order to read
the news to the unfortunates stretched out on the scaffold and then
had them killed,*[9] what did he answer when he was interrogated
at the bar of the National Convention by the only men in the
universe who had no right to find him guilty: *"I have had executed,*

5. *Notice on the life of Sieyès by himself.*
6. Mably, cited by the translation of Needham, Vol. I, p. 21.
7. *Social Contract,* Bk. II, Ch. IX.
8. *Social Contract,* Bk. II, Ch. XII; Bk. III, Ch. VIII.
9. *Nouvelles politiques nationales et étrangères,* 1795, No. 272, p. 1088.

he said, *some terrible laws, some laws which have made you turn pale. I was wrong. . . . One can treat me as I have treated others. When I met men of principles, I let myself be led by them.* IT IS ESPECIALLY THE PRINCIPLES OF J. J. ROUSSEAU THAT HAVE KILLED ME."[10]

He was right. The tiger who rends is plying his trade: the true culprit is the one who unmuzzles him and lets him loose on society. Do not believe that you absolve yourselves through your feigned lamentations on Marat and Robespierre. Listen to a truth: wherever you will be and people will have the misfortune to believe you, there will be similar monsters, for every society contains scoundrels who, to tear it apart, await only to be rid of the restraint of the laws; but, without you, Marat and Robespierre would have done no damage at all, because they would have been contained by this restraint that you have broken.

[Monarchy and Aristocracy]

The monarchy is a *centralized* aristocracy. In all times and in all places the aristocracy rules. Whatever form one gives to governments, birth and wealth always place themselves in the first rank and nowhere do they rule more harshly than where their empire is not founded on the law. But in the monarchy the king is the center of this aristocracy: it is indeed they who command as everywhere; but they command in the name of the king, or, if you prefer, it is the king informed by the enlightenment of the aristocracy [who commands].

"It is a sophism very familiar to publicists for royalty," Rousseau says again, "to assign liberally to that magistrate [the king] all the virtues he would need, and to suppose always that the prince is what he should be."[11]

I do not know what royal publicist made this strange supposition: Rousseau should certainly have cited him. As he read very little, it is probable that he took this assertion for granted, or that he took it from some dedicatory epistle.

But, while always avoiding exaggerations, one can say with assurance that the government of one man is that in which the vices of the sovereign have the least influence on the people governed.

A very remarkable truth was recently spoken at the opening of

10. Session of July 6, 1795. *Quotidienne ou Tableau de Paris*, No. 139, p. 4.
11. *Social Contract*, Bk. III, Ch. VI.

the republican Lycée of Paris: "In absolute governments,[12] the faults of the master can hardly ruin everything all at once, because his will alone cannot do everything; but a republican government is obliged to be essentially reasonable and just, because the general will, once misdirected, involves everything."[13]

This observation has the greatest exactitude: it is infinitely far from being the case that the will of the king does everything in the monarchy. It is considered as doing everything, and that is the great advantage of this form of government; but, in reality, it scarcely does more than centralize advice and knowledge. Religion, laws, customs, opinion, and the privileges of the orders and corporate bodies contain the sovereign and hinder him from abusing his power; it is even very remarkable that kings are accused much more often of lacking will than of abusing it. It is always the prince's council that directs affairs.

But the *pyramidal* aristocracy that administers the state in monarchies has particular characteristics that merit our whole attention.

In all countries and in all the possible governments, the great positions will always belong (with a few exceptions) to the aristocracy; that is to say, to the nobility and to wealth, usually united. Aristotle, in saying that the situation *must be thus*, states a political axiom whose simple good sense and the experience of all the ages leave in no doubt. This privilege of the aristocracy is really a natural law. [Footnote omitted.]

Now it is one of the great advantages of monarchical government that in it the aristocracy loses, as much as the nature of things permits, all its capacity for being offensive to the lower classes. It is important to understand the reasons for this.

(1) This kind of aristocracy is legal; it is an integral part of the government, all the world knows it, and it does not arouse in the mind of anyone the idea of usurpation and of injustice. In republics, on the contrary, distinctions between persons exist as in monarchies; but they are harsher and more insulting because they are not the work of the law, and because popular opinion regards

12. The word should have been *arbitrary:* for every government is absolute.
13. Speech pronounced at the opening of the republican Lycée, December 31, 1794, by M. de la Harpe. (*Journal de Paris*, 1795, No. 114, p. 461.)
    In the portion just read, the Lycée professor spoke a terrible truth to the Republic, and he strongly resembles an intelligent man who has been converted.

them as a persistent insurrection against the principle of equality admitted by the constitution.

There was perhaps as much distinction of persons, arrogance, and *aristocracy*, in the real sense of the word, in Geneva as in Vienna. But what a difference in both cause and effect!

(2) When the influence of hereditary aristocracy is inevitable (the experience of all the centuries leaves no doubt on this point), the best imaginable way to remove from this influence its tendency to irritate the pride of the lower classes is for it not to constitute an insurmountable barrier between the families of the state, and for none of them to be humiliated by a distinction that it can never enjoy.

Now that is precisely the case of a monarchy founded on good laws. There is no family that cannot, through the merit of its head, pass from the second order into the first, even independently of that prestigious assemblage, when, before it has acquired through time the influence that is equivalent to the price of acceptance in the higher rank, all the positions in the state—or at least a great many positions—are open to merit, to replace, for this family, hereditary distinctions and draw it closer to them. [Footnote omitted.]

This movement of general ascension that pushes all the families toward the sovereign and constantly fills all the vacuums left by those who die; this movement, I say, maintains a salutary emulation, animates the flame of honor, and diverts all private ambitions toward the welfare of the state.

(3) And that order of things will appear still more perfect if one thinks that the aristocracy of birth and offices, already made very attractive by the right of every family and every individual to enjoy in his turn the same distinctions, loses the remainder of what could be too offensive to the lesser social orders through the universal supremacy of the monarch before whom no citizen is more powerful than another; the man of the people, who finds himself too little in comparison with a great lord, compares the latter to the sovereign, and this title of *subject* that subjects them both to the same power and the same justice is a form of equality that quiets the inevitable sufferings of pride. . . .

48. September, 1796:
Théoanthropophile Manual

J. B. Chemin-Dupontès was a bookseller who himself wrote a number of books on morality and religion in the period of the Thermidorian reaction and the Directory. His *Manuel des Théoanthropophiles, ou adorateurs de Dieu, et amis des hommes; contenant l'exposition de leurs dogmes, de leur morale et de leurs pratiques religieuses. Publié par C.* (Paris, 1796, 51 pp.), a pamphlet in tiny format, of which the first part, containing, in the author's words, "the whole religion of the Théoanthropophiles," has been translated below, first appeared in September, 1796, and had new editions in 1797 and 1799, and was also translated into Italian. The strange name, taken from the Greek for "who loves God and man," soon gave way to the more melodious "Théophilanthrope," itself rather strange, which has since served to identify the unofficial deistic cult. Chemin's little book and the cult it illustrates enjoyed a certain popularity among educated people and had the support of a number of prominent political leaders of the Directory, particularly the Director Louis La Révellière-Lépeaux, who lectured on Theophilanthropy to the Institute on May 1, 1797, and later in the year participated in the coup of 18 Fructidor against the royalists. The moderate revolutionaries of the Thermidorian Convention and the Directory were still faced with the problem illustrated earlier in this collection by Robespierre's speech of May 7, 1794: they wanted to associate with their politics a set of religious and moral principles that would provide guidance and inspiration. They had come by a tortuous route to associate the traditional Catholic religion and its institutions with counter-revolution, but their own restrained and rational views, satisfying to a narrow circle of educated people, did not resolve the problem of fitting religion into the new social order in a manner acceptable to the great majority. Theophilanthropy, like the official *culte décadaire* promoted by the Directory, failed to penetrate very far into the French population. What follows is the first part, pp. 5–30, of Chemin's book.

Manual of the Théoanthropophiles,
or Adorers of God, and Friends of Men;
Containing the Exposition of Their Dogmas,
Their Ethics and Their Religious Practices

FIRST PART. DOCTRINE OF THE THÉOANTHROPOPHILES.
IT EMBRACES TWO OBJECTIVES: DOGMAS AND ETHICS

CHAPTER I. DOGMAS OF THE THÉOANTHROPOPHILES.
THEY CAN BE REDUCED TO TWO: THE EXISTENCE OF GOD AND
THE IMMORTALITY OF THE SOUL

The spectacle of the universe attests to the existence of a superior Being.

Our faculty of being able to think assures us that we have in ourselves a principle, superior to matter, which survives the disintegration of our bodies.

The existence of God and the immortality of the soul do not need lengthy demonstrations: they are intuited truths that each finds in his heart if he examines it in good faith. Only the wicked seek to doubt them, because the idea of a just God troubles their criminal enjoyments.

This twofold belief is necessary for the maintenance of society; for an aggregation of individuals who did not recognize God, and who believed that their crimes were buried forever in the tomb, would soon be a troop of ferocious beasts.

What God is, what the soul is, how God rewards the good and punishes the evil—the Théoanthropophiles do not carry out indiscreet researches concerning these matters: they are convinced that there is too great a distance between God and a created being for the latter to lay claim to knowing Him. They content themselves with knowing, from the magnificence and order of the universe, from the testimony of all peoples and of their own consciences, that there exists a God, that one cannot conceive of a God without the idea of every possible perfection; that consequently this God is good, that He is just; that therefore virtue will be recompensed, and vice punished. There is their whole theology. It is sufficient to make them good people. They regard all other questions as useless and dangerous, as tending to divide men and to make persecutors and victims such as there have already been in too great numbers because of religious opinions.

It is easy to deceive oneself or to be deceived. Our opinions depend on so many circumstances over which we are not in control that the Théoanthropophiles are convinced that God, being just and good, will not judge us from our opinions but from our actions. They take good care therefore not to hate, even less to persecute their fellowmen for opinions they do not share. They only seek, if they believe them to be in error, to disabuse them by gentle persuasion. If they persist, they keep the same sentiments of friendship for them. They have a feeling of horror only for criminal actions; they pity the guilty, and use all their efforts to bring them back to the good.

CHAPTER II. ETHICS OF THE THÉOANTHROPOPHILE.
IF THEIR DOGMAS ARE SIMPLE, THEIR ETHICS ARE NO LESS SO.
THEY ARE BASED ON A SINGLE PRECEPT:
WORSHIP GOD, CHERISH YOUR FELLOWMEN,
MAKE YOURSELF USEFUL TO THE PATRIE

This principle is the result of the existence of God. Since He is the supreme director of the universe, since we hold everything from Him, we owe Him the homage of gratitude. We owe friendship to our fellowmen, who are, like each one of us, His children. The obligation to cherish our fellows includes that of loving our native land, of making ourselves useful to our fellow citizens, with whom we have more relationships than with inhabitants of other parts of the world, and who protect our existence more immediately.

Any ethics which agree with this great principle are good in the eyes of the Théoanthropophiles. It serves as a rule in all their actions, and they derive all their duties from it.

1. Worship God

To worship God is to lift one's thoughts toward Him, to thank Him for His benefits and not complain about events which we regard as misfortunes but to profit from them to strengthen our souls and make them independent of all that is outside of us and accustom us to associate the idea of good only with wisdom and virtue and the idea of evil only with crime and madness.

To worship God is above all to obey His law, which He has clearly explained to us through that inner feeling which inclines us toward good, and turns us away from evil, and which is called *conscience*. Who can fail to recognize its voice? Some unfortunates seek in vain to stifle it by growing used to crime. It cries out to them always: *You are doing wrong.* The satisfaction we experience in doing good is the approbation of conscience. A bad deed is always accompanied and followed by its reproaches. We have no surer guide. It is through it that God teaches men what they must do and what they must avoid.

II. Cherish Your Fellows

To cherish one's fellows is to love them like oneself. He who cherishes his fellows does to others everything that he would want others to do to him.

He does to no one what he would not want done to him.

He is neither a slanderer nor a scandalmonger.

He does not put off to the morrow the service he can render at once.

He does not oppress those who are weaker than he. He lends them his support to defend them against oppression.

He consoles, he comforts the unhappy.

He pardons others the evil they do.

He does not seek vengeance. He forgets injuries. He avoids the wicked if he cannot reform them.

He helps widows and orphans.

He does not lend at usury.

He does not refuse what he owes: he does not make the indigent wait for their wages.

He does not turn his eyes away from the poor.

He gives with discrimination, and does not favor the lazy poor.

He does not prevent those who wish to do good from doing so; and he does good himself whenever he can.

He honors old age.

He respects the unfortunate.

He is hospitable to strangers.

He does not favor the rich to the prejudice of the poor.

He does not deceive; he does nothing contrary to fairness and good faith.

He is not envious of the success of the respectable man (he imitates his industrious probity); even less that of the rascal: ill-acquired wealth is one more misfortune for the wicked.

He checks his anger: he does not incite quarrels by his rages; he appeases them with his gentleness.

He avoids all excesses which confuse reason and lead to violence.

He endures the faults of others, well knowing that he has some of his own, which others see better than he and are obliged to bear.

He does not without reason entertain distrust or evil suspicions. He does not heed gossip, which is often ill-founded; he avoids everything that tends to impede the good understanding which should exist between brothers.

He is patient, mild, beneficent; he does not swell up with pride; he is not disdainful, or egoistic, or ambitious; he does not take offense and does not become soured easily; he does not rejoice in lies and injustice; he loves only the truth.

He does good without ostentation and without growing weary.

He loves his enemies; he does good to those who hate him, who persecute him and slander him.

What merit would he have if he loved only his friends and rendered service only to those who rendered it to him? He does good to all, even to the ungrateful, and disinterestedly.

He does not judge others more severely than he judges himself.

The sun never sets on his anger.

If he has subordinates, he treats them with mildness.

If he himself is a subordinate, he gives his superiors respect and affection; he fulfills his duties with precision and without need of supervision.

III. Make Yourself Useful to the Patrie

To make oneself useful to one's country is a duty whose necessity is not difficult to demonstrate. Apart from the fact that it is included, as already noted, in the obligation to cherish one's fellows, our interest requires it. It is to the coming together of the men around us that we owe our security and all the advantages that we enjoy in society. Man, who has such a long and feeble infancy, would nearly always perish from hunger or from the teeth of ferocious beasts if he were isolated or reduced to such ineffective defense as his father and mother could manage.

A society can only exist through the propensity of all its members to conserve it. On its suffering or well-being depends directly the suffering or well-being of every individual. We must therefore, as much from gratitude as from interest, cooperate in furthering the well-being of the society in which we were born, and which has raised us; that is, we must make ourselves useful to our country.

He who wishes to make himself useful to his country, if he has children, instructs them and accustoms them from an early age to virtue, in order that they in their turn may be useful to society. In this he will find his own happiness and glory, whereas the badly raised child is the shame of his father and mother; the well-brought up child honors his progenitors, obeys them. He comforts them in their old age; he carefully avoids all that could sadden them. For the child who pains his father and his mother is infamous and unhappy. The well brought-up child regards as a second father and second mother those who give him an education.

The good citizen is hard-working. Like the ant which during the summer makes provision for the winter, he contrives, while he is young, the means for existing in old age. The laborious man always gathers an abundance; but the lazy are always poor; indigence overtakes them like a man walking with great strides. In order to be independent, it is necessary to work. Laziness begets worries; it is the mother of all vices. Industriousness, on the contrary, brings about all pleasures; it is the support of good morals: it makes nations and individuals rich and powerful. Thus the laborious man is at the same time useful to his country, to his family, and to himself.

Is the country in danger? We must, without hesitating, rush to its defense. It is this absolute devotion that alone assures the safety of the state in general and of each citizen in particular. Let us make vows so that all men will at last consider themselves brothers and will cease to destroy each other. But if our country is attacked, the only way to have a firm peace is to offer a vigorous defense. Without that, all inhabitants would be victims of the enemy. All are therefore obligated, as much by interest as by duty, to unite their efforts in order to repulse him.

It is indispensable to the maintenance of the country that each individual comply with the laws and pay the state the taxes that are due it.

Each member of society owes the entire society the example of his respect for the customs, laws, magistrates, and generally accepted practices that do not offend morality; the example, in a word, of all the virtues that make the good son, husband, father, and citizen. . . .

49. September 19, 1797:
Bonaparte to Talleyrand About Sieyès

Shortly after the coup d'état of 18 Fructidor, An V (September 4, 1797), to which Napoleon, from Italy, had contributed military aid, and which revealed more starkly than ever the ruin facing France's effort to establish representative political institutions, Napoleon wrote the following letter to Talleyrand. Napoleon had already met Sieyès and was aware of some of his ideas, as was Mme. de Staël, who had conversed with them at a dinner party and whose political reflections on the problems facing France will be given in the final document. The source of Napoleon's letter is *Correspondance de Napoléon Ier, publiée par ordre de l'Empereur Napoléon III,* Vol. III (Paris, 1859), pp. 417–420.

Headquarters, Passariano, 3rd Day
Complementary, An V [September 19, 1797]
To the Minister of Foreign Relations

I have received, Citizen Minister, your confidential letter of 22 Fructidor relative to the mission that you wish to give Sieyès in Italy. I in fact believe, as you do, that his presence will be as necessary in Milan as it would have been in Holland, and as it is in Paris.

In spite of our pride, our thousand and one brochures, our endless and loquacious harangues, we are very ignorant in moral and political science. We have not yet defined what is meant by executive, legislative, and judicial powers. Montesquieu gave us false definitions, not that this celebrated man would not really have been capable of doing so, but his work, as he himself says, is only a kind of analysis of what existed or was existing; it is a résumé of notes made in his travels or in his reading.

He fixed his attention on the government of England; he defined, in general terms, the executive, legislative and judicial powers.

Actually, why would one regard the right of war and of peace and the right of determining the amount and nature of taxes as an attribute of legislative power?

The constitution has rightly entrusted one of these prerogatives to the House of Commons, and it has acted very well, because the

English constitution is only a charter of privileges: it is a ceiling all in black, but bordered in gold.

As the House of Commons is the only one which, after a fashion, represents the nation, it alone must have the right to tax; it is the only barrier that one has been able to find to modify the despotism and the insolence of the courtiers.

But in a government where all authority emanates from the nation, where the sovereign is the people, why classify among the attributes of the legislative power things which are alien to it?

In the last fifty years, I see only one thing that we have defined well, and that is the sovereignty of the people; but we have not been any more fortunate in the fixing of what is constitutional than in the assignment of the different powers.

In fact, therefore, the organization of the French people is still only roughly sketched.

The power of the government, in all the latitude that I give it, should be considered as the true representative of the nation, which should govern according to the constitutional charter and the organic laws; it is separated, it seems to me, naturally into two very distinct magistratures, one of which surveys but does not act, and to which what we call today the executive power would be obliged to submit important measures, if I may express myself in this way, the legislation of the execution: this high magistrature would be truly the great council of the nation; it would have all that part of the administration or of the execution that is entrusted by our Constitution to the legislative power.

By this means, the power of the government would consist of two magistratures, named by the people, one of which would be large in numbers, where only men who had already fulfilled some of the functions that give men maturity on the matters of government could be admitted.

The legislative power would, first, make all the organic laws; would change them, but not in two or three days, as is done, for once an organic law would be in process of execution, I do not believe that it could be changed before four or five months of discussion.

This legislative power, with no rank in the Republic, impassive, without eyes or ears for what surrounds it, would have no ambition and would no longer inundate us with a thousand laws decreed for the occasion which all alone annul themselves by their very absurdity, and which make us a lawless nation with three hundred folio volumes of laws.

There you have, I believe, a complete code of politics, which the circumstances in which we find ourselves render pardonable. It is such a great misfortune for a nation of thirty million inhabitants, and in the eighteenth century, to be obliged to have recourse to bayonets to save the *patrie!* Violent remedies accuse the legislator; for a constitution that is given to men must be planned for men.

If you see Sieyès, kindly transmit this letter to him; I urge him to write me that I am wrong; and believe me, you will give me much pleasure if you can contribute to the bringing to Italy of a man whose talents I esteem and for whom I have a very special friendship. I will support him with all my means, and I want us, by uniting our efforts, to be able to give to Italy a constitution more analogous to the customs of its inhabitants, to local circumstances, and perhaps even to true principles than that which we have given it. In order to avoid a complete innovation in the midst of the commotion of war and passions, it was difficult to do otherwise.

I sum up:

Not only do I reply to you confidentially that I want Sieyès to come to Italy, but I even think, and that very officially, that if we do not give to Genoa and to the Cisalpine Republic a constitution that suits them, France will draw no advantage from them; their legislative corps, bought with foreign gold, will be entirely at the disposition of the Austrian dynasty and of Rome. It will thus be, in the last analysis, like Holland.

Since the present letter is not an affair of tactics, or a plan of a campaign, I beg you to keep it for yourself and for Sieyès, and to use, if you judge it fitting, only what I have just told you about the unsuitableness of the constitutions that we have given to Italy.

You will see in this letter, Citizen Minister, the complete confidence that I have in you, and the answer to your last.

I greet you.

BONAPARTE

50. February or March, 1799:
Mme. de Staël on
Constitutionalism and Dictatorship

Mme. de Staël, daughter of the former Minister of Finances, Necker, became a celebrated literary critic and writer who combined talent with an irrepressible personality and a life that provided one of the most privileged vantage points from which to observe the era. Her mother's literary salon in the old regime, her marriage at twenty to the Baron de Staël-Holstein, Swedish Ambassador to France, her father's fame, and her own salon in the early revolutionary years provided a beginning. Then, between 1792 and 1795, came residence in Switzerland, where the wealthy Necker family had a home, and in England, and her return to Paris in 1795: too soon, for the Directory feared the political effects of her reopened salon and forced her to retire to Switzerland, from which she returned to Paris and the thick of things in 1797. All this gave her voracious intelligence unexampled opportunities for reflection. Her future was to see more exile and much travel, thanks to Napoleon, who could not stand aggressive female intellectuals and, more important, distrusted Mme. de Staël's circle of moderate liberal friends, including Benjamin Constant, with whom she had a liaison that lasted from 1794 until 1808. She was to be in Russia when Napoleon invaded in 1812, and was to return to France with the Restoration, heralded by works that were to assure her a lasting place in French literature. In early 1799, Mme. de Staël was thirty-three, living in Paris, and, with her penchant for devouring the best ideas of the best available minds, was fully aware of the perilous condition of the republic and of liberty. In an effort to point out the dangers, she wrote an essay, *Des circonstances actuelles qui peuvent terminer la révolution et des principes qui doivent fonder la république en France*, which in the absence of good documentation of the ideas of Sieyès, who hated to write things down, is perhaps the most significant statement about France made on the eve of the Napoleonic dictatorship and is a good example of a current of moderate liberalism that was to persist in France. Napoleon's coup of 18 Brumaire came before the book could be published, and it remained with Mme. de Staël's papers, to be edited by John Viénot (Paris, 1906). From this book, pp. 161–182, the following unfinished chapter on the constitution has been translated. Several paragraphs have been omitted to save space, but all of the principal arguments have been retained.

. . . In Europe, where all states are equally civilized, the little associations of men have no emulation, no riches, no fine arts, and no great men, and never would a Frenchman consent to renounce all that he shares of the glory and pleasure of his large association in order to obtain in exchange a perfect liberty in a small space, far from the world's gaze and from the pleasures of wealth. This opinion, which I believe to be very reasonable, nevertheless entails the obligation to reduce liberty, in the sense of having a right to deliberate on everything, to the power to choose one man out of a hundred thousand to pronounce, in the name of the nation, on all its interests. One has consented in advance to modify one's liberty in order to conserve the grandeur and brilliance of the empire. The maintenance of property in a country such as France also requires some sacrifice of the metaphysical principle of liberty since, to conserve it, power must be placed in the hands of the proprietors; finally, the republicans find with reason that the public spirit has not yet in France acquired that firm direction that long usage of liberty can alone give. The republicans base the necessity for revolutionary laws on the impossibility of yet entrusting to the nation the defense of its liberty.

In France, until the day comes when public instruction will have prepared a new generation for liberty, it will be necessary to prolong the hold of the republicans upon some portions of the trusteeship of power.

You have to choose between the dictatorship of institutions and that of individuals, and I very much prefer the first. You can democratize the Constitution in proportion to the progress of the public spirit. Everything that is done in conformity with opinion is maintained by it, but as soon as one precedes it or combats it, one is forced to have recourse to despotism. France in 1789 wanted a limited monarchy. Terror was not needed for its establishment. The Republic was proclaimed fifty years before people's minds were ready for it. Terror has been resorted to in order to establish it. But, this cruel means being far from capable of establishing anything, the reaction of that time, before the eighteenth of Fructidor, had forced the retreat of philosophical enlightenment to a point well before the first revolution. Voltaire, Helvétius, and Rousseau were looked upon as Jacobins, and the superstitions were professed by ambitious clairvoyants.

I ask of the enlightened republicans, is the nation well enough supplied with the love and the science of liberty to entrust all of the powers to the risk of annual elections? The republicans know so well that the outcome of elections left to themselves would be very unfavorable to the maintenance of the Republic that they supplement the public spirit with a multitude of improvised laws which subject the majority to the minority.

Nothing in the world is better calculated to discredit the representative system in the minds of the people than to proclaim the unlimited principles of liberty upon which it is based and then to have recourse to all sorts of sophisms and to all sorts of arbitrary acts in order to control the elections. It would be better to form a conservative corps, strengthen and continue the existence of the Council of Elders, make places in it for all outgoing members of the Directory and always choose from among them the new ones, grant them the right to propose laws, finally guarantee by an invincible barrier the stability of the constitutional bases of the Republic and of the principles of the Revolution, and then allow complete liberty in the election of the Council of Five Hundred. There would be neither duplicity nor violence in this order of things. Elections would be free and revolutions impossible. One could change and not upset; there would be at the same time liberty of motion and sureness of direction, whereas, in the present circumstances, the balance of the powers of our Constitution is maintained by an annual revolution that alternates between the royalists and the terrorists. In a given year one kills one group, in another year one deports the other, and it would be wrong to accuse the Directory of this, for since the Constitution does not give it sufficient prerogatives, and does not provide it with a point of support in an intermediary and independent corps, placed between two dangers, it saves the vessel from shipwreck, but cannot steer it to port (Sieyès). The Council of Elders, such as it is, renewed at the same times as the Council of Five Hundred, elected in the same manner, being absolutely nothing but a section of the same chamber, gives a faint suggestion of being conservative only because it has been given the name "Elders." But this institution is exactly calculated to irritate the revolutionary torrent and not to stop it.

The Council, such as it is, will be overthrown by the Five Hundred or will submit to collating its decrees like a copyist.

"What," someone will say to me, "can one not rely on the courage of virtue?" One must never calculate en masse except on the basis of personal interest.

Put men in a situation that promises them independence, fortune, and a certain degree of power for their whole lives, and you may be assured that they will defend, at the risk of their lives, the order of things which, if they preserve it, will care for that whole lifetime.

But if you give men three years of a rather feeble existence guaranteed by nothing and whose renewal is very uncertain, they will for the most part accept all the risks of change, and above all will not expose themselves to any danger to avoid it.

This French nation has given at one and the same time an example of fearlessness in its armies and of the most inconceivable weakness in internal affairs. The same men would have been intrepid warriors and ineffective deputies.

That is because in the army the path of interest was clearly and distinctly the same as that of glory and because in civil troubles, no one being sure of what he wanted, everyone avoided danger as the nearest and most positive inconvenience.

There are some exceptions to this inconceivable weakness, and you will find all of them among men whose past actions bound them invincibly to defend a certain opinion.

It would be necessary for the Council of Elders to be for life, at least for the present generation, for it to be from its ranks that the Five Hundred were obliged to choose the list of candidates for the Directory, for it to recruit its own replacements in the future from among the deputies of the Five Hundred, for it to be in the beginning composed of 150 members of the three national assemblies of France, of 50 men chosen from among the new deputies, the Institute, the most enlightened thinkers of France, and of 300 of the military who have best distinguished themselves in this war. It would above all be necessary for them to be assured by a considerable revenue, whether from the treasury or from the national properties, not only of independence but also of the consideration attached to wealth.

"What," some will cry, "Republicans seeking a fortune!"

You want the institution of property to be preserved. No social order can do without it: well, then, it is necessary for you to secure for your cause the influence of property.

France is being ruined by a few passages of Roman history which many men cite because they are wholly astounded at being able to do so, but the poverty of several famous republicans of Greece and Rome is not at all applicable to our social order and, I will repeat it ceaselessly, to our association of thirty million men. There were in Rome the most pronounced distinctions between patricians and plebeians. In Greece, the Lacedemonians did not know property.

The Athenian people, assembled in their entirety in the public square, could be governed only by the small number of eloquent men who knew how to talk to them. In France, one must hope, without doubt talent will have the prime places, but talent is the exception; but men, in relation to knowledge, are or believe themselves to be more on the same level than formerly, and it is in wealth that the customary and constant influence and consideration will for the most part be located. One must not therefore place government in opposition to this natural order of things; government must protect property instead of rivaling it.

Someone will hasten to tell me that if property has been persecuted, it is because it had come into the hands of enemies of the present order. It is always through lack of intelligence that one has recourse to violence. An institution requires thought, a revolutionary law anger: that is why we have so few institutions and so many revolutionary laws.

It is absurd, when one wishes to establish a constitution, when one has completed the confiscations deemed necessary, to continue, under whatever pretext, the war on property holders, and Babeuf, in wanting the agrarian law, is much more consistent than the legislators who tolerate property as a sort of onerous privilege which time will reform. When the legislators are not busying themselves with property, they take action concerning individuals. It is necessary that those who govern be proprietors, that a large fortune be attached to the 250 places of the Council of Conservators, the permanent corps in the state, from which members of the Executive Directory will be chosen, and to which they will return after having occupied public office. Then the gradations necessary to order will have been established; fortune united with power will have advantage over fortune without official standing. You will have raised the new institutions above the remembrance of the old; you will have created and therefore you will have destroyed, for men always need to exercise all their faculties, and if you do not replace the objects of these sentiments, they follow the same course; that is why the traveler perceives traces of ruins in all the places where new structures have not been put up. At present, power is on one side and fortune on the other. Consequently property is at war with legislation. Esteem is separate from official standing; opinion struggles against the government because official standing acts only upon the small number of men who concern themselves with public affairs and because esteem has an effect on the entire nation. Put power and fortune together; you will not yet have done everything unless you add to them virtue and enlightenment; but whereas individuals have need of personal merit, an association, a corps of any kind, may be judged by its circumstances. One always assumes that a certain number are motivated by their interests, and among 250 proprietors one holds it to be certain that a love of order and tranquillity will possess the majority.

"These," I will be told, "are the kinds of reasonings with which one could support all the prejudices that we have destroyed. Does the institution that you propose conform to the principle?" It does so in the same manner as the Constitution of 1795. The great principle of the Revolution, nonheredity, is preserved in it, selection instead of chance, election instead of privilege. And why would election every three years be more mathematically true than that every twenty years, or, what is worth even more, for life? Has nature indicated periodic replacements every three years? Why not every year, why not every day, why not whenever the people want them?

Property and the association of thirty million men are positive conditions which, rightly, one does not permit theorizing to dispose of. These two great modifications of natural liberty require, first of all, representative government instead of personal democracy, and require also the division into two chambers and the strong action of the Directory. Therefore there is not, properly speaking, democracy in the Constitution of France. It is a natural aristocracy as opposed to an artificial aristocracy; it should be the government of the best; it is always, however one behaves, the power of everyone placed in the hands of a very small number. One must therefore study the principles of this kind of government which consecrates natural inequality the better to destroy artificial inequality. It has its principle; it has its theory; it is an entirely new political system and one misinterprets it when one confuses it with the laws of democracy. What it has in common with it is a people who are one people without castes or privileged individuals. But Rousseau said, and that can be demonstrated as a mathematical truth, that there is no democracy where it is necessary to have a representative government. And so, therefore, neither the chamber for life that I propose, nor the two chambers of the present constitution, nor the single chamber of the Constitution of 1793, none of these institutions can be called democratic, and this designation has never been made except in hypocritical speeches justifying despotic and demented actions.

Certainly nothing seems to me better in itself than a perfect democracy and, for whoever renounces the glory of his *patrie*, and progress in science, the arts, and genius, true happiness lies there.
But let us learn then, in France, to understand the representative
system, of which neither the principle nor the correct evaluation
has yet been given.

The objective of the representative system is for the will of the
people, in other words the interests of the nation, all to be
defended and protected as if the nation itself could do it by
assembling in the public square.

It is thus not on varying the proportion of deputies, a proportion
which always depends on the size of the country, it is not upon this
proportion, I say, that the representative system depends. Without
doubt, in a thousand different ways, the larger a country grows, the
more of its liberty it loses; that does not depend on the proportion
of representatives to the represented, for you will not make a great
country freer by doubling the number of its representatives; you
will foster confusion, factions, divisions within the legislative corps
and, as all these misfortunes encourage despotism, by having
increased the proportion of deputies you will have destroyed the
effect of representation; that is to say, the will of the people will
have ceased to have representatives in the legislative corps, and
from the moment that you organize a legislative corps in a manner
that encourages factions there, you no longer have representation,
which is to say that the will of the people no longer has an
interpreter or no longer dominates. From that moment, men are
freed to devote themselves completely to their personal interests, for
the dangers and hopes of factions are always at the very least
foreign to the general will of the nation. It is necessary, therefore,
in order to have a representative government and to be faithful to
the principle of this government, to make, as it were, a reduced
image of the general will according to the proportions of the sum
total of public opinion. It is necessary for the legislature to be
organized in such a way that independence of views will have
nothing to fear and the ambition of the factions nothing to hope for;
and, finally, for the two distinct interests of societies to be represented.

In developing this idea, we will prove even more forcefully that
the conservative institution proposed in the constitution is not only
useful in practice but is an essential part of the abstract theory of
representative government. I compare it to the proof in arith-

metical rules: it demonstrates what usage had taught and makes known the cause whose result experience has shown.

In the era of privileged castes, the latter always had themselves represented by individuals of their orders. It has been proposed, in our day, to divide the representation into merchant deputies, farmer deputies, deputies who are men of letters, and so on, and this idea would have been good if the estates of society had been rigidly separated. Men have always sensed that it was interests that needed representation. They have disagreed on the basis, on the mode of elections, and on the number of deputies, but each of the various interests has always wanted to have its defender in the public powers.

There are two great interests—two fundamental interests, so to speak—which share the world: the need to acquire and the need to conserve. The proprietors, the nonproprietors, the generation in middle life, the generation beginning its career, the innovating spirits, the tranquil spirits—all gravitate to one or another of these two interests; finally, nature herself seems to present the same idea, with its change and its duration. Continuity of development and invariability of direction compose both its action and its existence. Nothing, then, is more true, according to the most widely diffused principles, than the necessity of representing in government the two interests upon which society rests.[1]

In placing the principal authors of the Revolution in a conservative institution, you are combining almost conflicting advantages: you place democratic principles under the safeguard of aristocratic forms and, as the partisans of prejudices have always taken great precautions to preserve themselves from upheavals, you use against them some of their own fortifications.

Among the authors of the Revolution, there are ardent men disposed to factionalism and, consequently, to anarchy; by giving them an honorable and permanent place in the state, you make use of their energy and you annul their defects by appealing to their interests. At first the Five Hundred, freely elected, will be more aristocratic in their principles than the Elders, because the frightful memories of the revolutionary regime will have made their strongest impression on the young and enthusiastic. But after a few years popular innovation will be the principal motivation of the elected

1. Mme. de Staël adds in a note in the mss.: "Put there what Godwin said about morality and legislative power."—Editor.

Council, and preservation of the constitution will be that of the permanent Council; finally, if opinion were to become well enough informed, if education were to be better disseminated, one would witness such changes as the extent of the increased enlightenment of the nation warranted. But at least there must be established in some branch or other of the government a free election, and that is what we have not yet seen. Although the present state of affairs is patterned more closely after the principle of representative government than the one I propose, it is entirely destructive of it. The terrorists and the royalists take turns dominating the electoral assemblies. Forms of liberty are established for the elections but in practice tyranny prevails, and in all parts of the government *compelled volunteers* are necessary. Everything must be done freely, on condition that one has a certain wish, and this mixture of hypocrisy and despotism provides all the disadvantages of tyranny. Tyrants command; popular chieftains lead instead of commanding.

But all virtues and sentiments are, so to speak, jumbled together if you are called a slave when you resist force and are called free when you join with those in power to oppress weakness; finally, in controlling the elections, as is being done, one destroys respect for republican government in the minds of the people. It would be better to allow them only the choice of the tribunes, as at Rome, and to deprive them openly of their rights than to make them play at elections like children playing at being adults, legalizing what the minority does, excluding from the assemblies, by force or by law, all of those who displease, and finally attacking ceaselessly the elementary principle of every representative government: total liberty in the assemblies which elect and in the nature of the choices which they make.

"With this system," I will be told, "you will return to us the elections which brought on the eighteenth of Fructidor. It is because, by your own admission and that of all observers, the nation, upon emerging from several centuries of monarchy, has not yet enjoyed liberty long enough to have the sentiment of it, because the generation born under kings has not yet passed, that it is necessary to place at the center of the government an immovable corps around which new recruits gather but whose strength is such that it can both combat and convert every spirit contrary to its own. When the entire nation will have risen to the level of republican opinions and enlightenment, when public education will have made of all men, if that is possible, wise and enlightened friends of liberty, then not only will you be able to make everything subject to election but almost, so to speak, do without government altogether."

But the republicans recognize the necessity of doing by violence what I propose that they establish legally. They agree that it is necessary to restrict choices to a small number of men who are profoundly republican. They annul elections, they deport people en masse, they banish a multitude of men falsely inscribed on the list of émigrés; they deprive people of political rights unconstitutionally; they threaten still more violence, and when one asks them what can give them the courage to commit so many injustices, they respond that the nation is not yet generally republican enough to justify unqualified reliance on the will of the masses.

In this respect they are right, but if a dictatorship is necessary—that is to say, a suspension of the exercise of the will of all—why not look for it in legal institutions instead of abandoning it to arbitrary violence? Which is better? To establish, so to speak, each year an 18 Fructidor against the royalists, and the following year a 9 Thermidor against the terrorists, or to establish a good organization based on two chambers! . . .

When you will have restored full liberty to the election of the Council of Five Hundred, not only will you be assured, by the existence of the permanent Council, that you have nothing to fear from a terrorist or royalist faction even if it should seize the Council of Five Hundred, but you may also be almost certain that such factions will never be elected. It is through hope of success that all such passions arise, and revolutionary furors will cease when there is no longer a possibility that they will serve someone's ambitions. Eventually, the people will grow disgusted with useless choices, and seeing the terrorists and the royalists equally break themselves against a stable government, they will choose men whose republican opinions serve the interests of the constitution instead of hampering it. Finally, if the free election of the Council of Five Hundred should, for some time yet, be anti-republican, the prerogatives that must be added to the executive power would still provide the necessary cohesion among all parts of the government. As an eloquent thinker has said, it is the union of the powers that must be sought, and people are always confusing the necessary separation of functions with a separation of powers which inevitably makes them enemies of one another. The Directory must have a suspensive veto from one session to another; it must have the right to dissolve the Council of Five Hundred and call for a new election by the people. What is the eighteenth of Fructidor? All parties are going to answer you: one, it is an atrocious conspiracy thwarted; another, it is a tyrannical act of a barbarous faction. I myself would answer: it is the necessary effect of a bad constitution, it is the breaking of a machine that was not calculated for action. . . .

. . . "What power," someone is going to cry, "what power you are going to give to the Executive Directory!" Infinitely less than it has at this moment, for it must govern illegally in order to maintain itself, in order to make the government work. Which do you prefer, a suspensive veto, the power to dissolve while appealing to the people through new elections, or 18 Fructidor, or its necessary appendage, 9 Thermidor? On the morrow of a constitutional act, all the powers and all individuals are in their places. On the morrow of a crisis, what tyrant, what factionist does not conceive criminal hopes? What innocent person is tranquil, what man is happy? . . .

[The chapter is not finished. The right-hand side of leaf 195 is made up of the following note, which leaves off abruptly.]

There are, in the present Constitution of France—or, to say it better still, in the spirit of the Revolution—three principles which are the secret of its strength and also its objective, three principles which one could not abandon without abandoning Republican government: the division of the executive power into several parts, because in France any man who was not king would not be tolerated alone at the head of the government, and because any man who would be allowed there would wish to become king; election by the people of the Council of Five Hundred, because on that depends the whole representative system; and the nonheredity of the powers, because it was through equality that the Revolution was made and through it that it has influence, and because finally the destruction of the privileges of the classes and castes is the conquest of the human spirit at this time. But, in conserving these three principles which are . . .

The Republican and Gregorian Calendars

		I 1792	II 1793	III 1794	IV 1795	V 1796	VI 1797	VII 1798	VIII 1799	IX 1800	X 1801	XI 1802	XII 1803	XIII 1804	XIV 1805
1 *vendémiaire* Lat. *vindemia* vintage	SEPT.	22	22	22	23	22	22	22	23	23	23	23	24	23	23
1 *brumaire* Lat. *bruma*, winter Fr. *brume*, mist	OCT.	22	22	22	23	22	22	22	23	23	23	23	24	23	23
1 *frimaire* Fr. *frimas* heavy fog	NOV.	21	21	21	22	21	21	21	22	22	22	22	23	22	22
1 *nivôse* Lat. *nivosus* snowy	DEC.	21	21	21	22	21	21	21	22	22	22	22	23	22	22
		1793	1794	1795	1796	1797	1798	1799	1800	1801	1802	1803	1804	1805	1806
1 *pluviôse* Lat. *pluvia* rain	JAN.	20	20	20	21	20	20	20	21	21	21	21	22	21	
1 *ventôse* Lat. *ventosus* windy	FEB.	19	19	19	20	19	19	19	20	20	20	20	21	20	
1 *germinal* Lat. *germen* embryo, bud	MARCH	21	21	21	21	21	21	21	22	22	22	22	22	22	

		20	20	20	20	20	20	20	21	21	21	21	21	21
1 *floréal* Lat. *flos, floris* flower	APRIL													
1 *prairial* Lat. *pratum*; Fr. *pré* field, meadow	MAY	20	20	20	20	20	20	21	21	21	21	21	21	21
1 *messidor* Lat. *messis*, harvest Gr. *dôron*, gift	JUNE	19	19	19	19	19	**19**	20	20	20	20	20	20	20
1 *thermidor* Gr. *thermos*, warm Gr. *dôron*, gift	JULY	19	19	19	19	19	19	20	20	20	20	20	20	20
1 *fructidor* Lat. *fructus*, fruit Gr. *dôron*, gift	AUG.	18	18	18	18	18	18	19	19	19	19	19	19	19

Example: *1 thermidor, an II* = July 19, 1794; *9 thermidor* would be 8 days later, on July 27, 1794. The republican calendar, which opened with September 22, 1792 (retroactively, by vote of the National Convention on November 24, 1793), was abandoned as of January 1, 1806, by *senatus consultum* of September 9, 1805. Each month had three ten-day weeks, each *décadi*, or tenth day, being a day of rest. The five days left over from the Gregorian calendar came between *fructidor* and *vendémiaire* and therefore do not have a place on the above chart; they were called *sans-culottides*, and were festival days; there was a sixth supplementary day in leap years. This non-Christian calendar was intended for universal adoption but Fabre d'Eglantine's poetic nomenclature would not have worked for the Southern Hemisphere, where *thermidor* would have come in midwinter.

Chronology

1787

February 22–May 25   First Assembly of Notables.
November 19   Royal session of the Parlement of Paris.

1788

May 8   Judicial reform, including Cour Plénière.
August 8   Estates General called and Cour Plénière suspended.
September 21   Parlement of Paris stipulates forms of 1614 for Estates General.
November 6–December 12   Second Assembly of Notables.
December 27   *Résultat du Conseil* announcing doubling of representation of Third Estate and admission of lower clergy to electoral assemblies of clergy; nothing said about vote by order or by head.

1789

March   Beginning of elections to Estates General.
April 27–28   Réveillon riots in Faubourg Saint-Antoine.
May 5   Royal session opening Estates General.
June 17   Deputies of Third Estate adopt proposition of Sieyès and constitute selves National Assembly.
June 19   Vote of majority of clergy to join Third.
June 20   Tennis Court Oath using Mounier's formula: not to separate until constitution is established.
June 21   Royal council meeting rejects Necker's compromise plan.
June 23   Royal session of Three Estates; failure of king to impose his program; Mirabeau and others express defiance.
June 27   Louis XVI orders clergy and nobles to join with deputies of Third.
July 1   Substantial military reinforcements to Paris region.
July 11   Dismissal of Necker.

July 12   Disorders in Paris; some military side with people; Parisian electoral assemblies for Estates General begin to assume control of the city.

July 13   Parisian electors establish central committee and form bourgeois militia.

July 14   Fall of the Bastille; Paris abandoned by royal troops.

July 16   Necker recalled.

July 17   Louis XVI visits Paris. Emigration begins.

July 20   Start of the Great Fear.

August 4   Evening session of National Constituent Assembly, lasting until 2 A.M. of the fifth, abolishes "feudal" dues and all sorts of personal and regional privileges, with certain property rights to be redeemed.

August 26   Adoption of Declaration of the Rights of Man and of the Citizen.

September 10   Assembly votes against having an upper chamber.

September 11   Assembly votes that king shall have only a suspensive veto.

October 5   Crowd of Parisians, including many women, marches to Versailles; Louis XVI agrees to sanction Declaration of Rights and legislation of August 4–11; Lafayette and National Guard arrive rather late.

October 6   At dawn crowds break into palace, endanger lives of royal family; guards massacred; royal family returns to Paris with crowds, to Tuileries Palace.

October 10   Assembly decrees Louis XVI "King of the French" (in place of "King of France"); Talleyrand proposes confiscation of Church property; Mounier goes home to Dauphiné; Dr. Guillotin proposes new method of execution.

November 2   Assembly decrees that Church properties belong to nation, which is responsible for upkeep of Church and aid to poor.

November 7   Assembly (thinking of Mirabeau) excludes its deputies from positions as ministers.

December 9   Division of France into departments accepted in principle.

December 19   Creation of *assignats* in large denominations bearing interest and usable for purchase of former Church properties.

1790

February 13   Monastic vows forbidden; religious orders suppressed except for teaching and charity.

April 27   Cordeliers Club opens.

May 10   First of the series of memorandums to Louis XVI from Mirabeau.

May 12   Society of 1789 created as rival to Jacobins by Lafayette, Sieyès, Talleyrand, Bailly, and others.

May 21   48 "sections" of Paris created by Assembly to replace the 60 electoral districts used in electing Estates General.

May 22   Assembly decrees renunciation of wars of conquest.

June 19   Assembly decrees abolition of titles of hereditary nobility.

July 12   Final vote of Civil Constitution of the Clergy.

July 14   Fête de la Fédération on Champ-de-Mars.

September 29   *Assignats* made into paper money without interest.

October 23   Louis XVI initiates overtures to foreign courts concerning their conditions for intervention in France.

October 28   Report of Merlin de Douai concerning possessions of German princes in Alsace advances idea of self-determination of peoples in opposition to traditional idea of dynastic properties.

November 27   Assembly orders clergy to take public oath of loyalty to the nation, the law, and the king.

November   Publication of Burke's *Reflections on the Revolution in France.*

1791

March 2   Abolition of guilds and masterships and privileged manufactures.

March 10   Pius VI issues pastoral letter condemning Civil Constitution of the Clergy and principles of the Declaration of the Rights of Man.

April 2   Death of Mirabeau.

May 16   National Assembly, urged by Robespierre, decrees that its members may not be elected to the next legislature.

June 14   Chapelier law on abolition of corporate bodies and illegality of strikes and labor organizations.

June 20   Flight of king and royal family.

June 21   Royal family arrested at Varennes.

June 25   Royal family is returned to Tuileries Palace. Assembly decrees that Louis XVI is suspended from his functions.

July 16   Assembly decrees that Louis XVI's suspension shall end when the constitution is finished and he has accepted it.

Feuillants formed as Jacobins split over what to do about the king.

July 17   Champ-de-Mars massacre as National Guard led by Lafayette fires on crowds.

August 5   Assembly decrees that French nation will never make wars of conquest or attack the liberties of any people.

August 27   Declaration of Pillnitz by emperor of Austria and king of Prussia pledges action vs. revolution if other powers will join.

National Assembly abolishes *marc d'argent* requirement for holding office as legislator but increases property qualification for voting.

September 14   Louis XVI appears before National Assembly and swears to uphold the constitution.

Assembly declares Avignon and the Comtat-Venaissin to be part of France, using plebiscites as basis of decision.

September 27   Citizenship rights voted for all Jews.

September 30   Final session of National Constituent Assembly.

October 1   First meeting of Legislative Assembly.

1792

March 10   Legislative Assembly forces Louis XVI's ministers to resign by threatening investigations.

March 15   Louis XVI appoints "Brissotin" ministry. (Jacobins still included both Brissotins and Robespierrists.)

April 20   France declares war on Hapsburg emperor as Legislative Assembly accepts king's proposal of war.

April 25   Rouget de Lisle, at Strasbourg, composes the song that will later be known as "La Marseillaise."

June 12   Louis XVI dismisses Brissotin ministers; replaces them with Feuillants in next few days.

June 20   Crowd invades Tuileries but fails to get king to make concessions.

June 28   Lafayette appears before Legislative Assembly and demands measures against the Jacobins.

June 29   Lafayette seeks but fails to get public support for coup to stabilize regime on a more conservative basis.

July 25   Brunswick Manifesto threatens punishment of Paris if rebels do not submit to their king.

August 10   Insurrection of Paris sections attacks Tuileries, massacres Swiss guards, sets up new city government (Commune); royal family takes refuge with Legislative Assembly, which decrees suspension of king and decides to call a convention.

August 11   Legislative Assembly chooses new ministers, e.g., Danton (justice), Roland (interior), and gives directions for election of constitutional convention to be chosen by manhood suffrage in two stages.

August 19   Lafayette, having failed in attempt to lead his army against Paris, surrenders to Austrians, who imprison him.

August 25   Legislative Assembly suppresses seigneurial dues without indemnity.

September 2   "September massacres" of persons in overcrowded Parisian prisons begins as news arrives of Prussian siege and capture of Verdun.

Danton makes celebrated speech in Legislative Assembly, rallying the country for resistance to invasion, but does not control the hysterical massacres in Paris, which last until September 5.

September 20   French victory over Brunswick's Prussians at Valmy.

September 21   In first full session of National Convention, royalty is decreed abolished but word "republic" is not used.

September 22   Convention uses word "republic" in ordering that henceforth all acts be dated from the Year I of the French Republic.

September 27   Danton and Roland resign as ministers in order to accept election to Convention. (Roland later reverses his decision and resigns his Convention seat in order to remain Minister of the Interior.)

October 11   Convention names largely Brissotin Constitutional Committee, of which Condorcet, considered an independent and a mediator, is to be secretary.

November 6   French victory over Austrians at Jemappes, in Belgium, notable for being done by new-style revolutionary army and for resulting prestige of French General Dumouriez.

November 13   In opening of debate on question of trial of Louis XVI, Saint-Just, speaking for first time in Convention, launches powerful attack on the king.

November 19   Convention decrees "that it will accord fraternity and aid to all peoples who wish to recover their liberty and that it charges the executive to give to the generals the necessary orders to bring aid to these peoples and defend citizens who have been or could be persecuted for upholding the cause of liberty."

November 20   Discovery in Tuileries of *armoire de fer* with documents incriminating to king; Roland to be criticized for not having witnesses present at time of removal of papers.

December 15   Convention approves Cambon report on policies to be followed in occupied countries, such as suppression of tithes and seigneurial dues, seizure of properties of princes, issue of *assignats*, encouragement of elections from which aristocrats have been excluded, and generally making expansion of the revolution pay for itself.

1793

January 15   Louis XVI voted guilty of conspiracy against the public liberty (707-0); ratification of this decision by the people voted down (424-287).

January 16–17   24 hours of voting (accompanied by explanatory statements) on subject of what punishment. Results: death (387–334); but some deputies have demanded reprieve.

January 18   Another vote on punishment. Result: death (361–360).

January 19–20   Vote on question of reprieve. Result: reprieve defeated (380–310).

Montagnard deputy Lepeletier de Saint-Fargeau murdered by a royalist on January 20.

January 21   Louis XVI (technically Louis Capet) guillotined.

February 1   Convention declares war on king of England and stadtholder of Netherlands.

February 15   Condorcet presents "Girondin" constitutional project to Convention.

February 17   Dumouriez invades Holland.

March 1   Dumouriez's position threatened by enemy offensive in Belgium.

March 7   Convention declares war on king of Spain.

March 9   Convention decides to send representatives on mission (from its own membership) into the provinces and to the military fronts.

March 10   Revolutionary Tribunal founded (at first called Extraordinary Criminal Tribunal).

March 11   Beginning of war in Vendée.

March 18   Dumouriez defeated at Neerwinden, in Belgium.

Convention decrees death to anyone proposing the agrarian law "or any other subversion of . . . property."

April 4   Dumouriez fails to get his army to march against Paris and takes refuge with Austrians.

April 6   Convention creates Committee of Public Safety, with Danton as a member.

April 24   Marat acquitted by Revolutionary Tribunal and carried in triumph to Convention, whose moderate majority had earlier voted his accusation.

May 4   First "maximum"; i.e., fixing of grain prices.

May 18   "Girondins" get Convention to decree Commission of Twelve to investigate Commune of Paris.

May 31   Insurrection, planned for several days, of Paris sections surrounds Convention and demands abolition of Commission of Twelve, exclusion of leading Girondins, more price-fixing, a tax on the rich, etc. Convention suppresses Commission of Twelve.

June 2   After further pressure from sections on June 1, Convention is forced by sans-culottes and National Guard to continue their session (after they had tried to leave), to expel Girondin deputies, and to arrest many of them.

June 3   Convention decides to break up properties of émigrés into small plots for sale to nonrich.

June 7   Widespread rebellion in sympathy with Girondins, e.g. in Bordeaux, against Convention's authority.

June 9   Jacobin constitutional project presented to Convention by Hérault de Séchelles.

Opening of big Vendée offensive against government.

June 24   Constitution of the Year I adopted by Convention.

June 25   Jacques Roux, who has been agitating at Cordeliers and elsewhere against the shortcomings of the constitution and has previously been kept from speaking to Convention, leads a delegation to Convention and speaks to a hostile audience.

June 30   Robespierre, Hébert, and others get Roux expelled from Cordeliers.

July 8   Condorcet decreed subject to arrest for his published protest against Jacobin Constitution; forced into hiding, where he writes *Esquisse d'un tableau historique des progrès de l'esprit humain.*

July 10   Reshuffle of Committee of Public Safety; Danton dropped; Saint-Just and Couthon added, with others.

July 13   Marat assassinated by Charlotte Corday.

July 27   Robespierre elected to Committee of Public Safety.

August 1   Adoption of metric system.

August 4   Ratification of constitution completed.

August 23   *Levée en masse* decreed by Convention: principle of universal service.

August 27   Mediterranean port and naval base of Toulon taken by the English.

September 5   Popular effervescence of sans-culottes comes to climax in surrounding of Convention and entry of delegation led by officials of Commune of Paris, with demands that Terror be the order of the day, suspects be arrested, a revolutionary army be formed, a general maximum for prices be established, the Revolutionary Tribunal be recast, etc. Convention adopts Terror as order of the day, and agrees in principle to the other demands.

September 17   Law of Suspects adopted by Convention.

September 22   Start of Year II of the Republic, according to republican calendar adopted later (October 5).

September 29   General Maximum on essential products and on wages decreed by Convention.

October 10   Revolutionary government proclaimed; i.e., government according to constitution postponed until peacetime.

October 16   Marie Antionette guillotined.

October 31   Execution of Brissot, Gensonné, Vergniaud, and other Girondins condemned by Revolutionary Tribunal.

November 7   Constitutional Bishop Gobel leads movement of abandonment of the priesthood before Convention.

Philippe Égalité, former Duke of Orléans, father of future King Louis Philippe (who left France with Dumouriez), guillotined.

November 10   Festival of Liberty and Reason celebrated at Notre-Dame, renamed Temple of Reason.

November 17   Robespierre's major report on foreign policy; arrest of some of Danton's associates.

November 20   Danton's return from semiretirement to take up campaign for an easing of the Terror, the making of peace, and constitutional revision.

December 4   Law of 14 Frimaire, An II, consolidating the revolutionary government.

December 19   French retake Toulon; Captain Napoleon Bonaparte contributes to the victory.

Adoption of principle of free, obligatory primary education.

December 23   Victory over Vendée army; end of large-scale warfare there, though guerrilla activity continues.

1794

February 4   Abolition of slavery in French colonies without indemnity.

February 5   Robespierre's major report to Convention on the principles of political morality.

February 26 (8 Ventôse, An II)   Saint-Just introduces first of the laws of Ventôse, and it is voted.

March 3 (13 Ventôse, An II)   Saint-Just introduces further laws of Ventôse, and they are voted.

March 21   Trial of Hébertists opens.

March 24   Execution of Hébertists and various militant sans-culottes, foreigners, former aristocrats, etc., who have been "amalgamated" with them in the trial and condemnation.

March 28   Suicide of Condorcet, arrested the day before.

April 2   Trial of Dantonists opens, various others being amalgamated with Danton and his friends.

April 5   Execution of Dantonists.

April 22   Couthon gets Convention to decree that a member of the Committee of Public Safety be charged with the writing of a code for "social institutions." Saint-Just's *Institutions républicaines*, an unfinished manuscript not published until long after the revolution, may have been the start of this project. It contains very drastic social proposals, e.g. the separation of children from their parents and their upbringing by the State.

May 7 (18 Floréal, An II)   Following Robespierre's major report on religious and moral ideas, the Convention decrees that the French people recognize the existence of the Supreme Being and the immortality of the soul; and the Convention institutes public festivals, the first to be to the Supreme Being.

June 8 (20 Prairial, An II)   Festival of the Supreme Being, presided over by Robespierre.

June 10 (22 Prairial, An II)   Following Couthon's report on the Revolutionary Tribunal, and some opposition which Robespierre dominates by demanding an immediate unanimous vote, the Convention passes the law of Prairial which almost eliminates judicial guarantees for the accused. The Great Terror dates from this law.

June 26   Victory of Fleurus, in Belgium, over the Austrians.

June 29   Following quarrel in Committee of Public Safety, Robespierre walks out; he is not to return until July 23, but does meanwhile attend Jacobin Club.

July 23   Joint meeting of committees of Public Safety and General Security, arranged the day before, for purposes of conciliation; Robespierre present; uneasy compromises agreed upon.

Publication of new maximum on wages arouses discontent.

July 26 (8 Thermidor, An II)   Robespierre's last speech to Convention, prepared without consulting anyone, calls for government reorganization and purge. Opposition gets order to print speech rescinded.

Evening: Robespierre repeats speech to sympathetic Jacobin Club; all forces prepare for struggle the next day in Convention.

July 27 (9 Thermidor, An II)   Opposition interrupts Saint-Just and Robespierre in Convention, which finally orders arrest of Robespierrists. Insurrection by Commune and refusal of prisons to receive Robespierrists enable latter to assemble at Hôtel de Ville, where they take no action. Supporting crowds dwindle; more radical sections have not supported Robespierrists, who are outlawed by Convention and captured about 2:30 A.M. on July 28.

July 28 (10 Thermidor, An II)   Robespierrists guillotined.

August 1   Law of Prairial rescinded; many prisoners to be released in days to come.

August 24   Government reorganized into 16 committees.

September 18   Republic will no longer pay the expenses of any form of worship.

October 30   Decree establishing normal schools.

November 12   Jacobin Club closed.

December 8   Many Girondin deputies return to Convention.

December 24   Abolition of the maximum.

1795

January 22   French capture Dutch fleet, iced in.

February 21   Freedom of worship and separation of Church and State decreed in France.

April 1 (12 Germinal, An III)   Sans-culotte insurrection against Convention; suppressed by military following day.

April 5   Peace of Basel with Prussia.

May 16   Peace of La Haye with Holland; France recognizes Batavian Republic, a "sister republic."

May 20 (1 Prairial, An III)   Sans-culotte insurrection that is to be suppressed on May 23.

May 31   Suppression of Revolutionary Tribunal.

June 8   Death of Louis XVII, a prisoner in the Temple.

July   Louis XVIII's Declaration of Verona published in France and England.

July 21   Defeat of émigré forces that had landed on Quiberon Peninsula in Brittany.

July 22   Peace of Basel with Spain.

August 22   Convention adopts Constitution of the Year III.

August 30   Two-thirds decree requiring voters to choose two-thirds of the members of the new legislature from the ranks of the Convention.

September 23   Proclamation of Constitution of the Year III.

October 1   Annexation of Belgium.

October 5 (13 Vendémiaire, An IV)   Royalist insurrection in Paris put down by troops, with Napoleon Bonaparte in charge of artillery.

October 12   Start of elections under new constitution.

October 26   Dissolution of the National Convention.
Place de la Révolution becomes Place de la Concorde.

1796

February 19   Suspension of issue of *assignats*.

March 2   Napoleon Bonaparte made General in Chief of Army of Italy.

March 9   Napoleon Bonaparte marries Josephine de Beauharnais.

March 30   Babeuf and a few others form an insurrectional committee.

May 10   Arrest of Babeuf and his associates.
Napoleon's victory at Lodi, near Milan, that contributes to the taking of Lombardy and to his reputation for bravery and leadership.

December 16   Failure of French expeditionary force under Hoche as bad weather prevents landing at Bantry Bay on southwest coast of Ireland and United Irish are unready.

1797

March 21   First stage of elections for renewal of a third of the legislature; elections are to be royalist and moderate victory, calling into question control of France by makers of Constitution of 1795.

May 20   First meeting of Councils of Elders and Five Hundred after elections.

May 27   Babeuf guillotined.
June 6   Ligurian Republic founded from former Republic of Genoa.
July 7   Opening of Anglo-French peace talks at Lille.
July 9   Cisalpine Republic established.
September 4 (18 Fructidor, An V)   Coup of the Executive Directors against the newly elected legislative councils with the aid of the military.
September 19   Failure of Lille peace talks.
September 30   First of two measures (second is December 14) amounting to virtual repudiation of two-thirds of outstanding government debts.
October 17   Treaty of Campo Formio with Austria.
October 26   Decision of Directory to create Army of England under command of Bonaparte.
November 16   Opening of Congress of Rastatt, as agreed at Campo Formio, to dispose of left bank of Rhine.

1798

February 13, 14   French troops take Berne, including its treasury.
February 15   Proclamation of Roman Republic.
March 24   Conclusion of elections to Elders and Five Hundred: replacement of one-third of deputies, as called for by constitution, and also of those excluded by Fructidor coup in 1797; victory for democrats.
April   Organization of Helvetic Republic.
April to December   Formation of Second Coalition against France.
May 11 (22 Floréal, An VI)   Coup of 22 Floréal by which Directors quash elections of 106 deputies to legislature and of various judges and other officials.
May 19   Departure of Napoleon's Egyptian expedition.
July 21   Napoleon's victory in Battle of the Pyramids.
August 1   Nelson's victory over French fleet at Aboukir Bay.
August   Landing of French General Humbert with 1,000 troops in western Ireland, too late to help United Irish; Humbert eventually forced to surrender.
September 5   Military service law instituting conscription for ages 20–25 if called.

1799

January 23   French take Naples, where on January 26 they support proclamation of a Parthenopean Republic.
February 16   Referendum (contested) favors annexation of Piedmont to France.

March 12   Directory declares war on Austria.

April 9   Second stage of elections for Elders and Five Hundred; strengthening of democratic and Jacobin minority; majority still moderates of Thermidorian type, but a good many of them dislike Directory's past interference with legislature.

April 10   Pope transferred to France.

April 27   Russians under Suvorov defeat French near Milan, an event which leads to General Moreau's evacuation of Lombardy.

April 28   Plenipotentiaries of the French at Congress of Rastatt are sabered by Austrian hussars, and two of the French die.

May 16   Sieyès chosen to fill vacancy in Directory; he is known to favor revision of Constitution of the Year III.

May 17   Napoleon lifts siege of Saint-Jean-d'Acre; within days he retreats from Syria.

June 18 (30 Prairial, An VII)   Councils of Elders and Five Hundred, after several days of pressure, reshape Directory by forcing resignations.

July 12   Law of Hostages opens way for arrest and deportation of relatives of émigrés, former nobles, and persons opposing government.

July 25   Napoleon defeats Turkish force at Aboukir.

August 6   Implementation of forced loan hitting well-to-do worked out in detail.

August 13   Jacobin Club closed despite recent cooperation of democrats and moderates.

August 15   French defeated by Russians under Suvorov at Novi, north of Genoa.

August 23   Bonaparte leaves Egypt.

August 27   English and Russians land in Holland.

September 13   Debate in Council of Five Hundred over whether to declare the *patrie* in danger; decision on following day negative.

September 25–27 French General Masséna drives Russians out of Zurich; prelude to withdrawal of Russians from Switzerland a month later.

October 9   Bonaparte lands at Fréjus on the coast of Provence.

October 14   Bonaparte arrives in Paris.

October 18   Anglo-Russian force agrees to evacuate Holland.

November 9 (18 Brumaire, An VIII)   Councils transferred to Saint-Cloud by order of Elders; Bonaparte named commander of troops in Paris: Sieyès, Barras, and Ducos resign and the other two Directors are powerless with Bonaparte in command of the military forces.

November 10 (19 Brumaire, An VIII)   Confused sessions of Elders and Five Hundred, with troops dispersing majority of Five Hundred; in the evening Provisional Consulate organized by remaining deputies, with Bonaparte, Sieyès, and Roger Ducos as consuls and two commissions to work on revision of constitution.

Selected References

The following will, it is hoped, direct persons desirous of further information toward some of the principal works in French and English. The suggestions for each category will be held to a minimum.

I. Bibliography; Introduction to Research

Jacques Godechot's *Les Révolutions (1770–1799)* (Paris, 1965) will lead to all kinds of sources and to the principal books in several languages. It also contains a brief factual résumé and a discussion of the state of research. More numerous suggestions in the English language will be found in the bibliographies of recent editions of Crane Brinton's *A Decade of Revolution* and Leo Gershoy's *The French Revolution and Napoleon*. For a more detailed introduction to French archives and publications, see the manual by Pierre Caron. For writings during the revolution, see the volumes edited by A. Martin and G. Walter, and also the set edited by A. Monglond. For parliamentary debates and documents, the best starting point is the *Archives parlementaires* with its many volumes, including a few very recent ones on the revolution, and the *Moniteur*, usually available in the United States in the form of the *Réimpression de l'ancien Moniteur*. Both of these sources are described in detail by Godechot. The *Annales historiques de la Révolution française* is the specialized journal in France; its files are an immense repository of articles, documents, and book reviews. In the United States, the journal *French Historical Studies* already provides an accumulation of articles and bibliographical suggestions.

II. General Histories

One may find a succession of twentieth-century classics in the works of Alphonse Aulard, Albert Mathiez, and Georges Lefebvre, who, in that order, taught the subject at the Sorbonne and produced many specialized studies as well as their general histories. Marcel Reinhard, who after an interval succeeded Lefebvre, produced many valuable monographs without writing a general history; anything by him is meticulous and imaginative. The present holder of the chair at the Sorbonne, Albert Soboul, has already written a useful general history that has gone through a number of editions, as well as works based on his personal research that will be referred to below. Jacques Godechot, already mentioned, is another of this group of learned and prolific twentieth-century French historians of the revolution; as in the case of the others, his publications form a valuable bibliography. The same may be said of C. E. Labrousse. The general histories of Aulard, Mathiez, and Lefebvre have been translated into English, as have some of the works of Soboul and Godechot. Among the Americans who have written general histories of the revolution, Louis Gottschalk, Leo Gershoy, and Crane Brinton were already well known in the 1930s and have continued to write and be read. Robert R. Palmer is the most distinguished addition to this group since World War II. As in the case of the French, these names should be consulted for specialized studies as well as for syntheses. Among English historians of the revolution who have written general histories, J. M. Thompson has been followed, chronologically, by A. Goodwin, Norman Hampson, George Rudé, and M. J. Sydenham. Alfred Cobban, who comes into the category for his history of France since 1715, has been influential through his original research and interpretive essays. The best-known general history in German is by Martin Goehring. Among books of documents, that of John Hall Stewart is in many ways a general history of the revolution. Two recent collections of documents are those of J. M. Roberts and R. C. Cobb and of P. Dawson. The most useful chronology of the revolution is that of J. Massin. Frank A. Kafker and James M. Laux have published a set of interpretive essays on various topics by historians of the revolution.

III. Histories, by Periods

Leaving aside a number of studies that come under other headings, one may recommend the following:

On the Background of the Revolution

In French, works by C. E. Labrousse on the economy, by
G. Lefebvre, P. Bois, E. Le Roy-Ladurie, A. Poitrineau, and P. de
Saint-Jacob on the peasants, by J. Meyer on the nobles, by
R. Mousnier, P. Goubert, R. Mandrou, and H. Méthivier on the
structure of the *ancien régime*, by D. Mornet on the intellectual
origins of the revolution, and by J. Egret on the political background and outbreak; in English, Alexis de Tocqueville's classic on
the old regime, Marc Bloch's classic on rural life, and monographs
by E. Barber (bourgeoisie), F. L. Ford (nobles), R. Forster
(nobles), V. R. Gruder (intendants), G. Matthews (tax farmers),
J. H. Shennan (Parlement of Paris), L. S. Greenbaum, J. McManners (the church), B. Hyslop (*cahiers*), and P. Gay (philosophes); historical essays edited by R. Greenlaw (economic background) and W. F. Church (intellectual origins).

On the year 1789

In French, J. Egret (on politics), J. Godechot (the Bastille),
P. Kessel (the night of August 4), G. Lefebvre (the Great Fear);
in English, G. Lefebvre (the year 1789), S. Herbert (the fall of
feudalism).

On Later Events

In French, A. Mathiez (on August 10, 1792), P. Caron (the
September massacres), L. Saurel (9 Thermidor), K. D. Tønnesson
(revolts of sans-culottes against the Thermidorian Convention); in
English, E. Thomson (National Assembly), L. Gottschalk and
M. Maddox (on Lafayette in 1789), R. R. Palmer (the Terror),
D. Greer (statistical studies of Terror and emigration), J. L. God-
frey (justice under the Terror), G. Lefebvre (Thermidorians,
Directory), R. Bienvenu (ed.) (9 Thermidor), D. Thomson
(Babeuf plot), H. Mitchell (attempts at counterrevolution vs.
Directory), W. Fryer (alternatives to Directory).

IV. The Political Institutions and Spectrum

Books, in French, by J. Godechot (all institutional changes
1789–1815), M. Deslandres (political institutions), J. J. Chevallier
(political institutions), and J. Ellul (all institutions, brief); by

G. Bonno (English influences); in English, by F. Acomb (hostility to English ideas), J. McDonald (Rousseau's influence).

On Absolutists and aristocrats

In French, J. Godechot (counterrevolution), E. Vingtrinier (émigrés), de Castries (émigrés); in English, P. H. Beik (absolutists, aristocrats), D. Greer (statistics on emigration).

On Anglophiles

In French, J. Egret (on Mounier and his circle), C. DuBus (on Clermont-Tonnerre); *on Mirabeau*, in French, J. J. Chevallier, duc de Castries; in English, O. Welch; *on Feuillants*, in French, G. Michon (Duport and others), L. Gottschalk and M. Maddox (Lafayette), J. J. Chevallier (Barnave); *on Sieyès*, in French, P. Bastid.

On Girondins

In English, R. Brace, M. J. Sydenham, J. S. Schapiro (Condorcet), E. Ellery (Brissot).

On the Mountain

In French, *on the Committee of Public Safety*, M. Bouloiseau; *on Danton*, J. Herissay, L. Barthou; *on Marat*, J. Massin; *on Robespierre*, J. Massin, M. Bouloiseau, G. Walter, *Actes du colloque Robespierre, XIIe Congrès international des Sciences historiques* (Paris, 1967); recent volumes of Robespierre's *Oeuvres*, with all the speeches; *on the Jacobins*, in English, C. Brinton, I. Woloch; *on Robespierre*, in English, J. M. Thompson, essays by A. Cobban reprinted in *Aspects of the French Revolution*, G. Rudé (ed.), *Robespierre*; *on Saint-Just*, in French, A. Ollivier; in English, E. Curtis, G. Bruun.

On Barère

In English, L. Gershoy; *on Carnot*, in French, M. Reinhard.

On the Enragés

In English, R. B. Rose; *on Hébert*, in French, L. Jacob; *on Babeuf*, in French, C. Mazauric, M. Dommanget; in English, D. Thomson, John A. Scott (ed.) (on Babeuf's trial).

V. Aspects of the Society and the Economy

In French, besides authors mentioned earlier, books and articles by A. Soboul on the sans-culottes; sans-culotte documents edited by W. Markov and A. Soboul; work on sans-culottes after Thermidor by K. Tønnesson; work on revolutionary army and on problems of subsistence and on revolutionary mentalities by R. Cobb; work on demography by M. Reinhard, M. Bouloiseau, P. Clémendot; work on finances and money by F. Braesch, M. Marion; B. Hyslop (properties of Philippe Égalité); J. Sentou (social groups at Toulouse).

In English, N. Hampson (on social aspects of the revolution), G. Rudé (behavior of revolutionary crowds), S. E. Harris (*assignats*), G. A. Williams (French sans-culottes and English artisans).

VI. Religion, Intellectual Life

On religion, in French, works by A. Aulard, A. Mathiez, P. de La Gorce, A. Latreille, J. Leflon, M. Reinhard (excellent mimeographed Sorbonne course); on intellectual life, in French, L. Trénard (intellectual life at Lyon), P. Ariès (attitudes); F. Brunot (on the French language), J. Godechot (documents on ideas of revolutionaries).

On religion, in English, translations of Aulard; J. McManners (on Church before and in revolution), B. C. Poland (Protestantism); on intellectual life, D. Dowd (studies of arts, especially role of David), H. T. Parker (influences of the classics).

VII. Foreign Policy and the International Revolution

In French, R. Fugier (diplomatic history), J. Godechot (books on French expansionist tendencies and on the revolutionary movements in other countries); in English, R. R. Palmer (revolutionary tendencies in Europe and America, France included but seen as part of larger picture; two editions, one in two volumes and one in a single volume); J. Godechot (English translation of part of his work); C. L. Lokke (on colonial policies), P. Amann (ed.) (readings on problems posed by idea of an international revolution.)

Index

DOCUMENTARY HISTORY OF WESTERN CIVILIZATION
Edited by Eugene C. Black and Leonard W. Levy

ANCIENT AND MEDIEVAL HISTORY OF THE WEST

Morton Smith: ANCIENT GREECE *

A. H. M. Jones: A HISTORY OF ROME THROUGH THE FIFTH CENTURY
Vol. I: The Republic
Vol. II: The Empire

Deno Geanakoplos: BYZANTINE EMPIRE *

Marshall W. Baldwin: CHRISTIANITY THROUGH THE THIRTEENTH CENTURY

Bernard Lewis: ISLAM TO 1453 *

David Herlihy: HISTORY OF FEUDALISM

William M. Bowsky: RISE OF COMMERCE AND TOWNS *

David Herlihy: MEDIEVAL CULTURE AND SOCIETY

EARLY MODERN HISTORY

Hanna H. Gray: CULTURAL HISTORY OF THE RENAISSANCE *

Florence Edler de Roover: MONEY, BANKING,
AND COMMERCE, THIRTEENTH THROUGH SIXTEENTH CENTURIES *

V. J. Parry: THE OTTOMAN EMPIRE *

Ralph E. Giesey: EVOLUTION OF THE DYNASTIC STATE *

J. H. Parry: THE EUROPEAN RECONNAISSANCE: Selected Documents

Hans J. Hillerbrand: THE PROTESTANT REFORMATION

John C. Olin: THE CATHOLIC COUNTER REFORMATION *

Orest Ranum: THE CENTURY OF LOUIS XIV *

Thomas Hegarty: RUSSIAN HISTORY THROUGH PETER THE GREAT *

Marie Boas Hall: NATURE AND NATURE'S LAWS

Barry E. Supple: HISTORY OF MERCANTILISM *

Geoffrey Symcox: IMPERIALISM, WAR, AND DIPLOMACY, 1550-1763 *

Herbert H. Rowen: THE LOW COUNTRIES *

C. A. Macartney: THE HABSBURG AND HOHENZOLLERN DYNASTIES
IN THE SEVENTEENTH AND EIGHTEENTH CENTURIES

Lester G. Crocker: THE AGE OF ENLIGHTENMENT

Robert and Elborg Forster: EUROPEAN SOCIETY IN THE EIGHTEENTH CENTURY

REVOLUTIONARY EUROPE, 1789-1848

Paul H. Beik: THE FRENCH REVOLUTION
David L. Dowd: NAPOLEONIC ERA, 1799-1815 *
René Albrecht-Carrié: THE CONCERT OF EUROPE
John B. Halsted: ROMANTICISM
R. Max Hartwell: THE INDUSTRIAL REVOLUTION *
Mack Walker: METTERNICH'S EUROPE
Douglas Johnson: THE ASCENDANT BOURGEOISIE *
John A. Hawgood: THE REVOLUTIONS OF 1848 *

NATIONALISM, LIBERALISM, AND SOCIALISM, 1850-1914

Eugene C. Black: VICTORIAN CULTURE AND SOCIETY
Eugene C. Black: BRITISH POLITICS IN THE NINETEENTH CENTURY
Denis Mack Smith: THE MAKING OF ITALY, 1796-1870
David Thomson: FRANCE: Empire and Republic, 1850-1940
Theodore S. Hamerow: BISMARCK'S MITTELEUROPA *
Eugene O. Golob: THE AGE OF LAISSEZ FAIRE *
Roland N. Stromberg: REALISM, NATURALISM, AND SYMBOLISM:
Modes of Thought and Expression in Europe, 1848-1914
Melvin Kranzberg: SCIENCE AND TECHNOLOGY *
Jesse D. Clarkson: TSARIST RUSSIA: Catherine the Great to Nicholas II *
Philip D. Curtin: IMPERIALISM *
Massimo Salvadori: MODERN SOCIALISM

THE TWENTIETH CENTURY

Jere C. King: THE FIRST WORLD WAR *
S. Clough, T. and C. Moodie : ECONOMIC HISTORY OF EUROPE:
Twentieth Century
W. Warren Wagar: SCIENCE, FAITH, AND MAN:
European Thought Since 1914
Paul A. Gagnon: INTERNATIONALISM AND DIPLOMACY BETWEEN THE WARS, 1919-1939 *
Henry Cord Meyer: WEIMAR AND NAZI GERMANY *
Michal Vyvyan: RUSSIA FROM LENIN TO KHRUSHCHEV *
Charles F. Delzell: MEDITERRANEAN FASCISM, 1919-1945
Donald C. Watt: THE SECOND WORLD WAR *

* In preparation

BIBLIOGRAPHY OF
BRITISH HISTORY
STUART PERIOD, 1603–1714

BIBLIOGRAPHY OF
BRITISH HISTORY
STUART PERIOD, 1603–1714

ISSUED UNDER THE DIRECTION OF THE ROYAL HISTORICAL SOCIETY
AND THE AMERICAN HISTORICAL ASSOCIATION

EDITED BY

GODFREY DAVIES

Assistant Professor of Modern History
in the University of Chicago

OXFORD
AT THE CLARENDON PRESS
1928

OXFORD
UNIVERSITY PRESS
LONDON: AMEN HOUSE, E.C.4
EDINBURGH GLASGOW LEIPZIG
COPENHAGEN NEW YORK TORONTO
MELBOURNE CAPETOWN BOMBAY
CALCUTTA MADRAS SHANGHAI
HUMPHREY MILFORD
PUBLISHER TO THE
UNIVERSITY

Printed in Great Britain

CONTENTS

INTRODUCTION

THE late H. R. Tedder read a paper on 19 March 1914 before the Royal Historical Society on ' The forthcoming bibliography of modern British History ', and his authoritative account is the basis of the following summary of the progress of the undertaking until the appointment of the present editor.

In 1909 the American Historical Association and the Royal Historical Society both named committees to discuss the question of co-operating in order to continue Gross's Sources and Literature of English History from the Earliest Times to about 1485. They planned a series of three volumes, each in two parts. The first was to be general, comprising an introduction on the scope and arrangement of the work, accounts of publications of learned societies and historical periodicals, &c., and lists of authorities covering the whole period 1485–1910. The second was to contain the special authorities for 1485–1714, and the third those for 1714–1910. In 1912 the late Sir George Prothero became general editor and committees were appointed for both the Tudor and Stuart periods. Much work had been performed by 1914, when the outbreak of war completely suspended it. Sir George Prothero was never again able to give much attention to it, and his death in July 1922 left it unfinished. A special committee of the Royal Historical Society sat in that year to discuss the continuance of the bibliography, and a change of plan was adopted. In view of the length of time which had elapsed since the project was first mooted, it was imperative to complete at least a part of it as speedily as possible. As the preparations for the original volume two were the most advanced, it was decided to proceed with it. Now the Tudor and Stuart periods were each to be allotted a separate volume. A committee of American scholars, with E. P. Cheyney as chairman, has charge of the Tudor volume, which is nearing completion.

I was nominated editor of the volume covering 1603–1714 in February 1923, but other literary commitments prevented my assuming my duties for more than a year. Owing to the urgency, as well as the extent of the work still to be accomplished, the original idea of including manuscripts was abandoned, although considerable information about them is incorporated in the notes. The indefinite postponement of the general introductory volume, and the impossibility of referring to it or to the Tudor volume, have necessitated the insertion in this book of a number of works not confined to the period. It is now designed to be complete in itself. Otherwise the contents correspond to the scheme prepared by Sir George Prothero and the committee of 1912, except that whereas they contemplated about 2,500 titles, there are now over 3,800 numbered, besides 1,500 to 2,000 in the footnotes.

It is my pleasant task to express the profound gratitude of the Royal Historical Society to the late Sir George Prothero and to those who have assisted in the production of this volume. It is most unfortunate that owing to the change of editorship there is neither a complete list of the original contributors nor a precise record of their services. So far as is known the following compiled the whole or parts of the sections which are inserted in brackets after their names, and in a number of cases have recently revised them : C. H. Collins Baker (Art) ; E. A. Benians (Voyages and Travels) ; Arthur Berry (Science) ; Sir Reginald Blomfield (Architecture) ; the late P. Hume Brown (Scotland) ; R. Dunlop (Ireland) ; the late H. E. Egerton (Colonies) ; Lord Ernle (Agriculture) ; the Bishop of Truro [W. H. Frere] (Anglican Church to 1660) ; Sir Henry Hadow (Music) ; B. L. K. Henderson (Economic and Social History) ; H. D. Hazeltine (Legal Sources) ; the late A. M. Hyamson (Judaism) ; the late Colonel E. M. Lloyd (Military) ; J. E. Lloyd (Wales) ; H. E. Malden (Local History) ; J. G. Muddiman (Newspapers) ; the late Sir A. E. Shipley (Science) ; W. T. Whitley (Nonconformity).

It is possible to specify more particularly the debt of gratitude due to those whose assistance dates from 1923. E. R. Adair took charge of Administration, read the typescripts of the political and constitutional and the economic sections, and made many improvements ; W. H. Burgess dealt with Unitarianism ; the late E. H. Burton with Roman Catholicism ; Miss E. Jeffries Davis virtually compiled all the entries on London ; A. H. Dodd and J. G. Edwards added many titles to the Welsh bibliography ; D. Hay Fleming doubled the size of the section on Scotland and subjected what had already been done to a very fruitful revision ; C. S. S. Higham assumed control of Voyages and Travels and the East and West Indies, and wrote their introductions ; M. W. Jernegan lent me his notes on the American colonies and made many valuable suggestions ; Norman Penney revised and considerably augmented Quakerism ; W. G. Perrin made himself responsible not only for the contents but also for the arrangement of the Naval section ; H. G. Richardson revised Agriculture so systematically as to transform it, and penned its introduction ; and W. R. Scott dealt with foreign trade and wrote part of the introduction to economic history.

One name deserves especial mention. Sir Charles Firth compiled the section on ballads, but this was the least of his services. He has assisted at every stage of the growth of this bibliography : his library and unrivalled stores of knowledge were always open to me. He has read the typescripts and the proofs, and encouraged me in every way. Nevertheless the final responsibility rests on my shoulders, not on his.

In spite of all this assistance, however, it is certain that much remains still to be accomplished. I have only been able to devote my leisure hours to this volume, and these perforce were mainly employed in compiling not less than a third of the entries. Consequently I am only too conscious that I have neglected many of my editorial duties. Yet those whose opinion is far weightier than mine believe that the interests of historical scholarship will be better served by the appearance of this volume now with all its imperfections than by delaying it for further revision. After all, the absence of such improvements as I could effect will matter little, if scholars will note such errors as they find and communicate them to the Honorary Secretary of the Royal Historical Society, 22 Russell Square, London, W.C. 1, by whom they will be acknowledged. Subjected to the revision of all who study the Stuart period, this book in a second edition will become more worthy of the two great historical bodies under whose direction it is issued.

In a bibliography of this kind the two main difficulties are those of selection and arrangement. In deciding what works to include or omit, the necessity of covering the whole field has been the ruling principle. In each section the aim has been to ensure that every aspect of its subject-matter shall be presented however inadequate the means may be. In dealing with controversial questions an attempt has been made to give fair representation to opposing schools of opinion whether contemporary or modern. Care has been taken to provide a selection of the historical literature of succeeding generations, so that the reader may trace the progress of knowledge and the different interpretations of events in each age. It has been impossible to include many pamphlets, but usually at least one tract of a prolific writer has been listed, so that his name can be turned up in the catalogue of a library such as the British Museum in order to discover what else he wrote. Most space has been devoted to the normal activities of the inhabitants of Stuart Britain. In the more specialized topics, such as art or science, the first consideration has been the needs of the general historian, in the hope that when he has occasion to tread these unfrequented paths he may find the guidance he requires.

The arrangement has been dictated by the avoidance of repetition and convenience of reference. Thus the desire not to do the same thing twice is responsible for putting peers in the alphabetical order of their titles in biographical sub-sections, since they are listed under their family names in the index. The usual arrangement of each section is to enumerate first the bibliographies, then the sources, and finally the later works. These all follow the chronological order of the date of the first edition unless there is an obvious reason for a deviation from this rule. Instances of such deviations are biographies arranged alphabetically, regimental histories which conform to the order of the Army List, or local histories which are arranged geographically. In a few small sub-sections, as in foreign relations or naval history, sources and later works are grouped together to save space, but such instances are rare. To keep the size of the bibliography within moderate limits certain devices have been adopted. Cross references, which are enclosed in round brackets, are only given when their absence cannot be supplied by the index. Many works have been inserted in footnotes—occasionally some strange bedfellows appear—but the more important are all indexed. Descriptions of books are necessarily brief. No distinction is made between small, medium, and large quartos. All others are octavos, or, if shorter, duodecimos, if taller, folios. Whenever possible the number of volumes, the size, the place and the date of publication of the first edition of each work is given, but no attempt is made to enumerate all later editions. The ideal has been, however, to note later editions whenever the rarity of the first, or the superior utility of the later, editions makes this desirable. When the format of the later edition is similar to the first, the description has not been repeated but the date alone is supplied. Thus an entry of the type 1 vol. 8vo. Lond. 1672 and 1701, would imply that the edition of 1701 was identical with that of 1672 in its format. On the other hand, if any detail of the description of the later volume is different, then all are repeated.

As regards the index, all authors and all editors, when there are no authors, are included, and the relatively few subject-matter entries are intended merely to supplement the table of contents. Titles are only inserted for anonymous works for which no subject-matter entry easy of reference could be found. When a book has both author and editor, the editor is only indexed if he has contributed materially to its value, or if there seems to be a reasonable chance that the reader will seek for it under the editor's name rather than under the author's. In short, practical utility has in all things been the chief guide of the editor.

I. ENGLISH POLITICAL AND CONSTITUTIONAL HISTORY

1. General and Miscellaneous.
2. Central Administration.
3. Parliamentary History.
4. Legal History.
5. Foreign Relations.
6. Biographies.

MORE detailed study has been devoted to the years 1603–1714 than to any period of English history of equal length, but it has been unevenly distributed. The works of Gardiner (219–20) and Firth (244) supply an elaborate survey of the years 1603–58, and have facilitated the production of a host of monographs. Macaulay (204) dealt with the fifteen years following the accession of James II on an unprecedented scale, but this era has attracted few later historians. Full histories of the years 1658–85 and 1697–1714 remain to be written. At present Guizot (207) has not been superseded for the restoration, and Ranke (214) remains the best history of the reign of Charles II. The reign of Anne has received more attention, and the works of Stanhope (211), Wyon (217), and Leadam (245) furnish a satisfactory outline.

There is no adequate bibliography, but the sections on sources in the three relevant volumes of the Political History of England (240, 245, 246) enumerate the chief authorities with useful comments, and are thus more valuable than the lists of titles in the Cambridge Modern History (239) and elsewhere. Since the output of new material is now exceeding the capacity of historians to absorb it, classified and annotated bibliographies should replace the mere lists of authorities appended to most modern studies. The value of the works of the chief narrative historians is estimated by Firth (21), and the lives of many historians and antiquaries in the Dictionary of National Biography contain valuable criticisms, but the historiography of the 17th century has not yet been treated as a whole.

¶ 1. GENERAL AND MISCELLANEOUS

(a) Bibliographies, Guides, and Sources.
(b) Later Works.

(a) BIBLIOGRAPHIES, GUIDES, SOURCES

1. A catalogue of the most vendible books in England orderly and alphabetically digested. By W. London. 1 vol. 4to. Lond. 1658.

The first English bibliography.

2. Catalogi librorum manuscriptorum Angliae et Hiberniae in unum collecti cum indice alphabetico. By E. Bernard. 2 pts. in 1 vol. fol. Oxf. 1697.

3. Catalogue of a collection of printed broadsides in the possession of the Society of Antiquaries. Ed. by R. Lemon. 1 vol. 4to. Lond. 1866.

4. Index expurgatorius anglicanus, or a descriptive catalogue of the principal books printed or published in England which have been suppressed or burnt by the common hangman. By W. H. Hart. 5 pts. 8vo. Lond. 1872–84.
Stops in 1684.

5. A transcript of the registers of the company of stationers of London, 1554–1640. Ed. by E. Arber. 5 vols. 4to. Lond. 1875–94.
Continued in : A transcript of the registers of the worshippful company of stationers from 1640–1708. Ed. by H. R. Plomer. 3 vols. fol. Lond. 1913–14.

6. Catalogue of books in the library of the British Museum printed in England, Scotland and Ireland and of books in English printed abroad to . . . 1640. 3 vols. 8vo. Lond. 1884.

7. An index to the Archaeologia or miscellaneous tracts relating to antiquity, from volume I to volume L inclusive. Ed. by M. Stephenson. 1 vol. 4to. Lond. 1889.
Other guides to Archaeologia, which has much 17th century material, are Gomme (2784) and Gerould (25) where the items are separately noticed.

8. A guide to the principal classes of documents preserved in the Public Record Office. By S. R. Scargill-Bird. 1 vol. 8vo. Lond. 1891 ; 2nd ed. 1896 ; 3rd ed. 1908.
Cf. M. S. Giuseppi : A guide to the MSS. preserved in the Public Record Office. 2 vols. 8vo. Lond. 1923–4, which largely supersedes the above.

9. The early Oxford press. A bibliography of printing and publishing at Oxford ' 1468 '–1640. By F. Madan. 1 vol. 8vo. Oxf. 1895. Illus.
Cf. the same author's A bibliography of printed works relating to the University and City of Oxford [1450–1640] or printed or published there [1641–50]. 1 vol. 8vo. Oxf. 1912. Illus.

10. Bibliotheca Lindesiana. Catalogue of English broadsides 1505–1897. 1 vol. 4to. s.l. 1898.

11. Book auctions in England in the seventeenth century [1676–1700] with a chronological list of the book auctions of the period. By J. Lawler. 1 vol. 8vo. Lond. 1898.

12. The sources and literature of English history from the earliest times to about 1485. By C. Gross. 1 vol. 8vo. Lond. 1900 ; 2nd revised ed. 1915.
Many general items are useful for later periods.

13. Early English printed books in the University Library Cambridge [1475–1640]. By C. E. Sayle. 4 vols. 8vo. Camb. 1900–7.

14. A bibliography of the historical works of Dr. Creighton . . . Dr. Stubbs . . . Dr. S. R. Gardiner and . . . Lord Acton. Ed. by W. A. Shaw. 1 vol. 8vo. Lond. 1903.

15. The term catalogues 1668–1709 with a number for Easter term 1711. Ed. by E. Arber. 3 vols. 4to. Lond. 1903–6.
Classified lists of published books with a good index.

16. General index of articles, notes, documents and selected reviews of books in the English Historical Review. Vols. i–xx, 1886–1905 and vols. xxi–xxx, 1906–15. 2 vols. 8vo. Lond. 1906, 1916.

17. Catalogue of the pamphlets, books, newspapers, and manuscripts relating to the civil war, the commonwealth and restoration collected by George Thomason, 1640–1661 [in the British Museum]. Ed. by G. K. Fortescue, 2 vols. 8vo. Lond. 1908.

Cf. A compleat catalogue of all the stitch'd books and single sheets printed since the first discovery of the popish plot. With A continuation, and A second continuation these cover Sept. 1678–Michaelmas 1680. [3 vols. 4to. ? Lond. 1680] Reissued together as A general catalogue of the stitch'd books &c., in 1680.

18. A catalogue of pamphlets, tracts, proclamations, speeches, sermons, trials, petitions from 1506 to 1700 in the library of . . . Lincoln's Inn. 1 vol. 8vo. Lond. 1908.

19. A dictionary of printers and booksellers in England, Scotland and Ireland, and of foreign printers of English books 1557–1640. Ed. by R. B. McKerrow. 1 vol. 4to. Pr. for the Bibliographical Soc. Lond. 1910.

Continued in : A dictionary of the booksellers and printers who were at work in England, Scotland and Ireland from 1641–1667. 1 vol. 4to. Lond. 1907. Ed. by H. R. Plomer, Biblio. Socy. who also compiled a work with a similar title extending from 1668–1725, 1 vol. 4to. Oxf. 1922, ed. by A. Esdaile.

20. Historical and political writings. I. State papers and letters. II. Histories and Memoirs. By Sir A. W. Ward. Camb. Hist. of Eng. Lit. vii. 1911, chs. viii, ix.

Extend to *c.* 1660. Similar articles for the later period are in *ibid.* ix. 1912, chs. vii and viii. The bibliographies are valuable so far as they go.

21. The development of the study of seventeenth century history. By Sir C. H. Firth. Royal Hist. Soc. Trans. 1913, 1914.

The first paper surveys existing works, the second suggests lines for future research.

22. A repertory of British archives. Part I. England. Compiled for the Royal Hist. Soc. by H. Hall. 1 vol. 8vo. Lond. 1920.

Designed ' to assist historical students in locating such documents as may be useful for their studies '.

23. The reports of the historical MSS. commission. By R. A. Roberts. Helps for students of history series. 1 vol. 12mo. Lond. 1920.

Contains an analysis of the contents of MSS. collections reported on to date.

24. A student's guide to the manuscripts of the British Museum. By J. P. Gilson. Helps for students of history series. 1 vol. 12mo. Lond. 1920.

25. Sources of English history of the seventeenth century 1603–1689 in the University of Minnesota library, with a selection of secondary material. Ed. by J. T. Gerould. 1 vol. 8vo. Minneapolis, 1921.

The best guide. Enumerates the separate items in collections of pamphlets &c.

26. A student's guide to the manuscripts relating to English history in the seventeenth century in the Bodleian Library. By G. Davies. Helps for students of history series. 1 vol. 12mo Lond. 1922.

27. List and index of the publications of the Royal Historical Society 1871–1924 and of the Camden Society 1840–1897. Ed. by H. Hall. 1 vol. 8vo. Lond. 1925.

28. A banquet of jeasts, or change of cheare. By A. Armstrong. Pt. I. 8vo. Lond. 1630, 4th ed. 1634. Pt. II. 1 vol. 12mo. Lond. 1633. Both pts. 12mo. Lond. 1639. Best ed. 1 vol. 8vo. Edin. 1872. Ed. by T. H. Jamieson.
The source of many historical ancedotes. Jamieson's reprint is from the 6th ed. 1640.

29. Annales or a generall chronicle of England. By J. Stow and E. Howes. 1 vol. fol. London. 1631.
Stow's chronicle was augmented and continued by Howes 1600–31.

30. A chronicle of the kings of England, from the time of the Romans government, unto the death of King James the First. By Sir R. Baker. 1 vol. fol. Lond. 1641. Later eds. 1665 and 1733.
Eds. after 1660 have a continuation by E. Phillips which is a valuable authority for 1658–60 and based on the lost papers of Sir Thomas Clarges, Monck's brother-in-law. In eds. later than that of 1674 this continuation is increasingly abridged. Ed. of 1733 has a continuation to 1727, but it is of slight value. Cf. T. Blount's Animadversions upon Sir Richard Baker's chronicle and its continuation. 1 vol. 12mo. Oxf. 1672.

31. Epistolae Ho-Elianae. Familiar letters domestic and forren, divided into six sections . . . By J. Howell. 1 vol. 4to. Lond. 1645. Later ed. 2 vols. 8vo. Lond. 1890–2. Ed. by J. Jacobs.
Untrustworthy : see Dict. Nat. Biog. *sub* Howell.

32. A declaration of the engagements, remonstrances, representations . . . from His Excellency Sir Tho: Fairfax and the generall councel of the army. 1 vol. sm. 4to. Lond. 1647.
Often called the Book of Army declarations : a useful collection.

33. Jonah's cry out of the Whale's belly or certaine epistles writ by Lieu. Col. J. Lilburne unto Lieu. Gen. Cromwell. 1 vol. 4to. Lond. 1647.
A bibliography of Lilburne by E. Peacock in Notes and Queries, 7th ser. vol. v.

34. Putney projects. Or the old serpent in a new forme. Presenting to the view of all the well affected in England the serpentine deceit of their pre-tended friends in the armie. By J. Wildman. 1 vol. sm. 4to. Lond. 1647.
One of the best-known Leveller pamphlets.

35. Elenchi motuum nuperorum in Anglia. Pars prima ; simul ac juris regis ac parlamentarii brevis enarratio. By G. Bate. 1 vol. 12mo. Paris. 1649.
A second part to 1660 was added in 1661, 8vo. Lond., and a third part called Motus compositi by T. Skinner in 1676. A trans. of the three parts appeared in 1685, 8vo. Lond. called Elenchus motuum nuperorum in Anglia or a short historical account of the rise and progress of the late troubles in England. A trans. of part i. was ed. by Edward Almack in the Stuart Library, 1 vol. 8vo. Lond. 1902 as A short narrative of the late troubles in England. Cf. Pugh's Elenchus elenchi : sive animadversiones in Georgii Batei, Cromwelli parricidae aliquando protomedici elenchum motuum nuperorum in Anglia [8vo. Paris. 1664] ; and Clarke Papers (150), iv. 274–6.

36. Reliquiae sacrae Carolinae. The workes of that great monarch and glorious martyr King Charles the 1st. both civil and sacred. 2 pts. in 1 vol. 8vo. The Hague. 1649.

Pt. I contains the king's state letters, proclamations &c. Pt. ii Eikon Basilike and other theological pieces.

37. The court and character of King James. By Sir A. Weldon. 1 vol. 12mo. London. 1650.

Repr. in Secret History (104). In ed. of 1651 The court of King Charles is added. Cf. Aulicus Coquinariae, 1650, an answer to the above attributed to Sir W. Sanderson.

38. The history of Great Britain, being the life and reign of King James the First. By A. Wilson. 1 vol. fol. Lond. 1653.

Repr. in Kennet (179). Cf. Wilson's autobiography in Peck (81) ii. 460; and the intro. to Wilson's play The Swisser, 1 vol. 8vo. Paris. 1904. ed. by A. Feuillerat. Useful but prejudiced : to be used with caution.

39. Cabala sive scrinia sacra : mysteries of state and government in letters of . . . great ministers of state . . . in the reigns of King Henry the Eighth . . . King Charles. 2 pts. sm. 4to. Lond. 1654. Later eds. 1 vol. fol. Lond. 1663, and 1691.

Miscellaneous state letters, many addressed to Buckingham. Ed. of 1691 is the best.

40. Historia rerum Britannicarum ut et multarum Gallicarum, Belgicarum et Germanicarum . . . ab anno 1572 ad annum 1628. By R. Johnston. 1 vol. fol. Amsterdam. 1655.

41. The reign of King Charles : an history faithfully and impartially delivered and disposed into annals [to 1641]. By H. L'Estrange. 1 vol. fol. Lond. 1655, and 1656.

Ed. of 1656 said to be ' revised and somewhat enlarged '. Cf. P. Heylyn's Observations [1656]; Extraneus Vapulans [1656]; and Examen Historicum [1659], all against L'Estrange.

42. A compleat history of the lives and reigns of Mary Queen of Scotland, and of her son . . . James the Sixth . . . in vindication of him against two scandalous authors [Sir Anthony Weldon and A. Wilson]. By Sir W. Sanderson. 2 pts. fol. Lond. 1656.

43. A compleat history of the life and raigne of King Charles from his cradle to his grave. By Sir W. Sanderson. 1 vol. fol. Lond. 1658.

Cf. P. Heylyn's Examen historicum [1 vol. 8vo. Lond. 1659], which includes A short survey of Mr. Sanderson's long history of the life and reign of King Charles.

44. Bibliotheca regia, or the royall library. 1 vol. 8vo. Lond. 1659.

A collection of letters, speeches and other documents of, or relating to, Charles I

45. Historical collections of private passages of state, weighty matters in law, remarkable proceedings in five parliaments . . . 1618 . . . 1629. By J. Rushworth. 7 vols. fol. Lond. 1659–1701. Ports. Later ed. 8 vols. fol. Lond. 1721. Ports.

Title is from first volume ; subsequent volumes extended the collection to the year 1649. Valuable storehouse of material : see Dict. Nat. Biog. *sub* Rushworth, John.

46. England's black tribunall. 1 vol. 8vo. Lond. 1660. 6th ed. 1737.

Ed. of 1660 has the trial of Charles I : ed. of 1737 adds : The loyal martyrology ; an historical register of the lords, knights, and gentlemen who were slain in defence of their king and country ; the loyal confessors . . . the most eminent sufferers by imprisonment, banishment or in estate.

47. A collection of several letters and declarations . . . sent by General Monk unto the Lord Lambert . . . 2 pts. in 1 vol. 4to. Lond. 1660. Later ed. 1 vol. 8vo. Lond. 1714.

Ed. of 1714 was issued, together with The art of restoring, as a warning against a second restoration.

48. A brief chronicle of the late intestine warr [1637–63]. By J. Heath. 1 vol. 8vo. Lond. 1663. Ports. Later ed. 1 vol. fol. Lond. 1676.

Ed. of 1676 has a continuation by J. Phillips, 1662–75.

49. The historians guide. In two parts . . . Second. England's remembrancer, being a summary of the actions . . . in his Majesties dominions [1600–75.] By S. Clarke. 1 vol. 8vo. Lond. 1676. Later ed. 1 vol. 12mo. Lond. 1690.

A detailed date-book. 1st part Chronology of the world from the Creation to this present age. The late eds. omit the Chronology, and have continuations to date.

50. Behemoth, or an epitome of the Civil Wars of England from 1640 to 1660. By T. Hobbes. 1 vol. 12mo. Lond. 1679. Later ed. 1 vol. 8vo. Lond. 1889. Ed. by F. Tönnies.

Repr. in Maseres (1158) and in Molesworth (2746 n.). Tönnies restores passages previously suppressed.

51. The mystery and method of his Majesty's happy Restauration. By J. Price. 1 vol. 8vo. Lond. 1680.

Repr. in Maseres (1158). Valuable as Price accompanied Monck. MSS. of this work are in Worcester College, Oxford [no. 54 in the catalogue] and amongst the Hunterian MSS. in the library of the University of Glasgow [no. 58].

52. The connexion, being choice collections of some principal matters in King James his reign. 1 vol. 12mo. Lond. 1681.

Proclamations, law cases &c.

53. A short view of the late troubles in England . . . To which is added a . . . narrative of the Treaty of Uxbridge in 1644. By Sir W. Dugdale. 1 vol. fol. Oxf. 1681.

Useful for exact dates.

54. The annals of King James and King Charles the First [1612–42]. By T. Frankland. 1 vol. fol. Lond. 1681.

55. Memorials of the English affairs . . . from the beginning of the reign of King Charles the First to King Charles the Second his happy restauration. By B. Whitelocke. 1 vol. fol. Lond. 1682. Later ed. 4 vols. 8vo. Oxf. 1853.

Has some personal memoirs, but mainly a compilation from newspapers—useful for the Commonwealth and Protectorate. Cf. Clarendon and Whitlock compar'd, by J. Oldmixon, 1727, which called forth answers from J. Davys, F. Curll, and J. Burton. There are Whitelock MSS. Brit. Mus. Add. MSS. 37341–7, and Hist. MSS. Comm. iii. 202.

56. An impartial collection of the great affairs of state from the beginning of the Scotch rebellion in the year 1639 to the murther of King Charles I . . . Ed. by J. Nalson. 2 vols. fol. Lond. 1682–3.

Intended as an antidote to Rushworth. Prints many documents from public records [see intro. to Portland MSS. vol. i], but only extends to 1642.
Partial in narrative, but useful for its documents.

57. A true copy of the journal of the high court of justice for the tryal of King Charles I. By J. Nalson. 1 vol. fol. Lond. 1684. Illus.

58. A true account and declaration of the horrid conspiracy to assassinate the late King . . . together with copies of the informations as they were ordered to be printed by his late majesty. By T. Sprat. 1 vol. 8vo. Lond. 1685. Later ed. 3 vols. 8vo. Edin. 1886, forming vol. xiv of Collectanea Adamantaea.

Official account of the Rye House plot.

59. A collection of papers relating to the present juncture of affairs in England. 12 pts. sm. 4to. Lond. 1688–9.

Issued separately as A collection, A second collection &c.

60. The history of the desertion or an account of all the publick affairs in England. [Sept. 1688–12 Feb. 1689.] By E. Bohun. 1 vol. sm. 4to. Lond. 1689.

Many useful documents.

61. An exact diary of the late expedition of . . . the Prince of Orange from The Hague to . . . his arrival at Whitehall. By J. Whittle. 1 vol. sm. 4to. Lond. 1689.

A useful daily record of events by one of William's army chaplains. Cf. The march of William of Orange through Somerset . . . 1688. By E. Green, 1 vol. 4to. Lond. 1892.

62. The secret history of the reigns of King Charles II and King James II. 1 vol. 12mo. [? Lond.] 1690.

Cf. The blatant beast muzzled or reflections on a late libel entitled The secret history [12mo. 1691].

63. Truth brought to light : or, the history of the first 14 years of King James I. 1 vol. 8vo. Lond. 1692.

Includes an account of the royal revenue, with the receipts, issues &c. The less complete ed. of 1651 has title : The narrative history of King James . . . for the first fourteen years. Repr. in Somers Tracts, 2nd ed. (89), vol. ii.

64. State tracts : in two parts. The first being a collection of several treatises relating to the government, privately printed in the reign of King Charles II ; the second part consisting of a further collection . . . 1660 to 1689. 2 pts. Fol. Lond. 1692–3.

Pt. I publ. 1689 separately.

65. The history of the late conspiracy against the king . . . with a particular account of the Lancashire plot. 1 vol. 8vo. Lond. 1696.

The official account of the Assassination plot.

66. The secret history of White-Hall from the restoration of Charles II down to the abdication of the late K. James. By D. Jones. 6 pts. 8vo. Lond. 1697. 2nd ed. 2 vols. 12mo. Lond. 1717.

A continuation . . . to . . . 1696 was publ. 8vo. Lond. 1697 and included in ed. of 1717.

67. Memoirs of the most material transactions in England for the last hundred years [to 1688]. By J. Welwood. 1 vol. 8vo. Lond. 1700. Later ed. 1820. Ed. by F. Maseres.

68. Miscellanea Aulica : or a collection of state-treatises. Ed. by T. Brown. 1 vol. 8vo. Lond. 1702.

Contains letters of Charles II and James, Duke of York, and documents illustrating foreign relations and Scottish history after 1660.

69. The history of the rebellion and civil wars in England. By E. Hyde, Earl of Clarendon. 3 vols. fol. Oxf. 1702–4. Later eds. 7 vols. 8vo. Oxf. 1849. Ed. by B. Bandinel. 6 vols. 8vo. Oxf. 1888. Ed. by W. D. Macray.

The reprint of 1849 includes the History of the Rebellion in Ireland, and Warburton's notes. For estimates of History see Ranke (214) vi, and C. H. Firth in Eng. Hist. Rev. xix. 1904. For the history of the MS. see Macray, Annals of the Bodleian [1 vol. 8vo. Oxf. 1890], p. 225.

70. History of the reign of Queen Anne digested into Annals [1703–13]. By A. Boyer. 11 vols. 8vo. Lond. 1703–13.

71. A collection of state tracts, publish'd on occasion of the late revolution in 1688 and during the reign of King William III. 3 vols. fol. Lond. 1705–7.

Cf. A choice collection of papers relating to state affairs during the late revolution. 1 vol. 8vo. Lond. 1703. Repr. as A collection of scarce and valuable papers, 1712.

72. The Phenix ; or, a revival of scarce & valuable pieces from the remotest antiquity down to the present times. 2 vols. 8vo. Lond. 1707–8.

Repr. in 1721 as A collection of choice, scarce and valuable tracts.

73. Some memoirs of the most remarkable passages and translations on the late happy revolution in 1688. By H. Speke. 1 vol. 12mo. Dublin. 1709.

74. Memoirs relating to the impeachment of Thomas Earl of Danby . . . in . . . 1678 . . . with an appendix containing the proceedings in parliament. 1 vol. 8vo. Lond. 1710.

75. The political state of Great Britain. Being an impartial account of the most material occurrences ecclesiastical, civil and military. In a monthly letter to a friend in Holland [1711–40]. By A. Boyer. 60 vols. 8vo. Lond. 1711–40.

The volumes dealing with 1711–14 were subsequently published in a 2nd and improved ed. in 1718 (8 vols. in 4) under the title Quadriennium Annae postremum.

75 A. The wisdom of looking backward to judge the better of one side and t' other by the speeches, writings, actions . . . for the four years last past. By W. Kennet. 1 vol. 8vo. Lond. 1715.

Valuable analysis of pamphlets &c. Cf. A collection of tracts written by J. Asgill [1700–15]. By J. Asgill. 1 vol. 8vo. Lond. 1715.

76. Bishop Burnet's history of his own time. By G. Burnet. 2 vols. fol. Lond. 1724–34. Later eds. 7 vols. 8vo. Oxf. 1823. 6 vols. 8vo. Oxf. 1833. Ed. by M. J. Routh. 2 vols. 8vo. Oxf. 1897 [to 1685 only]. Ed. by O. Airy.

For a bibliography see Clarke and Foxcroft (1498), pp. 551–2; for critical estimates, Ranke, vi. 45–87, and C. H. Firth in intro. to Clarke and Foxcroft. The original draft is publ. so far as it exists, in A supplement to Burnet's history of my own time . . . his autobiography, his letters to Admiral Herbert and his private meditations. Ed. by H. C. Foxcroft [1 vol. 8vo. Oxf. 1902]. Burnet's History of the reign of James II was separately ed. by Routh. 1 vol. 8vo. Oxf. 1852.

77. An impartial examination of Bishop Burnet's History of his own times. By T. Salmon. 2 vols. 8vo. Lond. 1724.

One of many answers to Burnet. See Lowndes, pp. 320–1.

78. Bishop Parker's history of his own time [1660–80]. In four books. Faithfully translated from the Latin original. By S. Parker. Trans. by T. Newlin. 1 vol. 8vo. Lond. 1727.

Trans. of De rebus sui temporis, 1726.

79. A register and chronicle ecclesiastical and civil, . . . with . . . notes and references towards discovering and connecting the true history of England from the restauration of King Charles II. By W. Kennet, Bishop of Peterborough. 1 vol. fol. Lond. 1728.

Very useful for 1660–2. The materials for this register, plus other materials for a continuation to 1679 are in Lansdowne MSS. 1002–10 &c. Brit. Mus.

80. Phoenix Britannicus being a miscellaneous collection of scarce and curious tracts . . . collected by J. Morgan. 1 vol. 4to. Lond. 1732.

81. Desiderata curiosa or a collection of divers scarce and curious pieces relating chiefly to matters of English history; consisting of choice tracts. memoirs, letters, wills, epitaphs etc. Ed. by F. Peck. 2 vols. fol. Lond. 1732–5. Later ed. 2 vols. la. 4to. Lond. 1779. Illus.

Miscellaneous papers, many from Nalson MSS. (151 n.)—valuable c. 1645–60.

82. Revolution politicks : being a compleat collection of all the reports, lyes and stories which were the forerunners of the great revolution in 1688. 8 pts. in 1 vol. sm. 4to. Lond. 1733.

83. The Earl of Strafforde's letters and despatches with an essay towards his life by Sir George Radcliffe . . . Ed. by W. Knowler. 2 vols. fol. Lond. 1739. Ports.

Correspondence to August 1639. MSS. in possession of Earl Fitzwilliam. Cf. Camd. Soc. Misc., vols. viii and ix, for other Strafford Papers.

84. Examen : or an enquiry into the credit and veracity of a pretended complete history . . . together with some memoirs occasionally inserted. All tending to vindicate the honour of the late King Charles the Second. By R. North. 1 vol. 4to. Lond. 1740.

A Tory criticism of Kennet's Complete History (179). The original matter is valuable but should be used with caution. The materials used are in Brit. Mus. Add. MSS. 32518–20, 32525.

85. A collection of the state papers of John Thurloe Esq., secretary first to the council of state and afterwards to the two Protectors. Ed. by T. Birch. 7 vols. fol. Lond. 1742. Port.

From Bodleian Library Rawlinson MSS. A, vols. 1–73, with papers from other sources including Brit. Mus. Add. MSS. 415–19. Main authority for Protectorate.

86. Original letters and papers of state addressed to Oliver Cromwell concerning the affairs of Great Britain from the year 1649–1658, found among the political collection of . . . John Milton. Ed. by J. Nickolls. 1 vol. fol. Lond. 1743.

MSS. in possession of the Society of Antiquaries.

87. The Harleian miscellany or a collection of scarce, curious and entertaining pamphlets and tracts . . . found in the late Earl of Oxford's Library. 8 vols. 4to. Lond. 1744–6. Ed. by W. Oldys. Later eds. 12 vols. 8vo. Lond. 1808–11. Ed. J. Malham ; 10 vols. 4to. Lond. 1808–13. Ed. T. Park.

Cf. Contents of the Harleian Miscellany with an index. 1 vol. 4to. Sydney. 1885.

88. Letters and memorials of state in the reigns of Queen Mary, Queen Elizabeth, King James, King Charles I, part of the reign of King Charles II, and Oliver's usurpation . . . from the originals at Penshurst . . . and from his majesty's Office of Papers. Ed. by A. Collins. 2 vols. fol. Lond. 1746.

Commonly called ' Sydney Papers ' : a valuable collection of letters of members of this family. Cf. Sydney papers, consisting of a Journal of the Earl of Leicester 1646–61, and Original letters of Algernon Sydney [1659–61], ed. R. W. Blencowe [1 vol. 8vo. Lond. 1825]. A brief description of MSS. at Penshurst in Hist. MSS. Comm. iii. 227–9.

89. Collection of scarce and valuable tracts . . . selected from . . . public as well as private libraries, particularly that of the late Lord Somers. 16 vols. 4to. Lond. 1748–52. Later ed. 13 vols. 4to. Lond. 1809–15. Ed. by Sir W. Scott.

Later ed. ' revised, augmented and arranged.'

90. Letters between Col. Robert Hammond . . . and the committee . . . at Derby House . . . relating to King Charles I while he was confined in Carisbrooke Castle. Ed. by T. Birch. 1 vol. 8vo. Lond. 1754.

91. The secret history of the Rye-House plot and of Monmouth's rebellion written by Ford Lord Grey in 1685. Now first published from a manuscript signed by himself before the Earl of Sunderland. 1 vol. 8vo. Lond. 1754.

92. The history of the last four years of the Queen Anne . . . published from the last manuscript copy corrected and enlarged by the author's own hand. By J. Swift. 1 vol. 8vo. Lond. 1758.

Best ed. in Temple Scott's Prose works of Jonathan Swift (2450), vol. x. This ed. should be consulted for Swift's other historical writings.

93. The life of Edward, Earl of Clarendon. Being a continuation of the History of the Great Rebellion from the restoration to his banishment in 1667. By E. Hyde, Earl of Clarendon. 1 vol. fol. Oxf. 1759. Later ed. 2 vols. 8vo. Oxf. 1857.

Original in Bodl. Libr. Clarendon MS. 123. Includes those portions of the Life not incorporated into the History, and an account of Clarendon's ministry and second exile.

94. State papers collected by Edward, Earl of Clarendon commencing from the year 1621. Ed. by R. Scrope and T. Monkhouse. 3 vols. fol. Oxf. 1767–86.

A valuable selection from the Clarendon MSS. Bodleian Libr. extending to 1660, The Calendar of the Clarendon state papers [3 vols. 8vo. Oxf. 1869–76, ed. by O. Ogle, W. H. Bliss, and W. D. Macray] extends to 1657. A continuation by F. J. Routledge is in progress.

95. Nugae antiquae, being a collection of original papers in prose and verse. By Sir J. Harington. Ed. by H. Harington. 2 vols. 12mo. Lond. 1769–75. Later ed. 2 vols. 8vo. Lond. 1804. Ed. by T. Park.

Ed. of 1804 repr. *inter alia* Harington's A brief view of the state of the Church of England as it stood in Queen Elizabeth's and King James' his reigns to the yeere 1608 [12mo. Lond. 1653].

96. Memoirs of Great Britain and Ireland [1681–92]. By Sir J. Dalrymple. 2 vols. 4to. Lond. and Edin. 1771–3. Later ed. 3 vols. 8vo. Lond. 1790.

Volume II of 1st ed. consists of documents, selected mainly from the correspondence of French ambassadors in the Archives des Affaires Étrangères at Paris, and from the domestic state papers now in the Public Record Office. A valuable collection : the first ed. is the best.

97. Original papers containing the secret history of Great Britain [1660–1714]. Ed. by J. Macpherson. 2 vols. 4to. Lond. 1775.

Contains extracts from the Life of James II, ed. J. S. Clarke [see Ranke, vi. 29–45], Jacobite correspondence 1688–1714 mainly from the Nairne Papers among the Carte MSS. Bodl. Libr. and Hanover Papers 1702–14, on which see J. F. Chance's Corrections to . . . original Papers, Eng. Hist. Rev. xii. 1898. Cf. J. Macpherson and the Nairne papers, by Arthur Parnell, Eng. Hist. Rev. xii. 1897 ; an attempt to disprove the authenticity of the Nairne Papers ; and an answer by G. Davies, *ibid.* xxxv. 1920.

98. Miscellaneous State Papers [Hardwicke State Papers], from 1501–1726. Ed. by P. Yorke, Earl of Hardwicke. 2 vols. 4to. Lond. 1778.

Valuable. Includes papers relating to the Spanish Match and the marriage of Charles I, letters of Charles I to Buckingham, and William III to Heinsius, and various statesmen to Somers, with documents relating to the Bishops' Wars 1637–41, and Monmouth's rebellion. Originals in Public Record Office or Brit. Mus. A Supplement to State Papers [s. l., s. a.] includes letters of James I, of Argyle [1641–42], and account of conferences between Portland and Boufflers 1697.

99. Collectanea Curiosa. Ed. by J. Gutch. 2 vols. 8vo. Oxf. 1781.

Useful for the reign of James II, especially for the trial of the seven bishops. Most of these papers are pr. from the Tanner MSS. Bodl. Libr.

100. Collection of original royal letters written by King Charles the First and Second, King James the Second . . . Ed. by Sir G. Bromley. 1 vol. 8vo. Lond. 1787.

Also letters of Palatine family.

101. Illustrations of British history . . . in the reigns of Henry VIII . . . and James I exhibited in a series of original papers selected from the manuscripts of the noble families of Howard, Talbot and Cecil [in the College of

Arms]. Ed. by E. Lodge. 3 vols. 4to. Lond. 1791. Illus. 2nd ed. 3 vols. 8vo. Lond. 1838.

Reign of James I, iii. 155–404.

102. Letters and correspondence, public and private, of . . . Henry St. John, Lord Viscount Bolingbroke, during the time he was Secretary of State [1710–14]. Ed. by G. Parke. 4 vols. 8vo. Lond. 1798 and 2 vols. 4to. Lond. 1798.

103. Cromwelliana. A chronological detail of events in which Oliver Cromwell was engaged from . . . 1642 to . . . 1658. Ed. by M. Stace. 1 vol. fol. Westminster. 1810. Plates.

Extracts from newspapers becoming more detailed after 1649.

104. Secret history of the court of James the First. Ed. by Sir W. Scott. 2 vols. 8vo. Edin. 1811.

Comprises : F. Osborne's Some traditionall memoyres on the raigne of King James the First [1 vol. 12mo. Lond. 1658]. Sir A. Weldon's The character of King James, whereunto is added The court of King Charles continued unto the beginning of these unhappy times [1651] ; A perfect description of the people and country of Scotland [1659] ; Aulicus coquinariae or a vindication in answer to . . . the court and character of King James [by Weldon, *supra*] [1 vol. 12mo. Lond. 1650]. Sir E. Peyton's The divine catastrophe of the kingly family of the house of Stuarts [1 vol. 12mo. Lond. 1652]. The court and kitchin of Elizabeth, commonly called Joan Cromwell, the wife of the late usurper [1 vol. 12mo. Lond. 1664]. All these to be used cautiously.

105. Tixall letters ; or the correspondence of the Aston family . . . during the seventeenth century. With notes and illustrations. Ed. by A. Clifford. 2 vols. 8vo. Lond. 1815.

Cf. Tixall Poetry [1 vol. 4to. Lond. 1813] by the same author.

106. A memorial offered to . . . the Princess Sophia . . . containing a delineation of the constitution and policy of England. . . . By [G. Smythe]. Ed. by J. G. H. Feder. 1 vol. 8vo. Lond. 1815.

Erroneously ascribed to Gilbert Burnet on the title-page.

107. Epistolary curiosities ; consisting of unpublished letters . . . illustrative of the Herbert family. Ed. by R. Warner. 2 vols. in 1. 8vo. Bath. 1818.

The first series mainly concerns the Herbert family in the 17th century, the second deals with the early 18th century and includes many letters from Shrewsbury, Cardonnel, Cresset, &c.

108. Smeeton's historical & biographical tracts. 2 vols. 4to. Westminster. 1820.

Facsimile reprints, among others of Weldon's Court and character of James I ; The history of the gunpowder treason ; Vicars' England's worthies. See list in Lowndes, p. 2416.

109. Private and original correspondence of Charles Talbot, Duke of Shrewsbury, with King William, the leaders of the Whig party . . . from the family papers . . . of . . . the duchess of Buccleuch. Ed. by W. Coxe. 1 vol. 4to. Lond. 1821.

Extremely valuable for the reign of William III, especially for 1694–8. Cf. Buccleuch MSS. Montagu House, II (278).

110. Original letters illustrative of English history . . . from autographs in the British Museum. Ed. by Sir H. Ellis. 11 vols. 8vo. Lond. 1825–46. Ports.

A good selection. 1st series, 3 vols. 2nd and 3rd series, 4 vols. each.

111. The Ellis correspondence : letters written during the years 1686–88 and addressed to John Ellis esq., secretary to the commissioners of his majesty's revenue in Ireland. . . . Ed. by Hon. G. J. W. Agar-Ellis, Lord Dover. 2 vols. 8vo. Lond. 1829. Ports. Later ed. 2 vols. 8vo. Lond. 1831.

MS. in Brit. Mus. Add. MS. 4194. Other Ellis papers *ibid.* 28875–956.

112. Letters of the Duke and Duchess of Buckingham chiefly addressed to King James I of England. Publ. and possibly ed. by T. G. Stevenson, 1 vol. 8vo. Edinburgh. 1834.

113. The Loseley manuscripts . . . from the reign of Henry VIII to that of James I. Preserved . . . at Loseley House, in Surrey. Ed. by A. J. Kempe. 1 vol. 8vo. Lond. 1836.

Has some letters of James I, and some documents illustrating Sir George Chaworth's embassy to the Infanta Isabella Clara Eugenia [1621]. Cf. Hist. MSS. Comm. Rep. vii. 1879. pp. 596 *seq.* for an account of these and other papers.

114. The correspondence of Sir Thomas Hanmer . . . with a memoir of his life. Ed. by Sir H. Bunbury. 1 vol. 8vo. Lond. 1838.

Useful for 1710–14.

115. The court of King James the First . . . to which are added letters .. of the most distinguished characters of the court. By G. Goodman. Ed. by J. S. Brewer. 2 vols. 8vo. Lond. 1839. Ports.

MS. in Bodl. Libr. Cf. Original letters of Godfrey Goodman together with materials for his life. Ed. J. E. B. Mayor. Camb. Antiq. Soc. ii. 1864.

116. The Egerton papers : a collection of public and private documents chiefly illustrative of the times of Elizabeth and James I. . . . Ed. by J. P. Collier. 1 vol. Camd. Soc. 1840.

MSS. accumulated by Sir T. Egerton, Lord Chancellor under James I. Cf. Hist. MSS. Comm., Rep. xi, App. vii, Bridgewater Trust Office MSS.

117. Letters illustrative of the reign of William III from 1696 to 1708 addressed to the Duke of Shrewsbury . . . by J. Vernon, Secretary of State. Ed. by G. P. R. James. 3 vols. 8vo. Lond. 1841.

Valuable, especially for 1696–1702.

117 A. Reprints of rare tracts & imprints of ancient manuscripts &c. chiefly illustrative of the history of the northern counties and prints at the press of M. A. Richardson. 7 vols. 8vo. Newcastle. *c.* 1843–8.

Mainly relating to Newcastle in the 17th century, especially *c.* 1639–45.

118. Letters of the kings of England. Ed. by J. O. Halliwell. 2 vols. 8vo. Lond. 1846.

Vol. ii contains many letters of James I and Charles I.

119. The court and times of James the First; illustrated by authentic and confidential letters. Ed. by R. F. Williams. 2 vols. 8vo. Lond. 1848.

Mainly the newsletters of J. Chamberlain and J. Mead, pr. from transcripts made by T. Birch; originals now among the Domestic State Papers in the Public Record Office. Cf. E. P. Statham's A Jacobean letter-writer. The life and times of John Chamberlain [1 vol. 8vo. Lond. *c.* 1920].

120. The court and times of Charles the First; illustrated by authentic and confidential letters . . . including memoirs of the mission in England of the Capuchin friars by Father Cyprien de Gamache. Ed. by R. F. Williams. 2 vols. 8vo. Lond. 1848.

Mainly newsletters written by or to J. Mead, pr. from transcripts made by T. Birch: originals in Public Record Office. Cf. No. 1827.

121. Memoirs of the reign of Charles the First [Fairfax Correspondence, i and ii, to 1642]. Ed. by G. W. Johnson. 2 vols. 8vo. Lond. 1848.

See No. 1160 for vols. iii and iv of the Fairfax correspondence.

122. Letters to and from Henry Savile, envoy at Paris and vice-chamberlain to Charles II and James II. Including letters from . . . George Marquess of Halifax. Ed. by W. D. Cooper. Camd. Soc. 1857.

Savile's letters from Paris cover 1679–82, those of Halifax 1679–86. The letters were drawn mainly from a MS. in the Duke of Devonshire's possession and from the secretary of state's letter-books in the Public Record Office. See also No. 171 n.

123. A brief historical relation of state affairs from September 1678 to April 1714. By N. Luttrell. 6 vols. 8vo. Oxf. 1857.

From MS. in library of All Souls, Oxford. A daily record of public events, extracted from newsletters &c. Valuable as a guide to what the general public knew of contemporary politics.

124. Calendar of State Papers, Domestic series.

James I. 4 vols. 1857–9, with Addenda vol. 1580–1625, 1872; Charles I, 22 vols. 1625–49, 1858–93 with addenda vol. 1625–49, 1897; 1649–60, 13 vols. 1875–86; 1660–81, 22 vols. 1860–1921; 1689–96, 7 vols. 1895–1913; 1702–4, 2 vols. 1916–24. Cf. S. C. Lomas, The state papers of the early Stuarts and the interregnum. Trans. Royal Hist. Soc., 2nd series, xvi.

125. Letters from George Lord Carew to Sir Thomas Roe. Ed. by Sir J. Maclean. Camd. Soc. 1860.

Forms a diary of public events, Jan. 1615–Jan. 1618. Originals in P.R.O. Dom. S.P.

126. On four letters from Lord Bacon to Christian IV King of Denmark [16 June 1619–13 Jan. 1621] together with observations on the part taken by him in the grants of monopolies made by James I. Ed. by S. R. Gardiner. Archaeologia xli. 1867.

127. On certain letters of Diego Sarmiento de Acuna, Count of Gondomar giving an account of the affair of the Earl of Somerset, with remarks on the career of Somerset as a public man. Ed. by S. R. Gardiner. Archaeologia xli. 1867.

128. Notes on the treaty carried on at Ripon between King Charles I and the convenanters of Scotland, 1640, taken by Sir J. Borough, Garter King of Arms. Ed. by J. Bruce. Camd. Soc. 1869.

129. Historical notices of the reign of Charles I [1630–46]. By N. Wallington. Ed. by R. Webb. 2 vols. 8vo. Lond. 1869.

Notices of events arranged under subjects and compiled from newsletters and newspapers.

130. Les derniers Stuarts à Saint-Germain en Laye. By La Marquise Campana de Cavelli. 2 vols. fol. Paris. 1871. Illus.

Contains numerous documents from many foreign archives to illustrate the lives of James II and Mary of Modena 1673–89. An article in the Edinburgh Review for April 1882, pp. 291–321, brings out its importance, especially for 1685–89. Cf. The Stuart papers relating chiefly to Queen Mary of Modena and the exiled court of King James II. Ed. by F. Madan. 2 vols. Roxburghe Club. 1889. Pr. from Bodl. Libr. MSS. Add. *C.* 106–7.

131. The Fortescue papers ; consisting chiefly of letters relating to state affairs, collected by J. Packer, secretary to George Villiers, [first] Duke of Buckingham. Camd. Soc. 1871. Ed. by S. R. Gardiner.

Pr. from MS. in the possession of the Hon. J. M. Fortescue.

132. Trevelyan Papers. Parts II and III. Ed. by J. P. Collier, Sir W. C. Trevelyan, and Sir C. E. Trevelyan. 2 vols. Camd. Soc. 1872–3.

A family correspondence of very varied interest : mainly relating to the Western counties.

133. Wilhelm III von Oranien und Georg Friedrich von Waldeck. Ed. by P. L. Muller. 2 vols. 8vo. The Hague. 1873.

Contains correspondence, in French, of William and Waldeck 1675–92. Valuable for English history 1688–90.

134. De La Warr MSS. Hist. MSS. Comm., Rep. IV, 1873, pp. 276–317.

Includes correspondence of Lionel Cranfield, Earl of Middlesex. Cf. Sackville MSS. *ibid.* Rep. vii, Pt. I. 1879

135. Letters addressed from London to Sir Joseph Williamson . . . 1673 and 1674. Ed. by W. D. Christie. 2 vols. Camd. Soc. 1874.

Newsletters written from the secretary of state's office.

136. Sutherland MSS. Hist. MSS. Comm., Rep. V. 1876.

Valuable series of newsletters for the interregnum and restoration.

137. Pine Coffin MSS. Hist. MSS. Comm., Rep. V. 1876.

Newsletters, *c.* 1685–1700.

138. Correspondence of the family of Hatton being chiefly letters addressed to Christopher, first Viscount Hatton 1601–1704. Ed. by E. M. Thompson. 2 vols. Camd. Soc. 1878.

Pr. from Brit. Mus. Add. MSS. 29548–29596. Valuable for 1660–1700.

139. An index of the names of the royalists whose estates were confiscated during the commonwealth. 1 vol. 4to. Index Soc. 1879. By M. G. W. Peacock.

Cf. Index nominum to the royalist composition papers, vol. i. A. to F. By W. P. W. Phillimore. Index Library. 1889.

140. Ashburnham MSS. Hist. MSS. Comm., Rep. VIII, Pt. III. 1881.

An artificial collection with many 17th-century official papers : now among the Stowe MSS. in Brit. Mus.

141. A secret negociation with Charles the First 1643–1644. Ed. by B. M. Gardiner. Camd. Soc. Misc. viii. 1883.

Pr. from Tanner MS. Bodl. Libr.

142. The Wentworth papers 1705–1739 selected from the . . . correspondence of Thomas Wentworth Lord Raby created in 1711 Earl of Strafford. Ed. by J. J. Cartwright. 1 vol. 8vo. Lond. 1883.

Selected from MSS. in the Brit. Mus.

143. Catalogue of the collection of autograph letters and historical documents formed . . . by Alfred Morrison. Ed. by A. W. Thibaudeau. 6 vols. la. 4to. s.l. 1883–92.

Many 17th-century items. Often letters are reproduced in full, some in facsimile. The arrangement is alphabetical. Valuable newsletters [1667–75] are summarized as The Bulstrode papers [1897] in one of a second series of 6 vols. Cf. Hist. MSS. Comm., Rep. IX, Pt. II, 1895.

144. The Nicholas papers. Correspondence of Sir Edward Nicholas secretary of state. Ed. by Sir G. F. Warner. Camd. Soc. 4 vols. 1886–1920.

1641–60. Selected from Brit. Mus. Egerton MSS.

145. Cowper MSS. I–III. Hist. MSS. Comm. 1888–9.

I and II contain papers of Sir John Coke 1603–44. Valuable for his secretaryship of state 1625–39, and for naval affairs. III has letters to Thomas Coke temp. Anne.

146. Rutland MSS. I and II. Hist. MSS. Comm. 1888, 1891.

Mainly Manners family papers, covering the whole period, and rich in ladies' letters. The Earl of Rutland's diary for 1639 is useful for the Scottish war.

147. The constitutional documents of the Puritan revolution. 1628–1660. Ed. by S. R. Gardiner. 1 vol. 8vo. Oxf. 1889. Later eds. 1899 and 1906.

Second and third ed. include documents of the opening years of Charles I's reign. Title altered to read ' 1625–60 '. Valuable alike for documents and introduction.

148. Le Fleming MSS. Hist. MSS. Comm. 1890.

A valuable series of newsletters *c.* 1660–1700 : also extracts from Sir Daniel Fleming's book of accounts 1656–88.

149. Beaufort MSS. Hist. MSS. Comm. 1891.

Contains letters of Charles I to the Marquis of Worcester 1639–45 ; journal of the siege of Colchester, family letters temp. Charles II, and a parliamentary diary 18 Dec. 1680–8 Jan. 1681.

150. Clarke Papers. Selections from the papers of William Clarke, secretary to the Council of the army 1647–9 and to General Monck and the commanders of the army in Scotland 1651–60. Ed. by C. H. Firth. 4 vols. Camd. Soc. 1891–1901.

MSS. at Worcester College, Oxford. Especially valuable for the debates of the Army Council.

151. Portland MSS. I–IX. Hist. MSS. Comm. 1891–1923.

I : originally House of Lords papers borrowed by J. Nalson, important for 1641–60 ; II : Cavendish papers, Newcastle's correspondence temp. Anne, letters of Nathaniel Harley 1682–1720, and Thomas Baskerville's tours in England ; III : Harley family papers 1603–1700 ; IV, V, VI : Harley's official correspondence temp. Anne ; VII : letters from W. Stratford, Canon of Christ Church, 1710–1729 ; VIII : official petitions to Harley 1700–08, and to Queen Anne 1704–08 ; IX : letter-book of Sir J. Holles, temp. James I, letters to and from J. Vernon, envoy to Copenhagen 1704–07, and Strafford's letters from the Hague and Utrecht, 1711–14.

152. Some sources of history for the Monmouth Rebellion and the Bloody Assizes. By A. L. Humphreys. Somersetshire Arch. and Natural Hist. Soc. Proc. 1892. pp. 312–26.

153. Fitzherbert MSS. Hist. MSS. Comm. 1893.
Contains letters to Sir George Treby 1671–1700 (mainly legal for William III's reign); and papers relating to the Popish Plot [1674–9].

154. Lonsdale MSS. Hist. MSS. Comm. 1893.
Contains : parliamentary diaries 24 Apr.–12 June 1626 and 4 June 1628–25 Feb. 1629 ; a tour in Scotland 1629 ; miscellaneous correspondence 1639–1711.

155. Select statutes and other constitutional documents illustrative of the reigns of Elizabeth and James I. Ed. by Sir G. W. Prothero. 1 vol. 8vo. Oxf. 1894. Later eds. 1898, 1906, and 1913.
Late eds. contain a few corrections and additions. Valuable for documents and intro.

156. Lindsey MSS. Hist. MSS. Comm. 1895.
Mainly papers of Sir Thomas Osborne, Earl of Danby 1667–88. Other Danby papers are briefly noticed in Leeds MSS. Hist. MSS. Comm. 1888. Most of Danby's papers are in Brit. Mus. Add. MSS. 28040–54, 28071–94, 38849 B. In the Retrospective Review, Series II, vol. ii, 1828, is an article on the letters of Charles Bertie to Arlington when envoy to Denmark 1670–2.

157. Correspondence of Henry Earl of Clarendon and James Earl of Abingdon, chiefly relating to the Monmouth insurrection [1683–85]. Ed. by C. E. Doble. Oxf. Hist. Soc., Collectanea, III. 1896. Illus.

158. Foljambe MSS. Hist. MSS. Comm. 1897.
Contains letters from James Duke of York to William Prince of Orange. 29 Oct. 1678–27 Nov. 1679.

159. Somerset MSS. Hist. MSS. Comm. 1898.
Correspondence of the Seymour family, relating to the civil war in the west, or to Anne's reign.

160. Ailesbury MSS. Hist. MSS. Comm. 1898.
Family correspondence from *c.* 1650–1714, and letters of Edward Cooke from Ireland, temp. Charles II.

161. Leyborne-Popham MSS. Hist. MSS. Comm. 1899.
Has naval papers of Edward Popham temp. Commonwealth, W. Clarke's papers 1650–61, the autobiography of G. Clarke, useful for Williamite wars in Ireland, and Mysteria Revelata by J. Collins, an account of the Restoration.

162. Montagu of Beaulieu MSS. Hist. MSS. Comm. 1900.
Mainly Montagu family correspondence during the first half of the seventeenth century.

163. Rariora : being notes of some of the printed books, manuscripts, historical documents, medals, engravings . . . collected 1858–1900 by John Eliot Hodgkin. 3 vols. 4to. Lond. 1902.
See Eng. Hist. Rev. 1903, xviii. 390–2, for a notice of some of the items. Cf. Eliot Hodgkin MSS. Hist. MSS. Comm. 1897, which describes this artificial collection covering the whole period.

164. Calendar of the Stuart papers . . . at Windsor Castle. Hist. MSS. Comm. 1902.

Jacobite papers of little value before 1712.

165. Stuart Tracts. 1603–1693. Ed. by C. H. Firth. 1 vol. 8vo. Westminster. 1903.

Repr. *inter alia* Fairfax, Short Memorials, A true relation of Major-General Sir Thomas Morgan's progress in France and Flanders [1699] ; A relation of the great sufferings and strange adventures of Henry Pitman [1689]. Cf. Later Stuart Tracts. Ed. by G. A. Aitken. 1 vol. 8vo. Westminster. 1903, contains Petty's Political Arithmetic [1690] and various pieces of Defoe and Arbuthnot. Both vols. originally formed part of Arber's An English Garner, 8 vols. 8vo. Lond. 1877–96.

166. Wombwell MSS. Hist. MSS. Comm., Various II, 1903.

Papers of Lord Fauconberg after the Restoration, including some on his mission to Italy in 1669–70 ; otherwise relates to family affairs or to Yorkshire.

167. Royal & loyal sufferers. Ed. by C. Deedes. 1 vol. 8vo. Lond. 1903.

Repr. Electra of Sophocles presented to . . . the Lady Elizabeth. By C. Wase [The Hague, 1649] ; An exact narrative . . . of his . . . majesties escape from Worcester [1660] ΕΙΚΩΝ ΒΑΣΙΛΙΚΗ or the true pourtraiture of . . . Charles II [1660] ; The loyal sacrifice . . . Sir Charles Lucas and Sir George Lisle [1648]. Only the second is repr. in full.

168. Harford MSS. Hist. MSS. Comm., Various II, 1903.

Mainly letters from exiled royalists to Sir Marmaduke Langdale, 1650–60.

169. Select statutes cases and documents to illustrate English constitutional history 1660–1832, with a Supplement from 1832–1894. Ed. by C. G. Robertson. 1 vol. 8vo. Lond. 1904 and 1913.

Later ed. has introductory notes.

170. Stopford-Sackville MSS. I. Hist. MSS. Comm. 1904.

Has letters on Monmouth's rebellion.

171. Bath MSS. I–III. Hist. MSS. Comm. 1904–8.

I : Harley's correspondence, valuable for Anne's reign, accounts of the siege of Brampton Bryan 1643, and miscellaneous correspondence ; II : miscellaneous, including Holles papers, useful for the royalists in exile, and letters from H. Savile 1677–9 ; III : Prior papers, valuable for the treaty of Ryswick and English embassy at Paris 1698–9. A brief description of the Bath MSS. is in Hist. MSS. Comm., Rep. III, pp. 193–4, and a catalogue of Henry Coventry's official foreign correspondence *ibid.* Rep. IV, pp. 228–51.

172. Ormonde MSS. New series, IV, pp. 374–598. Hist. MSS. Comm. 1906.

These letters of Sir R. Southwell to Ormonde from Sept. 1677–Feb. 1680 form practically a continuous diary of English politics, and illustrate the proceedings of the council. Cf. No. 3286.

173. Verulam MSS. Hist. MSS. Comm. 1906.

Mainly papers of Sir H. Grimston : an inventory, 1644, is valuable for social history.

173 A. Letters of Philip Gawdy 1579–1616. Ed. by J. H. Jeayes. Roxburghe Club. 1906.

Pr. from Brit. Mus. Add. MSS. 27395–9 and Egerton MSS. 2713–22. Cf. Gawdy MSS. Hist. MSS. Comm. 1885, a private family correspondence covering the seventeenth century.

174. Some unpublished letters of Gilbert Burnet the historian. Camd. Soc. Misc. xi. 1907. Ed. by H. C. Foxcroft.

Newsletters addressed to Halifax, Jan.–Sept. 1680. From an 18th-century transcript in the possession of Earl Spencer.

175. Magdalene College MSS. Pepys MSS. Hist. MSS. Comm. 1911.

Mainly royalist papers, 1644–51.

175 A. Finch MSS. Hist. MSS. Comm. 1913, 1922.

Vol. i has correspondence of Winchelsea during his Turkish embassy, 1660–68, vol. ii has private and official correspondence of the first and second Earls of Nottingham, the latter being valuable for 1689–90.

176. Harvey Bruce MSS. Hist. MSS. Comm., Various VII, 1914.

Mainly letters addressed to Sir G. Clifton during the first half of the seventeenth century. Has a description of Scotland in 1617.

177. Extracts from Jacobite correspondence 1712–14. Eng. Hist. Rev. xxx. 1915. By L. G. W. Legg.

From Arch. des. Aff. Étr., Paris.

178. Downshire MSS. I, Pts. I and II. Hist. MSS. Comm. 1924.

Comprises the correspondence of Sir W. Trumbull 1683–1714, including many state papers temp. William III.

(b) LATER WORKS

179. A complete history of England with the lives of all the kings and queens thereof [to William III]. By W. Kennet, Bishop of Peterborough. 3 vols. fol. Lond. 1706. 2nd ed. 1719.

Vols. i and ii comprise histories collected and edited by J. Hughes, including Camden's Annals of James I and Wilson's History of King James (38). 2nd ed., corrected with additions to vol. iii. Kennet's account 1660–1702 is useful. Cf. North (84).

180. The history of England from the first entrance of Julius Caesar [to 1688]. By L. Echard. 3 vols. fol. Lond. 1707–18. 3rd ed. 2 vols. fol. Lond. 1720.

Ed. of 1720 has additions. Cf. An Appendix to the three volumes of . . . Echard's History of England, consisting of several explanations and amendments . . . apologies and vindications, by the same author [sm. fol. Lond. 1720]. Echard also wrote : The history of the revolution and the establishment of England in 1688. 1 vol. 8vo. Lond. 1725.

181. The history of the revolutions in England under the family of the Stuarts [1603–90]. By P. J. D'Orléans. Trans. by J. Stevens. 1 vol. 8vo. Lond. 1711. Later ed. 1722.

Trans. of Histoire des révolutions d'Angleterre, 4to. Paris. 1693–4. Intro. by L. Echard. A Catholic history.

182. History of the life and reign of Queen Anne, illustrated with all the medals struck in this reign . . . and other useful and ornamental cuts. By A. Boyer. 1 vol. fol. Lond. 1722. Later ed. 1735.

Appendix of papers, and annual list of persons dying in this reign, with characters. Based on Annals but incorporated later material. Very useful, especially for parliamentary history.

183. The critical history of England. By J. Oldmixon. 2 vols. 8vo. Lond. 1724–6.

Criticizes Clarendon and Echard, but defends Burnet.

184. The history of England, written in French by Mr. Rapin de Thoyras. Translated into English with additional notes [and a continuation to the accession of George II] by N. Tindal. 28 vols. 8vo. Lond. 1726–47. Maps. Engravings : Medals. 3rd ed. in fol. 5 vols. fol. Lond. 1743–5.

Vols. i and ii of fol. ed. end in 1688 ; vols. iii–v (vol. iv being in two parts, which are generally separately lettered IV and V) form the continuation, 1689–1727. A bibliography of the French editions is in Raoul de Cazenove's Rapin-Thoyras, sa Famille, sa Vie et ses Œuvres, 4to. Paris. 1866 ; and there are bibliographical notes in Lowndes, p. 2047 (where is a list of illustrations of the fol. ed.) and in Dict. Nat. Biog. xvi. 740. A careful and valuable work.

185. The history of England, during the reigns of the royal house of Stuart. By J. Oldmixon. 1 vol. fol. Lond. 1730.

Led to a controversy with Atterbury. Oldmixon also wrote : The history of England during the reigns of King William and Queen Mary, Queen Anne, King George I, being the sequel of the reigns of the Stuarts. 1 vol. fol. Lond. 1735. Cf. his The secret history of Europe in four parts compleat . . . for 50 years past, with . . . original papers [8vo. Lond. 1712–15].

186. The history of England during the reigns of King William, Queen Anne and King George I, with an introductory review of the reigns of the royal brothers, Charles and James. By J. Ralph. 2 vols. fol. Lond. 1744–6.

Vol. i. 1660–88, ii. 1689–1702 (only). A careful compilation, giving authorities. Excellent use made of pamphlets, Ralph having obtained possession of collection formed by Somers.

187. A general history of England . . . from the earliest times [to 1654]. By T. Carte. 4 vols. fol. Lond. 1747–55.

188. The history of Great Britain. By D. Hume. 2 vols. 4to. Edin. and Lond. 1754–7. Later ed. 8 vols. 4to. Lond. 1770.

1st ed. covers only 1603–88. Later ed. is entitled ' The history of England from the invasion of Julius Caesar to the Revolution in 1688 '. T. Smollett and others published continuations of Hume.

189. The history of Great Britain from the restoration to the accession of the house of Hanover. By J. Macpherson. 2 vols. 4to. Lond. 1775.

190. The history of Great Britain from the revolution to the accession of George I. By A. Cunningham. Ed. by W. Thomson. 2 vols. fol. Lond. and Edin. 1787.

Trans. from Latin. Full of interesting anecdotes, but to be used with caution.

191. Transactions during the reign of Queen Anne from the Union to the death of that princess. By C. Hamilton. 1 vol. 8vo. Edin. 1790.

A few original documents illustrating Jacobite intrigues : otherwise of little value.

192. The history of political transactions and of parties from the restoration of King Charles the Second to the death of King William. By T. Somerville. 1 vol. 4to. Lond. 1792.

Cf. the same author's The history of Great Britain during the reign of Queen Anne. With . . . original papers [1 vol. 4to. Lond. 1798]. This is still useful.

193. A history of the early part of the reign of James the Second. By C. J. Fox. Ed. by V. Fox, Lord Holland. 1 vol. 4to. Lond. 1808.

App. has the correspondence of Barillon, the French ambassador at London, Dec. 1684–Dec. 1685.

194. Observations on the historical work of . . . Charles James Fox, with a narrative of . . . the enterprise of the Earl of Argyle, in 1685, by Sir P. Hume. By G. Rose. 1 vol. 4to. Lond. 1809.

Hume's narrative is important. Cf. S. Heywood's Vindication of Mr. Fox's history, 1811.

195. A history of England to 1688. By J. Lingard. 8 vols. 4to. Lond. 1819–30. Later ed. 10 vols. 8vo. Lond. 1854–5 and several reprints, with an abridgement and continuation by H. N. Birt [Lond. 1903 and 1912].

A careful survey from a moderate Roman Catholic point of view.

196. A history of the British empire from the accession of Charles I to the restoration. By George Brodie. 4 vols. 8vo. Edin. 1820. Later ed. 3 vols. 8vo. Lond. 1866.

Title of 1866 ed. : ' A constitutional history &c.' Criticism of Hume.

197. History of the commonwealth of England. From its commencement to the restoration of Charles the Second. By W. Godwin. 4 vols. 8vo. Lond. 1824–8.

Stops in 1658 ; useful for pamphlet literature.

198. Histoire de la révolution de 1688 en Angleterre [1660–1688]. By F. A. J. Mazure. 3 vols. 8vo. Paris. 1825.

Useful for extracts from French ambassador's dispatches.

199. The constitutional history of England from the accession of Henry VII to the death of George II. By H. Hallam. 2 vols. 4to. Lond. 1827. 8th ed. 3 vols. 8vo. Lond. 1855.

Has a steady Whig bias.

200. Commentaries on the life and reign of Charles I. By Isaac D'Israeli. 5 vols. 8vo. Lond. 1828–31. Later ed. 2 vols. 8vo. Lond. 1851. Ed. by B Disraeli aft. Earl of Beaconsfield.

201. Essays and orations. By Sir H. Halford. 1 vol. 8vo. Lond. 1831.

Contains ' An account of the opening of the tomb of King Charles I at Windsor ' in 1813.

202. History of the revolution in England in 1688, comprising a view of the reign of James II, from his accession to the enterprise of the prince of Orange. By Sir J. Mackintosh. 1 vol. 4to. Lond. 1834. Later ed. 2 vols. 8vo. Paris. 1834.

Chs. i–xi, only by Mackintosh. A careful piece of work, to which is appended a selection from the dispatches of the papal nuncio D'Adda, and other documents. The materials collected are in Add. MSS. 34487–526. The ed. of 1836–40 (in Lardner's Cabinet Cyclopaedia, 8vo. Lond.) has a continuation by William Wallace and Robert Bell. Macaulay's review (repr. in his Essays) is useful.

203. Critical and historical essays contributed to the Edinburgh Review. By T. Lord Macaulay. 3 vols. 8vo. Lond. 1843. Later ed. 1903. Ed. by F. C. Montague.

204. The history of England, from the accession of James II. By T. B. Macaulay. 5 vols. 8vo. Lond. 1849–61. Later eds. 1 vol. 4to. Lond. 1907. Ed. by T. F. Henderson. 6 vols. 8vo. Lond. 1913–15. Illus. Ed. by Sir C. H. Firth.

Ed. of 1907 has many useful notes added. Ed. of 1913–15 has nearly a thousand illustrations of every kind. There is a good review of Macaulay's account of foreign relations by J. M. Kemble in Frazer's Magazine for Feb. 1856.

205. History of Charles the First and the English revolution [1625–49]. By F. P. G. Guizot. Trans. by A. R. Scoble. 2 vols. 8vo. Lond. 1854. Later ed. 1 vol. 8vo. Lond. 1856. Trans. by W. Hazlitt.

Appendix has a few original documents.

206. History of Oliver Cromwell and the English commonwealth [1649–58]. By F. P. G. Guizot. Trans. by A. R. Scoble. 2 vols. 8vo. Lond. 1854.

Still useful for documents from French and Spanish archives. A trans. of Histoire de la république d'Angleterre et de Cromwell. 2 vols. 8vo. Paris. 1854.

207. History of Richard Cromwell and the restoration. By F. P. G. Guizot. Trans. by A. R. Scoble. 2 vols. 8vo. Lond. 1856.

Has many dispatches of the French ambassador.

208. The English constitution to the reign of King Charles the Second. By A. Amos. 1 vol. 8vo. Lond. 1857.

209. Studies and illustrations of the great rebellion. By J. L. Sanford. 1 vol. 8vo. Lond. 1858.

Includes essays on : Early life of Oliver Cromwell ; Constitutional returns to the Long Parliament ; Strafford and Pym ; Parliamentary Royalism ; The Earl of Essex ; Long Marston Moor ; Cavalier and Roundhead letters 1645 [mainly from Tanner MS. 60. Bodl. Libr.]. Still useful.

210. Omitted chapters of the history of England from the death of Charles I to the battle of Dunbar. By A. Bisset. 2 vols. 8vo. Lond. 1864–7.

2nd ed. History of the Commonwealth of England from the death of Charles I to the expulsion of the Long Parliament. 2 vols. 8vo. Lond. 1867.

211. History of England comprising the reign of Queen Anne until the peace of Utrecht, 1701–1713. By Philip Henry, 5th Earl Stanhope. 1 vol. 8vo. Lond. 1870. 4th ed. 2 vols. 8vo. Lond. 1872.

Sound and useful.

212. Europäische Geschichte im achtzehnten Jahrhundert. By C. von Noorden. 3 vols. 8vo. Düsseldorf. 1870–82.

213. Paradoxes and puzzles. By J. Paget. 1 vol. 8vo. Edin. 1874.

Includes a 2nd ed. of The New Examen (originally published in Blackwood's Magazine) in which Macaulay's accounts of Marlborough, the Massacre of Glencoe, the Highlands of Scotland, Dundee and William Penn, are adversely criticized.

214. A History of England principally in the seventeenth century. By L. von Ranke. 6 vols. 8vo. Oxf. 1875.

A trans. of Englische Geschichte (Berlin, 1859–69) ; has important appendices consisting of critical studies and documents, including the dispatches in French of the Brandenburg agent 1690–5, and William's letters in Dutch to Heinsius 1692–1702.

215. Der Fall des Hauses Stuart und die Succession des Hauses Hannover [1660–1714]. By O. Klopp. 14 vols. 8vo. Vienna. 1875–88.

The best account of English foreign relations, especially from about 1678.

216. The first two Stuarts and the Puritan revolution, 1603–1660. By S. R. Gardiner. Epochs of Modern History, 1876.

217. The History of Great Britain during the reign of Queen Anne. By F. W. Wyon. 2 vols. 8vo. Lond. 1876.

Useful.

218. Secret history of Charles II. By J. E. E. D. Lord Acton. The Home and Foreign Review, July 1882.

Mainly concerned with James de la Cloche. Repr. in Acton's Historical Essays and studies, ed. by J. N. Figgis and R. V. Laurence [1 vol. 8vo. Lond. 1907].

219. History of England from the accession of James I to the outbreak of the civil war, 1603–42. By S. R. Gardiner. 10 vols. 8vo. Lond. 1883–4. Maps. Plans.

This is the second and revised edition of the History first published as follows : History of England from the accession of James I to the disgrace of Chief-Justice Coke, 1603–16, 2 vols. 1863 ; Prince Charles and the Spanish marriage, 1617–23, 2 vols. 1869 ; History of England under the Duke of Buckingham and Charles I, 1624–8, 2 vols. 1875 ; The personal government of Charles I, 1628–37, 2 vols. 1877 ; The fall of the monarchy of Charles I, 1637–42, 2 vols. 1882. The standard history. The introductions in the first edition contain accounts of the authorities used which are omitted in the second edition. Cf. Usher (249).

220. History of the great civil war, 1642–9. By S. R. Gardiner. 3 vols. 8vo. Lond. 1886–91. Maps. Plans. Later ed. 4 vols. 8vo. Lond. 1893. Maps. Plans.

Ed. of 1893 revised. Continued in his History of the commonwealth and protectorate [1649–56]. 3 vols. 8vo. Lond. 1894–1901. Maps. Plans. Later ed. 4 vols. 8vo. Lond. 1903. Maps. Plans. Ed. of 1903 has a number of corrections and references to new authorities by C. H. Firth.

221. Some verdicts of history reviewed. By W. Stebbing. 1 vol. 8vo. Lond. 1887.

Has studies of Shaftesbury, Cowley, Prior, Bolingbroke, and New England and Virginia.

222. Cromwell and the insurrection of 1655. By Sir C. H. Firth. Eng. Hist. Rev. iii. 1888.

Ibid. 1889 for a reply by R. F. D. Palgrave and a reply by Firth. This controversy proves the reality of the plot against the protectorate. Cf. No. 872 n.

223. Side-lights on the Stuarts. By F. A. Inderwick. 1 vol. 8vo. Lond. 1888. Later ed. 1891. Illus.

The essay on Monmouth's rebellion supplies statistics from gaol-books &c. The other essays are on : Lady Arabella Stuart (with many letters) ; Witchcraft ; King Charles I ; The regicides ; Merrie England ; The king's healing.

224. The constitutional experiments of the commonwealth : a study of the years 1649–1660. By E. Jenks. 1 vol. 8vo. Camb. 1890.

Reviewed by C. H. Firth in Eng. Hist. Rev. vi. 1891.

225. The interregnum [1648–1660] : studies of the commonwealth, legislative, social and legal. By F. A. Inderwick. 1 vol. 8vo. Lond. 1891. Facsimiles of coins.

226. A student's manual of English constitutional history. By D. J. Medley. 1 vol. 8vo. Oxf. 1894. 6th ed. 1925.

A very useful summary of constitutional history as a whole.

227. Geschichte des letzten Ministeriums Königin Annas von England [1710–14] und der englischen Thronfolgefrage. By F. Salomon. 1 vol. 8vo. Gotha. 1894.

Prints in appendices documents from foreign archives and from MSS. in Brit. Mus.

228. Cromwell's major-generals. By D. W. Rannie. Eng. Hist. Rev. x. 1895.

229. Historical sketches of notable persons and events in the reigns of James I and Charles I. By T. Carlyle. Ed. by A. Carlyle. 1 vol. 8vo. Lond. 1898.

230. Geschichte der Revolution in England. By A. Stern. 1 vol. 8vo. Berlin. 1898.

231. The relations of Defoe and Harley [1703–11]. Ed. by T. Bateson. Eng. Hist. Rev. xv. 1900.

232. The development of political parties during the reign of Queen Anne. By W. F. Lord. In Trans. of Royal Hist. Soc., N.S., xiv. 1900.

233. English public opinion after the Restoration. By G. B. Hertz. 1 vol. 8vo. Lond. 1902.

Attempts to give ' the people's idea of politics ' 1660–1702.

234. Cromwell and the crown. By Sir C. H. Firth. Eng. Hist. Rev. xvii. 1902, xviii. 1903.

235. The valet's tragedy and other studies. By A. Lang. 1 vol. 8vo. Lond. 1903. Illus.

Includes essays on The mystery of James de la Cloche and The mystery of Sir Edmund Berry Godfrey.

236. James I and Sir Edward Coke. By R. G. Usher. In Eng. Hist. Rev. xviii. 1903.

Sets other accounts against Coke's own and concludes that Coke did not ' successfully beard the king '.

237. The failure of the humble petition and advice. By R. C. H. Catterall. Amer. Hist. Rev. ix. 1903–4.

238. England under the Stuarts. By G. M. Trevelyan. 1 vol. 8vo. Lond. 1904. Maps. Bibl. 12th ed. 1925.

239. The Cambridge Modern History, vols. iii, iv, v. Ed. by Sir A. W. Ward, Sir G. W. Prothero, and S. Leathes. 8vo. Camb. 1905–8.

List of authorities for each volume. English History in vol. iii. 1603–25 ; iv. 1625–60 ; v. 1660–1714.

240. The history of England 1603–1660. By F. C. Montague. Pol. Hist. of England. vii. 1 vol. 8vo. Lond. 1907. Maps. Bibl.

241. The junto. By T. Merz. 1 vol. 8vo. Newcastle. 1907. Ports.
Mainly on lives and personalities of Somers, Wharton, Russell, Montague, and Spencer. Intro. by W. F. Lord.

242. A history of modern liberty, vol. iii. The struggle with the Stuarts [1603–47]. By J. Mackinnon. 1 vol. 8vo. Lond. 1908.
Practically a general history of England and Scotland.

243. The constitutional history of England. By F. W. Maitland. Ed. by H. A. L. Fisher. 1 vol. 8vo. Camb. 1908.
Contains surveys of the constitution in 1625 and 1727.

244. The last years of the protectorate. By Sir C. H. Firth. 2 vols. 8vo. Lond. 1909. Bibl. note.
A continuation of Gardiner (220) on the same scale.

245. The history of England 1702–1760. By I. S. Leadam. Pol. hist. of England. ix. 1 vol. 8vo. Lond. 1909. Maps. Plans. Bibl.
Probably the best history of Anne's reign.

246. The history of England 1660–1702. By Sir R. Lodge. Pol. hist. of England. viii. 1 vol. 8vo. Lond. 1910. Maps. Bibl.

247. Four lectures on the Puritan revolution. By T. H. Green. Ed. by K. N. Bell. 1 vol. 8vo. Lond. 1912.
Also in Green's Collected Works [1888].

248. The suspension of the Habeas Corpus Act and the revolution of 1689. By C. C. Crawford. Eng. Hist. Rev. xxx. 1915.

249. A critical study of the historical method of Samuel Rawson Gardiner with an excursus on the historical conception of the puritan revolution from Clarendon to Gardiner. By R. G. Usher. 1 vol. 8vo. Washington Univ. Studies. St. Louis. 1915.
For a discussion of Gardiner's historical methods see Times Literary Supplement, 25 Sept. to 18 Dec. 1919.

250. The Derwentdale plot, 1663. By H. Gee. Trans. Roy. Hist. Soc., 3rd Ser. xi. 1917.

251. English political parties and leaders in the reign of Queen Anne 1702–1710. By W. T. Morgan. 1 vol. 8vo. New Haven. 1920. Bibl.
Based on much research. Cf. his : The ministerial revolution of 1710 in England. Political Science Quarterly, xxxvi, 1921.

252. A history of the Tory party 1640–1714. By K. Feiling. 1 vol. 8vo. Oxf. 1924.
Other similar works are by : C. B. R. Kent [1908] and M. Woods [1924]. Cf. The history of party, vol. i. 1666–1714. By G. W. Cooke. 8vo. Lond. 1836.

¶ 2. CENTRAL ADMINISTRATION

(i) General and Miscellaneous.
(ii) Privy Council : (*a*) General. (*b*) Cabinet Council.
(iii) Star Chamber.

Since the Privy Council was the mainspring of the whole central administration, Adair (275) supplies a guide to the materials, both printed and manuscript, for administrative history. Gerould (25) and other general bibliographies will also be found useful, while the more specialized bibliography in Mrs. Higham's Principal Secretary of State (274) should not be neglected.

But there was hardly an aspect of English life in which the hand of the central administration was not felt, and a student of its activities should consult works dealing with local government, the control of the press and of the drama, the development of social or economic life, the enforcement of the national religion, and other similar topics. As the Star Chamber stands on the border-line between administration and law, recourse should be made also to the legal section. For those branch establishments by which certain provincial areas were governed, the Councils of the North and of Wales, the books by Miss Reid (271) and Miss Skeel (3439) provide ample bibliographies.

(i) GENERAL AND MISCELLANEOUS

(*a*) Sources. (*b*) Later Works.

(*a*) SOURCES

253. A collection of ordinances and regulations for the government of the royal household, from Edward III to King William and Queen Mary. 1 vol. 4to. Lond. 1790.

Published for the Society of Antiquaries.

254. Order for his Highnes Court, given at Richmond the 16th of October 1610. Archaeologia xiv. Lond. 1803.

This is an order for the regulation of the household of Prince Henry.

255. A true collection as well of all the Kinges Majesties offices and fees in any the courtes at Westminster as of all the offices and fees of His Majesties honorable household. Archaeologia vol. xv. Lond. 1806.

A list for the year 1606.

256. Issues of the Exchequer ; being payments made out of His Majesty's revenue during the reign of King James I. Ed. by F. Devon. 1 vol. 4to. Lond. 1836.

Extracts from the records in the Pell office.

257. Notes of materials for a history of the public departments. By F. S. Thomas. 1 vol. fol. Lond. 1846.

Valuable for the history of the secretary of state and of the Signet Office.

258. The secret service expenses of Chsrles II and James II [1679–88]. By J. Y. Akerman. Camd. Soc. 1851.

259. Documents on the State Paper Office. Ed. by W. Noel Sainsbury. 30th Report of Dep. Keeper of Public Records App. 212–93. Lond. 1869.

260. Account of the English Court in 1704. By E. von Spanheim. Eng. Hist. Rev. vol. ii. 1887.

Best text pr. in French as an app. to Relation de la cour de France en 1690. Ed. by E. Bourgeois. 1 vol. 8vo. Paris. 1900.

261. An index to bills of privy signet, commonly called Signet bills 1584 to 1596 and 1603 to 1624 with a calendar of writs of privy seal 1601 to 1603. Ed. by W. P. W. Phillimore. British Record Soc. Index lib. 1 vol. 8vo. Lond. 1890.

There is also a calendar of Privy Seals 1–7 Charles I in the 43rd Report of the Deputy Keeper (App. pp. 1–205), and 8–11 Charles I in the 48th Report (App. pp. 451–560).

262. Maxims and instructions for ministers of state. By Daniel Defoe. Ed. by G. F. Warner. Eng. Hist. Rev. xxii. 1907.

From Brit. Mus. Lansdowne MS. 98 pp. 223–46. Describes the functions of government about 1704.

263. Bibliotheca Lindesiana. A bibliography of royal proclamations of the Tudor and Stuart sovereigns and others published under authority 1485–1714. Ed. by R. R. Steele. 2 vols. 4to. Oxf. 1910.

I. England and Wales.   II. Scotland and Ireland.   Has extremely good indexes and a valuable introduction.

(b) Later Works

264. Thomas Scot's services as intelligencer during the Commonwealth. By T. Scot. Ed. by C. H. Firth. Eng. Hist. Rev. vol. xii. 1897.

265. Thurloe and the Post Office. By C. H. Firth. Eng. Hist. Rev. vol. xiii. July 1898. Lond. 1898.

Cf. The secrecy of the post. By E. R. Turner. Eng. Hist. Rev. xxxiii. July 1918.

266. Cromwell's constitutional experiments. By J. P. Wallis. 19th Century, vol. xlvii. March 1900.

267. The history of the British Post Office. By J. C. Hemmeon. Harvard Economic Studies vii. 1 vol. 8vo. Camb. Mass. 1912.

Cf. H. Joyce, The history of the Post Office. 1 vol. 8vo. Lond. 1893 ; and J. W. Hyde, The early history of the post in grant and farm [to 1685]. 1 vol. 8vo. Lond. 1894.

268. The establishment of the committee of both kingdoms. By W. Notestein. Amer. Hist. Rev. xvii. Apr. 1912.

269. The lords justices of England. By E. R. Turner. Eng. Hist. Rev. xxix. July 1914.

270. The establishment of the great farm of the English customs. By A. P. Newton. Trans. of R. Hist. Soc. 4th Ser. vol. i. 1918.

Describes the system in use in 1600 and the great reform of 1604–5. Cf. A list of Records of the Greencloth extant in 1610. By A. P. Newton. Eng. Hist. Rev. Apr. 1919. vol. xxxiv.

271. The King's Council of the North. By R. R. Reid. 1 vol. 8vo. Lond. 1921. Bibl.

The bibliography is an excellent guide to the sources for the history of the government of the north to 1640.

272. The dispensing power and the defense of the realm. By E. F. Churchill. Law Quarterly Review, vol. xxxvii. Oct. 1921.

273. The dispensing power of the crown in ecclesiastical affairs. By E. F. Churchill. Law Quarterly Review, vol. xxxviii. July and Oct. 1922.

See also an article by the same author on ' Dispensations under the Tudors and Stuarts ' (Eng. Hist. Rev. vol. xxxiv. July 1919) which gives the tariff for ecclesiastical dispensations.

274. The principal secretary of state. A survey of the office from 1558 to 1680. By F. M. G. Evans (Mrs. C. S. S. Higham). 1 vol. 8vo. Manchester. 1923. Bibl.

A valuable study ; it contains an excellent account of the original records of the secretary's office.

(ii) PRIVY COUNCIL

(a) GENERAL

275. The sources for the history of the council in the sixteenth and seventeenth centuries. By E. R. Adair. 1 vol. 8vo. Lond. 1924.

Has many references to MSS. as well as to pr. sources. A Russian study of the council 1547–1649 by B. Alexandrenko was publ. Warsaw. 1890.

276. Notes which passed at meetings of the privy council between Charles II and the Earl of Clarendon [1660–7]. Ed. by W. D. Macray. 1 vol. 4to. Roxburghe Club. Lond. 1896. Facsimiles.

From Bodl. Libr. Clarendon MSS. 100–1.

277. Appeals from colonial courts to king in council with especial reference to Rhode Island. By H. D. Hazeltine. 1 vol. 8vo. Papers from the Historical Seminary of Brown Univ. No. 7. 1896.

This is based on J. F. Macqueen : A Practical Treatise on the appellate jurisdiction of the House of Lords and Privy Council. 1 vol. 8vo. Lond. 1842.

278. Buccleuch MSS. at Montagu House. II. Pts. I and II. Hist. MSS. Comm. 1903.

Has valuable minutes of meetings of committees of privy council 1694–8. Cf. No. 109.

279. Colonial administration under Lord Clarendon. By P. L. Kaye. 1 vol. 8vo. Johns Hopkins Univ. Studies in Historical and Pol. Science No. 23. Baltimore. 1905.

An earlier work by the same author ' The colonial executive prior to the Restoration ' (Johns Hopkins Univ. Studies in Historical and Pol. Sci. No. 18. 1900) is also of some value for the colonial control exercised by the home government.

280. British committees, commissions, and councils of trade and plantations, 1622–1675. By C. M. Andrews. 1 vol. 8vo. Johns Hopkins Univ. Studies in Hist. and Pol. Sc. vol. 26. Baltimore. 1908.

Prof. Andrews in his work on ' Colonial Self-Government 1652–89 ' (The American Nation Series, vol. 5 : 1904 Bibliogr. deals again with this subject, and the books of

Mr. G. L. Beer on ' The Origins of the British Colonial System [1908] and the Old Colonial System [2 vols. 1912] add further information. Cf. Amer. Hist. Ass. Rep. for 1911, pp. 393–528.

281. The board of trade at work. By M. P. Clarke. 1911. Amer. Hist. Rev. vol. xvii. Oct. 1911.

This subject is also dealt with by Mr. O. M. Dickerson in 'American Colonial Government 1696–1765'. 1 vol. 8vo. Cleveland 1912, a fine study.

282. Colonial appeals to the privy council. By A. M. Schlesinger. Political Science Quarterly, vol. xxviii. pp. 279–97, 433–50. 1913.

283. The review of American colonial legislation by the king in council. By E. B. Russell. 1 vol. 8vo. Columbia Univ. Studies in History, Economics, and Public Law. lxiv. 2. New York. 1915.

Ch. i deals with the period down to 1696.

284. The privy council registers. By E. R. Adair. Eng. Hist. Rev. vol. xxx. 1915.

There is another article by the same author on ' The rough copies of the privy council register ' in E.H.R. vol. xxxviii. pp. 410–22. July 1923.

285. The lords of trade and plantations 1675–1696. By R. P. Bieber. 1 vol. 8vo. Allentown. Pa. 1919.

This subject is also dealt with by W. T. Root in ' The lords of trade and plantations 1675–96 ' (A.H.R. vol. 23, pp. 20–41 Oct. 1917). Mr. Bieber has also published an article on ' The British plantation councils of 1670–4 ' describing their activities in detail (E.H.R. vol. xl. pp. 93–106, Jan. 1925.)

286. Acts of the privy council of England 1613–1617. 3 vols. 8vo. Lond. 1921–27.

Other volumes are in preparation ; those portions of the 17th and 18th century registers of the privy council that refer to the colonies were published by W. Grant and J. Munro (3554). The introductions to these volumes (especially vols. i and ii) are most valuable for the working of the privy council. There is a list of privy councillors for the period in the Addendum to vol. v. Extracts from the privy council registers concerning the drama have been printed by E. K. Chambers and W. W. Greg. Dramatic records from the privy council register 1603–42. (The Malone Society's Collections, Pts. IV and V, pp. 370–95. 1911.)

(b) CABINET COUNCIL

287. The private diary of William First Earl Cowper. Ed. by E. C. Hawtrey. 1 vol. 4to. Roxburghe Club, 1833.

Cowper's Diary is very valuable for the history of the cabinet during the period 1703 to 1710.

288. History of cabinets from the Union with Scotland to the acquisition of Canada and Bengal. By W. MacC. Torrens. 2 vols. 8vo. Lond. 1894.

Chapter I (pp. 1–85) covers period 1688–1714 ; general and rather out of date.

289. The development of cabinet government in England. By M. T. Blauvelt. 1 vol. 8vo. N.Y. 1902.

The Stuart period is covered in chapters 1–5. This is now decidedly out of date.

290. Queen Anne's defence committee.   By Sir J. S. Corbett. Monthly Rev. May 1904. pp. 55–65.

Examines Nottingham's notes, May 1702–Jan. 1703 in Brit. Mus. Hatton-Finch MSS. (Add. MS. 29591).

291. Committees of council under the earlier Stuarts [1603–40].   By E. I. Carlyle.   In Eng. Hist. Rev. vol. xxi. Oct. 1906.

Mr. Carlyle continued this study in a second article ' Clarendon and the privy council 1660–7 ' (*Ibid.* vol. xxvii. Apr. 1912).

292. Inner and outer cabinet and privy council 1697–1783.   By H. W. V. Temperley.   Eng. Hist. Rev. vol. xxvii. Oct. 1912.

This article was followed by an appendix of ' Documents illustrative of the powers of the privy council in the 17th century ' (*Ibid.* vol. xxviii. Jan. 1913).

293. Die Entstehung der Kabinettsregierung in England.   By W. Michael. Zeitschrift für Politik, vi. pp. 549–93. 1913.

294. The cabinet in the seventeenth and eighteenth centuries.   By Sir W. R. Anson.   Eng. Hist. Rev. xxix. pp. 56–78. Jan. 1914.

295. Council and cabinet 1679–88.   By G. Davies. Eng. Hist. Rev. xxxvii. Jan. 1922.

296. The origin of the cabinet council [to 1640].   By E. R. Turner.   Eng. Hist. Rev. xxxviii. Apr. 1923.

Other articles by Prof. Turner dealing with the history of the cabinet are : Committees of the council and the cabinet 1660–88. (Amer. Hist. Rev. vol. xix. July 1914.)
The privy council of 1679. (Eng. Hist. Rev. vol. xxx. Apr. 1915.)
The development of the cabinet 1688–1760. (Amer. Hist. Rev. vol. xviii. vol. xix. July and Oct. 1913.)
Privy council committees 1688–1760. (Eng. Hist. Rev. vol. xxxi. Oct. 1916.)
The lords of the committee of the council. (Amer. Hist. Rev. vol. xxii. Oct. 1916.)

(iii) STAR CHAMBER

297. A speech delivered in the star chamber, on Wednesday the XIV of June, MDCXXXVII, at the censure of John Bastwick, Henry Burton, and William Prinn.   By W. Laud.   1 vol. 4to. Lond. 1637.

Repr. in the Harleian Miscellany (87).

298. A treatise on the court of star chamber.   By W. Hudson.   Ed. by F. Hargrave.   In Hargrave's Collectanea Juridica, vol. ii. pp. 1–240. 2 vols. 8vo. Lond. 1792.

Written *c.* 1620 : the Treatise exists in many versions, probably the best is Add. MS. 11681. See also Scofield ' A study of the court of star chamber ' Bibliog. p. vi ; and An outline of the history of the star chamber [Archaeologia xxv. 1834] by John Bruce, which is derived from Hudson. A similar treatise by Isaac Cotton written in 1622 is in Brit. Mus. Stowe MS. 418.

299. The star chamber : notices of the court and its proceedings.   By J. S. Burn, 1 vol. 8vo. Lond. 1870.

300. Speech of Sir Robert Heath, attorney general, in the case of Alexander Leighton in the star chamber, 4 June 1630.   By Sir R. Heath.   Ed. by S. R. Gardiner. Camd. Soc. Misc. vii. 1875.

Printed from State Papers Domestic CLXVIII.   Preface by J. Bruce.

301. Documents relating to the proceedings against William Prynne in 1634 and 1637. Ed. by J. Bruce and S. R. Gardiner. Camd. Socy. New Ser. 18. 1 vol. 4to. Lond. 1877.

Pr. from MSS. in Brit. Mus. and P.R.O. App. contains a list of Prynne's works.

302. Reports of cases in the courts of star chamber and high commission. Ed. by S. R. Gardiner. Camd. Soc. 1886.

From Harl. MS. 4130, and Rawlinson, A 128 ; Star chambers cases Easter Term 1631 to Trinity Term 1632 ; high commission cases Oct. 1631 to June 1632 ; shows ordinary course of business in these courts. There are reports of other Star chamber cases 1625–8 in Rushworth, vol. ii, Pt. II.

303. Les Reportes del cases in camera stellata 1593–1609. By J. Hawarde. Ed. by W. P. Baildon. 1 vol. 8vo. Lond. 1894.

304. Star chamber proceedings against the Earl of Suffolk and others. By A. P. Keep. In Eng. Hist. Rev. vol. xii. Oct. 1898.

Gives account of Proceedings in 1619 against Suffolk and his wife and Sir John Bingley. Based on contemp. MS. in possession of Pye family.

305. A study of the court of star chamber largely based on manuscripts in the British Museum and the Public Record Office. By C. L. Scofield. 1 vol. 8vo. Chicago. 1900. Bibl.

A careful treatise (though in some respects superseded), with valuable bibliography of both manuscript and printed sources.

306. The court of star chamber. By E. P. Cheyney. Amer. Hist. Rev. vol. xviii. July 1913.

Good account of Star Chamber procedure.

¶ 3. PARLIAMENTARY HISTORY

     (i) General and Miscellaneous.
     (ii) Elections.
     (iii) Lists of members.
     (iv) Proceedings and debates :
          (*a*) General collections.
          (*b*) Individual parliaments.
     (v) Collections of statutes.

There is neither a bibliography for the general parliamentary history of the period nor for any of its separate aspects. The best general guides are Gerould (25) and the Cambridge Modern History. The introduction to Notestein and Relf (398) has an admirable discussion of the sources for the first half of the seventeenth century.

In addition to the works listed in this section, general histories, especially constitutional, should be consulted together with the biographies and writings of members of either house of parliament. Most tracts are excluded from lack of space, although they form important sources. There is no complete catalogue of them, but guidance should be sought in the Thomason Tracts (17), Knuttel (721 n.), and the printed catalogue of the British Museum Library, where pamphlets on a subject are often grouped together. Unprinted MSS. for the period to 1642 are being investigated by Professor Notestein and his corroborators, but there is no list even for the later period.

(i) GENERAL AND MISCELLANEOUS
(*a*) Sources. (*b*) Later Works.

(*a*) Sources

307. The prerogative of Parliaments in England : proved in a dialogue . . . between a councillor of state and a justice of peace. . . . By Sir W. Raleigh. 1 vol. 4to. Midelburghe. 1628.

308. The History of the Parliament of England which began November 3 1640, with a short and necessary view of some precedent years. By T. May. 1 vol. fol. Lond. 1647.

Based on newspaper and official manifestoes. For estimate see D.N.B. *sub* May. Repr. with an appendix of documents, by F. Maseres. 4to. 1812 and 8vo. Oxf. 1854. The last ed. restored the original text which Maseres amended.

309. The commoners liberty : or the English-Mans birthright. By Sir R. Twysden. 1 vol. 4to. [Lond.] 1648.

310. A plea for the Lords, or a short yet full and necessary vindication of the judiciary and legislative power of the House of Peeres. . . . By W. Prynne. 1 vol. 4to. Lond. 1648. Later ed. 1658.

The 2nd ed. is practically a new work. The work is largely antiquarian.

311. Cottoni posthuma : divers choice pieces of that renowned antiquary, Sir Robert Cotton. Ed. by J. Howell. 1 vol. 8vo. Lond. 1651. Later eds. 1672 and 1679.

A collection of tracts, mostly of constitutional importance.

312. The ancient method and manner of holding Parliaments in England. By H. Elsynge. 1 vol. 8vo. Lond. 1660. Later ed. 1675.

An account of established parliamentary procedure : drawn largely from the *Modus tenendi Parliamenti* but (especially in the ed. of 1675) with much new matter.

313. The grand question concerning the judicature of the House of Peers stated and argued, and the case of Thomas Skinner . . . faithfully related. By D. Holles. 1 vol. 8vo. Lond. 1669.

Vindicates jurisdiction of peers.

314. The case stated of the jurisdiction of the House of Lords in the point of impositions. By D. Holles. 1 vol. 8vo. Lond. 1676.

Supports Lords' claims to moderate, though not to institute or increase, rates on merchandise voted by Commons.

315. Honesty's best policy ; or penitence the sum of prudence : Being a brief discourse in honour of the Right Honourable Anthony Earl of Shaftsbury's humble acknowledgment and submission for his offences upon his knees, at the Bar of the House of Lords, on the 25th of Febr. 1677[–78]. Together with the several proceedings of the said Right Honourable House, in order to his Lordships late discharge from imprisonment. 1 vol. 4to. s.a. [1678].

Satirical advice to Shaftesbury. Important account of the rise of the Country party.

316. A letter from Amsterdam to a friend in England. 1 vol. 4to. Lond. 1678.

Court party satire on the Country party and the Scottish Covenanters. Dated 18 Apr. 1678.

317. The constitution of Parliaments in England deduced from the time of King Edward the Second, illustrated by King Charles the Second in his Parliament summoned 18 Feb. 1661 and dissolved 24 Jan. 1679. By J. Pettus. 1 vol. 8vo. Lond. 1680.

Incomplete : treats only of the Lords.

318. The antient right of the commons of England asserted. By W. Petyt. 1 vol. 8vo. Lond. 1680.

319. Miscellanea Parliamentaria : containing presidents (1) of Freedom from Arrests, (2) of Censures. . . . besides other Presidents. By W. Petyt. 1 vol. 8vo. Lond. 1680.

320. English liberties, or, The free-born subject's inheritance. Containing I. Magna Charta, the Petition of Right, the Habeas Corpus Act ; and divers other most useful statutes, with large comments upon each of them. II. The proceedings in appeal of murther ; the work and power of Parliament. . . . Plain directions for all persons concerned in ecclesiastical courts. III. All the laws against conventicles and Protestant Dissenters with notes. By [H. Care] 1 vol. 12mo. Lond. [1680 ?] Later eds. 1 vol. 12mo. Lond. 1691. 4th ed. 1 vol. 8vo. Lond. 1719.

The 4th ed. is altered and enlarged.

321. A perfect copy of all summons of the nobility to the Great Councils and Parliaments of the Realm, from the XLIX of King Henry the IIIrd. until these present times. By Sir W. Dugdale. 1 vol. fol. Lond. 1685.

322. The power, jurisdiction and priviledge of Parliament ; and the antiquity of the House of Commons asserted. By Sir R. Atkyns. 1 vol. fol. Lond. 1689.

323. Of the judicature in Parliaments, a posthumous treatise : wherein, the controversies and precedents belonging to that title, are methodically handled. By J. Selden. 1 vol. 8vo. Lond. [?1690].

324. A vindication of the proceedings of the late Parliament of England, A.D. 1689 . . . By [J. Lord Somers]. 1 vol. 4to. Lond. 1690.

325. The original institution, power and jurisdiction of Parliaments . . . with a Declaration of the House of Commons concerning their privileges. . . . By Sir M. Hale. 1 vol. 8vo. Lond. 1707.

Hale's authorship is very doubtful.

326. A short history of the Parliament. 1 vol. 8vo. Lond. 1713.

This was attributed to Sir R. Walpole. There were 3 other editions in 1713.

327. Of the antiquity, power and decay of Parliaments. Being a general view of government, and civil policy, in Europe : with other historical Observations relating thereunto. By T. Rymer. 1 vol. 8vo. Lond. 1714.

328. Jus Parliamentarium : or the ancient power, jurisdiction, rights and liberties of the most high Court of Parliament. . . . By W. Petyt. 1 vol. fol. Lond. 1739.

329. Precedents of proceedings in the House of Commons. By J. Hatsell. 4 vols. 4to. Lond. 1781. Later eds. 1785, 1796, 1818.

The 4th ed. 1818 has additions by Charles Abbot, Lord Colchester.

330. The jurisdiction of the Lords House, or Parliament considered according to antient records. By Sir M. Hale. Ed. by F. Hargrave. 1 vol. 4to. Lond. 1796.

331. Catalogue of the printed books and manuscripts in the Library of the Inner Temple. 1 vol. 8vo. Lond. 1833.

This contains a moderately detailed list of the Petyt MSS. which are very valuable for parliamentary history. See also 'Report on the MSS. on the Library of the Inner Temple' by the Hist. MSS. Comm. (11th Rep. App. VII. 1888).

332. The debates on the Grand Remonstrance, November and December 1641. With an Introductory Essay. . . . By J. Forster. 1 vol. 8vo. Lond. 1860.

Marked by a strong parliamentary bias. Based on MSS. in P.R.O. D'Ewes' Journal in Harleian MSS. [162–6], as well as on printed material, but biased in favour of the parliament. Cf. his : Arrest of the Five Members by Charles the First : a Chapter of English History re-written. 1 vol. 8vo. Lond. 1860.

333. Eliot MSS. 1st Report of Hist. MSS. Comm. App. pp. 41–4. 1870.

These MSS. contain a great deal of material that is valuable for Parliamentary history.

334. Braye MSS. Hist. MSS. Comm. Abergavenny MSS. 1887.

Mainly papers of John Browne, Clerk to the Parliaments c. 1621–60. Some correspondence of John Mordaunt with royalists 1658–9.

335. Letters concerning the dissolution of Cromwell's last Parliament, 1658. By J. Hobart. Ed. by C. H. Firth. Eng. Hist. Rev. vol. vii. 1892.

From correspondence of John Hobart among Tanner MSS. in Bodleian Library.

(b) Later Works

336. The parliamentary privilege of freedom from arrest, and Sir Thomas Shirley's Case 1604. By G. W. Prothero. Eng. Hist. Rev. vol. viii. Oct. 1893.

Reviews the case and prints—for the first time—two Acts passed on it, which, being regarded as private Acts, are not included in the Statutes of the Realm.

337. A constitutional history of the house of lords. By L. O. Pike. 1 vol. 8vo. Lond. 1894.

Valuable, especially for legal side.

338. The Barebone Parliament and the religious movements of the 17th century culminating in the protectorate system of church government. By H. A. Glass. 1 vol. 8vo. Lond. 1899. Ports.

339. The genesis of the grand remonstrance from parliament to King Charles I. By H. L. Schoolcraft. 1 vol. 4to. Urbana. 1902.

Almost wholly from printed sources.

340. Karl II. und sein Konflikt mit seinem unduldsamen anglikanischen Parlament. By A. Zimmermann. Historisches Jahrbuch 1905. Band xxvi. Heft 3.

341. The Long Parliament of Charles II. By W. C. Abbott. In Eng. Hist. Rev. vol. xxi. pp. 21–56 and pp. 254–85. Jan. and Apr. 1906.

342. The religious factors in the Convention Parliament. By L. F. Brown. Eng. Hist. Rev. vol. xxii. pp. 51–63. Jan. 1907.

343. The Declaration of Indulgence 1672. By F. Bate. 1 vol. 8vo. Lond. 1908. Bibl.

344. Women petitioners and the Long Parliament. By E. A. McArthur. Eng. Hist. Rev. xxiv. Oct. 1909.

345. The High Court of Parliament. By C. H. McIlwain. 1 vol. 8vo. New-haven (Conn.) and Lond. 1910.

346. The House of Lords during the Civil War [1603–60]. By C. H. Firth. 1 vol. 8vo. Lond. 1910.

347. The speakers of the house of commons from the earliest times to the present day with . . . a brief record of the principal constitutional changes during seven centuries . . . with . . . a portrait of every speaker where one is known to exist. By A. I. Dasent. 1 vol. 8vo. Lond. 1911. Illus.

348. The Petition of Right. By F. H. Relf. 1 vol. 8vo. University of Minnesota. Studies in the Social Sciences, No. 8. Minneapolis. 1917.
Also serves as a useful guide to the sources for the history of the session of 1628.

349. The royal veto under Charles II. By C. E. Fryer. Eng. Hist. Rev. xxxii. Jan. 1917.

350. The Expulsion of the Long Parliament. By C. H. Firth. History, vol. ii. Nos. 7 and 8, pp. 129–143, 193–206. Oct. 1917, Jan. 1918.
This is a full examination of the sources for the account of this event. He criticizes Prof. W. Michael's article on the same subject (' Oliver Cromwell und die Auflösung des langen Parlaments ') in the Historische Zeitschrift for 1889 (vol. 63. pp. 57–78). See also ' Cromwell and the Expulsion of the Long Parliament in 1653 ' (Eng. Hist. Rev. vol. viii. July 1893) where Firth prints some original documents.

351. In the time of Sir John Eliot : (1) Eliot and the case of John Nutt, a pirate. (2) The parliament of 1621. (3) Negotium Posterorum and the parliament of 1625. By M. B. Fuller. 1 vol. 8vo. Smith College Studies in History, vol. iv. No. 2. Northampton. Mass. 1919.

352. The origin of English political parties. By W. C. Abbott. Amer. Hist. Rev. xxiv. Apr. 1919.

353. History of English parliamentary privilege. By C. Wittke. 1 vol. 8vo. Ohio State Univ. Studies : Contributions in History and Political Science. No. 6. Columbus. 1921.
Not wholly abreast of modern research in this subject.

354. Writs of assistance. By E. R. Adair and F. M. G. Evans. Eng. Hist. Rev. vol. xxxvi. July 1921.

Deals with the position of those summoned to attend the House of Lords as assistants.

355. The winning of the initiative by the house of commons. By W. Notestein. Repr. from Proc. Brit. Acad. 8vo. Lond. 1926.

Supersedes The institutional history of the house of commons 1547–1641. By R. G. Usher. Washington Univ. Studies xi. Humanistic series. 1924.

(ii) ELECTIONS

356. A brief register, kalendar, and survey . . . of Parliamentary Writs. By W. Prynne. 4 vols. 8vo. Lond. 1659–64.

357. A collection of debates, reports, orders, and resolutions of the house of commons, touching the right of electing members to serve in parliament for the several counties, cities, boroughs, and towns corporate in England and Wales. By W. Bohun. 1 vol. fol. Lond. 1702.

‘ Most of the cases reported fall within the years 1674–1700.’ Gross, A Bibliography of British municipal history, [8vo. N.Y. 1897] p. 61, where there is a list of the boroughs concerned.

358. All the proceedings in relation to the Aylesbury men committed by the house of commons and the report of the lords journal and reports of the conferences. 1 vol. fol. Lond. 1704.

359. Ashby and White : or, the great question whether an action lies at common law for an elector, who is deny’d his vote for members of parliament ? 1 vol. 8vo. s.l. 1705.

360. An historical account of the rights of elections of the several counties, cities, and boroughs of Great Britain ; collected from public records and the journals of parliament to . . . [1754]. By T. Carew. 2 pts. fol. Lond. 1755.

‘ For the period covered [c. 1600–1754] this is the most exhaustive parliamentary history of boroughs.’ Gross, p. 62, where there is a list of the boroughs concerned.

361. Reports of certain cases, determined and adjudged by the commons in parliament, in the twenty-first and twenty-second years of the reign of King James the First. By J. Glanville. Ed. by J. Topham. 1 vol. 8vo. Lond. 1775.

362. The representative history of Great Britain and Ireland. By T. H. B. Oldfield. 6 vols. 8vo. Lond. 1816.

This supersedes the same author’s, An entire and complete history of the boroughs of Great Britain [3 vols. 1792].

363. The unreformed house of commons. Parliamentary representation before 1832. By E. Porritt and A. G. Porritt. 2 vols. 8vo. Camb. 1903 and 1909.

Vol. I. England and Wales. II. Scotland and Ireland. A comprehensive work.

364. The Elections to the Exclusion Parliaments 1679–1681. By E. Lipson. Eng. Hist. Rev. xxviii. January 1913.

365. An 18th century Election in England [1710]. By W. T. Morgan. Political Science Quarterly, vol. xxxvii. 1922.

366. The Elections for the Long Parliament, 1640. By R. N. Kershaw. Eng. Hist. Rev. vol. xxxviii. Oct. 1923.

This account of the composition of the Long Parliament is carried on by an article by the same author in History (vol. viii. no. 31. pp. 169–79. Oct. 1923) entitled ' The Recruiting of the Long Parliament 1645–7 '.

(iii) LISTS OF MEMBERS OF PARLIAMENTS

367. Notitia Parliamentaria. By Browne Willis. 3 vols. 8vo. Lond. 1715–50.

Vols. I and II deal with parliamentary representation in a very detailed way—taking the counties alphabetically—but reaches only as far as Durham : Vol. iii gives brief notes for cities sending members to parliament, and lists of speakers and M.P.s from 1542 to 1660. Browne Willis is occasionally useful, but often unreliable.

368. Return of the names of every member returned to serve in each parliament. 2 vols. fol. s.l. 1878.

Pr. from writs and returns in the P.R.O. The indexes, publ. *c*. 1891, contain valuable addenda et corrigenda. Commonly called Official returns of members of parliament. Cf. W. W. Bean's The parliamentary returns of members of the House of Commons. Notices of various errors and omissions in the above-named work [1663–1830]. 8vo. Lond. *c*. 1883.

369. Cumberland and Westmorland M.P.'s from the restoration to the reform bill of 1867. By R. S. Ferguson. 1 vol. 8vo. Lond. & Carlisle. 1871.

370. The parliamentary representation of Yorkshire from the earliest authentically recorded elections to the present time [Edward I to 1886]. By G. R. Park. 1 vol. 8vo. Hull. 1886.

371. Parliamentary representation of Lancashire, county and borough, 1258–1885. By W. D. Pink and A. B. Beaven. 1 vol. 8vo. Lond. 1889.

372. The parliamentary representation of Cornwall to 1832. By W. P. Courtney. 1 vol. 8vo. Lond. 1889

373. The parliamentary representation of the six northern counties of England . . . and their cities and boroughs, from 1603 to . . . 1886. With lists of members and biographical notices. By W. W. Bean. 1 vol. 8vo. Hull. 1890.

374. Knights of the shire for Kent. 1275–1831. By J. Cave-Brown. Archaeologia Cantiana xxi. 1895.

375. The parliamentary history of the county of Gloucester, including the cities of Bristol and Gloucester (1213–1898) . . . with biographical and genea-logical notices of the Members. By W. R. J. Williams. 1 vol. 8vo. Hereford. 1898.

The same author has also produced similar parliamentary histories of the counties of Hereford [Brecknock 1896], Oxford [Brecknock 1899], Worcester [Hereford 1897] and the Principality of Wales 1541–1895 [Brecknock 1895], together with the Official Lists of the Duchy and County Palatine of Lancaster [Lond. 1901].

376. Staffordshire parliamentary history from the earliest times to the pre-sent day. By J. C. Wedgwood. 2 vols. 8vo. William Salt Soc. Lond. 1919–20.

1603–1714 is in vol. ii. Supplies many valuable notes on M.P.s

(iv) PARLIAMENTARY PROCEEDINGS AND DEBATES

(a) GENERAL COLLECTIONS

377. Journals of the house of lords 1578–1714 [vols. ii–xix]. 18 vols. fol. s.l. s.a.

Of the greatest value for the civil war, supplying copies of bills, letters, and other documents. Generally gives a list of the peers present each day, the date when a peer first took his seat, as well as each day's proceedings.

378. Journals of the house of commons 1547–1714 [vols. i–xvii]. 17 vols. fol. s.l. s.a.

379. Remembrances of some methods, orders, and proceedings heretofore used and observed in the House of Lords, extracted out of the Journals of that House. By H. Scobell. 1 vol. 12mo. Lond. 1657.

380. Rules and customs which by long and constant practice have obtained the name of orders of the House. . . . By H. Scobell. 1 vol. 12mo. Dublin. 1692.

381. A complete collection of protests made in the house of lords . . 1641–1737. 1 vol. 8vo. 1737.

Cf. A complete collection of all the protests . . . from 1641 to . . . 1745 [Lond. 1745].

382. The history and proceedings of the house of lords from the restoration in 1660 to the present time. 8 vols. 8vo. Lond. 1742–3.

Often referred to by the publisher's name Timberland. Vol. i covers the period 1660–97.

383. The history and proceedings of the house of commons from the restoration to the present time. 14 vols. 8vo. Lond. 1742–4.

Often referred to by the publisher's name, Chandler. The first 4 vols. cover the period 1660–1713. Cf. a similar series publ. by J. Torbuck, 1740–2.

384. The parliamentary or constitutional history of England from the earliest times to the restoration of Charles II. 24 vols. 8vo. Lond. 1751–62.

Commonly known as the Old parliamentary history. Valuable, especially for the copious extracts quoted from contemporary pamphlets during 1642–60, but must be used with great care owing to the wholly uncritical methods of its compilation.

385. The parliamentary history of England. Ed. by William Cobbett. 36 vols. 8vo. Lond. 1806–20.

Vols. i–vi cover the period down to 1714. At the end of vols. iv and v some interesting pamphlets of the later 17th century are repr.

386. The protests of the lords, including those which have been expunged . . . with historical introductions. By J. E. T. Rogers. 3 vols. 8vo. Oxf. 1875. Vol. i, 1624–1741.

387. The manuscripts of the house of Lords.

Some of these papers came into the custody of the lords either because they were addressed to the speaker of the lords or because they were secured for the purpose of a parliamentary inquiry. Since the lords always demanded the original documents, and refused copies, their value is the greater. There are also minute books, drafts of bills with amendments marked, copies of bills which never became law and much other material, all of which illustrates the Journals.   These volumes are of the greatest importance for constitutional history, but they often contain information of the highest value for nearly every branch of English history.   They were calendared by the Hist. MSS. Comm. down to 1693, the calendar to 1678 being contained in the 9 fol. reports and from 1678–93 in four vols. [8vo. Lond. 1887–94].   For 1693–1710 the calendar has been continued in a new series by the house of lords itself, vols. i–viii (8vo. Lond. 1900–23).   For an account of them as a whole see the app. to Report I. (Hist. MSS. Comm.) pp. 1–4, but no general description can explain the wealth of detail often to be found in them.

388. French reports of British parliamentary debates in the 18th century. By P. Mantoux.   Amer. Hist. Rev. vol. xii. Jan. 1907.

Valuable as indicating the existence of detailed reports of parliamentary proceedings in the 17th century among the Correspondance politique : Angleterre, of the French Foreign Office.   He quotes a report of some of the proceedings of the session of 1679. Transcripts of most of the Fr. ambassador's dispatches during the 17th century are deposited in the Public Record Office.

389. Proceedings and debates of the British parliaments respecting North America.   Vol. i, 1542–1688 ; vol. ii, 1689–1702.   Ed. by L. F. Stock.   8vo. Washington. 1924–7.

(b) Separate Parliaments, arranged in the chronological order of the Parliaments

390. Parliamentary debates in 1610 . . . from the notes of a member of the house of commons.   Ed. by S. R. Gardiner.   Camd. Soc. 1862.

From B. Mus. Add. MS. 4210, with illustrative papers from Harleian and Lansdowne MSS.

391. Proceedings and debates of the house of commons in 1620 and 1621, collected by a member of that house. . . . By [E. Nicholas].   Ed. by T. Tyrwhitt.   2 vols. 8vo. Oxf. 1766.

From MSS. in library of Queen's College, Oxford.   Nicholas's notes of the Parliamentary proceedings on March 14 to 16, and Nov. 20 to Dec. 19, 1621 are S.P. Dom. Jas. I, vol. cxxv.   (Calendar 1619–23, p. 332.)   Further notes by Nicholas for the sessions of 1624 are S.P. Dom. Jas. I. clxvi (Calendar 1623–4, p. 263) and of 1628 (March 21–June 11) and 1629 (Jan. 26–March 2) are S.P. Dom. Chas. I. xcvii and cxxxiv (Calendar 1628–9, pp. 31, 466 printed in full in Notestein and Relf Commons' Debates for 1629, pp. 107–72.

392. Notes of the debates in the house of lords, officially taken by Henry Elsing, clerk of the parliaments, A.D. 1621.   Ed. by S. R. Gardiner.   Camd. Soc. 1870.

Edited from MSS. at Crowcombe Court once in possession of Lieutenant-Col. Carew.

393. Notes of the debates in the house of lords officially taken by Henry Elsing, clerk of the parliaments, A.D. 1624 and 1626.   Ed. by S. R. Gardiner. Camd. Soc. 1879.

From Crowcombe Court MSS.

394. Debates in the house of commons in 1625, edited from a MS. in the library of Sir Rainald Knightley, bart.   Ed. by S. R. Gardiner.   Camd. Soc. 1873.

From MS. at Fawsley, Northants.   Notes by Richard Knightley, M.P., an active opponent of the Court.

395. A diary of the parliament of 1626. By W. A. J. Archbold. Eng. Hist. Rev. vol. xvii. Oct. 1902.

Gives extracts from diary in Camb. Univ. Library (MSS. DD. 12, 20–2). Writer possibly Bulstrode Whitelocke. Cf. Lonsdale MSS. (154) for parliamentary diaries 24 April–12 June 1626, 4–26 June 1628, 20 Jan.–25 Feb. 1629.

396. Documents illustrating the impeachment of Buckingham in 1626. Ed. by S. R. Gardiner. Camd. Soc. 1889.

Copies of documents relating to five of the charges brought against Buckingham : from papers in P.R.O. and Harleian MSS. Cf. The earl of Bristol's defence of his negotiations in Spain. Camd. Soc. Misc. vi. 1871.

397. Ephemeris parliamentaria ; or A faithfull register of the transactions in parliament, in the third and fourth years of the reign of King Charles. Ed. by T. Fuller. 1 vol. fol. Lond. 1654. Later eds. 1657 and 1660.

A collection of legal arguments and speeches probably first issued as separates. A version of the True Relation for 1629 is also included. The eds. of 1657 and 1660 have a different title : The sovereigns prerogative and the subjects priviledge.

398. The commons' debates for 1629. Ed. by W. Notestein and F. Relf. 1 vol. 8vo. Univ. of Minnesota : Studies in the Social Sciences, No. 10. Minneapolis. 1921.

Prints the 'True Relation', the notes of Sir Edward Nicholas, and the diary of Sir Richard Grosvenor. An excellent introduction discussing the whole question of sources for history of the debates of the house of commons in the first half of the 17th century.

399. The proceedings and debates of the house of commons in the sessions of parliament 20 Jan.–10 March 1628, also the examination of several members. . . . By Sir T. Crew. Ed. by J. Parkhurst. 1 vol. 8vo. Lond. 1707.

Really one of the copies of the 'True Relation' for the session of 1629. See Notestein and Relf : Commons' debates for 1629, pp. xv–xix, 273–5.

400. The diurnall occurrences of every dayes proceeding in parliament . . . which ended 10 March Anno Dom. 1628. With the arguments of the members of the house then assembled. 1 vol. 4to. Lond. 1641.

One of the numerous versions of the 'True Relation' for the session of 1629. See Notestein and Relf : Commons' debates for 1629, pp. xv–xix, 273–5.

401. The journal of Sir Simonds D'Ewes. Ed. by W. Notestein. 1 vol. 8vo. Yale Historical Publications MSS. and Edited Texts VII. New Haven, Conn. 1923.

D'Ewes' journal of the long parliament from Nov. 3, 1640 to March 20, 1641 derived from Harl. MSS. 162, 164, 165 in the British Museum and collated with several other diaries of the Parliament.

402. A narrative of some passages in, or relating to, the long parliament. By a person of honour. 1 vol. 8vo. Lond. 1670.

Attributed to Francis North, Lord Guilford.

403. A diary of the early days of the long parliament. By W. A. J. Archbold. Eng. Hist. Rev. vol. xvi, Oct. 1901.

Includes extracts from MS. in Camb. Univ. Library (Nk. 6. 38) being notes by Geoffrey Palmer, M.P. for Stamford, as to proceedings in the commons from Nov. 3 to Dec. 18, 1640, and on Jan. 4, 1641.

404. Note book of Sir John Northcote sometime M.P. for Ashburton and afterwards for the county of Devon, containing memoranda of the proceedings in the house of commons during the 1st session of the long parliament. Ed. by A. H. A. Hamilton.   1 vol. 8vo. Lond. 1877.

From MSS. in possession of the Northcote family.   Notes extend from 24 Nov. to 28 Dec. 1640.   There are also some memoranda concerning session 18 May to 21 June 1661.

405. The diurnall occurrences, or dayly proceedings of both houses, in this great and happy parliament, from the third of November 1640, to the third of November 1641.   1 vol. 4to. Lond. 1641.

There is a full account of the nature of this publication in Notestein and Relf : Commons' Debates for 1629, pp. xlii-lv.

406. Speeches and passages of this great and happy parliament from 3. Nov. 1640 to June 1641 . . . according to the most perfect originals.   1 vol. 4to. Lond. 1641.

407. Verney papers : Notes of proceedings in the long parliament temp. Charles I, printed from original pencil memoranda taken in the House by Sir Ralph Verney.   Ed. by J. Bruce.   Camd. Soc. 1845.

Notes extending from Dec. 1640 to 27 June 1642, with a paper (App. I) of uncertain date.

408. Proceedings, principally in the County of Kent in connection with the parliaments called in 1640 and especially with the committee of religion.   Ed. by L. B. Larking.   Camd. Soc. 1862.

From the papers of Sir Edward Dering.   Relates mainly to proceedings in commons respecting Archbishop Laud's administration.

409. The tryal of Thomas, Earl of Strafford, . . . upon an impeachment of high treason by the commons . . . with some special arguments in law relating to a bill of attainder.   By J. Rushworth.   1 vol. fol. Lond. 1680.   Port.

Based mainly on notes taken by Rushworth during the trial, at which he was present every day.

410. Novissima Straffordii.   By Abraham Wright.   Ed. by P. Bliss and B. Bandinel.   1 vol. 4to. Roxburghe Club : Historical Papers.   Lond. 1846.

An account of the proceedings against Strafford with an English translation made by J. Wright.   Cf. A briefe and perfect relation of the answers and replies of Thomas Earle of Stratford.   By S. R.   1 vol. 4to. Lond. 1647.   Of greater value than Wright.

411. Diary of Thomas Burton Esquire, member in the parliaments of Oliver and Richard Cromwell from 1656 to 1659. . . . with an introduction containing an account of the parliament of 1654.   Ed. by J. T. Rutt.   4 vols. 8vo. Lond. 1828.

From Burton's note-books now in British Museum (Add. MSS. 15859-64) and Goddard's Journal (Add. MSS. 5138).

412. The complete works in prose and verse of Andrew Marvell M.P. for the first time fully collected.   Ed. by A. B. Grosart.   4 vols. 4to. s.l. 1872-5.   Ports.

Vol. ii consists mainly of letters to Hull giving accounts of Parliamentary proceedings 1660-78.

413. The proceedings in the house of commons touching the impeachment of Edward, late Earl of Clarendon, Lord High-Chancellour of England, Anno 1667. With the many debates and speeches in the house . . . 1 vol. 8vo. [? Lond.] 1700.

This important collection was apparently made at the time of the impeachment, and had a wide circulation in MS. Utilized by Cobbett, *Parliamentary History*, vol. iv.

414. Debates of the house of commons from the year 1667 to the year 1694, collected by Hon. Anchitel Grey Esq, who was thirty years member for the town of Derby, &c. 10 vols. 8vo. Lond. 1769.

Valuable.

415. A relation of the most material matters handled in parliament : relating to religion, property, and the liberty of the subject . . . 1 vol. 4to. ? Lond. 1673.

Repr. in State Tracts (64), pp. 26–36. Proceedings on various days in Feb., March, Oct., and Nov. 1673, together with a list of pensioners &c. Written by a country party extremist.

416. Votes and addresses of the honourable house of commons assembled in parliament, made this present year 1673, concerning popery and other grievances. 1 vol. 4to. 1673.

Commons' proceedings 29 Mar. and 20 Oct.–4 Nov. 1673.

417. A Journal of the proceedings of the house of commons the last session of parliament beginning Jan. 7. Anno Dom. 1673. And ending Feb. 24, 1673. Containing all the publick transactions of the house of commons. To which are added four of the grand bills prepared to be enacted that session. Printed at Rome by the especial command of his Holinesse, at the request of his Highnesse the Duke of York. 1 vol. 4to. Probably in Holland. 1674.

Full reports of proceedings of a political nature for the 1673/4 session. Texts of bills for improvement of writs of habeas corpus, for a test in religion, for preventing illegal exaction of money from the subject, and for preventing imprisonment in illegal prisons or beyond seas. Reasons for the prorogation—evidently drawn up by a supporter of the country party. Certain details in the typography, which is very beautiful, point to a Dutch origin.

418. Two seasonable discourses concerning this present parliament. 1 vol. 4to. Oxf. 1675.

Report of debate in the house of commons 20 Nov. 1675, giving the arguments for a dissolution.

This may have been published with T.E., *A Letter from a Parliament Man* &c. The two are State Tracts (64) pp. 65–9.

419. A letter from a parliament man to his friend, concerning the proceedings of the house of commons this last sessions, begun the 13th of October, 1675. By T. E. 1 vol. 4to. s.l. 1675.

Gives the composition of the House of Commons. See above, *Two seasonable discourses.*

420. Two speeches. I. The Earl of Shaftsbury's speech in the house of lords, the 20th of October, 1675. II. The D. of Buckingham's speech in the house of lords, the 16th of November, 1675. Together with the protestation, and reasons of several lords for the dissolution of this parliament ;

entered in the lords journal the day the parliament was prorogued, Nov. 22nd, 1675. 1 vol. [? 4to]. Amsterdam [Probably Lond.] 1675.

Repr. in State Tracts (64) pp. 57–64. Important as illustrating the country party's manœuvres.

421. A letter from a person of quality, to his friend in the country. 1 vol. 4to. 1675.

Reports of Lords' debates and proceedings; also statement of country party attitude. Probably written under Shaftesbury's supervision. Repr. in *State Tracts* (64), pp. 41–56—and in Cobbett's Parliamentary History. An answer by Marchamont Nedham appeared in 1676: A pacquet of advices and animadversions, sent from London to the men of Shaftesbury.

422. A narrative of the cause and manner of the imprisonment of the lords : now close prisoners in the Tower of London. By J. E. 1 vol. 4to. Amsterdam [probably Lond.] 1677.

Important reports of Lords' proceedings, 15 Feb. and following days, 1676/7 ; also reports of some speeches.

423. A collection of some memorable and weighty transactions in parliament in the year 1678, and afterwards, in relation to the impeachment of Thomas, Earl of Danby. 1 vol. 4to. Lond. 1695.

424. Historical collections or a brief account of the most remarkable transactions of the two last parliaments. 1 vol. 8vo. Lond. 1681.

425. An exact collection of the debates of the house of commons held at Westminster October 21, 1680 . . . with the debates of the house of commons at Oxford. 1 vol. 8vo. Lond. 1689.

426. A collection of the debates and proceedings in parliament in 1694 and 1695 upon the enquiry into the late briberies and corrupt practices.

427. The history of the last parliament began at Westminster the tenth day of February. . . . 1700 [–1]. 1 vol. 8vo. Lond. 1702.

428. A state[ment] of the proceedings in the house of commons with relation to the impeached lords, and what happened thereupon between the two houses. Anon. 1 vol. fol. Lond. 1701.

Report from journals, printed by order of the house.

429. The bill entituled an act for preventing occasional conformity with the amendments made by the Lords . . . and the reports of the several conferences . . . and the proceedings thereupon. 1 vol. fol. Lond. 1702.

Pr. by order of the house of commons.

430. An account of the proceedings of the house of peers upon the observations of the commissioners for taking, examining, and stating the publick accounts . . . together with the papers referred to in these proceedings. 1 vol. fol. Lond. 1702.

431. The proceedings of the house of lords concerning the Scottish conspiracy and the papers laid before that house by her majesties command relating thereunto. 1 vol. fol. Lond. 1704.

432. The report of the lords committees appointed to take into consideration the report of the commissioners . . . for . . . examining . . . the publick accompts . . . so far as relates to the accompts of . . . Edward Earl of Orford, late treasurer of the navy.   1 vol. fol. Lond. 1704.

433. Report of the commissioners for taking examining and stating the public accounts of the kingdom with the examinations and depositions relating thereunto.   1 vol. fol. Lond. 1712.

(v) STATUTES

General and individual collections.

434. The statutes at large from Magna Carta to 1806.   46 vols.   Ed. by D. Pickering.   8vo. Camb. 1762–1807.

Vol. i covers the period.   For the numerous other eds. see Lowndes, Bibliographer's Manual, 2499–2500.

435. Statutes of the realm.   Published by command of King George III. Ed. by Sir T. E. Tomlins and others.   11 vols. fol. s.l. [Lond.] 1810–24.

Vols. 10 and 11 are chronological and alphabetical indexes.

436. Anno regni Iacobi regis Angliae . . . 21 at the parliament begun . . . 19 . . . February in the 21 yeere of the reigne . . . and . . . continued vntill the 29 day of May following.   1 vol. fol. Lond. 1624.

Text of statutes passed.   An example of many similar publications.

437. The lawes resolutions of womens rights ; or the lawes provision for women.   A methodicall collection of such statutes . . . as doe properly concern women.   1 vol. 8vo. Lond. 1632.

438. An exact collection of the remonstrances, declarations . . . and other remarkable passages between the kings most excellent Majesty and his high court of parliament. . . . Dec. 1641 . . . March the 21 1643.   1 vol. 4to. Lond. 1643.

Pr. for E. Husband.

439. A collection of all the publicke orders, ordinances and declarations of both houses of parliament from 9 March 1642 untill December 1646, together with severall of his Majestie's proclamations &c. . . . 1 vol. fol. Lond. 1646.

Pr. for Edward Husband, printer to the house of commons, under order of the House to him.

440. A collection of the several acts of parliament from the 16 of January 1649 to the 8 of April 1653.   2 vols. fol. Lond. 1649–53.

Pr. for Edward Husband and really a collection of separate original acts bound up together with a title-page.

441. A collection of several acts of parliament published in the years 1648–1651 . . . whereunto are added some ordinances of parliament.   Ed. by H. Scobell.   1 vol. fol. Lond. 1651.

442. A collection of all the proclamations, declarations . . . passed by his Highness the Lord Protector and his Council and by their special command published, beginning December 16, 1653, and ending September 2, 1654. 1 vol. fol. Lond. 1654.

Pr. by H. Hills.

443. An exact abridgment of publick acts and ordinances of parliament made from the year 1640 to the year 1656. As also divers ordinances and publick orders made by his Highness the Lord Protector. Ed. by W. Hughes. 1 vol. 4to. Lond. 1657.

444. A collection of acts and ordinances . . . made in the parliament . . . 1640 to 1656. Ed. by H. Scobell. 2 vols. fol. Lond. 1658.

Not a complete collection ; also some of acts and ordinances are not printed in full. There is a good article based on Scobell in the Quarterly Review (vol. 145, pp. 449–74, Apr. 1878) under the title ' The Legislation of the Commonwealth '.

445. Acts and ordinances of the Interregnum 1642–1660. Ed. by C. H. Firth and R. S. Rait. 3 vols. 8vo. Lond. 1911.

Vol. iii contains an Introduction by Professor Firth giving account of sources, chronological table, and index.

¶ 4. LEGAL HISTORY

(*a*) Bibliographies and Sources.
(*b*) Later Works.

The nature of legal sources is clearly explained by Holdsworth (456) and Winfield (457), and there are a number of comprehensive lists. Holdsworth (588) provides a detailed history of law, and Jenks (591) a valuable sketch. For the semi-political activities of lawyers the general histories will be found useful. Thus Gardiner (219) has much to say about Coke, Macaulay (204) of Jeffreys.

(*a*) BIBLIOGRAPHIES AND SOURCES

446. A catalogue of the common and statute law-books of this realm . . . with an account of the best editions. By T. Bassett. 1 vol. 12mo. Lond. 1670. Later ed. 1682.

447. Bibliotheca legum Angliae Part i, or a catalogue of the common and statute law books. . . . Part ii containing a general account of the laws and law-writers of England . . . to . . . Edw. III . . . together with . . . the principal works upon the law and constitution. By J. Worrall and E. Brooke. 2 vols. 12mo. Lond. 1788.

Vol. i, pp. 234–54 has a good list of reports.

448. A short view of legal bibliography. By R. W. Bridgman. 1 vol. 8vo. Lond. 1807.

449. A general catalogue of law books. By J. and H. Butterworth. 1 vol. 8vo. Lond. 1815. 5th ed. 1 vol. 12mo. Lond. 1836.

Title of 1850 ed. is : Butterworth's general catalogue of law books including all the reports.

450. Bibliotheca legum or complete catalogue of the common and statute law-books of the United Kingdom.   By J. Clarke and T. H. Horne.   1 vol. 8vo. Lond. 1819.

451. The reporters arranged and characterized with incidental remarks. By J. W. Wallace.   1 vol. 8vo. Philadelphia. 1845.   4th ed. 1 vol. 8vo. Boston (Mass.) 1882. Ed. by F. F. Heard.

452. Legal bibliography : or a thesaurus of American, English, Irish, and Scotch law books ... interspersed with critical observations upon their various editions and authority.   By J. G. Marvin.   1 vol. 8vo. Philadelphia. 1847.

453. Catalogue of the printed books in the library of ... Lincoln's Inn.   Ed. by W. H. Spilsbury.   1 vol. 8vo. Lond. 1859.

Cf. No. 18.

454. Bibliotheca legum.   A catalogue of law books, including all the reports in the various courts of England, Ireland and Scotland : to 1865.   By H. G. Stevens and R. W. Haynes.   1 vol. 8vo. Lond. 1865.   Later ed. 1 vol. 12mo. Lond. 1906.

Ed. of 1906 has supplement to 1905.

455. Legal literature.   By F. J. C. Hearnshaw.   Camb. Hist. of Eng. Lit. viii. 1912.

456. Sources and literature of English law.   By W. S. Holdsworth.   1 vol. 8vo. Lond. 1925.

457. The chief sources of English legal history.   By P. H. Winfield.   1 vol. 8vo. Camb. (Mass.) 1925.

458. Les reports de Edward Coke.   By Sir E. Coke.   13 vols. fol. Lond. 1600-15, 1656, 1659.

The first four volumes are mainly concerned with the reign of Elizabeth and the fifth with the ecclesiastical cases of that reign. In the later volumes Jacobean cases gradually predominate over Elizabethan.   The 12th and 13th volumes were posthumously published and in English.   The former contains much about the ecclesiastical controversies in the law courts.   For later eds. see Lowndes, pp. 489-90.   In 1606 Thomas Ashe printed ' Un perfect table a touts les severall livers del reportes de Sir Edw. Coke : Ouesque un catalogue de touts les cases in larguments de les principall cases la remembre, et in le temps le raigne et adjudges, mes iammes deuant imprimee.' [1 vol. 8vo. Lond.], and in 1652 ' A generall table to all the severall bookes of the reports of the late Sir Edward Coke ' [1 vol. 8vo. Lond.].

459. A parallele or conference of the civil law, the canon law, and the common law of this realm. Wherein the agreement and disagreement of these three lawes are opened and discussed. Digested in sundry dialogues. At the end is a table of the matters handled in every dialogue.   By W. Fulbecke.   1 vol. 4to. Lond. 1601.   Later ed. 1618.

The second part of the parallele appeared in 1602 (vol. i. 4to. Lond.).

460. The order of keeping a court leet and a court baron ... By T. Wight. 1 vol. 8vo. Lond. 1603.   Later ed. 1625.

461. Institutiones juris Anglicani ad methodum et seriem institutionum imperialium compositae et digestae. By J. Cowell. 1 vol. 8vo. Camb. 1605. [Transl. into English by W. G. Lond. 1651.]

462. The Interpreter : or book containing the signification of words, wherein is set foorth the true meaning of all, or the most part of such words and termes, as are mentioned in the law writers or statutes of this kingdome, requiring any exposition or interpretation. By J. Cowell. 1 vol. 4to. Camb. 1607. Later ed. 1 vol. fol. Lond. 1701 [and many other editions].

Notable for enhancement of royal prerogative in certain definitions. Ed. of 1701 ' continued ' by T. Manley to the year 1684, and ' further augmented and improved ' by Kennet ; definitions in Cowell frequently abbreviated or modified.

463. A view of the civile and ecclesiasticall law : And wherein the practice of them is streitned and may be relieved within this land. By Sir T. Ridley. 1 vol. 4to. Lond. 1607. Later ed. 1 vol. 4to. Oxf. 1634.

464. Jani Anglorum facies altera. By J. Selden. 1 vol. 8vo. Lond. 1610, and 1681.

465. De pace regis et regni, viz. a Treatise declaring which be the great and generall offences of the realme, and the chiefe impediments of the peace of the King and the Kingdome, as treasons, homicides, and felonies [etc.]. By F. Pulton. 1 vol. fol. Lond. 1610.

466. Nomotechnia, c'est a scavoir un description del common leys d'Angleterre solonque les rules del art. Parallelees ove les Prerogatives le Roy. Ovesque auxy le substance et effect de les Estatutes per le quels le Common Ley est abridge, enlarge, ou ascunment alter, del commencement de Magna Charta fait 9 H.3 tanque a cest jour. By Sir H. Finch. 1 vol. fol. Lond. 1613.

Finch also wrote a work entitled ' Law, or discourse Thereof, in foure bookes '. Written in French and done into English by the Author [1 vol. 8vo. Lond. 1627, 2nd ed. 1636]. It resembles Nomotechnia but is a larger work.

467. A booke of entries : Containing perfect and approved presidents of coants, declarations, informations, pleints . . . By Sir E. Coke. 1 vol. fol. Lond. 1614.

Contains a number of documents about prohibitions and other ecclesiastical causes.

468. De laudibus legum Angliae written by Sir J. Fortescue. Hereto are added the two Sums of Sir R. de Hengham. [Notes by Selden both on Fortescue and Hengham are added.] By J. Selden. 1 vol. 8vo. Lond. 1616. Later ed. 1672.

469. A treatise conteining divers benefits and priviledges, and the power and authoritie granted to the patentee, who hath his Maiesties licence or grant of charter warren under the Great Seale of England. By Sir H. Yelverton. 1 vol. 4to. None. 1617.

470. Fasciculum florum, or a handfull of flowers, gathered out of the severall Bookes of Sir Edw. Coke. By T. Asche. 1 vol. 8vo. Lond. 1618.

471. The historie of tithes. That is, the practice of payment of them. The positive laws made for them. The opinions touching the right of them. A review of it is also annext. By J. Selden. 1 vol. 4to. [Lond.] 1618.

For later books on the controversy on this subject see the bibliography in R. G. Usher's Reconstruction of the Church of England. Richard Tillesley published certain 'Animadversions upon Mr. Selden's History of Tithes' in 1619 (1 vol. 4to.). Lond.

472. A treatise . . . concerning the office and authoritie of coroners and sherifes . . . court leet, court baron, hundred court etc. By J. Wilkinson. 1 vol. 12mo. Lond. 1618. Later eds. 1628 and 1638.

473. The countrey justice, containing the practice of the justices of the peace out of their sessions. Newly corrected and enlarged. By M. Dalton. 1 vol. fol. Lond. 1622, and 1705.

474. Officium vicecomitum. The office and authoritie of the sherifs. Gathered out of the statutes, and bookes of the common lawes of this kingdome. By M. Dalton. 1 vol. fol. Lond. 1623.

475. Archaeologus. In modum glossarii ad rem antiquam posteriorem continentis Latino-barbara, percgrina, obsoleta, quae, in ecclesiasticis profanisque scriptoribus, variarum item gentium legibus antiquis, chartis et formulis occurrunt. By Sir H. Spelman. 2 vols. fol. Lond. 1626-64.

Dugdale ed. vol. 2.

476. The attornies almanacke. Provided and desired for the use of all such as shall have occasion to remove any person, cause or record, from an inferiour court to any the higher courts at Westminster. By T. Powell. 1 vol. 4to. 1627.

Powell also wrote ' The attorneys academy : or the manner and forme of proceeding practically, upon any suite, in any court of record whatsoever within this Kingdome ' (1 vol. 4to. Lond. 1630).

477. The first-fourth part of the Institutes of the lawes of England. Or a Commentarie upon Littleton. By E. Coke. 4 vols. fol. Lond. 1628-44.

Part 4 : concerning the jurisdiction of Courts : deals with composition, jurisdiction, and procedure of Parliament (at some length), Council, Star Chamber, High Commission, Courts of Equity and Common Law, Ecclesiastical Courts of Special Jurisdiction, Local Courts. William Prynne published in 1669 (1 vol. fol. Lond.) his ' Brief animadversions on . . . The Fourth part of the Institutes '.

478. The lawyers light : or a due direction for the study of the law. To which is annexed another treatise, called The use of the law. By Sir J. Doderidge. 1 vol. 4to. Lond. 1629.

479. Les termes de la ley : or certaine difficult and obscure words and termes of the common lawes of this realme expounded. Now newly imprinted, and much inlarged and augmented. By J. Rastell. 1 vol. 8vo. Lond. 1629. Later eds. 1636 and 1641.

480. Descriptio juris et judicii feudalis, secundum consuetudines Mediolani et Normanniae. Pro introductione ad studium jurisprudentiae Anglicanae. By R. Zouche. 1 vol. 8vo. Oxf. 1634.

481. Elementa jurisprudentiae definitionibus, regulis et sententiis selectiori-
bus juris civilis illustrata. Quibus accessit descriptio juris et judicii temporalis
secundum consuetudines feudales et Normannicas, Necnon descriptio juris
et judicii ecclesiastici secundum Canones et constitutiones Anglicanas. By
R. Zouche. 1 vol. 4to. Oxf. 1636.

482. A briefe declaration for what manner of speciall nusance concerning
private dwelling houses, a man may have his remedy by assise, or other
action. Unfolded in the arguments and opinions of four famous sages of
the common law; together with the power and extent of customes in cities,
towns and corporations concerning the same. Whereunto is added the
justices of assise their opinion concerning statute law for parishes : and the
power of justices of the peace, churchwardens and constables. 1 vol. 4to.
Lond. 1639.

483. Concilia, decreta, leges, constitutiones, in re ecclesiarum orbis Britan-
nici. Ab initio Christianae ibidem Religionis ad nostram usque aetatem. By
Sir H. Spelman. 2 vols. fol. Lond. 1639–64.

Vol. 2, ed. Dugdale 1664.

484. The complete copy-holder. By Sir E. Coke. 1 vol. 4to. London.
1641. Later eds. 1 vol. 4to. Lond. 1650. 1 vol. 8vo. Lond. 1668. 1 vol. 8vo.
Lond. 1673.

The 1650 ed. has added to it ' The relation between the lord of a mannor and
the copy holder his tenant ' by Charles Calthrop. The 1668 and 1673 eds. have an
anonymous ' Supplement by way of additions to and amplifications of the foregoing
treatise '.

485. The arguments of Sir Richard Hutton . . . and Sir George Croke . . .
together with the certificate of Sir John Denham . . . upon a scire facias
brought by the King's Majesty in the court of exchequer against John
Hampden Esquire. As also the several votes of the commons and peeres in
parliament . . . touching ship-money. 1 vol. 4to. Lond. 1641.

486. A treatise of the principall grounds and maxims of the lawes of this
kingdome. By W. N[oy]. 1 vol. 4to. Lond. 1641.

487. The court-keepers guide, or a plain and familiar treatise needfull
and usefull for the helpe of many that are imployed in the keeping of lawdayes.
By W. Sheppard. 1 vol. 12mo. Lond. 1641. Later eds. 1656 and several
others to 1791.

One of the most popular and useful manuals for stewards of manors during the 17th
and 18th centuries. The edition of 1791 was the eighth or ninth.

488. The touchstone of common assurances : or a plain and familiar
treatise, opening the learning of the common assurances or conveyances of
the kingdom. By W. Sheppard. 1 vol. 4to. Lond. 1641. Later eds. 1 vol.
fol. Lond. 1784. 2 vols. 8vo. Lond. 1820. Ed. by R. Preston.

Sheppard produced two other works dealing with common assurances : ' precedent of
precedents, or one general precedent for common assurances ' (1 vol. 4to. Lond. 1655,
2nd ed. 8vo. Lond. 1825 ed. by T. W. Williams), and ' The law of common assurances, touching deeds in general : viz. feoffments, gifts, grants, leases ' (1 vol. fol.
Lond. 1669).

489. The reading in Lincolnes-Inne, Feb. 28, 1641, upon the statute of 25 E. 3. Cap. 2, being the statute of treasons. By Sir R. Holborne. 1 vol. 4to. Oxf. 1642.

490. A treatise of the antiquity etc. of the ancient courts of leet . . . with a large explication of the old oath of allegiance. . . . By R. Powell. 1 vol. 12mo. Lond. 1642. Later ed. 1688.

491. A short treatise of the lawes of England : with the jurisdiction of the high court of parliament with the liberties and freedomes of the subjects. By W. Mantell. 1 vol. 4to. Lond. 1644.
Repr. Harleian Misc. iv. ed. 1810.

492. Justice revived being the whole office of a country justice of the peace. By E. Wingate. 1 vol. 12mo. Lond. 1661.

493. Topicks in the laws of England. Containing media, apt for argument, and resolution of law cases : also an exposition of severall words, not touched by former glossaries. By J. C[layton]. 1 vol. 8vo. Lond. 1646.

494. The reading of the famous and learned Robert Callis upon the statute of sewers, 23 Henry VIII. c. 5. as it was delivered by him at Gray's Inn, in August 1622. 1 vol. 4to. Lond. 1647. 5th ed. 1 vol. 8vo. Lond. 1824. Ed. by W. J. Broderip.

495. Lex terrae. By D. Jenkins. 1 vol. 4to. [Lond.] [1647].
Deals largely with constitutional law.

496. The larger treatise concerning tithes, long since written and promised by Sir H. Spelman. Together with some other tracts of the same authour, and a fragment of Sir Francis Bigot, all touching the same subject. Ed. by J. Stephens. 1 vol. 4to. Lond. 1647.

497. Sergeant Thorpe . . . his charge to the grand-jury at Yorke Assizes the twentieth of March 1648, clearly epitomizing the statutes belonging to this nation, which concerns the severall estates and conditions of men. By F. Thorpe. 1 vol. 4to. Lond. 1649.

498. The transactions [and proceedings] of the high court of chancery, both by practice and president. By W. Tothill. 1 vol. 8vo. Lond. 1649. Later ed. 1671.
In the 1671 edition the Proceedings are at the beginning of the volume instead of the end.

499. The corruption and deficiency of the laws of England, soberly discovered : Or, Liberty working up to its just height. By J. Warr. 1 vol. 4to. Lond. 1649.
Printed also in Harleian Miscellany vol. iii. 1809 ed. Cf. Certaine proposals in order to a new modelling of the lawes. By H. Robinson. 1 vol. 4to. Lond. 1653.

500. Juris et judicii fecialis, sive juris inter gentes, et quaestionum de eodem explicatio. Qua quae ad pacem et bellum inter diversos principes, aut populos spectant, ex praecipuis historico-jure-peritis, exhibentur. By R.

Zouche. 1 vol. 4to. Oxf. 1650. Later eds. 1 vol. Leyden. 1651. 1 vol. The Hague. 1659. 1 vol. Mainz. 1661. 1 vol. Frankfort. 1666.

Republ. with translation by J. L. Brierly (1 vol. 4to. Washington. 1911) ed. by T. E. Holland.

501. The elements of law natural and politic. By T. Hobbes. Later ed. 1 vol. 8vo. Lond. 1889. Ed. by F. Tönnies.

This originally appeared in two parts : ' Humane nature ; or the fundamental elements of Policie ' (1 vol. 12mo. Lond. 1650, 2nd ed. in 1651) and ' De corpore politico. Or elements of law, moral, and politick '. (1 vol. 12mo. Lond. 1650). Tönnies has collated the printed with the MS. versions of both these works.

502. The order of keeping a court leet and a court baron. . . . By W. Lee and D. Pakeman. 1 vol. 4to. Lond. 1650.

503. Certaine observations concerning the office of lord chancellor. By Thomas Egerton, Lord Ellesmere. 1 vol. 8vo. Lond. 1651.

504. The faithfull councellor : or the marrow of the law in English. In two parts. By W. Sheppard. 1 vol. 4to. Lond. 1651, and 1653.

Part I deals with common law actions, part II with the jurisdiction and procedure of the Chancery.

505. Whole office of the country justice of the peace. By W. Sheppard, Serjeant at Law. 1 vol. 16mo. Lond. 1652.

Deals with the duties of justices of the peace and describes what evils they will encounter in their office and suggests remedies.

506. Cases and questions resolved in the civil-law. By R. Zouche. 1 vol. 8vo. Oxf. 1652.

507. Solutio quaestionis veteris et novae. By R. Zouche. 1 vol. 4to. Oxf. 1657. Later eds. 1 vol. 4to. Cologne. 1662. 1 vol. 4to. Berlin. 1669. 1 vol. 4to. Jena and Lond. 1717.

Discusses question of liability of criminal sovereigns and ambassadors to local jurisdiction.

508. New survey of the justice of the peace his office. By W. Sheppard. 1 vol. 12mo. Lond. 1659.

A criticism written to amend existing conditions. Cf. the same author's : A rure guide for his majesties justice of peace. 1 vol. 8vo. Lond. 1663.

509. De usu et authoritate juris civilis Romanorum, in dominiis principum christianorum libri duo. By A. Duck. 1 vol. 8vo. Lond. 1653.

510. The parsons guide : or the law of tithes. By W. S[heppard]. 1 vol. 4to. Lond. 1654.

511. The body of the common law of England : as it stood in force before it was altered by statute, or acts of parliament, or state. Together with an exact collection of such statutes as have altered or concern the same. Whereunto is also annexed certain tables concerning a summary of the whole law, for the help of such students as affect method. By E. Wingate. 2nd ed. 1 vol. 12mo. Lond. 1655.

In 1658 he produced his ' Maximes of reason : or the reason of the common law of England ' (Lond. fol. 1 vol.).

512. Survey of the county judicatures commonly called the county court, hundred court and court baron. By W. Sheppard. 1 vol. 12mo. Lond. 1656.

513. The grounds of the lawes of England ; extracted from the fountaines of all other learning : and digested methodically into cases for the use and benefit of all practicers, and students. With a commixtion of divers scattered grounds concerning the reasonable construction of the law. By M. Hawke. 1 vol. 8vo. Lond. 1657.

514. Pacis consultum ; a directory to the publick peace, briefly describing the antiquity, extent etc. of several countrey corporation courts, especially the court leet. Also some difficult questions of law proposed unto and resolved by Judge Jenkyns. By D. Jenkins. 1 vol. 8vo. Lond. 1657.

515. The law of laws : or the excellency of the civil law, above all other humane laws whatsoever. Shewing of how great use and necessity the civil law is to this nation. By R. Wiseman. 1 vol. 4to. Lond. 1657.

516. Maximes of reason : or the reason of the common law of England. By E. Wingate. 1 vol. fol. Lond. 1658.

517. Of corporations, fraternities, and guilds. Or, a discourse wherin the learning of the law touching bodies-politique is unfolded. With forms and presidents, of charters of corporation. By W. Sheppard. 1 vol. 8vo. Lond. 1659.

518. The grand abridgment of the law continued. Or, a collection of the principal cases and points of common law of England, from the first of Elizabeth to this present time. By W. Hughes. 1 vol. 4to. Lond. 1660.

519. The antiquity, legality, reason, duty and necessity of prae-emption and pourveyance for the king. By F. Philipps. 1 vol. 4to. Lond. 1663.

Cf. Dict. Nat. Biog. for his other numerous legal treatises.

520. An abridgment of the three vols. of Reports of Sir George Croke of such select cases as were adjudged in the courts of king's bench and common bench during the reigns of Queen Elizabeth, King James and King Charles the First. By W. Hughes. 1 vol. 8vo. Lond. 1665.

521. Origines juridiciales, or historical memorials of the English laws, courts of justice, forms of tryall, punishment in cases criminal, law writers, law books, grants and settlements of estates, degree of serjeant, inns of court and chancery. Also a chronology of the lord chancellors, justices [etc.]. By W. Dugdale. 1 vol. fol. Lond. 1666.

522. The authority, jurisdiction and method of keeping county courts . . . courts leet, courts baron. . . . By W. Greenwood. 1 vol. 8vo. Lond. 1668. Later ed. 1730.

The edition of 1730 (the ninth) has considerable additions.

523. Un abridgment des plusieurs cases et resolutions del common ley. By H. Rolle. 1 vol. fol. Lond. 1668,

524. A law dictionary and glossary, interpreting such difficult and obscure words and terms as are found either in our common or statute, ancient or modern, laws. By T. Blount. 1 vol. fol. Lond. 1670. Third ed. 1717.

525. A brief discourse touching the office of lord chancellor of England. By J. Selden. Ed. by W. Dugdale. 1 vol. fol. Lond. 1672. Later ed. 1 vol. 8vo. Lond. 1677.

526. Parsons law : or a view of advowsons. By W. Hughes. 3rd ed. 1 vol. 8vo. Lond. 1673.

527. England's independency upon the papal power historically and judicially stated, by Sir John Davis and by Sir Edw. Coke, in two Reports selected from their greater volumes. With a preface by Sir J. Pettus. 1 vol. 4to. Lond. 1674.

528. The orphans legacy : or a testamentary abridgement. In three parts. I. Of last wills and testaments. II. Of executors and administrators. III. Of legacies and devises. Wherein the most material points of law, relating to that subject are succinctly treated, as well according to the common and temporal, as ecclesiastical and civil laws of this realm. Illustrated with great variety of select cases in the law of both professions. By J. Godolphin. 1 vol. 4to. Lond. 1674. Later eds. 1677 and 1685.

529. Actions upon the case for deeds, viz. contracts, assumpsits, deceipts, nusances, trover and conversion etc. collect out of the many great volumes of law already extant. By W. Sheppard. 2nd ed. 1 vol. 8vo. Lond. 1674.

530. Les reports de Henry Rolle, de divers cases en le court del' banke le roy, en le temps del' Reign de roy Jaques colligees par luy mesme et imprimées par l'original. By H. Rolle. 1 vol. fol. Lond. 1675.

531. A grand abridgment of the common and statute law of England. By W. Sheppard. 3 vols. 4to. Lond. 1675.

532. The parson's counsellor, with the law of tithes and tithing. In two books. By Sir S. Degge. 1 vol. 8vo. Lond. 1676. Later eds. 1677, 1685, 1695, and 1820.

533. The office and duty of executors ; or a treatise of wills and executors. To which is added an appendix by J. M[anley]. By T. Wentworth. 1 vol. 8vo. Lond. 1676. Later eds. 1763, 1774, 1829.

534. A compendious and accurate treatise of recoveries upon writs of entry in the post, and fines upon writs of covenant. By W. Brown. 1 vol. 8vo. Lond. 1678.

535. The entring clerk's vade mecum. Being an exact collection of precedents for declarations and pleadings in most actions. By W. Brown. 1 vol. 8vo. Lond. 1678.

536. Repertorium canonicum : or an abridgment of the ecclesiastical laws of this realm, consistent with the temporal. . . . By J. Godolphin. 1 vol. 4to. Lond. 1678.
A good summary of the existing practice of ecclesiastical law.

537. The common law epitomiz'd : with directions how to prosecute and defend personal actions.   To which is annexed the nature of a writ of error. By W. Glisson and A. Gulston.   2nd edition revised and enlarged.   1 vol. 8vo. Lond. 1679.

538. Marriage by the morall law of God vindicated against all ceremoniall laws of popes and bishops destructive to filiation aliment and succession, and the government of familyes and kingdomes.   By W. Lawrence.   1 vol. 4to. [Lond.] 1680.

539. The excellency and preheminence of the law of England, above all other humane lawes in the world asserted in a learned reading upon the statute of 35 H. 8. cap. 6 concerning trials by jury, and tales de circumstantibus : II. Mr. Risdens Reading upon the statute of 21 H. 8. chap. 19 of Avowries.   III. Judge Hale's Opinion in some select cases.   IV. Certain cases which have been formerly mooted by the Society of Gray's Inn.   By T. Williams.   1 vol. 8vo. Lond. 1680.

540. A tryal of witches, at the assizes held at Bury St. Edmonds 10 March, 1664 before Sir M. Hale.   By Sir M. Hale.   1 vol. 8vo. Lond. 1682.

541. Quaestionum juris civilis centuria in decem classes distributa.   By R. Zouche.   3rd ed. 1 vol. 12mo. Lond. 1682.
1st ed. 1 vol. 12mo. Oxf. 1660.

542. A short treatise touching sheriffs' accompts.   To which is added, A tryal of witches, at the assizes at Bury St. Edmonds, 10 March 1664, before Sir M. Hale.   By Sir M. Hale.   1 vol. 8vo. Lond. 1683.

543. An assistance to justices of peace, for the easier performance of their duty.   By J. Keble.   1 vol. fol. Lond. 1683.

544. The Duke of Norfolk's case : or the doctrine of perpetuities fully set forth and explained.   1 vol. fol. [Lond.] 1688.

545. A compendium of the several branches of practice in the court of exchequer at Westminster.   By W. Brown.   1 vol. 8vo. Lond. 1688.

546. Conveyances : being select precedents of deeds and instruments concerning the most considerable estates in England.   2nd ed. carefully corrected.   By Sir O. Bridgman.   2nd ed. 1 vol. fol. Lond. 1689.   5th ed. 1 vol. fol. Lond. 1725.

547. An enquiry into the power of dispensing with penal statutes.   Together with some animadversions upon a book by Sir Edw. Herbert entituled, A short account of the authorities in law upon which judgment was given in Sir Edw. Hale's case.   By Sir R. Atkyns.   1 vol. fol. Lond. 1689.

548. A discourse concerning the ecclesiastical jurisdiction in the realm of England : occasioned by the late commission in ecclesiastical causes.   By Sir R. Atkyns.   1 vol. fol. Lond. 1689.

549. Remarks upon the tryals of Edw. Fitzharris, Stephen Colledge, Count Coningsmark.   The Lord Russel [etc.] as also on the Earl of Shaftes-

burys grand jury, Wilmore's homine replegiando and the award of execution against Sir Tho. Armstrong. By J. Hawles. 1 vol. fol. Lond. 1689.

550. A true narrative of the proceedings against the lord bishop of London, in the council chamber at Whitehall, by the lords commissioners. . . . 1 vol. fol. Lond. 1689.

Simple report of the proceedings against Compton without comment.

551. A display of tyranny or remarks upon the illegal and arbitrary proceedings in the courts of Westminster and Guild-hall London from . . . 1678 to . . . 1688. In which time the rule was, quod principi placuit lex esto. 2 vols. 12mo. Lond. 1689–90.

552. Regula placitandi : a collection of special rules for pleading in actions real, personal and mixt. Also directions for laying of actions, and etc. 1 vol. 8vo. Lond. 1691.

553. Praxis almae curiae cancellariae : A collection of precedents by bill and answer, plea and demurrer, in causes of the greatest moment which have been commenced in the high court of chancery for more than thirty years last past. With appeals to the house of peers. Also, a compleat collection of all the writs and process concerning the same. By W. Brown. 1 vol. 8vo. Lond. 1694.

The volume contains a preliminary discourse upon the practice of the chancery in equity cases.

554. The clerks tutor in chancery. Giving true directions by authentick precedents, how to draw affidavits, petitions, interlocutory-orders, reports before masters, bills, answers, pleas and demurrers ; with such process, proceedings and other instruments relating thereunto as are now in use. By W. Brown. 2nd ed. 1 vol. 8vo. Lond. 1694.

The introduction contains notes and observations upon proceedings in chancery and abstracts of recent cases and orders.

555. Lex custumaria, or a treatise of copy-hold estates. . . . S. Carter. 1 vol. 8vo. Lond. 1696. Later eds. 1701 and 1796.

556. Reliquiae Spelmannianae. The posthumous works of Sir H. Spelman relating to the laws and antiquities of England. With the life of the author. 1 vol. fol. Oxf. 1698.

557. The practice of courts leet and courts baron . . . By Sir W. Scroggs. 1 vol. 8vo. Lond. 1702. 4th ed. 1728.

The edition of 1728 has many additions.

558. The Lord Chancellor Egerton's Observations on the Lord Coke's reports : particularly in the debate of causes relating to the rights of the church ; the power of the king's prerogative ; the jurisdiction of courts ; or the interest of the subject. Ed. by G. Paul. 1 vol. fol. Lond. [1710].

Preface arguing for Egerton's authorship, which, however, is doubtful.

559. The history and analysis of the law. Written by a learned hand [Sir M. Hale]. 1 vol. 8vo. Lond. 1713. 3rd ed. 1 vol. 8vo. Lond. 1733. 6th ed. 2 vols. 8vo. Lond. 1820.

The history and analysis were also publ. separately.

560. The compleat court keeper, or land steward's assistant. By G. Jacob. 1 vol. 8vo. Lond. 1713. Later eds. 1724, 1764, and 1819.

The last (eighth) edition, revised by ' a barrister ', has many additions.

561. Opera omnia. By J. Selden. Ed. by D. Wilkins. 3 vols. fol. Lond. 1726.

562. Historia placitorum coronae. The history of the pleas of the crown. Now first published from his lordship's original MS., and the several references to the records examined by the originals. With large notes. By S. Emlyn. By Sir M. Hale. 2 vols. fol. Lond. 1736. Later ed. 2 vols. 8vo. Lond. 1800. Ed. by T. Dogherty.

Hale's Pleas of the Crown [1 vol. 8vo. Lond. 1678] with many reprs. is a much slighter work.

563. Law Tracts. By F. Bacon. 1 vol. 8vo. Lond. 1737.

Contains : A proposition for compiling and amending of our laws. An offer of a digest of the laws. The elements of the common laws of England. The use of the law for preservation of our persons, goods and good names. Case of treason, felony, præmunire, prerogative of the king, of the office of a constable. Arguments in law in certain great and difficult cases. Grievances in chancery. Reading on the statute of uses. All Bacon's professional works of permanent value are repr. in vol. vii. of Bacon's Works ed. by D. D. Heath (816).

564. Law tracts. By Sir E. Coke. Ed. by W. Hawkins. 1 vol. 8vo. Lond. 1764.

Repr. The compleat copyholder ; Reading on 27 Edw. the first called the statuta de finibus levatis ; A treatise of bail and main prize. There is an elaborate bibliography in Coke's life in the Dict. Nat. Biog.

565. Cobbett's complete collection of state trials and proceedings for high treason and other crimes and misdemeanors from the earliest period to the present time. 34 vols. 8vo. Lond. 1809–28.

Vol. ii begins in 1603. Mainly a repr. of pamphlets and other material already in print.

566. A series of precedents and proceedings in criminal causes . . . from . . . 1475 to 1640 extracted from act books of ecclesiastical courts in the diocese of London. By W. H. Hale. 1 vol. 8vo. Lond. 1847.

With introductory essay on English ecclesiastical law, and jurisdiction of ecclesiastical courts.

567. The Jacobite trials at Manchester in 1694. Ed. by W. Beamont. Chetham Soc. 1853.

The narrative of an anonymous spectator.

568. Liber famelicus of Sir James Whitelocke, a judge of the court of king's bench in the reigns of James I and Charles I. Ed. by J. Bruce. Camd. Soc. 1858.

Has interesting notices of judges and legal matters temp. James I.

569. A brief memoir of Mr. Justice Rokeby comprising his religious journal and correspondence. Ed. by J. Raine. Surtees Miscellanea, 1861.

The letters begin in 1665, the journal in 1688.

570. I. The narrative of Richard Abbott, a servant of Caryll Lord Moly-neux (1689–91); II. An account of the tryalls at Manchester October 1694. Ed. by A. Goss. 1864.

Both illustrate the so-called ' Lancashire Plot '.

571. Notes of the judgment delivered by Sir George Croke in the case of ship-money. From a MS. in the possession of the Earl of Verulam. Ed. by S. R. Gardiner. Camd. Soc. Misc. vii. 1875.

572. The records of the honourable society of Lincoln's Inn. The Black Books. II. 1568–1660. III. 1660–1775. Ed. by J. D. Walker and W. P. Baildon. 2 vols. (4 in all). Lond. 1898–9.

The minute book of the ruling body.

573. Middle Temple records. Ed. by C. H. Hopwood. 4 vols. 8vo. Lond. 1901–5.

Minutes of Parliament of Middle Temple 1501–1703. Cf. The history of the Temple, London . . . to the close of the Stuart period. By J. B. Williamson. 1 vol. 8vo. Lond. 1924. Illus. Valuable.

574. The pension book of Gray's Inn 1569–1669 ; 1669–1800. Ed. by R. J. Fletcher. 2 vols. 4to. Lond. 1901–10.

' The earliest extant minute book of the ruling body.'

(b) LATER WORKS

575. Memoirs of the life of Judge Jeffreys. By H. W. Woolrych. 1 vol. 8vo. Lond. 1827.

Cf. the same writer's The life of Sir Edward Coke. (1 vol. 8vo. Lond. 1826.)

576. The lives of the lord chancellors and keepers of the great seal of England . . . till the reign of King George IV. By J. Campbell. 7 vols. 8vo. Lond. 1845–7. 4th ed. 10 vols. 8vo. Lond. 1856–7.

Useful but inaccurate : has a strong whig bias.

577. The equitable jurisdiction of the court of chancery ; comprising its rise, progress, and final establishment. By G. Spence. 2 vols. 8vo. Lond. 1846–9.

References to the Stuart period will be found at various places.

578. The great oyer of poisoning. By A. Amos. 1 vol. 8vo. Lond. 1846.

The trial of Somerset for poisoning Overbury.

579. The judges of England. By E. Foss. 9 vols. 8vo. Lond. 1848–64.

Very useful. There is a handy abridgement in 1 vol. entitled Biographia juridica 1066–1870 (8vo. Lond. 1870).

580. The lives of the chief justices of England . . . till the death of Lord Mansfield. By J. Campbell. 3 vols. 8vo. Lond. 1849–57. Later ed. 4 vols. 8vo. Lond. 1874.

Useful but inaccurate.

581. A history of crime in England. By L. O. Pike. 2 vols. 8vo. Lond. 1873–6.

582. A history of the criminal law of England. By Sir J. F. Stephen. 3 vols. 8vo. Lond. 1883.

583. The order of the coif. By A. Pulling. 1 vol. 8vo. Lond. 1884. Later ed. 1887.

This is the best account of the serjeants-at-law.

584. Land in fetters, or the history and policy of the laws restraining the alienation and settlement of land in England [Yorke Prize Essay for 1885]. By T. E. Scrutton. 1 vol. 8vo. Camb. 1886.

Chaps. vi, viii, and ix deal especially with the Stuart period. Cf. No. 2063.

585. The history of the doctrine of consideration. By E. Jenks. 1 vol. 8vo. Lond. 1892.

Chap. ii, entitled ' The period of the abridgements ', deals with the period from the close of the year-books to the accession of George III.

586. The life of Judge Jeffreys. By H. B. Irving. 1 vol. 8vo. Lond. 1898. Illus. Bibl.

An ingenious, but unconvincing defence.

587. The story of habeas corpus. By E. Jenks. Law Quart. Rev. vol. 8. pp. 64–77.

588. A history of English law. By W. S. Holdsworth. 3 vols. 8vo. Lond. 1903–9. Later ed. 9 vols. 8vo. Lond. 1922–7.

589. Select essays in Anglo-American legal history. Ed. by E. Freund, W. E. Mikell, J. H. Wigmore. 3 vols. 8vo. Boston, Mass. 1907–9. Tables. Bibl.

A valuable collection of scattered essays in regard to English and American legal history from the earliest times to the present day. The following essays in vol. i deal, *inter alia*, with the Stuart period. Roman law influence in chancery, church courts, admiralty and law merchant. By T. E. Scrutton.
The history of the canon law in England. By W. Stubbs.
The development of the law merchant, and its courts. By W. S. Holdsworth.
A comparison of the history of legal development at Rome and in England. By J. Bryce.
The English common law in the early American colonies. By P. S. Reinsch.
The theory of the extension of English statutes to the [American] plantations. By St. G. L. Sioussat.
The influence of colonial conditions as illustrated in the Connecticut intestacy law. By C. McL. Andrews.
Anticipations under the commonwealth of changes in the law. By R. Robinson.
The five ages of the bench and bar of England. By J. U. Zane.
Vols. ii and iii contain fifty-five essays on sources, the courts, procedure, equity, commercial law, contracts, torts, property (in general), wills, descent, marriage. Many of these essays are concerned in part with the law of the Stuart period.

590. The collected works of Frederic William Maitland. Ed. by H. A. L. Fisher. 3 vols. 8vo. Camb. 1911.

English legal history of the Stuart period is dealt with, *inter alia*, in the following papers :
The mystery of seisin (vol. i).
The beatitude of seisin (vol. i).

The survival of archaic communities (vol. ii).
Records of the honourable society of Lincoln's Inn (vol. iii).
The corporation sole (vol. iii).
The crown as corporation (vol. iii).

591. A short history of English law. By E. Jenks. 1 vol. 8vo. Lond. 1912. Bibl.

Chaps. vi–xii deal with the period from 1272–1660 and chaps. xiii–xix with the period from 1660–1911. A valuable survey.

592. Lectures on legal history. By J. B. Amos. 1 vol. 8vo. Camb. (Mass.) 1913. Bibl.

Traces the history of actions and of doctrines of common law and equity. Law of Stuart period referred to at various places. A valuable work.

593. The trial of Sir Walter Raleigh. By Sir H. L. Stephen. Trans. Royal Hist. Socy. 4th series, ii, 1919.

594. The history of conspiracy and the abuse of legal procedure. By P. H. Winfield. 1 vol. 8vo. Camb. 1921.

595. Sir Matthew Hale. By W. S. Holdsworth. Law Quart. Rev. Oct. 1923.

There is a contemporary life of Sir M. Hale by G. Burnet, 1 vol. 12mo. Lond. 1682. Repr. at Oxford 1806 and 1856 with Fell's life of Hammond [1661].

596. Defamation in the 16th and 17th centuries. By W. S. Holdsworth. Law Quart. Rev. July 1924.

¶ 5. FOREIGN RELATIONS

    (i) General.
    (ii) France.
    (iii) Germany.
    (iv) Italy.
    (v) Northern Powers.
    (vi) Spain, Portugal, and the Low Countries.
    (vii) Switzerland.
    (viii) United Provinces.

There is no work on a large scale devoted to foreign policy during the Stuart period, although Seeley (619) supplies a basis. Gardiner was the first English historian fully to investigate the subject and to demonstrate its influence upon domestic history, and his works (219, 220) should be used for 1603–56. For the rest of the period Ranke (214) and Klopp (215) are the best guides. The series initiated by the Royal Historical Society should ultimately cover foreign relations with all European powers after 1688. The only calendar of the dispatches of any foreign representative is the Venetian (683), but copious extracts have been published from the correspondence of various French ambassadors, who during 1660–88, were often the confidential advisers of the crown, and the Austrian representatives' dispatches were systematically employed by Klopp. Much of the published material is contained in foreign works, of which only a few are here listed. Others should be sought in bibliographies such as Bourgeois and André for France and Dahlmann and Waitz for Germany. The best guide to the treaties of the period is Myers (599).

(i) GENERAL
(*a*) Guides. (*b*) Sources. (*c*) Later Works.

(*a*) GENERAL GUIDES

597. List of volumes of state papers foreign preserved in the Public Record Office. 1547–1782. Lists and indexes xix. fol. Lond. 1904.

598. Materials for English diplomatic history 1509–1783 calendared in the reports of the historical manuscript commission, with references to similar materials in the British Museum. By F. G. Davenport. Hist. MSS. Comm. Eighteenth Rep. 1917.

599. Manual of collections of treaties and of collections relating to treaties. By D. P. Myers. 1 vol. 8vo. Camb. (Mass.) 1922.

(*b*) GENERAL SOURCES

600. Finetti Philoxenis : some choice Observations of Sir John Finett . . . touching the reception . . . of forren ambassadors. Ed. by J. Howell. 1 vol. 12mo. Lond. 1656.

Valuable for diplomatic etiquette.

601. Interest of the princes and states of Europe. By S. Bethel. 1 vol. 8vo. Lond. 1680. Later ed. 1 vol. 8vo. Lond. 1681 (with additions).

Also contains ' Brief narrative of . . . that pretended parliament called by Richard Cromwel ', originally published in 1659 and reprinted in Somers' Tracts, vol. vi.

602. Several treaties of peace and commerce concluded between the late king . . . and other princes and states. . . Reprinted and published by his majesties especial command. 1 vol. 8vo. Lond. 1686.

The first English collection of treaties.

603. Lettres historiques : contenant ce qui se passe de plus important en Europe. Janvier 1692–Décembre 1736. Ed. by J. Dumont and H. Basnage. 90 vols. 12mo. The Hague. 1692–1736.

604. Letters of state written by Mr. John Milton to most of the sovereign princes and republicks of Europe. From the year 1649 till the year 1659. Ed. by E. Phillips. 1 vol. 12mo. Lond. 1694.

Cf. Masson, vi. 791. seq. for earlier eds. &c.

605. Actes et mémoires des négociations de la paix de Ryswick. Ed. by J. Bernard. 4 vols. 12mo. The Hague. 1699. 2nd ed. 5 vols. 12mo. The Hague. 1707, and 3rd ed. 1725.

606. Foedera, conventiones, literae, et cujuscunque generis acta publica, inter reges Angliae et alios quovis imperatores, reges, pontifices, principes, vel communitates ab . . . anno 1101, ad nostra usque tempora, habita aut tractata ; ex autographis . . . fideliter exscripta . . . Ed. by T. Rymer for vols. 1–15 and R. Sanderson 16–20. 20 vols. fol. Lond. 1704–32.

Collection carried to 1654, period from 1603 being covered in vols. 16–20. See Sir T. D. Hardy's Syllabus [3 vols. 8vo. Lond. 1869–85] for later eds., contents, index &c. and life of Rymer. A better version of the Dutch correspondence is in Thurloe.

607. The conduct of the allies, and of the late ministry, in beginning and carrying on the present War. By J. Swift. 1 vol. 8vo. Lond. 1711. Cf. No. 2450.

608. Report from the committee of secrecy appointed by order of the house of commons to examine several books and papers laid before the house relating to the late negociations of peace and commerce . . . reported on the 9th of June 1715 by . . . Robert Walpole. 1 vol. fol. Lond. 1715.

Prints many valuable state papers. Repr. in Cobbett (385) vii. Appendix.

609. The life of Sir Leoline Jenkins . . . ambassador and plenipotentiary for the general peace at Cologn and Nimeguen, and secretary of state to K. Charles II and a compleat series of letters from the beginning to the end of those two important treaties. By W. Wynne. 2 vols. fol. Lond. 1724.

The letters are extremely numerous.

610. Mémoires pour servir a l'histoire du XVIII siècle contenant les négociations traitez, resolutions et autres documens authentiques. Ed. by G. de Lamberty. 14 vols. 4to. The Hague and Amsterdam. 1724–40. 2nd ed. 1731–40.

A collection of state papers extracted from Gazettes &c. covering *c.* 1700–18. Vols 11–14 form supplements for the years 1700–7.

611. Corps universel diplomatique du droit des gens ; contenant un receuil des traitez d'alliance, de paix . . . faits en Europe depuis le regne de l'Empereur Charlemagne jusques à présent. By J. Dumont. 8 vols. fol. Amsterdam and The Hague. 1726–31.

A Supplément au Corps universel diplomatique . . . continué jusqu'à présent was ed. by J. Rousset de Missy. 5 vols. fol. Amsterdam and The Hague. 1739.

612. Historical and political memoirs containing letters written by sovereign princes, state ministers . . . from almost all the courts in Europe [1697–1708] . . . illustrated with treaties memorials . . . instructions for ambassadors. Ed. by C. Cole. 1 vol. fol. Lond. 1735.

Mainly letters to and from Manchester at Paris 1697–1701, and at Venice in 1707–8. Cf. Hist. MSS. Comm. Rep. viii. Pt. ii. 1881, and No. 778.

613. A collection of all the treaties of peace, alliance and commerce between Great Britain and other powers [1648–1783]. By Charles Jenkinson, 1st Earl of Liverpool. 3 vols. 8vo. Lond. 1785.

Jenkinson ed. an early volume with the same title extending from 1619 to 1734 [1 vol. 8vo. Lond. 1781]. He gives translations only.

614. A collection of treaties between Great Britain and other powers. Ed. by G. Chalmers. 2 vols. 8vo. Lond. 1790.

615. State papers and correspondence, illustrative of the social and political state of Europe (1686–1707). Ed. by J. M. Kemble. 1 vol. 8vo. Lond. 1857.

Mainly about Germany, and from German sources.

616. Les grands traités du règne de Louis XIV. By H. Vast. 3 pts. 8vo. Paris. 1893–9.

Has valuable bibliographical notes for each treaty.

(c) GENERAL LATER WORKS

617. The peace of Utrecht. By J. W. Gerard. 1 vol. 8vo. N.Y. 1885.

618. Der Friede von Utrecht. Verhandlungen zwischen England, Frankreich, dem Kaiser und den General-staaten 1710–1713. By O. Weber. 1 vol. 8vo. Gotha. 1891.

619. The growth of British policy. By Sir J. R. Seeley. 2 vols. 8vo. Camb. 1895. Later ed. 1 vol. 1922.

There is an introductory sketch by Sir A. W. Ward in Cambridge History of British foreign policy. Vol. i. 8vo. Camb. 1922.

620. The Protestant interest in Cromwell's foreign relations. By J. N. Bowman. 1 vol. 8vo. Heidelberg. 1900.

621. The Fallen Stuarts. By F. W. Head. 1 vol. 8vo. Camb. 1901.

A study of the influence of European politics upon the fortunes of the Stuarts, 1660–1748.

622. Die Friedensbestrebungen Wilhelms III von England in den Jahren 1694–1697. Ein Beitrag zur Geschichte des Rijswijker Friedens. By G. Koch. Ed. by W. Michael. 1 vol. 8vo. Tübingen and Leipzig. 1903.

Cf. Die Flugschriften-Literatur zu Beginn des spanischen Erbfolgekriegs. By Carl Ringhoffer. 1 vol. 8vo. Berlin. 1881.

623. The attempts to establish a balance of power in Europe during the second half of the seventeenth century [1648–1702]. By E. M. G. Routh. Trans. Royal Hist. Socy. N.S., xviii. 1904.

624. The life and letters of Sir Henry Wotton. By L. P. Smith. 2 vols. 8vo. Oxf. 1907. Illus.

A valuable contribution to the history of foreign policy. App. I contains a complete list of Wotton's letters and dispatches. Cf. Letters and dispatches from Sir Henry Wotton . . . 1617–1620. 1 vol. Roxburghe Club 1850 and Sir Henry Wotton by A. W. Ward. 1 vol. 8vo. Westminster. 1898.

625. The peace of Utrecht and the supplementary pacifications. By Sir A. W. Ward. Cambridge Modern History V. 1908. Bibl.

626. Parliament and foreign affairs, 1603–1760. By E. R. Turner. Eng. Hist. Rev. xxxiv. 1919.

(ii) FRANCE

SOURCES AND LATER WORKS

627. Lists of French ambassadors &c. in England . . . 1509–1714 with remarks on their correspondence. By A. Baschet. Rep. of the Deputy Keeper, xxxvii. 1876.

See *ibid.* xl–xlvii for Baschet's accounts of his transcripts of documents in French archives.

628. Notes on the diplomatic relations of England and France 1603–1688. Lists of ambassadors from England to France and from France to England. Ed. by Sir C. H. Firth and S. C. Lomas. 1 vol. 8vo. Oxf. 1906.

A similar list for 1689–1763 was compiled by L. G. W. Legg [1 vol. 8vo. Oxf. 1909] Both have full references to published dispatches.

629. Les sources de l'histoire de France XVIIIᵉ siècle 1610–1715.   Ed. by E. Bourgeois and L. André.   4 vols. 8vo. Paris. 1913–24.

I. Géographie et histoires générales ; II. Mémoires et lettres ; III. Biographies ; IV. Journaux et pamphlets.

630. British diplomatic instructions 1689–1789.   Volume II.   France 1689–1721.   Ed. by L. G. W. Legg.   Royal Hist. Soc. Lond. 1925.

631. Ambassades du Maréchal de Bassompierre en Espagne, en Suisse et en Angleterre [1626].   By F. de Bassompierre.   4 vols. 12mo Cologne. 1668.

Cf. Memoirs of the embassy of the Marshal de Bassompierre to the court of England in 1626, trans. by J. W. Croker [1 vol. 8vo. Lond. 1819].

632. Lettres, mémoires et négociations de M. le comte d'Estrades.   By Godefroy, Comte d'Estrades.   5 vols. 12mo. Brussels. 1709.   Later ed. 9 vols. 12mo. Lond. 1743.

Cf. Bourgeois and André (629), ii. 262–4.

633. Copies and Extracts of some letters written to and from The Earl of Danby [1676–8] . . . with particular Remarks upon some of them.   Ed. by Thomas Osborne Earl of Danby and Duke of Leeds.   1 vol. 8vo. Lond. 1710.

Danby's defence : illustrate foreign policy, particularly towards France.   See Hist. MSS. Comm. Eliot Hodgkin MSS.

634. The sale of Dunkirk to the late French King Lewis XIV in the year 1662.   Taken from the letters . . . of Count d'Estrades.   By E. Combe.   1 vol. 12mo. Lond. 1728.

Cf. S. A. Swaine, The English acquisition and loss of Dunkirk.   Trans. Royal Hist. Socy. N.S. i.

635. An historical view of the negociations between the courts of England, France and Brussels from the year 1592 to 1617.   Extracted, chiefly from the MS. State papers of Sir Thomas Edmondes.   By T. Birch.   1 vol. 8vo. Lond. 1749.

636. Ambassades de M. de la Boderie en Angleterre sous le règne d'Henri IV et la minorité de Louis XIII [1606–11].   By A. L. de La Boderie. 5 vols. 12mo. [Paris]. 1750.

For an earlier ed. see Firth (628), pp. 29–30.

637. Négociations du comte d'Avaux en Hollande.   By J. A. de Mesmes, comte d'Avaux.   6 vols. 12mo. Paris. 1752–3.

English trans. Lond. 1754.   Valuable for preparations of William of Orange 1687–8. Cf. No. 3253.

638. Mémoires de Monsieur De [Torcy] pour servir à l'histoire des négociations depuis le traité de Ryswyck jusqu'à la paix d'Utrecht.   By J. B. Colbert, Marquis de Torcy.   3 vols. 8vo. The Hague. 1756.   Later ed. 3 vols. 8vo. Lond. 1757.

Repr. in Petitot, 2nd series, lxvii–viii ; and in Michaud et Poujoulet, 3rd series, viii. For Torcy's other memoirs and correspondence see Bourgeois and André (629), ii, pp. 191–2, 400–1.

639. Négociations relatives à la succession d'Espagne sous Louis XIV. Ed. by F. A. M. Mignet. 4 vols. 4to. Paris. 1835–42.

Ends 1679 : has many valuable extracts from French ambassadors' despatches.

640. Letters of William III and Louis XIV and of their ministers [1697–1700]. Ed. by P. Grimblot. 2 vols. 8vo. Lond. 1848.

Important, especially for the Spanish Succession question.

641. Histoire des luttes et rivalités politiques entre les puissances maritimes et la France dans la dernière moitié du XVIIᵉ siècle. By C. F. S. de Grovestins. 8 vols. 8vo. Paris. 1851–4. Later ed. 1868.

In ed. of 1868 the words ' Guillaume III et Louis XIV.' were prefixed to the title.

642. Mémoires inédits du Comte Leveneur de Tillières ambassadeur en Angleterre sur la cour de Charles Iᵉʳ et son mariage avec Henriette de France. Ed. by C. Hippeau. 1 vol. 8vo. Paris. 1863.

643. L'ambassade de M. de Blainville à la cour de Charles Iᵉʳ, roi d'Angleterre. By M. Houssaye. Revue des questions hist. 1878.

644. Graham MSS. Hist. MSS. Comm. Rep. VII. Pt. I. 1879.

Comprises Lord Preston's letters, mainly from Paris, 1682–8.

645. Louis XIV et Guillaume III. Histoire des deux traités de partage. By H. Reynald. 2 vols. 8vo. Paris. 1883.

646. La diplomatie Française et la succession d'Espagne. By A. Legrelle. 4 vols. 8vo. Ghent. 1888–92. Later ed. 6 vols. 8vo. Braine-le-Comte. 1895–1900.

Later ed. has continuation. Cf. his Notes et documents sur la paix de Ryswick. 1 vol. 8vo. Lille. 1894.

647. A French ambassador at the court of Charles the Second. Le Comte de Cominges from his unpublished correspondence. By J. J. Jusserand. 1 vol. 8vo. Lond. 1892. Ports.

An app. contains the original text of the extracts from French dispatches quoted. An amusing and instructive work.

648. Une Négociation inconnue entre Berwick et Marlborough, 1708–9. By A. Legrelle. 1 vol. 8vo. Ghent. 1893.

649. Mission de Christophe de Harlay Comte de Beaumont [1602–05]. By P. P. Laffleur de Kermaingant. 2 vols. 8vo. Paris. 1895.

Belongs to the series L'Ambassade de France en Angleterre sous Henri IV. Vol. i is narrative, ii is documents.

650. Cromwell and Mazarin in 1652. By S. R. Gardiner. Eng. Hist. Rev. xi. 1896.

651. The journal of Joachim Hane containing his escapes and sufferings during his employment by Oliver Cromwell in France from November 1653 to February 1654. Ed. by Sir C. H. Firth. 1 vol. 8vo. Oxf. 1896.

MS. at Worcester College, Oxf.

652. Cromwell's instructions to Colonel Lockhart in 1656. Ed. by Sir C. H. Firth. Eng. Hist. Rev. xxi. 1906.

653. An unknown treaty between England and France, 1644. By D. A. Bigby. Eng. Hist. Rev. xxvii. 1913.

654. Torcy's account of Matthew Prior's negotiations at Fontainebleau in July 1711. By L. G. W. Legg. Eng. Hist. Rev. xxviii. 1914.

Pr. from Arch. des Aff. Étran., Corr. Pol. Angleterre, vol. 233.

(iii) GERMANY

655. Quellenkunde der deutschen Geschichte. By F. C. Dahlmann and G. Waitz. 1 vol. 8vo. Göttingen. 1830. Later ed. 1 vol. 8vo. Leipzig. 1912. Ed. by P. Herre.

Apparently Waitz was first associated with this work in the 3rd ed. 1869.

656. Notes on the diplomatic relations of England and Germany. List of diplomatic representatives and agents, England and North Germany 1689–1727. By J. F. Chance. Ed. by Sir C. H. Firth. 1 vol. 8vo. Oxf. 1907.

657. An account of the courts of Prussia and Hanover sent to a minister of state in Holland. By J. Toland. 1 vol. 8vo. Lond. 1705.

658. A brief history of the poor Palatine refugees lately arriv'd in England. 1 vol. 8vo. Lond. 1709.

659. Briefe aus England [1674–78] in Gesandtschafts-Berichten des Ministers Otto von Schwerin des Jüngern an den Grossen Kurfürsten Friedrich Wilhelm. Ed. by L. von Orlich. 1 vol. 8vo. Berlin. 1837.

Cf. Eng. Hist. Rev. xiv. 1899, p. 609.

660. The Lexington papers ; or, some account of the courts of London and Vienna at the conclusion of the seventeenth century. Extracted from the official and private correspondence of Robert Sutton, Lord Lexington, British minister at Vienna, 1694–8. Ed. by H. Manners Sutton. 1 vol. 8vo. Lond. 1851.

The letters to Lexington come from nearly every court in Europe.

661. Urkunden und Aktenstücke zur Geschichte des Kurfürsten Friedrich Wilhelm von Brandenburg. Ed. by B. Erdmannsdorffer and others. 21 vols. 8vo. Berlin. 1864–1915.

662. Letters and other documents illustrating the relations between England and Germany at the commencement of the Thirty years' war [1618–20]. Ed. by S. R. Gardiner. 2 vols. Camd. Soc. 1865.

663. The Hanover papers [1695–1719]. By P. M. Thornton. Eng. Hist. Rev. i. 1886.

A description of vols. in Brit. Mus. Stowe MSS.

664. Franz Paul Freiherr von Lisola 1613–1674. By A. F. Pribram. 1 vol. 8vo. Leipzig. 1894.

Cf. H. Reynald, Le Baron de Lisola, sa jeunesse et sa première ambassade en Angleterre, Revue Historique, xxvii.

665. Great Britain and Hanover. By Sir A. W. Ward. 1 vol. 8vo. Oxf. 1899.

666. The Electress Sophia and the Hanoverian succession. By Sir A. W. Ward. 1 vol. 4to. Lond. and Paris. 1903. Illus. Later ed. 1 vol. 8vo. Lond. 1909.

Valuable : ed. of 1909 has an important introductory survey of the authorities. Cf. Eng. Hist. Rev. i. 1886 for an article on the same subject.

667. König Wilhelm III, Bayern und die Grosse Allianz, 1701. By G. F. Preuss. Hist. Zeitschrift, xciii. 1904.

668. Österreichische Staatsverträge. England, Bd. I. 1526–1748. By A. F. Pribram. 1 vol. 8vo. Innsbruck. 1907.

669. The relations between England and Germany, 1660–88. By C. Brinkmann. Eng. Hist. Rev. xxiv. 1909.

670. The mission of Sir Thomas Roe to Vienna 1641–2. By R. B. Mowat. Eng. Hist. Rev. xxv. 1910.

Cf. E. A. Beller : The mission of Sir Thomas Roe to the conference at Hamburg, 1638–40. Eng. Hist. Rev. xli. 1926.

671. Brandenburg and the English revolution of 1688. By H. L. King. Oberlin. 1914.

672. England and Austria in 1657. Ed. by Sir C. H. Firth. Eng. Hist. Rev. xxxii. 1917.

Deals with Cromwell's attempt to prevent the election of a Hapsburg as emperor.

673. The negotiations of Sir Stephen Le Sieur 1584–1613. By E. A. Beller. Eng. Hist. Rev. xl. Jan. 1925.

(iv) ITALY

Sources and Later Works

674. History of the evangelical churches of the valleys of Piedmont. By Sir S. Morland. 1 vol. fol. Lond. 1658. Illus.

Cf. Vaughan's Pell and Morland correspondence (718).

675. Memoires of the transactions in Savoy during this war. Wherein the duke of Savoy's foul play with the allies and his secret correspondence with the French king are . . . demonstrated . . . Made English from the original. Translated by J. Savage. 1 vol. 12mo. Lond. 1697.

676. Traités publics de la royale maison de Savoie avec les puissances étrangères depuis la paix de Château-Cambresis jusqu'à nos jours publiés par ordre du Roi. 8 vols. 8vo. Turin. 1836–61.

Cf. Manuale di storia diplomatica. Cronologia dei principali trattati internazionali di pace [1496 B.C.–A.D. 1885]. 1 vol. 8vo. Turin. 1886.

677. The diplomatic correspondence of . . . Richard Hill envoy extraordinary . . . to the duke of Savoy . . . from July 1703 to May 1706. Ed. by W. Blackley. 2 vols. 8vo. Lond. 1845.

678. Relazioni degli Stati Europei. Lettere al Senato dagli ambasciatori Veneziani nel Secolo decimo settimo. III Ser. Italia e Inghilterra. Ed. by N. Barozzi and G. Berchet. 1 vol. 8vo. Venice. 1861.

679. Storia del regno di Vittorio Amadeo II. By D. Carutti. 1 vol. 8vo. Firenze. 1863.

680. Cromwell e la Repubblica di Venezia. By G. Berchet. 1 vol. 8vo. Venice. 1864.

681. Oliviero Cromwell dalla battaglia di Worcester alla sua morte. Ed. by C. Prayer. 1 vol. 8vo. Genoa. 1882.

Reprint of the Genoese ambassador's dispatches.

682. Skrine MSS. Hist. MSS. Comm. 1887.

Eng. trans. of the correspondence of Salvetti, Tuscan agent in England, 11 Apr. 1625–16 Dec. 1628.

683. Calendar of state papers and manuscripts relating to English affairs existing in the archives and collections of Venice and in other libraries of northern Italy, vols. x–xxvi. 1603–1643. Ed. by H. F. Brown and A. B. Hind. 17 vols. 8vo. Stationery Office. 1900–25.

684. Denbigh MSS. v. Hist. MSS. Comm. 1911.

Has correspondence of Basil Feilding, Earl of Denbigh, at Venice 1634–9. Cf. Hist. MSS. Comm. Rep. vi. Pt. i. 1877, Rep. viii. Pt. i. 1881.

(v) NORTHERN POWERS

685. Notes on the diplomatic relations of England with the north of Europe. List of English diplomatic representatives and agents in Denmark, Sweden and Russia, and of those countries in England 1689–1762. By J. F. Chance. Ed. by Sir C. H. Firth. 1 vol. 8vo. Oxf. 1913.

686. British Diplomatic Instructions 1689–1789. Volume I–Sweden. Ed. by J. F. Chance. Royal Hist. Soc. Lond. 1922.

Mainly from Foreign Entry Books, Public Record Office.

687. British diplomatic instructions 1689–1789. Volume III–Denmark. Ed. by J. F. Chance. Royal Hist. Soc. Lond. 1926.

688. A relation of three embassies from . . . Charles II to the Grand Duke of Muscovy, the King of Sweden and the King of Denmark performed by the Earl of Carlisle in the years 1663 and 1664. By G. Miège. 1 vol. 8vo. Lond. 1669.

For repr. see Dict. Nat. Biog. *sub* 'Miège'.

689. Narrative of the principal actions in the war between Sweden and Denmark before and after the Roschild Treaty. By Sir P. Meadowe. 1 vol. 12mo. Lond. 1677.

690. An account of Denmark as it was in the year 1692. By Robert Viscount Molesworth. 1 vol. 8vo. Lond. 1694.

Repr. in Harris (3454) ii. A bitter attack on the Danish government as tyrannical, which provoked answers by W. King, Animadversions. . . . 1694; and Denmark vindicated, attributed to Jodocus Crull. [1 vol. 8vo. Lond. 1694.]

691. An account of Sweden. By J. Robinson. 1 vol. 8vo. Lond. 1694.

692. An account of Russia as it was in the year 1710. By Charles, Lord Whitworth. 1 vol. 8vo. Strawberry Hill Press. 1758.

693. A journal of the Swedish embassy in the years 1653 and 1654. By B. Whitelocke. Ed. by C. Morton. 2 vols. 4to. Lond. 1772. Later ed. 2 vols. 8vo. Lond. 1855. Ed. by H. Reeve.
MS. in Brit. Mus. 4902.

694. Riks-rödet Frih. Christer Bondes Ambassad till England 1655. By Kalling. 1 vol. 8vo. Upsala. 1851.

695. Letters relating to the mission of Sir Thomas Roe to Gustavus Adolphus 1629–30. Ed. by S. R. Gardiner. Camd. Misc. vii. 1875.

696. Some correspondence of Thurloe and Meadowe. Ed. by E. Jenks. Eng. Hist. Rev. vii. 1892.

697. The diplomatic relations between Cromwell and Charles X Gustavus of Sweden. By G. Jones. 1 vol. 8vo. Lincoln. Nebraska. 1897.

698. The meeting of the duke of Marlborough and Charles XII at Altranstadt [1707]. By A. E. Stamp. Trans. Royal Hist. Soc. N.S. xii. 1898.

699. Sverige och England 1655–Aug. 1657. By J. L. Carlbom. 1 vol. 8vo. Göteborg. 1900.

700. England and Sweden in the time of William III and Anne. By J. F. Chance. Eng. Hist. Rev. xvi. 1901.

701. England and Denmark, 1660–1667. By H. L. Schoolcraft. Eng. Hist. Rev. xxv. 1910.

702. The relations between England and the northern powers, 1689–1697. Part I. Denmark. By M. Lane. Trans. Royal Hist. Soc. 3rd ser. v. 1911.

703. A project for the acquisition of Russia by James I. By I. Lubimenko. Eng. Hist. Rev. xxviii. 1914.

704. Letters illustrating the relations of England and Russia in the seventeenth century. By I. Lubimenko. Eng. Hist. Rev. xxxii. 1917.
Cf. the same writer's The correspondence of the first Stuarts with the first Romanovs. Trans. Royal Hist. Soc. 4th series I. 1918 ; and *ibid.* vii. 1924 for The struggle of the Dutch with the English for the Russian market in the seventeenth century.

(vi) SPAIN, PORTUGAL, AND THE LOW COUNTRIES

705. Bibliographie de l'histoire de Belgique. Catalogue . . . des sources et des ouvrages principaux relatifs à l'histoire de tous les Pays-Bas jusqu'en 1598 et à l'histoire de Belgique jusqu'en 1830. By H. Pirenne. 1 vol. 8vo. Ghent. 1893. Later ed. 1 vol. 8vo. Ghent. 1902.

706. Original letters written [in 1674] to the Earl of Arlington by Sir R. Bulstrode envoy at the court of Brussels. Ed. by E. Bysshe. 1 vol. 8vo. Lond. 1712.

707. Original letters and negotiations of . . . Sir Richard Fanshaw, the Earl of Sandwich, the Earl of Sunderland and Sir William Godolphin . . . wherein divers matters . . . between the three crowns of England, Spain and Portugal from . . . 1663 to 1678 are set in a clearer light than is any where else extant. 2 vols. 8vo. Lond. 1724.

Cf. Heathcote MSS. Hist. MSS. Comm. 1889 for Fanshaw's correspondence as ambassador in Portugal and Spain, 1661–6 ; and Memoirs (890).

708. The history of the revolutions of Portugal . . . to 1667 with letters of Sir Robert Southwell, during his embassy there, to the duke of Ormond. By T. Carte. 1 vol. 8vo. Lond. 1740.

Southwell's letters cover June to Dec. 1667.

709. The history of the reign of Philip the Third. By R. Watson. Ed. by W. Thomson. 1 vol. 4to. Lond. 1783. Later eds. 2 vols. 8vo. Lond. 1786 and 1 vol. 8vo. Lond. 1839.

Later eds. have diary of peace conference at Somerset House, 1604.

710. Collecção dos tratados . . . entre a coroa de Portugal e as mais potencias desde 1640 até ao presente. Ed. by José Ferreira, Visconde de Borges de Castro. 8 vols. 8vo. Lisbon. 1856–8.

Vols. i and ii. 1400–1749. A Supplemento ed. by J. F. J. Biker was issued as vols. ix–xxx of the preceding 8vo. Lisbon. 1872–80. Vols. ix and x cover 1629–1737.

711. Narrative of the Spanish marriage treaty. By Fray Francisco de Jesus. Ed. by S. R. Gardiner. Camd. Soc. 1869.

Translation of a Spanish narrative, of which a copy is in Brit. Mus. Add. MS. 14043.

712. The earl of Bristol's defence of his negotiations in Spain. From MSS. in the Bodleian Library and the Public Record Office. Ed. by S. R. Gardiner. Camd. Soc. 1871.

713. Un gran diplomático español : el conde de Gondomar en Inglaterra. By M. A. S. Hume. Revista Nuestro Tiempo. Madrid. 1902.

714. D. Antonio de Sousa de Macedo, residente de Portugal em Londres [1642–46]. By E. Prestage.

Cf. the same writer's Duas cartas do D. Antonio de Sousa de Macedo. Both repr. from the Bulletin of the Academia das sciencias of Lisbon, x. 1916.

715. Beginnings of the oldest European alliance : England and Portugal, 1640–1661. By G. Jones. Annual Rep. Amer. Hist. Ass. 1916. 1 vol. 8vo. Washington. 1919.

716. Correspondance de la Cour d'Espagne sur les affaires des Pays-Bas. Ed. by H. Lonchay and J. Cuvelier. fol. Brussels. 1923.

717. The diplomatic relations of Portugal and England from 1640 to 1668. By E. Prestage. 1 vol. 8vo. Watford. 1925.

(vii) SWITZERLAND

718. The protectorate of Oliver Cromwell and the state of Europe . . . illustrated in a series of letters between Dr. John Pell, resident ambassador with the Swiss cantons, Sir Samuel Morland, Sir William Lockhart, Mr. Secretary Thurloe. Ed. by R. Vaughan. 2 vols. 8vo. Lond. 1839.

719. Oliver Cromwell und die evangelischen Kantone der Schweiz. By A. Stern. Hist. Zeit. xl. 1878.

(viii) UNITED PROVINCES

720. Bibliotheca Historico-Neerlandica. Catalogue des livres et manuscrits concernant l'histoire et la topographie des Pays-Bas. By M. Nijhoff. 1 vol. 8vo. The Hague. 1871. Later ed. 1899.

A bookseller's catalogue. Cf. his Bibliotheca juridica ; catalogus van alle boeken sedert 1837 in het Koningrijk der Nederlanden verschenen, 8vo. 1874.

721. Lijst van Engelsche vlugschriften, betrekking hebbende op de Nederlandsche geschiedenis tot 1640. By W. P. C. Knuttel. 1886.

Cf. The same editor's Catalogus van de pamfletten-verzameling berustende in de Koninklijke Bibliotheek [9 vols. 4to. The Hague. 1889–1920] ; L. D. Petit, Bibliotheek van Nederlandsche pamfletten [2 vols. 4to. The Hague. 1882–84 ; in the Bibliotheca Thysiana at Leyden] ; and J. C. van der Wulp, Catalogus van de tractaten, pamfletten . . . in de bibliotheek van I. Meulman [3 vols. 4to. Amsterdam. 1866–8 ; in the University Library, Ghent].

722. Verslag van een onderzoek in Engeland naar Archivalia, belangrijk voor de geschiedenis van Nederland, in 1892 op last der Regeering ingesteld. By H. Brugmans. 1 vol. 8vo. The Hague. 1895.

723. List of authorities on British relations with the Dutch 1603–1713. By G. N. Clark. 1 vol. 8vo. s.l. 1920.

724. Observations upon the United Provinces of the Netherlands. By Sir W. Temple. 1 vol. 8vo. Lond. 1673.

Repr. in works (986).

725. The right honourable the Earl of Arlington's letters to Sir W. Temple from July 1665 . . . to Sept. 1670 . . . giving a perfect and exact account of the treaties of Munster, Breda, Aix-la-Chapelle and the Triple Alliance. Ed. by T. Bebington. 1 vol. 8vo. Lond. 1701.

726. Original letters from King William III then Prince of Orange to King Charles II, Lords Arlington, &c. Translated. Ed. by R. Sanderson. 1 vol. 8vo. Lond. 1704.

727. Memorials of affairs of state in the reigns of Queen Elizabeth and King James I, collected chiefly from the original papers of . . . Sir Ralph Winwood. Ed. by E. Sawyer. 3 vols. fol. Lond. 1725.

Covers 1590–1614. Important for Anglo-Dutch relations 1603–13. Other Winwood papers are in Buccleuch MSS. Montagu House. Hist. MSS. Comm. vol. i. 1899.

728. Letters to and from Sir Dudley Carleton during his embassy in Holland [Jan. 1616–Dec. 1620]. Ed. by Philip Yorke, 2nd Earl of Hardwicke. 1 vol. 4to. Lond. 1757. Later ed. 1780.

Cf. Sir Dudley Carleton's state letters during his embassy at the Hague, 1627. Ed. by Sir Thomas Phillipps. [1 vol. 4to. s.l. 1841.]

729. Nederland en Cromwell. By G. W. Vreede. 1 vol. 8vo. Utrecht. 1853.

730. Archives ou correspondance inédite de la maison d'Orange-Nassau.

2nd series 1584–1688, ed. by G. Groen van Prinsterer [5 vols. 8vo. The Hague and Utrecht. 1858–62]; 3rd series 1689–1702, ed. by F. J. L. Krämer [3 vols. 8vo. Leyden. 1907–09]. Both series are valuable, the second especially for the correspondence of William III and Heinsius.

731. History of the United Netherlands from the death of William the Silent to the Synod of Dort. By J. L. Motley. 4 vols. 8vo. Lond. 1860–7 and 1869–70.

Cf. his: The life and death of John of Barneveld, advocate of Holland [2 vols. 8vo. Lond. 1874].

732. Verbaal van de Buitengewone ambassade van Jacob van Wassenaar-Duivenvoorde, Arnout van Citters en Everard van Weede van Dijkveld naar Engeland in 1685. 1 vol. 8vo. Utrecht. 1863.

733. Verbaal van de ambassade van Aerssen, Joachimi en Burmania naar Engeland 1625. 1 vol. 8vo. Utrecht. 1867.

734. Englisch-Niederländische Unionsbestrebungen im Zeitalter Cromwell's. By G. Mitsukuri. 1 vol. 8vo. Tübingen. 1891.

735. De Verwikkelingen tusschen de Republiek en Engeland [1660–5]. By N. Japikse. 1 vol. 8vo. Leiden. 1900.

Cf. the same writer's Louis XIV et la Guerre Anglo-Hollandaise de 1665–7. Revue Historique, xcviii. 1908.

736. Charles II and the Bishop of Munster in the Anglo-Dutch war of 1665–66. By C. Brinkmann. Eng. Hist. Rev. xxi. 1906.

737. Secretary Thurloe on the relations of England and Holland. By J. Thurloe. Ed. by Sir C. H. Firth. Eng. Hist. Rev. xxi. 1906.

Drawn up by Thurloe for Hyde's instruction. MS. in Brit. Mus. Add. MS. 4200, fo. 113.

738. The capture of New Amsterdam. By H. L. Schoolcraft. Eng. Hist. Rev. xxii. 1907.

Proves from Anglo-Dutch relations 1654–64 that the capture was not unprovoked.

739. Anglo-Dutch rivalry during the first half of the seventeenth century. By G. Edmundson. 1 vol. 8vo. Oxf. 1911. Bibl.

The Ford Lectures delivered at Oxford in 1910.

740. A relation of the present state of affairs in the United Provinces 1675. By M. Lane. Eng. Hist. Rev. xxx. 1915.

Pr. from P.R.O. S.P. For. Holland, 198.

741. Die Gesandtschaft der protestantischen Schweiz bei Cromwell und den Generalstaaten der Niederlande 1652–54. By T. Ischer. 1 vol. 8vo. Bern. 1916.

742. The Dutch alliance and the war against French trade 1688–97. By G. N. Clark. 1 vol. 8vo. Manchester. 1923.

Based on printed and manuscript Dutch and English sources.

743. The Anglo-Dutch alliance of 1678. By C. L. Grose. Eng. Hist. Rev. xxxix. 1924.

744. Anglo-Dutch relations . . . to the death of William III. By J. F. Bense. 1 vol. 8vo. Lond. 1925.

¶ 6. BIOGRAPHIES

(*a*) Collective biographies, and biographiana.
(*b*) Biographies, personal narratives, and collected works of individuals.

This section includes only the lives and writings of those personages who figure in the political and constitutional history of England, or whose careers were too varied to be included elsewhere. Genealogies are not cited, but may be traced through G. W. Marshall's The genealogist's guide [1 vol. 8vo. Lond. 1879. Last ed. 1 vol. 8vo. Guildford. 1903]. Heraldry is omitted but may be studied in J. Guillim's A display of heraldry [1610 ; 6th ed. 1724].

The Dictionary of National Biography should always be consulted, not only for the lives but also for the authorities cited. Its publication made biography the easiest form of historical writing, and has resulted in the compilation of many works of slight value. No effort has been made to cite all these, but occasionally an indifferent life has been included in default of anything better. Care has been taken, however, to insert all the works containing documentary matter, and, what is much rarer though most valuable, information about the literary remains and correspondence of the subject of the biography.

The value of memoirs as sources for political history has been reduced by the modern scientific methods of historians. Nevertheless if their limitations are realized they are important in this respect as showing what the writer thought of current events or how he wished his actions to be judged. By revealing the spirit of the age they correct the common tendency to judge the past too exclusively by the standards of to-day. Their value is succinctly explained by Firth in an article in the Scottish Historical Review for July 1913.

(*a*) COLLECTIVE BIOGRAPHIES, AND BIOGRAPHIANA

745. England's worthies. Select lives of the most eminent persons of the English nation from Constantine the Great to the death of Oliver Cromwell. By W. Winstanley. 1 vol. 8vo. Lond. 1660. Later eds. 1 vol. 8vo. Lond. 1684.

Ed. of 1684 contains 15 new lives ending with Rupert, but omits Cromwell.

746. A compleat collection of the lives, speeches . . . of those persons lately executed. By W. S. 1 vol. 8vo. Lond. 1661.

Brief lives of executed regicides. Cf. the same writer's Rebels no saints : or a collection of the speeches . . . of those persons lately executed. 1 vol. 8vo. Lond. 1661.

747. Memorials of worthy persons. By C. Barksdale. 5 vols. 12mo. Lond. or Oxf. 1661–70.

748. The history of the worthies of England endeavoured by Thomas Fuller. 1 vol. fol. Lond. 1662. Port. Later eds. 2 vols. 4to. Lond. 1811. Ed. by J. Nichols ; 3 vols. 8vo. Lond. 1840. Port. Ed. by P. A. Nuttall.

Consult J. E. Bailey's Life of Thomas Fuller, 1874.

749. A new book of loyal English martyrs and confessors. By J. Heath.
1 vol. 12mo. Lond. 1663.

Royalist martyrology. Cf. No. 46.

750. State worthies or The statesmen and favourites of England since the
Reformation. By D. Lloyd. 1 vol. 8vo. Lond. 1665. Later eds. 2 vols. 8vo.
Lond. 1766. Ed. by C. Whitworth.

Lloyd also compiled Memoires of the Lives . . . of those . . . personages that suffered . . .
for the Protestant religion and . . . allegiance to their soveraigne . . . from 1637 to 1660,
and from thence continued to 1666.   fol. Lond. 1668.

751. The lives of Dr. John Donne, Sir Henry Wotton, Mr. Richard Hooker,
Mr. George Herbert . . . [The Life of Dr. Sanderson . . .] By I. Walton.
2 vols. 8vo. Lond. 1670, 1678. Ports. Later eds. 2 vols. 8vo. York. 1817. Ed.
by T. Zouch ; 2 vols. 8vo. Lond. 1898. Ed. by A. Dobson.

This is the first collected ed. of these four lives ; and the first ed. of the life of Sanderson.

752. A genealogical history of the kings of England [1066–1677]. By F.
Sandford. 1 vol. fol. Lond. 1677. Ports. Plates. Later ed. 1 vol. fol. Lond.
1707. Ed. by S. Stebbing.

Ed. of 1707 has additions and continuation to date.

753. The lives of sundry eminent persons in this later age. In two parts.
I. of divines. II. of nobility and gentry of both sexes . . . to which is added his
own life. By S. Clarke. 1 vol. fol. Lond. 1683. Ports.

Characters, rather than biographies, of pious men and women.

754. Succinct genealogies of the noble and ancient houses of . . . Mordaunt
of Turvey. By R. Halstead, pseudonym for Henry Mordaunt, 2nd Earl of
Peterborough. 1 vol. fol. Lond. 1685.

Of extreme rarity : useful for Peterborough's own life and times.

755. Danmonii orientales illustres : or the worthies of Devon. By J.
Prince. 1 vol. fol. Exeter. 1701. Later ed. 1 vol. 4to. Lond. 1810.

756. The western martyrology or bloody assizes containing the lives, trials
and dying-speeches of all those eminent protestants that suffered in the west of
England . . . with the life and death of George L[ord] Jeffreys. The fifth
edition. By T. Pitts. 1 vol. 8vo. Lond. 1705.

This is the usual title and permanent form.   The 1st ed. has not been found, probably
it was entitled A collection of the dying speeches, &c. [See Term Catalogue, ii. 258.]
The 3rd ed. is A new martyrology . . . life and death of George Lord Jeffrey [1 vol. 8vo.
1689 ; 4th ed. 1693].

757. A sermon preached at the funeral of . . . William Duke of Devonshire
. . . with some memoirs of the family of Cavendish. By W. Kennet. 1 vol. 8vo.
Lond. 1708.

758. Memoirs British and foreign of the lives . . . of the most illustrious
persons who dy'd in . . . 1711. By J. Le Neve. 1 vol. 8vo. Lond. 1712.

A similar collection for 1712 was pr. by Le Neve as The lives and characters of . . .
persons &c. [1 vol. 8vo. Lond. 1714.]

759. The history of the lives of the most noted highwaymen, footpads, housebreakers . . . for above fifty years past. By A. Smith. 1 vol. 8vo. Lond. 1714.

760. Mr. William Lilly's true history of King James the First and King Charles the First. 1 vol. 8vo. Lond. 1715.

Has interesting comments on Charles's character : otherwise valueless. Cf. Monarchy or no monarchy in England . . . passages upon the life and death of the late King Charles [1 vol. 4to. Lond. 1651].

761. Monumenta anglicana; being inscriptions of the monuments of several eminent persons deceased [1600–1718]. By J. Le Neve. 5 vols. 8vo. Lond. 1717–19.

An earlier work is : Ancient funerall monuments of Great Britain, Ireland and the isles adiacent. By J. Weever. 1 vol. fol. Lond. 1631.

762. The history of king-killers . . . containing the lives of thirty one fanatick saints famous for treason. 1 vol. 8vo. Lond. 1719.

763. Memoirs of the secret services of John Macky during the reigns of King William, Queen Anne and King George I. By J. Macky. 1 vol. 8vo. Lond. 1733. Repr. for Roxburghe Club, 1895.

Mainly characters of personages living in Anne's reign.

764. A general history of the lives and adventures of the most famous highwaymen, murderers, street-robbers, etc . . . and of the most notorious pyrates. By C. Johnson. 1 vol. fol. Lond. 1734. Later eds. 1 vol. fol. Lond. 1742. 1 vol. 8vo. Lond. 1839.

Repr. with No. 759 and other pieces in The complete Newgate calendar. Ed. by J. L. Rayner and G. T. Crook. 5 vols. 8vo. Navarre Soc. 1926. Illus. Cf. A bibliography of the works of Captain Charles Johnson. By P. Gosse. 4to. 1927.

765. Parentalia or Memoirs of the Family of the Wrens ; viz: of Matthew Bishop of Ely, Christopher Dean of Windsor, &c. but chiefly of Sir Christopher Wren. . . . By C. Wren. Ed. by S. Wren. 1 vol. fol. Lond. 1750. Ports.

The biography of Bp. Wren occupies pp. 1–134 ; the greater part is an Appendix of records. Cf. No. 2579.

766. Historical collections of the noble families of Cavendish, Holles, Vere, Harley, and Ogle. By A. Collins. 1 vol. fol. Lond. 1752.

767. Memoirs of several ladies of Great Britain who have been celebrated for their writings or skill in the learned languages, arts and sciences. By G. Ballard. 1 vol. 4to. Oxf. 1752. Later ed. 1 vol. 8vo. Lond. 1775.

768. A history of three of the judges of Charles I, Major-General Whalley, Major-General Goffe, and Colonel Dixwell. By E. Stiles. 1 vol. 12mo. Hartford. (Conn.) 1794.

769. The lives of the English regicides. By M. Noble. 2 vols. 8vo. Birmingham. 1798.

770. Brief lives, chiefly of contemporaries, set down by John Aubrey, between the years 1669 and 1696. By J. Aubrey. 2 vols. 8vo. Lond. 1813. Later ed. 2 vols. 8vo. Oxf. 1890. Port. Ed. by A. Clark.

Cf. Eng. Hist. Rev. xi. 1896, for a note by Mr. Clark on Aubrey's Biographical collections. The ed. of 1813 is entitled : Letters written by eminent persons . . . and lives of eminent men. The letters are pr. from Ballard and other MSS. in the Bodleian.

771. Memoirs of the Protector, Oliver Cromwell, and of his sons, Richard and Henry. Illustrated by original letters and other family papers. By Oliver Cromwell. 1 vol. 4to. Lond. 1820. Ports.

772. Portraits of illustrious personages of Great Britain. By E. Lodge. 12 vols. fol. Lond. 1823–34. 240 ports. Later ed. 12 vols. 8vo. Lond. 1835. Ports.

773. Collection des Mémoires relatifs a la Révolution d'Angleterre. Ed. by F. P. G. Guirot. 25 vols. 8vo. Paris. 1827.

The prefaces were publ. separately as Portraits politiques des hommes des différents partis [1851 and 1874] and trans. by A. R. Scoble as Monk's contemporaries [1851].

774. Lives of the queens of England. By A. Strickland. 12 vols. 8vo. Lond. 1840–8. Later eds. 6 vols. 8vo. Lond. 1864–5. 16 vols. 8vo. Philadelphia. 1907. Ed. by J. F. Kirk.

Useful but uncritical.

775. The lives of the princesses of England, from the Norman Conquest [to Charles I]. By M. A. E. Green. 6 vols. 8vo. Lond. 1849–55.

Useful, though the lives vary in value.

776. Lives of the friends and contemporaries of Lord Chancellor Clarendon: illustrative of portraits in his gallery. By Lady Theresa Lewis. 3 vols. 8vo. Lond. 1852.

777. The Howard papers with a biographical pedigree and criticism. By H. Kent Staple Causton. 1 vol. 8vo. Lond. *c.* 1862.

Includes a lengthy sketch of the chief members of the Howard family.

778. Court and society from Elizabeth to Anne. Edited from the papers at Kimbolton. By the Duke of Manchester. 2 vols. 8vo. Lond. 1864. Ports.

Virtually a history of the various branches of the Montagu family. Prints letters to and from Manchester at Paris and then at Venice *c.* 1697–1708. Cf. Hist. MSS. Comm. Report viii.

779. The great governing families of England. By J. L. Sanford and M. Townsend. 2 vols. 8vo. Edin. 1865 and 1885.

780. Three English Statesmen : A course of lectures on the political history of England. By Goldwin Smith. 1 vol. 8vo. Lond. 1867. Later ed. 1 vol. sm. 4to. Lond. 1868.

Pym, Cromwell and William Pitt the Younger.

781. Althorp memoirs, or biographical notices of Lady Denham, the Countess of Shrewsbury, the Countess of Falmouth, Mrs. Jenyns, the Duchess of Tyrconnel and Lucy Walter. By G. S. Steinman. 1 vol. 8vo. s.l. 1869.

782. Yorkshire diaries and autobiographies in the seventeenth and eighteenth century. 2 vols. Surtees Soc. 1877–86.

I. contains diaries &c. of Adam Eyre, John Shaw, James Fretwell, John Hobson, and Heneage Dering ; II. of Jonathan Priestley, Sir Walter Calverley.

783. The house of Cromwell and the story of Dunkirk. A genealogical history of the descendants of the Protector, with anecdotes and letters. By J. Waylen. 1 vol. 8vo. Lond. 1880. Later ed. 1 vol. 8vo. Lond. 1897. Ed. by J. G. Cromwell.

784. History of the Wrays of Glentworth 1523–1852. By C. Dalton. 2 vols. 8vo. Lond. 1880–1. Ports.

785. Complete peerage of England, Scotland, Ireland, Great Britain and the United Kingdom. Ed. by G. E. Cokayne. 8 vols. 8vo. Exeter. 1887–98.

New ed. in progress. Other useful peerages are by : Sir William Dugdale [3 vols. fol. Lond. 1675–6] ; Arthur Collins [best ed. by Sir S. E. Brydges, 1812], and J. E. Doyle, 1886, who omits the barons.

786. The lives of the Right Hon. Francis North, Baron Guilford, the Hon. Sir Dudley North ; and the Hon. and Rev. Dr. John North. By the Hon. R. North, together with the Autobiography of the author. Ed. by A. Jessopp. 3 vols. 8vo. Lond. 1890.

Guilford's Life separately pr. in 1742, 4to. ; Sir D. North's and J. North's Lives in 1744, 4to. These three lives were pr. together, ed. H. Roscoe, 1826. 3 vols. 8vo. The Autobiography was privately pr. in 1887, 4to. ed. Dr. Jessopp. Both Guilford's Life and R. North's Autobiography are of great value for the history of law and politics during the latter part of Charles II's reign : Sir D. North's Life is important for the history of trade. The MSS. of the Lives, together with various drafts, are in Brit. Mus. Add. MSS. 32506–17.

787. Notes on the history of the family of Rumbold in the seventeenth century. Trans. Royal Hist. Socy. N.S.W. 1892. By Sir H. Rumbold.

Mainly about Henry Rumbold.

788. Memoirs of the Verney family from the letters . . . at Claydon House. Vols. 1 and 2 by Frances Parthenope, Lady Verney, vols. 3 and 4 by Margaret Maria, Lady Verney. 4 vols. 8vo. Lond. 1892–9. Illus.

A valuable history of a county family during the 17th century. There is a Report on the MSS. in Part I of the Seventh Report of the Historical MSS. Commission—Some of the papers were printed in vols. 31 and 56 of the first Camd. Ser., edited by J. Bruce.

789. Lives of twelve bad men. Ed. by T. Seccombe. 1 vol. 8vo. Lond. 1894.

Includes, Matthew Hopkins, George Jeffreys, Titus Oates, Simon Fraser, Lord Lovat, Colonel Francis Charteris.

790. The Whartons of Wharton Hall. By E. R. Wharton. 1 vol. 8vo. Oxf. 1898.

Slight. Cf. Memoirs of the life of . . . Thomas, late Marquess of Wharton . . . to which is added his . . . character by Sir Richard Steel [8vo. Lond. 1715].

791. Complete baronetage. By G. E. Cokayne. 6 vols. 8vo. Exeter. 1900–9.

Arranged alphabetically, 1611–1800, with index vol.

792. History of Burley-on-the-Hill, Rutland, with a short account of the owners and extracts from their correspondence and catalogue of the contents of the house. By P. Finch. 2 vols. 4to. Lond. 1901.

Has some excellent illustrations and useful documents. Vol. ii is the catalogue referred to above.

793. The history of the house of Percy from the earliest times to the present century. By G. Brenan. Ed. by W. A. Lindsay. 2 vols. 8vo. Lond. 1902.

794. Rochester, and other literary rakes of the court of Charles II, with some account of their surroundings, by the author of ' The life of Sir Kenelm Digby ' [T. Longueville]. 1 vol. 8vo. Lond. 1902. Ports. Later ed. 1 vol. 8vo. Lond. 1903.

795. Five Stuart Princesses. Margaret of Scotland, Elizabeth of Bohemia, Mary of Orange, Henrietta of Orleans, Sophia of Hanover. Ed. by R. S. Rait. 1 vol. 8vo. Lond. 1902 and 1908. Ports.

796. The knights of England. A complete record . . . of the knights of all the orders of chivalry in England, Scotland and Ireland, and of knights bachelors. By W. A. Shaw. 2 vols. 8vo. Lond. 1906.

797. Some beauties of the seventeenth century. By A. Fea. 1 vol. 8vo. Lond. 1906. Illus.

798. The house of Howard. By G. Brenan and E. P. Statham. 2 vols. 8vo. Lond. 1907. Illus.

799. North Country Diaries. Ed. by J. C. Hodgson. 2 vols. Surtees Soc. 8vo. Durham. 1910–15.

A number of short diaries, of which John Ashton's (vol. i) gives some details about the Bishops' war, 1639. The Journal of Sir Wm. Brereton [1635] is reprinted in vol. ii.

800. The Cavendish family. By F. Bickley. 1 vol. 8vo. Lond. 1911. Illus.

801. The Seymour family. By A. A. Locke. 1 vol. 8vo. Lond. 1911. Illus.

802. Markham memorials, being a new edition of the ' History of the Markham family ' by David F. Markham. By Sir C. Markham. 2 vols. 4to. Lond. 1913. Illus.

803. The history of the Evelyn family. By H. Evelyn. 1 vol. 8vo. Lond. 1915. Illus.

Includes both the Wotton and Godstone branches.

804. Royalist father and Roundhead son ; being the memoirs of the first and second earls of Denbigh, 1600–1675. By Cecilia Mary Feilding, Countess of Denbigh. 1 vol. 8vo. Lond. 1915. Illus.

805. History of the family of Maunsell (Mansell, Mansel). Compiled chiefly from data collected . . . by Colonel Charles O. Maunsell. By E. P. Statham. 2 vols. in 3, 4to. Lond. 1917–20.

806. Memoirs of the family of Guise of Elmore, Gloucestershire [and] Autobiography of Thomas Raymond. Ed. by G. Davies. Camd. Soc. 1917.

Guise memoirs pr. from transcript in the Bodl. Libr. Raymond from Bodl. Lib. Rawl. MS. D. 1150.

(b) BIOGRAPHIES, PERSONAL NARRATIVES, AND COLLECTED WORKS OF INDIVIDUALS

AILESBURY, THOMAS BRUCE, 2ND EARL OF.

807. Memoirs. Ed. by W. E. Buckley. 2 vols. Roxburghe Club. 1890.

Vivid recollections written long after the events described.

ALBEMARLE, CHRISTOPHER MONCK, DUKE OF.

808. Christopher Monck, Duke of Albemarle. By E. F. Ward. 1 vol. 8vo. Lond. 1915. Illus.

ANGLESEY, ARTHUR ANNESLEY, EARL OF.

809. Memoirs of . . . Arthur Earl of Anglesey late lord privy seal intermixt with moral political and historical observations. Ed. by Sir P. Pett. 1 vol. 8vo. Lond. 1693.

Anglesey's diary 1671–5 is in Hist. MSS. Comm. 13th Rep. pt. vi. 261–78 : a continuation to 1684 is in Brit. Mus. Add. MS. 18730.

ANNE, QUEEN.

810. Queen Anne. By H. W. Paul. 1 vol. 4to. Lond. N.Y. and Paris. 1906. Illus. Later ed. 1 vol. 8vo. Lond. 1912.

ARLINGTON, HENRY BENNET, EARL OF.

811. Henry Bennet, Earl of Arlington. By V. Barbour. Amer. Hist. Assoc. 1 vol. 8vo. Washington. 1914. Bibl.

ARUNDEL, THOMAS HOWARD, 2ND EARL OF.

812. The life, correspondence and collections of Thomas Howard, Earl of Arundel. By M. F. S. Hervey. 1 vol. 8vo. Camb. 1921.

ASHBURNHAM, JOHN.

813. A Narrative by John Ashburnham of his attendance on King Charles the First . . . to which is prefixed A Vindication of his character and conduct. 2 vols. 8vo. Lond. 1830.

Ashburnham attended Charles 1646–8 : the vindication is an answer to Clarendon's criticisms. The appendices include, Memoirs of Sir John Berkley.

ASHMOLE, ELIAS.

814. Memoirs of the life of that learned antiquary Elias Ashmole drawn up by himself by way of diary with an appendix of original letters. Ed. by C. Burman. 1 vol. 12mo. Lond. 1717.

Repr. in The lives of those eminent antiquaries Elias Ashmole and William Lilly [8vo. Lond. 1774]. The MS. together with other autobiographical matter is in Bodl. Libr. Ashmole MS. 1136. Cf. A. L. Humphreys : Elias Ashmole. Repr. from the Berks. Bucks. and Oxon Arch. Journal. 1 vol. 8vo. Reading, 1925. A good short sketch. Ashmole's, The institution, laws and ceremonies of the most noble Order of the Garter appeared in 1 vol. fol. Lond. 1672 with engravings by Hollar.

ASSHETON, NICHOLAS.

815. The Journal of Nicholas Assheton of Downham in the County of Lancaster [1617–18].   Ed. by F. R. Raines.   Chetham Soc. 1848.

The diary of a sporting gentleman.

BACON, FRANCIS, VISCOUNT ST. ALBANS.

816. [Collected Works, with his letters and life].   Ed. by J. Spedding, R. L. Ellis, D. D. Heath.   14 vols. 8vo. Lond. 1857–74.

Cf. Spedding's An account of the life and times of Francis Bacon [2 vols. Boston. 1880] and Evenings with a reviewer [a defence of Bacon against the charges of Macaulay in his Essay on Bacon.   2 vols. Lond. 1881.]

817. Bacon.   By R. W. Church.   English Men of Letters.   1 vol. 8vo. Lond. 1884.

Cf. Edwin Abbott Abbott's Bacon and Essex [1 vol. 8vo. Lond. 1877] and Francis Bacon [1 vol. 8vo. Lond. 1885].

BARNES, AMBROSE..

818. Memoirs of the life of Mr. Ambrose Barnes, late merchant and some-time alderman of Newcastle upon Tyne.   Ed. by W. H. D. Longstaffe. Surtees Soc. 1867.

Dedication by M.R. dated 1716.

BLOOD, THOMAS.

819. Colonel Thomas Blood, Crown-stealer.   By W. C. Abbott.   1 vol. 12mo. Oxf. 1911.

Repr. in his Conflicts with Oblivion [1 vol. 8vo. New Haven. Conn. 1924] which also contains essays on the serious Pepys, the fame of Cromwell, Sir John Wentworth and Col. John Scott.

BOLINGBROKE, HENRY ST. JOHN, VISCOUNT.

820. Memoirs of the life and ministerial conduct . . . of the late Lord Viscount Bolingbroke.   1 vol. 4to. Lond. 1752.

821. Bolingbroke and his times.   By W. Sichel.   2 vols. 8vo. Lond. 1901–2.

Vol. i extends to 1714.   Other lives are by : G. W. Cooke [2 vols. 8vo. Lond. 1835] ; T. Macknight [1 vol. 8vo. Lond. 1863] A. Hassall [1 vol. 8vo. Lond. 1889 and Oxf. 1915].   Bolingbroke's philosophical works were ed. by D. Mallet [5 vols. 8vo. Lond. 1754 ; 11 vols. 1786 and 8 vols. 1809].   Cf. No. 102 for his official correspondence.

BRAMSTON, SIR JOHN.

822. The Autobiography of Sir John Bramston of Skreens, in the hundred of Chelmsford.   Ed. by Lord Braybrooke.   Camd. Soc. 1845.

Notices of public affairs as well as the history of a country gentleman's family.

BRISTOL, GEORGE DIGBY, EARL OF.

823. George Digby, 2nd Earl of Bristol.   By D. Townshend.   1 vol. 8vo. Lond. 1924.

Cf. H. M. Digby's Sir Kenelm Digby and George Digby, Earl of Bristol [1 vol. 8vo. Lond. 1912].

BRISTOL, JOHN HARVEY, FIRST EARL OF.

824. The diary of John Harvey, first Earl of Bristol, with extracts from his book of expenses 1688 to 1742. 1 vol. 4to. Wells. 1894.

His letter-books and Sir T. Harvey's letters were publ. 3 vols. 4to. Wells. 1894.

BUCKINGHAM, GEORGE VILLIERS, DUKE OF.

825. George Villiers, second Duke of Buckingham, 1628–1687. By Winifred Gardner, Lady Burghclere. 1 vol. 8vo. Lond. 1903. Ports.

BUCKINGHAM, JOHN SHEFFIELD, DUKE OF.

826. [Memoirs of his grace John Duke of Buckingham]. By John Sheffield, Earl of Mulgrave, Marquis of Normandy and Duke of Buckingham.

Includes (*a*) Memoirs (mainly about service in navy against the Dutch) ; (*b*) Memoirs in the reign of Charles II (mainly about Monmouth) ; (*c*) Some Account of the Revolution. (*a*) and (*b*) are pr. in the Works of John Sheffield . . . Duke of Buckingham, (*c*) was separately pr. at the Hague, 4to. 1727, and (under title ' The Castrations ') is bound up with some copies of The Works, 2nd ed. 1729. Cf. No. 2377.

BULSTRODE, SIR RICHARD.

827. Memoirs and reflections upon the reign and government of King Charles the 1st and K. Charles the IId. By Sir R. Bulstrode. 1 vol. 8vo. Lond. 1721.

Cf. Sir C. Firth's article on Bulstrode's Memoirs in Eng. Hist. Rev. x. 1895, which shows that this work contains some genuine memoirs plus additions from Clarendon and Warwick.

CAESAR, SIR JULIUS.

828. Life of Sir Julius Caesar, a privy councillor to Kings James and Charles, the First, With memoirs of his family and descendants. By E. Lodge. 1 vol. 4to. Lond. 1827. Ports.

CATHERINE OF BRAGANZA.

829. Catherine of Braganza, infanta of Portugal and queen-consort of England. By L. C. Davidson. 1 vol. 8vo. Lond. 1908.

CHANDOS, JAMES BRYDGES, DUKE OF.

830. The princely Chandos : a memoir of James Brydges, paymaster-general to the forces abroad . . . 1705–1711, afterwards the first Duke of Chandos. By J. R. Robinson. 1 vol. 8vo. Lond. 1893. Illus.

CHARLES I.

831. The tablet, or moderation of Charles I the martyr. By J. Arnway. 1 vol. 12mo. The Hague. 1649. Later ed. 1 vol. 8vo. Lond. 1661. Ed. by W. Rider.

832. The none-such Charles his character. 1 vol. 12mo. Lond. 1651.

Published by authority and attributed to Balthazar Gerbier ; cf. The life and reign of King Charles or the pseudo-martyr discovered [1 vol. 12mo. Lond. 1651] : both are very hostile to Charles I.

833. Iter Carolinum; being a succinct relation of the necessitated marches, retreats, and sufferings of his Majesty Charles the First (Jan. 1642–9). By T. Manley. 1 vol. 1660.

States in which places Charles stayed and for how many nights. Repr. in Gutch's Collectanea Curiosa II. Somers' Tracts, ed. Scott, vol. v. and (down to Feb. 1647) from the original MS. in Hereford Library in Royalist Revelations, by H. S. Wheatly-Crowe, 8vo. Lond. 1922.

834. Charles I in 1646. Letters of King Charles the First to Queen Henrietta Maria. Ed. by J. Bruce. Camb. Soc. 1856.

835. Charles I. By Sir J. Skelton. 1 vol. la. 4to. Lond. & Paris. 1898. Illus.

836. Memoirs of the martyr king, being a detailed record of the last two years of the reign of Charles I [1646–9]. By A. Fea. 1 vol. fol. Lond. 1905. Illus.

CHARLES II.

837. ΕΙΚΩΝ ΒΑΣΙΛΙΚΗ or the true pourtraiture of his sacred majestie Charles the II . . . wherein is interwoven a compleat history of the high-born Dukes of York and Gloucester. By D. Lloyd. 1 vol. 8vo. Lond. 1660.

Cf. W. Winstanley's England's triumph. A . . . history of his majesties escape after the battle of Worcester [1 vol. 8vo. Lond. 1660].

838. Boscobel or the history of his most sacred majesty's most miraculous preservation after the battle of Worcester. By T. Blount. 2 pts. 12mo. Lond. 1660–2. Plates. Later eds. 2 pts. in 1. 12mo. Lond. 1680–1. 1 vol. 8vo. Lond. 1894. Bibl. Ed. by C. G. Thomas (subsequently Thomas-Stanford).

Repr. in The Boscobel Tracts (841) and in After Worcester Fight (843n). For bibliography see The Royal Miracle (847). This is the best contemporary account of the king's escape.

839. ΕΙΚΩΝ ΒΑΣΙΛΙΚΗ ΔΕΥΤΕΡΑ The pourtraieture of his sacred majesty King Charles II with his reasons for turning Roman Catholick, published by K. James. 1 vol. 8vo. s.l. 1694.

840. An account of the preservation of King Charles II after the battle of Worcester . . . to which are added his letters to several persons. Ed. by S. Pepys. 1 vol. 8vo. Lond. 1766. Later ed. 1 vol. 8vo. Lond. 1803. Ports. Ed. by David Dalrymple, Lord Hailes.

Charles's own account to Pepys. From Magdalene College, Cambridge. Repr. in The Boscobel Tracts (841); After Worcester Fight (843n) &c. For bibliography see the Royal Miracle (847).

841. The Boscobel tracts relating to the escape of Charles the Second after the Battle of Worcester. Ed. by J. Hughes. 1 vol. 8vo. Edin. & Lond. 1830. Illus. Later ed. 1857.

Reprints : (i) An Account of His Majesty's Escape . . . dictated to Mr. Pepys [MS. in Brit. Mus. Add. MS. 31955]. (ii) Boscobel Parts I and II by Thomas Blount. (iii) Claustrum Regale Reseratum ; or, King Charles the Second's concealment at Trent by Mrs. Anne Wyndham [1667]. There are also extracts from contemporary authorities.

842. Charles the Second in the Channel Islands. By S. E. Hoskins. 2 vols. 8vo. Lond. 1854.

Based on Chevalier's Journal, on which see Hist. MSS. Comm. Rep. II. pp. 158–64.

843. The flight of the king : being a full . . . account of the miraculous escape of King Charles II after the battle of Worcester. By A. Fea. 1 vol. 8vo. Lond. 1897. Illus. Later ed. 1908.

Repr. A true narrative and relation of his majesty's miraculous escape [1660] ; A summary of occurrences relating to the miraculous preservation of . . . King Charles II [1688], Captain Alford's narrative ; the last act in . . . his Majesties escape, by Colonel George Gounter, the last two items being pr. in Cary's Memorials (1159). The same author's After Worcester Fight [1 vol. 8vo. Lond. 1905. Illus.] repr. the narratives in the Boscobel Tracts (841).

844. Charles II. By O. Airy. 1 vol. 4to. Lond. 1901. Illus. Later ed. 1 vol. 8vo. Lond. 1904.

845. Charles II and his court. By A. C. A. Brett. 1 vol. 8vo. Lond. 1910. Ports.

846. The king in exile. The wanderings of Charles II from June 1646 to July 1654. By E. Scott. 1 vol. 8vo. Lond. 1905. Ports.

Cf. the same author's The travels of King Charles II in Germany and Flanders 1654–1660 [1 vol. 8vo. Lond. 1907. Ports.].

847. The royal miracle. A collection of rare tracts, broadsides, letters, prints and ballads concerning the wanderings of Charles II after the battle of Worcester with . . . bibliography and illustrations. Ed. by A. M. Broadley. 1 vol. 4to. Lond. 1912.

Valuable. Repr. many scarce items.

848. A bibliography of the literature relating to the escape and preservation of King Charles II after the battle of Worcester 3rd September 1651. Ed. by W. A. Horrox. 1 vol. 4to. Aberdeen. 1924.

CHESTERFIELD, PHILIP STANHOPE, SECOND EARL OF.

849. Letters of Philip, second Earl of Chesterfield . . . with some of their replies. 1 vol. 8vo. Lond. 1837.

Interesting private letters, mainly 1656–89.

CHETHAM, HUMPHREY.

850. Life of Humphrey Chetham. Founder of the Chetham Hospital and Library, Manchester. By F. R. Raines and C. W. Sutton. 2 vols. Chetham Soc. 1903. Illus. Bibl.

CLARENDON, EDWARD HYDE, EARL OF.

851. Life and administration of Edward, first Earl of Clarendon. By T. H. Lister. 3 vols. 8vo. Lond. 1838.

Third vol. comprises correspondence from Clarendon MSS. Bodl. Libr., most of it 1660–7. Still the best life.

852. The life of Edward, earl of Clarendon. By Sir H. Craik. 2 vols. 8vo. Lond. 1911. Ports.

Cf. Edward Hyde, Earl of Clarendon. A lecture by C. H. Firth. 1 vol. 8vo. Oxf. 1909.

CLEVELAND, BARBARA, DUCHESS OF.

853. A memoir of Barbara, Duchess of Cleveland. By G. S. Steinman. 1 vol. 8vo. Oxf. 1871.

Addenda, 1874 and 1878.

CLIFFORD, LADY ANNE.

854. The diary of the Lady Anne Clifford [1590–1676]. Ed. by V. Sackville-West. 1 vol. sm. 4to. Lond. 1923. Ports.

Diary extends from 1603–19.

COAD, JOHN.

855. A memorandum of the wonderful Providences of God. By J. Coad. 1 vol. 12mo. Lond. 1849.

A narrative of one of Monmouth's supporters transported to Jamaica. A similar narrative by H. Pitman in Stuart Tracts (165).

COKE, ROGER.

856. Detection of the court and state of England during the last four reigns. By R. Coke. 2 vols. 8vo. Lond. 1694. Later ed. 3 vols. 8vo. Lond. 1719.

Has some family memoirs and remarks on trade : otherwise unreliable gossip. Ed. of 1719 has a continuation to 1714.

COLSTON, EDWARD.

857. Edward Colston, the philanthropist, his life and times. By T. Garrard. 1 vol. 8vo. Bristol. 1852.

CORNWALLIS, JANE, LADY.

858. The private correspondence of Jane, Lady Cornwallis ; 1613–1644. From the originals in the possession of the family. 1 vol. 8vo. Lond. 1842.

Contains some interesting anecdotes and occasional notices of public affairs.

COURTHOP, SIR GEORGE.

859. The memoirs of Sir George Courthop [1616–85]. By Sir G. Courthop. Camd. Soc. Misc. xi. 1907.

Edited from an 18th-century transcript in G. J. Courthope's possession.

CROMWELL, OLIVER.

860. The perfect politician, or a full view of the life and actions, military and civil, of O. Cromwell. By [H. Fletcher]. 1 vol. 8vo. Lond. ? 1660.

' The only early life of any value.' Dict. Nat. Biog.

861. Flagellum or the life . . . of O. Cromwel. By J. Heath. 1 vol. 8vo. Lond. 1663. Later ed. 1679.

The extreme Royalist view.

862. The life of Oliver Cromwell . . . Impartially collected from the best historians and several original manuscripts. By [I. Kimber]. 1 vol. 8vo. [? Lond.] 1724 and 1778.

863. A short critical review of the political life of Oliver Cromwell. By J. Banks. 1 vol. 8vo. Lond. 1739.

864. Oliver Cromwell's letters and speeches, with elucidations. By T. Carlyle. 2 vols. 8vo. Lond. 1845. Later ed. 3 vols. 8vo. Lond. 1904. Ed. by S. C. Lomas.

Ed. of 1904 has an introduction by C. H. Firth on Carlyle as an editor, and on the 'Squire Papers'. On the latter cf. notes by W. A. Wright, S. R. Gardiner and W. Rye in Eng. Hist. Rev. i, and Sir C. Firth's The early history of the Ironsides. Cf. No. 1169.

865. Numismata Cromwelliana; or, the medallic history of Oliver Cromwell illustrated by his coins, medals and seals. By H. W. Henfrey. 1 vol. 4to. Lond. 1873-7.

866. Oliver Cromwell und die puritanische Revolution. By M. Brosch. 1 vol. 8vo. Frankfort on Main. 1886.

867. The two Protectors: Oliver and Richard Cromwell. By Sir R. Tangye. 1 vol. 8vo. Lond. 1899. Illus.

868. Oliver Cromwell. By S. R. Gardiner. 1 vol. 4to. Lond. 1899. Illus. Later ed. 1 vol. 8vo. Lond. 1901.

Cf. the same author's Cromwell's place in history [1 vol. 8vo. Lond. 1897].

869. Oliver Cromwell. By John, Viscount Morley. 1 vol. 8vo. Lond. & N.Y. 1900. Illus.

870. Oliver Cromwell and the rule of the Puritans in England. By Sir C. H. Firth. Heroes of the Nations. 1 vol. 8vo. N.Y. 1901 and 1923. Illus.

The best life.

871. Speeches of Oliver Cromwell, 1644-1658. Ed. by C. L. Stainer. 1 vol. 8vo. Lond. 1901.

872. Cromwell. By W. Michael. 2 vols. 8vo. Berlin. 1907. Ports.

Valuable for Cromwell's foreign policy. Other lives are by: J. A. Picton [1 vol. 8vo. Lond. 1882]; F. Harrison [1 vol. 8vo. Lond. 1888]; Sir R. F. D. Palgrave [1 vol. 8vo] Lond. 1890. He also wrote Oliver Cromwell . . . and the royalist insurrection . . . March 1655 [1 vol. 8vo. Lond. 1903]; S. H. Church [1 vol. 8vo. N.Y. and Lond. 1894]; T. Roosevelt [1 vol. 8vo. N.Y. and Westminster. 1900.]

CROMWELL, RICHARD.

873. Correspondence of Richard Cromwell. [c. 1675-1708.] Ed. by A. S. Burn. Eng. Hist. Rev. xiii. 1898.

DE LA PRYME, ABRAHAM.

874. The diary of Abraham de la Pryme, the Yorkshire antiquary. Ed. by C. Jackson. Surtees Soc. 1870.

DERBY, JAMES STANLEY, EARL OF.

875. Private devotions and miscellanies of James, seventh Earl of Derby, with a prefatory memoir and an appendix of documents. Ed. by F. R. Raines. Chetham Soc. 3 vols. 1867.

The introduction is a full biography.

DERBY, CHARLOTTE, COUNTESS OF.

876. Charlotte de La Trémoille, Comtesse de Derby (1599–1664). By L. Marlet. 1 vol. 8vo. Paris. 1895.

An earlier life by H. de Witt called The Lady of Lathom appeared in 1869.

D'EWES, SIR SIMONDS.

877. The autobiography [to 1636] and correspondence [to 1649] of Sir Simonds D'Ewes during the reigns of James I and Charles I. By Sir S. D'Ewes. Ed. by J. O. Halliwell. 2 vols. 8vo. Lond. 1845.

The autobiography of a puritan antiquary. Valuable. Contains also The Secret history of the reign of King James I (Harl. MS.), and An account of the journey of the Prince's servants into Spain, A.D. 1623, by Sir R. Wynne.

DIGBY, SIR KENELM.

878. Private memoirs of Sir Kenelm Digby, gentleman of the bedchamber to King Charles the First. Written by himself. Now first published . . . Ed. by Sir N. H. Nicholas. 1 vol. 8vo. Lond. 1827. Port.

Mainly a defence of Venetia Stanley in a fictitious form. MS. in Brit. Mus. Harl. MS. 6758.

879. The life of Sir Kenelm Digby. By T. Longueville. 1 vol. 8vo. Lond. & N.Y. 1896.

DOWNING, SIR GEORGE.

880. The godfather of Downing Street. Sir G. Downing, 1623–1684. By J. Beresford. 1 vol. 8vo. Lond. 1925. Illus.

Cf. Downing and the regicides. By R. C. H. Catterall. Amer. Hist. Rev. vol. xvii.

DUGDALE, SIR WILLIAM.

881. The life, diary [1643–86] and correspondence [1635–86] of Sir William Dugdale. Ed. by W. Hamper. 1 vol. 4to. Lond. 1827.

DUNTON, JOHN.

882. The life and errors of John Dunton . . . written by himself in solitude . . . with the lives and characters of more than a thousand contemporary divines, and other persons of literary eminence. By J. Dunton. 1 vol. 8vo. Lond. 1705. Later ed. 2 vols. 8vo. Lond. 1818. Ed. by J. B. Nichols.

ELIOT, SIR JOHN.

883. Sir John Eliot : a Biography. By J. Forster. 2 vols. 8vo. Lond. 1864. Ports.

Makes use of MSS. at Port Eliot. Valuable though uncritical. Comments are in various notes in Gardiner's History of England. Eliot's An Apology for Socrates [i.e. a vindication of himself] and Negotium posterorum [an account of the parliamentary opposition and his own share in it] were ed. by A. B. Grosart [2 vols. 4to. s.l. 1881].

ELIZABETH, PRINCESS PALATINE.

884. Elizabeth, Princess Palatine [1618–80]. By Sir A. W. Ward, in Owens College Historical Essays. Ed. T. F. Tout and J. Tait. 1 vol. 8vo. Lond. 1902.

ELIZABETH, ELECTRESS PALATINE.

885. Elizabeth Electress Palatine and Queen of Bohemia. By M. A. E. Green. Ed. by S. C. Lomas. 1 vol. 8vo. Lond. 1909.

A thorough revision of one of the series of Lives of the Princesses of England.

EVELYN, JOHN.

886. Memoirs illustrative of the life and writings of John Evelyn, comprising his Diary from the year 1641 to 1705–6, and a selection from his familiar letters [1642–1704]. By J. Evelyn. Ed. by W. Bray. 2 vols. 8vo. Lond. 1818. Later ed. 4 vols. 8vo. Lond. 1879. Ports. Ed. by H. B. Wheatley. 3 vols. 8vo. Lond. 1906. Ports. Plans. Ed. by A. Dobson.

Most eds. of the diary contain correspondence of Charles I and Charles II with Sir E. Nicholas [1641–55], letters between Hyde and Sir R. Browne [1646–59], and other correspondence of Browne [1640–51].

887. The miscellaneous writings of John Evelyn. Ed. by W. Upcott. 1 vol. 4to. Lond. 1825.

FALKLAND, LETTICE VISCOUNTESS.

888. The holy life and death of the Lady Letice Vi-Countess Falkland. By J. Duncon. 1 vol. 12mo. Lond. 1648. Later eds. 1653 and 1 vol. 8vo. Lond. 1908.

Duncon was Lady Falkland's chaplain.

FALKLAND, LUCIUS CARY, VISCOUNT.

889. The life and times of Lucius Cary Viscount Falkland. By Sir J. A. R. Marriott. 1 vol. 8vo. Lond. 1907. Illus. Bibl. Later ed. 1908.

FANSHAWE, ANN, LADY.

890. Memoirs of Lady Fanshawe, wife of . . . Sir Richard Fanshawe, ambassador . . . to the Court of Madrid in 1665. To which are added Extracts from the correspondence of Sir Richard Fanshawe. Ed. by C. R. Fanshawe. 1 vol. 8vo. Lond. 1829. Later ed. 1907. Ed. by H. C. Fanshawe.

The ed. of 1907 has new notes as well as a better text.

FERGUSON, ROBERT.

891. Robert Ferguson the Plotter. By J. Ferguson. 1 vol. 8vo. Edin. 1887.

Important for Rye House Plot and Jacobite intrigues temp. William and Mary.

FOX, SIR STEPHEN.

892. Memoirs of the life of Sir Stephen Fox. 1 vol. 8vo. Lond. 1717.

FULLER, WILLIAM.

893. The whole life of Mr. William Fuller . . . together with a true discovery of the intrigues for which he lies now confin'd. By W. Fuller. 1 vol. 8vo. Lond. 1703.

A perjurer's autobiography. Includes A brief discovery of the true mother of the pretended Prince of Wales, and A further confirmation that Mary Grey was the true mother of the pretended Prince of Wales (both by Fuller). Cf. The life of William Fuller, 2 pts. 1 vol. 8vo. Lond. 1701.

FYTTON, ANNE AND MARY.

894. Gossip from a muniment room [at Arbury]. Being passages in the lives of Anne and Mary Fytton, 1574 to 1618. Ed. by Lady Newdigate-Newdegate. 1 vol. 4to. Lond. 1897. Illus.

GODOLPHIN, MRS.

895. The life of Mrs. Godolphin. By J. Evelyn. Ed. by S. Wilberforce, Lord Bishop of Oxford. 1 vol. 8vo. Lond. 1847. Later ed. 1 vol. 12mo. Lond. 1904. Ed. by Sir I. Gollancz.

The character-sketch of a maid of honour untainted by the vices of Charles II's court.

GODOLPHIN, SIDNEY, EARL.

896. The life of Sidney, Earl Godolphin, lord high treasurer of England, 1702–1710. By H. F. H. Elliot. 1 vol. 8vo. Lond. 1888.

GRAFTON, HENRY, DUKE OF.

897. Henry Duke of Grafton 1663–1690. By Sir A. Fitzroy. 1 vol. 8vo. Lond. 1921. Ports.

GRAMMONT, COUNT DE.

898. Memoirs of the life of Count de Grammont : containing in particular the amorous intrigues of the Court of England in the reign of King Charles II. By A. Hamilton. Translated by A. Boyer. 1 vol. 8vo. Lond. 1714. Later eds. 2 vols. 8vo. Lond. 1811. Ed. by Sir W. Scott. 2 vols. 8vo. Lond. 1903. Ed. by G. Goodwin.

This work appeared originally in French, 1713.

GWYN, NELL.

899. The story of Nell Gwyn and the sayings of Charles II. By P. Cunningham. 1 vol. 8vo. Lond. 1852. Later eds. 1892. Ed. by H. B. Wheatley, and 1 vol. 12mo. Lond. 1903. Illus. Ed. by G. Goodwin.

First appeared in the Gentleman's Magazine for 1851.

HALIFAX, SIR GEORGE SAVILE, FIRST MARQUIS OF.

900. The life and letters of Sir George Savile, Bart., first Marquis of Halifax. With a new edition of his works. By H. C. Foxcroft. 2 vols. 8vo. Lond. 1898. Ports.

One of the best biographies of the period. Vol. ii contains a bibliography, as well as a reprint of his works, and his notes of conversations with William III. The works of Halifax were separately ed. by Sir W. Raleigh [1 vol. 8vo. Oxf. 1912].

HALIFAX, CHARLES, EARL OF.

901. The works and life of . . . Charles late Earl of Halifax. 1 vol. 8vo. Lond. 1715.

HALKETT, ANNE LADY.

902. The autobiography of Anne, Lady Halkett. Ed. by J. G. Nichols. Camd. Soc. 1875.

Important for the duke of York's escape and for royalist activities in Scotland, 1649–54. There is an interesting article on Lady Halkett in Blackwood's Magazine, Nov. 1924.

HAMPDEN, JOHN.

903. Some memorials of John Hampden, his party and his times. By George Nugent Grenville, Lord Nugent. 2 vols. 8vo. Lond. 1832. Ports. Later ed. 1 vol. 8vo. Lond. 1854.

Macaulay's review is repr. in his Essays.

HARLEY, LADY BRILLIANA.

904. Letters of the Lady Brilliana Harley, wife of Sir Robert Harley. Ed. by T. T. Lewis. Camd. Soc. 1854.

Covers 1625–43. Most interesting letters of a presbyterian, mainly written to her son at Oxford. Other letters and narratives of the sieges of Brampton Castle, 1643–4, are in Bath MSS. i. (171).

HENRIETTA, DUCHESS OF ORLEANS.

905. Madame. A life of Henrietta, daughter of Charles I and Duchess of Orleans. By J. Cartwright [Mrs. Henry Ady]. 1 vol. 8vo. Lond. 1894. Ports. Later ed. 1903.

Contains letters of Charles II to his sister from Les Arch. des Aff. étrangères. Cf. Henriette-Anne d'Angleterre, duchesse d'Orléans, sa vie et sa correspondance avec son frère Charles II, by Comte de Baillon [1 vol. 8vo. Paris. 1886].

HENRIETTA MARIA.

906. Letters of Queen Henrietta Maria including her private correspondence with Charles the First. Ed. by M. A. E. Green. 1 vol. 8vo. Lond. 1857.

907. Henriette-Marie de France Reine D'Angleterre. Étude Historique... suivi de ses lettres inédites. By Charles, Comte de Baillon. 1 vol. 8vo. Paris. 1877.

The letters include many from MSS. in the Arch. des Aff. étr. and other archives. Other lives are by I. A. Taylor [2 vols. 8vo. Lond. 1905. Illus.] and H. Haynes [1 vol. 8vo. Lond. 1912. Illus.].

908. Lettres de Henriette-Marie de France reine d'Angleterre à sa soeur Christine Duchesse de Savoie. Ed. by H. Ferrero. 1 vol. 8vo. Turin, Rome. 1881.

Cover 1628–66.

909. Memoir by Madame de Motteville on the life of Henrietta Maria. Ed. by M. G. Hanotaux. Camd. Soc. Misc. viii. 1883.

HENRY, PRINCE OF WALES.

910. The life of Henry Prince of Wales, eldest son of King James I. By T. Birch. 1 vol. 8vo. Lond. 1760.

HERBERT, EDWARD, LORD HERBERT OF CHERBURY.

911. The life of Edward Lord Herbert of Cherbury written by himself. Ed. by H. Walpole. 1 vol. 4to. Strawberry Hill Press. 1764. Later eds. 1 vol. 8vo. Lond. 1824. Ed. by Sir W. Scott. 1 vol. 8vo. Lond. 1886. Ed. by Sir S. Lee. 1 vol. 8vo. Lond. & N.Y. 1907. Ed. by Sir S. Lee.

Extends to 1624.

HERBERT, SIR THOMAS.

912. Memoirs of the two last years of the reign of . . . King Charles I. By Sir T. Herbert. 1 vol. 8vo. Lond. 1702. Later ed. 1813. Ed. by W. Nicoll.

Includes also narratives by Col. Edward Cooke, Major Huntingdon, and Henry Firebrace. Herbert's narrative was first published in 1678 with the title ' Threnodia Carolina '.

HINTON, SIR JOHN.

913. Memoires by Sir John Hinton physitian in ordinary to his majesties person. 1 vol. 8vo. s.l. 1679.

Slight : mainly personal adventures during 1642–60. Cf. Munk (2739) ed. 1861, i. 309–16.

HOLLES, DENZIL, LORD.

914. Memoirs of Denzil, Lord Holles (1641–8). By Denzil, Lord Holles. 1 vol. 8vo. Lond. 1699.

Mainly an attack on the conduct of Cromwell and the army in 1647. Repr. in Maseres' Select Tracts. Cf. W. L. Grant, A Puritan at the court of Louis XIV, in Bulletin of the Department of History . . . Queen's University, Kingston, Ontario. July 1913. A pamphlet on the embassy of Holles at Paris, 1663–6.

HOPKINS, EDWARD.

915. Memoirs of . . . Edward Hopkins, M.P. for Coventry. Ed. by M. D. Harris. Eng. Hist. Rev. xxxiv. 1919.

Mainly William III to Anne.

ISHAM, SIR JUSTINIAN.

916. The diaries (home and foreign) of Sir Justinian Isham, 1704–1735. By Sir J. Isham. Ed. by H. I. Longden. Trans. Royal Hist. Soc. 3rd series I. 1907.

JAMES THE FIRST.

917. An historical and critical account of the life and writings of James the First, King of Great Britain. After the manner of Mr. Bayle. By W. Harris. 1 vol. 8vo. Lond. 1753.

Harris wrote similar lives of Charles I [1758], Oliver Cromwell [1762], and Charles II [2 vols. 1766]. Their sole value lies in the copious references and quotations in the footnotes. A new ed. of these lives, 5 vols. 8vo. Lond. 1814.

JAMES THE SECOND.

918. The life of James the Second. By [? D. Jones]. 1 vol. 4to. Lond. s.a. [c. 1702].

Has a few documents : otherwise valueless.

919. Life of James II . . . collected out of memoirs writ of his own hand . . . Published from the original Stuart MSS. in Carlton House. Ed. by J. S. Clarke. 2 vols. 4to. Lond. 1816.

For a critical examination of the value of the Life see Ranke, History of England, (translation, Oxford, 1875) vi. 29. James's Papers of Devotion were ed. by G. Davies for the Roxburghe Club, 1925.

920. The adventures of King James II of England. By T. Longueville.
1 vol. 8vo. Lond. 1904. Illus.

Cf. James II and his wives, by A. Fea [1 vol. 8vo. Lond. 1908. Illus.].

LEEDS, THOMAS OSBORNE, EARL OF DANBY, DUKE OF.

921. Thomas Osborne, Earl of Danby and Duke of Leeds. By A. Browning.
Stanhope Prize Essay, Oxf. 1 vol. 8vo. Oxf. 1913.

App. III has notes on authorities, MSS. as well as pr.

LILLY, WILLIAM.

922. History of his life and times. By W. Lilly. 1 vol. 8vo. Lond. 1715.
Later ed. 1 vol. 8vo. Lond. 1822. Ports.

Curious autobiography of an astrologer.

LISTER, JOSEPH.

923. Autobiography of Joseph Lister of Bradford in Yorkshire to which is
added a contemporary account of the defence of Bradford and capture of Leeds
by the parliamentarians in 1642. Ed. by T. Wright. 1 vol. 8vo. Lond. 1842.

LONSDALE, JOHN LOWTHER, VISCOUNT.

924. Memoir of the reign of James II. By John Lowther, Viscount Lonsdale. 1 vol. 4to. York. 1808.

A continuation in Eng. Hist. Rev. xxx. 1915. ed. Sir C. H. Firth, from Brit. Mus. Add.
MS. 34516.

LUDLOW, EDMUND.

925. Memoirs of Edmund Ludlow. 3 vols. 8vo. Vivay in Bern. 1698–9.
Later ed. 2 vols. 8vo. Oxf. 1894. Ed. by Sir C. H. Firth.

The autobiography of a republican. Ed. of 1894 has many documents and elaborate
notes.

MARLBOROUGH, SARAH, DUCHESS OF.

926. An account of the conduct of the Dowager Duchess of Marlborough,
From her first coming to court, to the year 1710. 1 vol. 8vo. Lond. 1742.

The duchess's defence : includes many letters between Anne and herself. Although
written in the first person it is generally attributed to Nathaniel Hooke. Answered by
James Ralph in The other side of the question : or an attempt to rescue the characters
of Q. Mary and Q. Anne [1 vol. 8vo. Lond. 1742 and 1744].

927. Private correspondence of Sarah Duchess of Marlborough illustrative
of the court and times of Queen Anne . . . and the select correspondence of
her husband. 2 vols. 8vo. Lond. 1838.

Mainly letters addressed to the duchess ; and pr. from Coxe's Transcripts of papers
at Blenheim. Cf. Mrs. A. T. Thomson's Memoirs of Sarah Duchess of Marlborough
[2 vols. 8vo. Lond. 1839] ; F. Molloy's The Queen's comrade [2 vols. 8vo. Lond. 1901.
Illus.] ; Mrs. A. Colville's Duchess Sarah [1 vol. 8vo. Lond. 1904. Illus.].

928. Letters of Sarah Duchess of Marlborough . . . published from the
original manuscripts at Madresfield Court. 1 vol. 8vo. Lond. 1875.

Written in Anne's reign, chiefly to a relative Sarah Jennings.

929. John and Sarah, Duke and Duchess of Marlborough. By S. J. Reid. 1 vol. 8vo. Lond. 1914. Illus.

A vindication, mainly, of the duchess, based on unpublished MSS. at Blenheim.

MARTEN, HENRY.

930. Henry Marten. By J. Forster.

Vol. iv of Lardner's Cabinet Cyclopaedia, 1838.

MARY II.

931. Essay on the memory of the late Queen [Mary]. By G. Burnet. 1 vol. 8vo. Lond. 1695. Later ed. 1 vol. 8vo. Edin. 1842.

Contains also letters and Burnet's sermon of 16 July 1690, whose title is ' Memorials of Mary . . .' Cf. Memoirs . . . of . . . Queen Mary, by E. Fowler. 2nd ed. 1 vol. 12mo. Lond. 1712.

932. Lettres et Mémoires de Marie Reine D'Angleterre Épouse de Guillaume III. Ed. by Mechtild, Comtesse Bentinck. 1 vol. 8vo. Hague. 1880.

Contains correspondence of James II and Mary in 1687–8, of Anne and Mary 1688 [an English version in Dalrymple's Memoirs], and letters of Mary to Electress Sophia and others 1689–93. The memoirs relate to 1688 and 1691.

933. Memoirs of Mary Queen of England [1689–93]. Ed. by R. Doebner. 1 vol. 8vo. Lond. and Leipzig. 1886.

Includes letters from Mary, James II, and William III to the Electress Sophia.

934. Maria II Stuart Gemalin van Willem den Derden. By F. J. L. Krämer. 1 vol. 8vo. Utrecht. 1890.

935. Princess and Queen of England. Life of Mary II. By M. F. Sandars. 1 vol. 8vo. Lond. 1913. Illus.

Uncritical, but contains a little new material.

936. Letters of two queens. Ed. by A. B. Bathurst. 1 vol. 8vo. Lond. 1924. Illus.

Mainly letters of Queen Mary II, *c.* 1673–88, with some of Anne.

MARY OF MODENA.

937. Queen Mary of Modena. Her life and letters. By M. Haile. 1 vol. 8vo. Lond. 1905. Ports.

Based on unpublished materials in foreign archives.

MAYNWARING, ARTHUR.

938. The life and posthumous works of Arthur Maynwaring. Ed. by J. Oldmixon. 1 vol. 8vo. Lond. 1715.

MONMOUTH, ROBERT CAREY, EARL OF.

939. Memoirs of the life of Robert Carey [to 1626] . . . written by himself. Ed. by John, Earl of Cork and Orrery. 1 vol. 8vo. Lond. 1759. Later eds. 1 vol. 8vo. Edin. 1808. Ed. by Sir W. Scott. 1 vol. 16mo. Lond. 1905. Ed. by G. H. Powell.

MONMOUTH, JAMES, DUKE OF.

940. The life, progresses and rebellion of James, Duke of Monmouth . . . with a full account of the Bloody Assize, and copious biographical notices. By G. Roberts. 2 vols. 8vo. Lond. 1844. Illus.

941. King Monmouth : being a history of the career of James Scott ' the Protestant duke '. By A. Fea. 1 vol. 8vo. Lond. 1902. Illus.

Cf. Camd. Soc. Misc. viii for letters of Monmouth after his capture in 1685 [from Rawl. MSS. Bodl. Libr.] ed. by Sir G. Duckett.

MORICE, WILLIAM.

942. William Morice and the restoration of Charles II. By M. Coate. Eng. Hist. Rev. xxxiii. 1918.

MYDDELTON, JANE.

943. Some particulars contributed towards a memoir of Mrs. Myddelton, the great beauty of the time of Charles II. By G. S. Steinman. 1 vol. 8vo. s.l. 1864.

NEWDIGATE, SIR RICHARD.

944. Cavalier and puritan in the days of the Stuarts compiled from the private papers and diary of Sir Richard Newdigate . . . with extracts from MS. news-letters addressed to him between 1675 and 1689. By Lady Newdigate-Newdegate. 1 vol. 8vo. Lond. 1901.

OSBORNE, DOROTHY.

945. Letters from Dorothy Osborne to Sir William Temple 1652–54. Ed. by E. A. Parry. 1 vol. 8vo. Lond. 1888. Later ed. 1 vol. 12mo. Lond. 1914.

Cf. Julia G. Longe's Martha, Lady Giffard. Her life and correspondence (1664–1722). A sequel to the Letters of Dorothy Osborne [1 vol. 8vo. Lond. 1911. Ports.].

OXFORD, ROBERT HARLEY, EARL OF.

946. Robert Harley, Earl of Oxford. By E. S. Roscoe. 1 vol. 8vo. Lond. 1902. Ports.

Very slight.

PEPYS, SAMUEL.

947. Memoirs of Samuel Pepys, Esq. comprising his diary from 1659 to 1669, deciphered by the Rev. John Smith from the original shorthand manuscript in the Pepysian Library, and a selection from his private correspondence. Ed. by Richard, Lord Braybrooke. 2 vols. 4to. Lond. 1825. Later eds. 6 vols. 8vo. Lond. 1875–9. Ed. by M. Bright, and 10 vols. 8vo. Lond. 1893–9. Ed. by H. B. Wheatley.

Wheatley's edition includes a full Index and a volume of Pepysiana.

948. The life, journals, and correspondence of Samuel Pepys . . . including a narrative of His voyage to Tangier. Ed. by J. Smith. 2 vols. 8vo. Lond. 1841.

Includes letters written to, as well as by, Pepys. Printed from MSS. Rawl. A. 170–95. Bodl. Libr.

949. Samuel Pepys and the world he lived in. By H. B. Wheatley. 1 vol. 8vo. Lond. 1880. Later eds. 1889 and 1907.

950. Mr. Pepys. By J. R. Tanner. 1 vol. 8vo. Lond. 1925.
Cf. the same writer's Pepys and the Popish Plot. Eng. Hist. Rev. vii. 1892. Other studies of Pepys are by E. H. Moorhouse and by P. Lubbock [each 1 vol. 8vo. Lond. 1909. Illus.].

951. Private correspondence and miscellaneous papers of Samuel Pepys, 1679–1703. Ed. by J. R. Tanner. 2 vols. 8vo. Lond. 1926. Illus.

POCOCK, EDWARD.

952. The life of Dr. Edward Pocock, the celebrated orientalist. By L. Twells.
In vol. i of 2 vols. entitled The lives of Dr. Edward Pocock, &c. [1816].

PORTER, ENDYMION.

953. Life and letters of Mr. Endymion Porter. By D. Townshend. 1 vol. 8vo. Lond. 1897. Illus.
The life of a courtier temp. Charles I.

PORTLAND, WILLIAM BENTINCK, EARL OF.

954. William Bentinck and William III (Prince of Orange). The life of Bentinck, Earl of Portland from the Welbeck correspondence. By M. E. Grew. 1 vol. 8vo. Lond. 1924. Illus.

PORTSMOUTH, LOUISE DE KÉROUALLE, DUCHESSE DE.

955. Louise De Kéroualle Duchesse De Portsmouth 1649–1734. Ed. by H. Forneron. 1 vol. 8vo. Paris. 1886.
Based on French archives but rather slight. The English trans. 1887 is untrustworthy.

PRIDEAUX, HUMPHREY.

956. Letters of Humphrey Prideaux sometime dean of Norwich to John Ellis sometime under-secretary of state. 1674–1732. Ed. by E. M. Thompson. Camd. Soc. 1875.
Pr. from Add. MS. 28929 Brit. Mus. Gives much amusing gossip, especially about Oxford 1674–85. The life of Prideaux, attributed to T. Birch, is useful. 1 vol. 8vo. Lond. 1748. For other letters of Prideaux see Pine Coffin MSS. (137).

PRIOR, MATTHEW.

957. The life of Matthew Prior. By F. Bickley. 1 vol. 8vo. Lond. 1914.

958. Matthew Prior : a study of his public career. By L. G. W. Legg. 1 vol. 8vo. Camb. 1921. Bibl.
A careful study.

PYM, JOHN.

959. John Pym. By C. E. Wade. 1 vol. 8vo. Lond. 1912.

RADCLIFFE, SIR GEORGE.

960. The life and original correspondence of Sir George Radcliffe . . . the friend of the Earl of Strafford. By T. D. Whitaker. 1 vol. 4to. Lond. 1810.
Contains letters from Radcliffe to his mother and wife as well as the letters he received from Strafford.

RALEGH, SIR WALTER.

961. The works of Sir Walter Ralegh . . . political, commercial and philosophical, together with his letters and poems. . . . To which is prefixed a new account of his life by Tho. Birch. 2 vols. 8vo. Lond. 1751. Later ed. 8 vols. 8vo. Oxf. 1829.

See T. N. Brushfield's Bibliography of Sir Walter Ralegh [2nd ed. Exeter, 1908] and Cambridge Hist. of Eng. Lit. iv. 450-2.

962. The life of Sir Walter Raleigh, together with his letters. By E. Edwards. 2 vols. 8vo. Lond. 1868.

963. Sir Walter Ralegh. By W. Stebbing. 1 vol. 8vo. Oxf. 1891. Later ed. 1 vol. 8vo. Oxf. 1899. Bibl.

Other biographies are by A. Cayley [2 vols. 1805]; L. Creighton [1877 and 1882]; Sir E. W. Gosse [1886]; H. de Sélincourt [1908].

964. Sir Walter Raleigh's History of the World. By Sir C. H. Firth. Proc. British Academy. 1 vol. 8vo. Oxf. 1919.

Raleigh's History of the World was publ. in fol. 1614.

RAWDON, MARMADUKE.

965. The life of Marmaduke Rawdon of York. Anon. Ed. by R. Davies. Camd. Soc. 1863.

Of importance for trade with the Canary islands.

RERESBY, SIR JOHN.

966. The memoirs of Sir John Reresby [1634-89]. 1 vol. 4to. Lond. 1734. Later ed. 1 vol. 8vo. Lond. 1875. Ed. by J. J. Cartwright. 1 vol. 8vo. Lond. 1904. Ed. by A. Watt. Ports.

Interesting record of a Yorkshire M.P., a moderate Tory, and friend of Halifax. MS. in Brit. Mus.

RICHMOND, FRANCES THERESA, DUCHESS OF.

967. La belle Stuart . . . court and society in the times of Frances Theresa, Duchess of Richmond. By C. H. Hartmann. 1 vol. 8vo. Lond. 1924.

ROBINSON, MATTHEW.

968. Autobiography of Matthew Robinson. Ed. by J. E. B. Mayor. 1 vol. 12mo. Camb. 1856.

Robinson was a Fellow of St. John's College, Cambridge, and Vicar of Burneston, Yorks.

ROCHESTER, JOHN WILMOT, EARL OF.

969. Some passages of the life and death of John Earl of Rochester, written by his own direction on his death-bed. By G. Burnet. 1 vol. 8vo. Lond. 1680. Later ed. 1 vol. 8vo. Lond. 1875. Port. Ed. by Lord Ronald Gower.

ROMNEY, HENRY SIDNEY, EARL OF.

970. Diary of the times of Charles the Second by Henry Sidney, including his correspondence with the Countess of Sunderland and other distinguished persons. Ed. by R. W. Blencowe. 2 vols. 8vo. Lond. 1843.

Diary covers 1679-82, correspondence 1679-81 and 1684-9. The diary is in Brit. Mus. Add. MSS. 32682 : the correspondence in 32680-1.

RUSSELL, RACHAEL WRIOTHESLEY, LADY.

971. Some account of the life of Rachael Wriothesley, Lady Russell . . . followed by a series of letters from Lady Russell to Lord Russell [1672–82] together with some miscellaneous letters to and from Lady Russell. To which are added eleven letters from Dorothy Sidney Countess of Sunderland to George Saville Marquis of Hallifax in the year 1680. By M. Berry. 1 vol. 4to. Lond. 1819.

Originals in the possession of the Duke of Devonshire. There have been many editions of Lady Russell's letters before and after 1819. The most complete edition, with new letters, is Lord John Russell's, 2 vols. 8vo. Lond. 1853. Illus.

RUSSELL, WILLIAM LORD.

972. Life of William Lord Russell. By Lord John Russell. 1 vol. 4to. Lond. 1819. 4th ed. 1 vol. 8vo. Lond. 1853.

More a history of the times than a biography.

SALISBURY, ROBERT CECIL, EARL OF.

973. A life of Robert Cecil, first Earl of Salisbury. By A. Cecil. 1 vol. 8vo. Lond. 1915.

SHAFTESBURY, ANTHONY, EARL OF.

974. The compleat statesman, demonstrated in the life, actions and politicks of that great minister of state Anthony, Earl of Shaftesbury. 1 vol. 8vo. Lond. 1683.

There is another life, Rawleigh redivivus [1 vol. 8vo. Lond. 1683] : a note on both by J. R. Tanner. Eng. Hist. Rev. i. 1886.

975. The life of Anthony Ashley Cooper, first Earl of Shaftesbury, from original documents in the possession of the family. By B. Martyn and A. Kippis. 1 vol. 4to. [? Lond.] [? 1790]. Later ed. 2 vols. 8vo. Lond. 1836. Ed. by G. Wingrove Cooke.

Inaccurate, but includes material now missing.

976. Memoirs, letters and speeches of A. A. Cooper, first Earl of Shaftesbury . . . with other papers illustrating his life. Ed. by W. D. Christie. 1 vol. 8vo. Lond. 1859.

Mostly incorporated into the Life. See Reports of the deputy-keeper of the Public Record Office, xxxiii, xxxiv, xxxix. 1871–7, for Shaftesbury's MSS.

977. A Life of Anthony Ashley Cooper, first Earl of Shaftesbury, 1621–1683. By W. D. Christie. 2 vols. 8vo. Lond. 1871. Ports.

Based mainly on Shaftesbury papers now in Public Record Office, Locke papers in possession of Earl of Lovelace, Thynne papers at Longleat, Archives of French Foreign Office, and Domestic State papers at P.R.O., Appendices of letters, speeches, &c.

SYDNEY, ALGERNON.

978. The life and times of Algernon Sydney 1622–1683. By A. C. Ewald. 2 vols. 8vo. Lond. 1873.

Other lives are : by G. W. Meadley [1 vol. 8vo. Lond. 1813]; and by G. M. I. Blackburne [1 vol. 8vo. Lond. 1885]. The works of Algernon Sidney [1 vol. 4to. Lond. 1772] contain letters as well as his philosophical works. His Letters . . . to the Honourable H. Savile 1679 were publ. 1 vol. 8vo. Lond. 1742.

SMITH, MATTHEW.

979. Memoirs of secret service. By M. Smith. 1 vol. 8vo. Lond. 1699.

Smith was employed to hunt for Jacobite conspirators. Cf. his Remarks upon the D[uke] of S[hrewsbury]'s letter to the house of lords concerning Capt. Smyth. 1700.

STRAFFORD, THOMAS WENTWORTH, EARL OF.

980. The Life of Thomas Wentworth Earl of Strafford. By E. Cooper. 2 vols. 8vo. Lond. 1874.

A few new letters : otherwise of little value. For Strafford's Private letters . . . to his third wife, see Philobiblon Soc. Misc. i. 1854, ed. R. M. Milnes, Lord Houghton. Cf. No. 84 for Strafford's Correspondence.

981. Prose life of Strafford. By R. Browning. Ed. by Sir C. H. Firth and F. J. Furnivall. 1 vol. 8vo. Lond. 1892.

Originally published under the name of J. Forster in 1836 in vol. ii of the Lives of Eminent British Statesmen in Lardner's Cabinet Cyclopaedia.

SACHEVERELL, WILLIAM.

982. The first Whig. An account of the parliamentary career of William Sacheverell. By Sir G. Sitwell. 1 vol. 8vo. Scarborough. 1894. Illus.

Cf. The same author's Letters of the Sitwells and Sacheverells [2 vols. 4to. Scarborough. 1900–1] which contains much identical with the above.

STUART, LADY ARABELLA.

983. Life and letters of Lady Arabella Stuart, including numerous original and unpublished documents. By E. Cooper. 2 vols. 8vo. Lond. 1866.

Other lives by E. T. Bradley, with a collection of her letters [1 vol. 8vo. Lond. 1889]; M. Lefuse [1 vol. 8vo. Lond. 1913. Illus.]; B. C. Hardy [1 vol. 8vo. Lond. 1913. Illus.].

SUNDERLAND, DOROTHY SIDNEY, COUNTESS OF.

984. Sacharissa; some account of Dorothy Sidney, Countess of Sunderland, her family and friends, 1617–1684. By J. Cartwright (Mrs. H. Ady). 1 vol. 8vo. Lond. 1893 and 1901.

TASWELL, WILLIAM.

985. Autobiography and anecdotes by William Taswell . . . 1651-1682. Ed. by G. P. Elliott. Camd. Soc. Misc. II. 1853.

Contains a vivid description of the fire of London, but little else.

TEMPLE, SIR WILLIAM.

986. The works of Sir William Temple, Bart., . . . to which is prefix'd some account of the Life and Writings of the Author. Ed. by J. Swift. 2 vols. fol. Lond. 1720. Port. Later eds. 4 vols. 8vo. Edin. 1754. 4 vols. 8vo. Lond. 1814.

Swift ed. Temple's letters 1700–3, essays 1705–8, the memoirs, 1709.

987. Memoirs of the life, works and correspondence of Sir William Temple, Bart. By T. P. Courtenay. 2 vols. 8vo. Lond. 1836.

THORESBY, RALPH.

988. The diary of Ralph Thoresby (1677–1724) [and] Letters of eminent men addressed to Ralph Thoresby. Ed. by J. Hunter. 4 vols. 8vo. Lond. 1830–2.

989. Ralph Thoresby the topographer; his town and times. By D. H. Atkinson. 2 vols. 8vo. Leeds. 1885.

THORNTON, ALICE.

990. The autobiography of Mrs. Alice Thornton of East Newton, co. York. Surtees Soc. 1875.

Covers 1629–69.

THURLOE, JOHN.

991. Die Politik des Protectors Oliver Cromwell in der Auffassung und Thätigkeit seines Ministers des Staats-Secretärs John Thurloe. By Sigismund Freiherr von Bischoffshausen. 1 vol. 8vo. Innsbruck. 1899.

Has appendix of documents.

TWYSDEN, SIR ROGER.

992. Sir Roger Twysden's journal. From the Roydon Hall MSS. Ed. by L. B. Larking. From Archaeologia Cantiana i–iv. 1858.

Written by Twysden to expose the persecution he endured from Parliament, 1641–8.

VANE, SIR HENRY.

993. The life of young Sir Harry Vane. By J. K. Hosmer. 1 vol. 8vo. Boston & Lond. 1888.

Other lives by J. Forster [vol. iv. of Lardner's Cabinet Cyclopaedia 1838]; W. W. Ireland [1 vol. 8vo. Lond. 1905], and J. Willcock [1 vol. 8vo. Lond. 1913. Illus.].

WALLER, SIR WILLIAM.

994. Vindication of the character and conduct of Sir William Waller. By Sir W. Waller. 1 vol. 8vo. Lond. 1793.

A vague and verbose defence of his conduct in 1647. Waller's recollections, which are scattered anecdotes, are printed at the end of The Poetry of Anna Matilda, 1788. MS. in Wadham College Library, Oxford.

WALPOLE, SIR ROBERT.

995. Memoirs of the life and administration of Sir Robert Walpole. By W. Coxe. 3 vols. 4to. Lond. 1798. Illus.

Vol. i, narrative, ii and iii, text of documents. The bulk of the correspondence before 1714 relates to 1710.

WARCUP, EDMUND.

996. The journal of Edmund Warcup 1676–84. Ed. by K. Feiling and F. R. D. Needham. Eng. Hist. Rev. xl. Apr. 1925.

WARD, JOHN.

997. Diary of the Rev. John Ward ; Vicar of Stratford-upon-Avon (1648–79). Ed. by C. Severn. 1 vol. 8vo. Lond. 1839.

Very curious extracts from common-place books, many relating to medical or surgical cases, and some to famous characters.

WARWICK, MARY RICH, COUNTESS OF.

998. Autobiography of Mary [Rich] Countess of Warwick. Ed. by T. C. Croker. 1 vol. 8vo. Lond. 1848.

Illustrates social life and religion. Lives by : C. F. Smith [1 vol. 8vo. Lond. 1901. Illus.] and M. E. Palgrave [1 vol. 8vo. Lond. 1901. Illus.].

WARWICK, SIR PHILIP.

999. Memoires of the reign of King Charles I . . . with a continuation to the happy restauration of King Charles II. By Sir P. Warwick. 1 vol. 8vo. Lond. 1702. Later ed. 1 vol. 8vo. Edin. 1813. Ed. by Sir W. Scott.

A royalist memoir, MS. in Add. MS. 34714.

WELDON, ANTHONY.

1000. To the Parliament of England and Army. The Declaration of Colonel Anthony Weldon. 1 vol. sm. 4to. s.l. 1649.

Included as a specimen of many similar complaints of unfair treatment by county committees.

WHISTON, WILLIAM.

1001. Memoirs of the life and writings of William Whiston . . . written by himself. 1 vol. 8vo. Lond. 1749.

WHITELOCKE, BULSTRODE.

1002. Memoirs, biographical and historical, of Bulstrode Whitelocke. By R. H. Whitelocke. 1 vol. 8vo. Lond. 1860.

WILBRAHAM, SIR ROGER.

1003. The journal of Sir Roger Wilbraham, solicitor-general in Ireland and master of requests, 1593–1617, together with notes in another hand . . . 1642–1649. Ed. by H. S. Scott. Camd. Soc. Misc. x. 1902.

Pr. from MS. in the possession of the Earl of Lathom.

WILLIAM III.

1004. The history of the most illustrious William, Prince of Orange. 1 vol. 8vo. s.l. 1688.

1005. The History of King William the Third. By A. Boyer. 3 vols. 8vo. Lond. 1702–3.

1006. The life and times of William the Third. By Arthur Hill Trevor, 3rd Viscount Dungannon. 2 vols. 8vo. Lond. 1835–6.

Another life by H. D. Traill, Twelve Eng. Statesmen series, 1888.

WORTHINGTON, JOHN.

1007. The diary and correspondence of Dr. John Worthington, Master of Jesus College, Cambridge, Vice-chancellor. . . . By J. Worthington. Ed. by J. Crossley and R. C. Christie. Chetham Soc. 3 vols. 1847–86.

Mainly from Harl. MS. 7045. Covers 1632–7. Correspondence includes letters from S. Hartlib and others from Baker MSS. Camb. Univ. Libr., and Add. MS. 32498 Brit. Mus. Cf. A Bibliography of the works written and edited by Dr. J. Worthington, Chetham Soc. ed. R. C. Christie, 1888.

YONGE, WALTER.

1008. Diary of Walter Yonge, Justice of the Peace and M.P. for Honiton . . . from 1604 to 1628. Ed. by G. Roberts. Camd. Soc. 1843.

Has some interesting notices of public events.

YORK, ANNE HYDE, DUCHESS OF.

1009. Anne Hyde, Duchess of York. By J. R. Henslowe. 1 vol. 8vo. Lond. c. 1915.

II. MILITARY HISTORY

1. General.
2. Discipline, Drill, Equipment, and Tactics.
3. Narratives and Histories of Campaigns.
4. Regimental Histories.
5. Biographies and Personal Narratives, (*a*) 1603–1660, (*b*) 1660–1714.
6. Civil War : (*a*) General sources, (*b*) General later Works, (*c*) Local Sources and later Works.

THERE is no military bibliography covering the period 1603–1714. The best guides are the catalogue of the War Office Library (8vo. 1906, with annual supplements); the catalogue of the Library of the Royal United Service Institution (2nd ed. 1908), and the British Museum catalogue (*sub* England, Army). Apart from Cockle (1020) there are no bibliographies for the period before 1660. After that useful bibliographies will be found in Clifford Walton (1016), Atkinson (1053), Parnell (1052), and Taylor (1145). Otherwise recourse must be made to bibliographies in general histories, to the footnotes to accounts of campaigns embedded in general histories, and to the bibliographies attached to the lives of soldiers in the Dictionary of National Biography.

Considerations of space compel the omission of all but a very few foreign works, although they often throw light upon the operations of English armies. These should be sought for in the bibliographies mentioned in the section dealing with foreign affairs.

Scottish military books are here included, but those dealing with Ireland will be found under Ireland.

¶ 1. GENERAL

1010. A short history of standing armies in England. By J. Trenchard, 1 vol. small 4to. Lond. 1698.

Repr. with other similar pieces in No. 71 n.
This pamphlet and Defoe's ' Argument showing that a standing army is inconsistent with a free government ' (1697) gave rise to a sharp controversy. See Macaulay (204) ch. xxiii.

1011. The British army : its origin, progress and equipment. By Sir S. D. Scott. 3 vols. 8vo. Lond. 1868–80.

Antiquarian. The third volume deals with 1660–89.

1012. The military forces of the crown : their administration and government. By C. M. Clode. 2 vols. 8vo. Lond. 1869.

Legal enactments and administrative orders relating to the army.

1013. English army lists and commission registers, 1661–1714. By C. Dalton. 6 vols. 8vo. Lond. 1892–1904.

These are invaluable guides to the personnel of the army. Cf. the same author's The Blenheim roll. Ed. and annotated. 1 vol. 8vo. Lond. 1907.

1014. Irish Army lists 1661–1685. By C. Dalton. 1 vol. 8vo. Lond. 1907.
Cf. his The Scots army 1661–1688, with memoirs of the commanders in chief. 1 vol.
8vo. Edin. and Lond. 1909.

1015. The standards and colours of the army from the Restoration (1661 to
1881). By S. M. Milne. 1 vol. 8vo. Leeds. 1893.

1016. History of the British standing army, 1660–1700. By C. Walton.
1 vol. large 8vo. Lond. 1894.
Very complete, with an appendix of documents.

1017. Medals and decorations of the British army and navy. By J. H.
Mayo. 2 vols. 8vo. Lond. 1897.
With extracts from general orders, royal warrants, &c., relating to their issue. Well
illustrated.

1018. A history of the British army, vol. i (to 1713). By J. W. Fortescue.
8vo. Lond. 1899. Plans. 2nd ed. 1910.
Deals with the formation, administration and operations of the army.

1019. List of war office records preserved in the Public Record Office.
Vol. i, Lists and Indexes. xxviii. 1908.

¶ 2. DISCIPLINE, DRILL, EQUIPMENT, AND TACTICS

There is no comprehensive work on these subjects. Lloyd (1034) has a
valuable sketch of the general development of infantry tactics in Europe.
The most useful works are for the period 1603–42 Cockle (1020); for 1642–60,
Elton (1025) and Firth (1170); for 1660–1702, The Official Abridgement
(1030) and Clifford Walton (1016); and for 1702–13, Bland (1031) and
Fortescue (1018).

1020. A bibliography of English military books up to 1642, and of contemporary foreign works. By M. J. D. Cockle. 1 vol. 4to. Lond. 1900. Illus.
A model bibliography. It contains books on the art of war, but only a few historical
works.

1021. The gunner, showing the whole practice of artillerie, with all the
appurtenances thereunto belonging. By R. Norton. 1 vol. fol. Lond. 1628.
Plates.

1022. Military discipline, or the young artillery-man, wherein is discoursed
and showne the postures both of musket and pike. By W. Bariffe. 1 vol. 4to.
Lond. 1635. 3rd ed. 1643. 6th ed. 1661.
The 3rd ed. is revised and enlarged.

1023. The principles of the art militarie, practised in the warres of the
United Netherlands . . . represented by figure. By H. Hexham. 1 vol. fol.
Lond. 1637. 2nd ed. 1 vol. fol. Delft. 1642.

1024. Anima' adversions of warre, or a militarie magazine of the truest rules and ablest instructions for the managing of warre. By R. Ward. 1 vol. fol. Lond. 1639. Illus.

Based on wars in the Netherlands and Germany. Important.

1025. The compleat body of the art military illustrated with a varietie of figures. By R. Elton. 1 vol. fol. Lond. 1650. 2nd ed. 1659. 3rd ed. 1668.

Mainly concerned with infantry drill. The author served in the Parliamentary forces. 3rd ed. has a supplement by T. Rudd, chief engineer to Charles I.

1026. Observations upon military and political affairs. By George Monck (Duke of Albemarle). Ed. by J. Heath. 1 vol. fol. Lond. 1761 (with plates). 2nd ed. 1 vol. 8vo. Lond. 1796 (with plates).

1027. Military and maritime discipline . . . Book I. Military observations or tacticks put into practice for the exercise of horse and foot [by T. Venn]. Book II. An exact method of military architecture rendred into English out of the works of . . . Andrew Tacquet . . . Book III. The compleat gunner, translated out of Casimir, Diego, Uffano, and Hexam. 1 vol. fol. Lond. 1672.

1028. Treatise of the art of war. By Roger Boyle, Earl of Orrery. 1 vol. fol. Lond. 1677. Diagrams.

Gives some personal experiences in Ireland.

1029. Pallas armata : military essays of the ancient Grecian, Roman and modern art of war. By Sir J. Turner. 1 vol. fol. Lond. 1683.

Written in 1670 and 1671.

1030. Abridgment of the English military discipline. Printed by his majesty's special command for the use of his majesty's forces. 1 vol. 12mo. Lond. 1686.

Containing also Rules and articles for the better government of the land forces. This is the commonest of these manuals, of which the earliest I have seen is dated 1678. (16mo. Lond.) Cf. The exercise of the foot, with the evolutions . . . By their majesties' command. 1 vol. 12mo. Lond. 1690.

1031. A treatise of military discipline. By H. Bland. 1 vol. 8vo. Lond. 1727. 9th ed. 1762.

Bland served under Marlborough, and his book is the best account of British drill and discipline then.

1032. Military antiquities respecting a history of the English army from the conquest to the present time. By F. Grose. 2 vols. 4to. Lond. 1786–8. 2nd ed. 2 vols. 1801. 3rd ed. 1812.

The 2nd ed. includes a treatise on ancient armour and weapons with 61 plates, published separately in 1785.

1033. A history of the dress of the British soldier, from the earliest period to the present time. Illustrated with fifty drawings. By J. Luard. 1 vol. 8vo. Lond. 1852.

1034. A review of the history of infantry. By E. M. Lloyd. 1 vol. 8vo. Lond. 1908.

¶ 3. NARRATIVES AND HISTORIES OF CAMPAIGNS

See also the general histories of the period. These are arranged in the chronological order of the campaigns described.

1035. Monro his expedition with the worthy Scots regiment (called Mac-Keyes regiment) levied in August 1626 . . . to which is annexed the abridgement of exercise and divers practical observations, for the youngest officer his consideration. By R. Monro. 1 vol. fol. Lond. 1637.

Levied for service with Christian IV of Denmark and served under Gustavus Adolphus.

1036. Memoirs of military transactions, 1683–1718, in Ireland and Flanders. By R. Parker. 1 vol. 8vo. Lond. 1747.

The author was present at Blenheim, Malplaquet, &c. Much identical with Kane. Cf. Hist. MSS. Comm. Rep. i, p. 129.

1037. Iter Bellicosum. Adam Wheeler. His account of 1685. Ed. by H. E. Malden. Camd. Misc. xii. 1910. Map.

The narrative of a soldier who served against Monmouth.

1038. Frankland-Russell-Astley MSS., Hist. MSS. Comm. 1900.

Has Cutts and Revett papers 1687–1708, which are important for the Marlborough wars.

1039. Campaigns of King William and Queen Anne ; from 1689 to 1712. Also a new system of military discipline for a battalion of foot in action. By R. Kane. 1 vol. 8vo. Lond. 1745. 2nd ed. 1 vol. 1747. Plans.

A later ed. has title : A system of camp discipline. . . . To which is added General Kane's campaigns improved from the late Earl of Craufurd's and Colonel Dunbar's copies. Continued to 1757. Seems to be a kind of cram book for the Royal Academy of Woolwich.

1040. An imperial relation of all the transactions between the army of the confederates and that of the French king in their last summer's campaign in Flanders. . . . By W. Sawle. 1 vol. 8vo. Lond. 1691.

1041. A relation of the most remarkable transactions of the last campaigne . . . in the Spanish Netherlands, 1692–7. By E. D'Auvergne. 6 pts. 8vo. Lond. 1693–8.

The title for the years 1693–4 is : The History of the last campagne in the Spanish Netherlands ; for 1695–7, The History . . . in Flanders. The author was chaplain to the Scots Guards. Valuable for a soldier's daily life and habits. Gives lists of regiments, winter-quarters, &c.

1042. Wilhelm III von England und Max Emanuel von Bayern im Niederländischen Kriege, 1692–7. By K. von Landmann. 1 vol. 8vo. Munich. 1901.

1043. A compleat history of the late war in the Netherlands, together with an abstract of the treaty at Utrecht. By T. Brodrick. 1 vol. 8vo. Lond. 1713. Maps. Plans.

1044. A compendious journal of all the marches, &c. . . . [of the allied armies 1701–12]. By J. Millner. 1 vol. 8vo. Lond. 1733.

A daily record of marches, &c. Very useful.

1045. An impartial enquiry into the management of the war in Spain, by the ministry at home and into the conduct of those generals to whose care the same has been committed abroad. Collected from many original letters and councils of war, never published before. 1 vol. 8vo. Lond. 1712.

'Repr. in 1726 with a new title-page : " The history of the last war in Spain from 1702 to 1710 ", is based on the Annals, and may have been written by Boyer himself '. Dict. Nat. Biog., *sub* Massue de Ruvigny, Henri de.

1046. The history of the campaign in Germany for the year 1704 under the command of his grace John Duke of Marlborough. 1 vol. 4to. Lond. 1705.

1047. Letters, describing the battles of Blenheim, Ramillies and Malplaquet. By George Hamilton, Earl of Orkney. Ed. by H. H. E. Craster. English Hist. Rev. xix. 1904.

1048. The history of the campaign in Flanders in the year 1708. . . . To which is prefixed a map of Lille and the adjacent countries. 1 vol. 4to. Lond. 1709.

A few documents.

1049. Journal of the campaign in Flanders 1708. By J. M. Deane. 1 vol. 8vo. s.l. 1846.

1050. The conduct of his grace the Duke of Ormonde in the campagne of 1712. 1 vol. 4to. Lond. 1715.

A vindication with letters.

1051. History of the war of the succession in Spain. By Philip Henry Stanhope, Lord Mahon (aft. Earl Stanhope). 1 vol. 8vo. Lond. 1832.

An appendix containing further extracts from General Stanhope's letters appeared in 1833, and is bound up with the History in the issue of that year. Cf. Mr. Stanhope's Answer to the report of the commissioners sent into Spain. 1714.

1052. The war of succession in Spain during the reign of Queen Anne, 1702–1711. By A. Parnell. 1 vol. 8vo. Lond. 1888. Bibl.

Based on many both printed and unprinted sources, but too positive in tone and unduly depreciatory of Peterborough.

1053. The wars of the Spanish succession. By C. T. Atkinson. Camb. Modern Hist. v. 1908.

Has a good bibliography.

¶ 4. REGIMENTAL HISTORIES

For bibliographies of regimental histories see the note to Cannon (1054).

1054. Regimental records of the British army, comprising the history of every regiment. Ed. by R. Cannon.

These regimental histories number about sixty and were officially compiled during 1835–51. A useful list of these and other regimental histories is in the printed catalogue of the Brit. Mus. Library (under England, army), in F. J. Hudleston's Catalogue of the War Office Library, part iii. Subject index (8vo. Lond. 1912, with annual supplements), and in the catalogue of the Library of the Royal United Service Institution (8vo. Lond. 1890). The series ed. by Cannon contains some useful information but is disappointing.

1055. The British army : its regimental records, badges, devices. By J. H. Lawrence-Archer. 1 vol. 8vo. Lond. 1888.

1056. The records and badges of every regiment and corps in the British army. By H. M. Chichester and G. B. Short. 1 vol. 8vo. Lond. 1895. Illus. 2nd ed. 1900. Illus.
Contains useful notes on the services of each regiment and lists of regimental histories.

1057. Papers illustrating the history of the Scots Brigade in the service of the United Netherlands (1572–1782) from the archives at the Hague. By J. Ferguson. 3 vols. 8vo. Scottish Hist. Soc. Edin. 1899–1901.
The third volume contains a metrical account of the war in Flanders by John Scot, a soldier in Hepburn's regiment. Cf. Historical account of the British regiments employed in the formation and defence of the Dutch republic, particularly of the Scotch brigade. 1 vol. 8vo. Lond. 1795.

1058. The regimental records of the British army. A historical resume chronologically arranged of titles, campaigns, honours, uniforms, facings, badges, nicknames. By J. S. Farmer. 1 vol. 4to. Lond. 1901.

1059. The story of the Household Cavalry. By Sir G. C. A. Arthur. 2 vols. 4to. Lond. 1909. Maps. Plans. Illus.
Fairly full for 1660–1714.

1060. An historical record of the royal regiment of Horse Guards or Oxford Blues. By E. Packe. 1 vol. 8vo. Lond. 1834. Illus.

1061. Historical record of the First or the Royal Regiment of Dragoons. By C. P. de Ainslie. 1 vol. 8vo. Lond. 1887. Illus.

1062. The story of a regiment of horse being the regimental history from 1685 to 1922 of the 5th Princess Charlotte of Wales' Dragoon Guards. By R. L. Pomeroy. 2 vols. 4to. Edin. and Lond. 1924. Illus.

1063. History of the Honourable Artillery Company, with maps and illustrations. By G. A. Raikes. 2 vols. 8vo. Lond. 1878–9.
Gives particulars of the London trained bands in the civil war. Cf. The ancient vellum book of the Honourable Artillery Company, being the roll of members, 1611–82 (8vo. Lond. 1890).

1064. The origin and history of the First or Grenadier Guards. By Sir F. W. Hamilton. 3 vols. 8vo. Lond. 1874. Illus.
Corrigenda and addenda issued 8vo. Lond. 1877.

1065. Origin and services of the Coldstream Guards [to 1815]. By D. Mackinnon. 2 vols. 8vo. Lond. 1833.
There is an appendix of original documents.

1066. The early history of the Coldstream Guards. By G. Davies. 1 vol. 8vo. Oxf. 1924. Illus. Bibl. Note.
Preface by Brigadier-General H. W. Studd, and introduction by J. W. Fortescue. Appendices of documents.

1067. Mackay's Regiment : A narrative of the principal services of the regiment now known as the Royal Scots. By J. Mackay. 1 vol. 8vo. Inverness. 1879.

1068. The regimental records of the Royal Scots (the First or the Royal Regiment of Foot). By J. C. Leask and H. M. McCance. 1 vol. 4to. Dubl. 1915. Illus.
Useful.

1069. The story of the Royal Scots (the Lothian Regiment) formerly the First of the Royal Regiment of Foot. By L. Weaver. Preface by the Earl of Rosebery. 1 vol. 8vo. Lond. *c.* 1916. Illus.

1070. History of the Second Queen's Royal Regiment, now the Queen's (Royal West Surrey) Regiment. By J. Davies. 6 vols. 8vo. Lond. 1887–1906.
Vols. i and ii go down to 1715, the first dealing entirely with Tangier. The most detailed and best regimental history for the period.

1071. Historical records of the Buffs (East Kent Regiment), 3rd Foot, formerly designed the Holland Regiment. . . . Vol. i. (1572–1704). By H. R. Knight, 1 vol. 8vo. Lond. 1905. Maps and Plans.

1072. The story of the Royal Warwickshire Regiment (formerly the Sixth Foot). By C. L. Kingsford. 1 vol. 8vo. Lond. 1921. Maps.

1073. The history of the Norfolk Regiment, 1685–1918. By F. L. Petre. 2 vols. 4to. Norwich. *c.* 1924. Illus. Bibl.

1074. History of the 12th (Suffolk Regiment), 1685–1913. By E. A. H. Webb. 1 vol. 4to. Lond. 1914. Illus.

1075. A History of the services of the 17th (the Leicestershire) Regiment, containing an account of the formation of the regiment in 1688 and of its subsequent services, revised and continued to 1910. By E. A. H. Webb. 1 vol. 8vo. Lond. 1911. Illus.

1076. The campaigns and history of the Royal Irish Regiment from 1684 to 1902. By G. Le M. Gretton. 1 vol. 8vo. Edin. & Lond. 1911. Maps.

1077. History of the 21st Royal Scots Fusiliers . . . now known as the Royal Scots Fusiliers . . . 1678–1895. By P. Groves. 1 vol. 8vo. Edin. & Lond. 1895. Illus.

1078. History of Thos. Farringtons' Regiment subsequently designated the 29th (Worcestershire) Foot. 1694 to 1891. By H. Everard. 1 vol. 4to. Worcester. 1891. Illus.
Has some extracts from MSS. Records.

1079. The First Highland Regiment. The Argyllshire Highlanders (1689–97). By R. MacK. Holden. Scot. Hist. Rev. iii. 1905. Repr. 8vo. Glasgow. 1905.

¶ 5. BIOGRAPHIES AND PERSONAL NARRATIVES

(*a*) 1603–1660. (*b*) 1660–1714

(*a*) 1603–1660

ALBEMARLE, GEORGE MONCK, DUKE OF.

1080. The life of General Monck, Duke of Albemarle.   By T. Gumble.
1 vol. 8vo. Lond. 1671.

Gumble was Monck's chaplain and is valuable for 1659–60.

1081. Life of General Monck, late Duke of Albemarle.   By T. Skinner.
Ed. by W. Webster.   1 vol. 8vo. Lond. and Dubl. 1723–4.

A mere compilation.

1082. Monck : or the fall of the republic and the restoration of the
monarchy.   By F. P. G. Guizot.   1 vol. 8vo. Lond. 1851.

This trans. by A. R. Scoble contains dispatches of Bordeaux, May 1659–July 1660;
another by J. Stuart Wortley [1838] has useful notes but no dispatches.   Original
French ed. 1837.

1083. Monk.   By Sir J. S. Corbett.   English Men of Action.   1 vol. 8vo.
Lond. 1889.

BELASYSE, JOHN LORD.

1084. A briefe relation of the life and memoires of John Lord Belasyse.   By
J. Moone.   Hist. MSS. Comm. Ormonde MSS. N.S. 11, 1903.

BIRCH, COLONEL JOHN.

1085. Military Memoir of Colonel John Birch, written by his secretary
[Roe].   Ed. by J. Webb & T. W. Webb.   Camd. Soc. 1873.

CHOLMLEY, SIR HUGH.

1086. The memoirs of Sir Hugh Cholmley . . . in which he gives some
account of his family and the distresses they underwent in the civil wars, how
far he himself was engaged in them.   1 vol. 4to. s.l. 1787.   Repr. 1870.

CROMWELL, OLIVER.

1087. Der Reitergeneral, Feldherr und Staatsmann (1599–1658);   ein
Beitrag zur Kriegsgeschichte des XVII. Jahrhunderts.   By F. Hoenig.   4 parts
in 3 vols. 8vo. Berlin 1887–9. Plans.   2nd ed. 3 vols. 8vo. Leipzig. 1911.   Ports.
Maps.

Interesting as the work of a distinguished military critic, but often wrong as to facts.

1088. Cromwell as a soldier.   By T. S. Baldock.   1 vol. 8vo. Lond. 1899.

For other biographies of Cromwell see Nos. 860–72.

ESSEX, ROBERT DEVEREUX, EARL OF.

1089. Lives and letters of the Devereux, Earls of Essex, in the reigns of
Elizabeth, James I, and Charles I.   1540–1646.   By W. B. Devereux.   2 vols.
8vo. Lond. 1853.   Illus.

Most of the letters of the last earl, the parliamentarian, are pr. in the Cal. of State
Papers, Dom., or in the Lords' Journals.

FAIRFAX, THOMAS LORD.

1090. A short memorial of the northern actions in which I was engaged [1642–44]; [and] Short Memoirs of some things to be cleared during my command [1645–50]. By Thomas, Lord Fairfax. Ed. by B. Fairfax. 1 vol. 12mo. Lond. 1699.

Reprinted in the Antiquarian Repertory, iii. 1808; Somers' Tracts (89) v; Maseres (1158) ii; and Stuart Tracts (165).

1091. Life of the great Lord Fairfax, commander-in-chief of the army of the parliament of England. By Sir C. R. Markham. 1 vol. 8vo. Lond. 1870. Plans.

GRANVILLE, SIR RICHARD.

1092. The king's general in the west. The life of Sir Richard Granville, 1600–59. By R. Granville. 1 vol. 8vo. Lond. 1908. Illus.

GWYNNE, JOHN.

1093. Military memoirs of the great civil war, being the memoirs of J. Gwynne, and an account of the Earl of Glencairn's expedition [1653–4]. Ed. by Sir W. Scott. 1 vol. 4to. Edin. 1822.

Many extracts from Mercurius Politicus for 1653–4.

HAMILTON, JAMES AND WILLIAM HAMILTON, DUKES OF.

1094. Memoirs of the lives and actions of James and William, Dukes of Hamilton. By G. Burnet. 1 vol. fol. Lond. 1677. 2nd ed. 1 vol. 8vo. Oxford. 1852.

Cf. Robert Dewar's ' Burnet on the Scottish troubles ', Scot. Hist. Rev. iv, and H. C. Foxcroft's ' An early recension of Burnet's memoirs of the Dukes of Hamilton ' (in Brit. Mus. Add. MSS. 33259), Eng. Hist. Rev. xxiv. 1909.

HARRISON, THOMAS.

1095. Thomas Harrison Regicide and Major-General. By C. H. Simpkinson. 1 vol. 8vo. Lond. 1905. Illus.

Reprints nineteen Letters of Harrison. Cf. Sir C. H. Firth's ' The life of Thomas Harrison ' in Proc. Amer. Anti. Soc. April 1893. Illus. Worcester, Mass.

HEPBURN, SIR JOHN.

1096. Memoirs and adventures of Sir John Hepburn. . . . marshal of France under Louis XIII and commander of the Scots Brigade under Gustavus Adolphus. By J. Grant. 1 vol. 8vo. Edin. 1851.

HODGSON, CAPTAIN JOHN.

1097. Autobiography of Captain John Hodgson of Coley Hall near Halifax. 1 vol. 8vo. Edin. 1806. Later ed. 1 vol. 8vo. Brighouse. 1882. Ed. by J. H. Turner.

In the edition of 1806 it was coupled with extracts from the diary of Sir H. Slingsby, under the title ' Original memoirs written during the great civil war . . . .' Letters and pamphlets on the operations of the English army in Scotland in 1650 were added (pp. 203–367).

HUTCHINSON, COLONEL JOHN.

1098. Memoirs of the Life of Colonel John Hutchinson, Governor of Nottingham, by his widow [Lucy Hutchinson]. Ed. by J. Hutchinson. 1 vol. 4to. Lond. 1806. Later ed. 1 vol. 8vo. Lond. 1906. Ed. by Sir C. H. Firth.

LEVEN, ALEXANDER LESLIE, EARL OF.

1099. The life and campaigns of Alexander Leslie, first Earl of Leven. By C. S. Terry. 1 vol. 8vo. Lond. 1899.

MELVILL, SIR ANDREW.

1100. Memoirs of Sir Andrew Melvill, translated from the Trench. Ed. by Ameer-Ali Torick. 1 vol. Lond. 1918. Illus.

This autobiography of a soldier of fortune was first published at Amsterdam in 1704 as Mémoires de M. Chevalier de Melvill. Of dubious authenticity.

1101. The Monckton papers. By Sir P. Monckton. Ed. by E. Peacock. 1 vol. sm. 4to. *c.* 1884.

Practically memoirs of the first and second Civil Wars. Appendix contains An impartial and true relation of the great victory . . . of Col. Edw. Rossiter . . . July 5, 1648.

MONTROSE, JAMES GRAHAM, MARQUIS OF.

1102. The memoirs of James, Marquis of Montrose, 1639–50. Translated with introduction, notes, appendices and the original Latin. By G. Wishart. Ed. by A. D. Murdock & H. F. M. Simpson. 1 vol. 4to. Lond. 1893.

The first part (to 1646) was published in Latin in 1647, probably at Amsterdam, and was translated in 1648 ; a portion of a translation of part two appeared in 1720. The ed. of 1893 is the only complete one.

1103. Memorials of Montrose and his times. By M. Napier. Maitland Club. 2 vols. 4to. Edin. 1848–50.

The documentary evidence on which the following item is based.

1104. Memoirs of the Marquis of Montrose. By M. Napier. 2 vols. 8vo. Edin. 1856.

An earlier work, Montrose and the Covenanters [1838] contains Montrose's poems.

1105. Montrose. By M. Morris. English Men of Action Series. 1 vol. 8vo. Lond. 1892.

1106. The Marquis of Montrose. By J. Buchan. 1 vol. 8vo. Lond. 1913.

NEWCASTLE, DUKE OF.

1107. The life of . . . William Cavendish, Duke of . . . Newcastle. . . . By Margaret Cavendish, Duchess of Newcastle. 1 vol. fol. Lond. 1667. Later eds. 1 vol. 8vo. Lond. 1886 and 1907. Both ed. by Sir C. H. Firth.

RUPERT, PRINCE.

1108. Memoirs of Prince Rupert and the cavaliers, including their private correspondence, from the original MSS. By E. B. G. Warburton. 3 vols. 8vo. Lond. 1849.

The MSS. used are now in the British Museum, Add. MSS. 18980–2. Other letters addressed to Rupert *temp.* civil war are in the Pythouse papers, ed. by W. A. Day (1 vol. 8vo. Lond. 1879).

1109. Prince Rupert's Journal in England ; from September 5, 1642, to July 4, 1646. Ed. by Sir C. H. Firth. Eng. Hist. Rev. xiii. 1898.

A Journal of his marches, from Clarendon MSS. xxviii. 129.

1110. Rupert, Prince Palatine. By E. Scott. 1 vol. 8vo. Lond. 1899. Illus. 2nd ed. 1904.

SLINGSBY, SIR HENRY.

1111. The diary of Sir Henry Slingsby. Ed. by D. Parsons. 1 vol. 8vo. Lond. 1836.

An abridged version of this diary was published at Edin. in 1806, with Hodgson's autobiography under the title Original memoirs during the Civil War. The MSS. belongs to the Duke of Northumberland. See Hist. MSS. Comm. 3rd Rep., p. 121.

SMITH, SIR JOHN.

1112. Britannicae virtutis imago or . . . the life . . . of . . . Major-General Smith. By E. Walsingham. 1 vol. sm. 4to. Oxf. 1644.

Walsingham also wrote : Alter Britannicae heros or the life of . . . Sir Henry Gage (1 vol. sm. 4to. Oxf. 1645) ; and life of Sir John Digby [1605–45], printed in Camd. Misc. xii. 1910, ed. by G. Bernard.

TURENNE, VISCOUNT DE.

1113. The history of Henry de la Tour d'Auvergne, Viscount de Turenne. By A. M. Ramsay (Chevalier de Ramsay). 2 vols. 8vo. Lond. 1735.

The second volume contains the authorities including Turenne's own Memoirs (1643–58) and those of the Duke of York (1652–9). A French edition was published at the same time in two volumes 4to. In 1909 the Société de l'Histoire de France began the publication of a new edition of Turenne's Memoirs.

TURNER, SIR JAMES.

1114. Memoirs of his own life and times [1632–70]. Ed. by I. Thomson. 1 vol. 4to. Edin. 1829. Bannatyne Club.

He served under Gustavus Adolphus and in the civil war. Cf. ' Dugald Dalgetty : and Scottish soldiers of fortune,' by J. D. Mackie. Scot. Hist. Rev. xii.

VERE, SIR FRANCIS.

1115. Commentaries, being diverse pieces of service wherein he had command. Ed. by W. Dillingham. 1 vol. fol. Camb. 1657. Maps. Ports.

Repr. in Stuart Tracts (165).

1116. ' The fighting Veres '; lives of Sir Francis Vere . . . and of Sir Horace Vere . . . Baron Vere of Tilbury. By Sir C. R. Markham. 1 vol. 8vo. Lond. 1888.

WHETHAM, COLONEL NATHANIEL.

1117. History of the life of Colonel Nathaniel Whetham. By C. D. Whetham & W. C. D. Whetham. 1 vol. 8vo. Lond. 1907. Illus.

WIMBLEDON, EDWARD CECIL, VISCOUNT.

1118. Life and times of General Sir Edward Cecil, Viscount Wimbledon (1572–1638). By C. Dalton. 2 vols. 8vo. Lond. 1885.

Valuable.

(b) 1660–1714

BERNARDI, MAJOR JOHN.

1119. A short history of the life of Major John Bernardi, written by himself in Newgate. 1 vol. 8vo. Lond. 1729.

In the English brigade in Dutch service from 1674, and afterwards with James II in Ireland.

BERWICK, JAMES FITZJAMES, DUKE OF.

1120. (a) James II and the Duke of Berwick. (b) The Duke of Berwick, Marshal of France, 1702–1734. Both by C. T. Wilson. 1 vol. 8vo. Lond. 1876, and 1 vol. 8vo. Lond. 1883.

Berwick's Mémoires were ed. by l'Abbé L. J. Hooke, 2 vols. 12mo. Paris. 1778, 2nd ed. 8vo. Paris. 1819. Petitot collection. The abbé de Margon (Guillaume, Plantavit de la Pause) compiled ' Mémoires du Maréchal de Berwick ', 12mo, The Hague, 1737 : but the edition of 1778 was the first authentic one. The editor added notes and a continuation from 1716 to 1734. A translation was published in Lond. in 1779, 2 vols. 8vo.

BISHOP, MATTHEW.

1121. The life and adventures of Matthew Bishop of Deddington in Oxfordshire. Containing an account of several actions by sea, battles and sieges by land, in which he was present from 1701 to 1711. 1 vol. 8vo. Lond. 1744.

Many incidents illustrate the life of a private soldier and methods of recruiting. Cf. The Retrospective Review, 2nd series [1828] ii. 42 for a useful article on the above.

BLACKADER, JOHN, LIEUTENANT-COLONEL.

1122. The life and diary of Lieutenant Colonel John Blackader of the Cameronian Regiment. Ed. by A. Crichton. 1 vol. 8vo. Edin. 1824.

Useful for the war in Flanders in Anne's reign. Has superseded Select passages from the diary and letters of J. Blackader, with a preface by J. Newton, 8vo. 1806.

CARLETON, GEORGE.

1123. Military memoirs of Captain George Carleton, from the Dutch war, 1672, in which he served, to the conclusion of the peace at Utrecht, 1713. 1 vol. 8vo. Lond. 1728. 5th ed. 1 vol. 8vo. Edin. 1809 (with preface by Sir W. Scott).

Original title : The memoirs of an English officer. Has been attributed to Defoe, also to Swift. See Dict. Nat. Biog., Parnell (1048), Appendix C, and Eng. Hist. Rev. vol. vi. p. 97 ; Percival A. Carleton, Memorials of the Carletons ; and Arthur Wellesley Secord's Studies in the narrative method of Defoe [Univ. of Illinois Studies in Language and Literature, Urbana, 1924, deals with Robinson Crusoe, Singleton, and Carleton], where the conclusion is that Defoe compiled from contemporary sources a fictitious narrative woven round a genuine personage.

DAVIES, CHRISTIAN.

1124. The life and adventures of Mrs. Christian Davies, commonly call'd Mother Ross. 1 vol. 8vo. Lond. 1740.

An abridged version appeared in 1742 with the title The British heroine, by J. Wilson. See N. and Q. 5th series, vi. 511. Contains some personal adventures of a woman who served in the ranks and then became a sutler. Largely fiction, but throws much light on provisioning the army.

DRAKE, PETER.

1125. The memoirs of Captain Peter Drake; containing an account of many strange and surprising events. 1 vol. 8vo. Dubl. 1755.

Drake served in the Irish, English, and French armies, and his adventures reveal the seamy side of military life.

DUNDEE, JOHN GRAHAM OF CLAVERHOUSE, VISCOUNT.

1126. Letters of John Grahame of Claverhouse, Viscount Dundee, with illustrative documents, 1678–1689. Ed. by G. Smythe. Bann. Club. 1 vol. 4to. Edin. 1826. 2 ports.

1127. Memorials and letters illustrative of the life and times of John Graham of Claverhouse, Viscount Dundee. By M. Napier. 3 vols. 8vo. Edin. 1859–62.

1128. John Graham of Claverhouse, Viscount of Dundee, 1648–89. By C. S. Terry. 1 vol. 8vo. Lond. 1905.

1129. Clavers, the despots champion. A Scots biography. By a southern. 1 vol. 8vo. Lond. 1889.

1130. Grahame of Claverhouse, Viscount Dundee. By M. Barrington. 1 vol. 4to. Lond. 1911. Maps. Ports.

Cf. Claverhouse's last letter, Scot. Hist. Rev. v. and criticisms by C. S. Terry and J. Anderson, *ibid.* vi.

GALWAY, HENRI DE RUVIGNY, EARL OF.

1131. Henri de Ruvigny, Earl of Galway. By D. C. A. Agnew. 1 vol. 4to. Edin. 1864.

GORDON, PATRICK.

1132. Passages from the diary of General Patrick Gordon of Auchleuchries, 1635–99. Ed. by J. Robertson. 1 vol. 4to. Aberdeen. 1859. Spalding Club.

Gordon was a soldier of fortune in Russian service.

HALKETT, JAMES.

1133. Diary of Sir James Halkett.

Deals with the siege of Tangiers, 1680. Pr. from MS. in the Signet Library. Journal of the Society of Army Historical Research, Dec. 1922 (special number).

MACKAY, HUGH.

1134. Life of Lieut.-General Hugh Mackay (1640 ?–1692). By J. Mackay. 1 vol. 4to. Edin. 1836. 2nd ed. 1 vol. 8vo. Lond. 1842. Bannatyne Club.

The author has also edited General Mackay's ' Memoirs of the war carried on in Scotland and Ireland ' 1689–91, with an appendix of original papers (Bannatyne Club). 4to. Edin. 1833. Cf. Brit. Mus. Add. MS. 33264.

MARLBOROUGH, JOHN CHURCHILL, DUKE OF.

1135. The conduct of the Duke of Marlborough during the present war, with original papers. By F. Hare. 1 vol. 8vo. Lond. 1712.

A defence of the Duke. Hare was Chaplain-General to the army in Flanders in 1704. Some of Hare's letters, 1704–11, are in the Hist. MSS. Comm. Hare MSS. *apud* Buckinghamshire MSS. 1895.

1136. Histoire militaire du Prince Eugène de Savoy, du Prince et duc de Marlborough et du Prince de Nassau . . . où l'on trouve un détail des principales actions de la dernière guerre.   By J. Dumont & J. Rousset de Missey.   3 vols. fol. The Hague. 1729–47.

Translated in part by P. Chamberlain as The military history of Prince Eugene &c. Fol. Lond. 1736.

1137. Life of John, Duke of Marlborough, illustrated with maps, plans of battles, sieges, and medals and a great number of original letters and papers. By T. Lediard.   3 vols. 8vo. Lond. 1736.   2nd ed. 2 vols. 8vo. 1843.

Still useful for documents.

1138. The military history of the late Prince Eugene of Savoy and of the late John Duke of Marlborough . . . collected from the best authors in all languages. . . . From 1701 to 1706.   By [J. Campbell].   2 vols. fol. Lond. 1736–7.   2nd ed. 1 vol. fol. 1742.

Plates engraved by C. du Bosc.

1139. Histoire de Jean Churchill duc de Marlborough.   By N. Madgett & H. Dutems.   3 vols. 8vo. Paris. 1805–6.

1140. Memoirs of the Duke of Marlborough, with his original correspondence.   By W. Coxe.   3 vols. & atlas. 4to. Lond. 1818–19.   2nd ed. 6 vols. 8vo. Lond. 1820.   3rd ed. 3 vols. 8vo. Lond. 1847–8. Ed. by J. Wade. Bohn's Library.

Transcripts of documents at Blenheim made by Coxe are in Brit. Mus. Add. MSS.   A description, with some extracts, of the papers at Blenheim is in Hist. MSS. Comm. Rep. viii. 1–62.   Coxe's work is still the best biography for Marlborough's political career.

1141. Letters and despatches of John Churchill, Duke of Marlborough. [1702–12].   Ed. by Sir G. Murray.   5 vols. 8vo. Lond. 1845.

1142. The military life of John, Duke of Marlborough, by Sir A. Alison. 1 vol. 8vo. Edin. 1848.   Plans.   2nd ed. 2 vols. 8vo. Edin. 1852.   Ports.

Originally published in Blackwood's Magazine in 1845–6.   The 2nd ed. is re-written on a larger scale (see Alison's Autobiography, 1883, i. 563, ii. 3), with the title The life of John, Duke of Marlborough.

1143. The life of John Churchill, Duke of Marlborough, to the accession of Queen Anne.   By Garnet Joseph, Viscount Wolseley.   2 vols. 8vo. Lond. 1894.   Maps.   Plans.

Cf. E. M. Lloyd's Marlborough and the Brest expedition 1694, Eng. Hist. Rev. ix. 1894.

1144. The life of the Duke of Marlborough.   By E. Thomas.   8vo. Lond. 1915.

1145. The wars of Marlborough.   By F. Taylor.   Ed. by G. W. Taylor. 2 vols. 8vo. Oxf. 1921.   Maps.

Mainly devoted to 1702–9.

1146. Marlborough and the rise of the British army.   By C. T. Atkinson. 1 vol. 8vo. N.Y. 1921 and 1924.   Maps.   Illus.

PETERBOROUGH, CHARLES MORDAUNT, EARL OF.

1147. Account of the Earl of Peterborough's conduct in Spain, chiefly since the raising of the siege of Barcelona, 1706. To which is added the campagne of Valencia. With original papers. By J. Freind. 1 vol. 8vo. Lond. 1707.

Freind was in Spain with Peterborough as his physician and wrote on his behalf. Cf. The comparison or Accounts on both sides fairly stated. 1711; and Letters from the Earl of Peterborough to General Stanhope in Spain [1705-7] from the originals at Chevening. Not publ. 1 vol. 8vo. Lond. 1834.

1148. A memoir of Charles Mordaunt, Earl of Peterborough . . . with selections from his correspondence. By G. Warburton. 2 vols. 8vo. Lond. 1853.

1149. The Earl of Peterborough and Monmouth. By F. S. Russell. 2 vols. 8vo. Lond. 1887. Plans. Ports.

Embodies new material but is rather uncritical.

1150. Peterborough. By W. Stebbing. English Men of Action Series. 1 vol. 8vo. Lond. 1890.

An impartial account of Peterborough's action in Spain, and of the controversies connected with it.

ST. PIERRE, COLONEL DE.

1151. Military journal of Colonel de St. Pierre (Royal Dragoons) and other manuscripts relating to the war of the Spanish succession, 1703-13. Ed. by J. E. Renouard James. 1 vol. 8vo. Chatham. 1882.

Repr. from the Royal Engineers' Journal. It deals with the operations in Spain and Portugal.

SCHOMBERG, FRIEDRICH VON.

1152. Leben Friedrichs von Schomberg oder Schoenburg. By J. F. A. Kazner. 2 vols. 8vo. Mannheim. 1789.

Contains Schomberg's diary.

¶ 6. CIVIL WAR

(*a*) General Sources.
(*b*) General Later Works.
(*c*) Local Sources and Later Works.

Both for the general outlines of the Civil War, a knowledge of which is necessary for the critical study of any part of it, and also for their footnotes referring to authorities, Gardiner (220) and Firth (1171) are throughout indispensable. The same may be said of the notes in the Dictionary of National Biography and in the biographies mentioned in 4 (*a*), *supra*. Owing to the nature of a civil war, and to the intervention in politics by the New Model Army, military history is often inseparable from political, and both the general sources and later works 1603-60 should be consulted. It should not be forgotten that the most important sources for the Civil War are pamphlets and newspapers (2470-2484), and it is essential to examine the collection of both formed by Thomason and now in the British Museum (17).

(*a*) General Sources

1153. England's parliamentarie chronicle. 3 vols. sm. 4to. Lond. 1643–6. By J. Vicars.

Comprises : Jehovah Jireh. God in the mount (1641–Oct. 1642). God's arke over-topping the worlds waves (July 1643–July 1644) ; the Burning-bush not consumed (Aug. 1644–July 1646). Cf. The same writer's England's worthies, under whom all the bloudy warres since anno 1642 to anno 1647 are related. (1 vol. 12mo. Lond. 1647. Ports.)

1154. Anglia rediviva ; England's recovery : being the history of the motions, actions, and successes of the army under . . . Sir Thomas Fairfax. By J. Sprigge. 1 vol. 8vo. Lond. 1647. 2nd ed. 1 vol. 8vo. Oxf. 1854.

A history of the new model army by Fairfax's chaplain, who is said to have been helped by Colonel Fiennes. The list of officers at the end can be supplemented, as far as the Colonels are concerned, from Notes & Queries, 18 Nov. 1893 and 3 March 1894.

1155. A list of officers claiming to the sixty thousand pounds . . . granted by his . . . majesty for the relief of his truly loyal and indigent party. 1 vol. 4to. Lond. 1663.

A long, though incomplete, list of royalist officers. The names of many others can be found in A most true relation of the present state of his majesties army (4to. Lond. 1642). Cf. The loyal indigent officer being a brief description of the truly loyal commissioned officer which hath faithfully served his late majesty of ever blessed memory and his majesty that now is. By Charles Hammond. 1 vol. sm. 4to. Lond. s.a. For com-missions issued at Oxford see William Henry Black's Docquets of letters patent . . . passed under the great seal of King Charles I at Oxford (1642–46). Not published. 8vo. Lond. 1838.

1156. Historical discourses upon several occasions ; with copies of all votes, letters, etc., relating to the treaty at Newport 1648. By Sir E. Walker. 1 vol. fol. Lond. 1705.

Walker was secretary to Charles I at Newport. He wrote narratives of the campaigns of 1644 and 1645 and of 1650 in Scotland.

1157. Ormonde Papers. A collection of original letters and papers con-cerning affairs of England, 1641–60, found among the Duke of Ormonde's papers. Ed. by T. Carte. 2 vols. 8vo. Lond. 1739.

Originals among the Carte MSS. in the Bodleian Library.

1158. Select tracts relating to the civil wars in England in the reign of King Charles the first. Ed. by Francis, Bacon Maseres. 2 vols. 8vo. Lond. 1815 and 1826.

1159. Memorials of the great civil war, 1646–52 ; edited from original letters in the Bodleian. Ed. by H. Cary. 2 vols. 8vo. Lond. 1842.

Selected letters from the Tanner MSS. in the Bodleian Library which contain many others not printed relating to the war during 1642–6.

1160. Memorials of the civil war ; correspondence of the Fairfax family with personages in that contest. Ed. by R. Bell. 2 vols. 8vo. Lond. 1849.

These form vols. iii and iv of the Fairfax correspondence. Cf. No. 121.

1161. Letters of a subaltern officer of the Earl of Essex's army written in
... 1642. By N. Wharton. Ed. by Sir H. Ellis. Archaeologia, xxxv. 1853.
Also slightly abridged in Cal. S. P. Dom. 1641–3. Gives a lively picture of the experiences of a parliamentary soldier during the opening stages of the Civil War.

1162. Diary of the marches of the royal army during the great civil war
[1644–5]. By R. Symonds. Ed. by C. E. Long. Camd. Soc. 1859.
Pr. from Brit. Mus. Add. MS. 17062 ; Harl. MSS. 911, 939, 944.

1163. The army lists of the roundheads and cavaliers, containing the names
of the officers in the royal and parliamentary armies of 1642. Ed. by E. Peacock.
1 vol. 4to. Lond. 1863. 2nd ed. 1874.
Second ed. has an index. A reprint of contemporary pamphlets merely with a few
notes. Cf. Lord Dillon's MS. List of the officers of the London trained bands in 1643,
in Archaeologia, vol. lii.

1164. Ruthven correspondence. Letters and papers of Patrick Ruthven,
Earl of Forth and Brentford, and of his family (1615–1662), with an appendix
of papers relating to Sir John Urry. Ed. by W. D. Macray. 1 vol. 4to. Lond.
Roxburghe Club. 1868.

1165. Documents relating to the quarrel between the Earl of Manchester
and Oliver Cromwell. Ed. by J. Bruce & D. Masson. 1 vol. Camd. Soc. 1875.
Throws light on the campaign of 1644. Cf. Camd. Soc. Misc. viii for a letter from
Manchester on Cromwell's conduct. For other Civil War papers now in the Pub. Rec.
Off. see Manchester MSS. Hist. MSS. Comm., Rep. viii, Part ii.

1166. Bellum civile : Hopton's narrative of his campaign in the west
[1642–4] and other papers. By Sir R. Hopton. Ed. by C. E. H. Chadwyck-
Healey. 1 vol. 4to. Somerset Record Soc. Lond. 1902.

(b) General Later Works

1167. Cromwell et Mazarin, Deux campagnes de Turenne en Flandre :
La bataille des Dunes. By J. Bourelly. 1 vol. 8vo. Paris. 1886.

1168. Military engineering during the great civil war, 1642–9. By W. G.
Ross. In Occasional Papers of the Corps of Royal Engineers. vol. xiii. 1 vol.
8vo. Lond. 1887.
Deals with fortification, ordnance, and sieges, and has fifteen plates.

1169. Oliver Cromwell and his 'Ironsides' as they are represented in the
so-called 'Squire Papers'. By W. G. Ross. 1 vol. 8vo. Chatham. 1889.
An account of the controversy about these papers with additional evidence of their
spuriousness. See also vols. i and ii of the Eng. Hist. Rev. (1886–7), and Walter Rye's
Two Cromwellian myths viz. the alleged royal descent of Oliver Cromwell and the
Squire letters. 1 vol. 8vo. Norwich. 1925.

1170. The raising of the Ironsides. By Sir C. H. Firth.
The later history of the Ironsides is a sequel. Both are in Trans. of the Royal Hist.
Soc. xiii and xv, 1899, 1901.

1171. Cromwell's army : A history of the English soldier during the civil
wars, the commonwealth and the protectorate (Ford Lectures 1900–1). By

Sir C. H. Firth. 1 vol. 8vo. Lond. 1902. 2nd ed. 1 vol. 8vo. Lond. 1912.
3rd ed. 1 vol. 8vo. Lond. 1921. Illus.

An invaluable storehouse of facts relating to the art of war, 1603–60.

1172. Royalist and Cromwellian armies in Flanders, 1657–1662. By Sir
C. H. Firth.

App. contains new material. In Trans. of the Royal Hist. Soc. xvii. 1903.

(c) Local Histories and Sources

In addition to the items enumerated below, articles and notes on the Civil
War in different localities may be found in the proceedings of local antiquarian societies. These articles are very numerous and the few here included should be regarded as specimens only. They can be often traced in the
bibliographies mentioned in the local history section (XI) or, if printed not
later than 1890, in Gomme (2766).
For the Civil War in Wales see No. 3408.

BERKSHIRE.

1173. The first and second battles of Newbury and the siege of Donnington
Castle (1643–6). By W. Money. 1 vol. 8vo. Lond. 1881. 2nd ed. 1 vol. 8vo.
Lond. 1884.

With plans of the battles and of the siege.

CHESHIRE.

1174. Memorials of the civil war in Cheshire and the adjacent counties.
By T. Malbon. Ed. by J. Hall. Record Society of Lancashire and Cheshire.
1 vol. 8vo. Lond. 1889.

1175. Tracts relating to the civil war in Cheshire. 1641–59. Ed. by
J. A. Atkinson. Chetham Soc. 1909.

Reprint of thirty-seven pamphlets.

1176. The siege of Chester 1643–1646. By R. H. Morris. Ed. by P. H.
Lawson. 1 vol. 8vo. Chester. 1924. Illus.

Pr. many extracts from authorities.

CUMBERLAND.

1177. A narrative of the siege of Carlisle in 1644 and 1645. By I. Tullie.
Ed. by S. Jefferson. 1 vol. 8vo. Carlisle. 1840.

See also R. S. Ferguson in Cumberland and Westmorland Antiq. and Arch. Soc. xi ;
cf. *ibid.* vii. 48–63.

DERBYSHIRE.

1178. Pole-Gell MSS. Hist. MSS. Comm. Rep. ix. Pt. ii. 1884.

Has papers of Sir John Gell relating to the civil war in Derbyshire. Others are in app.
to Stephen Glover's Derbyshire. 8vo. Derby. 1829.

DEVONSHIRE.

1179. Barnstaple and the northern part of Devonshire during the great civil war [1642–6]. By R. W. Cotton. 1 vol. 8vo. s.l. 1889.

Good use made of pamphlets.

DORSET.

1180. The story of Corfe Castle and of many who have lived there. By G. Bankes. 1 vol. 8vo. Lond. 1853.

Cf. Hist. MSS. Comm., Rep. viii, Pt. i, Bankes MSS.

1181. The great civil war in Dorset [1642–60]. By A. R. Bayley. 1 vol. 8vo. Taunton. 1910. Bibl.

Prints Edward Drake's Diary of the siege of Lyme Regis and other documents.

ESSEX.

1182. A most true relation of the expedition of Kent, Essex, and Colchester. By M. Carter. 1 vol. 8vo. Lond. 1650.

Carter was a royalist and took part in the defence of Colchester against Fairfax. There are diaries and other papers of the siege of Colchester in Hist. MSS. Comm., Round MSS., *apud* Buckinghamshire MSS., 1895, and in Hist. MSS. Comm., Beaufort MSS., 1891 ; cf. J. H. Round's The case of Lucas and Lisle, Trans. Royal Hist. Soc., N.S. viii. 1894.

GLOUCESTERSHIRE.

1183. Bibliotheca Gloucestrensis ; a collection of . . . tracts relating to the county and city of Gloucester during the civil war. Ed. by J. Washbourne. 1 vol. 4to. Gloucester. 1825.

Published in three parts in 1823–5, then in one vol.

1184. Sieges of Bristol during the civil war. By (Richard ?) Robinson. 1 vol. 8vo. Bristol. 1868.

HAMPSHIRE.

1185. The civil war in Hampshire [1642–5] and the story of Basing House. By G. N. Godwin. 1 vol. small 4to. Lond. 1882. 2nd ed. 1 vol. 4to. Lond. 1904. Illus.

HEREFORDSHIRE.

1186. Memorials of the civil war . . . as it affected Herefordshire and the adjacent counties. By J. Webb. Ed. by T. W. Webb. 2 vols. 8vo. Lond. 1879.

Appendix of documents.

HERTFORDSHIRE.

1187. Hertfordshire during the civil war and long parliament. By A. Kingston. 1 vol. 8vo. Lond. 1894.

Cf. East Anglia and the civil war, by the same author. 1 vol. 8vo. Lond. 1897. Illus.

KENT.

1188. The storm of Maidstone by Fairfax in 1648. By H. E. Malden. Eng. Hist. Rev. vii. 1892.

LANCASHIRE.

1189. Tracts relating to military proceedings in Lancashire during the civil war. Ed. by G. Ormerod. 1 vol. 4to. Chetham Soc. Lond. 1844.

1190. A discourse of the civil war in Lancashire. By E. Robinson. Ed. by W. Beamont. 1 vol. small 4to. Chetham Soc. Lond. 1864.

1191. The great civil war in Lancashire [1642–51]. 1 vol. 8vo. Manchester. 1910. Bibl. By E. Broxap.

LEICESTERSHIRE.

1192. Leicester during the civil war. By J. F. Hollings. 1 vol. 8vo. Leicester. 1840. Plan.

1193. The battle of Naseby. By W. G. Ross. Eng. Hist. Rev. iii. 1888.

1194. Loughborough during the great civil war. By E. W. Hensman. 1 vol. 8vo. Loughborough. *c.* 1921.

The same author wrote : The East Midlands and the second Civil War, May to July 1648. Trans. Royal Hist. Soc. 1923.

NORTHUMBERLAND.

1195. The siege of Newcastle-upon-Tyne by the Scots in 1644. By C. S. Terry.

In Archaeologia Aeliana, vol. xxi. Cf. *ibid.* The visits of Charles I to Newcastle in 1633, 1639, 1641, 1646–7, with some notes on contemporary local history ; and The Scottish campaign in Northumberland and Durham between January and June 1644.

SHROPSHIRE.

1196. Letters and papers of Thomas Mytton of Halston 1642–1655. Ed. by S. Leighton. 1 vol. 8vo. 1875.

Reprinted for the Powysland Club from Montgomeryshire Collections, vii and viii. Useful for the Civil War in and around Shropshire.

SOMERSETSHIRE.

1197.

Articles on various incidents in the civil war by Emanuel Green are in Somerset Arch. and Nat. Hist. Soc. xiv, xxiii–xxv ; others are in Proc. Bath Field Club, iii, iv, vi.

SUSSEX.

1198. Sussex in the great civil war and the interregnum, 1642–60. By C. Thomas-Stanford. 1 vol. 8vo. Lond. 1910. Illus.

Cf. W. H. Blaauw in Sussex Arch. Coll. v.

WARWICKSHIRE.

1199. Edgehill : the battle and battlefields : together with some notes on Banbury and thereabouts. By E. A. Walford. 1 vol. 8vo. Banbury. 1886. Bibl. 2nd ed. 1 vol. sm. 4to. Banbury. 1904. Illus. Bibl.

Cf. Notes on the battle of Edgehill, by T. Arnold and by W. G. Ross, in the Eng. Hist. Rev. ii. [1887] and an article by G. Davies, *ibid.*, xxxvi [1921]. All have bibliographical notes, and the last prints some new material.

WORCESTERSHIRE.

1200. The civil war in Worcestershire [1642–6], and the Scotch invasion of 1651. By J. W. Willis Bund. 1 vol. 8vo. Birmingham. 1905. Illus.

1201. Diary of Henry Townshend of Elmley Lovett 1640–1663. Worcestershire Hist. Soc. 2 vols. 4to. Lond. 1920. Ed. by J. W. Willis Bund.

Issued in 4 pts., the last being a valuable introduction. Important as showing how the royalists administered a friendly county.

YORKSHIRE.

1202. A journal of the first and second sieges of Pontefract Castle 1644–45 . . . with an appendix of evidences relating to the third siege. By N. Drake. Ed. by W. H. D. Longstaffe. Surtees Misc. 1861.

Drake was a volunteer during the sieges. Cf. The sieges of Pontefract Castle 1644–48, ed. by R. Holmes (8vo. Pontefract 1887. Illus.), in which Drake's and other narratives are printed.

1203. The Hull letters. Documents from the Hull records. 1625–46. Ed. by T. T. Wildridge. 1 vol. 8vo. Hull. 1886.

1204. The battle of Marston Moor. By Sir C. H. Firth.

Has an elaborate bibliography and new accounts. In Trans. of the Royal Hist. Soc. xii.

1205. The sieges of Hull during the great civil war. By E. Broxap. Eng. Hist. Rev. July 1905.

1206. Sir Hugh Cholmley's narrative of the siege of Scarborough 1644–5. Ed. by Sir C. H. Firth. Eng. Hist. Rev. xxxii. 1917.

From Bodl. Libr. Clarendon MSS. 1669.

SCOTLAND.

1207. Letters from roundhead officers written from Scotland to Captain Adam Baynes 1650–1660. Ed. by J. Y. Akerman. 1 vol. 4to. Bann. Club. Edin. 1856.

A selection from 10 vols. in Brit. Mus. Add. MSS. For further extracts from Baynes correspondence see Proc. Soc. Antiq. ii. 1849–53 and iii. 1853–6; and Tait's Edinburgh Magazine, xvii–xviii. 1850–1. Many of the Magazine letters are repr. in Surtees Soc. Misc. i. 1860.

1208. Cromwell's Scotch campaigns : 1650–51. By W. S. Douglas. 1 vol. 8vo. Lond. 1899.

1209. The battle of Dunbar. By Sir C. H. Firth.

Has bibliography and Payne Fisher's picture-plan of the battle. In Trans. of the Royal Hist. Soc. xiv. 1900.

1210. Papers relating to the army of the Solemn League and Covenant 1643–7. Ed. by C. S. Terry. 2 vols. Scot. Hist. Soc. Edin. 1917.

Deals with the equipment, payment, personnel, &c., of the army, not with operations. Cf. The Solemn League and Covenant of the three kingdoms, by Lord Guthrie, Scot. Hist. Rev. xv.

III. NAVAL HISTORY

1. Bibliographies.
2. General Sources and Later Works.
3. Administration and Policy.
4. Art of War.
5. Biographies and Personal Narratives.
6. Maritime Law.
7. Operations at Sea.
8. Seamanship and Navigation.
9. Construction and Descriptions of Ships.
10. Voyages in Men-of-war, including Shipwrecks.

THE serious study of naval history is comparatively modern, and owes much to the inspiration of Mahan (1276) and Laughton, whose lives of sailors in the Dictionary of National Biography form a valuable series. The only modern studies covering the whole period are Clowes (1229) and Corbett (1235), who confines himself to the Mediterranean. Administration is well treated by Oppenheim (1269) and by Tanner in his various Pepysian studies, but there is nothing better for the rest of the period than Burchett (1217–18). The documents published by the Navy Records Society are essential, and there is valuable material for the Dutch wars in Colenbrander (1346).

Many sources and later works enumerated elsewhere have important references to the navy. Among them the Calendar of State Papers, Domestic (124), and the House of Lords Papers (387) deserve particular mention, the latter being an indispensable source after the Revolution.

¶ 1. BIBLIOGRAPHIES

1211. List of Admiralty records preserved in the Public Record Office. Vol. i. Lists and indexes. xviii. Lond. 1904.

1212. Admiralty Library. Subject catalogue of printed books. Part I. Historical Section. Ed. by W. G. Perrin. 1 vol. 4to. Lond. 1912.
The best general bibliography for naval history.

1213. British sources of naval history in the seventeenth century. By A. C. Dewar.
Rep. of a paper read at the International Congress of History, London. 1913.

1214. Bibliotheca Pepysiana. A descriptive catalogue of the library of Samuel Pepys (Magdalene College, Cambridge). Ed. by J. R. Tanner, and others. 3 pts. sm. 4to. Lond. 1914.

1215. Bibliography of naval history. Part I. The Historical Association. By G. A. R. Callender. Lond. 1924.

¶ 2. GENERAL SOURCES AND LATER WORKS

1216. Judicious and select essayes and observations . . . upon the first invention of shipping; the misery of invasive warre, the navy royall and sea service; with his apologie for his voyage to Guiana. By Sir W. Raleigh. 1 vol. 12mo. Lond. 1650.

1217. Memoirs of transactions at sea during the war with France [1688–97]. By J. Burchett. 1 vol. 8vo. Lond. 1703.

Burchett was Secretary to the Admiralty, and in this work and in his Complete history supplies what is still in many respects the best naval history for 1688–1713. Cf. Luke Lillington's Reflections on Mr. Burchet's memoirs, or remarks on his second account of Captain Wilmot's expedition to the West Indies (1 vol. 8vo. Lond. 1704); answered in Mr. Burchett's Justification (1 vol. 8vo. Lond. 1704).

1218. A complete history of the most remarkable transactions at sea . . . to the conclusion of the last war with France [to 1712]. By J. Burchett. 1 vol. fol. Lond. 1720. Maps.

1219. Columna Rostrata; A critical history of the English sea-affairs. . . . By S. Colliber. 1 vol. 8vo. Lond. 1727. Later eds. 1739; 1742.

1220. The naval history of England . . . from . . . 1066 to . . . 1734. By T. Lediard. 2 vols. in 1. fol. Lond. 1735.

1221. A new naval history. By J. Entick. 1 vol. fol. Lond. 1757.
Useful for occasional documents.

1222. History of merchant shipping and ancient commerce. By W. S. Lindsay. 4 vols. 8vo. Lond. 1874–6.

1223. History of the Indian navy 1613–1863. By C. R. Low. 2 vols. 8vo. Lond. 1877.

1224. Correspondence of the family of Haddock 1659–1719. Ed. by Sir E. M. Thompson. Camd. Soc. Misc. viii. 1883. Pr. from Brit. Mus. Egerton MSS. 2520–32.

1225. Dartmouth MSS. Vols. i and iii. Hist. MSS. Comm. 1887, 1896.
Vol. i contains papers relating to (a) Tangier, and (b) Naval events in 1688, which are important. Vol. iii has valuable papers on the Dutch War, 1672–4.

1226. Cowper MSS. Hist. MSS. Comm. 3 vols. 1888–9.
Many naval documents throughout the period.

1227. Les ouvriers de la onzième heure. Les Anglais et les Hollandais dans les mers polaires et dans la mer des Indes. By J. P. E. J. de la Gravière. 2 vols. 8vo. Paris. 1890.

1228. The historical records of the royal marines. By L. Edye. 1 vol. 8vo. Lond. 1893.
Only 1 vol. published; covers period 1664–1701.

1229. The royal navy. A history. By W. L. Clowes and others. Lond.
The second vol. [1897] deals with 1603–1714.

1230. Eliot Hodgkin MSS. Hist. MSS. Comm. 1897.
Has naval papers addressed to or written by Pepys temp. Charles II.

1231. The British merchant service ; being a history of the British mercantile marine. . . . By R. J. C. Jones. 1 vol. 8vo. Lond. 1898. Illus.

1232. A short history of the royal navy. By D. Hannay. 2 vol. 8vo. Lond 1898–1909.
Vol. i, 1217–1688 ; vol. ii, 1688–1815.

1233. Leyborne-Popham MSS. Hist. MSS. Comm. 1899.
Useful for naval operations under the Commonwealth.

1234. The naval tracts of Sir William Monson ; in 6 books. Navy Records Society. Ed. by M. Oppenheim. 5 vols. 8vo. Lond. 1902–14.
Useful for reign of James I. First repr. in Churchill's Collection of voyages, vol. iii, 1704.

1235. England in the Mediterranean; a study of the rise and influence of British power within the Straits, 1603–1713. By Sir J. S. Corbett. 2 vols. 8vo. Lond. 1904.
Valuable.

1236. Seekriege und Seekriegswesen in ihrer weltgeschichtlichen Entwicklung. By R. Rittmeyer. 2 vols. fol. Berlin. 1907–11.
Vol. i to 1740.

1237. Extracts from a commissioner's note book 1691–94. Navy Records Soc. Misc. ii, 1912. Ed. by Sir J. K. Laughton.

1238. The navy under the early Stuarts and its influence on English history. By C. D. Penn. 1 vol. 8vo. Leighton Buzzard & Manchester. 1913. Illus. Bibl. Later ed. 1 vol. 8vo. Lond. 1920.
Covers 1603–49.

1239. The old Scots navy from 1689 to 1710. Ed. by J. Grant. 1 vol. 8vo. Navy Records Soc. vol. xliv. Lond. 1914.

1240. The navy of the Restoration from the death of Cromwell to the treaty of Breda. By A. W. Tedder. 1 vol. 8vo. Camb. 1916. Maps. Bibl.

1241. Der erste Englisch-Holländische Seekrieg 1652–1654. . . . By C. Ballhausen. 1 vol. 8vo. The Hague. 1923. Illus.
Useful collection of documents.

¶ 3. ADMINISTRATION AND POLICY

1242. An advice of a seaman. By N. Knott. s.l. 1634.

1243. The speech or declaration of Mr. St. John . . . 1640 . . . concerning ship-money. 1 vol. 8vo. Lond. 1641.

1244. An humble remonstrance to his majesty against the tax of ship-money imposed. 1 vol. 12mo. s.l. 1641.

1245. Englands outguard or Englands royall navie surveyed and lamented. By A. Burrell. 2 Pts. sm. 4to. Lond. 1646.

Cf. The answer of the commissioners of the navie to a scandalous pamphlet published by Mr. Andrewes Burrell. 1 vol. sm. 4to. 1646. Burrell also wrote ' A Memorable Sea Fight &c.' giving an account of the fight in the Downs, 1639, between Van Tromp and Oquendo. 1 vol. sm. 4to. Lond. 1649.

1246. A declaration in vindication of . . . Parliament and the committee of the navy. By G. Greene. 1 vol. 8vo. Lond. 1647.

By a leading member of the Committee of the Navy which dealt with naval administration, 1642–53.

1247. A cordiale for the calenture : or a declaration advising how England's sea honour may be regained. By A. Burrell. 1 vol. 12mo. Lond. 1648.

1248. A letter from the commanders and officers of the fleet : unto General Monck in Scotland. 5 pp. sm. 4to. Lond. 1659.

1249. The interest of England in the present war with Holland. 1 vol. 8vo. Lond. 1672.

1250. Memoires relating to the state of the royal navy of England 1679–88. By S. Pepys. 1 vol. 12mo. Lond. 1690. Later ed. 1 vol. 8vo. Oxf. 1906. ed. by J. R. Tanner.

Deals with Naval Administration.

1251. The late plot on the fleet detected, with the Jacobites memorial to the French king and an account of those gentlemen who invited the French fleet to invade our English coasts. 1 vol. 8vo. Lond. 1690.

1252. Naval speculations and maritime politicks : being a modest and brief discourse on the royal navy of England . . . a projection for a royal marine hospital. Also necessary measures in the present war with France. By H. Maydman. 1 vol. 12mo. Lond. 1691.

1253. The pathway to peace and profit : or a sure and certain way for the more speedy and effectual building and repairing their majesties' royal navy. By G. Everett. 1 vol. sm. 4to. Lond. 1694.

1254. England's interest or a discipline for seamen wherein is proposed a sure method for raising qualified seamen. By G. St. Lo. 1 vol. sm. 4to. Lond. 1694.

One of several similar works by St. Lo.

1255. A rough draft of a new model at sea, 1694. By George Savile, Marquis of Halifax. 1 vol. 4to. Lond. 1694.

Repr. in Foxcroft's Life of Halifax, ii. 454, and elsewhere.

1256. Justice perverted and innocence and loyalty oppressed. By R. Crosfield. 1 vol. 4to. Lond. 1695.

On the maladministration of the navy. Cf. Brit. Mus. Catalogue for Crosfield's other works.

1257. Great Britain's groans : or an account of the oppression ruin and destruction of the loyal seamen of England in the fatal loss of their pay. By W. Hodges. 1 vol. sm. 4to. s.l. 1695.

1258. The seaman's opinion of a standing army in England, in opposition to a fleet at sea.   2nd ed.   1 vol. 8vo. Lond. 1699.

1259. Remarks on the present conditions of the navy : in which 'tis clearly proved that the only security of England consists in a good fleet.   1 vol. 12mo. Lond. 1700.

1260. An essay on the navy.   By J. Dennis.   1 vol. 8vo. Lond. 1702.

1261. The present condition of the English navy.   1 vol. 8vo. Lond. 1702.

1262. An historical and political treatise of the navy.   1 vol. 8vo. Lond. 1703.

1263. The report of the Lords committees appointed to take into consideration the report of the commissioners ; so far as relates to the accounts of the Rt. Hon. Edward, Earl of Orford, late treasurer of the navy.   1 vol. fol. Lond. 1704.
Cf. The answers of the Earl of Orford, to the observations made by the hon. commissioners of accompts (1 vol. fol. Lond. 1704).

1264. The oeconomy of his majesty's navy office.   1 vol. 12mo. Lond. 1717.
The instructions for the Navy Board drawn up by Pepys and issued by the Duke of York.

1265. Memoirs of the English affairs : chiefly naval from ... 1660 to 1673. By James, Duke of York.   1 vol. 8vo. Lond. 1729.
Orders and instructions issued by James, Duke of York, as Lord High Admiral.

1266. Documents illustrating the impeachment of the Duke of Buckingham in 1626.   Ed. by S. R. Gardiner.   Camd. Soc. 1889.

1267. Naval commissioners . . . 1660–1760.   Compiled from the original warrants and returns.   By Sir G. Jackson and Sir G. F. Duckett.   1 vol. 8vo. (Lewes) 1889.

1268. A list of the lords high admiral and commissioners for executing that office . . . since the year 1660.   1 vol. fol. Admiralty. Lond. 1892.   Later ed. 1915.

1269. A history of the administration of the royal navy and of merchant shipping in relation to the navy from 1509 to 1660.   By M. Oppenheim. 1 vol. 8vo. Lond. 1896.
Valuable.   Cf. The lord high admiral and the board of admiralty, by W. G. Perrin, and The naval administration of the interregnum by A. C. Dewar, both in the Mariner's Mirror, April and October, 1926.

1270. Two discourses of the navy, 1638 and 1659, by J. Hollond ; also a discourse of the navy 1660 by Sir R. Slyngsbie.   Ed. by J. R. Tanner.   1 vol. 8vo. Navy Records Soc. Lond. 1896.

1271. The administration of the navy from the Restoration to the Revolution.   By J. R. Tanner.   Eng. Hist. Rev. xii–xiv. 1897–9.
Subsequently expanded to form the General Introduction to the Catalogue of Pepysian MSS., vol. i.

1272. A descriptive catalogue of the naval manuscripts in the Pepysian Library at Magdalene College, Cambridge. Ed. by J. R. Tanner. 4 vols. 8vo. Navy Records Society. Lond. 1903–23.

Vol. i, General Introduction, register of ships and of sea officers ; ii and iii, Admiralty letters ; iv, Minutes of the admiralty commission, 1 Jan. 1674–21. Apr. 1679. Further volumes in preparation. Cf. Samuel Pepys's naval minutes. Ed. J. R. Tanner for Navy Records Soc. 1926.

1273. Samuel Pepys and the royal navy—Lees Knowles Lectures delivered at Trinity College in Cambridge, Nov. 1919. By J. R. Tanner. 1 vol. 8vo. Cambridge. 1920.

¶ 4. ART OF WAR

1274. L'Art des armées navales. By P. Hoste. 1 vol. fol. Lyons. 1697.

An important treatise on tactics, based on the naval actions of the preceding fifty years.

1275. The sailing and fighting instructions or signals. By J. Greenwood. 1 vol. 12mo. s.l. 1714. Diagrams.

1276. The influence of sea-power upon history, 1660–1783. By A. T. Mahan. 1 vol. 8vo. Lond. s.a. [1896].

The study of British naval actions and naval policy that first drew attention to the vital importance of sea-power.

1277. Naval warfare. Its ruling principles and practice historically treated. By P. H. Colomb, Vice Admiral. 1 vol. 8vo. Lond. 1891. 2nd ed. 1895 ; 3rd ed. 1899.

A naval history on strategical lines containing many plans.

1278. Fighting instructions 1530–1816. Ed. by J. S. Corbett. 1 vol. 8vo. Navy Records Soc. Lond. 1905.

¶ 5. BIOGRAPHIES AND PERSONAL NARRATIVES

1279. The lives of the admirals and other eminent British seamen. By J. Campbell. 4 vols. 8vo. 1742–4, later ed. 8 vols. 8vo. Lond. 1812–17. Illus. Ed. by H. R. Yorke.

Cf. Campbell's The naval history of Great Britain . . . including the history and lives of the British admirals. 8 vols. 8vo. Lond. 1818. Illus. This is virtually another ed. of the above.

1280. Biographia navalis or impartial memoirs of the lives and characters of officers of the navy . . . from . . . 1660 to the present time. By J. Charnock. 6 vols. 8vo. Lond. 1794–8. Illus.

BADILEY, RICHARD.

1281. A life of Richard Badiley vice admiral of the fleet. 1 vol. 8vo. Lond. 1899. By T. A. Spalding.

Chiefly operations in the Mediterranean, 1652–4.

BLAKE, ROBERT.

1282. Robert Blake, admiral and general at sea. Based on family and state papers. By W. H. Dixon. 1 vol. 8vo. Lond. 1852. Later ed. 1885. Illus.

Another life by David Hannay. 1 vol. 8vo. Lond. 1886. Cf. John Oldmixon's The history and life of Admiral Blake. 2nd ed. 8vo. 1746.

DEANE, RICHARD.

1283. The life of Richard Deane, major-general and general-at-sea in the service of the commonwealth. By J. B. Deane. 1 vol. 8vo. Lond. 1870.

FAIRFAX, ROBERT.

1284. Life of Robert Fairfax of Steeton, vice-admiral, alderman and member for York ... 1666–1725. By Sir C. R. Markham. 1 vol. 8vo. Lond. 1885. Illus.

LEAKE, SIR JOHN.

1285. Life of Sir John Leake rear admiral of Great Britain. By S. M. Leake. Priv. pr. 1750. 2nd ed. 2 vols. Navy Records Soc. 1920. Port. Plans. Ed. by G. A. R. Callender.

Leake's service at sea covers 1673–1712.

MAINWARING, SIR HENRY.

1286. The life and works of Sir Henry Mainwaring. By G. E. Manwaring. 2 vols. Navy Records Soc. 1920–2.

Vol. i, life; vol. ii, works. Repr. Of the beginnings, practices and suppression of pirates and The seaman's dictionary.

MARTIN, STEPHEN.

1287. Life of Captain Stephen Martin 1666–1740. Ed. by Sir C. R. Markham. 1 vol. Navy Records Soc. 1895. Illus.

Compiled from Martin's journals by his son. Intro. contains an account of the constitution and condition of the navy.

PENN, SIR WILLIAM.

1288. Memorials of ... Sir William Penn, admiral and general of the fleet 1644 to 1670. By G. Penn. 2 vols. 8vo. Lond. 1833.

Important : has many documents.

PETT, PHINEAS.

1289. The autobiography of Phineas Pett. Ed. by W. G. Perrin. 1 vol. Navy Records Soc. 1918.

Covers 1570–1638. Valuable for the history of shipbuilding in England. Intro. contains a history of the shipwrights' company.

RAINBOROWE, THOMAS.

1290. Notes on the life of Thomas Rainborowe, officer in the army and navy in the service of the parliament of England. By E. Peacock. Archaeologia, xlvi.

SANDWICH, EDWARD MOUNTAGU, EARL OF.

1291. The life of Edward Mountagu, K.G., first Earl of Sandwich (1625–1672). By F. R. Harris. 2 vols. 8vo. Lond. 1912. Illus.

TORRINGTON, ARTHUR HERBERT, EARL OF.

1292. An impartial account of some remarkable passages in the life of Arthur, Earl of Torrington, together with some modest remarks on his tryal and acquitment. 1 vol. 4to. Lond. 1691.

Herbert's correspondence, including letters of William III and Burnet, at the time of the Revolution, is in Eng. Hist. Rev. i. 1886. Ed. by Sir E. M. Thompson.

TORRINGTON, GEORGE BYNG, LORD.

1293. Memoirs relating to the Lord Torrington. Ed. by Sir J. K. Laughton. Camd. Soc. 1889.

Life of Byng, cr. Viscount Torrington 1721, with an account of his sea service 1678–1705. Pr. from Brit. Mus. Add. MS. 31958.

¶ 6. MARITIME LAW

1294. Abridgment of all sea lawes. By W. Welwod. 1 vol. 4to. Lond. 1613. Later ed. 1 vol. 8vo. 1636.

1295. Mare Clausum seu de Dominio Maris. By J. Selden. 1 vol. fol. Lond. 1635. Later ed. 1652. Trans. by M. Nedham.

1296. The soveraignty of the British seas proved. By Sir J. Boroughs. 1 vol. 12mo. Lond. 1651.

1297. A view of the admiral jurisdiction. By J. Godolphin. 1 vol. 8vo. Lond. 1661.

1298. The jurisdiction of the admiralty of England. By R. Zouch. 1 vol. sm. 8vo. Lond. 1663.

1299. The maritime dicaeologie, or sea jurisdiction of England. By J. Exton. 1 vol. fol. Lond. 1664.

1300. De jure maritimo et navali : or a treatise of affairs maritime and of commerce By C. Molloy. 1 vol. 8vo. Lond. 1676. 4th ed. 1 vol. 8vo. Lond. 1688. 6th ed. 1 vol. 8vo. Lond. 1707. 8th ed. 1 vol. 8vo. Lond. 1744. 9th ed. 2 vols. 8vo. Lond. 1769.

Long remained a standard work.

1301. Observations concerning the dominion and sovereignty of the seas, being an abstract of the marine affairs of England. By Sir P. Medows. 1 vol. sm. 4to. Lond. 1689.

1302. A general treatise of the dominion and laws of the sea . . . and particularly that excellent body of sea-laws lately published in France . . . with a collection of the marine treaties concluded during the last century. By A. Justice. 1 vol. 4to. Lond. 1705.

Third ed. with large additions, no date (*c.* 1710).

1303. A collection of all statutes and parts of statutes as in any way relate to the admiralty, navy and ships of war . . . down to the 14th year of King George the Second.   1 vol. 4to. Lond. 1742.

Similar volumes were published in 1768 and 1810.

1304. The statutes relating to the admiralty, navy shipping and navigation of the United Kingdom from 9 Hen. III. to 3 Geo. IV. inclusive . . . collected and arranged under the authority of the lords commissioners of the admiralty. Ed. by J. Raithby.   1 vol. 4to. Lond. 1823.

1305. The orders in council at present in force and some of the acts of parliament for the regulation of the naval services (27 Aug. 1663–2 Feb. 1842). 1 vol. 8vo. Lond. 1842.   Later ed. 1856.

Cf. General index to orders in council from 1663 to 1902 ; and some of the acts of Parliament for the regulation of the naval service (1 vol. 8vo. Lond. 1904).

1306. The admiralty statutes : being the public statutes actually in force . . . from . . . 1552 to . . . 1874 . . . Under the authority of the lords commissioners of the admiralty.   Ed. by A. V. Dicey.   1 vol. 8vo. Lond. 1875.   Later eds. 1 vol. 8vo. Lond. 1886. Ed. by A. V. Dicey and J. L. Goddard.   2 vols. 8vo. Lond. 1905. Ed. by A. T. Carter.

1307. Early prize jurisdiction and prize law in England.   Part II, 1603–40 ; III, 1643–98. By R. G. Marsden. Eng. Hist. Rev. xxv. 1910 ; xxvi. 1911.

1308. The sovereignty of the sea, an historical account of the claims of England to the dominion of the British seas and of the evolution of the territorial waters. By T. W. Fulton. 1 vol. 8vo. Lond. 1911.

1309. Naval courts martial. By D. Hannay. 1 vol. 8vo. Camb. 1914.

1310. The law and custom of the sea.   Vol. i, 1205–1648 ;   vol. ii, 1649–1767. By R. G. Marsden. Navy Records Soc. 1915–17.

A valuable collection of documents relating to prize, piracy, &c., mostly from the public records.

1311. The freedom of the seas, or, the right which belongs to the Dutch to take part in the East Indian trade. By H. de Groot. Translated with a revision of the Latin text of 1633 by R. Van D. Magoffin. Carnegie Endowment for International Peace, Division of Int. Law. Ed. by J. B. Scott. 8vo. New York. 1916.

1312. Doctor's Commons and the old court of admiralty. By W. Senior. 1 vol. 8vo. Lond. 1922.

1313. A history of the English prize court. By E. S. Roscoe. 1 vol. 8vo. Lond. 1924.

¶ 7. OPERATIONS AT SEA

1314. A journall of all the proceedings of the Duke of Buckingham in the Isle of Ree. . . . 2 pts. 4to. Lond. 1627.

1315. A true journall of the Sallee fleet. . . . By J. Dunton. 1 vol. 4to. Lond. 1637.

See Churchill's Collection of voyages, vol. viii.

1316. Expeditio in ream insulam.   By Edward Herbert, Lord of Cherbury.
1 vol. 8vo. Lond. 1656.   Trans. publ. by Philobiblon Soc.   1 vol. 4to. Lond.
1860.   Ed. by Edward James Herbert, third Earl of Powis.

1317. A true narrative of the engagement between his majesties Fleet and
that of Holland begun June the first, 1666.   1 vol. Lond. 1666.

1318. A true and perfect relation of the happy successe and victory obtained
against the Turks of Algiers at Bugia, by his majesty's fleet . . . 1 vol. 4to.
Lond. 1671.

1319. An exact relation of the several engagements and actions of his
majesties fleet.   Anno 1673.   1 vol. 8vo. Lond. 1673.

1320. A just vindication of the principal officers of his majesties ordnance
from the scandalous aspersions laid upon them in . . . an exact relation of the
several engagements.   1 vol. 12mo. Lond. 1674.

1321. Relation de ce qui s'est passé entre les armées navales de France et
d'Angleterre et celle de Hollande pendant les années 1672 et 1673. 1 vol.
12mo. Paris. 1674.

1322. The Netherland-historian, containing a true and exact relation of
the late warrs between the king of Great Britain, and the French king against
the United Provinces, from 1671 to 1674.   Trans. by S. Swart.   1 vol. 12mo.
Amsterdam. 1675.   Plates.
Mainly devoted to military history, but has useful information of naval operations.

1323. A list of several ships belonging to English merchants taken by
French privateers since Dec. 1673, also a brief account touching what applications hath been made for redress.   1 vol. 4to. Amsterdam.   1677.

1324. A plain relation of the late action at sea between the English and
Dutch and the French fleets.   By [E. Stephens].   1 vol. sm. 4to. Lond. 1690.

1325. An account given by Sir John Ashby vice-admiral and Reere
Admiral Rooke to the lords commissioners of the engagement at sea between
the English, Dutch, and French fleets, June 30th, 1690.   1 vol. sm. 4to. Lond.
1691.

1326. Adml. Russell's letter to the Earl of Nottingham containing an
exact and particular relation of the late happy victory and success against the
French fleet.   1 vol. fol. Lond. 1692.

1327. An account of the late great victory obtained at sea against the
French. . . . May 1692.   1 vol. 4to. Lond. 1692.

1328. A journal of the Brest expedition.   By Peregrine Osborne, Marquis
of Caermarthen.   1 vol. 8vo. Lond. 1694.

1329. An impartial account of all the material transactions of the grand
fleet and land forces from their first setting out from Spithead June 29 till . . .
the Duke of Ormond's arrival at Deal, Nov. 7th, 1702.   By an officer that was
present.   1 vol. 4to. Lond. 1703.

1330. Memoirs of the British fleets and squadrons that acted in the Mediterranean 1708 and 1709. By N. Taubman. 1 vol. 8vo. Lond. 1710. Later ed. 1714.

Taubman was a naval chaplain.

1331. Two original journals of Sir R. Granville of the expedition to Cadiz anno 1625, of the expedition to the Isle of Rhee . . . anno 1627. 2 pts. 8vo. Lond. 1724.

1332. A narrative of the victory obtained by the English and Dutch fleet . . . over that of France, near La Hogue 1692. 1 vol. 8vo. Lond. 1744.

From the journal of R. Allyn, the chaplain of the ' Centurion '.

1333. M. de Bonrepaus, la marine et le désastre de la Hougue. By A. de Boislisle. 1 vol. 8vo. Paris. 1877.

1334. The voyage to Cadiz in 1625. Being a journal written by John Glanville, secretary to the lord admiral. By J. Glanville. Ed. by A. B. Grosart. Camd. Soc. 1883.

Pr. from Sir John Eliot's MS. at Port Eliot.

1335. Naval preparations of James II in 1688. By J. R. Tanner. Eng. Hist. Rev. viii. 1893.

1336. Journal 1700–1702. By Sir G. Rooke, Admiral. Ed. by O. Browning. 1 vol. 8vo. Navy Records Soc. Lond. 1897.

Covers the expedition to the Sound in 1700 and the attacks in Cadiz and Vigo in 1702. Cf. Eng. Hist. Rev. xiii. 1898.

1337. Letters and papers relating to the first Dutch war 1652–54. Ed. by S. R. Gardiner, and C.T. Atkinson. 5 vols. 8vo. Navy Records Soc. Lond. 1898–1912.

1338. The capture of Santiago in Cuba by Captain Myngs, 1662. By C. H. Firth. Eng. Hist. Rev. July 1899.

1339. La bataille de la Hougue (29 Mai 1692). By G. Toudouze. 1 vol. 8vo. Paris. 1899.

1340. Prince Rupert at Lisbon (1649–50). Ed. by S. R. Gardiner. Camd. Soc. Misc. x. 1902.

Pr. from Add. MS. 35251. Brit. Mus.

1341. Blake and the battle of Santa Cruz. By Sir C. H. Firth. Eng. Hist. Rev. xx. 1905.

Cf. A narrative of the battle of Santa Cruz, written by Sir Richard Stayner, rear-admiral of the Fleet, ed. by Sir C. H. Firth from Add. MS. 32093. Navy Records Soc. Miscellany II. 1912.

1342. A note on the drawings in the possession of the Earl of Dartmouth illustrating the battle of Sole Bay, May 28, 1672, and the battle of the Texel, Aug. 11, 1673 (with the drawings in a case). By Sir J. S. Corbett. 1 vol. 8vo. Navy Records Soc. Lond. 1908.

1343. Naval wars in the Baltic, 1522–1850. By R. C. Anderson. 1 vol. 8vo. Lond. 1910. Maps and plans.

1344. The operations of the English fleet 1648–52. By R. C. Anderson.
Eng. Hist. Rev. xxxi. 1916.

App. has list of ships belonging to, or taken by, the Royalist fleet, 1648–53.

1345. Bescheiden uit vreemde archieven omtrent de groote Nederlandsche
Zeeoorlogen, 1652–1676. By Dr. H. T. Colenbrander. 2 vols. 8vo. The
Hague. 1919.

A collection of documents from English and French archives, with a few from Swedish
and Danish sources, elucidating the history of the three naval wars between England and
Holland.

1346. The voyages of Captain William Jackson. Ed. by V. T. Harlow.
Camd. Soc. Musc. xiii. 1924.

1347. Stukken betrekking hebbende op den tocht naar Chatham en berustende op het Record Office te Londen. By P. Geyl.

Bijdragen en Mededeelingen van het Historisch Genootschap. Deel xxxviii.

¶ 8. SEAMANSHIP AND NAVIGATION

1348. The light of navigation, wherein are declared all the coasts & havens
of the west, north & east seas. By W. Johnson (Janszoon). 1 vol. 4to.
Amsterdam. 1625.

1349. An accidence, or the path-way to experience necessary for all young
seamen, showing the phrases, offices and words of command belonging to the
building, ridging and sayling a man of warre. By J. Smith. 1 vol. 4to. Lond.
1626.

Describes the duties of mariners and their necessary outfit. An enlarged ed. entitled
' A sea grammar ' was published in 1627–8. There were further eds. in 1653, 1691, &
1692, and the 1626 ed. was repr. in 1636, in each case with slightly different titles.
Repr. in vol. ii. ' John Smith's Travels ', Glasgow, 1907.

1350. The navigator ; shewing and explaining all the chiefe principles and
parts . . . in the . . . art of navigation. By C. Saltonstall. 1 vol. 4to. [Lond.?]
1642. 3rd ed. 1 vol. 4to. [Lond.?] 1660.

1351. The seaman's practice. By R. Norwood. 1 vol. 4to. Lond. 1637.
Later ed. 5th vol. sm. 4to. Lond. 1662.

1352. The seamans dictionary. By Sir H. Mainwaring. 1 vol. sm. 4to.
Lond. 1644. Later eds. 1667 ; 1670.

The early printed editions are imperfect, the best edition formed by collation of the
original MSS. is included in vol. ii of the Life and works of Sir H. M. (Navy Records
Soc., vol. lvi). See also Boteler ' Six Dialogues. . . .' No. 1366.

1353. Pathway to perfect sailing. By R. Potter. 1644.

1354. The sizes and lengths of rigging for all his majesty's ships and
frigates. By E. Hayward. 1 vol. fol. Lond. 1660.

1355. A short compendium of the . . . sea book ; or pilots sea-mirror . . .
newly enlarged and amended and now translated into English. By L. Childe.
1 vol. 4to. Lond. 1663.

1356. The mariners magazine. By S. Sturmy. 1 vol. fol. Lond. 1669.
Later eds. 1679 ; 1700, ed. by J. Colson.

1357. The boat-swains art ; or the complete boat-swain, wherein is shewed
a true proportion for the masting, yarding and rigging of any ship. By H.
Bond. 1 vol. 4to. Lond. 1670. Later ed. 1704.
 Ed. of 1704 entitled : The art of apparelling and fitting of any ship.

1358. The English pilot : the first book describing the northern navigation :
the second book describing the southern navigation : the second book Pt. II
describing the Mediterranean Sea. By J. Seller. 3 vols. fol. Lond. 1671–7.
Many subsequent eds.
 Sailing directions and charts, largely from Dutch sources.

1359. Atlas maritimus : or a book of charts describing the sea coasts . . . in
most of the knowne parts of the world. . . . By J. Seller. 1 vol. fol. Lond. 1675.

1360. The seaman's tutor. By P. Perkins. 1 vol. 12mo. Lond. 1682.

1361. Norwoods system of navigation teaching the whole art. By M.
Norwood. Lond. 1685.

1362. Great Britain's coasting pilot : being a survey of the sea coast of
England from the river Thames to the westward . . . By G. Collins. 1 vol.
fol. Lond. 1693. Later eds. 1744, 1753, 1792.
 The first scientific survey of the English coast : it does not extend to the east coast.

1363. The whole art of navigation. By D. Newhouse. 1 vol. 4to. Lond.
1701.

1364. The mariner's jewel. By J. Love. 5th ed. 1 vol. 12mo. Lond. 1705.
6th ed. 1724. 7th ed. 1735.

1365. A treatise on rigging written about the year 1625. From a MS. at
Petworth. Ed. by R. C. Anderson. 1 vol. 4to. Lond. 1921.

¶ 9. CONSTRUCTION AND DESCRIPTIONS OF SHIPS

1366. Six dialogues about sea services. By N. Boteler. 1 vol. 8vo. Lond.
1685. Later ed. 1688.
 Printed from one of the early MSS., written *c.* 1625 : the best MS. is probably Sloane
2449, revised and re-written *c.* 1635. The 2nd ed. is entitled ' Colloquia maritima,
or sea dialogues'. The dialogues are concerned principally with administration and
seamanship.

1367. Architectura navalis. By J. Furtenbach. 2 vols. Ulm. 1629.

1368. A true description of his majesties royal ship built 1637 at Woollwitch
in Kent. By T. Heywood. 1 vol. 4to. Lond. 1637.
 Repr. with additions in 1653 as The common-wealths great ship.

1369. The compleat ship-wright. By E. Bushnell. 1 vol. 4to. Lond. 1664.
Diagrams. 5th ed. 1688.

1370. Navigation improved, or the art of rowing ships of all rates, in calms with a more easy, swift and steady motion than oars can. By T. Savery. 1 vol. 4to. Lond. 1698. Repr. 1880.

1371. The ship-builders assistant, or marine architecture. By W. Sutherland. 1 vol. 4to. Lond. 1711. Plans. Later ed. 1784, 1794.

He also publ. a larger work, Britain's glory or shipbuilding unvail'd. 2 pts. fol. Lond. 1717.

1372. History of marine architecture. By J. Charnock. 3 vols. 4to. Lond. 1800–2. Plans.

Contains many documents and much historical matter, but to be used with caution.

1373. Sailing ship models. By R. M. Nance. 1 vol. 4to. Lond. 1924.

1374. Old ship figure-heads and sterns. A survey of the development of ship ornamentation. By L. G. C. Laughton. 1 vol. 4to. Lond. 1925.

Numerous illustrations by Cecil King. An invaluable study of the course of development of the outer form of ships of war from the 15th cent.

¶ 10. VOYAGES IN MEN-OF-WAR, INCLUDING SHIPWRECKS

1375. A new voyage round the world. By W. Dampier. 1 vol. 8vo. Lond. 1697. Later eds. 2nd, 3 vols. 8vo. Lond. 1697–1709. 4th ed., 4 vols. 8vo. Lond. 1699–1729.

For the additions in later eds. see Dict. Nat. Biog., *sub* Dampier.

1376. A cruising voyage round the world ; begun in 1708 and finished in 1711. By W. Rogers. 1 vol. 8vo. Lond. 1712. Later ed. 1 vol. 8vo. Lond. 1718.

Cf. Life aboard a British privateer in the time of Queen Anne. Being the journal of Captain W. Rogers, with notes and illustrations : Ed. by R. C. Leslie, 8vo. 1889.

1377. The diary of Henry Teonge, chaplain on board H.M.S. Assistance, Bristol, & Royal Oak. 1675–79. By H. Teonge. 1 vol. 8vo. Lond. 1825. New ed. 1 vol. 8vo. Lond. 1927. Ed. by G. E. Manwaring.

Account of life on board ship in seventeenth century during two voyages to Mediterranean.

1378. Journal of a voyage into the Meditterranean A.D. 1628. By Sir K. Digby. Ed. by J. Bruce. Camd. Soc. 1868.

1379. The shipwreck of Sir Cloudesley Shovell on the Scilly Islands in 1707, from . . . documents hitherto unpublished. By J. H. Cooke. 1 vol. 4to. Gloucester. 1883. Map. Port.

From the Proceedings of the Society of Antiquaries ; gives pedigree of Shovell's descendants.

1380. Sir John Penningtons' naval journal for 1631, 1633–36. Muncaster MSS. *apud* Westmorland MSS. Hist. MSS. Comm. 10th Report, app. iv. 1885, reissued 1906, pp. 275–96.

IV. RELIGIOUS HISTORY

1. General and Miscellaneous.
2. Anglican Church.
3. Nonconformity.
4. Quakerism.
5. Unitarianism.
6. Judaism.
7. Roman Catholicism.

¶ 1. GENERAL AND MISCELLANEOUS

ECCLESIASTICAL historians deal too exclusively with particular bodies, and Stoughton (1393) has not been superseded as a general history of the religious development of England. There are, however, valuable studies of tendencies of religious thought during the Stuart period. Thus the growth of rationalism is adequately treated by Lecky (1391) and Tulloch (1392), and the theory of toleration by Russell Smith (1399) and Seaton (1399 n.).

1381. The authorised version of the English Bible, 1611. 1 vol. fol. Lond. 1611. Later ed. 5 vols. 8vo. Camb. 1909. Ed. by W. A. Wright.

Cf. A. W. Pollard's Records of the English Bible. The documents relating to the translation and publication of the Bible in English, 1525–1611. 1 vol. 8vo. Oxf. 1911.

1382. Liberty of conscience or the sole means to obtain peace and truth. 1 vol. 4to. 1643.

Probably by Henry Robinson. See Eng. Hist. Rev. ix. 715. See the index to Thomason Tracts under Liberty of conscience for similar pamphlets.

1383. The bloudy tenent of persecution for cause of conscience discussed in a conference betweene truth and peace. . . . By R. Williams. 1 vol. 4to. Lond. 1644.

Repr. by Hansard Knollys Soc. in a vol. entitled Tracts on liberty of conscience and persecution, 1614–1661. Ed. by E. B. Underhill. 8vo. Lond. 1848.

1384. A discourse of the liberty of prophesying, shewing the unreasonableness of prescribing to other mens faith, and the iniquity of persecuting differing opinions. By J. Taylor. 1 vol. 4to. Lond. 1647.

1385. Epistola de tolerantia. . . . By J. Locke. 1 vol. 8vo. Tergou. 1689.

Translated into English by W. Popple, and published in London in the same year (1689). A second, and a third, letter concerning toleration, were published in London, 4to. in 1690 and 1692. His The reasonableness of Christianity as delivered in the scriptures was publ. 1 vol. 8vo. 1695.

1386. Christianity not mysterious : or, a treatise shewing there is nothing in the Gospels contrary to reason nor above it. By J. Toland. 1 vol. 8vo. [? Lond.] 1696.

Started the deist controversy.

1387. A new catalogue of all the small tracts lately printed for the promoting Christian knowledge and practise in all sorts of people . . . with the prices of them single and by the hundred. 1 vol. fol. s.l. s.a.

Pr. for W. Hawes *c.* 1705.

1388. Pietas Londinensis : or the present ecclesiastical state of London, containing an account of all the churches and chapels of ease . . . the set times of their public prayers . . . the names of the present dignitaries ministers and lecturers. By J. Paterson. 1 vol. 8vo. Lond. 1714.

Cf. Richard Newcourt's Repertorium ecclesiasticum parochiale Londinense. An ecclesiastical parochial history of the diocese of London [2 vols. fol. Lond. 1708–10] ; and George Hennessy's Novum Repertorium parochiale Londinense [1 vol. 4to. Lond. 1898].

1389. Ecclesiastical biography . . . from the . . . Reformation to the Revolution. Ed. by C. Wordsworth. 6 vols. 8vo. Lond. 1810. Later eds. 1818 ; and 4 vols. 8vo. Lond. 1853.

Contents. Vol. v : Sir Henry Wotton, reprinted entire from Walton's Lives ; Nicholas Ferrar, from the Life by Dr. Peck and with large additions from a manuscript in the Lambeth Library ; Bishop Hall, reprinted entire from Observations, &c. by himself. 1660. 4to ; Doctor Henry Hammond, repr. entire from his Life by Bishop Fell, ed. 2d. 1662 ; Bishop Sanderson, repr. entire from Walton's Lives ; Richard Baxter, extracted from his Life and times written by himself. Vol. vi : Sir Matthew Hale, repr. entire from his Life by Burnet, ed. 1682 ; Philip Henry, repr. entire from his Life by Matthew Henry, ed. 1699 ; Earl of Rochester, repr. entire from Burnet's Some passages &c., ed. 1680 ; Archbishop Tillotson, abridged from his Life, 8vo. 1717.

1390. The literature of the Sabbath question. By R. Cox. 2 vols. fol. Edin. 1865.

1391. The history of the rise and influence of the spirit of rationalism in Europe. By W. E. H. Lecky. 2 vols. 8vo. Lond. 1865.

1392. Rational theology and Christian philosophy in England in the 17th century. By J. Tulloch. 2 vols. 8vo. Edin. 1872. Later ed. 1874.

1393. History of religion in England. I. The church of the civil wars. II. The church of the commonwealth. III & IV. The church of the restoration. V. The church of the revolution. By J. Stoughton. 8 vols. 8vo. Lond. 1881.

Originally publ. in parts, vols. i–iv, 1867–70, and v–vi, in 1878.

1394. Dictionary of hymnology. Ed. by J. Julian. 1 vol. 8vo. Lond. 1892.

Cf. Hymns ancient and modern . . . historical edition with notes on the origin of both hymns and tunes . . . illustrated with facsimiles and portraits. 1 vol. 8vo. Lond. 1909 ; and The English hymn, its development and use in worship. By L. F. Benson. 1 vol. 8vo. N.Y. 1915.

1395. The English government and the relief of Protestant refugees. By W. A. Shaw. Eng. Hist. Rev. ix. 1894.

1396. Die Unionstätigkeit John Duries unter dem Protektorat Cromwells. Ein Beitrag zur Kirchengeschichte des siebzehnten Jahrhunderts. By K. Brauer. 1 vol. 8vo. Marburg. 1907.

1397. Religious toleration in England. By H. M. Gwatkin. Cambridge Modern History. v. 1908. Bibl.

1398. Latitudinarianism and Pietism. By M. Kaufmann. Cambridge Modern History, v. 1908. Bibl.

1399. The theory of religious liberty in the reigns of Charles II and James II. By H. F. Russell Smith. 1 vol. 8vo. Camb. 1911. Bibl.
Cf. Alexander Adam Seaton's The theory of toleration under the later Stuarts. [1 vol. 8vo. Camb. 1911. Bibl.]

1400. Der Toleranzgedanke im England der Stuarts. By A. O. Meyer. Historische Zeitschrift, cviii. 1912.

1401. Platonists and latitudinarians. By J. B. Mullinger. Camb. Hist. of Eng. Lit. viii. 1912. Bibl.

1402. Caritas Anglicana, or, an historical inquiry into those religious and philanthropical societies that flourished in England between the years 1678 and 1740. By G. V. Portus. 1 vol. 8vo. Lond. 1912.

¶ 2. ANGLICAN CHURCH

> (*a*) General Sources.
> (*b*) General Later Works.
> (*c*) Collective Biographies.
> (*d*) Biographies, Personal Narratives, and
>   Collected Works of Individuals.

The mass of material for the doctrinal and liturgical history of the Anglican Church is enormous, and is accessible in the collected works of eminent divines. The contents of many of these voluminous collections are enumerated in James Darling's Cyclopaedia Bibliographica [2 vols. 8vo. Lond. 1854], a valuable work of reference. Documents illustrating the constitutional history of the Church are provided mainly by Cardwell, and Makower (1464) furnishes a useful outline.

There is an elaborate study for the years 1640–60 by Shaw (1466), and Frere (1469) and Hutton (1468) are the best summaries for the whole period from the Anglo-Catholic standpoint. On the whole the period especially after the restoration has been comparatively neglected by ecclesiastical historians, and there is no adequate bibliography. No successful attempt has yet been made to estimate the influence of the Anglican Church upon the political and social development of England during the period in modern times when its power was greatest, although eighty years have elapsed since Macaulay pointed out that the pulpit was the main organ of public opinion. There are, however, many useful hints on the decline of clerical influence in the first volume of Lecky's History. Generally speaking, biographies unduly preponderate over more general studies.

(*a*) SOURCES

1403. The summe and substance of the conference, which it pleased his excellent maiestie to have . . . at Hampton Court, January 14, 1603. By W. Barlow. 1 vol. 8vo. Lond. 1604.
Repr. in Cardwell, History of conferences.

1404. Constitutions and canons ecclesiasticall treated upon by the Bishop of London president of the Convocation for the province of Canterbury and the rest of the bishops and clergie . . . and agreed upon with the kings . . . licence. 1 vol. sm. 4to. Lond. 1604. Later eds. 1 vol. 12mo. Lond. 1869. Ed. by C. H. Davis. 1 vol. 8vo. Oxf. and Lond. 1874. Ed. by M. E. C. Walcott.

1405. Reasons for refusal of subscription to the booke of Common Prayer under the handes of certaine ministers of Devon and Cornwall. By T. Hutton. 2 parts. 4to. Oxf. 1605. Later ed. part 2. 4to. Lond. 1606.

This produced a considerable controversy. Note The removal of certaine imputations laid upon the Ministers of Devon and Cornwall by one M. T. H. . . . 4to. s.l. 1606. T. Sparke : A brotherly Perswasion to Unitie . . . 4to. Lond. 1607. [S. Heiron] A Defence of the Ministers' Reasons . . . against T. Hutton . . . W. Covel . . . T. Sparke. 4to. s.l. 1607–8.

1406. Of the consecration of the bishops in the Church of England . . . as also of the ordination of priests and deacons. Five bookes—wherein they are cleared from the slanders . . . of Bellarmine Sanders . . . and other Romanists. By F. Mason. 1 vol. fol. Lond. 1613.

Also in Latin, 1625.

1407. Doctrina et politia Ecclesiae Anglicanae . . . quibus ejusdem Ecclesiae apologia praefigitur. By R. Mocket. 1 vol. 8vo. Lond. 1617.

Contains esp. Jewel's ' Apology ', the Prayer Book Catechism, A more advanced Catechism, The 39 Articles—with summary of two books of homilies. The ordinal and Ecclesiae Anglicanae disciplina et politia, an account of the organization of the Church of England, authority of king, jurisdiction of bishops, &c.

1408. A defence of the Innocencie of the three ceremonies of the Church of England. viz. the surplice, crosse after Baptisme, and kneeling at the receiving of the blessed sacrament. By T. Morton. 1 vol. 4to. Lond. 1619.

This provoked [W. Ames'] A reply to Dr. Morton's generall defence . . 1622 ; and also J. Burges' An answer rejoyned to . . . A Reply . . . 1631.

1409. Defensio Ecclesiae Anglicanae contra M. Antonii de Dominis . . . iniurias. By R. Crakanthorp. Ed. by J. Barkham. 1 vol. fol. Lond. 1625.

Reprint in Anglo-Catholic Library, 1847.

1410. Appello Caesarem. A iust appeale from two uniust informers. By R. Mountagu. 1 vol. 4to. Lond. 1625.

The central work of the controversy which raged round Mountagu. For details see Dict. Nat. Biog.

1411. The holy table, name and thing, more anciently, properly and literally used under the New Testament, than that of an altar. Written long ago by a minister in Lincolnshire, in answer to D. Coal, a judicious divine of Q. Maries dayes. By J. Williams. 1 vol. sm. 4to. Printed for the dioc. of Lincoln. 1637.

Cf. Peter Heylyn's Antidotum Lincolniense or an answer to a book entituled The Holy Table. 1 vol. sm. 4to. Lond. 1637.

1412. An humble remonstrance to the high court of parliament by a dutifull sonne of the Church. By J. Hall. 1 vol. sm. 4to. Lond. 1640.

This provoked ' An answer ' by Smectymnuus, 1641. q. v. Bishop Hall replied with ' A defence of the humble remonstrance ' 1641. Smectymnuus issued ' A vindication

of the answer.' . . . To this, and to a further reply to the ' Defence ' called ' Animadversions upon the remonstrants defence ' by Milton, Hall responded with (1) A short
answer to the tedious vindication . . . 1641. (2) A modest confutation of . . . animadversions . . . 1642. For the controversy see further in Hall's Works, especially ' Episcopacie by divine right ', 1640 ; and Masson's Life of Milton, ii. 213.

1413. A remonstrance against Presbitery. Exhibited by divers of the
nobilitie, gentrie, ministers and inhabitants of the county palatine of Chester.
. . . Together with a short survey of the Presbyterian discipline. . . . By Sir T.
Aston. 1 vol. sm. 4to. [Lond.] 1641.

Includes (1) the Chester remonstrance to the House of Lords against Presbyterian
government, with (2) A letter in support of it, and (3) A petition against it.

1414. Certaine grievances, or the errours of the service-booke plainely layd
open . . . By L. Hewes, 1 vol. sm. 4to. s.l. 1641.

A summary of Puritan objections with interesting illustrative matter.

1415. The first century of scandalous, malignant priests made and admitted
into benefices by the prelates. . . . By J. White. 1 vol. sm. 4to. Lond. 1643.

An account of sequestrated clergy, mainly in Essex, by the chairman of committee of
inquiry.

1416. The church history of Britain [to 1648]. By T. Fuller. 6 parts. fol.
Lond. 1655. Later eds. 6 vols. 8vo. Oxf. 1845. Ed. by J. S. Brewer. 3 vols.
8vo. Lond. 1868. Ed. by J. Nichols.

In ed. of 1845 vols. v and vi contain the reigns of James I and Charles I. Appendices
include : (A) Sir Thomas Herbert's memoirs ; (B) Bishop Cosin and his accusers ;
(C) Bishop Montague and his accusers.

1417. A rationale upon the book of common prayer. By A. Sparrow.

The date of the earliest edition is doubtful. There are copies of that of 1657 at the
Bodleian Library and at Queens' College, Cambridge. After the revision of the Prayer
Book in 1662 the Rationale was altered accordingly and appeared in many editions.

1418. Ecclesia vindicata or the Church of England justified. By P. Heylyn.
1 vol. 4to. Lond. 1657.

This includes The historie of episcopacie, published by the author in 1642 under the
pseudonym of Theophilus Churchman.

1419. An exposition of the creed. By John Pearson. 1 vol. 4to. Lond.
1659. Later eds. 1 vol. fol. Lond. 1710. Ed. by W. Bowyer. 1 vol. 8vo. Oxf.
1890. Ed. by S. Burton.

Cf. The minor theological works of . . . John Pearson, 1659–82, ed. by E. Churton
[2 vols. 8vo. Oxf. 1844].

1420. A collection of articles, injunction, canons, orders, ordinances, and
constitutions ecclesiastical, with other publick records of the Church of
England chiefly in the times of K. Edward VIth, Q. Elizabeth, and K. James.
. . . Ed. by [A. Sparrow]. 1 vol. sm. 4to. Lond. 1661. Arms of the Bps. of
England. Later ed. 1 vol. 8vo. Lond. 1699.

Pref. by Sparrow. Most of the material is now more easily found in the publications of
Cardwell.

1421. The grounds and occasions of the contempt of the clergy and religion
enquired into. By J. Eachard. 1 vol. 8vo. Lond. 1670.

Repr. in Critical essays and literary fragments (2351). Cf. An answer to a letter of enquiry into the grounds &c. [8vo. Lond. 1671]; Some observations upon the answer to an enquiry [by Eachard. 8vo. Lond. 1671]; A vindication of the clergy from the contempt imposed upon them by the author of the grounds &c. [8vo. Lond. 1672 and 1686]; An answer to two letters of T. B. [i.e. John Eachard. 8vo. Lond. 1673]; Hieragonisticon or Corah's doom, being an answer to two letters of enquiry &c. [8vo. Lond. 1672].

1422. Speculum crape-gownorum or a looking-glass for the young academicks . . . with reflections on some late high flown sermons. By J. Phillips. 2 pts. 4to. Lond. 1682.

1423. Bishop Overall's convocation-Book MDCVI concerning the government of God's catholick church and the kingdoms of the whole world. By J. Overall. 1 vol. 4to. Lond. 1690. Later ed. 1 vol. 8vo. Oxf. 1844.

1424. The case of the allegiance due to soveraign powers stated and resolved according to scripture and reason and the principles of the Church of England. By W. Sherlock. 1 vol. sm. 4to. Lond. 1691.

Cf. Macaulay (204) for a summary of this controversy, pp. 457–9, 543 [ed. 1907].

1425. Valor beneficiorum, or a valuation of all ecclesiastical preferment in England and Wales. 1 vol. 8vo. Lond. 1695.

1426. The authority of Christian princes over their ecclesiastical synods asserted with particular respect to the convocations of the clergy of the realm and Church of England. By W. Wake. 1 vol. 8vo. Lond. 1697.

This provoked a lively controversy. Cf. Atterbury's The rights, powers and privileges of an English convocation stated and vindicated [1 vol. 8vo. Lond. 1700]. Wake replied in The state of the Church and clergy of England in their councils, synods, convocations . . . historically deduced from the conversion of the Saxons to the present times [1 vol. fol. Lond. 1703]. There is a useful bibliographical note on this controversy in Hutton (1468), pp. 280–1.

1427. Synodus anglicana, or the constitution and proceedings of an English convocation shewn from the acts and registers thereof to be agreeable to the principles of an episcopal church. By E. Gibson. 1 vol. 8vo. Lond. 1702. Later eds. 1730. 1 vol. 8vo. Oxf. 1854. Ed. by E. Cardwell.

1428. The memorial of the Church of England, humbly offer'd to the consideration of all true lovers of our church and constitution. By J. Drake. 1 vol. 4to. Lond. 1705. Later ed. [with life] 1 vol. 8vo. Lond. 1711.

1429. Two treatises, one of the Christian priesthood, the other of the dignity of the episcopal order. By G. Hickes. 1 vol. 8vo. Lond. 1707. Later eds. 2 vols. 8vo. Lond. 1711. 3 vols. 8vo. Oxf. 1847–8.

1430. An ecclesiastical history of Great Britain from the first planting of Christianity to the end of the reign of King Charles II. By J. Collier. 2 vols. fol. Lond. 1708–14. Later ed. 9 vols. 8vo. Lond. 1852. Ed. by T. Lathbury.

1431. An attempt towards recovering an account of the numbers and sufferings of the clergy of the Church of England who were sequestered, harassed &c. in the grand rebellion. By J. Walker. 1 vol. fol. Lond. 1714.

Walker's MS. collections which formed the basis of the above work are in the Bodleian, and contain a mass of biographical material which appears only in part in the above work. G. B. Tatham's Dr. John Walker and the sufferings of the clergy [1 vol. 8vo. Camb. 1911] supplies a study of Walker's work and a catalogue of his MSS.

1432. The history of St. Paul's Cathedral. By Sir W. Dugdale. 2nd ed. enlarged and corrected by the author. 1 vol. fol. Lond. 1716. Ed. by E. Maynard. Later ed. 1818. Ed. by H. Ellis.
Originally published in 1685.

1433. Concilia Magnae Britanniae et Hiberniae [446-1717]. Ed. by D. Wilkins. 4 vols. fol. Lond. 1731.
The latter part of vol. iv deals with the 17th century.

1434. Letters . . . to and from William Nicolson, successively Bishop of Carlisle, and of Derry ; and Archbishop of Cashell. 2 vols. in 1, 8vo. Lond. 1809.

1435. Documentary annals of the reformed Church of England ; being a collection of injunctions, declarations, orders, articles of inquiry . . . from the year 1546 to the year 1716, with notes, historical and explanatory. Ed. by E. Cardwell. 2 vols. 8vo. Oxf. 1839. Later ed. 1844.

1436. Synodalia. A collection of articles of religion, canons and proceedings of convocations in the province of Canterbury from . . . 1547 to . . . 1717. By E. Cardwell. 2 vols. 8vo. Oxf. 1842.

1437. Enchiridion theologicum anti-Romanum. 3 vols. 8vo. Oxf. 1852.
Repr. of tracts by Jeremy Taylor, Isaac Barrow, Wake, Patrick, Stillingfleet and others against Roman Catholicism.

1438. The marriage, baptismal and burial registers of the collegiate church or abbey of St. Peter Westminster. Harleian Soc. 1 vol. 8vo. Lond. 1876. Ed. by J. L. Chester.
The footnotes are elaborate and valuable.

1439. The manner of the coronation of King Charles the First of England at Westminster, 2 February, 1626. Ed. by C. Wordsworth. 1 vol. 8vo. Lond. 1892.
Henry Bradshaw Soc., vol. ii.

1440. Documents illustrative of English church history [314-1701]. Ed. by H. Gee and W. J. Hardy. 1 vol. 8vo. Lond. 1896.

1441. Documents relating to the history of the cathedral church of Winchester in the seventeenth century. Ed. by W. R. W. Stephens and F. T. Madge. 1 vol. 8vo. Hampshire Record Soc. Lond. 1897.
Cf. The statutes governing the cathedral church of Winchester given by King Charles I. Ed. by A. W. Goodman and W. H. Hutton. 1 vol. 4to. Oxf. 1925.

1442. Ecclesiae Londino-Batavae Archivum III. Epistulae et tractatus cum Reformationis tum ecclesiae Londino-Batavae historiam illustrantes. I. 1523–1631 ; II. 1631–1874. Ed. by J. H. Hessels. 2 vols. Camb. 1897.
Cf. Eng. Hist. Rev. xv. 1900, pp. 788–800.

1443. English coronation records. Ed. by L. G. W. Legg. 1 vol. 8vo. Westminster. 1901. Illus.
From the earliest times to the coronation of Queen Victoria.

1444. The coronation order of King James I. By J. W. Legg. 1 vol. 12mo. Lond. 1902.

The coronation order of William and Mary is in the same writer's Three coronation orders. 8vo. Henry Bradshaw Soc. Lond. 1900.

1445. The records of the northern convocation [1279–1710]. Ed. by G. W. Kitchin, Dean of Durham. 1 vol. 8vo. Surtees Soc. Durham. 1907.

1446. Extracts from the papers of Thomas Woodcock (ob. 1695). Ed. by G. C. Moore Smith. Camd. Soc. Misc. xi. 1907.

Mainly anecdotes about ecclesiastics, beginning about 1636.

1447. The rector's book, Clayworth, Notts. 1672–1701. Ed. by H. Gill and E. L. Guilford. 1 vol. 8vo. Nottingham. 1910. Illus.

1448. English orders for consecrating churches in the 17th century, together with forms for the consecration of churchyards. By J. W. Legg. 1 vol. 8vo. Henry Bradshaw Soc. Lond. 1911.

Cf. the same writer's On the form and consecration of the church and churchyard of Fulmer in 1610, as used by William Barlow, Bishop of Lincoln, in Trans. St. Paul's Ecclesiastical Soc. vi. 1907.

(b) LATER WORKS

1449. An impartial history of the occasional conformity and schism bills, containing the rise and progress of those two bills, with all the debates. . . . By [A. Boyer]. 1 vol. 8vo. Lond. 1717.

Advocates repeal.

1450. The history and antiquities of the cathedral church of Canterbury. By J. Dart. 1 vol. fol. Lond. 1726.

1451. Westmonasterium : the history and antiquities of the abbey church of St. Peter's, Westminster. By J. Dart. 2 in 1 vol. fol. Lond. *c*. 1742. Many plates of monuments.

Cf. H. F. Westlake's Westminster Abbey, 2 vols. illus. Lond. 1923.

1452. A history of conferences and other proceedings connected with the revision of the Book of Common Prayer from the year 1558 to the year 1690. By E. Cardwell. 1 vol. 8vo. Oxf. 1840.

1453. A history of the convocation of the Church of England . . . to . . .1742. By T. Lathbury. 1 vol. 8vo. Lond. 1842. Later ed. 1853.

1454. A history of the non-jurors, their controversies and writings. By T. Lathbury. 1 vol. 8vo. Lond. 1845.

1455. Mr. Macaulay's character of the clergy in the latter part of the seventeenth century considered. By C. Babington. 1 vol. 8vo. Camb. 1849.

Cf. The errors of Lord Macaulay in his estimation of the squires and parsons of the seventeenth century. P. H. Ditchfield in Trans. Royal Hist. Soc., 3rd series, ix. 1915 ; and The social status of the clergy in the seventeenth and eighteenth century. By C. H. Mayo. Eng. Hist. Rev. xxxvii. Apr. 1922.

1456. The history of the Church of England from the death of Elizabeth to the present time. By G. G. Perry. 3 vols. 8vo. Lond. 1861–4.

1457. The annotated Book of Common Prayer. By J. H. Blunt. 1 vol. 4to. Lond. 1866. Bibl. Later eds. 1884; 1 vol. 8vo. Lond. 1903. Bibl.

1458. Essays historical and theological. By J. B. Mozley. 2 vols. 8vo. Lond. 1878.

Parts of vol. i only refer to period.

1459. The English church in the eighteenth century. By C. J. Abbey and J. H. Overton. 2 vols. 8vo. Lond. 1878.

1460. The Somerset diocese, Bath and wells. By W. Hunt. 1 vol. 12mo. Lond. 1885.

For the other vols. in this series of diocesan histories see Gross, The sources and literature of English history to 1485, No. 820b.

1461. Life in the English church [1660–1714]. By J. H. Overton. 1 vol. 8vo. Lond. 1885. Bibl.

1462. The restoration settlement of the English church. By N. Pocock. Eng. Hist. Rev. i. 1886.

1463. Troubles in a city parish under the protectorate [i.e. St. Botolph without Aldgate]. By J. Dodd. Eng. Hist. Rev. x. 1895.

1464. The constitutional history and constitution of the Church of England. Translated from the German of F. Makower. 1 vol. 8vo. Lond. 1895.

1465. Church briefs or royal warrants for collections for charitable objects. By W. A. Bowes. 1 vol. 8vo. Lond. 1896.

1466. A history of the English church during the civil wars and under the commonwealth 1640–1660. By W. A. Shaw. 2 vols. 8vo. Lond. 1900.

With full reference to and account of sources and valuable appendixes of documents.

1467. A new history of the Book of Common Prayer. By F. Procter and W. H. Frere. 1 vol. 8vo. Lond. 1901.

1468. The English church from the accession of Charles I to the death of Anne. By W. H. Hutton. 1 vol. 8vo. Lond. 1903. Bibl. notes.

1469. The English church in the reigns of Elizabeth and James I. By W. H. Frere. 1 vol. 8vo. Lond. 1904. Bibl. notes.

1470. The sale of episcopal lands during the Civil Wars and Commonwealth. By G. B. Tatham. Eng. Hist. Rev. xxiii. 1908.

Has valuable tables from the P.R.O. Close Rolls, 1647–59.

1471. The reconstruction of the English church. By R. G. Usher. 2 vols. 8vo. Lond. and N.Y. 1910. Bibl.

Deals chiefly with the work and times of Bancroft. Appendixes of documents and studies.

1472. The parish registers of England. By J. C. Cox. 1 vol. 8vo. Lond. 1910. Illus.

Appendixes contain lists of early, and of printed, parish registers. Other works on the same subject are by J. S. Burn [1829 and 1862] ; E. C. Waters [1870 and 1883] ; G. W. Marshall [1900] ; A. M. Burke [1908]. The last two have valuable lists.

1473. The importance of the reign of Queen Anne in English church history. By F. W. Wilson. 1 vol. 8vo. Oxf. 1911. Bibl.

1474. The relation of the Church of England to the other reformed churches. By H. H. Henson. 1 vol. 8vo. Edin. 1911.

1475. Caroline divines. By W. H. Hutton. Camb. Hist. of Eng. Lit. vii. 1911. Bibl.

Continued in his Divines of the Church of England 1660–1700. By W. H. Hutton. Camb. Hist. of Eng. Lit. viii. 1912. Bibl.

1476. A dictionary of English church history. Ed. by S. L. Ollard and G. Crosse. 1 vol. 8vo. Lond. and Oxf. 1912. Bibl. notes.

1477. The Puritans in power [1640–60]. By G. B. Tatham. 1 vol. 8vo. Camb. 1913.

Deals with the ejected clergy, the visitation of the universities, and the disposal of church property.

1478. Churchwarden's accounts from the fourteenth century to the close of the seventeenth century. By J. C. Cox. 1 vol. 8vo. Lond. 1913. Illus.

Cf. Eng. Hist. Rev. xv. 1900 for a list of printed churchwarden's accounts by Elsbeth Philipps.

1479. The rise and fall of the high commission. By R. G. Usher. 1 vol. 8vo. Oxf. 1913. Bibl.

(c) COLLECTED BIOGRAPHIES

1480. Life of Seth [Ward] Lord Bishop of Salisbury . . . with a brief account of Bishop Wilkins, Dr. Isaac Barrow, Mr. Lawrence Rooke, Dr. Turberville and others. By W. Pope. 1 vol. 8vo. Lond. 1697.

1481. Fasti Ecclesiae Anglicanae : or, an essay towards deducing a regular succession of all the principal dignitaries in each cathedral, collegiate church or chapel . . . in . . . England and Wales . . . to this present year 1715. By J. Le Neve. 1 vol. fol. Lond. 1716. Later ed. 3 vols. 8vo. Oxf. 1854. Ed. by T. D. Hardy.

Ed. of 1854 corrected and continued to 1854.

1482. The lives of the English bishops from the Restauration to the Revolution. By N. Salmon. 1 vol. 8vo. Lond. 1733.

A useful compilation containing seventy-four lives. Originally publ. in three parts, 1731–3. It was anonymous. Cf. John Le Neve, The lives and characters . . . of all the protestant bishops of the Church of England since . . . 1559 [1 vol. 8vo. Lond. 1720]. Only has lives of archbishops.

1483. Lives of the bishops of Bath and Wells from the earliest to the present period. By S. H. Cassan. 2 vols. 8vo. Lond. 1829–30.

Cassan wrote similar works for Sherborne and Salisbury [8vo. Salisbury. 1824], and for Winchester [2 vols. 8vo. Lond. 1827].

1484. Lives of the archbishops of Canterbury [to Juxon]. By W. F. Hook. 12 vols. with index. 8vo. Lond. 1860–75.

1485. Typical English churchmen from Parker to Maurice. A series of lectures. Ed. by W. E. Collins. 1 vol. 8vo. Lond. 1902.

Includes Chillingworth, Usher, Bramhall, Jeremy Taylor, Burnet.

(d) BIOGRAPHIES, PERSONAL NARRATIVES, AND COLLECTED WORKS

ANDREWES, LANCELOT.

1486. [Works]. By L. Andrewes. Ed. by J. P. Wilson and J. Bliss. 9 vols. 8vo. Oxf. 1841–54.

Includes Tortura Torti sive ad Matthai Torti librum responsio. fol. Lond. 1609 ; Responsio ad Apologiam Cardinalis Bellarmini . . . fol. Lond. 1610 ; being two important parts of the controversy about the oath of allegiance ; and, among the ' Minor Works ', An exact narration of the life & death of . . . Lancelot Andrewes . . . faithfully collected by Henry Isaacson. Lond. 1650 ; and Two answers to Cardinall Perron, and Two speeches in the Starr-Chamber by . . . Lancelot late Bishop of Winchester. Lond. 1629.

1487. Memoirs of the life and works of . . . Lancelot Andrewes, Lord Bishop of Winchester. By A. T. Russell. 1 vol. 8vo. Camb. 1860.

1488. Lancelot Andrewes. By R. L. Ottley. 1 vol. 8vo. Lond. 1894. Port.

ATTERBURY, FRANCIS.

1489. Memoirs and correspondence of Francis Atterbury Bishop of Rochester. Ed. by F. Williams. 2 vols. 8vo. Lond. 1869.

Useful though meandering.

1490. Francis Atterbury. By H. C. Beeching. 1 vol. 8vo. Lond. 1909. Illus. Bibl.

BARLOW, THOMAS.

1491. The genuine remains of . . Thomas Barlow, late lord bishop of Lincoln. 1 vol. 8vo. Lond. 1693.

BARROW, ISAAC.

1492. The theological works of . . . Isaac Barrow. Ed. by A. Napier. 9 vols. Camb. 1859.

BARWICK, JOHN.

1493. The life of . . . John Barwick . . . successively dean of Durham and St. Paul's . . . with . . . an appendix of letters from King Charles I in his confinement, and King Charles II and . . . Clarendon in their exile, and other papers . . . from . . . St. John's College [Cambridge]. By P. Barwick. Trans. by H. Bedford. 1 vol. 8vo. Lond. 1724.

Original Latin ed. Vita Johannis Barwick. 1 vol. 8vo. Lond. 1721

BEVERIDGE, WILLIAM.

1494. The works of . . . William Beveridge, Lord Bishop of St. Asaph. With a memoir of the author by T. H. Horne. 9 vols. 8vo. Lond. 1824. Later ed. 12 vols. 8vo. Oxf. 1842–8.

BLAKE, MARTIN.

1495. The life and times of Martin Blake (1593–1673) vicar of Barnstaple and prebendary of Exeter Cathedral. By J. F. Chanter. 1 vol. 8vo. Lond. 1910. Illus.

BRAMHALL, JOHN.

1496. The works of the most reverend John Bramhall, D.D., sometime Lord Archbishop of Armagh . . . Ed. by A. W. H. Later ed. 5 vols. 8vo. Oxf. 1842–5. Port.

Cf. No. 3334. Defends Anglican and royalist views against Romanists, sectaries, and Hobbes—with sermons, letters, and a life of the author.

BULL, GEORGE.

1497. The works of George Bull, Lord Bishop of St. David's, collected and revised by Edward Burton. To which is prefixed the Life of Bishop Bull by Robert Nelson. 8 vols. 8vo. Oxf. 1827. Later ed. 1846.

BURNET, GILBERT.

1498. A life of Gilbert Burnet, Bishop of Salisbury. By T. E. S. Clarke and H. C. Foxcroft. Intro. by Sir C. H. Firth. 1 vol. 8vo. Camb. 1907. Bibl.

BUSHNELL, WALTER.

1499. A narrative of the proceedings of the commissioners appointed by O. Cromwell for ejecting scandalous and ignorant ministers in the case of Walter Bushnell . . . vicar of Box in the county of Wilts. By W. Bushnell. 1 vol. 8vo. Lond. 1660.

Specimen of the attacks on Cromwell's ecclesiastical settlement.

CARTWRIGHT, THOMAS.

1500. The diary of Dr. Thomas Cartwright, Bishop of Chester [1686–87]. Ed. by J. Hunter. Camd. Soc. 1843.

CASAUBON, ISAAC.

1501. Isaac Casaubon 1559–1614. By M. Pattison. 1 vol. 8vo. Lond. 1875. Bibl.

CHILLINGWORTH, WILLIAM.

1502. The works of William Chillingworth. 3 pts. fol. Lond. 1727. Later eds. 1742. Ed. by T. Birch and 3 vols. 8vo. Oxf. 1838.

Cf. Historical and critical account of the life of William Chillingworth. By P. Des Maizeaux. 1 vol. 8vo. Lond. 1725.

COMPTON, HENRY.

1503. Episcopalia or letters . . . to the clergy of his diocese. By H. Compton. 1 vol. 12mo. Lond. 1686. Later ed. 1 vol. 12mo. Oxf. 1842. Ed. by S. W. Cornish.

COSIN, JOHN.

1504. The works of the Right Reverend father in God John Cosin, Lord Bishop of Durham. Ed. by J. Sansom. 5 vols. 8vo. Oxf. 1843–55. Bibl.

1505. The correspondence of John Cosin, Lord Bishop of Durham, together with other papers illustrative of his life and times. Ed. by G. Ornsby. 2 vols. 8vo. Surtees Soc. Durham. 1869–72.

Cf. A life of John Cosin, Bishop of Durham. By P. H. Osmond. 1 vol. 8vo. Lond. 1913. Illus.

LORD CREWE.

1506. Memoirs of Nathaniel, Lord Crewe. Ed. by A. Clark. Camd. Soc. Misc. ix. 1895.

MS. at Bamborough Castle. A flattering biography by an early 18th-century writer. An examination of the life and character of Nathaniel Crewe was publ. 8vo. Lond. 1790.

DAVENANT, JOHN.

1507. The life, letters, and writings of John Davenant, D.D. 1572–1641, Lord Bishop of Salisbury. By M. Fuller. 1 vol. 8vo. Lond. 1897. Port.

Gives considerable quotations from writings, as well as letters.

DODWELL, HENRY.

1508. The life of Henry Dodwell with an account of his works. By F. Brokesby. 1 vol. 8vo. Lond. 1715.

DONNE, JOHN.

1509. The works of John Donne . . . with a memoir of his life. Ed. by H. Alford. 6 vols. 8vo. Lond. 1839.

Cf. E. M. Simpson's A study of the prose works of J. Donne [1 vol. 8vo. Lond. 1924], which includes new letters. His Poems were ed. by A. B. Grosart [2 vols. 8vo. 1872–3], by E. K. Chambers, with an intro. by G. Saintsbury [2 vols. 8vo. Lond. 1896], and by H. J. C. Grierson [2 vols. 8vo. Oxf. 1912. Ports.]. For a bibliography see Cambridge Hist. of Eng. Lit. iv. 488–90 ; and G. L. Keynes, Bibliography of the works of Dr. John Donne.

1510. John Donne—sometime Dean of St. Paul's, A.D. 1621–1631. By A. Jessopp. 1 vol. 8vo. Lond. 1897. Ports.

1511. The life and letters of John Donne, Dean of St. Paul's . . . By E. W. Gosse. 2 vols. 8vo. Lond. 1899.

FERRAR, NICHOLAS.

1512. Nicholas Ferrar. Two lives by his brother John and by Doctor Jebb. Ed. by J. E. B. Mayor. 1 vol. 8vo. Camb. 1855.

1513. Nicholas Ferrar—his household and his friends. Anon. Ed. by T. T. Carter. 1 vol. 8vo. Lond. 1892. Port.

FLEETWOOD, WILLIAM.

1514. A compleat collection of the sermons tracts and pieces of all kinds that were written by . . . William Fleetwood late lord bishop of Ely. 1 vol. fol. Lond. 1737. Later ed. 3 vols. 8vo. Oxf. 1854.

FRAMPTON, ROBERT.

1515. The life of Robert Frampton, Bishop of Gloucester. Deprived as a non-juror 1689. Ed. by T. S. Evans. 1 vol. 8vo. Lond. 1876.

FULLER, THOMAS.

1516. The life of Thomas Fuller, with notices of his books, his kinsmen, and his friends. By J. E. Bailey. 1 vol. 8vo. Lond. 1874. Ports. Bibl.

A full and documented biography and not superseded by later efforts. For a bibliography see Camb. Hist. of Eng. Lit. vii, 1911, pp. 462–3.

GRANVILLE, DENIS.

1517. The remains of Denis Granville, Dean . . . of Durham, being a further selection from his correspondence, diaries and other papers. Ed. by G. Ornsby. Surtees Soc. 1 vol. 8vo. Durham. 1865.

The first selection was published in the society's volume of Miscellanies, 1860.

HACKET, JOHN.

1518. An account of the life and death of . . . John Hacket, late Lord Bishop of Lichfield and Coventry. By T. Plume. Later ed. 1 vol. 12mo. Lond. 1865. Ed. by M. E. C. Walcott.

Originally prefixed to the Century of sermons, by Hacket, which Plume publ. in 1675.

HALES, JOHN.

1519. Works . . . now first collected together. By J. Hales. Ed. by Sir David Dalyrmple, Lord Hailes. 3 vols. 8vo. Glasgow. 1765.

Cf. An account of the life and writings of John Hales, by Peter des Maizeaux [8vo. Lond. 1719]. Hales's Golden remains were first publ. 1659, 4to.

HALL, JOSEPH.

1520. The Works of Joseph Hall . . . 1 vol. fol. Lond. 1625. Later eds. : 10 vols. 8vo. Lond. 1808. Ed. by J. Pratt; 12 vols. 8vo. Oxf. 1837–9. Ed. by P. Hall ; and 10 vols. 8vo. Oxf. 1863. Ed. by P. Wynter.

Hall's complete poems were ed. by A. B. Grosart [1 vol. 4to. Manchester. 1879]. Cf. Camb. Hist. of Eng. Lit. iv. 519.

HAMMOND, HENRY.

1521. The life of . . . Dr. H. Hammond. By J. Fell. 1 vol. 12mo. Lond. 1661. Later ed. 1 vol. 8vo. Oxf. 1856 [with Burnet's life of Sir Matthew Hale].

HERBERT, GEORGE.

1522. The complete works in prose and verse of George Herbert. Ed. by A. B. Grosart. 3 vols. 8vo. Edin. 1868.

With biography by B. Oley. For bibliography see Camb. Hist. of Eng. Lit.

HEYLYN, PETER.

1523. The life of . . . Dr. Peter Heylyn, chaplain to Charles I, and Charles II. By G. Vernon. 1 vol. 12mo. Lond. 1682.

HORNECK, A[NTHONY].

1524. The life of . . . A[nthony] Horneck. By R. Kidder. 1 vol. 8vo. Lond. 1698.

Cf. Bibliotheca Hornecciana : a catalogue of the library of A. H. 1 vol. 4to. Lond. 1697.

HUTTON, MATTHEW.

1525. The correspondence of Dr. Matthew Hutton, Archbishop of York
. . . of Sir Timothy Hutton his son, and Matthew Hutton his grandson.   Ed.
by J. Raine.   Surtees Soc. 1 vol. 8vo. Lond. *c.* 1844.
Contains some interesting accounts of expenses at Cambridge University temp. James I.

JACKSON, T[HOMAS].

1526. A collection of the works of . . . T[homas] Jackson . . . with the life
of the author by E. V[aughan].   Ed. by B. Oley.   3 pts. fol. Lond. 1653-7.
Later ed. 12 vols. 8vo. Oxf. 1844.

JOHNSON, SAMUEL.

1527. The works of . . . Samuel Johnson.   1 vol. fol. Lond.   1710.   Later
ed. 1713.

JOSSELIN, RALPH.

1528. The diary of the Rev. Ralph Josselin, 1616–1683.   Ed. by E. Hock-
liffe.   Camd. Soc. 1908.
Illustrates the life of the country clergy.

JUXON, WILLIAM.

1529. Memoirs of Archbishop Juxon and his times, with a sketch of the
archbishop's parish Little Compton.   By W. H. Marah.   1 vol. 8vo. Oxf. 1869.

KEN, THOMAS.

1530. The life of Thomas Ken, Bishop of Bath and Wells.   By E. H.
Plumptre.   2 vols. 8vo. Lond. 1888.   Illus.
A detailed life, printing eighty-five of Ken's letters. It supersedes all earlier lives, as
that by W. Hawkins [1713] and that by ' A Layman ' [i.e. J. L. Anderdon] [1851].   Cf.
The prose works of . . . Thomas Ken, ed. by W. Benham [1877–89].

KENNET, WHITE.

1531. The life of . . . White Kennet, late Lord Bishop of Peterborough, with
several original letters of the late Archbishop . . . Tennison . . . and some
curious original papers and records, never before published.   By W. Newton.
1 vol. 8vo. Lond. 1730.

KETTLEWELL, JOHN.

1532. A compleat collection of the works of . . . John Kettlewell . . . to
which is prefix'd the life of the author . . . compiled from the collection of
G. Hicks and R. Nelson.   2 vols. fol. Lond. 1719.
Cf. T. T. Carter's Life and times of John Kettlewell, 1895.

LAUD, WILLIAM.

1533. Canterburies doome, or The first part of a compleat history of the
commitment, charge, tryall, condemnation, execution of William Laud, late
Arch-bishop of Canterbury. . . . By W. Prynne.   1 vol. sm. fol. Lond. 1646.
A collection of the documents and of the proceedings. It has the Hollar frontispiece
in a very worn state and without the explanatory table. For Prynne's other writings
against Laud see the bibliographies in the Dict. Nat. Biog., *sub* ' Prynne', and ' Bruce '
(301).

1534. Cyprianus Anglicus; or the history of the life and death of . . . William [Laud] . . . Archbishop of Canterbury . . . Also the ecclesiastical history of . . . England, Scotland and Ireland, from his first rising till his death. By P. Heylyn. Ed. by H. Heylin. 1 vol. fol. Lond. 1668.

1535. The works of . . . William Laud, sometime Lord Archbishop of Canterbury. Ed. by W. Scott and J. Bliss. 7 in 9 vols. 8vo. Oxf. 1847–60.

Vol. i, Sermons; ii, Conference with Fisher; iii and iv, A summary of devotions, the history of the troubles and trial [written by Laud], including the diary, and Rome's masterpiece; v, Pt. i. History of Laud's chancellorship at Oxford; v, Pt. ii. Laud's annual accounts of his province, and constitutions and canons of 1640; vi and vii, Letters to and from Laud, which are of great importance for the reign of Charles I. Papers relating to Laud's visitations 1634 are in Hist. MSS. Comm. Rep. iv, 124–59.

1536. William Laud. By W. H. Hutton. 1 vol. 8vo. Lond. 1895. Port.

1537. Lectures on Archbishop Laud, together with a bibliography of Laudian literature and the Laudian exhibition catalogue. Ed. by W. E. Collins. 1 vol. 8vo. Lond. 1895.

The most useful work on Laud.

1538. Life of William Laud. By W. L. Mackintosh. 1 vol. 8vo. Lond. 1909. Ports.

LAW, WILLIAM.

1539. The works of William Law. 9 vols. 8vo. Lond. 1753–76.

1540. William Law, nonjuror and mystic. By J. H. Overton. 1 vol. 8vo. Lond. 1881.

Earlier lives by R. Tighe [1813] and C. Walton [1854].

LESLIE, CHARLES.

1541. The theological works of . . . Charles Leslie. 2 vols. fol. Lond. 1721. Later ed. 7 vols. 8vo. Oxf. 1832.

MORE, HENRY.

1542. The life of . . . Dr. Henry More, late fellow of Christ's College in Cambridge, to which are annex'd divers of his useful and excellent letters. By R. Ward. 1 vol. 8vo. Lond. 1710.

NELSON, ROBERT.

1543. Memoirs of the life and times of the pious Robert Nelson. By C. F. Secretan. 1 vol. 8vo. Lond. 1860.

PATRICK, SYMON.

1544. The auto-biography of Symon Patrick, Bishop of Ely. 1 vol. 12mo. Oxf. 1839.

Repr. with Patrick's Works [9 vols. 8vo. Oxf. 1858], ed. by A. Taylor.

PRESTON, JOHN.

1545. Life of the renowned Doctor Preston writ by his pupil Master Thomas Ball in the year 1628. Ed. by E. W. Harcourt. 1 vol. 8vo. Oxf. 1885.

RAINBOW, EDWARD.

1546. The life of . . . Edw[ard] Rainbow, late Lord Bishop of Carlisle. By [J.] [Banks]. 1 vol. 8vo. Lond. 1688.

ROUS, JOHN.

1547. Diary of John Rous, incumbent of Santon Downham, Suffolk, from 1625 to 1642. Ed. by M. A. E. Green. Camd. Soc. 1856.

SACHEVERELL, HENRY.

1548. A bibliography of Dr. Henry Sacheverell. Extracted from the Bibliographer 1883–4 with additions. Ed. by F. Madan. 1 vol. 8vo. Oxf. 1884.

SANCROFT, WILLIAM.

1549. The Life of William Sancroft, Archbishop of Canterbury. By G. D'Oyly. 2 vols. 8vo. Lond. 1821. Later ed. 1 vol. 8vo. Lond. 1840.
Based on Tanner MSS. Bodl. Libr.

SANDERSON, ROBERT.

1550. The works of Robert Sanderson. Ed. by W. Jacobson. 6 vols. 8vo. Oxf. 1854.

SHARP, JOHN.

1551. The life of John Sharp . . . Archbishop of York . . . collected from his diary, letters. . . . By T. Sharp. Ed. by T. Newcome. 2 vols. 8vo. Lond. 1825.
Important for Anne's reign. Sharp's Works were publ. in 7 vols. 12mo. Lond. 1754.

SHELDON, GILBERT.

1552. The life and times of Gilbert Sheldon, sometime Warden of All Souls College, Oxford, Bishop of London, Archbishop of Canterbury, and Chancellor of the University of Oxford. By V. Staley. 1 vol. 8vo. Lond. 1913.

SHERLOCK, WILLIAM.

1553. Discourses preached . . . on several occasions. By W. Sherlock. 4 vols. 8vo. Oxf. 1812.

SOUTH, ROBERT.

1554. Memoirs of the life and writings of . . . R. South. 7 vols. 8vo. Oxf. 1823. Later ed. 2 vols. 8vo. Lond. 1865.
Mainly repr. of Sermons preached upon several occasions. 11 vols. 8vo. Lond. 1737–44.

STEWARD, RICHARD.

1555. Life of Richard Steward. By N. Pocock. Ed. by T. I. Pocock. 1 vol. 8vo. Lond. 1908.
Life of a royalist divine in exile.

STILLINGFLEET, EDWARD.

1556. The life and character of . . . Edward Stillingfleet, Lord Bishop of Worcester . . . with some account of the works he has published. 1 vol. 8vo. Lond. 1710. Later ed. 1735.

TAYLOR, JEREMY.

1557. The whole works of . . . Jeremy Taylor . . . with a life of the author. Ed. by R. Heber. 15 vols. 8vo. Lond. 1822. Later ed. 10 vols. 8vo. Lond. 1847–54. Ed. by C. P. Eden.

Cf. E. H. May's A dissertation on the life, theology and times of . . . Jeremy Taylor. 1 vol. 8vo. Lond. 1892.

TENISON, THOMAS.

1558. Memoirs of the life and times of . . . Thomas Tenison, late Archbishop of Canterbury. 1 vol. 8vo. Lond. *c.* 1716.

THORNDIKE, HERBERT.

1559. The theological works of . . . Herbert Thorndike. 9 vols. in 6. 8vo. Oxf. 1844–56.

His Epilogue to the tragedy of the Church of England. fol. Lond. 1659 contains the ablest defence of Anglican church polity at the time of the Commonwealth. Vols. v and vi include other valuable controversial treatises with letters and a life.

TILLOTSON, JOHN.

1560. The works of Dr. John Tillotson late archbishop of Canterbury. With the life of the author. 10 vols. 8vo. Lond. 1820.

The above-mentioned life, by T. Birch, had been previously published separately [2nd ed. 1 vol. 8vo. Lond. 1753].

USHER, JAMES.

1561. The life of . . . James Usher, late Lord Arch-Bishop of Armagh, Primate and Metropolitan of All Ireland. By R. Parr. 1 vol. fol. Lond. 1686.

Life—with appendix vindicating the Abp.'s orthodoxy, and 300 letters to and from famous persons at home and abroad.

1562. The whole works of . . . J. Usher. With a Life of the author . . . Ed. by C. R. Elrington and J. M. Todd. 17 vols. 8vo. Dublin. 1847–64.

For the literary history of his Reduction of episcopacie see D.N.B.

1563. The life and times of James Usher, Archbishop of Armagh. By J. A. Carr. 1 vol. 8vo. Lond. 1896. Port.

WALTON, BRIAN.

1564. Memoirs of the life and writings of Brian Walton, Bishop of Chester. By H. J. Todd. 2 vols. 8vo. Lond. 1821.

WILLIAMS, JOHN.

1565. Scrinia reserata : a memorial offer'd to the great deservings of John Williams, D.D. . . . containing A series of the most remarkable occurrences and transactions of his life. . . . By J. Hacket. 1 vol. fol. Lond. 1693. Port.

In two parts, paged separately.

1566. Letters of Archbishop Williams and others addressed to him [and] Letters . . . with materials for his life. By J. E. B. Mayor. Camb. Antiq. Soc. ii. & iii. 1864.

WILSON, THOMAS.

1567. The works of Thomas Wilson . . . with his life. 2 vols. 4to. Bath. 1781. Later ed. 7 vols. 8vo. Oxf. 1847–63. Ed. by J. Keble.

¶ 3. NONCONFORMITY

(a) General, Bibliographies, and Sources.
(b) General Later Works.
(c) Collective Biographies.
(d) Biographies, Personal Narratives, and Collected Works of Individuals.
(e) Local. 1. General. 2. County.

This section includes English Presbyterians, Independents, and Baptists, who were often collectively called the 'old dissent'.

The literature dealing with these sects is enormous, and new sources are continually being published, especially in the historical societies of the Baptists, Congregationalists, and Presbyterians. The Dr. Williams Library, Gordon Square, London, is the central storehouse for both manuscripts and later works. There is a model, detailed, Baptist bibliography, ed. by Whitley in progress (1569); that of Dexter (1568) is valuable for congregationalism; but there is no similar work for Presbyterianism. For the period before the civil war the best guide is Champlin Burrage (1617); for 1640–60 probably Masson's Life of Milton (2417) is as useful as any one work; Hanbury (1586) is important for both periods. For 1660–88 Baxter (1627), Calamy (1621), and Lyon Turner (1595) are essential, and Bate (343) is the chief authority for the declaration of indulgence. For 1689–1714 there are valuable materials in Calamy (1636) and Heywood (1644), and Gordon (1625) examined minutely the effect of the act of toleration during 1690–2, but the reign of Anne has not attracted nonconformist historians. Of the general historians Neal and his critics (1596) are still useful, and Whitley (1619) and Dale (1615) are the best studies of the Baptists and Congregationalists respectively within moderate compass.

In addition to the books enumerated here, works in other sections should often be consulted, for many nonconformist laymen are important in other than ecclesiastical history, as Cromwell or Milton. Similarly the position of nonconformity was always a political question during the Stuart period and is dealt with in secular histories.

(a) GENERAL, BIBLIOGRAPHIES, AND SOURCES

1568. The Congregationalism of the last three hundred years, as seen in its literature. By H. M. Dexter. 1 vol. 8vo. Lond. 1879 and 1880.

The bibliography has 7,250 titles, more than half American, and is more valuable than the lectures.

1569. A Baptist bibliography, being a register of the chief materials for Baptist history, whether in manuscript or in print. Ed. W. T. Whitley. 2 vols. 4to. Lond. 1916, 1922.

Vol. i, 1526–1776; ii, 1777–1837. Gives the titles &c. of all books by or relating to Baptists in the chronological order of publication, and of MSS. under the years in which their contents begin, with many notes. Extremely valuable.

1570. An appeal to the parliament, or Sions plea against the prelacie. By A. Leighton. 1 vol. 4to. Lond. [1628].

This led to Leighton's citation before the Star Chamber.

1571. An answer to a booke entitled, an humble remonstrance in which, the originall of

Liturgy

Episcopacy

is discussed. By Smectymnuus, i. e. S[tephen] M[arshall], E[dmund] C[alamy], T[homas] Y[oung], M[atthew] N[ewcomen], W[illiam] S[purestowe]. 1 vol. sm. 4to. Lond. 1641.

For the controversy which followed see Masson, Life of Milton, ii. 219 *et seq.*

1572. A small treatise of baptisme or dipping. By E. Barber. 12mo. Lond. 1642.

Cf. Daniel Featley's καταβαπτισται καταπτυστοι, The dippers dipt [4to. Lond. 1645].

1573. An apologeticall narration. By T. Goodwin, P. Nye, and others. 1 vol. 4to. Lond. 1643.

A defence of Independency, answered by T. E. and others. Cf. Masson, Life of Milton, iii. 23 *et seq.*

1574. The confession of faith of those churches which are commonly (though falsly) called Anabaptists ; presented to the view of all that feare God to examine by the touchstone of the word of truth : as likewise for the taking off those aspersions which are frequently both in pulpit and print (although unjustly) cast upon them. 1 vol. 4to. Lond. 1644. Later eds. 1646 and 1651.

Opponents of the English churches usually supposed that they were akin to the German Anabaptists of the sixteenth century, so quoted largely from continental historians rather than observed what was around them. Both connexion and name were repudiated by these Calvinists. Alternative names appeared. ' Baptists ' in 1644, ' Antipaedobaptists ' in 1646.

1575. A Directory for the publique worship of God, throughout the three kingdoms of England, Scotland and Ireland. Together with an ordinance of parliament for the taking away of the Book of Common-Prayer. sm. 4to. Lond. 1644[-5]. 2nd ed. 4to. Edin. 1645.

Drawn up by the Westminster Assembly : repr. in the Book of Common Order of the Church of Scotland, 1868. The other pieces of work have proved even more enduring : The metrical version of the Psalms, 1646 ; The Confession of Faith, 1647 ; The two Catechisms, 1648.

The Minutes of the Westminster Assembly of divines were ed. by A. F. Mitchell and J. Struthers, 1874. A good account of the assembly, with bibl. by W. A. Shaw. Camb. Mod. Hist. iv. 1906.

1576. Heresiography : or A description of the heretickes and sectaries of these latter times. By E. Pagitt. 1 vol. sm. 4to. Lond. 1645. 6th ed. 1 vol. 8vo. Lond. 1661. Ports.

An unfriendly account of Anabaptists, Brownists, Independents, Familists, Adamites, Antinomians, Arminians, Socinians, Antitrinitarians, Millenaries, Hetheringtonians, Antisabbatarians, Traskites, Jesuits.

Successive editions added to the material and some cuts of heresiarchs were introduced. The 6th ed. is the closing form of the book.

1577. Gangraena or a catalogue and discovery of many of the errours, heresies, blasphemies and pernicious practices of the sectaries of this time,

vented and acted in England in these four last years.   By T. Edwards.
3 parts. sm. 4to. Lond. 1646.

A bitter attack on sectaries by a Puritan, with many curious details of their proceedings.

1578. The compleat history of Independency 1640–60.   By C. Walker.
1 vol. sm. 4to. Lond. 1660–1.

Made up of various parts : 1. Title-page.   2. Relations and observations . . . 1648.
3. The history of Independency . . . 1648.   4. An appendix to the history . . . 1648.
5. Anarchia Anglicana : or the history of Independency.   The second part . . . by Theodorus Verax. 1649.   6. The High Court of Justice. . . . Being the third part of the
History of Independency Written by the same Author. 1660.   7. The history of Independency The fourth and last part. . . . By T. M. Esquire, . . . 1660.

1579. A compleat collection of farewell sermons preached by London &
countrie ministers August 17th, 1662.   1 vol. sm. 4to. Lond. 1663.

1580. Aerius Redivivus or the history of the Presbyterians . . . from 1536 to
1647.   By P. Heylyn.   1 vol. fol. Oxf. 1670.

1581. A confession of faith, put forth by the elders and brethren of many
congregations of Christians (baptized upon profession of their faith) in London
and the country.   1 vol. 4to. Lond. 1677.

A Baptist revision of the Westminster Confession.   Still acknowledged by the Strict
and Particular Baptists of England and Australia.   Revised 1742 at Philadelphia, and
still acknowledged widely in America.

1582. Christianismus primitivus : or, the ancient Christian religion.   By
T. Grantham.   1 vol. fol. Lond. 1678.

In four parts, with separate title-pages and pagination.   Incorporating earlier pamphlets, especially the 1660 confession which long remained standard among the General
Baptists who originated in 1609.

1583. The unreasonableness of separation, or an impartial account of the
history . . . of the present separation from the communion of the Church of
England.   By E. Stillingfleet.   1 vol. 4to. Lond. 1681.

1584. A defence of moderate non-conformity.   By E. Calamy.   3 vols. 8vo.
Lond. 1703–5.

1585. Vindiciae fratrum dissentientium.   By J. Peirce.   1 vol. 8vo. Lond.
1710.

Trans. as Vindication of the dissenters in answer to Dr. William Nichols' Defence . . .
of the Church of England [8vo. Lond. 1717–18].

1586. Historical memorials relating to the Independents and Congregationalists from their rise to the restoration . . . 1660.   Ed. by B. Hanbury.
3 vols. 8vo. Lond. 1839–44.

Very valuable for literature : consists of lengthy extracts from scarcer early Independent works.

1587. The records of a church of Christ, meeting in Broadmead, Bristol.
1640–1687.   Ed. for the Hanserd Knollys Soc. with an historical introduction,
by E. B. Underhill.   1 vol. 8vo. Lond. 1847.

Dr. Underhill's introduction deals with the rise of dissent in the Tudor period.
Cf. his Records of the churches of Christ gathered at Fenstanton, Warboys, and Hexham, 1644–1720.   1 vol. 8vo. Lond. 1856.

1588. Open communion and the Baptists of Norwich. Ed. G. Gould. 1 vol. 8vo. Norwich, 1860.

Text has important legal arguments and judgments. Intro. discusses critically the origin of Baptists in England.

1589. Documents relating to the settlement of the Church of England by the Act of Uniformity of 1662. Ed. G. Gould. 1 vol. 8vo. Lond. 1862.

Intro. by P. Bayne.

1590. The Nonconformist register of baptisms, marriages, and deaths, compiled by the Revs. O. Heywood & T. Dickenson, 1644–1702, 1702–1752, generally known as the Northowram or Coley register. Ed. J. H. Turner. 1 vol. 8vo. Brighouse. 1881. Illus.

1591. The creeds and platforms of Congregationalism. Ed. W. Walker. 1 vol. 8vo. N.Y. 1893.

Mainly documents showing the principles of Congregationalists at different times.

1592. Vestiges of Protestant dissent, being lists of ministers, sacramental plate, registers . . . pertaining to most of the churches. . . . of Unitarian, Liberal Christian, Free Christian, Presbyterian . . . congregations. Ed. G. E. Evans. 1 vol. 8vo. Liverpool. 1897.

1593. Minutes of the General Assembly of the General Baptist churches in England, with kindred records ; Edited with introduction and notes for the Baptist Historical Society. Vol. i. 1654–1728. Vol. ii. 1731–1811. Ed. W. T. Whitley. 8vo. Lond. 1909–10.

1594. Baptist confessions of faith, ed. W. J. McGlothlin. 1 vol. 12mo. Phila. 1910.

Continental, English, American. Supersedes similar collection of 1854.

1595. Original records of early Nonconformity. Ed. G. L. Turner. 3 vols. 8vo. Lond. 1911.

Vols. i and ii are documents relating to the persecution of Nonconformists during the first half of the reign of Charles II : vol. iii is a commentary.

(b) GENERAL LATER WORKS

1596. The history of the Puritans or Protestant Nonconformists from the Reformation 1517 to the Revolution in 1688. By D. Neal. 4 vols. 8vo. Lond. 1732–8. Later eds. 2 vols. 4to. Lond. 1754, ed. by N. Neal. 5 vols. 8vo. Bath. 1793–7, ed. by J. Toulmin. 3 vols. 8vo. Lond. 1837.

The supplementary chapters in the ed. of 1793–7 comprise the history of the English Baptists and Quakers, and form two appendices to vol. iii in the ed. of 1837. Vol. i of Neal called forth an answer from Isaac Maddox, A vindication of the government, doctrine and worship of the Church of England established in the reign of Queen Elizabeth against . . . Neal (8vo. Lond. 1733 & repr. 1740). Vols. ii, iii, and iv of Neal were subjected to 'An impartial examination ' by Zachary Grey in 3 vols. Lond. 1736–9. Grey's last two vols. contain valuable documents from the collection of state papers used by Nalson, and described in the intro. to vol. i of the Portland MSS. (Hist. MSS. Comm.), Neal replied in A review of the principal facts objected to the first volume of the History of the Puritans (8vo. Lond. 1734).

1597. The history of the English Baptists, from the Reformation to the beginning of the reign of King George I. By T. Crosby. 4 vols. 8vo. Lond. 1738–40.

Based on MS. collections by J. Stennett and B. Stinton to be seen at Dr. Williams's Library and in the Angus Library at the Baptist College, formerly at Regent's Park, now in course of transference to Oxford. See Transactions of the Baptist Historical Society, i. 193; vi. 712.

1598. History of Dissenters from the revolution in 1688 to the year 1808. By D. Bogue and J. Bennett. 4 vols. 8vo. Lond. 1808–12. Later ed. 3 vols. 8vo. Lond. 1833–9.

1599. A history of the English Baptists : including an investigation of the history of baptism in England from the earliest period to which it can be traced to the close of the seventeenth century. By J. Ivimey. 4 vols. 8vo. Lond. 1811, 1814, 1823, 1830.

Vols. i and ii are inaccurate in many details : the later vols. come down to 1820.

1600. An historical view of the state of the Protestant dissenters in England from the revolution to the accession of Queen Anne. By J. Toulmin. 1 vol. 8vo. Bath. 1814.

1601. The history of the English General Baptists. In two parts. Part first : the English General Baptists of the seventeenth century. Part second : The New Connexion of General Baptists. By A. Taylor. 2 vols. 8vo. Lond. 1818.

1602. History of the Westminster assembly of divines. 1 vol. 8vo. Edin. 1843. By W. M. Hetherington. Later ed. Edin. 1878. Ed. by R. Williamson.

1603. History of the early Puritans from the reformation to . . . 1642. By J. B. Marsden. 1 vol. 8vo. Lond. 1850.

Continued in : History of the later Puritans (1642–62). 1 vol. 8vo. Lond. 1852.

1604. History of the Free Churches of England 1688–1851 [with a continuation to 1891 by C. S. Miall in the second edition]. By H. S. Skeats. 1 vol. 8vo. Lond. 1868. 2nd ed. [1891].

1605. Congregational history. By J. Waddington. 5 vols. 8vo. Lond. 1869–80.

Vol. i, 1200–1567 ; ii, 1567–1700 ; iii, 1700–1800 ; iv, 1800–1850 ; v, 1850–1880.

1606. Bye-paths in Baptist history : a collection of interesting, instructive, and curious information, not generally known, concerning the Baptist denomination. By J. J. Goadby. 8vo. Lond. 1871.

1607. Annals of English Presbytery from the earliest period to the present time. By T. McCrie. 1 vol. 8vo. Lond. 1872.

1608. Baptist history : from the foundation of the Christian church to the present time. By J. M. Cramp. 8vo. Lond. 1875. Ports.

Publ. in the Nova Scotia *Christian Messenger* as a series of letters, 1856–8 ; revised and issued separately in Nova Scotia, 1868 ; standard form in 1875. Practically ends with 1750.

1609. A history of the Baptists ; traced by their vital principles and practices, from the time of our Lord and Saviour Jesus Christ to the year 1886. By T. Armitage. 1 vol. 8vo. N.Y. 1887. Ports.

1610. History of the Presbyterians in England, their rise, decline and revival. By A. H. Drysdale. 1 vol. 8vo. Lond. 1889.

1611. A short history of the Baptists. By H. C. Vedder. 8vo. Philadelphia. 1892. Later ed. 1907. Ports.
Edition of 1907 re-written, and doubled in size. Based on original research and study of sources.

1612. English Baptist reformation. (From 1609 to 1641 A.D.) By G. A. Lofton. 8vo. Louisville. Ky. 1899.

1613. A short history of the Free Churches. By J. A. Houlder. 8vo. Lond. 1899.

1614. The church covenant idea : its origin and its development. By C. Burrage. 8vo. Phila. 1904.
Chiefly 16th and 17th century.

1615. History of English Congregationalism. By R. W. Dalc. Ed. by Sir A. W. W. Dale. 1 vol. 8vo. Lond. 1907.

1616. The political activities of the baptists and fifth monarchy men in England during the interregnum. By L. F. Brown. 1 vol. 8vo. Washington. 1912. Bibl.

1617. Early English dissenters in the light of recent research [1550–1641]. By C. Burrage. 2 vols. 8vo. Camb. 1912. Illus.
Vol. i is history, vol. ii documents. There is a critical introduction on authorities. A valuable study.

1618. A history of the Baptists together with some account of their principles and practices. By J. T. Christian. 1 vol. 8vo. Nashville. Tenn. 1922.
Really a history of immersion. A second vol. deals mainly with America.

1619. A history of British Baptists. By W. T. Whitley. 1 vol. 8vo. Lond. 1923.

(c) COLLECTIVE BIOGRAPHIES

1620. A general martyrologie . . . from the creation to our present times. By S. Clarke. 1 vol. fol. Lond. 1651. 3rd ed. 1 vol. fol. Lond. 1677.
Ed. of 1677 has added : The lives of thirty-two English divines . . . most of them sufferers in the cause of Christ, and cuts.

1621. Abridgement of Mr. Baxter's History of his life and times, with a particular account of the ministers . . . ejected after the restauration. By E. Calamy. 1 vol. 8vo. Lond. 1702. Later eds. 2 vols. 1713, and 1727.
In ed. of 1713 the Account forms a separate volume : in ed. of 1727 there is a Continuation of the Account which consists of emendations. Samuel Palmer condensed and rearranged these works in 1775 under the title ' The Nonconformists' memorial ', improved ed. 3 vols. 1802–3, with many portraits. Palmer cannot be implicitly trusted, and reference should be made to Calamy's originals.

1622. The lives of the Puritans, containing a biographical account of those divines who distinguished themselves in the cause of religious liberty from the reformation under Queen Elizabeth to the Act of Uniformity in 1662. By B. Brook. 3 vols. 8vo. Lond. 1813.

MSS. for a second ed. are in the Congregational Library, Lond.

1623. English puritanism and its leaders : Cromwell, Milton, Baxter, Bunyan. By J. Tulloch. 1 vol. 8vo. Edin. 1861.

1624. Baptist and Congregational pioneers. By J. H. Shakespeare. 1 vol. 8vo. Lond. 1906.

1570–1646.

1625. Freedom after ejection. By A. Gordon. 1 vol. 8vo. Manchester. 1917.

' A report on the condition of the nonconformist clergy in 1690–2, setting forth the names, the character, and the stipends of about 760 ministers . . the index is a biographical dictionary of the 760 ministers.' C. H. Firth.

(d) BIOGRAPHIES, PERSONAL NARRATIVES, AND COLLECTIVE WORKS OF INDIVIDUALS

ALLEINE, JOSEPH.

1626. Joseph Alleine : his companions & times ; a memorial of ' Black Bartholomew ', 1662. By C. Stanford. 1 vol. 8vo. Lond. 1861.

BAXTER, RICHARD.

1627. Reliquiae Baxterianae, or Mr. Richard Baxter's narrative of the most memorable passages of his life and times faithfully published from his own original manuscript. Ed. by M. Sylvester. 1 vol. fol. Lond. 1696.

1628. The practical works of . . . with a life of the author and a critical examination of his writings. Ed. by W. Orme. 23 vols. 8vo. Lond. 1830.

1629. A life of the Reverend Richard Baxter, 1615–1691. By F. J. Powicke. 2 vols. 8vo. Lond. 1924–7.

Has new material from the Baxter MSS. in Dr. Williams's Library, Gordon Square, Lond. First vol. ends with 1662, the second closes with Baxter's death.

BROWNE, ROBERT.

1630. The true story of Robert Browne (1550 ?–1633), Father of Congregationalism, including . . . an extended and improved list of his writings. By C. Burrage. 1 vol. 8vo. Oxf. 1906.

Cf. Robert Browne's ancestors and descendants ; New facts relating to Robert Browne ; Robert Browne and the Achurch parish register ; The later years of Robert Browne. By F. I. Cater. Trans. Congregational Hist. Soc. ii and iii. 1905–8.

1631. Robert Browne, pioneer of modern congregationalism. By F. J. Powicke. 1 vol. 8vo. Lond. 1910.

An excellent short biography.

BUNYAN, JOHN.

1632. Grace abounding to the chief of sinners, or a brief and faithful relation of the exceeding mercy of God in Christ to his poor servant John Bunyan . . . all which was written by his own hand, &c. 1 vol. 12mo. Lond. [1666].

Ed. of 1692 supplemented to complete the story.

1633. The works of that eminent servant in God . . . John Bunyan. 1 vol. fol. Lond. 1692. Ed. by C. Doe.

The first completed works of Bunyan were ed. by G. Offor [3 vols. 8vo. Glasgow. 1855]. The first critical ed. of the text of The pilgrim's progress [1678 and 1682] was Offor's [Hanserd Knollys Soc. 1847].

1634. John Bunyan : his life, times and work. By J. Brown. 1 vol. 8vo. Lond. 1885.

The definitive life : contains a list of Bunyan's works.

BURTON, HENRY.

1635. A narrative of the life of Mr. Henry Burton . . . written with his own hand. 1 vol. 4to. [? Lond.] 1643.

CALAMY, EDMUND.

1636. An historical account of my own life. Ed. by J. T. Rutt. 2 vols. 8vo. Lond. 1829.

CAWTON, THOMAS.

1637. The life and death of Mr. Thomas Cawton. By his son T. Cawton. 1 vol. 8vo. Lond. 1662.

CLARKE, SAMUEL.

1638. Historical memoirs of the life and writings of Dr. Samuel Clarke . . . to which is added . . . I. Dr. Sykes, Elogium of Dr. Clarke. II. Mr. [Thomas] Emlyn's Memoirs of the life and sentiments of Dr. Clarke. By W. Whiston. 3rd ed. 1 vol. 8vo. Lond. 1748.

CLEGG, JAMES.

1639. Extract from the diary and autobiography of the Rev. James Clegg, nonconformist minister and doctor of medicine, 1679–1755. Ed. by H. Kirke. 1 vol. 8vo. Buxton. 1899.

His account of his youth is valuable for the history of education.

DELAUNE, THOMAS.

1640. A narrative of the tryal and sufferings of Thomas Delaune, for writing and publishing a late book called ' A plea for the Nonconformists ' . . . with some modest reflections thereon. 1 vol. 4to. Lond. 1684.

GOODWIN, THOMAS.

1641. Works. 5 vols. fol. Lond. 1681–1704. Later ed. 11 vols. 8vo. Edin. 1861–4. Ed. by T. Smith.

The ed. of 1861–4 has preface by J. C. Miller and memoir by R. Halley.

HENRY, PHILIP.

1642. The life of . . . Philip Henry with funeral sermons for Mr. and Mrs. Henry. By M. Henry. 1 vol. 8vo. Lond. 1825.

I have not been able to find the 1st ed. dated either 1697 or 1698. The 3rd ed. [1712] was the last corrected by the author.

1643. The diaries and letters of Philip Henry of Broad Oak, Flintshire [1631–96]. Ed. by M. H. Lea. 1 vol. 8vo. Lond. 1882.

Diary covers 1657–96 with gaps.

HEYWOOD, OLIVER.

1644. The whole works of the Rev. O. Heywood . . . with memoirs of his life. 5 vols. 8vo. Idle. 1827.

1645. The Rev. Oliver Heywood, B.A. 1630–1702, his autobiography, diaries. . . . Ed. by J. H. Turner. 4 vols. 8vo. Brighouse, 1882–5. Illus.

Cf. The rise of the old dissent exemplified in the life of Oliver Heywood . . . 1630–1702. By J. Hunter. 1 vol. 8vo. Lond. 1842.

HOWE, JOHN.

1646. Memoirs of the life of the late Revd. Mr. John Howe. By E. Calamy. 1 vol. 8vo. Lond. 1724.

Cf. The life and character of John Howe, by H. Rogers, 1836, new ed. 1863. The works of Howe were ed. by J. Hunt in 8 vols. 8vo. 1810–22.

JESSEY, HENRY.

1647. The life and death of Mr. Henry Jessey, who, having finished his testimony, was translated, 4 Sept. 1663 &c. by E. W[histon ?] 12mo. Lond. 1671.

JOLLY, THOMAS.

1648. The note book of the Rev. Thomas Jolly, 1671–1693. Extracts from the church book of Altham and Wymondhouses, 1649–1725. Ed. by H. Fishwick. Chetham Soc. 1894.

The spiritual reflections of a Nonconformist.

KIFFIN, WILLIAM.

1649. Remarkable passages in the life of William Kiffin : written by himself. Ed. by W. Orme. 1 vol. 8vo. Lond. 1823.

KNOLLYS, HANSERD.

1650. Hanserd Knollys, 'a minister and witness of Jesus Christ', 1598–1691. By J. Culross. 8vo. Lond. 1895.

NEWCOME, HENRY.

1651. The diary of the Rev. Henry Newcome from September 30, 1661, to September 29, 1663. Ed. by T. Heywood. 1 vol. Chetham Soc. 4to. 1849.

The journal of a Lancashire minister. Cf. The autobiography of Henry Newcome. Ed. by R. Parkinson. Chetham Soc. 2 vols. 1852. The autobiography covers *c.* 1627–95, and is only an abstract of a lost diary.

OWEN, JOHN.

1652. Memoirs of the life, writings and religious connexions of John Owen. By W. Orme. 1 vol. 8vo. Lond. 1820.

Useful : has list of Owen's works.

PETERS, HUGH.

1653. A memoir or defence of Hugh Peters. By J. Felt. 1 vol. 8vo. Boston. U.S.A. 1851.

ROBINSON, JOHN.

1654. The works of John Robinson, pastor of the Pilgrim Fathers, with a memoir and annotations. By R. Ashton. 3 vols. sm. 4to. Lond. & Boston (Mass.) 1851.

Among the more important reprints are: A iustification of separation from the Church of England [4to. Lond. 1610]. Of religious communion private & publique [4to. Lond. 1614]. The peoples plea for the exercise of prophesie [sm. 4to. s.l. 1618]. A defence of the doctrine propounded by the synode at Dort [4to. s.l. 1624]. A iust and necessarie apologie of certain Christians . . . called Brownists or Barrowists [4to. Lond. 1625].

1655. Pastor of the Pilgrim Fathers : A study of his life and times. By W. H. Burgess. 1 vol. 8vo. Lond. 1920.

ROGERS, JOHN.

1656. Some account of the life and opinions of a Fifth-Monarchy-Man. Chiefly extracted from the writings of John Rogers, preacher. By E. Rogers. 1 vol. 4to. Lond. 1867.

SMYTH, JOHN.

1657. John Smith the se-baptist, Thomas Helwys, and the first Baptist church in England, with fresh light upon the Pilgrim Fathers' church. By W. H. Burgess. 1 vol. 8vo. Lond. 1911.

There are interesting comments on this work in Burrage's Early English dissenters, i. x–xiii.

1658. The works of John Smyth, fellow of Christ's College 1594–8 . . . with notes and biography by W. T. Whitley. 2 vols. 8vo. Camb. 1915.

(e) LOCAL

(1) GENERAL

1659. A brief history of the Western [Baptist] Association, from its commencement, about the middle of the seventeenth century, to . . . 1823. By J. G. Fuller. 1 vol. 8vo. Bristol [1843].

1660. History of the Baptist churches in the north of England, from 1648 to 1845. By D. Douglas. 12mo. Lond. 1846.

1661. History of the Berks, South Bucks, and South Oxon Congregational churches. By W. H. Summers. 1905.

1662. Records of an Old Association, being a memorial volume of the 250th anniversary of the Midland, now the West Midland, Baptist Association, formed in Warwick, May 3rd 1655. Ed. by R. Gray, J. Ford, and J. M. G. Owen. 8vo. Birmingham. 1905.

Covers Stafford, Worcester, Gloucester, Oxford, Leicester.

1663. Baptists in Yorkshire, Lancashire, Cheshire and Cumberland. By E. C. Shipley and T. W. Whitley. 1 vol. 8vo. Lond. 1913.

(2) Counties, arranged in Alphabetical Order

1664. Gleanings from forgotten fields Being the story of the Berks Baptist Association 1652–1907. By H. R. Salt. 8vo. Reading [1907 n.d.].

Prints the earliest minutes, from MS. in the Gould collection, Regent's Park College.

1665. Historical sketches of Nonconformity in the County Palatine of Chester. By W. Urwick, Sen. 1 vol. 8vo. Lond. 1864. 1 map.

1666. The ejected of 1662 in Cumberland and Westmorland : their predecessors and successors. By B. Nightingale. 2 vols. 8vo. Manchester. 1911.

Reproduces many documents.

1667. The story of the Congregational churches of Dorset. By W. Densham and J. Ogle. 1 vol. 8vo. Bournemouth. 1899.

1668. Annals of Evangelical Nonconformity in the county of Essex . . . with memorials of the Essex ministers who were ejected . . . in 1660–2. By T. W. Davids. 1 vol. 8vo. Lond. 1863.

1669. Nonconformity in Herts. By W. Urwick [Jun.] 1 vol. 8vo. Lond. 1884.

1670. Lancashire Nonconformity, or sketches historical and descriptive of the Congregational and old Presbyterian churches in the county. By B. Nightingale. 6 vols. 8vo. Manchester. 1890–3.

Has entirely superseded R. Halley's Lancashire, its Puritanism and Nonconformity.

1671. Minutes of the Manchester Presbyterian Classis [1646–60]. Ed. by W. A. Shaw. 3 vols. Chetham Soc. 1890–1.

' Probably the most perfect of the surviving records of Presbyterianism ' for the period it covers. Cf. Materials for an account of the provincial synod of the county of Lancaster, 1646–1660. By W. A. Shaw. 8vo. Priv. Pr. Manchester. 1890.

1672. Minutes of the committee for the relief of plundered ministers and of the trustees for the maintenance of ministers, relating to Lancashire and Cheshire 1643–1660. Ed. by W. A. Shaw. 2 vols. Lancashire and Cheshire Record Soc. 1893.

1673. Minutes of the Bury Presbyterian Classis, 1647–1657. 2 vols. Chetham Soc. 1896–8. Ed. by W. A. Shaw.

App. I : Minutes of the Nottingham Classis, 1656–60. App. II : Minutes of the Cornwall Classis, 1655–8. App. III : Minutes of the Cambridge Classis, 1657–8.

1674. Record of the Provincial Assembly of Lancashire and Cheshire. By G. E. Evans. 1 vol. 4to. Manchester. 1896.

1675. The history and antiquities of Dissenting churches and meeting houses in London, Westminster, and Southwark, including the lives of their ministers, from the rise of Nonconformity to the present time. By W. Wilson. 4 vols. 8vo. Lond. 1808–14.

The materials used are in Dr. Williams's Library, Lond., as also the preparation for an enlarged edition.

1676. History of Congregationalism and memorials of the churches in Norfolk and Suffolk. By J. Brown. 1 vol. 8vo. Lond. 1877.

1677. Memorials of the Independent churches in Northamptonshire. By T. Coleman. 1 vol. 8vo. Lond. 1853.

1678. The history of Friar Lane Baptist Church, Nottingham, being a contribution towards the history of the Baptists in Nottingham. Illustrated with portraits, views, plans, facsimiles of autographs. By J. T. Godfrey and J. Ward. 8vo. Nottingham. 1903.

By skilled antiquaries. A fine specimen of a large class of local histories.

1679. The Congregational churches of Staffordshire, with some account of the Puritans and Quakers. By A. G. Matthews. 1 vol. 8vo. Lond. 1924.

1680. Independency in Warwickshire; a brief history of the Independent or Congregational churches in that county. By J. Sibree and M. Caston. 1 vol. 8vo. Coventry, 1855.

¶ 4. QUAKERISM

(*a*) Bibliographies.
(*b*) General Histories.
(*c*) Biographies, Personal Narratives, and Collected Works of Individuals.

George Fox, the founder of the Quakers, early impressed upon his followers the importance of the use of the pen as well as of the voice in the propagation of their Gospel message. The result was that, according to a modern computation, some four thousand different works were published previous to 1718. Many of them are of permanent importance, not only for the history of Quakerism, but also for the picture they afford of the middle and lower classes.

John Whiting (1681) produced the earliest ecclesiastical bibliography in 1708, which formed the basis for the elaborate work by Joseph Smith (1682). The Journal of George Fox is the classic of Quakerism and should be studied in the edition prepared by Norman Penney (1699). Next in importance are the Works of William Penn (1711). There are valuable short histories by Emmott (1688, 1692), Harvey (1687), and Brayshaw (1691), and an elaborate one by Braithwaite (1689), a work difficult to praise too highly.

The Friends' Reference Library, established in 1673, is attached to the headquarters of the Society of Friends, Friends House, Euston Road, London, N.W.1, and has the largest collection of Quaker literature in existence. The corresponding collection in America is at Haverford College, Pennsylvania.

(*a*) BIBLIOGRAPHIES

1681. A catalogue of Friends books; written by many of the people called Quakers from the . . . first appearance of the said people. By J. Whiting. 1 vol. 8vo. Lond. 1708.

One of the earliest English bibliographies.

1682. A descriptive catalogue of Friends' books or books written by members of the society of Friends . . . from their first rise to the present time. By J. Smith. 2 vols. 8vo. Lond. 1867.

Vol. i, A–I; vol. ii, J–Z. Cf. Supplement to a descriptive catalogue, by J. Smith [1 vol. 8vo. Lond. 1893]. These and the next item are all valuable.

1683. Bibliotheca anti-Quakeriana, or a catalogue of books adverse to the Society of Friends . . . together with the answers. By J. Smith. 1 vol. 8vo. Lond. 1873.

(b) GENERAL HISTORIES

1684. The history of the rise, increase and progress of the Christian people called Quakers . . . with several remarkable occurrences, written originally in Low Dutch by William Sewel and by himself translated into English. By W. Sewel. 1 vol. fol. Lond. 1722. Later eds. 1 vol. fol. Lond. 1725.

Originally publ. in Dutch [fol. Amsterdam 1717] : Histori van de Opkomste, Aanwas, en Voortgang der Christenen bekend by den naam van Quakers. Valuable.

1685. A collection of the sufferings of the people called Quakers [1650–89]. By J. Besse. 2 vols. fol. Lond. 1753.

Besse also wrote : Abstract of the Sufferings &c. 1733–8 ; Brief account of many of the prosecutions &c. 1736. His various works form an invaluable storehouse of biographical facts.

1686. The inner life of the religious societies of the Commonwealth. By R. Barclay. 1 vol. 8vo. Lond. 1876, and later eds. 1877, 1879.

1687. The rise of the Quakers. By T. E. Harvey. 1 vol. 8vo. Lond. 1905. 6th impression, 1921.

1688. The story of Quakerism. By E. B. Emmott. 1 vol. 8vo. Lond. 1908. reprinted.

1689. The beginnings of Quakerism. By W. C. Braithwaite. Intro. by R. M. Jones. 1 vol. 8vo. Lond. 1912.

Covers 1650–60. This and the following form the best general history. Continued in his : The second period of Quakerism [1660–1725], Intro. by R. M. Jones, 1 vol. 8vo. Lond. 1919.

1690. Quaker women, 1650–90. By M. R. Brailsford. 1 vol. 8vo. Lond. 1915.

1691. The Quakers : their story and message. By A. N. Brayshaw. 1 vol. 8vo. Lond. 1921. 2nd ed. enlarged 1927.

1692. A short history of Quakerism [to 1725]. By E. B. Emmott. 1 vol. 8vo. Lond. 1923.

1693. The Quakers in peace and war. By M. E. Hirst. 1 vol. 8vo. Lond. 1923.

(c) BIOGRAPHIES, PERSONAL NARRATIVES, AND COLLECTED WORKS OF INDIVIDUALS

DEWSBURY, WILLIAM.

1694. The life of William Dewsbury. By E. Smith. 1 vol. 8vo. Lond. 1836.

ELLWOOD, THOMAS.

1695. The history of the life of Thomas Ellwood . . . written by his own hand. Ed. by J. Wyeth. 1 vol. 8vo. Lond. 1714. Ed. by C. G. Crump 1900. Ed. by S. Graveson 1906.

FELL, MARGARET.

1696. A brief collection of remarkable passages and occurrences relating to . . . Margaret Fell, but by her second marriage, Margaret Fox. Together with sundry of her epistles, books and Christian testimonies. 1 vol. 8vo. Lond. 1710.

1697. Margaret Fox of Swarthmoor Hall. By H. G. Crosfield. 1 vol. 8vo. Lond. *c.* 1913. Illus.

FISHER, SAMUEL.

1698. The testimony of truth exalted by the collected labours of . . . Samuel Fisher. 1 vol. fol. s.l. 1679.

Mainly a repr. of Rusticus ad academicos . . . The rustick's alarm to the rabbies or the country correcting the university and clergy, publ. separately in 1660 and 1677.

FOX, GEORGE.

1699. A journal or historical account of the life, travels, sufferings . . . of . . . George Fox. Intro. by W. Penn. 1 vol. fol. Lond. 1694. Later eds. 2 vols. 8vo. Camb. 1911 ; 1 vol. 8vo. Lond. 1924. Both ed. by N. Penney.

The first ed. was prepared by T. Ellwood and other Friends. The Cambridge edition first gives the original manuscript verbatim. For addenda and corrigenda of ed. 1911 see the Journal of the Friends' Hist. Soc. ix–xxi. 1912–24. The short journal of George Fox was ed. by N. Penney. 1 vol. 8vo. Camb. 1925.

1700. A collection of epistles. By G. Fox. 1 vol. fol. Lond. 1698.

1701. Gospel truth demonstrated in a collection of doctrinal books given forth . . . by George Fox . . . containing principles essential to Christianity held among the people called Quakers. 1 vol. fol. Lond. 1706.

The above books are repr. with many others in The works of George Fox [8 vols. 8vo. Philadelphia. 1831].

1702. George Fox. By T. Hodgkin. 1 vol. 8vo. Lond. 1896.

The best short life. Other biographies of Fox are by : J. Marsh [1 vol. 8vo. Lond. 1847] ; S. M. Janney [1 vol. 8vo. Philadelphia. 1853] ; W. Tallack [1 vol. 8vo. Lond. 1868] ; A. C. Bickley [1 vol. 8vo. Lond. 1884] ; H. G. Wood [1 vol. 8vo. Lond. 1912] ; R. M. Jones [1 vol. 8vo. 1919 and 1922] ; Rachel Knight [1 vol. 8vo. Lond. 1922].

HOOTON, ELIZABETH.

1703. Elizabeth Hooton, first Quaker woman preacher (1600–72). By E. Manners. Intro. by N. Penney. 1 vol. 8vo. Lond. 1914.

Deals with her experiences in New England as well as in England. This forms Supplement 12 of the Journal of the Friends' Hist. Soc.

HOWGIL, FRANCIS.

1704. The dawnings of the gospel-day and its light and glory discovered by . . . Francis Howgil. Ed. by E. Hooks. 1 vol. fol. s.l. 1676.

A reprint of Howgil's tracts, including The heart of New England hardened through wickedness, Lond. 1659. Cf. Memoirs of Francis Howgill, by J. Backhouse [1 vol. 8vo. York. 1828].

LURTING, THOMAS.

1705. The fighting sailor turn'd peaceable Christian. By T. Lurting. 1 vol. 8vo. Lond. 1710. Later eds. 1 vol. 12mo. Lond. 1813. 1 vol. 12mo. Lond. 1842.

Ed. of 1842 has title, A narrative of Thomas Lurting.

NAYLER, JAMES.

1706. A true narrative of the examination, tryall and sufferings of James Nayler. 1 vol. sm. 4to. Lond. *c.* 1657.

Cf. Memoirs of the life, ministry, tryal and sufferings of . . . James Nailer [1 vol. 8vo. Lond. 1719]. There are lives by J. G. Bevan, 1 vol. 8vo. 1800, and by H. Tuke, in vol. ii of Biographical notices of members of the society of friends. 12mo. York. 1815 and 1826. The latest and best life is by M. R. Brailsford. 8vo. Lond. 1927.

PARNELL, JAMES.

1707. A memoir of James Parnell with extracts from his writings. By H. Callaway. 1 vol. 12mo. Lond. 1846.

Cf. James Parnell. By C. Fell-Smith. 1 vol. sm. 8vo. Lond. 1906.

PENNS & PENINGTONS.

1708. The Penns & Peningtons of the seventeenth century in their domestic and religious life, illustrated by original family letters. By M. Webb. 1 vol. 8vo. Lond. 1867. Illus. repr. 1891.

The same authoress wrote, The Fells of Swarthmoor Hall and their friends [1 vol. 8vo. Lond. 1865].

PENINGTON, ISAAC.

1709. Works of the long mournful and sorely distressed Isaac Penington. By I. Penington, son of Sir I. Penington, Lord Mayor of London. 2 parts. fol. Lond. 1680–1. Later eds. 2 vols. 4to. Lond. 1761. 4 vols. 8vo. Lond. 1784.

Cf. Letters of Isaac Penington, ed. by J. Barclay [1 vol. 8vo. Lond. 1828].

1710. Memoirs of the life of Isaac Penington, to which is added a review of his writings. By J. G. Bevan. 1 vol. 8vo. Lond. 1807. Later ed. 1 vol. 12mo. Lond. 1830.

PENN, WILLIAM.

1711. A collection of the works of William Penn. To which is prefixed a journal of his life with many original letters. 2 vols. fol. Lond. 1726. Later ed. 5 vols. 8vo. Lond. 1782.

Ed. of 1782 is entitled : The select works of William Penn [with the author's life]. Among the more important works repr. are : The sandy foundation shaken [1668] ; The people's ancient and just liberties asserted in the trial of William Penn and William Mead [1670] ; No cross, no crown; A treatise of oaths ; The great case of liberty of conscience debated [1670] ; Travels in Holland and Germany [1677] ; A general description of the province of Pennsylvania [1683] ; Some fruits of Solitude [1693] ; A brief account of the rise and progress of the people called Quakers [1694].

1712. Memoirs of the public and private life of William Penn. By T. Clarkson. 2 vols. 8vo. Lond. 1813. Bibl. Later ed. 1 vol. 8vo. Lond. 1849.

The ed. of 1849 has a preface by W. E. Forster, replying to the charges against Penn made by Macaulay in his History of England. This preface was publ. separately in Philadelphia, 1850, as ' William Penn and Thomas B. Macaulay '.

1713. William Penn : an historical biography, founded on family and state papers. By W. H. Dixon. 1 vol. 8vo. Lond. 1851. Later ed. 1 vol. 8vo. Lond. 1872.

The ed. of 1872 has the title : History of William Penn.

1714. William Penn. By J. W. Graham. 1 vol. 8vo. Lond. 1916.

A good popular life. Other biographies are by S. M. Janney [1 vol. 8vo. Philadelphia. 1851 and 1852. Illus.] ; J. Stoughton [1 vol. 8vo. Lond. 1882].

ROBERTS, JOHN.

1715. Some memoirs of the life of John Roberts. By D. Roberts. 1 vol. 8vo. Exeter. 1746. Later ed. 1 vol. 8vo. Lond. 1898. Illus. Bibl. Ed. by E. T. Lawrence.

The ed. of 1898 is called : A Quaker of the olden time, and contains, in addition to a repr. of the Life, The Roberts Family from the time of Queen Elizabeth to the present day.

SANSOM, OLIVER.

1716. An account of . . . the life of Oliver Sansom. By O. Sansom. 1 vol. 12mo. Lond. 1710. Later ed. 1 vol. 12mo. Lond. 1848.

STORY, THOMAS.

1717. Journal of the Life of Thomas Story, containing an account of his remarkable convincement of . . . truth as held by the people called Quakers, also his travels and labours in the service of the Gospel. 1 vol. fol. Newcastle-on-Tyne. 1747.

Abridged by J. Kendall, 1786, and by W. Alexander, 1832.

WHITEHEAD, GEORGE.

1718. The Christian progress of . . . George Whitehead, historically relating his experience, ministry, sufferings . . . in defence of the truth and God's persecuted people commonly called Quakers. 4 pts. in 1 vol. 8vo. Lond. 1725.

A very detailed autobiography. Cf. George Whitehead . . . compiled from his autobiography, by W. Beck [1 vol. 8vo. Lond. 1901. Illus.].

WHITEHEAD, JOHN.

1719. The written Gospel-labours of . . . John Whitehead. Preface by W. Penn. 1 vol. 8vo. Lond. 1704.

Cf. The life and writings of John Whitehead, by T. Chalk [1 vol. 8vo. Lond. 1852].

WHITING, JOHN.

1720. Persecution expos'd in some memoirs relating to the sufferings of John Whiting and many others of the people called Quakers . . . in the west of England. 1 vol. 4to. Lond. 1715. Later ed. 1 vol. 8vo. Lond. 1791.

¶ 5. UNITARIANISM

(a) Bibliography and Sources.
(b) Later Works.

As Unitarians stood outside the protection of the law in Great Britain for the period 1603–1714, they were unable to form any lasting organization or to gather congregations for worship. The regular press was closed against them. Except for a brief period under the Commonwealth, publications favouring Unitarian opinions were anonymous and surreptitious and often printed abroad. Materials for the study of Unitarianism in that century are therefore scanty. The story of the Unitarian movement in this period is, accordingly, the story, in the main, of individual thinkers and writers. It must be studied through biography.

The Dictionary of National Biography gives the lives of most of these Unitarian pioneers, mainly from the hand of Rev. Alexander Gordon.

The history of many of the Protestant Dissenting congregations which advanced to Unitarianism is set out in special monographs dealing with particular churches. Most of these congregations were founded prior to 1714 and the earlier chapters of their story fall well within the period covered by this Bibliography.

(a) BIBLIOGRAPHY AND SOURCES

1721. Antitrinitarian biography, or sketches of the lives and writings of distinguished antitrinitarians, exhibiting a view of the state of the Unitarian doctrine and worship in the principal nations of Europe from the Reformation to the close of the seventeenth century : to which is prefixed a history of Unitarianism in England during the same period. By R. Wallace. 3 vols. 8vo. Lond. 1850.

1722. A confession of faith touching the Holy Trinity according to the Scriptures. By J. Biddle. 1 vol. 8vo. Lond. 1648. Later ed. 1 vol. 4to. Lond. 1691.

Cf. Biddle's The testimonies of Irenaeus, Justin-Martyr, Tertullian, Novatianus, Theophilus Origen . . . concerning that one God and the persons of the Holy Trinity. 1 vol. 8vo. Lond. c. 1650. Repr. 1653 and 1691.

1723. The Racovian catechisme, wherein you have the substance of the confession of those churches which in the kingdom of Poland . . . do affirm that no other save the Father of our Lord Jesus Christ is that one God of Israel. 1 vol. 8vo. Amsterdam (Lond. ?) 1652. Later ed. 1 vol. 12mo. Lond. 1818. Ed. by T. Rees.

1724. Two books touching one God the Father. English version. By J. Crellins. 1 vol. 4to. (Amsterdam or Lond.). 1665.

Some copies have a rubricated title-page, but these are rare.

1725. Brief history of the Unitarians, called also Socinians. In four letters. [By S. Nye.] 1 vol. 8vo. Lond. 1687. Later ed. 1 vol. 4to. Lond. 1691.

1726. A short account of the life of John Biddle. 1691.

Cf. Joannis Bidelli ... vita. 1 vol. 12mo. Lond. 1682 ; and A review of the life, character and writings of ... John Biddle. By J. Toulmin. Lond. 1791.

1727. The life of Mr. Thomas Firmin, late citizen of London. 1 vol. 8vo. Lond. 1698. Later ed. 1 vol. 12mo. 1791.

Ed. of 1791 one of the Tracts, printed and published by the Unitarian Society. (13 vols. 12mo. Lond. 1791–1802.)

1728. Last thoughts on the Trinity, extracted from his posthumous work entitled ' A treatise on Christian doctrine '. By J. Milton. 1 vol. 8vo. Lond. 1828.

(b) LATER WORKS

1729. An historical view of the state of Unitarian doctrine and worship from the Reformation to our own times. By T. Lindsey. 1 vol. 8vo. Lond. 1783.

1730. A history of the Presbyterian and General Baptist churches in the west of England ; with memoirs of some of their pastors. By J. Murch. 8vo. Lond. 1835.

Deals only with those churches usually called Unitarian.

1731. Unitarianism exhibited in its actual condition ; consisting of essays by several Unitarian ministers and others ; illustrative of the rise, progress and principles of Christian Anti-Trinitarianism in different parts of the world. Ed. by J. R. Beard. 1 vol. 8vo. Lond. 1846.

1732. Early sources of English Unitarian Christianity. By G. Bonet-Maury. 1 vol. 8vo. Lond. 1884.

Has a valuable introductory survey by J. Martineau and appendix of documents.

1733. Unitarianism, its origin and history. By J. H. Allen, A. P. Peabody, B. Herford, and others. 1 vol. 8vo. Boston (Mass.). 1890.

16 lectures delivered in Boston, 1888–9, by the above-mentioned and others.

1734. Heads of English Unitarian history, with appended lectures on Baxter and Priestley. By A. Gordon. 1 vol. 8vo. Lond. 1895.

Lays bare ' the framework of the subject as a guide to learners '. Gives valuable references ' to publications presumed to be fairly accessible '.

1735. Dukinfield Chapel. By A. Gordon. 1 vol. 8vo. 1896.

Other typical studies of Unitarian congregations whose history in an earlier phase of theology goes back to the seventeenth century are : Matthew Henry and his chapel, 1662–1900, by H. D. Roberts. 8vo. Liverpool. 1901 ; History of the Free Christian Church, Horsham, by E. Kensett. 8vo. Horsham. 1921 ; The story of Dean Row Chapel, Cheshire, by W. H. Burgess, 8vo. Hull. 1924.

1736. Vestiges of Protestant dissent, being list of ministers, sacramental plate, registers, antiquities and other matters pertaining to most of the churches . . . included in the National Conference of Unitarian, Liberal Christian . . . congregations. By G. E. Evans. 1 vol. 8vo. Liverpool. 1897.

Valuable for local history. Has references to authorities, MSS. and registers, relating to Unitarian congregations.

1737. The story of Protestant dissent and English Unitarianism. By W. Lloyd. 1 vol. 8vo. London. 1899.

1738. A short history of Unitarianism. By F. B. Mott. 1 vol. 8vo. Lond. 1906.

1739. Unitarianism. By W. G. Tarrant. 1 vol. 8vo. Lond. 1912.
A good outline : traces the relationship between Unitarianism and the ' old dissent '.

1740. The Arian movement in England. By J. H. Colligan. 1 vol. 8vo. Manchester. 1913.

1741. Transactions of the Unitarian Historical Society. Issued annually to subscribers. 1917—. Ed. by W. H. Burgess.

1742. Addresses biographical and historical. By A. Gordon. 1 vol. 8vo. Lond. 1922.
Many of these addresses relate to the Unitarian movement.

¶ 6. JUDAISM

In addition to the works here listed, there is a good general sketch in A. M. Hyamson's History of the Jews in England, 1908. The Jewish Historical Soc. Trans. contain other relevant articles for which no room could be found. The Mocatta library of Jewish works is in the custody of the University of London.

1743. Bibliotheca Anglo-Judaica. A bibliographical guide to Anglo-Jewish history. By J. Jacobs and L. Wolf. 1 vol. 8vo. Lond. 1888.

1744. A short demurrer to the Jews long discontinued remitter into England. By W. Prynne. 2 pts. 4to. Lond. 1656.

1745. Anglia Judaica: or the history and antiquities of the Jews in England. By D'Blossiers Tovey. 1 vol. 4to. Oxf. 1738.

1746. The question whether a Jew, born within the British dominions, was before the making the late act of parliament a person capable by law to purchase and hold lands . . . fairly stated and considered. By P. C. Webb. 1 vol. 8vo. Lond. 1753.

1747. Crypto-Jews under the Commonwealth. By L. Wolf. Trans. Jewish Hist. Soc. vol. i. 1895.
Cf. his : Cromwell's Jewish Intelligencers. 1 vol. 8vo. Lond. 1891. 2nd ed. in Jewish Literary Annual. 1904.

1748. The first English Jew. Notes on Antonio Fernandez Carvajal. By L. Wolf. Jewish Hist. Soc. Trans. vol. ii.

1749. Menasseh Ben Israel's mission to Oliver Cromwell. Being a reprint of the pamphlets published by Menasseh Ben Israel to promote the re-admission of the Jews to England, 1649–56. Ed. by L. Wolf. 1 vol. 4to. Lond. 1901.

1750. The Jewry of the Restoration, 1660–1664. By L. Wolf. 1 vol. 8vo. Lond. 1902.

Cf. his Status of the Jews in England after the resettlement. Trans. Jewish Hist. Soc. vol. iv. 1903.

1751. The return of the Jews to England. By H. S. Q. Henriques. 1 vol. 8vo. Lond. 1905.

1752. The Jews and the English law. By H. S. Q. Henriques. 1 vol. 8vo. Lond. 1908.

1753. The first synagogue of the resettlement [Creechurch Lane], founded in 1657. By W. S. Samuel. 1 vol. 4to. Lond. 1924. Illus.

¶ 7. ROMAN CATHOLICISM

(*a*) General Histories.
(*b*) Societies, excluding Jesuits.
(*c*) Jesuits.
(*d*) Nuns.
(*e*) Martyrology and Persecution.
(*f*) Gunpowder Plot.
(*g*) Popish Plot.
(*h*) Miscellaneous : (1) Sources.
　　　　　　　　　　　 (2) Later Works.

Owing to the circumstances of the Catholics in England during the seventeenth century comparatively little of an historical character was published, though the devotional and controversial literature is considerable in extent. With the foundation of the Catholic Record Society in 1904 a beginning has been made in the task of printing MSS. of purely historical interest. The Church History published by Dodd (Hugh Tootell) and Bishop Challoner's ' Memoirs of Missionary Priests ' long remained the chief sources of information during the eighteenth century, and continue to be of great importance. Tierney's unfinished edition of Dodd is indispensable for the period 1603–25 because he supplemented the text with a wealth of original contemporary documents. Since his time two valuable sources of information have appeared. The one is Joseph Gillow's ' Bibliographical Dictionary of English Catholics ' in five volumes : from A to P the work is fairly exhaustive ; from R to Z it is practically useless, except for a few lists of works of particular writers. The second work referred to is Foley's ' Records of the English Province of the Society of Jesus ', which incidentally deals with the whole body of Catholics as well as the Jesuits themselves. In recent years most of the other orders, Benedictines, Dominicans, Franciscans, Carmelites, and various bodies of Nuns, have published lists of their members, obituaries, and records which abound in genealogical as well as historical matter. College lists, and in some cases annals, for Douay, Rome, Lisbon, and Paris have been published, but those for Valladolid, though in existence, have not yet been printed. Biographies for this period are rare, and those which were contemporary in character are frequently brief. The history of English Catholics in the seventeenth century as a whole yet remains to be written.

(a) GENERAL HISTORIES

1754. The church history of England from . . . 1500 to . . . 1688. By C. Dodd. 3 vols. fol. Brussels 1737–42. Later ed. 5 vols. 8vo. Lond. 1839–43. Ed. by M. A. Tierney.

The ed. of 1839–43 has valuable additions and notes. Vol. v, 1603–25, has appendix of documents. For bibliographical note see Gillow v. 546 ; and for the MSS. collected for Tierney's ed. now in the custody of the Bishop of Southwark, see Hist. MSS. Comm., 3rd Rep., p. 233.

1755. Historical memoirs respecting the English, Irish and Scottish Catholics from the Reformation. By C. Butler. 4 vols. 8vo. Lond. 1819–21.

1st ed. ' In two volumes '—1819. Vols. iii and iv were issued as Additions to the historical memoirs in 1821. 3rd ed. With further additions. 4 vols. Lond. 1822.

1756. A history of the Church in England, from the earliest period to the re-establishment of the hierarchy in 1850. By T. Flanagan. 2 vols. 8vo. Lond. 1857.

1757. The Episcopal succession in England, Scotland and Ireland, A. D. 1400–1875. With appointments to monasteries and extracts from consistorial acts taken from MSS. in public and private libraries in Rome, Florence, Bologna, Ravenna, and Paris. By W. M. Brady. 3 vols. 8vo. Rome. 1876–7.

Important. Ireland, vol. ii. Vol. iii was reissued separately under title Annals of the Catholic Hierarchy in England and Scotland, A. D. 1585–1876, with Dissertation on Anglican Orders. Rome. 1877 ; Lond. 1883.

1758. A literary and biographical history or bibliographical dictionary of the English Catholics from the breach with Rome in 1534 to the present day. By J. Gillow. 5 vols. 8vo. Lond. and N.Y. *c.* 1885–1902.

Vol. i, A–C ; ii, D–Grad ; iii, Grah–Kem ; iv, Kem–Met ; v, Mey–Zoo. Valuable though incomplete. Gives lists of writings of each Catholic. Fairly complete down to end of P. The rest was massacred because publishers refused an extra volume.

1759. Clemens VIII und Jakob I von England. By A. O. Meyer. 1 vol. 4to. Rome. 1904.

Cf. his : Charles I and Rome. Amer. Hist. Rev. xix. 1913.

(b) SOCIETIES, EXCLUDING JESUITS

1760. Notices of the English colleges and convents established on the continent after the dissolution of religious houses in England. By E. Petre. Ed. by F. C. Husenbeth. 1 vol. 4to. Norwich. 1849.

A convenient summary.

1761. Chronological notes, containing the rise, growth and present state of the English congregation of the Order of St. Benedict drawn from the archives of the houses of the said congregation at Douay in Flanders, Dieulwart in Lorraine, Paris in France, and Lambspring in Germany, where are preserved the Authentic Acts and original deeds &c. An. 1709. By B. Weldon. Ed. at St. Gregory's Priory, Downside. 1 vol. 4to. Lond. 1881.

History of Eng. Benedictines in 17th century. Lists of monks and obituaries.

1762. Necrology of the English congregation of the order of St. Benedict from 1600 to 1883. By T. B. Snow. 1 vol. 8vo. Lond. 1883. Later eds. 1 vol. 8vo. Privately printed 1913. Ed. by H. N. Birt.

Intro. Chronological lists of Monks, Laybrothers, and Nuns. The second edition has a new title : ' Obit book of the English Benedictines from 1600 to 1912, being the Necrology of the English congregation of the order of Benedict from 1600 to 1883. Compiled by Abbot Snow.'

1763. The Franciscans in England, 1600–1850, being an authentic account of the second English province of Friars Minor. By Father Thaddeus. 1 vol. 8vo. Lond. 1898. Port.

Includes valuable citations from contemporary accounts. List of Friars is now largely superseded by the official lists published by Catholic Record Society, vol. xxiv.

1764. The English black monks of St. Benedict. By E. L. Taunton. 2 vols. 8vo. Lond. 1898.

1765. La conservation providentielle du Catholicisme en Angleterre ou histoire du Collège Anglais, Douai (1563–78), Reims (1578–93), Douai (1593–1793). By A. Haudecoeur, Curé de Pouillon. Reims. 1898.

The only outline of the entire history of the College, 1568–1793. English names frequently misprinted.

1766. Carmel in England : a history of the English mission of the Discalced Carmelites 1615 to 1849, drawn from documents preserved in the archives of the Order. By B. Zimmerman. 1 vol. 8vo. Lond. 1899.

Full for 17th century—less material for 18th. Throws much light on general state of English Catholics.

1767. Historical account of Lisbon College. With a register compiled by J. Gillow. By J. Kirk. Ed. by W. Croft. 1 vol. 8vo. Barnet. 1902. Several ports.

The Register is indispensable for 17th-century Lisbonian priests.

1768. Memoir of Edmund Mathew, alias Poins at St. Omers College, 1667. Ed. by J. H. Pollen. Catholic Record Soc. Misc. iii. 1906.

' Perhaps the earliest English account of a Catholic boy of his years which we possess.' Preface.

1769. Notices sur les établissements religieux Anglais, Ecossais et Irlandais fondés à Paris avant la Révolution. In ' Mémoires de la Société de l'Histoire de Paris et de l'Ile de France ', vols. xxxvii [1910] and xxxix [1912]. By G. Daumet. 2 vols. 4to. Paris. 1910–12.

Contains information nowhere else available.

1770. The Douay College diaries, third, fourth, and fifth, 1598–1654. Ed. by E. H. Burton and T. L. Williams. Catholic Record Soc. x, xi. 2 vols. 8vo. 1911. Illus.

Text in Latin : a summary in English is appended to each vol. Vol. i goes down to 1637, vol. ii to 1654.

1771. The English Catholic refugees on the continent, 1558–1795. Vol. i. The English colleges and convents in the Catholic Low Countries. By P. Guilday. 1 vol. 8vo. Lond. 1914.

1772. The register book of St. Gregory's Seminary at Paris, 1667–1786. Ed. by E. H. Burton.   Catholic Record Soc. Misc. xi. 1917.

(c) JESUITS

1773. Historia provinciae anglicanae societatis Iesu [1580–1635].   By H. More.   1 vol. fol. [Saint-Omer] 1660.

In Latin : valuable.

1774. Collections towards illustrating the biography of Scotch, English and Irish members, S[ocietatis] J[esu].   By G. Oliver.   1 vol. 8vo. Exeter. 1838.

For other works illustrating the history of the Catholics in the west of England see T. N. Brushfield's The bibliography of the Rev. George Oliver [8vo. s.l. *c.* 1886], repr. from Trans. Devonshire Association for the advancement of science, literature, and art, 1885.

1775. The discovery of the Jesuits' College at Clerkenwell in March 1627–8. Ed. by J. G. Nichols.   Camd. Soc. Misc. ii. 1853.

Cf. Camd. Soc. Misc. iv for a supplementary note.

1776. Records of the English province of the Society of Jesus.   Historic facts illustrative of the labours and sufferings of its members in the sixteenth and seventeenth centuries.   By H. Foley.   6 vols. 8vo. Lond. 1875–80.   Illus. Later ed. 7 vols. 8vo. Lond. 1882.

Collections from printed and MS. sources, ' arranged . . . in order of time and according to the ancient divisions of the English province into districts'.   Vol. vi of 1st ed. contains the diary of the English college at Rome (1579–1773) and the pilgrim book of the ancient English hospice attached to the college (1580–1656).   Valuable.

1777. The history of the Jesuits in England 1580–1773.   By E. L. Taunton. 1 vol. 8vo. Lond. 1901.   Illus.

Not reliable.

(d) NUNS

1778. The chronicle of the English Augustinian canonesses regular of the Lateran at St. Monica's Louvain (now at St. Augustine's Priory, Newton Abbot, Devon).   Ed. by A. Hamilton.   2 vols. 8vo. Edin. 1904.   Several Ports.

Much genealogical information and several excellent pedigrees.   Vol. i, 1548–1625; vol. ii, 1626–44.

1779. Abbess Neville's annals of five communities of English Benedictine nuns in Flanders, 1598–1687.   Contributed by the Lady Abbess of St. Scholastica's Abbey, Teignmouth.   By M. Neville.   Ed. by M. J. Rumsey. Catholic Record Soc. Misc. v. 1909.

1780. The diary of the ' Blue nuns ' or order of the immaculate conception of our Lady at Paris 1658–1810.   Ed. by J. Gillow and R. Trappes-Lomax. 1 vol. 8vo. Catholic Record Soc. viii. Lond. 1910.

1781. Registers of the English Poor Clare nuns at Gravelines, with notes of foundations at Aire, Dunkirk, and Rouen, 1608–1837.   Ed. by W. M. Hunnybun and J. Gillow.   Catholic Record Soc. Misc. ix. 1914.

1782. Records of the English canonesses of the Holy Sepulchre at Liège, now at New Hall, Essex, 1652–1793. Ed. by A. J. Kendal and R. Trappes-Lomax. Catholic Record Soc. Misc. x. 1915. Illus.

1783. Obituary notices of the English Benedictine nuns of Ghent in Flanders, and at Preston, Lancashire, 1627–1811. Ed. by A. L. Ward. Catholic Record Soc. Misc. xi. Lond. 1917.

1784. The English Franciscan nuns, 1619–1821, and the Friars Minor of the same province, 1618–1761. Ed. by R. Trappes-Lomax. Catholic Record Soc. xxiv. 1922.

(e) MARTYROLOGY AND PERSECUTION

1785. Histoire de la persécution présente des Catholiques en Angleterre. By F. de Marsys. 3 pts. 4to. Paris. 1646.

1786. Draconica : or an abstract of all the penal laws touching matters of religion, and the several oaths and tests thereby enjoyned. . . . By H. Care. 1 vol. fol. Lond. 1689.

Advocates abrogation of the penal laws.

1787. Memoirs of missionary priests and other Catholics of both sexes that have suffered death in England on religious accounts, from the year 1577 to 1684, carefully collected from the accounts of eye-witnesses. . . . By R. Challoner. 2 vols. 8vo. Lond. 1741–2. Later eds. 2 vols. 8vo. Manchester. 1803. 2 in 1 vol. 4to. Edin. and Lond. 1878. Illus. Preface by T. Graves Law. 1 vol. 8vo. Lond. 1924. Ed. by J. H. Pollen.

Vol. i, 1577–1603 ; ii, 1603–84[–5]. Particulars of various editions in Burton's ' Life and times of Bishop Challoner ', ii. 329–30 ; and chap. x (vol. i, 160 *seq.*) on this work, its sources and later influence. Valuable.

1788. A guide to the laws of England affecting Roman Catholics. By T. C. Anstey. 1 vol. 8vo. Lond. 1842.

Includes the 17th-century laws—classified and digested. Cf. The history of the penal laws enacted against Roman Catholics. By R. R. Madden. 1 vol. 8vo. Lond. 1847.

1789. A calendar of the English [Catholic] martyrs of the sixteenth and seventeenth centuries. Ed. by T. G. Law. 1 vol. 8vo. Lond. 1876.

For a complete list of contemporary martyrologies see J. H. Pollen in Cath. Rec. Soc. v. 1–7. Other useful lists are Henry Foley's Alphabetical catalogue of members of the English province, S.J. who assumed aliases or by-names, together with the said aliases [8vo. Manresa Press, 1875] ; and W. Gumbley's Provincial priors and vicars of the English Dominicans, 1221–1916, Eng. Hist. Rev. xxxiii. 1918.

1790. Penal laws and Test Act. By Sir G. F. Duckett. 2 vols. 8vo. 1882–3.

Pr. from Bodl. Lib. MS. Rawl. A. 139A : contains the replies sent by deputy lieutenants and others to the three questions James II propounded about the repeal of the Test Act, &c.

1791. Faithful unto death. An account of the sufferings of the English Franciscans during the 16th and 17th centuries, from contemporary records. By J. M. Stone. 1 vol. 8vo. Lond. 1892.

1792. A Benedictine martyr in England.   By B. Camm.   1 vol. 8vo. Lond. 1897.

The life of John Roberts, executed in 1610.

1793. The life and martyrdom of Mr. Maxfield, 1616.   With portrait and facsimile letter of the martyr.   Ed. by J. H. Pollen.   Catholic Record Soc. Misc. iii. Lond. 1906.

1794. A list of convicted recusants in the reign of King Charles II.   Ed. by J. Gillow and J. S. Hansom.   Catholic Record Soc. Misc. v. 1909.

Repr. from Brit. Mus. Add. MS. 20739.

1795. Tower bills 1585–1681, with gatehouse certificates 1592–1603.   Ed. by J. H. Pollen.   Catholic Record Soc. Misc. iv. 1907.

From P.R.O. Exch. of Receipt, Misc. bundle 342.

1796. A narrative of the martyrdom of the Ven. Thomas Holland, S.J. 1642.   Ed. by E. R. James.   Catholic Record Soc. Misc. viii. 1913.

A repr. with translation of a Portuguese pamphlet, publ. at Lisbon in 1643—Relacão da Ditosa morte do Padre Thomas Hollanda . . . Escrivoa hũ Inglez Catholico que se achou presente.

1797. A century of persecution under Tudor and Stuart sovereigns from contemporary records.   By St. G. K. Hyland.   1 vol. 8vo. Lond. 1920.

Has information about Catholics under James I and Charles I from the Loseley MSS.

(f) GUNPOWDER PLOT

1798. A true and perfect relation of the whole proceedings against the late most barbarous traitors.   1 vol. 4to. Lond. 1606.

The official account.

1799. A true and perfect relation of the whole proceedings against . . . Garnet, a Jesuite, and his confederats.   1 vol. 4to. Lond. 1606.

Publ. by authority and answered in Apologia pro Henrico Garneto ad actionem proditoriam E. Coqui Andreae Eudaemon Joannis Cydonii [i. e. the Jesuit L'Heureux] [12mo. Cologne. 1610], to answer which Robert Abbot was commissioned, and wrote Antilogia adversus apologiam Andreae Eudaemon Joannis [1 vol. 4to. Lond. 1613]. This produced a rejoinder Eudaemon-Joannes : Responsio . . . ad antilogiam [1 vol. 8vo. s.l. 1615].

1800. The tryal and execution of Father H. Garnet collected by R. W. Printed in Latin in 1616 . . . and thence translated.   Fol. Lond. 1679.

1801. A narrative of the Gunpowder Plot.   By D. Jardine.   1 vol. 8vo. Lond. 1857.

Cf. The identification of the writer of the anonymous letter to Lord Monteagle in 1605 [4to. Lond. 1916, with facsimiles].

1802. The condition of Catholics under James I.   Father Gerard's Narrative of the Gunpowder Plot.   Ed. by J. Morris.   1 vol. 8vo. Lond. 1871. Later eds. 1872 and 1881.

Life of Fr. Gerard, S.J., consisting mainly of extracts from his autobiography (cclxiii pp.), followed by his narrative of the Gunpowder Plot.

1803. The life of Father John Gerard of the Society of Jesus. By J. Morris, S.J. 1 vol. 8vo. Lond. 1881.

Though described as a third edition of ' The Condition of Catholics under James I ' it is so re-written and enlarged that it became a new book and has a new title.

1804. The life of a conspirator ; being a biography of Sir Everard Digby, by one of his descendants. By T. Longueville. 1 vol. 8vo. Lond. 1895. Illus.

1805. What was the Gunpowder Plot ? The traditional story tested by original evidence. By J. Gerard. 1 vol. 8vo. Lond. 1897. Illus.

An unsuccessful attempt to prove the Plot to be chiefly a fiction made up by Salisbury. Answered by S. R. Gardiner (1806), to whose work a rejoinder appeared in The Month. No. 399. Cf. Eng. Hist. Rev. xii. 1897, pp. 791–5.

1806. What Gunpowder Plot was. By S. R. Gardiner. 1 vol. 8vo. Lond. 1897.

A reply to the above. Ch. I has a valuable discussion on the nature of historical evidence.

1807. Contributions towards a Life of Father Henry Garnet, S.J. By J. Gerard. 8vo. Lond. 1898.

(g) POPISH PLOT

1808. Mr. Langhorn's memoires, with some meditations and devotions of his, during his imprisonment, as also his petition to his majesty and his speech at his execution. 1 vol. fol. s.l. 1679.

1809. The compendium, or a short view of the late tryals in relation to the present plot against his majesty and government, with the speeches of those that have been executed. 1 vol. 4to. Lond. 1679.

1810. A true narrative of the horrid plot and conspiracy . . . against . . . his sacred majesty the government and the Protestant religion. By T. Oates. 1 vol. fol. Lond. 1679.

Pr. by order of Parliament. Cf. A vindication of the Inglish Catholiks from the pretended conspiracy against the life and government of his sacred majesty discovering the chief falsities & contradictions in the narrative of Titus Oates [1 vol. sm. 4to. Antwerp. 1680].

1811. A collection of letters and other writings relating to the horrid Popish Plot. Printed from the originals in the hands of Sir George Treby, chairman of the committee of secrecy of the . . . house of commons. Published by order. 2 pts. sm. 4to. Lond. 1681.

Important. Cf. Hist. MSS. Comm., Fitzherbert MSS., 1893.

1812. The history of Popish—Sham—Plots from the reign of Queen Elizabeth to this present time. Particularly of the present Popish plot. 1 vol. 8vo. Lond. 1682.

1813. A brief history of the times, &c. in a preface to the third volume of Observators. By R. L'Estrange. 3 parts. 8vo. Lond. 1687–8.

A Tory history of the Popish Plot.

1814. The Popish Plot. By J. Pollock. 1 vol. 8vo. Lond. 1903. Bibl.

Deals with the designs of the Roman Catholics, the death of Sir Edmund Berry Godfrey, the politics of the plot and trials for treason. The appendices contain illustrative matter. An ingenious but not wholly convincing work, reviewed by A. Lang [in A. Valet's Tragedy] and by J. Gerard [The Popish Plot and its newest historian, 1903].

1815. Who killed Sir Edmund Berry Godfrey ? By A. Marks. 1 vol. 8vo. Lond. 1905.

Argues that Godfrey committed suicide. Reviewed by J. Pollock in the Law Quarterly Review, Oct. 1906, to whom the author replied in The Month, Jan. 1907.

(*h*) MISCELLANEOUS

(1) SOURCES

1816. A catalogue of the collection of tracts for and against Popery (published in or about the reign of James II) in the Manchester Library founded by Humphrey Chetham, in which is incorporated . . . Peck's list of the tracts in that controversy. Ed. by T. Jones. 2 vols. Chetham Soc. 1859–65.

Francis Peck's list is entitled A complete catalogue of all the discourses written, both for and against Popery, in the time of King James II. 4to. Lond. 1735. These two vols. have many bibliographical notes.

1817. A supplication to the kings most excellent maiestie. Anon. 1 vol. sm. 4to. s.l. 1604.

A Catholic plea for toleration.

1818. An ansuuere to the fifth part of reportes lately set forth by Syr Edward Cooke knight . . . Imprinted wuith licence, Anno Domini 1606. By a Catholicke Deuyne [R. Parsons]. 1 vol. sm. 4to. s.l. 1606.

A useful summary of the historical argument of the Roman Catholic controversialist at the beginning of the 17th century, with some special references to Garnet's case.

1819. Mr. George Blackwel, (made by Pope Clement 8. Archpriest of England) his answeres upon sundry his examinations : together with his approbation and taking of the oath of allegeance : and his letter written to his assistants . . . 1 vol. sm. 4to. Lond. 1607.

Cf. a large examination taken at Lambeth . . . of M. George Blackwell . . . upon occasion of a certain answere of his . . . to a letter . . . from Cardinall Bellarmine. sm. 4to. Lond. 1607.

1820. The Popes brief or Romes inquiry after the death of their Catholiques here in England during these times of warre . . . with a catalogue of the vicars generall and archdeacons. 1 vol. sm. 4to. Lond. 1643.

A parliamentary pamphlet.

1821. The popish royall favourite or a full discovery of his majesties extraordinary favours to . . . Papists, priests, Jesuits . . . manifested by sundry letters of grace, warrants. Ed. by W. Prynne. 1 vol. 4to. Lond. 1643.

Valuable : publ. by order of parliament.

1822. Certamen seraphicum provinciae Anglaie pro sancta Dei ecclesia in quo breviter declaratur, quomodo FF. Minores Angli calamo et sanguine pro fide Christi sanctaque ejus ecclesia certarunt. By R. Mason. 1 vol. sm. 4to. Douay. 1649. 5 ports. Later ed. 1 vol. 8vo. Quaracchi. 1885.

The larger part of the book relates to the first half of the 17th century. The 1885 edition was probably edited by the late Father D. Fleming. The five portraits were reproduced in ' The Franciscans in England ' by Thaddeus.

1823. Mutatus polemo. The horrible stratagems of the Jesuits . . . during the civil wars. By A. B. 1 vol. sm. 4to. Lond. 1650.

1824. The catholique apology. By Roger Palmer, Earl of Castlemaine. 3rd ed. 1 vol. 12mo. s.l. 1674.

A reasoned defence : contains a list of Catholics who died or suffered for the royalist cause during the civil wars.

1825. An abstract of the transactions relating to the English secular clergy. By J. Sergeant. 1 vol. 16mo. Lond. 1706. Later ed. 1 vol. 8vo. Lond. 1853. Ed. by W. Turnbull.

2nd ed. is styled An account of the chapter erected by William, titular Bishop of Chalcedon and Ordinary of England and Scotland. ' This most valuable little work.' Gillow.

1826. The memoirs of Gregorio Panzani—giving an account of his agencies in England in . . . 1634, 1635, 1636. By J. Berington. 1 vol. 8vo. Birmingham. 1793.

Introduction gives account of fortunes of Roman Catholics in England from 1558. Supplement carries it to 1793. Transcript in Brit. Mus. Add. MSS. 15389. Cf. Hist. MSS. Comm., 3rd Rep., pp. 234–6 ; and The Pope's nuntioes or the negotiation of Seignior Panzani, Seignior Con [1634–6], [sm. 4to. Lond. 1643].

1827. Memoirs of the mission in England of the capuchin friars of the province of Paris from the year 1630 to 1669. By C. de Gamaches.

Trans. The court and times of Charles I, vol. ii (120). The French text was ed. by Apollinaire de Valence as Mémoires de la mission &c. 1 vol. 8vo. Paris. 1881. See Bourgeois and André (625), ii. 57–8, for criticism.

1828. List of Roman Catholics in the county of York [in 1604]. Ed. by E. Peacock. 1 vol. 8vo. Lond. 1872.

From Bodl. Libr.

1829. The Tyldesley diary. Personal records of Thomas Tyldesley . . . during the years 1712–13–14. Ed. by J. Gillow and A. Hewitson. 1 vol. 4to. Preston. 1873. Illus.

The diary of a Lancashire Roman Catholic.

1830. Crosby records. A cavalier's note book being notes, anecdotes & observations of William Blundell . . . captain of dragoons under Maj.-Gen. Sir Thos. Tildesley in the Royalist army of 1642. By W. Blundell. Ed. T. E. Gibson. 1 vol. 4to. Lond. 1880.

This and the following two items supply a valuable picture of the fortunes of a Lancashire Catholic family through four generations. (1) Crosby records : a chapter of Lancashire recusancy, containing a relation of troubles and persecutions sustained by William Blundell of Crosby Hall [1560–1638] and an account of an ancient burial ground for recusants, called the Harkirke. Chetham Soc. 1887. Ed. by T. E. Gibson. (2) Crosby records : Blundell's diary, comprising selections from the diary of Nicholas Blundell from 1702 to 1728. Ed. by T. E. Gibson. 1 vol. 4to. Liverpool 1895.

1831. Diario del viaggio fatto in Inghilterra nel 1638 dal Nunzio Pontificio [Carlo] Rossetti. Scelta di curiosita letterarie. No. 212. 8vo. Bologna. 1885.

1832. The note-book of John Southcote from 1623 to 1637. Ed. by J. H. Pollen. Catholic Record Soc. Misc. i. 1905.

Brief but interesting. MS. in the possession of the Bishop of Southwark, amongst the Tierney MSS.

1833. The Huddleston obituaries. By J. Huddlestone. Ed. by J. Gillow. Catholic Record Soc. Misc. i. 1905.

Obituaries of Catholics dying chiefly *c.* 1639–63.

1834. Records relating to Catholicism in the South Wales Marches, 17th and 18th centuries. Ed. by J. H. Matthews. Catholic Record Soc. Misc. i. 1906.

Repr. of Domestic S.P., James I, xiv, nn. 52, 53 (1605), and Recusant Papers, 1688–1717, Monmouthshire and Herefordshire, P.R.O.

1835. Bedingfeld papers. Ed. by J. H. Pollen. Catholic Record Soc. Misc. vi. 1909. Illus.

Selected from MSS. at Oxburgh Hall to illustrate the life of a Catholic family during the penal times. The diary of Thomas Marwood (1699–1703) gives interesting details of English Catholics living abroad.

1836. The archpriest controversy. Ed. by R. Stanfield. Catholic Record Soc. Misc. xii. 1921.

Covers 1621–33.

(2) LATER WORKS.

1837. The state and behaviour of English Catholics from the Reformation to the year 1781, with a view of their present number, wealth, character, &c. By J. Berington. 2 vols. 8vo. Lond. 1780. Later ed. 2 vols. sm. 4to. Lond. 1781.

Outline of 17th century. Fuller for 18th century.

1838. The life of Philip Thomas Howard, cardinal of Norfolk, grand almoner to Catherine of Braganza. By C. F. R. Palmer. 1 vol. 8vo. Lond. 1867.

1839. The life of Mary Ward [1585–1645]. By M. C. E. Chambers. Ed. by H. J. Coleridge. 2 vols. 8vo. Lond. 1882–5. Illus.

Other lives by M. Salome [1 vol. 8vo. Lond. 1901] and F. A. Gasquet [1 vol. 8vo. Lond. 1909].

1840. The condition of English Catholics under Charles II. By the Comtesse R. de Courson. Translated and amplified from original sources. Ed. by Mrs. R. Raymond-Barker. 1 vol. 8vo. Lond. 1899.

1841. Catholic London missions from the Reformation to the year 1850. By J. H. Harting. 1 vol. 8vo. Lond. 1903. Ports.

Much curious and valuable information—especially about Catholic Chapels Royal and Embassy Chapels. But contains many inaccuracies.

1842. A history of the post-reformation Catholic missions in Oxfordshire. By Mrs. Bryan Stapleton. 1 vol. 8vo. Lond. 1906.

Arranged topographically.

1843. Biographies of English Catholics in the eighteenth century. Ed. by J. Kirk, J. H. Pollen, and E. H. Burton. 1 vol. 8vo. Lond. 1909. 6 ports.

As in title ; but with many late 17th-century worthies.

V. ECONOMIC HISTORY

1. Industry and Commerce.
   (*a*) Bibliographies and Sources. (*b*) Later Works.
2. Banking and Finance.
   (*a*) Sources. (*b*) Later Works.
3. Poor Law.
   (*a*) Sources. (*b*) Later Works.
4. General Agriculture.
   (*a*) Bibliographies and Sources. (*b*) Later Works.
5. Horses, Cattle, and Sheep.
   (*a*) Sources.
6. Enclosures.
   (*a*) Sources. (*b*) Later Works.
7. Draining.
   (*a*) Sources. (*b*) Later Works.

THE only survey of the whole field is Cunningham (1905), but there are admirable studies of special subjects, such as Scott, Daniels, Heaton, and Hamilton (1928, 1933, 1934, 1936), whose bibliographies are all important. The articles in Palgrave (1847) vary in value, but usually indicate the main authorities; the best guide to the sources is still McCulloch (1844), whose reprints of tracts are indispensable. Many other economic treatises are in collections of pamphlets, especially in the Harleian miscellany (87). The economic literature dealing with trade is concerned with the dominance and decline of mercantilism, maritime expansion and the foundation of new trading stations, plantations or colonies, and foreign rivalry, particularly Dutch. Many works are general and mainly descriptive, showing the nature of various foreign trades, and dealing with the commodities exported and imported, foreign currencies and the exchange. To this class belong the treatises and pamphlets of Malynes, Misselden, Lewis Roberts, Robinson, Fortrey, Yarranton, Justice, and Charles King. In the second half of the century the implications of mercantilism were being tested, and there is another group of writers whose works, while also general, are less descriptive, and aim at seeking general tendencies of foreign trade. Within this category may be placed Mun, Child, Roger Coke, Barbon, Sir Dudley North, and Charles Davenant. It has only been possible to indicate the chief authorities on special aspects of overseas trade where either a bibliography or references will show the sources of data on that special subject. In certain cases where such authority is not available, a selection from the contemporary sources is given. Industrial conditions in England attracted less notice, but can be studied in Unwin (1916, 1920) and Clark (1932). Banking is adequately treated by Thorold Rogers, Andreades, and others, but there is no satisfactory account of taxation for the whole period, though Dowell is useful. Gardiner (219, 220) supplies valuable notices, but no connected account of finance in the first half of the century exists. From 1660–89 Shaw's (1958) prefaces are indispensable;

Macaulay (204) is excellent for the reign of William III; and Leadam (1975) is a good outline for that of Anne.   As regards the poor, contemporaries are usually more interested in theoretical remedies than in actual conditions : to their theories Eden (1991) is a useful guide.   There are sound modern studies by Nicholls (1992) and Leonard (1994).

Agriculture is the subject of a separate preface, but a number of sources in the subsection, industry and commerce, are important, especially Houghton (1870).

¶ 1. INDUSTRY AND COMMERCE

(a) BIBLIOGRAPHIES AND SOURCES

1844. The literature of political economy. By J. R. McCulloch. 1 vol. 8vo. Lond. 1845.

A valuable bibliography, with extracts and descriptive notes.

1845. Two select bibliographies. 1. A classified list of works relating to the study of English palaeography and diplomatic. II. A classified list of works relating to English manorial and agrarian history . . . to . . . 1660. By M. F. Moore. 1 vol. 8vo. Lond. 1912.

1846. A select bibliography for the study, sources and literature of English mediaeval economic history. Ed. by H. Hall. 1 vol. 8vo. Lond. 1914.

Many items contain material for modern as well as mediaeval times.

1847. Dictionary of political economy. Ed. by Sir R. H. I. Palgrave. 3 vols. 8vo. Lond. 1891-9. Later eds. 1908-15, 1925-6.

The articles and biographies contain short bibliographies.

1848. A treatise of commerce, wherein are shewed the commodies arising by a wel ordered. . . . trade such as that of Merchantes Adventurers is proved to bee. By J. Wheeler. 1 vol. 4to. Middleburgh. 1601. Later ed. Lond. 1601.

A short history of the Merchants Adventurers and their methods and operations at home and abroad. Wheeler defends the Company against the Hanseatic Merchants and others.

1849. The replie, or second apologie. That is to say, an annswer to a confused treatise of publicke commerce, printed at Midlebourghe and London in favour of the private Society of Merchants Adventurers. By T. Milles. Ed. by I. Roberts. 1 vol. 4to. Lond. 1604.

1850. A declaration of the estate of clothing now used within this realme of England. By J. May. 1 vol. 4to. Lond. 1613.

Deals with the growth and present condition of the wool trade ; its abuses and how to remedy them.

1851. A discourse consisting of motives for enlargement and freedome of trade . . . engrossed by a company of private men who stile themselves Merchant Adventurers. 1645.

In Brit. Mus. [712g. 16 (2) and 1102. h. 1 (3).] For other attacks see Cat. of Thomason Tracts, i. 417, 500.

1852. Declaration from the poor oppressed people of England, directed to all that call themselves or are called lords of manors. 1 vol. 4to. [Lond.] 1649.
Brit. Mus. 1027, i. 16 (3). Against the cutting down of timber on commons.

1853. Englands grievance discovered in relation to the coal trade ; with a map of the river of Tine and situation of the town and corporation of Newcastle. By R. Gardiner. 1 vol. 4to. Lond. 1655. Plates. Later ed. 1 vol. 8vo. Newcastle. 1796. Plates.
Cf. M. A. Richardson's Reprints of old tracts, vol. iii : ibid., vol. vii, repr. The compleat collier or the whole art of sinking, getting and working coal-mines as is now used in the northern parts, by J. C. [Lond. 1708].

1854. The golden fleece. By W. S. 1 vol. 8vo. Lond. 1656.
Describes the several branches of the wool trade and officers connected therewith.

1855. Reasons offered by the Merchant Adventurers of England and Eastland Merchants residing at Hull for the preservation of their societies and regulations as being reasonable, just and necessary to the liberal and profitable vent of our native manufactures in the forreign parts. 1 vol. fol. Lond. 1661.

1856. The trade and fishing of Britain displayed. By J. Smith. 1 vol. 4to. Lond. 1661.

1857. An essay for recovery of trade, viz. i. for regulating the manufacture of wool. ii. against the corruptions practised upon Tin and Lead. iii. for the advancement of Fishing and Plantations. By W. Smith. 1 vol. fol. Lond. 1661.

1858. Englands Interest and improvement consisting in the increase of the store and trade of this kingdom. By S. Fortrey. 1 vol. 8vo. Camb. 1663. Later eds. Lond. 1713, and 1744 (4th ed.).
Also repr. by McCulloch (1883), and by J. H. Hollander, Baltimore, 1907.

1859. England's treasure by forraign trade. By T. Mun. 1 vol. 8vo. Lond. 1664.
Probably written 1635–40 : a classic. Repr. by McCulloch (1883) and ed. Sir W. J. Ashley. 8vo. N.Y. 1895.

1860. Discourse upon trade. By J. Child. 8vo. Lond. 1668. Later ed. 1690.
The 1690 ed. was published with additions under the title ' The new discourse of trade '.

1861. England's interest by trade asserted, wherein is discovered that many hundred thousand pounds might be gained to the king and kingdom by the improvement of the product thereof, more particularly by wool and the evil consequences of its exportation unmanufactured. By W. Carter. 1 vol. 4to. Lond. 1669.
Cf. England's interest asserted in the improvement of its native commodities and more especially the manufacture of wool [1669].

1862. Discourse of trade. By R. Coke. 2 pts. in 1 vol. 4to. Lond. 1670.
One of many economic tracts by Coke.

1863. Fodinae regales : or the history, laws and places of the chief mines and mineral works in England, Wales. By Sir J. Pettus. 1 vol. fol. Lond. 1670. Plates.

1864. Reasons of the increase of the Dutch trade wherein is demonstrated from what causes the Dutch govern and manage trade better than the English; whereby they have so far improved their trade above the English. By R. Coke. 1 vol. 4to. Lond. 1671.

1865. A treatise wherein is demonstrated that the church and state of England are in equal danger with the trade of it. By R. Coke. 1 vol. 4to. Lond. 1671.

A close inquiry into current trade conditions.

1866. A proposal for the advancement of trade upon such principles as must necessarily enforce it. By R. Murray. 1 vol. fol. Lond. 1676.

He also wrote other economic tracts, of which a list will be found in the Dict. Nat. Biog.

1867. England's improvement by sea and land. By A. Yarranton. 2 vols. 4to. Lond. 1677–81. Maps. Plates.

1868. Britannia languens ; or, a discourse of trade, shewing that the present management of trade in England is the true reason of the decay of our manufactures and the late great fall of land-rents . . . Wherein is demonstrated that the East-India Company, as now managed, has nearly destroyed our trade with these parts, as well as with Turkey. 1 vol. 8vo. Lond. 1680 and 1689.

Repr. by McCulloch (1890).

1869. Certain considerations relating to the Royal African Company of England. s.l. 1680.

Brit. Mus. 712. f. 19. (1). There is also a volume of tracts relating to the African trade, Brit. Mus. 8223. 1. 4.

1870. A collection of letters for the improvement of husbandry and trade. By J. Houghton. 2 vols. 4to. Lond. 1681–3.

Houghton also started a weekly paper, A collection for improvement of husbandry and trade, 1691–1703, of which the leading articles were repr. by R. Bradley [4 vols. 8vo. Lond. 1727–8], and the stock and share list is repr. in Scott, Joint stock companies, vol. i. There is an account of the paper in Rogers (1967).

1871. The compleat miner ; or a collection of the laws, liberties, ancient customs . . . of the several mines and miners in the counties of Derby, Gloucester and Somerset. Ed. by T. Houghton. 3 pts. 12mo. Lond. 1688.

Pt. i is a duplicate of Rara avis in terris, or the compleat miner [1 vol. 12mo. Lond. 1681]. Cf. The compleat miner . . . with the liberties, laws and customs of lead mines within the wapentake of Wirksworth in Derbyshire, repr. in A collection of scarce and valuable treatises upon metals, mines and minerals, 1740.

1872. Reasons humbly offered by the governor assistants and fellowship of Eastland Merchants against giving a general liberty to all persons whatsoever to export the English woollen manufacture whither they please. By N. Tench. 1 vol. Lond. 1689.

Brit. Mus. 712. 8. 16. (25).

3285

1873. Discourse of trade. By N. B[arbon]. 1 vol. 8vo. Lond. 1690. Later ed. Baltimore. 1905. Ed. by J. H. Hollander.

1874. Discourses upon trade, principally directed to the cases of the interest, coynage, clipping, increase of money. By Sir D. North. 1 vol. 8vo. Lond. 1691. Later ed. Baltimore. 1907. Ed. by J. H. Hollander.

1875. Essays on trade and navigation, in five parts. The first part. By Sir F. Brewster. 1 vol. 8vo. Lond. 1695.

1876. An essay upon the probable methods of making a people gainers in the ballance of trade. By C. Davenant. 1 vol. 8vo. Lond. 1699.

1877. A discovery of indirect practices in the coal trade. . . . To which are added some proposals for the improvement of trade and navigation in general and of the colliery-trade to Newcastle in particular. By C. Povey. 1 vol. 4to. Lond. 1700.

1878. Unhappiness of England as to its trade by sea and land truly stated. By C. Povey. 1 vol. 8vo. Lond. 1701.

1879. Proposals and reasons for constituting a council of trade. 1 vol. 8vo. Edinburgh. 1701.

1880. A general discourse of commerce. By A. Justice. 1 vol. 4to. Lond. 1707.
Deals mainly with the foreign exchanges.

1881. Reflections upon the constitution and management of the trade to Africa through the whole course and progress thereof, from the beginning of the last century to this time. 1 vol. fol. Lond. 1709.

1882. A survey of trade in four parts. I. The great advantages of trade . . . II. The marks of a beneficial trade . . . III. The great advantages of our colonies and plantations to Great Britain . . . IV. Some considerations on the disadvantages our trade at present labours under. By W. Wood. 1 vol. 8vo. Lond. 1718.

1883. The British merchant or commerce preserv'd. By C. King. 3 vols. 8vo. Lond. 1721.
The Earl of Sunderland, when he was First Lord of the Treasury, ordered a copy of this work to be sent to every parliamentary borough for the use of the inhabitants.

1884. The laws and customs of the stannaries in Cornwall and Devon. Ed. by T. Pearce. 1 vol. fol. Lond. 1725.

1885. A Plan of the English commerce, being a complete prospect of the trade of this nation, as well the home trade as the foreign. By D. Defoe. 1 vol. 8vo. Lond. 1728. Later ed. 1730.

1886. Chronicon rusticum-commerciale, or memoirs of wool. By J. Smith. 2 vols. 8vo. Lond. 1747, and 4to. 1757.
In this collection a number of papers relating to the woollen trade in the 17th century are printed.

1887. Observations touching trade and commerce with the Hollander, and other nations. By Sir W. Raleigh.

In Raleigh's Miscellaneous works 1751, repr. in Select collection of scarce and valuable tracts on commerce, ed. J. R. McCulloch, London, 1859. A comparison of English trade with that of Holland and suggestions for advancing the former.

1888. The political and commercial works of . . . Charles D'Avenant relating to the trade and revenue of England . . . Collected and revised . . . [with] a copious index. Ed. by Sir C. Whitworth. 5 vols. 8vo. Lond. 1771.

Vol. i. contains : An essay upon ways and means ; An essay on the East India trade ; Discourses on the public revenues and on the trade of England in two parts [first on credit, public revenue and debts, second on foreign trade]. Vol. ii : Discourses continued. Part ii [on the plantation and East India trade] ; An essay upon the probable methods of making a people gainers in the balance of trade. Vol. iii : A discourse upon grants and resumptions [of royal lands and especially of Irish forfeitures] ; An essay upon the balance of power ; An essay upon the right of making war, peace and alliances. Vol. iv : An essay upon universal monarchy ; The true picture of a modern Whig ; Essays upon peace at home and war abroad. Vol. v : Essays upon peace contd. ; Reflections upon the constitution and management of the trade to Africa.

1889. A select collection of scarce and valuable economical tracts. Ed. by J. R. McCulloch. 1 vol. 8vo. Lond. 1859.

Repr. An apology for the builder : or a discourse shewing the cause and effects of the increase of building [1685] ; Defoe's Giving alms no charity and employing the poor a grievance to the nation [1704].

1890. A select collection of scarce and valuable tracts on commerce. By J. R. McCulloch. 1 vol. 8vo. Lond. 1859.

Items separately noticed.

1891. The laws of the Mercers Company of Lichfield [1624]. Trans. Royal Hist. Soc., N.S. vii. 1893. Ed. by W. H. Russell.

' Typical of the ordinances . . . made for industrial regulation.' Intro. by W. Cunningham.

1892. Extracts from the records of the Merchant Adventurers of Newcastle-upon-Tyne. Ed. by J. W. Boyle and F. W. Denby. 2 vols. Surtees Soc. Durham. 1895–9.

Cf. The York Mercers and Merchant Adventurers, 1356-1917. Ed. by M. Sellers. Surtees Soc. 1918.

1893. The economic writings of Sir William Petty, together with the Observations upon the bills of mortality more probably by Captain John Graunt. Ed. by C. H. Hull. 2 vols. 8vo. Camb. 1899. Bibl.

Among the reprints are : A treatise of taxes and contributions [1662] ; The political anatomy of Ireland . . . to which is added verbum sapienti or an account of the wealth and expences of England [1691] ; Political arithmetick or a discourse concerning the extent and value of lands, people, buildings, husbandry &c. . . . of Great Britain [1690] ; Natural and political observations . . . upon the bills of mortality [1662] ; Quantulumcunque concerning money [1682] ; A treatise of Ireland, 1687.

1894. The acts and ordinances of the Eastland Company. Ed. by M. Sellars. 1 vol. 4to. Royal Hist. Soc. 1906.

1895. Select charters of trading companies, A. D. 1530–1707. Ed. by C. T. Carr. 1 vol. 8vo. Selden Soc. Lond. 1913.

The editor's Introduction (pp. xi-cxxxvi) contains, *inter alia*, a valuable account of the incorporation of trading companies.

(b) LATER WORKS

1896. An historical and chronological deduction of the origin of commerce. By A. Anderson. 2 vols. fol. Lond. 1764. Later ed. 4 vols. 4to. Lond. 1787–9, ed. by W. Combe.

Much important material in the form of annals. Cf. D. Macpherson's Annals of commerce, manufactures, fisheries and navigation [4 vols. 4to. Lond. 1805], which is a continuation of Anderson to 1800.

1897. An estimate of the comparative strength of Great Britain during the present and four preceding reigns and of the losses of her trade from every war since the revolution. By G. Chalmers. 1 vol. 4to. Lond. 1782. Later ed. 1 vol. 8vo. Lond. 1794 and 1804.

Eds. of 1802 and later include G. King's Natural and political observations upon the state and condition of England, 1696.

1898. A compendious history of the cotton manufacture. By R. Guest. 1 vol. 4to. Manchester. 1823.

1899. History of the cotton manufacture in Great Britain with a notice of its early history in the east. By Sir E. Baines. 1 vol. 8vo. Lond. 1835.

1900. A comprehensive history of the woollen and worsted manufactures and the natural and commercial history of sheep. By J. Bischoff. 2 vols. 8vo. Lond. 1842.

1901. The history of the worsted manufacture in England. By J. James. 1 vol. 8vo. Lond. 1857.

1902. Industrial biography. Iron workers and tool makers. By S. Smiles. 1 vol. 8vo. Lond. 1863 and 1879.

1903. The linen trade, ancient and modern. By A. J. Warden. 1 vol. 8vo. Lond. 1864 and 1867.

1904. The history of Lloyds and of marine insurance in Great Britain. By F. Martin. 1 vol. 8vo. Lond. 1876. Bibl.

1905. The growth of English industry and commerce in modern times. By W. Cunningham. 1 vol. 8vo. Camb. 1882. Bibl. Later ed. 2 vols. 1919. Bibl.

There is a full bibliography of Cunningham's works in his Growth of capitalism.

1906. A history of coal mining in Great Britain. By R. L. Galloway. 1 vol. 8vo. Lond. 1882. Later ed. 1898.

Cf. E. R. Turner, English coal industry in the seventeenth and eighteenth centuries. Amer. Hist. Rev. xxvii. 1921–2.

1907. Memoirs of Thomas Papillon of London, merchant (1623–1702). 1 vol. 8vo. Reading. 1887. Ports. By A. F. W. Papillon.

Important for trade and politics in London temp. Charles II.

1908. The history of wool and wool combing—with illustrations and portraits. By J. Burnley. 1 vol. 8vo. Lond. 1889.

1909. English trade and finance chiefly in the seventeenth century. By W. A. S. Hewins. 1 vol. 8vo. Lond. 1892. Bibl.

1910. An account of the fire insurance companies . . . in Great Britain and Ireland during the 17th and 18th centuries including the Sun Fire Office : also of Charles Povey. By F. B. Relton. 1 vol. 8vo. Lond. 1893.

Based on considerable research : includes a bibliography of Povey's writings.

1911. The life of Sir William Petty 1623–1687. One of the first fellows of the Royal Society, sometime secretary to Henry Cromwell, maker of the ' Down Survey ' of Ireland, author of ' Political arithmetic ', &c. By Lord E. G. Fitzmaurice. 1 vol. 8vo. Lond. 1895. Map. Ports.

List of works in appendix. Cf. W. L. Bevan, Sir William Petty : a study in English economic literature. American Econ. Assoc. Baltimore, 1894. Bibl.; and M. Pasquier, Sir William Petty. Ses idées économiques. 1 vol. 8vo. Paris. 1903.

1912. The early chartered companies. By G. Cawston and A. H. Keane. By 1 vol. 8vo. Lond. 1896. Plate of arms.

Contains documents.

1913. The mercantile system and its historical significance . . . being a chapter from the Studien über die wirthschaftliche Politik Friedrichs des Grossen, 1884. By G. Schmoller. 1 vol. 8vo. N.Y. and Lond. 1896.

1914. History of corn-milling. By R. Bennett and J. Elton. 4 vols. 8vo. Lond. 1898–1904.

1915. Die staatliche Regelung der englischen Wollindustrie [15th to 18th centuries]. By F. Lohmann. Staats- und socialwissenschaftliche Forschungen. Bd. xviii. Leipsic. 1900.

1916. A seventeenth century trade union. By G. Unwin. Economic Jour. x. 1900.

1917. The Great Company [Hudson's Bay], 1667–1871. By B. Willson. 2 vols. 8vo. Lond. 1900. Map. Ports. Illus.

Other histories are by G. Bryce [1 vol. 8vo. Lond. 1900. Bibl.] and Sir W. Schooling [4to. 1920. Illus.]

1918. The internal organisation of the merchant adventurers of England. By W. E. Lingelbach. Trans. Royal Hist. Soc. 1902.

The same author ed. J. Wheeler's The lawes, customes and ordinances of the . . . Merchantes Adventurers 1608, Univ. of Pennsylvania Translations and reprints from the original sources of European history, 2nd ser. vol. ii. 1902.

1919. The history of the society of Merchant Venturers of the city of Bristol. By J. Latimer. 1 vol. 8vo. Bristol. 1903.

1920. Industrial organization in the 16th and 17th centuries. By G. Unwin. 1 vol. 8vo. Oxf. 1904.

1921. De Merchant Adventurers in de Nederland. By C. Te Lintum. 1 vol. 8vo. The Hague. 1905.

1922. The manor and manorial records. By N. J. Hone. 1 vol. 8vo. Lond. 1906. Illus.

1923. The history of the wine trade in England. By A. L. Simon. 3 vols. 8vo. Lond. 1906–09. Illus.

Vol. iii deals with the 17th century. Valuable.

1924. The commercial relations of England and Portugal. By V. M Shillington and A. B. W. Chapman. 1 vol. 8vo. Lond. 1907.

1925. England and the Hanse under Charles II. By C. Brinkmann. Eng Hist. Rev. xxiii. 1908.

1926. The early history of the Levant Company [to 1640]. By M. Epstein 1 vol. 8vo. Lond. *c.* 1908.

Appendices include, the charter of 1605, lists of governors, ambassadors, consuls ships, ports, impositions &c. For later relations with Turkey, both economic and political, see G. F. Abbott, Under the Turk in Constantinople. A record of Sir John Finch's embassy 1674–81 [1 vol. 8vo. Lond. 1920] ; and A. C. Wood, The English embassy at Constantinople 1660–1762. Eng. Hist. Rev. xl. 1925.

1927. The stannaries : a study of the English tin mines. By G. R. Lewis. 1 vol. 8vo. Boston, N.Y., and Oxf. 1908. Bibl.

1928. The constitution and finance of English, Scottish and Irish joint-stock companies to 1720. By W. R. Scott. 3 vols. 8vo. Camb. 1912. 1 Map. Bibl.

Vol. i deals with the general development of the joint-stock system, vols. ii and iii with individual companies, vol. ii containing those relating to overseas trade. Extremely valuable.

1929. Middlemen in English business, particularly between 1660 and 1760. By R. B. Westerfield. Trans. Connecticut Academy of Arts and Sciences, 1915.

1930. The Canary Company [1665–67]. By C. A. J. Skeel. Eng. Hist. Rev. xxxi. 1916.

1931. The Company of Royal Adventurers trading into Africa [1662–72]. By G. F. Zook. 1919.

Reprint from the Journal of Negro History.

1932. Working life of women in the seventeenth century. By A. Clark. 1 vol. 8vo. Lond. 1919. Bibl.

App. has list of wage-assessments.

1933. The early English cotton industry. By G. W. Daniels. Intro. by G. Unwin. 1 vol. 8vo. Manchester. 1920.

1934. The Yorkshire woollen and worsted industries from the earliest times up to the industrial revolution. By H. Heaton. 1 vol. 8vo. Oxf. 1920.

1935. Some remarks on British forest history. II. The sixteenth and seventeenth centuries. By H. G. Richardson. Trans. Royal Scottish Arboricultural Soc. xxxvi.

Has valuable references in footnotes. Cf. Forests and sea-power : the timber problem of the royal navy, 1652–1862. By R. G. Albion. 1 vol. 8vo. Camb. (Mass.) 1926.

1936. The English copper and brass industries to 1800. By H. Hamilton. Intro. by Sir W. Ashley. 1 vol. 8vo. Lond. 1926.

¶ 2. BANKING AND FINANCE

(a) SOURCES

1937. A contribution to the bibliography of the Bank of England.   By T. A. Stephens.   1 vol. 8vo. Lond. 1897.

1937 A. Lists of the records of the treasury, the paymaster-general's office, the exchequer and audit department and the board of trade to 1837 preserved in the Public Record Office.   Lists and indexes. xlvi. 1921.

1938. A treatise of usurie.   By R. Fenton.   1 vol. 4to. Lond. 1612.

1939. Tract against usurie.   By Sir T. Culpepper.   1 vol. 4to. Lond. 1621
Written against the importation of money for the purposes of usury.

1940. Quaestio quodlibetica or a discourse whether it be lawfull to take use for money.   By Sir R. Filmer.   1 vol. 12mo. Lond. 1653.
An examination of Fenton's Treatise on usury, q.v.

1941. An appeal to Caesar, wherein gold and silver is proved to be the kings majesties royal commodity, &c.   By T. Violet.   2 vols. 4to. Lond. 1660.
Complaints of the action of some merchants to obtain an act of Parliament to make gold and silver a merchandize and transport it freely at their pleasure.   His 'Humble declaration . . . touching the transportation of gold and silver 1643' was reprinted at Hull about 1812.   See Shaw's English monetary history, 1896, p. 83.

1942. Discourse of coin and coinage.   By R. Vaughan.   1 vol. 12mo. Lond. 1675.

1943. Consideration of the consequences of the lowering of interest and raising the value of money.   By J. Locke.   1 vol. 8vo. Lond. 1692.
Repr. in J. R. McCulloch's Principles of political economy, 1870.

1944. A brief account of the intended Bank of England.   1 vol. 4to. Lond. 1694.
'The Bank will lay a foundation for trade, security and greatness within this Kingdom for the present and succeeding ages.'

1945. A report containing an essay for the amendment of the silver coins.   By W. Lowndes.   1 vol. 8vo. Lond. 1695.
An inquiry as to whether it is needful to re-establish the currency for the benefit of commerce.   Repr. in J. R. McCulloch's Select tracts on Money.   Lowndes also wrote : A further essay . . . [1 vol. 4to. Lond. 1695].

1946. Further considerations concerning raising the value of money; wherein Mr. Lowndes's arguments for it in his late report concerning 'An essay for the amendment of the silver coins' are particularly examined.   By J. Locke. 1 vol. 8vo. Lond. 1695.
An inquiry into the silver currency.   Cf. No. 2765 for Locke's works.

1947. Review of the universal remedy for all diseases incident to coin 1696 with application to our present circumstances.   1 vol. Lond. 1696.

1948. A proposal for the more easie advancing to the crown any fixed sum of money to carry on the war against France ; and payment of the debts contracted thereby. By R. Murray. 1 vol. 4to. Lond. 1696.

1949. An essay upon projects. By D. Defoe. 1 vol. 8vo. Lond. 1697.

This essay did not appear till 1698. It contains suggestions for a national bank, a system of assurance, for friendly societies, ' pension offices ' or savings banks, idiot asylums, and so on.

1950. Chronicon preciosum : or, an account of English money. By W. Fleetwood. 1 vol. 8vo. Lond. 1707.

Repr. in A compleat collection of the sermons tracts and pieces of all kinds that were written by . . . Dr. William Fleetwood late lord bishop of Ely. [1 vol. fol. Lond. 1737.]

1951. An essay upon publick credit. By Robert Harley, Earl of Oxford. 8vo. s.l. 1710.

The only relevant item in A select collection of scarce and valuable tracts . . . on the national debt. Ed. by J. R. McCulloch [1 vol. 8vo. Lond. 1857].

1952. A select collection of scarce and valuable tracts on money. By J. R. McCulloch. 1 vol. 8vo. Lond. 1856.

Repr. A discourse of coin and coinage, by Rice Vaughan [1675] ; A speech made by Sir Robert Cotton . . . touching the alteration of coin . . . 1626 [1651] ; Advice of his majesty's council of trade concerning the exportation of gold and silver in foreign coins and bullion. Concluded 11th December 1660 ; Sir William Petty his Quantulumcunque concerning money [1695] ; A report containing an essay for the amendment of the silver coins. By W. Lowndes [1695].

1953. Calendar of treasury papers. Ed. by J. Redington. 6 vols. 8vo. Lond. 1868–89.

Miscellaneous papers addressed to the Treasury.

1954. Return. Public income and expenditure. Part I. fol. s.l. 1869.

Compiled by order of the House of Commons. Begins 1688/9.

1955. Calendar of the proceedings of the Committee for Advance of Money, 1642–1656. Ed. by M. A. E. Green. 3 vols. 8vo. Lond. 1888.

1956. Calendar of the proceedings of the Committee for Compounding, 1643–60. Ed. by M. A. E. Green. 5 vols. Lond. 1889–92.

1957. Select tracts and documents illustrative of English monetary history, 1626–1730. Ed. by W. A. Shaw. 1 vol. 8vo. Lond. 1896.

Repr. A speech made by Sir Rob. Cotton . . . touching the alteration of coyn [1651] ; H. Robinson's England's safety [1641], and Certain proposals [1652] ; A selection of Commonwealth state papers, 1649–51 ; Sir R. Temple's Some short remarks upon Mr. Locke's book in answer to Mr. Lounds [1696] ; Sir I. Newton's mint reports, 1701–25.

1958. Calendar of Treasury books, 1660–1689. Ed. by W. A. Shaw. 8 vols. 8vo. Lond. 1904–23.

The introductions furnish a valuable survey of financial history.

(b) LATER WORKS

1959. The royal treasury of England, or an historical account of all taxes. By J. Stevens. 1 vol. 8vo. Lond. 1725. Later ed. 1733.

1960. The history of the public revenue of the British Empire . . . from the remotest periods. By Sir J. Sinclair. 3 pts. 4to. Lond. 1785–90. Later ed. 3 vols. 8vo. Lond. 1803–4.

1961. An inquiry concerning the rise and progress, the redemption and present state and the management of the national debt of Great Britain and Ireland. By R. Hamilton. 1 vol. 8vo. Edin. 1813 and 1818.

1962. Annals of the coinage of Britain and its dependencies. By R. Ruding. 3 vols. 4to. Lond. 1817–19. Plates. Later ed. 6 vols. 8vo. Lond. 1819 (including 4to vol. of plates). 3 vols. 4to. Lond. 1840. Plates.
 Still useful.

1963. Temple Bar, or some account of ' ye Marygold ', No. 1 Fleet Street. By F. G. Hilton Price. 1 vol. 8vo. Lond. 1875.
 A sketch of the banking-house of Messrs. Child & Co.

1964. A handbook of London bankers with some account of their predecessors, the early goldsmiths. By F. G. Hilton Price. 1 vol. 8vo. Lond. 1876. Later ed. 4to. 1890–1.

1965. A history of taxation and taxes in England from the earliest times to the present day. By S. Dowell. 4 vols. 8vo. Lond. 1884 and 1885.

1966. A history of the custom-revenue in England from the earliest times to . . . 1827. By H. Hall. 2 vols. 8vo. Lond. 1885.

1967. The first nine years of the Bank of England. By J. E. T. Rogers. 1 vol. 8vo. Oxf. 1887.

1968. ' The Grasshopper ' in Lombard Street. By J. B. Martin. 1 vol. 4to. Lond. 1892. Illus.
 Contains useful information about early banking and bankers, especially of the families of Martin, Duncombe, and Backwell. App. repr. in facsimile, The mystery of the new fashioned goldsmiths or bankers, 1676.

1969. The history of currency, 1252–1894. By W. A. Shaw. 1 vol. 8vo. Lond. 1895.
 Cf. T. H. B. Graham, The re-coinage of 1696–1697. Repr. from the Numismatic Chronicle, 4th series. vol. vi.

1970. The beginnings of the national debt. By W. A. Shaw.
 In Historical essays by members of the Owens College, Manchester, ed. by T. F. Tout and J. Tait [1 vol. 8vo. Lond. 1902 and Manchester 1907].

1971. The Houblon family, its story and times. By Lady A. Archer Houblon. 2 vols. 8vo. Lond. 1907.
 Vol. i sketches the history of a family of merchants and bankers in the 17th century.

1972. English finance under the Long Parliament. By W. O. Scroggs. Quarterly Jour. of Economics, vol. xxi. 1907.

1973. History of the Bank of England. By A. Andréadès. Pref. by H. S. Foxwell. 1 vol. 8vo. Lond. 1909.
 A trans. of Histoire de la Banque d'Angleterre, 2 vols. 1904.

1974. The collection of ship money in the reign of Charles I. By M. D. Gordon. In Trans. Royal Hist. Soc. 3rd Ser. iv. 1910.

Based on A. O. Declared Accounts, assessments in Council Register, and Letters of instructions to sheriffs. Deals with amounts raised, methods of collection, &c.

1975. The finance of Lord Treasurer Godolphin. By I. S. Leadam. Trans. Royal Hist. Soc. 3rd Ser. iv. 1910.

1976. The rise of the London money market, 1640–1826. By W. R. Bisschop. Preface by H. S. Foxwell. 1 vol. 8vo. Lond. 1910.

1977. English taxation, 1640–1799; an essay on policy and opinion. By W. Kennedy. 1 vol. 8vo. Lond. 1913.

¶ 3. POOR LAW

(a) SOURCES

1978. Greevous grones for the poore done by a well-willer who wisheth that the poore of England might be so provided for as none should neede to go a begging. By M. S. 1 vol. 4to. Lond. 1621.

The work is quoted by Eden (1991), vol. i, p. 154 ct seq.

1979. Stanleye's remedy, or the way how to reform wandring beggers, theeves, high-way robbers and pick-pockets. 1 vol. 4to. Lond. 1646.

This work purports to be from the pen of a repentant Elizabethan highwayman.

1980. Unum necessarium or the poore man's case : being an expedient to make provision for all poore people in the kingdome. By J. Cooke. 1 vol. sm. 4to. Lond. 1648.

1981. The poore man's advocate. By P. Chamberlen. 1 vol. 4to. Lond. 1649.

An appeal for the alleviation of poverty, and proposals for the employment of the poor, with an inquiry into public expenditure.

1982. Clear and evident way for enriching the nations of England and Ireland and for setting very great numbers of poore on work. By I. D. 1 vol. 4to. Lond. 1650.

Urging that the poor may be employed in the fishing industries.

1983. Proposals for building in every county, a working-almshouse or hospital, as the best expedient to perfect the trade and manufactory of linen cloth. By R. Haines. 1 vol. 4to. Lond. 1677.

Repr. in the Harleian Miscellany, vol. iv, p. 489.

1984. Some proposals for the imployment of the poor and for the prevention of idleness. By T. Firmin. 1 vol. sm. 4to. Lond. 1678. Later ed. 1681.

1985. A discourse touching provision for the poor. By Sir M. Hale. 1 vol. 12mo. Lond. 1683.

1986. Bread for the poor or, a method shewing how the poor may be maintained. By R. D[unning]. 1 vol. sm. 4to. Exeter. 1698.

1987. An account of the proceedings of the corporation of Bristol, in execution of the act of Parliament for the better employing and maintaining the poor of that city. By J. Cary. 1 vol. 8vo. Lond. 1700.

For other works on this corporation of Bristol see Webb, English local government : statutory authorities (2793), p. 114, n. 1.

1988. Giving alms no charity, and employing the poor a grievance to the nation. By D. Defoe. 1 vol. 4to. Lond. 1704.

1989. A discourse of the poor, shewing the pernicious tendency of the laws now in force for their maintenance and settlement. By R. North. 1 vol. 8vo. Lond. 1753.

(b) LATER WORKS

1990. The history of the poor-laws. By R. Burn. 1 vol. 8vo. Lond. 1764.

1991. The state of the poor, or a history of the labouring classes in England, from the conquest to the present period, with respect to diet, fuel, and habitations. By Sir F. M. Eden. 3 vols. 4to. Lond. 1797.

Valuable for the documents, and extracts from pamphlets, &c. quoted.

1992. A history of the English poor law. By Sir G. Nicholls. 2 vols. 8vo. Lond. 1854. Later ed. 3 vols. 1898–9, ed. by H. G. Willink and T. Mackay.

1993. A history of vagrants and vagrancy and beggars and begging. By C. J. Ribton-Turner. 1 vol. 8vo. Lond. 1887.

Deals with : England, 1603–1713, chs. vi and vii ; Scotland, 968–1885, ch. xv ; Ireland, 450–1885, chs. xvi and xvii. Extracts from various writers illustrating the habits and impostures of beggars, 1610–1875, are in chs. xxx–xxxi.

1994. The early history of English poor relief. By E. M. Leonard. 1 vol. 8vo. Camb. 1900.

Cf. The relief of the poor by the state regulation of wages. Eng. Hist. Rev. xiii. 1898.

1995. A history of English philanthropy from the dissolution of the monasteries to the taking of the first census. By B. K. Gray. 1 vol. 8vo. Lond. 1905.

¶ 4. GENERAL AGRICULTURE

Although the seventeenth century produced a large number of works on agriculture and allied matters, these are, as a whole, unoriginal and often shameless plagiarisms. To what extent they reflect agricultural practice is a difficult question : presumably, since a good many of the works seem to have commanded a ready sale, there was something to be learned from them. But it is probably true to say that where they are most original they are most untrustworthy.

Agricultural changes in a broad sense are reflected in the books and pamphlets on enclosures and drainage, and something may be learned from contemporary local histories and from general descriptions of the kingdom. In the former class mention may be made of Richard Carew's Survey of Cornwall (2800), Plot's Natural Histories of Oxfordshire and Staffordshire (2844, 2851),

Aubrey's Natural Remarques in the County of Wilts (2859) and Charles Leigh's Natural History of Lancashire (2824) : such works vary greatly in value but there are gleanings in them all. In the second class such works as Richard Blome's *Britannia* [1 vol. fol. Lond. 1673] are occasionally of service.

What literature gives us very inadequately is a knowledge of actual farming practice. The way to this knowledge is to be found in account books and similar documents : but little enough of this nature has been published. Although the manorial system was lapsing into decay, the aspect of agriculture and rural life which the records of manor courts present is important and requires to be taken into account. Occasionally churchwarden's accounts shed some light on the subject : not only were there parish lands to be managed, but the parish was increasingly taking over functions anciently performed by the manor. The records of commissioners of sewers cover very much wider areas than the marshlands reclaimed in the 17th century; they are concerned with the maintenance of drainage and defensive works which had existed continuously from early in the Middle Ages. Some information regarding these records will be found in the Report of the Royal Commission on Public Records (1910–19), volumes ii and iii (2788), and in S. and B. Webb, English Local Government : Statutory Authorities, ch. i (2793 n.).

(a) BIBLIOGRAPHIES AND SOURCES

1996. Tracts on practical agriculture and gardening with a chronological catalogue of English authors on agriculture. By R. Weston. 1 vol. 8vo. Lond. 1769 and 1773.

Contains many errors, but still useful.

1997. Agricultural biography : containing a notice of the life and writings of the British authors on agriculture, from the earliest date in 1480 to the present time. By J. Donaldson. 1 vol. 4to. Lond. 1854.

1998. Agricultural writers from . . . 1200–1800. Reproductions in facsimile and extracts from their actual writings . . . to which is added an exhaustive bibliography. By D. Mcdonald. 1 vol. 8vo. Lond. 1908.

Valuable. For other bibliographies see Ernle (2039) ; H. G. Aldis in Camb. Hist. of Eng. Lit. iv. ch. xvii. 1909 ; E. S. Rohde, The old English gardening books, 1 vol. 8vo. Lond. 1924 ; G. E. Fussell, English printed books on agriculture, Bookman's Journal, beginning June 1925 ; Rothamsted experimental station library : catalogue of the printed books on agriculture [1471–1840] with notes by M. S. Aslin. 1 vol. 8vo. s.l. s.a. [*c.* 1926]. Photographs of title-pages.

1999. Profitable instructions for the manuring, sowing, and planting of kitchen gardens. By R. Gardiner. 2nd ed. 1 vol. 4to. Lond. 1603. 1st ed. 1599.

2000. The surveiors dialogue, very profitable for all men to peruse, but especially for gentlemen, farmers, and husbandmen, by J. Norden. 1 vol. 4to. Lond. 1607. Later eds. 1610 and 1618.

The first four books deal with surveys of manors and the relations between lords of manors and their tenants. The fifth book treats of ' the different natures of ground '.

In the third ed. a sixth book is added on the points necessary to be considered by a purchaser of land.

Other works on Surveying are : W. Folkingham, Feudigraphia the synopsis or epitome of surveying methodised, 1610 ; A. Rathbone, The surveyor, in foure books, 1616 ; O. Wallinby, Planometria, or the whole art of surveying of land, 1650 ; G. Attwell, The faithfull surveyor, 1662.

2001. The feminine monarchie : or, a treatise concerning bees, and the due ordering of them by C. Butler. 1 vol. 8vo. Oxf. 1609. Later ed. 1 vol. sm. 4to. Oxf. 1634.

One of the most popular treatises on bee-keeping, then a very important industry. The edition of 1634 adopts phonetic spelling. It was translated into Latin under the title of Monarchia foeminina, sive apum historia, interprete R. Ricardi [Lond. 8vo. 1673].

Other works on Bees are : John Levett, The ordering of bees, 1634 ; R. Remnant, A discourse or historie of Bees &c., 1637. J. Gedde, A new discovery of an excellent method of bee houses and colonies, &c., 1675 (later eds. 1676, 1722), reissued in an expanded form as The English apiary, 2 pts. 1721–2 ; M. Rusden. A further discovery of bees, 1679, 2nd ed. 1685. See also works by J. Worlidge and S. Hartlib.

2002. Most approved and long experienced water works. Containing the manner of winter and summer drowning of medow and pasture. By R. Vaughan. 1 vol. 4to. Lond. 1610. Later ed. 1 vol. 8vo. Lond. 1897. Ed. by E. B. Wood.

A record of experience in the irrigation of grasslands.

2003. The commons' complaint. Wherein is contained two speciall grievances. The first is the generall destruction and waste of woods. . . . The second grievance is the extreame dearth of victuals &c. By A. Standish. 1 vol. 4to. Lond. 1611.

2004. The English husbandman. By G. Markham. 2 Parts 4to. Lond. 1613 : 1615.

A miscellaneous compilation.

2005. An advice how to plant tobacco in England. By C. T. 1 vol. 4to. Lond. 1615.

2006. Paradisi in sole, paradisus terrestris or a garden of . . . flowers . . . with a kitchen garden . . . and an orchard. By J. Parkinson. 1 vol. fol. Lond. 1629, and 1656.

2007. A direction to the husbandman in a new cheape and easie way of fertiling [sic] and inriching areable grounds, by a mixture of certain native materialls in small quantities with the seed to sow, and strowing the same upon the ground sowed &c. Anonymous. 1 vol. 4to. Lond. 1634.

2008. A discovery of infinite treasure hidden since the world's beginning in the way of husbandry. By G. Plattes. 1 vol. 4to. Lond. 1639.

2009. The profitable intelligencer, containing many rare secrets and experiments in agriculture. By G. Plattes. 8 pp. 4to. Lond. 1644.

This is an advertisement of a book entitled The treasure house of nature unlocked, which does not seem to have been printed. There are also attributed to Plattes A treatise of husbandry, 1638 (which cannot be traced), and The countryman's recreation or three books of planting, graffing, and gardening (1640 : 1654). The latter is an anonymous compilation, also attributed to Thomas Barker.

2010. A way to get wealth : containing six principall vocations or callings in which every good husband or housewife may lawfully imploy themselves. By G. Markham.

A compilation comprising : (i) The natures, ordering . . . of all sorts of catell and fowle. 6th ed. 1631. (ii) The knowledge, use and laudable practise of all the recreations meete for a gentleman. 5th ed. 1633. (iii) The office of a housewife, in physicke, surgery . . . cookerie . . . distillations . . . malting brewing baking and the profit of oates. 1637. (iv) The enrichment of the weald in Kent. 1636 [1 vol. 4to. Lond 1625]. (v) The husbanding and enriching of all sorts of barren grounds. 4th ed. 1638. [Otherwise Farewell to husbandry. 1 vol. 4to. Lond. 1620. Many later eds.] (vi) The making of orchards, planting and grafting, the office of gardening . . . with the best husbanding of bees 1638. [1 vol. 4to. Lond. 1618.] With this is repr. The Husbandman's faithful orchard, by N. F., [1 vol. 4to. Lond. 1608, 2nd ed. 1609] apparently a new ed. of The fruiterer's secrets [Lond. 1604]. i–v by Markham, vi by W. Lawson.

2011. The English improver : or, a new survey of husbandry &c. By W. Blith. 1 vol. sm. 4to. Lond. 1649. Later eds. 1649, 1652, 1653.

The ' third Impression much augmented ' 1652, which appeared as The English improver improved : or The survey of husbandry surveyed, contains ' six newer Peeces of Improvement ', among which was the introduction of clover and sainfoin. The best treatise on 17th-century agriculture. On Markham and Blith see The English improvers, by Sir William Ashley, in Mélanges d'histoire offerts à Henri Pirenne, Brussels, 1926.

2012. A discours of husbandrie used in Brabant and Flanders : shewing the wonderfull improvement of land there ; and serving as a pattern for our practice in this commonwealth. By Sir R. Weston. Ed. by S. Hartlib. 1 vol. sm. 4to. Lond. 1650. Later eds. 1652 and 1742.

Of first-rate importance, especially for sheep-farming. Repr. by G. Reeve [1670 and 1674] as Directions left by a gentleman to his sons for the improvement of barren and heathy land. Reprinted, with additions by R. Child and C. Dymock, as Samuel Hartlib his legacie, 1651 : later eds. 1652, 1655. Hartlib was a copious editor or publisher of the work of others whose names are a matter of uncertainty : among these are : Essay on the advancement of husbandry and learning, with propositions for erecting a college of husbandry [1651] ; The reformed husbandman [1651] ; Design for plenty, by a universal planting of fruit trees [1652] ; Discovery for division or setting out of waste land . . . for Direction . . . of the Adventurers and Planters in the Fens [1653] ; Reformed commonwealth of bees . . . with the reformed Virginian silk worm [1655] ; The complete husbandman [1659].

2013. A treatise of fruit trees, showing the manner of planting, grafting, pruning, and ordering of them in all respects according to rules of experience, gathered in the space of thirty-seven years, &c. By R. Austen. 1 vol. sm. 4to. Oxf. 1653. Later eds. 1 vol. sm. 4to. Oxf. 1651 and 1 vol. 12mo. Oxf. 1665.

In 1658 Austen published his Observations upon some parts of Sr. Francis Bacon's Natural history as it concerns fruit-trees, fruits, and flowers. The ' Observations ' were added to the Treatise of fruit-trees in 1665.

2014. Certaine plaine and easie demonstrations of divers easie wayes and meanes for the improving of any manner of barren land. By J. Sha. 1 vol. 4to. Lond. 1657.

2015. Adam out of Eden ; or, an abstract of divers excellent experiments touching the advancement of husbandry, &c. By Adolphus (? Adam) Speed. 1 vol. 12mo. Lond. 1659 (?).

2016. The history of the propagation and improvement of vegetables, by the concurrence of art and nature. By R. Sharrock. 1 vol. 8vo. Oxf. 1660. 2nd ed. (enlarged) 1672. Re-issued under title An improvement to the art of gardening. 8vo. Lond. 1694.

2017. The great improvement of lands by clover. By A. Yarranton. 1 vol. 8vo. Lond. 1663.

2018. England's happiness increased : or a sure and easie remedie against all succeeding dear years : by a plantation of the roots called potatoes. By J. Forster. 1 vol. 4to. Lond. 1664.

The first plea for the field-cultivation of potatoes.

2019. The compleat gardener's practice. By S. Blake. 1 vol. 4to. Lond. 1664.

2020. The compleat vineyard. By W. Hughes. 1 vol. 4to. Lond. 1665. Later eds. 1670 and 1 vol. 12mo. Lond. 1683.

The extension of the cultivation of the vine on the continental model was a favourite project among literary farmers. The second edition of the Compleat vineyard was enlarged above half. The third edition appears as The flower garden and compleat vineyard.

2021. Systema agriculturae, being the mystery of Husbandry discovered and layd open. By J. W[orlidge]. 1 vol. fol. Lond. 1669. Later eds. 1 vol. 8vo. Lond. 1675, 1681, 1687, and 1716.

The most systematic work on agriculture yet published. In addition to a description of the operations, crops, and implements of the farm, it contains a calendar of monthly directions for husbandmen, and a Dictionarium rusticanum ; or the interpretation of rustick terms. The 3rd edition (1681) was ' carefully corrected and amended, with one whole section ' added, and ' many large and useful additions throughout the whole work '. The Treatise of Husbandry, 1675, attributed to Worlidge is presumably the second edition of this work. Other works by Worlidge are : Vinetum Britannicum ; or a treatise of cider &c. 1 vol. 8vo. Lond. 1676. Later eds. 1678, 1691. Apiarium ; or a discourse on bees. 1 vol. 8vo. Lond. 1676. Systema Horti-culturae ; or the art of gardening in three books. Illus. 1 vol. 8vo. Lond. 1677. The most easie method for making the best cider. Pamphlet 4to. Lond. 1687. The compleat bee master ; or a discourse of bees &c. 1 vol. 8vo. Lond. 1698.

2022. The epitome of the art of husbandry. Comprizing all necessary directions for the improvement of it &c. By J. B[lagrave]. 1 vol. 12mo. Lond. 1669.

A popular compilation which went through many editions [16mo. Lond. 1670; 8vo. Lond. 1675, 1678, 1685].

2023. The shepheard's legacy; or John Clearidge, his forty years experience. By J. Claridge. 1 vol. 8vo. Lond. 1670.

Afterwards reprinted as The Shepherd of Banbury's rules to judge the changes of the weather.

2024. A short and sure guide in the practice of raising and ordering of fruit trees. By F. Drope. 1 vol. 8vo. Oxford. 1672.

Other works on fruit-trees are : The planters manual, by C. Cotton. 1675, frequently reprinted in collected works. The manner of raising, ordering and improving forest and fruit trees, by M. Cook. 1676 and later eds. Plaine instructions to raise all sorts of fruit-trees that prosper in England, by T. Langford, 1681 : 2nd ed. 1696.

2025. Nurseries, orchards, profitable gardens and vineyards encouraged. In several letters out of the country, directed to Henry Oldenberg Esq., Secretary to the Royal Society. By A. Lawrence and J. Beale. 1 vol. 4to. Lond. 1677.

See also Herefordshire orchards, a pattern for all England. Written in an epistolary address to S. Hartlib, Esq., by I[ohn] B[eale]. 1 vol. 8vo. Lond. 1657.

2026. The Scots gardner. 2 pts. By J. Reid. 1 vol. 4to. Edinburgh. 1683. 2nd ed. 8vo. 1721.

Reprinted with several additional tracts under title The Scots gardener for the climate of Scotland. 4to. 1766.

2027. England's improvement and seasonable advice to all gentlemen and farmers, how to prepare the ground fit for sowing hemp and flax-seed. Anonymous. 1 vol. 4to. Lond. 1691.

2028. The mystery of husbandry : or arable, pasture and woodland improved by L. Meager. 1 vol. 12mo. Lond. 1697.

Wrote also The English Gardener 1670, of which eleven editions appeared by 1710, as well as a revised version The new art of gardening 1697, and later eds.

2029. Husbandry anatomized ; or an enquiry into the present manner of tilling and manuring the ground in Scotland. 2 pts. By J. Donaldson. 1 vol. 12mo. Edin. 1697–8.

The best contemporary picture of Scottish farming.

2030. Campania foelix : or, a discourse of the benefits and improvements of husbandry : . . . With some considerations upon I. Justices of the peace . . . II. On inns and alehouses. III. On servants and labourers. IV. On the poor, &c. By T. Nourse. 1 vol. 8vo. Lond. 1700. Later ed. 1706.

2031. The whole art of husbandry: or, the way of managing and improving of land &c. By J. M[ortimer], Esq. 1 vol. 8vo. Lond. 1707. Later eds. 1 vol. 8vo. Lond. 1708–12. 2 vols. 8vo. Lond. 1721. 2 vols. 8vo. Lond. 1761.

This is the best and most complete work on practical farming which had yet appeared. The second edition [1708–12] has a second part ' containing such additions as are proper for the husbandman and gardiner' &c., and a ' Countryman's kalendar, what he is to do every month in the year '. The fifth edition [1721] is in two volumes : the sixth [1761] was enlarged and revised by T. Mortimer.

2032. Rural economy in Yorkshire in 1641, being the farming and account books of Henry Best, of Elmswell in the East Riding of the county of York. Ed. by C. B. Robinson. 1 vol. 8vo. Newcastle. 1857.

A valuable record of farm-management, published by the Surtees Soc. (vol. 33). Cf. The account book of a Kentish estate, 1616–1704. Ed. by E. C. Lodge. 1 vol. 8vo. Oxf. 1927.

2033. History of agriculture and prices in England, 1259–1793. By J. E. T. Rogers. 7 vols. 8vo. Oxf. 1866–1902.

Vols. v and vi cover 1583–1702, vii 1703–93.

2034. Common rights at Cottenham & Stretham in Cambridgeshire. Ed. by W. Cunningham. Camd. Misc. xii. 1910.

Early 17th century.

2035. Sixteen old maps of properties in Oxfordshire (with one in Berkshire) illustrating the open-field system [1605–1768]. By J. L. G. Mowat. 1 vol. fol. Oxf. 1888.

(b) LATER WORKS

2036. History of the English landed interest, its customs, laws, and agriculture. By R. M. Garnier. 2 vols. 8vo. Lond. 1892–3. Later ed. 2 vols. 8vo. Lond. 1908.

Vol. i goes down to the beginning of the 18th century. Garnier also wrote Annals of the British peasantry [8vo. Lond. 1895].

2037. The disappearance of the small landowner. By A. H. Johnson. 1 vol. 8vo. Oxf. 1909. Maps.

2038. The agrarian problem in the sixteenth century. By R. H. Tawney. 1 vol. Lond. 1912. 6 maps.

Contains incidentally some useful information about the 17th century. One of the maps belongs to 1620.

2039. English farming past and present. By R. E. Prothero, Lord Ernle. 1 vol. 8vo. Lond. 1912. Bibl. Later eds. 1917, 1922, 1927.

Supersedes, The pioneers and progress of English farming.

2040. The English cornmarket, xii–xviii centuries. Harvard University Press. By N. S. B. Gras. 1 vol. 8vo. Oxf. 1915.

2041. A short history of English agriculture. By W. H. R. Curtler. 1 vol. 8vo. Oxf. 1909.

Cf. Evolution of the English farm. By M. E. Seebohm. 1 vol. 8vo. Lond. 1927.

2042. English field systems. By H. L. Gray. 1 vol. Cambridge, Mass. 1915. 18 maps.

Contains much important material from 17th-century records. See also G. N. Clark, Open fields and inclosure at Marston, Oxfordshire. 1 vol. 8vo. Oxf. 1925.

2043. Rural Northamptonshire under the Commonwealth. Oxford Studies in Social and Legal History, v. By R. Lennard. 1 vol. 8vo. Oxf. 1916. Maps.

2044. The enclosure and redistribution of our land. By W. H. R. Curtler. 1 vol. 8vo. Oxf. 1920.

Contains a chapter on the 17th century.

¶ 5. HORSES, CATTLE, AND SHEEP

For bibliography see No. 2080.

(a) SOURCES

2045. Cavalarice : or, The English horseman, contayning all the arte of horsemanship, as much as is necessary for any man to understand, whether he be horse-breeder, horse-ryder, horse-hunter, horse-runner, horse-ambler, horse-farrier, horse-keeper, coachman, smith, or sadler, &c. By G. Markham. 1 vol. 4to. Lond. 1607.

The most important of Markham's many books on horses. To the seven books of the first and second (1616–17) editions an eighth book was added in the edition of 1625.

Markham had previously published Discourse on horsemanshippe, 1593, and How to chuse, ride, train and diet both hunting horses and running horses, 1599 : the substance of these is included in Cavalarice.   See also his Countrey contentments, 1615, and later eds.

2046. Cheape and good husbandry for the well-ordering of all beasts and fowles, and for the generall cure of their diseases &c. By G. Markham. 1 vol. 4to. Lond. 1614. Later eds. 1621, 1623, and 1633.

This popular treatise passed through many editions. The ninth edition forms the first of the ' Vocations or Callings in which every good Husband or Huswife, may lawfully Imploy themselves ' which are collected in A way to get wealth [No. 2010]. See also Markham's maister piece : contaying all knowledge belonging to a smith, farrier, or horse Leech, 1614 ; Markham's methode, 1616 ; Faithful farrier, 1638 ; Complete farrier, 1639 ; Perfect horseman, 1655.

2047. The country-man's instructor . . . containing many remedies for the diseases commonly befalling to horses, sheepe, and other cattle, &c. By J. Crawshey. 1 vol. 4to. Lond. 1636.

The fifth edition appeared under the title of The good husband's jewel, or, plain directions how to know the means whereby horses, beasts, sheep, come to have diseases, and the way to cure them [1 vol. 8vo. York. 1661]. In 1636 also appeared The English farrier or country-man's treasure (anonymous) and The honest and plaine dealing farrier, by T. Grymes.

2048. The complete horse-man, and expert ferrier. By Thomas De la Gray or De Grey. 1 vol. 4to. Lond. 1639.

The work continued to be repr. till the close of the century. Later works on Farriery include : The perfect and experienced farrier, by R. Barrett, (?) 1660 ; The English horseman and complete farrier, by R. Almond, 1673 ; The experienced farrier, by E. R. (?) 1691, 4th ed. 1720.

2049. La methode et invention nouvelle de dresser les chevaux. By William Cavendish, 1st Duke of Newcastle. 1 vol. fol. Antwerp. 1658. Plates. Later ed. 1 vol. fol. Lond. 1737.

Trans. in A general system of horsemanship [2 vols. fol. 1743]. Newcastle wrote a second work : A new method and extraordinary invention to dress horses [1 vol. fol. Lond. 1667 ; 2nd ed. 1677, with many repr.].

2050. The herds-man's mate ; or, a guide for herdsmen, teaching how to cure all diseases in bulls, oxen, cows, and calves, &c. By M. Harward. 1 vol. 8vo. Dubl. 1673.

2051. The countryman's treasure; shewing the nature, cause and cure of all diseases incident to cattel. 1 vol. 8vo. Lond. 1676 : 2nd ed. 1683.

Frontispiece showing bull, sheep, and swine. See also The country-man's companion, by Philotheos Physiologus (i. e. Thomas Tryon). 1700.

2052. A treatise of oxen, sheep, hogs and dogs . . . How to chuse, govern and preserve them in health. 1 vol. 8vo. Lond. 1683.

Describes best kind of cattle to buy for various purposes.

2053. The gentleman's recreation. In two parts. The first being an encyclopedy of the arts and sciences . . . The second treats of horsemanship, hawking &c. By R. Blome. 1 vol. fol. Lond. 1686.

Interesting passages, especially about the different breeds of sheep, their qualities, and locality.

2054. The husbandman, farmer and graziers' compleat instructor. By A. S. 1 vol. 12mo. Lond. 1697.

Attributed uncertainly to Ad. Speed. Deals with buying, selling, breeding, and fattening cattle.

¶ 6. ENCLOSURES

(a) SOURCES

2055. To the king's most excellent majestie. The humble petition of two sisters ; the Church and Commonwealth : for the restoring of their ancient commons and liberties. By F. Trigge. 1 vol. 8vo. Lond. 1604.

Trigge's Petition against the enclosure of commons belongs to the sheep-breeding, pasture-farming movement of the reign of Elizabeth.

2056. Depopulation arraigned, convicted, and condemned by the lawes of God and man. &c. By R. Powell. 1 vol. 8vo. Lond. 1636.

Powell complains that the evil of inclosures was never more ' monstrous ' than at the time when he wrote. See on the other side G. Plattes' Discovery of infinite treasure (2008).

2057. Inclosure thrown open ; or, depopulation depopulated, not by spades and mattocks, but by the word of God, the laws of the land, and solid arguments. By H. Halhead. 1 vol. 4to. Lond. 1650.

The work is prefaced by ' an address to the reader ' by J. Sprigge of Banbury. It probably belongs to a group of pamphlets dealing with the midland counties, where enclosure was again extremely active.

2058. Common good, or, the improvement of commons, forrests & chasses by inclosure &c. (An appendix, shewing the chiefe cause of wandring poor in England.) By S. Taylor. 1 vol. 4to. Lond. 1652.

' The two great nurseries of idleness and beggery ', says Taylor, ' are ale-houses and commons.'

2059. Wast land's improvement, or certain proposals made and tendred to the consideration of the honorable committee appointed by Parliament, &c. By E. G. 1 vol. 4to. Lond. 1653.

The writer considers that ' robberies, thefts, burglaries, rapes, and murders receive their nourishment and encouragement ' from unenclosed wastes.

2060. Bread for the poor, and advancement of the English nation, promised by enclosure of the wastes and common-grounds of England. By A. Moore. 1 vol. 4to. Lond. 1653.

Moore regards the commons as ' nurseries of thieves and horse-stealers '.

2061. The crying sin of England, of not caring for the poor, wherein inclosure . . . is arraigned, convicted, and condemned by the word of God. By J. Moore. 1 vol. 4to. Lond. 1653.

This treatise provoked a war of pamphlets. It was answered by ' Pseudomisius ' in Considerations concerning common-fields and inclosures . . . partly to answer some passages in another discourse by Mr. J. Moore under the title of The crying sinne &c. [1 vol. 4to. Lond. 1654]. Moore replied with A scripture-word against Inclosures, viz. such as doe un-people townes and un-corne fields &c. [1 vol. 4to. Lond. 1656]. This second treatise was partly an answer to Joseph Lee (q.v.). Pseudomisius again replied in A vindication of considerations concerning common-fields and inclosures ; or a rejoinder unto that reply which Mr. Moore hath pretended to make unto these considerations [1 vol. 4to. Lond. 1656].

2062. Εὐταξία τοῦ Αγροῦ or a vindication of a regulated inclosure. Wherein is plainly proved, that inclosure of commons in general, and the inclosure of Catthorpe . . . in particular, are both lawful and laudable. By J. Lee. 1 vol. 4to. Lond. 1656.

In this treatise Lee defends the enclosure of Catthorpe Common.

(b) LATER WORKS

2063. Commons and common fields, or the history and policy of the laws relating to commons and inclosures in England. By T. E. Scrutton. 1 vol. 8vo. Cambridge. 1887.

Cf. No. 584.

2064. The midland revolt and the inquisitions of depopulation of 1607. By E. F. Gay. Trans. Royal Hist. Soc., N.S. xviii. 1904.

2065. The inclosure of common fields in the seventeenth century. By E. M. Leonard. Trans. Royal Hist. Soc., N.S. xix. 1905.

2066. Common land and inclosure. By E. C. K. Gonner. 1 vol. 8vo. Lond. 1912.

Valuable. Cf. Eng. Hist. Rev. xxiii. 1908, for the same author's The progress of inclosure during the seventeenth century, with a map showing the enclosed roads in 1675.

¶ 7. DRAINING
(a) SOURCES

2067. A true report of certaine wonderfull overflowings of waters, now lately in Summerset-shire, Norfolke, and other places of England. Anonymous. 1 vol. 4to. Lond. 1607.

Second ed. with additions, More strange newes of wonderfull accidents &c. Lond. n.d.

2068. A discourse concerning the dreyning of fennes and surrounded grounds in the sixe counteys of Norfolke, Suffolke, Cambridge, with the Isle of Ely, Huntingdon, Northampton, and Lincolne. By H. C. 1 vol. 4to. Lond. 1629.

The author describes the condition of the ' drowned lands ' of the Fens, and urges the Government to undertake their reclamation.

2069. A discourse concerning the great benefit of drayning and embanking. . . . By J. L. 1 vol. 4to. [Lond.] 1641.

2070. A briefe relation discovering plainely the true causes why the great levell of fennes . . . have been drowned. By A. Burrell. 1 vol. 4to. Lond. 1642.

Burrell, who was employed by the Earl of Bedford on fen drainage, criticizes the engineering works. He refers more particularly to Vermuyden's work in his Exceptions against Sir C. Virmudens discourse for the drainage of the great fennes &c. [1 vol. 4to. Lond. 1642].

2071. Discourses touching the drayning of the great fennes lying within the several counties of Lincolne, Northampton, Huntingdon, Norfolke, Suffolke, Cambridge, and the Isle of Ely. By Sir C. Vermuïden (or Vermuyden). 1 vol. 8vo. Lond. 1642.

Vermuyden, who was the engineer employed to drain the fens for the ' Undertakers ', in this work defends his methods. See also The anti-projector or the history of the fen project : Lond. 1646 ; and A narrative of all the proceedings in the draining of the great level of the fens, by N. N. Lond. 1661, repr. in Social England illustrated (ed. 1903), pp. 407 ff.

2072. A remonstrance of some decrees and other proceedings of the Commissioners of Sewers for the upper levels in the counties of Kent and Sussex. By Sir N. Powell. 1 vol. 4to. Lond. 1659.

Thomas Harlachenden ' published ' but apparently did not print Animadversions on several material passages in this book : to which Powell replied with The Animadverter animadverted, 4to. Lond. 1663. Both books contain copious extracts from records.

2073. History of imbanking and drayning of divers fennes and marshes, both in forein parts and in this kingdom, and of the improvements thereby. By Sir W. Dugdale. 1 vol. fol. Lond. 1662. Later ed. 1772. Ed. by C. N. Cole.

A valuable collection of material. The ed. of 1772 was revised and corrected, and adds three indices. Dugdale's Diary, while making a tour of the district in 1657, remains unpublished (Lansdowne MSS. 722). Among the collections of material which he made, the Survey of the Fens (possibly by R. Atkins), drawn up in July 1605, is preserved in the Harleian MSS. 5011.

2074. History or narrative of the great level of the fens called Bedford Level : with a large map of the said level, as drained, surveyed, and described. By Sir J. Moore. 1 vol. 8vo. Lond. 1685.

As surveyor of the drainage works Moore speaks with authority.

2075. A collection of laws which form the constitution of the Bedford Level Corporation. Ed. by C. N. Cole. 1 vol. 8vo. Lond. 1761. Later ed. 1803.
Valuable for texts of documents.

(b) LATER WORKS

2076. Historical account of the great level of the fens. By W. Elstobb. 1 vol. 8vo. Lynn and London. 1793.

A posthumous work : Elstobb had been employed as engineer by John, 4th Duke of Bedford.

2077. The history of the drainage of the great level of the fens, called Bedford Level ; with the constitution and laws of the Bedford Level Corporation. By S. Wells. 2 vols. 8vo. Lond. 1828–30.

2078. A history of the fens of South Lincolnshire. By W. H. Wheeler. 1 vol. 8vo. Boston and London. 2nd ed. [1897].
Supersedes 1st ed. 1868. Bibliography and list of Statutes.

VI. SOCIAL

1. General and Miscellaneous.
   (a) Bibliographies and Sources. (b) Later Works.
2. Descriptions of England, Travels, &c.
3. Education.
   (a) Sources. (b) Later Works.

IN a sense nearly everything written in the seventeenth century illustrates
its social history, and many of the best sources are not to be found in this
section. Letters, diaries and memoirs, together with household accounts,
furnish the most trustworthy illustrations of the daily habits of the upper and
middle classes, and casual allusions in the drama and other forms of literature
are often valuable. The observation of foreign travellers supply important
generalizations as well as details ignored by native writers. The history of the
inarticulate masses must be sought mainly from trials, especially from quarter
sessions records, and from ephemeral literature, particularly ballads. The
numerous guides to deportment published during this period are largely
based on French models, and merely influenced the higher ranks.

Shakespeare's England (2445) gives the best picture of social conditions at
the beginning of the period, and its bibliographies describe the sources. There
is no similar study for its close. Macaulay (204) sketched the state of England
in 1685, and Lecky in the first volume of his History of England in the
eighteenth century has some useful comments. There are a number of 'social
histories' dealing with the period as a whole or with considerable sections of it,
but the mass of material embodied in such periodicals as the Tatler and Spectator, or in the writings of Defoe and Swift, has never been properly utilized,
though John Ashton made a systematic collection of extracts [Social life in the
reign of Queen Anne. Lond. 1883]. Social historians in general tend to
concentrate unduly on life in London and to ignore the rest of England.

¶ 1. GENERAL AND MISCELLANEOUS

(a) BIBLIOGRAPHIES AND SOURCES

2079. Bibliotheca piscatoria. A catalogue of books on angling, the fisheries
and fish-culture, with bibliographical notes. Ed. by T. Westwood and T.
Satchell. 1 vol. 8vo. Lond. 1883.

Valuable : a supplement was published in 1901 as a List of books . . . to supplement
the Bibliotheca piscatoria.

2080. Works on horses and equitation. A bibliographical record of hip-
pology. By F. N. Huth. 1 vol. 8vo. Lond. 1887.

2081. Bibliotheca accipitraria. A catalogue of books ancient and modern
relating to falconry. By J. E. Harting. 1 vol. 8vo. Lond. 1891. Illus.

A very well arranged bibliography, which includes foreign as well as English books.

2082. A bibliography of fishes.   Ed. by B. Dean, C. R. Eastman, E. W. Gudges, and A. W. Henn.   3 vols. 8vo. New York.   1916–23.

2083. The wonderfull discoveries of witches in the countie of Lancaster . . . 1612.   By T. Potts.   1 vol. 8vo. Lond. 1613.

Repr. Chetham Soc., ed. J. Crossley, 1845.

2084. Falconry or the Faulcon's lure and cure.   By S. Latham.   1 vol. sm. 4to. Lond. 1615.   Later ed. 1633.

2085. Countrey contentments, in two bookes : The first containing the whole art of riding . . . the second intituled the English huswife.   By G. Markham.   1 vol. 4to. Lond. 1615.

Extracts from The English huswife were ed. by Constance, Countess De La Warr [8vo. Lond. *c.* 1908].

2086. Essayes and characters of a prison and prisoners.   By G. Mynshul. 1 vol. 4to. Lond. 1618.   Later ed. 1 vol. 8vo. Edin. 1821.

Cf. The compters common wealth, or a voiage made to an infernall iland . . . long since discovered.   By W. Fennor.   1 vol. 4to. Lond. 1617 ; and W. Bagwell, The merchant distressed, his observations when he was a prisoner for debt in London in 1637.   Verse. 1 vol. 4to. 1644.

2087. The kinges majesties declaration to his subiects concerning lawfull sports to be used.   1 vol. 4to. Lond. 1618.   Later ed. 1633.

Commonly called The book of sports, to which Puritans strongly objected.   Repr. in Somers' Tracts.   Cf. The declaration of sports for Lancashire [1617], by J. Tait, Eng. Hist. Rev. xxxii. 1917 ; and L. A. Govett's The kings book of sports.   A history of the declarations of King James I, and King Charles I . . . with a reprint of the declarations and a description of the sports then popular.   1 vol. 8vo. Lond. 1890.

2088. An approved treatise of hawkes and hawking.   Divided into three books.   By E. Bert.   1 vol. sm. 4to. Lond. 1619.   Later ed. 1891. Ed. by J. E. Harting.

2089. The compleat gentleman, fashioning him absolute in the most necessary and commendable qualities concerning minde or bodie that may be required in a noble gentleman.   By H. Peacham.   1 vol. 4to. Lond. 1622. Later ed. 1 vol. 4to. Oxf. 1906.   Ed. by G. S. Gordon.

For a companion vol. written about 1729 see Daniel Defoe's The compleat English gentleman.   1 vol. 8vo. Lond. 1890.   Ed. by K. D. Bülbring.

2090. Healthes sicknesse, or a discourse proving the drinking of healthes to be sinfull.   By W. Prynne.   1 vol. 4to. Lond. 1628.

2091. The unloveliness of love-locks.   By W. Prynne.   1 vol. 4to. Lond. 1628.

Cf. Thomas Hall, Comarum ἀκοσμεια.   The loathsomenesse of long haire . . . with an appendix against painting, spots, naked breasts.   1 vol. 8vo. Lond. 1654.

2092. Microcosmography ; or a piece of the world discovered in essays and characters.   By J. Earle.   1 vol. 8vo. Lond. 1628.   Later eds. 1 vol. 8vo. Lond. 1811. Ed. by P. Bliss.   1 vol. 4to. Bristol. 1897.   Ed. by S. T. Irwin.

Owing to the bibliographies in the eds. of 1811 and 1897 many similar character-books are omitted.

2093. The English gentleman, containing sundry excellent rules ... tending to direction of every gentleman. By R. Brathwait. 1 vol. sm. 4to. Lond. 1630.

2094. The English gentlewoman . . . expressing what habilliments doe best attire her, what ornaments doe best adorne her, what complements doe best accomplish her. By R. Brathwait. 1 vol. sm. 4to. Lond. 1631.

2095. Tom of all trades, or the plaine path-way to preferment ... in all professions, trades, arts and mysteries. By T. Powell. 1 vol. 4to. Lond. 1631.

2096. Annalia Dubrensia. [Poems] upon the yeerely celebration of Mr. Robert Dovers' Olimpick games upon Cotswold-Hill. 1 vol. sm. 4to. Lond. 1636. Later ed. 1 vol. 4to. Manchester. 1877. Ed. by A. B. Grosart.

2097. The ladies cabinet opened ; wherein is found hidden severall experiments in preserving and conserving, physicke and surgery, cookery and huswifery. 1 vol. 4to. Lond. 1639.

2098. The academy of complements. Wherein ladyes, gentlewomen schollers and strangers may accommodate their courtly practice with most curious ceremonies. 1 vol. 12mo. Lond. 1640 and 1650.

For similar works see Brit. Mus. Pr. Cat., *sub* Academy. The ed. of 1685 has title : The academy of complements or a new way of wooing [1 vol. 8vo. Lond. 1685].

2099. Youths behaviour, or decency in conversation amongst men . . . newly turned into English. Trans. by F. Hawkins. 11th ed. 1 vol. 12mo. Lond. 1672.

1st ed. is said to be about 1641. See Dict. Nat. Biog. A second part, Youths' behaviour, or decency in conversation amongst women, was added in the 1664 ed.

2100. The English dancing-master, or plain and easie rules for the dancing of country dances, with the tune to each dance. By J. Playford. 1 vol. 4to. Lond. 1650. 2nd ed. 1 vol. 12mo. Lond. 1652. 17th ed. 1 vol. 12mo. Lond. 1721.

The second part of the Dancing-master was publ. 1 vol. 12mo. Lond. 1691. 4th ed. 1728.

2101. The vaulting master, or the art of vaulting reduced to a method . . . illustrated by examples. By W. Stokes. 1 vol. 8vo. Oxf. 1652.

2102. The compleat angler, or the contemplative man's recreation. By I. Walton. 1 vol. 8vo. Lond. 1653. 5th ed. 1 vol. 8vo. Lond. 1676. 100th ed. 2 vols. 4to. Lond. 1888. 54 photogravures. Ed. by R. B. Marston.

The ed. of 1676 is the first in which C. Cotton's The compleat angler ... Part ii (12mo. Lond. 1676) and R. Venables's The experienc'd angler (8vo. Lond. 1662) are joined to Walton's Treatise, with the common title, The universal angler. The 100th ed. has a complete bibliographical note . . . Cf. The chronicle of the ' Compleat Angler ' of Izaak Walton and Charles Cotton, being a bibliographical record. By T. Westwood [1 vol. 4to. Lond. 1864].

2103. The academy of eloquence formula's . . . to speak and to write fluently. By T. Blount. 1 vol. 12mo. Lond. 1654. 5th ed. 1 vol. 12mo. Lond. 1683.

2104. God's plea for Nineveh, or London's precedent for mercy delivered, in certain sermons within the city of London.   By T. Reeve.   1 vol. fol. Lond. 1657.

A specimen of Puritan sermons affording matter for social history.

2105. Advice to a daughter in opposition to the advise to a sonne.   By J. Heydon.   1 vol. 12mo. [Lond]. 1658.   2nd ed. 1659.

2106. The accomplisht cook, or the art and mystery of cookery, wherein the whole art is revealed &c.   By R. May.   1 vol. 8vo. Lond. 1660.   Later eds. 1671, 1675, 1678.

Illustrated.   5th ed. with additions. &c. 8vo. Lond. 1685.   Cf. The receipt book of Mrs. Ann Blencowe A.D. 1694.   Intro. by G. Saintsbury.   1 vol. 8vo. Lond. 1925.

2107. The refin'd courtier, or a correction of several indecencies crept into civil conversation.   By N. W.   1 vol. 12mo. Lond. 1663.

2108. The English rogue described in the life of Meriton Latroon, a witty extravagant, being a compleat history of the most eminent cheats of both sexes.   By R. Head and F. Kirkman.   4 parts. 8vo. Lond. 1665–80.   Illus.

2109. Angliae speculum morale ; the moral state of England with the several aspects it beareth to virtue and vice.   1 vol. 8vo. Lond. 1670.

2110. The rules of civility, or certain ways of deportment observed in France amongst all persons of quality upon several occasions.   1 vol. 12mo. Lond. 1671.   Later ed. 1678.

The art of complaisance, or the means to oblige in conversation, 2nd ed. 1677, is recommended by the publisher as ' very fit to be bound with this '.

2111. Remarques on the humours and conversations of the town.   Written in a letter to Sir T. L.   1 vol. 12mo. Lond. 1673.

Cf. Remarks upon remarques : or, a vindication of the conversations of the town [1 vol. 12mo. Lond. 1673].

2112. The works of Francis Osborne.   7th ed. 1 vol. 8vo. Lond. 1673.   11th ed. 2 vols. 12mo. Lond. 1722.

The ed. of 1673, though called the 7th (? of Advice to a son) is probably the 1st collected ed. of Osborne's works.   Ed. of 1722 is the last and best, containing Osborne's letters to Col. William Draper, 1653–7.   His advice to a son . . . under these general heads, 1. Studies, 2. Love and Marriage, 3. Travel, 4. Government, 5. Religion, 1st publ. in two parts 1656 and 1658, was ed. by E. A. Parry.   1 vol. 8vo. Lond. 1896.

2113. The ladies calling.   Later eds.   2 pts. 8vo. Oxf. 1673.   7th ed. 2 pts. 8vo. Oxf. 1700.

Said to be by the author of The whole duty of man, i. e. ? R. Allestree, see Dict. Nat. Biog., *sub* Pakington, Dorothy.

2114. The compleat gamester, or instructions how to play at billiards, trucks, bowls and chess . . . cards . . . dice.   By C. Cotton.   1 vol. 8vo. Lond. 1674.   5th ed. 1 vol. 12mo. Lond. 1725.

2115. The gentleman's recreation : in four parts, viz., hunting, hawking, fowling, fishing.   Collected from ancient and modern authors . . . illustrated with sculptures.   By N. Cox.   1 vol. 8vo. Lond. 1674.   Plates.   4th ed. 1 vol. 8vo. Lond. 1697.

2116. Proteus redevivus : or the art of wheedling or insinuation obtain'd by general conversation. By R. Head. 1 vol. 8vo. Lond. 1675.

2117. The compleat servant-maid, or the young maiden's tutor. 1 vol. 12mo. Lond. 1677. 4th ed. 1 vol. 12mo. Lond. 1685.

2118. The compleat gentleman. By J. Gailhard. 2 vols. 8vo. Lond. 1678.

2119. Sadducismus triumphatus, or a full and plain evidence concerning witches and apparitions. By J. Glanvil. 1 vol. 8vo. Lond. 1681. Later ed. 1 vol. 8vo. Lond. 1726.

2120. The wonders of the female world . . . to which is added a pleasant discourse of female pre-eminence or the dignity and excellency of that sex above the male. 1 vol. 12mo. Lond. 1683.
Cf. The woman as good as the man, or the equality of both sexes. Trans. by A. L. 1 vol. 12mo. Lond. 1677.

2121. A treatise against drunkenness, described in its nature, kindes, effectes and causes, especially that of drinking healths. By M. Scrivener. 1 vol. 12mo. Lond. 1685.

2122. The academy of armory, or a storehouse of armory and blazon. By R. Holme. 1 vol. fol. Chester. 1688.

2123. The cry of the oppressed, being a true and tragical account of the unparallel'd sufferings of multitudes of poor imprisoned debtors in most of the gaols in England. By M. Pitt. 1 vol. 12mo. Lond. 1691. Plates.

2124. The ladies dictionary; being a general entertainment for the fair sex. 1 vol. 8vo. Lond. 1694.
Publ. by J. Dunton, who may be its author.

2125. An essay in defence of the female sex, in which are inserted the characters of a pedant, a squire, a beau, a vertuoso, a poetaster, a city-critick, &c. By M. Astell. 1 vol. 8vo. Lond. 1696.
Cf. A farther essay relating to the female sex, containing six characters and six perfections [1 vol. 8vo. Lond. 1696]. There is a good essay on Mary Astell, by K. D. Bülbring, repr. from the Journal of Education, April and May 1891.

2126. An account of the societies for reformation of manners in London and Westminster and other parts of the kingdom. 1 vol. 8vo. Lond. 1699.
One of several pamphlets on this subject.

2127. Several letters between two ladies ; wherein the lawfulness and unlawfulness of artificial beauty, in point of conscience are nicely debated. Ed. by C. G. 1 vol. 12mo. Lond. 1701.

2128. The compleat caterer, or instructions how to chuse the best of provisions. 1 vol. 12mo. Lond. 1701.

2129. Sensus communis ; an essay on the freedom of wit and humour. In a letter to a friend. By Anthony Ashley Cooper, 3rd Earl of Shaftesbury. 1 vol. 8vo. Lond. 1709.

2130. An essay towards an history of dancing. By J. Weaver. 1 vol. 8vo. Lond. 1712.

Cf. his Orchesography, or the art of dancing by characters and demonstrative figures . . . being an exact translation from the French of Monsieur Feuillet. 1 vol. 4to. Lond. 1706 and 1710. Diagrams.

2131. The new academy of complements erected for ladies, gentlewomen, courtiers, gentlemen . . . with an exact collection of the newest and choicest songs a la mode. 1 vol. 12mo. Lond. 1713.

2132. Προγυμνάσματα. The inn-play; or, Cornish-hugg-wrestler. By Sir T. Parkyns. 1 vol. 4to. Nottingham. 1713. 2nd ed. corrected with large additions. 1714. 3rd ed. 1714. Last ed. 1 vol. 12mo. Lond. [? 1800].

2133. Memoirs of the lives, intrigues and comical adventures of the most famous gamesters and celebrated sharpers in the reigns of Charles II, James II, William III and Queen Anne. By T. Lucas. 1 vol. 12mo. Lond. 1714.

2134. An historical essay concerning witchcraft. By F. Hutchinson. 1 vol. 8vo. Lond. 1718.

2135. The postman robb'd of his mail: or, the packet broke open. By C. Gildon. 1 vol. 8vo. Lond. 1719.

Cf. C. G[?ildon's] The post-boy robb'd of his mail . . . letters of love and gallantry. [1 vol. 12mo. Lond. 1692; 2nd ed. 8vo. Lond. 1706]. See J. Nichols, John Dunton (882), i. 201. According to the Term Catalogue, ii. 466, a second vol. of the Postboy was issued in 1693.

2136. Miscellaneous anecdotes illustrative of the manners and history of Europe during the reigns of Charles II, James II, William III, and Q. Anne. By J. P. Malcolm. 1 vol. 8vo. Lond. 1811.

Quotations, mainly from English newspapers.

2137. The progresses, processions and magnificent festivities of King James the First, his royal consort, family and court; collected from original manuscripts, scarce pamphlets . . . comprising forty masques and entertainments; ten civic pageants; numerous original letters; and annotated lists of the peers, baronets and knights who received those honours during the reign of King James. By J. Nichols. 4 vols. 4to. Lond. 1828. Illus.

2138. Satirical songs and poems on costume from the 13th to the 19th century. Ed. by F. W. Fairholt. Percy Soc. 1849.

2139. Extracts from the journal and account book of Timothy Burrell, 1683 to 1714. Ed. by R. W. Blencowe. Sussex Arch. Coll. iii. 1850.

Cf. A 17th-century account book [of William Freke at Oxford and elsewhere 1619–30]. Ed. G. W. Prothero. Eng. Hist. Rev. vii. 1892; and The account-book of James Wilding 1682–8. Ed. by E. Gordon Duff. Oxf. Hist. Soc. Collectanea. 1st series. 1885.

2140. Extracts from the diary of John Richards of Warmwell in Dorsetshire [1697–1702]. The Retrospective Review. Series III, vol. i. 1853.

2141. A relation of some abuses which are committed against the Commonwealth ... composed especiallye for the benefit of this countrie of Durhame, December the xxvjth, 1629. Ed. by Sir F. Madden. Camd. Soc. Misc. 1855.

The abuses were the ' waste of woods,—the pulling down of castles and fortresses—the decay of martial discipline—and the vanities of the people in drinking, smoking, and apparel '. Intro.

2142. The house and farm accounts of the Shuttleworths of Gawthorpe Hall, in the county of Lancaster, at Smithils and Gawthorpe, from September 1582 to October 1621. Ed. by J. Harland. Chetham Soc. 4 vols. 1856–8.

2143. Books of characters, illustrating the habits and manners of Englishmen from the reign of James I to the Restoration. Ed. by J. O. Halliwell. 1 vol. 4to. Lond. 1857.

Repr. The wandering Jew telling fortunes to Englishmen [1649]; The man in the moone telling strange fortunes, or the English fortune teller [1609]; Essayes and characters, ironicall and instructive, by J. Stephens [1615]; London and the countrey carbonadoed and quartred into severall characters, by D. Lupton [1632].

2144. The old book collector's miscellany : or, a collection of readable reprints of literary rarities ... during the sixteenth and seventeenth centuries. Ed. by C. Hindley. 3 vols. 8vo. Lond. 1871–3.

Minor literary pieces mainly illustrating social history.

2145. Fugitive tracts written in verse which illustrate the condition of religious and political feeling in England and the state of society there during two centuries. Second series, 1600–1700. Ed. by W. C. Hazlitt. 1 vol. 8vo. s.l. 1875.

2146. Selections from the household books of the Lord William Howard of Naworth Castle, 1612–40. Ed. by G. Ornsby. Surtees Soc. 1878.

Appendix has illustrative documents.

2147. The oeconomy of the Fleete, or an apologiticall answere of Alexander Harris (late Warden) unto xix articles sett forth against him by the prisoners. Ed. by A. Jessopp. Camd. Soc. 1879.

2148. Humour, wit and satire of the seventeenth century. Ed. by J. Ashton. 1 8vo. Lond. 1883. Illus.

Mainly a repr. of ballads.

2149. Playing cards of various ages and countries. Selected from the collection of Lady Charlotte Schreiber. Vol. i, English and Scottish, Dutch and Flemish (143 plates). 1 vol. fol. Lond. 1892.

A catalogue of this collection, now in the Brit. Mus., was made by F. M. O'Donoghue, 8vo. Lond. 1901. Cf. Playing and other cards [in the Brit. Mus.], a catalogue, by W. H. Willshire. 8vo. Lond. 1876–7.

2150. Catalogue of the collection of fans and fan-leaves, presented to the trustees of the British Museum by the Lady Charlotte Schreiber. By L. Cust. 1 vol. 8vo. Lond. 1893.

2151. Social England illustrated. A collection of xviith. century tracts. Intro. by A. Lang. 1 vol. 8vo. Westminster. 1903.

Repr. from An English garner.

2152. Letters of denization and acts of naturalization for aliens in England and Ireland, 1603–1700. By W. A. Shaw. 1 vol. 4to. Lymington. 1911.

Intro. explains the history of the law and documentary sources. Cf. J. S. Burn, History of French, Walloon, Dutch and other foreign protestant refugees settled in England from the reign of Henry VIII to the revocation of the edict of Nantes. 1 vol. 8vo. Lond. 1846; W. D. Cooper's Lists of foreign protestants and aliens resident in England 1618–1688 [Camd. Soc. 1862]; Protestant exiles from France in the reign of Louis XIV; or, the Huguenot refugees and their descendants in Great Britain and Ireland. By D. C. A. Agnew [1 vol. 4to. s.l. 1866. Plates. Later ed. 3 vols. 4to. Lond. and Edin. 1871–4]; and A bibliography of works relating to the Huguenot refugees, whence they came and where they settled. By E. E. Stride [1 vol. 8vo. Lymington. 1886].

2153. The household account book of Sarah Fell, of Swarthmoor Hall. Ed. by N. Penney. 1 vol. 8vo. Camb. 1920.

Printed *verb. et lit.* from the original MS. The entries date from 1673 to 1678.

(b) LATER WORKS

2154. A complete view of the dress and habits of the people of England . . . to the present time. By J. Strutt. 2 vols. 4to. Lond. 1796–9. Illus.

2155. Glig-Gamena Angel-Deod, or the sports and pastimes of the people of England . . . from the earliest period to the present time, illustrated by engravings. By J. Strutt. 1 vol. 4to. Lond. 1801. Later eds. 1 vol. 8vo. Lond. 1875. Ed. by W. Hone. 1 vol. 4to. Lond. 1903. Ed. by J. C. Cox.

2156. Anecdotes of the manners and customs of London from the Roman invasion to the year 1700. By J. P. Malcolm. 2 vols. 4to. Lond. 1811. Plates. Later eds. 3 vols. 8vo. Lond. 1811. Plates.

Many useful quotations from ephemeral literature.

2157. Costumes in England : a history of dress from the earliest period till the close of the eighteenth century. By F. W. Fairholt. 1 vol. 8vo. Lond. 1846. Illus. Later ed. 2 vols. 8vo. Lond. 1885. Ed. by H. A. Dillon.

2158. The social history of the people of the southern counties of England in past centuries. By G. Roberts. 1 vol. 8vo. Lond. 1856.

Has quotations from Dorsetshire, and other local records.

2159. Tobacco : its history and associations. By F. W. Fairholt. 1 vol. 8vo. Lond. 1859. Later ed. 1 vol. 8vo. Lond. 1876.

Cf. W. Bragg's Bibliotheca nicotiana [Birmingham. 1880]; and W. J. Hardy, Tobacco culture in England during the seventeenth century. Archaeologia. li. 157–66. 1888.

2160. Memoirs of Bartholomew fair. By H. Morley. 1 vol. 8vo. Lond. 1859. Illus.

2161. Social amusements under the Restoration. By R. Bell. The Fortnightly Review, 1865.

2162. The annals of tennis. By J. Marshall. 1 vol. 4to. Lond. 1878. Plates.

2163. Schools and masters of fence from the middle ages to the eighteenth century. By E. Castle. 1 vol. 4to. Lond. 1885. Bibl. Later ed. 1 vol. 8vo. Lond. 1892. Bibl.

2164. The curiosities of ale and beer. By J. Bickerdyke (C. H. Cook). 1 vol. 8vo. Lond. 1886.

2165. The history of Newmarket and the annals of the turf : with memoirs and biographical notices of the habitués of Newmarket. . . . to the end of the seventeenth century. By J. P. Hore. 3 vols. 8vo. Lond. 1886. Illus.
Detailed : contains many extracts from state papers, memoirs, &c.

2166. Old cookery books and ancient cuisine. By W. C. Hazlitt. 1 vol. 8vo. Lond. 1886.
Prints some extracts and supplies a bibliographical note, pp. 79–81.

2167. Social life in England from the Restoration to the Revolution, 1660–1690. By W. C. Sydney. 1 vol. 8vo. Lond. 1892.

2168. The early history of coffee houses in England, with some account of the first use of coffee and a bibliography of the subject. By E. F. Robinson. 1 vol. 8vo. Lond. 1893. Illus.

2169. A history of English lotteries. By J. Ashton. 1 vol. 8vo. Lond. 1893. Illus.

2170. The traditional games of England, Scotland and Ireland. By Alice Bertha, Lady Gomme. 2 vols. 8vo. Lond. 1894–8.

2171. Social England. A record of the progress of the people in religion, laws, learning, arts, industry, commerce, science, literature and manners. vol. iv, 1603–1714. Ed. by H. D. Traill. 1 vol. 8vo. Lond. 1895. Later ed. 1 vol. 8vo. Lond. 1903. Illus. Ed. by J. S. Mann.
The work of many hands : second ed. profusely illustrated.

2172. Fencing and duelling as practised by all European nations from the middle ages to the present day. With bibliography of the art of fence. By C. A. Thimm. 1 vol. 8vo. Hampton Hill. 1897.

2173. The history of gambling in England. By J. Ashton. 1 vol. 8vo. Lond. 1898.

2174. A history of dancing from the earliest ages to our own times. By G. Vuillier. 2 vols. 4to. Lond. 1898. Illus.
A trans. Ch. xiv deals with English, ch. xv with Irish and Scottish dancing. Cf. R. St. Johnston, A history of dancing [1 vol. 8vo. Lond. 1906. Illus.] ; C. J. Sharp and H. C. Macilwaine, The Morris book [1 vol. 8vo. Lond. 1907 and 1911. Illus.] ; A. M. Cowper Coles, Old English country dance steps [1 vol. 8vo. Lond. 1909. Illus.].

2175. Home Life under the Stuarts, 1603–1649. By E. Godfrey [Jessie Bedford]. 1 vol. 8vo. Lond. 1903. Illus.

2176. Life and letters at Bath in the 18th century. By A. Barbeau. 1 vol. 8vo. Lond. and N.Y. 1904. Illus. Bibl.
Includes the reign of Anne. A trans. of Une ville d'eaux Anglaise &c. Paris. 1904.

2177. The digger movement in the days of the Commonwealth as revealed in the writings of Gerrard Winstanley, the digger. By L. H. Berens. 1 vol. 8vo. Lond. 1906.

2178. The England and Holland of the Pilgrims. By H. M. Dexter. Ed. by M. Dexter. 1 vol. 8vo. Lond. & Boston (Mass.) 1906.
A valuable study.

2179. Old English sports. By F. W. Hackwood. 1 vol. 8vo. Lond. 1907. Illus.

2180. Jewellery (The connoisseur's library). By H. Clifford Smith. 1 vol. 8vo. Lond. 1908.

2181. A history of witchcraft in England from 1558 to 1718. By W. Notestein. Amer. Hist. Assoc. 1 vol. 8vo. Washington. 1911. Bibl.
Based on thorough research.

2182. Carriages and coaches. Their history and their evolution. 1 vol. 8vo. Lond. 1912. Illus. Ed. by R. Straus.

2183. The Anglo-French entente in the seventeenth century. By C. Bastide. 1 vol. 8vo. Lond. 1914. Illus.
Deals with French influence on England : entertaining and instructive. Virtually a translation of the same author's Anglais et Français du dix-septième siècle.

2184. Social life in Stuart England. By M. Coate. 1 vol. 8vo. Lond. 1924. Bibl.

¶ 2. DESCRIPTIONS OF ENGLAND, TRAVELS, &c.

2185. The road-books and itineraries of Great Britain, 1570 to 1850. A catalogue, with an introduction and a bibliography. By Sir H. G. Fordham. 1 vol. 4to. Camb. 1924.

2186. Theatre of the empire of Great Britaine. By J. Speed. 1 vol. fol. Lond. 1611.
A series of 50 or more maps of English counties. There are notes on this and other works of Speed in Lowndes, Bibliographical manual, p. 2472.

2187. England. An intended guyde for English travailers, shewing in generall, how far one citie & many shire-townes in England, are distant from other. By J. Norden. 1 vol. 4to. Lond. 1625.

2188. Itinerarii Galliae et Magnae Britanniae. By M. Zeiller [or Zeiler]. 2 pts. 8vo. Strasburg. 1634.

2189. A character of England as it was lately presented in a letter to a noble man of France. By J. Evelyn. 1 vol. 12mo. Lond. 1659. 3rd ed. 1659.
Repr. in Miscellaneous writings (887). Cf. Gallus Castratus. An answer to a slanderous pamphlet called the character of England [1 vol. 12mo. Lond. 1659]. 3rd ed. has reflections upon Gallus Castratus.

2190. Relation d'un voyage en Angleterre, où sont touchées plusieurs choses qui regardent l'état des sciences et de la religion et autres matières curieuses. By S. de Sorbière. 1 vol. 8vo. Paris. 1664.

A trans. was published [Lond. 1709] with the title, A voyage to England containing many things relating to the state of learning &c. Cf. T. Sprat's Observations on M. de Sorbières voyage [1 vol. 12mo. Lond. 1665] ; and J. J. Jusserand, A French ambassador, &c., pp. 62–4.

2191. Angliae notitia ; or, the present state of England. By E. Chamberlayne. 1 vol. 12mo. Lond. 1669.

A sort of Whitaker's Almanack : very useful. Went through 22 eds. from 1669–1707, being continued by J. Chamberlayne from 1704 onwards. In 1708 and afterwards the title is changed to Magnae Britanniae notitia. The 38th and last ed. is 1755. Ref. to N. and Q. 6th series, 12 ; 7th series, 1 and 2. There was a rival publication by Guy Miège, The present state of England. 1 vol. 12mo. Lond. 1683. After 1707 the title changes to The present state of Great Britain.

2192. Le voyageur d'Europe où sont les voyages de France . . . d'Angleterre. . . . By A. Jouvin de Rochefort. 6 vols. 12mo. Paris. 1672. Maps.

The section relating to England and Ireland was trans. and pr. in The Antiquarian Repertory, ed. 1809, iv. 549–622.

2193. Britannia, or a geographical description of the kingdoms of England, Scotland and Ireland, with the isles and territories [i. e. plantations]. By R. Blome. 1 vol. fol. Lond. 1673. Maps of counties.

Part of the above was privately repr. in folio, 1892, as An alphabetical account of the nobility and gentry of England and Wales.

2194. Britannia. Or an illustration of the kingdom of England and the dominion of Wales by a geographical and historical description of the principal roads. By J. Ogilby. 1 vol. fol. Lond. 1675. Maps.

Cf. Ogilby's The traveller's guide, or a most exact description of the roads of England [1 vol. 8vo. Lond. 1699. Map], and his An actual survey of all the principal roads of England and Wales, described by one hundred maps . . . improved and corrected by C. J. Senex [2 vols. 4to. Lond. 1719].

2195. The kingdome of England and principality of Wales exactly described . . . in six mappes . . . useful for all commanders and quartering of souldiers. By W. Hollar. 6 sheets 4to. Lond. 1676.

The first general maps marking the roads. 1st ed. 1644.

2196. Index villaris, or an alphabetical table of all the cities, market-towns, parishes, villages and private seats in England and Wales. By J. Adams. 1 vol. fol. Lond. 1680.

In ed. of 1690 [fol. Lond.] a list of the nobility and their seats is added.

2197. Memoires et observations faites par un voyageur en Angleterre. By H. Misson de Valbourg. 1 vol. 8vo. The Hague. 1698. Illus.

Apparently Misson visited England in 1697. An English trans. by Ozell appeared in 1719.

2198. Anglia rediviva : being a full description of all the shires, cities, principal towns and rivers in England. By S. Dunstar. 1 vol. 8vo. Lond. 1699.

2199. Travels over England, Scotland and Wales, giving a true and exact description of the chiefest cities, towns and corporations. By J. Brome. 1 vol. 8vo. Lond. 1700. Later ed. 1707.

Mainly antiquarian.

2200. A journey through England in familiar letters from a gentleman here to his friend abroad. By J. Macky. 2 vols. 8vo. Lond. 1714–22.

The intro. to vol. ii explains that the delay in its appearance was due to political reasons, and that it was now publ. to refute Misson's Memoirs (2197). A third vol., A journey through Scotland, appeared in 1723, 2nd ed. 1729, both eds. in 8vo. Lond.

2201. Lettres sur les Anglais et les Français. By B. L. Muralt. 1 vol. 8vo. Cologne. 1725. Later ed. 1 vol. 8vo. Bern. 1897. Ed. by O. von Greyerz.

A description of England temp. William III. Trans. as Letters describing the character and customs of the English and French nations [1 vol. 8vo. Lond. 1726].

2202. Itineraries. By J. Ray.

Pr. in Selected remains of . . . John Ray . . . with his life by W. Derham [1 vol. 8vo. Lond. 1760].

2203. Natural and political observations and conclusions upon the state and condition of England, 1696. By G. King. 1 vol. 8vo. Lond. 1810. Ed. by G. Chalmers.

Cf. No. 1897.

2204. Travels of Cosmo, the third Grand Duke of Tuscany, through England [in 1669] . . . translated from the Italian manuscript in the Laurentian library at Florence. By Count Lorenzo Magalotti. 1 vol. 4to. Lond. 1821. Views.

2205. Travels in Holland, the United Provinces, England, Scotland, and Ireland, 1634–1635. By Sir W. Brereton. Ed. by E. Hawkins. Chetham Soc. 1844.

2206. England as seen by foreigners in the days of Elizabeth and James the First. By W. B. Rye. 1 vol. 4to. Lond. 1865.

2207. Through England on a side saddle in the time of William and Mary, being the diary of Celia Fiennes. By C. Fiennes. Ed. by E. W. Griffiths. 1 vol. 8vo. Lond. 1888.

2208. Foreign visitors in England, and what they have thought of us : being some notes on their books and their opinions during the last three centuries. By E. Smith. 1 vol. 8vo. Lond. 1889.

2209. Thomas Baskerville's journeys in England, temp. Car. II. In Hist. MSS. Comm. Portland MSS. ii. 1893.

2210. A relation of a short survey of 26 counties observed in a seven weeks journey begun on August 11, 1634 by a captain, a lieutenant and an ancient. Ed. by L. G. W. Legg. 1 vol. 8vo. Lond. 1904.

MS. in Lansdowne MS. 213, Brit. Mus.

2211. Roads in England and Wales in 1603. Ed. by G. S. Thomson. Eng. Hist. Rev. xxxiii. 1918.

Lists of roads to London from different localities.

2212. Travel in England in the seventeenth century. By J. Parkes. 1 vol. 8vo. Lond. 1925. Illus. Bibl.

¶ 3. EDUCATION

(a) SOURCES

2213. The curriculum and text books of English schools in the first half of the seventeenth century. By F. Watson. Trans. of the Bibliographical Soc., vol. vi. Pt. ii. 1903.

A full bibliography. Cf. The same author's Notices of some early English writers on education, 1578–1603. United States Bureau of education, ch. viii. 8vo. Washington. 1905. This contains many items in use in the seventeenth century.

2214. The two bookes of Francis Bacon of the advancement and proficiencies of learning, divine and humane. By Francis Bacon, Viscount St. Albans. 1 vol. 4to. Lond. 1605.

The above ed. is the first in English. Cf. No. 816.

2215. Ludus literarius : or, the grammar schoole. By J. Brinsley. 1 vol. sm. 4to. Lond. 1612 and 1627. Later ed. 1 vol. 8vo. Liverpool. 1917. Ed. by E. T. Campagnac.

2216. Ἡγεμὼν εἰς τὰς Γλῶσσας id est Ductor in Linguas. The Guide into Tongues. By J. Minsheu. 1 vol. fol. Lond. 1617.

2217. An apologie for schoolemasters, tending to the advancement of learning and the vertuous education of children. By T. Morrice. 1 vol. 8vo. Lond. 1619.

2218. A reformation of schools, designed in two excellent treatises . . . [and continuation]. By S. Hartlib. 1 vol. 4to. Lond. 1642–8.

2219. Of education. To Master Samuel Hartlib. By J. Milton. 1 vol. 4to. Lond. 1644. Later ed. 1 vol. 8vo. Camb. 1895. Ed. by O. Browning.

2220. The advice of W.P. to Mr. S. Hartlib for the advancement of some particular parts of learning. By Sir W. Petty. 1 vol. 4to. Lond. 1648.

2221. The reformed school. By J. Durie [or Dury]. 1 vol. 12mo. Lond. [1649 ?].

Cf. Dury's The reformed libraree-keeper. With a supplement to The reformed school [1 vol. 12mo. Lond. 1650].

2222. Academiarum examen, or the examination of academies wherein is discussed . . . academick and scholastick learning. By J. Webster. 1 vol. sm. 4to. Lond. 1654.

Advocates university reform. Cf. S. Ward's Vindiciae academiarum, containing some briefe animadversions upon Mr. Webster's book [1 vol. sm. 4to. Oxf. 1654].

2223. A true and ready way to learne the Latine tongue . . . By S. Hartlib.
1 vol. 4to. Lond. 1654.

2224. The history of the University of Cambridge. By T. Fuller. Lond.
1655. Later ed. 1 vol. 8vo. Lond. 1840. Ed. by J. Nichols.
Originally part v. of Fuller's Church history (1416).

2225. A new discovery of the old art of teaching schoole, in four small
treatises. By C. Hoole. 1 vol. 8vo. Lond. 1660. Later ed. 1 vol. 8vo. Liverpool. 1913. Bibl. index. Ed. by E. T. Campagnac.

2226. A discourse concerning schools and schoolmasters. By M. Nedham.
1 vol. 4to. 1663.

2227. An essay to revive the ancient education of gentlewomen in religion,
manners, arts and tongues. By B. Makin. 1 vol. 4to. 1673.

2228. Of education, especially of young gentlemen. In two parts. By O.
Walker. 1 vol. 8vo. Oxf. 1673. Later ed. 1687.

2229. Considerations concerning the free schools as settled in England. By
C. Wase. 1 vol. 8vo. Oxf. 1678.
Has much information about grammar schools.

2230. The lady's new-years gift or advice to a daughter. By George
Savile, Marquis of Halifax. 1 vol. 12mo. Lond. 1688.
For a bibliography and annotated reprint see H. C. Foxcroft's Life of Halifax, ii.
379–424.

2231. Athenae Oxonienses. An exact history of all the writers and bishops
who have had their education in the University of Oxford. To which are
added the Fasti or annals of the said University. By Anthony à Wood.
2 vols. fol. Lond. 1691–2. Later eds. 1721 ; and 4 vols. 4to. Lond. 1813–20.
Ed. by P. Bliss.
A series of short biographies. Valuable, but needs revision from Wood's MSS. in the
Bodl. Libr.

2232. Some thoughts concerning education. By J. Locke. 1 vol. 8vo.
Lond. 1693. Later ed. 1 vol. 8vo. Camb. 1898. Ed. by R. H. Quick.
Repr. together with Of the conduct of the understanding, in The educational writings
of John Locke, ed. by J. W. Adamson [1 vol. 8vo. Lond. 1912].

2233. Reflections upon ancient and modern learning. By W. Wotton.
1 vol. 8vo. Lond. 1694. 2nd ed. 1 vol. 8vo. Lond. 1697.
The 2nd ed. is prefixed to the first ed. of Bentley's Dissertation upon the epistles of
Phalaris.

2234. The most natural and easie way of institution ; containing proposals
for making a domestic education less chargeable to parents, and more easie
and beneficial to children. By R. Ainsworth. 1 vol. 4to. Lond. 1698.

2235. A letter from a country divine to his friend in London concerning the
education of dissenters in their private academies in several parts of this
nation. By S. Wesley. 1 vol. 4to. Lond. 1702.
Written in 1693. This produced an answer from S. Palmer, A defence of the dissenters
education, 1703, and Wesley's rejoinder A defence of a letter, 1704.

2236. Reliquiae Bodleianae or some genuine remains of Sir Thomas Bodley containing his life, the first draught of the statutes of the publick library at Oxford (in English) and a collection of letters. 1 vol. 8vo. Lond. 1703.

2237. An account of charity-schools in Great Britain and Ireland : with the benefactions thereto. Anon. 1704. 13th ed. with additions 1 vol. 8vo. Lond. 1714.

Has useful lists. The first ed. is appended to A sermon preached in the parish of St. Andrews, Holborn, June 8, 1704, by R. Willis. Cf. An account of the methods whereby the charity-schools have been erected and managed.

2238. Two dialogues . . . on education and on the respect due to age. By Edward Hyde, Earl of Clarendon. 1727.

First appeared in Clarendon's Miscellaneous works, 1 vol. fol. Lond. 1727. 2nd ed. 1751.

2239. Life and literary remains of Ralph Bathurst, Dean of Wells and President of Trinity College in Oxford. By T. Warton. 1 vol. 8vo. Lond. 1761.

2240. Thoughts on education. Now first published from an original manuscript. By G. Burnet, Bp. of Salisbury. 1 vol. 8vo. Lond. 1761.

Written about 1668. Cf. Bishop Gilbert Burnet as educationist, being his thoughts on education, with notes and life of the author. By J. Clarke. 8vo. Aberdeen. 1914.

2241. The history and antiquities of the University of Oxford. By Anthony à Wood. Ed. by J. Gutch. 3 vols. 4to. Oxf. 1792–6.

First publ. in Latin as Historia et antiquitates, &c. in 1674. The Latin ed. ended in 1649, the English in 1660.

2242. Annals of Cambridge. By C. H. Cooper. 5 vols. 8vo. Camb. 1842–1908.

Vols. iii and iv cover 1603–1714.

2243. Documents relating to the University and colleges of Cambridge. 3 vols. 8vo. Lond. 1852.

2244. Statutes of the colleges of Oxford with royal patents of foundation ; injunction of visitors . . . 3 vols. 8vo. Oxf. and Lond. 1853.

2245. Cambridge University transactions during the Puritan controversies of the 16th and 17th centuries. Ed. by J. Heywood and T. Wright. 2 vols. 8vo. Lond. 1854.

Mainly official documents ending *c.* 1661.

2246. Athenae Cantabrigienses. I. 1500–85. II. 1586–1609. III. 1609–11. By C. H. Cooper and T. Cooper. 3 vols. 8vo. Camb. 1858–1913.

2247. The register of the visitors of the University of Oxford, 1647–1658 . . . with some account of the state of the University during the Commonwealth. Ed. by M. Burrows. 1 vol. Camd. Soc. 1881.

2248. Remarks and collections of Thomas Hearne. By T. Hearne. Ed. by C. E. Doble, D. W. Rannie, and H. E. Salter. 11 vols. 8vo. Oxf. Hist. Soc. Oxf. 1885–1918.

' Contains fragments of the materials ' Hearne used in his historical works and ' memoranda on any subject that attracted his attention at the moment '. Preface, vol. i. Covers 1705–35. A selection of the material was publ. by P. Bliss [2 vols. 8vo. Oxf. 1857 ; and 3 vols. 8vo. Lond. 1869].

2249. Statutes of the University of Oxford codified in the year 1636 under the authority of Archbishop Laud. Ed. by J. Griffiths and C. L. Shadwell. 1 vol. 4to. Oxf. 1888.

For Laud's account of his chancellorship see Works (1530) vol. v. It was first pr. in vol. ii of H. Wharton's ed. of Laud's Remains, 1700.

2250. Magdalen College and King James II, 1686–1688. A series of documents. Ed. by J. R. Bloxam. 1 vol. 8vo. Oxf. Hist. Soc. Oxf. 1886. Bibl. of MSS.

Comprehensive, but its utility is diminished by the way in which narratives are split up to illustrate what happened on particular days.

2251. Register of the University of Oxford. Vol. ii, 1571–1622. Ed. by A. Clark. 4 pts. 8vo. Oxf. Hist. Soc. Oxf. 1887–9.

2252. Alumni Oxonienses, being the matriculation register of the university 1500–1714. Ed. by J. Foster. 4 vols. 8vo. Oxf. 1891–2.

Cf. The historical register of the University of Oxford . . . an alphabetical record of University honours and distinctions completed to . . . 1900. 1 vol. 8vo. Oxf. 1900.

2253. The life and times of Anthony Wood, antiquary, of Oxford, 1632–95, described by himself. Ed. by A. Clark. 5 vols. 8vo. Oxf. Hist. Soc. Oxf. 1891. Illus.

Vol. i, 1632–63 ; ii, 1664–81 ; iii, 1682–95 ; iv. Addenda (including a catalogue of MS. authorities) ; v, Indexes.

2254. Early Yorkshire schools. Ed. by A. F. Leach. Yorkshire Archaeological Soc. Record Series, xxvii, xxxiii, 1898, 1903.

Prints some 17th-century documents.

2255. The Flemings in Oxford, being documents selected from the Rydal papers in illustration of the lives and ways of Oxford men, 1650–1700. Ed. by J. R. Magrath. 3 vols. 8vo. Oxf. Hist. Soc. Oxf. 1904–24. Illus.

Vol. i, 1650–80 ; ii, 1680–90 ; iii, 1691–1700.

2256. Letters of Dorothy Wadham, 1609–18. Ed. by R. B. Gardiner. 1 vol. Lond. 1904.

2257. Endowments of the University of Cambridge. Ed. by J. W. Clark. 1 vol. 8vo. Camb. 1904.

Valuable.

2258. Cambridge under Queen Anne, illustrated by memoir of Ambrose Bonwicke and diaries of Francis Burman and Zacharias Conrad von Uffenbach. By J. E. B. Mayor. Preface by M. R. James. 1 vol. 8vo. Camb. 1911.

The memoir of Bonwicke was publ. separately as Life of Ambrose Bonwicke, by his father [1 vol. 8vo. Camb. 1870].

2259. Educational charters and documents 598 to 1909. Ed. by A. F. Leach. 1 vol. 8vo. Camb. 1911.

2260. Enactments in Parliament specially concerning the Universities of Oxford and Cambridge and halls therein and the colleges of Winchester, Eton and Westminster. Ed. by L. L. Shadwell. 4 vols. 8vo. Oxf. Hist. Soc. Oxf. 1912.

Vol. i, 37 Edward III–13 Anne.

2261. Documents illustrating early education in Worcester, 685 to 1700. Ed. by A. F. Leach. Worc. Hist. Soc. 4to. 1913.

Introduction is valuable.

2262. Alumni Cantabrigienses, a biographical list of all known students, graduates and holders of office at the University of Cambridge. Part I. From the earliest times to 1751. By J. Venn and J. A. Venn. 4to. Camb. 1922. In progress.

Cf. The same author's The book of matriculation and degrees : a catalogue of those who have been matriculated or been admitted to any degree in the University of Cambridge from 1544 to 1659 [1 vol. 8vo. Camb. 1913] ; and J. R. Tanner's The historical register of the University of Cambridge . . . a record of university honours and distinctions to the year 1910 [1 vol. 8vo. Camb. 1917].

(b) LATER WORKS

2263. The history of the colleges of Winchester, Eton and Westminster, with the Charter-house, the schools of St. Paul's, Merchant Taylors, Harrow and Rugby and the free-school of Christ's Hospital. By R. Ackermann. 1 vol. 4to. Lond. 1816.

The same author also wrote : History of the University of Oxford [2 vols. 4to. Lond. 1814], and History of Cambridge, its colleges, halls and public buildings [2 vols. 4to. Lond. 1815].

2264. A concise description of the endowed grammar schools in England and Wales, ornamented with engravings. By N. Carlisle. 2 vols. 8vo. Lond. 1818.

2265. The life of Richard Bentley, Master of Trinity College [Cambridge]. By J. H. Monk. 1 vol. 4to. Lond. 1830. Later eds. 2 vols. 8vo. Lond. 1833.

Cf. Sir R. C. Jebb's Bentley in the English Men of Letters series [1882] ; and Richard Bentley, D.D., a bibliography of his works and of all the literature called forth by his acts or writings, ed. by A. T. Bartholomew, with intro. by J. W. Clark [1 vol. 8vo. Camb. 1908].

2266. College life in the time of James I as illustrated by an unpublished diary of Sir Symonds D'Ewes. Ed. by J. O. Halliwell-Phillipps. 1 vol. 8vo. Lond. 1851.

2267. The great schools of England : an account of the foundation endowments and discipline of the chief seminaries of learning in England. By H. Staunton. 1 vol. 8vo. Lond. 1865.

2268. History of the college of St. John [Cambridge]. By T. Baker. Ed. by J. E. B. Mayor. 2 vols. 8vo. Camb. 1869.

In addition to the series of College histories published by Robinson *c*. 1900–6 [1 vol. 8vo. Lond. for each college], there are also : Admissions to the college of St. John, ed. J. E. B. Mayor [2 vols. 8vo. Camb. 1882–93], Biographical history of Gonville and Caius college, 1349–1897, ed. by J. Venn [4 vols. Camb. 1897–1912] ; Biographical register of Christ's College, 1505–1905, ed. J. Peile [2 vols. 8vo. Camb. 1910–13] ; Admissions to Trinity College, ed. by W. W. Rouse Ball and J. A. Venn [5 vols. 8vo. Lond. 1911–16] ; Admissions to Peterhouse, ed. T. A. Walker [1 vol. 8vo. Camb. 1912].

2269. Lives of the founders of the British Museum ; with notices of its chief augmentors and other benefactors 1570–1870. By E. Edwards. 1 vol. 8vo. Lond. 1870.

2270. The University of Cambridge. By J. B. Mullinger. 3 vols. 8vo. Camb. 1873–1911.

Vol. ii covers 1535–1625 ; vol. iii, 1626–*c*. 1670.

2271. Social life at the English universities in the eighteenth century. By C. Wordsworth. 1 vol. 8vo. Camb. 1874.

Cf. The same author's Scholae academicae : some account of the studies at the English universities in the eighteenth century [1 vol. 8vo. Camb. 1877]. Both these works have useful materials for the 17th century.

2272. A history of Eton College, 1440–1875. By Sir H. C. Maxwell Lyte. 1 vol. 8vo. Lond. 1875. Illus. 4th ed. 1911.

2273. Schools, school-books and schoolmasters. By W. C. Hazlitt. 1 vol. 8vo. Lond. 1888.

Much miscellaneous information. Cf. the same author's Farther contributions towards a history of earlier education in Great Britain. The Antiquary, No. 109, new series. Jan. 1899–July 1900.

2274. The colleges of Oxford : their history and traditions. Ed. by A. Clark. 1 vol. 8vo. Lond. 1891.

In addition to a series of College histories published by Robinson *c*. 1900 [1 vol. 8vo. Lond. for each college] the following histories should be noted : Merton, by G. C. Brodrick ; Corpus Christi, by T. Fowler ; and Pembroke, by D. Macleane [all publ. by the Oxf. Hist. Society in 1885, 1893, and 1897 respectively] ; Brasenose College quatercentenary monographs [3 vols. 8vo. Oxf. 1909–10. Illus.] ; and The Queen's College, by J. R. Magrath [2 vols. 4to. Oxf. 1921. Illus.]. There are also : A register of the presidents, fellows, demies . . . of Magdalen College, ed. by J. R. Bloxam and W. D. Macray [15 vols. 8vo. 1853–1915] ; Register of the rectors and fellows, scholars, exhibitioners . . . of Exeter College . . . with illustrative documents, ed. by C. W. Boase [1 vol. 4to. Exeter. 1879 ; later ed. called Registrum Collegii Exoniensis, 1 vol. 8vo. Oxf. 1894] ; The registers of Wadham College, Part i. from 1613 to 1719, ed. by R. B. Gardiner [1 vol. 8vo. Lond. 1889] ; Registrum Orielense, an account of the members of Oriel College, ed. by C. L. Shadwell [2 vols. 8vo. Lond. 1893–1902].

2275. Memoir of Richard Busby (1606–95), with some account of Westminster School during the 17th century. By G. F. R. Barker. 1 vol. 8vo. Lond. 1895. 2 ports.

Cf. A True and perfect narrative of the differences between Mr. Busby and Mr. Bagshawe, the first and second masters of Westminster School. 1 vol. 4to. Lond. 1659.

2276. Two hundred years : the history of the society for promoting Christian knowledge, 1698–1898. By W. O. B. Allen and E. McClure. 1 vol. 8vo. Lond. 1898.

2277. Annals of Westminster School. By J. Sargeaunt. 1 vol. 8vo. Lond. 1898.

2278. A history of Winchester College. By A. F. Leach. 1 vol. 8vo. Lond. 1899. Illus.

2279. The state and education during the Commonwealth. By F. Watson. Eng. Hist. Rev. xv. 1900.

2280. State intervention in English education [to 1833]. By J. E. G. De Montmorency. 1 vol. 8vo. Camb. 1902.

Has useful information, which is also true of the same writer's The progress of education in England [1 vol. 8vo. Lond. 1904].

2281. Early nonconformity and education. By A. Gordon. 1 vol. 8vo. Manch. 1902.

2282. Pioneers of modern education. 1600–1700. By J. W. Adamson. 1 vol. 8vo. Camb. 1905. Bibl.

2283. The English grammar schools to 1660, their curriculum and practice. By F. Watson. 1 vol. 8vo. Camb. 1908.

2284. Schola regia Cantuariensis. A history of Canterbury school, commonly called the king's school. By C. E. Woodruff and H. J. Capes. 1 vol. 8vo. Lond. 1908.

2285. The beginnings of the teaching of modern subjects in England. By F. Watson. 1 vol. 8vo. Lond. 1909.

The bibliographical notes are of the utmost value.

2286. English grammar schools. By J. B. Mullinger. Camb. Hist. of Eng. Lit. vii. 1911. ch. xiv.

The bibliography includes a list of the chief public schools [to 1650] and of histories of them.

2287. Scholars and scholarship, 1600–60. By F. Watson. Camb. Hist. of Eng. Lit. vii. 1911.

The bibliography is very detailed and valuable.

2288. Education. By J. W. Adamson. Camb. Hist. of Eng. Lit. ix. 1912. ch. xv.

Covers *c*. 1660–1760 : a useful bibliography is appended.

2289. Scholars and antiquaries. I. Bentley and classical scholarship. II. Antiquaries. By J. D. Duff and H. G. Aldis. Camb. Hist. of Eng. Lit. ix. 1912. ch. xiii.

The bibliographies are valuable. Cf. Sir John Edwin Sandys, A history of classical scholarship, vol. ii. From the revival of learning to the end of the eighteenth century [8vo. Camb. 1908].

2290. Early collegiate life. By J. Venn. 1 vol. 8vo. Camb. 1913.

2291. Dissenting academies in England. By I. Parker. 1 vol. 8vo. Camb. 1914. Bibl.

App. I has list of academies.

2292. The old grammar schools. By F. Watson. 1 vol. 8vo. Camb. 1916. Illus. Bibl.

2293. The teaching and cultivation of the French language in England during Tudor and Stuart times. By K. Lambley. 1 vol. 8vo. Manchester Univ. Press. 1920.

An excellent piece of research.

2294. The learned lady in England, 1650–1760. By M. Reynolds. 1 vol. 8vo. Camb. (Mass.). 1920.

Valuable for education of women : a good bibliography.

2295. Samuel Hartlib. A sketch of his life and his relations to J. A. Comenius. By G. H. Turnbull. 1 vol. 8vo. Oxf. 1920.

Cf. H. Dircks, A biographical memoir of Samuel Hartlib . . . with bibliographical notices of works published by him. 1 vol. 8vo. Lond. 1865.

2296. A history of the University of Oxford. By Sir C. E. Mallet. 2 vols. 8vo. Lond. 1924. Illus.

Vol. i, The mediaeval university ; vol. ii, The 16th and 17th centuries.

VII. LITERATURE, BALLADS, AND JOURNALISM

1. General Bibliographies and Sources.
2. General Later Works.
3. Collections of Plays, Poems, and other Literary Pieces.
4. Biographies and Works of Individuals.
5. Ballads.
6. Journalism.
    (*a*) Newspapers. (*b*) History of Journalism.

LITERARY periods do not correspond with political. The year 1603 does not mark the close of 'the Elizabethan Age ' : 1714 falls within the ' Augustan Age '. To this difficulty arising from the vagueness of chrono- logical limits is added the relative paucity of titles that can be here included. Therefore the selection becomes exceptionally arbitrary. All that has been attempted with regard to the sources is to indicate the most complete editions of the works of the chief writers, and the most useful bibliographies of, and commentaries on, their writings. The principles adopted in selecting the later works are two : to endeavour to cover a very wide field by the inclusion of at least one work on each branch of literature, and to prefer works containing bibliographies. Since literary bibliographies are both numerous and detailed, it is hoped that this section will provide historians with adequate guidance to the literature of the seventeenth century. Its existence in an historical biblio- graphy calls attention to the interdependence of history and literature. Neither can be profitably studied in any detail without an adequate knowledge of the other.

¶ 1. GENERAL BIBLIOGRAPHIES AND SOURCES

2297. A dictionary of old English plays . . . to the close of the seventeenth century. By J. O. Halliwell. 1 vol. 8vo. Lond. 1860.

2298. Collections and notes. By W. C. Hazlitt. 7 vols. 8vo. Lond. 1876– 1903.

After vol. i the title is Second [or Third or Fourth] series of bibliographical collections and notes on early English literature.

2299. A bibliographical account of English theatrical literature. From the earliest times to the present day. By R. W. Lowe. 1 vol. 8vo. Lond. 1888.

2300. A list of English plays written before 1643 and printed before 1700. By W. W. Greg. 1 vol. 4to. Lond. 1900.

Cf. A list of masques, pageants . . . written before 1643 and printed before 1700, 1902, by the same author. Both works were publ. by the Bibliographical Soc.

2301. A list of English tales and prose romances printed before 1740. By A. Esdaile. 1 vol. 4to. Lond. 1912.

2302. [Catalogue of] the Ashley Library . . . collected by T. J. Wise. 8 vols. 4to. Lond. 1921–6.

An elaborate work with many facsimiles : index still to appear.

2303. [Annual] bibliography of English language and literature. Compiled by members of the Modern Humanities Research Association. Ed. by A. C. Paues [2–5] and D. Everett [6]. Camb. 1921. In progress.

The best current bibliography.

2304. A bibliography of English character-books 1608–1700. By G. Murphy. 1 vol. 4to. Oxf. 1925.

2305. An apology for actors. By T. Heywood. 1 vol. 4to. Lond. 1612.

Repr. in Somer's Tracts, ed. 1809–15, vol. iii. 574–600, and ed. J. P. Collier for the Shakespeare Soc. 1841.

2306. Histrio-mastix. The players scourge or actors tragaedie, divided into two parts. . . . By W. Prynne. 1 vol. 4to. Lond. 1633.

For bibliographies of Prynne's writings see Wood's Athenae Oxonienses, 3rd ed., ed. P. Bliss, vol. iii, pp. 844 ff. ; and Documents relating to the proceedings against Prynne, 1634 and 1637, ed. by S. R. Gardiner, Camd. Soc. 1877.

2307. Theatrum redivivum ; or the theatre vindicated in answer to Mr. Prynne's Histrio-Mastix. By Sir R. Baker. 1 vol. 8vo. Lond. 1662.

2308. Theatrum poetarum, or a compleat collection of the poets. By E. Phillips. 1 vol. 12mo. Lond. 1675.

2309. The lives of the most famous English poets. By W. Winstanley. 1 vol. 8vo. Lond. 1687.

2310. A short view of tragedy. By T. Rymer. 1 vol. 8vo. Lond. 1693.

Cf. Rymer's The tragedies of the last age considered and examined. 1 vol. 8vo. Lond. 1678, and 1692.

2311. A short view of the immorality and profaneness of the English stage. Together with the sense of antiquity upon this argument. By J. Collier. 1 vol. 8vo. Lond. 1698.

For a bibliography of the controversy on the immorality of the English stage see Camb. Hist. of Eng. Lit., vol. viii, pp. 432 ff. ; also J. Ballein, Jeremy Collier's Angriff auf die Englische Bühne. Marburg, 1910; and J. W. Krutch, Comedy and conscience after the restoration. 1 vol. 8vo. N.Y. 1924.

2312. The lives and characters of the English dramatick poets. Also an exact account of all the plays that were ever yet printed in the English tongue [to 1698]. By G. Langbaine. Ed. by C. Gildon. 1 vol. 8vo. Lond. 1699.

Said to be ' begun by Mr. Langbain, improved and continued by a careful hand ', i. e. Gildon. First publ., without Gildon's revision, in 1691.

2313. Historia histrionica. By J. Wright. 1 vol. 8vo. Lond. 1699.

Repr. in Dodsley's Old plays, ed. Hazlitt, xv, and in Lowe's ed. of Cibber's Apology.

2314. Roscius Anglicanus, or an historical review of the stage from 1660 to 1706. By J. Downes. 1 vol. 8vo. Lond. 1708.

Repr. in facsimile 1886.

2315. The English drama and stage under the Tudor and Stuart princes, 1543–1664. Illustrated by a series of documents, treatises and poems. Ed. by W. C. Hazlitt. 1 vol. 4to. s.l. 1869.

2316. The dramatic records of Sir Henry Herbert, master of the revels, 1623–1673. Ed. by J. Q. Adams. 1 vol. 8vo. Yale University Press. 1917.
Cf. The seventeenth century accounts of the masters of the revels. By C. C. Stopes. 1 vol. 8vo. Lond. 1922.

2317. Characters from the histories and memoirs of the seventeenth century with an essay on the character. Ed. by D. N. Smith. 1 vol. 8vo. Oxf. 1920.

¶ 2. GENERAL LATER WORKS

2318. The companion to the play-house. By D. E. Baker. 2 vols. 12mo. Lond. 1764. Later ed. 3 vols. 8vo. Lond. 1812. Ed. by S. Jones.
The later eds. are entitled Biographia dramatica, or a companion to the playhouse.

2319. Prefaces biographical and critical to the works of the English poets. By S. Johnson. 10 vols. 12mo. Lond. 1779–81. Later eds. 3 vols. 8vo. Lond. 1854. Ed. by P. Cunningham. 3 vols. 8vo. Oxf. 1905. Ed. by G. B. Hill.
Known as Lives of the English poets.

2320. Essays illustrative of the Tatler, Spectator, and Guardian. By N. Drake. 3 vols. 16mo. Lond. 1805.

2321. Literary anecdotes of the eighteenth century. By J. Nichols. 9 vols. 8vo. Lond. 1812.
Cf. the same writer's Illustrations of the literary history of the eighteenth century [8 vols. 8vo. Lond. 1817]. Both have 17th-century material, especially the Anecdotes.

2322. History of fiction. By J. C. Dunlop. 3 vols. 8vo. Edinburgh. 1814. Later ed. 2 vols. 8vo. Lond. 1888. Ed. by H. Wilson.

2323. Some account of the English stage from the Restoration in 1660 to 1830. By J. Genest. 10 vols. 8vo. Bath. 1832.
An attempt to discover the date when each play was first acted.

2324. Histoire de la littérature anglaise. By H. A. Taine. 4 vols. 8vo. Paris. 1863–4. Later ed. 5 vols. 8vo. Paris. 1892–5. With index.
Trans. by H. Van Laun. 2 vols. 8vo. Edin. 1871 and 1872.

2325. History of English dramatic literature down to Queen Anne. By Sir A. W. Ward. 2 vols. 8vo. Lond. 1875. Later ed. 3 vols. 8vo. Lond. 1899.

2326. Le public et les hommes de lettres en Angleterre au dix-huitième siècle, 1660–1744. By A. Beljame. 1 vol. 8vo. Paris. 1881. Bibl. Later ed. 1 vol. 8vo. Paris. 1897. with index and Bibl.

2327. Seventeenth century studies. By E. Gosse. 1 vol. 8vo. Lond. 1883. Later ed. 1 vol. 8vo. Lond. 1913.
Essays on Thomas Lodge, John Webster, Samuel Rowlands, Dover's Cotswold games, Robert Herrick, Richard Crashaw, Abraham Cowley, The Matchless Orinda, Sir George Etherege.

2328. A history of Elizabethan literature. By G. Saintsbury. 1 vol. sm. 8vo. Lond. 1887.

Covers the period 1560–1660.

2329. Le roman au temps de Shakespeare. By J. J. Jusserand. 1 vol. 8vo. Paris. 1887.

Tr. by E. Lee under title The English novel in the time of Shakespeare, 8vo. Lond. 1890, 3rd ed. 1899.

2330. A chronicle history of the London stage 1559–1642. By F. G. Fleay. 1 vol. 8vo. Lond. 1890.

2331. A biographical chronicle of the English drama, 1559–1642. By F. G. Fleay. 2 vols. 8vo. Lond. 1891.

2332. The child and his book. Some account of the history and progress of children's literature in England. By E. M. Field. 1 vol. 8vo. Lond. 1891.

2333. Histoire littéraire du peuple anglais. By J. J. Jusserand. 2 vols. 8vo. Paris. 1894–1904.

Trans. as A literary history of the English people [3 vols. 8vo. Lond. 1906–09. Illus.]. Vols. ii and iii are entitled : From the Renaissance to the Civil War.

2334. History of English poetry. By W. J. Courthope. 6 vols. 8vo. Lond. 1895–1910.

Vols. iii. and iv cover the 17th century.

2335. La littérature comparée. Essai bibliographique. By L. P. Betz. 1 vol. 8vo. Strasburg. 1900.

Includes a bibliography of works on Anglo-French literary relations.

2336. Puritan and Anglican : studies in literature. By E. Dowden. 1 vol. 8vo. Lond. 1900.

2337. The collected works of William Hazlitt. Ed. by A. R. Waller and A. Glover. 12 vols. 8vo. Lond. and N.Y. 1902–4. Index. vol. 1906.

Includes Lectures on the comic writers.

2338. The English heroic play. A critical description of the rhymed tragedy of the Restoration. By L. N. Chase. 1 vol. 8vo. N.Y. 1903. Bibl.

2339. The temper of the seventeenth century in English literature. By B. Wendell. 1 vol. 8vo. Lond. 1904.

2340. L'influence française en Angleterre au xviie siècle. La vie sociale— la vie littéraire. By L. Charlanne. 1 vol. 8vo. Paris. 1906.

Cf. No. 2183.

2341. The literature of roguery. By F. W. Chandler. 2 vols. 8vo. Lond. 1907. Bibl.

2342. The French influence in English literature from the accession of Elizabeth to the Restoration. By A. H. Upham. 1 vol. 8vo. N.Y. 1908. Bibl.

2343. Elizabethan drama 1558–1642. By F. E. Schelling. 2 vols. 8vo. Lond. and Boston (Mass.) 1908. Bibl.

2344. Les masques anglais. Étude sur les ballets et la vie de cour en Angleterre 1512–1640. By P. Reyher. 1 vol. 8vo. Paris. 1909.

2345. The Cambridge history of English literature. Ed. by Sir A. W. Ward and A. R. Waller. 14 vols. 8vo. Camb.

Vol. iv. 1909 : Prose and poetry, Sir Thomas North to Michael Drayton. Vols. v and vi. 1910 : The drama to 1642. Vol. vii. 1911 : Cavalier and Puritan. Vol. viii : The age of Dryden. Vol. ix. 1912 : From Steele and Addison to Pope and Swift. Each volume has valuable and, generally, detailed and classified bibliographies.

2346. English tragicomedy, its origin and history. By F. H. Ristine. 1 vol. 8vo. N.Y. 1910. Bibl.

2347. The rise of the novel of manners. A study of English prose fiction between 1600 and 1740. By C. E. Morgan. 1 vol. 8vo. N.Y. 1911. Bibl.

2348. The Mary Carleton narratives, 1663–1673 : a missing chapter in the history of the English novel. By E. Bernbaum. 1 vol. 8vo. Camb. (Mass.), 1914.

2349. The academ roial of King James I. Proc. Brit. Academy. vii. 1916. By E. M. Portal.

2350. A contribution to the history of the English Commonwealth drama. By H. E. Rollins.

Reprinted from Studies in Philology, July 1921.

2351. The Elizabethan stage. By E. K. Chambers. 4 vols. 8vo. Oxf. 1923. Illus. Bibl.

2352. A history of Restoration drama, 1660–1700. By A. Nicoll. 1 vol. 8vo. Camb. 1923. Bibl.

Valuable : Continued in his : A history of early eighteenth century drama, 1700–1750. 1 vol. 8vo. Camb. 1925. Bibl.

2353. Histoire de la littérature anglaise. By E. Legouis and L. Cazamian. 1 vol. 8vo. Paris. 1925. Bibl.

Trans. of pt. I by H. D. Irvine as A history of English literature . . . Volume one. The Middle Ages and the Renascence (650–1660). 1 vol. 8vo. Lond. 1926.

2354. Boileau and the French classical critics in England [1660–1830]. 1 vol. 8vo. Paris. 1925.

¶ 3. COLLECTIONS OF PLAYS, POEMS, AND OTHER LITERARY PIECES

2355. The works of the Earls of Rochester, Roscomon and Dorset ; the Dukes of Devonshire, Buckinghamshire . . . 2 vols. 12mo. Lond. 1731. Later ed. 1 vol. 12mo. Lond. 1885.

2356. A select collection of old plays. Ed. by R. Dodsley. 12 vols. 12mo. Lond. 1744. 2nd ed. 12 vols. 8vo. Lond. 1780. Ed. by I. Reed. 3rd ed. 13 vols. 8vo. Lond. 1825-8. Ed. by J. P. Collier. 4th ed. 15 vols. 8vo. Lond. 1874-6. Ed. by W. C. Hazlitt.

Cf. Robert Dodsley, poet, publisher and playwright, by R. Straus, 1 vol. 8vo. Lond. and N.Y. 1910, with bibliography.

2357. The poets of Great Britain complete from Chaucer to Churchill. Ed. by J. Bell. 109 vols. 12mo. Edin. 1776–83.

Cf. Bell's British theatre, consisting of the most esteemed English plays. 20 vols. 12mo. Lond. 1776–8, and 34 vols. 8vo. Lond. 1791–7.

2358. The works of the English poets. Ed. by S. Johnson. 68 vols. 12mo. Lond. 1779–81.

2359. A complete edition of the poets of Great Britain. Ed. by R. Anderson. 13 vols. 8vo. Lond. 1792–4.

2360. The works of the English poets [Chaucer to Cowper]. By A. Chalmers. 21 vols. 8vo. Lond. 1810.

2361. Old English plays, being a selection from the early dramatic writers. Ed. by C. W. Dilke. 6 vols. 8vo. Lond. 1814–15.

Contents listed in Lowndes, p. 1883.

2362. The dramatic works of Wycherley, Congreve, Vanbrugh, and Farquhar, with biographical and critical notices. By J. H. Leigh Hunt. 1 vol. 8vo. Lond. 1840 and 1875.

2363. Dramatists of the Restoration. 14 vols. 8vo. Edin. 1872–9. Ed. by J. Maidment and W. H. Logan.

Repr. the plays of Cokain, Crowne, Davenant, Lacy, Marmion, Tatham, and Wilson.

2364. The Mermaid series : the best plays of the old dramatists. 27 vols. Lond.

Contain generally select plays but sometimes the complete plays of the following : Beaumont and Fletcher, Chapman, Congreve, Dekker, Dryden, Farquhar, Ford, Greene, Heywood, Jonson, Marlowe, Massinger, Middleton, Otway, Shadwell, Shirley, Steele, Vanbrugh, Webster, and Wycherley.

2365. Critical essays and literary fragments. Intro. by J. Churton Collins. 1 vol. 8vo. Westminster. 1903.

Repr. from An English garner.

2366. Minor poets of the Caroline period. Ed. by G. Saintsbury. 3 vols. 8vo. Oxf. 1905–21.

Reprints of the works of 18 poets.

2367. Seventeenth century critical essays. Ed. by J. E. Spingarn. 3 vols. 8vo. Oxf. 1908–9. Bibl.

Extracts and reprints of 17th-century essays, prefaces, &c. Cf. J. Haslewood's Ancient critical essays upon English poets and poesy [2 vols. 4to. 1811–15].

¶ 4. BIOGRAPHIES AND WORKS OF INDIVIDUALS

ADDISON, JOSEPH.

2368. The works of Joseph Addison. Ed. by T. Tickell. 4 vols. 4to. Lond. 1721. Later eds. : 6 vols. 8vo. Lond. 1811. Ed. by R. Hurd. 6 vols. 8vo. Lond. 1854–56 and 1893. Ed. by H. G. Bohn.

For bibliography see Camb. Hist. of Eng. Lit. ix. 1912, pp. 434–8.

ARBUTHNOT, JOHN.

2369. The life and works of John Arbuthnot. By G. A. Aitken. 1 vol. 8vo. Oxf. 1892.

BEAUMONT, FRANCIS, AND FLETCHER, JOHN.

2370. The comedies and tragedies written by Francis Beaumont and John Fletcher, gentlemen. Never printed before. And now published by the authours originall copies. Ed. by J. Shirley. 1 vol. fo. Lond. 1647. Port. Later eds.: 11 vols. 8vo. Lond. 1843–6. Ed. by A. Dyce. 10 vols. 8vo. Camb. 1905–12. Ed. by A. Glover and A. R. Waller.

Cf. A bibliography of Beaumont and Fletcher, by A. C. Potter, Camb. Mass. 1890 ; and Camb. Hist. of Eng. Lit. vi. 435–41.·

BEHN, APHRA.

2371. The works of Aphra Behn. Ed. by M. Summers. 6 vols. 8vo. Lond. 1915.

Her histories and novels were publ. 8vo. Lond. 1696, 7th ed. 2 vols. 8vo. Lond. 1722 ; her plays 2 vols. 8vo. Lond. 1702. An ed. of both was publ. in 6 vols. 8vo. Lond. 1871. The novels were separately ed. by E. A. Baker, 1 vol. 8vo. Lond. 1905.

BETTERTON, THOMAS.

2372. Thomas Betterton. By R. W. Lowe. 1 vol. 8vo. Lond. 1891.

BROWN, THOMAS.

2373. The works of Mr. Thomas Brown, serious and comical, in prose and verse [with J. Drake's life of T. B.]. 3 vols. 8vo. Lond. 1707–8. 5th ed. 5 vols. 12mo. Lond. 1719–21. 9th ed. 4 vols. 12mo. Lond. 1760.

BROWNE, SIR THOMAS.

2374. Sir Thomas Browne's works, including his life and correspondence. Ed. by S. Wilkin. 4 vols. 8vo. Lond. 1835–6. Later ed. 3 vols. 8vo. Lond. 1852–80.

See C. Williams's The bibliography of the Religio Medici (2 vols. 8vo. Norwich, ed. 1907) ; and G. Keynes, A bibliography of Sir Thomas Browne, 1 vol. Camb. 1924.

BROWNE, WILLIAM.

2375. The poems of William Browne. Ed. by G. Goodwin. 2 vols. 8vo. Lond. 1894.

BUCKINGHAM, GEORGE VILLIERS, 2nd DUKE OF.

2376. The Rehearsal, as it was acted at the Theatre Royal. By George Villiers, 2nd Duke of Buckingham. 1 vol. 4to. Lond. 1672. Later eds.: 1 vol. 12mo. Lond. 1868. Ed. by E. Arber. 1 vol. 8vo. Stratford-on-Avon, 1914. Illus. Ed. by M. Summers.

BUCKINGHAMSHIRE, JOHN SHEFFIELD, DUKE OF.

2377. The works of . . . John Sheffield, late Duke of Buckingham. Ed. by J. Henley. 1 vol. 8vo. Lond. 1721. Port. Later eds. : 2 vols. 4to. Lond. 1723. 2 vols. 8vo. Lond. 1729 and 1753.

See the article in the Dict. Nat. Biog. on the various editions of his works and the censorship of them by the government. Cf. No. 826.

BURTON, ROBERT.

2378. The anatomy of melancholy, what it is, with all the kindes, causes, symptoms, prognosticks, and several cures of it. By R. Burton. 1 vol. 4to. Oxf. 1621. Later ed. 3 vols. 8vo. Lond. 1893. Ed. by A. H. Bullen and A. R. Shilleto.

See Camb. Hist. of Eng. Lit. iv. 496–9.

BUTLER, SAMUEL.

2379. Hudibras. By S. Butler. 3 parts. 8vo. Lond. 1663–78. Later eds. : 2 vols. 8vo. Camb. 1744. Illus. by Hogarth. Ed. by Zachary Grey. 1 vol. 8vo. Camb. 1905. Ed. by A. R. Waller.

The genuine remains in verse and prose of Mr. Samuel Butler, ed. by R. Thyer, were publ. 2 vols. 8vo. Lond. 1759, and 2 vols. 12mo. Lond. 1893, Bibl., ed. by R. B. Johnson. His characters and passages from note-books were ed. by A. R. Waller, 1 vol. 8vo. Camb. 1908.

CAREY, PATRICK.

2380. Trivial poems and triolets. Written . . . 1651. By P. Carey. Ed. by Sir W. Scott. 1 vol. 4to. Lond. 1820.

CHAPMAN, GEORGE.

2381. The works of George Chapman. 3 vols. 8vo. Lond. 1873. Later eds. 3 vols. 8vo. Lond. 1874–5 and 1889. Ed. by R. H. Shepherd.

In ed. of 1874–5, vol. i is Plays ; ii, Poems (with an introduction by A. C. Swinburne) ; iii, Iliad and Odyssey.

CIBBER, COLLEY.

2382. An apology for the life of Mr. Colley Cibber, comedian. By C. Cibber. 1 vol. 4to. Lond. 1740. Later ed. 2 vols. 8vo. Lond. 1889. Illus. Ed. by R. W. Lowe.

The ed. of 1889 repr. A brief supplement to Colley Cibber, Esq. ; his lives of the late famous actors and actresses. By A. Aston [1 vol. 8vo. ? Lond. ? 1748].

2383. The dramatic works of Colley Cibber. 5 vols. 12mo. Lond. 1736. Later ed. 1777.

CLEVELAND, JOHN.

2384. The poems of John Cleveland. Ed. by J. M. Berdan. 1 vol. 8vo. N.Y. 1903. Later ed. 1 vol. 8vo. New Haven. 1911. Bibl.

Cleveland's works, including poems, orations, and epistles, were publ. 1 vol. 8vo. Lond. 1687. The character of a London diurnall [1644], A character of a diurnal-maker [1654], and The character of a moderate intelligencer [s.a.], are of interest for the history of journalism.

CONGREVE, WILLIAM.

2385. The . . . works of Mr. William Congreve. 3 vols. 8vo. Lond. 1710. Later eds. : 2 vols. 8vo. Lond. 1895. Ed. by G. S. Street. 4 vols. 8vo. Lond. 1923. Ed. by M. Summers.

2386. Life of William Congreve. By E. Gosse. 1 vol. 12mo. Lond. 1888. Later ed. 1 vol. 8vo. Lond. 1924.

COWLEY, ABRAHAM.

2387. The works of Mr. Abraham Cowley. Ed. by T. Sprat. 1 vol. fol. Lond. 1668. Later ed. 2 vols. 4to. Blackburn. 1876–81. Ed. by A. B. Grosart.

A. R. Waller ed. Cowley's Poems, miscellanies, &c. [1 vol. 8vo. Camb. 1905] and his Essays, plays, and verses [1 vol. 8vo. Camb. 1906].

CRASHAW, RICHARD.

2388. The complete works of Richard Crashaw. Ed. by W. B. Turnbull. 1 vol. 8vo. Lond. 1858. Later ed. 2 vols. 8vo. [? Blackburn]. 1872–3. Ed. A. B. Grosart.

Poems, ed. by A. R. Waller, 1904.

DANIEL, SAMUEL.

2389. The complete works in verse and prose of Samuel Daniel. Ed. by A. B. Grosart. 5 vols. 8vo. Aylesbury. 1885.

Poeticall essayes publ. 1599.

D'AVENANT, SIR WILLIAM.

2390. The works of Sir William D'Avenant, Kt. Consisting of those which were formerly printed and those which he designed for the press, now published out of the author's originall copies. 1 vol. fol. Lond. 1673. Port. Later ed. 5 vols. 8vo. Edin. 1872–4. Ed. by J. Maidment and W. H. Logan.

For bibliography see Camb. Hist. of Eng. Lit. vi, pp. 454, 489 and viii, 1912, pp. 417–18.

DEFOE, DANIEL.

2391. A true collection of the writings of the author of the True Born Englishman. By D. Defoe. 2 vols. 8vo. Lond. 1703–5. Later eds. 20 vols. 8vo. Oxf. 1840. 16 vols. 8vo. Lond. 1895–6. Ed. by G. A. Aitken.

The ed. of 1703–5 contains early pamphlets and political works : it also appeared as The genuine works of Mr. Daniel Defoe [2 vols. *c.* 1705]. The ed. of 1840 is the most complete collection of Defoe's works. The ed. of 1895–6 gives the romances and shorter narratives. See the bibliographies in Camb. Hist. of Eng. Lit. ix. 418–33, and in the lives separately mentioned.

2392. Memoirs of the life and times of Daniel Defoe. By W. Wilson. 3 vols. 8vo. Lond. 1830. Bibl.

Cf. W. Lee, Daniel Defoe. His life and recently discovered writings [3 vols. 8vo. Lond. 1869. Bibl.] ; and T. Wright, The Life of Daniel Defoe [1 vol. 8vo. Lond. 1894. Bibl.]. Cf. Daniel de Foe et ses Romans. By Paul Dottin. 3 vols. 8vo. Paris. 1924. The bulk of Defoe's letters are in vols. iv. and v of the Portland MSS. 1897, 1899.

DEKKER, THOMAS.

2393. The dramatic works of Thomas Dekker now first collected with illustrative notes. 4 vols. 8vo. Lond. 1873.

His non-dramatic works were ed. by A. B. Grosart [5 vols. 8vo. 1884–6. Huth Library]. For bibliography see Camb. Hist. of Eng. Lit. iv. 526–8.

DENNIS, JOHN.

2394. John Dennis, his life and criticism. By H. G. Paul. 1 vol. 8vo. N.Y. 1911.

His Miscellanies in verse and prose were publ. 1 vol. 8vo. Lond. 1693 ; his Select works, 2 vols. 8vo. Lond. 1718 ; and his Original letters, familiar, moral and critical, 2 vols. 8vo. Lond. 1721.

DRAYTON, MICHAEL.

2395. The works of Michael Drayton . . . now first collected. 1 vol. fol. Lond. 1748. Later eds. 4 vols. 8vo. Lond. 1753. 3 vols. 1876. Ed. by R. Hooper.

The poems were ed. by J. P. Collier for the Roxburghe Club, 1856 ; the minor poems by C. Brett [1 vol. sm. 4to. Oxf. 1907]. For bibliographies see O. Elton's Michael Drayton. A critical study with a bibliography [1 vol. 8vo. Lond. 1905] ; and Camb. Hist. of Eng. Lit. iv. 487–8.

DRUMMOND OF HAWTHORNDEN, WILLIAM.

2396. The works of William Drummond of Hawthornden. 2 pts. in 1 vol. fol. Edin. 1711. Later ed. 2 vols. 8vo. Manchester. 1913. Illus. Ed. by J. Sage, T. Ruddeman, and L. F. Kastner.

His poems were first pr. 1 vol. sm. 4to. Edin. 1616. Cf. David Masson's Drummond of Hawthornden : the story of his life and writings [1 vol. 8vo. Lond. 1873].

DRYDEN, JOHN.

2397. The works of John Dryden. Ed. by Sir W. Scott. 18 vols. 8vo. Edin. 1808 and 1821. Later ed. 1882–93. Ed. by G. Saintsbury.

Dryden's critical and miscellaneous prose works were ed. by E. Malone [3 vols. in 4, 8vo. Lond. 1800], his Essays by W. P. Ker [2 vols. 8vo. Oxf. 1900], and his Poems by W. D. Christie [1 vol. 8vo. Lond. 1870], and by John Sargeaunt [1 vol. 8vo. Oxf. 1910]. For a bibliography see Camb. Hist. of Eng. Lit. viii. 1912, pp. 391–406.

D'URFEY, THOMAS.

2398. A study of the plays of Thomas D'Urfey, with a reprint of A fool's preferment. By R. S. Forsythe. 2 vols. 8vo. Cleveland, Ohio. 1916–17.

ETHEREGE, SIR GEORGE.

2399. The works of Sir George Etherege, containing his plays and poems. 1 vol. 8vo. Lond. 1704. Later ed. 1888. Ed. by A. W. Verity.

Cf. Sir George Etheredge, sein Leben, seine Zeit und seine Dramen, by Vincenz Meindl. 8vo. Vienna. 1901.

FARQUHAR, GEORGE.

2400. The dramatick works of George Farquhar. 2 vols. 8vo. Lond. 1736. Later ed. 1892. Ed. by A. C. Ewald.

Cf. George Farquhar, sein Leben und seine Original-Dramen. By D. Schmid. 1 vol. 8vo. Vienna, 1904.

FORD, JOHN.

2401. The dramatic works of John Ford. Ed. by H. Weber. 2 vols. 8vo. Edin. 1811. Later eds. 2 vols. 8vo. Lond. 1827. Ed. by W. Gifford. 3 vols. 8vo. Lond. 1869 and 1895. Ed. by A. Dyce.

[?GAUDEN, ?JOHN]

2402. Eikon Basilike. εικων βασιλικη. The pourtraicture of his sacred majestie in his solitudes and sufferings. By [? J. [?Gauden]. 1 vol. 8vo. [Lond.]. 1648–9. Port.

See Edward Almack's Bibliography of Eikon Basilike, 4to. 1896 ; and Henry John Todd's A letter to his grace the Archbishop of Canterbury concerning the authorship of ΕΙΚΩΝ ΒΑΣΙΛΙΚΗ [1 vol. 8vo. Lond. 1825].

GAY, JOHN.

2403. The works of John Gay. 4 vols. 8vo. Dubl. 1770. Later ed. 6 vols. 8vo. Lond. 1795.

The poetical works of John Gay were ed. by J. Underhill, 2 vols. 12mo. Lond. 1893 and 1905.

HERBERT, GEORGE.

2404. The complete works in verse and prose of George Herbert. 3 vols. 4to. Blackburn. 1874. Ed. by A. B. Grosart. Later ed. 3 vols. 8vo. Lond. 1905. Ed. by G. H. Palmer.

Cf. G. H. Palmer's A Herbert bibliography [1 vol. 8vo. Camb. (Mass.) 1911].

HERRICK, ROBERT.

2405. Hesperides, or the works both humane and divine of Robert Herrick. 1 vol. 8vo. Lond. 1648. Later eds. 2 vols. 12mo. Lond. 1869. Ed. by W. C. Hazlitt. 3 vols. 8vo. Lond. 1876. Ed. by A. B. Grosart. 2 vols. 8vo. Lond. 1891. Ed. by A. W. Pollard. 1 vol. 8vo. Oxf. 1915. Ed. by F. W. Moorman.

Bibliography in Camb. Hist. of Eng. Lit. vii, 1911, pp. 398–9.

HEYWOOD, THOMAS.

2406. The dramatic works of Thomas Heywood. 6 vols. 8vo. Lond. 1874.

See Camb. Hist. of Eng. Lit. vi. 430–4 ; and Oxford Bibliographical Society Proceedings and Papers, 1925, where there is a full bibliography by A. M. Clark.

JONSON, BEN.

2407. The workes of Benjamin Jonson. fol. Lond. vol. i. 1616, vol. ii. 1631–41. Later eds. 9 vols. 8vo. Lond. 1816, ed. by W. Gifford ; 1875, ed. by F. Cunningham ; and 2 vols. 12mo. Lond. and N.Y. 1910, ed. by F. E. Schelling.

Notes of Ben Jonson's conversations with William Drummond of Hawthornden, 1619, were publ. 1 vol. 8vo. Lond. 1842 and 1906. For bibliography see Camb. Hist. of Eng. Lit. vi. 413–20. New ed. of the works ed. by C. H. Herford and P. Simpson in progress. Vols. i and ii, 8vo. Oxf. 1925, contain an elaborate life and documents.

LEE, NATHANIEL.

2408. The works of . . . Nathaniel Lee. 2 vols. 8vo. Lond. 1713. Later ed. 3 vols. 12mo. Lond. 1733–4.

LOVELACE, RICHARD.

2409. The poems of Richard Lovelace. Ed. by C. H. Wilkinson. 2 vols. 4to. Oxf. 1925.

A sumptuous ed. with many illustrations and facsimiles.

MANDEVILLE, BERNARD.

2410. The fable of the bees. By B. Mandeville. Ed. by F. B. Kaye. 2 vols. 8vo. Oxf. 1924.

Has a valuable intro.

MARSTON, JOHN.

2411. The workes of Mr. J. Marston, being tragedies and comedies. 1 vol. 8vo. Lond. 1633. Later eds. 3 vols. 8vo. Lond. 1856. Ed. by J. O. Halliwell. 3 vols. 8vo. Lond. 1887. Ed. by A. H. Bullen.

MARVELL, ANDREW.

2412. The complete works in verse and prose of Andrew Marvell. Ed. by A. B. Grosart. 4 vols. 4to. Blackburn. 1872–5.

Vol. i, Verse : ii, Letters : iii and iv, Pamphlets. This supersedes the ed. of 3 vols. 4to. Lond. 1776, ed. by E. Thompson. Marvell's Poems and satires were also ed. by G. A. Aitken [2 vols. 8vo. Lond. 1892. Bibl.].

MASSINGER, PHILIP.

2413. The dramatic works of Philip Massinger. Ed. by T. Coxeter. 4 vols. 8vo. Lond. 1761. Later eds. 4 vols. 4to. Lond. 1779. Ed. by J. M. Mason. 4 vols. 8vo. Lond. 1805. Ed. by W. Gifford. 1 vol. 8vo. Lond. 1871. Ed. by F. Cunningham.

Works, ed. T. Coxeter, 4 vols. 1759. Cf. S. R. Gardiner, The political element in Massinger, Contemporary Review, Aug. 1876. Bibl. Camb. Hist. of Eng. Lit. vi. 442-4.

MIDDLETON, THOMAS.

2414. The works of Thomas Middleton. Ed. by A. H. Bullen. 8 vols. 8vo. Lond. 1885–6.

MILTON, JOHN.

2415. The poetical works of John Milton [with] some account of [his] life and writings. By H. J. Todd. 1 vol. 8vo. Lond. 1801. Later ed. 1861.

2416. The works of John Milton in verse and prose. Ed. by J. Mitford. 8 vols. 8vo. Lond. 1851.

For bibliography see Camb. Hist. of Eng. Lit. vii, 1911, pp. 413–23.

2417. The life of John Milton, narrated in connexion with the political, ecclesiastical and literary history of his time. By D. Masson. 7 vols. 8vo. Camb. and Lond. 1859–94. Ports.

Exhaustive and valuable as a history of the times in which Milton lived.

2418. Milton. By M. Pattison. English Men of Letters, 1879.

A good short sketch.

2419. A lexicon to the English poetical works of John Milton. By L. E. Lockwood. 1 vol. 8vo. Lond. and N.Y. 1907.

Cf. A concordance to the poetical works of John Milton, by J. Bradshaw [1 vol. 8vo. Lond. 1894].

2420. [Papers on] The tercentenary of Milton's birth. Proc. Brit. Academy, 1908 : also issued in a portfolio, Oxf. 1908.

MORE, HENRY.

2421. Philosophicall Poems. . . . By H. More. 1 vol. 8vo. Camb. 1647. Later ed. 1 vol. 4to. Blackburn. 1878. Ed. by A. B. Grosart.

For an article on, and bibliography of, Platonists and latitudinarians see Camb. Hist. of Eng. Lit. viii, 1912. Cf. The philosophical writings of Henry More, by Flora I. Mackinnon, 1 vol. 8vo. N.Y. 1925.

NEWCASTLE, MARGARET CAVENDISH, DUCHESS OF.

2422. The first Duchess of Newcastle and her husband as figures in literary history. By H. Ten Eyck Perry. 1 vol. 8vo. Boston and Lond. 1918.

Cf. T. Longueville's The first Duke and Duchess of Newcastle-upon-Tyne. 1 vol. 8vo. Lond. 1910. Illus.

OLDHAM, JOHN.

2423. Satyrs upon the Jesuits : written in the year 1679 upon occasion of the plot. Together with the satyr against vertue and some other pieces by the same hand. By J. Oldham. 1 vol. 8vo. Lond. 1681.

The works of Mr. John Oldham, together with his remains. 4 pts. 8vo. Lond. 1686. 3 vols. 8vo. Lond. 1770. Ed. by E. Thompson.

ORRERY, ROGER BOYLE, EARL OF.

2424. Dramatic works. By Roger Boyle, Earl of Orrery. 2 vols. 8vo. Lond. 1739.

Cf. Roger Boyle, Earl of Orrery und seine Dramen, by E. Siegert [1 vol. 8vo. Vienna. 1906].

OTWAY, THOMAS.

2425. The works of Mr. Thomas Otway . . . consisting of his plays poems and love-letters. 2 vols. 12mo. Lond. 1712. Later ed. 3 vols. 8vo. Lond. 1813. Ed. by T. Thornton.

OVERBURY, SIR THOMAS.

2426. A wife now the widow of Sir Thomas Overbury, being a most exquisite and singular Poem of the choice of a wife. Whereunto are added many witty characters and concerted news written by himself and other learned gentlemen his friends. 1 vol. 4to. Lond. 1614. Later ed. 1 vol. 8vo. Lond. 1856. Port.

An enlarged ed. appeared in 1616.

PHILLIPS, EDWARD and JOHN.

2427. Lives of Edward and John Phillips, nephews and pupils of Milton, including various particulars of the literary and political history of their times. To which are added I. Collections for the life of Milton by John Aubrey. II. The life of Milton. By E. Phillips. Printed in the year 1694. Ed. by W. Godwin. 1 vol. 4to. Lond. 1815.

POPE, ALEXANDER.

2428. The works of Alexander Pope. Ed. by W. Elwin and W. J. Courthope. 10 vols. 8vo. Lond. 1871–89.

Vols. i–iv, Poetry ; v, Life, and index ; vi–x, Letters. Cf. G. A. Aitken's Notes on the bibliography of Pope [1 vol. sm. 4to. Lond. 1914] ; and R. H. Griffiths, Alexander Pope, a bibliography. i. Pope's own writings, 1709–34. Austin (Texas) 1922.

PRIOR, MATTHEW.

2429. Poems on several occasions ; and Dialogues of the dead. By M. Prior. Ed. by A. R. Waller. 2 vols. 8vo. Camb. 1905–7.

Prior's poems were also publ. 1 vol. fol. Lond. 1718. 2 vols. 12mo. Lond. 1779. Ed. T. Evans. 2 vols. 8vo. Lond. 1892. Ed. R. B. Johnson. See Nos. 957–8 for lives.

ROWE, NICHOLAS.

2430. The dramatick works of Nicholas Rowe. 2 vols. 12mo. Lond 1720 and 1736. Later eds. 2 vols. 8vo. Lond. 1747. 2 vols. 8vo. Lond. 1792.

His poetical works were publ. in 1720 and repr. in Bell (2357), Johnson (2358), Anderson (2359), and Chalmers (2360).

SAINT-ÉVREMOND, CHARLES DE MARGUETEL DE SAINT-DENIS DE.

2431. Oeuvres. Ed. by P. Silvestre and P. Des Maizeaux. 2 vols. 4to. Londres. 1705. Later ed. 3 vols. 8vo. Paris. 1865. Ed. by C. Giraud.

At least one pirated ed. preceded that here described. Cf. The works of Mr. de St. Evremont translated from the French, 2 vols. 8vo. Lond. 1700 ; another trans. 3 vols. 8vo. Lond. 1714 ; W. M. Daniels, Saint Evremond en Angleterre. 1 vol. Versailles. 1907.

SEDLEY, SIR CHARLES.

2432. The works of . . . Sir Charles Sedley. 2 vols. 12mo. Lond. 1722. Later ed. 2 vols. 8vo. Lond. 1778.

Cf. Sir Charles Sedley's Leben und Werke, by K. Max Lissner. 1 vol. 8vo. Halle. 1905.

SELDEN, JOHN.

2433. Table-Talk, being the discourses of John Selden, Esq., or his sense of various matters of weight and high consequence relating especially to religion and state. 1 vol. 4to. Lond. 1689. Later eds. 1 vol. 8vo. Lond. 1847. Ed. by S. W. Singer. 1 vol. 8vo. Oxf. 1892. Ed. by S. H. Reynolds. 1 vol. 4to. Lond. 1927. Ed. by Sir F. Pollock.

Ed. of 1927 includes an account of Selden and his work by the late Sir Edward Fry.

SETTLE, ELKANAH.

2434. Elkanah Settle his life and works. By F. C. Brown. 1 vol. 8vo. Chicago. 1910. Illus.

SHADWELL, THOMAS.

2435. The dramatick works of Thomas Shadwell. 4 vols. 12mo. Lond. 1720.

SHAFTESBURY, ANTHONY ASHLEY COOPER, 3rd EARL OF.

2436. Characteristics of men, manners, opinions, times. By Anthony Ashley Cooper, 3rd Earl of Shaftesbury. 3 vols. 8vo. Lond. 1711. Later ed. 2 vols. 8vo. Lond. 1900. Ed. by J. M. Robertson.

SHAKESPEARE, WILLIAM.

2437. Mr. William Shakespeare's Comedies, histories, and tragedies. Published according to the true originall copies. 1 vol. fol. Lond. 1623.

The first folio was reproduced by the Clarendon Press in 1902. The second, third and fourth folios [1632, 1664, and 1685], together with the first, were all reproduced in facsimile by Messrs. Methuen & Co. Lond. fol. in 1909, 1905, 1904 and 1910 respectively.

2438. The plays and poems of W. S. with the corrections and illustrations of various commentators. . . . Ed. by E. Malone. 21 vols. 8vo. Lond. 1821.

This ed. was completed by Jas. Boswell from Malone's notes.

2439. The life of William Shakespeare. By J. O. Halliwell-Phillipps. 1 vol. 8vo. Lond. 1848.

Cf. Outlines of the life of Shakespeare [1 vol. 8vo. Brighton. 1881 ; 7th ed. 2 vols. 8vo. Lond. 1887].

2440. A new variorum edition of Shakespeare. Ed. by H. H. Furness. 20 vols. la. 8vo. Lond. and Philadelphia. 1871–1919.

' Contains a collation of the ancient copies and of the best modern critical eds., with notes, criticisms, and illustrations . . .'

2441. The Cambridge Shakespeare. Ed. by W. A. Wright. 2 vols. 8vo. Lond. 1891–2.

2442. The diary of Master William Silence. A study of Shakespeare and of Elizabethan sport. By D. H. Madden. 1 vol. 8vo. Lond. 1897 and 1907.

2443. A life of William Shakespeare. By Sir S. Lee. 1 vol. 8vo. Lond. 1898. Illus. Bibl. 7th ed. 1915.

The bibliographical chapters supply the best summary guide to the various eds. of Shakespeare's works.

2444. Shakespeare Bibliography ; a dictionary of every known issue of Shakespeare's writings and of recorded opinions therein in the English language. By W. Jaggard. 8vo. Stratford. 1911.

2445. Shakespeare's England, being an account of the life and manners of his age. Ed. by Sir S. Lee. 2 vols. 8vo. Oxf. 1916. Illus.

Each chapter has valuable bibliographical notes.

2446. Mr. William Shakespeare. Original and early editions of his quartos and folios, his source books and those containing contemporary notices. By H. C. Bartlett. 1 vol. 8vo. New Haven. 1922.

SHIRLEY, JAMES.

2447. Dramatic Works and Poems. Ed. by A. Dyce. 6 vols. 8vo. 1833.

Cf. James Shirley dramatist. By A. H. Nason. 1 vol. 8vo. N.Y. 1915. Bibl.

STEELE, RICHARD.

2448. The life of Richard Steele. By G. A. Aitken. 2 vols. 8vo. Lond. 1889.

The best short life is by H. Austin Dobson. 1 vol. 8vo. Lond. 1886.

SUCKLING, SIR JOHN.

2449. Fragmenta aurea. A collection of all the incomparable pieces written by Sir John Suckling. 1 vol. 8vo. Lond. 1646. Port. Later ed. 2 vols. 8vo. Lond. 1874 and 1892. Port. Ed. by W. C. Hazlitt.

SWIFT, JONATHAN.

2450. The works of Jonathan Swift. Ed. by Sir W. Scott. 19 vols. 8vo. Edin. 1814 and 1824.

The prose works were separately ed. by Temple Scott, 12 vols. 8vo. Lond. 1897–1908 ; the Poems by William Ernst Browning, 2 vols. 8vo. Lond. 1910 ; the Correspondence by T. Elrington Ball, 6 vols. 8vo. Lond. 1910–14. Cf. E. Pons : Swift, Les années de jeunesse et le ' Conte du tonneau '. 1 vol. Strasbourg, 1925.

TAYLOR, JOHN.

2451. All the workes of John Taylor the water-poet. 1 vol. fol. Lond. 1630. Wood-cuts. Later ed. 3 vols. 1863–9.

The ed. of 1863–9 was publ. by the Spenser Soc., which also publ. the works not included in the folio in 5 vols. 1870–8. A selection from Taylor's tracts published prior to 1630 was ed. by C. Hindley, 1 vol. 4to. Lond. 1872.

VANBRUGH, JOHN.

2452. Plays written by Sir John Vanbrugh. 2 vols. 12mo. Lond. 1734–5. Later ed. 2 vols. 8vo. Lond. 1893. Ed. by W. C. Ward.

Cf. John Vanbrughs Leben und Werke, by Max Dametz, 1 vol. 8vo. Vienna. 1898.

VAUGHAN, HENRY.

2453. The works in verse and prose of Henry Vaughan. 4 vols. 4to. Blackburn. 1870–1. Ed. by A. B. Grosart.

His Poems [1646] were ed. by E. K. Chambers, 2 vols. 8vo. Lond. 1896 and 1905.

WALLER, EDMUND.

2454. Poems &c. written by Mr. Edmund Waller. 1 vol. 12mo. Lond. 1645. Later eds. 1664, and 1893, ed. by G. Thorn Drury.

Bibliography in Camb. Hist. of Eng. Lit. vii, 1911, pp. 409–11.

WEBSTER, JOHN.

2455. The works of John Webster. Ed. by A. Dyce. 4 vols. 8vo. Lond. 1830.

Cf. F. E. Pierse, John Webster, the periods of his work, N.Y. 1909. Camb. Hist. of Eng. Lit. v. 445–7.

WITHER, GEORGE.

2456. [Works] repr. by the Spenser Society. 20 vols. 4to. Manchester. 1870–83.

Poems, ed. J. M. Gutch. 3 vols. 8vo. Bristol. 1820.

WOTTON, SIR HENRY.

2457. Reliquiae Wottonianae, or a collection of lives, letters, poems, with characters of sundry personages, and other incomparable pieces of language and art, by the curious pensil of . . . Sir Henry Wotton. 1 vol. 12mo. Lond. 1651. Port.

See No. 624 for his Life and Letters, by L. Pearsall Smith.

WYCHERLEY, WILLIAM.

2458. The works of the ingenious Mr. William Wycherley. I vol. 8vo. Lond. 1713. Later eds.: I vol. 8vo. Lond. 1888. Ed. by W. C. Ward. 4 vols. 8vo. Lond. 1924. Ed. by M. Summers.

These are eds. of the plays : the poems have been publ. from 1704 onwards.

¶ 5. BALLADS

2459. Catalogue of an unique collection of ancient English broadside ballads printed entirely in the black letter . . . on sale by John Russell Smith. I vol. 8vo. Lond. 1856.

A list of 408 ballads mainly of the 17th century. This collection, now known as the Euing Ballads, is in the library of the University of Glasgow.

2460. Bibliotheca Lindesiana. Catalogue of a collection of English ballads. I vol. 4to. Privately pr. 1890.

A list of 1466 ballads (17th and 18th centuries, mostly black letter) in the possession of the Earl of Crawford, admirably indexed.

2461. An analytical index to the ballad-entries 1557–1709 in the Register of the Stationers Company of London. By H. E. Rollins. I vol. 8vo. Univ. of N. Carolina Press. 1924.

2462. Political merriment, or truths told to some tune. By a lover of his country. 3 pts. 12mo. Lond. 1714–15.

Cf. A pill to purge state melancholy, or a collection of excellent new ballads. 3rd ed. 12mo. 1716.

2463. Wit and mirth, or pills to purge melancholy, being a collection of the best merry ballads and songs. By T. Durfey. 6 vols. 8vo. Lond. 1719–20.

A modern repr. in the same format is undated.

2464. A collection of old ballads, corrected from the best and most ancient copies extant, with introductions historical, critical, or humorous. 3 vols. 8vo. Lond. 1723–5.

Ambrose Philips is said to have been the editor.

2465. Reliques of ancient English poetry, consisting of old heroic ballads, songs and other pieces of our earlier poets (chiefly of the lyric kind), together with some few of later date. Ed. by T. Percy. 3 vols. 8vo. Lond. 1765.

Repr. and ed. with all the many variants of later eds. by A. Schröer, 2 vols. 8vo. Berlin, 1903. Cf. Bishop Percy's Folio manuscript [3 vols. 8vo. Lond. 1868] and supplement, Loose and humorous songs [1 vol. 8vo. Lond. 1868], both ed. by F. J. Furnivall and J. Hales. From this early 17th-century MS. Percy derived 45 of the 176 pieces pr. in his Reliques : it contains many ballads 1600–50.

2466. The Rump ; or an exact collection of the choicest poems and songs relating to the late times. By the most eminent wits from anno 1639 to anno 1661. 2 vols. in 1, 8vo. Lond. 1662. Repr. 2 vols. 8vo. Lond. 1874.

Mainly pr. from contemporary broadsides, with additions from books : reissued with a few additions in 1731 in 2 vols. 12mo. as A collection of loyal songs written against the Rump parliament.

2467. Poems on affairs of state.   5th ed. 8vo. Lond. 1703-7.

This collection of political poems and satires includes a number of ballads and songs publ. between 1660 and 1704.   It was originally publ. in 1689 in 4 pts. 4to., and between 1698 and 1707 five eds. in 4 vols. 8vo. followed.   An index to this and to five smaller collections of the same nature pr. in Notes and Queries, 5th Ser. vol. vi. Nov. 18—Dec. 30, 1876.

2468. Whig and Tory, or wit on both sides—a collection of state poems upon all remarkable occurrences from the change of ministry to this time. 1 vol. 8vo. Lond. 1713.

Reissued in 1715 as A Tory pill to purge Whig melancholy.

2469. Ballads and other fugitive poetical pieces chiefly Scottish from the collections of Sir James Balfour.   Ed. by J. Maidment. 1 vol. 4to. Edin. 1834.

Cf. Ballads on the Bishops' wars, 1638-40, Scot. Hist. Rev. Apr. 1906 ; and Ballads illustrating the relations of England and Scotland during the 17th century, ibid. Jan. 1909.   Both by C. H. Firth.

2470. A collection of national English airs.   By W. Chappell.   2 vols. fol. Lond. 1838-40.

Reissued as Popular music of the olden time in 1855-9, and as Old English popular music, ed. by H. Ellis Wooldridge, 2 vols. 8vo. Lond. 1893.

2471. Political ballads published in England during the commonwealth. Ed. by T. Wright.   8vo. Percy Soc. 1841.

Selection from the broadsides in the Thomason collection, Brit. Mus.

2472. Poems and songs relating to George Villiers, Duke of Buckingham and his assassination by John Felton.   Ed. by F. W. Fairholt.   8vo. Percy Soc. 1850.

2473. Political ballads of the seventeenth and eighteenth centuries [beginning 1641].   Ed. by W. W. Wilkins.   2 vols. 8vo. Lond. 1860.

2474. The Roxburghe ballads.   Ed. by W. Chappell [i–iii] and J. W. Ebsworth [iv–ix].   9 vols. 8vo. Hertford. 1871-97.

Two smaller selections from this collection are : A book of Roxburghe ballads, ed. by J. P. Collier, 1 vol. 4to. Lond. 1847 ; and Roxburghe ballads, ed. C. Hindley, 2 vols. 8vo. Lond. 1873-4.

2475. Westminster drolleries, with an introduction on the literature of the drolleries.   Ed. by J. W. Ebsworth.   1 vol. 8vo. Boston. Lincs. 1875.

Cf. his Merry drollery complete and Choice drollery . . . with the extra songs of merry drollery, 8vo. Boston, 1875 and 1876.

2476. The Bagford ballads : illustrating the last years of the Stuarts.   Ed. by J. W. Ebsworth.   2 vols. 8vo. Hertford. 1878.

2477. The English and Scottish popular ballads.   Ed. by F. J. Child. 5 vols. 4to. Boston (Mass.) 1882-98.

2478. The Shirburn ballads, 1585-1616.   Ed. by A. Clark.   1 vol. 8vo. Oxf. 1907.

From MS. in possession of the Earl of Macclesfield at Shirburn Castle, Oxfordshire. See Notes on the Shirburn ballads, by H. E. Rollins, Journal of American Folk Lore, 1917.

2479. Naval songs and ballads. Ed. by C. H. Firth. 1 vol. 8vo. Navy Records Soc. 1908.

Cf. Early naval ballads of England, ed. by J. O. Halliwell. 8vo. Percy Soc. 1851.

2480. Old English ballads, 1553–1625. Ed. by H. E. Rollins. 1 vol. 8vo. Camb. 1920.

Illustrates the struggle between Protestants and Catholics. He also ed. A Pepysian Garland. Black-letter broadside ballads of the years 1595–1639, chiefly from the collection of Samuel Pepys [1 vol. 8vo. Camb. 1922], and Cavalier and Puritan. Ballads and broadsides illustrating the period of the Great Rebellion, 1640–1660 [1 vol. 8vo. N. Y. 1923]. All have valuable introductions and notes.

2481. Ballad history of the reigns of James I and Charles I. By C. H. Firth. Trans. Royal Hist. Soc. 3rd Ser. v. vi. 1911, 1912.

2482. Martin Parker, ballad monger. By H. E. Rollins. Modern Philology, Jan. 1919.

2483. The black-letter broadside ballad. By H. E. Rollins. Publications of the Modern Language Association of America, xxxiv, 1919.

¶ 6. JOURNALISM
(a) NEWSPAPERS

2484. The Kingdomes Weekly Intelligencer. . . . 27 Dec. 1642/3 Jan. 1643 —9 Oct. 1649. By R. C. Sm. 4to.

Presbyterian.

2485. Mercurius Aulicus . . . 8 Jan. 1643—7 Sept. 1645. By Sir J. Berkenhead. Sm. 4to.

Royalist and satirical.

2486. Mercurius Civicus . . . 11 May 1643—10 Dec. 1646. By R. C. Sm. 4to.

Presbyterian.

2487. A Perfect Diurnall of some passages in Parliament . . . 27 June 1643— 8 Oct. 1649. By S. Pecke. Sm. 4to.

Neutral. By the earliest and most well-informed writer.

2488. Mercurius Britanicus . . . 29 August 1643—18 May 1646. By T. Audley (to No. 51) and M. Nedham. Sm. 4to.

Parliamentary and satirical.

2489. The Moderate Intelligencer . . . 6 March 1645—May 1649. By John D[illingham]. Sm. 4to.

Presbyterian royalist. A new series continued it 1649–54.

2490. Perfect Occurrences . . . 8 Jan. 1647—12 Oct. 1649. By H. Walker [Luke Harruney, anagram]. Sm. 4to.

2491. Mercurius Pragmaticus . . . 21 Sept. 1647—28 May 1650. (Variations in title.) By [? J. Cleveland] (until 1648) and M. Nedham. Sm. 4to.

Royalist. Various authors used the same title in 1649 and 1650.

2492. The Moderate . . . 29 June 1648—25 Sept. 1649. By G. Mabbot. Sm. 4to.

The Levellers' chief organ. First no. = No. 171. In opposition to Presbyterian periodicals of similar titles.

2493. A briefe relation. . . . 2 Oct. 1649—22 Oct. 1650. By W. Frost. Sm. 4to.

By the Secretary of the Council of State.

2494. Severall (or ' Perfect ') Proceedings. . . . 9 Oct. 1649—27 Sept. 1655. By H. Walker. Sm. 4to.

At first official [1649,] afterwards semi-official.

2495. A Perfect Diurnall of . . . the armies . . . 17 Dec. 1649—24 Sept. 1655. By S. Pecke. Sm. 4to.

At first official, afterwards semi-official.

2496. Mercurius Politicus . . . 13 June 1650—12 April 1660. By M. Nedham, and J. Canne [1659]. Sm. 4to.

Official.

2497. The Publicke Intelligencer . . . 8 Oct. 1655—9 April 1660. By M. Nedham, and J. Canne [1659]. Sm. 4to.

Official.

2498. The Parliamentary (with 1661 the ' Kingdoms ') Intelligencer . . . 26 Dec. 1659—31 August 1663. By H. Muddiman. Sm. 4to.

2499. Mercurius Publicus . . . 5 Jan. 1660—31 August 1663. By H. Muddiman and G. Dury (April—June 1660). Sm. 4to.

2500. The Intelligencer . . . 31 Aug. 1663—29 Jan. 1666. By Sir R. L'Estrange. Sm. 4to.

2501. The Newes . . . 3 Sept. 1663—29 Jan. 1666. By Sir R. L'Estrange Sm. 4to.

2502. The Oxford Gazette 16 Nov. 1665, which became with No. 24, Monday 5 Feb. 1666, The London Gazette. Still exists. By H. Muddiman (to No. 25 inclusive). Fol.

2503. ' Domestick Intelligence '. . . . No. 56. ' The Protestant (Domestick) Intelligence ' . . . 7 July 1679—15 April 1681. By B. Harris. Fol.

Anabaptist. In support of Oates.

2504. The True Protestant Mercury. 28 Dec. 1680—18 Oct. 1682. By T. Vile. Fol.

In support of Oates and Shaftesbury.

2505. Heraclitus Ridens, or a dialogue between jest and earnest concerning the times. 1 Feb. 1681—22 Aug. 1682. By T. Flatman. Fol. Later ed. Repr. 2 vols. 12mo. Lond. 1713.

A satirical opponent of Oates. Reprinted in 1713, with an index.

2506. The Merchants Remembrancer. 23 May 1681 to about 1700? By J. Whiston. Fol.
Of great value for trade and prices. Existing sets very incomplete.

2507. The Loyal Protestant . . . 9 March 1681—20 March 1683. By N. Thompson. Fol.
In opposition to Oates and the 'Associators'. Later numbers licensed.

2508. The Observator . . . 13 April 1681—9 March 1687. By Sir R. L'Estrange. Fol.
Satirical opponent of Oates and Shaftesbury. Licensed by both Secretaries of State.

2509. Mercurius Reformatus . . . (continued as M. Britannicus). 15 May 1689—1694. By J. Welwood. Fol.

2510. The Post-Man (commenced as, 'Account of the Publick transactions in Christendom, 11 Aug. 1694, afterwards becoming both the 'Post-Man' and 'Post Boy'). No. 72, 24 Oct. 1695. By various.
Tory and Jacobite.

2511. The Post Boy (same origin as the Post Man). 1695—1735. By various.
Jacobite.

2512. The Flying Post. 17 May 1695—1731? By various.
Whig.

2513. Dawks's News-Letter. (Half printed in imitation of hand-writing, the rest filled in by hand. At first without this title.) 3 Jan. 1698—1708(?) By J. Dawks. Fol.

2514. The London Post. (Commenced as 'The London Slip of News' 6 June 1699.) 9 June 1699—1705. By B. Harris (and others).
Whig.

2515. The Daily Courant. 11 March 1702—1735. By various.
Non-partisan (?)

2516. The Observator. 1 April 1702–1712. By J. Tutchin.

2517. A Weekly Review of the affairs of France. [19 Feb. 1704—1712.] By D. Defoe.
After several changes of name this becomes The Review from 2 August 1712.

2518. The Rehearsal. [5 Aug. 1704—23 March 1709.] By C. Leslie.

2519. The Dublin Gazette, 1705—present day.
Official.

2520. The Edinburgh Courant. 19 Feb. 1705—20 March 1710.

2521. The Edinburgh Gazette. 25 March 1707—present day. (Previous unofficial issues in 1699 and 1706.)
Official.

2522. The Scots Postman. Sept. 1708—26 June 1713. Anon.

2523. The Scots Courant. [Date of origin disputed and given variously, as ' September 1705 ', ' 2 March 1710 ' &c.] 1710–20 ?

2524. The Examiner. 3 Aug. 1710—1714. By various.
Tory. Cf. The prose works of Jonathan Swift (2450 n.). ix. 69.

2525. The Medley. 5 Oct. 1710—7 Aug. 1712. By various. Ed. by A. Maynwaring and J. Oldmixon.
Whig.

2526. The Tatler. By I. Bickerstaff, Esq. By R. Steele. Fol. Lond. 12 Apr. 1709—May 1711. Later ed. 4 vols. Lond. 1898–9. Ed. by G. A. Aitken.
Consult G. A. Aitken's Life of Steele (2 vols. 1889), which contains a full bibliography.

2527. The Spectator. By J. Addison. Fol. Lond. 1 March 1711—6 Dec. 1712. Later ed. 8 vols. 8vo. Lond. 1898. Ed. by G. A. Aitken.
Revived 18 June—29 Sept. 1714. Cf. Camb. Hist. English Lit. ix. 436.

2528. Mercator ; or commerce retrieved. 1 May 1713–1714.

2529. The Guardian. 12 March 1713—1 Oct. 1713. By R. Steele.
Whig.

2530. The Englishman. 6 Oct. 1713—Feb. 1714. By R. Steele.
Whig.

(b) HISTORY OF JOURNALISM

2531. The miscellaneous works of Charles Blount . . . to which is prefixed the life of the author. 1 vol. 12mo. Lond. 1695.
Includes Blount's A just vindication of learning and the liberty of the press.

2532. The present state of wit in a letter to a friend. By J. Gay. 1 vol. 8vo. Lond. 1711.

2533. Memoirs of the press, historical and political, from 1710 to 1740. By J. Oldmixon. 1 vol. 8vo. Lond. 1742.

2534. The diary and autobiography of Edmund Bohun . . . with an introductory memoir, notes and illustrations. Ed. by S. Wilton Rix. 1 vol. 4to. Beccles. 1853.
Bohun was licenser of the press 1692–3.

2535. Catalogue of a collection of early newspapers and essayists formed by the late John Thomas Hope and presented to the Bodleian Library. 1 vol. 8vo. Oxf. 1865.

2536. English newspapers : chapters in the history of journalism. By H. R. F. Bourne. 2 vols. 8vo. Lond. 1887.

2537. Bibliotheca Lindesiana. Collations and notes, No. 5. Catalogue of English newspapers, 1641–1666. 1 vol. la. 4to. Aberdeen. 1901.

2538. A history of English journalism to the foundation of the Gazette. By J. B. Williams. 1 vol. 8vo. Lond. 1908. Illus. Bibl.
Cf. the same writer's The newsbooks and letters of news of the Restoration. Eng. Hist. Rev. xxiii. 1908.

2539. The Edinburgh periodical press . . . vol. i, Introduction and bibliography, 1642–1711 ; vol. ii, Bibliography, 1711–1800.   By W. J. Couper. 2 vols. 8vo. Stirling. 1908.   Facsimiles.
A detailed account.

2540. The beginnings of English journalism.   By J. B. Williams.   Camb. Hist. of Eng. Lit. vii. 1911.   Bibl.

2541. Sir Roger L'Estrange.   A contribution to the history of the press in the seventeenth century.   By G. Kitchin.   1 vol. 8vo. Lond. 1913.   Illus.   Bibl.
A solid piece of work.

2542. Party politics and English journalism.   By D. H. Stevens.   1 vol. 8vo. Menasha, Wisconsin. 1916.   Bibl.

2543. Tercentenary handlist of English and Welsh newspapers, magazines and reviews.   By [J. G. Muddiman].   1 vol. 8vo. Lond. 1920.

2544. The king's journalist, 1659–1689.   By J. G. Muddiman.   1 vol. 8vo. Lond. 1923.   Ports. and Illus.
Virtually a life of Henry Muddiman.

VIII. FINE ARTS AND MUSIC

1. Fine Arts excluding Architecture.
2. Architecture.
   (*a*) Sources. (*b*) Later Works.
3. Music.
   (*a*) Sources. (*b*) Later Works.

¶ 1. FINE ARTS EXCLUDING ARCHITECTURE

2545. Sculptura, or the history and art of chaleography and engraving in copper. By J. Evelyn. 1 vol. 8vo. Lond. 1662. Later eds. 1 vol. 8vo. Lond. 1755; 1 vol. 8vo. Oxf. 1906. Ed. by C. F. Bell.

Repr. in Miscellaneous writings (887).

2546. The heads of illustrious persons of Great Britain engraven by Houbraken and Vertue, with their lives and characters. By T. Birch. 2 vols. fol. Lond. 1743.

2547. Anecdotes of painting in England, with some account of the principal artists; and incidental Notes on other Arts ; collected by the late Mr. George Vertue. And now digested and published from his original MSS. By Mr. H. Walpole. Printed by Thomas Farmer at Strawberry Hill. 4 vols. 4to. Strawberry Hill 1762–71. Ports. and Plates. Later eds. 4 vols. 4to. Strawberry Hill 1765–71. Ed. by Sir W. Musgrave; 5 vols. 8vo. Lond. 1826. Plates. Ports. Ed. by J. Dallaway ; 3 vols. 8vo. Lond. 1849. Ports. and Plates. Ed. by R. Wornum.

Vol. iv includes The history of the modern taste in gardening, by H. Walpole, and was printed by T. Kirgate at Strawberry Hill. Largely based on G. Vertue's Common-place books, now Brit. Mus. Add. MSS. 23068–74, and 21114. Cf. George Vertue's note-books relating to the history of art in England. By L. Cust and A. M. Hind. Walpole Soc. iii. 1914– .

2548. The English connoisseur : containing an account of whatever is curious in painting, sculpture, &c. in the palaces and seats of the nobility and principal gentry of England. By T. Martyn. 2 vols. 12mo. Lond. 1766.

2549. A biographical dictionary ; containing an historical account of all the engravers from the earliest period to the present time and a list of their most esteemed works. By J. Strutt. 2 vols. 4to. Lond. 1785. Plates.

2549A. Catalogue of the Sutherland collection [in the Bodleian Library]. By C. Sutherland. 2 vols. fol. Lond. 1837.

See W. D. Macray's Annals of the Bodleian ed. 1890, p. 331, for an account of this remarkable collection formed to illustrate Clarendon's History of the Rebellion and Burnet's History of his own Times.

2550. Catalogue of the first special exhibition of national portraits, ending with the reign of King James the Second, on loan to the South Kensington

K k

Museum, April 1866 [Introduction by S. Redgrave], Science and Art Department of the Committee on Education. 1 vol. 4to. Lond. 1866.

A separate illustrated catalogue, entitled A series of historical portraits selected from the National Portrait Exhibition, was published 10 vols. 4to. London. 1886–7. 1,030 photographs. Similar vols. for the same exhibition continued the collection to 1700 : Catalogue of the second special exhibition, &c. [1 vol. 4to. London. 1867] and A series of historical portraits, &c. 9 vols. 4to. London. 1867. 866 photographs. Together they form a unique collection.

2551. The ceramic art of Great Britain from prehistoric times down to the present day . . . illustrated with nearly two thousand engravings. By Ll. Jewitt. 2 vols. 8vo. Lond. 1878. Later ed. 1 vol. 8vo. Lond. *c.* 1883.

The later ed. is revised but slightly abridged.

2552. A descriptive catalogue of the engraved works of William Faithorne. By L. Fagan. 1 vol. fol. Lond. 1888.

2553. Burlington Fine Arts Club Exhibition of portrait miniatures, 1889. [Introduction by J. L. Propert.] 1 vol. 4to. Lond. 1889.

2554. [Catalogue of the] Exhibition of the Royal House of Stuart, the New Gallery, Regent Street. 1 vol. sm. 4to. Lond. 1889.

Portraits, miniatures, coins, and medals.

2555. Illustrated history of furniture from the earliest to the present time. By F. Litchfield. 1 vol. 4to. Lond. 1892. Plates.

Chapter IV covers the Stuart Period. The dictionary of English furniture from the Middle Ages to the late Georgian period, by P. Macquoid and R. Edwards, is in progress, fol. Lond. 1924– .

2556. Anthony van Dyck. An historical study of his life and works. By L. Cust. 1 vol. fol. Lond. 1900. Plates.

2557. The history of portrait miniatures. By G. C. Williamson. 2 vols. fol. Lond. 1904. Plates.

Cf. J. J. Foster, British miniature painters and their works. 1 vol. fol. Lond. 1898, his Samuel Cooper, 1914–16, and his Dictionary of painters of miniature 1525–1850. Ed. by E. M. Foster. 1 vol. 8vo. Lond. 1926.

2558. Illustrated catalogue of a loan collection of portraits of English historical personages who died between 1625 and 1714. Exhibited in the Examination School, Oxford, April and May 1905. Introduction by L. Cust. Ed. by C. F. Bell and Rachael Poole. 1 vol. 4to. Oxf. 1905. 2 Plates of facsimile signatures. 20 Plates.

A similar vol. for the period to 1625 appeared in the same format 1904.

2559. Some drawings of English women from Van Dyck to Kneller. By L. Binyon. Burlington Magazine, No. xliv, vol. x, pp. 74–81. Lond. Nov., 1906. Plates.

2560. The English miniatures painter. Illustrated by works in the Royal and other collections. Burlington Magazine, vol. viii. 4to. Lond., January, February, May, August, September, 1906. Plates.

N. Hilliard, I. Oliver, P. Oliver, J. Hoskins, S. Cooper.

2561. A history of tapestry from the earliest times until the present day. By W. G. Thomson. 1 vol. 8vo. Lond. 1906. Plates.

Contains an exhaustive treatise on the Mortlake tapestries.

2562. The Royal Stuarts in their connection with art and letters. By W. G. Blaikie Murdock. 1 vol. 8vo. Edin. 1908.

2563. Engraved British portraits. Ed. by F. M. O'Donoghue and H. M. Hake. 6 vols. 8vo. Oxford University Press for British Museum. 1908–25.

2564. Art in Great Britain and Ireland. By Sir W. Armstrong. 1 vol. sm. 8vo. London. 1909. Illustrations.

Architecture, Sculpture, Painting. Chaps. viii, ix, xiii especially treat the Stuart period.

2565. British portrait painting to the opening of the nineteenth century. By M. H. Spielmann. 2 vols. fol. Lond. 1910. Plates.

2566. Gilbert Jackson, portrait painter. By Rachael [Mrs. R. L.] Poole. Burlington Magazine, vol. xx, Lond. 1911. Plates.

Cf. Vol. xxi, p. 169 for an article by C. H. C. Baker.

2567. Tapestry weaving in England. 6 pts. By W. G. Thomson. Art Journal, 1911. Plates.

2568. Historical portraits. Vol. ii, 1600–1700 ; iii, 1700–1800. 4to. Oxf. 1911–19.

Portraits chosen by Emery Walker with intro. on the artists by C. F. Bell. Lives by C. R. L. Fletcher and H. B. Butler.

2569. Lely and the Stuart portrait painters, a study of English portraiture before and after Van Dyck. By C. H. C. Baker. 2 vols. 4to. Lond. 1912. 240 Ports.

The only modern work systematically dealing with the subject. Cf. his Lely and Kneller. 8vo. Lond. 1922.

2570. Catalogue of portraits in the possession of the university, colleges, city and county of Oxford. By Rachael [Mrs. R. L.] Poole. 3 vols. 8vo. Oxf. 1912–25.

Valuable introduction. Cf. English 17th-century portrait drawings in Oxford collections. By C. F. Bell. Walpole Soc. v. 1917.

2571. Gleanings from the records of James I and Charles I. By C. C. Stopes. Burlington Magazine, No. cxix, vol. xxii. Lond. February 1913.

Extracts from an ' uncalendared and hitherto unread series' of accounts.

2571A. Designs by Inigo Jones for masques and plays at court. A descriptive catalogue of drawings for scenery and costumes mainly in the collection of the Duke of Devonshire, with introduction and notes by P. Simpson and C. F. Bell. Publ. by the Walpole Soc. xii. 1924 [in conjunction with the Malone Soc.].

¶ 2. ARCHITECTURE

(a) SOURCES

2572. The elements of architecture. By Sir H. Wotton. 1 vol. 4to. Lond. 1624.

Also in Reliquiae Wottonianae ed. by I. Walton, 1672, 4th ed. 1685. Repr. in Somers Tracts, iii.

2573. Oxonia illustrata. By D. Loggan. 1 vol. fol. Oxf. 1675.

2574. The whole body of ancient and modern architecture, with L. B. Albert's treatise of statues . . . published for the benefit of builders, limners, and painters. By J. Evelyn. 1 vol. fol. Lond. 1680.

A translation of Roland Freart's Parallel, 1651. The licence to print Evelyn's translation was issued at Lambeth in 1663. Cf. An account of architects and architecture, repr. in Evelyn's Miscellaneous writings (887).

2575. Cantabrigia illustrata. By D. Loggan. 1 vol. fol. Camb. 1690.

2576. Britannia illustrata, or views of several of the Queens palaces, as also of the principal seats of the nobility and gentry of Great Britain, curiously engraven on 80 copper plates. By L. Knyff, draughtsman, J. Kip, engraver. 1 vol. fol. Lond. 1709, 1720.

Bird's-eye views of great value for the history of the laying-out of houses and grounds.

2577. Vitruvius Britannicus, or the British architect. By C. Campbell. 2 vols. fol. Lond. 1715.

Vols. i and ii were published in 1715, vol. iii in 1725, vols. iv and v by Wolfe and Gandon 1767–71, vols. vi–vii by Richardson 1802–8. Vols. i and ii are invaluable as illustrating most of the important buildings of Great Britain in the latter part of the 17th century, ' in 200 large folio Plates, engraven by the best hands, and drawn either from the buildings themselves or the original designs of the architects '.

2578. The designs of Inigo Jones. By W. Kent. 1 vol. fol. Lond. 1727. Repr. 1835 for J. B. Nichols.

(b) LATER WORKS

2579. Architectural remains of the reign of Elizabeth and James, from accurate drawings and measurements taken from existing specimens. By C. J. Richardson. 1 vol. fol. Lond. 1840.

Only 1 vol. seems to have been published.

2580. Inigo Jones—a life of the architect [with] Remarks on some of his sketches for masques and dramas by J. R. Planché. And Five Court masques, [ed.] by J. Payne Collier. By P. Cunningham. 1 vol. 8vo. Lond. 1848.

2581. Architecture of the seventeenth century, pts. 1–3 [no more published]. By A. W. Hakewill. 1 vol. fol. Lond. 1856.

2582. A history of the three cathedrals dedicated to S. Paul in London. By W. Longman. 1 vol. 8vo. Lond. 1873. 6 engravings in steel, 50 woodcuts.

2583. A complete account of buildings erected by Sir Thomas Tresham. By J. A. Gotch. 1 vol. fol. Northampton. 1883.

2584. The Renaissance and Italian styles of architecture in Great Britain ... during the period 1450–1700. By W. Papworth. 1 vol. 8vo. Lond. 1883.
A list of dated examples.

2585. Old halls in Cheshire. By W. Taylor. 1 vol. Manchester. 1884.

2586. The architectural history of the university of Cambridge and of the colleges of Cambridge and Eton. Ed. with large additions and brought up to the present time by J. W. Clark. By R. Willis and J. W. Clark. 4 vols. 8vo. Camb. 1886, with plans.

2587. The formal garden in England. By R. Blomfield. 1 vol. 8vo. Lond. 1892. 3rd ed. 1901.

2588. Architecture of the Renaissance in England. By J. A. Gotch assisted by W. T. Brown. 2 vols. fol. Lond. 1894. 145 plates, 180 illustrations in text.
A series of views and details from buildings erected between the years 1560–1635, with historical and critical text.

2589. London churches of the 17th and 18th centuries. By G. H. Birch. 1 vol. fol. Lond. 1896. 64 plates and other illustrations.
An account of churches erected in London between 1630 and 1730 from designs of Inigo Jones, Wren, Hawksmoor, and Gibbs. For a short list of other works see Journal of the London Soc. April 1924.

2590. A history of Renaissance architecture in England 1500–1800. By R. Blomfield. 2 vols. 8vo. Lond. 1897. 90 plates, 150 illustrations by author.
Later edn. 1900 is an abridgement: Short history of Renaissance architecture in England, 1500–1800. An account of the development of Neo-classical architecture in England from the time of Henry VIII till the Gothic revival.

2591. Later Renaissance architecture in England : a series of examples of the domestic buildings erected subsequent to the Elizabethan Period. By J. Belcher and M. Macartney. 2 vols. fol. Lond. 1901. 170 plates, 153 illustrations in text.

2592. Early Renaissance architecture in England. By J. A. Gotch. 1 vol. la. 8vo. Lond. 1901. 87 plates, 230 illustrations in text.
An account of the details of earlier Renaissance architecture prior to 1625.

2593. Sir Christopher Wren. By L. Milman. 1 vol. 8vo. Lond. 1908.
Cf. Parentalia (765). The Wren Society is publ. Wren's works [4to. Oxf. 1924-7]. So far there have appeared, Vols. 1–3, St. Paul's Cathedral; Vol. 4, Hampton Court Palace, 1689–1702. Both reproduce original Wren drawings. Eds. A. T. Bolton and H. Duncan Hendry.

2594. The growth of the English house. A short history of its architectural development from 1100 to 1800. By J. A. Gotch. 1 vol. 8vo. Lond. 1909. Illustrations.
Cf. his The English home from Charles I to George IV. Its architecture, decoration and garden design. 1 vol. 8vo. Lond. 1918. Illus.

¶ 3. MUSIC

(a) COLLECTIONS

2595. Catalogue of printed music, published 1487–1800, now in the British Museum. Ed. by W. Barclay Squire. 2 vols. 8vo. Oxford University Press for the British Museum. 1912.

Cf. A. Hughes-Hughes, Catalogue of MS. Music in the British Museum. Vol. i, Sacred vocal music ; ii, Secular vocal music ; iii, Instrumental music, treatises, &c. 8vo. 1906–9.

2596. A plaine and easie introduction to practical musicke. By T. Morley. 1 vol. fol. Lond. 1597. Later eds. 1 vol. 8vo. Lond. 1608 ; 1 vol. 4to. Lond. 1771.

In three parts : (1) on singing, (2) on descant, (3) on composition. The most important work in English on modal music. See Mr. G. E. P. Arkwright's article on Morley in Grove's Dictionary of Music and Musicians.

2597. Parthenia. By W. Byrd, J. Bull, O. Gibbons. 1 vol. fol. Lond. 1611. Later eds. 1613, 1635, and 1650.

The first collection of virginal music printed from engraved plates in England. It was printed by the celebrated engraver William Hole. A version ' translated into modern notation ' was edited by E. F. Rimbault for the Musical Antiquarian Society in 1847.

2598. A briefe discourse of the true (but neglected) use of charact'ring the degrees by their perfection, imperfection, and diminution in mensurable musicke. By T. Ravenscroft. 1 vol. 4to. Lond. 1614.

A treatise on the elements of music, with compositions by E. Peiss, J. Bennet, and T. Ravenscroft.

2599. The first book of selected church musick. Ed. by J. Barnard. 10 part-books. fol. Lond. 1641.

Post-Reformation anthems and services. No complete printed copy is known to exist. There is a complete set of MSS. parts, with an organ part collated by John Bishop of Cheltenham, in the British Museum : Add. MSS. 30085–7.

2600. A breif introduction to the skill of musick for song and viol. By J. Playford. 1 vol. 8vo. Lond. 1654.

In two ' books ' : (1) on the elements of music, (2) on instructions for playing the bass-viol and treble violin. To the edition of 1660 is added, with a separate title-page, Campion's treatise on The art of setting or composing musick in parts, with annotations by Christopher Simpson. The 12th ed. [1694] is corrected and amended by H. Purcell. The work went through 19 editions, the best of which is dated 1730.

2601. Musick's monument. By T. Mace. 1 vol. fol. Lond. 1676. Port.

In three parts : (1) on the singing of psalms in parochial churches, (2) on the lute, (3) on the viol. The best-known authority for the practice of lute-music.

2602. Orpheus Britannicus. By H. Purcell. Ed. by H. Playford. 2 vols. fol. Lond. 1698, 1702.

A collection of Purcell's songs.

2603. Cathedral music. Ed. by W. Boyce. 3 vols. fol. Lond. 1760–73.

A collection of services and anthems by English composers. All three volumes contain examples of 17th-century music.

2604. Cathedral music. Ed. by S. Arnold. 4 vols. fol. Lond. 1790.
Supplementary to Boyce.

2605. Publications of the Musical Antiquarian Society. 19 vols. fol. Lond. 1841–8.

Republications of old English music. Vol. iii consisted of Purcell's Dido and Qucas, ed. by G. A. Macfarren, 1842; vol. vii of Purcell's Bonduca, ed. by E. F. Rimbault, 1842; vol. x of Purcell's King Arthur, ed. by Edward Taylor, 1843; vol. xviii of Parthenia (an early collection of virginal music, of which the probable date is 1611), ed. by E. F. Rimbault, 1847; and vol. xix of Purcell's Ode for St. Cecilia's Day, ed. by E. F. Rimbault, 1848.

2606. Works by H. Purcell (Purcell Soc. edition). 24 vols. fol. London. 1878. In progress.

2607. The Fitzwilliam virginal book. Ed. by J. A. Fuller Maitland and W. Barclay Squire. 2 vols. fol. Lond. 1894–9.

The most important known collection of Elizabethan and Jacobean virginal music. See Mr. W. Barclay Squire's article on Virginal Music in Grove's Dictionary of music and musicians, 2nd ed., which gives an account of this collection and a table of its contents.

2608. The king's musick. By H. C. De Lafontaine. 1 vol. 8vo. Lond. 1909.

A transcript of records relating to musicians in the service of the English Court from 1460 to 1700. Based on The old cheque-book of the chapel royal from 1561–1744. Ed. E. F. Rimbault. Cam. Soc. 1872.

2608A. Other recent publications are : The English school of lutenist song writers. Transcribed, scored, and edited from the original editions by E. H. Fellowes. 15 parts. 4to. Lond. 1920–5. Second series in progress; English aiyres 1598–1612. Transcribed and edited from the original editions by P. Warlock [i.e. Philip Heseltine] and P. Wilson. 4 vols. 4to. Lond. 1922–5 [cf. P. Warlock's The English ayre, 8vo. Lond. 1926] ; The English madrigal school, ed. E. H. Fellowes. 36 vols. 8vo. Lond. 1913–24.

(b) LATER WORKS

2609. A general history of the science and practise of music. By Sir J. Hawkins. 5 vols. 4to. Lond. 1776. Ports. Later eds. 2 vols. 8vo. Lond. 1853 and 1875 with a supplementary vol. and portraits in each case.

2610. A general history of music. By C. Burney. 4 vols. 4to. Lond. 1776–89.

2611. Biographie universelle des musiciens. By F. J. Fétis. 8 vols. 8vo. Paris. 1835–44. Later ed. 10 vols. 8vo. Paris. 1860–80 corrected. Ed. by A. Pougin.

Ed. of 1860–80, includ. 2 vols. of Supplement by the editor (A. Pougin), dated respectively 1878 and 1880. The actual 2nd ed. of Fétis came out 1860–5 ; but Pougin's two volumes are always incorporated with it.

2612. Memoirs of musick. By R. North. Ed. by E. F. Rimbault. 1 vol. 4to. Lond. 1846.

History of music to beginning of 18th century. The probable date of the MS. is 1728. Chiefly valuable on the 17th century. Some memoranda about music, and another version of the above, are in Brit. Mus. Add. MSS. 32531–7.

2613. Musikalisches Konversations-lexikon. By H. Mendel. 11 vols. 8vo. Berlin. 1870–81.

2614. Dictionary of music and musicians. Ed. by Sir G. Grove. 4 vols. 8vo. Lond. 1879–90. 2nd ed. 5 vols. 8vo. Lond. 1904–10. Ed. J. A. Fuller Maitland.

2615. Purcell (Great Musicians Series). By W. H. Cummings. Ed. by F. Hueffer. 1 vol. 8vo. Lond. 1881.

Requires to be corrected by Mr. J. A. Fuller Maitland's article in Grove's Dictionary of music and musicians, 2nd ed. See also special articles on Purcell's Church music, by Mr. G. E. P. Arkwright, in the Musical Antiquary for Jan. 1910 and July 1910, and on Purcell's Dramatic music by Mr. W. Barclay Squire in the Sammelbände of the Internationale Musik Gesellschaft for Sept. 1904.

2616. Musiklexikon. By H. Riemann. 2nd ed. 1 vol. 8vo. Leipsic. 1882.

English translation from ed. 2 by J. S. Shedlock. 1 vol. 8vo. Lond. 1893–7. 2nd ed. 1902.

2617. Geschichte der Musik in England. By W. Nagel. 2 vols. 8vo. Strassburg, 1894.

Ends with Purcell. Vol. ii is specially valuable for the music of the 17th century.

2618. A history of English music. By H. Davey. 1 vol. 8vo. Lond. 1895.

2619. Biographisch-Bibliographisches Quellen-Lexikon der Musiker und Musikgelehrter. By R. Eitner. 10 vols. 8vo. Leipsic. 1900–4.

Chiefly valuable for its bibliography of composers, &c. It comes down to the middle of the 19th century.

2620. The music of the seventeenth century. By Sir C. H. H. Parry. 1 vol. 8vo. Oxf. 1902.

Vol. iii of the Oxford History of Music.

2621. Samuel Pepys : lover of music. By Sir F. Bridge. 1 vol. 8vo. Lond. 1903.

2622. The history of music to the death of Schubert. By J. K. Paine. Ed. by A. A. Howard. 1 vol. 8vo. Boston. 1907.

Contains two chapters on English music, one 16th century and one 17th century.

2623. A History of music in England. By E. Walker. 1 vol. 8vo. Oxf. 1907.

2624. A history of English Cathedral music, 1549–1889. By J. S. Bumpus. 2 vols. 8vo. Lond. 1908. Ports.

IX. SCIENCE AND MEDICINE

THE bibliographies of science are mostly catalogues, arranged alphabetically and covering many centuries, but valuable for reference. Probably the easiest approach to the subject is by means of such studies as Weld (2669), Sachs (2671), the Cambridge Modern History (2673), Cantor (2692), Bryant (2695), and Moore (2718, 2722). From such works a general knowledge of the leading scientists can be acquired, and then recourse is possible to the Dictionary of National Biography and the bibliographies here listed. The items in this section have been selected with a view to the needs of the general historian rather than of the scientific expert, but an attempt has been made to include at least one work or life of the leading scientists, and thus to facilitate further study.

¶ 1. GENERAL AND MISCELLANEOUS SCIENCE

(a) BIBLIOGRAPHIES AND SOURCES

2625. Catalogue of books on natural science in the Radcliffe Library at the Oxford University Museum up to December 1872. 1 vol. 4to. Oxf. 1877.
With annual supplements to date.

2626. Guide to the literature of botany, being a classified selection of botanical works. By B. D. Jackson. 1 vol. 8vo. Lond. 1881.
Has over 9,000 titles of English and foreign books.

2627. Catalogue of the books, manuscripts, maps and drawings in the British Museum (Natural History). 5 vols. 4to. Lond. 1903–15.
Vol. vi, Supplement A–I, 1922.

2628. Bibliotheca chemica : a catalogue of the alchemical, chemical and pharmaceutical books in the collection of the late James Young of Kelly and Durris. By J. Ferguson. 2 vols. 4to. Glasgow. 1906.

2629. Bibliotheca chemico-mathematica : catalogue of works in many tongues on exact and applied science, with a subject-index. By H. Zeitlinger and H. C. Sotheran. 2 vols. 8vo. Lond. 1921. Many plates.
A sale catalogue containing over 17,000 items with notes.

2630. The feminine monarchie, or a treatise concerning bees. By C. Butler. 1 vol. 8vo. Oxf. 1609.

An entertaining book, whose 3rd ed. [1634] is in phonetic spelling.

2631. Propositiones tentationum : sive propaedeumata de vitis et faecunditate compositorum naturalium. By T. Willis. 1 vol. 8vo. Lond. 1615.

2632. Novum organum. By Francis Bacon, Viscount St. Albans. 1 vol. fol. Lond. 1620. Later ed. 8vo. Oxf. 1890. Ed. by T. Fowler.

This was intended to be the second part of the Instauratio magna, though it was the first published.

2633. Sylva sylvarum : or a naturall historie. In ten centuries. By Francis Bacon, Viscount St. Albans. 1 vol. fol. Lond. 1627. Port.

Published after the author's death by W. Rawley. ' A miscellaneous collection of observations and experiments in natural history.' Many of them are puerile and even ridiculous, nevertheless ' it is probably the best and most complete collection of the kind that, up to that time, had been published '.

2634. Insectorum sive minimorum animalium theatrum : olim ab Edoardo Wottono, Conrado Gesnero, Thomaque Pennis inchoatum. By T. Muffet or Moffett, 1 vol. fol. Lond. 1634. Woodcuts.

Publ. thirty years after author's death. Trans. by John Rowland as The theater of insects, and app. to his reissue in 1658 of E. Topsell's Historie of foure-footed beasts [1 vol. fol. Lond. 1607] and Historie of serpents [1 vol. fol. Lond. 1608]. Moffett's Theatrum begins entomological science.

2635. Two treatises. In the one of which the nature of bodies ; in the other the nature of man's soule. By Sir K. Digby. 1 vol. fol. Lond. 1644.

2636. Phytologia Britannica. By W. How. 1 vol. 8vo. Lond. 1650.

The first British flora.

2637. Exercitationes de generatione animalium. By W. Harvey. 1 vol. 4to. Lond. 1651.

The publication of this was due to Dr. Ent. The account of the development of the duck is clear, good and laborious, and as far as the apparatus of the day permitted accurate, but until the invention of the compound microscope many details necessarily escaped observation.

2638. Arcana microcosmi: or the hid secrets of man's body discovered. With a refutation of Dr. Brown's vulgar errors, the Lord Bacon's Natural history, and Dr. Harvey's Book de generatione. By A. Ross. 1 vol. 8vo. Lond. 1652.

2639. Adam in Eden : or nature's paradise. The history of plants, fruits, herbs and flowers. By W. Coles. 1 vol. fol. Lond. 1657.

2640. A discourse concerning the vegetation of plants. By Sir K. Digby. 1 vol. 12mo. Lond. 1661.

The work of a gifted amateur and partly a quack. It is said that the importance of ' vital air ' (oxygen) to living plants was first noticed in this book.

2641. Sylva, or a discourse of forest-trees. By J. Evelyn. 1 vol. fol. Lond. 1664.

A classic and a standard work, which had a very direct and stimulating influence on planting.

2642. Micrographia. By R. Hooke. 1 vol. fol. Lond. 1665.

' A book full of ingenious ideas and singular anticipations.'

2643. Philosophical transactions of the Royal Society. 4to. Lond.

Vols. i–xxix cover 1665–1716. Cf. A general index, by P. H. Maty, publ. 4to. Lond. 1787 ; An abridgement to 1700, ed. by John Lowthorp, 1705 ; and another 1700–20, by H. Jones. For other abridgements, &c. see Lowndes, pp. 2143–7.

2644. The history of the Royal Society of London for the improving of natural knowledge. By T. Sprat. 1 vol. 4to. Lond. 1667.

Cf. H. Stubbe's A censure upon certain passages contained in the History of the Royal Society as being destructive to the established religion of the Church of England [4to. Oxf. 1670].

2645. Plus ultra, or the progress and advancement of knowledge since the days of Aristotle in an account of some of the most remarkable late improvements of practical, useful learning. By J. Glanvill. 1 vol. 8vo. Lond. 1668.

Deals with scientific discoveries. Cf. H. Stubbe's The Plus ultra reduced to a nonplus, or a specimen of some animadversions upon the Plus ultra of Mr. Glanvill [4to. Warwick. 1670]. Glanvill replied with A prefatory answer to Mr. Henry Stubbe, the doctor of Warwick [8vo. Lond. 1670]. For the rest of this controversy see E. Arber's The Term Catalogues, i. 67, 73, 79, &c.

2646. The natural history of nitre : or, a philosophical discourse of the nature, generation, place and artificial extraction of nitre. By W. Clarke. 1 vol. 8vo. Lond. 1670.

2647. Essays on several important subjects in philosophy and religion. By J. Glanvill. 1 vol. 4to. Lond. 1676.

The essays are : (i) Against confidence in philosophy ; (ii) Of scepticism and certainty ; (iii) Modern improvements of knowledge ; (iv) The usefulness of philosophy to theology ; (v) The agreement of reason and religion ; (vi) Against sadducism in the matter of witchcraft ; (vii) Antifanatick theologie and free philosophy.

2648. Ornithologiae libri tres. Totum opus recognovit . . . Joh. Raius. By F. Willughby. 1 vol. fol. Lond. 1676.

This records the first attempt to study birds scientifically, and the first effort at a rational scheme of classification.

2649. Exercitationes de differentiis et nominibus animalium. By W. Charleton. 2nd ed. 1 vol. fol. Oxf. 1677.

1st ed. was : Onomasticon zoicon, plerorumque animalium differentias et nomina propria pluribus linguis exponens. 1 vol. 4to. Lond. 1668.

2650. Philosophical dialogues concerning the principles of natural bodies. By W. Simpson. 1 vol. 8vo. Lond. 1677.

2651. Historiae animalium Angliae libri tres. By M. Lister. 1 vol. 4to. Lond. 1678.

2652. The ornithology of Francis Willughby. In three books. Translated and enlarged by J. Ray. 1 vol. fol. Lond. 1678.

2653. Aurifontina chymica : or, a collection of fourteen small treatises concerning the first matter of philosophers for the discovery of their (hitherto so much concealed) mercury. Ed. by [? W. Cooper]. 1 vol. 12mo. Lond. 1680.

2654. Plantarum historiae universalis Oxoniensis, ii and iii. By R. Morison. Ed. by J. Bobart. 2 vols. fol. Oxf. 1680–99. Port.

Apparently part i never appeared. Cf. Plantarum umbelliferarum distributio nova. 1 vol. fol. Oxf. 1672. Many plates.

2655. The anatomy of plants. By N. Grew. 1 fol. Lond. 1682.

In four books with numerous plates. Although a disputable point, it is believed by many that it was Grew who first observed the existence of sex in plants.

2656. Collectanea chymica: a collection of ten several treatises in chymistry, concerning the liquor alkahest, the mercury of philosophers, and other curiosities worthy the perusal. 1 vol. 8vo. Lond. 1684.

Partly repr. in Collectanea chymica; being certain select treatises on alchemy and hermetic medicine. Ed. by A. E. Waite. 1 vol. 8vo. Lond. 1893.

2657. De historia piscium libri quinque. Recognovit Joh. Raius. By F. Willughby. 2 vols. fol. Oxf. 1685–6.

Illus. and publ. at the expense of Bishop Fell and the Royal Society.

2658. Historia plantarum generalis. By J. Ray. 3 vols. fol. Lond. 1686–1704.

Sachs says this ' treats of the whole of theoretical botany in the style of a modern textbook '.

2659. Synopsis methodica stirpium Britannicarum. By J. Ray. 1 vol. 8vo. Lond. 1690 and 1724.

The earliest systematic account of British plants, widely used for many years.

2660. A natural history : containing many not common observations : extracted out of the best modern writers. By Sir T. P. Blount. 1 vol. 8vo. Lond. 1693.

2661. Synopsis methodica animalium. By J. Ray. 1 vol. 8vo. Lond. 1693. Port.

This book marked an epoch in the history of Zoology which had been practically at a standstill since Aristotle. The treatise has been described ' as the first classification of animals that can be reckoned both general and grounded in nature '.

2662. Musei Petiveriani centuria prima-decima rariora naturae continens viz. animalia fossilia plantas . . . By J. Petiver. 1 vol. 8vo. Lond. 1695–1703.

2663. Ourang-outang, sive homo sylvestris, or the anatomy of a pygmy. By E. Tyson. 1 vol. 4to. Lond. 1699.

This, which really deals with the chimpanzee and not with 'ourang', is one of a series of monographs relating to single species of animal. Tyson was the first to publish elaborate monographs on particular animals in this country.

2664. Methodus insectorum. By J. Ray. 1 vol. 8vo. Lond. 1705.

This, with his Historia insectorum [1 vol. 4to. Lond. 1710], threw a new light on the classification of insects.

2665. A collection of letters illustrative of the progress of science in England from the reign of Queen Elizabeth to that of Charles the Second. Ed. by J. O. Halliwell. 1 vol. 8vo. Lond. 1841.

2666. Correspondence of scientific men of the seventeenth century . . . printed from the originals in the collection of . . . the Earl of Macclesfield. Ed. by S. P. Rigaud and S. J. Rigaud. 2 vols. 8vo. Oxf. 1841–62.

Has valuable correspondence of Newton, Barrow, Wallis, and others.

(b) LATER WORKS

2667. The lives of the professors of Gresham College. By J. Ward. 1 vol. fol. Lond. 1740.

2668. The history of the Royal Society of London. By T. Birch. 4 vols. 4to. Lond. 1756–7.

2669. A history of the Royal Society, with memoirs of the presidents. By C. R. Weld. 2 vols. 8vo. Lond. 1848.

2670. The life, times, and scientific labours of the second Marquis of Worcester. By H. Dircks. 1 vol. 8vo. Lond. 1865.

Cf. Worcesteriana : a collection of literary authorities, affording historical biographical and other notices relating to Edward Somerset . . . second Marquis of Worcester. 1 vol. 8vo. Lond. 1866.

2671. History of botany, 1530–1860. By J. von Sachs. Trans. by H. E. F. Garnsey. 1 vol. 8vo. Oxf. 1890 and 1906.

Continuation by J. R. Green, 1909, has bibl.

2672. Joseph Glanvill. A study in English thought and letters of the seventeenth century. By F. Greenslet. 1 vol. 8vo. Oxf. and New York, 1900.

2673. European science in the seventeenth and earlier years of the eighteenth centuries. Camb. Mod. Hist. v. 1908. Bibl.

(i) Mathematical and physical science, by W. W. Rouse Ball ; (ii) Other branches of science, by Sir M. Foster. Cf. The progress of science, by A. E. Shipley, in Camb. Hist. of Eng. Lit. viii. 1912. Bibl.

2674. Early science in Oxford. By R. T. Gunther. Oxf. Hist. Soc. 2 vols. 8vo. Oxf. 1923. Illus.

Vol. i, Chemistry, mathematics, physics and surveying ; ii, Astronomy.

2675. Three centuries of chemistry. By I. Mason. 1 vol. 8vo. Lond. 1925. Illus.

¶ 2. MATHEMATICAL AND PHYSICAL SCIENCE

(a) SOURCES

2676. Mirifici logarithmorum canonis descriptio, ejusque usus, in utraque trigonometria ; ut etiam in omni logistica mathematica ; amplissimi facillimi et expeditissimi explicatio. By J. Napier, of Merchistoun. 1 vol. 4to. Edin. 1614. Diagr.

2677. Arithmetica logarithmica sive logarithmorum chiliades triginta, pro numeris . . . ad 20,000 et a 90,000 ad 100,000. . . . By H. Briggs. 1 vol. fol. Lond. 1624. Later ed. 1 vol. fol. Gouda. 1628, ed. by A. Vlacq.

Vlacq added the logarithms from 20,000 to 90,000 omitted by Briggs, as well as tables of trigonometrical functions. Substantially all modern tables of logarithms are based on this work.

2678. Artis analyticae praxis ... By T. Harriot.   Ed. by W. Warner.   1 vol. fol. Lond. 1631.

The best work on algebra and theory of equations of the time.

2679. Clavis mathematicae denuo limata, sive potius fabricata.   By W. Oughtred.   1 vol. 8vo. Lond. 1631.   4th ed. 4 pts. 12mo. Oxf. 1667.

The title is taken from ed. of 1667.   Original title was Arithmeticae in numeris et speciebus institutio.   A text-book of arithmetic and algebra.   Cf. W. Oughtred, by F. Cajori.   1 vol. 8vo. Chicago and Lond. 1916.

2680. New experiments physico-mechanicall touching the spring of the air and its effects (made for the most part in a new pneumatical engine), ... By R. Boyle.   1 vol. 8vo. Oxf. 1660.

Contains important experiment which led to the well-known ' Boyle's law '.   Boyle's Works, with his life by T. Birch, were publ. 5 vols. fol. Lond. 1744, later ed. 6 vols. 4to. Lond. 1772.

2681. The sceptical chymist : or chymico-physical doubts and paradoxes, touching the experiments whereby vulgar spagyrists are wont to endeavour to evince their salt, sulphur, and mercury, to be the true principles of things. ... By R. Boyle.   1 vol. 8vo. Oxf. 1661.

' Marks a turning-point in the history of chemistry.'   Sir Edward Thorpe.

2682. Lectiones xviii, *Cantabrigiae* in scholis publicis habitae ; in quibus opticorum phaenomenΩn genuinae rationes investigantur, ac exponuntur. Annexae sunt lectiones aliquot *Geometricae*.   By I. Barrow.   1 vol. sm. 4to. Lond. 1669.   Diagrams.

The ' Lectiones geometricae ' has a separate title-page dated 1670, and is separately paged.   His mathematical lectures were trans. by J. Kirkby [1 vol. 8vo. Lond. 1744], his geometrical lectures by E. Stone [1 vol. 8vo. Lond. 1735].

2683. Lectures de potentia restitutiva, or of spring, explaining the power of springing bodies ... By R. Hooke.   1 vol. 4to. Lond. 1678.

Contains the well-known ' Hooke's law '.

2684. Philosophiae naturalis principia mathematica.   By I. Newton. 1 vol. 4to. Lond. 1687.   Diagrams.   Later eds.: Camb. 1713, ed. by R. Cotes. Lond. 1726, ed. by H. Pemberton.

The second and third editions appeared during Newton's lifetime and were revised by him.   There are many later eds., complete or partial.   By far the most important book on physical science of the period and one of the greatest of all time.

2685. Opera mathematica.   By J. Wallis.   3 vols. fol. Oxf. 1695–9.   Diagr. Port.

2686. Astronomiae cometicae synopsis.   By E. Halley.   4to. Lond. 1705. Diagr.

Contains *inter alia* the prediction of the return of ' Halley's ' comet.   It is a paper in the Philosophical Transactions of the Royal Society for March, 1705, vol. 23 (pp. 1882–99).

2687. De mensura sortis, seu de probabilitate eventuum in ludis a casu fortuito pendentibus.   By A. De Moirre.   1 vol. 4to. Lond. 1711.

A paper in the Philosophical Transactions of the Royal Society for Jan., Feb., Mar. 1711, vol. 27, pp. 213–64.

2688. Isaaci Newtoni Opera quae exstant omnia. Ed. by S. Horsley. 5 vols. 4to. Lond. 1779–85. Diagr.

The only complete ed. of Newton's works.

2689. Correspondence of Sir Isaac Newton and Professor Cotes, including letters of other eminent men . . . other unpublished letters and papers by Newton. By J. Edleston. 1 vol. 8vo. Lond. 1850. Port.

(b) LATER WORKS

2690. History of physical astronomy from the earliest ages to the middle of the nineteenth century . . . By R. Grant. 1 vol. 8vo. Lond. 1852.

2691. Memoirs of the life, writings, and discoveries of Sir Isaac Newton. By D. Brewster 2 vols. 8vo. Lond. 1855. Diagr. Ports.

Cf. G. J. Gray, A bibliography of the works of Sir Isaac Newton, 1 vol. 8vo. Camb. 1888. Port.

2692. Vorlesungen über Geschichte der Mathematik. By M. Cantor. 4 vols. 8vo. Leipzig. 1880–1908. Diagr.

The standard modern history of mathematics. The Stewart period is contained in vols. ii and iii. Cf. F. Cajori, A history of Mathematics, 2nd ed. 1 vol. 8vo. N.Y. 1919.

2693. A history of the study of mathematics at Cambridge. By W. W. Rouse Ball. 1 vol. 8vo. Camb. 1889.

He also wrote : A short account of the history of mathematics. 1 vol. 8vo. Lond. 1888. 3rd ed. 1901.

2694. Great astronomers. By Sir R. S. Ball. 1 vol. 8vo. Lond. 1895. Illus. Later ed. 1907.

Brief lives of Isaac Newton, John Flamsteed, Edmund Halley.

2695. A history of astronomy. By W. W. Bryant. 1 vol. 8vo. Lond. 1907. Illus.

¶ 3. MEDICINE

(a) BIBLIOGRAPHIES AND GENERAL SOURCES

2696. Catalogus librorum . . . in Musaeo Harveano. By C. Merrett. 1 vol. 4to. Lond. 1660.

The earliest catalogue of the library of the Royal College of Physicians.

2697. Catalogue of the library of the Royal College of Surgeons in London. 1 vol. 8vo. Lond. 1831.

2698. Royal College of Physicians of London. Catalogue of the library. 1 vol. 8vo. Lond. 1912.

2699. Catalogue of the library of the Society of Apothecaries. By W. B. Taylor. Ed. by J. E. Harting. 1 vol. 8vo. Lond. 1913.

2700. Via recta ad vitam longam. By T. Venner. 1 vol. 4to. Lond. 1638.

2701. The surgeon's mate ; or military and domestique surgery. By J. Woodall. 4 pts. in 1 vol. fol. Lond. 1639. Plates.

2702. Certain necessary directions as well for the cure of the plague as for preventing the infection . . . set down by the College of Physicians. 1 vol. sm. 4to. Lond. 1665.

2703. A letter concerning the present state of physick and the regulation of the practice of it in this kingdom. By T. M. 1 vol. sm. 4to. Lond. 1665.

2704. A short view of the frauds and abuses committed by apothecaries as well in relation to patients as physicians. By C. Merrett. 1 vol. sm. 4to. Lond. 1669. Later ed. 1670.

Answered by Lex talionis sive vindiciae pharmacopaeorum, or a short reply to Dr. Merrett's book and others written against the apothecaries [sm. 4to. Lond. 1670]. Merrett replied in Self-conviction or an enumeration of the absurdities, railings, &c. against the college and physicians in general . . . and also an answer to the rest of lex talionis [sm. 4to. Lond. 1670].

2705. A discourse setting forth the unhappy condition of the practice of physick in London. By J. Goddard. 1 vol. sm. 4to. Lond. 1670.

2706. The family-physician and the house-apothecary. By G. Harvey. 1 vol. 12mo. Lond. 1676. 2nd ed. 1678.

One of many popular works by Harvey.

2707. Manuale medicum, or a small treaties of the art of physick. By H. Chamberlain. 1 vol. 12mo. Lond. 1685.

2708. The dispensary. A poem. By Sir S. Garth. 1 vol. 4to. Lond. 1699. Later ed. ed. by W. J. Leicht. 1 vol. 8vo. Heidelberg. 1905.

Cf. Dr. Johnson's Lives of the Poets, ed. G. B. Hill, vol. ii, *sub* Garth.

2709. The natural history of the chalybeat and purging waters of England, with their particular essays and uses. By B. Allen. 1 vol. 8vo. Lond. 1699 and 1711.

Cf. T. Venner, The baths of Bathe [1 vol. 4to. Lond. 1628 ; repr. Harl. Misc. iv.] ; E. Jorden, A discourse of naturall bathes and minerall waters [1 vol. 4to. Lond. 1631 and 1632] ; R. Peirce, Bath memoirs [8vo. Bristol. 1697], a 2nd ed. of which is apparently The history and memoirs of the Bath [12mo. Lond. 1713].

2710. Bellum medicinale, or the present state of doctors and apothecaries in London. 1 vol. 4to. Lond. 1701.

2711. Loimologia ; or, an historical account of the plague in London in 1665. By N. Hodges. 1 vol. 8vo. Lond. 1720.

2712. The plague pamphlets of Thomas Dekker. By F. P. Wilson. 1 vol. 8vo. Oxf. 1925.

See also F. P. Wilson's The plague in Shakespeare's London. 1 vol. 8vo. Oxf. 1927.

(b) LATER WORKS

2713. The illness and death of Henry Prince of Wales in 1612. A historical case of typhoid fever. By N. Moore. 1 vol. 8vo. Lond. 1882.

2714. Memorials of the craft of surgery in England. From materials compiled by J. F. South. Ed. by D'Arcy Power. 1 vol. 8vo. Lond. 1886. Plates.

2715. The annals of the barber-surgeons of London. By S. Young. 1 vol. 4to. Lond. 1890. Illus.

2716. A history of epidemics in Britain [664–1866]. By C. Creighton. 2 vols. 8vo. Camb. 1891–4.

2717. The history of the Society of Apothecaries of London. Illustrated by the author. By C. R. B. Barrett. 1 vol. 4to. Lond. 1905.

2718. The history of the study of medicine in the British Isles. By N. Moore. The Fitz-Patrick Lectures for 1905–6. 1 vol. 8vo. Oxf. 1908. Illus.
Lecture II. The education of physicians in London in the 17th century. iii and iv. The history of the study of clinical medicine in the British Islands.

2719. The last days of Charles II. By R. Crawfurd. 1 vol. 8vo. Oxf. 1909. Ports. Bibl.
An investigation of the causes of the king's death.

2720. The king's evil. By R. Crawfurd. 1 vol. 8vo. Oxf. 1911. Illus.
The best contemporary work is John Browne's Charisma Basilicon. 1 vol. 8vo. Lond. 1684.

2721. The growth of medicine from the earliest times to 1800. By A. H. Buck. 1 vol. 8vo. Yale Univ. Press, and Oxf. 1917. Illus.

2722. The history of St. Bartholomew's Hospital. Vol. ii. By N. Moore. 2 vols. 4to. Lond. 1918. Illus.
Much general information, especially in the chapters on Harvey, and The successors of Harvey.

(c) BIOGRAPHIES AND COLLECTED WORKS

CULPEPER, NICHOLAS.

2723. Culpeper's works enlarged . . . and improved, or the complete English family physician. By N. Culpeper. Ed. by G. A. Gordon. 3 vols. 8vo. Lond. 1802. Illus.

HARVEY, WILLIAM.

2724. Gulielmi Harveii opera omnia ; a Collegio Medicorum Londinensi edita. 1 vol. 4to. Lond. 1766. Later ed. 1847. Ed. by R. Willis.
Ed. of 1847 is a trans. from the Latin.

2725. Memorials of Harvey, including a letter and autographs in facsimile. Ed. by J. H. Aveling. 1 vol. 8vo. Lond. 1875.

2726. William Harvey. By D'Arcy Power. Masters of Medicine series. 1 vol. 8vo. Lond. 1897.

LOWER, RICHARD.

2727. Two Oxford physiologists. By F. Gotch. 1 vol. 8vo. Oxf. 1908.
Studies of Richard Lower [1631–91] and John Mayow [1643–79].

PARÉ, AMBROISE.

2728. The workes of that famous chirurgion A. Parey. Translated out of Latin and compared with the French. Ed. by T. Johnson. 1 vol. fol. Lond. 1634. Woodcuts. Later ed. 1665.

Much esteemed in seventeenth-century England. Cf. F. R. Packard, Life and times of Ambroise Paré [1510–90]. 1 vol. 8vo. Lond. 1922.

RADCLIFFE, JOHN.

2729. Some memoirs of the life of John Radcliffe. By W. Pittis. 1 vol. 8vo. Lond. 1715. 4th ed. 1736.

Ed. of 1736 has new app. of letters, and is styled, Dr. Radcliffe's life and letters.

2730. Dr. John Radcliffe, a sketch of his life [1650–1714], with an account of his fellows and foundations. By J. B. Nias. 1 vol. 8vo. Oxf. 1918.

SYDENHAM, THOMAS.

2731. Opera omnia. By T. Sydenham. Ed. by G. A. Greenhill. 1 vol. 8vo. Lond. 1846. Later ed. 2 vols. 8vo. Lond. 1848–50. Ed. by R. G. Latham.

Both publ. by the Sydenham Soc. The later ed. is an Engl. trans. of the 1st.

2732. Thomas Sydenham. By J. F. Payne. Masters of Medicine series. 1 vol. 8vo. Lond. 1900.

WILLIS, THOMAS.

2733. Opera omnia. 1 vol. 4to. Amsterdam. 1682.

Trans. as : Dr. Willis's practice of physick. fol. Lond. 1684. Plates.

WISEMAN, RICHARD.

2734. Richard Wiseman, surgeon & sergeant-surgeon to Charles II. By Sir T. Longmore. 1 vol. 8vo. Lond. 1891.

(d) ROYAL COLLEGE OF PHYSICIANS

2735. Pharmacopœa Londinensis in qua medicamenta antiqua et nova usitatissima, sedulo collecta, accuratissime examinata . . . discribuntur. Opera medicorum collegii Londinensis. 1 vol. fol. Lond. 1618.

There are many eds. and trans. Cf. A physicall directory, or a translation of the London dispensatory . . . with many hundred additions. By N. Culpeper [4to. Lond. 1649].

2736. The Colledge of Physicians vindicated and the true state of physick . . . represented in answer to a scandalous pamphlet entitled ' The corner stone '. By C. Goodall. 1 vol. 8vo. Lond. 1676.

2737. The Royal College of Physicians of London founded and established by law . . and an historical account of the college's proceedings against empiricks and unlicensed practisers. By C. Goodall. 1 vol. 4to. Lond. 1684.

2738. The statutes of the Colledge of Physicians in London. Anon. 1 vol. 8vo. Lond. 1693.

English and Latin. For supplement and new eds. of the above, and for lists of members, see Brit. Mus. Catalogue, *sub* Academies, London.

2739. The roll of the Royal College of Physicians of London, comprising biographical sketches of all the eminent physicians. By W. R. Munk. 2 vols. 8vo. Lond. 1861. Later ed. 3 vols. 8vo. Lond. 1878.

Ed. of 1861 covers 1518–1800 ; that of 1878, 1518–1825.

X. POLITICAL SCIENCE

1. Sources.
2. Later works.

OWING to the Stuart succession, the civil war, and the revolution, the seventeenth century witnessed much speculation about the nature of government. There are four movements in political thought : (i) the elaboration and decline of the theory of the divine right of kings ; (ii) the emergence during and after the civil war of democratic ideas ; (iii) the development of the theory of sovereignty by Hobbes ; and (iv) the growth of a theory by which the power of the monarch was to be limited by the terms of an original contract of which Locke was the ablest exponent. The first is treated by James I (2741), Filmer (2752), and Figgis (2770). The second must be sought in a host of pamphlets and treatises, to which Gooch (2771) and Pease (2776) provide guidance. For the third and fourth the sources are the works of Hobbes (2746) and Locke (2765), whose ideas find commentators in modern writers such as Graham (2772), Dunning (2773), and Sorley (2775, 2777).

The influence of these theories upon political and constitutional development during this period can only be estimated after examination of such sources as the debates in the army council in 1647 (150) or in the convention parliament of 1689. Writers on political science have explored the origin of theories but have neglected their effect on politics in Stuart England.

¶ 1. SOURCES

2740. A comparative discourse of the bodies natural and politique wherein . . . is set forth the true forme of a commonweale. By E. Forsett. 1 vol. 4to. Lond. 1606.

2741. The workes of the most high and mighty prince James. 1 vol. fol. Lond. 1616. Later ed. 4to. Camb. Mass. 1918, ed. by C. H. McIlwain.

2742. The divine right of government natural and politique. By M. Hudson. 1 vol. 4to. Lond. 1647.

2743. An historical discourse of the uniformity of the government of England . . . By N. Bacon. 2 vols. 4to. Lond. 1647–51.

2744. The legall fundamentall liberties of the people of England revived, asserted, and vindicated. By J. Lilburne. 1 vol. 8vo. Lond. 1649.
Cf. No. 33.

2745. The case of the Commonwealth stated. By M. Nedham. 1 vol. 4to. Lond. 1649.
He also wrote The excellency of a free state [12mo. Lond. 1656], which should be compared with the leading articles in Mercurius Politicus. It was repr. in 1767 [8vo. Lond.].

2746. Leviathan, or the matter, forme, and power of a commonwealth ecclesiastical and civil. By T. Hobbes. 1 vol. fol. Lond. 1651. Later eds.: 8vo. Camb. 1904. Ed. by A. R. Waller. 1 vol. 8vo. Oxf. 1909. Ed. by W. G. Pogson Smith.

Cf. The English works of Thomas Hobbes, now first collected and edited by Sir William Molesworth. 11 vols. 8vo. Lond. 1839–45. Clarendon's criticism [A brief view and survey, 4to. Oxf. 1676] was repr. in his Miscellaneous tracts (2238n.). There are lives of Hobbes by G. C. Robertson [12mo. Edin. 1886] and Sir L. Stephen [8vo. Lond. 1904]. Ferdinand Tönnies wrote: Hobbes Leben und Lehre (Frommanns Klassiker der Philosophie, vol. ii), 8vo. Stuttgart, 1896. 3rd ed. 1925; and Thomas Hobbes der Mann und der Denker, 1 vol. Osterwieck, 1912. Cf. No. 51.

2747. Modern policies taken from Machiavel, Borgia and other choice authors. By W. Sancroft. 1 vol. 12mo. [? Lond.] 1653.
Repr. from 7th ed. 1657 in D'Oyly (1549) and in Somers Tracts, vol. vii, 1809 ed.

2748. Commonwealth of Oceana. By J. Harrington. 1 vol. fol. Lond. 1656. Later eds.: 1700 [with life and other works]. Ed. by J. Toland. 8vo. 1883. Ed. by H. Morley. Lund. 1924. Ed. by S. B. Liljegren.

Cf. Harrington and his Oceana, by H. F. Russell Smith, 1 vol. 8vo. Camb. 1914.

2749. The divine right and originall of the civill magistrate from God. By E. Gee. 1 vol. 8vo. Lond. 1658.

2750. The readie and easie way to establish a free commonwealth, and the excellence thereof compared with the inconveniences and dangers of readmitting kingship in this nation. By J. Milton. 1 vol. 4to. Lond. 1660.
Cf. Nos. 2415–20.

2751. The common interest of king and people: shewing the original antiquity and excellency of monarchy compared with aristocracy and democracy, and particularly of our English monarchy. J. Nalson. 1 vol. 8vo. Lond. 1678.

2752. Patriarcha: or the natural power of kings asserted. 1 vol. 8vo. Lond. 1680. By Sir R. Filmer. Later eds.: 1685. Ed. by E. Bohun and Sir J. Tyrrell. 1884. Ed. by H. Morley.

Filmer also wrote: The free-holders grand inquest touching . . . the king and his parliament, to which are added observations upon forms of government. 1 vol. 4to. Lond. 1648; later ed. 3 pts. 8vo. Lond. 1679.

2753. Plato redivivus, or a dialogue concerning government. By H. Neville. 1 vol. 8vo. Lond. 1681. 4th ed. 1763.

2754. The great point of succession discussed, with a full and particular answer to the late pamphlet entitled a brief history of the succession, &c. By R. Brady. 1 vol. fol. Lond. 1681.
Defends hereditary right, and contends that exclusion of James would be unlawful.

2755. Jus regium or . . . monarchy . . . maintain'd against Buchannan, Naphtali, Dolman, Milton. By Sir G. Mackenzie. 2 pts. 8vo. Edin. 1684.

2756. A brief history of the succession of the crown of England, &c. collected out of the records and the most authentic historians. . . . By John, Lord Somers. 1 vol. fol. Lond. 1689.

2757. The history of passive obedience since the Reformation [with continuation]. By A. Seller. 3 pts. 4to. Amsterdam, 1689–90.

2758. The fundamental constitution of the English government, proving King William and Queen Mary our lawful and rightful King and Queen . . . By W. Atwood. 1 vol. fol. Lond. 1690.

An argument on behalf of the ' original contract ' theory.

2759. An argument proving that the abrogation of King James by the people of England from the royal throne . . . was according to the constitution . . . By S. Johnson. 1 vol. 4to. Lond. 1692.

2760. Bibliotheca politica : or an enquiry into the ancient constitution of the English government . . . wherein all the chief arguments as well against as for the late revolution are . . . considered. . . By J. Tyrell. 1 vol. 4to. Lond. 1694. Later ed. 1 vol. fol. Lond. 1727.

Valuable statement of Whig case.

2761. Discourses concerning government published from the author's original manuscript. By A. Sidney. 1 vol. fol. Lond. 1698.

Publ. posthumously. Cf. Nos. 88 n., 978.

2762. Anglia libera : or the limitation and succession of the crown of England explained and asserted. . . . By J. Toland. 1 vol. 8vo. Lond. 1701.

A defence of the Acts of 1689 and 1701.

2763. The original power of the collective body of the people of England. By D. Defoe. 3rd ed. 8vo. Lond. 1702.

2764. The judgement of whole kingdoms and nations concerning the rights, power, and prerogative of kings, and the rights, priviledges and properties of the people . . . 1 vol. 8vo. Lond. 1710. Later ed. 1771.

Authorship doubtful : possibly by Lord Somers, but more probably by Daniel Defoe.

2765. The works of John Locke. 3 vols. fol. Lond. 1714. 12th ed. 9 vols. 8vo. Lond. 1822.

His two treatises of government publ. 8vo. Lond. 1689 ; ed. H. Morley, 8vo. Lond. 1884. For bibl. see Camb. Hist. Eng. Lit. viii. 1912. Cf. Sir F. Pollock and A. C. Fraser in Proc. Brit. Acad. 1903–4 ; S. P. Lamprecht [The moral and political philosophy of John Locke. 8vo. N.Y. 1918] ; lives of Locke by Peter, Lord King [1 vol. 4to. Lond. 1829 ; 3rd ed. 1 vol. 8vo. Lond. 1858] and by H. R. Fox Bourne [2 vols. 8vo. Lond. 1876] ; and Original letters of Locke, Algernon Sidney, and Anthony, Lord Shaftesbury, ed. by T. Forster. 1 vol. 8vo. Lond. 1830 ; 2nd ed. 1847.

2766. Notes upon the king's writ for choosing members of Parlement, 13 Charles II, being disquisitions on the government of England by King, Lords, and Commons. By B. Whitelocke. Ed. by C. Morton. 2 vols. 4to. Lond. 1766.

2767. The complete works of George Savile first Marquess of Halifax. Ed. by Sir W. Raleigh. 1 vol. 8vo. Oxf. 1912.

Cf. No. 900, where the above are also repr.

¶ 2. LATER WORKS

2768. History of English thought in the eighteenth century.   By L. Stephen. 2 vols. 8vo. Lond. 1876. Later ed. 1902.

2769. Kommunistische und demokratisch-sozialistische Strömungen während der englischen Revolution des 17. Jahrhunderts.   In Die Geschichte des Sozialismus. Bd. i. By E. Bernstein and C. Kautsky. 8vo. Stuttgart, 1895.

2770. The theory of the divine right of kings. By J. N. Figgis. 1 vol. 8vo. Camb. 1896. Bibl. Later ed. 1914.

2771. The history of English democratic ideas in the seventeenth century. By G. P. Gooch. 1 vol. 8vo. Camb. 1898.

Cf. his Political thought in England from Bacon to Halifax, Home University Libr. 1914–15. See also Borgeand, The rise of democracy in old and new England. Trans. B. Hill. 1 vol. 8vo. Lond. 1894.

2772. English political philosophy from Hobbes to Maine. By W. Graham. 1 vol. 8vo. Lond. 1899.

2773. A history of political theories from Luther to Montesquieu. By W. A. Dunning. 1 vol. 8vo. New York. 1905. Bibl.

2774. English political philosophy in the seventeenth and eighteenth centuries. By A. L. Smith. Camb. Mod. Hist. vi. 1909. Bibl.

2775. Hobbes and contemporary philosophy. By W. R. Sorley. Camb. Hist. of Eng. Lit. vii, 1911.

Cf. *ibid.* viii, 1912, for the same writer's John Locke. Both articles have good bibliographies.

2776. The leveller movement, a study in the historical and political theory of the English great civil war. By T. C. Pease. 1 vol. 8vo. Washington and Oxf. 1916. Bibl.

2777. A history of English philosophy. By W. R. Sorley. 1 vol. 8vo. Camb. 1920. Bibl.

XI. LOCAL HISTORY

1. General Bibliographies and Guides.
2. General Later Works.
3. County and other Local Records arranged alphabetically under counties.
4. London.

HUMPHREYS (2788) is the best general bibliography, and Gross (2782) is valuable for municipalities. Hyett and Bazeley (2811) provide a model county bibliography. General county, municipal and parish histories, covering many centuries, have been omitted perforce, although they often include relevant sections of importance. Similarly parish registers are excluded, but lists are contained in the books mentioned in No. 1472. Of the books dealing more or less exclusively with the Stuart period, preference has been given to the main sources, but it is hoped that sufficient minor ones have been included to show the nature of the material available. There is no work on local government for the seventeenth century to correspond with the magnum opus of Sidney and Beatrice Webb (2792), which is mainly concerned with the following century, but the introductions to published county records are often valuable : that by Willis Bund (2861) is a fine specimen. The Victoria County History (2790), at present incomplete, is so comprehensive and systematic that it should always be consulted. The inventories of the royal commission on historical monuments [4to. Lond. 1910–   ] contain much historical and bibliographical matter. So far there are published : Hertfordshire, Buckinghamshire (2 vols.), Essex (4 vols.), Huntingdonshire and two of the London volumes.

Local histories of the civil war are listed in the military section, and those dealing with the ecclesiastical history of particular districts are in the religious section.

¶ 1. GENERAL BIBLIOGRAPHIES AND GUIDES

2778. British topography, or an historical account of what has been done for illustrating the topographical antiquities of Great Britain and Ireland. By R. Gough. 2 vols. 4to. Lond. 1780.

Originally publ. in 1768 in one vol. as Anecdotes of British topography.

2779. A bibliographical account of the principal works relating to English topography. By W. Upcott. 3 vols. 8vo. Lond. 1818.

2780. Calendar and inventory of parliamentary surveys preserved among the records of the augmentation office. Rep. of the Deputy Keeper, vii. 224 ; viii. 52. 1846–7.

2781. The book of British topography : a classified catalogue of the topographical works in . . . the British Museum relating to Great Britain and Ireland. By J. P. Anderson. 1 vol. 8vo. Lond. 1881.

2782. A bibliography of British municipal history. By C. Gross. 1 vol. 8vo. N.Y. 1897.

2783. Report of the committee appointed to enquire as to the existing arrangements for the collection and custody of local records.   Cd. 1335. 1 vol. fol. Lond. 1902.

Deals with England, Wales, Scotland, and Ireland.   App. III contains details of the nature and dates of records appertaining to counties, county boroughs, non-county boroughs, London vestries, bishoprics, cathedrals, archdeaconries, &c., together with useful information as to extracts, &c. printed from the same.

2784. Index of archaeological papers, 1665–1890 [with annual supplements to 1908].   Ed. by G. L. Gomme.   1 vol. 8vo. Lond. 1907.

Valuable but far from exhaustive : arranged under authors.

2785. Index of inquisitions preserved in the Public Record Office.   Vol. iii, James I ; iv, Charles I and later.   Lists and Indexes.   Nos. xxxi, xxxiii. 1909.

2786. A guide to the reports on collections of manuscripts of private families, corporations and institutions in Great Britain and Ireland issued by the royal commissioners for historical manuscripts.   Part I. Topographical.   1 vol. 8vo. Lond. 1914.

2787. Third report of the royal commission on public records appointed to inquire into and report on the state of the public records and local records of a public nature of England and Wales ... Vol. iii.   Cmd. 367.   3 pts. fol. Lond. 1916–19.

Summarizes the returns of 1800, 1837, and 1902, and adds more recent information about local records in local repositories.   This is the best guide to the various classes of local records.   The First and Second Reports [1912, 1914] should also be consulted.

2788. A handbook to county bibliography : being a bibliography of bibliographies relating to the counties and towns of Great Britain and Ireland.   By A. L. Humphreys.   1 vol. 4to. Lond. 1917.

¶ 2. GENERAL LATER WORKS

2789. The history of the boroughs and municipal corporations of the United Kingdom, from the earliest to the present time.   By H. A. Merewether and A. J. Stephens.   3 vols. 8vo. Lond. 1835.

See Gross, Bibliography of municipal hist., p. xxv seq.

2790. Victoria history of the counties of England.   Ed. by W. Page, H. A. Doubleday, and others.   Westminster. 1900.   In progress.

Deals with the political, ecclesiastical, social, and economic history, the geology, &c. of each county and of London on a large scale.

2791. The royal forests of England.   By J. C. Cox.   1 vol. 8vo. Lond. 1905. Illus.

2792. English local government from the Revolution to the Municipal Corporations Act : the parish and the county.   By S. and B. Webb.   1 vol. 8vo. Lond. 1906.

Other vols. in this series are : The manor and the borough [2 vols. 1908] ; The King's highway [1913] ; Statutory authorities for special purposes [1922] ; English prisons [1922].   All contain useful 17th-century material, and supply a valuable survey of conditions at the end of the Stuart period.

2793. Seventeenth century life in the country parish ; with special reference to local government. By E. Trotter. 1 vol. 8vo. Camb. 1919.

¶ 3. COUNTY AND OTHER LOCAL RECORDS ARRANGED ALPHABETICALLY UNDER COUNTIES

BERKSHIRE.

2794. Reading records. Diary of the corporation. Ed. by J. M. Guilding. 4 vols. 8vo. Lond. 1892–6.
Vols. ii–iv cover 1603–54.

CAMBRIDGE.

2795. A catalogue of books printed at or relating to the university, town and county of Cambridge from 1521 to 1893, with bibliographical and biographical notes. By R. Bowes. 1 vol. 8vo. Camb. 1894.

2796. Catalogue of the books and papers for the most part relating to the University, town and county of Cambridge bequeathed to the University by J. W. Clark. By A. T. Bartholomew. 1 vol. 8vo. Camb. 1912.

CHESHIRE.

2797. Bibliotheca Cestriensis, or a biographical account of books, maps, plates . . . relating to, printed or published in, or written by authors resident in Cheshire. By J. H. Cooke. 1 vol. fol. Warrington. 1904.

CORNWALL.

2798. Bibliotheca Cornubiensis : a catalogue of the writings, both MS. and printed, of Cornishmen, and of works relating to the county of Cornwall. By G. C. Boase and W. P. Courtney. 3 vols. 4to. Lond. 1874–82.
Cf. Boase's Collectanea Cornubiensia. 1 vol. 8vo. Truro. 1890.

2799. Carew's survey of Cornwall. By R. Carew. 1 vol. 4to. Lond. 1811.

DERBYSHIRE.

2800. Three centuries of Derbyshire annals as illustrated by the records of the quarter sessions. By J. C. Cox. 2 vols. 8vo. Lond. 1890.
Cf. Calendar of the records of the county of Derby. 1 vol. 8vo. Lond. 1899. These supply a valuable guide to the various kinds of county records.

DEVONSHIRE.

2801. Bibliotheca Devoniensis : a catalogue of the printed books relating to the county of Devon. By J. Davidson. 1 vol. 4to. Exeter. 1852.
A supplement was issued in 1861.

2802. Quarter sessions from Queen Elizabeth to Queen Anne : illustrations of local government and history drawn from original records [chiefly of county of Devon]. By A. H. A. Hamilton. 1 vol. 8vo. Lond. 1878.

DORSETSHIRE.

2803. Bibliotheca Dorsetiensis : being a carefully compiled account of printed books and pamphlets relating to . . . the county of Dorset. By C. H. Mayo. 1 vol. 8vo. Lond. 1885.

2804. The minute books of the Dorset standing committee . . . 1646 to . . . 1650. By C. H. Mayo.   1 vol. 8vo. Exeter. 1902.

For other Bankes MSS. see Hist. MSS. Comm. Rep. viii, Pt. I, 1881, pp. 208–13.

DURHAM.

2805. The Acts of the High Commission Court within the diocese of Durham. Ed. by W. H. D. Longstaffe.   1 vol. 8vo. Durham. 1858.

From Dr. Hunter's MSS. in the library of the dean and chapter of Durham.   Acts extend from 1628 to 1639.   Depositions from 1626 to 1638.

2806. Records of the committee for compounding with delinquent royalists in Durham and Northumberland, 1643–1660. Ed. by R. Welford.   Surtees Soc. 1905.

2807. Durham protestations, or the returns made to the House of Commons in 1641/2 for the maintenance of the Protestant religion for the county palatine of Durham. Ed. by H. M. Wood.   Surtees Soc. 1922.

ESSEX.

2808. Catalogue of books, maps and manuscripts relating to or connected with the county of Essex and collected by A. Cunnington.   1 vol. 4to. Braintree. 1902.

2809. Colchester during the Commonwealth. By J. H. Round.   Eng. Hist. Rev. xv. 1900.

Illustrates by extracts from the borough records Cromwell's dealings with corporations. Cf. The history and antiquities of Colchester Castle, 1 vol. 8vo. Colchester. 1882 ; and Cromwell and the electorate [i. e. charter of Colchester], Nineteenth Century, xlvi, 1899. Both by J. H. Round.

2810. A lieutenancy book for Essex, 1608 to 1631 and 1637 to 1639. By A. Clark.   The Essex Review, xvii, 1908.

Other papers *ibid*. xvii–xviii, 1908–9.   The Essex territorial force in 1608 ; Essex woollen manufactures, 1629 ; The Essex territorial force, 1625–38.

GLOUCESTERSHIRE.

2811. The bibliographer's manual of Gloucestershire literature. By Sir F. A. Hyett and W. Bazeley.   3 vols. 8vo. Gloucester. 1895–7.

Cf. Supplement to the bibliographer's manual ed. by Sir F. A. Hyett and R. Austin [2 vols. 8vo. Gloucester. 1915–16].

2812. Records of the corporation of Gloucester.   In Beaufort MSS. Hist. MSS. Comm. 1891.

Calendar of letter books, 1619–60.

2813. The annals of Bristol in the 17th century. By J. Latimer.   1 vol. 8vo. Bristol. 1900.

Based on the corporation records, Domestic State Papers, &c.

HAMPSHIRE.

2814. Bibliotheca Hantoniensis : a list of books relating to Hampshire. By H. M. Gilbert and G. N. Godwin.   1 vol. 8vo. Southampton. 1891

2815. Court leet records of Southampton. Vol. i. pt. 3. 1603–24. Ed. by F. J. C. Hearnshaw and D. M. Hearnshaw. Southampton Record Soc. 1908.

2816. The assembly books of Southampton. Vols. i–iv, 1602–16. Ed. by J. W. Horrocks. 8vo. Southampton Record Society, Southampton. 1917–25. In progress.

HERTFORDSHIRE.

2817. Hertford county records. Notes and extracts from the session rolls [1581–1894]. Ed. by W. J. Hardy. 3 vols. 8vo. Hertford. 1905–10.

Vol. i, 1581–1698 ; ii, 1699–1850 ; iii, 1851–94, with addenda 1630–1880.

HEREFORDSHIRE.

2818. Bibliotheca Herefordiensis ; or a descriptive catalogue of the books, pamphlets, maps, prints . . . relating to the county of Hereford. By J. Allen. 1 vol. 8vo. Hereford. 1821.

HUNTINGDONSHIRE.

2819. Catalogue of the Huntingdonshire books collected by Herbert E. Norris. By H. E. Norris. 1 vol. 8vo. Cirencester. 1895.

KENT.

2820. Bibliotheca Cantiana. A catalogue of a . . . collection of books and manuscripts relative to the county of Kent . . . offered for sale. By J. R. Smith. 1 vol. 8vo. Lond. 1837. Later ed. 1 vol. 8vo. Lond. 1851.

The ed. of 1851 includes Sussex and Surrey as well.

2821. A handbook to Kent records. Ed. by I. J. Churchill. 1 vol. 8vo. Kent Arch. Soc. Lond. 1914.

LANCASHIRE.

2822. The Lancashire library ; a bibliographical account of books on topography . . . and miscellaneous literature relating to the county palatine. By H. Fishwick. 1 vol. 4to. Lancs. 1875.

Cf. A. J. Hawkes. Lancashire printed books. A bibliography . . . down to . . . 1800. 8vo. Wigan. 1925.

2823. The natural history of Lancashire, Cheshire and the Peak in Derbyshire. By C. Leigh. 1 vol. fol. Oxf. 1700.

2824. The Norris papers. Ed. by T. Heywood. Chetham Soc. 1846.

Miscellaneous : mainly *c.* 1690–1708. Much about Liverpool. Cf. Liverpool in King Charles the Second's time. By Sir E. Moore [written 1667–8]. Ed. by W. F. Irvine. 1 vol. 4to. 1899. Plates. Maps.

2825. The Farington papers. Ed. by S. M. ffarington. Chetham Soc. 1856.

Contents are : (1) The shrievalty of William Farington, 1636. (ii) Civil war papers, 1638–49. (iii) Miscellaneous correspondence, 1547–1688. Cf. Hist. MSS. Comm. Rep. vi. 426.

2826. The Lancashire lieutenancy under the Tudors and Stuarts, Part II. Ed. by J. Harland. Chetham Soc. 1859.

A few documents relating to the Stuart period until 1642. Mainly from Shuttleworth MSS. at Gawthorpe Hall.

2827. Royalist composition papers, being the proceedings of the Committee for Compounding, A.D. 1643–1660, so far as they relate to the county of Lancashire. Ed. by J. H. Stanning. 4 vols. Chetham Soc. 1891–8.

2828. Minutes of the committee for the relief of plundered ministers, and of precepts for the maintenance of ministers, relating to Lancashire and Cheshire, 1643–1660. Ed. by W. A. Shaw. 2 vols. 8vo. Lancs. and Ches. Rec. Soc. 1893–7. Bibl.

From MSS. at Brit. Mus., Record Office, Bodleian, Sion College, and Lambeth. Introduction gives account of sources.

2829. The portmote or court leet records of the borough or town and royal manor of Salford (1597–1669). Ed. by J. G. de T. Mandley. 2 vols. Chetham Soc. 1902.

2830. Lancashire quarter sessions records [1590–1606]. Ed. by J. Tait. Chetham Soc. 1917.

The introduction is valuable.

LEICESTERSHIRE.

2831. Records of the borough of Leicester . . . [vol. iv] 1603–1688. By H. Stocks. 8vo. Camb. 1923.

LINCOLNSHIRE.

2832. Bibliotheca Lincolniensis. A catalogue of the books, pamphlets, &c. relating to the city and county of Lincoln . . . in . . . the city of Lincoln Public Library. Ed. by A. R. Corns. 1 vol. 4to. Lincoln. 1904.

NORFOLK.

2833. An index to Norfolk topography. By W. Rye. Index Soc., Publ. x, 1881.

2834. The Norwich rate book from Easter 1633 to Easter 1634. Ed. by W. Rye. 1 vol. 8vo. Lond. 1903.

2835. The records of the city of Norwich. Ed. by W. Hudson and J. C. Tingey. 2 vols. 8vo. Norwich. 1906. Map. Plan.

Vol. i, Government and administration ; ii, social and economic. Mainly medieval

2836. State papers relating to musters, beacons, shipmoney, &c. in Norfolk from 1626, chiefly to the beginning of the civil war. Ed. by W. Rye. 1 vol. 8vo. Norwich. 1907.

Intro. by Sir C. H. Firth : of value for local government and militia system. From MSS. in the possession of Mr. Rye.

2837. The official papers of Sir Nathaniel Bacon of Stiffkey, Norfolk, as justice of the peace 1580–1620. Ed. by H. W. Saunders. Camd. Soc. 1915.

NORTHAMPTONSHIRE.

2838. Bibliotheca Northantonensis. *c.* 1869. By J. Taylor.

See Humphreys (2788), p. 182.

2839. Tracts (chiefly rare and curious reprints), relating to Northampton-shire, with illustrations. [Two series.] Ed. by J. Taylor. 2 vols. 8vo. North-ampton. 1870–81.

Many 17th-century items, especially on witches.

2840. The records of the borough of Northampton. Ed. by C. A. Markham and J. C. Cox. 2 vols. 8vo. [? Northampton] 1898.

Vol. ii, 1550–1835.

NOTTINGHAMSHIRE.

2841. Nottinghamshire county records. Notes and extracts from the Nottinghamshire county records of the 17th century. Ed. by H. H. Copnall. 1 vol. 8vo. Nottingham. 1915. Facsimiles.

2842. Records of the borough of Nottingham. 6 vols. 8vo. Lond. and Nottingham. 1882–1914.

Vol. iv, 1547–1625, ed. by W. H. Stevenson ; v, 1625–1702, ed. by W. T. Baker ; vi, 1702–60, ed. by E. L. Guilford.

OXFORDSHIRE.

2843. The natural history of Oxfordshire. By R. Plot. 1 vol. fol. Oxf. 1677. Maps. Plates. Later ed. 1705. Ed. by J. Burman.

SHROPSHIRE.

2844. Shropshire county records. Orders of the Shropshire quarter ses-sions. Ed. by R. L. Kenyon and Sir O. Wakeman. 8vo. s.l. s.a.

Vol. i, 1638–1708 ; ii, 1709–26.

SOMERSETSHIRE.

2845. Bibliotheca Somersetensis : a catalogue of books, pamphlets, single sheets and broadsides in some way connected with the county of Somerset. By E. Green. 3 vols. la. 8vo. Taunton. 1902.

2846. Somersetshire parishes. A handbook of historical reference to all places in the county. By A. L. Humphreys. 2 vols. 4to. Lond. 1906.

2847. Quarter sessions records for the county of Somerset [1607–60]. Ed. by E. H. Bates-Harbin. 3 vols. 4to. Somerset Record Soc. [Lond.] 1907–12.

From county records at Taunton.

2848. A particular description of Somerset [1633]. By T. Gerard. Ed. by E. H. Bates. 1 vol. sm. 4to. Somerset Record Soc. Bath. 1900.

2849. A history of Dunster and of the families of Mohun and Luttrell. By Sir H. C. Maxwell Lyte. 2 vols. 8vo. Lond. 1909. Illus.

Much 17th-century material : a good specimen of local history.

STAFFORDSHIRE.

2850. The natural history of Staffordshire. By R. Plot. 1 vol. fol. Oxf. 1686.

SUFFOLK.

2851. County of Suffolk. Its history as disclosed by existing records and other documents, being materials for the history of Suffolk. Ed. by W. A. Copinger. 5 vols. 8vo. Lond. 1904–6.

2852. The journal of William Dowsing of Stratford, parliamentary visitor appointed . . . for demolishing the superstitious pictures . . . &c. within the county of Suffolk in the years 1643–1644. By W. Dowsing. Ed. by R. Loder. 1 vol. 4to. Woodbridge. 1786. Later ed. 1 vol. 4to. Ipswich. 1885. Ed. by C. H. Evelyn White.

2853. Suffolk in the seventeenth century : the breviary of Suffolk by R. Reyce, 1618, now published for the first time from the MS. in the British Museum, with notes. Ed. by Lord Francis Hervey. 1 vol. 8vo. Lond. 1902.

SURREY.

2854. The natural history and antiquities of the county of Surrey. By J. Aubrey. 5 vols. 8vo. Lond. 1718–19.

Cf. A catalogue of works relating to Surrey in the Minet Library, Camberwell. 8vo. 1901 ; Supplement, 1923. A valuable bibliography.

WARWICKSHIRE.

2855. The antiquities of Warwickshire. By Sir W. Dugdale. 1 vol. fol. Lond. 1656. Map and plates by Hollar. Later ed. 2 vols. fol. Lond. 1730. Ed. by W. Thomas.

Ed. of 1730 has continuation ' to this present time '

WESTMORELAND.

2856. Description of the county of Westmoreland [1671]. By Sir D. Fleming. Ed. by Sir G. F. Duckett. 1 vol. 8vo. Lond. 1882.

Cf. Fleming's Description of the county of Cumberland [1671] ed. by R. S. Ferguson [1 vol. 8vo. Kendal. 1889]. Both publ. for Cumberland and Westmoreland Arch. Soc. from MS. in Bodleian Library.

ISLE OF WIGHT.

2857. The Oglander memoirs : extracts from the MSS. of Sir J. Oglander . . . deputy-lieutenant of the Isle of Wight, 1595–1648. Ed. by W. H. Long. 1 vol. 4to. Lond. 1888.

Has some notices of Charles I in the Isle of Wight, 1627 and 1647–8: otherwise only of local interest.

WILTSHIRE.

2858. The natural history of Wiltshire. By J. Aubrey. 1 vol. 4to. Oxf. 1847. Ed. by J. Britten.

2859. The Commonwealth charter of the city of Salisbury, [12] September 1656. Ed. by H. Hall. In Camd. Misc. xii. 1907.

Incidentally ' furnishes the missing clue to the origin of the important Commonwealth Committee on municipal charters '. Cf. B. L. K. Henderson. The Commonwealth Charters, in Royal Hist. Soc. Trans. 1912.

WORCESTERSHIRE.

2860. Bibliography of Worcestershire. Part I. Acts of parliament relating to the county. Part II. Being a classified catalogue of books, and other printed matter relating to the county of Worcester. Ed. by J. R. Burton and F. S. Pearson. Worcs. Hist. Soc. 1898, 1903.

2861. Worcester county records : The quarter sessions rolls, 1591–1643. Ed. by J. W. Willis Bund. 2 pts. in 1 vol. 8vo. Worcs. Hist. Soc. Worcester. 1899–1900.

Notices 5870 documents from sessions rolls, mainly under James I and Charles I. Valuable for local government under early Stuarts.

YORKSHIRE.

2862. Catalogue of a collection of historical and topographical works, and civil war tracts relating to the county of York. By E. Hailstone. 1 vol. 8vo. Bradford. 1858.

2863. Chapters in the history of Yorkshire, being a collection of original letters, papers and public documents. By J. J. Cartwright. 1 vol. 8vo. Wakefield. 1872.

2864. The booke of entries of the Pontefract corporation, 1653–1726. Ed. by R. Holmes. 1 vol. 8vo. Pontefract. 1882.

2865. The North Riding Record Society. Quarter sessions records. Ed. by J. C. Atkinson. 9 vols. 8vo. Lond. 1884–92.

Intro. to each volume.

2866. The Hull letters, printed from a collection of original documents found among the borough archives in the Town Hall, Hull, 1884. Ed. by T. T. Wildridge. 1 vol. 8vo. Hull. [1887].

Letters and papers illustrating proceedings of king and Parliament, 1625–46. Among the letters are those of Peregrine Pelham, M.P., addressed to the Corporation.

2867. Royalist composition papers, or the proceedings of the committee for compounding with delinquents during the Commonwealth. Ed. by J. W. Clay. 3 vols. 8vo. s.l. [York.] 1893–6.

In Proceedings of Yorkshire Arch. Soc. : relates wholly to Yorkshire during the years 1645–53.

2868. York in the sixteenth and seventeenth centuries. By M. Sellers. Eng. Hist. Rev. xii. 1897.

Mainly about the cloth trade.

¶ 4. LONDON

(*a*) Periodicals. (*b*) Sources. (*c*) Later works.

As London was the stage on which much of English history was acted in the Stuart period, many general sources and later works are often of far greater importance for its history than works specifically devoted to that subject.

For bibliographies of the latter see Nos. 2778–88. All the rest of any value are in library or sale catalogues. By far the most complete is that of the Guildhall Library, which includes an elaborate subject index, on cards, as are those of the libraries of the London County Council, the Bishopsgate Institute, the University of London (Goldsmiths' Library at the University Offices, London section of the library at University College), which all have large general collections, while the libraries of the City of Westminster and most of the metropolitan Boroughs, and the Minet Library at Camberwell (covering all London south of the Thames) (2854 n.) have good local ones.

Sotheby's catalogue of the library of Edward Tyrrell, sold in April 1864, is the most valuable in that class : it gives the titles of many tracts. These, one of the most important sources for the history of London during the period, could not be included in the brief list given below : for them see, for 1640–60, the Brit. Mus. Catalogue of the Thomason Tracts ; before and after those dates the footnotes to Sharpe (2905) and the Victoria County History (2790), Bell's bibliographies (2912 and 2914), and the above library catalogues, with that of the London Institution [1835]. See also for these and other literary sources (especially plays) the bibliographies in the Cambridge History of English Literature. There is a useful list of statutes and charters prefixed to Pulling's Laws, customs . . . of London, 1842. For maps and views see Crace (2883).

(a) PERIODICALS

2869. London and Middlesex Archaeological Society. Transactions, i–vi, 1860–1890. New Series, i [1905] : in progress. Many maps, facsimiles, and other illustrations. Other publications include : Facsimile reproductions of Ogilby and Morgan's Map of the city, 1677, with Ogilby's description of it, ed. by C. Welch.

N.S. vol. iv (the last completed) contains *inter alia* a study of the Parliamentary surveys of crown lands, 1649–59, in London and Middlesex.

2870. (a) Middlesex and Hertfordshire Notes and Queries. Continued as (b) The Home Counties Magazine, devoted to the topography of London, Middlesex, Essex, Herts, Bucks, Berks, Surrey, and Kent. Ed. by W. J. Hardy (series (a) and vols. i–vi of (b)) and W. P. Baildon (vols. viii–xiv). (a) 4 vols. 8vo. Lond. 1895–8. (b) 14 vols. 8vo. Lond. 1899–1912. Many illustrations. Valuable lists of relevant works published during the period covered.

Includes some documents, e. g. the Parliamentary surveys of livings in Middlesex (Home Counties, vol. i). Much bibliographical matter.

2871. Publications of the London Topographical Society : in progress.

Include : (a) Annual Record, continued as London Topographical Record (in progress). (b) Facsimiles, from the best originals, of maps and views of London, among them Visscher's, Merian's and Hollar's views [1616, 1638 and 1647], and the maps by Faithorne and Newcourt [1658], Porter [1660], Ogilby and Morgan [1682]; A bird's-eye view of West Central London [c. 1648] ; ' Exact surveigh of the streets . . . within the ruines ' [1667] ; and seven drawing of buildings, by Hollar ; a plan of Whitehall, 1680, and view of the palace, 1683 ; Jonas Moore's map of the Thames, 1662 ; a plan of Ebury Manor [c. 1670] ; and two drawings (one by Wren) of Old St. Paul's.

The Record contains notes on all of these, and other important papers : a complete list of its contents and of all the society's publications is appended to the last volume, xiii [1923].

(*b*) SOURCES

2872. The survey of London . . . Begunne first by . . . Iohn Stow . . . afterwarde inlarged by . . . A. M. in the year 1618. And now completely finished by A. M[unday], H. D[yson], and others. 1 vol. fol. Lond. 1633. Later ed. 2 vols. fol. Lond. 1720. Maps. Plans (many). Ed. by J. Strype.

Both the 1633 edition and Strype's contain much additional matter, valuable for the history of London in the 17th century. For bibliographical notes see the introduction to the standard edition of Stow's original work, by C. L. Kingsford [Oxford, 1908], pp. xlii, lxxxv.

2873. Histoire de l'entree de la reine mere dans la Grande Bretagne. By J. P. de la Serre. 1 vol. fol. Lond. 1639. Later ed. 3 pts. 4to. Lond. 1755. Ed. by R. Gough.

Useful for its description of London. Repr. 1775 with Description des royaumes d'Angleterre et d'escosse composé par Estienne Perlin [1558], illustrated with notes in English.

2874. Reports of speciall cases touching severall customs and liberties of the city of London. Collected by Sir H. Calthrop Knight, sometimes Recorder . . . Whereunto is annexed divers ancient customes and usages of the said city. By Sir H. Calthrop. 1 vol. 12mo. London. 1655. Later ed. 1670.

In the edition of 1670 the last case (taxes on Wharfes) is omitted and the commission and articles of the Wardmote Inquest and other documents are appended to the second part. The latter, alone, is No. 2060 in Gross.

For Calthorpe (*sic*) see Dict. Nat. Biog., where, however, neither this work (nor the less important one described by Gross (2782) No. 2023) is mentioned. It is one of a series of books on the civic constitution, e.g., The city law [1647 and 1658], Camera regis (2876), and Lex Londinensis [1680]. See A. H. Thomas, Mayor's court rolls [1924], p. xxvi.

2875. Londinopolis. An historicall discourse or perlustration of the city of London . . . By J. Howell. 1 vol. fol. Lond. 1657. Port. Map.

Chiefly interesting as a panegyric, the historical part being borrowed from Stow's Survey. Another work of similar character is William Gough's Londinum triumphans [1682].

2876. Camera regis, or, A short view of London. Containing the antiquity . . . officers, courts, customs, franchises, &c. of that renowned city. By J. Brydall. 1 vol. sm. 8vo. Lond. 1676. Later ed. 1678.

See 2874 n. It gives copious references to Coke, whose 4th Institute (467) has an important section on the subject, and to other legal writers, statutes, and law reports. For the author see Dict. Nat. Biog.

2877. A collection of the names of the merchants living in and about the city of London . . . directing . . . to the place of their abode. (Hereunto is added an addition of all the goldsmiths that keep running cashes.) 1 vol. 12mo. Lond. 1677. Later ed. 1 vol. 16mo. Lond. 1863. Ed. by J. C. Hotten.

The reprint is entitled The Little London Directory of 1677.

2878. The royal charter of confirmation granted by King Charles II to the city of London. Wherein are recited *verbatim* all the charters to the said

city . . . Taken out of the records and exactly translated into *English*. By
S. G. Gent. 1 vol. 8vo. Lond. 1680. Later eds. 1738 and 1745.

The second edition by J. E. has the wording of the Epistle Dedicatory altered to suit Lord
Mayor Sir John Barnard [1737–8] instead of Sir Robert Clayton [1679–80], and contains no indication that it is not a new book ; it is therefore catalogued separately by the
British Museum, followed by Gross (2782); cf. his Nos. 2035 and 2032. It has additions,
as shown by the title : The charters of the city of London . . . taken verbatim out of the
records, exactly translated into English, with notes. . . . And the Parliamentary confirmation by K. William and Q. Mary. To which is annexed an abstract of the argu-
ings in the case of the Quo Warranto.

2879. The present state of London, or, Memorials comprehending a full
and succinct account of the ancient and modern state thereof. By T. De
Laune. 1 vol. 12mo. London. 1681. Later ed. 1690.

Mainly descriptive, with a good deal of miscellaneous information : e. g. pp. 345–59
are about the Post Office and penny post. The second edition ' continued to this present year by a careful hand ', was entitled Angliae Metropolis.

2880. The pleadings, arguments and other proceedings in the court of
King's Bench upon the Quo Warranto, touching the charter of the city of
London ; with the judgement entred thereupon. The whole pleadings
faithfully taken from the record. 1 vol. fol. Lond. 1690. Later ed. 1696.

Contains : (1) the entries relating to the case on the Coram Rege Rolls, including the
pleadings ; (2) the Report, beginning with an English summary of the pleadings, and
including all the arguments of counsel, and the judgement ; (3) a ' Postscript ', collecting precedents bearing on the question, whether a body corporate can surrender and
dissolve itself.

(1) and (2) are also printed, in the reverse order, with numerous additions and annotations, in State Trials (562), viii, 1039–1358 (which also reports, ix. 187, 299, the Trials
of the Sheriffs and of Sir Patience Ward, 1683) ; and the case is in Shower's Reports
(B.R.) ii. 262. The judgement was annulled by statute 2 Wm. and Mary, c. 8.

The Quo Warranto case led to the publication of a large number of pamphlets, frequently containing extracts from the pleadings and arguments and the charters.
Some are given by Gross (2782), Nos. 2024–6, 2029–30, 2033, 2039, 2045, 2051, 2054–5,
2057, 2059. Among others are : ' The Modest Enquiry . . .' [1683], ' A Defence of
the Charter and Municipal Rights of the City . . .', by Thomas Hunt [1683], and ' A
Display of Tyranny ', First part, 1689. The Second Part, 1690.

2881. Privilegia Londini : or, the laws, customs, and priviledges of the
city of London. Wherein are set forth all the charters . . . customs . . . The
nature of by-laws . . . and how pleadable . . . Together with the practice of
all the courts . . . 1 vol. 8vo. Lond. 1702. 3rd ed. 1723. Ed. by W. Bohun.

The best description of the civic constitution and customs at the end of the century.

2882. A collection of the yearly bills of mortality from 1657 to 1758,
inclusive. Together with several other bills of an earlier date. To which
are subjoined i. Observations on the bills of mortality by Capt. J. Graunt.
ii. Another Essay . . . concerning the growth of the City of London . . . by
Sir W. Petty. Ed. by T. Birch. 2 pts. 4to. Lond. 1759.

The original bills, weekly and general (or yearly), may be seen in the Guildhall
Library, and (from 1664 and 1658 respectively) at the British Museum. Facsimiles of
the bills for the week 13–20 Oct. 1603, and the year 1665, are in Ten years' growth of
the City, published by the Corporation (1891). The weekly bills for 1665 were republished that year by the Company of Parish Clerks, under the title London's dreadful

visitation, and also by John Bell, London's Remembrancer. The general bills are summarized and discussed by Maitland (2899).

The bills are useful for other than statistical purposes : e. g. the changes in the lists of parishes, and their arrangement, illustrate the development of the idea of what constituted the ' metropolis '. For general information about them see J. Christie, Parish Clerks, pp. 132 *et seq.*; Creighton, Epidemics (2700), i. 295 *et seq.*, and ch. x ; and Bell, Great Plague (2914), passim.

Graunt's essay was published in 1661, republished 1662, 1665 (twice), and 1676; Petty's published in 1683, republished 1686. The latter also wrote on the people, housing, hospitals, &c. of London and Paris (1686), and the cities of London and Rome (1687). For repr. of both Petty and Graunt see No. 1893.

2883. A Catalogue of maps, plans and views of London and Southwark, collected and arranged by F. Crace. Ed. by J. G. Crace. 1 vol. 8vo. Lond. 1878.

The collection was acquired by the British Museum in 1880. The catalogue is on the whole the best bibliography of the subject ; others are the catalogues of the Gardner Collection, sold at Sotheby's in Feb. and March 1923, Nov. 1923, and May 1924, and that included in Wenceslaus Hollar and his views of London, by A. M. Hinds (London, 1921). There are large collections of relevant London prints at the Guildhall, the London Museum, Sir John Soane's Museum, and the libraries of the Bishopsgate Institute and of the local authorities mentioned above.

2884. Analytical index to the series of records known as the Remembrancia [9 vols.] preserved among the archives of the city of London, A. D. 1579–1664. Ed. by W. H. and H. C. Overall. 1 vol. 8vo. Lond. 1878.

The Remembrancia books contain copies of correspondence between the civic authorities and the King, Privy Council, and private persons of importance. The ' Index ' is really a calendar, the letters being summarized with varying fullness. A few have been printed *in extenso* by the Malone Soc., Collections, i (1).

2885. Parish of St. Christopher le Stocks : The register book (1558–1780), 2 vols. Vestry minutes and other records (1559–1686); Churchwardens' accounts (1575–1685), 2 vols. Wills, leases and memoranda (to 1715). Ed. by E. Freshfield. 6 vols. 4to. Lond. 1882, 1886, 1885, and 1895.

One facsimile [1665] in the Register Book. At the end of the second volume of this are notes of collections, 1659–65.

2886. The historical charters and constitutional documents of the city of London. Ed. by an Antiquary [W. de Gray Birch]. 1 vol. 4to. Lond. 1884. Bibl. Later ed. 1 vol. 8vo. Lond. 1887.

Based upon the Appendix to John Noorthouck's New history of London, 1773. Includes Charles II's proclamation after the fire and his confirmation of the order of Common Council, May 1667 ; two other Acts, for Paving and Cleansing [1671] and regulating the Markets for Woollen Goods ; and the Statute [1690] vacating the judgements on the Quo Warranto. The charters have also been printed by J. Luffman [1793] and others. See No. 2878. In all these collections Latin documents are given in an English translation.

2887. The vestry minute book of the parish of St. Margaret Lothbury, 1571–1677. Ed. by E. Freshfield. 1 vol. 4to. Lond. 1887. 2 maps. Several plans.

Numerous small plans extracted from the reports of the surveyors who set out the new foundations of buildings after the Fire ; three facsimiles, one of 1643. Cf. the author's paper, with extracts from the records of the neighbouring parish of St. Stephen Coleman Street, in Archaeologia, l.

2888. A discourse on some unpublished records of the city of London. By E. Freshfield. 1 vol. 4to. Lond. 1887.

Indicates the general contents of London parochial records, and the extent to which they include material for the history not only of London but of England, in the 17th century. It is impossible to enumerate here those from which extracts have been printed : for some see V. C. H. London (2790) i, Appendix ; but that is confined to the City, Westminster, and Southwark, and only includes publications before 1908. For all the parish histories see the catalogue of the Guildhall Library. There is a list of the Registers published before 1897 in Middx. and Herts. N. & Q. iii. 99 ; many have been printed by the Harleian Society, which has also printed some London visitations of this period.

2889. Middlesex County Records : vols. ii–iv, sessions rolls, from 1603 ; vols. v–vi, sessions books, from 1689. Middlesex County Records Soc. continued by the Middlesex County Council. Vols. i–iv, ed. by J. C. Jeaffreson ; vols. v, vi, ed. by W. J. Hardy. 6 vols. 8vo. i–iii, Clerkenwell ; iv–vi, London. 1888–

The record kept by the clerk to the justices, now at the Middlesex Town Hall, Westminster. The calendar has been continued in typescript, and may be consulted there, or at the British Museum. A list of the extant county records, mainly of the 17th and 18th centuries, is prefixed to each vol.

2890. Calendar of wills proved and enrolled in the court of Husting . . . preserved among the archives of the Corporation . . . Part II, A. D. 1358–A. D. 1688. Ed. by R. R. Sharpe. 1 vol. la. 8vo. Lond. 1890.

Pp. 730–79 contain wills of the period. For other London wills see British Record Soc. : P.C.C. vols. v, vi.

2891. Memorials of Stepney . . . the vestry minutes from 1579 to 1662, to which is appended a reprint of Gascoyne's map of the parish, 1703. With introduction and notes. Ed. by G. W. Hill and W. H. Frere. 1 vol. 8vo. Guildford. 1890–1.

The parish of Stepney then extended from the Thames to Hackney.

2892. Parish of St. Bartholomew Exchange. Vestry minute books (1567–1676), account books (1596–1698). Ed. by E. Freshfield. 2 vols. 4to. Lond. 1890, 1895. 3 maps. 1 plan. 1 port.

2 facsimiles, one of 1644. The second vol. has an Appendix of extracts from minutes, 1676–9.

2893. Catalogue of books and documents belonging to the royal parish of St. Martin-in-the-Fields. By T. Mason. 1 vol. 8vo. Lond. 1895.

Printed for the vestry. The list is arranged as the documents were then numbered, and consequently (e. g. on p. 46) some of the 17th century occur among those of the 19th. The accounts to 1603 have been edited by J. V. Kitto [London, 1901], and extracts from later records are given in the history of the parish by John McMaster [London, 1916].

2894. A catalogue of Westminster records deposited at the Town Hall . . . in the custody of the vestry of St. Margaret and St. John, with introductory essay, illustrations and extracts. By J. E. Smith. 1 vol. 4to. Lond. 1900. Many facsimiles.

Includes important extracts from 17th-century accounts. The registers from 1539–1660 have since been edited by A. M. Burke : Memorials of St. Margaret's (London,

1914). Smith was vestry clerk, and his other works are valuable for the history of Westminster at this period.

2895. Survey of London, issued by the joint publishing committee representing the London County Council and the London Survey Committee ; in progress. Present general eds. Sir J. Bird, P. Norman. 4to. Lond. 1900. Copiously illus.

A sumptuous series, concerned mainly with buildings and antiquities, but having an historical section in each volume, and valuable bibliographical notes. Among the illustrations are many maps and plans. Of the volumes issued to date the following deal with London parishes included in the ' metropolis ' of the 17th century : iii and v, St. Giles-in-the-Fields ; viii, Shoreditch ; ix, St. Helen Bishopsgate. There is a companion series of monographs on individual buildings, several of the 17th century, published by the Survey Committee alone.

2896. The aldermen of the city of London temp. Henry III—1908. With notes on the parliamentary representation of the city, the aldermen and the livery companies, the aldermanic veto, aldermanic baronets, and knights. By A. B. Beaven. 2 vols. 8vo. Lond. 1908.

Contains much biographical material including (see vol. ii, p. cxvii) numerous corrections of the Dict. Nat. Biog. Cf. J. J. Baddeley, The aldermen of Cripplegate Ward. Lond. 1900.

2897. London citizens in 1651, being a transcript of Harleian MS. 4778. Ed. by J. C. Whitebrook. Lond. 1910.

List of signatures of members of 22 companies, with a repr. of a tract giving the names of the grand jury of the London quarter sessions, in Oct. 1681.

2898. Records of the Worshipful Company of Carpenters : vol. i, Apprentices' entry books, 1654–94. Ed. by Bower Marsh. 4to. Oxf. 1913.

The remaining 3 vols. contain earlier Records.

(c) LATER WORKS

2899. The history of London . . . including the several parishes. By W. Maitland and others. 1 vol. fol. Lond. 1739. Plates. Later ed. 2 vols. fol. Lond. 1756.

The 2nd ed. contains much additional material. Vol. i is a narrative history, cc. xxix–xlii (pp. 282–502) covering the 17th century ; it consists largely of documents arranged chronologically. Vol. ii is mainly descriptive, but includes a few documents of this period, e. g. (p. 813), the Commonwealth Act (1649) establishing the London Workhouse, which anticipated the Act of 1662. It also contains a useful list of the companies, with references to the Patent Rolls for their charters of incorporation, which are not given in Unwin's bibliographies (2910).

2900. History and description of the parish of Clerkenwell, embellished with numerous engravings, by J. and H. S. Storer. The historical department by T. Cromwell. 1 vol. 8vo. [Lond.]. 1828.

Gives extracts from the parish records, and is more valuable, for this period, than the better-known work by W. J. Pinks (Clerkenwell, 1865).

2901. Urkundliche Geschichte des Hansischen Stahlhofes zu London. By J. M. Lappenberg. 1 vol. 4to. Hamburg. 1851.

With this should be read a paper by P. Norman on the later history of the Steelyard, in Archaeologia, lxi [1909], based upon many additional documents.

2902. Chapters in the history of old St. Paul's; Gleanings from old St. Paul's; St. Paul's and old city life. By W. S. Simpson. 3 vols. 8vo. Lond. 1881, 1889, 1894. Illus.

A series of miscellanies, including valuable references to tracts, from which long extracts are given. The author was librarian of the Cathedral and edited Documents illustrating the History of St. Paul's (Nos. xx-xxxiii of the 17th century) for the Camd. Soc. (N.S. 26, 1880).

2903. London past and present: its history, associations and traditions. Based upon the Handbook of London by the late P. Cunningham. By H. B. Wheatley. 3 vols. 8vo. Lond. and N.Y. 1891.

A most useful topographical dictionary, giving taverns, coffee-houses, &c., as well as streets and notable buildings. The two editions of its predecessor, by Cunningham (1849, 2 vols. 1850, 1 vol.), are also useful for the 17th century.

2904. London during the great rebellion. Being a memoir of Sir Abraham Reynardson, sheriff . . . lord mayor of London (1648–9). By C. M. Clode. 1 vol. 8vo. Lond. 1892.

Should be compared with the author's Memorials of the Merchant Taylors (London, 1875).

2905. London and the kingdom: a history derived mainly from the archives at Guildhall. By R. R. Sharpe. 3 vols. 8vo. Lond. 1894–5. Facsimiles.

Vol. ii deals with the period 1603–1714; important documents 1603–83 are in vol. iii, app. The work is based upon the minutes ('Repertories' and 'Journals') of the Courts of Aldermen and Common Council, the most valuable material for the history of London during the period, and is the best existing guide to their contents. The author was Records Clerk to the Corporation.

2906. The history of St. James's Square and the foundation of the west end of London. By A. I. Dasent. 1 vol. 8vo. Lond. 1895. 2 maps. 2 plans. 1 port.

The author used the rate-books of the parish, and the family MSS. of the Duke of Norfolk and other owners of property there. Appendices: A. Lists of the successive owners and occupiers of each house in the square; B. Warrant for a crown lease, 1662, and the grant of the site to the Earl of St. Albans, 1665, both printed in full.

2907. Some account of the lord mayors and sheriffs of the city of London [1601–25]. By G. E. Cokayne. 1 vol. 8vo. Lond. 1897.

Some additional references are given by Beaven (2896).

2908. The old royal palace of Whitehall. By E. Sheppard. 1 vol. 8vo. Lond. 1902. 1 plan. Numerous ports. and other illustrations.

2909. London in the time of the Stuarts. By Sir W. Besant. 1 vol. 4to. Lond. 1903. 3 maps. 2 plans. Many ports.

Many illustrations, which, like the text (a novelist's compilation), vary much in value.

2910. The gilds and companies of London. By G. Unwin. 1 vol. 8vo. Lond. 1908.

Appendix B, 'List of sources for the history of the existing London companies,' is the best existing bibliography both of original materials and later works upon them.

More detailed references to MS. sources are in the same author's Industrial organization (1913). For those which have been published since 1908 see the card index of the Guildhall Library.

2911. History of the Worshipful Company of Drapers of London. By A. H. Johnson. 5 vols. 8vo. Oxf. 1914–22.

Vol. iii contains the history from 1603 ; vol. iv the Appendices to it, documents mostly of the 17th century ; vol. v the Index.

2912. The great Fire of London in 1666. By W. G. Bell. 1 vol. 8vo. Lond. 1920. Many illustrations. 1 map. 3 plans. Bibliogr. (valuable).

Largely derived from MS. and other sources hitherto unexplored. Appendices comprising documents, a reprint of the official account in The London Gazette, No. 85, Sept. 1666, and lists of the churches and halls destroyed and those preserved. Gives much information both about the state of London before the Fire and about the rebuilding. For a few additional references and conclusions see History, viii. 40–3.

2913. History of the Mansion House. By S. Perks. 1 vol. 8vo. Cambridge. 1922. Many plans.

Is really a history of the space in the centre of the city, now partly open, partly the site of the Mansion House. The author is the city surveyor, and was therefore able to include official plans of the area in the 17th century, and copious extracts from the City archives about the Stocks market, &c. Appendix on the rebuilding of London after the great Fire. See also on that subject his Essays on Old London. 1 vol. 4to. Camb. 1927.

2914. The great plague in London in 1665. By W. G. Bell. 1 vol. 8vo. Lond. 1924. Many illustrations, including facsimiles of bills of mortality, and several charts. 1 plan. 4 ports. Bibliogr.

Based entirely upon contemporary sources. It therefore supersedes all accounts published since Defoe's Journal of the plague year, which the author shows to be essentially a work of fiction, though it incorporates material from the Lord Mayor's orders and the bills of mortality. Cf. History, x. 65–7.

2915. The Westminster city fathers (the Burgess Court of Westminster), 1585–1901. By W. H. Manchée. 1 vol. 8vo. Lond. 1924. Numerous illustrations.

Includes extracts from minutes, 1610–15 : the other volumes of the period are lost. Should be compared with chap. iv, on Westminster, in Webb's Local Government (2792), vol. ii.

2916. The early history of Piccadilly, Leicester Square, Soho, and the neighbourhood. By C. L. Kingsford. 1 vol. 8vo. Camb. 1926. Illus.

Valuable. Cf. Mary Davies and the manor of Ebury, by C. T. Gatty. 2 vols. Lond. 1921.

XII. SCOTLAND

SCOTTISH history from 1560 to 1690 is mainly concerned with the establishment of presbyterianism, the attempts of successive Stuart kings to modify it by superimposing episcopacy, and its final re-establishment after the revolution. It is natural, therefore, that both the sources and later works are largely ecclesiastical in character, and tend to be biased by the religious preferences of their authors. Another feature of the period is the importance of the nobility, and thus national history is often bound up with the fortunes of individuals as Montrose or Argyle. Accordingly family histories are unusually important. Thanks to religious zeal on the one hand and family pride on the other it is probable that a larger proportion of the extant sources has been published than for the history of any other modern country.

Scotland is fortunate in possessing an excellent general history in moderate compass by Hume Brown (3100). In conjunction with Masson he edited the Scottish Privy Council Register (2112), the chief source for administrative history, and wrote the best account of the Union. For that event Defoe (2933) and Bruce (3067) are valuable for documents, and Mackinnon (3098) for references to pamphlets. Since the two relations of England and Scotland were so intimate, the works of English historians are often valuable for Scottish history, and Gardiner (219, 220), and Firth (244) are as indispensable as such sources as Thurloe (86) and the Clarke Papers (151).

The military history of England and Scotland is inextricably entwined, and is dealt with jointly. A number of books which are listed under England but which are important for Scotland are indexed under Scotland.

¶ 1. BIBLIOGRAPHIES AND SOURCES

2917. A bibliography of printed documents and books relating to the Scottish Company, commonly called the Darien Company. Ed. by J. Scott. 1 vol. 4to. Edin. 1904.

This work appears in part i of vol. vi of the Publications of the Edinburgh Bibliographical Society (1904). For some of Lieut. Robert Turnbull's Darien letters see Scottish Historical Review, vol. xi.

2918. A list of books printed in Scotland before 1700, including those printed furth of the realm for Scottish booksellers, with brief notes on the printers and stationers. By H. G. Aldis. 1 vol. 4to. Edin. Bibl. Soc. Edin. 1904.

2919. A guide to the public records of Scotland deposited in H. M. General Register House, Edinburgh. By M. Livingstone. 1 vol. 8vo. H. M. Stat. Office, Edin. 1905.

The State Papers relating to Scotland in the Public Record Office have been calendared only to 1603. 'Calendars of State Papers—Domestic' (124), however, contain valuable references to Scottish history.

The Edinburgh periodical press. See No. 2539.

2920. An index to the papers relating to Scotland, described or calendared in the Historical MSS. Commission's Reports. Ed. by C. S. Terry. 1 vol. 8vo. Glasgow. 1908.

2921. A catalogue of the publications of Scottish historical and kindred clubs and societies, and of the volumes relative to Scottish history issued by His Majesty's Stationery Office, 1780–1908, with a subject-index. Ed. by C. S. Terry. 1 vol. 8vo. Glasgow. 1909.

Invaluable.

2922. Scottish economic literature to 1800 [from 1124]. Ed. by W. R. Scott. 1 vol. 8vo. Glasgow and Edin. 1911.

Contains a list of authorities prepared for the Committee of early economic literature, Scottish Exhibition of National History, Art, and Industry, Glasgow, 1911. Cf. T. Keith's Bibliography of Scottish economic history. Scottish Historical Association's Pamphlets, No. 5 [1914].

2923. List of works relating to Scotland. Ed. by G. F. Black. 1 vol. 4to. New York. 1916.

Although only a list of works in New York Public Library on 31 Dec. 1914, it is ' of the highest reference value '. Scot. Hist. Rev. xiv, p. 286.

2924. Contribution to the bibliography of Scottish topography. Sir A. Mitchell and C. G. Cash. 2 vols. 8vo. Scottish Hist. Soc. Edin. 1917.

Vol. i, Topographical ; ii, Topical—Industries, Maps, Travellers, &c. Valuable.

2925. The Scottish Historical Review. Index to vols. 1–12, 1904–15. By A. Mill. 1 vol. 8vo. Glasgow. 1918.

SOURCES

2926. A large declaration concerning the late tumults in Scotland, from their first originalls : together with a particular deduction of the seditious practices of the prime leaders of the Covenanters : collected out of their owne foule acts and writings. . . . By the King. By [W. Balcanquhall]. 1 fol. Lond. 1639. 1 Port.

The official defence of the policy of Charles I by a Laudian.

2927. The history of the Church of Scotland, beginning the year of our Lord 203, and continued to the end of the reign of James VI. By J. Spottiswoode. 1 vol. fol. Lond. 1655. Later ed. 3 vols. 8vo. Spottiswoode Soc. and Bann. Club. Edin. 1847–1851. Ed. by M. Russell and M. Napier.

Of the first importance for the period, containing original documents—royalist and episcopal in sympathies, but moderate in tone. For proof that grave liberties have been taken with some documents see Proc. Soc. Antiq. of Scotland, lx. 317, 344–7.

2928. An apologeticall relation of the sufferings of ministers . . . since 1660. By J. Brown of Wamphray. 1 vol. s.l. 1665.

2929. Naphtali or the wrestlings of the Church of Scotland . . . from the Reformation . . . until 1667. By Sir J. Stewart and J. Stirling. 1 vol. 8vo. s.l. 1667. Several reprs., the last 8vo. Perth, and Kirkcudbricht 1845.

Andrew Honeymoir, Bishop of Orkney, wrote a reply in two parts : A survey of the insolent and infamous libel entituled Naphtali [4to. s.l. 1668] and Survey of Naphtali [4to. Edin. 1669].

2930. An apology for or vindication of the oppressed. By H. Smith. 1 vol. 8vo. s.l. 1677.

2931. The true history of the Church of Scotland From the beginning of the Reformation, unto the end of the reign of King James VI. . . . By D. Calderwood. 1 vol. fol. [Rotterdam]. 1678. Later ed. 8 vols. 8vo. Wodrow Soc. Edin. 1842–9. Ed. by T. Thomson.

The first ed. was a condensed history printed from a manuscript prepared by the author for the press. The Wodrow Society edit. is from the MS. in the Brit. Mus. Presbyterian : of the first importance for the contemporary documents it contains.

2932. Hind let loose, or an historical representation of the testimonies of the Church of Scotland. By A. Shields. 1 vol. 8vo. s.l. 1687. Later eds. : 1 vol. 8vo. Edin. 1744. 1 vol. 8vo. Glasgow. 1770 and 1797.

Represents the position of the extreme Covenanters. The first ed. pr. in Holland without the author's name.

2933. The history of the union of Great Britain. By D. Defoe. 1 vol. fol. Edin. 1709. Later ed. 4to. Lond. 1786. 1 Port.

Of the first importance. Defoe was commissioned by the English Government to reside in Edinburgh while the Treaty of Union was being discussed in the Scottish Parliament. Ed. of 1786 has An essay containing a few strictures on the Union, by J. L. de Lolme.

2934. The original papers and letters relating to the Scots Company, trading to Africa and the Indies : from the memorial given in against their taking subscriptions at Hamburgh, by Sir Paul Ricaut, His Majesty's resident there. . . . By Sir P. Rycaut. 1 vol. 8vo. s.l. 1700.

2935. A cloud of witnesses for the royal prerogatives of Jesus Christ, or the last speeches and testimonies of those who suffered for the truth in Scotland since the year 1680. 1 vol. 4to. s.l. 1714. Many later eds., the best 8vo. Edin. 1871. Ed. by J. H. Thomson.

2936. Memoirs of North Britain. By J. Oldmixon. 1 vol. 8vo. Lond. 1715. Useful for Glencoe and the Darien Company.

2937. Memoirs of the Church of Scotland in four periods . . . [From the Reformation to the Union] with an appendix of some transactions since the Union. By D. Defoe. 1 vol. 8vo. Lond. 1717. Later ed. 1 vol. 8vo. Edin. 1848.

The issue of 1848 is a reprint ; also printed in Perth in 1844 and ed. by W. Wilson, 8vo.

2938. The history of the sufferings of the Church of Scotland from the Restauration to the Revolution. . . . From the public records, original papers, and manuscripts of that time, and other well attested narratives. By R.

Wodrow. 2 vols. fol. Edin. 1721–2. Later ed. 4 vols. 8vo. Glasgow. 1828–30. 8 ports. Ed. by R. Burns.

Consists largely of transcripts from the Register of the Privy Council of Scotland relative to ecclesiastical affairs. The author was a zealous Presbyterian.

2939. The history of the troubles of Great Britain, containing a particular account of the most remarkable passages in Scotland, from the year 1633 to 1650. With an exact relation of the wars carried on . . . by . . . Montrose . . . To which is added The true causes . . . which contributed to the Restoration of King Charles II . . . by D. Riordan of Muscry. Translated into English by Capt. J. Ogilvie. By R. Menteth. 1 vol. Lond. 1735.

The 1st ed. is entitled Histoire des Troubles . . . par Messire Robert Mentet de Salmonet. 1 vol. fol. Paris, 1661. It also contains Riordan's Relation des veritables causes. . . . Royalist in sympathies. This ed. has a portrait of Menteth.

2940. The staggering state of the Scots statesmen . . . from 1550 to 1650. By Sir J. Scott of Scotstarvet. Ed. by [W. Goodall]. 1 vol. 12mo. Edin. 1754. Later ed. 1 vol. 8vo. Edin. 1872. Ed. by C. Rogers.

Cf. Scotstarvet's Trew relation, ed. G. Neilson, Scot. Hist. Rev. xi, xii, xiii, xiv.

2941. Secret history of Colonel Hooke's negociations in Scotland in 1707, being the original letters and papers. By N. Hooke. 1 vol. 8vo. Edin. 1760.

The original edition, 'Révolutions d'Ecosse et d'Irlande en 1707, 1708, et 1709 . . .' was published at the Hague in 1758. See Prefaces to Hooke's Correspondence (Roxburghe Club).

2942. Memorials and letters relating to the history of Britain in the reign of James the First. By Sir David Dalrymple, Lord Hailes. 1 vol. 8vo. Glasgow. 1762. Later ed. 1 vol. 8vo. Glasgow. 1766.

Mainly from Wodrow MSS. The 2nd ed. was ' corrected and enlarged '. From the Balfour MSS. in the Advocates' Library, Edinburgh.

2943. State papers and letters addressed to William Carstares, confidential secretary to K. William during the whole of his reign . . . relating to public affairs in Great Britain, but more particularly in Scotland, during the reigns of K. William and Q. Anne. Ed. by J. M'Cormick. 1 vol. 4to. Edin. 1774.

2944. The letters and journals of Robert Baillie, Principal of the University of Glasgow, 1637–1662. 2 vols. 8vo. Edin. 1775. Later ed. 3 vols. 4to. and 8vo. Bann. Club. Edin. 1841–2. Ed. by D. Laing.

First ed. has only a selection : that of Laing is complete. Supplies a vivid presentation of leading events and persons, English as well as Scottish, from a Presbyterian point of view. App. to vol. i has original papers 1633–9 ; ii, 1639–46 ; and iii, 1647–61.

2945. The history of Darien. Giving a short description of that country, an account of the attempts of the Scotch nation to settle a colony in that place . . . with some practical reflections upon the whole. By F. Borland. 1 vol. 12mo. Glasgow. 1779.

Borland accompanied the last expedition to Darien. His narrative, he says, was mostly written in 1700 in the ' American Regions '.

2946. Faithful contendings displayed, being an historical relation of the state and actings of the suffering remnant of the Church of Scotland, who subsisted in select Societies . . . 1681 to 1690. By M. Shields. Ed. by J. Howie. 1 vol. 8vo. Glasgow. 1780.

2947. The history of the troubles and memorable transactions in Scotland from the year 1624 to 1645. . . . From the original MS. of John Spalding, then commissary clerk of Aberdeen. 2 vols. 8vo. Aberdeen. 1792. Later eds. : 2 vols. 4to. Bann. Club. Edin. 1828–9. Maps and plans. Ed. by [J. Skene]. 2 vols. 4to. Spalding Club, Aberdeen. 1850–1. Ed. by J. Stuart.

The 1st ed. is unscholarly and incomplete. Spalding has strong royalist leanings. The ed. 1850–1, called Memorialls of the troubles in Scotland and in England, has the best text.

2948. The Acts of the Parliament of Scotland, 1593–1707. Vols. iv–xii ed. by T. Thomson and C. Innes. 12 vols. fol. H. M. Stationery Office. 1814–75.

Contains the proceedings as well as the Acts of Parliament. Vols. v and, especially, vi in the reissue are very much fuller than the first edition. Each vol. has an index of persons and places. Vol. xii is a most complete and reliable index to the whole work.

2949. Registrum magni sigilli regum Scotorum. The register of the great seal of Scotland [from 1306]. Ed. by T. Thomson, Sir J. B. Paul, J. Maitland Thomson, J. Horne Stevenson, and W. K. Dickson. Imp. 8vo. Edin. 1814–1914.

Vol. vi (1593–1608)—vol. xi. 1660–8.

2950. The secret and true history of the Church of Scotland from the Restoration to the year 1678, by the Rev. Mr. James Kirkton, to which is added an account of the murder of Archbishop Sharp, by James Russell, an actor therein. Ed. by C. K. Sharpe. 1 vol. 4to. Edin. 1817. 2 ports.

A vivid narrative written from the covenanting point of view, with notes from the opposite point. For a review by Principal Lee see Edinburgh Christian Instructor, xv. 333–53.

2951. Memorialls ; or The memorable things that fell out within this island of Brittain from 1638 to 1684, by the Rev. Mr. Robert Law. Ed. by C. K. Sharpe. 1 vol. 4to. Edin. 1818.

Interesting as reflecting the spirit of the time.

2952. Miscellanea Scotica. A collection of tracts, relating to the history, antiquities, topography and literature of Scotland. 4 vols. 12mo. Glasgow. 1818–20.

Vol. i contains Authentic narrative of the massacre of Glencoe, contained in a Report of the Commission given by his Majesty for inquiring into the slaughter of the men of Glencoe.

2953. Documents relative to the reception at Edinburgh of the kings and queens of Scotland 1561–1650. Ed. by Sir P. Walker of Coates. 1 vol. 4to. Edin. 1822.

2954. Chronological notes of Scottish affairs from 1680 till 1701, being chiefly taken from the diary of Lord Fountainhall. By Sir John Lauder, Lord Fountainhall. Ed. by Sir W. Scott. 1 vol. 4to. Edin. 1822.

From a small 12mo. vol. in Advocates' Library, Edin., compiled by Robert Mylne, who suppressed some passages and inserted others with ' perverse assiduity '. See

Scott's Introduction ; also Fountainhall's Historical notices, Bann. Club, vol. i, pp. x, xi.
Cf. Historical observes of memorable occurrents in church and state [1680–1686.
Bann. Club. 1 vol. 4to. Edin. 1840. Port.], ed. by A. Urquhart and D. Laing, and
Historical notices of Scottish affairs selected from the manuscripts of Sir J. Lauder of
Fountainhall [1661–1688. Bann. Club. 2 vols. 4to. Edin. 1848, ed. by David Laing] ;
and Journals of Sir John Lauder, Lord Fountainhall, with his observations on public
affairs and other memoranda, 1665–1676. Ed. by D. Crawford. Scot. Hist. Soc. 1 vol.
8vo. Edin. 1900. 4 ports. These works form a valuable criticism of the government by
a Presbyterian.

2955. The historical works of Sir James Balfour. . . . Lord Lyon King at
arms to Charles the First, and Charles the Second . . . from the original manuscripts . . . in the Advocates' Library. Ed. by J. Haig. 4 vols. 8vo. Edin. 1825.
1 port.

The last three vols. (1604–52) are valuable as the work of one who in his later years was
in close contact with the administration. Royalist in sympathies, but critical. Up to
1640 called by the author ' Annales ', and after ' Memories and passages of State ', the
volumes form a chronological whole.

2956. Report upon the settlement of the revenues of excise and customs in
Scotland A.D. 1656. By R. Tucker. Ed. by J. A. Murray. 1 vol. 4to. Bann.
Club. Edin. 1825.

2957. A diary of the proceedings in the Parliament and Privy Council of
Scotland, May 21, 1700—March 7, 1707, by Sir D. Hume of Crossrigg, one
of the senators of the College of Justice. 1 vol. 4to. Bann. Club. Edin. 1828.

See : Domestic Details of Sir David Hume of Crossrig . . . 1697 . . . 1707. 8vo. Edin.
1843. Ed. by W. B. D. D. T[urnbull].

2958. Siege of the castle of Edinburgh 1689. Ed. by R. Bell. 1 vol. 4to.
Bann. Club. Edin. 1828.

Cf. C. S. Terry's Siege of Edinburgh Castle in 1689, Scot. Hist. Rev. ii. The Le
Fleming MSS. Hist. MSS. Comm. 1890 has many newsletters from Edinburgh 1689–90.

2959. Letters from Archibald, Earl of Argyll, to John, Duke of Lauderdale
(1663–70). Ed. by [Sir G. Sinclair] and [C. K. Sharpe]. 1 vol. 4to. Bann. Club.
Edin. 1829. 1 port.

Appendix contains letters from Sir Andrew Ramsay to Lauderdale, 1663–7.

2960. A relation of proceedings concerning the affairs of the Kirk of
Scotland, from August 1637 to July 1638. By John Leslie, Earl of Rothes.
Ed. by J. Nairne and D. Laing. 1 vol. 4to. Bann. Club. Edin. 1830. 1 port.

Defends the proceedings of the Covenanters against Charles I. MS. in Advocates'
Library, Edinburgh.

2961. A selection from the papers of the Earls of Marchmont in the possession of the Right Honble. Sir George Henry Rose, illustrative of events from
1685–1750. Ed. by G. H. Rose. 3 vols. 8vo. Lond. 1831.

Sir Patrick Hume, 1st Earl of Marchmont (1641–1724), was Lord Chancellor of Scotland (1696–1702), and Lord High Commissioner in 1698 and 1702.

2962. Historical fragments relative to Scottish affairs from 1635–1664. Ed.
by [J. Maidment]. 3 pts. 8vo. Edin. 1832–3.

See the Bibliography of J. M. . . . from . . . 1817 to 1878. Priv. pr. 8vo. Edin. 1883.

2963. Ancient criminal trials in Scotland [1488–1624]. Ed. by R. Pitcairn. 3 vols. 4to. Bann. Club. Edin. 1833.

Compiled from the original records and MSS. with historical illustrations, &c.

2964. The Argyle papers (1640–1723). Ed. by J. Maidment. 1 vol. 4to. Edin. 1834.

2965. Analecta Scotica. Ed. by J. Maidment. 2 vols. 8vo. Edin. 1834–7.

2966. Letters to King James the Sixth from the Queen, Prince Henry, Prince Charles, the Princess Elizabeth and her husband, Frederick King of Bohemia. Ed. by A. Macdonald. 1 vol. 4to. Mait. Club. Edin. 1835. 35 facsimiles.

2967. Reports on the state of certain parishes in Scotland in 1627. 1 vol. 4to. Maitland Club. Edin. 1835.

2968. Miscellany of the Bannatyne Club, ii and iii. Ed. by D. Laing. 4to. Edin. 1836, 1855.

2969. Ecclesiastical records. Selections from the minutes of the presbyteries of St. Andrews and Cupar, 1641–98. Ed. by G. R. Kinloch. 1 vol. 4to. Abbotsford Club. Edin. 1837. 1 plan.

Similar volumes are : for the Synod of Fife, 1611–1687, pr. in 1837, and ed. by C. Baxter. 4to. Abbotsford Club, 3 plates ; presbytery of Lanark, 1623–1709, ed. by J. Robertson. Abbotsford Club. 1 vol. 4to. Edin. 1839.

2970. State papers and miscellaneous correspondence of Thomas [Hamilton], Earl of Melros. Ed. by J. Maidment. 2 vols. 4to. Abbotsford Club. Edin. 1837.

Mainly from Balfour MSS. in Advocates' Library, Edinburgh, consisting of letters of Privy Council to James VI and others, and chiefly relative to the period 1603–25.

2971. Miscellany of the Abbotsford Club. 1 vol. 4to. Edin. 1837.

2972. Records of the Kirk of Scotland, containing the acts and proceedings of the several assemblies from the year 1638 downwards, as authenticated by the clerks of assembly, with notes and historical illustrations [to 1654]. By A. Peterkin. 1 vol. 8vo. Edin. 1838.

2973. Letters and state papers during the reign of King James the Sixth (1578–1625). Ed. by J. Maidment. 1 vol. 4to. Abbotsford Club. Edin. 1838.

Chiefly from MSS. collected by Sir J. Balfour.

2974. Acts and proceedings of the general assemblies of the Kirk of Scotland from the year 1560–[1618]. Collected from the most authentic manuscripts. Ed. by T. Thomson. 3 vols. 4to. Edin. 1839–45.

Part iii, 1593–1618. The work is usually known as ' The Booke of the Universall Kirk of Scotland ', and was issued by both the Bann. Club and the Maitland Club. The latter issued an appendix 1597–1603. An ed. in one vol. 8vo., ed. by Alex. Peterkin, was published in 1839.

2975. Letters to the Argyll family (1520–1685). Ed. by A. Macdonald. 1 vol. 4to. Maitland Club. Edin. 1839. 15 facsimiles.

2976. Miscellany of the Maitland Club, vol. ii. Ed. by J. Dennistoun and A. Macdonald. 1 vol. 4to. Edin. 1840.

Part i has documents relative to schools, and part ii contains papers relative to Montrose.

2977. History of Scots affairs from 1637 to 1641. By J. Gordon, parson of Rothiemay. Ed. by J. Robertson and G. Grub. 3 vols. 4to. Spalding Club. Aberdeen. 1841.

Written from a royalist point of view.

2978. The historie of the Kirk of Scotland. 1558–1637, by John Row, minister at Carnock ; with additions and illustrations by his sons. . . . Ed. by B. Botfield. 1 vol. 4to. Maitland Club. [Edin.] 1842. Later ed. 1 vol. 8vo. Wodrow Soc. Edin. 1842. Ed. by D. Laing.

Covenanting : the Wodrow Soc. ed. has the better text.

2979. Correspondence of George Baillie of Jerviswood, 1702–1708. Ed. by Gilbert Elliot, second Earl of Minto. 1 vol. 4to. Bann. Club. Edin. 1842.

2980. Analecta, or materials for a history of remarkable providences ; mostly relating to Scotch ministers and Christians. By R. Wodrow, 4 vols. 4to. Maitland Club. Edin. 1842–3.

MS. in the Advocates' Library. [The prefatory notice, dated March 31st, 1843, is initialled ' M. L.' ; but Malcolm Laing the historian died in 1818.]

2981. Acts of the general assembly of the Church of Scotland, 1638–1842. Ed. by T. Pitcairn and others. 1 vol. 8vo. Church Law Society. Edin. 1843.

2982. Leven and Melville papers : letters and state papers chiefly addressed to George, Earl of Melville, Secretary of State for Scotland, 1689–1691. Ed. by W. L. Melville. 1 vol. 4to. Bann. Club. Edin. 1843.

The most important work for the period it covers.

2983. Extracts from the presbytery book of Strathbogie, 1631–1654. Ed. by J. Stuart. 1 vol. 4to. Spalding Club. Aberdeen. 1843.

2984. Short abridgement of Britane's distemper 1639–49. By P. Gordon. Ed. by J. Dunn. 1 vol. 4to. Spalding Club. Aberdeen. 1844.

2985. Spottiswoode Miscellany, ii. Ed. by J. Maidment. 1 vol. 8vo. Spot. Soc. Edin. 1845.

Contains many extracts from Mercurius Politicus, Aug. 1652—Apr. 1654.

2986. Papers illustrative of the political condition of the Highlands of Scotland, 1689–1696. Ed. by J. Gordon. 1 vol. 4to. Maitland Club. Glasgow. 1845.

2987. Certaine records touching the estate of the Kirk in the years 1605 and 1606. By J. Forbes. Ed. by D. Laing. 1 vol. 8vo. Wodrow Soc. Edin. 1846.

Valuable.

2988. Selections from the records of the kirk session, presbytery and synod of Aberdeen (1562–1681). Ed. by J. Stuart. 1 vol. 4to. Spalding Club. Aberdeen. 1846.

2989. A collection of letters addressed by prelates and individuals of high rank in Scotland and by two bishops of Sodor and Man to Sancroft, Archbishop of Canterbury, in the reigns of Charles II and James VII, ed. from the originals in the [Tanner MSS.] Bodleian Library, Oxford. Ed. by W. N. Clarke. 1 vol. 8vo. Edin. 1848.

2990. Extracts from the council register of the burgh of Aberdeen. Vol. ii, 1570–1625. Ed. by J. Stuart. 1 vol. 4to. Spalding Club. Aberdeen. 1848.

A work with the same title covers 1625–1747. Ed. by J. Stuart. 2 vols. 4to. Scottish Burgh Rec. Soc. Edin. 1871–2.

2991. The Darien papers : being a selection of original letters and official documents relating to the establishment of a colony at Darien by the Company of Scotland trading to Africa and the Indies, 1695–1700. Ed. by J. H. Burton. 1 vol. 4to. Bann. Club. Edin. 1849. 1 map.

Originals in Advocates' Library, Edinburgh.

2992. Original letters relating to the ecclesiastical affairs of Scotland, chiefly written by, or addressed to, His Majesty King James the Sixth, 1603–1625. Ed. by D. Laing. 2 vols. 4to. Bann. Club. Edin. 1851.

2993. Letters, illustrative of public affairs in Scotland, addressed by contemporary statesmen to George, Earl of Aberdeen, Lord High Chancellor of Scotland. 1681–4. Ed. by J. Dunn. 1 vol. 4to. Spalding Club. Aberdeen. 1851.

MSS. at Haddo House in possession of the Earl of Aberdeen.

2994. Selections from the family papers preserved at Caldwell [1496 to 1853]. Ed. by [? William] [? Mure]. 3 vols. 4to. Maitland Club. Glasgow. 1854.

2995. Munimenta almae universitatis Glasguensis : records of the University of Glasgow from its foundation till 1727. Ed. by C. Innes. 3 vols. 4to. Maitland Club. Glasgow. 1854.

2996. Minute-book kept by the war committee of the covenanters in the stewartory of Kirkcudbright in 1640 and 1641. 1 vol. 8vo. Kirkcudbright. 1855.

2997. Domestic annals of Scotland from the Reformation to the Revolution (vols. i and ii) [and] Domestic annals . . . to the rebellion of 1745 (vol. iii). By R. Chambers. 3 vols. 8vo. Edin. 1859–61. Third ed. 3 vols. 8vo. Edin. and Lond. 1874.

Consists of quotations from contemporaries.

2998. Facsimiles of national manuscripts of Scotland. Ed. by J. Robertson and C. Innes. 3 vols. fol. Ordnance Survey Office. Southampton. 1867–71.

Vol. iii (1488–1706).

2999. Royal letters, charters and tracts relating to the colonization of New Scotland, 1621–38. Ed. by D. Laing. 1 vol. 4to. Bann. Club. Edin. 1867. 1 port.

3285

3000. A book of Scotish pasquils, 1568–1715. Ed. by [J.] [Maidment]. 1 vol. 8vo. Edin. 1868.

3001. Correspondence of Colonel N. Hooke, agent from the court of France to the Scottish Jacobites in the years 1703–1707. Ed. by W. D. Macray. 2 vols. 4to. Roxburghe Club. Lond. 1870–1.

Ed. from transcripts in the Bodleian Library. See No. 2941.

3002. Records of the convention of the royal burghs of Scotland, 1597–1711 [vols. 2–4]. Ed. by Sir J. D. Marwick. 3 vols. 4to. Edin. 1870–80.

Valuable for the light the records throw on the institutions of the burghs with which they respectively deal. There is a separate index to all the five volumes [1295–1738], Edin. 1890.

3003. Scottish liturgies of the reign of James VI. Ed. by G. W. Sprott. 1 vol. 8vo. Edin. 1871. Later ed. 1 vol. 8vo. Edin. and Lond. 1901.

3004. Montrose MSS. at Buchanan Castle. Hist. MSS. Comm. (*a*) Rep. II. 165–177. (*b*) Rep. III. 368–402. Ed. by W. Fraser. 2 vols. fol. Lond. 1871–2.

(*a*) Chiefly letters and commissions to the first Marquis of Montrose, 1639–50; (*b*) a few 17th-century papers in the Lennox papers, pp. 395–6, and Menteith papers, pp. 399–402.

3005. Charters and documents relating to the burgh of Peebles, with extracts from the records of the burgh, 1165–1710. Ed. by W. Chambers. 1 vol. 4to. Scot. Burgh Rec. Soc. Edin. 1872.

Cf. The burgh of Peebles. Gleanings from its records, 1604–52. Ed. by R. Renwick. [2nd ed. 4to. Peebles. 1912]; and Extracts from the records of the burgh of Peebles, 1652–1714. Ed. by R. Renwick. Scot. Burgh Rec. Soc. [1 vol. 4to. Glasgow. 1910].

3006. Correspondence of Sir Robert Kerr, first Earl of Ancram, and his son William, third Earl of Lothian [1616–1667]. Ed. by D. Laing. Uniform with Bann. Club publications. 2 vols. 4to. Edin. 1875. 2 plates. 9 ports.

Kerr was a Covenanter and filled high offices of state while his party was in the ascendant. From the original letters preserved at Newbattle Abbey.

3007. Extracts from the records of the burgh of Glasgow. Ed. by Sir J. D. Marwick and R. Renwick. 4 vols. 4to. Scot. Burgh Rec. Soc. Glasgow. 1876–1908.

Vol. i, 1573–1642; ii, 1630–62; iii, 1663–90; iv, 1691–1717.

3008. The register of the Privy Council of Scotland. Ed. by J. H. Burton, D. Masson, P. H. Brown, and H. Paton. 8vo. Edin. H.M. Stationery Office. 1877–1924.

Vol. i begins with year 1545. Vols. vi (first series)—vol. ix, third series deal with the period to 1684. The register concludes with the year 1707, when the Privy Council of Scotland was abolished. The most valuable source of information regarding the administration under the successive reigns. The MS. is in the General Register House, Edinburgh.

3009. The Hamilton papers; being selections from original letters in the possession of His Grace the Duke of Hamilton and Brandon relating to the years 1638–1650. Ed. by S. R. Gardiner. Camd. Soc. Lond. 1880.

Originals preserved at Hamilton Palace. Cf. Cam. Soc. Misc. ix for other letters.

3010. Miscellany of the Scottish Burgh Record Society.   Ed. by Sir J. D. Marwick.   1 vol. 4to. Edin. 1881.

3011. The Lauderdale papers.   Vol. i, 1639–1667 ; vol. ii, 1667–1673 ; vol. iii, 1673–1679.   Ed. by O. Airy.   3 vols. 4to. Camd. Soc. Lond. 1884–5.

Important as containing the correspondence of those responsible for the administration.   Selected from British Museum Add. MSS. 23119–34, 35125.   Cf. Mr. Airy's letters addressed to the Earl of Landerdale [1660–69] in Camd. Soc. Misc. viii. 1883, and his articles on Lauderdale in Eng. Hist. Rev. July 1886, Quarterly Rev. July 1884, and on Archbishop Sharp in the Scottish Rev. July 1884.

3012. Eglinton MSS. : Hist. MSS. Comm.   Lond. 1885.

Mainly of social importance.

3013. The Earl of Stirling's register of royal letters relative to the affairs of Scotland and Nova Scotia from 1615 to 1635.   Ed. by C. Rogers.   2 vols. 4to. Edin. 1885.

William Alexander, Earl of Stirling, was Secretary of State for Scotland from 1626 till his death in 1640.   MSS. in General Register House and Advocates' Library, Edinburgh.

3014. The Arniston memoirs . . . 1571–1838.   Edited from the family papers.   Ed. by G. W. T. Omond.   1 vol. 8vo. Edin. 1887.   12 ports.

A few 17th-century documents, but mainly later.

3015. Hamilton MSS. : Hist. MSS. Comm.   Lond. 1887.

Of great importance for the Civil War period.

3016. Extracts from the records of the . . . burgh of Stirling, 1519–1752.   Ed. by R. Renwick.   2 vols. 4to. Glasgow. 1887–89.   1 plan.

Cf. The Stirling guildry book, 1592–1846.   Ed. by W. B. Cook and D. B. Morris [1 vol. 4to. Stirling. 1916].

3017. The Grameid : an heroic poem descriptive of the campaign of Viscount Dundee in 1689, and other pieces.   By J. Philip.   Ed. by A. D. Murdoch.   1 vol. 8vo. Scot. Hist. Soc. Edin. 1888.

Translation from the Latin.

3018. Fasti academiae mariscallanae Aberdonensis : selections from the records, 1593–1850.   Ed. by P. J. Anderson.   3 vols. 4to. New Spalding Club. Aberdeen. 1889–98.   16 ports.

Vol. iii is an index by J. F. K. Johnstone.   Cf. Officers and graduates of University and King's College, Aberdeen, 1893 ; and Roll of alumni in Arts University and King's College, 1596–1860, 1900 ; by the same editor ; and Fasti Aberdonenses : selections from the records of the University and King's College of Aberdeen, 1494–1854, ed. by C. Innes, 1854.

3019. Scottish national memorials.   A record of the historical and archaeological collection in the Bishop's castle, Glasgow, 1888.   Ed. by J. Paton. 1 vol. fol. Glasgow. 1890.   47 ports.

Cf. Scottish history and life [1 vol. fol. Glasgow. 1902.   25 ports.].

3020. The book of record : a diary written by Patrick, first Earl of Strathmore, and other documents relating to Glamis Castle, 1684–9. Ed. by A. H. Millar. 1 vol. 8vo. Scot. Hist. Soc. Edin. 1890. 1 port.

From MSS. at Glamis.

3021. Athole MSS. : Hist. MSS. Comm. Rep. Lond. 1891.

Includes correspondence of Murray, aft. 1st Duke, who held various offices *temp.* William and Anne.

3022. Early travellers in Scotland [to 1689]. Ed. by P. H. Brown. 1 vol. 8vo. Edin. 3 maps.

Contains the impressions of travellers from England and the continent. Cf. Sir A. Mitchell's List of travels and tours in Scotland [1296–1900], repr. from the Proceedings of the Society of Antiquaries of Scotland, vol. xxxv, Edin. 1902, and continued in vol. xxxix.

3023. Court book of the barony of Urie. 1604–1747. Ed. by D. G. Barron. 1 vol. 8vo. Scot. Hist. Soc. Edin. 1892. 1 map.

3024. Tours in Scotland, 1677 and 1681. By T. Kirk and R. Thoresby. Ed. by P. H. Brown. 1 vol. 8vo. Edin. 1892.

3025. Records of the commissions of the general assemblies of the Church of Scotland [1646–52]. Ed. by A. F. Mitchell and J. Christie. 3 vols. 8vo. Scot. Hist. Soc. Edin. 1892–1909. 1 port.

3026. Scotland before 1700, from contemporary documents. Ed. by P. H. Brown. 1 vol. 8vo. Edin. 1893. 2 maps.

3027. Extracts from the records of the . . . burgh of Lanark, with charters . . . 1150–1722. Ed. by R. Renwick. 1 vol. 4to. Glasgow. 1893. 1 plan.

3028. Miscellany of the Scottish History Society, I, II, III, 1893, 1904, 1919.

I has : Civil war papers, 1643–50 ; letters to Archbishop Sharp from the Duke and Duchess of Lauderdale and Lord Hatton ; diary of John Turnbull, 1657–1704 ; Masterman papers, 1660–1719. II has : Correspondence of George Graeme, Bishop of Dunblane and of Orkney, 1602–38 ; narratives of Hamilton's expedition in 1648 ; papers of Robert and Gilbert Burnet and Archbishop Robert Leighton. III has : Dundee court martial records, 1651 ; Bishop of Galloway's correspondence, 1679–85 ; diary of Sir James Hope, 1646–54 ; contributions to the distressed church of France, 1622 ; Forbes baron court book, 1659–78.

3029. The account book of Sir John Foulis of Ravelston, 1671–1707. Ed. by A. W. C. Hallen. 1 vol. 8vo. Scot. Hist. Soc. Edin. 1894.

Useful for social and economic history.

3030. Seafield MSS. : Hist. MSS. Comm. Lond. 1894.

Contains the correspondence of Seafield, Lord Chancellor *temp.* Anne.

3031. Letters and papers illustrating the relations between Charles the Second and Scotland in 1650. Ed. by S. R. Gardiner. 1 vol. 8vo. Scot. Hist. Soc. Edin. 1894.

Consists of extracts from the Brief Relation, the official organ of the Council of State, and from the State Papers in the Public Record Office, London, and from MSS. in the Bodleian.

3032. Scotland and the Commonwealth : letters and papers relating to the military government of Scotland from August 1651 to December 1653. Ed. by C. H. Firth.   1 vol. 8vo. Scot. Hist. Soc. Edin. 1895.

Mainly from Clarke Papers, Worcester College Library, Oxford, and from the Tanner MSS. and the Clarendon Papers in the Bodleian : has valuable introduction.   Continued to 1659 in his Scotland and the Protectorate.   Scot. Hist. Soc. 1899.   1 map. 3 plans.   Mainly from the Clarke and Clarendon papers.

3033. Records of the presbyteries of Inverness and Dingwall, 1643–1688. Ed. by W. Mackay.   1 vol. 8vo. Scot. Hist. Soc. Edin. 1896.

3034. Royal letters and other historical documents . . . from the family papers of Dundas of Dundas.   Ed. by W. Macleod.   1 vol. 4to. Edin. 1897.

3035. Revenue of the Scottish crown, 1681.   By Sir W. Purves.   Ed. by D. M. Rose.   1 vol. 4to. Edin. 1897.

An account of the rents due to the crown, with a comparison between the rental in 1681 and that of 1603.   Drawn up by the King's solicitor.

3036. Johnstone MSS.: Hist. MSS. Comm.   8vo. Lond. 1897.

Valuable for William III's reign.

3037. Drumlanrig MSS. I and II : Hist. MSS. Comm.   2 vols. 8vo. Lond. 1897, 1903.

Important for the suppression of Covenanters, 1676–85.

3038. Portland MSS. iv : Hist. MSS. Comm.   Lond. 1897.

Contain Defoe's letters to Harley, 1706–11, and Greg's 1705 : both were employed as confidential agents in Scotland.   Some letters from Defoe and others for 1711–13 are in Portland MSS. V.

3039. Compt buik of David Wedderburne, merchant of Dundee, 1587–1630, together with the shipping lists of Dundee, 1580–1618.   Ed. by A. H. Millar.   1 vol. 8vo. Scot. Hist. Soc. Edin. 1898.

3040. The diplomatic correspondence of Jean de Montereul and the brothers De Bellièvre, French ambassadors in England and Scotland, 1645–48.   Ed. by J. G. Fotheringham.   2 vols. 8vo. Scot. Hist. Soc. Edin. 1898–9.

Of great value for the period it covers.   From the original ciphered dispatches in the French Foreign Office.

3041. The rising of 1745, with a bibliography of Jacobite history, 1689–1788. Scottish History from Contemporary Writers. Ed. by C. S. Terry.   1 vol. 8vo. Lond. 1900.   2 maps, 5 plans, 1 port.   Later ed. 1903.

The later ed. has a revised and enlarged bibliography.

3042. The Chevalier de St. George and the Jacobite movements in his favour, 1701–1720.   Ed. by C. S. Terry.   1 vol. 8vo. Lond. 1901.   3 maps. 2 plans. 8 ports.   Later ed. 1 vol. 12mo. Lond. 1915.

Scottish History from Contemporary Writers, Series No. 4.

3043. Loyall dissuasive and other papers concerning the affairs of Clan Chattan, 1691–1705.   By Sir A. Macpherson.   Ed. by A. D. Murdoch.   1 vol. 8vo. Scot. Hist. Soc. Edin. 1902.   1 port.

3044. The Cromwellian Union : papers relating to the negotiations for an incorporating union between England and Scotland, 1651–1652, with an appendix of papers relating to the negotiations in 1670. Ed. by C. S. Terry. 1 vol. 8vo. Scot. Hist. Soc. Edin. 1902.

3045. Journey to Edenborough in Scotland. By J. Taylor. Ed. by W. Cowan. 1 vol. 8vo. Edin. 1903.

The journey took place in 1705.

3046. Buccleuch MSS. at Montagu House, II. pts. i and ii : Hist. MSS. Comm. 2 vols. 8vo. Lond. 1903.

Useful for 1689–95.

3047. Mar and Kellie MSS.: Hist. MSS. Comm. 1 vol. 8vo. Lond. 1904.
Valuable for the Union.

3048. Records of the sheriff court of Aberdeenshire. Ed. by D. Littlejohn. 3 vols. 4to. New Spalding Club. Aberdeen. 1904–7.

Vols. ii and iii give the records 1598–1660, with lists of officials to 1907.

3049. Records of the baron court of Stitchill, 1655–1807. Ed. by C. B. Gunn. 1 vol. 8vo. Scot. Hist. Soc. Edin. 1905.

3050. Records of a Scottish cloth manufactory at New Mills, Haddingtonshire, 1681–1703. Ed. by W. R. Scott. 1 vol. 8vo. Scot. Hist. Soc. Edin. 1905.
Valuable for development of cloth trade.

3051. Records of the proceedings of the Justiciary Court, Edinburgh, 1661–1678. Ed. by W. G. Scott-Moncrieff. 2 vols. 8vo. Scot. Hist. Soc. Edin. 1905.

MS. in possession of J. W. Weston. Political trials include those of the rebels in the Pentland rising in 1666.

3052. Memoirs of Scottish Catholics during the XVIIth and XVIIIth centuries, selected from hitherto inedited MSS. Ed. by W. F. Leith. 2 vols. 8vo. Lond. 1909. 8 ports.

3053. De unione regnorum Britanniae tractatus. By Sir T. Craig. Ed. by C. S. Terry. 1 vol. 8vo. Scot. Hist. Soc. Edin. 1909. 1 port.

A treatise on the proposed union written about 1604. MS. in Advocates' Library. Ed. with a translation.

3054. Edinburgh guilds and crafts [1616–1872]. Ed. by Sir J. D. Marwick. 1 vol. 4to. Scot. Burgh Rec. Soc. Edin. 1909.

3055. In defence of the regalia, 1651–2. Being selections from the family papers of the Ogilvies of Barras. Ed. by D. G. Barron. 1 vol. 8vo. Lond. 1910. 1 map and illus.

3056. The records of the Trades House of Glasgow, 1605–1678. Ed. by H. Lumsden. 1 vol. 4to. Glasgow. 1910.

Cf. A sketch of the rise and progress of the Trades' House of Glasgow, its constitution, funds, and bye-laws, by G. Crawford, 8vo. Glasgow. 1858. 1 plan ; and Inventory of charters, deeds, old minute books and other records belonging to the Trades House of Glasgow [1 vol. 4to. Glasgow. 1909].

3057. The household book of Lady Grisell Baillie, 1692–1733. Ed. by R. Scott-Moncrieff. 1 vol. 8vo. Scot. Hist. Soc. Edin. 1911. 11 ports.

3058. Seafield Correspondence [1685–1708]. Ed. by J. Grant. 1 vol. 8vo. Scot. Hist. Soc. Edin. 1912. 1 port.

Valuable. Cf. Scot. Hist. Rev. x, p. 47.

3059. The Clan Campbell : abstracts of entries relating to Campbells in the sheriff court books of Argyll, Perth, particular register of Sasines, books of council and session, register of deeds, parish registers, and miscellaneous. Ed. by H. Paton. 8 vols. 4to. Edin. 1913–22.

Vols. i and iii, sheriff court of Argyll ; ii, do. of Perth ; iv, miscellaneous ; v. particular register of Sasines ; vi, books of council and session, and register of deeds ; vii, parish registers ; viii, books of council and session, and acts and decreets.

3060. Highland papers. Ed. by J. R. N. Macphail. 3 vols. 8vo. Scot. Hist. Soc. Edin. 1914–20.

3061. Letters relating to Scotland in the reign of Queen Anne [1702–8]. Ed. by P. H. Brown. 1 vol. 8vo. Scot. Hist. Soc. Edin. 1915.

Mainly written by Seafield : valuable for the Union.

3062. Papers relating to the Scots in Poland, 1576–1793. Ed. by A. F. Steuart. 1 vol. 8vo. Scot. Hist. Soc. Edin. 1915.

Cf. The Scot abroad. By J. H. Burton. 1 vol. 8vo. Edin. and Lond. New edition 1881. Cf. also The Scots in Germany, 1 vol. 8vo. Edin. 1902. 3 ports. The Scots in . . . Prussia. 1 vol. 8vo. Edin. 1903. 7 ports. The Scots in Sweden, 1 vol. 8vo. Edin. 1907. 1 port. and 1 map. All by Th. A. Fischer.

3063. Correspondence of the Scots Commissioners in London, 1644–6. Ed. by H. W. Meikle. 1 vol. 4to. Roxburghe Club. Lond. 1917.

Letters from the representatives of Scotland in the Committee of both kingdoms.

3064. Free quarters in Linlithgow, 1642–7. Ed. by C. S. Terry. Scot. Hist. Rev. xiv. 1917.

3065. Register of the consultations of the ministers of Edinburgh and some other brethren of the ministry, 1652–1657. Ed. by W. Stephen. 1 vol. 8vo. Scot. Hist. Soc. Edin. 1921.

Illustrates the divisions between Resolutioners and Protesters.

¶ 2. LATER WORKS

3066. History of the church and state of Scotland from the accession of Charles I to the Restoration. By A. Stevenson. 3 vols. 8vo. Edin. 1753–7. Later ed. 1 vol. 8vo. Edin. 1840.

Both eds. stop in 1649.

3067. Report on the events and circumstances which produced the union of the kingdoms of England and Scotland ; on the effects of this great national event, on the reciprocal interests of both kingdoms . . . [with appendix]. By [J.] [Bruce]. 2 vols. 8vo. [Lond.] [1799].

Appendix contains original documents dealing with projected unions before 1707. A limited number only were pr. for official use.

3068. History of Scotland from the union of the crowns . . . to the union of the kingdoms. By M. Laing. 2 vols. 8vo. Lond. 1800. 3rd ed. 4 vols. 8vo. Lond. 1819.

2nd and 3rd eds. corrected.

3069. A treatise on the law of Scotland respecting tithes and the stipends of the parochial clergy, with an appendix containing illustrative documents not before published. By Sir J. Connell. 3 vols. 8vo. Edin. 1815. Later ed. 2 vols. 8vo. Edin. 1830.

The 2nd ed. is ' considerably enlarged '.

3070. Vindication of the Scottish Covenanters, consisting of a review of the first series of ' Tales of My Landlord ' extracted from the Christian Instructor for 1817. By T. M'Crie. 1 vol. 12mo. Glasgow. 1824.

This able review of 'Old Mortality' is more accessible in M'Crie's Miscellaneous Writings, 1841, and in vol. iv. of his works, 1857.

3071. The history of the Western Islands and Isles of Scotland, 1493–1625. By D. Gregory. 1 vol. 8vo. Edin. 1836. Later ed. 1 vol. 8vo. Lond. 1881.

The 2nd ed. is a reprint. The work draws largely on the Privy Council register, the register of the Privy Seal, and the Denmylne MS. in the Advocates' Library, Edinburgh.

3072. Annals of the persecution in Scotland from the Restoration to the Revolution. By J. Aikman. 1 vol. 8vo. Edin. 1842.

Cf. Glimpses of pastoral work in . . . covenanting times. By W. Ross. 1 vol. 8vo. Lond. 1877.

3073. History of the Church of Scotland from the Reformation. By T. Stephen. 4 vols. 8vo. Lond. 1843–5. 24 ports.

3074. A history of the Highlands and of the Highland clans [1815]. By J. Browne. 4 vols. 8vo. Glasgow. 1838. 1 map and 8 ports. Later eds. : 4 vols. 8vo. Lond. 1849. 1 map. 5 ports. 4 vols. 8vo. Edin. and Lond. s.a.

Contains a catalogue of Gaelic and Irish MSS. in the libraries of Great Britain and Ireland.

3075. History of Scotland. By J. H. Burton. 9 vols. 8vo. Lond. and Edin. 1853, 1867–1870. Later eds. 1873 and 1876.

Burton first wrote his History of Scotland [1689–1748] 1853 ; then his History of Scotland from Agricola's invasion to the revolution of 1688, 1867–1870. Cf. Scot. Hist. Rev. i.

3076. The church history of Scotland, from the commencement of the Christian era to the present century. By J. Cunningham. 2 vols. 8vo. Edin. 1859. 6 ports. Later ed. 1882.

A convenient summary.

3077. The fifty years struggle of the Scottish Covenanters, 1638–88. By J. Dodds. 1 vol. 8vo. Edin. 1860. 3rd ed. 1861.

3078. Lectures on the history of the Church of Scotland, from the Reformation to the Revolution settlement. By J. Lee. 2 vols. 8vo. Edin. 1860.

See also his Memorial for the Bible Societies of Scotland, 1 vol. 8vo. Edin. 1824 ; and Additional Memorial, 1 vol. 8vo. Edin. 1826.

3079. An ecclesiastical history of Scotland from the introduction of Christianity to the present time. By G. Grub. 4 vols. 8vo. Edin. 1861.
The writer was a Scottish Episcopalian. Moderate and accurate.

3080. Social life in former days, chiefly in the province of Moray. By E. D. Dunbar. 2 vols. 8vo. Edin. 1865–6.

3081. The law of creeds in Scotland. By A. T. Innes. 1 vol. 8vo. Edin. 1867. Later ed. 1902.

3082. History vindicated in the case of the Wigtown martyrs. By A. Stewart. 1 vol. 8vo. Edin. 1867. 2nd ed. 1869.

3083. The industries of Scotland : their rise, progress, and present condition. By D. Bremner. 1 vol. 8vo. Edin. 1869.
Repr. of newspaper articles revised and extended.

3084. The martyr graves of Scotland. By J. H. Thomson. 2 vols. 8vo. Edin. 1875, 1877. 2nd ed. 1 vol. 8vo. Edin. and Lond. 1903. Ed. by M. Hutchison, with introduction by D. H. Fleming.
On the monuments and epitaphs of the sufferers during the reigns of Charles II and James VII, originally printed as articles in a newspaper and magazine. The edition of 1903 is much enlarged, and contains a list, previously unprinted, of the Dunnottar prisoners.

3085. History of the burgh and parish schools of Scotland. By J. Grant. 1 vol. 8vo. Lond. 1876.
Deals only with burgh schools.

3086. The practice of the Court of Session. By A. J. G. Mackay. 2 vols. 8vo. Edin. 1877–9.
Vol. i, History, constitution and jurisdiction of the Court, and procedure in ordinary actions.

3087. The history of civilization in Scotland. By J. Mackintosh. 4 vols. 8vo. Aberdeen and Lond. 1878–88. Later ed. 4 vols. 8vo. Paisley and Lond. 1892–6.
An unscholarly work, but of use for its collection of facts. The 2nd ed. was revised and partly re-written, but is far from being immaculate.

3088. Ordnance gazetteer of Scotland : A survey of Scottish topography, statistical, biographical and historical. Ed. by F. H. Groome. 6 vols. 8vo. Edin. 1882–5. 33 maps. 5 plans. Later eds. : 6 vols. 8vo. Lond. 1894 [95] ; 3 vols. 8vo. Lond. 1903.
The notice of each important town is furnished with a bibliography.

3089. History of banking in Scotland. By A. W. Kerr. 1884. 3rd ed. 1 vol. 8vo. Lond. 1918.

3090. Social life in Scotland from early to recent times. By C. Rogers. 3 vols. 8vo. Grampian Club. Edin. 1884–6.

3091. Treasury of the Scottish covenant. By J. C. Johnston. 1 vol. 8vo. Edin. 1887.

3092. Merchant and craft guilds. A history of the Aberdeen incorporated trades. By E. Bain. 1 vol. 8vo. Aberdeen. 1887.

3093. History of the Catholic Church in Scotland. Vols. iii–iv, 1560–1878. By A. Bellesheim. Ed. by D. O. H. Blair. 4 vols. 8vo. Edin. 1887–90. 4 maps.

Transl. with some notes. Bibl. to whole work in vol. i. The translator has taken occasional liberties with the text.

3094. The castellated and domestic architecture of Scotland from the twelfth to the eighteenth century. By D. MacGibbon and T. Ross. 5 vols. 8vo. Edin. 1887–92. Numerous plans.

3095. Frankreichs Beziehungen zu dem Schottischen Aufstand 1637–40. By F. Salomon. 1 vol. 8vo. Berlin. 1890.

3096. The reformed presbyterian church in Scotland, 1680–1876. By M. Hutchison. 1 vol. 8vo. Paisley. 1893.

3097. History of the Scottish Church [from the introduction of Christianity until 1895]. By W. Stephen. 2 vols. 8vo. Edin. 1894–6.

3098. The union of England and Scotland, A study of international history. By J. Mackinnon. 1 vol. 8vo. Lond. 1896.

3099. The ecclesiastical architecture of Scotland from the earliest Christian times to the seventeenth century. By D. MacGibbon and T. Ross. 3 vols. 8vo. Edin. 1896–7. Numerous plans.

3100. History of Scotland to the present time. By P. H. Brown. 3 vols. 8vo. Camb. 1899–1905. 11 maps. 1 plan. Illus. Bibl. Later ed. 3 vols. 8vo. Camb. 1911. 12 maps. 47 illus. Bibl.

The standard authority.

3101. A history of Scotland from the Roman occupation. By A. Lang. 4 vols. 8vo. Edin. and Lond. 1900–7. 17 maps. 5 ports.

The 2nd ed. of vols. i and ii (1900, 1903) contains the author's corrections.

3102. Catalogue of the Scottish coins in the National Museum of Antiquities, Edinburgh [David I to Queen Anne]. By A. B. Richardson. 1 vol. sm. 4to. 1901. Illus.

3103. Politics and religion. A study in Scottish history from the Reformation to the Revolution [1550–1695]. By W. L. Mathieson. 2 vols. 8vo. Glasgow. 1902.

3104. Scottish portraits, with an historical and critical introduction and notes. By J. L. Caw. 2 vols. la. 4to. Edin. 1903. 132 ports.

Cf. Scottish painting past and present, 1620–1908 [1 vol. 8vo. Edin. 1908. 15 illus.].

3105. A literary history of Scotland [to 1901]. By J. H. Millar. 1 vol. 8vo. Lond. 1903. 1 port. Bibl.

See Hay Fleming's Critical reviews, relating chiefly to Scotland, pp. 518–23.

3106. The fiscal policy of Scotland before the Union. By W. R. Scott. Scot. Hist. Rev. i. 1903–4.

Cf. Scottish industrial undertaking before the Union. *Ibid.* i, ii, iii ; and Joint stock companies (1928).

3107. Story of the Scottish covenants in outline. By D. H. Fleming. 1 vol. 4to. Edin. 1904. Later ed. 1 vol. 8vo. Edin. 1904.

3108. Condition of the Border at the Union. Destruction of the Graham clan. By J. Graham. 1 vol. 8vo. Glasgow. 1905. Illus. 2nd ed. 1 vol. 8vo. Lond. 1907.

3109. The Pentland rising and Rullion Green. By C. S. Terry. 1 vol. 8vo. Glasgow. 1905. 2 maps.

Drummond's official dispatch is printed Scot. Hist. Rev. iii : Terry discusses it, *ibid.* iv.

3110. Scotland and the Union. A history of Scotland from 1695 to 1747. By W. L. Mathieson. 1 vol. 8vo. Glasgow. 1905.

3111. The Scottish Parliament, its constitution and procedure, 1603–1707. With an appendix of documents. By C. S. Terry. 1 vol. 8vo. Glasgow. 1905.

The documents are taken from the ' Acts of the Parliament of Scotland '. Cf. The Scottish Parliament, 1560–1707, by W. L. Mathieson, Scot. Hist. Rev. iv.

3112. Scottish social sketches of the seventeenth century. By R. M. Fergusson. 1 vol. 8vo. Stirling. 1907.

3113. The Covenanters of Teviotdale. By D. Stewart. 1 vol. 8vo. Galashiels. 1908.

3114. The Covenanters. A history of the Church in Scotland from the Reformation to the Revolution. By J. K. Hewison. 2 vols. 4to. Glasgow. 1908. 38 ports. Later ed. 2 vols. 4to. Glasgow. 1913.

The writer has strong Covenanting sympathies. Some errors have been corrected in the 1913 edition.

3115. A history of the University of Glasgow from its foundation in 1451 to 1909. By J. Coutts. 1 vol. 4to. Glasgow. 1909. Illus. 17 ports.

3116. Scottish staple at Veere : a study of the economic history of Scotland. By J. Davidson and A. Gray. 1 vol. 8vo. Lond. 1909. Bibl.

3117. A history of secondary education in Scotland [to 1908]. By J. Strong. 1 vol. 8vo. Oxf. 1909.

3118. Scottish education. School and University. From early times to 1908. By J. Kerr. 1 vol. 8vo. Camb. 1910. Later ed. 1913.

1913 ed. ' with an addendum 1908–1913 '.

3119. The Scottish staple in the Netherlands : an Account of the trade relations between Scotland and the Low Countries from 1292 till 1676, with a calendar of illustrative documents. By M. P. Rooseboom. 1 vol. 8vo. The Hague. 1910. Illus.

Draws on MS. material in the Low Countries.

3120. Commercial relations of England and Scotland 1603–1707. By T. Keith. 1 vol. 8vo. Camb. 1910. Bibl.

Cf. Economic condition of Scotland under the Commonwealth and the Protectorate, Scot. Hist. Rev. v ; Scottish trade with the plantations before 1707, *ibid.* vi ; Influence of the convention of the royal burghs of Scotland on the economic development of Scotland before 1707, *ibid.* x.

3121. Scottish prose of the seventeenth and eighteenth centuries. By J. H. Millar. 1 vol. 8vo. Glasgow. 1912. 4 ports.

See Hay Fleming's Critical reviews (3122), pp. 524–30.

3122. Critical reviews relating chiefly to Scotland. By D. Hay Fleming. 1 vol. 8vo. Lond. 1912.

3123. The legislative union of England and Scotland. By P. Hume Brown. 1 vol. 8vo. Oxf. 1914.

Appendix of documents in the Public Record Office and British Museum. Cf. Hume Brown's and W. L. Mathieson's articles in Scot. Hist. Rev. iv ; G. W. T. Omond's The early history of the Scottish Union Question, 2nd ed. 1906 ; and The Union of 1707, a survey of events, by various authors, intro. by P. Hume Brown, 1907.

3124. The Highland host of 1678. By J. R. Elder. 1 vol. 8vo. Glasgow. 1914.

3125. Some subscribed copies of the Solemn League and Covenant. By D. Hay Fleming. 1 vol. 4to. Edin. Bibl. Soc. Edin. 1918. 6 facsimiles.

A paper by D. Hay Fleming on The subscribing of the National Covenant in 1638, in W. M. Bryce's History of the Old Greyfriars Church, Edinburgh, 1912.

3126. Thoughts on the union between England and Scotland. By A. V. Dicey and R. S. Rait. 1 vol. 8vo. Lond. 1920.

A commentary on certain aspects of the Union. Cf. The constitutional necessity for the Union of 1707, by W. S. McKechnie, Scot. Hist. Rev. v.

3127. Scottish colonial schemes, 1620–1686. By G. P. Insh. 1 vol. 8vo. Glasgow. 1922. 2 ports.

Cf. Papers relating to the ships and voyages of the company of Scotland trading to Africa and the Indies, 1696–1707. Scottish Hist. Soc. 1924.

3128. The estate of the burgesses in the Scots parliament and its relation to the convention of royal burghs. By J. D. Mackie and G. S. Pryde. 1 vol. 8vo. St. Andrews. 1923.

¶ 3. COLLECTIVE BIOGRAPHIES AND BIOGRAPHIANA

3129. A large new catalogue of the bishops of the several sees . . . of Scotland down to the year 1688. By R. Keith. 1 vol. 4to. Edin. 1755. Later ed. 1 vol. 8vo. Edin. 1824. Ed. by M. Russell.

3130. Biographia Scoticana : or Scots worthies. By J. Howie. 1 vol. 8vo. Glasgow. 1775. Later ed. 1781, and many others.

3131. Memorie of the Somervilles ; being a history of the baronial house of Somerville. By J. Somerville, eleventh lord. Ed. by Sir W. Scott. 2 vols. 8vo. Edin. 1815. 2 ports.

Preface and notes by Scott. MS. in the possession of the family. The Introduction is dated 1679.

3132. Memoirs of Mr. William Veitch and George Brysson, written by themselves, with other narratives illustrative of the history of Scotland from the Restoration to the Revolution. Ed. by T. M'Crie. 1 vol. 8vo. Edin. and Lond. 1825.

Valuable for the accounts of the risings against the government.

3133. Select biographies. By R. Wodrow and others. Ed. by W. K. Tweedie. 2 vols. 8vo. Wodrow Soc. Edin. 1845–7.

Largely from MSS. in the Advocates' Library. The authors are various. A similar volume is, Selections from Wodrow's biographical collections : divines of the north-east of Scotland. New Spalding Club, 1890. 4to. 2 ports.

3134. Lives of Alexander Henderson and James Guthrie, with specimens of their writings. . . . By T. M'Crie and T. Thomson. 1 vol. 8vo. Edin. 1846.

3135. Catalogue of the graduates . . . of the University of Edinburgh, 1587–1858. Ed. by D. Laing. 1 vol. 8vo. Bann. Club. Edin. 1858.

3136. Fasti Ecclesiae Scoticanae. The succession of ministers in the parish churches of Scotland from the Reformation, 1560, to the present time. By H. Scot. 3 vols. (6 pts.) 4to. 1866–71.

New ed. 4to. 1915 in progress. Edin.

3137. Annals and correspondence of the Viscount and the first and second Earls of Stair. By J. M. Graham. 2 vols. 8vo. Edin. and Lond. 1875. 4 ports.

Part of vol. i has valuable original documents.

3138. The Earls of Middleton . . . and the Middleton family. By A. C. Biscoe. 1 vol. 8vo. Lond. 1876.

Rather slight.

3139. The Earls of Cromartie : their kindred country and correspondence. By W. Fraser. 2 vols. 4to. Edin. 1876. 15 ports.

The correspondence extends from 1662 to 1774. Some other histories of Scottish families by the same author are separately noticed. For a complete list see the first Supplement to the Dict. Nat. Biog., *sub* Fraser. Nearly all have 17th-century correspondence.

3140. The red book of Menteith. By Sir W. Fraser. 2 vols. 4to. Edin. 1880. Illus. 25 ports.

Vol. ii, Correspondence, many letters *temp*. Charles I, including about 80 of the king's.

3141. Members of Parliament, Scotland, 1357–1882. Ed. by J. Foster. 1 vol. 8vo. Lond. 1882. 2nd ed. 1882 ' revised and corrected '.

Has genealogical and biographical notes, and some additions to, and corrections of, the official returns. Repr. from Collectanea Genealogica.

3142. The Lord Advocates of Scotland from the close of the fifteenth century to the passing of the Reform Bill. By G. W. T. Omond. 2 vols. 8vo. Edin. 1883.

3143. The Douglas book. By Sir W. Fraser. 4 vols. 4to. Edin. 1885. Illus.
Vol. iv has some royal and family letters.

3144. Memorials of the family of Wemyss of Wemyss. By Sir W. Fraser. 3 vols. 4to. Edin. 1888.
Vol. iii, Correspondence, has many 17th-century letters of value.

3145. Memorials of the Earls of Haddington. By Sir W. Fraser. 2 vols. 4to. Edin. 1889. Illus. 2 ports.
Vol. ii includes about forty letters of James VI.

3146. The Melvilles, Earls of Melville, and the Leslies, Earls of Leven. By Sir W. Fraser. 3 vols. 4to. Edin. 1890. 14 ports.
Vol. ii, Correspondence, important for 1689–1714.

3147. Genealogical collections . . . made by Walter Macfarlane. 2 vols. 8vo. Scot. Hist. Soc. Glasgow. 1900.

3148. Six saints of the Covenant, Peden, Semple, Welwood, Cameron, Cargill, Smith, edited with illustrative documents. By P. Walker. Ed. by D. Hay Fleming and a Foreword by S. R. Crockett. 2 vols. 8vo. Lond. 1901.
Walker published the life of Peden in 1724 ; those of Semple, Welwood, and Cameron in 1727 ; those of Cargill and Smith in 1732. They were reprinted in 1827 in 2 vols. 8vo. (with the addition of the life of J. Renwick by A. Shields) under the title of Biographia Presbyteriana. For bibliography see Six saints, ii. 237.

3149. Men of the Covenant. By A. Smellie. 1 vol. 8vo. Lond. 1903. 24 ports.

3150. The Scots peerage, founded on Wood's edition of Sir Robert Douglas's Peerage of Scotland, containing an historical and genealogical account of the nobility of that kingdom. With armorial illustrations. Ed. by Sir J. B. Paul. 9 vols. 8vo. Edin. 1904–14.
Has full references to the sources.

3151. Chronicles of the Frasers . . . the true genealogy of the Frasers, 916–1674. By J. Fraser. Ed. by W. Mackay. 1 vol. 8vo. Scot. Hist. Soc. Edin. 1905.
Useful for the middle of 17th century.

3152. The Moderators of the Church of Scotland from 1690 to 1740. By J. Warrick. 1 vol. 8vo. Edin. 1913. 6 ports.

¶ 4. BIOGRAPHIES, PERSONAL NARRATIVES, AND COLLECTED WORKS OF INDIVIDUALS

ARGYLL, ARCHIBALD, 1st MARQUESS OF.

3153. The great Marquess. Life and times of Archibald, 8th Earl and 1st (and only) Marquess of Argyll (1607–1661). By J. Willcock. 1 vol. 8vo. Edin. and Lond. 1903. 7 ports.

ARGYLL, ARCHIBALD, 9th EARL OF.

3154. A Scots Earl of Covenanting times : being life and times of Archibald, 9th Earl of Argyll (1629–1685). By J. Willcock. 1 vol. 8vo. Edin. 1907. 1 Map. 8 ports.

ARGYLE, JOHN, DUKE OF.

3155. The life of the most illustrious Prince John, Duke of Argyle and Greenwich . . . the whole making a compendious abstract of the British history from the death of King William III to the present time. By R. Campbell. 1 vol. 8vo. Lond. 1745. 1 port.

BALCARRES, ANNA, COUNTESS OF.

3156. Memoir of Lady Anna Mackenzie, Countess of Balcarres, and afterwards of Argyll (1621–1706). By Alexander William Lindsay, Earl of Crawford and of Balcarres. 1 vol. 8vo. Edin. 1868. 1 port.

BALCARRES, COLIN LINDSAY, THIRD EARL OF.

3157. Memoirs touching the Revolution in Scotland [1688–90]. Presented to King James II at St. Germains [1690]. By Colin Lindsay, Earl of Balcarres. Ed. by Alexander William Crawford, Lord Lindsay. 1 vol. 4to. Bann. Club. Edin. 1841.

Two earlier eds.—one Lond. 1714, and the other Edin. 1754—from transcripts mutilated and interpolated repr. in Somers Tracts, vol. xi.

BLACKADDER, JOHN.

3158. Memoirs of the Rev. John Blackadder, composed chiefly from memoirs of his life and ministry written by himself. Ed. by A. Crichton. 1 vol. 12mo. Edin. 1832. Later ed. 1826.

Illustrates the fate of a minister *temp*. Charles II.

BLACKHALL [BLACKHAL], GILBERT.

3159. Breiffe narrative of the services done to three noble ladyes (1631–49). By G. Blackhall. Ed. by J. Stuart. 1 vol. 4to. Spalding Club. Aberdeen. 1844.

BLAIR, ROBERT.

3160. Life of Mr. Robert Blair, minister of St. Andrews, containing his autobiography, 1593–1636, with supplement . . . to 1680 by Mr. W. Row. Ed. by T. M'Crie. 1 vol. 8vo. Wodrow Soc. Edin. 1848.

BRODIE, ALEXANDER.

3161. Diary of Alexander Brodie, 1652–80, and of his son James Brodie, 1680–5. Ed. by D. Laing. 1 vol. 4to. Spalding Club. Aberdeen. 1863.
Extracts were published at Edin. in 1740.

CAMERON OF LOCHEIL, SIR EWEN.

3162. Memoirs of Sir Ewen Cameron of Locheil (1629–1696). By J. Drummond. Ed. by J. Macknight. 1 vol. 4to. Abbotsford and Maitland Clubs. Edin. 1842.
Rather uncritical : said to be written in 1733.

CAMERON, RICHARD.

3163. Richard Cameron. By Sir J. Herkless. Famous Scots Series. 1 vol. 8vo. Edin. 1896.

CARSTARES, WILLIAM.

3164. William Carstares : A character and career of the Revolutionary epoch (1649–1715). By R. H. Story. 1 vol. 8vo. Lond. 1874. 1 port.
Contains family papers in possession of Carstares's descendants. Carstares's letters to Harley, 1702–7, are in Portland MSS. viii, Hist. MSS. Comm.

CLERK, SIR JOHN.

3165. Memoirs of the life of Sir John Clerk of Penicuik, Baronet, baron of the Exchequer, extracted by himself from his own journals, 1676–1755. Ed. by J. M. Gray. 1 vol. 8vo. Scot. Hist. Soc. Edin. 1892. 7 ports.
Clerk was one of the Commissioners for the Union. MSS. at Penicuik House. Also repr. Roxburghe Club, 1895.

CUNNINGHAM, WILLIAM.

3166. Diary and general expenditure book of William Cunningham of Craigends (1673–80). Ed. by J. Dodds. 1 vol. 8vo. Scot. Hist. Soc. Edin. 1887.
Illustrates social and economic history.

ERSKINE, JOHN.

3167. Journal of the Hon. John Erskine of Carnock, 1683–7. Ed. by W. Macleod. 1 vol. 8vo. Scot. Hist. Soc. Edin. 1893.
Important for Argyll's insurrection in 1685.

FLETCHER OF SALTOUN, ANDREW.

3168. The political works of Andrew Fletcher, Esq. 1 vol. 8vo. Lond. 1732. Later ed. 1 vol. 8vo. Glasgow. 1749.
Fletcher was one of the most prominent members of the Scottish Parliament that concluded the Treaty of Union. See ' A Bibliography of Andrew Fletcher of Saltoun, 1653–1716 ', by R. A. S. Macfie. Edin. Bibl. Soc. Publications, vol. iv. 1901, and Fletcher of Saltoun, by G. W. T. Omond. Famous Scots Series. 1 vol. 8vo. Edin. [c. 1897].

FOX, GEORGE.

3169. George Fox in Scotland. An appreciation of the Society of Friends and its founder. By D. Butler. 1 vol. 8vo. Edin. 1913.

FRASER OF BRAE, JAMES.

3170. Memoirs of . . . James Fraser of Brae written by himself. 1 vol. 8vo. Edin. 1738. 7th ed. 1 vol. 8vo. Inverness. 1889.

GRIERSON, SIR ROBERT.

3171. The Laird of Lag. By A. Fergusson. 1 vol. 8vo. Edin. 1886.
A life of Sir Robert Grierson (d. 1733).

GUTHRY, HENRY.

3172. Memoirs of Henry Guthry, late Bishop of Dunkel, in Scotland: wherein the conspiracies and rebellion against King Charles I, to the time of the murther of that monarch, are briefly and faithfully related. 1 vol. 8vo. Lond. 1702. Later eds. 1 vol. 12mo. Glasgow. 1747 and 1748. Ed. by G. Crawfurd.
Guthry's sympathies are strongly Royalist. There were two second editions ; both published in Glasgow, one in 1747, the other in 1748. The 'advertisement' is omitted in the 1748 ed., the glossary is transferred to the end, a ' Life of the Author ' is added, and a new title-page is substituted. Otherwise the impression is the same.

HAY OF CRAIGNETHAN, ANDREW.

3173. Diary, 1659–60. Ed. by A. G. Rcid. 1 vol. 8vo. Scot. Hist. Soc. Edin. 1901.

HENDERSON, ALEXANDER.

3174. The life and times of Alexander Henderson, giving a history of the Church of Scotland and of the Covenanters during the reign of Charles I. By J. Aiton. 1 vol. 8vo. Edin. 1836. 1 port.
Cf. Alexander Henderson : churchman and statesman. By R. L. Orr. 1 vol. 8vo. Lond. 1919. 2 ports.

HOPE, SIR THOMAS.

3175. Diary of the correspondence of Sir Thomas Hope, 1633–45. Ed. by T. Thomson. 1 vol. 4to. Bann. Club. Edin. 1843.
Lord Advocate under Charles I and Lord High Commissioner in 1643. Letters of his are in Miscellany of Scot. Hist. Soc. i. Cf. Scot. Hist. Rev. iii.

JAFFRAY, ALEXANDER.

3176. Diary of Alexander Jaffray. Ed. by J. Barclay. 1 vol. 8vo. Lond. 1833. 3rd ed. 1 vol. 4to. Aberdeen. 1856.
A Scottish Commissioner to Charles II in 1649–50 ; afterwards a Quaker.

JOHNSTON, SIR ARCHIBALD.

3177. Diary of Sir Archibald Johnston of Wariston. Ed. by Sir G. M. Paul and D. Hay Fleming. 2 vols. 8vo. Scot. Hist. Soc. Edin. 1911–19.
A portion for 1639 with portrait is in vol. xxvi of Scot. Hist. Soc. The above includes 1632–54 with gaps. Mainly a record of the writer's spiritual experiences. From Lord Binning's MSS. preserved at Mellerstain.

KENNEDY, LADY MARGARET.

3178. Letters from Lady Margaret Kennedy to John, Duke of Lauderdale. 1 vol. 4to. Bann. Club. Edin. 1828. 3 plates, 1 port.

Gilbert Burnet's first wife : her letters are valuable for the years succeeding the Restoration.

KER OF KERSLAND, JOHN.

3179. The memoirs of John Ker of Kersland, in North Britain, Esq. Containing his secret transactions and negotiations in Scotland, England, the courts of Vienna, Hanover, and other foreign parts . . . Published by himself. 3 vols. 8vo. Lond. 1726. 1 map.

Ker was in the pay both of the Government and the Jacobites. Part 1, 3rd ed. Lond. 1727, contains one portrait and an additional ' postscript '. See D. Hay Fleming's Critical Reviews relating chiefly to Scotland.

LAMONT, JOHN.

3180. The diary of Mr. John Lamont of Newton, 1649–1671. Ed. by G. R. Kinloch. 1 vol. 4to. Maitland Club. Edin. 1830.

Of special value to the genealogist. An earlier incomplete edition, ed. by A. Constable, was publ. in Edin. in 1810, 4to.

LEIGHTON, ROBERT.

3181. The life and letters of Robert Leighton, Restoration Bishop of Dunblane and Archbishop of Glasgow. By D. Butler. 1 vol. 8vo. Lond. 1903. 1 port.

Cf. The whole works as yet recovered of Robert Leighton, vols. ii–vii (vol. i not publ.). 6 vols. 8vo. Lond. 1869–75. Ed. W. West. The best of several eds. Cf. Scot. Hist. Rev. ii. 452.

LOCKHART, GEORGE.

3182. The Lockhart Papers : containing memoirs and commentaries upon the affairs of Scotland from 1702 to 1715, by George Lockhart, Esq., of Carnwarth . . . Published from original manuscripts in the possession of Anthony Aufrere, Esq., of Hoveton, Norfolk. Ed. by [A. Aufrere]. 2 vols. 4to. Lond. 1817.

' The memoirs . . . from Queen Anne's accession . . . to . . . May, 1707 ' was published in 1714 (1 vol. 8vo. Lond.), without Lockhart's consent. The Introduction was written by Sir David Dalrymple. Valuable for Jacobitism.

MACKENZIE OF ROSEHAUGH, SIR GEORGE.

3183. Memoirs of the affairs of Scotland from the Restoration of King Charles II [1660–3 : 1669–77]. By Sir G. Mackenzie of Rosehaugh. Ed. by T. [Thomson]. 1 vol. 4to. Edin. 1821.

Narrates the events of the period from the point of view of the Government, under which he was Lord Advocate from 1677.

3184. Sir George Mackenzie, King's Advocate of Rosehaugh. His life and times, 1636 (?)–1691. By A. Lang. 1 vol. 8vo. Lond. 1909. 3 ports.

Cf. Scot. Hist. Rev. xiii.

MELVILLE, ANDREW.

3185. The life of Andrew Melville : containing illustrations of the ecclesiastical and literary history of Scotland, during the latter part of the sixteenth and beginning of the seventeenth century. With an appendix consisting of original papers. By T. M'Crie. 2 vols. 8vo. Edin. 1819. Later eds. 1824 and 1 vol. 8vo. Edin. 1856. Ed. by Thomas M'Crie.

The 1824 ed. was revised by the author ; that of 1856 contains additional editorial notes by his son. A work of the first importance for the period.

MORAY, SIR ROBERT.

3186. The life of Sir Robert Moray : soldier, statesman, and man of science (1608–1673). By A. Robertson. 1 vol. 8vo. Lond. 1922.

Note on MS. sources. Valuable.

NICOLL, JOHN.

3187. A diary of public transactions and other occurrences, chiefly in Scotland, from January 1650 to June 1667, by J. Nicoll. Ed. by D. Laing. 1 vol. 4to. Bann. Club. Edin. 1836.

From a MS. in Advocates' Library, Edinburgh.

NIMMO, JAMES.

3188. Narrative of Mr. James Nimmo, 1654–1709. 1 vol. 8vo. Scot. Hist. Soc. Edin. 1889.

The religious reflections of a Covenanter.

PATERSON, WILLIAM.

3189. The writings of William Paterson, founder of the Bank of England, with biographical notices of the author, his contemporaries and his race. Ed. by S. Bannister. 2 vols. 8vo. Lond. 1858. 2nd ed. 3 vols. 8vo. Lond. 1859.

The 1859 edit. ' With biographical notices, facsimiles, and portrait '.

3190. William Paterson, the merchant statesman, and founder of the Bank of England : his life and trials. By S. Bannister. 1 vol. 8vo. Edin. 1858. 2nd ed. 1859.

3191. A history of William Paterson and the Darien Company, with illustrations and appendices. By J. S. Barbour. 1 vol. 8vo. Edin. & Lond. 1907. 1 map. 1 plan. 1 port.

See Hiram Bingham's articles on the early history of the Company in Scot. Hist. Rev. vol. iii (1906).

PERTH, JAMES DRUMMOND, 4TH EARL OF.

3192. Letters from James, Earl of Perth . . . to his sister the Countess of Erroll, and other members of his family. Ed. by W. Jordan. Camd. Soc. 1845.

Covers Dec. 1688—Apr. 1696.

RENWICK, JAMES.

3193. The life and death of . . . James Renwick. By A. Shields. 1 vol. 8vo. Edin. 1724.

Renwick was the last of the martyrs of the Covenant publicly executed 1688. Reprinted in the second vol. of Biographia Presbyteriana in 1827 and 1837. Sixty-one of Renwick's letters are in ' A collection of letters ', Edin. 12mo. 1764.

RUTHERFORD, SAMUEL.

3194. Samuel Rutherford. A study, biographical and somewhat critical, in the history of the Scottish Covenant. By R. Gilmour. 1 vol. 8vo. Edin. and Lond. 1904.

Another life by T. Murray [1 vol. 12mo. Edin. 1828]. Cf. Rutherford's Lex Rex : the law and the prince [1 vol. 4to. Lond. 1644], reissued as : The pre-eminence of the election of kings, or a plea for the people's rights [1648].

STAIR, SIR JAMES DALRYMPLE, FIRST VISCOUNT.

3195. Memoir of Sir James Dalrymple, first Viscount Stair. A study in the history of Scotland and Scotch law during the seventeenth century. By A. J. G. Mackay. 1 vol. 8vo. Edin. 1873.

XIII. IRELAND

1. Bibliographies and Sources.
2. Later Works.

DURING the Stuart period the native Irish made two determined attempts to throw off the English yoke and to uproot the plantation system, and their history is mainly a record of rebellion and repression. The nationalist movement in Ireland during the civil war and during the war of the English succession became involved in a dynastic struggle, and was powerfully influenced in the first case by events in England, and in the second by the international issues at stake. Thus many sources as well as general histories listed under England have important references to Ireland. Among the former Strafford's Letters (84), Thurloe (85), Ludlow (925), the Clarendon State Papers (94), the Life of James II (919), and Bolingbroke's correspondence (102) are indispensable. Among the latter Gardiner (219, 220) and Firth (244) are valuable for the early Stuarts, while Klopp (215) explains most clearly the international importance of Ireland at the time of the Revolution.

From 1603–90 Bagwell (3366) has written an admirable history on an adequate scale, and the rest of the period is covered by Murray (3368). Both write from the English point of view: the other side is represented by Dalton (3363) or Prendergast (3319); Gilbert's many documentary publications are essential for the Irish rebellion and the Jacobite wars. They are supplemented by the papers and biographies of the first Duke of Ormonde (3298) and by Dunlop (3295), whose contributions to the Cambridge Modern History (239) and to the Dictionary of National Biography should not be neglected.

¶ 1. BIBLIOGRAPHIES AND SOURCES

3196. Books printed in Dublin in the 17th century. Ed. by E. R. McC. Dix and C. W. Dugan. 3 pts. 4to. Dubl. 1898–1902.

3197. Catalogue of the manuscripts in the library of Trinity College, Dublin, to which is added a list of the Fagel collection of maps in the same library. By T. K. Abbott. 1 vol. 8vo. Dubl. and Lond. 1900.

Cf. Hist. MSS. Comm. Reps. IV and VIII, and R. H. Murray's A short guide to some MSS. in the library of Trinity College, Dublin. Helps for students of history. 1 vol. 12mo. Lond. 1920.

3198. A guide to the records deposited in the Public Record Office of Ireland. By H. Wood. 1 vol. 8vo. Stationery Office, Dubl. 1919.

The Irish Record Office and its contents were destroyed by fire in June 1922, but the Guide is still useful for its references to printed sources. The three Reports of the Irish Record Commissioners [fol. 1810–25] and the fifty Reports of the Deputy Keeper of the Irish Records [8vo. 1869–1918] print, calendar or summarize documents that have perished.

3199. Ireland, 1603–1714. By R. H. Murray. Helps for students of history. 1 vol. 12mo. Lond. 1920.

A bibliographical guide. A short bibliography by Miss C. Maxwell was publ. by the Hist. Assoc. 1921.

3200. The road-books and itineraries of Ireland 1647 to 1850. A catalogue. By Sir H. G. Fordham. 1 vol. 8vo. Dubl. 1923.

3201. Le primer report des cases et matters en ley resolues et adiudges en les courts del roy en Ireland. By Sir J. Davies. 1 vol. fol. Dubl. 1615. Later eds.: 1 vol. fol. Lond. 1628 and 1674; 1 vol. fol. Dubl. 1762 [a translation]; 1 vol. 8vo. Edin. 1907 [The English Reports, vol. 80].

3202. The statutes of Ireland, beginning the third yere of K. Edward the Second, and continuing untill . . . the eleventh yeare of King James. Newly perused and examined with the Parliament Rolls. By Sir R. Bolton. 1 vol. fol. Dubl. 1621.

3203. His majesties directions for the ordering and setling of the courts, and course of justice, within his kingdom of Ireland. 1 vol. 4to. Dubl. 1622.

3204. The case of tenures upon the commission of defective titles, argued by all the judges of Ireland, with their resolution, and the reasons of their resolution. By J. Barry. 1 vol. fol. Dubl. 1637.

3205. A justice of peace for Ireland, consisting of two bookes : whereunto are added many presidents of indictments of treasons, felonies, [&c.] By Sir R. Bolton. 1 vol. fol. Dubl. 1638 and 1683.

3206. A remonstrance of divers remarkable passages concerning the church and kingdome of Ireland, to the honourable House of Commons in England. By H. Jones. 1 vol. 4to. Lond. 1642.

This remonstrance is based on the personal experience of Jones and on extracts out of the depositions preserved in Trinity College Dubl. Library.

3207. The whole proceedings of the siege of Drogheda in Ireland, with a thankful Remembrance of its wonderful delivery, raised with God's assistance by the prayers and sole valour of the beseiged, with a relation of such passages as have fallen out there, and in the parts near adjoining. By N. Bernard, Dean of Ardagh. 1 vol. 4to. Lond. 1642. Later ed. 1 vol. 4to. Dubl. 1736.

Ed. of 1736 has appended an account of the siege of Londonderry (by G. Walker). A vivid narrative with details of importance.

3208. Relation of the beginning and proceedings of the rebellion of county Cavan. By H. Jones, Bishop of Neath. 1 vol. 4to. Lond. 1642.

Repr. in Somers Tracts, vol. v ; and in Gilbert's Contemporary history.

3209. The Irish rebellion : or an history of the beginnings and first progress of the general rebellion, raised within the kingdom of Ireland, upon the three and twentieth day of October 1641. Together with the barbarous cruelties and bloody massacres which ensued thereupon. By Sir J. Temple.

2 pts. 4to. Lond. 1646.   Later eds.: 1 vol. 4to. Lond. 1674 ; 6th. 1 vol. 4to.
Lond. 1679 (best) ; 1 vol. 4to. Dubl. 1724.

The responsibility for publishing ed. of 1674 was disclaimed by Temple.   The ed. of
1679 'wherein several entire sentences, omitted in all the Irish editions, are truly
inserted ', is the best.   Ed. of 1724 has frontispiece exhibiting cruelties inflicted by
Catholics on the Protestants.   To which is added Sir H. Tichborne's History of the
siege of Drogheda in the year 1641 : as also the whole tryal of Connor Lord Maguire.
. . . Together with the Pope's bull to the confederate Catholics in Ireland.
Though still appealed to as an authority its position is rather that of a partisan pamphlet than an historical treatise.   Dict. Nat. Biog.

3210. A guide for strangers in the kingdome of Ireland.   Wherein the
high-wayes and roads . . . is truly set down.   By J. Woodhouse.   1 vol. 8vo.
Lond. 1647.   Later ed. 1 vol. 4to. Lond. 1683. Map.

3211. Ireland's naturall history.   Being a true and ample description of its
literation, greatness, shape, and nature ; of its hills, woods . . . heads or pro-
montories . . . of its metalls . . . and lastly its air and season. . . . By G. Boate.
1 vol. 8vo. Lond. 1652.   Later eds.: 1 vol. 4to. Dub. 1726, with folding plates
and illusts ; 1 vol. 8vo. Dubl. 1860.

French version : Histoire naturelle d'Irlande.   Paris, 1666.

3212. The great case of transplantation discussed.   By [V. Gookin].   1 vol.
4to. Lond. 1655.

On the authorship of the tract and Petty's supposed share in it see Lord E. Fitzmaurice's Life of Petty, p. 32, note 3, and Gardiner's The transplantation to Connaught
in Eng. Hist. Rev. Oct. 1899. The proper date of publication is 1654. Cf. R. Lawrence's
The interest of England in the Irish transplantation stated [1 vol. 4to. Lond. 1655].

3213. Reflections upon persons and things in Ireland by letters to and from
Dr. Petty with Sir Hierome Sankey's speech in Parliament.   By M. H.   1 vol.
12mo. Lond. 1660.

3214. Loyalty asserted, and the late remonstrance . . . of the Irish clergy and
layty confirmed. . . . By Raymond or Redmond Caron.   1 vol. 4to. Lond. 1662.

3215. Cambrensis eversus, seu potius historica fides in rebus Hibernicis
Giraldo Cambrensi abrogata . . . qui etiam aliquotres memorabiles Hibernicas
veteris et novae memoriae passim e re nata huic operi inseruit.   By [J. Lynch].
1 vol. fol. [St. Malo ?] 1662.   Later ed. 3 vols. 8vo. Dubl. (Celtic Soc.) 1848–52,
with Eng. trans. and notes. Ed. by M. Kelly.

' Lynch defends the Cessation of 1643, the peaces of 1646 and 1648, condemns the
nuncio and approves the general policy of Ormond.' Dict. Nat. Biog. Expresses the
views of the moderate or Anglo-Irish party in Ireland.

3216. Pii Antistibis Icon, sive de vita et morte R^{ml} D. F. Kirwani Alladen-
sis Episcopi &c.   By J. Lynch.   1 vol. 8vo. St. Malos [Maclorii]. 1669.   Later
ed. 1 vol. 8vo. Dubl. 1884. Ed. by C. P. Meehan.

Ed. of 1884 trans.   The portrait of a pious bishop : or the life and death of . . . Francis
Kirwan, Bishop of Killala.   (Lat. and Eng.)

3217. The history and vindication of the loyal formulary, or Irish remonstrance . . . received by his majesty . . . 1661, against all calumnies and censures
in several treatises.   With a true account . . . of the delusory Irish remonstrance

...framed ... by the National Congregation ... 1666 ... By P. Walsh. 1 vol. fol. Lond. 1674.

' I have never read over Walsh's History of the remonstrance, which is full of a sort of learning I have been little conversant in ; but the doctrine is such as would cost him his life if he could be found where the pope has power.' Ormond in 1680, Carte, App. ii. 114. See Dict. Nat. Biog.

3218. Life of Archbishop Bramhall, prefixed to his Works. By J. Vesey, Archbishop of Tuam. 1 vol. fol. Dubl. 1676. Later eds.: 1 vol. fol. Dubl. 1677; 1 vol. 8vo. Bury St. Edmonds. 1841. Ed. by G. Ingram.

Ed. of 1841 repr. from the Dublin edition of 1677 with notes and a memoir.

3219. The memoires of James Lord Audley, Earl of Castlehaven, his engagement and carriage in the wars of Ireland, from the year 1642 to the year 1651. 1 vol. 8vo. Lond. 1680. Later eds.: 1 vol. 8vo. Lond. 1681; 1 vol. 8vo. Lond. 1684. enlarged and corrected with Appendix; 1 vol. 8vo. Waterford. 1753. Ed. by C. O'Conor.

Attacked by Arthur Annesley, Earl of Anglesey, in A letter from a person of honour in the country.

3220. The history of the execrable rebellion traced from the grand eruption the 23 of October 1641, to the Act of Settlement 1662 ... to which are added letters ... from the original MSS. of Mr. Cliffe ... secretary to General Ireton. By E. Borlase. 1 vol. fol. Lond. 1680. Later ed. 1 vol. fol. Dubl. 1743.

A copy with the excisions of the licencer is in Brit. Mus. Sloane MS. 1008.
Ed. of 1743 contains some documents not in the original edition.

3221. A narrative of the late Popish plot in Ireland. By T. Samson. 1 vol. fol. Lond. 1680.

Cf. A true narrative of the late design of the papists [fol. Lond. 1679]; The information of John Macnamara ... touching the Popish plot in Ireland [fol. Lond. 1680] ; David Fitz Gerald's A narrative of the Irish Popish plot [*ib.* 1680] ; J. Carrol's A narrative of the Popish plot in Ireland [*ib.* 1681].

3222. The interest of Ireland in its trade and wealth stated. By R. Lawrence. 2 pts. in 1 vol. 12mo. Dubl. 1682.

3223. Hibernia Anglicana, or the history of Ireland, from the conquest thereof by the English to this present time. By Sir R. Cox. 2 vols. fol. Lond. 1689. Map. Ports.

Serviceable for the documents in the Appendix relating to the reign of Charles I.

3224. A true account of the whole proceedings of the parliament in Ireland, beginning March 25, 1689. 1 vol. 4to. Lond. 1689.

Cf. The journal of the proceedings of the parliament [1 vol. 4to. Lond. 1689]; A journal of the proceedings of the pretended parliament [Somers Tracts, iv. ed. 1750]. An exact list of the lords spiritual and temporal who sate in the pretended parliament [1 vol. 4to. Lond. 1689].

3225. An account of the transactions of the late King James in Ireland, wherein is contain'd the Act of Attainder passed at Dublin, in May 1689. 1 vol. 4to. Lond. 1690.

3226. Narrative of the siege of Londonderry, or the late memorable transactions of that city faithfully represented to rectify the mistakes and supply the omissions of Mr. Walker's account. By J. Mackenzie. 1 vol. 4to. Lond. 1690. Later ed. 1 vol. 8vo. Belfast. 1861, with notes and introduction. Ed. by W. D. Killen.

An anonymous writer attacked the ' Narrative ' in ' Mr. John Mackenzie's Narrative of the siege of Londonderry a false lible ' ; Mackenzie replied in ' Dr. Walker's Invisible champion foiled '. See No. 3285 for Walker's account.

3227. A true and impartial account of the actions of the Inniskilling men. By Captain W. M'Carmick. 1691. Later ed. 1 vol. 8vo. [? Belfast] 1896. Ed. by W. T. Latimer.

3228. The history of the wars in Ireland between their majesties army and the forces of the late King James. By an officer in the royal army. 1 vol. 12mo. Lond. 1690. 2nd ed. 1 vol. 12mo. Lond. 1691

2nd ed. has continuation.

3229. An exact description of Ireland, chorographically surveying all its provinces and counties. By L. Eachard. 1 vol. 12mo. Lond. 1691. Maps.

3230. The state of the Protestants of Ireland under the late King James's government : in which their carriage towards him is justified, and the absolute necessity of their endeavouring to be freed from his government, and of submitting to their present majesties is demonstrated. By [W. King], Archbishop of Dublin. 1 vol. 4to. Lond. 1691. 3rd ed. 1 vol. 8vo. Lond. 1692. 4th ed. 1 vol. 8vo. Lond. 1692, with additions.

Cf. Charles Leslie's An answer to a book intituled the state . . . [1 vol. 4to. Lond. 1692].

3231. The political anatomy of Ireland, with the establishment for that kingdom when the late Duke of Ormond was Lord Lieutenant. Taken from the records. To which is added Verbum sapienti ; or an account of the wealth and expenses of England, &c. By Sir W. Petty. 1 vol. 8vo. Lond. 1691. Later ed. 2 pts. 8vo. Lond. 1719.

Ed. of 1719 has additions. Reprinted in The economic writing of Sir William Petty, ed. by C. H. Hull. 2 vols. 8vo. Cambridge, 1889, vol. i, p. 121.

3232. A true and impartial history of the most material occurrences in the kingdom of Ireland during the two last years. With the present state of both armies written by an eyewitness to the most remarkable passages. By [G. Story]. 1 vol. 4to. Lond. 1691. Maps. Plans. Later ed. 1 vol. 4to. Lond. 1693 (with the continuation).

Ed. of 1691 goes down to Jan. 1691, the continuation to March 1692.

3233. Ireland's case briefly stated. By H. Reily. 2 pts. 12mo. s.l. 1695. Later eds. : 1 vol. 12mo. Lond. 1754 ; 1 vol. 12mo. Dubl. [1799].

Ed. of 1754 has title . . . ' The impartial history of Ireland . . . to which is annexed : The nobility and gentry of Ireland's remonstrance to King Charles the Second. . . . The speech and dying words of O. Plunket. Ed. of 1799 has title ' The genuin history of Ireland . . . The whole revised and brought down from 1676 to the present time.' The popularity of the book is due to no special merit, but to the fact that it was long almost the only printed argument in favour of the Irish Roman Catholics. Dict. Nat. Biog.

3234. The case of Ireland's being bound by Act of Parliament in England stated. By W. Molyneux. 1 vol. 12mo. Dubl. 1697 or 1698. Later ed. 1 vol. 12mo. Dubl. 1725. Port.

Ed. of 1725 : To which is added the case of tenures upon the commission of defective titles (Trin. 13 Caroli Regis), argued by all the judges of Ireland. With their resolutions and the reason.
The original autograph is in Trinity College, Dublin, No. 890 in Abbott's Cat.

3235. The report of the commissioners appointed by parliament to enquire into the Irish forfeitures . . . 15th of Dec. 1699. 1 vol. sm. fol. Lond. 1700.

Repr. in vol. ii of A collection of State tracts. Lond. 1705-7.

3236. The exemplary life and character of James Bonnell, Esq. late accountant-general of Ireland. By W. Hamilton. Dubl. 1703. Later eds. 1707, 1718, and many reprints.

3237. An essay towards improving the hempen and flaxen manufactures in the kingdom of Ireland. By L. Crommelin. 1 vol. 4to. Dubl. 1705. Diagrams.

3238. A journal of the life, travels, suffering . . . of . . . William Edmundson. 1 vol. 4to. Dubl. 1715. Many reprints.

A quaker's autobiography, useful for political, social as well as religious history.

3239. The history of the rebellion and civil wars in Ireland. By Edward Hyde, Earl of Clarendon. 1 vol. 8vo. Lond. 1719. Later ed. 1 vol. 8vo. Dubl. 1720. Port.

Incorporated in Bandinel's ed. of Clarendon's History of the rebellion (69) ; the ed. of 1720 is the more correct.

3240. The memoirs of G[eorge] L[eyburn]. Being a journal of his agency for Prince Charles in Ireland in the year 1647. Accompanied with original instructions and letters to the author from Prince Charles. . . . By G. Leyburn. 1 vol. 8vo. Lond. 1722.

3241. A collection of the state letters of . . . Roger Boyle, the first Earl of Orrery, Lord President of Munster in Ireland. Containing correspondence between the Duke of Ormonde and his Lordship. [1660-8.] Ed. by T. Morrice. 1 vol. fol. Lond. 1742. Later ed. 2 vols. 8vo. Dubl. 1743.

Life of Orrery prefixed.

3242. A history of the rise and progress of the people called Quakers in Ireland from 1653 to 1700 . . . To which is added a continuation . . . to . . . 1751 by J. Rutty. By T. Wight and J. Rutty. 1 vol. 4to. Dubl. 1751. Later ed. 1 vol. 8vo. Lond. 1800.

3243. The memoirs and letters of Ulick, Marquis of Clanricarde . . . Lord Lieutenant of Ireland and Commander in Chief of the forces of King Charles the First . . . during the rebellion. 1 vol. fol. Lond. 1757.

Pp. 1–443 contain letters covering Oct. 1641—Aug. 1643 ; then follow letters about the treaty with the Duke of Lorraine, 1651—Aug. 1652. This second section was separately pr. 1 vol. 8vo. Lond. 1722 as Memoirs of . . . Clanricarde . . . containing several original papers . . . relating to the treaty between the Duke of Lorraine and the Irish Commissioners.

3244. The state letters of Henry Earl of Clarendon, Lord lieutenant of Ireland during the reign of King James the Second and his worship's diary, 1687–90. 2 vols. 4to. Oxf. 1763. Later ed. 2 vols. 4to. Lond. 1828. Ed. by S. W. Singer.

Later ed. has many papers added, mostly referring to family affairs.

3245. Letters written by his excellency Arthur Capel, Earl of Essex, Lord Lieutenant of Ireland, in the year 1675. By Arthur Capel, Earl of Essex. 1 vol. 4to. Lond. 1770. Later ed. 1 vol. 8vo. Dubl. 1773.

Life prefixed. Cf. Essex papers, vol. i, 1672–5, ed. O. Airy ; vol. ii, 1675–7, ed. by C. E. Pike. Both vols. Camd. Soc. 1890, 1913. Both contain official and private correspondence from the Brit. Mus. Stowe MSS. There is a paper by C. E. Pike in Royal Hist. Soc. Trans. 3rd ser. v. 1911 on the intrigue to deprive the Earl of Essex of the Lord Lieutenancy of Ireland.

3246. Desiderata curiosa Hibernica : or A select collection of state papers ; to which are added some historical tracts. By [J. Lodge]. 2 vols. 8vo. Dubl. 1772.

Includes *inter alia* William Farmer's A chronicle of Lord Chichester's government of Ireland, 1612–15 [of which an earlier portion was pr. from Harl. MS. 3544 by C. L. Falkiner in Eng. Hist. Rev. xxii], and Henry McTully O'Neill's A journal of the most memorable transactions of General Owen O'Neill, 1641–50.

3247. Historical tracts : consisting of A discovery of the true causes why Ireland was never brought under obedience to the crown of England. By Sir J. Davies. Ed. by G. Chalmers. 1 vol. 8vo. Lond. 1786. Later ed. 1 vol. 8vo. Dubl. 1787.

Repr. in Works of Sir John Davies, ed. by A. B. Grosart, 3 vols. 8vo. 1869–76, and in Ireland under Elizabeth and James I, ed. by H. Morley. Lond. 1870 (Carisbrooke Library).

3248. Journals of the House of Lords of the kingdom of Ireland from 1634–1800. 8 vols. fol. Dubl. 1779–1800.

A journal from 17 March 1640—5 March 1641 with variations from the above is in Hist. MSS. Comm. Various viii. Clements MSS.

3249. The statutes at large passed in the parliament held in Ireland from the third Edw. II A.D. 1310 to the fortieth year of Geo. III A.D. 1800. 20 vols. fol. Dubl. 1786–1801.

Cf. A collection of all the statutes now in use in the kingdom of Ireland with notes in the margin . . . also a necessary table or kalendar to the whole work. 1 vol. fol. Dubl. 1678. Useful as containing the Acts of Settlement and Explanation.

3250. The history of the principal transactions of the Irish Parliament from the year 1634 to 1666. By H. R. Morres, Lord Mountmorres. 2 vols. 8vo. Lond. 1792.

Includes Sir Robert Southwell's life of the 1st Duke of Ormonde and some papers on finance and trade.

3251. The journals of the House of Commons of the kingdom of Ireland . . . 1613 to . . . 1800. 19 vols. App. and Index. 20 vols. fol. Dubl. 1796–1800.

3252. The Rawdon papers, consisting of letters on various subjects . . . to and from J. Bramhall, Primate of Ireland. Illustrated with notes. Ed. by E. Berwick. 1 vol. 8vo. Lond. 1819.

3253. Négociations de M. le Comte d'Avaux en Irlande, depuis 1689 jusqu'en 1690. By J. A. Mesmes, Count d'Avaux. 1 vol. 8vo. Lond. 1830.

Six copies printed privately at the expense of the Foreign Office.

3254. The Montgomery manuscripts. By W. Montgomery. Ed. by J. McKnight. 1 vol. 12mo. Belfast. 1830. Later ed. 1 vol. 4to. Belfast. 1869. Ed. by G. Hill.

A reprint of extracts published in the Belfast ' News Letter ' in 1785-6.
Ed. of 1869 is practically a new work owing to additions and notes. A vivid sketch of the Scottish settlements in co. Down and the history of Ulster from 1641 onwards.

3255. Journal of the Very Rev. Rowland Davies, Dean of Ross (and afterwards Dean of Cork) from March 8, 1689, to Sept. 29, 1690. By R. Davies. Ed. by R. Caulfield. Camd. Soc. 1837.

3256. Narratives illustrative of the contests in Ireland in 1641 and 1690. 1. The siege of Ballyally Castle in the county of Clare. By M. Cuffe, Esq. 2. Macariae excidium. Ed. by T. C. Croker. 1 vol. Camd. Soc. 1841.

3257. Macariae excidium, or the destruction of Cyprus, being a secret history of the war of the revolution in Ireland. By C. O'Kelly. Ed. by T. C. Croker.* Camd. Soc. 1841. Later eds.: 1 vol. 4to. Irish Arch. Soc. Dubl. 1850. Best ed. Ed. by C. O'Callaghan. 1 vol. 8vo. Dub. 1894. Ed. by Hogan E. Plunket (Count).†

* In Narratives illustrative of the contests in Ireland in 1641, &c.
† Under title The Jacobite war in Ireland (1688–1691), from a Clongowes Wood MS., with the cryptic names translated.

3258. La Nunziatura in Irlanda di Monsignor Giov. Battista Rinuccini, arcivescovo di Fermo negli anni 1645 a 1649, pubblicata per la prima volta sui MSS. originali della Rinucciniana. By G. Aiazzi. 1 vol. 8vo. Florence. 1844.

Eng. abridged trans. by A. Hutton under title The embassy in Ireland of Monsignor Rinuccini, 1645-1649. 1 vol. 8vo. Dubl. 1873. Cf. Hist. MSS. Comm., 9th Rep., Pt. II, 340-57, for Gilbert's description of the Earl of Leicester's Rinuccini MS.

3259. The historical works of [Nicholas French, Bishop of Ferns] now first collected. With an introduction containing notices historical and descriptive of the Irish colleges of Louvain. Ed. by S. H. Bindon. 2 vols. 12mo. Dubl. (Duffy's Lib.) 1846.

Including: 1. A Narrative of . . . Clarendon's settlement and sale of Ireland [publ. 1 vol. 4to. Louvain. 1668. and rep. 1 vol. 4to. Lond. 1704 under the title Iniquity displayed ; or, the settlement of the kingdom of Ireland. 2. The bleeding Iphigenia [Louvain. 1675]. 3. The vnkinde desertor of loyall men and true friends [1 vol. 8vo. Louvain. 1676]. The unkind desertor is Ormond.

3260. A repertory of the inrolments of the patent roles of Chancery, in Ireland ; commencing with the reign of King James I. Ed. by J. C. Erck. 1 vol. 8vo. Dubl. 1846.

Only the first part of this work was published.

3261. Life of Archbishop Ussher, prefixed to his complete Works (vol. i). By C. R. Elrington. 17 vols. 8vo. Dubl. 1847–64. Port. Later ed. 1 vol. 8vo. Dubl. 1848. Port.

A corrected copy of the life and vols. xv and xvi of the correspondence, with index by Bishop Reeves, is in the library of Trinity College, Dublin (see Abbott's Cat., nos. 1072–5). Cf. nos. 1561–3.

3262. A collection of tracts and treatises illustrative of the natural history, antiquities and the political and social state of Ireland. 2 vols. 8vo. Dubl. 1860.

Vol. i has Gerald Boate's Ireland's naturall history, Jacobi Waroei . . . de Hibernia, Sir John Davies, a discourse ; ii has Petty's The Political anatomy.

3263. The history of the survey of Ireland, commonly called The Down survey . . . A. D. 1655–6. Edited from a manuscript in the library of Trinity College, Dublin, with another in the possession of the most noble the Marquis of Lansdowne and one in the library of the King's Inns, Dublin. By Sir W. Petty. Ed. by T. A. Larcom. 1 vol. 4to. Irish Archaeol. Soc. Dubl. 1861.

3264. Memoir of the life and episcopate of William Bedell, Lord Bishop of Kilmore . . . Printed for the first time (with illustrative notes) from the original MS. in the Harleian Collection. By A. Clogy or Clogie. Ed. by W. W. Wilkins. 1 vol. 8vo. Lond. 1862. Later ed. 1902. Ed. by E. S. Shuckburgh.

Ed. of 1902 in Two biographies of William Bedell, Bishop of Kilmore ; the other biography is by W. Bedell Junr.: The true relation of the life and death of William Bedell. Ed. by T. W. Jones. Camd. Soc. 1872. Original in Bodl. Lib. Tanner MS. cclxxvii. This is the most trustworthy source. The life of Bishop Bedell, by Gilbert Burnet, based on information supplied by Clogy was publ. 1 vol. 8vo. Lond. 1685. 3rd ed. Dubl. 1758.

3265. Calendar of the patent and close rolls of Chancery in Ireland of the reign of Charles the First. First to eighth year inclusive. Ed. by J. Morrin. 1 vol. 8vo. Lond. 1863.

Sharply criticized in ' On the history, position, and treatment of the public records of Ireland ', by an Irish Archivist ; believed to be Sir J. T. Gilbert. 2nd ed. Lond. 8vo. 1864.

3266. Clerical and parochial records of Cork, Cloyne, and Ross, taken from diocesan and parish register MSS. By W. M. Brady. 3 vols. 8vo. Dubl. 1864.

3267. Mémoires inédits. By I. Dumont de Bostaquet. Ed. by C. Read and F. Waddington. 1 vol. 8vo. Paris. 1864.

Useful for war against William III.

3268. A true narrative of the rise and progress of the Presbyterian Church in Ireland (1623–70). [By Patrick Adair.] Also the History of the Church in Ireland since the Scots were naturalized. By the Rev. A. Stewart. Ed. by W. D. Killen. 1 vol. 8vo. Belfast. 1866.

On errors in this edition see Northern Whig, Oct. and Nov. 1867.

3269. The Hamilton manuscripts : containing some account of the settlement of the territories of the Upper Clandeboye, Great Ardes and Dufferin, in the county of Down . . . in the reigns of James I and Charles I ; with memoirs of him and of his son and grandson, James and Henry, the first and second

Earls of Clanbrassil. . . . By Sir J. Hamilton, Viscount Claneboye. Ed. by T. K. Lowry. 1 vol. 4to. Belfast. [1867].

3270. Carew manuscripts preserved in the archiepiscopal library at Lambeth, Calendar of the (1515–1624). Ed. by J. S. Brewer and W. Bullen. 6 vols. 8vo. Lond. 1867–73.

Vol. vi, entitled Miscellaneous and book of Howth, contains documents of an earlier period.

3271. Observations in a voyage through the kingdom of Ireland . . . in the year 1681. By T. Dineley. Ed. by J. Graves, with introduction by E. P. Shirley. 1 vol. 8vo. Dubl. 1870. Illus.

The vol. was published as Annuary of the Kilkenny Arch. Soc., 1865–7.

3272. Calendar of the state papers relating to Ireland, 1603–1670 [in the English Public Record Office]. Ed. by C. W. Russell, J. P. Prendergast, and R. P. Mahaffy. 13 vols. Lond. 1872–1910.

The introd. to vol. i. contains a valuable account of the sources. After 1670 Irish state papers are included in the English Calendar of State Papers, Domestic (125).

3273. The history of the warr of Ireland from 1641 to 1653. By a British officer of the regiment of Sir J. Clottworthy. Ed. with preface, notes, and appendix, by E. H[ogan]. 1 vol. 8vo. Dubl. 1873.

3274. De La Warr MSS., Hist. MSS. Comm., Reps. IV. 276–317 and VII. 249–60. 1873, 1879.

Papers *temp.* James I, collected by Lionel Craufield, Earl of Middlesex. Cf. *ibid.* viii. Manchester MSS. for other papers of the same period.

3275. Spicilegium Ossoriense : being a collection of original letters and papers, illustrative of the history of the Irish Church from the Reformation to the year 1800. By Cardinal P. F. Moran. 3 vols. 4to. Dubl. 1874–84.

3276. A contemporary history of affairs in Ireland, from A.D. 1641 to 1652 : containing the unique narrative, entitled an ' Aphorismical discovery of treasonable faction '—now for the first time published. Ed. by Sir J. T. Gilbert. 3 vols. in 6 pts. 4to. Dubl. Irish Arch. Soc. 1879. Ports. &c.

Printed from MS. F. 3. 28 in Trinity College, Dublin. The author P. S. styles himself secretary to Owen Roe O'Neill. The work was known to Carte but condemned as unworthy of credit.

3277. History of the Irish confederation and the war in Ireland, 1641–3. Containing a narrative of the affairs in Ireland from 1641 to 1643. By Sir R. Bellings. With original documents, correspondence of this confederation, and of the administration of English government in Ireland. Ed. by Sir J. T. Gilbert. 7 vols. 4to. Dubl. 1882–91.

Contains many documents drawn from the Carte Collection in the Bodleian. Cf. Desiderata curiosa Hibernica, ii (3246) for the Second and Third Books of the war in Ireland, by Sir Richard Bellings.

3278. Drogheda MSS., Hist. MSS. Comm. 1884.

Has Loftus papers, mainly about the quarrel of Adam Loftus, Viscount Loftus, with Strafford and the subsequent legal proceedings. Other similar papers are in Barrett Lennard MSS., Hist. MSS. Comm. Various, iii. 1904.

3279. Ireland in the seventeenth century, or the Irish massacres of 1641–2, their causes and results. Illustrated by extracts from the unpublished state papers, &c., relating to the plantations of 1610–39, depositions relating to the massacres, and the reports of the trials in the High Court of Justice in 1652–4, with a preface by J. A. Froude. By M. Hickson. 2 vols. 8vo. Lond. 1884. Facs.

Cf. Eng. Hist. Rev. i and ii (1886–7) for a controversy with R. Dunlop on the depositions and *ibid.* ii for Mr. Dunlop's The Forged Commission of 1641.

3280. Lismore papers. By Richard Boyle, Earl of Cork. Ed. by A. B. Grosart. 10 vols. 4to. Lond. 1886–8.

Preserved in Lismore Castle. The first series (5 vols.) contains the Earl of Cork's diary from 1611 to 1643. The second series contains letters to and from him.

3281. Cowper MSS., Hist. MSS. Comm. 1888.

Vols. i and ii contain Irish papers of Sir John Coke, secretary of state 1625–39.

3282. Two diaries of Derry in 1689, being Richard's diary of the fleet and Ash's journal of the siege, with introduction and notes. By T. Witherow. 1 vol. 8vo. [Lond. ?] 1888.

3283. Ancient records of Dublin in the possession of the municipal corporation of that city. Ed. [for earlier vols.] by Sir J. T. Gilbert. 13 vols. 8vo. Dubl. 1889–1907. Illus.

Vols. iii–vii deal with period. Brief description of Dublin records in Hist. MSS. Comm. i. 129. Gilbert also wrote A history of the city of Dublin. 3 vols. 8vo. Dublin, 1854–9. In its preface he describes the earlier histories by W. Harris [1766] and Warburton [1818].

3284. A Jacobite narrative of the war in Ireland, 1688–91 : with contemporary letters and papers, now published for the first time. Illustrated with facsimiles. By Sir J. T. Gilbert. 1 vol. 4to. Dubl. 1892.

The additional documents are valuable. The MS. is in the possession of the Earl of Fingal (see Hist. MSS. Comm., 10th Rept., App. V). The original title is ' A light to the blind '.

3285. The siege of Londonderry in 1689, as set forth in the literary remains of Colonel the Rev. George Walker, D.D., which are now first collected and comprise : 1. A true account of the siege ; 2. A vindication of the true account; 3. A letter on the treachery of Lundy ; 4. Other official letters ; 5. Sermons, prayers, and speeches during the siege. With notes, original and selected, from the best authorities on the subjects, and numerous illustrations. By G. Walker. Ed. by P. Dwyer. 1 vol. 4to. Lond. 1893. Maps. Plans. Ports.

Walker's A true account of the siege of Londonderry was originally published in 1689 and three editions were almost immediately exhausted. A German translation was published at Hamburg and a Dutch translation at Antwerp the same year. ' A vindication of the true account ' bears date Lond. 1689, though Mackenzie's Narrative, which was the cause of it, is dated 1690.

3286. Ormonde MSS., Hist. MSS. Comm. 10 vols. 8vo. Lond. 1895–1920.

An index to vols. i and ii was publ. in 1909. A new series began in 1902. The principal contents are :
Vol. i. Royal letters ; miscellaneous correspondence ; papers about the Irish army 1598–1686.
Vol. ii. Letters connected with the Deputy governor of Trim, 1646–9 ; list of trans-

ported Irish, 1655–9; Irish army papers, 1662–84; Ormonde's letters to Southwell, 1673–87; report on fortifications in Ireland, 1685; proclamations, &c., 1671–1714.

N.S. Vol. i. Ormonde correspondence relating to affairs in Ireland, *c.* 1641–50, and to royalists in exile, 1650–60.

Vol. ii. Letters of Irish lords justices and Privy Council, 1641–44; life of John Lord Belasyse.

Vol. iii. Miscellaneous correspondence, 1660–75; letters from the Duchess of Ormonde, 1668–73; and an account of the Irish revenue, 1661.

Vol. iv. Miscellaneous Irish and other Ormonde correspondence, 1675–9; letters from Sir R. Southwell to Ormonde, important for English politics, 1677–85; Ormonde letters as chancellor of the University of Oxford, 1675–84; Ormonde's household papers, 1675–84, Irish wool licences and licencees, 1678–81.

Vols. v, vi, and vii. Ormonde's miscellaneous correspondence, both English and Irish, 1679–81, 1681–3, and 1683–8. Vol. vii has inventories of his furniture, &c.

Vol. viii. Correspondence of the second Duke of Ormonde, 1688–1715, and a diary of events in Ireland, 1685–90. In addition there are general accounts and calendars of this collection, with some extracts, in the second, third, fourth, sixth, seventh, eighth, and ninth reports of the Hist. MSS. Comm. For the Ormonde MSS. in the Bodleian Library, Oxford, see the Reports of T. Duffus Hardy and J. S. Brewer, 1864, and of C. W. Russell and J. P. Prendergast, 1871, the latter being also pr. in Reports of the Deputy Keeper, xxxii.

3287. Some letters of Toby and James Bonnell [1660–90]. Ed. by C. L. Falkiner. Eng. Hist. Rev. xix. 1904.

3288. The registers of the parish of St. John, Dublin, 1619–99. Ed. by J. Mills. Parish Register Society of Dublin, 1906.

3289. Registers of Derry Cathedral . . . 1642–1703. Ed. by R. Hayes. Parish Register Society of Dublin, 1910.

3290. Egmont manuscripts, Hist. MSS. Commission. 2 vols. 8vo. Lond. 1905.

Has entry book of orders or decrees of the court of Castle Chamber, i. 1–60.

3291. Blake family records, 1600–1700 [second series]. A chronological catalogue with notes. Ed. by M. J. Blake. 1 vol. 8vo. Lond. 1905.

3292. Franciscan MSS. at the convent, Merchants' Quay, Dublin. Hist. MSS. Comm. 1906.

Mainly 1625–48, especially 1641 and later.

3293. Waterford during the civil war [1641–53]. Documents. By T. Fitzpatrick. 1 vol. 8vo. Waterford. 1912.

Repr. from the Waterford Journal of Archaeology.

3294. The journal of John Stevens, containing a brief account of the war in Ireland, 1689–91. By J. Stevens. Ed. by R. H. Murray. 1 vol. 8vo. Oxf. 1912. Bibl.

Pr. from Add. MS. 36296, Brit. Mus. Extracts in Ranke, vi.

3295. Ireland under the Commonwealth. Being a selection of documents relating to the government of Ireland from 1651 to 1659. With historical introduction and notes. By R. Dunlop. 2 vols. 8vo. Manchester. 1913.

3296. Stuart manuscripts at Windsor Castle, vi. Hist. MSS. Comm. 1916.

Contains Sheridan's narrative of events *temp.* James II.

3297. Alumni Dublinenses. A register of the students, graduates, professors and provosts of Trinity College in the University of Dublin [1593–1846]. By G. D. Burtchaell and T. U. Sadleir. 1 vol. 8vo. Lond. 1924. Illus.

¶ 2. LATER WORKS

3298. The life of James Duke of Ormond ; containing an account of the most remarkable affairs of his time, and particularly of Ireland under his government : with an appendix and a collection of letters. By T. Carte. 3 vols. fol. Lond. 1735–6. 2nd ed. best, 6 vols. 8vo. Oxf. 1851.

The title given is that to the 2nd ed. The title of the 1st ed. was ' An history of the life of James, Duke of Ormond, from his birth in 1610 to his death in 1688 '. An indispensable work for the period 1610–88.

3299. An inquiry into the share which King Charles I had in the transactions of the Earl of Glamorgan . . . in the years 1645 and 1646. By T. Birch. 1 vol. 8vo. Lond. 1747. Later ed. 1756.

Birch used the Rinuccini memoirs in the possession of the Earl of Leicester ; he issued An appendix to an enquiry &c. 8vo. Lond. 1755. J. Boswell replied in ' The case of the royal martyr considered with candour '. 1 vol. 8vo. Lond. 1758. Cf. S. R. Gardiner's Charles I and the Earl of Glamorgan. Eng. Hist. Rev. ii. 1887.

3300. The history of the life and reign of William-Henry, Prince of Nassau and Orange . . . King of England . . . In which the affairs of Ireland are more particularly handled . . . With an appendix containing original papers. By W. Harris. 1 vol. fol. Dubl. 1749. Maps. Plans. Ports.

First ed. Dublin 1747 abridged and, without the documents, published anonymously.

3301. The ancient and present state of the county and city of Cork. . . . To which are added . . . notes and observations . . . embellished with maps of the county and city, perspective views of the chief towns &c. By C. Smith. 2 vols. 8vo. Dubl. 1750. Maps. Plans. Later eds. : 2 vols. 8vo. Dubl. and Lond. 1774. Maps. Plans (with additions), and 2 vols. 8vo. Cork. 1893–4. Maps. Plans.

Ed. of 1893–4 has numerous additions from MSS. of the late Thomas Crofton Croker and Richard Caulfield. Repr. from the Cork Hist. and Arch. Society's Journal.

3302. The peerage of Ireland : or, a genealogical history of the present nobility of that kingdom with engravings of their paternal coats of arms. Collected from public records, authentic manuscripts, approved historians, well attested pedigrees, and personal information. By J. Lodge. 4 vols. 8vo. Dubl. 1754. Later ed. 7 vols. 8vo. Dubl. 1789. Ed. by M. Archdall.

Ed. of 1789 revised, enlarged, and continued to the present time. The peerage of G. E. C. (785) contains Irish peers.

3303. Histoire de l'Irlande, ancienne et moderne (Précis de l'histoire des quatre Stuarts sur le Trône Britannique). By J. MacGeoghegan. 3 vols. 4to. Paris. 1758–63. Eng. trans. 3 vols. 8vo. Dubl. 1831–2. Ed. by P. O'Kelly.

Vol. iii of 1st ed. was printed at Amsterdam.

3304. Historical memoirs of the Irish rebellion, in the year 1641 . . . in a letter to Walter Harris, Esq. ; occasioned by his answer to a late dialogue on the causes, motives and mischiefs of this rebellion. By M. R. 1 vol. 8vo. Lond. 1765.

Supplies some useful references and quotations ; otherwise of no great value.

3305. The history and antiquities of the city of Dublin . . . with an appendix, containing an history of the cathedrals of Christ Church and St. Patrick, the university, the hospitals, and other public buildings &c. By W. Harris. 1 vol. 8vo. Dubl. 1766. Map. Plans. Later ed. 1 vol. 8vo. Lond. 1766. Map. Plans.

3306. The history of the rebellion and civil war in Ireland [1641–60]. By F. Warner. 1 vol. 4to. Lond. 1767. Later ed. 1768.

Still useful.

3307. Vindiciae Hibernicae ; or Ireland vindicated. By M. Carey. 1 vol. 8vo. Phil. 1819. 2nd ed. 1823 enlarged and improved.

Attempts to refute English accounts of the massacre of 1641.

3308. History of the town and county of Galway ; with appendix, containing the principal charters and other original documents. By J. Hardiman. 1 vol. 4to. Dubl. 1820. Maps. Plans.

3309. Liber munerum publicorum Hiberniae ab an. 1152 usque ad 1827 ; or, the establishments of Ireland. By R. Lascelles. 2 vols. fol. Lond. 1824–30. 2nd ed. 1852 with introd. by F. S. Thomas.

The chief source for Irish official appointments. A partial index in the Ninth Report of the Deputy Keeper of the Public Records in Ireland. Dubl. 1877.

3310. History of the civil wars of Ireland from the Anglo-Norman invasion till the union of the country with Great Britain. By W. C. Taylor. 2 vols. 12mo. Edin. 1831. Later ed. 2 vols. 12mo. N.Y. 1833.

3311. History of the Presbyterian Church in Ireland, comprising the civil history of the province of Ulster from the accession of James the First : with a preliminary sketch . . . and an appendix, consisting of original papers. By J. S. Reid. 3 vols. 8vo. Belfast. 1834. Later ed. 1867. Ed. by W. D. Killen.

3312. History of the Church of Ireland from the Reformation to the Revolution ; With a preliminary survey, from the papal usurpation, in the twelfth century, to its legal abolition in the sixteenth. By R. Mant, Bishop of Down and Connor. 1 vol. 8vo. Lond. 1840.

A second vol., containing the History from the Revolution to the Union, was published at the same time. The book was intended to do for the Church of Ireland what Reid's had done for the Presbyterian Church.

3313. Military history of the Irish nation [1550–1750], comprising a memoir of the Irish brigade in the service of France, with official papers relative to the brigade. By M. O'Conor. 1 vol. 8vo. Dubl. 1845.

Cf. History of the Irish brigades in the service of France from the revolution in Great Britain and Ireland under James II to the revolution in France under Louis XVI. By J. C. O'Callaghan. 1 vol. 8vo. Glasgow. 1870.

3314. The confederation of Kilkenny. By C. P. Meehan. 1 vol. 12mo. Duffy's Lib. Dubl. 1846. Later ed. 1 vol. 8vo. Dubl. 1882.

Ed. of 1882 much enlarged.

3315. Illustrations, historical and genealogical, of King James's Irish army list [1689]. By J. D'Alton. 1 vol. 8vo. Dubl. 1855. Best ed. 2 vols. 8vo. Dubl. 1861.

Valuable for the history of the principal Roman Catholic families in Ireland.

3316. Memoirs of the Most Rev. Oliver Plunket, Archbishop of Armagh . . . compiled from original documents. By P. F., Cardinal Moran. 1 vol. 8vo. Dubl. 1861.

3317. The diocese of Meath, ancient and modern. By A. Cogan. 3 vols. 8vo. Dubl. 1862–70.

3318. History of the Catholic archbishops of Dublin [to 1641]. By P. F. Moran. 1 vol. 8vo. Dubl. 1864.

3319. The Cromwellian settlement of Ireland. By J. P. Prendergast. 1 vol. 8vo. Dubl. 1865. Maps. 2nd ed. 1875. 3rd ed. 1 vol. 8vo. Dubl. 1922.

3320. Limerick : its history and antiquities, ecclesiastical, civil, and military, from the earliest ages. By M. Lenihan. 1 vol. 8vo. Dubl. 1866. Maps. Plans.

Transcripts and notes made by Lenihan for this work are in the British Museum Add. MSS. 31878–88.

3321. Memoirs of the Earls of Granard. By J. Forbes. Ed. by George Arthur Hastings Forbes, Earl of Granard. 1 vol. 8vo. Lond. 1868.

Appendix of documents for Irish history. Cf. Hist. MSS. Comm., Rep. II. 210–17.

3322. The fate and fortunes of Hugh O'Neill, Earl of Tyrone, and Rory O'Donel, Earl of Tyrconnel ; their flight from Ireland and death in exile. By C. P. Meehan. 1 vol. 8vo. Dubl. (Lond.) 1868. Ports. Later eds. : 1 vol. 8vo. N.Y. 1868. Ports. and 1 vol. 8vo. Dubl. 1870. Ports.

3323. The rise and fall of the Irish Franciscan monasteries, and memories of the Irish hierarchy in the seventeenth century. By C. P. Meehan. 1 vol. 12mo. Dubl. (Lond.) 1869. 5th ed. 1 vol. 8vo. Dubl. [1877].

3324. The lives of the lord chancellors and keepers of the great seal of Ireland. By J. R. O'Flanagan. 2 vols. 8vo. Lond. 1870.

3325. An historical account of the MacDonnells of Antrim : including notices of some other septs, Irish and Scottish. By G. Hill. 1 vol. 4to. Belfast. 1873.

3326. The ecclesiastical history of Ireland from the earliest period to the present times. By W. D. Killen. 2 vols. 8vo. Belfast. 1875.

3327. Some account of Sir Audley Mervyn, his majesty's prime sergeant and speaker in the House of Commons in Ireland, from 1661 till 1666. By J. P. Prendergast. Trans. Roy. Hist. Socy. iii. 1875. 421–54.

3328. An historical account of the plantation in Ulster at the commencement of the 17th century, 1608–20. Compiled from state papers. By G. Hill. 1 vol. 4to. Belfast. 1877.

3329. History of the town of Belfast, from the earliest times to the close of the 18th century. By G. Benn. 2 (in 3) vols. 8vo. Belfast. 1877–80. Maps. Illus.
Vol. ii, ed. J. Carlisle.

3330. The Ulster civil war of 1641, and its consequences ; with the history of the Irish brigade under Montrose in 1644–6. By J. McDonnell. 1 vol. 8vo. Dubl. 1879.

3331. The history of the two Ulster manors of Finagh in the county of Tyrone, and Coole, otherwise Manor Atkinson, in the county of Fermanagh, and of their owners. By S. R. L. Corry, Earl of Belmore. 1 vol. 8vo. Dubl. (Lond.) 1881.

3332. Cromwell in Ireland. A history of Cromwell's Irish campaign. By D. Murphy. 1 vol. 8vo. Dubl. 1883. Maps. Plans. Illus.
Appendix of documents.

3333. Irish landed gentry when Cromwell came to Ireland ; or a supplement to Irish pedigrees. By J. O'Hart. 1 vol. 8vo. Dubl. 1884. Later ed. 1892.
Based on documents preserved in the Public Record Office, Dublin, viz. Books of survey and distributions and forfeiting proprietors listed.

3334. The reformed Church of Ireland [1537–1889]. By J. T. Ball. 1 vol. 8vo. Lond. 1886. Later ed. 1890.

3335. The repression of the woollen manufacture in Ireland. By W. Cunningham. Eng. Hist. Rev. i. 1886.

3336. Ireland from the Restoration to the Revolution, 1660 to 1690. By J. P. Prendergast. 1 vol. 8vo. Lond. 1887.

3337. Two chapters of Irish history : i. The Irish Parliament of James II. ii. The alleged violation of the treaty of Limerick. By T. D. Ingram. 1 vol. 8vo. Lond. 1888.
A clever bit of special pleading.

3338. Historical review of the legislative systems operative in Ireland from the invasion of Henry II to the union, 1172–1800. By J. T. Ball. 1 vol. 8vo. Lond. 1888. Later ed. 1 vol. 8vo. Dubl. 1889.

3339. The history of the university of Dublin from its foundation to the end of the 18th century. By J. W. Stubbs. 1 vol. 8vo. Dubl. 1889.

3340. History of Sligo, county and town, from the accession of James I to the Revolution of 1688. By W. G. Wood-Martin. 1 vol. 8vo. Dubl. 1889. Illus. Plans.

3341. Geschichte der Katholischen Kirche in Irland von der Einführung des Christenthums bis auf die Gegenwart. By A. Bellesheim. 3 vols. 8vo. Mainz. 1890–1. Bibl.

A portion of this work was trans. by W. McLoughlin (Dubl. 1908) as : The papal nuncio Archbishop Rinuccini among the Irish confederates (1645–9).

3342. The early history of Trinity College Dublin, 1591–1660, as told in contemporary records. By W. Urwick. 1 vol. 8vo. Lond. 1892.

3343. An officer of the Long Parliament and his descendants . . . Life and times of Colonel Richard Townsend. By R. and D. Townshend. 1 vol. 8vo. Lond. 1892. Pedigrees, &c.

3344. The patriot Parliament of 1689. By T. Davis. Ed. by Sir C. G. Duffy. 1 vol. 12mo. The New Irish Library. Lond. 1893.

Originally appeared in the Dublin Magazine in 1843. Cf. Ingram (3337).

3345. History and topography of the county of Clare from the earliest times to the beginning of the 18th century. By J. Frost. 1 vol. 8vo. Dubl. 1893.

3346. A history of the Irish Presbyterians. By W. T. Latimer. 1 vol. 8vo. Belfast [1893]. Later ed. 1902.

3347. The life of Sir William Petty, 1623–1687 . . . Chiefly derived from private documents hitherto unpublished. By Lord Edmond Fitzmaurice. 1 vol. 8vo. Lond. 1895. Map. Ports.

Cf. Works (1893).

3348. Life of Patrick Sarsfield, Earl of Lucan. With a short narrative of the principal events of the Jacobite war in Ireland. By J. Todhunter. 1 vol. 8vo. Lond. 1895.

In Duffy's New Irish Library, vol. vii.

3349. Owen Roe O'Neill. By J. F. Taylor. 1 vol. 8vo. Lond. 1896.

3350. Historical notices of old Belfast . . . With maps and illustrations. Selections from the MSS. collected by W. Pinkerton for his intended History of Belfast, O'Mellan's Narrative of the wars of 1641, &c. By R. M. Young. 1 vol. 8vo. Belfast. 1896. Maps. Illus.

3351. A Great Yorkshire divine of the 17th century. A sketch of the life and work of John Bramhall. By W. B. Wright. 1 vol. 8vo. Lond. 1899.

Cf. No. 1496.

3352. The king's and queen's corporation for the linen manufacture in Ireland [1690]. By W. R. Scott. Proc. Royal Soc. Antiq. of Ireland, xxxi. 1901.

3353. Immigration of the Irish Quakers into Pennsylvania, 1682–1750, with their early history in Ireland. By A. C. Myers. Swarthmore, Pennsylvania, 1902.

3354. A history of the county of Dublin : the people, parishes, and antiquities, from the earliest times to the close of the eighteenth century. By F. E. Ball. 4 pts. 8vo. Dubl. 1902–6. Maps. Plans. Ports.

3355. An epoch in Irish history. Trinity College Dublin, its foundation and early fortunes, 1591–1660. By J. P. Mahaffy. 1 vol. 8vo. Lond. 1903.

3356. The history of the commercial and financial relations between England and Ireland from the period of the Restoration. By A. E. Murray (Mrs. Radice). 1 vol. 8vo. Lond. 1903.

3357. The Bloody Bridge, and other papers relating to the insurrection of 1641. By T. Fitzpatrick. 1 vol. 8vo. Dubl. 1903.

3358. Illustrations of Irish history and topography, mainly of the seventeenth century. By C. L. Falkiner. 1 vol. 8vo. Lond. 1904. Maps.

3359. The life and letters of the great Earl of Cork. By D. Townshend. 1 vol. 8vo. Lond. 1904. Map. Ports.

3360. The war of William III in Ireland. Being a narrative of the campaigns of Duke Schomberg, of the king, and of General de Ginckel ; with some references to the regiments engaged therein. By Lt.-Col. E. Macartney-Filgate. 1 vol. 8vo. Military Soc. of Ireland. Dubl. 1905.

3361. Ireland to the settlement of Ulster. By R. Dunlop. Camb. Modern Hist. iii. ch. xviii. 1905.

Continued 1611–59, *ibid*. iv. ch. xviii. 1906 ; 1660–1700, *ibid*. v. ch. x [3] 1908 ; *ibid*. vi. ch. xiv. 1909. All are by R. Dunlop and have lengthy bibliographies.

3362. Die englische Kolonisation in Irland. By M. J. Bonn. 2 vols. 8vo. Stuttgart and Berlin. 1906.

Cf. Eng. Hist. Rev. 1906. xxi. 772–8.

3363. History of Ireland from the earliest times to the present day. Vol. ii. 1547–1782. By E. A. Dalton. 1 vol. 8vo. 1906. Later ed. 6 vols. 8vo. Lond. 1912.

3364. A great archbishop of Dublin, 1650–1729 ; his autobiography, family, and a selection from his correspondence. By Sir C. S. King. 1 vol. 8vo. Lond. 1906. Ports.

See Hist. MSS. Comm. Rep. II. 231 seq. ; III. 416 seq. A Latin autobiography of King was pr. Eng. Hist. Rev. xiii. 1898 ; a diary kept during his imprisonment 1689 was repr. from the Journal of Royal Soc. Antiq. of Ireland [1 vol. 8vo. Dubl. 1903], ed. by H. J. Lawlor.

3365. The origin of the regium donum. By C. E. Pike. Trans. Royal Hist. Soc. 3rd Series, iii. 1909.

Deals with Charles II's reign only.

3366. Ireland under the Stuarts [1603–90]. By R. Bagwell. 3 vols. 8vo. Lond. 1909–16. Maps.

The standard history.

3367. Stuart Ireland. By G. B. O'Connor. 1 vol. 8vo. Dubl. 1910.

3368. Revolutionary Ireland and its settlement, with an introduction by Rev. J. P. Mahaffy, D.D. By R. H. Murray. 1 vol. 8vo. Lond. 1911. Maps. Bibl.

3369. The battle of the Boyne. By D. C. Boulger. 1 vol. 8vo. Lond. 1911. Ports.

Based on research at Paris, but uncritical.

3370. Life of James Duke of Ormond. By Winifred Gardner, Lady Burghclere. 2 vols. 8vo. Lond. 1912. Ports.

3371. Little Jennings and fighting Dick Talbot; a life of the Duke and Duchess of Tyrconnel. By P. W. Sergeant. 2 vols. 8vo. Lond. 1913. Illus.

Rather better than its title might suggest.

3372. The colonization of Ulster. By C. Maxwell. History, i. 1916.

3373. The economic history of Ireland in the 17th century. By G. A. T. O'Brien. 1 vol. 8vo. Dubl. and Lond. 1919.

3374. The Irish rebellion of 1641, with a history of the events which led up to and succeeded it. By Lord Ernest William Hamilton. 1 vol. 8vo. Lond. 1920.

3375. The Puritans in Ireland, 1647–1661. By St. J. D. Seymour. 1 vol. 8vo. Oxf. 1921.

On the organization of the Puritan Church, with an appendix containing a list of ministers.

3376. Strafford and Ireland. The history of his vice-royalty, with an account of his trial. By W. H. A. O'Grady. 2 vols. 8vo. Dubl. 1923.

3377. The rise of the Irish linen industry. By C. Gill. 1 vol. 8vo. Oxf. 1925. Illus. Bibl.

XIV. WALES

1. Bibliographies and Sources.
2. Later Works.

THERE is no adequate history of Wales in the seventeenth century, but of recent years a number of monographs have appeared, which help to cover the ground.

Morrice (3381) has many useful bibliographical notes for the period, and valuable information is accessible in Rowlands (3378) and Jones (3383). Up to 1641 Skeel (3439) is indispensable, and for 1640–60 Phillips (3425) and Richards (3445, 3449) are adequate. The rest of the period is comparatively unexplored, although much can be gleaned from histories of localities.

¶ 1. BIBLIOGRAPHIES AND SOURCES

3378. Cambrian bibliography, containing an account of the books printed in the Welsh language or relating to Wales, from 1546 to 1800. By W. Rowlands. Ed. by D. Silvan-Evans. 1 vol. 8vo. Llanidloes. 1869.

Written in Welsh. Useful. A continuation by C. Ashton, also in Welsh, gives a list of books printed 1801–10. (Published by National Eisteddfod Association, Oswestry, 1908.)

3379. A catalogue of the manuscripts relating to Wales in the British Museum. By E. Owen. 4 pts. 8vo. Lond. 1900, 1903, 1908, 1922.

Cymmrodorion Record Series, 4.

3380. National Library of Wales . . . Catalogue of tracts of the Civil War and Commonwealth period relating to Wales and the borders. 1 vol. 8vo. Aberystwyth. 1911.

Issued by the National Library. It contains 264 items of the period 1640–61.

3381. Wales in the seventeenth century, its literature and men of letters and action. By J. C. Morrice. 1 vol. 8vo. Bangor. 1918.

Mainly biographical and bibliographical.

3382. National Library of Wales : Catalogue of Sir John Williams's Manuscripts. Additional MSS. vol. i. 1921.

3383. A history of printing and printers in Wales to 1810. By I. Jones. 1 vol. 8vo. Cardiff. 1925.

3384. The history of the ancient and modern estate of the principality of Wales, dutchy of Cornwall, and earldom of Chester. By Sir J. Doddridge. 1 vol. 4to. Lond. 1630. 1 vol. 8vo. Lond. 1714.

Written by Doddridge (1555–1628) in the early part of the reign of James I to urge the revival of the principality.

3385. Contemplations upon these times, or The Parliament explained to Wales. Written by . . . a cordiall well-wisher of his countries happinesse. By (J. Lewis of Glasgrug). 1 vol. 8vo. Lond. 1646. 1 vol. 4to. Cardiff. 1907. Issued by ' Cymdeithas Llen Cymru ' (Society of Welsh Literature).

An appeal to Wales on behalf of Parliament.

3386. Cambria triumphans.   Showing the origin and antiquity of that illustrious nation, the succession of their kings and princes, from the first to King Charles of happy memory.   The description of the country.   By P. Enderbie.   1 vol. fol. London. 1661.   Later ed. 1810.

' Enderbie hath done this work very meanly.' A. Wood.

3387. The bird in the cage, with an epistle to the Welsh churches, and a brief narrative.   By V. Powell.   1661.   Later ed. 12mo. Lond. 1662.

The ' Narrative ' is a defence of the proceedings of the commission of 1650 for the propagation of the Gospel in Wales.

3388. The life and death of Vavasor Powell.   1 vol. 12mo. s.l. 1671.

Contains Powell's autobiography.   The editor is thought to have been Edward Bagshaw the younger.   Cf. A. Griffith's Strena Vavasoriensis, or A hue and cry after Mr. Vavasor Powell, 1654, a hostile account ; and David Davies : Vavasor Powell : the Baptist evangelist of Wales in the seventeenth century.   1 vol. 8vo. Lond. 1896.

3388 A. An account of the convincement, exercises, services, and travels. of . . . Richard Davies with some relation of ancient friends and the spreading of truth in North-Wales.   1 vol. 12mo. Lond. 1710.   7th ed. 1844.

An interesting autobiography.   Cf. John Ap John and early records of Friends in Wales.   By W. G. Norris.   Ed. by N. Penney.   1 vol. 8vo. Lond. 1907. Illus.

3389. The history of the Gwydir family.   By Sir J. Wynn.   Ed. by Daines Barrington.   8vo. Lond. 1770.   Later eds. : 4to. Lond. 1781.   By Daines Barrington (in Miscellanies).   4to. Ruthin 1827.   Ed. by (Miss) A. Llwyd. 4to. Oswestry 1878. Ports. Ed. by W. W. E. Wynne and A. Roberts.

Written by the first baronet of Gwydir (1553–1626). Especially valuable for its picture of social conditions in North Wales c. 1600.

3390. The Cambrian register.   3 vols. 8vo. Lond. 1796–1818.   Plates.
Repr. documents, &c.

3391. The description of Pembrokeshire.   By G. Owen.   Ed. by R. Fenton.

Written in 1603.   In vol. ii of Cambrian register.   The best edition is that published by the Cymmrodorion Society in three parts, Lond. 1892–1906, ed. by H. Owen.   This edition includes a number of other tracts, &c., by G. Owen on the history of Pembrokeshire.

3392. Heraldic visitations of Wales, and part of the marches.   By L. Dwnn. Ed. by Sir S. R. Meyrick.   2 vols. 4to. Llandovery. 1846.

The fullest printed collection of Welsh pedigrees made by Dwnn as deputy herald at arms between 1586 and 1613.

3393. An ancient survey of Penmaenmawr [*temp*. Chas. I].   Ed. J. O. Halliwell. Lond. 1859.   Later ed. 8vo. Llanfairfechan. 1906. Ed. by W. B. Lowe.

3394. Records of Denbigh and its lordship. Vol. i. [all publ.]. Ed. by J. Williams. Wrexham. 1860.

Cf. his Ancient and modern Denbigh. 1 vol. Denbigh. 1856. Both have valuable excerpts from municipal archives.

3395. The official progress of . . . Henry . . . Duke of Beaufort through Wales in 1684. By T. Dineley. Ed. by C. Baker. 4to. Lond. 1864. Later ed. 4to. Lond. 1888. Ed. by R. W. Banks. The second edition reproduces Dineley's MS. in photo-lithography.

Beaufort was Lord President of the Council in Wales from 1672 to 1689.

3396. Collections historical and archaeological relating to Montgomeryshire and its borders. (Issued by the Powys-land Club.) 8vo. Lond. From 1868 until now.

Contain a great deal of material and articles, of varying value, dealing with the history of the districts at various periods.

3397. Bye-Gones, relating to Wales and the border counties. 23 vols. in two series. 4to. Oswestry. 1871–1919.

Contains masses of material of very varying value, including excerpts from newspapers of the Civil War period.

3398. Y Cwtta Cyfarwydd. By P. Roberts. Ed. by D. R. Thomas. 8vo. Lond. 1883.

A chronicle for the years 1607–46, kept by a St. Asaph public notary. Appended is the register note-book of T. Rowlands, Vicar-choral, for the years 1595–1607 and 1646–1653.

3399. The records of the corporation of Oswestry. Ed. by S. Leighton. 1 vol. 8vo. Oswestry. s.a.

Repr. from the Transactions of Shropshire Archaeological Society, 1879–83. (Though Oswestry itself is in Shropshire, the town is partly Welsh, and the above records contain a certain amount of material of interest to students of local Welsh genealogy.)

3400. Cardiff records, being materials for the history of the county borough from the earliest times. Ed. by J. H. Matthews. 6 vols. Cardiff. 1898–1911. Maps.

Contains much material relating to the history of Cardiff and the neighbourhood.

3401. Gweithiau Morgan Llwyd [The works of M.Ll.]. Ed. by T. E. Ellis (vol. i) and J. H. Davies (vol. ii). 2 vols. 8vo. Bangor. 1899 and 1908.

A complete edition of the Welsh and English works of the Puritan mystic of Wrexham (1619–59). The full (Welsh) introduction to vol. ii is an important study of the history of the period.

3402. The registers of the parish of Llansannan, 1667–1812. Ed. by R. Ellis. 1 vol. 4to. Liverpool. 1904.

3403. Llandaff records. 5 vols. 8vo. Cardiff and Lond. 1905–14.

Vol. i: Digest of parish registers of the diocese. Vols. ii, iii, iv, v: Acts of the bishops of Llandaff, 1660–1765. Vols. ii to iv. Ed. by J. A. Bradney. Vol. v. Ed. by R. Rickards.

3404. The taylors cussion. By G. Owen. Ed. by E. M. Pritchard. fol. Lond. 1906.

A photo-lithographic reproduction of the Commonplace book of George Owen, Lord of Cemais, Pembrokeshire (1552 ?–1613).

3405. Diary (1603–54). By W. Powell. Ed. by J. A. Bradney. 1 vol. 8vo. Bristol. 1907. Port.

Valuable for Monmouthshire local history.

3406. Chirk Castle accounts, A.D. 1605–1666. Ed. by W. W. Myddleton. 1 vol. 8vo. Privately printed. 1908.

Valuable for social and economic history.

3407. An Act for the propagation of the gospel in Wales, 1649 ; together with the proceedings of the commissioners for North Wales. Privately printed for ' Cymdeithas Llen Cymru ' (The Welsh Literature Society). 1 vol. 4to. Cardiff. 1908.

The proceedings are printed from Bodley MS. Rawlinson C. 261, the official minute-book.

3408. The statutes of Wales. Ed. by I. Bowen. 1 vol. 8vo. Lond. 1908.

A very useful collection of the statutes relating to Wales, 1215–1902.

3409. Genealogies of the Carmarthenshire sheriffs from 1539 to 1759. By J. Buckley. 2 vols. 8vo. Carmarthen. 1910–13.

3410. Llyfr Baglan. By J. Williams. 1 vol. 4to. Lond. 1910. Ed. by J. A. Bradney.

A book of Welsh pedigrees, compiled between 1600–7.

3411. Registra antiqua de Llantilio Crossenny et Penrhos in comitatu Monumethensi, 1577–1644. Ed. by J. A. Bradney. 1 vol. 8vo. London. 1916.

A copy of the original parish registers made by W. Powell, the author of the diary, 1603–54.

3412. Calendar of deeds and documents. Vol. i. The Coleman Deeds (Nat. Library of Wales). Ed. by F. Green. 1 vol. 8vo. Aberystwyth. 1921.

Relates chiefly to 16th–18th centuries. The deeds are of considerable value for genealogy and economic and social history.

¶ 2. LATER WORKS

3413. Historical account of the British or Welsh versions and editions of the Bible. By T. Llewelyn. 8vo. Lond. 1768.

Contains the dedications of Salesbury [1567], Morgan [1588], and Parry [1620].

3414. A history of the Baptist Association in Wales, from the year 1650 to . . . 1790. By J. Thomas. 1 vol. 8vo. Lond. 1795.

Pr. in J. Rippon's Baptist Annual Register, at intervals from 1791. Cf. his History of the Welsh Baptists from the time of the apostles to 1797. A MS. at Baptist College, Bristol, trans. into Welsh and publ. Pontypridd 1885.

3415. An historical tour in Monmouthshire. By W. Coxe. 2 vols. 4to. Lond. 1801. Plates. Repr. Brecon. 1904.

3416. A history of the county of Brecknock. By T. Jones. 2 vols. 4to. Brecknock. 1805–9. Plates. Repr. 1 vol. Brecon. 1898.

3417. The history and antiquities of the county of Cardigan. By Sir S. R. Meyrick. 1 vol. 4to. Lond. 1810. Illus. Repr. Brecon. 1907.

3418. A historical tour through Pembrokeshire. By R. Fenton. 1 vol. 4to. Lond. 1811. Plates. Repr. Brecon. 1903.

3419. History of the Welsh Baptists. By J. Davis. Pittsburg. 1835.

3420. A biographical dictionary of eminent Welshmen, from the earliest times to the present. By R. Williams. 1 vol. 8vo. Llandovery. 1852.

3421. The history of Radnorshire. By J. Williams. Repr. from Arch. Camb. 8vo. Tenby. 1859. Later ed. 4to. Brecknock, 1905.

3422. History of Protestant nonconformity in Wales from its rise in 1633 to the present time. By T. Rees. 1 vol. 8vo. Lond. 1861. Later ed. 1883.
A careful account written from the nonconformist point of view.

3423. Kalendars of Gwynedd: lists of lords-lieutenant, custodes rotulorum, sheriffs, and knights of the shire for Anglesey, Carnarvon, and Merioneth. By E. Breese. Notes by W. W. E. Wynne. 1 vol. 4to. Lond. 1873.

3424. The history of the diocese of St. Asaph. By D. R. Thomas. 1 vol. 8vo. Lond. 1874. 3 vols. 8vo. Oswestry, 1908–13.

3425. Memoirs of the Civil War in Wales and the marches, 1642–1649. By J. R. Phillips. 2 vols. 8vo. Lond. 1874.
Vol. i is narrative; vol. ii contains illustrative documents.

3426. Memorials of the parish and family of Hanmer. By Lord Hanmer. Chiswick Press. 1876.
History of a Flintshire family.

3427. The history of Powys Fadog. By J. Y. W. Lloyd. 6 vols. 8vo. Lond. 1881–7. Maps.
Contains a mass of material, especially genealogical : though ill-arranged, it is useful if cautiously employed.

3428. Towns, fields and folk of Wrexham in the time of James the first. By A. N. Palmer. 1 vol. Wrexham. 1883.
Based on Norden's survey, parish registers, and family papers.

3429. History of the old Nonconformity of Wrexham. By A. N. Palmer. 1 vol. 8vo. Wrexham. 1888.

3430. The history of Little England beyond Wales [i. e. South Pembrokeshire]. By E. Laws. 1 vol. 4to. Lond. 1888.

3431. The parliamentary history of the principality of Wales (1541–1895) ... comprising lists of the representatives with biographical ... notices of the members. By W. R. J. Williams. 1 vol. 8vo. Brecknock. 1895.

3432. The history of the great sessions in Wales, 1542–1830, together with the lives of the Welsh judges. By W. R. J. Williams. 1 vol. 8vo. Brecknock. 1899.

3433. Jesus College. By E. G. Hardy. 1 vol. 8vo. Lond. 1899.
The author used the material contained in the college muniments. Cf. The Life of Francis Mansell, Principal of Jesus College in Oxford. By Sir L. Jenkins. 1 vol. 8vo. Lond. 1854.

3434. The administration of English law in Wales and the marches. By H. Owen. 4to. Lond. 1900. Bibliogr.
A valuable sketch.

3435. The Welsh people. By J. Rhys and D. Brynmor-Jones. 1 vol. 8vo. Lond. 1900.

3436. Wales. Story of the Nations series. By O. M. Edwards. 1 vol. 8vo. Lond. 1901. Illus.

3437. Welsh Catholics on the continent. Transactions of the Honourable Society of Cymmrodorion for 1901–2. By W. Ll. Williams. 8vo. Lond. 1903.
With a series of appendices (illustrated by facsimiles) dealing with moot points. Cf. No. 1834.

3438. A history of Monmouthshire from the coming of the Normans into Wales down to the present time. By J. A. Bradney. 3 vols. fol. Lond. 1904.
In progress. 3 vols. in 6 parts completed to date. Contains a great deal of genealogical matter.

3439. The council in the marches of Wales. By C. A. J. Skeel. 8vo. Lond. 1904.
A careful and thorough study, covering the period 1471 to 1689.

3440. The Bible in Wales. By J. Ballinger. 1 vol. 8vo. Lond. 1906. Bibl.
Traces the history of the Welsh versions of the Bible to 1900, with a complete bibliography.

3441. Eminent Welshmen: a short biographical dictionary of Welshmen who have attained distinction from the earliest times to the present [1700–1900]. By T. R. Roberts. 1 vol. Cardiff. 1908. Ports.
Popular, but frequently gives useful references to periodicals.

3442. A history of Chirk Castle and Chirkland. By M. Mahler. 1 vol. 4to. Lond. 1912.

3443. Chronicles of Erthig on the Dyke. By L. A. Cust [Mrs. Wherry]. 2 vols. Lond. 1914.
History of a Denbighshire family c. 1661 until the present times, with many letters Valuable for social history and Welsh Jacobitism.

3444. An account of the kings court of great sessions in Wales. By W. L. Williams. 1 vol. 8vo. Lond. 1916.
A paper read before the Cymmrodorion Society in 1911.

3445. History of the puritan movement in Wales from 1639 to 1653. By T. Richards. 1 vol. 8vo. Lond. 1920.

Publ. by the National Eisteddfod Assoc.

3446. The Welsh woollen industry in the sixteenth and seventeenth centuries. By C. A. J. Skeel. Arch. Camb. Dec. 1922.

3447. The diocese of Bangor in the sixteenth century. A digest of the episcopal registers from 1512–1646. By A. I. Pryce. 1 vol. 8vo. Bangor. 1923.

3448. Religious developments in Wales 1654–62. By T. Richards. 1 vol. 8vo. Lond. 1923.

The fullest account of the religious history of the period. Publ. by the National Eisteddfod Assoc.

3449. The Puritan visitation of Jesus College, Oxford, and the principalship of Dr. Michael Roberts [1648–57]. By T. Richards. 1 vol. 8vo. Lond. 1924.

From the Trans. Cymmrodorion Soc. 1922–3.

XV. VOYAGES AND TRAVELS

1. Collections of Voyages arranged chronologically.
2. Individual Voyages arranged alphabetically.
3. General Later Works arranged alphabetically.

THE books included below are of two classes : (1) the voyages of discovery proper, and the travels to little known lands, and (2) the personal records of Englishmen travelling on the continent of Europe. The voyages of discovery of others than Englishmen are necessarily excluded, but a brief survey may be gained from Heawood (3540). The first subsection, in which the arrangement is chronological, is devoted to collections of voyages ; the most famous of which is Purchas (3450), and of the remainder Churchill's collection (3453) is perhaps the most important. Some of the collections are anonymous, and are usually cited by their publisher, e. g. Astley (3458), Knox (3463), or the Harleian collection (3457). An analysis of the contents of the chief collections will be found in Appendix I to the Catalogue of the Royal Geographical Society.

The next subsection consists of individual voyages of travellers, or voyages to a given place, and the arrangement is alphabetical, the name of the *traveller* rather than the editor being adopted : cross-references are given to the principal English collections, in which they may be found in whole or in part. The Harleian Miscellany contains some material [see Index (88)]. The Dictionary of National Biography should be consulted *sub nom.* of the chief explorers, and the authorities there noted. The Hakluyt Society is constantly publishing fresh material.

All English travellers are not included in this section, and search must also be made under the geographical heading, e. g. *West Indies* for J. Esquemelling's Buccaneers (3850), *America* for voyages or persons directly connected with the plantations such as Captain John Smith (3620), and the *East Indies* for a large section dealing with travel to, and residence in, the East.

For a study of the voyages the modern Admiralty Charts and the Pilot (Admiralty publication) of the various seas are very useful : 17th-century conditions of travel are best gathered from the narratives themselves. The British Museum Catalogue of Printed Maps serves as a guide to early maps and charts.

¶ 1. COLLECTIONS OF VOYAGES

3450. Hakluytus posthumus or Purchas his pilgrimes. . . . By S. Purchas. 4 vols. fol. Lond. 1625. Later ed. 20 vols. 8vo. Glasgow, 1905–7. Maps. Illus.

Purchas his pilgrimage, or relations of the world and the religions observed in all ages and places discovered . . . , folio 1613, reached its fourth ed. in 1626, and is usually added as a fifth volume to Purchas his pilgrimes. Ed. of 1905 has bibliographical note.

3451. A collection of curious travels and voyages, in two tomes . . . By J. Ray. 2 vols. 8vo. Lond. 1693.

Vol. i is translated from Dutch, vol. ii includes some English travels in Greece, Asia Minor, Egypt, &c.
Period : 16th and 17th centuries.

3452. A collection of original voyages, containing : I. Capt. Cowley's voyage round the globe. II. Capt. Sharpe's Journey over the isthmus of Darien . . . III. Capt. Wood's voyage thro' the Straights of Magellan. IV. Mr. Roberts's adventures among the Corsairs of the Levant. . . . By W. Hacke. 1 vol. 8vo. Lond. 1699. Maps.

Period : 17th century.

3453. A collection of voyages and travels. . . . Ed. by A. and J. Churchill. 4 vols. fol. Lond. 1704. Maps. Later eds.: 6 vols. fol. Lond. 1732. Maps. 8 vols. fol. Lond. 1744–7. Maps.

Contains a prefatory essay on the history of navigation. For vols. 7 and 8 see no. 3457.
Period : 16th and 17th centuries.

3454. Navigantium atque itinerantium bibliotheca : or, a compleat collection of voyages and travels. . . . Ed. by J. Harris. 2 vols. fol. Lond. 1705. Maps. Ports. Later ed. 1744–8. Ed. by J. Campbell.

The second edition revised with large additions.
Period : 15th to 18th century, but the work also contains some medieval travels.

3455. A new collection of voyages and travels into several parts of the world. . . . By [J. Stevens]. 2 vols. 4to. Lond. 1711.

Contains one English journey in vol. i ' A journal of a thousand miles travel among the Indians from South to North Carolina ', by Mr. Lawson, with map.
Period : 16th to 18th centuries

3456. A collection of voyages. . . . 4 vols. 8vo. Lond. 1729. Maps.

Contains (1) Captain William Dampier's Voyages round the world. (2) The Voyages of Lionel Wafer. (3) A Voyage round the world : an account of Captain Dampier's expedition into the South Seas by W. Funnell. (4) Capt. Cowley's Voyage round the globe. (5) Capt. Sharpe's Journey over the Isthmus of Darien. (6) Capt. Wood's Voyage through the Straights of Magellan. (7) Mr. Roberts's Adventures amongst the Corsairs of the Levant.
Period : later 17th century.

3457. A collection of voyages and travels . . . Compiled from the library of the late Earl of Oxford. 2 vols. fol. Lond. 1745. Later ed. 1747.

Known as the Harleian collection. The 1747 edition is numbered vols. vii and viii in continuation of the Churchill collection in 6 vols. (3453).

3458. A new general collection of voyages and travels. 4 vols. 4to. Lond. 1745–47. Maps. Plans. Illus.

Published by Thomas Astley, and usually known as the Astley collection.
Period : 15th to 18th century.

3459. Histoire des navigations aux terres Australes. . . . By C. de Brosses. 2 vols. 4to. Paris. 1756. Map.

3460. The world displayed, or a curious collection of voyages and travels selected from the writers of all nations : ... 20 vols. 12mo. Lond. 1759–61. Maps. Illus.

Period : 15th to 18th century.

3461. A collection of travels thro' various parts of the world ... By S. Derrick. 2 vols. 12mo. Lond. 1762.

In regard to English travels, vol. i contains The entertaining travels and various adventures of Capt. John Smyth ; vol. ii, The history of Mr. Joseph Pitt's slavery in Algiers, with his travels over some part of the continent.....

Period : 16th and 17th centuries.

3462. Terra Australis cognita : or, voyages to the Terra Australis, or southern hemisphere, during the sixteenth, seventeenth, and eighteenth centuries ... with a preface by the editor. Ed. by J. Callander. 3 vols. 8vo. Edin. 1766–8. Maps.

Based largely on de Brosses.

3463. A new collection of voyages, discoveries, and travels ... 7 vols. 8vo. Lond. 1767.

Published by J. Knox, and known as the Knox collection.

Period : 15th to 18th century.

3464. A new and complete collection of voyages and travels ... By J. H. Moore. 2 vols. fol. Lond. [1785 ?] Maps.

Period : 15th to 18th centuries.

3465. A general collection of the best and most interesting voyages and travels in all parts of the world. ... Ed. by J. Pinkerton. 17 vols. 4to. Lond. 1808–14. Maps. Bibl.

Vol. xvii contains an essay on the origin and progress of discovery and a bibliography of travel.

Period : 16th to 18th century.

3466. Historical account of the most celebrated voyages, travels, and discoveries. ... By W. F. Mavor. 20 vols. 12mo. Lond. 1795–1802. Later ed. 28 vols. 12mo. Lond. 1810.

The 1810 edition entitled ' General collection of voyages and travels '.

Period : 15th to 18th century.

3467. A general history and collection of voyages and travels ... Ed. by R. Kerr. 18 vols. 8vo. Edin. 1811–24. Maps.

Period : from the time of Alfred to the 18th century.

3468. Voyages and travels, mainly during the 16th and 17th centuries. ... Ed. by C. R. Beazley. 2 vols. 8vo. Westminster. 1903.

Repr. from An English garner. Vol. ii contains 17th-century voyages as follows : (1) Fight of Dolphin against Five Turk's Men of War. Jan. 12, 1616/7. (2) Capt. Robert Knox's captivity in Ceylon, 1660–1679. (3) Retaking of St. Helena, ? 1673.

3469. Early Dutch and English voyages to Spitsbergen in the 17th century. Ed. by W. M. Conway. 1 vol. 8vo. Lond. 1904. Maps. Facs. Bibl.

Chiefly translations of early Dutch accounts, but includes MSS. from P.R.O., S.P. Dom. Ch. i. Hakluyt Soc., Ser. ii, vol. ii.

¶ 2. INDIVIDUAL VOYAGES

3470. Remarks on several parts of Italy, &c. in the years 1701, 1702, 1703. . . . By J. Addison. 1 vol. 8vo. Lond. 1705. Later ed. 1 vol. 12mo. Lond. 1718.

See Mavor, vol. xiv (3466); Moore, vol. ii (3464); World Displayed, vol. xix (3460). For a discussion of the MSS. see Francis Harvey (bookseller), Catalogue of rare and valuable books [Lond. July 1887].

3471. An account of a voyage from Archangel in Russia in the year 1697. . . . By T. Allison. 1 vol. 8vo. Lond. 1699. Map.

See Pinkerton, vol. i (3465).

3472. The voyages of William Baffin. 1612–1622. . . . Ed. by C. R. Markham. 1 vol. 8vo. Lond. 1881. Maps. Ports.

Printed for the Hakluyt Soc., Series I, vol. lxiii. Contains various narratives of Baffin's voyages by J. Gatonbe, R. Fotherby, Baffin himself, and others. See Churchill, vol. vi, Pt. 2 (3453).

3473. The strange adventures of Andrew Battell of Leigh, in Angola and in adjoining regions. . . . By A. Battell. Ed. by E. G. Ravenstein. 1 vol. 8vo. Lond. 1901. Maps. Bibl.

' The earliest record of travels in the interior of this part of Africa.' Hakluyt Soc., Series II, vol. vi. See Astley, vol. iii (3458); Pinkerton, vol. xvi (3465); Purchas, Pt. 2 (3450).

3474. The travels of certaine Englishmen into Africa, Asia. . . . and into Syria. . . . begunne in the yeare of jubile 1600, and by some of them finished this yeare 1608. By W. Biddulph. Ed. by T. Lavender. 1 vol. 4to. Lond. 1609. Later ed. 1 vol. 4to. Lond. 1612. Ed. by T. Lavender.

Title of 1612 edition runs : ' The travels of foure English men . . . finished in the yeare 1611.' See Purchas, Pt. 2 (3450); Churchill, vol. vii (3453).

3475. The discovery of New Brittaine begun August 27 anno dom 1650 by Edward Bland. . . . From Fort Henry at the head of Appamatuck river in Virginia. . . . 1 vol. 4to. Lond. 1651. Maps.

3476. A voyage into the Levant. A brief relation of a journey . . . from England by the way of Venice, into Dalmatia, Sclavonia, Bosnah, Hungary, Macedonia, Thessaly, Thrace, Rhodes, and Egypt unto Gran Cairo : . . . By H. Blount. 1 vol. 4to. Lond. 1636.

See vol. xvii, Series II, Hakluyt Soc. Publ. for a bibliographical note on this book. See Churchill, vol. vii (3453), Pinkerton, vol. x (3465).

3477. Remarks in the grande tour of France and Italy. . . . By W. Bromley. 1 vol. 8vo. Lond. 1692.

An ed. of 1705 was unauthorized.

3478. Several years travels through Portugal, Spain, Italy, Germany. . . . By W. Bromley. 1 vol. 8vo. Lond. 1702.

3479. A brief account of some travels in divers parts of Europe, viz. Hungaria, Servia, Bulgaria, Macedonia, Thessaly, Austria, Styria, Carinthia,

Carniola, and Fruili, through a great part of Germany and Low Countries. By E. Browne.   Later ed. 1 vol. fol. Lond. 1685. Plans. Illus.

Browne published in 1673 'A brief account of some travels . . .', 4to; in 1677, 'An account of several travels through a great part of Germany . .', 4to; and in 1685 his collected travels in one volume.   See Harris, vol. ii (3454).

3480. A relation of a journey of . . . Lord H. Howard from London to Vienna and thence to Constantinople. . . . By J. Burbury. 1 vol. 12mo. Lond. 1671.

3481. Some letters containing an account of what seemed most remarkable in Switzerland, Italy, &c.   By G. Burnet.   1 vol. 12mo. Rotterdam. 1686. Later ed. 1 vol. 12mo. London. 1688.

The edition of 1688 includes 'Three letters concerning the present state of Italy, written in 1687'.   See Harris, vol. ii (3454).

3482. A voyage to the South Sea and round the world performed in the years 1708, 1709, 1710 and 1711. . . . By E. Cooke.   2 vols. 8vo. Lond. 1712. Maps.

3483. Coryats crudities, hastily gobled up in five moneths travells in France, Savoy, Italy, Rhetia, commonly called the Grisons country, Helvetia alias Switzerland, some parts of high Germany, and the Netherlands.   By T. Coryate.   1 vol. 4to. Lond. 1611.   Later eds.: 3 vols. 8vo. Lond. 1776, and 2 vols. 8vo. Glasgow. 1905.

Coryate's letters from India are added to the edition of 1776.   'The first, and for long . . . the only handbook for continental travel.'   See Kerr, vol. ix (3467) Purchas, Pts. 1 and 2.

3484. Early voyages and travels in the Levant.   I. The diary of Master Thomas Dallan, 1599–1600.   II. Extracts from the diaries of Dr. John Covel, 1670–1679. . . . Ed. by J. T. Bent.   1 vol. 8vo. Lond. 1893.   Ports.

Hakluyt Soc., Series I, vol. lxxxvii.   See B.M. Add. MSS. 22912–4 for Covel's diary.

3485. A true and almost incredible report of an Englishman . . . that . . . travelled by land throw many unknowne kingdomes and great cities. . . . By R. Coverte.   1 vol. 4to. Lond. 1612.

See Astley, vol. i (3458) ; Churchill, vol. viii (3453) ; Kerr, vol. viii (3467).

3486. I. A new voyage round the world . . . II. Voyages and descriptions. . . . A supplement of the voyage round the world. . . . Two voyages to Campeachy. . . . A discourse of Trade-winds.   III. A voyage to New Holland, &c. in the year 1699. . . . By W. Dampier.   3 vols. 8vo. Lond. 1697–1709.   Maps. Illus.   Later ed. 2 vols. 8vo. Lond. 1906. Maps. Illus. Port. Ed. by J. Masefield.

The MS. of 'The new voyage' is B.M. Sloane MS. 3236.   The ed. of 1906 includes : A vindication in answer to the chimerical relation of William Funnell [which was first published as a 4to volume in Lond. 1707] and other relevant documents.   See Callander, vol. ii (3462) ;   Collection of voyages, 1729, vols. i–iii (3456) ;   Early voyages to Terra Australis (3462) ;   Harris (3454) ;   Kerr, vol. x (3467) ;   Moore, vol. i (3464) ;   Pinkerton, vol. xi (3465) ;   World displayed, vol. vi (3460).

3487. The voyages and works of John Davis the navigator.   By J. Davis.
Ed. by A. H. Markham.   1 vol. 8vo. Lond. 1880.   Maps.   Illus.   Bibl.
Hakluyt Soc., Series I, vol. lix.

3488. Journal of a voyage into the Mediterranean by Sir Kenelm Digby,
A. D. 1628. . . . By K. Digby.   Ed. by J. Bruce.   Camd. Soc. Lond. 1686.
From an MS. in the possession of W. W. E. Wynne, Esq.

3489. Observations concerning the present state of religion in the Romanish
Church, with some reflections upon them made in a journey through some
provinces of Germany in the year 1698 ; as also an account of what seemed
most remarkable in those countries. By T. Dorrington. 1 vol. 8vo. Lond. 1699.

3490. A voyage to Sicily and Malta . . . in the years 1700 and 1701.   By
J. Dryden (junior).   1 vol. 8vo. Lond. 1776.

3491. The state of France as it stood in the ixth yeer of the present monarch
Louis XIII, written to a friend.   By J. Evelyn.   1 vol. 8vo. Lond. 1652.

3492. North-west Fox, or Fox from the North-west passage. . . . By
L. Foxe.   1 vol. 4to. Lond. 1635.   Map.   Later ed. 2 vols. 8vo. Lond. 1894.
Maps.   Ports.   Ed. by R. M. Christy.
' The voyages of Capt. Luke Foxe of Hull and Capt. Thomas James of Bristol in
search of a N.W. passage in 1631–2 . . . ' is the title of 1894 edit. Hakluyt Soc., Series I,
vols. lxxxviii, lxxxix, B.M. Add. MSS. 19302.

3493. A voyage round the world, containing an account of Captain Dampier's expedition into the South Seas in the ship St. George in the years 1703
and 1704 . . . together with the author's voyage from Amapalla on the west-
coast of Mexico to East India. . . . By W. Funnell.   1 vol. 8vo. Lond. 1707.
Maps.
See Callander, vol. iii (3462) ; Harris, vol. i (3454) ; Kerr, vol. x (3467). ' Captain
Dampier's vindication . . . with some observations . . . on Mr. Funnell's chimerical
relation of his voyage round the world . . .' appeared in 1707. [Lond. 4to.] See Dampier's Voyages [ed. Masefield, 1906] (3486).

3494. Subsidium peregrinantibus ; or, an assistance to a traveller in his
convers with Hollanders, Germans, Venetians, Italians, Spaniards and French.
By Sir B. Gerbier.   1 vol. 12mo. Oxf. 1665.

3495. A relation of a voyage to Guiana. . . . By R. Harcourt.   1 vol. 4to.
Lond. 1613.   Later ed. 1626.
Second ed. enlarged.   See Harleian Miscellany, vol. vi (88), Purchas, Pt. 4 (3450).

3496. A relation of some yeares travaile, begunne anno 1626, into Afrique
and the greater Asia. . . . By T. Herbert.   1 vol. fol. Lond. 1634.   Maps.   3rd
ed. 1665.   4th ed. 1 vol. fol. Lond. 1675. Maps. Ports.
The third and fourth editions much enlarged by the author.   See Harris, vol. i (3454);
Moore, vol. ii (3464).

3497. A full relation of two journeys : the one into the mainland of France,
the other into some of the adjacent islands.   By P. Heylyn.   1 vol. 4to. Lond.
1656.
Heylyn wrote also a satirical journal, ' France painted to the life ', which was published
without his consent, London, 1657.

3498. Instructions for forreine travell. By J. Howell. 1 vol. 12mo. Lond. 1642. Later ed. 1650.

See E. Arber, English Reprints, London, 1869. The ed. of 1650 contains an appendix on travel into Turkey and the Levant.

3499. Henry Hudson the navigator. The original document in which his career is recorded. . . . Ed. by G. M. Asher. 1 vol. 8vo. Lond. 1860. Maps. Bibl.

' An almost exhaustive account of all that is known of Hudson's career.' Hakluyt Soc., Series I, vol. xxvii.

3500. The voyage of Captain William Jackson (1642–5). Ed. by V. T. Harlow. Camd. Misc. xiii [1924].

Raids on the Spanish West Indies. B.M. Sloane MSS. 793 or 894.

3501. The strange and dangerous voyage of Captaine Thomas James in his intended discovery of the North-West passage into the South Sea. . . . By T. James. 1 vol. 4to. Lond. 1633. Map. Later ed. 2 vols. 8vo. Lond. 1894. Maps. Ports. Ed. by R. M. Christy.

The 1894 ed. printed for the Hakluyt Soc., Series I, vols. lxxxviii, lxxxix. See Churchill, vol. ii (3453); Harris, vol. ii (3454) ; World displayed, vol. x (3460) ; Mavor, vol. i (3466).

3502. The golden trade : or a discovery of the river Gambia, and the golden trade of the Aethipoians. . . . By R. Jobson. 1 vol. 4to. Lond. 1623. Later ed. 1 vol. 8vo. Teignmouth. 1904. Ed. by C. G. Kingsley.

The 1904 edition is in the Saracen's Head Library. See Purchas, Pt. 2 (3450) ; Astley, vol. ii (3458).

3503. An account of two voyages to New England. . . . By J. Josselyn. 1 vol. 12mo. Lond. 1674.

See Mass. Hist. Soc. Collections, Third Series, vols. iii, iv.

3504. Remarks on the government of several parts of Germany . . . but more particularly of the United Provinces, with some few directions how to travel in the States Dominions. By W. Ker. Later ed. 1 vol. 8vo. Lond. 1727.

Printed in ' The memoirs of John Ker . . .' [Lond. 1727].

3505. The voyage of Italy : or a compleat journey through Italy. . . . By R. Lassels. Ed. by S. Wilson. 1 vol. 12mo. Paris. 1670. Later ed. 1 vol. 8vo. Lond. 1698.

Second ed. has ' large additions by a modern hand '. See Harris, vol. ii (3454).

3506. Three diatribes or discourses. First of travel, or a guide for travellers into foreign parts. . . . By E. Leigh. 1 vol. 12mo. Lond. 1671.

See Harleian Miscellany, vol. x (88).

3507. A voyage into New England begun in 1623 and ended in 1624. . . . By C. Levett. 1 vol. 4to. Lond. 1628.

3508. A journey to Paris in the year 1698. By M. Lister. 1 vol. 8vo. Lond. 1699. Later ed. 1 vol. 8vo. Paris. 1873.

See Pinkerton, vol. iv (3465). Ed. of 1873 published with annotations by Société des

Bibliophiles Français. Satirized by S. de Sorbière [pseud.], A journey to London, in the year 1698, after the ingenuous method of that made by Dr. M. Lyster to Paris [1698. Lond.].

3509. The totall discourse of the rare adventures and painefull peregrinations of long nineteene yeares travayles from Scotland to the most famous kingdomes in Europe, Asia, and Africa . . . By W. Lithgow. 1 vol. 4to. Lond. 1614. Later eds.: 1632, and 1 vol. 8vo. Glasgow. 1906.

The 1614 ed. entitled ' A most delectable and true discourse of an admired and painefull peregrination. . . .' The later ed. contains further matter. See Purchas (3450).

3510. A journey from Aleppo to Jerusalem at Easter, A.D. 1697. By H. Maundrell. 1 vol. 8vo. Oxf. 1703. Later ed. 1714.

The 1714 ed. includes ' An account of the author's journey [April 1699] to the banks of Euphrates at Beer and to . . . Mesopotamia '. See Harris, vol. ii (3454); Pinkerton, vol. x (3465); Moore, vol. ii (3464); World displayed, vol. xi (3460).

3511. An itinerary . . . containing his ten yeeres travell through the twelve dominions of Germany, Bohmerland, Sweitzerland, Netherland, Denmarke, Poland, Italy, Turkey, France, England, Scotland and Ireland. . . . By F. Moryson. 1 vol. fol. Lond. 1617. Plan. Later ed. 4 vols. 8vo. Glasgow. 1907–8. Plan.

' Invaluable to the social historian.' The MS. of an unfinished part of this work is in the library of Corpus Christi College, Oxford, and parts of it were edited by Mr. C. Hughes and published in 1903 under the title of ' Shakespeare's Europe '.

3512. The travels of Peter Mundy in Europe and Asia, 1608–1667. . . . By P. Mundy. Ed. by R. C. Temple. 5 vols. 8vo. Camb. 1907. Maps. Plans. Illus. Bibl.

Vol. i, Europe, 1608–28; ii, Asia, 1628–34; iii, pt. 1, England, W. India, Achin, Macao, 1634–7; iii, pt. 2, Achin, Martinique, Madagascar, St. Helena, 1638. iv, Europe. Hakluyt Soc., Series II, vol. xvii, xxv, xlv, xlvi. From Bodleian Library, Rawl. MS. A 315; Brit. Mus. Harl. MS. 2286 : of great value.

3513. An account of several late voyages and discoveries . . . towards the Streights of Magellan, the South Seas . . . as also towards Nova Zembla. . . . 1 vol. 8vo. Lond. 1694. Maps.

Contains (1) Sir John Narbrough's voyage to the South Sea ; (2) Captain J. Tasman's Discoveries on the coast of the South Terra Incognita ; (3) Capt. J. Wood's attempt to discover a North-east passage to China; (4) F. Marten's observations made in Greenland, and other northern countries. See Callander, vol. ii (3462).

3514. Topographical descriptions with historico-political and medico-physical observations made in two several voyages through most parts of Europe. By J. Northleigh. 1 vol. 8vo. Lond. 1702.

See Harris, vol. ii (3454).

3515. Sir Thomas Overbury, his observations in his travailes upon the state of the XVII Provinces as they stood anno dom. 1609. 1 vol. 4to. Lond. 1626.

3516. God's power and providence : shewed in the miraculous preservation . . . of eight Englishmen, left by mischance in Greenland, anno 1630,

nine months and twelve days. . . . By E. Pellham.   1 vol. 4to. Lond. 1631.
Map.

Included in ' A collection of documents on Spitzbergen and Greenland . . .' ed.
Hakluyt Soc. by A. White, 1855, Series I, vol. xviii.   See Churchill, vol. iv (3453).

3517. A faithful account of the religion and manners of the Mahometans,
in which is a particular relation of their pilgrimage to Mecca.   By J. Pitts.
1 vol. 8vo. Exeter. 1704.   Later eds. 1717, 1719, and 1731.

The first Englishman to reach Mecca.

3518. Observations, topographical, moral, and physiological, made in a
journey through part of the Low Countries, Germany, Italy, and France. . . .
[also] A brief account of Francis Willughby, Esq: his voyage through a
great part of Spain.   By J. Ray.   1 vol. 8vo. Lond. 1673.   Later ed. 2 vols.
8vo. Lond. 1738.

See Harris, vol. ii (3454).

3519. An itinerary contayning a voyage through Italy in the years 1646–
1647.   By J. Raymond.   1 vol. 12mo. Lond. 1648.   Illus.

3520. The dangerous voyage and bold attempts of Captain Bartholomew
Sharp ; and others performed upon the coasts of the South Seas. . . . By
B. Ringrose.

See J. Esquemelling, Buccaneers of America (3856).

3521. A cruising voyage round the world : first to the South Seas, thence to
the East Indies, and homeward by the Cape of Good Hope.   Begun in 1708,
and finish'd in 1711. . . . By Woodes Rogers.   1 vol. 8vo. Lond. 1712.   Maps.
Later ed. 1 vol. 8vo. Lond. 1718.

See Callander, vol. iii (3462);   World displayed, vol. vi (3460) ;   Kerr, vol. x (3467);
Knox, vol. iii (3463).

3522. Narratives of voyages towards the north-west in search of a passage
to Cathay and India, 1496 to 1631. . . . Ed. by T. Rundall.   1 vol. 8vo. Lond.
1849.   Maps.

Printed for the Hakluyt Soc., Series I, vol. v.

3523. A relation of a journey begun an. dom. 1610.   Foure bookes containing a description of the Turkish empire, of Aegypt, of the Holy Land, of the
remote parts of Italy, and ilands adjoyning.   By G. Sandys.   1 vol. fol. Lond.
1615.   Maps. Port.   7th ed. 1 vol. fol. Lond. 1673. Maps.

Title of the 7th ed. is ' Travels, containing an history of the original and present state
of the Turkish empire, their laws, government, policy . . .' See Purchas, pt. ii (3450) ;
Harris, vol. i (3454).

3524. The three brothers, or the travels and adventures of Sir Anthony, Sir
Robert, and Sir Thomas Shirley in Persia, Russia, Turkey, Spain, &c.   1 vol.
8vo. Lond. 1825.   Ports.

Based on early tracts, &c.   See Purchas, pt. ii (3450); E. P. Shirley, The Shirley
brothers, an historical memoir . . . (Roxburghe Club, Lond. 1848), based largely on
MSS. in P. R. O. ; Journal R. Asiatic Soc., vol. vi [o.s.], p. 77 ; Gentleman's Mag., Nov.
and Dec. 1844.

3525. A voyage to the islands Madera, Barbados, Nieves, S. Christophers and Jamaica, with the natural history . . . of the last of these islands. . . . By Hans Sloane. 2 vols. fol. Lond. 1707–25. Maps.

3526. Sir Thomas Smithes voiage and entertainment in Rushia . . . Anon. 1 vol. 4to. Lond. 1605.

3527. The historie of travaile into Virginia Britannia. . . . By W. Strachey. Ed. by R. H. Major. 1 vol. 8vo. Lond. 1849. Maps. Illus.

Pr. for the Hakluyt Soc., Series I, vol. vi; B.M. Sloane MS. 1622; Ashmolean MS. 1754.

3528. An account of divers choice remarks, as well geographical, as historical, political, mathematical, physical, and moral; taken in a journey through the Low Countries, France, Italy, and part of Spain . . . as also a voyage to the Levant. . . . By E. Veryard. 1 vol. fol. Lond. 1701.

3529. The English Spanish pilgrime, or a new discoverie of Spanish popery and Jesuitical stratagems. . . . By J. Wadsworth. 1 vol. 4to. Lond. 1629. Later ed. 1630.

Wadsworth was an ex-Jesuit. The 2nd ed. contains a second part, ' Further observations . . . concerning Spaine.'

3530. A new voyage and description of the isthmus of America. . . . By L. Wafer. 1 vol. 8vo. Lond. 1699. Maps. Illus. Later eds.: 1704, and 1 vol. 8vo. Cleveland. 1903. Maps. Ed. by G. P. Winship.

To the second ed. is added Nathaniel Davis's Expedition to the gold mines, in 1702. Wafer's voyages is sometimes issued with vol. iii of Dampier's Voyages [ed. 1729]. See Callander, vol. ii (3462) ; Collection of voyages, 1729, vol. iii (3456).

3531. An answer to Captain Dampier's vindication of his voyage to the South Seas . . . with . . . observations on his . . . barbarous usage to his ship's crew. By J. Welbe. 1 vol. 4to. Lond. [1705].

3532. A journey into Greece . . . in company of Dr. Spon of Lyons. By G. Wheler [Wheeler]. 1 vol. fol. Lond. 1682. Maps. Plans.

See Dr. J. Spon's account of this journey published at Lyons, 1678, 2 vols. 12mo.

3533. A discourse and discovery of New-foundland . . . as also an invitation: and likewise certain letters sent from that countrey. By R. Whitbourne. 1 vol. 4to. Lond. 1622.

' Published by authority ', and contains the king's order to the archbishops to circulate the book and encourage church collections to defray its costs. See Westward Hoe for Avalon . . . [ed. T. Whitburn. Lond. 1870] for extracts.

¶ 3. GENERAL LATER WORKS

3534. A chronological history of voyages into the Arctic regions . . . By J. Barrow. 1 vol. 8vo. Lond. 1818. Maps.

3535. A chronological history of north-eastern voyages of discovery . . . By J. Burney. 1 vol. 8vo. Lond. 1819. Maps.

3536. A chronological history of the discoveries in the South Sea or Pacific Ocean. By J. Burney. 5 vols. 4to. Lond. 1803–17. Maps.

3537. Découvertes et explorations du XVIe au XIXe siècle . . . By E. Cat. 1 vol. 8vo. Paris. 1892.

3538. Nouvelle histoire des voyages et des grandes découvertes géographiques. . . . By R. Cortambert. 1 vol. 8vo. Paris. 1883. Illus.

3539. Handbook of Arctic discoveries. By A. W. Greely. Ed. by D. P. Todd. 1 vol. 8vo. Lond. 1896. Maps. Bibl. 4th ed. 1 vol. 8vo. Boston. 1909. Maps. Bibl.
No. iii Columbian Knowledge Series. The fourth ed. is entitled ' Handbook of Polar discoveries ', and is revised and enlarged.

3540. A history of geographical discovery in the seventeenth and eighteenth centuries. By E. Heawood. 1 vol. 8vo. Camb. 1912. Maps. Ports.
Cambridge Geographical Series.

3541. An historical account of all the voyages round the world performed by English navigators. . . . By D. Henry. 4 vols. 8vo. Lond. 1774. Maps. Ports.

3542. English travellers of the Renaissance. By C. Howard. 1 vol. 8vo. Lond. 1914. Illus.
Deals with 16th, 17th, and early 18th centuries.

3543. Seventeenth-century travel in Europe. By M. Letts. Notes and Queries. July 1915, Jan. Feb. Mar. Apr. 1916.
Valuable series of articles.

3544. The whole history of navigation from its original to this time [1704]. By J. Locke.
See Churchill, vol. i (3453) ; John Locke, Works, vol. x [10th ed. Lond. 1801] (2765).

3545. Historical account of discoveries and travels in Asia from the earliest ages to the present time. By H. Murray. 3 vols. 8vo. Edin. 1820. Maps.

3546. Historical account of discoveries and travels in North America ; including the United States, Canada, the shores of the Polar Sea, and the voyage in search of a North-west passage. . . . By H. Murray. 2 vols. 8vo. Lond. 1829. Map. Bibl.
Appendix : list of important works relating to America.

3547. Narrative of discovery and adventure in Africa from the earliest ages to the present time. . . . By H. Murray (and others). 1 vol. 12mo. Edin. 1830. Map.
In the Edin. Cab. Library, vol. ii.

3548. Historical account of discoveries and travels in Africa. By J. Leyden. Ed. by H. Murray. 2 vols. 8vo. Edin. 1817. Maps.
Enlarged and completed by H. Murray.

3549. Narrative of discovery and adventures in the Polar Seas. . . . By H. Murray (and others). 1 vol. 12mo. Edin. 1830. Maps.
In the Edin. Cab. Library, vol. i.

3550. William Dampier. By W. C. Russell. 1 vol. 8vo. Lond. 1889.
English Men of Action series.

XVI. COLONIAL HISTORY

1. General and Miscellaneous.
   (a) Sources and Guides.
   (b) Later Works.
2. American Colonies.
3. East Indies.
4. West Indies.

¶ 1. GENERAL AND MISCELLANEOUS

(a) SOURCES AND GUIDES

3551. The colonial entry-books. A brief guide to the colonial records in the Public Record Office before 1696. S.P.C.K. Helps for Students series, by C. S. S. Higham. 1 vol. 8vo. Lond. 1921.

Very useful summary guide.

3552. Calendar of state papers, colonial series, America and West Indies, 1574–1711. Ed. by W. N. Sainsbury, J. W. Fortescue, and C. Headlam. 20 vols. 8vo. Lond. 1860–1924.

Has a list of colonial entry books, 1606–88.

3553. Calendar of state papers, colonial series, East Indies, China, and Japan, 1513–1634. Ed. by W. N. Sainsbury. 5 vols. 8vo. Stationery Office, 1862–92.

3554. Acts of the Privy Council, colonial series. Ed. by W. L. Grant and J. Monro. 6 vols. 8vo. Stationery Office, 1908–12.

3555. Journal of the commissioners for trade and plantations 1704. (In progress.) Stationery Office, 1921.

(b) LATER WORKS

3556. The history of the Church of England in the colonies and foreign dependencies of the British empire. By J. S. M. Anderson. 3 vols. 12mo. Lond. 1845–55. Later ed. 1856.

3557. English intercourse with Siam in the seventeenth century. By J. Anderson. 1 vol. 8vo. Lond. 1890.

3558. Historical geography of the British colonies. Vol. iii. West Africa. By C. P. Lucas. 1 vol. 8vo. Oxf. 1894. Later ed. 8vo. Oxf. 1900.

3559. A history of Newfoundland from the English, colonial, and foreign records by D. W. Prowse. 1 vol. 8vo. Lond. 1895. Illus. Bibl. Later ed. 1 vol. 8vo. Lond. 1896. Illus.

Based on much research : the bibliography is omitted in 1896 ed.

3560. A short history of British colonial policy. By H. E. Egerton. 1 vol. 8vo. Lond. 1897, and 5th ed. 1918. Bibl.

3561. The old colonial system. By G. B. Hertz. 1 vol. 8vo. Manchester. 1905.

3562. Newfoundland. Vol. v, pt. iv, of Lucas's Historical geography of the British colonies. By J. D. Rogers. 1 vol. 8vo. Oxf. 1911.
Contains much learning within a small compass.

3563. Tangier, England's lost Atlantic outpost, 1661–84. By E. M. G. Routh. 1 vol. 8vo. Lond. 1912. Bibl.
The best account of the English occupation of Tangier.

3564. The colonizing activities of the English Puritans. The last phase of the Elizabethan struggle with Spain. . . . Introduction by C. M. Andrews. By A. P. Newton. 8vo.
Yale Historical Publ. Misc. No. 1. New Haven 1914.

3565. The colonial policy of William III and the West Indies. By G. H. Gutteridge. 1 vol. 8vo. Camb. 1922.

¶ 2. AMERICAN COLONIES

The existence of a number of detailed bibliographies to some extent atones for the relatively few entries which limitations of space permit. With regard to the sources an attempt has been made to show the kind of available material. In choosing the later works two principles have been adopted : to cover the wide field as adequately as possible, and to give fair representation to the different schools of American historians. Probably Larned (3577) is the most useful guide to begin with ; Channing, Hart and Turner (3575) is detailed enough for all but the most advanced research ; Griffin (3581) is invaluable for the publications of historical societies, and Grace Griffin (3584) for the annual output of historical literature.

Books dealing with the relations of the Colonies and the home government will be found in the section devoted to central administration.

(a) BIBLIOGRAPHIES AND GUIDES

3566. The history of printing in America. By I. Thomas. 2 vols. Worcester (U.S.) 1810. New ed. in Amer. Antiq. Soc., Arch. Americana, v, vi. Albany N.Y. 1874.

3567. A bibliographical and historical essay on the Dutch books and pamphlets relating to New Netherland and to the Dutch West India Company. . . . As also on the maps . . . of New Netherland, with facsimiles of the map of New Netherland by N. Y. Vischer, and of three existing views of New Amsterdam. By G. M. Asher. 2 pts. 4to. Amsterdam. 1854–67.

3568. Catalogue of the American books in the library of the British Museum at Christmas, 1856. By H. Stevens. 1 vol. 8vo. Lond. 1866.
The Catalogues of Additions have American sections, which continue the above.

3569. Dictionary of books relating to America from its discovery to the present time. By J. Sabin. 20 vols. 8vo. N.Y. 1868–92.

Stops in the letter S.

3570. A history of American literature. I. 1607–1676. II. 1676–1765. By M. C. Tyler. 2 vols. 8vo. N.Y. 1879 and 1897.

3571. Index to the first twenty volumes of the Proceedings of the Massachusetts Historical Society, 1791–1883. 1 vol. 8vo. Boston. 1887.

The index to the second series, 1884–1907, was publ. 1919. Each series of ten volumes of the Collections [1792–] has an index in the last volume. Cf. Griffin (3581).

3572. Check-list of the bibliographies, catalogues, reference-lists, and lists of authorities of American books and subjects. By P. L. Ford. 1 vol. 4to. Brooklyn. N.Y. 1889.

3573. Charlemagne Tower collection of American colonial laws. Phila. 1890.

The best bibliography of the codes of law : in the possession of the Pennsylvania Hist. Soc. Cf. The colonial assemblies and their legislative journals, by J. F. Jameson, Amer. Hist. Assoc. Rep., 1897, pp. 403–53.

3574. The history of historical writing in America. By J. F. Jameson. 1 vol. 8vo. Boston and N.Y. 1891.

Cf. The middle group of American historians. By J. S. Bassett. 1 vol. 8vo. N.Y. 1917.

3575. Guide to the study of American history. Ed. by E. Channing, A. B. Hart, and F. J. Turner [for 3rd ed.]. 1 vol. 8vo. Boston. 1896. 3rd ed. 1912.

3576. Guide to the items relating to American history in the reports of the English Historical Manuscripts Commission. Ed. by J. F. Jameson. Amer. Hist. Asso. Rep. 1898. Washington. 1899.

3577. Literature of American history : a bibliographical guide [with supplements]. Ed. by J. N. Larned. Boston. 1902.

3578. American bibliography. A chronological dictionary of all books, pamphlets, and periodical publications printed in the United States of America from . . . 1639 to 1820. By C. Evans. 9 vols. 4to. Chicago. 1903–25. In progress.

Vol. i, 1639–1729. Vol. ix, 1793–4. Cf. O. A. Roorback, Bibliotheca Americana. Catalogue of American publications, 1820–61. 4 vols. 8vo. 1852–61.

3579. An introduction to the records of the Virginia Company of London, with a bibliographical list of the extant documents. By S. M. Kingsbury. 1 vol. 4to. Washington. 1905.

3580. Materials for a bibliography of the public archives of the thirteen original states to 1789. By A. R. Hasse. Amer. Hist. Assoc. Rep. 1906, vol. ii. 243–572.

3581. Bibliography of American historical societies (the United States and the Dominion of Canada) [to 1905]. Ed. by A. P. C. Griffin. Amer. Hist. Assoc. Rep. 1905, vol. ii. 2nd ed. 1 vol. 8vo. Washington. 1907.

1st ed. 1895. Invaluable.

3582. Bibliographer's manual of American history, containing an account of all state, territory, town, and county histories. Ed. by T. L. Bradford and S. V. Henkels. 4 vols. with index. 8vo. Phila. 1907–10.

3583. Guide to the manuscript materials for the history of the United States to 1783 in the British Museum, in minor London archives, and in the libraries of Oxford and Cambridge. By C. M. Andrews and F. G. Davenport. 1 vol. 8vo. Washington. 1908.

3584. Writings on American history, 1906. A bibliography of books and articles on United States and Canadian history during the year. Ed. by G. G. Griffin. 4to. New Haven. 1908.

A vol. for 1902 was ed. by E. C. Richardson and A. E. Morse [Princeton, 1904]; for 1903 by A. C. McLaughlin, W. A. Slade, and E. D. Lewis, Washington, 1905. After 1906 an annual publication of great value.

3585. List of commissions and instructions to governors and lieutenant-governors of American and the West Indian colonies, 1609–1784. Amer. Hist. Assoc. Rep. 1911, i. 393–529.

Cf. Amer. Hist. Rev. 1898, iii. 170–6 and No. 3580.

3586. Guide to the materials for American history to 1783, in the Public Record Office of Great Britain. Vol. i. The state papers. By C. M. Andrews. 1 vol. 8vo. Washington. 1912.

Vol. ii, Departmental and miscellaneous papers, appeared in 1914, also ed. by C. M. Andrews.

3587. A history of American literature. Ed. by W. P. Trent, J. Erskine, S. P. Shirman, C. Van Doren. 4 vols. 8vo. Camb. 1918–21.

3588. A select bibliography of the Pilgrim Fathers of New England. Trans. Congregational Hist. Soc. Lond. 1920.

In writings on American history, 1920 (publ. 1923), items 568–685 deal with the Pilgrim Fathers.

(b) SOURCES

3589. Plaine dealing, or newes from New England. By T. Lechford. 1 vol. 4to. Lond. 1642. Later ed. 1 vol. 4to. Boston (Mass.) 1867. Ed. by J. H. Trumbull.

Lechford's note-book, 1638–41, was publ. in Trans. of Amer. Antiq. Soc. vii. 8vo. Camb. (Mass.) 1885.

3590. New Englands memoriall : or a brief relation of the most memorable and remarkable passages of the providence of God manifested to the planters of New England. By N. Morton. 1 vol. sm. 4to. Boston (Mass.) 1669. Later ed. 1 vol. 8vo. Boston. 1855.

3591. Magnalia Christi Americana; or the ecclesiastical history of New England [1620–98]. By Cotton Mather. 1 vol. fol. London. 1702. Later ed. 2 vols. 8vo. Hartford (Conn.) 1853. Ed. by T. Robbins.

The book has merits as illustrative of New England religious feeling, but according to Prof. M. C. Tyler, ' on no disputed question of fact is the unaided testimony of Mather of much weight.'

3592. The British empire in America, containing the history of the discovery, settlement, progress, and state of the British colonies on the continent and islands of America. By J. Oldmixon. 2 vols. 8vo. Lond. 1708. Maps. Later ed. 2 vols. 8vo. Lond. 1741. Maps.

3593. The laws of the British plantations in America relating to the church and the clergy, religion and learning. Ed. by N. Trott. 1 vol. fol. Lond. 1721.

3594. A journal of the transactions and occurrences in the settlement of Massachusetts and the other New England colonies from the year 1630 to 1644. By J. Winthrop. Ed. by N. Webster. 1 vol. 8vo. Hartford (U.S.A.) 1790. 2 vols. 8vo. Boston (U.S.A.) 1825–6 and 1853. Ed. by J. Savage. 2 vols. 8vo. N.Y. 1908. Orig. Narr. Series. Ed. by J. K. Hosmer.

The chief authority for the early history of Massachusetts. The first ed. contains only part of the original, all of which is incorporated in the later eds. Winthrop's papers, publ. in the Coll. Massa. Hist. Soc., 4th ser., vol. vi, 1863, are being re-edited for the same society. Cf. R. C. Winthrop, Life and letters of John Winthrop, 2 vols. 8vo. Boston. 1864–7 and 1869.

3595. The statutes-at-large, being a collection of the laws of Virginia. Ed. by W. W. Hening. 13 vols. 8vo. Richmond (Va.) 1819–23.

Vols. i–iii deal with the Stuart period. See No. 3573 for other sets of colonial laws.

3596. Tracts and other papers relating principally to the origin, settlement, and progress of the colonies in North America, from the discovery of the country to the year 1776. Ed. by P. Force. 4 vols. 8vo. Washington. 1836.

3597. Chronicles of the first planters of the colony of Massachusetts Bay from 1623 to 1636. By A. Young. 1 vol. 8vo. Boston. 1846.

Cf. his Chronicles of the Pilgrim Fathers . . . 1602 to 1625. 2nd ed. Boston. 1844.

3598. Collections concerning the early history of the founders of New Plymouth. Ed. by J. Hunter. 1 vol. 8vo. Lond. 1849.

Enlarged in 1854 as : Collections concerning the church or congregation of Protestant separatists formed at Scrooby in North Nottinghamshire in the time of King James I.

3599. Documentary history of the state of New York. By E. B. O'Callaghan. 4 vols. 4to. Albany. 1850–1.

Cf. his : Laws and ordinances of New Netherland. 8vo. N.Y. 1868 and No. 3606.

3600. The colonial records of Connecticut. Ed. by J. H. Trumbull and C. J. Hoadley. 15 vols. 8vo. Hartford. 1850–90.

Trumbull also ed. : The public records of the colony of Connecticut, 1636–1677, 3 vols. 8vo. Hartford (U.S.A.) 1850–9.

3601. Pennsylvania archives, selected and arranged from original documents in the office of the secretary. 91 vols. 8vo. Phila. 1852–1907.

The colonial records, 1683–1790, were publ. Phila. 1852–3. See Channing, Hart, and Turner, ed. 1912, pp. 144–5.

3602. Records of the governor and company of Massachusetts Bay, 1628–1686. Ed. by N. B. Shurtleff. 5 vols. fol. Boston. 1853–4.

The acts and resolves, public and private, of the province of the Massachusetts Bay : to which are prefixed the charters of the province. Ed. A. C. Goodell [vols. i–viii] and M. M. Bigelow [vol. ix]. Boston 1869– . Cf. Provincial and state papers of New Hampshire. 4to. Concord. 1867– . Ed. by N. Bouton, W. Hammond, and A. S. Batchellor.

3603. Records of the colony of New Plymouth in New England. Ed. by N. B. Shurtleff and D. Pulsifer. 12 vols. 4to. Boston. 1855–61.

3604. History of Plimouth plantation, containing an account of the voyage of the Mayflower, by W. Bradford. Ed. by C. Deane. Mass. Hist. Soc., 4th ser., vol. iii, 1856. Later eds. : 8vo. Boston. 1896. In facsimile. Ed. by J. A. Doyle. Orig. Narr. Series. 1908. Ed. by W. T. Davis. 2 vols. Boston. 1912. Ed. by W. C. Ford.

Bradford's letter-book was publ. in Coll. Mass. Hist. Soc., 1st ser., vol. iii.

3605. Records of the colony of Rhode Island and Providence plantations in New England. By J. R. Bartlett. 10 vols. 8vo. Providence. 1856–65.

3606. Documents relative to the colonial history of the state of New York. By E. B. O'Callaghan. 15 vols. 4to. Albany. 1856–87.

The 1st and 2nd vols. contain Holland documents and the 3rd the London documents from 1613 to 1692. The collection is more valuable for the 18th century and cannot be neglected for the 17th. The Paris documents in vol. ix are important for the early relations between the English and French colonies.

3607. Records of the colony of New Haven, 1638–1665. By C. T. Hoadley. 2 vols. 8vo. Hartford. 1857–8.

3608. A collection of original papers relative to the history of Massachusetts Bay. Ed. by T. Hutchinson. Prince Soc. Publications. 2 vols. 4to. Boston. 1865.

A standard collection of documentary matter.

3609. Letters written from New England, 1686. By J. Dunton. Ed. by W. H. Whitmore. Prince Soc. 1 vol. 4to. Boston. 1867.

3610. The Andros tracts ; being a collection of pamphlets and official papers. Ed. by W. H. Whitmore. 3 vols. 4to. Boston. 1868–74.

3611. The Clarendon papers. N.Y. Hist. Soc. Coll. ii. 8vo. N.Y. 1869.

Transcripts from MSS. in the Bodleian Library relating to New York and New England affairs during Clarendon's ascendancy.

3612. Historical collections relating to the American colonial church. Ed. by W. S. Perry. 5 vols. in 4. Hartford. 1870–8.

Documents from archives of the S.P.C., Lambeth, and Fulham.

3613. The original lists of persons of quality, emigrants &c. who went from Great Britain to the American plantations, 1600–1700. By J.C. Hotten. 1 vol. 4to. Lond. 1874.

3614. Calendar of Virginia state papers. Ed. by W. P. Palmer and H. W. Flournay. 11 vols. Richmond (Va.) 1875–1893.

Cf. Minutes of the council and general court of colonial Virginia, 1622–1683 (with gaps). Ed. by H. R. McIlwaine. fol. Richmond. 1924 ; and Journals of the house of Burgesses of Virginia i, 1619–59 ; ii, 1659–93 ; iii, 1703–12 ; iv, 1712–26. fol. Richmond (Va.) 1912–15.

3615. Diary : 1674–1729. By S. Sewell. Mass. Hist. Soc. Coll., 5th ser., vols. v–vii. 8vo. Boston. 1878–82.

The diary expresses 17th-century New England just as that of Pepys does the England of the Restoration. His Letter-book, *ibid*. 6th ser., i and ii, 1886–88.

3616. Colonial records of North Carolina. By W. L. Saunders. 10 vols. 8vo. Raleigh (N. Ca.) 1886–90.

Vol. i deals with the Stuart period.

3617. Archives of the state of New Jersey, 1631–1776. Ed. by W. A. Whitehead. 25 vols. 8vo. New Jersey Hist. Soc. Newark, N.J. 1880–1903.

Vols. i–iv deal with the Stuart period.

3618. Archives of Maryland. By W. H. Browne. 4to. Maryland Hist. Soc. Baltimore. 1883– . In progress.

3619. Works by John Smith. Ed. by E. Arber. 1 vol. 8vo. Birmingham. 1884. Later eds. 2 vols. 8vo. Lond. 1895, 1907, and 1910.

3620. Old south leaflets, 200 Nos. 8vo. Boston. 1888–1909.

Repr. of pamphlets, documents, extracts, &c. Cf. American history leaflets, 1892–, ed. by A. B. Hart and E. Channing.

3621. The Calvert papers. 3 vols. 8vo. Maryland Hist. Soc. Baltimore. 1889–99.

Of great importance in connexion with the beginnings of Maryland.

3622. The story of the Pilgrim Fathers [1606–23] as told by themselves, their friends, and their enemies. Ed. by E. Arber. 8vo. Boston. 1897.

Contains numerous contemporary documents relating to its subject.

3623. Some correspondence between the governors ... of the New England Company in London and the commissioners of the united colonies in America, the missionaries of the company, and others [1657–1712] ... to which are added the journals of ... Experience Mayhew [1713–14]. Ed. by J. W. Ford. 1 vol. 8vo. Lond. 1897.

3624. The Shaftesbury papers. 8vo. South Carolina Hist. Soc. Coll., vol. v. Charleston. 1897.

These transcripts of papers in the P.R.O. are useful for foundation of the Carolinas. List and abstracts of papers in the State Paper Office, London, relating to South Carolina, *ibid*. i and ii, 1857–8.

3625. Edward Randolph, including his letters and official papers. By R. N. Toppan. Prince Soc. Publs. 7 vols. 4to. Boston. 1898–1909.

These papers are the most vivid authority on the working of the old colonial system in the colonies from the point of view of a zealous English official. The two last supplementary volumes were edited by A. T. S. Goodrick.

3626. Select charters and other documents illustrative of American history, 1606–1775. Ed. by W. Macdonald. 1 vol. 8vo. N.Y. 1899 and 1904.

3627. Narratives of New Netherland, 1609–64. Ed. by J. F. Jameson. Orig. Narr. Series. 1 vol. 8vo. N.Y. 1906.

Other vols. in this series not enumerated elsewhere are : Edward Johnson's wonderworking providence [1910] ; Narratives of Early Carolina, ed. by A. S. Salley [1911] ; Narratives of the insurrections 1675–90, ed. by C. M. Andrews [1915] ; Early narratives of the north-west 1634–99, ed. by L. P. Kellog [1917].

3628. The records of the Virginia Company of London. The court book. By S. M. Kingsbury. 2 vols. 4to. Washington. 1906.

The first court book of the Virginia Company was destroyed or lost. Its records from 1619 to its dissolution are here printed from the MS. in the Library of Congress.

3629. Narratives of early Virginia, 1606–25. Ed. by L. G. Tyler. Orig. Narr. Series. 8vo. N.Y. 1907.

Includes Capt. J. Smith's ' Generale historie '.

3630. The federal and state constitutions, colonial charters, and other organic laws of the states. By F. N. Thorpe. 7 vols. 8vo. Washington. 1909.

3631. Narratives of early Maryland. Ed. by C. C. Hall. Orig. Narr. Series. 8vo. N.Y. 1910.

Contains Lord Baltimore's ' Instructions to the colonists ' and other documents of interest.

3632. Diary. By Cotton Mather. Ed. by W. C. Ford. Mass. Hist. Soc. Coll. 7th ser., vols. vii and viii. 8vo. Boston. 1912–13.

Supplements the diary of Judge Sewell, and throws much light upon the social conditions in Boston during a period of change and unrest.

3633. Journals of Dankers and Sluyter, 1679–80. Ed. by B. B. James and J. F. Jameson. Orig. Narr. Series. 8vo. N.Y. 1913.

Contemporary account of N.Y. by two Dutch observers.

3634. Narratives of early Pennsylvania, Delaware, and New Jersey, 1630–1708. Ed. by A. C. Myers. Orig. Narr. Series. 8vo. N.Y. 1913.

Cf. No. 3353.

3635. Narratives of the witchcraft cases, 1648–1706. Ed. by G. L. Burr. Orig. Narr. Series. 1914. Facs.

Cf. S. G. Drake, Annals of witchcraft in New England and elsewhere in the United States. 1 vol. 8vo. Boston. 1869.

3636. An abridgement of the Indian affairs contained in four folio volumes transacted in the colony of New York, from the year 1678 to the year 1751. By P. Wraxall. Ed. by C. McIlwain. 1 vol. 8vo. Camb. 1915.

3285   3 A

3637. Privateering and piracy in the colonial period : illustrative documents. Ed. by J. F. Jameson. 1 vol. 8vo. N.Y. 1923.

3638. Letters and papers of Roger Williams, 1629–1682. Facsimile repr. Massachusetts Hist. Soc. Fol. 1924.

Supersedes the ed. of J. R. Bartlett in the Narragansett Club Pub., vol. vi.

(c) LATER WORKS

3639. The history of New England, containing an impartial account of the civil and ecclesiastical affairs of the country to . . . 1700. By D. Neal. 2 vols. 8vo. Lond. 1720.

3640. History of the five Indian nations. By C. Colden. 8vo. N.Y. 1727. Later ed. 8vo. N.Y. 1866. Ed. by J. G. Shea.

3641. History of the first discovery and settlement of Virginia. By W. Stith. 2 pts. 8vo. Williamsburg. 1747.

The first instalment of an extended work which never appeared. It is throughout based on first-hand authority.

3642. History of the colony [and province] of Massachussets Bay. By T. Hutchinson. 8vo. Boston. 1764–7.

Vol. i, 1628–91 ; ii, 1691–1750.

3643. History of the colony of Nova Caesaria or New Jersey . . . to . . . 1721. By S. Smith. 2 vols. 8vo. Burlington (N.J.) 1765. Later ed. Trenton. 1877.

The author had access to material not now accessible.

3644. Materials towards a history of the Baptists in Pennsylvania. By M. Edwards. 1 vol. 12mo. Phila. 1770.

Cf. his similar vol. for New Jersey, 1 vol. 12mo. Phila. 1792.

3645. A history of New England, with particular reference to the denomination of Christians called Baptists. By I. Backus. 3 vols. 8vo. Boston. 1777–96.

An abridgement of 1804 has a chapter as to the origin in the southern states. Cf. D. Benedict, A general history of the Baptist denomination in America and other parts of the world. 2 vols. 8vo. Boston. 1813. Later ed. 1 vol. 8vo. N.Y. 1848, much enlarged with bibl. notes.

3646. Political annals of the present united colonies from their settlement to the peace of 1763. Vol. i [to 1689]. By G. Chalmers. 1 vol. 4to. Lond. 1780.

Three chapters of a second vol. have been published in N.Y. Hist. Soc. Coll. Public. Fund, vol. i. Chalmers had strong Tory prejudices, but his history is based on MS. material in the P.R.O.

3647. History of New Hampshire. By J. Belknap. 3 vols. 8vo. Phila. and Boston. 1784–92. Later ed. 3 vols. 8vo. Boston. 1813.

Vol. i deals with the Stuart period.

3648. History of Pennsylvania from 1681 till after the year 1742. By R. Proud. 2 vols. 8vo. Phila. 1797–8.

Still useful.

3649. History of Virginia from its first settlement to the present day. By J. Burk. 3 vols. 8vo. St. Petersburg (Va.) 1804–5.

Written under strong democratic bias ; but the author had access to records some of which are now lost and the book contains valuable appendices.

3650. Complete history of Connecticut, civil and ecclesiastical, from the emigration of the first planters . . . to the close of the Indian wars. By B. Trumbull. 2 vols. 4to. New Haven (U.S.A.) 1818.

Still useful.

3651. History of the United States. By G. Bancroft. 10 vols. 8vo. Boston. 1834–74. Later ed. 6 vols. 8vo. N.Y. 1883–5.

Ed. of 1885 the author's last revision.

3652. History of Maryland, 1633–60. By J. L. Bozman. 2 vols. 8vo. Baltimore. 1837.

Based throughout on first-hand authority. Cf. J. Macsherry, The history of Maryland from its first settlement in 1634 . . . 1648. 12mo. Baltimore. 1849. Ed. and contd. by B. B. James, 8vo. Baltimore. 1904.

3653. History of New Netherland or New York under the Dutch. By E. B. O'Callaghan. 2 vols. 8vo. N.Y. 1845–8.

3654. League of the Ho-de-No-San-nee or Iroquois. By L. H. Morgan. 1 vol. 8vo. Rochester (U.S.A.) 1851. Later ed. 2 vols. 8vo. N.Y. 1902. Ed. by H. M. Lloyd.

A standard work.

3655. History of the Society of Friends in America. By J. Bowden. 2 vols. 8vo. Lond. 1851–4 and 1861.

3656. History of the state of New York, 1609–91. By J. R. Brodhead. 2 vols. 8vo. N.Y. 1853–71.

Still a standard book.

3657. History of Virginia. By R. Beverly. Repr. from the author's 2nd rev. ed. of 1727, with an introd. by C. Campbell. 8vo. Richmond (Va.) 1855.

The history comes down to 1707 and is still a standard authority.

3658. The ecclesiastical history of New England ; comprising not only religious but also moral and other relations. By J. B. Felt. 2 vols. 8vo. Boston (Mass.) 1855–62.

3659. A history of the Presbyterian church in America, from its origin until the year 1760. By R. Webster. 1 vol. 8vo. Phila. 1857.

Cf. E. H. Gillett, History of the Presbyterian church in the United States of America. 2 vols. 12mo. Phila. 1864. Later ed. 2 vols. 12mo. Phila. 1873.

3660. History of North Carolina. By F. L. Hawks. 3 vols. 8vo. Fayetteville (N.C.) 1857–8.

Vol. i deals with the Roanoke settlement, 1584–91. Vol. ii covers the proprietary period, 1663–1729, and contains many original documents.

3661. History of New England during the Stuart dynasty. By J. G. Palfrey 3 vols. 8vo. Boston (Mass.) 1858–64.

Contains much documentary matter in its notes. Continued in History of New England from the Revolution of the 17th century to the Revolution of the 18th century. 2 vols. 8vo. Boston (Mass.) 1875–90.

3662. History of the state of Rhode Island, 1636–1790. By S. G. Arnold. 2 vols. 8vo. N.Y. 1859–60.

The standard history of Rhode Island.

3663. Count Frontenac and New France under Louis XIV. By F. Parkman. 8vo. Boston. 1877. Numerous subsequent eds. in U.S.A. and in England.

3664. The history of the American episcopal church [1587–1883]. By W. S. Perry. 2 vols. Boston (Mass.) 1885.

3665. The English in America. By J. A. Doyle. 3 vols. 8vo. Lond. 1882, 1887.

Vol. i deals with Virginia ; ii and iii with the Puritan colonies.

3666. Narrative and critical history of America. By J. Winsor. 8 vols. Boston. 1884–9.

Much bibliographical material.

3667. Introduction to the local constitutional history of the United States. By G. E. Howard. Johns Hopkins Univ. Studies, extra vols. 4. 8vo. Baltimore. 1889.

Maintains with much learning the Germanic origin of the township, hundred, and shire.

3668. Sir Ferdinando Gorges and his province of Maine. By J. P. Baxter. 3 vols. 4to. Boston. 1890.

An exhaustive study of an Elizabethan adventurer born some thirty years too late.

3669. The genesis of the United States. By A. Brown. 2 vols. 8vo. Lond. 1890.

A narrative of the history of Virginia, 1605–16, set forth by new MS. material. Continued to 1625 in his : The first republic in America. 1 vol. 8vo. Boston. 1898.

3670. Economic and social history of New England, 1620–1789. By W. B. Weeden. 2 vols. 8vo. Boston. 1890.

The greater part of vol. i deals with the Stuart period.

3671. The American race. By D. G. Brinton. 1 vol. 8vo. N.Y. 1891.

A work of great learning, but discursive and unsatisfactory by reason of omissions.

3672. Three episodes of Massachusetts history : the settlement of Boston Bay, the Antimonian controversy, a study of church and town government. By C. F. Adams. 2 vols. 8vo. Boston. 1892.

A vivid study of the New England character.

3673. The discovery of America. By J. Fiske. 2 vols. Boston. 1892.

Cf. the same writer's Old Virginia and her neighbours [2 vols. 1897] ; The beginnings of New England [1 vol. 8vo. Boston. 1889] ; The Dutch and Quaker colonies in America [2 vols. 8vo. Boston. 1899].

3674. A half-century of conflict. By F. Parkman. 2 vols. 8vo. Boston. 1892. Many subsequent eds., both in U.S.A. and in England.

The first portion of the first volume belongs to the period before 1715.

3675. Massachusetts, its historians and its history. By C. F. Adams. 1 vol. 8vo. Boston and N.Y. 1893.

A trenchant indictment of the pious New England view of the past history.

3676. Cartier to Frontenac. By J. Winsor. 1 vol. 8vo. Boston. 1894.

An account of geographical discovery in the interior of North America in its historical relations, 1534–1700. Cf. his : The Mississippi basin and the struggle in America between England and France, 1697–1763. 1 vol. 8vo. Boston. 1895.

3677. A history of the congregational churches in the United States. By W. Walker. 1 vol. 8vo. N.Y. 1894.

3678. Economic history of Virginia in the seventeenth century. By P. A. Bruce. 2 vols. 8vo. Lond. 1896 and 1907.

A most elaborate and careful work, based on an immense amount of MS. material. Cf. his : Social life of Virginia in the seventeenth century [1 vol. 8vo. Richmond (Va.) 1907], and Institutional history of Virginia in the seventeenth century [2 vols. 8vo. N.Y. and Lond. 1910]. All three are valuable.

3679. The suppression of the African slave trade to the United States of America, 1638–1870. By W. E. B. Du Bois. 1 vol. 8vo. Camb. (Mass.) 1896 and 1916.

3680. The beginners of a nation. By E. Eggleston. 1 vol. 8vo. N.Y. 1896. Maps.

Cf. his : The transit of civilization from England to America. 1 vol. 8vo. N.Y. 1901.

3681. History of South Carolina under the proprietory government, 1670–1719. By E. McCrady. 1 vol. 8vo. N.Y. and Lond. 1897.

An earlier work is : J. W. Rivers, Sketch of the history of South Carolina. 1 vol. 8vo. Charleston. 1856.

3682. The provincial governor in the English colonies of North America. By E. B. Greene. 1 vol. 8vo. Harvard Hist. Studies. Camb. 1898.

3683. A history of the Baptists in the middle states. By H. C. Vedder. 1 vol. 8vo. Phila. 1898.

3684. History of Quaker government in Pennsylvania. By I. Sharpless. 2 vols. 8vo. Phila. 1898–9.

3685. Maryland as a proprietary province. By N. D. Mereness. 8vo. N.Y. and Lond. 1901.

3686. The Anglican episcopate and the American colonies. By A. L. Cross. 1 vol. 8vo. N.Y. 1902. Bibl.

3687. New Jersey as a colony and as a state. By F. B. Lee. 4 vols. N.Y. 1902.

3688. Rhode Island, its making and meaning [1636–83]. By I. B. Richman. 2 vols. 8vo. N.Y. 1902. 2 vols. in 1. 1907.

There is an elaborate bibliography by C. S. Brigham in E. Field's State of Rhode Island, and publ. separately 1902.

3689. A history of the United States. By E. Channing. 6 vols. 8vo. N.Y. 1903– . In progress.

Vol. i, 1000–1660 ; ii, 1660–1760.

3690. The beginnings of Maryland. By B. C. Steiner. Johns Hopkins Univ. Studies in Hist., series xxi, No. 8–10. Baltimore. 1903.

The first attempt to trace minutely the beginnings of Maryland since the publication of the archives.

3691. The Cambridge modern history. Vol. vii. The United States. Ed. by Sir A. W. Ward and others. 1 vol. 8vo. Camb. 1903.

Has useful lists of authorities.

3692. Colonial self-Government, 1652–1689. By C. M. Andrews. The American nation, vol. v. 1 vol. 8vo. N.Y. and Lond. 1904. Maps. Bibl.

An admirable introduction to more detailed history. The previous vol. in this series is : England and America, 1580–1652. By L. G. Tyler.

3693. Basis of American history. By L. Farrand. The American nation, vol. iv. 8vo. N.Y. and Lond. 1904. Bibl.

The chapters on the distribution of the Indians describe the different geographical groups and the Indian characters, life, business, and religion.

3694. The American colonies in the seventeenth century. By H. L. Osgood. 3 vols. 8vo. N.Y. 1904–7.

Valuable especially for institutional and religious history. The colonies are grouped institutionally. Continued in his : The American Colonies in the eighteenth century. 4 vols. 8vo. N.Y. 1924.

3695. Provincial America, 1690–1740. By E. B. Greene. The American nation, vol. vi. 8vo. N.Y. and Lond. 1905.

Deals mainly with the general imperial British system in connexion with the economic and social life of the time. Has a very useful selected bibliography.

3696. France in America, 1497–1763. By R. G. Thwaites. The American nation, vol. vii. 8vo. N.Y. and Lond. 1905. Maps.

Deals with the relations of New France and the New England states.

3697. The origins of the British colonial system, 1578–1660. By G. L. Beer. 1 vol. 8vo. N.Y. 1908 and 1922.

The work is based throughout on material in the P.R.O., and is of special value on the economic side. Continued in his : The old colonial system, 2 vols. 8vo. N.Y. 1912 ; and The commercial policy of England towards the American colonies. Columbia Univ. Studies in History, vol. iii, 1893.

3698. A documentary history of American industrial society. Vol. i and ii. Plantation and frontier. Ed. by J. R. Commons and U. B. Phillips. 11 vols. 8vo. Cleveland (Ohio) 1910–11.

3699. The public life of Joseph Dudley. A study of the colonial policy of the Stuarts in New England, 1660–1715. By E. Kimball. 1 vol. 8vo. N.Y. and Lond. 1911.

3700. Maryland under the Commonwealth. Johns Hopkins Univ. Studies, xxix. 1911. By B. C. Steiner.

3701. The first explorations of the trans-Allegheny region by the Virginians, 1650–74. By C. W. Alvord and L. Bidgood. 1 vol. 8vo. Cleveland. 1912. Map. Facsimiles.
Establishes by original documents the claim of the English explorers to the discovery of that region. A scholarly introduction.

3702. Daniel Gookin, 1612–1687, assistant and major-general of the Massachusetts Bay Company. By F. W. Gookin. 1 vol. 8vo. Chicago. 1912.

3703. The relations of Pennsylvania with the British government, 1696–1765. By W. T. Root. 8vo. Phila. 1912.
A careful and able study of colonial conditions in relation to the British executive and parliaments. Contains a valuable bibliographical note.

3704. Cyclopedia of American Government. By A. C. McLaughlin and A. B. Hart. 3 vols. N.Y. 1913. Many Bibls.

3705. Virginia under the Stuarts. By T. J. Wertenbaker. 1 vol. 8vo. Princeton. 1914.
Cf. his : The planters of colonial Virginia, 1 vol. 8vo. Princeton. 1922.

3706. Beginnings of the American people. By C. L. Becker. 1 vol. 8vo. Boston and N.Y. 1915.

3707. History of domestic and foreign commerce of the United States. Ed. by E. R. Johnson. 2 vols. 8vo. Washington. 1915.

3708. Household manufactures in the United States, 1640–1860. By R. M. Tryon. 1 vol. 8vo. Chicago. 1917.
Other works are : J. L. Bishop, History of American manufactures from 1608 to 1860 [2 vols. Phila. 1861–4], and V. S. Clark, History of manufactures in the United States, 1607–1860. With a bibl. [8vo. Washington, 1916].

3709. The pilgrims and their history. By R. G. Usher. 1 vol. 8vo. N.Y. 1918. Facs.
For other similar works see No. 3588.

3710. The quit-rent system in the American colonies. By B. W. Bond. 1 vol. 8vo. New Haven. 1919. Bibl.

3711. The founding of New England. By J. T. Adams. 1 vol. 8vo. Boston. 1921. Illus.
Continued in his Revolutionary New England, 1691–1776. Port. and Facs. 1 vol. 8vo. Boston. 1923.

3712. Pioneers of the old south. By M. Johnston. The Chronicles of American series. 8vo. New Haven. 1921.

3713. The frontier in American history. By F. J. Turner. 1 vol. 8vo. N.Y. 1921.

Has a study of the first official frontier of the Massachusetts Bay.

3714. The foundations of American nationality [to 1789]. By E. B. Greene. 1 vol. 8vo. N.Y. 1922. Illus.

3715. The dominion of New England. A study in British colonial policy. By V. F. Barnes. 1 vol. 8vo. New Haven. 1923. Bibl.

3716. Colonial background to the American Revolution. By C. M. Andrews. 1 vol. 8vo. Yale Univ. Press. 1924.

¶ 3. EAST INDIES

(*a*) Bibliographies, Guides, and Sources.
(*b*) Later Works.

The following bibliography is limited to the English in India, and the activities of the East India Company during the seventeenth century, though a few books are included which throw light on the condition of India during that period. The great Dutch collections of documents have been omitted, but reference may be made to W. H. Moreland, Dutch Sources for Indian History (3727) and note. The travel section includes only the English travellers ; and for such wide voyagers as Peter Mundy (3512) reference must be made to the general section on Voyages. Some light on the English in India may be gained from foreign travellers such as J. B. Tavernier's Travels in India [ed. Bell. London. 1889. 2 vols.], and for a survey of such works see E. F. Oaten, European Travellers in India (3773). Indian historians may be approached through H. M. Eliott, The History of India as told by its own Historians (3719). The mass of pamphlets called forth by the struggle between the two companies at the end of the century has never been adequately catalogued, but useful lists will be found in the bibliography and footnotes to W. R. Scott's Joint Stock Companies to 1720 (1928), in the B. M. Printed Catalogue *sub* E. I. Trade, and E. I. Company, and in the Catalogue of the Library of the Hon. E. I. C. (3717) *sub* Tracts : a representative selection has been included below. The recent development of historical research in India on the part of Indian students is reflected in the institution of Historical series by some of the Universities and of the Journal of Indian History [1919 onwards]. There is an Indian Historical Records Commission, with annual Proceedings, while the annual reports of the Indian Archaeological Survey also yield gleanings. The Journals of the Royal Asiatic Society of Great Britain [Index vols., vol. xx, pt. iv, Lond. 1888 ; and Index 1889–1903, Lond. 1904], and of its affiliated societies, the Bengal branch, the Ceylon branch [Index to Nos. 1–41, 1845–1890, by J. F. W. Gore, Colombo, 1895], and the Straits Branch [Index to Nos. 1–50, 1878–1908, by W. D. Barnes, Singapore, 1909] occasionally afford matter.

The bulk of the MS. records in England are in the India office [see W. Foster's guide (3723)] ; they are now made available by two series of current Calendars, E. B. Sainsbury's Calendar of Court Minutes (3771), and W.

Foster's English Factories in India (3770), which is a continuation in calendar form of the letters received by the E.I.C. from its servants in the East (3763). Documents in the P.R.O. were formerly dealt with in separate Calendars, but are now included in the India Office series of MSS. still preserved in India ; those at Madras are the most accessible in print, see H. Dodwell's Report (3718 n), and the extensive publication commenced in 1910 under title Records of Fort St. George (3774). For Bombay there is A. F. Kindersley's Handbook (3725), and G. W. Forrest's Selections from the State Papers preserved in the Bombay Secretariat (3757). The MSS. at Calcutta are of comparatively small importance for the 17th century. For St. Helena see H. R. Janisch's Extracts (3756). Lastly, Mr. John Murray's Indian Records Series should be noticed.

(a) BIBLIOGRAPHIES, GUIDES, AND SOURCES

3717. A catalogue of the library of the Hon. East-India Company. 2 vols. 8vo. Lond. 1845–51.

Vol. ii is : A supplement to the catalogue . . . Notes many pamphlets.

3718. Handbook to the Madras records, being a report on the public records preserved in the Madras Government Office previous to 1834. By J. T. Wheeler. 1 vol. 8vo. Madras. 1861.

Cf. H. Dodwell's Report. 1 vol. Madras. 1916.

3719. The history of India as told by its own historians. The Muhammadan period. Ed. from the posthumous papers of Sir H. M. Elliot. Ed. by J. Dowson. 8 vols. 8vo. Lond. 1867–77.

Gives some guidance to the native historians of India. First projected as Bibliographical Index to the historians on Mohammedan India. [1 vol. only, 1849.]

3720. Report on the miscellaneous old records of the India Office, November 1, 1878. By Sir G. C. M. Birdwood. 1 vol. fol. Lond. Maps. For private use. Later eds. 1890, 1891.

Contains Note on the discovery of the passage to India by the Cape of Good Hope, and on the early settlements of the European nations in the eastern seas.

3721. Press list of India Office records from the earliest date to 1630, including also notices of all documents extant in India for the same period. 1 vol. fol. s.l. 1891.

3722. List of marine records of the late East India Company, preserved in the Record Department of the India Office. Ed. by F. C. Danvers. 1 vol. fol. Lond. 1895.

Lists of ships' journals, logs, and other miscellaneous papers. Useful introduction.

3723. A guide to the India Office records, 1600–1858. By W. Foster. 1 vol. 8vo. Lond. 1919.

Valuable introduction on the record system, calendars, guides, press-lists, &c. For 17th-century records see the press-lists of the Factory records [1897].

3724. Proceedings of the [first] meeting of the Indian Historical Records Commission . . . In progress, annual volume. fol. Calcutta. 1919– .

3725. A handbook of the Bombay Government records. By A. F. Kindersley. 1 vol. 8vo. Bombay. 1921.

See G. W. Forrest Alphabetical catalogue of the contents of the Bombay Secretarial records (1630–1780) [Bombay 1887] ; contains little of 17th century.

3726. Sources for the history of British India in the seventeenth century. By Shafaat Ahmad Khan. 1 vol. 8vo. Bombay. 1926.

A bibliography of Documents in the British Museum, the Public Record Office, Chancery Lane, the Bodleian Library, All Souls College, the India Office, the Guildhall Library, the Archiepiscopal Library at Lambeth, the Privy Council Registers, and the Indian Record Offices ; the last Section is less complete than the others.

3727. Dutch sources for Indian history, 1590 to 1650. By W. H. Moreland. Journal of Indian History, No. 5, 1923, pp. 222–32. Bibl.

See Journal of Asiatic Society of Gt. Britain, vol. i, O.S., 345, 353, for Materials for an account of the Dutch in India.

3728. A true and large discourse of the voyage of the whole fleete of ships set forth the 20 of April 1601 . . . wherein is set doune the order and manner of their trafficke. 1 vol. 4to. Lond. 1603.

See also A letter . . . to the governors and assistants of the East India merchants in London, containing the estate of the East Indian fleete . . . [London 1603] ; and C. R. Markham, The voyages of Sir James Lancaster (3753).

3729. The last East-Indian voyage. 1 vol. 4to. Lond. 1606. Later ed. 1 vol. 8vo. Lond. 1855. Maps. Plans. Illus. Bibl. Ed. by B. Corney.

Ed. of 1855, Hakluyt Soc., Series I, vol. xix, is entitled : The voyage of Sir Henry Middleton to Bantam. It is the second voyage of the East India Company, and the only East-Indian voyage of the 17th century of which a separate narrative was published. See Purchas, Pt. 1 (3450).

3730. A letter of instructions from the East Indian Company to its agent, circ. 1614. Ed. by W. G. Maxwell, in Journal of the Straits Branch of the Royal Asiatic Society [No. 54], pp. 63–98 [Singapore. 1910].

Prints in full, with geographical annotations, B.M. Cotton MS. Otho E. VIII, ff. 231–40.

3731. A true relation of the unjust cruel and barbarous proceedings against the English at Amboyna. . . . 1 vol. 4to. Lond. 1624. Illus.

Contains also the Dutch ' True declaration . . .', and the E.I.C. reply. See Churchill, Collection of voyages, vol. viii, p. 277 (3454). For the various editions, and corresponding Dutch pamphlets, see B.M. Catalogue of printed books, *sub* Amboyna. For criticism of these documents see W. W. Hunter, History of British India, vol. i, ch. x (3789).

3732. A remonstrance . . . of the directors of the Netherlands East India Company . . . touching . . . Amboyna. Together with the acts of processe, against the said English. And the reply of the English East India Company. . . . 1 vol. 4to. Lond. 1632.

Sub-title to the Acts of processe : ' An authentick copy of the confessions & sentences against Mr. Towerson.' See Churchill, Collection of voyages, vol. viii, p. 313 (3454).

3733. An East India colation ; or, A discourse of travels ; set forth in sundry observations, briefe and delightfull ; collected by the author in a voyage

he made unto the East Indies, of almost foure yeares continuance. By F. C.
1 vol. 12mo. Lond. 1633.

Voyage of March 1614 with Capt. Nicholas Downton.

3734. A voyage to East India. By E. Terry. 1 vol. 8vo. Lond. 1655. Maps.
Ports. Later ed. 1777.

Terry was chaplain to Sir T. Roe. See E. Havers's translation of Della Valle's Travels
[1665]; Purchas (pt. 2), Hakluyt Soc., Series II, vol. i, for bibliographical information.

3735. A relation of the retaking of the Island of St. Helena, and three Dutch
East India ships. Anon. 1 vol. fol. Lond. 1673.

Repr. Arber's English garner : Voyages and travels, vol. ii, p. 431 (3468).

3736. The East India trade a most profitable trade to this kingdom. 1 vol.
Lond. 1677. Later ed. 1 vol. 4to. Lond. 1690.

Written at instance of T. Papillon ; ed. of 1690 is ' A treatise concerning the East India
trade : being a most profitable . . .' Mercantilist reply to attacks such as : Two letters
concerning the East India Company [1676]. Compare an answer to two letters concerning the E. I. C. [1676].

3737. A treatise wherein is demonstrated : I. That the East India trade
is the most national of all foreign trades. II. That the clamours . . . against the
present East India Company are sinister. . . . By Philopatris pseud. [i. e.
Josiah Child]. 1 vol. 4to. Lond. 1681. Later ed. 1689 [2 editions].

Repr. Somers Tracts, viii. 455 (90). One ed., 1689, is an abstract entitled ' A discourse concerning trade, and that in particular of the East Indies : the other is : A supplement, 1689, to a former treatise. . . . See the reply : A discourse concerning the
East India trade in Somers Tracts, x. 634. Compare (1) Companies in joynt-stock unnecessary and inconvenient . . . [Lond. 1691] ; (2) A regulated company more material
than a joint-stock in the East India trade . . . [Lond.? 1700]. See also Child's New
discourse of trade (1860).

3738. The allegations of the Turky Company . . . against the East India
Company relating to the management of the trade . . . 1 vol. fol. Lond. 1681.

See Answer of the East India Company to the allegations of the Turky Company
[1681].

3739. An historical relation of the island Ceylon in the East Indies : together with an account of the detaining in captivity the author and divers of
the Englishmen now living there, and of the author's miraculous escape. By
R. Knox. 1 vol. fol. Lond. 1681. Maps. Illus. Later ed. 1 vol. 8vo. Glasgow.
1911. Ed. by J. Ryan.

Ed. of 1911 also contains Knox's autobiography [MS. Bod. Lib. Fol. A 623] ? The
first account of Ceylon in the English language.

3740. The argument of the lord chief justice . . . concerning the great case
of monopolies between the East India Company . . . and Thomas Sandys . . .
1 vol. fol. Lond. 1689.

For Sandys' case see Cobbett, State trials (566), x. 372–554.

3741. An account of some transactions in . . . the House of Commons and
before the Privy Council . . . relating to the East India Company. 1693.
Somers Tracts, x. 618.

See also : (1) A collection of debates and proceedings in Parliament in 1694 and 1695 upon the inquiry into the late briberies, and, Supplement to ... [Lond. 1695]. (2) The examinations and informations upon oath of Sir Thomas Cooke ... [Lond. 1695]. (3) Abstract of proceedings in the House of Commons in relation to the East India Company and trade [Lond. 1698].

3742. A voyage to Suratt, in the year 1689 ... likewise a description of Madeira, St. Jago. ... By J. Ovington. 1 vol. 8vo. Lond. 1696. Plans.

Ovington also published : An essay upon the nature and qualities of tea ... [Lond. 1699].

3743. An essay on the East-India-Trade. By the author of the Essay upon wayes and means. By C. Davenant. 1 vol. 8vo. Lond. 1696.

Repr. in Davenant's Discourses on the publick revenues ... [1698], and political and commercial works [Lond. 1771], vol. i (1888). Provoked in reply : (1) An answer to a late tract entituled ... [Lond. 1697]. (2) England and East India inconsistent in their manufactures, being an answer ... [Lond. 1697]. (3) Some reflections on a pamphlet ... [Lond. 1696]. (4) S.T., a weaver in London, Reasons humbly offered for having a bill for the hindering the home consumption of the East India silks ... and an answer [Lond. 1697].
See also : (1) S.T., The profit and loss of the East India trade stated [Lond. 1700]. (2) C. N., a weaver of London. The great necessity and advantage of preserving our own manufactures [Lond. 1697]. (3) Some reflections on a pamphlet entituled, England and East India inconsistent in their manufactures [Lond. 1696].

3744. A new account of East-India and Persia, in eight letters, being nine years travels, begun 1672, and finished 1681. By J. Fryer. 1 vol. fol. Lond. 1698. Maps. Plans. Ports. Later ed. 3 vols. 8vo. Lond. 1909–15. Maps. Plans. Ports. Bib. Ed. by W. Crooke.

The 1909 ed. printed for the Hakluyt Soc., Series II, vols. xix, xx, xxxix.

3745. The case of William Kaling, chief of the factory at Tonqueen in China, belonging to the old East India Company. ... 1 vol. fol. Lond. ?1698.

The closing of the factory at Tonquin.

3746. A true relation of what passed between the English company trading to the East Indies, and the governor and company of merchants trading to the East Indies, touching an agreement between both companies. 1 vol. fol. Lond. ?1699.

Story continued in ' An account of what passed in the treaty between the old and new East India Companies, towards an agreement ' [Lond. ?1699]. See also : (1) A letter from a gentleman to an East India merchant [concerning a union of the Companies] [Lond. 1698]. (2) John Toland, Propositions for uniting the two East India Companies. ... [Lond. 1701].

3747. Considerations upon the East India trade. By [D. North]. 1 vol. 8vo. Lond. 1701. Later eds. 1720 and 1856.

Sometimes attributed to W. Martin. Repr. 1720 under title : ' The advantages of the East India trade to England consider'd. ... ' Included in A select collection ... of English tracts [1856].

3748. An account of the trade in India ... with descriptions of Fort St. George, Acheen. ... By C. Lockyer. 1 vol. 8vo. Lond. 1711.

Practical advice to traders and journal of a voyage ' from Canton in China to Gombroom in Persia ',

3749. Belga-Britannus ; or the Hollander always in the English interest . . . to which is added, the affair of Amboyna set in a true light by one that lived on the spot, in answer to a pamphlet called Dutch alliances, &c. . . . By A. Van Golt.   1 vol. 2 pts. 8vo. Lond. 1712.

3750. A voyage to and from the island of Borneo . . . with a description of the re-establishment of the English trade there on . . . 1714 . . . By D. Beeckman.   1 vol. 8vo. Lond. 1718.   Maps.

See Pinkerton, vol. ii (3465).

3751. A new account of the East Indies, being the observations and remarks of Capt. Alexander Hamilton, who spent his time there from the year 1658 to 1723. . . . By A. Hamilton.   2 vols. 8vo. Edin. 1727.

See Pinkerton, vol. viii (3465).

3752. Memorials of the empire of Japan in the sixteenth and seventeenth centuries.   Ed. by T. Rundall.   1 vol. 8vo. Lond. 1850.   Maps.

Part II.   The letters of William Adams, 1611 to 1617.   Printed for the Hakluyt Soc., Series I, vol. viii, from MSS. in India Office.

3753. The voyage of Sir James Lancaster, Kt. to the East Indies, with abstracts of journals of voyages to the East Indies, during the seventeenth century, preserved in the India Office, and the voyage of Captain John Knight (1606) to seek the North-West passage.   Ed. by C. R. Markham.   1 vol. 8vo. Lond. 1877.

Pr. for the Hakluyt Soc., Series I, vol. lvi, from Purchas, and from MSS. in the India Office, of which an account is given in the Introd.   See Purchas, Pt. 1.

3754. Early records of British India : a history of the English settlements in India, as told in the government records, the works of the old travellers. . . . By J. T. Wheeler.   1 vol. 8vo. Lond. 1878.

Preface explains destruction of early Calcutta records in storm of 1737.

3755. Diary of Richard Cocks, Cape merchant in the English factory in Japan 1615–22, with correspondence.   Ed. by E. M. Thompson.   2 vols. 8vo. Lond. 1883.

Pr. for the Hakluyt Soc., Series I, vols. lxvi and lxvii, from B.M. Add MSS. 31300, 31301.   See Astley, vol. i (3458), Purchas, Pt. 1 (3450).

3756. Extracts from the St. Helena records. . . . By H. R. Janisch.   Ed. by B. Grant.   1 vol. 8vo. St. Helena. 1885.

See also E. L. Jackson, St. Helena (3790) for more particulars of these records.

3757. Selections from the letters, despatches, and other state papers, preserved in the Bombay Secretariat. . . . Ed. by G. W. Forrest.   4 vols. 4to. Bombay. 1885–99.

Maratha Series, 1 vol., contains 18th-century papers.   Homes Series, 2 vols. vol. i, contains 17th-century papers ; vol. iv, index.

3758. The dawn of British trade to the East Indies as recorded in the court minutes of the East India Company, 1599–1603.   Containing an account of . . .

Waymouth's voyage in search of the North-West passage. . . . By H. Stevens. I vol. 8vo. Lond. 1886.

A verbatim reprint of the first Court book of the E.I.C. [MS. in India Office], with an introduction by G. Birdwood. For Waymouth's Journal see Purchas.

3759. The diary of William Hedges, Esq. . . . during his agency in Bengal ; as well as on his voyage out and return overland [1681–87]. By W. Hedges. Ed. by R. F. Barlow and H. Tule. 3 vols. 8vo. Lond. 1887–9. Maps. Ports.

Pr. for the Hakluyt Soc., Series I, vols. lxxiv, lxxv, lxxviii. Vol. i contains the diary, vols. ii and iii illustrative extracts from unpublished records. MSS. of diary in India Office.

3760. The register of letters, &c. of the governors and company of merchants of London trading into the East Indies, 1600–1619. Ed. by G. Birdwood and W. Foster. I vol. 8vo. Lond. 1893.

The first letter-book of the E.I.C. MS. in India Office.

3761. Selections from the consultations of the agent governor and council of Fort St. George. . . . Ed. by A. T. Pringle. 5 vols. 8vo. Madras. 1893–5.

Continued (vol. ii) under title : The diary and consultation book of the . . . Vol. i contains selections, vols. ii–v are verbatim (1681–5). For period 1670–80 see Extracts from the government records in Fort St. George (Madras. 1871).

3762. The early annals of the English in Bengal, being the Bengal Public consultations for the first half of the eighteenth century. . . . By C. R. Wilson. 3 vols. 8vo. Lond., Calcutta. 1895–1917. Maps.

Vol. i contains extracts from the Bengal consultation books, 1704–10 (MS. in India Office), and from Governor Thomas Pitt's correspondence. Narrative introduction of the early period.

3763. Letters received by the East India Company from its servants in the east. . . . Ed. by F. C. Danvers [vol. i] and W. Foster [vols. ii to vi]. 6 vols. 8vo. Lond. 1896–1902.

Transmitted from an ' Original correspondence ' series of the India Office records, 1602–17.

3764. Charters relating to the East India Company from 1600 to 1761. . . . Ed. by J. Shaw. I vol. 4to. Madras. 1887.

Repr. with preface and additions from an earlier collection ; Charters granted to the East India Company . . . [Madras ?1774]. Preface explains that the original documents have disappeared.

3765. The embassy of Sir Thomas Roe to the court of the Great Mogul, 1615–19. . . . By T. Roe. Ed. by W. Foster. 2 vols. 8vo. Lond. 1899. Maps. Ports.

Roe's journal, letters, and other documents. Hakluyt Soc., Series II, vols. i and ii. B.M. Add. MSS. 6115, 19277. For bibliography of voyage see Introd. lxiii–lxviii. See Purchas, Pt. I (3450); Harris, vol. i (3454); Churchill, vol. i (3453); Pinkerton, vol. viii (3465).

3766. The voyage of Captain John Saris to Japan 1613. . . . By J. Saris. Ed. by E. M. Satow. I vol. 8vo. Lond. 1900. Maps. Ports.

Pr. for the Hakluyt Soc., Series II, vol. v. MS. in India Office, Marine Records, No. xiv. For further documents see Riess (3800).

3767. The journal of John Jourdain, 1608–1617, describing his experiences in Arabia, India, and the Malay Archipelago. Ed. by W. Foster. 1 vol. 8vo. Camb. 1905. Maps. Bibl.

Pr. for the Hakluyt Soc., Series II, vol. xvi. B.M. Sloane MS. 858.

3768. A geographical account of countries round the Bay of Bengal, 1669 to 1679. By T. Bowrey. Ed. by R. C. Temple. 1 vol. 8vo. Camb. 1905. Maps. Illus. Bibl.

Printed for the Hakluyt Soc., Series II, vol. xii. MS. in the possession of Mr. Eliot Howard.

3769. Old Fort William in Bengal. A selection of official documents dealing with its history. By C. Wilson. 2 vols. 8vo. Lond. 1906. Plan. Ports.

John Murray's Indian Records Series.

3770. The English factories in India . . . a calendar of documents in the India Office, British Museum, and Public Record Office. Ed. by W. Foster. 8vo. Oxf. 1906–   . In progress.

Continues the series ' Letters received by the E.I.C.' (3763) in calendar form from 1618.

3771. A calendar of the court minutes, &c. of the East India Company . . . Ed. by E. B. Sainsbury. 8vo. Oxf. 1907–   . In progress.

Intro. and notes by W. Foster. In addition to court minutes contains abstracts of documents in East Indies series at P.R.O. and references to Indian affairs in S.P. Dom. For court minutes before 1835 see Calendar S.P. East Indies.

3772. Relics of the honourable East India Company. By W. Griggs and G. Birdwood. 1 vol. fol. Lond. 1909. Map. Illus.

Facsimile reproductions of early documents : plan of Bombay harbour in 1626.

3773. European travellers in India during the fifteenth, sixteenth, and seventeenth centuries : the evidence afforded by them with respect to Indian social institutions, and the nature and influence of Indian Governments. By E. F. Oaten. 1 vol. 8vo. Lond. 1909.   Bibl.

See Camb. Hist. of Eng. Lit. xiv, p. 331, for article by same writer on Anglo-Indian literature.

3774. Records of Fort St. George . . . Ed. H. Dodwell. fol. Madras. 1910–   . In progress.

Systematic publication of Madras records *in extenso*. The following are the series for the 17th century : (1) Consultations, 1672–81, 1686–94. (2) Despatches from England, 1670–7, 1680–6. (3) Despatches to England, 1694–6. (4) Letters from Fort St. George to subordinate factories, 1679, 1688, 1689, 1697. (5) Letters to Fort St. George from ditto, 1681–2, 1684–5, 1686–7, 1688. (6) Sundry books, 1677–8, 1680–1, 1686. There are also miscellaneous volumes and a Dutch series, Press lists of ancient documents in Fort St. George, 47 vols. (1891–1910), may be consulted.

3775. The diaries of Streynsham Master, 1675–1680, and other contemporary papers relating thereto. Ed. by R. C. Temple. 2 vols. 8vo. Lond. 1911. Map. Ports.

John Murray's Indian Records Series. MS. in India Office. Records of journeys of inspection for E.I.C.

3776. Vestiges of old Madras, 1640–1800. By H. D. Love. 4 vols. 8vo. Lond. 1913. Maps. Plans. Ports. Bibl.

John Murray's Indian Records Series. Vol. i contains 17th-century matter ; vol. iv, index.

3777. Early travels in India, 1583–1619. Ed. by W. Foster. 1 vol. 8vo. Oxf. 1921. Maps. Illus. Bibl.

Reprints travels of Fitch, Mildenhall, Hawkins, Finch, Wittington, Coryat, Terry, with intro.

3778. President Fremlen's Journal, 1638–39. By W. Foster. Journal of Indian History, No. 6, pp. 307–16.

Extracts from Journal of President of Surat, recently found among Orme MSS. at India Office. (For other 17th-century finds see Hill, Catalogue of Orme MSS., p. 55.)

(b) LATER WORKS

3779. Historical fragments of the Mogul empire, the Morrattoes, the English concerns in Industan from the year 1659. By R. Orme. 1 vol. 4to. Lond. 1782. Maps. Later ed. 1805.

The 1805 edition contains an additional essay : On the origin of the English establishment at . . . Broach and Surat.

3780. Annals of the honourable East-India Company from 1600 to 1707–8. By J. Bruce. 3 vols. 4to. Lond. 1810.

Bruce was historiographer to the H.E.I.C. and had charge of their official records. See J. Bruce, historiographer. By W. Foster. Scot. Hist. Rev. ix. 366.

3781. The history of European commerce with India. By D. Macpherson. 1 vol. 4to. Lond. 1812. Map.

3782. History of the Indian Archipelago. By J. Crawfurd. 3 vols. 8vo. Edin. 1820. Map. Illus.

Some remarks on Dutch and English in the Far East.

3783. A history of the Mahrathas. By J. G. Duff. 3 vols. 8vo. Lond. 1826. Maps. Illus.

The classical history of the Mahrathas based on materials, some of which have since disappeared.

3784. China. An outline of the . . . British and foreign embassies to, and intercourse with that empire. By P. Auber. 1 vol. 8vo. Lond. 1834.

Contains chapter on British intercourse with China.

3785. Historical record of the honourable East India Company's first Madras European regiment. . . . By ' Staff Officer ' (pseud.). 1 vol. 8vo. Lond. 1843. Plans. Ports.

Contains a few pages on the origins of the regiment in the 17th century. See H. Dodwell, Sepoy recruitment in the old Madras army (Calcutta. 1922).

3786. The English in Western India, being the history of the factory at Surat, of Bombay, and the subordinate factories on the western coast. By P. Anderson. 1 vol. 8vo. Lond. 1854.

3787. Madras in the olden time . . . compiled from original records. By J. T. Wheeler. 3 vols. 4to. Madras. 1861-2. Plan. MS. Facsimiles.

Vol. i deals with period 1639–1702, based on Madras records. For a modification of the early history see W. Foster, The Founding of Fort St. George [1 vol. 8vo. Lond. 1902].

3788. The Imperial Gazetteer of India. Ed. by W. W. Hunter. 9 vols. 8vo. 1881. Maps. Later eds.: 14 vols. 8vo. 1885–7. Maps. Ed. by W. W. Hunter. 25 vols. 8vo. Oxf. 1907–9. Maps. Ed. anon.

Hunter's article on India was revised and issued separately in 1893 as : The Indian empire : its peoples, history and products. Vol. ii of 1907 is historical ; vol. xxv, index ; vol. xxvi, atlas. There is also historical material in Gazetteer of the Bombay Presidency.

3789. A history of British India. By W. W. Hunter. 2 vols. 8vo. Lond. 1899–1900. Maps.

Vol. ii completed with bibliographical introduction by P. E. Roberts. The standard history of the period, based throughout on original material : vol. i to 1629 ; vol. ii, 1623–1708. Other histories are by : J. Mill [9 vols. 8vo. Lond. 1840–8, ed. by H. H. Wilson] ; J. T. Wheeler [1 vol. 8vo. Lond. 1886] ; B. Willson [called Ledger and Sword &c. 2 vols. 8vo. Lond. 1903. Map. Ports.] ; P. E. Roberts [2 vols. 8vo. Oxf. 1916. Maps] ; V. A. Smith [1 vol. 8vo. Oxf. 1919 and 1923. Maps. Plans. Ports. Bibl.].

3790. St. Helena : the historic island from its discovery to the present date. By E. L. Jackson. 1 vol. 8vo. Lond. 1903. Ports.

Contains a section on the St. Helena records, with excerpts and facsimiles.

3791. Charles I and the East India Company. By W. Foster. Eng. Hist. Rev. xix. 1904.

3792. Bombay in the making. Being mainly a history of the origin and growth of judicial institutions in the Western Presidency, 1661–1726. By P. B. M. Malabari. 1 vol. 8vo. Lond. 1910. Plan. Bibl.

3793. An English settlement in Madagascar in 1645–46. By W. Foster. Eng. Hist. Rev. xxviii. 1912.

3794. History of Aurangzib. Mainly based on Persian sources. By Jadunath Sarkar [Jadunātha Sarkār]. 8vo. Calcutta. 1912. In progress.

Introd. on authorities.

3795. Shivágí the Maráthá : his life and times. By H. G. Rawlinson. 1 vol. 8vo. Oxf. 1915. Map. Ports.

First English life of Shivagi : it is based on Indian chronicles and records. Useful bibliographical introduction, and survey of literature about the Marathas.

3796. The life of Thomas Pitt. By C. N. Dalton. 1 vol. 8vo. Camb. 1915. Plan. Ports.

See H. Yule, Documentary contributions to a biography of Thomas Pitt [Hakluyt Soc., Series I, vol. lxxviii. 1889].

3797. Keigwin's rebellion (1683–4). An episode in the history of Bombay. By R. and O. Strachey. 1 vol. 8vo. Oxf. 1916. Bibl. note.

3798. Akbar, the Great Mogul. 1542–1605. By V. A. Smith. 1 vol. 8vo. Oxf. 1917. Map. Plan. Ports. Bibl.

An important monograph with valuable critical bibliography, dealing with records written in Persian and Turkish, as well as European accounts.

3799. A history of the Maratha people. By C. A. Kincaid and Rao Bahadur D. B. Parasnis. 3 vols. 8vo. Bombay. 1918-1925. Ports.

Contains some reference to relations of Shivagi with the East India Company.

3800. History of the English factory at Hirado [1613–22], with an introductory chapter on the origin of English enterprise in the Far East. By L. Riess. Trans. of the Asiatic Soc. of Japan, vol. xxvi, pp. 1–114.

An appendix (pp. 163–218) contains original documents.

3801. British beginnings in Western India, 1579–1657. An account of the early days of the British factory of Surat. By H. G. Rawlinson. 1 vol. 8vo. Oxf. 1920. Map. Illus.

Contains appendix of documents.

3802. India at the death of Akbar. An economic study. By W. H. Moreland. 1 vol. 8vo. Lond. 1920. Maps. Bibl.

A careful study of the economic conditions of India at the time of the arrival of the E.I.C.

3803. Anglo-Portuguese negotiations relating to Bombay, 1660–1677. By Shafaat Ahmad Khan. 1 vol. 8vo. Oxf. Univ. Press (Indian Branch). 1922.

Repr. from Jour. of Indian History (Sept. 1922). Contains a list of pamphlets.

3804. From Akbar to Aurangzeb. A study in Indian economic history. By W. H. Moreland. 1 vol. 8vo. Lond. 1923. Maps. Bibl.

Valuable study of the economic reaction in India of the arrival of European trading companies.

3805. The East India trade in the seventeenth century, in its political and economic aspects. By Shafaat Ahmad Khan. 1 vol. 8vo. Oxf. 1903.

Deals only with the trade between India and England. Notes contain references to many contemporary pamphlets on East Indian trade.

3806. The East India House. Its history and associations. By W. Foster. 1 vol. 8vo. Lond. 1924. Plans. Ports.

See Foster's articles in Home Counties Magazine [Mar. and Sept. 1912] and his East India Company at Crosley House, 1621–1638 [London Topographical Records, vol. viii. 1913].

3807. The Chronicles of the East India Company trading to China, 1635–1834. By H. B. Morse. 4 vols. 8vo. Oxf. 1926. Illus.

¶ 4. WEST INDIES

(a) General Bibliography.
(b) General sources.
(c) General accounts.
(d) General monographs.
(e) Bahamas.
(f) Barbados.

(g) Bermudas.
(h) Jamaica.
(i) Leeward Islands.
(j) Surinam.
(k) Buccaneers.

The most important MSS. are in the P.R.O., and the Calendars of State Papers, Colonial [America and West Indies], give very useful précis. The various Guides to MSS. issued by the Carnegie Institution of Washington are valuable for MSS. in the P.R.O., the B.M., &c.: a special guide to West Indian archives is at present being prepared. The Acts P.C. (Colonial) and the Register P.C. Scotland give access to the Privy Council minutes: The Historical Manuscript Commission reports are now rendered much more useful by the general geographical index, but no collection in this series is of outstanding value for West Indian affairs. Thurloe's State Papers contain several West Indian letters. Pamphlets, &c. will be found reprinted in Purchas's Pilgrims, Arber's English Garner, Somers' Tracts, and the Harleian Miscellany. John Smith's True Travels should be consulted.

The Historical Reviews, and the Proceedings of various historical societies, repay examination; and the lesser-known journals, e.g. Journal of Negro History, the Proceedings of the American Jewish History Soc., and of the similar society in London, should not be neglected.

A number of bibliographies are included below: attention may be called to those issued by the Institute of Jamaica. A very scholarly bibliography is that by Jacques de Dampierre. Though it deals specifically with authorities for French colonization, the French and English plantations were so closely related that many of the early authorities are of common interest. Note must therefore be taken of S. L. Mim's Colbert's West Indian Policy [New Haven 1912], and the authorities he cites; while the French technical journals contain useful articles, some of which are noticed below W. Westergaard, The Danish West Indies under Company rule, 1671–1754 [N.Y. 1917], throws a little light on English colonies; while F. W. Pitman, The development of the British West Indies, 1700–1763 [New Haven 1917], has some valuable statistics.

The islands appear more or less inaccurately in the various printed maps of the West Indies. Maps of separate islands may often be discovered among the MS. collections. For maps of *Jamaica* see the excellent list in F. Cundall, Bibliographia Jamaicensis, pp. 65–76, and his note on cartography (with four reproductions of 17th-century maps from Spanish archives) in Jamaica under the Spaniards. For *St. Christopher* we have maps in du Tertre, Histoire generale (see below), and one published in 1696 by F. de Witt [Brit. Mus. Maps. 86 d. 10 (140)]. J. Thornton, Atlas Maritinus [1700], prints a map 'being an actual survey', scale 1 in. to a mile. *Antigua* also appears in Thornton's Atlas, while *Barbados* has a fine map in Ligne's History (see below). For general use Thomas Jeffrey, The West Indian Atlas [Lond. 1775], is good. Weather conditions are best studied in The West India Pilot [London : Admiralty publication].

For works on the Scottish expedition to Darien, see under Scotland.

(*a*) GENERAL BIBLIOGRAPHY

3808. Essai sur les sources de l'histoire des Antilles Françaises (1492–1664). By J. de Dampierre. 1 vol. 8vo. Paris. 1904.

Vol. vi of Mémoires et documents publiés par la Société de l'École des Chartes. Very detailed critical examination of the great 17th-century French writers, who are invaluable for the history of the English West Indies.

3809. Bibliography of the West Indies (excluding Jamaica). By F. Cundall. 1 vol. 8vo. Kingston, Jamaica. 1909. Later eds. (supplements) 1915 and 1919. Ed. F. Cundall.

Very useful : non-critical ; hand-list arranged in chronological order of publication under geographical headings. *Index nominum* refers also to Cundall, Bibliographia Jamaicensis [Kingston, 1902] and Supplement [1908]. None claims to be exhaustive.

3810. List of works in the New York Public Library relating to the West Indies. 1 vol. 8vo. N.Y. 1912.

In vol. xvi of Bulletin of the New York Public Library.

(*b*) GENERAL SOURCES

3811. The groans of the plantations. 1 vol. 8vo. Lond. 1689.

A pamphlet written by a Barbadian ; notable for the remark : ' They have a great advantage over us in regard we have none to represent us in Parliament. 'Tis true we have not : but we hope we may have them.'

3812. Monumental inscriptions of the British West Indies from the earliest date ; with genealogical and historical annotations . . . illustrative of the histories and genealogies of the 17th-century. Ed. by J. H. Lawrence-Archer. 1 vol. 4to. Lond. 1875. Coat of arms.

The title is misleading : there is much more material for the 18th and 19th centuries than for the 17th.

3813. Caribbeana, being miscellaneous papers relating to the history, genealogy, topography, and antiquities of the British West Indies. Ed. by V. L. Oliver. 6 vols. 8vo. Lond. 1910–19. Maps. Plans. Ports.

A quarterly magazine containing a valuable if miscellaneous collection of transcripts of original MSS., both public and private, parish registers, genealogical trees, &c. Much material for 17th century. The volumes were made up every second year, and contain eight quarterly parts. Publication ceased with Pt. IV of vol. vi.

(*c*) GENERAL ACCOUNTS

3814. The English American, his travail by sea and land : or A new survey of the West Indies. By T. Gage. 1 vol. fol. Lond. 1648. Later ed. 1 vol. 8vo. Lond. 1699.

Personal description of travels in Mexico : a very popular book, which is believed to have influenced Cromwell's West Indian policy.

3815. Histoire générale des Antilles habitées par les François. By J. B. du Tertre. 4 vols. 4to. Paris. 1667–71. Maps. Plates.

Invaluable for early relations of French and English in West Indies up to 1668. Many documents quoted at length. [Du Tertre made several voyages to the West Indies.] His first work was published in 1654 under the title : Histoire generale des isles de S. Christophe, de la Guadaloupe. For critical discussion see de Dampierre.

3816. Relation de ce qui s'est passé dans les Isles et Terre-Ferme de l'Amerique. By J. Clodoré. 2 vols. Paris. 1671.

Useful for English loss of Surinam.

3817. America, being the latest and most accurate description of the New World ... with the several European plantations in those parts. By J. Ogilby. 1 vol. fol. Lond. 1671. Maps. Plates. Later ed. 1 vol. 8vo. Kingston, Jamaica. 1851. Map. Ed. by W. W. Anderson.

With much worthless ancient American history contains a good deal of geographical and historical information on the English colonies in the 17th century. The repr. of 1851 is entitled : A description and history of Jamaica, and is extracted from the earlier ed., with chapter added to bring it down to date.

3818. An historical account of the rise and growth of the West India collonies, and of the great advantages they are to England, in respect to trade. By T. Dalby. 1690.

Typical mercantilist argument. Repr. in Harl. Misc.

3819. Nouveau voyage aux isles de l'Amerique contenant ... les guerres et les événemens singuliers qui y sont arrivez pendant le long séjour que l'auteur y a fait. By J. B. Labat. 6 vols. 12mo. Paris. 1722. Maps. Plans. Plates.

Labat went to the West Indies in 1694 and lived there for eleven years : his book is very interesting, and particularly valuable for Anglo-French relations during that period and for illustrated descriptions of sugar-making, indigo works, &c.

3820. The history, civil and commercial, of the British colonies in the West Indies. By B. Edwards. 3 vols. 8vo. Lond. 1793. Maps. Plans. Ports. Later ed. (5th) 5 vols. 8vo. Lond. 1819. Maps. Plans. Ports.

Though the 'standard history', it has little of value for the 17th century. 'C'est surtout le récit des événements révolutionnaires qui a fait la vogue de l'ouvrage, à une époque où cette histoire n'était pas encore faite du côté français ' [de Dampierre].

3821. Chronological history of the West Indies. By T. Southey. 3 vols. 8vo. Lond. 1827.

A dull but useful compilation ; quotes treaties and other documents, but generally from secondary authorities.

3822. A historical geography of the British colonies. Vol. ii : The West Indies. By C. P. Lucas. 1 vol. 8vo. Oxf. 1890. Maps. Later ed. 1905. Ed. by C. Atchley.

The best popular account of the British West Indies.

3823. Government of the West Indies. By H. Wrong. 1 vol. 8vo. Oxf. 1923. Map. Bibl.

Deals mainly with the constitutional changes of the 19th century, and present-day problems : some reference to 17th-century history.

(d) GENERAL MONOGRAPHS

3824. Guillaume d'Orange et les origines des Antilles Françaises. Etude historique d'après les chroniques de l'époque et de nombreux documents inédits. By le Vicomte du Motey. 1 vol. 8vo. Paris. 1908.

Based partly on MS. sources, but largely on du Tertre. Throws some light on Anglo-French relations up to the Peace of Breda. See also G. St. Yves, Les premières relations des Antilles françaises et des Antilles anglaises [Paris, 1902, repr. from Bull. Hist. Géographique], and G. Servant, Les Compagnies de Saint-Christophe et des Îles de l'Amérique (1626–53) [Rev. Hist. Col. Franç. i, pp. 385–482, 1913].

3825. English colonies in Guiana and on the Amazon, 1604–1668. By J. A. Williamson. 1 vol. 8vo. Oxf. 1923.

3826. The colonial agents of the British West Indies. A study in colonial administration, mainly in the eighteenth century. By L. M. Penson. 1 vol. 8vo. Lond. 1924. Bibl.

Traces the rise of the agents in the 17th century. Lists of agents. Appendix of illustrative documents, and note on authorities.

3827. The Caribee islands under the proprietary patents. By J. A. Williamson. 1 vol. 8vo. Lond. 1926.

(e) BAHAMAS

3828. Company of Adventurers for the plantation of the islands of Eleutheria, formerly called Bahama : articles and orders. Lond. 1647.

See also : Company of Adventurers for the plantation of the islands called Eleutheria. . . . articles and orders [Lond. 1647].

3829. The Bahama Islands : notes on an early attempt at colonization. By J. T. Hassam. 1 vol. 8vo. Boston (Mass.) 1899. Map.

Deals with the history of the islands in the 17th century, and quotes original documents. In Mass. Hist. Soc. Proc., Series 2, vol. xiii.

3830. List of documents relating to the Bahama Islands in the British Museum and the Record Office, London. By H. Malcolm. 1 vol. Nassau. 1910.

(f) BARBADOS

3831. A briefe relation of the late horrid rebellion acted in the island Barbados. . . . Acted by the Waldronds and their abettors, anno 1650. By N. Foster. 1 vol. 8vo. Lond. 1650. Later ed. 1879.

A number of pamphlets were called forth by the Cavalier v. Roundhead struggle in the Barbados. Thence there is a steady stream all through the century. See F. Cundall, Bibl. of West Indies, p. 1.

3832. A true and exact history of the island of Barbados, illustrated with a map of the island. By R. Ligon. 1 vol. fol. Lond. 1657. Map. Plans. Plates.

Rather a description of the island than a history. Ligon spent three years in Barbados, and wrote this vivid picture of West Indian society in a London debtor's prison. Contains a description of early sugar-planting.

3833. The laws of Barbadoes, collected in one volume. Ed. by W. Rawlin. 1 vol. 1699.

A 17th-century collection of Acts made by the clerk to the Assembly. There are several later collections of Acts of Assembly, but they usually only print *in extenso* those laws which are still in force.

3834. Some memoirs of the first settlement of the island of Barbadoes. . . . Extracted from ancient records, papers, and accounts. . . . Also remarks on the laws and constitution of Barbados. 1 vol. 1741.

For critical discussion of the value of this book see J. A. Williamson (3827).

3835. The history of Barbados, comprising a geographical and statistical description of the island ; and a sketch of the historical events since the settlement. By R. H. Schomburgk. 1 vol. 8vo. Lond. 1840. Maps. Plates.

A book of great learning and authority, though recent research has added much to our knowledge of the early history of Barbados ; *vid.* V. T. Harlow's A history of the Barbadoes 1625–85. 1 vol. 8vo. Oxf. 1926   Maps.

3836. The Cavaliers and Roundheads of Barbados, 1650–1652, with some account of the early history of Barbados. By N. D. Davis. 1 vol. 8vo. Georgetown, Br. Guiana. 1887.

One of the first modern attempts to deal critically with English West Indian history. Several pamphlets and magazine articles, as well as MS. notes by this author, are preserved in the Royal Colonial Institute, London.

(g) BERMUDAS

3837. Acts of assembly made and enacted in the Bermuda or Summer Islands from 1690 to 1713–14. 1 vol. fol. Lond. 1719.

3838. Memorials of the discovery and early settlement of the Bermudas or Somers Islands, 1515–1685, compiled from colonial records and other sources. By J. H. Lefroy. 2 vols. 8vo. Lond. 1877–9.

An exhaustive treatment of the subject, with a reprint of early descriptions and official documents.

3839. The historye of the Bermudaes or Summer Islands. Ed. by J. H. Lefroy. 1 vol. 8vo. Lond. 1882. Plan. Ports.

Reprints Brit. Mus. MS. Sloane 750. Preface discusses authorship. Reproduces early portrait of Sir John Somers. Hakluyt Soc. Pub., No. 65.

(h) JAMAICA

3840. A description of the island of Jamaica with the other isles and territories in America. . . . Taken from the notes of Sir Thomas Linch . . . governor of Jamaica and other experienced persons. . . . Ed. by R. Blome. 1 vol. 8vo. Lond. 1672. Later ed. 1 vol. 8vo. Lond. 1678. Maps.

The Rylands copy of 1687 is : The present state of His Majesty's isles and Territories in America . . (map). For other 17th–century accounts of Jamaica see Cundall, Bibl. Jamaica, pp. 14–16.

3841. Laws of Jamaica : passed by the Assembly and confirmed by his Majesty in Council, April 17th, 1684. To which is added the State of Jamaica, as it now is under the government of Sir Thomas Lynch. 1 vol. Lond. 1684. Map.

In 1698 a second volume was published : The continuation of the Laws of Jamaica . . . confirmed . . . December 26th 1695. See also : Acts of the Assembly passed in the island of Jamaica from 1681 to 1737 inclusive [1 vol. fol. Lond. 1738].

3842. The history of Jamaica, or General survey of the ancient and modern state of that Island. By [E. Long]. 3 vols. 4to. Lond. 1774. Maps. Plans. Plates.

Displays strong prejudice, but is of permanent value.

3843. Journals of the Assembly of Jamaica, 1663–1826. 15 vols. Jamaica. 1811–29.

3844. The causes of Cromwell's West Indian expedition. By F. Strong. 1 vol. 8vo. New York. 1899.

In Am. Hist. Rev. vol. iv, p. 228 : maintains view that the West Indian expedition was part of a far-seeing deliberate policy.

3845. The narrative of General Venables, with an appendix of papers relating to the expedition to the West Indies and the conquest of Jamaica. Ed. by C. H. Firth. Camd. Soc. 1900.

Preface by C. H. Firth. Ed. for Royal Hist. Soc. [Camd. Soc. Publications, 1900.] See also : The English conquest of Jamaica, an account of what happened in the island . . . [from 20 May 1655 to 3 July 1656]. . . by Captain Julian de Castilla, trans. from the MS. and ed. with introd. by I. A. Wright [Camd. Misc., vol. xiii, Lond. 1923] and Narratives of the English attack on St. Domingo. Trans. and ed. by I. A. Wright. Camd. Soc. Misc. xiv. 1926. A valuable account from the Spanish side. For other pamphlets see Cundall, Bibl. Jamaica, p. 2. On Venables himself see Some acccount of General Robert Venables, together with the . . . diary of his widow, Elizabeth Venables. Chetham Soc. Misc. iv. 1872.

3846. Jamaica under the Spaniards, abstracted from the archives of Seville. Ed. by F. Cundall and J. L. Pietersz. 1 vol. 8vo. Kingston, Jamaica. 1919. Maps.

A selection from the original documents preserved in the Archivo de Indios at Sevilla, which have been transcribed for preservation in the Institute of Jamaica. Reproductions of MS. maps with a commentary. About half the booklet deals with the period 1656–60. Further documents are being transcribed, and it is hoped to publish a translation *in extenso*.

(i) LEEWARD ISLANDS

3847. The history of the Caribby-Islands . . . with a Caribbian vocabulary, rendered into English by John Davies of Kidwelly. By J. Davies. 1 vol. fol. Lond. 1666. Plates.

Chiefly deals with natural history, but has some details about the early relations of French and English in St. Christopher. A translation from the 2nd ed. of César de Rochefort, Histoire naturelle et morale des îles Antilles de l'Amérique . . . (Rotterdam. 1665). See de Dampierre.

3848. Les particularitez de la défaite des Anglois . . . dans l'Isle de S. Cristophe, en l'Amérique, par les François. 1 vol. Paris. 1666.

The first of several pamphlets printed in Paris with news of the Anglo-Dutch war. See Cundall, Bibl. of West Indies, p. 14.

3849. A briefe account of the sufferings of the servants of the Lord called Quakers : from their first arrival in the island of Antegoa, under the several governours ; from 1660 to 1695. By J. Langford. 1 vol. 1706.

See also the sections on Antigua and Nevis in Besse, Sufferings of the Quakers.

3850. Acts of Assembly passed in the Charibbee Leeward Islands, from 1690 to 1730. 1 vol. fol. Lond. 1734.

Consists of two parts : Acts of the General (federal) Assembly, 1690–1705, and Acts of Antigua, 1668–1730. Only those acts which were in force at the time of publication are printed *in extenso*. Similar collections were printed for each of the other Leeward Islands, but they suffer from the same defect.

3851. A young squire of the seventeenth century, from the papers [1676–86] of Christopher Jeaffreson of Dullingham House, Cambridgeshire. Ed. by J. C. Jeaffreson. 2 vols. 8vo. Lond. 1878.

A valuable but uncritical edition of the MS. letter-book of C. Jeaffreson, settler in

St. Kitts, and later agent for the island. The MS. is at present in the possession of Mrs. J. C. Jeaffreson.

3852. The History of the island of Antigua. By V. L. Oliver. 3 vols. fol. Lond. 1894, 1896, 1899.

The work is preceded by a short historical introduction, arranged in strict chronological order, and consisting almost entirely of transcripts of documents. The book itself is a genealogical record of families connected with Antigua : précis of all important wills are printed with their reference number.

3853. The development of the Leeward Islands under the Restoration, 1660–1688. By C. S. S. Higham. 1 vol. 8vo. Camb. 1921. Maps. Bibl.

Compare C. S. S. Higham, The early days of the church in the West Indies, in Church Quart. Rev., vol. xcii ; The accounts of a colonial governor in the seventeenth century, in Am. Hist. Rev., vol. xxviii ; Some Treasurer's accounts of Monserrat, 1672–1681, in Eng. Hist. Rev., vol. xxxviii ; and The general assembly of the Leeward Islands, *ibid.* xli, Apr.–July, 1926.

(*j*) SURINAM, &c.

3854. Surinam justice . . . being a publication of that perfect relation of the . . . disturbances in the colony . . . set forth by W. Byam . . . couched in answer thereto by Robert Sanford. By R. Sanford. Lond. 1662.

Reprints an extremely rare pamphlet by Governor Byam, A narrative of the late troubles in Surinam. For further pamphlets on Surinam, with criticism, see Williamson, The English in Guiana, p. 150. Cf. Cundall, Bibl. of West Indies, p. 72.

3855. English colonies in Guiana and on the Amazon, 1604–1668. By J. A. Williamson. 1 vol. 8vo. Oxf. 1923. Map.

Critical discussion of authorities. For further discussion of contemporary authorities see G. Edmundson, The Dutch in Western Guiana, and The Dutch on the Amazon, in Eng. Hist. Rev., vols. xvi and xviii.

3856. Colonising expeditions to the West Indies and Guiana 1623–1667. Ed. by V. T. Harlow. 1 vol. Hakluyt Soc. 1925. Maps. Illus.

(*k*) BUCCANEERS

3857. Bucaniers of America, or a true account of the most remarkable assaults committed of late years upon the coasts of the West Indies by the bucaniers of Jamaica and Tortuga . . . especially . . . the exploits of Sir Henry Morgan. By J. Esquemeling. Lond. 1684. Map. Later eds. 1 vol. 8vo. Lond. 1699 and 1911. Maps. Ports.

Much light on local affairs of West Indian colonies. Esquemelin's book was originally published in Dutch in 1674 : it has become the source of numerous later compilations and translations. The English edition of 1699, entitled The History of the Bucaniers, . . . contains much additional matter. The ed. of 1911 is the best available modern reprint. For full critical discussion see de Dampierre and Haring, The buccaneers in the West Indies.

3858. The buccaneers in the West Indies in the seventeenth century. By C. H. Haring. 1 vol. 8vo. Lond. 1910. Maps. Plans. Bibl.

Brings out the connexion between the buccaneers and the English W. Indian colonies. Critical bibliography discusses Esquemelin. Cf. Violet Barbour's Privateers and Pirates of the West Indies. Amer. Hist. Rev. xvi. Apr. 1911.

INDEX OF AUTHORS, BOOKS, ETC.

3 I

Torrington, Earl of: v. Herbert, Arthur.
Torrington, Lord: v. Byng, George.
Tothill, William:
court of chancery, 498.
Touchet, James, Earl of Castlehaven:
memoirs, 3219.
Toudouze, Georges:
La Hogue, 1339.
Toulmin, Joshua:
ed. Neal's history of puritans, 1596.
view of protestant dissenters, 1600.
life of Biddle, 1726.
Tovey, D'Blossiers:
Anglia judaica, 1745.
Townsend, Meredith:
governing families, 779.
Townsend, Richard:
life, 3343.
Townshend, Dorothea:
life of Digby, 823.
life of Porter, 953.
life of Richard Townsend, 3343.
life of the Earl of Cork, 3359.
Townshend, Henry:
diary, 1201.
Traill, Henry Duff:
ed. social England, 2171.
Trappes-Loman, Richard:
ed. diary of the blue nuns, 1780.
ed. English canonesses, 1782.
ed. Franciscan nuns, 1784.
Treatise of oxen: 2052.
Treby, Sir George:
collection of letters, 1811.
Trenchard, John:
short history of standing armies, 1010.
Trent, William Peterfield:
American literature, 3587.
Tresham, Sir Thomas:
buildings erected by, 2583.
Trevelyan, Sir Charles Edward:
ed. Trevelyan papers, 132.
Trevelyan, George Macaulay:
England under the Stuarts, 238.
Trevelyan, Sir Walter Calverley:
ed. Trevelyan papers, 132.
Trevor, Arthur Hill, Viscount Dun-
cannon:
William III, 1006.
Trigg, Francis:
petition, 2055.
Trott, Nicholas:
laws of the British plantations, 3593.
Trotter, Eleanor:
life in the country parish, 2793.
True account of the parliament in Ire-
land: 3224.
True and large discourse of the voyage,
A: 3728.
True and perfect relation of the happy
successe: 1318.
True and perfect relation of the whole
proceedings: 1798.
True collection of offices and fees: 255.
True narrative of the engagement: 1317.

True report of certaine wonderfull over-
flowings: 2067.
Trumbull, Benjamin:
history of Connecticut, 3650.
Trumbull, James Hammond:
ed. Lechford's Plaine dealing, 3589.
ed. records of Connecticut, 3600.
Truth brought to light: 63.
Tryon, Rolla Milton:
household manufactures, 3708.
Tucker, Robert:
Scottish excise and customs, 2956.
Tullie, Isaac:
siege of Carlisle, 1177.
Tulloch, John:
rational theology, 1392.
puritanism, 1623.   [vergne.
Turenne, Viscount de: v. La Tour d'Au-
Turnbull, G. H.:
Samuel Hartlib, 2295.
Turner, Edward Raymond:
secrecy of post, 265 n.
lord justices, 269.
articles on cabinet, 296 and n.
parliament and foreign affairs, 626.
coal industry, 1906 n.
Turner, Frederick Jackson:
ed. guide to American history, 3575.
frontier in American history, 3713.
Turner, G. Lyon:
ed. original records of early nonconformity, 1595.
Turner, Sir James:
Pallas armata, 1029.
memoirs, 1114.
Turner, James Horsfall:
ed. nonconformist register, 1590.
ed. Hodgson, 1097.
ed. Heywood, 1645.
Tutchin, John:
the Observator, 2516.
Tweedie, William K.:
ed. Wodrow's select biographies, 3133.
Twells, Leonard:
life of Pocock, 952.
Two seasonable discourses: 418.
Twysden, Sir Roger:
commoners liberty, 309.
journal, 992.
Tyldesley, Thomas:
diary, 1829.
Tyler, Lyon G.:
ed. narratives of early Virginia, 3631.
England and America, 3692 n.
Tyler, Moses Coit:
American literature, 3570.
Tyrell, James:
bibliotheca politica, 2760.
Tyson, Edward:
ourang-outang, 2663.

Underhill, Edward Bean:
ed. tracts on liberty of conscience,
1383 n.
ed. records of a church, 1587.

INDEX OF SUBJECTS

PRINTED IN ENGLAND AT THE UNIVERSITY PRESS, OXFORD
BY JOHN JOHNSON, PRINTER TO THE UNIVERSITY